A Companion to the Cantos of Ezra Pound

A Companion to the Cantos of Ezra Pound

by

Carroll F. Terrell

Published in Cooperation with
The National Poetry Foundation
University of Maine at Orono
Orono, Maine

UNIVERSITY OF CALIFORNIA PRESS
Berkeley · Los Angeles · London

Published in Cooperation with
The University of Maine at Orono
Orono, Maine

University of California Press
Berkeley and Los Angeles, California

University of California Press, Ltd.
London, England

First Paperback Printing 1993

ISBN: 0-520-08287-7
Library of Congress Catalog Card Number: 78-054802

Printed in the United States of America

1 2 3 4 5 6 7 8 9

The paper used in this publication meets the minimum requirements of American National Standard for Information Sciences—Permanence of Paper for Printed Library Materials, ANSI Z39.48–1984. ∞

Contents

Preface

I

Early in life Ezra Pound dedicated himself to the art of poetry, for him the most exalted vocation possible to man. His approach was programmatic: he would take twenty-five years to learn and practice all that was known about the craft of poetry; he would use as models only the best work of the greatest masters [Homer, Dante, Chaucer, Shakespeare, Browning] or of minor poets whose discoveries had advanced the art [Sappho, Ovid, Catullus, Propertius, the Provençal poets, Waller, Laforgue, et al.]. He also realized early on that if he was to be numbered among the greatest himself, his masterwork would have to be of epic proportions. For more than a dozen years (1908-1921) Pound contemplated possible forms and structures for his "poem of some length." After making several false starts he had moments of despair. One such moment occurred in Venice in 1908, when he was tempted to throw the page proofs of *A Lume Spento* into the San Vio Canal and take up a different vocation. He did not yield to the temptation. Other moments of doubt occurred during the period 1915-1920 while he was reading the manuscripts of *Ulysses*: he had fears that the age of poetry was over and that the verbal arts of the future would have to be in prose. The wide variation in tone of the cantos written and published during these years shows these fears. Some passages reflect a Cavalcanti-Dante attitude; others show that Pound had adopted Browning's tone, diction, and toughness of texture as most appropriate to the twentieth century.

Then, around 1922, something happened to Pound: he started *The Cantos* anew, adapting some passages from earlier versions but discarding much more, and from that moment on he never wavered. There is no uncertainty as to form, content, or direction; an ambience of confident control informs each canto and the way each canto articulates with the whole. Whether 100 or 120 cantos would be needed fully to realize the design was a decision left for the future, but all the themes to be developed were known to him in July 1922, when he wrote to Felix Schelling:

> Perhaps as the poem goes on I shall be able to make various things clear. Having the crust to attempt a poem in 100 or 120 cantos long after all mankind has been commanded never again to attempt a poem of any length, I have to stagger as I can.
>
> The first 11 cantos are preparation of the palette. I *have to* get down all the colours or elements I want for the poem. Some perhaps too enigmatically and abbreviatedly. I hope, heaven help me, to bring them into some sort of design and architecture later [*L*, 180].

Over the years Pound made a number of other statements about the form and content of *The Cantos*. Among the most important is this excerpt from a letter: "Afraid the whole damn poem is rather obscure, especially in fragments. Have I ever given you outline of main scheme . . . or whatever it is? 1. Rather like, or unlike subject and response and counter subject in fugue. A.A. Live man goes down into world of Dead. C.B. the 'repeat in history.' B.C. the 'magic moment' or moment of metamorphosis, bust thru from quotidien into 'divine or permanent world.' Gods, etc." [*L*, 210]. He also called *The Cantos* "the tale of the tribe" and "a poem containing history." Pound and others have drawn some parallels with *The Divine Comedy*, but not to suggest the neat categories of Hell, Purgatory, and Paradise perceived in Dante's time. In 1928 Yeats tried to convey his understanding of Pound's explanations of the poem's form: "He has scribbled on the back of an envelop certain sets of letters that represent emotions or archetypal events–I cannot find any adequate definition–ABCD and then JKLM, and then each set of letters repeated, and then ABCD inverted and this repeated, and then a new element XYZ . . . and all set whirling together" [Yeats, *A Packet for Ezra Pound*, 1928, 4-5]. Pound is on record as saying that Yeats's explanation did more harm than good because he had as little idea of a fugue as he had of a frog. The significance of the quotation is less in its accurate description than in Yeats's conviction that Pound knew exactly what he was doing and why, whether anyone else did or not. Yeats added: "He has shown me upon the wall a photograph of a Cosimo Tura decoration in three compartments, in the upper the Triumph of Love and the Triumph of Chastity, in the middle Zodiacal signs, and in the lower certain events in Cosimo Tura's day." The parallels between the panels and Dante's structure are clear: the upper panel suggests Paradise, the middle one Purgatory, and the lower one Hell.

Although it is not possible now–nor will it ever be–to make a complete statement about all the themes in *The Cantos*, it is possible to posit a hypothesis that can help the reader, a hypothesis he can alter to his own bent as his experience dictates. To me, *The Cantos* is a great religious poem. The tale of the tribe is an account of man's progress from the darkness of hell to the light of paradise. Thus it is a revelation of how divinity is manifested in the universe: the process of the stars and planets, the dynamic energy of the seed in motion (*semina motuum*), and the kind of intelligence that makes the cherrystone become a cherry tree. Hell is darkness ["there is only the darkness of ignorance"]; thus the highest manifestation of divinity flows from the mind and the spirit of man. Whatever gods there be act through man's mind and perceptions and are revealed in (1) his intelligence, (2) his ethical sense and his thirst for perfectibility, (3) his power to love (*amo ergo sum*), (4) his perception of beauty (*tò kalón*), (5) his sense of mystery, (6) his power and urge to be a maker (in music, painting, sculpture, poetry, prose), and (7) his aspiration to create a paradise on earth. These are the major ways divinity is manifested in the mind, spirit, and heart of man. But there are obverse cues: (1) hatred of injustice and tyranny over people, (2) disgust with moneymongers and those who lust for possessions ("hoggers of harvest are the curse of the people"), and (3) revulsion from the ooze of the material hell many men create and happily wallow in.

The hundreds of people who inhabit *The Cantos* were all born into the darkness of hell. From then on they fall into three groups: (1) those who enjoy their hellish state and remain the same; (2) those who experience a metamorphosis and, desiring to get out of darkness, are drawn to follow a vision of fire and light; and (3) the highly endowed few who become leaders of the mass moving toward the land of light (*paradiso terrestre*). Toward the end of the poem Pound says that it was his dream to create this special group, but by the end of the poem he had lost his love ("what do I love and / where are you?"), and he had lost his "center / fighting the world. The dreams clash / and are shattered– / and that I tried to make a paradiso/ terrestre" [802]. The last line of this fragment is an appeal to mankind: "To be men not destroyers." Men, we assume, are those who dedicate themselves to the betterment of the human condition; the destroyers do not. Thus, the central conflicts and tensions of the poem are the same as those of all other great epics, prose or poetry, of the past: the eternal struggle of the forces of good against the forces of evil.

If the major import of the poem can be stated so simply, why then has the text bewildered so many? The reasons are many, but they are also simple: although traditional moral values of the West–say the seven deadly sins of the Christians and the lists of primary virtues–are all to be found in the poem, their order of importance is quite different. Also, that Pound opted for a musical thematic structure rather than the more traditional historical or narrative structure has made even so basic a statement less than clear to most readers. Finally, the extreme concentration of his gists and piths, which comes from an impulse to present a great deal in a small space, makes the text difficult to adjust to.

In spite of the difficulties few critics these days would dissent from the view that Ezra Pound is one of the most significant men of letters of the twentieth century and that his influence on poets of all nations has been pervasive and formative. His own place as an individual poet in the tradition is, however, quite another question. In the end, whether Pound will be assigned a place in the hierarchy as a major poet will depend on a fuller if not a final critical evaluation of *The Cantos*. Before that can be accomplished the text must be made more broadly accessible.

Although hundreds of books, articles, and reviews have been written about Pound and his work and continue to be written with increasing frequency, there has been no tradition of literary criticism, for three quite understandable reasons. First, Pound has been identified as a partisan on the wrong side in the most violent upheavals of a violent century. In the mind of the public he is a man who endorsed and promoted the Fascist cause; who sponsored and propagandized for bizarre theories of economics, money, and banking; who was identified as a rabid anti-Semite of the Henry Ford–Father Coughlin kind; who made pejorative statements about organized religions, including Christianity (both Catholic and Protestant) and Buddhism; and who became a henchman of Mussolini and used all the means at his disposal in seeking the defeat of the Allies in World War II and was therefore guilty of treason. A decade of war propaganda, which still lingers in the minds of those who lived through it, has made it almost impossible to get past the public image of the poet formed in those years so as to consider what he really believed in and thought he was doing or to get past the mythical man to consider the work–especially *The Cantos*–as an object of art. Indeed, since many critics insist that one cannot and should not consider the work apart from the poet, most published criticism about *The Cantos* has been less than evenhanded; articles have been either defenses written by the poet's fans or castigations written by his detractors. The result is a series of apologetics or animadversions rather than temperate evaluation.

Second, no final literary criticism about *The Cantos* could begin until after 1970 when the complete text was published in one volume. Although serious critical inquiry about the work of other major writers of the twentieth century, such as T. S. Eliot and James Joyce, began in the 1920s, thoughtful examination of Pound's ideas and methods did not begin until 1951 with the publication of Hugh Kenner's *The Poetry of Ezra Pound*. This book opened up new worlds and set the reader high on a peak in Darien. But even such astute critics and interpreters as Kenner, Eva Hesse, Clark Emery, Forrest Read, Guy Davenport, and Walter Baumann (to list but a few) could deal only with parts of the poem or special themes until the whole was available in one volume.

Third, serious literary evaluation of *The Cantos* has been impossible for most critics because of the difficulty of the text. Before a genuine dialogue is possible, the text of *The Cantos* must be made more easily comprehensible to a sizable audience of students and professors as well as critics. Although some progress has been made, it becomes clearer, as time goes on, that the problems are not so much in the abstruse levels of thinking as in the extraordinary and wide-ranging fields of reference. The "luminous details" or "gists and piths" or "ideas in action" which Pound gives us in his epic are drawn from sources quite outside the humanist tradition in which literary scholars have been trained; hence the need for *A Companion to the Cantos*.

By far the most important work published to date to help readers has been *The Annotated Index to the Cantos of Ezra Pound* by John Hamilton Edwards and William W. Vasse, with the assistance of John J. Espey and Frederic Peachy (University of California Press, 1957). The *Index* lists alphabetically and annotates all proper names and foreign phrases of the cantos (1-84) then in print. At that time little exegesis and even fewer source studies had been done. In the more than twenty years since the appearance of the *Index*, a great deal of basic work has been published, though much remains to be done. Furthermore, after the poem was completed through the fragments to Canto 120, the *Index* became dated, and requests to update it with an alphabetical supplement or to replace it by redoing the whole, canto by canto, became clamorous. I started an alphabetical supplement in 1972, but at the Pound conference held in Orono, Maine, in 1975, the decision to redo the whole in two volumes was finally made. In philosophy and design, the *Companion* was conceived to be the logical step between the *Index* of 1957 and the definitive variorum edition of *The Cantos* which would be the function of the future.

The most time-consuming if not the most difficult part of the work has been the constant readjustments of design. To bring the final text to publishable form, original manuscripts were pruned of several kinds of information which I had hoped it would be possible to include; the following guiding statement was finally adopted:

> Practical considerations dictate what the *Companion* must be and what it must not be. It is not being prepared for Pound scholars who do not need it. It is being prepared as a handbook for new students of *The Cantos* who need it badly. Therefore it is not designed as a complete compendium of present knowledge about *The Cantos*, with exegeses and analyses of the text; such a 10-volume work must be left to the future. The projected 2-3 volume work (I:1-71; II:74-120) must be budgeted to not more than 800 pages.
>
> The book is designed for the beginner so as to (1) answer his first and most immediate questions; (2) tell him where to go next for exegesis and comment; and (3) tell him where to go to find the sources EP used. The text will be based on the edition of 1975 published by New Directions and Faber.
>
> Certain kinds of information were finally pruned from the glosses: (1) textual variants from one edition to another, (2) citations from sources which did not contribute to the meaning; (3) cross-references except for the most important; (4) dates of composition which have not been precisely established.

Procedures for preparing the manuscript have been systematic. First, the information contained in the *Index* was converted to glosses for each canto. Although the data from the *Index* were supplemented with additional information from Pound's sources, and although the number of glosses was doubled to cover materials other than those to which this work was limited, my most important debt for the *Companion* is to the *Index*. Although I have rewritten and expanded most entries, a few translations or parts of sentences have been used verbatim. Efforts to indicate all such exact quotations had to be abandoned as confusing and space-consuming; I make this general acknowledgment instead.

The *Companion* is indebted, too, to the dozens of Pound scholars who since 1957 have done basic exegetical studies on the text. The list of abbreviations of books on Pound stresses the importance of such works as Kenner's *The Pound Era*, Davie's *Poet as Sculptor*, and Hesse's *New Approaches* for numerous glosses. The unpublished doctoral dissertation of Achilles Fang, "Materials for the Study of Pound's Cantos" (Harvard University, 1958) has been extremely valuable in locating numerous sources. A very special debt is owed to a few scholars who have made direct contributions to the text: Eva Hesse (Cantos I-XI); Ben Kimpel and T. Duncan Eaves (Cantos XLII-XLIV, L); John Nolde (Cantos LII-LXI); Frederick Sanders (Cantos LXIII-LXVIII); James Wilhelm (Italian and Provençal, passim); John Espey, (passim).

Eva Hesse not only corrected a number of errors in the drafts I sent her for Cantos I-XI, but she also made additions that literally doubled the length of the text. During the years she spent in translating *The Cantos* into German, she gathered one of the most complete files available of Pound's original sources; she thus possesses information known only to her and the scholars with whom she has shared it. She was in fact so generous with both her time and her knowledge that, as early plans had to be modified because of the exigencies of time, money, and space, some of her materials, especially of the interpretive kind, had to be deleted. Nevertheless, the final glosses for these cantos carry Eva Hesse's very substantial authority, although all infelicities of expression must be attributed to me. Since she worked with an earlier version of the Faber text, some instances may be found in places where adjustments to the 1975 common text were made.

The text for the three Leopoldine cantos [XLII-XLIV] is almost exactly in the form submitted by Ben Kempel and T. Duncan Eaves. My additions were mostly of the cross-referencing and apparatus-dictated kind. I am indebted to them also for checking all the glosses for Cantos XXV-XXX against the original (mostly Italian) sources; I followed their advice in a number of places and quite often used their phrasing as a more accurate reflection of Pound's idea about the significance of some "luminous detail" in the source than my own. The glosses for Canto L are based in large part on their source article (*Paideuma*, VII, 2-3).

John Nolde, who is in process of completing detailed studies of the Mailla sources for Cantos LIII-LXI, has given careful scrutiny to the glosses for these cantos and in particular has standardized the transliteration of all Chinese characters and names according to the Wade-Giles Tables. When the historical data used by Pound are inaccurate, Nolde has so indicated. Frederick Sanders, author of *John Adams Speaking: Pound's Sources for the Adams Cantos*, started with the drafts based on the *Index* and made substantial contributions to the glosses for the six central Adams cantos, LXIII-LXVIII. Thereafter, in a reverse role, I added glosses not covered by proper names. James Wilhelm, who had already provided coded glosses for all Italian and Provençal materials in Cantos LXXXV-CXX, also gave me annotated translations for such materials in the earlier cantos. Wilhelm must not, however, be held responsible for any deficiencies in the final text. Although Pound expressed satisfaction with most of the work in the *Index* he had no enthusiasm for idiomatic translations of Italian. Because of that the method of translating Italian, especially medieval and Renaissance, has been a controversial issue. It is not a question of scholarly knowledge as opposed to dilettante knowledge; those who know most about the documents and locutions involved disagree. In this dilemma I have chosen the translation that seemed closest to the Poundian spirit, and a few times, in a spirit of complete abandon, I rejected them all and used my own. In such decisions I have been guided by Pound's rendition of *Tan mare fustes* ("You came at a bad moment") or of *J'en ai marre* ("I'm fed up") [*L*, 210]. I say "rendition" because "translation," in any literal sense, is hardly involved. Pound preferred to use colloquial expressions in English which would satisfy the emotional attitudes found in the original. Over the years his attitude changed; in expressing his idea of *Tan mare fustes* to his father in 1927, he would more likely have said: "This is a hell of a time to show up." Thus neither Wilhelm, nor the other experts who have advised me in Italian and Provençal, such as Eva Hesse, John Espey, and Ben Kimpel, can be held responsible. Although their interpretations have varied they have all been quite correct.

We all owe a particular debt to John Espey, who made major contributions to the *Index* and has kept current with all problems of sources and glosses. If the present text is relatively free from error, it is because of a final check he gave to the entire manuscript against the original sources and a final accuracy test of almost all numbers. Other scholars who should be mentioned include Stephen Fender, University College, London, with whom I exchanged material for Canto XXXVIII, and who Xeroxed and forwarded all of Pound's contributions to the *New English Weekly*; Hugh Witemeyer who read many of the early manuscript for errors and made many suggestions for alterations and additional glosses, which I meticulously followed; Forrest Read and Herbert Schneidau who read the early drafts for Cantos XII-XX; Hugh Kenner who convinced me I should do this job and who has been ready with valuable advice on editorial procedures; Mary de Rachewiltz, Donald Gallup, Donald Davie, and David Gordon who have helped resolve some especially difficult problems. The list could go on but I must end with a general acknowledgment to the dozens of scholars who during the last thirty years have contributed to my knowledge of the cantos. Otherwise, credits are given under the heading "Exegeses," a standard unit in the prefatory matter for each canto. It is here that the value of the contributions made by the *Analyst* and the authors of exegetical work in *Paideuma*, as well as in a number of books and journals, is acknowledged.

II

After completing the glosses for this volume of the *Companion*, I read again the preface to Volume I to see if the premises and hypotheses about the poem expressed there still seem valid. Since the work on this volume has revealed nothing but support for those premises, none of that material is repeated here. Also since cross-references continuously require that this volume be read with Volume I at hand, the tables of Abbreviations and other apparatus will not be repeated either. But a supplementary bibliography of works that have appeared since 1979 will be found at the end of this volume, along with an index to *The Cantos*.

With slight modifications, the procedures adopted for Volume I are the same also. In that volume, for people whose names occurred often in the text, the information available was distributed among the several glosses in order to alleviate the textual aridity of nothing but a series of cross-references. But for such people as Antoninus Pius who is mentioned eighteen times in the poem, this procedure was given up for Volume II. I have used the space saved to develop a few fairly long glosses in order to show the extraordinary significance one or two words in the text often has. For example, "Wolverine" [103:57] might have been glossed briefly: "An ironclad ship built in the early 1840s in order to achieve naval parity with Canada on Lake Erie." But, the reader might be satisfied with that and miss Pound's point of mentioning it at all. The central issue involves the wisdom of Millard Fillmore, a vastly and *unjustly* underrated American statesman. Most of the people who inhabit *Thrones* are there because they have been neglected or mistreated by historians either deliberately or carelessly. Since they tried to improve the human condition, justice [96:headnote] requires that at last they be honored as they deserve.

Again, "prana" [94:18] might have been dealt with in one sentence: "The energy principle of Hatha Yoga in occult Hinduism." But since the hypothesis of the *Companion* is that *The Cantos* is a great religious poem, such a gloss would have misled by default. Pound practiced prana at St. E's: that is, continuously over the years he literally did some of the breathing, sitting, and meditation exercises. To his mind, Richard of St. Victor [*SP*, 71-72] would have done no less. But he also practiced some of the rituals of a number of other religions including Confucianism (with incense burning), the Bahai, and even the rites of some Christian sects–if the Quakers can be so-called. In fact he finds the rites of celebration, reverence, and rejoicing of all religions to be intracompatible: the practices of Hatha Yoga might well be cheered by the Bahai, a point to be emphasized because Pound had a lifelong interest in the Bahai [46:22; 96:93]. Still more, his personal religious beliefs and life style are better expressed by some ideas of the Bahai than they are by any other religious creed.

For, as did Pound, the Bahai believe "that God can be known to man through manifestations, that have come at various states of human progress. . . . Bahaists believe in the unity of all religions, in universal education, in world peace, and in the equality of men and women. . . . Emphasis is laid upon simplicity of living and upon service to suffering fellow men" [CE]. Pound would not start a new religion; he would rather a person were true to the vision of the founder of his own. He would not talk as a religious, he would rather be religious. For Pound, "the essence of religion is the present tense" [*SP*, 70]. He said, "The religious man communes every time his teeth sink into a bread crust" [ibid]. By this, he meant something disarmingly simple: the religious man prays every time he eats, or does anything else for that matter. He said, "he who works prays" [91:6]. He also said: he who loves prays; he who lusts prays; he who procreates prays; he who sings, dances, paints, or writes poetry prays, and so on, minute by minute, because in all these things it is "the still small voice" or the divinity, or the "intimate essence" in the mind and heart of man that is being expressed: "nothing is either good or bad but thinking makes it so." The most terrible results may come when what one thinks is good is evil or what one thinks is evil is in reality good. Wherefore create no dogma to coerce the acts of others and thereby create destructive fanaticisms [*SP*, 70, 150]. Believing these things, Pound might well have responded in the way Abdul Baha did to the man who wanted to "speak of religion." Said Abdul, "I must dance" [46/232]. Indeed, the Bahai would endorse the intent of all the great religious thinkers celebrated in *The Cantos* such as Averroes, Avicenna, St. Anselm, Lord Herbert of Cherbury and Erigena. They are there not because Pound had an interest in curious and arcane historical figures, but because he believed what they said is true: true enough to live by. Thus, glosses for some of these people, such as St. Anselm [105:16, 18, 31, 37, etc.], have been longer than most.

Extended glosses have sometimes been written for other reasons. For "DROIT FAIT" [108:7], I might have written, "part of traditional formula by which English monarchs made acts of parliament legal." That is true enough. But behind this "gist" or "pith" or "luminous detail" lies one of the most dramatic moments in English history. In the days before the moment arrived, a hundred strong men had literally been reduced to tears. Although space did not allow the development of very many such moments, the reader can be assured that behind many a phrase and the brief gloss given for it there lies a dramatic story of great religious, historical, economic, and ethical interest: in *The Cantos* all four are always at issue, a sort of rhyme with the Four Tuan, a recurrent theme in the poem.

Most of the time Pound acts only as a recorder, putting down what the hundreds of characters in the poem actually did and said. He believes that professional historians have mythified and falsified the past. Thus he goes always to the original records and documents. If the fact exists, he will find it. During the St. E.'s years he had a team of people hunting down data at the Library of Congress. Their research was pointed, never random. They went armed with precise directions such as, "I want to know exactly what Benton said about the motion to clear the United States Senate, after passage of the motion to expunge, and exactly the hour of the night he said it" [89:258]!

Pound did his best to obtain the best authority available and never falsifies the records. But sometimes his use of the record is biased. This aspect of the poem is perhaps expressed best with his attitude toward Disraeli and the Rothschilds. The events Pound refers to in the poem are well documented. But one would have to be passionately anti-British not to believe that both Disraeli and the Rothschilds acted brilliantly, with loyalty to the crown, and in good faith [86:56, 61].

The whole poem is colored by Pound's passionately held beliefs: in fact much of its power and intensity derive from this very passion which becomes the power in the shape of the poetic line and the great harmonic rhythms of the poem as a whole. But otherwise, Pound intruded personally into the text only a few times: e.g., at 24/112; 62/350; 76/458 with such words as "ego scriptor" [76:129]. His intent in such intrusion is to remind the reader that the poem is being written by a living person, a responsible "I" with a name and address [78:48]; by one who was there and can testify, or can remember; or to suggest that the kind of thing that went on at some critical moment in the past is still going on [103:46]. For similar reasons, I have intruded into the text of the *Companion* several times to show that the glosses are written by a living person, who expects to be responsible for what is said and done, or to spell out an irony that might otherwise be missed [97:153; 113:30].

III

A great deal of the work on the glosses for the later cantos was done between 1972 and 1975. In 1972, I started collecting materials for an alphabetical supplement to the old *Index* to cover Cantos 85-120. A part of the work was farmed out to various experts. James Wilhelm completed cards for all the Italian and Provençal materials. Latin source materials were divided between James D. Neault who did the first half of the text and John Espey who did much of the last half. To these people, I am much indebted. But in June of 1975, when the decision to do the *Companion*, canto by canto from the beginning, was made that work was put aside. Considerations of space (my firm belief that the *Companion* should not exceed the length of the poem) made it necessary to reduce a lot of their early work, especially quotes from the original languages, to much briefer forms.

The numerous scholars who have done exegetical work on *The Cantos* in *Paideuma* and other journals have been given credit in individual glosses and the headnotes for each canto. But three people must be mentioned in particular. Although quite a lot of the work on the Chinese sources of *Rock-Drill* had been done by 1975, Thomas Grieve's thesis [*Pai*, 2 & 3, 361-508] became very helpful: his work saved much space in locating exact sources and reduced the need for continuous documentation. Special credit too should be given to Charles Watts whose thesis on the sources of Cantos 88 and 89 saved much time. But most of all I am indebted to David Gordon who has been a helper and an adviser in numerous ways. His work on *The Sacred Edict* cantos (98-99) has been a *sine qua non*. Especially for the *Companion*, he spent time at the Beinecke studying Pound's annotations of the *Wen-li* text and prepared a 185-page manuscript recording his discoveries which will be published as soon as possible. Almost all the glosses of Canto 99 are based on this work. Also the study he did on the Coke Cantos [*Pai*, 4-2 & 3, 223-229] was a great help. Other people who knew Pound at St. E's have also been helpful. The notes provided by Reno Odlin, William French, or Sheri Martinelli have been recognized by their initials in brackets: RO, WF, or SM. Mary de Rachewiltz, Marcella Spann Booth, and Hugh Kenner read the manuscripts for the *Pisan Cantos* and *Rock-Drill*. Mary de R. caught several errors because of her firsthand knowledge of the Italian scene; for example, I had glossed Vecchia [76/452] as "I, old lady." Mary could say that "the old road under St. Pantaleo at St. Ambrogio is meant." And so on. With the notes of Marcella Booth I've used two procedures. During Pound's last year at St. E's, she asked him numerous questions about the cantos through *Rock-Drill* which were in print at that time. Some times she copied into the margin of her text exactly what he said in quotes. Sometimes, she summarized what he said in her own words or by writing a brief cue. In the *Companion*, I've preserved this distinction. At the end of my gloss I've inserted her comments after the initials MSB either in quotes [74:176] or without [74:197]. Similarly Hugh Kenner could make a number of corrections or additions to the text based on notes he obtained from Pound directly or on his detailed knowledge of the text. His additions are discriminated as coming from Pound himself or his own knowledge, and accompanied by the initials: H. K. Then there is Colin McDowell of Victoria, Australia, who in 1982 dropped by and was immediately put to work checking manuscripts for *Thrones*, a section of the poem he had been working on for some years. He made several valuable contributions.

In translating names from Arabic, western authorities disagree on forms. Except for quotes from sources, I use Mohammed as standard for the Prophet. But for Abd-el-Melik, there is no clear preference established by custom. Thus, where Pound's major source uses Abd-l-melik as in Canto 96, I use that form, but when the source uses Abd-el-melik as in Canto 97, I do, too.

IV

As I've indicated, the *Companion* is conceived to be a logical and necessary step on the way to a variorum edition of *The Cantos*. But much work remains to be done before that task can be started. First the text of both volumes of the *Companion* must be tested, corrected, and authenticated by the scholars who use it. Then revisions must be made, making use of new scholarly work that can be expected to appear continuously. In time, a deficiency of the present texts can, I hope, be resolved. Some of the information in the glosses I had gathered for my own use over the years. Those notes do not always tell who first made important discoveries. It would be most helpful if any scholars whose work has not been recognized would send me documentary information so that future editions can give them appropriate acknowledgment.

Other acknowledgments I can now make with great pleasure. I am much indebted to the National Endowment for the Humanities for a grant that gave me two-thirds released time from teaching for three semesters and provided other support during that time. Without that assistance, the preparation of Volume Two would certainly have taken several additional years. And along with all Pound scholars, I owe many thanks to Donald Gallup of the Beinecke Library at Yale and to those who preside over the Pound archives there.

Administrative officers of the University of Maine at Orono have given me continued support over a number of years, Presidents Howard Neville and Paul Silverman, Vice Presidents Frederick Hutchinson and Kenneth Allen, Deans Gordon Haaland and Karl Webb in particular, as have Professors Joseph Brogunier, and Burton Hatlen of the English Department. The whole staff of the Folger Library at Orono have been most helpful, but I want to thank in particular Charlotte Huntley, Thomas Patterson, and Margaret Menchen of the Reference Department and Carol Curtis and Dorothy Hutchins of Interlibrary Loan. The work could never have reached its present state of completeness without them.

To my own office staff and assistants I am most indebted. To Nancy Nolde, my main research and administrative assistant, who since 1975 has kept all the dozens of parts of the project in order; to Marilyn Emerick who has done a yeoman's amount of typing; and to Dirk Stratton, a graduate assistant, who has spent hours alone and in team work with Nancy in making my handwriting intelligible to typists, in checking quotes against sources, and in checking the numbers in cross-references, dates, and documentation. Barbara Ramsay-Strout deserves much credit for detailed work on the Index, and Steve Boardway for organizing the Chinese part of the Index. In addition I owe much to the faculty at large which, as with any university faculty, is likely to have someone who can be consulted with profit about almost anything in human history. And finally, we are all indebted to the remarkable editorial team in the Los Angeles office of the University of California Press which made our task less difficult.

In its final form Volume I has 4,772 numbered glosses and Volume II, 5,649 for a total of 10,421. Although I accept the responsibility for writing and testing the accuracy of all of them, the acknowledgments here and throughout the text of the *Companion* should indicate that the work is the product of dozens of Pound scholars, worldwide, done over a period of fifty years.

Abbreviations

WORKS BY POUND

ABCE . . . . . . *ABC of Economics*
ABCR . . . . . *ABC of Reading*
ALS . . . . *A Lume Spento and Other Early Poems*
ATH . . . . . . *Antheil and The Treatise on Harmony*
CEP . . . . *Collected Early Poems*
CNTJ . . . . . . *Classic Noh Theatre of Japan*
CON . . . . . . *Confucius*
GB . . . . *Gaudier-Brzeska: A Memoir*
GK . . . . *Guide to Kulcher*
HSM . . . . . . *Hugh Selwyn Mauberley*
HSP . . . . *Homage to Sextus Propertius*
IMP . . . . *Impact*
J/M . . . . *Jefferson and Mussolini*
L . . . . *Letters of Ezra Pound*, ed. D. D. Paige
LE . . . . *Literary Essays*
LPJ . . . . *Letters Pound/Joyce*, ed. F. Read
MIN . . . . *Make It New*
NPL . . . . Postscript to *Natural Philosophy of Love*
P, 1909 . . . . . *Personae*
P . . . . *Personae: Collected Shorter Poems*
PD . . . . *Pavannes and Divagations*
PE . . . . *Polite Essays*
PM . . . . *Patria Mia*
SP . . . . *Selected Prose*, ed. W. Cookson
SR . . . . *Spirit of Romance*
T . . . . *Translations*
WT . . . . *Sophocles: Women of Trachis*
YC . . . . Yale Collection, American Literature, early letters from Pound to parents

WORKS ABOUT POUND
(For complete citations see bibliography.)

Index . . . . *Annotated Index to the Cantos of Ezra Pound*
WB, *Rose* . . . . Baumann, Walter, *The Rose in the Steel Dust*
CB-R, *ZBC* . . . . Brooke-Rose, Christine, *A ZBC of Ezra Pound*

R. Bush, *Genesis*	Bush, Ronald, *The Genesis of Ezra Pound's Cantos*
Davis, *Vision*	Davis, Earle, *Vision Fugitive*
DD, *Ezra*	Davie, Donald, *Ezra Pound*
DD, *Sculptor*	Davie, Donald, *Ezra Pound: Poet as Sculptor*
Dekker, *Cantos*	Dekker, George, *Sailing after Knowledge: The Cantos of Ezra Pound*
CE, *Ideas*	Emery, Clark, *Ideas into Action: A Study of Pound's Cantos*
JE, *Mauberley*	Espey, John, *Ezra Pound's Mauberley: A Study in Composition*
EH, *Approaches*	Hesse, Eva, ed., *New Approaches to Ezra Pound*
EH, *B.E.P.*	Hesse, Eva, *Beckett. Eliot. Pound. Drei Textanalysen*
HK, *Poetry*	Kenner, Hugh, *The Poetry of Ezra Pound*
HK, *Era*	Kenner, Hugh, *The Pound Era*
LL, *Motive*	Leary, Lewis, ed., *Motive and Method in the Cantos of Ezra Pound*
DP, *Barb*	Pearlman, Daniel S., *The Barb of Time*
M de R	Rachewiltz, Mary de, *Discretions*
NS, *Exile*	Stock, Noel, *Poet in Exile: Ezra Pound*
NS, *Life*	Stock, Noel, *The Life of Ezra Pound*
NS, *Reading*	Stock, Noel, *Reading the Cantos*
JW, *Later*	Wilhelm, James, *The Later Cantos of Ezra Pound*
JW, *Epic*	Wilhelm, James, *Dante and Pound: The Epic of Judgement*

Authors Frequently Cited

MB	Massimo Bacigalupo
MSB	Marcella Spann Booth
GD	Guy Davenport
JE	John Espey
WF	William French
DG	David Gordon
EH	Eva Hesse
HK	Hugh Kenner
BK	Ben Kimpel
HM	Harry Meacham
EM	Eustace Mullins
JN	John Nolde
RO	Reno Odlin
OP	Omar Pound
M de R	Mary de Rachewiltz
FR	Forrest Read
NS	Noel Stock
CFT	Carroll F. Terrell
JW	James Wilhelm

Standard Reference Works

CE	*Columbia Encyclopedia*
EB	*Encyclopedia Britannica*, 1911
HMS	History of Monetary Systems
L&S	Liddell & Scott's Greek-English Lexicon
Loeb	Loeb Classical Library
OBGV	*Oxford Book of Greek Verse*
OCD	Oxford Classical Dictionary
OCM	Oxford Companion to Music

Languages

A .... Arabic
Af.D. .... African Dialect
AS .... Anglo-Saxon
C .... Chinese
D .... Dutch
F .... French
G .... German
H .... Greek
I .... Italian
J .... Japanese
L .... Latin
LSc .... Lowland Scottish
ME .... Middle English
MF .... Middle French
ML .... Medieval Latin
NF .... Norman French
NK .... Na-Khi
OE .... Old English
OF .... Old French
PG .... Portuguese
P .... Provençal
R .... Russian
S .... Spanish
Scot .... Scottish
SGae .... So. Gaelic

Other abbreviations follow MLA style conventions.

OTHER EDITORIAL CONVENTIONS

Cross-references to other glosses are given in brackets with number of the canto followed by a colon and the number of the gloss. Thus [12:16] means gloss 16 of Canto 12. But [81/517] refers not to a numbered gloss but to Canto 81, page 517, of the text of *The Cantos*. A cross-reference to a gloss in the same canto is given as either [cf. 12 above] or [see 75 below]. To save space, proper names have not been repeated in the glosses unless the name in the text is (1) incomplete, (2) misspelled, or (3) a variant from standard usage: for example, the gloss for *Robert Browning* [2:1] repeats neither name; the gloss for *Divus* [1:21] is given as "Andreas D."; *Cabestan* [4:10] is followed by "Guillems de Cabestanh or Cabestaing" to give the more usual designation; and *So-shu* [2:4] is followed by "Corruption of Shiba Shōjo . . ." to give needed explanation. As with *So-shu*, a few glosses have been expanded to review scholarship, if confusion of names is possible.

In the headnotes, under the heading "Sources," all titles have been spelled out, but in the text itself standard abbreviations are often used: *Od.* for *Odyssey* and *Meta.* for Ovid's *Metamorphoses*. Also in the glosses *Inf.*, *Pur.*, and *Par.*, followed by Roman numerals for canto and Arabic numbers for lines, are used for the *Commedia* (e.g., *Inf.* V, 28). The names of some historical characters who appear often in certain cantos are sometimes abbreviated, as SM for Sigismundo Malatesta, JA for John Adams, and TJ for Thomas Jefferson.

CANTO I

Sources

Homer, *Odyssey* XI: the Nekyia passage in which the ghosts of the dead are called up and consulted about the future, in the ML translation of Andreas Divus of Justinopolis (Capodistria) and the First and Second Homeric Hymns to Aphrodite and the First Hymn to Hermes in the ML interpretation of Georgius Dartona of Crete, all published in the volume entitled *Homeri Odyssea ad verbum translata*, Andrea Divo Justinopolitano interprete, *Eiusdem Hymni Deorum XXXII*, Georgio Dartona Cretense interprete, Parisiis, In officina Christiani Wecheli, 1538.

Background

EP, Discarded Cantos: "Three Cantos" (1), *Poetry*, X, 5, 1917, "The Fourth Canto," *Dial*, LXVIII, 1920, "Three Cantos" (2), *Dial*, LXXI, 1921; *P*, "Mauberley I," "The Seafarer"; Cantos 23, 39, 47, 82, 90; *L*, 210 (to Homer Pound) and 274 (to W. H. D. Rouse); *LE* "Early Translators of Homer," "Notes on Elizabethan Classicists"; J. G. Frazer, *The Golden Bough*.

Exegeses

E. Glenn, *Analyst* I and VIII; Dekker, "Myth and Metamorphosis," JE, "The Inheritance of Tò Kalón," CB-R, "Lay me by Aurelie," GD, "Persephone's Ezra," Rachewiltz, "Pagan and Magic Elements in Ezra Pound's Works," HK, "Blood for the Ghosts," FR, "Pound, Joyce, and Flaubert: The Odysseans," all in EH, *Approaches*; CE, *Ideas*; HK, *Era*, 361.

Glossary

1. **Circe**: Goddess living on fabulous island of Aeaea who is powerful in magic; sister of Acoetes; daughter of Helios and Perse [*Od.* X, 210 ff.] . Witch-goddess, particularly associated with sexual regeneration and degeneration. Circe, Aphrodite, and Persephone form the archetypal triad of feminine deity: sorceress, lover, girl–identities "compenetrans." Also Circe Titania, Kirké, Kirkh.

2. **Kimmerian lands**: Territory of the Cimmerians, a people whose city and land were perpetually shrouded in mist and cloud [*Od.* XI, 14-19] .

3. **Perimedes**: One of Odysseus's crew.

4. **Eurylochus**: "Great-hearted and godlike Eurylochus" was Odysseus's second-in-command. He was the leader of the first band of men who sought out Circe.

5. **pitkin**: Word invented by Pound: "little pit."

6. **Ithaca**: Island kingdom of Odysseus near coast of Hellas in Ionian Sea. Countertheme to Troy, the archetypal city that Odysseus helped to destroy. The epic "nostos" [return journey] of *The Cantos* is thus polarized between the destruction and the rediscovery of civilization and sovereignty.

7. **Tiresias**: Given the power of prophecy by Zeus, Tiresias was the Theban seer "Who even dead, yet hath his mind entire!" [cf. 47/236]. Associated with house of Cadmus and the founding of Thebes [cf. Sophocles, *Oedipus*; *Od.* X, XI; Ovid, *Meta.* III].

8. **Erebus**: Dark place through which souls must pass on way to Hades.

9. **dreory**: AS, "blood-dripping."

10. **Pluto**: God of Hades, the underworld or hell. Also called Hades or Dis. Consort of Persephone for the winter months. Also the god of wealth, particularly of gold and all precious metals and stones below the earth's surface [cf. 16, 31 below].

11. **Proserpine**: Daughter of Zeus and Demeter. She was condemned to live half the year in the underworld, but the Eleusinian rites brought her and all nature back to life in the spring. Also known as Persephone, Flora, Kore. She divides her time between Dis and Demeter, between the realm of death and the realm of vegetation. As the chthonic Persephone she is a goddess of death. The rising [*anodos*] of Persephone from the underworld was associated with the rising of Aphrodite from the sea in the Greater Eleusinian Mysteries. Persephone and Aphrodite were also closely linked in the myth of Adonis, who was the consort of chthonic Persephone for one-third of the year and of Aphrodite for the other two-thirds.

12. **Elpenor**: Youngest of Odysseus's men; drunk when Odysseus left Aeaea, he fell down a ladder, broke his neck, and "his spirit went down to the house of Hades" [Loeb]. Stands for luckless incidental companion of the hero (or poet) whose only fame after death rests in the fact that the hero has placed his name on record.

13. **ingle**: Inglenook. LSc, "chimney corner," ingle being derived from SGae *aingeal*, "fire." Pound is using the vocabulary of Gavin Douglas's translation of *Aeneid* where, however, "ingle" by itself always means "fire."

14. **Avernus**: Pound's Ovidian translation of Andreas Divus's *infernus*. Homer's Hades, "A deep lake near Puteoli. . . . its reputed immense depth, and its situation amid gloomy-looking woods and mephitic exhalations inspired the belief that it led to the underworld" [*OCD*].

15. **Anticlea**: Mother of Odysseus. She died during his absence.

16. **golden wand**: A double of the golden bough, key to the underworld, and of the caduceus with which Hermes summoned the souls of the dying to the underworld. The golden bough belongs to the artificial vegetation of Persephone's underground garden [cf. 10 above and 31 below; *Aeneid* VI, 141 ff.].

17. **"A second time?"**: Pound's translation of Andreas Divus's Latin translation of the Greek word διγονος which was apparently printed in place of the now accepted διογενὲς in line 92 of Book XI of the *Odyssey*. Divus was probably using a corrupt Renaissance edition of the Greek text. Scholarly regularized editions still place this line in square brackets to indicate restoration of a corrupt text. Whereas δίγονος means twice-born or double, διογενὲς means "sprung from Zeus" or, in a general sense, "noble," as used in the above line with reference to Laertes [cf. *LE*, 262; 48/241, 74/425, 449, 77/472; also Virgil, *Aeneid* VI, 134 ff.] [EH].

18. **fosse**: ME, "ditch."

19. **bever**: LSc, "drink" [cf. beverage].

20. **Neptune**: Roman god of water identified with the Greek Poseidon, whose son, Polyphemus, held Odysseus and his men captive in a cave. Odysseus blinded Polyphemus while he was in a drunken sleep in order to escape [*Od.* IX, 106 ff.]. Neptune, for ven-

geance, sought to oppose Odysseus's homecoming in every way.

21. **Divus**: Andreas D. of Justinopolis (originally Aegida, renamed J after Justinian I; now Capodistria) [cf. *LE*, 259].

22. **In officina Wecheli**: ML "In the workshop of Wechelus," Paris publisher of Divus.

23. **Homer**: Greek epic poet regarded by Pound as the originator of the epic tradition he sought to continue with *The Cantos*.

24. **Sirens**: Inhabitants of island near Scylla and Charybdis. Sailors lured by their song land and perish. In ancient times they were depicted as harpies or bird-women waiting to carry off the souls of men. Pound, however, sees them as mermaids. The specific lure of their song becomes clear in 79/488 ("as the fish-tails said to Odysseus"): it is praise for his past achievements. Pound is thinking of the line [*Od*. XII, 189] which he has also quoted in *Mauberley* ("we shall tell you of all that happened at Troy") [cf. *Od*. XII, 39 ff., 142-200].

25. **Venerandam**: ML, "worthy of veneration." Beginning of Georgius Dartona's ML interpretation of the Second Homeric Hymn to Aphrodite [*LE*, 266].

26. **Aphrodite**: Goddess of love, beauty, and fertility. Born of blood and seafoam. She supported the Trojans against the Greeks until the end of the war, opposing Athena, defender of the Greeks. Also called Kypris after her island of Cyprus, Cytherea after her island of Cythera, as well as Venus, Venere, and Dione/Diona (i.e., the daughter of Dione and Zeus invoked in the *Pervigilium Veneris* as the spring goddess of vegetation) [cf. *SR*, 19-20, 39/195]. Her birth [*anados*] from the sea rhymes with Persephone-Kore's ascent from the earth's nether regions celebrated at Eleusis and the original of the late canto motif of "Reina" rising from the deeps [91/610]. She was also the mother of Aeneas who, after Troy's fall, set out like Odysseus to found the archetypal city anew under her protection. Her voyage in *The Cantos* is a double of that of Odysseus, but unlike his it is undertaken in a spirit of serene confidence.

27. **Cypri munimenta sortita est**: ML, [who] "held sway over [all] the Cyprian heights." Continuation of Georgius Dartona's ML interpretation [*LE*, 266]. The reference is still to Aphrodite, later referred to in *The Cantos* as the Cyprian goddess.

28. **mirthful**: Pound's translation of Georgius Dartona's *hilariter*.

29. **orichalchi**: ML, "of copper." The Latin word for copper is *Cyprium*, the "Cyprian metal," which takes its name from the island of Cyprus, center of the Aphrodite cult. In his ML interpretation of the Second Homeric Hymn to Aphrodite, Georgius Dartona uses the word *orichalchi* with reference to Aphrodite's earrings. Pound later uses it to describe the color of her eyes as being of "copper and wine" [cf. 25, 26 above and 102/730 ff., 93/631, 97/675].

30. **with golden / Girdles and breast bands, thou with dark eyelids**: Pound's translation of Georgius Dartona's "Collum autem molle, acpectora argentea / Monilibus aureis ornabant"; the "dark eyelids" come from Dartona's interpretation *nigras . . . palpebras* for the Greek *elikoblephare*, a word of uncertain meaning which is generally taken to mean "flashing eyes."

31. **Bearing the golden bough of Argicida**: Pound's mistranslation of Georgius Dartona's *habens auream virgam Argicida* in his interpretation of the First Hymn to Aphrodite (v. 117), where Aphrodite relates that she has been abducted by *chrusórrapis 'Argeîphóntes*, i.e., 'Argeiphóntes (Slayer of Argos, the epithet for Hermes) with the golden bough or wand. Dartona translates *'Argeîphóntes* as "Argicida," the epithet for Mercury which likewise has the literal meaning "Slayer of Argos." The golden bough later came to be associated with Aeneas, who was required to find one as an offering for Proserpine before he could descend to Hades (*Aeneid* VI); still later it reappeared as the Golden Bough of Aricia, a region in the Alban Hills south of Rome consisting of a grove and a lake (now known as Nemi) asso-

ciated with Diana Nemorensis (Diana of the Wood) [4:16].

32. **Argicida**: L, "Slayer of Greeks" as in Greek term *'Argeiphóntes*. A reference to Aphrodite's championship of the Trojans and especially of Aeneas against Greeks and against Odysseus. The epithet indicates that Aphrodite is associated with Persephone as the goddess of death.

CANTO II

Sources

Ovid, *Meta*. III, 511-733; X, 560-707; Euripides, *Bacchae*; Homeric Hymn to Dionysos; R. Browning, *Sordello*; Homer, *Od.* XI, 235-259; *Iliad* III, 139-160; *Mabinogion*; Aeschylus, *Agamemnon*; Arthur Golding, *P. Ovidius Naso: The XV Books, entytuled Metamorphosis*; Camille Chabaneau, *Les Biographies des Troubadours en Langue Provençale*, Toulouse, 1885; Fenollosa Notebooks (inedit.), University of Virginia Library.

Background

EP, *SR*, 16, 132; *Quia Pauper Amavi*; "Three Cantos, II," *Poetry*, 1917 [Discarded Cantos]; "Famam Librosque Cano," "Mesmerism" in *P*; Dante, *Pur*. 6, 7; Mary de Rachewiltz, *Discretions*, Boston and Toronto, 1971; La Chronique de Rains, in *Three Old French Chronicles of the Crusades*, trans. E. Noble Stone, Seattle, 1939.

Exegeses

E. Glenn, *Analyst* XVIII; N. C. de Nagy, "Pound and Browning," and Dekker, "Myth and Metamorphosis," both in EH, *Approaches*; CE, *Ideas*; EH, *Pai*, 7, 1 & 2, 179-180.

Glossary

1. **Robert Browning**: 1812-1889, author of the epic poem, *Sordello*, based on the life of the Italian troubadour of that name who wrote in Provençal. Browning gives an unconventional image of the troubadour as a lyrical persona or mask of himself (a "dramatic monologue"), just as Pound later uses him and other historical characters. The point is that there is no way of seeing the personality of Sordello objectively but only of seeing subjective perspectives of the facts. Browning's *Sordello* is, for Pound, the last

instance of the epic tradition in the English language, which he intends to take up from there on. Pound traces his personal literary lineage back to Browning in *L* [letter to R. Taupin of May 1928 ("Und überhaupt ich stamm aus Browning. Pourquoi nier son père?")], but he intends to include the mythological dimension as well. In introducing the persona "Sordello" and the epic of Browning, he is recycling material from the discarded cantos which is now subsumed into the persona of Odysseus and the epic of Homer [cf. *SR*, 132; *LE*, 33; *ABCR*, 78, 188-191; and letter to W. C. Williams, *L*, 7].

2. **Sordello**: ?1180-?1255, Italian troubadour, son of a poor cavalier, who came to the court of Count Ricciardo de San Bonifazzio, fell in love with the count's wife, Cunizza da Romano, and abducted her at the behest of her brothers. He then lived with Cunizza and was forced to flee to Provence. Later on he performed military service for Charles I of Anjou, Naples, and Sicily, who rewarded him with five castles which, however, he returned, considering himself far richer through his poetry [cf. *LE*, 97-98; Browning's *Sordello*; *Pur*. 6, 7].

3. **Lo Sordels . . .** : P, "Sordello is from Mantua." Direct translation from a *vida* (P, "life") of Sordello in Chabaneau, which begins "Lo Sordels si fo de Mantoana, de Sirier, fils d'un paubre cavallier que avia nom sier el Cort. E deletava se en cansos aprendre & en trobar, e briguet com los bons homes de cort, & apres tot so qu'el poc; e fetz coblas e sirventes. E venc s'en a la cort del comte de San Bonifaci; el coms l'onret molt; & enamoret se de la moiller del comte a forma de solatz, & ella de lui. Et avenc si quel coms estet mal com los fraires d'ella, e si s'estranjet d'ella. E sier Icellis e sier Albrics, li fraire d'ella, si la feiren envolar al comte a sier Sordel; e s'en venc estar com lor en gran benanansa. E pois s'en anet en Proensa, on el receup grans honors de totz los bos homes, e del comte e de la comtessa, que li deron un bon castel e moiller gentil." For Pound's translation, see *LE* 97 ff. [EH].

4. **So-shu**: Corruption of Shiba Shōjo, Japanese name for Chinese Han dynasty poet, Ssu-ma Hsiang-ju (179-117), a representative of the rhyme-prose school criticized by Li Po in an allegory from which the line quoted is derived via a translation by Fenollosa in the Fenollosa Notebooks (inedit.). Li Po scouts Ssu-ma Hsiang-ju, an imitator of Ch'u Yüan, for creating foam instead of waves. Pound quotes from Fenollosa's notes: "Yoyu and Shojo stirred up decayed (enervated) waves. Open current flows about in bubbles, does not move in wave lengths" [*Affirmations*, Jan. 28, 1916]. Not to be confused with "So-shu" in "Ancient Wisdom, Rather Cosmic" (*P*), which is a Japanese transliteration of the name of the Chinese philosopher Chuang Chou (more commonly known as Chuang Tzu), or with "So Shu, king of Soku," in *J/M* (p. 100), where "So Shu" is an incorrect Japanese transliteration of the Chinese name Ts'an Ts'ung, the first king of Shu (now Szechwan) in W China, earlier referred to as "Sanso, King of Shoku," in the motto to Li Po's poem "Leave-taking near Shoku" in *Cathay* [*P*, 138] [EH].

5. **Lir**: Old Celtic sea-god. Pound regards seals as being Lir's daughters [cf. chapter "Branwen the Daughter of Llyr" in *Mabinogion*, where Branwen means "White Crow"].

6. **Picasso**: The reference to Picasso's seal's eyes evokes the artist's faculty for changing the shape of the things he sees. In ancient mythology the seal is the animal most closely linked with Proteus, who among other things used to assume the shape of a seal [cf. 30 below].

7. **Eleanor**: Helen of Troy, also Elena, Tellus-Helena, Helen of Tyre, Tyndarida. Also Eleanor of Aquitaine [cf. 9 below].

8. **ἑλέναυς and ἑλέπτολις!**: H, *helenaus* and *heleptolis*, "ship-destroying and city-destroying." Aeschylus's puns on the name of Helen in *Agamemnon*, 689.

9. **Eleanor**: E. of Aquitaine, 1122-1204. Like Helen of Troy, Eleanor was the archetype of the femme fatale, inspiring both strife and poetry. She was the granddaughter

of Guillaume of Poitiers, 1071-1127, 9th Duke of Aquitaine, who, according to Pound, superimposed the music of Moresco Spain upon the poetry of S France, an important cultural synthesis of different ethnic elements such as Eleanor was also destined to bring about and which Pound too had hoped to achieve for America. Eleanor married Louis VII of France and accompanied him on a crusade to the Holy Land, where she allegedly had an affair with Saladin, the great Kurdish Moslem warrior, a tale invented by her enemies and spread, for instance, in the Chronique de Rains. Louis divorced her and a few months later she married Henry II of England, bringing him all Aquitaine as dowry. When Henry II proved untrue and even held Eleanor captive, she turned her sons, notably the "young king" Henry and Richard (later the Lion-Heart), against their father. Her political activities and the legal tangles resulting from her two marriages were the cause of the Hundred Years War between England and France. Thus, she was truly a "Helen," agent of both love and death.

10. Let her go . . .: [*Iliad* III, 139-160]. The fear that the elders of Troy, the old men (the husks of life), experienced when confronted with Helen's living but death-bringing beauty [7:3, 5, 32, 35, 37].

11. Schoeney . . .: Schoeneus, father of Atalanta who, like Helen, through her beauty caused the death of many men. Pound is misremembering Arthur Golding's spelling, Schoenyes, in his translation of Ovid [*Meta*. X, 566-707]. For Pound an instance of the metamorphosis and transmission of beauty by translation. Refractions of ephemeral beauty through time [cf. *LE*, 235-236; 7:29; 102/730].

12. Tyro: Daughter of Salmoneus. She became enamored of the divine river, Enipeus. Poseidon, at the mouth of the river, took on Enipeus's form, shed sleep upon her, and, while a dark wave rose like a mountain to screen him, raped her [*Od*. XI, 235-259].

13. Scios: Ancient Chios, modern Scio, Aegian island about 70 miles north and slightly east of Naxos.

14. Naxos: Largest island of the Cyclades, famous for its wine. The island was a center of the Dionysus cult [cf. *Meta*. III, 636-637, and Homeric Hymn to Dionysos].

15. young boy: The young god, Bacchus, Dionysus, Zagreus, Iacchus, Lyaeus, originally Cretan, god of wine, fertility, and ecstasy whose cult arose to challenge that of Apollo. He is on his way to Naxos.

16. vine-must: New wine.

17. King Pentheus: Grandson of Cadmus. Refusing to worship Dionysus he was torn to pieces by Dionysus's followers, the Maenads, led by Pentheus's mother, who wrenched off his head and carried it home in triumph. Acoetes is telling the story of his crew's attempt to kidnap the god as a warning to Pentheus.

18. Acoetes: A Lydian of humble parents, skilled in navigation, captain of the ship.

19. Lyaeus: Refers to Dionysus in his function as the god of wine and ecstasy.

20. Olibanum: L, "frankincense." The Romans believed Bacchus responsible for the use of incense in ritual [cf. Ovid, *Fasti* III, 727].

21. Lycabs and Medon: Other members of Odysseus's crew. Ovid lists more names.

22. dory: The *Zeus faber*, a kind of fish.

23. Tiresias: Theban seer. In Euripides' *Bacchae*, he appears with Cadmus on the way up the mountain to join the women in *orgia* and worship of the god. Given the power of prophecy, he advises Pentheus to worship the god also. Pentheus pays no heed [1:7].

24. Cadmus: Son of Phoenician King Agenor. Europa, sister of Cadmus, was carried off by Zeus, who took the form of a bull. Sent by his father to find her, Cadmus wandered as far as the oracle at Delphi, where he was given directions which led to the founding of Thebes. According to the myth the stones of the walls of Thebes rose to the rhythm of the music Amphion played on his lyre. The walls are conceived as the magical protective walls around the archetypal city which were traced in the air by ritual dance, music, and incantation, as were also the walls of the Knossian labyrinth, the walls of Troy, and the walls of Alba Longa [*Aeneid* V, 583-602]. Grandfather of Pentheus and father of Ino ["Ino Kadmaia" at 98/685, 102/728, 109/774; 4:4].

25. **Ileuthyeria**: Apparently an inadvertent conflation of Eileithyia, the goddess of childbirth, with *Eleutheria*, H, "freedom," a marine organism of the genus of bisexual jellyfishes. On Greek amphoras, where the goddess is sometimes depicted in company with Hermes, Apollo, and Ares attending Zeus as he is about to give birth to Dionysus, she is variously identified in Greek letters as Ileíthya [HIΛEIΘΥA] (cf. Eduard Gerhard, *Auserlesene griechische Vasenbilder*, Vol. I, Pl. IV, Berlin, 1840) and Ilíthyia, as she also appears in Horace, *Carm. Sec*. 14, and Ovid, *Meta*. IX, 283 [EH].

26. **Dafne**: Daphne, daughter of Peneus, a river-god. In headlong flight from the amorous Apollo, she invoked the aid of Peneus who transformed her into a laurel tree [*Meta*. I, 546-552]. Pound said: "a theme of Ovid—Dafne, my own myth, not changed into a laurel but into coral" [cf. Mary de Rachewiltz, *Discretions*, 159].

27. **So-shu**: [cf. 4 above].

28. **Poseidon**: Greek god of the sea. The reference is to the rape of Tyro [cf. 12 above].

29. **Hesperus**: Evening star sacred to Aphrodite. Always associated in Pound's mind with the nuptial hymns of Sappho and Catullus [cf. 79/488, 492].

30. **Proteus**: Sea-god who had power of metamorphosis and knowledge of past and future. In Aristophanes' *The Frogs* Dionysus and his servant Xanthias, descending into Hades in search of a "good poet," are greeted by the thunderous chorus of infernal frogs, which they try to drown out. Dionysus, first dressed up as Heracles, goes through a series of quick disguises. Speciality of Aristophanes' comedies: the hemichant, setting one part of the chorus against the other. That Pound was aware of the function of the hemichant in Aristophanes' plays, as well as in the Eleusinian Mysteries, is documented by an early poem: "Salve O Pontifex—for Swinburne; an hemi chaunt." In *LE*, 293-294, he praises S. for his "surging and leaping dactyllics" and "rhythm-building faculty," the very faculty that represents the horse or goat hindquarters of poetry, the centaur [cf. *LE*, 52].

CANTO III

Sources

R. Browning, *Sordello* III; *Cantar de mio Cid* (anon.); Luiz de Camoëns, *Os Lusíadas* III; G. D'Annunzio, *Notturno*, Milan, 1921; Catullus LXIV, 17-18; LXI, 13.

Background

EP, *SR*, 67-68, 218; "Cavalcanti" in *LE*, 149-160; "Terra Italica" in *SP*, 54-60; "Three Cantos" (2), in *Poetry*, X, 5, 1917, and in *Quia Pauper Amavi*; "Burgos: A Dream City of Old Castile" in *Book News Monthly*, Oct. 1906; "Lettere E 9 Cartoline Inedite" in *Nuova Corrente*, 5/6, 1956.

Exegeses

E. Glenn, *Analyst* XXV; CE, *Ideas*, 86-91 and passim; HK, *Era*, passim; GD, "Persephone's Ezra," and FR, "Pound, Joyce, and Flaubert: The Odysseans," both in EH, *Approaches*.

Glossary

1. **Dogana**: Customhouse in Venice. Gives striking view across the Grand Canal to buildings surrounding St. Mark's [see photograph, HK, *Era*, 418]. In earlier version, Pound responds to Browning's "I muse this on a ruined palace-step / At Venice" [*Sordello* III, 675] by "Your palace steps? / My stone seat was the Dogana's vulgarest curb."

2. **that year**: Prob. 1908, the year Pound went into exile. His lack of funds introduces the economic problem as a theme for the first time.

3. **"those girls"**: Echo of Browning's "Let stay those girls" [*Sordello* III, 698].

4. **one face**: Unidentified. Earlier version reads: "there was one flare, one face. / 'Twas all I ever saw, but it was real . . . . / And I can no more say what shape it was . . . / But she was young, too young."

5. **Buccentoro**: Bucentoro or Bucintoro, meaning "Golden Bark," a rowing club situated around the corner from the Dogana; originally, for some eight centuries, the name of the barge used by the Doges of Venice for the ceremony in which they "married" Venice to the sea by the act of dropping a ring into the Adriatic. In 1908 Pound heard the club members singing traditional Venetian songs [cf. 27/129].

6. **Stretti**: I, "in close embrace." From "La spagnuola" [I, "The Spanish Girl"], a Neapolitan song by Vicenzo de Chiara which was popular in the first half of the 20th century: "Stretti, stretti / nell'estasi d'amor / La spagnuola sa amar cosi / bocca a bocca la notte e il di" ["In close embrace, in close embrace / in love's ecstasy / the Spanish girl is that way when in love / mouth to mouth, night and day"] [cf. 26/121; 27/130].

7. **Morosini**: Aristocratic Venetian family. Name of a square and a palace. Earlier version reads: "And at Florian's under the North arcade / I have seen other faces, and had my rolls for breakfast. / Drifted at night and seen the lit, gilt crossbeams. / Glare from the Morosini."

8. **Koré's house**: In 1922 (*Dial*, Nov.) Pound translated a D'Annunzio line "La casa di Corè è abitata dai pavoni bianchi" in *Notturno* as: "In Koré's house there are now only white peacocks." D'Annunzio appears to refer thus to the neglected grounds of the Palazzo dei Leoni on the Grand Canal, which had become a rookery. (See *Notturno*, 105, 410, 443, 449, 480) Kore(H) daughter, i.e. Persephone, daughter of Demeter.

9. **Gods float in the azure air**: One of the "three sorts of blue" to which Pound at-

tached special significance, the azure stands for the continuum in which the gods exist, i.e., collective memory; sapphire, for personal memory; and cobalt, for oblivion [cf. 5:8; "Blandula, Tenella, Vagula"; and *Mauberley* in *P*].

10. Panisks: H, Paniskos. Little woodland Pans, half human and half goat [cf. "goatfoot" at 4/13].

11. dryas: L, ME, oak tree nymph that dies when the tree dies. Also dryad [cf. 76/452; 83/530].

12. maelid: H, *maliades* or *meliades,* nymphs of the apple tree [cf. 4/13; 79/489, 491].

13. The silvery . . . nipple: Not Poggio's exact words but an image easily evoked by a scene he witnessed at the baths in Baden, Switzerland, in the spring of 1416 and recorded in the well-known letter to his friend Niccolò de'Niccoli. Pound's imitation of this letter appeared under the title "Aux étuves de Weisbaden, A.D. 1451" [sic] in the *Little Review*, July 1917 [rpt. in *PD*, 98-103], indicating perhaps that he had read the French translation of the original. The ML text runs [*Opera Omnia*, Basle, 1538], with the ligatures omitted: "Quotidie ter aut quater balnea intrant, maiorem in his diei partem agentes, partim cantando, partim potando, partim choreas exercendo. Psallunt & iam in aquis paululum subsidendo. In quo iocundissimum est videre puellas iam maturas viro, iam plenis nubilās annis, facie splendida ac liberali, in Dearum habitum ac formam psallentes, modicas vestes retrorsum trahunt desuper aquam fluitantes, ut alteram Venerem extimares." ["They (members of both sexes who are privileged by family connections or high favor) go to the pools three or four times daily, dividing their time among singing, drinking, dancing. Even in the water they play an instrument. There is nothing more delighful than to watch the young ladies, some just turning nubile and others in full bloom, with their beautiful faces, frank looks, shaped and draped like the goddess, playing an instrument while leaning back in the water with their shift, which they have pulled back slightly, floating behind them so that they look like a winged Venus." Like all ML, the text contains various ambiguities. In particular, *habitus* can alternatively mean "status" or "bearing." Since Pound's figures, however, are not reclining in the water, he may have conflated Poggio's young ladies with the nude Nereids rising up out of the spindrift in Catullus LXIV, 18 [HK, *Era*, 143]: "viderunt . . . mortales oculis nudato corpore Nymphas / nutricum tenus extantes e gurgite cano" [EH].

14. Poggio: Gian Francesco P. Bracciolini, 1380-1459, Renaissance Italian humanist who rediscovered many of the lost Latin classics.

15. gray steps: From Discarded Canto I (June 1917): "gray gradual steps / Lead up beneath flat sprays of heavy cedars, / Temple of teak wood, and the gilt-brown arches / Triple in tier, banners woven by wall, / Fine screens depicted, sea waves curled high, / Small boats with gods upon them, / Bright flame above the river!" The steps lead to the ancestral temple, dedicated to the Duke of Chou, which Confucius entered for the first time at the beginning of his service with the Chi family, which ruled the principality of Lu, his native state [cf. *Lun-yü* III, 15; 13/58] [EH].

16. My Cid . . . Burgos: S, my "commander" or "Lord," a title given by the Moors to Ruy Díaz (Rodrigo Díaz de Bivar, 1040?-1099), hero of the Spanish epic, *Cantar de mío Cid*, ca. 1140. Díaz was exiled by Alfonso VI for bearing false witness against him. Pound quotes from Part I ("The Exile") of the epic. Like Odysseus and Sigismundo Malatesta, Ruy Díaz was resourceful, adventurous, and cunning: "a live man among duds," a "glorious bandit," the factive personality. He lived and was buried in Burgos, capital of Burgos Province in Old Castile.

17. **Una niña . . .** : S, "a little girl nine years old." An incident from the biography of El Cid conflated with personal memory of Pound's 1906 visit to Spain [cf. "Burgos: A Dream City of Old Castile," *Book News Monthly*, Oct. 1906; 80/493, 95/645].

18. **voce tinnula**: L, "with ringing voice." From Catullus LXI, 13 [cf. 4/15; 28/137].

19. **Bivar**: Or Vivar, variant of name of the Cid.

20. **Raquel and Vidas**: Two Jewish moneylenders. The Cid, in order to pay his knights and followers, tricked the moneylenders into believing that two trunks, loaded with sand, really contained gold. They lent him 600 marks, accepting the trunks, which they promised not to open, for security.

21. **menie**: ME, "retinue," but here referring to a private army.

22. **Valencia**: A region of E Spain occupied by the Moors from 714 to 1094, when they were expelled by the Cid.

23. **Ignez da Castro**: Inés de Castro, d. 1355. Pedro, son and heir of Alphonso IV of Portugal, secretly married Inés after his wife Constance died. Pound writes: "Her position was the cause of jealousy, and of conspiracy; she was stabbed in the act of begging clemency from the then reigning Alphonso IV. When Pedro succeeded to the throne, he had her body exhumed, and the court did homage, the grandees of Portugal passing before the double throne of the dead queen and her king, and kissing that hand which had been hers. A picture of the scene hangs in the new gallery at Madrid, in the series of canvasses which commemorate the splendid horrors of the Spanish past" [*SR*, 218]. Inés is a Kore figure untimely forced into Hades, representing the overlapping of the past into the present, a discrepancy between the fine image held in the mind and the actual fact of the rotting corpse from the past, as may occur when time, for a mind like Pedro's, has stood still. [cf. 30/148; Camoëns, *Os Lusíadas* III].

24. **Drear waste**: Decay of the splendors of the Renaissance during 400 or more years of an increasingly usurious civilization.

25. **Mantegna**: Andrea M., 1431-1506, Renaissance painter who spent his last years in Mantua under the patronage of the Gonzagas, painting the frescoes in the ducal palace and in the countryside at Goito, whence the Sordello family came. Mantegna also painted the fresco of "Gonzaga and his heirs and concubines" mentioned in the Usura Canto [45/229] as a prime example of the quality of art in a nonusurious era.

26. **Nec Spe Nec Metu**: L, "neither by hope nor by fear"– to achieve anything, you must act. Motto in the rooms of Isabella d'Este Gonzaga, 1474-1539, in the ducal palace at Mantua.

CANTO IV

Sources

Euripides, *Troades*, opening scene; Virgil, *Aeneid* II, III; Pindar, *Olympian* II; Catullus LXI; Sappho 93D, 117D; Ovid, *Meta.* II, III, IV, V, VI, XII; Horace, *Odes* IV, xii, 5; Camille Chabaneau, *Les Biographies des Troubadours en Langue Provençale*, Toulouse, 1885; Arnaut Daniel, "Lancan son passat li giure"; R.

Browning, *Sordello* V, 163; Fenollosa Notebooks (inedit.), University of Virginia Library, "Takasago" and "Sō Gyoku" (= Sung Yü); Herodotus, *Historiae* I, 8-14 and 98; Guido Cavalcanti, Sonnet 35.

Background

EP, *ABCR*, 47-48, 56; *PM*, 56; *P*, "The Coming of War: Actaeon," "Provincia Deserta," "The Unmoving Cloud"; *LE*, 49, 52; *SR*, 44, 87-100; *T*, 95, 221-222, 246-247, 269 ff.; *L*, 178 (to F. E. Schelling); J. G. Frazer, *The Golden Bough*; Virgil, *Eclogues*; Philip Grover, *Ezra Pound: The London Years*, Sheffield University Library, 1976.

Exegeses

E. Glenn, *Analyst* I and addenda in II, III, IV; WB, *Rose*; CB-R, GD, Dekker, and B. de Rachewiltz, all in EH, *Approaches*; HK, *Era*, 6-7, 215, 375, 417; R. Bush, *Genesis*, 145; EH, *Pai*, 7.

Glossary

1. **Palace . . .** : Scene at the opening of Euripides' *The Trojan Women* recalling the burning of the archetypal city [cf. also *Aeneid* II, 309-310, 431; III, 3—Aeneas setting out to rebuild destroyed Troy].

2. **Anaxiforminges**: H, from *Anaxiphormigges hymnoi*, "Hymns that are lords of the lyre," beginning of Pindar's "Olympian Ode II," the power of poetry and recorded words. The double gamma was pronounced "ng."

3. **Aurunculeia**: Vinia A., bride praised in Catullus, *Epithalamium* LXI, 86-87. Catullus's marriage hymns echo Sappho's *Epithalamia* [cf. 5/17].

4. **Cadmus of Golden Prows**: Eponymous hero and founder of Thebes [2:24]. Like Odysseus, Cadmus set out into the unknown. He was sent by the king, his father, to discover the fate of his sister Europa, who had been abducted by Zeus. The walls of lower Thebes rose to the sound of Amphion's lyre [cf. 62:33; 90/605; 93/630; 107/761].

5. **Beat, beat, . . .** : Variation on the line in Whitman's "Drum Taps": "Beat, beat, whirr, pound . . ." [cf. Sappho 93D].

6. **Choros . . .** : L, "Chorus of nymphs" [Sappho 93D].

7. **black cock**: The cockcrow announces the rebirth of Aphrodite from the sea-foam and a rebirth of the Renaissance [FR].

8. **Ityn**: H, Itys, son of Procne and Tereus, king of Thrace [Ovid, *Meta*. VI, 652 ("Ityn huc accersite!")]. Procne killed her son Itys in order to cook and feed him to Tereus after she had discovered that he had raped Philomela, her sister, and cut out her tongue so that she could not tell what he had done. Procne and Philomela afterward escaped the vengeance of Tereus by turning respectively into a swallow and a nightingale. Philomela, the nightingale, is said to cry out the name Itys, whose death she had caused: "Itu! Itu!" [Ovid, *Meta*. VI, 426-674; cf. 78/477; 82/525].

9. Et ter flebiliter: L, "And thrice with tears" [see Horace, *Odes* IV, xii, 5].

10. Cabestan: Guillems de Cabestanh or Cabestaing, an ascetic troubadour to whom, ironically, an ancient Celtic legend was attached according to which he became the lover of the Lady Seremonda, wife of Ramon, lord of the castle of Rossillon, whom he served. According to Chabaneau, Pound's source, Raymond killed Cabestanh and served his cooked heart to Seremonda [cf. *SR*, 44]. The original legend was also attached to the Châtelain de Couci in France and the German minnesinger Reinmar von Brennenberg; see also Boccaccio, *Decamerone* IV, 9 [EH].

11. Rhodez: Earlier spelling of Rodez, a high plateau overlooking the sinuous river Aveyron. It has a cathedral whose original structure was built in 1274, and two towers remaining from the old fortification. Pound visited R on July 2, 1912, and a second time with his wife Dorothy sometime between June 6 and August 15, 1919 [cf. "The Gypsy" in *P*, 119].

12. Actaeon: By accident while hunting, he came upon the naked Diana bathing in the pool of Gargaphia. She changed him into a stag in which form he was pursued and killed by his own companions and dogs.

13. Poictiers: Refers to the church of St. Hilaire in Poitiers [cf. *GK*, 109]. Visited by Pound in 1912.

14. Diana: Or "Delia," virgin goddess of Delos, called *kallĭastrágălos* ["with fine ankles"]; the Greek Artemis; "Lucina," goddess of childbirth; "Selena," goddess of the moon; of Cretan origin. Goddess of the moon, mountains, mountain lakes, woods, the hunt, and of all wildlife, the incarnation of untamed nature and its self-healing powers of renewal (hence associated with *hsin* in 110/780). Like Persephone (with whom she is associated at 76/457), Diana is also the goddess of the double gates of birth and death. Her images at Ephesus do not show her as the chaste virgin goddess, but as the Great Mother [cf. *SR*, 95-96] suckling the newborn dead at her numerous breasts. This Ephesian image of Diana later merges into the image and cult of the Virgin Mary [cf. 80/500-501], who is also depicted standing on the moon's sickle with the baby in her arms. The tradition of virgin birth is likewise linked with Artemis, who annually renewed her virginity by bathing in the pool of Gargaphia. What the "Artemis type" meant to Pound personally is expressed in *PM*, 56.

15. Vidal: The troubadour Peire Vidals of Tolosa [cf. "Piere Vidal Old" in *P*]. He dressed in wolfskins to woo his lady, Loba of Penautier, an Albigensian noblewoman. *Loba* translates as "she-wolf." Like Actaeon, Vidal in pursuit of his love becomes the prey of his own hounds. Pound translates the legend from the Provençal *vida* of Chabaneau. His English version is in *SR*, 178.

16. Pergusa: A lake [see Ovid, *Meta.* V, 386]. A deep pool suggestive of the underworld near Enna (Sicily), where Persephone was carried off by Dis [1:14, "Avernus"]. Also a parallel to Lake Nemi, where there was a temple dedicated to Diana [cf. 74/438; 77/467; *The Golden Bough*].

17. Gargaphia: A deep valley and spring in Boeotia, where Artemis was surprised by Actaeon while bathing [Ovid, *Meta.* III, 156].

18. Salmacis: [Ovid, *Meta.* IV, 285-388]. Spring near Halikarnassos (Asia Minor) belonging to the water nymph Salmacis, who attempted unsuccessfully to rape the boy Hermaphroditos.

19. The empty armour . . . cygnet moves: Cygnus or "swan," the son of Neptune, comes up against Achilles, son of Thetis (a marine goddess), when defending Troy. Under the spell of Neptune, Cygnus proves invulnerable even to Achilles. But when Achilles finally throws him to the ground, crushing him bodily, his battered armor is found to be empty, Cygnus having escaped in the guise of a swan.

20. e lo soleills plovil: P, "thus the light rains." From Pound's rendering of Arnaut Daniel's *on lo soleills plovil*, from the last line of the song "Lancan son passat li giure," which he had earlier given as "where the rain falls from the sun" [*LE*. 122-123]. There it is meant to pinpoint an absurdity. For Pound, however, it turns into the important canto motif of the light-water-stone progression which finally ends in crystal, i.e., the transmutation of the fluid transparency of subjective experience into the objective solidity of stone through poetry, or, in another relevant terminology, the alchemist's fabrication of the philosopher's stone by palingenesis [cf. *LE*, 49; *SR*, 93-94; 23/109; 54/449; 76/456-457, 459; 91/611-613, 617; 116/795].

21. Ply over ply: A recurrent simile in Pound's poetry and prose originating superficially in Browning's *Sordello* V, 161-172: "The other was a scaffold. See him stand / Buttressed upon his mattock, Hildebrand / Of the huge brainmask welded ply o'er ply / As in a forge; it buries either eye / White and extinct, that stupid brow; teeth clenched, / The neck tight-corded, too, the chin deep-trenched, / As if a cloud enveloped him while fought / Under its shade, grim prizers, thought with thought / At dead-lock, agonizing he, until / The victor thought leap radiant up, and Will, / The slave with folded arms and drooping lids / They fought for, lean forth flame-like as it bids." It should be noted, however, that Browning's image of the skull of Gregory VII welded "ply o'er ply" within the scaffolding has little in common with Pound's, which recalls the layers of cloud described in "To-Em-Mei's 'The Unmoving Cloud' " (*P*, 142, a poem by T'ao Ch'ien, which begins: "The clouds have gathered, and gathered, / and the rain falls and falls, / The eight ply of the heavens / are all folded into one darkness." HK (in *Spectrum*, IX, 1967, 35-36) has shown that the last two lines derive from Fenollosa's mistranslation of *hachi hoi do kon* as "eight surface same dark," where "eight surface" should read "eight points of the compass." Proceeding from here it is not too difficult to see how the mistake may have crept in. *Hachi hoi* (*pa mien* in the original Chinese text) is written 八面. Fenollosa correctly translated 八 as "eight" and 面 as "surface," overlooking, however, that the two characters, used together, form a compound expression meaning "eight points of the compass." Pound's rendering "ply over ply" echoes Mallarmé's *pli selon pli* in *Rémemoration d'amis belges* and *Autre Éventail*, where it describes the unfolding and folding of a fan [EH.]

22. Takasago: The title of a Japanese Nō play named after the legendary pine tree growing on the shore of Takasago Bay in S Honshu. The subject of the play is a Philemon and Baucis story of a couple growing old together, the couple being symbolized by two pine trees, one growing at Takasago and the other at Sumiyoshi [cf. 21/99: the "old man sweeping leaves"]. Pound, following Fenollosa, sees the Japanese Nō play as a parallel to the Greek drama [cf. *T*, 222, 246-247, 269 ff.] [EH].

23. Isé: A bay famous for its pine grove at Ano, mentioned toward the end of the Japanese Nō play entitled *Tamura*. Because of its association with pine trees, Pound confuses Isé with Sumiyoshi in Settsu Province, which is mentioned in the Nō play *Takasago* (see above) as the location of the legendary pine tree which forms a pair with the one growing at Takasago [EH].

24. The water whirls: Pound wrote in 1913: "We might come to believe that the thing that matters in art is a sort of energy, something more or less like electricity or radioactivity, a force transfusing, welding, and unifying. A force rather like water when it spurts up through very bright sand and sets it in swift motion" [*LE*, 49].

25. "Tree of the Visages": Apparently a mistranslation of *seimei zyu* (生命樹), meaning "trees of life," a synonym for "pine trees" used in the Nō play *Takasago*. Fenollosa would seem to have misread the second character 命 as 臉, meaning "face," which would explain Pound's "Visages" [cf. 22 above] [EH].

26. **Gourdon**: Another recollection of Pound's walking tour through Provence in 1912 as recorded in "Provincia Deserta" ["I have seen the torch-flames, high-leaping"].

27. **Hymenaeus Io . . .** : L, "Hymen, hail! Hymen, hail Hymen!" [Catullus LXI; cf. 3 above; 2:29]. Hymen is the god of marriage and saffron is his color.

28. **Aurunculeia**: [cf. 3 above].

29. **scarlet flower**: Fragment of another wedding hymn. This image of the virgin's loss of maidenhood on her wedding night is paralleled by the much used topos of Provençal and other medieval poetry of the knight being reminded of his beloved by blood drops in the snow [cf. 6/23; Sappho 117D].

30. **So-Gyoku**: Sō Gyoku. Japanese form of name of Chinese poet, Sung Yü, 4th century B.C., author of "Rhymeprose on the Wind" (Wen-Hsûan VII, 13, la) in which King Hsiang of Ch'u and the poet discuss the difference between the male and the female wind. Pound's source was the Fenollosa Notebooks. Arthur Waley's translation is to be found in *170 Chinese Poems*, 1922, 41.

31. **Hsiang**: King of Ch'u referred to in Sung Yü, "Rhymeprose on the Wind," noted above.

32. **Ecbatan**: Founded by the Median Deïoces (Herodotus I, 98), the city of Ecbatana (Agbatana, now Hamadan) was meticulously mapped out to correspond in every detail with the plan of the universe, esp. the firmament. Ecbatana is archetypal as a concept of perfect human order, a reconciliation of nature and civilization, as paralleled in other cantos by Ithaca, Troy, Mt. Segur, Thebes, Rome, Wagadu, and later Trinovant (= London). The building of the terraces of Ecbatana in correspondence with the seven planets reflects the late megalithic concept of the Mesopotamian ziggurat (or Tower of Babylon) [cf. 5/17; 74/425, 434; 80/510].

33. **Danaë**: Acrisius, king of Argos and father of Danaë, also tried to manipulate and control the elemental forces of nature. Having been told by an oracle that his daughter's son would kill him, he imprisoned Danaë at the top of a bronze tower. But Zeus, seeing her from above, visited her in a shower of golden light that poured into her lap [cf. 92/619]. As a result, Danaë bore him a son, the culture-hero Perseus. Learning of the birth, Acrisius cast Danaë and Perseus adrift in a sea chest. After many adventures Perseus returns and accidentally kills his grandfather. At the back of this myth is the prehistorical memory, recorded by Greek mythologists, of the transition from the fertility rites of the earth to the later cult of heaven (light = sun, moon, and stars), the great goddess representing the earth religion and the later male deities the sky religions of light [cf. 5/17]. This transition is reflected architectonically in the Tower of Babylon (the Mesopotamian ziggurat). To symbolize the new concept of the ritual consummation of a marriage of heaven and earth, a young girl was placed at the top of the tower to await the coming of the god. The golden rain of light into Danaë's lap thus symbolized the sexual consummation of the marriage of earth and heaven in the form of rain and light [cf. 32 above].

34. **grey stone posts**: [3:15.]

35. **Père Henri Jacques**: According to Pound, "a French priest (as a matter of fact he is a Jesuit)" [*L*, 180.]

36. **Sennin**: J, Japanese word for Chinese *hsien*, a genie or genies. Pound in re *sennins*: "I don't see that they are any worse than Celtic Sidhe" [*L*, 180]. The literal Chinese translation of *sennin* is, however, *hsin-jen*, meaning a hermit or "philosopher" (sing. or pl.) who has attained immortality by resisting desire [cf. "Sennin Poem by Kakuhaku," *P*, 139].

37. Rokku: Wrongly transcribed Japanese translation of a Chinese place-name, poss: Taipeh (Taihoku) in Taiwan. According to Pound, "either a mountain or an island" [*L*, 180].

38. Polhonac: Viscount Heraclius III of Polhonac, fl. 1180, was persuaded by the troubadour Guillems de San Leidier (also known as Guilhem de Saint Didier) to sing to his wife a love song he had composed for her after she had refused to accept him as her knight except at the invitation of her husband. Pound comments: "Guillaume St. Leider even went so far as to get the husband of his lady to do the seductive singing" [*LE*, 94]. Ironically, in the *trobar clus* tradition, the husband did not know he was assisting in the seduction of his wife.

39. Gyges: Bodyguard of King Candaules who, for cause, killed the king and married the queen at her behest [Herodotus I, 8-14]. Gyges is a subject rhyme to the story of Polhonac, although without a happy ending, the motivation being different. Candaules, king of Lydia, secretly introduced Gyges into his bedroom so that he could admire the naked beauty of his wife. But his wife, on discovering his scheme to show her off possessively as a sex object, was offended; she seduced Gyges and made him kill Candaules and marry her.

40. Thracian platter: The platter calls to mind the story of Tereus, king of Thrace [cf. 8, 9, above].

41. Garonne: River in Provence recollected from Pound's walking tour in 1919.

42. "Saave! . . . sa'ave Regina!": L. "Hail! . . . hail Queen!" Pound, in a letter to his father (ca. 1919): "This worm of the procession had three large antennae, and I hope to develop the motive later, text clearly states that this vermiform object circulated in the crowd at the Church of St. Nicholas in Toulouse. No merely mediaeval but black central African superstitution [sic] and voodoo energy squalling infant, general murk and epileptic religious hog wash with chief totem magnificently swung over whole" [YC].

43. Adige: Italian river that rises in the Alps and flows into the Adriatic N of the Po delta.

44. Stefano: S. da Verona, ca. 1374-1451, painter of the *Madonna in hortulo*.

45. Madonna in hortulo: I, "Madonna in the Little Garden," a painting by Stefano seen by Pound in 1912 in the Palazzo Laveozzola Pompei, situated "across the Adige" from San Zeno. It is now in the Castel Vecchio at Verona. Confused by Pound with Cavalcanti's lady of Sonnet 35 [cf. *T*, 95], in which Cavalcanti explains that the miracles worked by the painting of the Madonna of San Michele in Orto (in Florence) are owing to her having been painted with his lady's face.

46. Cavalcanti: Guido C., 1250-1300, Tuscan poet and friend of Dante [cf. *LE*, 149-200; 36/177 ff.; *SR* 91]: "The rise of Mariolatry, its pagan lineage, the romance of it, find modes of expression which verge overeasily into the speech . . . of Our Lady of Cyprus . . . as we see so splendidly in Guido's 'Una figura della donna miae [sic].' " Pound corrected *miae* to *mia* in *T*, 94.

47. Centaur: Symbol of the enduring presence of the pagan elemental gods and demigods–as in Cavalcanti's sonnet. [cf. *LE*, 52: "Poetry is a centaur. The thinking word-arranging, clarifying faculty must move and leap with the energizing, sentient, musical faculties. It is precisely the difficulty of this amphibious existence that keeps down the census record of good poets"].

48. arena: The arena at Verona, to which Pound refers in order to define his position as onlooker throughout the ages and levels of time [cf. also 11/50; 12/53; 29/145; 78/481; 80/505].

CANTO V

Sources

Herodotus, Historiae I, 96-103; Dante, *Par.* XVIII, 100, 108, *Inf.* V, 107, *Rime* I, 1; John Heydon, *The English Physitians Guide: or a Holy Guide*, 1662; J. A. Symonds, *In the Key of Blue*, 1893; Giordano Bruno, *De gli eroici furori* I, V, and II, I; Catullus LXI, 86, 131; LXII, 20, 26, 32, 35; Sappho/Aldington, 98D, 120D, 132aD, 133D, 137D; F. J. M. Raynouard, *Biographie des troubadours*, 1820, Vol. V of *Choix des poésies originales des troubadours*; Ida Farnell, *The Lives of the Troubadours*, London, 1896; Camille Chabaneau, *Les Biographies des Troubadours en Langue Provençale*, Toulouse, 1885; Robert Browning, "Meeting at Night" and "Parting at Morning"; A. H. Mathew, *The Life and Times of Rodrigo Borgia, Pope Alexander VI*, 1910; Benedetto Varchi, *Storia Fiorentina* (1527-1538), III, 262-263; Aeschylus, *Agamemnon*, 1344-1345; Homer, *Iliad* I, 159, 225; William Roscoe, *The Life and Pontificate of Leo the Tenth*, 1893; Martial V, 37.

Background

EP, *P*, "Coitus," "Phanopoeia," "Provincia Deserta," "Near Perigord, II," "Ἱμέρρω," "Horae Beatae Inscriptio," "Blandula, Tenella, Vagula"; *Mauberley* (Envoi, Medallion, The Age Demanded, IV); *ABCR*, 47-48; *GK*, 128, 223, 225; *LE*, 95-97, 99, 240; Iamblichus, *On the Mysteries of the Egyptians, Chaldeans, and Assyrians*, trans. Thomas Taylor, 3d ed., London, 1968; Porphyry, *De Occasionibus*, in Marsilio Ficino, *Opera Omnia* II, Paris, 1641, fol. 1931.

Exegeses

D. H. Tritschler, *Analyst* V; J. Drummond in *Ezra Pound* (symposium, ed. P. Russell); JE, *Mauberley*, 78; D. R. Stuart, "Modernistic Critics and Translators," *Princeton University Library Chronicle*, XI; HK, *Era*, 58, 64-66; F. Moramarco, "Schiavoni . . . ," and EH, "Schiavoni . . . ," *Pai*, 4-1; S. M. Libera, "Casting His Gods Back into the NOUS," *Pai*, 2-3; CFT, in *Pai*, 6-3, 359.

Glossary

1. **Ecbatan**: Ecbatana (Agbatana, now Hamadan), on the Iranian plateau in N Media, founded, according to Herodotus I, 98, by Deioces as capital of Median Empire [4:32].

2. **The bride** [4:33]. The additional relevance here is that the transition from the fertility rites of the earth cult to the cult of the sky and the heavenly bodies marks the beginnings of astronomy and the creation of the calendar, i.e., the measuring of time by observing the stars.

3. **viae stradae**: L, "streets."

4. **and North was Egypt . . . water-wheels**: As it leaves the Nubian Desert on its way northward to Egypt, the Nile cuts through flat barren land which is irrigated to support a small nomadic population.

5. **Iamblichus**: fl. 4th century A.D.; Greek, Neoplatonic light philosopher, his light denoting the oneness, the single principle from which the plurality of things derive ("measureless seas and stars"). Presumed author of *On the Mysteries of the Egyptians, Chaldeans and Assyrians* (trans. Thomas Taylor, Chiswick, 1821; London, 1968). "Iamblichus' light" refers to his teaching: " . . . the whole world being partible, is divided about the one and impartible light of the Gods. But this light is everywhere one and the same whole and is impartibly present with all things that are able to participate of it" [ibid., 46]. The idea of human participation in divine creativity outlined here provides a justification of divination in Iamblichus's teaching and also has important sexual implications for *The Cantos*: "We say that the erection of the *phalli* is a certain sign of prolific power, which, through this, is called forth to the generative energy of the world. On which account, also, many *phalli* are consecrated in the spring, because then the whole world receives from the gods the power which is productive of all generation" [ibid., 53].

6. **ciocco**: I, "log." The game of striking a burning log and counting the sparks that fly up was used in fortune-telling, i.e., foretelling the future as a safeguard against time's treachery [cf. *Par.* XVIII, 100].

7. **Et omniformis**: L, "and omniform." From "Omnis intellectus est omniformis" ["Every intellect is capable of assuming every shape"], the caption of the 3-line item 10 in Marsilio Ficino's [21:10] interpretation of Porphyry's *De Occasionibus, sive causis ad intelligibilia nos ducentibus*, in Ficino, *Opera Omnia* II, fol. 1931. Pound implies in Discarded Canto 3 (1917) that he came across the quotation in John Heydon's *Holy Guide*: "Let us hear John Heydon! / '*Omniformis* / Omnis intellectus est'—thus he begins, by spouting half of Psellus. / (Then comes a note, my assiduous commentator: / Not Psellus *De Daemonibus*, but Porphyry's *Chances*, / In the thirteenth chapter, that 'every intellect is omniform')" [cf. 74/425-426, 430; 80/499; *Pai*, 6 (1977), 360] [EH].

8. **Topaz**: For Pound the color of Hymen, just as gold, yellow, saffron, amber, and orange symbolize erotic love and sexual union. The three sorts of blue represent three different dimensions of time: azure stands for the continuum in which the gods exist, i.e., the collective memory; sapphire, for personal memory; cobalt, for oblivion [cf. *P*, *Mauberley*: Envoi, Medallion, The Age Demanded, IV; "Blandula, Tenella, Vagula," "Horae Beatae Inscriptio"; and Canto III]. The "three sorts of blue" is a literal quotation from J. A. Symonds, *In the Key of Blue* (1893), where the author describes how he makes Augusto, his young Venetian friend, pose "dressed in three sorts of blue," which inspires him to write a series of poems to Augusto as "a symphony in

blues," referred to variously as "triple blues" and "triple azures." Symonds, however, appreciates the colors esthetically, whereas Pound uses them symbolically [see 1:29, "Orichalchi"; 3:9, "azure"].

9. **barb of time**: Perhaps an allusion to Giordano Bruno's motto *vincit instans* ("the instant triumphs"), of which Bruno says that the creative instant or inspiration is a barb of light which pierces the mind to give one a totally new perception beyond all mere logic chopping. This links up with Pound's notions regarding the "luminous detail" [cf. *SP*, 21-23].

10. **fire . . . and vision**: Reference to *Par.* XVIII, 108, the vision coming from the fire and sparks forming the head of the eagle, symbol of the so-called Holy Roman Empire and of Justice. According to Iamblichus [cf. 5 above], the sign of divine possession, and therefore also of poetic inspiration, is a divine fire: "the presence of the fire of the gods, and a certain ineffable species of light, externally accede to him who is possessed, . . . they wholly fill him, have dominion over and circularly comprehend him on all sides, so that he is not able to exert any one proper energy" [op. cit., 125; cf. *GK*, 223-224: "Iamblichus on the fire of the gods, tou ton theon pyros, etc. which comes down into a man and produces superior ecstasies, feelings of regained youth, super-youth and so forth"; cf. also 23/107, "God's fire"].

11. **gold-yellow, saffron. . . . The roman shoe**: [cf. 8 above, 4:3; Catullus LXI].

12. **shuffling feet**: [Catullus LXI].

13. **Da nuces!**: L, "Give nuts!" [Catullus LXI, 131]. An implied reference to the bridegroom's betrayal of his former boy concubine, who is now summarily told to "give nuts" to the young boys. The distribution of nuts in the street to celebrate a marriage was an old Roman custom.

14. **Sextus**: Prob. a reference to *Homage to Sextus Propertius* VII, suggesting that Catullus and S. Propertius, being contemporaries, may both have known Aurunculeia.

15. **Hesperus**: L, "evening star" [Catullus LXII, 20, 26, 32, 35; 2:29].

16. **older song**: [cf. Sappho 120D, 132aD, 133D, which are older than the Catullus references noted above]. Pound repeatedly associates the poetic techniques of Sappho and Catullus so that their names often crop up together.

17. **Lydia . . . Sardis**: Cf. Sappho 98D and 137D via translation of Aldington, where Atthis is denounced for having turned from Sappho to Andromeda.

18. **"In satieties"**: [cf. Sappho 137D]. "Atthis, you grew fed up with being with me in your thoughts" [cf. HK, *Era*, 54-71].

19. **Atthis unfruitful**: [cf. Sappho 98D]. Sappho is betrayed by her lover Atthis. The word "unfruitful" is owing to Richard Aldington's translation, in which the Aeolian ἀγάνας ["gentle"] is misread as ἄγονος ["unfruitful"] [cf. *P*, Ἰμέρρω].

20. **Mauleon**: Savaric de M., d. 1236, seneschal of Peiteu [F, Poitou], professional soldier and poet, patron of Gausbertz de Poicebot and other troubadours [cf. *LE*, 95, 99; 48/243].

21. **Poicebot . . .** : Gausbertz de Puegsibot [F, Poicebot], a monk who became a troubadour. Roaming in search of sexual adventures, he believes his wife to be safely at home with the rest of his possessions, but finds her drifting like himself, the first to offer herself to him in a brothel, matching his betrayal with her own. "And for this grief he ceased to sing and to compose" [cf. *LE*, 96; 48/243].

22. **romerya**: P, *romeria*, lit. "pilgrimage," fig. "roaming, roving" ("for desire of woman he [the monk Poicebot] went forth from the monastery") [*LE*, 95].

23. **Lei fassa furar a del**: P, wrong transcription of *se laisset ad el* ("yielded herself to

him"), a line referring to Peire de Maensac in Raynouard's *Biographie*. Pound conflates two stories: Gausbertz de Poicebot's wife was seduced by an English knight who, after abducting her, "let her go to the dogs," whereas Peire de M. seduced the wife of Bernart de Tierci who "let herself go" ("yielded herself / furar ad el"). The juxtaposition points up the opposing attitudes of the two troubadours to sex and property: the possessive Gausbertz de Poicebot, whose concern for property was already indicated in the part of the story referring to Savaric de Mauleon, loses all, including his creative powers, whereas Peire de M., careless of property, gains all and also keeps the woman he abducted [cf. *LE*, 96-97].

24. **Sea-change**: Another symbol of time. Perhaps an echo of "Suffer a sea-change / Into something rich and strange" [*Tempest*, I, ii, 464].

25. **Hard night, and parting at morning**: A combination of the titles of Browning's two poems, "Meeting at Night" and "Parting at Morning."

26. **Pieire de Maensac**: Peire de M. Peire and his brother Austors had too small a patrimony for both to live on, so they agreed, by means unknown (Pound invents the story of the tossed coin), that Austors should take the castle and Peire should become a troubadour [cf. "Provincia Deserta," where Peire "set on the high way to sing"]. The theme of possessiveness versus the free unencumbered poetic spirit is thus exemplified in the story of the two brothers [cf. *LE*, 96-97; 23/108-109].

27. **dreitz hom**: P, "an upstanding fellow" [*LE*, 97].

28. **Troy in Auvergnat**: The drama of ancient Troy paralleled on a smaller scale in Auvergnat, the territory of the Dalfin of Alvernhe, who protected Peire de Maensac and the wife of Bernart de Tierci from her irate husband [cf. 23, 26, 29, 30, 31]. Not a reference to Troyes in Département Aube.

29. **Menelaus**: Helen of Troy's husband, here used with reference to Bernart de Tierci.

30. **Tyndarida**: H, "Daughter of Tyndareus." The wife of Bernart de Tierci is here compared with Helen of Troy, daughter of Leda and Zeus, Leda being wife to Tyndareus, king of Sparta [2:8; "Provincia Deserta"; 23/108-109].

31. **Dauphin**: The Dalfin of Alvernhe, who protected de Maensac and the wife of de Tierci from her husband when he came after them "in the manner of the golden Menelaus" [cf. *LE*, 97].

32. **John Borgia**: Giovanni B., Duke of Gandia, son of Pope Alexander VI and Vanozza Catanei ("Vanoka" in 20/95), and younger brother of Cesare and Lucrecia Borgia. He was murdered on the night of June 14, 1497, in Rome and his body was thrown into the Tiber [cf. *Pai*, 4-1, 101 ff]. The element of treason arises here between brothers, Cesare having been suspected (wrongly) of having had Giovanni murdered.

33. **Varchi**: Benedetto V., 1503-1565, Italian classical scholar, wrote a history of Florence covering the years 1527-1538 [*Storia Fiorentina*, first printed 1721], in which the ruling Medici come in for objective criticism. Varchi is here turning over in his mind the possible motive behind the near-fratricidal murder of Alessandro Medici by his libertarian friend and cousin Lorenzo Medici. The juxtaposition of the Borgia and Medici murders is linked in turn with the murder of Caesar by Brutus, his protégé and supposed friend.

34. **Brutus**: Lorenzo was compared with the tyrannicide Brutus by his contemporaries.

35. **Σίγα μαλ' αὖθις δευτὲραν!**: H, "Silence once more a second time." Lines 1344-1345 of Aeschylus's *Agamemnon* jumbled together: "*Leader of chorus*: Silence! Hark! Who cries he has been struck a mortal blow? *Agamemnon*: Again, I have been struck a

second time." Agamemnon, returning home to his wife Clytemnestra after the long war years before Troy, gets into the warm bath she has prepared. There she stabs him ["bumped off in his bath," 96/652] [see also "Atreides" (Agamemnon, being of the line of Atreus) at 8/32, 82/523, 89/602].

36. **"Dog-eye!!"**: A reference to Achilles' description of Agamemnon as "dog-eyed" or "dog-faced" (*Iliad* I, 159, 225). The tyrannicide Lorenzo, who was compared by contemporaries with Brutus, is compared here with Achilles; Alessandro is compared with Agamemnon [cf. *LE*, 250, "the dog-faced, chicken-hearted Agamemnon"].

37. **Benedetto**: B. Varchi [cf. 33 above].

38. **Se pia? O empia?**: I, "Whether noble / Or ignoble?" [Varchi III, 262; cf. 58 below].

39. **Lorenzaccio**: The name of abuse generally used for Lorenzo Medici by his contemporaries and frequently by Varchi. Also called Lorenzo and Lorenzino [cf. 7/27; 26/126].

40. **Alessandro**: A. Medici [cf. 33 above; 7/27].

41. **O se credesse**: I, "Or himself believed" [cf. 45 below].

42. **Caina attende**: I, "Caina is waiting" [*Inf.* V, 107]. Words addressed by Francesca da Rimini to Dante to transmit to her husband, Gianciotto Malatesta, who had murdered her and her lover, his own brother Paolo. Caina, named after the Cain who slew his brother Abel, is the first of the four divisions of the ninth circle of Hell. It is pictured as a frozen lake and reserved for traitors to kindred.

43. **dreamed out beforehand**: Alessandro had been forewarned of his impending assassination three times in his own dreams as well as by the horoscope worked out by the astrologer Giuliano del Carmine. Perugia is the capital of Umbria in C Italy.

44. **abuleia**: Abulia, a mental state characterized by the impairment of volition, so that the subject is pathologically irresolute [cf. 54/285; 93/627].

45. **O se morisse, credesse caduto da sè**: I, "Or if he were killed, believe he had fallen by himself." Pound's variation of Varchi III, 262, which reads: "One night he was tempted to push him from a wall, but he feared that either he would not be killed or, if killed, it would not be believed he had fallen by himself ("ma ebbe paura o che egli non morisse, o che pure morendo, *non si credesse lui esser caduto da se*"). Varchi is reporting Lorenzo's own account of his hesitations before the actual murder, which attest to the depth of his pathological hatred for Alessandro [cf. 7/27].

46. **Schiavoni**: I, "Slavonians." The reference is to the man on the wood barge, Giorgio of the Slavonians, a colony of Dalmatian refugees who had been allowed by Pope Sixtus IV to settle in the quarter around the Church of S. Girolamo degli Schiavoni. Giorgio had seen the body of Giovanni Borgia, Duke of Gandia, thrown into the Tiber late at night on June 14, 1497.

47. **Barabello**: Baraballo of Gaeta, a society poet during the papacy of Leo X who aspired to be crowned, like Petrarch, with a wreath of laurels at the Capitol. Leo X placed at his disposal the white elephant he had received as a gift from the king of Portugal. Attired in a toga palmata and latus clavus like an ancient Roman, the venerable sexagenarian set off for the Capitol on the back of the elephant. At the bridge of S. Angelo the animal was frightened by the fireworks celebrating the festival of the saints Cosmo and Damian and refused to go farther, so Baraballo was forced to descend.

48. **Mozarello**: Giovanni Mozzarello or Muzarelli, a talented young Mantuan poet and scholar who wrote in elegant Latin and Italian under the names Arelius Mutius and

Arelio Mutio. Leo X (1513-1521) made him governor of the fort of Mondaino, near Rimini, as a sinecure that would allow him to continue his studies. Before he could finish his epic poem *Porsenna* he was pushed by resentful local residents down a well together with his mule, where after a search lasting more than a month both were found suffocated. Ariosto placed him among the foremost scholars of his age in *Orl. Fur. Cant.* 42, st. 87: *Uno elegante Castiglione, e un culto Mutio Arelio*. The phrase "a poet's ending" could be intended to recall Horace, *Ars poetica*, 478-481.

49. Sanazarro: Sannazzaro, 1458-1530, a poet of Naples who composed a famous epigram on the murder of the Duke of Gandia implying incest as a motive: "Piscatorem hominum ne te non, Sexte, putemus, / Piscaris natum retibus, ecce, tuum" ["Sextus, let us not think that you are a fisher of men, / Behold, you catch your own son with nets"].

50. Fracastor: Girolamo Fracastoro, 1483-1553, physician and poet, author of *Syphilis sive de morbo gallico* which describes in symbolic form the symptoms, development, and treatment of the "French disease" to which he gave the name "syphilis." Escaped death as a baby in his mother's arms when she was killed by lightning. The story also recalls the birth of Zagreus/Dionysus, when Zeus appeared to the pregnant Semele as a flash of lightning.

51. Cotta: Giovanni Cotta, 1480-1510, Italian poet and scholar and a friend of Fracastoro's. Helped the general Bartolomeo D'Alviano to found an academy of the arts.

52. Ser D'Alviano: Bartolomeo D'Alviano, 1455-1515, a general in the service of the Orsini, suspected for a time of the murder of the Duke of Gandia. Founded an academy of the arts with the aid of Giovanni Cotta.

53. Al poco giorno ed al gran cerchio d'ombra: I, fig., "In the small hours with the darkness describing a huge circle" [Dante, *Rime* I, 1; the line is repeated at 116/797]. Dante was here imitating the style of Arnaut Daniel. [EH].

54. Navighero: Andreas Navagerius or Andrea Navagero, 1483-1529, a Venetian poet who wrote in Latin and Italian. When a gathering of poets praised his verses for being in the vein of Martial, he was so indignant that he publicly burned them, later recording his resentment in four distichs. According to some accounts the ceremonial burning of imitation Martials was repeated annually.

55. slavelet . . . vain: Martial mourns the death of the little slave girl, Erotion, in the three poems V, 34, 37 and X, 61. Martial's Erotion appears to have something in common with the nymphet Erotion in a poem by Lukillios in the Greek Anthology: "When a gnat kidnapped Erotion for a lark / The nymphet chirruped: 'Right on, Papa Zeus, if it's me you want' " [EH].

56. Nine wounds: The nine wounds found on the body of the Duke of Gandia in addition to his throat having been cut [cf. 32 above].

57. "Four men, white horse . . . thing!:" Testimony of Giorgio of the Schiavoni who saw the body of the Duke of Gandia thrown into the Tiber [cf. 32, 46, above].

58. Se pia, . . . O empia, ma risoluto e terribile deliberazione: Source has *risoluta*. I, "Whether noble or ignoble, certainly a resolute and terrible decision" [Varchi III, 262]. Varchi leaves the question as to Lorenzo's good or evil motives for the murder open [7:44].

59. Ma se morisse: I, "But if he were killed." Words of Lorenzo as reported by Varchi except that Pound has substituted *ma* ("but") for *o* ("or").

CANTO VI

Sources

Camille Chabaneau, *Les Biographies des Troubadours en Langue Provençale*, Toulouse, 1885; Ida Farnell, *The Lives of the Troubadours*, London, 1896; Carl Appel, *Bernart von Ventadorn*, Halle, 1915; Cesare de Lollis, *Vita e Poesie di Sordello di Goito*, Halle, 1896.

Background

EP, *P*, "Planh for the Young English King," "Provincia Deserta," "Sestina Altaforte," "Near Perigord"; *SR*, 41-42; *LE*, 34-35, 97-99, 158; *PM*, 28; *T*, 427; Giambattista Verci, *Storia degli Ecelini*, III, Bassano, 496-498; Dante, *Inf.* XII, 110, XXVIII, 134, *Pur.* VI, 58, *Par.* IX, 25 ff.; R. Browning, *Sordello*; Wace, *Brut*; Benoit de Sainte-Marie, *Roman de Troie*; William of Newburgh (chronicle of Eleanor's divorce); Richard Howlett, ed., *The Chronicle of Robert of Torigni*, London, 1889, 318-319; Lionel Landon, *The Itinerary of King Richard I*, London, 1935, 220-222; G. P. R. James, *A History of the Life of Richard Coeur-de-Lion*, London, 1864, II, 254-255; Alfred Jeanroy, *Les Chansons de Guillaume IX, Duc d'Aquitaine*, Paris, 1913, lines 8-13; Amy Kelly, *Eleanor of Aquitaine and the Four Kings*, Cambridge, Mass., 1951.

Exegeses

Thelma C. Balagot, *Analyst* III, R. Schneideman, *Analyst* IV, 1954; Dekker, *Sailing*, 51-52, 132-133; HK, *Era*, 339 ff.; CB-R, *Approaches*, 254; DD, *Approaches* 198-214; for a translation of "La Chronique de Rains," see *Three Old French Chronicles of the Crusades*, trans. E. Noble Stone, Seattle, 1939; JW, *Later*; JE, *Pai*, 8, 298.

Glossary

1. **"What have you done, Odysseus"**: Possibly a reworking or an echo of the sirens' song [*Od.* XII, 185 ff.; 1:24]. The similarity between the careers of Odysseus and Guillaume de Poitou is pinpointed by referring to the ancient biographical note on Guillaume reprinted in Chabaneau, p. 213: "Lo Coms de Peitieus si fo uns dels majors cortes del mon, e dels majors trichadors de dompnas; e bons cavalliers d'armas, e larcs de dompneiar. E saup ben trobar e cantar; & anet lonc temps per lo mon per enganar las domnas." ["The Count of Poitou was one of the foremost courtiers in the world, one of

the foremost deceivers of women; and a good knight at arms and free with women. And was a good troubadour and singer; and long roamed the world for the sake of duping women."]

2. Guillaume: William IX, 1071-1127, 9th Duke of Aquitaine and 7th Count of Poitou. His participation in the First Crusade (1101) with a large retinue of women turned into a hilarious but disastrous joyride. The canto reference appears to relate to his pilgrimage to Santiago di Compostela, whence he "brought the song up out of Spain" [cf. 8/32], thus becoming the first troubadour and the real instigator of Provençal poetry. The reference to ground rents indicates Guillaume's readiness to fritter away his fortune in order to finance his escapades. Raymond of Poitou was his second son [cf. 12 below] and Eleanor, his granddaughter. In relation to Eleanor there is the special irony that one of Guillaume's few extant songs consists of a passionate denunciation of the practice of locking up women who have given reason for jealousy. He was an "inventor" in the sense defined in *ABCR*, 39 [cf. *LE*, 94; *SR*, 39, 53; 8/32; 91/610; 100/721; 105/750].

3. Eleanor: [2:7, 9; 7:1].

4. Tant . . . vetz: Direct quotation of lines 79-80 of poem by Guillaume beginning *Farai un vers, pos mi somelh* ("I'll write a verse and take a nap"), telling of his meeting two women of noble birth who, believing him to be a mute, invited him to a week-long orgy. The lines say: "I fucked them, as you will hear, 100 + 4 x 20 + 8 times."

5. Stone . . . death year: An invocation of the prehistorical concept of kingship, where the cycle of life and death, running from sexual prowess to sacrificial regicide, is linked with the fertility of the earth just as Pound links Guillaume's sexuality with the initiation of a culture in which architecture emerges as "the first of the arts" [*PM*, 27: "Architecture consists of fitting a form to a purpose"; cf. DD, *Approaches*, on Pound's idea of "the stone alive"]. The architecture of Poitiers is to assume a special significance for Pound later on [cf. 90/605].

6. Louis . . . Eleanor: Louis VII of France, ?1121-1180, and Eleanor of Aquitaine married on July 25, 1137, in Bordeaux, Eleanor being 15 and Louis 16 [for Eleanor, 2:7, 9; 7:1].

7. Duchess of Normandia: Since Eleanor became Duchess of Normandy and Countess of Anjou through her second marriage to Henry Plantagenet, Pound's source is in error. For "Duchess of Normandia" read "daughter of the Countess of Châtellerault," who had been one of Guillaume's more notorious mistresses. Eleanor was known as the Duchess of Normandy in her home country because she acquired that title on marrying Henry Plantagenet in 1152. Henry P. did not become Henry II of England until 1154, when he and Eleanor were crowned at Westminster. She was called the "Duchess of N." because the domain of her suzerain lord, Louis VII, was negligible and poor (the Ile-de-France, Orleans, and a part of Berry) compared with Eleanor's domain, which included the duchy of Aquitaine, the county of Poitiers, the duchy of Gascogne, and nineteen "départements" (in present parlance), combined with Henry's duchy of Normandy and the county of Anjou. From the Indre to the Basses-Pyrénées, it was all "her" territory.

8. e maire del rei jove: *P*, "and mother to the young king." The "jove rey" Henry, 1155-1183, son of Eleanor and Henry, was commonly praised as having all the virtues desirable for a ruler [cf. Pound's adaptation of Bertrans de Born's *planh* ("lament"), "Si tuit li dol e·lh plor e·lh marrimen," in *P*, 36-37]. The younger Henry was called the "young king" because Henry II had him and his young wife, Margaret (daughter of Louis), crowned in 1172, during his own reign, in order to placate Louis for the murder of young Henry's tutor and friend, Thomas à Becket. Young Henry was supposed to be king in name only, but he did not see it that way. Bertrans de Born was his friend and follower whom Dante placed in

Hell for having made strife between young Henry and his father [*Inf.* XXVIII, 134]. Altogether Eleanor bore Henry nine children, of whom only her firstborn son, William, died in childhood; all the others, daughters as well as sons, were exceptionally gifted and played major roles in history or the arts [cf. also "Near Perigord" in *P*, 151-156].

9. **Went over sea . . .** : An echo of the *Odyssey*. But Louis and Eleanor (aged 25), on this Second Crusade, took the land route through Hungary, Bulgaria, Byzance, and Adalia (Satalia), and traveled by sea only from there to Antioch (1147). The journey, lasting ten months and filled with hardship and mishaps, soured their relationship. Now estranged, Eleanor and Louis returned by sea separately via Sicily and Italy, where in Tusculum Pope Eugenius III (1149) temporarily patched up their marital differences.

10. **Acre**: Important port in all crusades, belonging to the kingdom of Jerusalem. Eleanor and Louis did not land at Acre but at Saint Siméon, the small harbor of the city of Antioch, situated at the foot of the mountain range called Jebel Accra [cf. 94/640-641].

11. **Ongla, oncle**: *P*, lit. "fingernail, uncle," a sexual double-entendre. From Arnaut Daniel's sestina beginning *Lo ferm voler qu'el cor m'intra* ["The longing that pierces my heart"], the first line of its three-line tornada reading "Arnautz tramet sa chansson d'ongla e d'oncle" ["Arnaut transmits his song of fingernail and uncle"].

12. **Her uncle . . .** : Raymond of Toulouse, younger brother of Eleanor's father, a handsome and romantic figure who had become prince of Antioch. A special relationship developed between Eleanor and Raymond, who was only eight years older than she and had been her playmate in childhood. This relationship was strengthened because the language spoken at Antioch was her native langue d'oc (incomprehensible to Louis and his men) and because Raymond had brought troubadours to the city.

13. **Theseus, son of Aegeus**: The exploits of Raymond, son of Guillaume, are compared here with those of Theseus, because Theseus also owed much of his success to his involvements with women. Raymond had been invited to the Holy Land by Fulco, king of Jerusalem, in order to marry the Princess Constanza, heiress to the principality of Antioch, then ruled by her widowed mother Alix. Raymond gained the confidence of the mother by first pretending he wanted to marry her, not her daughter.

14. **Louis . . . not at ease**: During this time Eleanor was first heard to say that she thought she had married a monk. She took to the oriental atmosphere like a fish to water, while Louis's ascetic nature was revolted by life in Antioch. Raymond pleaded for a campaign to regain Edessa, whose fall had been the real reason for the Second Crusade, but Louis insisted on continuing his pious pilgrimage to Jerusalem. Seeing the value of Raymond's strategic considerations, Eleanor strongly seconded his argument. Louis invoked his marital authority. In response Eleanor said that their marriage was null and void in the eyes of the church because of their consanguinity. The further development of the crusade bore out Raymond's argument. Louis and Eleanor returned home by sea with nothing achieved; in June Raymond had been killed by Nureddin (commander of the infidel forces) and his head cut off and sent to the caliph of Bagdad.

15. **Cimier**: F, "helmet." A baseless myth invented or at least recorded by the anonymous minstrel of Reims in *La Chronique de Rains*. It was Nureddin who commanded the infidel forces; Saladin at that time was a boy of 12 who was destined to reconquer Jerusalem in 1187 and to play a major role in the life of Eleanor's son Richard. Pound himself has attached Eleanor's scarf to Saladin's helmet as a luminous detail.

16. **Divorced her**: Another baseless myth; the opposite was true. Eleanor insisted on the annulment of her marriage on the

grounds of consanguinity, as correctly recorded by the chronicler William of Newburgh. Eleanor and Louis had had only two children, Marie and Alix, in 15 years of marriage. Thus Louis lost not only Aquitaine but also, through Eleanor's marriage with Henry Plantagenet, the entire western region of his realm. Eleanor married Henry in May 1152, only two months after the annulment without the legally required permission of Louis, who was still the suzerain lord of both Eleanor and Henry.

17. Henry Plantagenet: 1133-1189, Henry II of England.

18. (that had dodged . . . suitors): After her separation from Louis had become final, Eleanor and a small train of followers took to the road to return to Poitiers. On her way she was set upon by various minor nobles who hoped to kidnap her and force her into marriage.

19. Et quand . . . fasché: F, "And when King Louis heard it he was much riled."

20. Nauphal: Territory with fort forming part of dowry of Margaret, daughter of Louis VII and his second wife, for her marriage with Henry, son of Henry II and Eleanor. Now known as Néaufles.

21. Vexis: Vexin, a territory along the border of Normandy and France, long in dispute between the two countries. To improve Franco-Norman relations and in pursuit of their common policy of uniting all the great powers of Europe through strategic marriages with their children, Henry II and Eleanor arranged for their son Henry to marry Margaret, daughter of Louis VII by a second marriage. The scheme was conceived because Louis had not as yet produced a male heir and Margaret was preceded in her claim to the French throne only by Eleanor's two daughters, Marie and Alix. Margaret's dowry included the Vexin territory and the fortresses of Nauphal, Gisors, and Neufchastel [now Neufchâtel]. Margaret was betrothed to Henry as a baby of six months and shipped to England to be reared by her husband's family, Louis's only stipulation being that Eleanor should have no say in her upbringing. The wedding ceremony was performed when Margaret was two. Henry and Eleanor then jointly seized the Norman Vexin. Since the Templars guarding Gisors saw no reason not to surrender the keys, Louis expelled their order from Paris. When Henry, the "young king," died, Margaret was married to the king of Hungary and her dowry went to her sister Adelaide, another of Louis's daughters, who had been betrothed to Richard in 1169.

22. joven: P, "young," referring to the young king, Henry [cf. 8 above].

23. Gisors: A commanding fortress on the river Epte in Normandy. Part of Margaret's dowry [cf. 21 above].

24. Neufchastel: Neufchâtel, a fortress in the region of Rouen and part of Margaret's dowry.

25. Alix: Pound's source is in error. Alix, daughter of Louis and Eleanor, could hardly have married her half brother Richard, son of Henry and Eleanor. It was Adelaide [see 21 above] who was betrothed to Richard and shipped to England at the age of eight to become the ward of Henry II, who subsequently got her with child. Eleanor was again excluded from having any hand in the upbringing of the child. Thus Richard, now heir apparent, refused to marry Adelaide, while the French king demanded the return of either the princess or the fortress of Gisors. Estranged from his father on account of this scandal, Richard sided with the French king, now Philip II, son of Louis VII, saying: "What heretofore I could not believe, emerges now as clear as day." The French king eventually realized the need for the betrothal between Adelaide and Richard to be dissolved, and the marriage contract was annulled at Messina in 1191. Pound quotes from a text in which the scribe wrongly recorded the name of Alix in place of Adelaide.

26. Richard Plantagenet: Known as Richard Coeur de Lion, 1157-1199 [cf. 25 above; 7:1; also *P*, "Near Perigord," "Provincia Deserta," "Sestina Altaforte"; 97/671].

27. domna jauzionda: P, "radiant lady," from line 52 of the poem "Tant ai mo cor ple de joya" addressed by Bernart de Ventadour to Eleanor upon her return to Provence after her separation from Louis VII at the age of 30. Bernart, having been banished from the court of Eblis, went to Poitiers, where Eleanor had just arrived. From now on his poems are addressed to her.

28. Malemort, Correze: The ruins of Malemort Castle, which Pound and his wife Dorothy appear to have visited after passing the "river-marsh" of the river Corrèze and a "galleried church-porch" on July 24, 1919, during their walking tour of Provence. Occupied in 1177 by free lances and their wives and children, the castle was attacked by the combined forces of the suzerain lord of Limousin and the bishop. Those who survived the onslaught were taken prisoner and slaughtered in cold blood. The castle was henceforth given the name Malemort or Malamort, meaning "malign death." Shortly afterward it became the residence of the Lady Audiart (Na Audiart) of Malemort, the subject of the poem by Bertrans de Born translated by Pound in *P*, 8-9 [4:26, 41; "Provincia Deserta," *P*, 121-123; "Near Perigord," *P*, 151-156] [EH].

29. My Lady of Ventadour: Margarida of Torena married Eblis III of Ventadour in 1148, who shut her up in a dungeon out of jealousy. He repudiated her in 1150 in order to marry Alice of Montpellier, while she in turn married Guilhem IV of Angoulême the same year.

30. Nor watch fish rise to bait: Suggested by line 8 (*Aissi co·l peis qui s'eslaiss' el cadorn*) ["Like the fish that rises to the bait"] in the poem of Bernart beginning *Be m'an perdut lai enves Ventadorn* ["My friends around Ventadorn have surely seen the last of me"], probably addressed to Alaiz de Montpellier, second wife of Eblis III.

31. Que la lauzeta mover: P, "Quan(t) vei la lauzeta mover / de joi sas alas contral rai, / que s'oblid' e's laissa chazer / per la doussor c'al cor li vai." A poem by Bernart de Ventadour which Pound translates [*SR*, 41]: "When I see the lark a-moving / For joy his wings against the sunlight, / Who forgets himself and lets himself fall / For the sweetness which goes into his heart." It is with this poem that Bernart is said to have won the heart of Margarida, first wife of Eblis III.

32. E lo Sordels . . . : [2:3].

33. Sier Escort: Sier El Cort, father of Sordello. Pound has misread the letter *l* as a long *s*.

34. Cunizza da Romano: 1198-1279, married (ca. 1232) Ricciardo di San Bonifazio, the Bonifazi being the leading Guelphs of the region. Her brother, Ezzelino da Romano II, 1194-1259, podesta of Verona and one of the most homicidal rulers in Italian history, is said to have been responsible for more than 50,000 executions which in many instances wiped out entire noble families. One year after Ezzelino's death, Cunizza's brother Alberic was forced by hunger to surrender unconditionally the castle of San Zeno. His sons and daughters were tortured and killed before his eyes, and he himself was dragged to his death tied to a horse. Cunizza left her husband for Sordello. Her act of releasing her brother's slaves on April 1, 1265, symbolizes for Pound her freedom from possessiveness.

35. Masnatas et servos: ML, "Domestics and slaves." "Cunizza soror Ecelini de Romano emancipat, & libertati donat Masnatas & servos fratrum suorum" [cf. Verci, III, 496].

36. Picus de Farinatis . . . : Pichinus de F., Don Elinus, and Don Lipus, mentioned in the document of manumission by which Cunizza freed her brother's slaves, were sons of Farinata degli Uberti (d. 1264), head of the Ghibelline faction, who reconquered Florence from the Guelphs in 1260. His daughter Beatrice married Guido Cavalcanti [cf. *Inf.* X]. Pound surmises that Dante consigned the elder Cavalcanti to hell because the rather free table talk in the Uberti household had shocked his orthodox mind [cf. *LE*, 158]. The descent of his Fascist friend, Admiral Ubaldo degli Uberti [78/480], from this family impressed Pound deeply.

37. A marito . . . .concubuisse: L, Sordello "took her away from her husband and is supposed to have slept with her." Direct quotation from Rolandini chronicle, lib. V, cap 3, in Chabaneau: "Sordellus de ipsius familia dominam ipsam latenter a marito subtraxit, cum qua in patris curia permanente, dictum fuit ipsum Sordellum concubuisse" ["Sordello stealthily detached from her husband and family the lady with whom he is said to have slept at her father's official residence"].

38. "Winter and Summer . . . / . . . remember her.": An adaptation of lines 2, 5, 6 and 8 of Sordello's poem beginning "Atretan deu ben chantar finamen": "D'invern com fatz d'estiu, . . . (2) / Quar la rosa senbla lei de cui chan, (5) / Aultresi es la neus del sieu senblan: (6) / Tant fort mi fai . . . el neu menbrar (8).

39. Cairels was of Sarlat: Pound's translation from the Provençal biographical notice on the troubadour Elias Cairel, fl. 1220-1230, beginning "Elias Cairels si fo de Sarlat," given by Chabaneau. Pound translates the entire notice in *LE*, 98-99: "Elias Cairels was of Sarlat; ill he sang, ill he composed, ill he played the fiddle and worse he spoke, but he was good at writing out words and tunes. And he was a long time wandering, and when he quitted it, he returned to Sarlat and died there."

40. Theseus from Troezene: Theseus, having grown up in Troezene with his mother Aethra, was not known to his father Aegeus. Before leaving Aethra, Aegeus buried a sword and sandals under a rock, telling Aethra that his son should join him in Athens as soon as he was strong enough to lift the rock. When Theseus eventually got to Athens, he was not recognized by his father but only by Medea, whom his father had married in the interim. Jealous of the interests of Medus, her son by Aegeus, as heir apparent, Medea persuaded Aegeus that Theseus was a spy or an assassin and plotted with Aegeus to have him poisoned. But when Theseus was invited to the feast at the Dolphin Temple, where a beaker of wine poisoned with wolfsbane was set before him, Aegeus noticed from the Erechtheid serpents carved in the guest's ivory sword hilt that it had to be his son and thereupon dashed the poison to the floor.

CANTO VII

Sources

Aeschylus, *Agamemnon*, 689-690; Homer, *Iliad* III, 151-160, I, 34; Sextus Propertius; Ovid, *Ars Amatoria* I, 151, *Elegies* II, XVI, 43-46; Bertrans de Born, "B'em platz lo gais temps de Pascor"; Dante, *Inf.* IV, 112, III, 64, XII, 110, *Pur.* VI, 63, *Par.* XVIII, 100, II, 1; Flaubert, *Un Coeur Simple*; J. Joyce, *Ulysses*, Ithaca; Virgil, *Aeneid* I, IV; H. James, *The Jolly Corner*, *The Sense of the Past*; E. and J. de Goncourt, *Germinie Lacerteux*; Ovid, *Meta.* X,

586 ff.; Arthur Golding, *P. Ovidius Naso: The XV Bookes, entytuled Metamorphosis*, X, 586 ff.; Luiz de Camoëns, *Os Lusíadas* II, xcvii, 3-4; Arnaut Daniel, "Doutz brais et critz"; Benedetto Varchi, *Storia Fiorentina*, III.

Background

EP, *LE*; *SR*; *NPL*; *P*; "Stele," "Moeurs Contemporaines VII," "Ione, Dead the Long Year," "Dance Figure," "Liu Ch'e"; *L*, 274 (to W. H. D. Rouse); "Conversations in Courtship," *Criterion*, Jan. 1923; *Dial*, Nov. 1922, 554; *LPJ*; J. Joyce, *Ulysses*; T. S. Eliot, *The Waste Land*, "Gerontion"; Matthew Arnold, *The Study of Celtic Literature*; H. James, *The Beast in the Jungle*, *The Spoils of Poynton*; René Descharmes, *Autour de Bouvard et Pécuchet*, 1921; Flaubert, *Bouvard et Pécuchet*, 1881; R. de Gourmont, *NPL*, 154-155; University of Chicago Library, MSS, Dec. 3, 1912; *Observer*, London, Feb. 23, 1969; YC, no. 538; *Chelsea Mail*, London, Aug. 9, 1912; U. A. Canello and R. Lavaud, *Les Poésies d'Arnaut Daniel*, Halle, 1893; A. Stimming, *Bertrans de Born*, Halle, 1892.

Exegeses

Schneideman, *Analyst* IV and VI, 1954; Dekker, *Sailing*, 15-28 and passim; FR in *Approaches*; EH, *B. E. P.*, 99-131; HK, *Era*, 119-120, 338-339; JE, *Mauberley* (chapter on H. James and R. de Gourmont); Norman, *EP*, 114-115; CB-R, *ZBC*; Peter Makin, *Provence and Pound*.

Glossary

1. **Eleanor (she spoiled in a British climate)**: Since this remark is in no way supported by the evidence of Eleanor's creative and active life up to the age of 82, it could perhaps be intended as (*a*) an ironical expression of the general vacuity of public opinion, which preferred Henry Plantagenet's paramour, Rosamond Clifford (Giraut de Barrie's *Rose immonde*, "impure rose"), to the emancipated and intellectual foreigner, Eleanor; (*b*) a reference to the 15 years during which Eleanor was held in durance by Henry following their break after 15 years of dynamic teamwork, in the course of which, besides bearing him seven children, she was constantly traveling between England and her own domain, Aquitaine, and shared fully in all political decision making. The break occurred because Henry found profligacy more amusing than Eleanor's Provençal concept of "creative love," which had up to then defined their relationship. After the beginning of Henry's affair with Rosamond, which coincided with the birth of his and Eleanor's youngest son, John, Eleanor returned with all her children except John, her children-in-law, and her two daughters by Louis, to Poitiers, where for 8 years she maintained a center of poetry and music. Her children, not without cause [2:9], sided with Louis VII against their father. Henry thereupon attacked Poitiers with an army of

mercenaries and laid waste the land. Fleeing disguised as a page, Eleanor was recognized by Henry's men and dragged off to England for a long period of enforced inactivity. Free again at the age of 67, she ruled both England and Aquitaine for her son Richard, remaining a positive force in European affairs and culture until her death in 1204. The more likely explanation for the line is, however, Pound's sudden disregard for historical facts and justice occasioned by his disillusionment with England, which had forced him to emigrate to Paris in the winter of 1920-21, the approximate date of this canto's origin [6:2, 7; *Analyst* III, IV].

2. Ἑλανδρος and Ἑλέπτολις: H, "man-destroying and city-destroying," a repetition of the traditional puns on the name of Helen of Troy, which Pound here extends to Eleanor [2:8]. The line fixes the origin of the literature inspired by Helen's beauty: the *Iliad* and the *Odyssey*.

3. poor old Homer . . . : The first literary reflection of beauty via the sensibility of Homer, who transmitted it for all ages even though he never saw it with his own eyes but only "echoes it" in the terrified chatter of the old men at the Skaian gate when confronted with Helen's person. The beauty that set off all the echoes in literature is therefore actually but an echo of an echo. At the same time the episode introduces in this canto the theme of the rejection of life by the living dead [cf. *Iliad* III, 151-152].

4. Ear, ear for the sea-surge: A reference to the "magnificent onomatopoeia, as of the rush of the waves on the sea-beach and their recession" [*LE*, 250; *L*, 274, viz. the *polyphloisboio* in *Iliad* I, 34; cf. also "Stele," *P*, 181; 74/427; 92/620].

5. Rattle of old men's voices . . . : Here Pound is trying, in turn, to recapture the "authentic cadence" of the Homeric original as described in *LE*, 250 [cf. *Analyst* IV]. The Homeric passage compares the old men's voices to the chirpings of cicadas [cf. "words like locust-shells"; cf. 13, 32, 35, 37 below].

6. And then the phantom Rome: Homer's sonorous cadence echoing the sea surge is superseded by Ovid's sophisticated table talk. Roman mythology, architecture, art, and literature are commonly regarded as second-rate imitations of the Greek prototypes, but Pound finds something added to the art of writing: "we may suppose that the Romans added a certain sophistication; at any rate, Catullus, Ovid, Propertius, all give us something we cannot find now in Greek authors" [*LE*, 27].

7. "marble narrow for seats": Ovid advises the reader to pick out a shapely girl as she is about to enter the theater and follow her to a seat where they will be forced to sit squeezed together [*Ars amatoria* I, 133-142].

8. "Si pulvis nullus . . . : L, "If no dust." "And if a speck of dust should fall into your lady's lap, flick it off with your fingers; if there be no speck of dust, well, flick it off anyway" [ibid., 149-151].

9. Then file and candles, e li mestiers ecoutes: [Read *escoutes* for *ecoutes*] P, "and harkened to the crafts" or "to the mysteries." The word *mestiers* has a variety of meanings, the two most probable of which in the given context are "crafts" and "mysteries." Insofar as Pound is seeking to depict either a personally witnessed or a painted scene, the "file and candles" could refer to a file of people bearing candles in a religious procession or, as for instance in Sicily and other parts of Italy, to a detachment of craftsmen bearing candles and a large replica of a file as the emblem of their craft in a religious procession on some saint's day. Otherwise Makin (*Provence and Pound*, p. 38) could be correct in regarding the "file" (L, *lima*) as the traditional implement used by the Latin poets for polishing their verses, and the "candles" as a means of lucubration for poets too poor to afford an oil lamp.

10. y cavals armatz . . . : [Read *e* for *y*] P, "and horses in armor" (i.e. neck guard, chamfron, poitrel, flancards, rump piece). A quotation from Bertrans de Born's sirventes beginning "Be·m platz lo gais temps de Pascor [*T*, 426], in which the last line of the first stanza runs: *Chavaliers e chavals armatz* ["Knights and horses in armor"]. Cf. *SR*, 47: "Well pleaseth me the sweet time of Easter" . . . "and great joy have I / When I see o'er the campagna knights armed and horses arrayed." Bertrans welcomed the arrival of spring as the season when knights can resume their warlike activities. Loving strife for its own sake, he even sang of his "Lady Battle" [*SR*, 44]. A footnote added to p. 48 of the revised edition of *SR* (1952) likens the pageantry in the above poem to the paintings of Simone Martini and Paolo Uccello that appear to be characterized by the definition "Not mere successions of [brush-] strokes, sightless narration" in the next line.

11. ciocco: I, "log" [5:6, 10]. Dante's image of the souls rising like sparks from the fifth circle (of Mars, god of war) to the sixth (of Jupiter, the sky-god) marks the transition from the medieval chronicle to Dante's *Divina Commedia*. We now leave the inventors for the "masters" [*ABCR*, 47-48]. The era of chronicled action is superseded by Dante's "imaginative vision" [*SR*, 157]. Dante's work is another reflection of Homer's for just as Virgil in the *Aeneid* was "translating" the *Odyssey* into the mentality and idiom of his time, Dante in turn was "translating" the *Aeneid* with Virgil as guide. In medieval times Virgil was commonly referred to as the "translator" of Homer. Dante, like his direct antecedents, Homer and Virgil, is seeking to present the full range of human knowledge in his age and for the first time touches critically on some of the evils of its culture. But this intellectual analysis or criticism is still caught up and neutralized by the quality of his "emotional synthesis."

12. Un peu moisi . . . baromètre: F, "A little musty . . . the floor being below garden level . . . Against the wainscot . . . a wicker armchair, . . . an old piano . . . and under the barometer" [Flaubert, *Un Coeur Simple*, par. 4]. "Un vestibule étroit séparait la cuisine de la salle où Mme. Aubain se tenait tout le long du jour, assise près de la croisé dans un *fauteuil de paille. Contre le lambris*, peint en blanc, s'alignaient huit chaises d'acajou. *Un vieux piano* supportait, *sous un baromêtre*, un tas pyramidal de boîtes et de cartons. Deux bergères de tapisserie flanquaient la cheminée en marbre jaune et de style Louis XV. La pendule, au milieu, représentait un temple de Vesta,–et tout l'appartement sentait *un peu* le *moisi*, car le *plancher* était *plus bas que le jardin*." Such objects begin to assume for Flaubert a dead weight that arrests the subjective movement of the mind. His genius and creative urge come up against a materialist civilization of alienation, which subsists solely on the "interest" yielded by the cultural assets of former times. Thus, Flaubert has to achieve his effects by a "greater heaping up of factual data" [*LE*, 26], as demonstrated in these lines. Flaubert's writings represent here the caesura between the epic tradition and prose, i.e. "the instinct of negation" [*LE*, 324; cf. *LE*, 31-32; FR in *Approaches*].

13. Old men's voices: [cf. 5 above and 32, 35, 37 below]. Another echo of Homer. The passage is concerned with Henry James, of whom Pound has written that although James does not "feel" as solid as Flaubert [*LE*, 305], he is sensitive to things that Flaubert did not see. James was a recorder of "atmospheres, nuances, impressions of personal tone and quality" [*LE*, 324]; his sensitivity was attuned to the "feel of the place or to the tonality of the person" [*LE*, 306]. But the action of his stories is a mere "excuse" for writing up his impressions of people so as to "show what acts, what situations, what contingencies would befit or display certain characters. We are hardly asked to accept them as happening" [*LE*, 299]. The ghostly impression of the plot thus conveyed explains James's "need of opacity" [*LE*, 321], leading among other things to his "damn'd fuss about furniture" [*LE*, 308], as demonstrated in this canto passage, and "a thickening, a chiaroscuro is needed, the long sentence" [*LE*, 304]. Hence, Pound's main criticism of James: "It is too much as if he were depicting stage scenery, not *as* stage scenery, but as nature" [*LE*, 325]. The house described in this passage is an almost compulsive leitmotif in James's writings: the "great gaunt shell of a house." It can be variously identified as (*a*) Lamb House in Surrey, where James spent his later years (Pound comments on James's bad taste in painting [*LE*, 307], but note also "a thickening, a chiaroscuro is needed'" [LE, 304]); (*b*) the London Polytechnic Institute, where Pound held his lectures on Provençal poetry in 1910 (this interpretation would explain "the old men's voices" and the "dry professorial talk"); (*c*) Leopold Bloom's Ideal Home in *Ulysses* (Ithaca), with its invented 99-year lease listing among other things the "stepped up panel dado, dressed with camphorated wax," the point being that the house remains unreal by "three squares" (panels) in spite of all of James's "thickening" [*LE*, 324; cf. *LE*, 31-32, 45, 210, 399, 403; FR in *Approaches*].

14. **Con gli . . . grave incessu**: I, L, "with eyes honest and slow," "solemn movement" [*Pur.* VI, 63, *Inf.* IV, 112]. The first quotation refers to Sordello; the second is a variation of Dante's *Genti veran con occhi tardi e gravi* [I, "I saw men approaching with slow and solemn eyes"], describing Homer, Horace, and Ovid, three of the four great shades of antiquity approaching Dante and Virgil (Virgil himself was the fourth). The variation incorporates Virgil's *vera incessu* [cf. *Aeneid* I, 405; *LE*, 246; 74/435]: "and from her manner of walking" and "a great goddess, Aeneas knew her forthwith" [cf. also in "Conversations in Courtship," *T*, 401]; James is thus directly associated with the grand tradition recalled from Orage's dictum: "James will be quite comfortable after death, as he had been dealing with ghosts all his life" [*LE*, 302]. The passage also sums up Pound's personal memories of James as in *LE* [295, 311] and "*Moeurs Contemporaines* VII," where James's remark, "Oh! Abelard," regarding the castrated medieval scholar, gives the key biological clue to the indirectness of James's responses, to his perennial theme of the unlived life, and to the underlying motivation of his circuitous sentences, his oblique method, and his constant "dealing with ghosts."

15. **We also . . .** : Pound is referring to himself in the first person, revisiting after seven years a Paris house in search of "buried beauty," using allusively the motif of the old house, the "shell of life" in James's writings, with particular reference to *The Jolly Corner* and *The Sense of the Past*. This visit to the house of the past marks Pound's transition from the past to the present and is the first time that the present enters *The Cantos* in any real and sustained sense. Yet the "ghostly visit" emphasizes the ambivalence of what is normally called "reality" and "fact": the remembered experience has far more solidity than the objective drab shell of life, the concierge, and so on. The "flimsy partition" harks back to Flaubert's observation [cf. 12 above].

16. **Empire handle**: The handle of the door knocker was designed in the Empire style of Napoleon I.

17. **Ione, dead the long year**: Cf. Pound's poem "Ione, Dead the Long Year" [*P*, 112], first published in *Poetry and Drama* (London, Dec. 1914), seven years before the first publication of Canto VII. It has been variously pointed out that Landor used the name "Ione" as a pseudonym for a Miss Nancy Jones and also that "Ione" was the petrified maiden in Bulwer Lytton's *Last Days of Pompeii*. There was, however, among the *New Freewoman* group a beautiful 19-year-old French-born dancer, Jeanne Heyse, who used the alias Joan Hayes and the professional name Ione de Forest. She committed suicide at her home in Chelsea, London, on August 2, 1912, which can be

fairly described as a "long year" before the first publication of Pound's obituary poem. She reappears in *Dance Figure* [*P*, 91; cf. Chicago MSS, Dec. 3, 1912] before its publication in *Poetry* II, 1 (April 1913), 1-12, and in *New Freewoman* I, 5 (Aug. 15, 1913), 87-88 [EH].

18. Liu Che's lintel: A reference to the poem "Lo-yeh ai-ch'an ch'ü" by Liu Che, a Chinese emperor canonized as Wu-ti, 156-187. In the Chinese poem the emperor's dead mistress, having passed through the various phases of natural decay, ends as a dead leaf clinging to the threshold, from which lowly position Pound elevates her to the lintel, the supporting beam spanning the top of the doorway. In "Liu Ch'e" [*P*, 108] she was still clinging to the threshold [EH].

19. Elysée . . . : Hotel de l'Elysée, 9 rue de Beaune in Paris, where Pound had stayed and also arranged for James Joyce and his family to stay. The name is an echo of the Elysium of antiquity, the abode of the Happy Dead. The presence of the "masters," Pound and Joyce, at this hotel would, to Pound's mind, have reinforced the association. Joyce might not have appreciated this to the same degree. The bus transports Pound back to the present [cf. FR, *LPJ*, 173, 176].

20. Erard . . . : Érard, a famous French make of pianos. The lines following describe Vanderpyl's Paris flat [cf. 21 below] in the style of Flaubert, using the passage from *Un Coeur Simple* (see 12 above) as a parallel just as the house in the previous passage was described in the style of Henry James. Thus "ply over ply": the present is overlapped by the past.

21. Beer bottle . . . : Another indication of the present, when the artist is confronted with the problem of the industrial mass production of artifacts and the reproduction of earlier styles. The statues in the Jardin du Luxembourg as viewed from the windows of Vanderpyl's flat are for the most part in the abominable fake style of the 19th century based on copies from antiquity and therefore examples of "dogmatized form."

22. Fritz: Fritz-René Vanderpyl, 1876-? , a Dutch writer living at 13 rue Gay-Lussac [cf. 74/435; 80/510; *L*, 151 (to John Quinn); Vanderpyl's letter in *Analyst* VI]. Vanderpyl, who knew both Pound and Joyce in Paris, was an avant-garde novelist, poet, and art critic. In his letter he writes: "I then mixed all kinds of languages in my verses . . . . In those days I took myself for a very emancipated being."

23. Smaragdos, chrysolithos . . . : L, "Emeralds, topazes." From Sextus Propertius, *Elegies* II, xvi, 43-46. S. P. is saying here that he would like to see all the modish finery, which Cynthia takes to wearing as she feels herself to be growing older, swept away by the forces of nature: "emeralds, topazes, clothes made of the finest stuffs, all of this I should like to see swept into nothingness by raging storms. Oh that they would be turned into water and dust by some sleight of the gods."

24. De Gama: Vasco da Gama, ca. 1469-1524, Portuguese navigator and explorer who discovered the sea route to India [cf. 35/175] via Africa. Allusions to the *Lusiads* of Luiz de Camoëns, 1524-1580, the tenth canto of which celebrates da Gama and other Portuguese heroes, while the second canto (xcviii, 3-4) describes da Gama's bloomers as being slashed with gold in the fashion of the time. "Mountains of the sea gave birth to troops" may parody Camoëns' grandiloquent style [*SR*, 214ff.].

25. Le vieux . . . acajou: F, "The old mahogany chest." The French should read "La vieille commode." Possibly a reference to the already quoted passage from Flaubert's *Un Coeur Simple*: "Contre le lambris, peint en blanc," taken together with later references to "un socle d'acajou" and "la commode, couverte d'un drap comme un autel"; or to E. and J. de Goncourt, *Germinie Lacerteux* (1864), fourth par. of Ch. I: "Sur la commode d'acajou, d'un style

Empire, un Temps en bronze noir et courant, sa faux en avant, servait de porte-montre à une petite montre au chiffre de diamants sur émail bleu entouré de perles."

26. **Tyro**: [2:12]. Tyro, Helen, Eleanor, Atalanta, "Nicea," and Dido represent here the timeless beauty of naked humanity in the sense that Pound has ascribed to Gourmont. All are manifestations of Eros juxtaposed with the period-bound ephemera of civilization. The "But *is* she dead... In seven years?" appears to refer to the seven years between the death of Ione [cf. 17 above] in 1912 and the composition of Canto VII in 1919 [Pound wrote to his father on Dec. 13, 1919: "done cantos 5, 6, 7" (YC, no. 538)]. The line marks the transition to Gourmont's theme of poetry as "emotional synthesis."

27. **'Ε***λέναυς*... : H, "ship-destroying" [2:8]. A reiteration of the original theme of beauty as reflected in the arts.

28. **The sea runs**: The sea and its tides, shaking the shingle [cf. 4 above re Homer's *polyphloisboio* (*LE*, 250) and "the turn of the wave and the scutter of receding pebbles" (*L*, 274), are here used to symbolize both permanence and change, analogous to the "permanent elements in human nature," one of which is for Pound the creative passion for beauty as exemplified by Eleanor's sustained impact on literature, while another is translation.

29. **The scarlet curtain**... : Arthur Golding's English version of Ovid's *Meta*., particularly the passage X/586 ff. describing how, during her race with Hippomenes, Atalanta's naked beauty was enhanced by her body taking on a ruddy hue as she grew hot. Golding translates: "As when a scarlet curtaine streynd against a playstred wall / Dooth cast like shadowe, making it seem ruddye therewith all." The theme of the reflections of beauty thus enters into the image itself. This theme is emphasized where Pound [*LE*, 235] asks if Golding's translation is not "a mirror" of Chaucer, whose work in turn "mirrors" Ovid: "Or is a fine poet ever translated until another his equal invents a new style in a later language? . . . Is there one of us so good at his Latin . . . that Golding will not *throw upon his mind shades and glamours* inherent in the original text. . . . *Or is not a new beauty created, an old beauty doubled* when the overchange is well done?" The series of echoes do not in that case fade out but intensify [cf. 102/730].

30. **Lamplight at Buovilla... e quel remir**: A reference to the troubadour Arnaut Daniel, who loved the wife of Guillem de Bouvila, supposedly in vain. But his poem "Doutz brais e critz" suggests otherwise. "E quel remir" ["and that I may gaze upon her"] is from lines 31-32: "Quel seu bel cors baisan rizen descobra / E quel remir contral lum de la lampa" ["and that she should kiss me and laughingly expose her body / and I might gaze upon her in the light of the lamp"]. Pound returns here to the theme of the desire to discard the accouterments of civilization [cf. 23 above] and return to bare humanity. At the same time he is echoing the image from Ovid in the preceding line [cf. *SR*, 34; *LE*, 111, 137; 20/90].

31. **Nicea**... : A recollection of the dancer, Ione [cf. 17 above, 36 below], here likened to the graceful statue of Nike of Samothrace at the Louvre. Another contrast to the fake echoes in the Jardin du Luxembourg.

32. **Thin husks**... : "Shelley, Yeats, Swinburne, . . . Remy de Gourmont, when he says that most men think only husks and *shells of the thoughts that have been already lived over by others*, have shown their very just appreciation of the *system of echoes*, of the general vacuity of public opinion" [*LE*, 371]. This sentence may be regarded as seminal for Canto VII. The other motifs, such as the fancy dress of history, the old men ("dry casques of departed locusts"), the "great gaunt shell of a house," the dogmatized forms, the "*idées reçues*," the reifications of life, and the consequent alienation of the living dead all hark back to this passage and

to the Waste Land motif of sexual frustration, aridity, and stasis.

33. Sham Mycenian: Walls supposedly in imitation of the architectural style of Mycenae, the ancient Greek city of Argolis, seat of the kingdom of Agamemnon.

34. "Toc" sphinxes, sham Memphis columns: F (patois), *toc*, "sham, ugly." Memphis was an ancient Egyptian city said to have been built in 3110 B. C. by Menes, first king of Egypt, on the west bank of Nile about 12 miles from the present location of Cairo. It was destroyed in the 7th century A. D. by Arabs, who quarried the ruins to build al-Fustât (now Cairo).

35. Shell of the older house . . . House expulsed by this house: [cf. 32 above]. The passage is strongly reminiscent of Matthew Arnold's reference to the *Mabinogion* in *The Study of Celtic Literature*, 1867, where the *Mabinogion* myths are described as "a detritus . . . of something far older." The compilation of these tales, Arnold says [57 and 54], may be compared with the "peasant building his hut on the site of Halicarnassus or Ephesus; he builds, but what he builds is full of materials of which he knows not the history, or knows by a glimmering tradition merely—stones 'not of this building,' but of an older architecture, greater, cunninger, more majestical" [EH].

36. Square even shoulders . . . dancing woman: Another recollection of Ione [cf. 17, 31, above], dating back to 1909, three years before her suicide and exactly "ten years gone" since the canto was composed.

37. Still the old dead dry talk . . . petrifaction of air: An echo of the talk of the old men of Troy confronted with Helen's living beauty, here reflected in academic efforts to mummify the beauties of the classics, whereby they are emptied of their original content and placed under a glass dome which neutralizes the biological function of beauty by denying access to it.

38. O voi che siete: I, *Par.* II, 1, which Pound translates: "Oh you, in the dinghy astern there" [93/631; 109/774]. Dante is addressing his readers who have up to now followed the course of his big ship, telling them that from here on only the few who have applied themselves to the study of the greatest mysteries will be able to understand his meaning. Pound is picking up the original Odyssean theme of the sea voyage in order to link this canto with the preceding six.

39. Dido . . . : The Roman *Aeneid* is an echo of the Greek *Odyssey* in that Aeneas too sets out after the fall of the archetypical city of Troy to found a new city and kingdom, Rome [1:16]. After seven years of wandering he and his remaining seven ships reach the African port of Carthage, where Dido, still grieving for her murdered husband Sichaeus, is queen. Aeneas becomes her lover ("new Eros"), but he leaves her in order to set sail for Italy. In her fresh grief Dido commits suicide [*Aeneid* I, 341 ff., IV].

40. solid as echo: In the echelonned unrealities that constitute present-day life, the echo or reverberation of an "emotional synthesis" once experienced is often more solid than reality.

41. Eros: [cf. 39 above].

42. Passion to breed . . . : Pound sees Eros as the motive force of both procreation and the artist's urge to create new forms: "The power of the spermatozoid is precisely the power of exteriorizing a form" [*NPL*, 149].

43. The live man . . . : Identified by Pound in the margin of the Faber edition of *The Cantos* as Desmond Fitzgerald, 1890-1947, London-born Irish member of T. E. Hulme's circle who took part in the 1916 Easter rising in Dublin, for which he was sentenced by the English to life imprisonment. Released on the conclusion of the treaty with England, he was appointed minister for publicity in the Irish Free State government and shortly afterward minister of external affairs (1922) and later minister of defense (1931). Fitzgerald, like Hulme, was an extreme reactionary in politics. Reviewing Fitzgerald's memoirs (1969), Christopher Hollis wrote:

"Even at the time of the rising he [Fitzgerald] violently reacted against anyone who drew a parallel between Ireland's fight and the French Revolution and in later years was to attack any smallest abridgment of the principles of absolute capitalism with a savagery that I have never heard equalled" [*Observer*, London, Feb. 23, 1969; cf. 95/644].

44. Lorenzaccio . . . : [5:39, 45, 58, 59]. The allusion is to *Inf.* III, 64, i.e., to the spirits of those "who were never alive" because they "lacked energy to sin or to do good, fit neither for Hell or Heaven" [*SR*, 129].

45. the tall indifference . . . : [5:44 "abuleia"].

46. Ma . . . morisse: [5:59].

47. E biondo . . . : I, "he is blond" [*Inf.* XII, 110]. Next to the dark head of Ezzelino, Cunizza's brother [6:34], the blond head of Obizzo d'Este (d. 1293) appears in the mire of Hell. Obizzo had been one of the most homicidal tyrants in Italy. Pound has now come back full circle to the real events that "carve a trace" in time in the same way as does the work of a poet. Action that springs from such passionate depths constitutes a "poem . . . written with deeds; . . . art becomes necessary only when life is inarticulate and when art is not an expression, but a mirroring, of life; it is necessary only when life is apparently without design . . . . *Art that mirrors art* is unsatisfactory . . . . No poem *can have as much force as the simplest narration of the events themselves*" [*SR*, 218]. Thus, Canto 7 leads to the straightforward account [Cantos 7-11] of the deeds of Sigismundo Malatesta, a Renaissance Odysseus.

CANTOS VIII-XI
THE MALATESTA CANTOS

Sources

C. E. Yriarte, *Un Condottière au XVe siècle*, Paris, 1882; Edward Hutton, *Sigismundo Pandolpho Malatesta, Lord of Rimini* (a novel), London and New York, 1906, and *Ravenna* (a study), London and New York, 1913; L. A. Muratori, *Annali d'Italia*, IX, 1763; Platina, *The Lives of the Popes from the time of our Savior J. C. to the reign of Sixtus IV, trans. and contd. from the year 1471 to the present time by P. Rycaut*, London,1685; A. Battaglini, "Della corte letteraria di Sigismondo Pandolfo Malatesta," F. G. Battaglini, "Della vita e dei fatti di Sigismondo Malatesta," in *Basinii Parmensis Poetae Opera Praestantiora*, II, 43-255, 259-698, Rimini, 1794; Luigi Tonini, *Storia Civile e Sacra Riminese*, II, Rimini, 1882; Luciano Banchi, *La Guerra de' Senesi col Conte di Pitigliano*, Archivio Storico Italiano, ser. 4, III, 1879; Niccolò Machiavelli, *Istorie Fiorentine*, VII; Fritz Schultze, *Georgios Gemistos Plethon und seine reformatorischen Bestrebungen*, Jena, 1874; Dante, *Inf.* V,

73-142; XXVII, 44-48, 79-90; Horace, *Odes* III, 3; Virgil, *Aeneid* VI; Plato, *Platonic Epistles* VII; W. S. Landor, "To Ianthe"; T. S. Eliot, *The Waste Land*, v, 430.

Background

EP, *GK* frontispiece and 159-160; T. S. Eliot, "Gerontion"; Adrian Stokes, *The Quattro Cento*, London, 1932, and *Stones of Rimini*, London, 1934, 19-20; Byron, "Parisina," 1816; G. D'Annunzio, *Francesca* (drama); Enea Silvio Piccolomini (Pius II), *Commentarii rerum memorabilium*, Rome, 1584, and *Vatican Codex Reginensis*, no. 1995; *The Commentaries of Pius II*, trans. Florence A. Gragg with introduction and notes by Leona Gabel, Smith College Studies in History, XXII, XXV, XXX, XXXV, XLIII, 1939-1951; Corrado Ricci, *Il Tempio Malatestiano*,Milan and Rome, 1925; Alberto Ricci, *Sigismondo e Isotta*, Milan, 1929; Cesare Clementini, "Vita di Sigismundo Pandolfo," *Raccolto Istorico della Fondatione di Rimino e dell' Origine e Vite de' Malatesti*, II, Rimini, 1627 (facsimile in *Historiae Urbium et Regionum Italiae Rariores*, XXXVIII, pt. 2, Bologna, 1969); Lorenzo de' Medici, *Scritti Scelti*, Introduzione e note de Egidio Bellorini, Turin, 1922; Roberto Valturio, *De Re Militarii*, X; Basinio de Basini, *Le poesie liriche*, Turin, 1925; Alfonso Lazzari, *Ugo e Parisina nella realtà storica*, Florence, 1915 (expanded and reissued as *Parisina*, Florence, 1949); Giovan Battista Pigna, *Historie de' principi di Este*, Ferrara, 1570; G. Boccaccio, story of Paolo and Francesca; E. Gibbon, *Decline and Fall of the Roman Empire*, Modern Library, 1932, chap. 66; Joseph Jay Deiss, *Captains of Fortune: Profiles of Six Italian Condottieri*, London, 1966; Willibald Block, *Die Condottieri: Studien über die sogenannten "unblutigen Schlachten*," Berlin, 1913; Geoffrey Trease, *The Condottieri: Soldiers of Fortune*, London, 1970; Piero Zama, *I Malatesti*, Faenza, 1956.

Exegeses

R. Mayo, *Analyst* V; A. Fang, J. Palmer, R. Ellmann, et al., *Analyst* VI; R. Mayo and S. Wuletich, *Analyst* VII; A. Manganaris-Descavalles, *Analyst* XI; R. Mayo, *Analyst* XIII; John Drummond, "Italian Background to the Cantos," in *Ezra Pound*, ed. P. Russell, 104-113; FR, *P/J*, 272; DD, *Sculptor*.

Glossary Canto VIII

1. These fragments you have . . . . : The "you" refers to T. S. Eliot, who some months before the composition of Canto VIII had submitted to Pound a manuscript containing a collection of independent poems and verse fragments for his appraisal [cf. *L*, p. 169]. Pound indicated how many of the poems could be strung together to form a cohesive group, which subsequently came to be published under the title *The Waste Land*. Pound's own "fragments" are of course the still inchoate *Cantos*.

2. **Calliope**: The Muse of epic poetry. Her quarrel with "Truth" refers to the persistent denigration that has followed Sigismundo for centuries, owing mainly to the campaign of character assassination initiated against him by Pius II in his *Commentaries* [9:21; 10:25, 28].

3. **sous les lauriers**: F, "under the laurels."

4. **Alessandro**: A. de' Medici, 1511-1537, son of Pope Clement VII and a Moorish slave [5:33, 43].

5. **Malatesta/Sigismund**: Sigismundo Pandolfo Malatesta, 1417-1468, Lord of Rimini, Fano, and Cesena, famous condottiere, military engineer, and patron of the arts, for Pound the "factive personality." Malatesta da Verrucchio, 1212-1312, known as Mastin (the Mastiff), the first Lord of Rimini [cf. 49 below], was his great-great-grandfather, and Pandolfo Malatesta, 1377-1427, famous condottiere and patron of the arts and sciences, his father. During Pandolfo's lifetime, Pope Martin V, influenced by the Pesaro line of the Malatesta family [cf. 40 below], had dragged out his suit to have his three natural sons declared legitimate. On his death in 1427 the lordship of Rimini was taken over by his brother Carlo Malatesta [cf. 51 below] in behalf of the three young nephews. In order to plead Pandolfo's still pending suit, Carlo personally went to Rome in 1428, accompanied by Niccolò d'Este on a similar mission (cf. *tre cento bastardi* at 24/112). This time the pope, in return for certain lands and fortresses, declared legitimate the elder nephew, Galeotto, noted for his extreme piety. But within only a few months after Carlo's death in 1429 he sent troops to reclaim Rimini for the Holy See on the pretext of Carlo's failure to pay the annual levy due the Church. Though only 13 at the time, Sigismundo with his small force succeeded in dispersing the papal troops. This incident marked the beginning of a lifelong struggle to defend his domain against all comers, a struggle that reached climactic points during the reigns of Pius II and Paul II. Above all, Pius II, a partisan of the house of Aragon against the house of Anjou, conceived a deep personal dislike for Sigismundo which is eloquently reflected in the many references to him, usually characterized by an extreme vulgarity of style, in his *Commentaries*. Sigismundo, although in many ways a heroic figure in his lifelong struggle against superior odds, was by no means without blemishes of character which can even be discerned between the lines of the Malatesta Cantos, but up to Pound's day Pius II's paranoically biased misrepresentation of him, which was parroted by later historians without the slightest attempt at verification, was still being taught in the schools even though a popular attempt to straighten the record had been undertaken by Yriarte in 1882 followed by Edward Hutton in 1906, which appears to have been the first to catch Pound's attention [cf. *GK*, 115, 159-160, 194, 261, 301].

6. **Frater . . . carissime**: ML, "Brother, as it were, and most dear companion."

7. **Tergo**: ML, "Written on the back."

8. **Giohanni . . . Medici**: Giovanni de' Medici, 1421-1463, youngest son of Cosimo de' Medici [10:22]. The words, which spell out "Giohanne de Medicis Fiorentia," have been partly obliterated by the wax wafer depicting Sigismundo's profile as shown facing the title page of *GK* inserted between the sheets of parchment.

9. **Gianozio**: Messer G., a dignitary (from Florence?) with whom Sigismundo was dealing; perhaps chancellor to Sigismundo.

10. **King of Ragona**: "El re de Ragona," i.e., Alphonso I of Sicily and Naples, king of Aragon (1385-1458). On the death of the Duke of Milan, Philippe Maria de Visconti, in 1447, Alphonso claimed Milan because the duke, being without male issue, had

appointed him his heir. Milan was, however, also claimed both by Venice and by Francesco Sforza, while the city proclaimed itself a republic and hired Francesco Sforza [see 15], but as condottiere to defend its independence. Sigismundo had been engaged by Alphonso as condottiere to enforce his claim, but he broke the agreement by going over to the side of Florence and Venice.

11. **Maestro di pentore**: I, "Master of painting," prob. Piero della Francesca, ?1420-1492 [9:4].

12. **buttato via**: I, "chucked away" [Yriarte, 381].

13. **affatigandose . . . mai**: I; Pound translates: "Can work as he likes, / Or waste time as he likes / . . . / never lacking provision" [Yriarte, 385].

14. **In campo . . . Cremonam**: ML, "In the field of the most illustrious masters of Venice, the 7th day of April 1449, outside Cremona." Sigismundo writing, now as the leader of the Venetian forces against Sforza, and besieging Cremona, which Sforza had left in the hands of his wife Bianca Maria Sforza (a natural daughter of the late Visconti, Duke of Milan), whom he had married in 1441.

15. **Duke of Milan**: At the time of the agreement referred to, the duke was Francesco Sforza, 1401-1466, a peasant turned condottiere. Although lacking the military genius and versatility of Sigismundo, he succeeded in all his ventures because of his ruthless ambition. Throughout the Malatesta Cantos his career counterpoints the defeats and humiliations suffered by Sigismundo. Thanks largely to the unwavering support of the Medicis, who used him as an instrument with which to offset the power of Venice, Sforza finally achieved his ambition to become Duke of Milan in 1450 and founded a ducal dynasty [9:45; 10:17, 54].

16. **Agnolo della Stufa**: Negotiator sent by Florence to engage Sigismundo's services to defend the city against Alphonso's troops, which had invaded Tuscany in 1452. Sigismundo thus suddenly found himself fighting on the side of his enemy Francesco Sforza, who was allied with Florence.

17. **ten of the baily**: "Dieci della Balia." The Balìa was the emergency council of Florence, appointed during wars and rebellions when the ordinary citizen's rights were suspended.

18. **gente . . . pie**: I; Pound translates: "horsemen and footmen" [Yriarte, 383].

19. **Penna and Billi, . . . Carpegna, . . . Marecchia**: Penna and Billi are high rocks near Rimini; Carpegna is a nearby mountain; Marecchia is a river flowing into the Adriatic Sea near Rimini.

20. **Lyra**: An indication that the following verse should be sung to the accompaniment of a lyre.

21. **"Ye spirits . . . Batsabe"**: Lines adapted from a poem by Sigismundo in praise of his mistress (later his third wife), Isotta degli Atti [cf. 9:59]. Pound takes the lines "O Spreti che gia fusti in questi regny / Voi ciaschaduno dalo Amor pcosso" and "Che in ver di me l'amor nascosa" and includes isolated references to *Lauti* (lutes), *Betzabé*, and *Hellena* [9:81]; Yseut is Iseult (lover of Tristan) and Batsabe is Bathsheba, one of the wives of King David.

22. **Magnifico . . . carissime**: ML, "most dear and honored compatriot," from a letter Sigismundo wrote to Giovanni de' Medici.

23. **Johanni**: Giovanni de' Medici [cf. 8 above]. Excerpt from a letter from Sigismundo dated March 4, 1449, written "in the field, outside Cremona."

24. **fiorini di Camera**: I, "florins of the treasury," prob. meaning coins of full weight. The gold florin of the Republic of Florence had become the basic monetary standard of Europe.

25. **bombards**: Early cannon for hurling rocks and other missiles. Sigismundo was renowned for his invention of military

engines as well as for his ingenuity as a strategist and tactician [9:6, 10].

26. **Under the plumes . . .** : The siege of Cremona, which was defended by Bianca Visconti, wife of Francesco Sforza, in 1449, will have recalled to Sigismundo's mind his former alliance and friendship with Francesco Sforza. Sforza and Bianca Visconti, after their marriage in the fall of 1441, had visited Rimini in May 1442 on their way to Ancona and been received with the festivities here described. Sigismundo had in the same year married Francesco Sforza's daughter, Polissena [cf. 40 below]; Cremona was part of the dowry given to Bianca by her father, Philippo Maria de Visconti, Duke of Milan. Sigismundo had allied himself with Sforza against Sforza's father-in-law and the pope (Nicholas V), all of whom were trying to wrest the Marches of Ancona from Sforza's control. For two years (1442-1444) the two had fought unsuccessfully against Sforza's enemies, the agreement between them being that Sforza would as quid pro quo help Sigismundo regain Pesaro, a city of great strategic importance for him and part of the hereditary domain of the Malatestas which had been split off and awarded to another line of his family.

27. **baldachino**: I, "canopy."

28. **la pesca . . . godeva molto**: I, "fishing, in which he took great pleasure."

29. **And the Greek emperor**: John Paleologus (reign 1425-1448), who devoted his life's effort to saving Greece from the Turks, an aim that could have been accomplished only if all the European powers had combined to help the Greeks expel the Turks from Europe. But the European states were preoccupied with other interests. On May 29, 1453, Constantinople fell, ending a thousand years of Greek rule. The last Greek emperor was killed defending the city. In 1438 John Paleologus made a futile bid to enlist the aid of the Italian princes by agreeing to heal the split between the Church of Rome and the Greek Church. Thus, the unprecedented Council of Ferrara was called into being [26:39].

30. **Ferrara**: The remarkable meeting between the pope (Eugenius IV) and the patriarch of the Eastern Church took place when the latter debarked at Venice [25:44]. The council was attended by Sigismundo, Cosimo de' Medici, Francesco Gonzaga, and many other dignitaries. The pope planned to house and conduct the council at Ferrara because it was a central location and not subject to the pressures of any one of the strong city-states. But in 1439, when Ferrara was struck by the plague, the council was moved to Florence.

31. **Gemisthus Plethon**: Gemistus P., 1355?-1450?, the Byzantine Neoplatonist philosopher who attended the council at Ferrara and Florence as a delegate of the Eastern Church. Eighty-three at the time, he was steeped in Greek mythology and a Christian in name only. Under his influence Cosimo set up the Platonic Academy of Florence, which became a center of humanistic learning and of the revival of Greek studies in the Western world [*GK*, 160]. Gemistus returned to Greece and diëd there some ten years later. When the Venetians sent a military expedition to the Peloponnesus (Morea) under Sigismundo in 1464-1466 in order to counter the Turkish invasion, the expedition failed but Sigismundo brought back the ashes of Gemistus and had them reinterred in one of the sarcophagi decorating the outside walls of the Tempio at Rimini. His brother Novello [9:5; 11:18, 20, 27] brought back hundreds of Greek manuscripts by ship for his newly founded library, the Bibliotheca Malatestiana, at Cesena [cf. 55 below], texts that would otherwise have been lost to the Western world [cf. 26/123; 83/528; 98/685, 688, 690; *GK*, 224-225].

32. **Delphos**: One of the most sacred places of ancient Greece which Gemistus repeatedly mentioned in his conversation. He dreamed of grafting polytheistic myths onto the Christian religion, an aim with which Pound was in sympathy [9:80; 11:26, 27].

33. Poseidon: The Greek god of water [also as Neptune in 83/528; 96/795]. Gemistus's own hierarchy of the Greek gods placed Zeus first and Poseidon next in a certain correlation to the Neoplatonic hierarchy of values. Pound associates the water/stone motifs, which are so characteristic of Sigismundo's Tempio, with Gemistus's teaching about the god of water [*GK*, 224-225; DD, *Sculptor* 126 ff.].

34. concret Allgemeine: G, the "concrete universal." Pound is quoting from Fritz Schultze [p. 159], who described Gemistus Plethon as a "realist" in the medieval sense, that is, as taking the position of the *universalia in re* represented by Aristotle: "generals are known by particulars" [cf. 74/441], or as Pound [quoting Aquinas] said: "nomina sunt consequentia rerum"—not abstract and arbitrary labels pinned onto concrete things as the Nominalists would have it. A definition introduced by Hegel in order to differentiate between universals which are concrete and those which are abstract.

35. Dionysius: Dionysius I, 430-367 B.C. tyrant of Syracuse. Plato stayed at his court for a time in 388 as tutor to Dionysius the Younger, but his efforts to turn the son into a "philosopher king" failed [cf. *Platonic Epistles* 7]. Sigismundo's veneration of Gemistus is being compared by implication with Dionysius II's respect for Plato.

36. Ancona: City in the Romagna [cf. 26 above]. The described episode prob. took place during the two years of Sigismundo's alliance with Sforza.

37. church against him: Although Pope Martin V had originally tended to support the claims of the legitimate Pesaro line of the Malatesta family, he was eventually induced to accept Galeazzo, Sigismundo's elder brother, as Lord of Rimini on the death of their uncle, Carlo Malatesta of Rimini. The next pope, Eugene IV (1431-1447), similarly accepted Sigismundo as Lord of Rimini following the death of Galeazzo. In 1438 Sigismundo was even appointed chief commander of the papal forces, while in 1445 he was invited to Rome, where he was received with full papal honors and awarded the Sword and the Hat of the Holy See. It was not until the papacy of Enea Silvio Piccolomini, as Pius II (1458-1464), that Sigismundo found the "church against him," for the simple reason that he was a supporter of the Angevine cause, whereas the material interests of Pius II lay with the Aragonese.

38. Medici bank: Cosimo de' Medici, 1389-1464, based his power on his monetary policies. By withdrawing all his capital from the market in 1464, he forced both Naples and Venice to conclude a peace with Florence. The Medici policy consisted of supporting Sforza in Milan in order to offset the power of Venice. Sigismundo had been on his own ever since Milan had fallen to Sforza in 1450. This event marked the end of 30 years of war in northern Italy, which had led to a balance of power among Venice, Milan, Florence, Naples, and the Holy See. At any rate the freedom of movement of the condottieri and minor despots was sharply restricted from 1450 on [cf. 9:48; 10:22; 21/96, 97; 26/123, 124; 93/624; 94/633].

39. wattle Sforza: A reference to the somewhat pendulous fleshy nose of Sforza [cf. 15 above].

40. Pèsaro: [cf. 26 above]. Pesaro had been part of the hereditary domain of the Malatesta family founded by Mastin [cf. 49 below]. It now belonged to Sigismundo's cousin Galeazzo, called the "Inept," who had no heirs. In order to regain Pesaro for himself, Sigismundo formed an alliance with Sforza and even married his illegitimate daughter Polissena [9:23]. But Galeazzo sold Pesaro to Sforza for 20,000 florins so that his niece Constanza could marry Sforza's brother Alessandro, who was to become Lord of Pesaro. At the same time (1445) Galeazzo sold Fossombrone to Federigo d'Urbino [11:12, 14], Sigismundo's archenemy [cf. 5 above].

41. Broglio: Gaspare B., comrade-in-arms of Sigismundo, author of "Cronaca", an unpublished account of Malatesta's campaigns [10:16].

42. bestialmente: I, 'bestially, meanly." Broglio maintained that Galeazzo had no right to sell territory that belonged to the Malatesta family collectively [cf. 40 above and 9:15].

43. templum aedificavit: ML, "he built a temple," from the *Commentaries* of Pius II [9:80], referring to the Tempio which Sigismundo had built as a monument to himself and his mistress. Pound said the Tempio at Rimini is both "an apex and in verbal sense a monumental failure" [*GK*, 159]. In order to build the Tempio, which was officially dedicated to St. Francis, Sigismundo employed the greatest artists of the age: Leon Battista Alberti, Matteo da Pasti, Simone Ferucci, Agostino di Duccio. The church was begun in 1445 and consecrated in 1450. In 1455 the work was interrupted, leaving the front incomplete and the roof not even begun. Only seven of the fourteen sarcophagi intended for the remains of humanists and philosophers were filled. The Tempio was partly destroyed in the Allied bombing raids of December 28, 1943, and January 29, 1944 [cf. 76/459; 80/497; 83/528; 90/605; 92/621; 107/758].

44. with the game lost: Prob. refers to Sigismundo's lost hopes of regaining Pesaro and Fossombrone in 1445.

45. and never quite lost till '50: The year when the treacherous Francesco Sforza became Duke of Milan [cf. 10, 15, 38 above].

46. and never quite lost . . . Romagna: Where there was life, there was always hope for the indomitable Sigismundo. But in 1468 he again fell ill of the fever he had contracted in Morea [11:21] and died at Rimini in the Romagna a few months later. He had been excommunicated in 1460 and deprived of all his possessions except Rimini in 1463 [11:15, 21, 34].

47. Poictiers: Guillaume Poitiers, Duke of Aquitaine [6:2], believed to be the composer of the earliest troubadour lyrics extant and to have introduced troubadour music to France.

48. viels: MF, *viell(e)s*: medieval "viols": stringed instruments of the lute family.

49. Mastin: I, "Mastiff." Nickname of Malatesta da Verrucchio, 1212-1312, great-great-grandfather of Sigismundo. The "Old Mastiff" had been the original founder of the Malatesta dynasty and became the first Lord of Rimini in 1293. Earlier he had lived at Verrucchio, which had been awarded to him for his services to the city of Rimini [cf. *Inf*. XXVII, 44-46; 5 above].

50. Paolo il Bello: I, "Paul the Handsome," ?1247-1283?, second son of the "Old Mastiff." His elder brother Gianciotto was deformed and had been married to Francesca, daughter of Guido Vecchio da Polenta. Paolo and Francesca fell in love with each other and were killed by the enraged Gianciotto. Boccaccio says that Paolo tried to escape but his mantle caught on a nail [cf. *Inf*. V, 73-142; also the line *che paion' si al vent* ("who appeared so light on the wind") at 110/777].

51. Parisina: Daughter of Carlo Malatesta and cousin to Sigismundo [cf. 5 above]. In 1418 she married Niccolò d'Este, Lord of Ferrara, when she was 14 and he was 34. In 1425, after Parisina had borne him two daughters, Niccolò suspected her of adultery with his favorite son Ugo, who was of the same age, and had them both beheaded. Pound tells the story in some detail in 20/90, 91 [cf. 24/110-112; *L*, 210 to Homer Pound].

52. Atreides: H, "sons of Atreus." The violence in the house of Malatesta is compared with the internecine strife in the house of Atreus.

53. was twelve at the time: Sigismundo was 12 when Carlo Malatesta, his uncle and tutor, died. His "elder brother gone pious" was Galeotto, who had entered the Franciscan order. Wearing a monk's habit he devoted himself to prayer, fasting, and self-flagellation.

54. fought in the streets: After having become Lord of Rimini at 15, Sigismundo had been attacked on the streets of Rimini by a band of peasants led by a sixty-year-old priest, Don Matteo, who combined his support for their grievances with a desire to place the city under the jurisdiction of the Holy See. Sigismundo afterward had the priest defrocked by three friendly bishops and hanged in public on the piazza.

55. Cesena: In 1432, after Sigismundo had succeeded the dead Galeotto as Lord of Rimini, Carlo Malatesta of Pesaro (head of the legitimate side of the family), supported by the Count of Urbino, attempted to seize Rimini. Warned of the approaching forces, Sigismundo rode to Cesena, another of his possessions, where he gathered a force of 400 foot soldiers and 300 mounted men. Returning to Rimini with this force he challenged the troops of his relative outside the city walls, demanding to know whether they came as friend or foe. They said they came as friends and thereupon withdrew. Shortly afterward Sigismundo appointed his younger brother, Domenico (Novello/Novvy), governor of Cesena [9:5; 11:18, 20].

56. Foglia: The alacrity with which Galeotto was obeying the orders of the new pope, Eugenius IV (1431-1447), to harass the Jews and investigate the practice of concubinage among the clergy gave rise to the fear among the legitimate branch of the Malatesta, headed by Carlo Malatesta of Pesaro, that Rimini would shortly be handed over to the Holy See as a gift. With the support of the Count of Urbino he decided to forestall any such action by seizing the town along with Fano, which also belonged to the illegitimate side of the family. Not long after his troops had left Pesaro and had camped for the night near Serra Ungarina, they were attacked and dispersed by a small force under the 13-year-old Sigismundo, who had crossed the Foglia (a river flowing into the Adriatic near Pesaro) at dusk.

Glossary Canto IX

1. one year . . . : The introductory lines give an impressionistic account of specific episodes in Sigismundo's career. They are also reminiscent of the lines in T. S. Eliot's description of the factive personality in *Gerontion* ("Nor fought in the warm rain / Nor knee deep in the salt marsh, heaving a cutlass / Bitten by flies, fought"). The episodes concern the flood of 1440 during which Rimini was encircled by water like Venice; the winter of 1444 when Sigismundo set out in a snowstorm and, for the sake of Sforza, caused Monte Gaudio to surrender [8:26]; the hailstorm of 1442 which wrought great destruction in Rimini and the surrounding countryside [*Analyst* VII; Hutton, 106, 129, 118].

2. Astorre Manfredi: Lord of Faenza, a condottiere like Sigismundo but an ally of the Duke of Urbino and a hereditary enemy of the Malatestas. The lines refer to an incident when Sigismundo had to cross Astorre's territory and was ambushed by him. Sigismundo escaped the pursuing hounds by standing in marsh water up to his neck, an incident that took place near Astorre's castle of Russi on the road from Mantua to Rimini.

3. Fano: Town in the marshes of central Italy, part of the hereditary domain of the Malatestas but eventually lost to the Holy See, whence the inscription there: *Olim de Malatestis* ["Once of the Malatestas"]. Fano, originally *fanum* ["temple"], had in Roman times been the site of a temple in honor of Caesar Augustus, whence *Fano Caesaris*. It also has a triumphal arch (*l'arco d'Augusto*) left over from Roman times and thus once more associates Sigismundo with the heroes of antiquity. The incident here mentioned refers to the trouble young Sigismundo experienced in assuming lordship over the cities of Rimini, Fano, and Cesena against the resistance of their inhabitants [8:40, 54; 11:12; 11/50; 30/148, 149; 76/462; 80/501, 502; 83/529].

4. **Emperor**: Sigismund V, 1368-1437, Holy Roman emperor (1433-1437) of the house of Luxemburg. In the fall of 1433 he was crowned emperor in Rome by the pope. On his way back north he stopped at Rimini where, being received with elaborate ceremony, he knighted both Sigismundo and his youngest brother Domenico. Piero della Francesca depicted the event in a fresco in the Chapel of Relics of the Tempio.

5. . . . **knighted us**: Sigismundo's youngest brother Domenico, called "Malatesta Novello," or "Novvy," by Pound, 1418–1465. He governed Cesena for Sigismundo and founded the library there [8:31; 10:58; 11:18; 16/69; 23/107].

6. **wooden castle**: A wooden castle designed by Sigismundo was built for use in the tourneys during the three-day fiesta celebrating his marriage to Ginevra in 1433 [cf. 8 below]. This feat of military engineering prefigures the building of La Rocca [cf. 10 below].

7. **Basinio**: Basinio de Basini, 1425-1457, Italian poet and humanist patronized by Sigismundo. His *L'Isottaeus*, 30 epistles in the manner of Ovid's *Heroides*, celebrates Sigismundo's love of Isotta degli Atti. After he had entered the service of Sigismundo he was challenged to a literary duel by a rival poet at the court, one Porcellio Pandone, 1405-1485, who had written a poem on the same theme, *De amore Iovis in Isottam* ["Of Jupiter's love of Isotta"]. The event, presided over by Sigismundo and Isotta, took place in the courtyard of La Rocca. Porcellio defended the thesis that one could write good Latin verse without having studied Greek (hence "the anti-Hellene"). But Basinio, who had studied Greek (a rare accomplishment at the time), defended Greek studies by showing the dependence of Latin literature upon Greek (a view shared by Pound) and the importance of Greek scholarship in the new humanistic Renaissance. Basinio was declared victor in the debate. He remained at Rimini and is buried in one of the sarcophagi outside the Tempio [cf. 82/524; 104/740].

8. **Madame Ginevra**: Daughter of Parisina and Niccolò d'Este, became Sigismundo's first wife in 1434 when she was 16 and he was 17. In 1437 she bore him a son who lived only a year. Unwell after the birth of the child, she died at the age of 22. Sigismundo had been away in the field during most of their marriage. Pius II [10:25] later accused him of having poisoned her.

9. **Capitan**: In 1437 Sigismundo, then only 20 years old, was engaged as captain by the Venetians [cf. 25 below].

10. **Rocca**: In the same year Sigismundo began building La Rocca, a fortress, at Rimini, a project that was to take nine years (1437-1446). Its design and execution were largely undertaken by Sigismundo himself, and the fortress was one of the main achievements of his life. In its day La Rocca was considered one of the marvels of Italy. During the past century it has been altered beyond recognition.

11. **Monteluro**: Site of a battle where in 1444 Sigismundo won a victory for the cause of Francesco Sforza, his father-in-law [8:26, 40]. But this victory accomplished little for Sigismundo because a few months later he broke with Sforza over the sale of Pesaro [cf. Hutton, 128].

12. **Sforza**: [8:15, 39].

13. **March 16th**: The date in 1445 when the agreement was executed between Francesco Sforza and his brother Alessandro Sforza, Federigo d'Urbino, and Galeazzo Malatesta under which Pesaro was sold to Alessandro and Fossombrone to Federigo [Tonini, v, 152; 8:40].

14. **Federicho d'Orbino**: Medieval spelling of Federigo d'Urbino, i.e., Federigo da Montefeltro, 1422-1482, first Duke of

Urbino, a great Italian condottiere and politician and patron of the arts. According to Pound, Federigo was "Sigismundo's Amy Lowell" [*GK*, 159].

15. **bestialmente**: [8:41, 42]. The account is by Gaspare Broglio.

16. **per capitoli**: I, "by agreement."

17. **out of the Marches**: Sigismundo now joined the alliance against Sforza and, in a brilliant two-year campaign, drove his enemies out of the Marches of Ancona.

18. **King o' Ragona**: [8:10]. Sigismundo had been engaged by Alphonso of Aragon, king of Naples, in 1447 to enforce his claim to Milan. For his services to Alphonso, Sigismundo had already received 25,000 ducats out of the 32,400 agreed upon, when the Florentines persuaded him to take service with them instead. This Sigismundo did, keeping the money already paid to him, on the advice of Valturio. For his treachery he earned the undying hatred of Alphonso [cf. F.G. Battaglini, 399].

19. **Valturio**: Roberto Valturio, ?1414-1489, Italian engineer and author of *De Re Militari*, 1472, one of the books in Leonardo da Vinci's library; first secretary and adviser to Sigismundo, charged with building La Rocca. He is buried in one of the sarcophagi of the Tempio.

20. **haec traditio**: ML, "this treachery." Pound eliminates the charge of treachery against Sigismundo by translating *traditio* as "change-over," as though the word were Latin rather than Medieval Latin [EH].

21. **old bladder**: Aeneas Sylvius (Enea Silvio de) Piccolomini, 1404-1464, as Pius II (1458-1462) [10:25]. Pound refers to him as *old bladder* because he suffered from gallstones [10:36].

22. **rem eorum saluavit**: L, "saved their cause," from the *Commentaries* of Pius II: "There is no doubt that Sigismundo's treachery saved the Florentine Cause."

23. **Polixena**: Polissena Sforza, natural daughter of Francesco Sforza. Sigismundo married her barely a year after the death of his first wife in return for her father's promise to help him regain Pesaro. In the following year she bore Sigismundo a son who died in his first year. Sigismundo abandoned her for his successive mistresses Vanetta Toschi and Isotta degli Atti. When the plague was ravaging Rimini in 1449, she fled to the Convent of Scolca in the hills where she choked to death one night and was hastily buried in an unmarked grave; it may thus be inferred that she fell victim to the plague. Ten years later Pius II accused Sigismundo of having strangled her [cf. 8:26, 40; 10:23].

24. **old Wattle-wattle**: Francesco Sforza finally entering Milan as duke in 1450 [8:15, 39].

25. **Feddy**: Federigo d'Urbino [cf. 14 above]. When Sforza entered Milan, Sigismundo was still in the service of Venice and therefore enjoyed a high status, since the rich republic employed only the most daring condottieri. In order to separate him from Venice, Sforza again used Pesaro as bait and induced Federigo d'Urbino to pretend that he would help Sigismundo take Pesaro from Alessandro Sforza. But when Sforza's forces came up from the rear and were welcomed in Urbino, Sigismundo knew that he had been tricked [Hutton, 197-199].

26. **Foscari**: Francesco Foscari, ?1372-1457, Doge of Venice (1423-1457).

27. **Caro mio**: I, "my dear man." Foscari writing to Sigismundo, offering to help him regain Pesaro in order to dissuade him from leaving Venetian service.

28. **Classe**: Refers to the great basilica of S. Apollinare in Classe, Ravenna, the most important Byzantine church in Italy, dating back to 534, the same period in which the tomb of Galla Placidia and San Vitale were built, both of which Pound praises and contrasts with the "monumental failure" of the Tempio. Sigismundo stripped the basilica of

its marble decorations (porphyry, serpentine) for use in his Tempio [*Analyst* VII; Yriarte, 193-194; Hutton, *Ravenna*, 204-205; F. G. Battaglini, 431-432]. Pound's "Sant Apollinaire" comes from Yriarte's "San Apollinaire," but the original Italian form is "S. Apollinare."

29. Casus est talis: L, "that's the way it is." Sigismundo is excusing his actions to Foscari. The citizens of Ravenna, outraged at the spoliation, complained to Foscari, since Ravenna was then under the jurisdiction of a Venetian podesta. Upon pressure from the doge, the Benedictine abbot of S. Apollinare [cf. 34 below] and the commune of Ravenna agreed to accept 200 gold florins from Sigismundo in compensation for the loss. Another attempt by Sigismundo to avail himself of the treasures of the basilica, as though it were a stone quarry, took the form of obtaining a papal bull transferring jurisdiction over the Abbey of S. Apollinare to his own canon at Rimini. This caused the outraged Venetian senate to prohibit any move to take possession of the abbey. Pound has reversed the chronological order of the two events [cf. 35 below].

30. Filippo: F. Calandrini, Cardinal Bishop of Bologna, who had become "commendatary" of the Abbey of S. Apollinare. Sigismundo approached him and "easily obtained his authority to remove as much as he desired" [F. G. Battaglini, 431-432], Pound's insinuation here being that the cardinal had received "four hundred ducats" for his acquiescence, which is not borne out by the records.

31. quadam nocte: L, "on a certain night."

32. Santa Maria in Trivio: [8:43]. Name of the older church built in honor of the Madonna dell'Acqua but replaced by the Tempio Malatestiano, which was officially dedicated to St. Francis. The great Renaissance architect, Leon Battista Alberti, had decided not to destroy the older church with the tombs of Sigismundo's ancestors but to superimpose the Tempio upon it, so showing a respect for earlier achievements obviously missing in Sigismundo [cf. 54 below]. Thus the Tempio incorporates cultural layers from various periods (the Gothic church, the Renaissance shell, the Byzantine marbles), as Pound does in *The Cantos*. Pound's defense of Sigismundo from the charge of stealing is therefore not devoid of a self-serving element.

33. plaustra: L, "wagons, carts."

34. Aloysius Purtheo: Fl. 1450. Prob. Benedictine abbot of S. Apollinare in Classe.

35. corn-salve: The hasty sally of "an hundred two-wheeled oxcarts" to strip S. Apollinare overnight presumably caused considerable damage to the fields and crops. The lines are intended to show Sigismundo's concern for the peasants and the integrity of his arrangement with the abbot [cf. 29 above].

36. German-Burgundian female: The great Italian historian, Ludovico Antonio Muratori, writes in his *Annali d'Italia*: "Whether he was indeed guilty of this outrage I am unable to say, for in spite of all the investigations undertaken by the perspicacious Venetians, they were unable to discover the culprit." Pius II, on the other hand, presents the story in his *Commentaries* in the lurid denunciatory language of a cheap journalist: "Meeting not far from Verona a noble lady who was going from Germany to Rome in the jubilee year, he [Sigismundo] assaulted her (for she was very beautiful) and when she struggled, left her wounded and covered with blood" [167]. Pound, in a letter to John Quinn dated August 10, 1922, garbles both accounts and adds some trimmings of his own invention: "Authorities differ as to whether Sigismundo Malatesta raped a german girl in Verona, with such vigor that she 'passed on,' or whether it was an Italian in Pesaro, and the pope says he killed her first and raped her afterwards: . . . in fact all the *minor* points that might aid one in forming an historic rather than a fanciful idea of his character seem 'shrouded in mystery' or rather lies" [YC] [EH].

37. Poliorcetes: H, "Taker of cities," epithet linked with the exploits of Demetrius, king of Macedonia, 294-288 B.C. Demetrius's military career and his feats of military engineering show parallels with Sigismundo's. The legend on the medallions of Sigismundo executed by Pisanello read: "Poliorcetes et semper Invictus" [H, L, "Taker of cities, and always victorious"].

38. POLUMETIS: H, "many-minded," that is, versatile, stock Homeric epithet for Odysseus [*Od.* I, 1] here applied to Sigismundo [cf. 11:29; *GK*, 146].

39. Feddy: Federigo d'Urbino [cf. 14, 25 above].

40. Alessandro: A. Sforza, Lord of Pesaro [cf. 8:40, 25 above].

41. Broglio: [8:41].

42. m'l'ha calata: I [slang], "he's tricked me" [Tonini, 198-203]. Pound uses the phrase again in his translation of Sophocles' *Trachiniae*.

43. Istria: Peninsula at N end of Adriatic. Istrian marble was used in building the city of Venice [17/79]. Sigismundo had ordered a large quantity of marble from Istria for his Tempio; the delayed delivery is mentioned in Pietro di Genari's [cf. 53 below] letter [cf. Adrian Stokes, *Stones of Rimini*, 19-20; DD, *Sculptor*, 127-131].

44. Silk war: Prob. a war between Venice and Ragusa (now Dubrovnik) in Dalmatia [17/79; 77/394]. Venice and Ragusa were traditional enemies, Ragusa being the only town along the Adriatic coast that was long able to maintain its independence against Venice and to rival it in the silk industry. Venice assumed the lead in the silk industry in the 15th century. In 1423 the doge mentioned 1,600 silk weavers working there. Pandolfo Malatesta, Sigismundo's father, had unsuccessfully led the Venetians against Ragusa in 1420.

45. Wattle: Francesco Sforza. Prob. refers to the invasion of Tuscany by Alphonso d'Aragon in 1452. Since Sigismundo had entered the service of Florence [8:10, 16], he now found himself supporting Florence and Milan, i.e., F. Sforza [8:15], against Venice and Naples.

46. Vada: Scene of one of Sigismundo's military successes. In 1453 he used his bombards to take the supposedly impregnable fortress of Vada manned by Alphonso of Aragon's troops.

47. bombards: Sigismundo is credited with the invention of various military engines, including a catapult or cannon for firing incendiary projectiles in the form of bronze balls filled with powder and fused with dry burning tinder [Valturio, 267].

48. Siena: The jobs available for Sigismundo and other condottieri were becoming scarce, forcing him to serve minor powers such as Siena, which he apparently did not take very seriously. He had been engaged by Siena to attack the Count of Pitigliano (Aldobrandino Orsini), who had seized several strongholds belonging to the commune. Sigismundo besieged his castle of Sorano: the *two lumps of tufa* describe the insignificance of the affair in Sigismundo's eyes. Venice, an ally of Siena, sent along an army under the command of Carlo Gonzago to assist him while Siena, seeing that the siege was dragging on into the winter, engaged yet another condottiere, Ghiberto da Correggio. The command was thus divided and wracked by secret hostilities, causing Siena and particularly the bishop, Enea Silvio Piccolomini [later Pius II], to suspect Sigismundo of double-dealing [8:37; 10:1, 2, 5, 6].

49. postbag: In 1454, when a breach was finally made in the fortifications of Sorano, Sigismundo, without consulting the commune, made a truce with the count and raised the siege. The commune, convinced now of Sigismundo's treachery, raided his headquarters and tried to arrest him. Sigismundo escaped, but his postbag containing the letters he had received in five months, about 50 in all, fell into the hands of the Sienese. The following are extracts from eight of these letters, discovered in the Archives of Siena in the nineteenth century. They illustrate the preoccupations of Sigismundo's mind [cf. *Analyst* VII; Yriarte, 419-423, 396-397, 443-444, 406-407].

50. Ex Arimino . . . singularissime: ML, "From Rimini, 22 December 1454, Magnificent and powerful master to me most extraordinary." This letter is written by Matteo Nuti of Fano, an architect whom Novello had lent to Sigismundo, and runs through to "roof and. . . ." The chief architect of the Tempio, Alberti, had been recalled to Rome and the plans he had left behind were giving the builders some difficulty, so Nuti was brought in to clarify them [cf. 54 below].

51. Alwidge: Luigi Alvise, overseer of carpenters and masons at work on the Tempio.

52. Magnifice . . . Mio: I, "Magnificent Excellency, My Lord" [Letter 2, dated Dec. 21, 1454]. Excerpt runs from "JHesus" to "rite." It is from Giovane, son of the overseer Alvise, who is writing at his father's dictation.

53. Genare: Pietro di Genari, Sigismundo's chancellor.

54. Albert: Leon Battista Alberti, 1404-1472, the architect of the Tempio. He was one of the universal men of the century: inventor, astronomer, athlete, poet, sculptor, painter, and Latinist, but best known as an architect. He was a Florentine and Sigismundo is thought to have met him in Florence in 1435. Alberti was under the patronage of Pope Nicholas V and it was through the pope that Sigismundo was able to obtain Alberti's services. Alberti, however, had been recalled to Rome by his patron.

55. Sagramoro: Jacopo S. da Soncino, counselor and secretary to Sigismundo. Postscript to Letter 2 saying that Sagramoro had examined all the works.

56. Illustre . . . mio: I, "My dear sir." Letter 3, dated December 21, 1454, addressed to Alberti and signed by Pietro di Genari and Matteo da Pasti. It lists material needed for the construction of the Tempio.

57. Monseigneur: Letter 4, dated December 21, 1454, addressed to Sigismundo by "D. de M.," considered by some to have been dictated by Isotta. It reports on the visit made by Isotta [cf. 59 below] to a young girl with whom Sigismundo was probably having an affair. Isotta was at that time still only Sigismundo's mistress.

58. S. Galeazzo's: Galeazzo was prob. the father of the girl who had been seduced by Sigismundo.

59. Madame Isotta: Isotta degli Atti, ?1430-1470, Sigismundo's mistress and later (1456) his third wife [8:21]. His love for her is celebrated all over the Tempio, especially in her monumental tomb, by the intertwined initials S and I. She bore him at least two sons, both before marriage: Sallustio (1448) and Valerio (1453) [cf. 61, 79, 80, 81 below].

60. Mi pare . . . chossia: I; Pound translates: "I think [she] very nearly exhausted the matter."

61. All the children: At least seven illegitimate children of Sigismundo were living in 1454. Two of them were Isotta's; Lucrezia, one of the older of the other five, was made legitimate by the pope in 1453.

62. Sagramoro: [cf. 55 above].

63. Messire Malatesta: Sigismundo's young son Sallustio, 1448-1470. Letter 5, dated December 20, 1454, signed Lunarda da Palla [cf. 66 below]. Sallustio was murdered by, or at the behest of, his half brother Roberto Malatesta [cf. 11:9; 20/94; 74/448].

64. Chateau: The fortress of Sorano [cf. 48 above].

65. Georgio Rambottom: G. Ranbutino, a stonemason.

66. Lunarda: L. da Palla, Sallustio's tutor.

67. Magnifice ac potens: ML, "to the magnificent and powerful," opening of Letter 1.

68. Malatesta . . . suum: ML, "from Malatesta of Malatestis to his magnificent Lord and Father." Letter 6, dated December 22, 1454, written by Sallustio, then six years old, to his father.

69. Ex[so] **. . . General**: ML, "Excellent Lord, my Lord, and also Lord Sigismundo Pandolpho of the Malatesti, Captain General." Inscription on the outside of Sallustio's letter.

70. Gentilino da Gradara: Unknown agent of Sigismundo's.

71. Illustrious Prince: Letter 7, dated December 18, 1454, written by Iacopo Trachulo ("Servulus Trajatus"), a court poet of Sigismundo's. The advice given to Sigismundo in this letter to establish his own party in Siena and eventually take over the city must, in Pound's opinion, have clinched the matter and confirmed the Sienese in their suspicions of Sigismundo [10:2].

72. Hannibal: Famous general who led the forces of Carthage against Rome, crossing the Alps with his elephants. Sigismundo claimed to have been descended from Hannibal, so Trachulo is here addressing Sigismundo, who often used elephants as his emblem.

73. Magnifice . . . premissa: ML, "Magnificent and powerful Lord, my most particular Lord, I send you my most humble greetings." Letter 8 written by Pietro di Genari [cf. 53, 56 above], dated December 18, 1454, reporting on a shipment of marble which had at last arrived and the progress of the work on the Tempio and La Rocca.

74. defalcation: Embezzlement.

75. aliofants: I, "elephants." The conventional Italian form being *elefante*, *aliofant* may have been used by Pound to emphasize the resemblance between Matteo da Pasti's black porphyry elephant heads and garlic cloves [I, *aglio*], no one there at that time having ever set eyes on an elephant. These sculptured elephants support the columns of the Tempio [cf. HK, *Era*, 429].

76. Antonio: A. degli Atti, brother of Isotta, who had been knighted by the Emperor Sigismund.

77. Ottavian: Ottaviano, a painter commissioned to illuminate the papal bull allowing Sigismundo to erect an altar in the church of St. Sigismund.

78. Agostino: A. di Duccio, 1418-1481, Florentine sculptor who worked on the sarcophagus dedicated to Sigismundo's ancestors and on the bas-reliefs of the Tempio [cf. DD, *Sculptor*, 127-131; 20/90; 45/229; 51/250; 74/425].

79. et amava . . . decus: I, ML, "And he loved Isotta degli Atti to distraction / and she was worthy of it / constant in purpose / She delighted the eye of the prince / lovely to look at / pleasing to the people (and the ornament of Italy)." This tribute to Isotta is a composite of several sources: Pius II, *Commentaries*; a 15th-century chronicle of Rimini; *constans in proposito* [L] is from Horace, *Odes* III, 3; Pound also uses it in relation to J. Q. Adams [cf. 34/171]: *Constans proposito / Justum et tenacem* ["Constant in purpose, just and enduring"] from *The Diary of John Quincy Adams*, 568 [cf. *Pai*, 6-2, 231].

80. and built a temple: From the *Commentaries* of Pius II [8:37, 43; 21 above]. The Tempio, although dedicated to St. Francis, is devoid of Christian symbols. All the allegorical figures are classical and Sigismundo himself is enthroned among Olympian deities. The temple is likewise a monument to the love of Sigismundo and Isotta; the tomb in the chapel of S. Michael Archangel is inscribed: "D. ISOTTAE ARIMINENSI. B.M. MCCCCL," where the "D" may stand for either "DIVAE" or "DOMINAE" [ML, "Sacred to the Blessed Memory of the Goddess (Lady?) Isotta of Rimini, 1450"]. Pound reads it as *Divae* [cf. *Divae Ixottae* in 76/459].

81. **"Past ruin'd Latium"**: An echo of the line "Past ruined Ilion Helen lives" from the poem "To Ianthe" by W. S. Landor which Pound quotes to align Isotta with the archetypal Helen [8:21].

82. **San Vitale**: Byzantine church in Ravenna dating back to the 6th century, like S. Apollinare, and similarly full of marble, mosaics, and carved columns [cf. 28 above]. Pound compares the quiet dignity of the old sarcophagi outside San Vitale to the conglomeration of styles in the Tempio.

Glossary Canto X

1. **Sorano**: Sigismundo laid siege to this castle in the winter of 1454-55 [9:48, 64] while in the service of Siena. To Pound, the Siena venture was another turning point in Sigismundo's fortunes because he incurred the enmity of Enea Silvio Piccolomini [later Pius II], who was then Bishop of Siena [9:21]. According to Pound, there was no "deceit, conspiracy, treachery, slander" Piccolomini would not stoop to in order to destroy Sigismundo.

2. **Orsini**: Aldobrandino O., Count of Pitigliano [9:48]. From his stronghold Orsini wrote Sigismundo a taunting letter containing the same suggestions as those already made by Trachulo, namely that he abandon the siege and make himself master of Siena instead. From Sigismundo's strange truce with Orsini after he had actually breached the fortress [9:49], it would appear that he accepted Orsini's suggestions.

3. **Trachulo**: [9:71].

4. **Fanesi**: Citizens of Fano. This unknown and improbable incident, for Fano belonged to Sigismundo's own territory, was poss. invented by Pound to indicate the trivial nature of the tasks now left to Sigismundo, who had served the great powers of Naples, Florence, and Venice [8:38].

5. **three men**: Carlo Gonzago, Ghiberto da Correggio, and Sigismundo, officers in command of the three armies serving the Sienese [9:48].

6. **Careggi**: Ghiberto da Correggio, the second officer called in by the Sienese, naturally saw himself as Sigismundo's rival for the favor of the commune.

7. **Carmagnola**: Francesco Bussone da C., 1380-1432, one of the most distinguished condottieri of the century. In 1432 he offered his daughter in marriage to the then 15-year-old Sigismundo. The offer was accepted, but because of Carmagnola's execution shortly thereafter Sigismundo reneged on the marriage, though keeping the dowry. Bussone had long been in the service of the noble family of the Visconti of Milan, from whom he had received the title of count. In 1424 he shifted to the service of Venice, whose citizens traditionally hired professional soldiers to do their fighting while they themselves followed exclusively mercantile interests. But they were always careful to stipulate that no condottiere should ever enter Venice with his troops. The condottieri were of course little interested in bringing any armed conflict to a speedy conclusion and Carmagnola, who had been procrastinating like Sigismundo at Sorano, was therefore suspected by the Venetians of having been bribed by the Visconti. In order to set a warning example, the council summoned Carmagnola to Venice (i.e., "invited [him] to lunch") to give a progress report. On his arrival on May 5, 1432, he was seized and summarily executed, an event that left an indelible mark on other soldiers of fortune.

Thus, when Sigismundo was invited to Siena to discuss the situation, he recalled the fate of Carmagnola and declined the "invitation to lunch" [17:31].

8. **the two columns**: The columns (one red, one gray), brought from Syria in 1128, were set up at the Piazetta, the sea entrance to Venice and also the traditional site of executions. The red column is surmounted by a marble statue of the first patron saint of Venice, St. Theodorus, and his emblem, the crocodile [26/121], while the gray column is surmounted by his more prestigious successor, the evangelist St. Mark, and his emblem, a bronze winged lion, reputedly an ancient Chinese or Babylonian artefact. Since St. Theodorus had belonged to the lowly Eastern Church, the Venetians replaced him as their patron saint at the first opportunity (838) by St. Mark, whose remains they had pressured the padres of an Alexandrinian monastery into relinquishing to them for the trifling sum of 50 zecchini. His bones were smuggled out of the harbor under sides of bacon, which it was correctly surmised would ward off the curiosity of the Moslem officials. Thus the execution site itself came to signify a betrayal.

9. **Et . . . Sigismundo**: ML, I, "they've got the better of Sigismundo," from a letter by Filippo Strozzi dated December 31, 1454 [Luciano Banchi in *Archivio Storico Italiano*, ser. IV, iii, 184-197] giving an account of Sigismundo's retreat after the Sienese raid on his headquarters [9:49]. Sigismundo, finding all escape routes blocked, finally requested permission from Florence to pass through its territory at Campiglia, which was granted as predicted in Strozzi's letter.

10. **Filippo Strozzi**: 1426-1491, member of the famous Florentine family driven into exile in 1434. Filippo became a banker in Naples, amassing a huge fortune. Later he was allowed to return to Florence. Zan Lottieri is Zanobi Lottieri [ibid.].

11. **Florence . . . Pitigliano**: I, "Italian Historical Archives. . . . The War of the Sienese against the Count of Pitigliano," i.e., Banchi's record of the Sienese affair. Identification of source of three foregoing lines.

12. **Carlo Gonzago**: [9:48]. Leader of the Venetian forces supporting Siena against Pitigliano; he had also outraged the commune by forcibly entering Orbetello with his troops with the intention of staying there over the winter. The Venetians had only just assuaged the Sienese on this count when Sigismundo turned up, requesting permission to take refuge at Orbetello. It certainly was an unpropitious moment.

13. **Orbetello**: Town situated in the middle of a muddy lagoon ca. 100 km S of Siena, whence "mud-frog."

14. **Caro Mio**: I, "My dear man." Gonzago addressing Sigismundo.

15. **Broglio**: [cf. 16 below; 8:41].

16. **Gorro Lolli**: Nephew of the Bishop of Siena [later Pius II, cf. 1 above], an influential man in Sienese affairs who had always defended Sigismundo. As Sigismundo had been offended by the distrust of the Sienese, Broglio had suggested that the commune placate him with the gift of a valuable charger with trappings; the horse was formally presented to him by Gorro Lolli. When Sigismundo, forgetting his upbringing, neglected to give the bearer a small present in return as custom required, the latter was deeply offended.

17. **Piccinino**: Giacomo P., d. 1465, a powerful condottiere released from Venetian service after the Treaty of Lodi (1454), was hanging around with his private army in the hope of establishing a dynasty as other condottieri had done (e.g., Francesco Sforza). Thus he was a constant threat to anyone in power in Italy up to the year of his death, a fact recorded by Machiavelli [quoted in 21/97: *E non avendo stato* . . ., i.e., "And as Piccinino had no property / or state, / anyone who had, felt threatened by him"]. Piccinino married Drusiana [cf. 23 below], another daughter of Francesco Sforza, at Milan and was invited to celebrate the event

(another "invitation to lunch") at Naples by Alphonso of Aragon's son Ferrante [Ferdinand; cf. 44, 46, 48 below; 8:10]. Ferrante feasted Piccinino for 27 days and then had him thrown into a dungeon and strangled, afterward spreading the rumor that Piccinino had fallen out a window. This crime shocked all Italy. But it is doubtful that Francesco Sforza was a party to the plot [Muratori, IX, 236-237; 21/97].

18. **the old row with Naples**: [8:10; 9:18]. Alphonso of Aragon had turned Piccinino against Sigismundo, but Piccinino was diverted from his attempt to seize Rimini. Alphonso's son Ferdinand [Ferrante, 1458-1494], who succeeded Alphonso after his death in 1458, continued the old feud with Sigismundo.

19. **Mantua**: The most serious problem confronting Piccolomini when he became Pius II in 1458 was the Moslem threat to Europe. In 1453 Constantinople had fallen to the Turks [8:29], who had since overrun the whole of Peloponnesus (Morea), Attica, and Corinth. Hence Pius II called an international congress at Mantua in 1459. All the delegates agreed that the countries nearest the Turks should do the fighting, while the Italians should supply the funds. Sigismundo alone proposed the opposite on two grounds: (1) the countries nearest the Turks, having been defeated, were already demoralized; (2) the Italians, being more quick-witted and also better fighters, should do the fighting, while the others should foot the bill [Pius II, *Commentaries* III; 11:21; 26/125].

20. **Borso**: B. d'Este, 1413-1471, natural son of Niccolò d'Este [8:51], Lord of Ferrara and Modena, patron of learning and the arts, and dedicated to keeping the peace. Because of Borso's peaceful diplomacy, Ferrara was known throughout Italy during his rule as *la terra della pace* ["the domain of peace"]. Since he always strove to maintain neutrality in all conflicts, he was frequently called upon by his neighbors to arbitrate their quarrels and "keep the peace." At the same time he succeeded in increasing his own territory without bloodshed. He was a friend of Sigismundo's [8:5] and in 1456, when Rimini was under heavy pressure, tried to mediate between Sigismundo and one of his worst enemies, Federigo d'Urbino [cf. 9:14, 25, 39; 17/78, 79; 20/91, 21/96; 24/114; 26/121].

21. **Bel Fiore**: Borso had arranged a meeting between Federigo d'Urbino, who was passing through Ferrara, and Sigismundo. They dined together and the next day repaired to Borso's villa Belriguardo (Pound's *Bel Fiore*). All present sought to persuade them to make peace and become friends, but according to Battaglini [468] they came close to blows instead. The exchange of vituperations given by Pound: Sigismundo: "Te cavero . . ." ["I, I'll tear your guts out"]; Federigo, "el Conte levatosi" ["the count rising"], says: "Io te . . ." ["I'll tear your liver out"] [9:14; 81/518].

22. **Cosimo**: C. de' Medici, 1389-1464, Florentine banker, patron of the arts, founder of the elder branch of the family, called Pater Patriae by his fellow citizens. It was his policy to work in close association with Francesco Sforza [cf. 8:15, 38; 21/96, 97; 26/123, 124].

23. **Drusiana**: One of Francesco Sforza's illegitimate daughters, all of whom he used to further his own political ends [cf. 17 above]. Another, Polissena, was Sigismundo's second wife [8:40; 9:23]. Yet another was married to Federigo d'Urbino. Drusiana married Piccinino in 1465, which pleased Cosimo as the alliance made Piccinino less of a threat to Florence. Drusiana, however, was soon to be widowed.

24. **un sorriso malizioso**: I, "a malicious smile."

25. **INTEREA . . . FLAGRAVIT**: ML. Quoted by Yriarte from the *Commentaries* of Pius II, this passage concerns the auto-da-fé at which Sigismundo was burned in effigy. Florence A. Gragg translates: "Meantime in front of the steps of St. Peter's there was built a great pyre of dry wood, on top

of which was placed an effigy of Sigismundo imitating the [wicked and accursed] man's features and dressed so exactly that it seemed a real person rather than an image. But that no one should make any mistake about it, an inscription issued from the figure's mouth, which read: SIGISMUNDO MALATESTA, SON OF PANDOLFO, KING OF TRAITORS, HATED OF GOD AND MAN, CONDEMNED TO THE FLAMES BY VOTE OF THE HOLY SENATE. This writing was read by many. Then, while the populace stood by, fire was applied to the pyre and the image, which at once blazed up." The events leading up to this incident were the following: Sigismundo, surrounded by enemies, had ultimately been forced to come to terms with Pius II, agreeing to a treaty under which he was to pay an indemnity to Naples for his betrayal, surrender some of his strongholds to Federigo d'Urbino and Pius II, and undertake to abstain from all military activities for ten years. Sigismundo broke the treaty the following year by seizing two fortresses from Federigo d'Urbino and attacking Sinigaglia. Pius II immediately excommunicated him, declaring all his possessions forfeit and instituting legal proceedings against him. Shortly afterward (1461) the pope sent a large army against Sigismundo, who completely routed the superior papal forces [cf. 60 below]. Pius II thereupon renewed the charges against Sigismundo and issued a total interdict against anyone helping him or communicating with him; the pope also summoned Sigismundo to Rome to be burned alive (not even a pretense at an "invitation to lunch"). Since Sigismundo did not show up, Pius had two effigies made of him (the first one not having shown a sufficient resemblance) "costing 8 florins 48 bol," to be burned on the steps of St. Peter's.

26. **Andreas Benzi**: Of Siena; d. 1460. Fiscal agent of Pius II ordered by the latter to present the case against Sigismundo before the consistory of cardinals.

27. **Papa Pio Secundo** . . . : I, "Pope Pius II / Aeneas Silvius Piccolomini / of Siena," Piccolomini was short and stout and had a puffed face of ashen complexion which turned livid at the slightest indisposition [cf. 36 below].

28. **bear's-greased latinity**: Pius II was generally known for his elegant Latin, although most of his references to Sigismundo were characteristically vulgar, for which reason some of them were omitted from the official edition of his *Commentaries* [*Commentarii rerum memorabilium*, Rome, 1584] and are only to be found in the *Vatican Codex Reginensis*, no. 1995. Pound suggests that he had cooperated in writing the text of Benzi's list of charges, losing all sense of style through his personal animosity toward Sigismundo. Pius even went to the extreme of "canonizing" Sigismundo as "a devil in hell," thereby rather exceeding his sphere of jurisdiction.

29. **Stupro . . . concubinarius**: ML; the text of the indictment runs: "Ravisher, butcher, adulterer / murderer, parricide, and perjurer, / killer of priests, reckless [one], lecher, / . . . fornicator and assassin, / traitor, rapist, committer of incest, arsonist, and keeper of concubines."

30. **and that he rejected**: All present at the consistory agreed with Benzi's list of charges, but Federigo d'Urbino and Alessandro Sforza added that Sigismundo also "rejected not one or two articles of the Catholic faith but the entire Catholic Creed" and had no sense of religion. In his *Commentaries* Pius II even claimed that Sigismundo was in the pay of the Turks and had betrayed the cause of Christianity. Pound found the charge concerning Sigismundo's belief about ownership of Church property and use of temporal power in Pius's *Epistolae*. Perhaps he intended to show his ideas were far ahead of his age, prefiguring the criticism later to be leveled against the Church by the Reformation.

31. **nisi forsitan epicureae**: L, "unless perhaps a follower of Epicurus" [?342-270 B.C.]. For Pound this Greek philosopher represented an enlightened mind [cf. 31/156 where John Adams and Jefferson agree on

this point in their old age, at the same time bringing up the very arguments touched upon by Sigismundo's enemies].

32. chiexa: I, *chiesa*, "church." The account of these juvenile pranks illustrates both Sigismundo's high spirits [11:34] and his enemies' lack of humor.

33. "Whence that his . . .: Pound's imitation of Benzi's rhetoric.

34. Lussorioso . . . uxoricido: I, "Lustful indulger in incest, perfidious, filthpot and glutton, / assassin, greedy, grabbing, arrogant, untrustworthy / counterfeiter, sodomite, wife-killer," Benzi's charges against Sigismundo [cf. 29 above] are here repeated with trimmings in Italian.

35. Orationem . . . filii: ML, "We have heard a most elegant and highly ornate speech of our reverend brother in Christ and most beloved son." Thus Pius II praises Benzi's indictment of Sigismundo.

36. Testibus idoneis: ML, "with fit witnesses," these being ironically Sigismundo's archenemies, Federigo d'Urbino and Alessandro Sforza. Pound associates these words with Pius's proverbial gallstones (he calls him "old bladder" [9:21]), reading *testibus* as "testicles."

37. cardinale di San Pietro in Vincoli: The cardinal at that time was Nicolas Cusanus, 1401-1464, whom Pius II had instructed to try Sigismundo *in absentia*. The adjective "kid-slapping" could refer to his recent ill-tempered behavior as Bishop of Brixen, where he banned parish fairs on feast days and ordered the excommunication of persons seen dancing in public. As a wheeler-dealer in papal politics, he amassed a fortune early by exploiting the inhabitants of church benefices awarded him in the archdiocese of Trèves and later again as Bishop of Brixen. On the other hand he was also an important philosopher who rebelled against syllogistic or Aristotelian logic by introducing the concept of the *coincidentia oppositorum*, was the first to declare the existence of a plurality of worlds and to claim that the earth rotates around the sun (ideas later taken up by Giordano Bruno [cf. 114/791]), and also the first to denounce the Pseudo-Isidorus and the Constantine Donation as a forgery, for which argument Lorenzo Valla provided in 1440 the scholarly substantiation later published as *De falso credita et ementita Constantini donatione declamatio* (Basle, 1950) [cf. 89/602; *GK*, 160; *LE*, 192; *Versa prosaici*, 17] [EH].

38. tanta novità: I, "such oddities." Borso is voicing the general opinion in Italy at the time that the auto-da-fé of Sigismundo violated the humanistic spirit of the age.

39. stuprum, raptum: ML, "debauchery, rape," part of the list of charges against Sigismundo.

40. I.N.R.I. . . . Proditorum: ML, *Iesus Nazarenus, Rex Iudaeorum*, the inscription over the Cross of Jesus, here ironically placed over the head of Sigismundo's effigy: "Jesus of Nazareth, King of the Jews, General Sigismundo, King of Traitors."

41. Old Pills: Ugolino de'Pili, Sigismundo's old tutor. Benzi charged Sigismundo with having Ugolino and his sons imprisoned and murdered. The falsity of the charge was proved when Ugolino emerged alive from jail (where he had been put for conspiring against Sigismundo's life).

42. Et les angloys . . . : MF, "And the English unable to eradicate . . . poison of hatred." Poss. refers to the burning of Joan of Arc by the English 30 years before the burning in effigy of Sigismundo. The paranoiac treatment of Joan of Arc by the English reflected the hatred engendered by the Hundred Years War (1337-1453); the hatred is still evident in Shakespeare's treatment of Joan as a "Minister of Hell" in *Henry VI*, I, a play winding up with the marriage of Henry to the "she-wolf of Anjou," i.e., René of Anjou's daughter Margaret, 1430-1480 [cf. 44 below; Pound's interest in Joan of

Arc is also manifest in 80/503; 91/617; 93/630].

43. Gisors . . . : [6:21, 23]. The possession of Gisors and the Norman Vexin was one of the crucial factors in the Hundred Years War. The French regained Gisors from the English "Angevins," the Plantagenets being descended from Godfrey V, Count of Anjou.

44. Angevins: Members of the house of Anjou, here referring to the French line and particularly to René of Anjou, 1408-1480, Duke of Lorraine [cf. 42 above], whose claim to the throne of Naples and Sicily was as legitimate as that of Alphonso of Aragon [8:10]. In sending emissaries to René of Anjou in 1458, urging him to send an army to Italy to reclaim the throne of Naples, Sigismundo fatefully initiated centuries of war between Aragon and Anjou in S Italy as well as the prolonged occupation of the region by the French, Spanish, and Austrians, which accounts for the present still underdeveloped state of the S as well as its virtual separation from the rest of Italy. The "we" in "we dragged in the Angevins" refers to Machiavelli's charge in *Il Principe* that the condottieri in general were responsible for the inroads made by the French and Spanish on Italian territory.

45. Louis Eleventh: King of France, 1461-1483. Sigismundo had sought the aid of Louis against Pius II, but when Louis urged Pius II to support the Angevin cause in Naples, Sigismundo's ploy failed [18/81].

46. tiers Calixte: MF, "the third Calixtus." Pope Calixtus III and Alphonso of Aragon both died in 1458. Calixtus was succeeded by Pius II [9:21] and Alphonso by his natural son Ferrante (Ferdinand), both implacable enemies of Sigismundo [cf. 18 above].

47. this Aeneas: Pius II. Aeneas Sylvius Piccolomini chose the name "Pius" in recollection of the reference to *pius Aeneas* in Virgil's *Aeneid*, IX:21.

48. Ferdinando: King of Naples after the death of his father Alphonso of Aragon [cf. 18, 46 above].

49. Piombino: Refers to Sigismundo's defeat of Alphonso of Aragon at Piombino in 1448, Sigismundo then being in the service of the Florentine Republic. Alphonso retreated, leaving Ferdinand to drag out the war.

50. Piccinino: [cf. 17 above].

51. marriage: Alphonso once proposed that his niece marry Sigismundo's son, Roberto; on another occasion he offered Sigismundo the command of his army in the N. Both offers were declined.

52. Mantua: [cf. 19 above].

53. Tolfa: In 1462 vast deposits of alum, a mineral essential for the dyeing of wool, were discovered in the Papal States, giving the Church a virtual monopoly. Tolfa is still a center of alum mining. The discovery greatly increased the wealth of the Church, which had hitherto spent some 300,000 ducats a year to import alum from the Turks. Pius II [Pio] described the discovery as "a victory over the Turks." Pound's suggestion here is that this uncanny luck must have been the work of the devil [93/624].

54. Francesco: F. Sforza describing his interest in the division of the Malatesta territories in 1464 [8:46; 11:15, 16]. Actually Sforza disapproved of the liquidation of the Malatesta domain as a dangerous precedent that might one day jeopardize his own newly achieved status.

55. mal hecho: S, "badly done."

56. Pasti: Matteo da P., d. 1468 [9:56, 75]. Pasti, who had been commissioned by Sigismundo to paint a portrait of the Ottoman Sultan Mohammed II (1430-1481), was arrested by the Venetians on suspicion of being in league with the Turks, but he was ultimately released [21/98; 26/121; 74/437].

57. Borso: [cf. 20 above and 17/78, 79].

58. Novvy: [8:30; 9:5]. Sigismundo's youngest brother Domenico, called "Malatesta Novello," was friendly with Giacomo Piccinino and at one time promised to make him his heir [11:18]. The suggestion here that Domenico was party to a conspiracy against Sigismundo is without historical foundation.

59. Count Giacomo: I.e., Piccinino [cf. 17 above].

60. E gradment . . . annutii: I, *Grandemente li antichi e valenti romani davano fed a questi annuntii chiamati augurii* ["The ancient Roman knights put great faith in such omens"]. Pound is transcribing Broglio's Italian without heeding his diacritical marks. The clue to this address of Sigismundo to his captains before sending them into battle against superior papal forces in the spring of 1461 [cf. 25 above] is its allusion to the number of homosexuals among the ecclesiastical legates under the command of the Bishop of Corneto: "Though they outnumber us in heads, we have more men."

Glossary Canto XI

1. **E gradment . . . annutii**: [10:60].

2. **Bernardo Reggio . . .** : A Homeric roster of Sigismundo's officers in the battle near Vitelleschi in 1461. Piero della Bella is called a "gay bird" because the Italian (Broglio's chronicle, given by Tonini) reads *il gagliardo Piero della Bella*, where *gagliardo* can have the meaning "sturdy" or "gay." "Roberto" refers to Sigismundo's eldest son [cf. 8, 9 below; 9:61, 63; 10:51].

3. **dilly cavalli tre milia**: I, "of horses, three thousand," Sigismundo had only 1,300 cavalry and 500 foot soldiers to the pope's 3,000 cavalry and 2,000 foot soldiers. For *dilly* read *delli*, poss. intended as a pun.

4. **mille tre cento . . .** : I, "Thirteen hundred horses / . . . and barely 500 / foot."

5. **spingard**: I, *spingarda*, "battering ram."

6. **mille . . . cavalli**: I, "one thousand five hundred horses." A reference to Sigismundo's booty.

7. **E li . . . trecento**: I, "And the men of Messer Sigismundo were barely one thousand three hundred."

8. **next August**: After having taken Sinigaglia in 1462 [10:25], Sigismundo withdrew but was forced into an engagement at Mondolfo (near plains of Fano) on August 24, which he lost. Leaving his son Roberto to defend Fano he then sought to obtain help by the sea route from his Angevin allies in the south [10:44]. *August* could also refer to the defeat of the Angevin forces at Troya [cf. 10 below].

9. **Roberto**: R. Malatesta, 1442-1482, Sigismundo's eldest son, made legitimate by Pope Nicholas V. At the age of 21 Roberto led the defense of Fano against Federigo d'Urbino in a manner that won the admiration of his enemies. Pius II, with heavy sarcasm, called him "a child worthy of his father." But Roberto was forced to surrender Fano in 1463. He was later disinherited by Sigismundo in favor of Sallustio, his son by Isotta. As a result Sallustio was murdered in 1470, presumably by, or at the behest of, his half brother Roberto [8:52; 9:63].

10. **Tarentum**: Dominant seaport of the Gulf of Taranto. Unable to withstand the superior forces of his enemies, Sigismundo turned south to seek aid via the sea from his allies, the Angevins, one of whom was the prince of Taranto [cf. 8 above]. Taranto was claimed by René of Anjou [10:44], represented by his son John, Duke of Calabria, who had been severely beaten at Troya on August 18, 1462, by Ferrante and Alessandro Sforza.

11. **Anti-Aragons**: [10:44].

12. **Feddy**: Federigo d'Urbino was beleaguering Roberto in Fano. His profile as depicted by Piero della Francesca in the bas-relief at the Bargello in Florence shows his

"nick-nose." The *s.o.b.* is an allusion to Federigo's dubious parentage [9:14].

13. **Par che . . . mundo**: I [pun], "He seems lost to the . . . Sigis . . . world."

14. **They say he dodders** . . . : Refers to the siege of Rimini begun by Federigo in the winter of 1462-63 but lifted in 1463 because the plague had broken out in both the city and the countryside. The lines express the hope that Sigismundo might himself have fallen a victim to the plague.

15. **rottenes' peace**: Although Federigo in 1463 had taken neither Rimini nor the famous La Rocca [9:10], the peace dictated by Pius II all but ruined Sigismundo Malatesta [8:5].

16. **Quali lochi** . . . : I, "These are the places in question." Under the peace treaty dictated by Pius II in 1463 Federigo d'Urbino was awarded the lion's share of the Malatesta domain, which had once extended across the Marches of Ancona and included many towns and fortified places. The rest were shared among Pius II's followers and captains, as well as Antonio Piccolomini, his nephew. The places listed are from a document drawn up in the name of a distant relative of Sigismundo's, Carlo de' Malatesti, a supporter of Pius II, from whom he expected to receive them as an award [F.G. Battaglini, 659].

17. **salt heaps**: The above list further recalls the loss of Cervia with its lucrative salt industry. Cervia had been awarded to Novello [10:58] in 1443 by the German emperor. By 1463 he had found himself forced to sell it to Venice.

18. **lame Novvy**: Novello was lamed in an accident at age 29, and his condition was made worse by medical treatment. He was retiring and quite unlike his warlike brother. But under the treaty of 1463 he was allowed to retain the city of Cesena for life with the proviso that if he died without issue it should revert to the Holy See, which it did in 1465 [8:31, 55; 9:5; 10:58].

19. **Piero . . . Vanni.** These anecdotes come from an article by C. Grigioni in *La Romagna*, August–September, 1910, pp. 367–83, who found them in the unpublished *Cronaco* of Gaspare Broglio at the Gambalunga Library in Rimini. Zuliano is Guiliano Agulante, a poor subject of Sigismundo; Robert is Giuliano's bastard son. Vanni is Giovanni Riccio. The anecdotes are meant to illustrate Sigismundo's concern for his poor subjects.

20. **Sub annulo** . . . : ML, "Under the seal of the pope, the palace and council chamber, once of the Malatesta . . . Cesena of the beautiful columns." The "z" sound and the elided "11" are supposed to reproduce Sigismundo's Romagnole accent. The inscription OLIM DE MALTESTIS ["once of the Lords Malatesta"] in the "long room over the arches" at Fano is frequently cited by Pound [30/149; 76/462; 80/501; 83/529]. The beautiful columns of Cesena are those of the Hospital of the Holy Cross built by Novello, who also built the magnificent library.

21. **Morea**: I.e., Peloponnesus [8:29, 31; 10:19]. Refers to the campaign of 1464-1466, when Sigismundo's services were once more enlisted by the Republic of Venice to recover Peloponnesus from the Turks. Sigismundo, leading an army of 7,000 which was soon reduced to 5,000, was hopelessly outnumbered by the 25,000 Turks. Frustration, defeat, and the plague forced him to disengage at Lacedaemon and go into winter quarters at a place N of Sparta, where he fell ill and was reported dead [8:46]. Hopelessly short of men and disgusted by the intrigues and suspicions at home, he sought permission to withdraw and returned to Rimini in 1466.

22. **And we sit here** . . . : Pound and companions watching events and historical characters of all ages as if staged in the arena at Verona [cf. 4:45; 12:1; 29:41; 78/481; 80/505].

23. And they trapped him . . . : [9:1, 2; 10:9].

24. And the poor devils . . . : [9:48, 49; 10:1].

25. Vogliamo . . . : I, "It is our desire that the women. . . ." Sigismundo had early decreed that the womenfolk residing in his domains should dress up in all their finery. His command was in sharp contrast with the petty restrictions on the attire of women imposed in other parts of Italy at that time [cf. 22:31] in order to maintain the class barrier between aristocracy and commoners. The rising wealth and power of the commercial classes were already beginning to vex the increasingly impoverished aristocracy, especially in the republics of Florence and Venice.

26. Platina: Bartolomeo Sacchi, 1421-1481, a celebrated humanist known by his assumed Latin name, Platina. Pius II had made him a member of the College of Abbreviators. The college was dissolved by Pius's successor, Paul II [cf. 28 below], an act that brought him a letter of protest from Platina, who was thereupon thrown into jail for four months. Platina later became a member of the Accademia Romana [cf. 27 below]. When an alleged conspiracy against Paul II was discovered in 1468, Platina was once more cast into jail and interrogated under torture. He later avenged himself on Paul II in his *History of the Popes*. After Sigismundo arrived in Rome hoping for a chance to assassinate Paul II, he visited Platina. Later, when Platina was asked under torture whether he had conspired with Sigismundo against the pope and what they had talked about, he gave the answer translated in 29 below.

27. Accademia Romana: L, "Roman Academy." Being passionately devoted to the classics, the academy was accused of worshiping pagan deities such as Zeus. Like Sigismundo in his Tempio [9:32, 80] and Gemistus Plethon [8:31, 32, 33], they visualized a synthesis between the Christian religion and Greek polytheism, an idea to which Pound subscribed [cf. *L*, 30, 182, 345]. Being also confirmed republicans with regard to church authority [10:37], they were opposed to the pope's wielding absolute power. Paul II ultimately dissolved the academy, imprisoned several of its members, and declared any mention of its name to be a heresy.

28. fatty Barbo: Pietro B., 1417-1471, Pope Paul II (1464-1471), who succeeded Pius II. On election he chose the name "Formosus" [L, "Handsome"], which was rejected by the cardinals because it could be understood as an allusion to his good looks, a detail that to Pound pinpoints his fatheaded conceit. When Sigismundo returned from Morea in 1466 [cf. 21 above] Paul awarded him the Golden Rose as a "Champion of Christendom," an act that seemed to indicate a total reversal of the policy of Pius II. But the following year Paul, who disliked the idea of troops in the pay of Venice being stationed in Rimini, proposed that Sigismundo should exchange Rimini, the sole remaining possession he had inherited from his ancestors, for the lordships of Spoleto and Foligno. Deeply offended, Sigismundo rode to Rome firmly resolved to kill Paul II. But the pope, suspecting his intentions, summoned seven cardinals "whom he could trust" to stand by him, thus upsetting Sigismundo's plan [Tonini, 314-315, citing Broglio].

29. de litteris . . . : ML, "about scholarship and war, and men of outstanding genius." In a letter to John Quinn dated August 10, 1922, Pound comments: "He [S. de M.] was in Rome towards the end, the whole existence of his state depending on negotiations. . . . [He] spent most of his time in the papal library, and when they asked the librarian, Platina, what they had talked about he said 'We talked about books, and fighting, and unusual intelligence, both in the ancients, and in men of our own time, in short the things one wd naturally talk about' " [YC]. [Cf. 34/165, where the idea is used to characterize J. Q. Adams; 80/512; 83/528; Rome broadcast entitled "James Joyce: To His Memory," FR, *LPJ*, 272.]

30. sexaginta . . . plures: For *tentatur* read *teneatur*. ML, "Sixty-four, nor is he to have more." The agreement that Paul II drew up for Sigismundo the following year (1468) allowed him a company of only 64 soldiers and an annual payment of only 8,000 florins, a vast comedown from the rates he had been used to. Since Paul as vicar of Rimini had the right to garrison the town himself, Sigismundo was allowed to station only half of his own company there. Paul II was eager to have his own men in Rimini in order to keep an eye on Venice, the Vatican's traditional enemy.

31. Formosus: Pope Paul II [cf. 28 above].

32. Montefiore: A stronghold in the Malatesta domain. A reference to Sigismundo's return from Morea some time between 1466 and 1468 [cf. 21 above]. Paul II, who had taken Montefiore into his own hands, is warned by the castellan to keep Sigismundo out of the district because he and his family are popular heroes. The cries of "Pandolfo" would not have been meant for Sigismundo personally, but for his whole dynasty from Pandolfo I (d. 1326) on.

33. Henry: Enrico Aquadelli, steward to Sigismundo.

34. Actum . . . : ML, "Executed at the castle of Sigismundo . . . in the presence of Roberto of Valturio . . . freely and in clear understanding . . . to Henry of Aquabello." This notarization of who was entitled to play a practical joke on whom once more illustrates Sigismundo's unquenchable spirit even in adversity. Sigismundo died at the age of 51, only three and a half months after signing the agreement with Paul II on October 7, 1466.

CANTO XII

Sources

Mostly nonliterary and personal experience. *Odyssey* I, 3.

Background

EP, "Indiscretions or Une Revue de Deux Mondes" and "Stark Realism," in *PD; SP*, 61; B. L. Reid, *The Man from New York: John Quinn and His Friends*, Oxford, 1968; NS, *Life*.

Exegeses

CE, *Ideas*, 32, 55, 114-115, 158; EH, *Approaches*, 141, 172, 264; HK, *Era*, 344, 390, 417, 425-426.

Glossary

1. **Arena romana**: L, "The Roman Arena." Pound alludes to the Theatrum in the Baths of Diocletian, situated at the junction of the Quirinal and Viminal hills in Rome, but the arena of the *Cantos* is at Verona [4:48], where Pound began his meditations on history. He used the arena as a symbolic stage where many a dramatic or significant moment of human history, past and present, is acted out. At 4/16, "there in the arena" leads into the historical events of Canto V. At 29/145, "toward sundown by the arena / (les gradins)," a linkage is established by repeating "les gradins," suggesting steps up a metaphorical Mt. Purgatory on the way to a terrestrial paradise [cf. also 78/481].

2. **les gradins . . . calcaire**: F, "the steps / forty-three tiers made of limestone." At 91/614, "the steps" are 44. [Asked about the disparity in 1972, Pound affirmed 44, which would include the arena pavement. FR; cf. also picture: HK, *Era*, 344.]

3. **Baldy Bacon**: Francis S. B., fl. 1910, American businessman whom Pound met at the old Weston boardinghouse at 24 East 47th Street during his 1910 visit to America. "Baldy" was a "jobber . . . living on the fringes of the business world." Pound became enthusiastic about a business proposition Baldy outlined and tried to get his father and Aunt Frank to invest in it [NS, *Life, 90*].

4. **Un centavo . . .** : S, "One cent, two cents."

5. **Henry and Castano**: Private references to persons unknown. Identified in the Italian translation by Mary de Rachewiltz as "Henry Longfellow." *Index* suggests in addition to Longfellow either Henry James or Henry Newbolt as possible [cf. 74/433, and especially 80/507, where Newbolt's inverted word order is mocked].

6. **Guardia regia**: S, "royal guard."

7. **Pollon d'anthropen iden**: H, "And of many men he saw" [the cities, and knew their mind] [*Od.* I, 3].

8. **Hermes**: Messenger and herald of the gods; patron of merchants and thieves and the god of luck and wealth. Suggests Baldy arrived quickly "on the wings of Hermes [Mercury]."

9. **angelos**: H, "messenger."

10. **Habitat cum Quade**: L, "Lives with Quade."

11. **Mons Quade**: An associate of Baldy Bacon's. In "Stark Realism" [*Pavannes*] Pound wrote about Quade: "This little American went to the great city Manhattan. He made two dollars and a half per week. He saw the sheeny girls on the East Side who lunch on two cents worth of bread and sausages, and dress with a flash on the remainder. He nearly died of it. Then he got a rise. He made fifteen dollars per week selling insurance. He wore a monocle with a tortoise-shell rim. He dressed up to 'Bond St.' No lord in The Row has surpassed him. He was a damn good fellow."

12. **Dos Santos**: Prob. a Portuguese merchant. The "spoiled maize & sucking pigs" story has long been seen as an example of money lust or "usury." But since Dos Santos [S, "Two Saints"] used credit imaginatively to create real wealth [food], the story makes him a minor hero, quite in contrast with the usurious bankers in Jim X's story which follows.

13. **Tagus**: River in Spain and Portugal.

14. **nemo obstabat**: L, "nobody prevented it."

15. **e tot lo sieu aver**: P, "and all his possessions."

16. **undsoweiter**: G, "and so forth."

17. **Apovitch**: Prob. an invented name.

18. Jim X: John Quinn, 1870-1924; American lawyer; authority on modern Irish literature and drama; collector and patron of modern art.

19. S.A: South American.

20. Stambouli: Stamboul, the oldest part and main Turkish residential section of Istanbul. Although the idea of shocking the stuffed-shirt bankers with the bawdy story emphasizes the humor of the scene, the story may have another significance. Dos Santos used nature to create wealth, while the bankers, "*alias* usurers in excelsis," worked "contra naturam" with destructive effects "whining over their 20 p.c." And about sodomy, Pound wrote: "In theology, as Dante knew it, the usurer is damned with the sodomite. Usury judged with sodomy as 'contrary to natural increase,' contrary to the nature of live things" [*SP*, 61; see also *SP*, 265].

CANTO XIII

Sources

Doctrine de Confucius: Les Quatre livres de philosophie morale et politique de la Chine, Paris, 1841, Traduits du Chinois par M. G. Pauthier. Pound uses the canonical books *Le Lun-Yu* [*The Analects*], *Le Ta Hio* [*Ta Hsüeh, The Great Digest*], and *Tchoung-Young* [*Chung Yung, The Unwobbling Pivot*]; Chuang Tzu, XXXI. [When the standard Wade-Giles transliteration is different from Pauthier's, it is given after the Pauthier as an alternate form.]

Background

EP, *Confucius: The Great Digest, The Unwobbling Pivot, The Analects; PD*, 72-73 (EP's lively, condensed prose translation of *Le Lun-Yu*, XI, 25) "Confucius and Mencius," *SP*, 73-97; HK, *Era* 445-459; *The Complete Works of Chuang Tzu*, trans. Burton Watson, New York, Columbia University Press, 1968.

Exegeses

Little exegesis for Canto XIII exists in the published record. The indexes of most of the major books on Pound contain passing references, most of them repeating the same points. Angela Palandri, *Pai*, 3-3, 301 ff., contains new and interesting ideas; also, see David Wand, *Pai*, 3-1, 10. The lines Pound used were located by David Gordon.

Glossary

1. **Kung**: Kung Fu-tse (Confucius), 551-479 B.C., Chinese philosopher and teacher. Kung carries most of the ethical content of the *Cantos* [cf. 52/258: "Between KUNG and Eleusis"] : that is, Western ethical precepts from Aristotle on are measured against the precepts of Kung and are often found wanting. Canto 13 consists of a montage of quotations from Pauthier's translations rendered into English by Pound, who uses the French transliteration of the Chinese characters rather than the standard Wade-Giles tables. In the glosses the Wade-Giles form is given first.

2. **the cedar grove**: "the gray steps lead up under the cedars" [cf. 3/11] rhymes with "the tiered steps of the arena," the Western locus at Verona [4:48].

3. **Khieu**: Ch'iu, designation of Zan Yu, a disciple of Kung's [*Le Lun-Yu*, XI, 25; *The Analects*, 242].

4. **Tchi**: Ch'ih, surnamed Kung-hsi and styled Tsze-hwa, disciple of Kung's [*Le Lun-Yu*, XI, 25; *The Analects*, 242].

5. **Tian**: [Tien], Tsang Hsi, father of Tsang Shan, disciple of Kung's [*Le Lun-Yu*, XI, 25; *The Analects*, 242].

6. **"we are unknown"**: "Nous ne sommes pas connus" [*Le Lun-Yu*, XI, 25; *The Analects*, 242].

7. **"You will take up . . . archery?"**: "Prendrai-je l'état de voiturier, ou apprendrai-je celui d'archer? Je serai voiturier." ["Shall I take up charioteering? or shall I learn to be an archer? I will be a charioteer."] [*Le Lun-Yu*, IX, 2; *The Analects*, 228.]

8. **practice of public speaking**: No specific passage in Pauthier, but Confucius frequently condemns ornate speech and mere rhetoric.

9. **Tseu-lou**: Tze-Lu, designation of the disciple Chung Yu, often styled Yü, [*Le Lun-Yu*, XI, 25; *The Analects*, 242].

10. **". . . defences . . ."**: ". . . je pourrais faire en sorte que le peuple de ce royaume reprit un courage viril. . . ." ["I could try to make the people of this kingdom show a manly courage."] [*Le Lun-Yu*, XI, 25; *The Analects*, 242].

11. **"If I were lord . . ."**: ". . . soit préposé à son administration, en moins de trois ans je pourrais faire en sorte que le peuple eût le suffisant" ["...might propose to his administration, in less than three years I would see to it that the people were provided for"] [*Le Lun-Yu*, XI, 25; *The Analects*, 242.]

12. **"I would prefer . . . ritual"**: "Lorsque se font les cérémonies du temple des ancêtres, et qu'ont lieu de grandes assemblées publiques, revêtu de ma robe d'azur et des autres vêtements propres à un tel lieu et à de telles cérémonies, je voudrais y prendre part en qualité d'humble fonctionnaire." ["Rather than performing the ceremonies at the ancestral temples and other places of great public assemblies, adorned with my blue robe and other vestments proper for such a place and such ceremonies, I would like to take part in the rank of a humble functionary."] [*Le Lun-Yu*, XI, 25; *The Analects*, 242.]

13. **Tian said . . . mandolins**: "Le disciple ne fit plus que de tirer quelques sons rares de sa guitare; mais ces sons se prolongeant, il la déposa, et, se levant, il répondit respectueusement: Mon opinion diffère entièrement de celles de mes trois condisciples. . . . Le printemps n'étant plus, ma robe de printemps mise de côté, mais coiffé du bonnet de virilité, accompagné de cinq ou six hommes et de six ou sept jeunes gens, j'aimerais à aller me baigner dans les eaux de l'Y, à aller prendre le frais dans ces lieux touffus où l'on offre les sacrifices au ciel pour demander la pluie. . . ." ["The disciple did no more than to pluck a few occasional

notes on his lute; but with the notes still echoing, he set it down, and, rising, he answered respectfully: My opinion differs completely from those of my three codisciples. . . . Spring being past, my spring gown put aside, but covered with my man's hat, accompanied by five or six men and six or seven youths, I would like to go and bathe in the waters of the Y, to take the fresh air in those leafy places where one offers sacrifices to heaven to ask for rain. . . ."] [*Le Lun-Yu*, XI, 25; *The Analects*, 242-243.]

14. **And Kung smiled**: "Le Philosophe, applaudissant à ces paroles par un soupir de satisfaction, dit: Je suis de l'avis de Tian." ["The philosopher praised these words by a gratified sigh and said: I agree with Tian."] [*Le Lun-Yu*, XI, 25; *The Analects*, 243.]

15. **Thseng-sie**: Tsang Hsi, another name for Tian [cf. 5 above].

16. **Which . . . nature**: "Que doit-on penser des paroles de ces trois disciples? Le Philosophe dit: Chacun d'eux a exprimé son opinion; et voilà tout." ["What should one think about the words of these three disciples? The philosopher said: Each one has expressed his opinion; and that's all."] [*Le Lun-Yu*, XI, 25; *The Analects*, 243.]

17. **Yuan Jang**: Yüan Jang. "Youan-jang (un ancien ami du Philosophe), plus âgé que lui, etait assis sur le chemin les jambes croisées. Le Philosophe lui dit: Etant enfant, n'avoir pas eu de déférence fraternelle; dans l'âge mûr, n'avoir rien fait de louable; parvenu à la vieillesse, ne pas mourir: c'est être un vaurien. Et il lui frappa les jambes avec son bâton (pour le faire lever)." ["Yuan Jang, an old friend of the philosopher, older than he himself, was seated by the road, his legs crossed. The philosopher said to him: 'Being a child, not to have had brotherly respect; in maturity to have done nothing praiseworthy; having arrived at old age not to die: that's to be a good-for-nothing.' And he rapped his legs with his cane to make him get up."] [*Le Lun-Yu*, XIV, 46; *The Analects*, 262.]

18. **And Kung said** . . . : "Le Philosophe dit: Dès l'instant qu'un enfant est né, il faut respecter ses facultés; la science qui lui viendra par la suite ne ressemble en rien à son état présent. S'il arrive à l'âge de quarante ou de cinquante ans sans avoir rien appris, il n'est plus digne d'aucun respect." ["The philosopher said: From the time that a child is born, one must respect his faculties; the knowledge that will come to him in the course of time will be nothing like his present state. If he lives to be forty or fifty years old without doing anything at all, he is no longer worthy of anyone's respect." [*Le Lun-Yu*, IX, 22; *The Analects*, 232.]

19. **"When the prince** . . .": ". . . dès l'instant qu'il aura attiré près de lui tous les savants et les artistes, aussitôt ses richesses seront suffisamment mises en usage." ["From the moment that he (the Prince) has gathered about him all the savants and artists his riches will be sufficiently put to use."] [*Tchoung-Young*, XX, 12; *The Unwobbling Pivot*, 155-156.]

20. **And Kung said, and wrote** . . . : "Les tablettes en bambou des anciennes. . . ." ["The bamboo tablets of the ancients. . . ."] [*Ta Hio*, 1, 7; *The Great Digest*, 35.]

21. **If a man have not** . . . : ". . . ceux qui désiraient bien gouverner leurs royaumes s'attachaient auparavant à mettre le bon ordre dans leurs familles; ceux qui désiraient mettre le bon ordre dans leurs familles s'attachaient auparavant à se corriger euxmêmes; ceux qui désiraient se corriger euxmêmes. . . ." ["Those who desired to govern their kingdoms well dedicated themselves first to bring good order into their families; those who desired to bring good order into their families dedicated themselves first to rectify themselves; those who desired to rectify themselves. . . ."] [*Ta Hio*, 1, 4; *The Great Digest*, 29, 31.]

22. **"brotherly deference"**: "La piété filiale, la déférence fraternelle, dont nous avons parlé, ne sont-elles pas le principe fonda-

mental de l'humanité ou de la bienveillance universelle pour les hommes?" ["The filial piety and fraternal deference of which we spoke, are they not the fundamental principle of humanity or the universal benevolence for men?"] [*Le Lun-Yu*, 1, 2; *The Analects*, 195.]

23. "life after death": "Quand on ne sait pas encore ce que c'est que la vie, comment pourrait-on connaître la mort?" ["When one still does not know what life is, how can he know about death?"] [*Le Lun-Yu*, XI, 11; *The Analects*, 239.]

24. "Anyone can run . . . ": "Dépasser, c'est comme ne pas atteindre." ["To go beyond is like not hitting."] [*Le Lun-Yu*, XI, 15; *The Analects*, 240.]

25. ". . . hard to stand . . . ": "L'invariabilité dans le milieu est ce que constitue la vertu; n'en est-ce pas le faîte même? Les hommes rarement y persévèrent." ["To stand unwaveringly in the middle is what constitutes *Vertu*; is it not even the summit? Men rarely attain it."] [*Le Lun-Yu*, VI, 27; *The Analects*, 218.]

26. commit murder: ". . . le père cache les fautes de son fils, le fils cache les fautes de son père. La droiture et la sincérité existent dans cette conduite." ["The father should hide the defects of the son, the son hide the defects of the father. Rectitude and sincerity exist in such conduct."] [*Le Lun-Yu*, XIII, 18; *The Analects*, 251.]

27. Kong-Tch'ang: Kung Yeh Ch'ang, disciple and later son-in-law of Kung. "Le Philosophe dit que Kong-tchi-tchang (un de ses disciples) pouvait se marier, quoiqu'il fût dans les prisons, parce qu'il n'était pas criminel; et il se maria avec la fille du Philosophe." ["The philosopher said that Kung Yeh Ch'ang could get married although he had been in prisons, because he was not a criminal; and he married the daughter of the philosopher."] [*Le Lun-Yu*, V, 1; *The Analects*, 209.]

28. Nan-Young: Nan Yung, disciple of Kung's. "Le Philosophe dit à Nan-Young . . . que si le royaume était gouverné selon les principes de la droite raison, il ne serait pas repoussé des emplois publics; que si, au contraire, il n'était pas gouverné par les principes de la droite raison, il ne subirait aucun châtiment: et il le maria avec la fille de son frère ainé." ["The Philosopher said to Nan Yung . . .that if the kingdom was governed by the principles of right reason Nan Yung would not be fired from public office; that if, on the contrary, the kingdom was not governed by the principles of right reason, he would receive no punishment: and he married Nan Yung to the daughter of his [Confucius'] elder brother." *Le Lun-Yu*, V, 1; *The Analects*, 209.]

29. Wang: Wu Wang: 1169-1115 B.C., title under which Fa, son of Wen Wang, was canonized. Wu continued his father's battles against Cheou-Sin, assembled a huge army, and defeated him at Meng-chin in Honan and thereby ended the Shang (or Yin) dynasty. Wu ruled (1122-1115) as the first emperor of the Tcheou (Chou) dynasty. Kung said: "Les lois gouvernementales des rois Wen et Wou sont consignées tout entières sur les tablettes de bambou. Si leurs ministres existaient encore, alors leurs lois administratives seraient en vigueur . . . ." ["The governmental laws of kings Wen and Wu are completely written out on the bamboo tablets: If their ministers still existed, then their laws of administration would be in force . . . ."] [*Tchoung-Young*, XX, 2; *The Unwobbling Pivot*, 147.]

30. "And even I . . .": "Le Philosophe dit: J'ai presque vu le jour où l'historien de l'empire laissait des lacunes dans ses recits (quand il n'était pas sûr des faits); où celui qui possédait un cheval, le prêtait aux autres pour le monter; maintenant ces moeurs sont perdues." ["The Philosopher said: I almost saw that time when the imperial historian left blanks in his writings (when he was not sure of the facts); when a person who owned a horse lent it to others to ride; now these customs are lost."] [*Le Lun-Yu*, XV, 25; *The Analects*, 267.]

31. **"Without character"**: "Être homme, et ne pas posséder les vertus que comporte l'humanité, comment jouerait-on dignement de la musique?" ["Being man and not having the virtues appropriate to a human being, how would one play music worthily?"] [*Le Lun-Yu*, III, 3; *The Analects*, 201.]

32. **"blossoms of the apricot"**: Chapter 31 of the Chuang Tzu starts: "Confucius, after strolling through the Black Curtain Forest, sat down to rest on the Apricot Altar." [Watson, p. 345. A footnote explains: "the word altar here refers to a mesa or flat-topped hill rising out of the lowland."] The apricot orchard, believed to be a place where Kung lectured, is now "marked by a pavilion enclosing a stone slab with the seal characters of *Hsing T'an* ('Apricot Temple') . . . in front of the Confucian Temple in present day Ch'iu-fu of Shantung, Confucius' home town." Apricot blossoms "symbolize at once cultural florescence and Confucian teachings" [Palandri, *Pai*, 3-3, 301]. These concluding lines suggest Pound's efforts to keep Confucian thought alive and flowing from the Orient to the Occident.

CANTOS XIV-XV

The Hell Cantos

Sources

Dante, *Inf.* V, 28; Edward FitzGerald, *The Rubáiyát of Omar Khayyám*; Horace, *Ars Poetica* V, 173.

Background

EP, "The Serious Artist," *LE*, 42, and "Hell," 201-213; *L*, 191 (to Wyndham Lewis), 239 (to John Drummond), 293 (to John Lackay Brown), 210 (to his father): Preface to *CON: SR*, 127-135; *SP*, 207, 210; *A Visiting Card*, Peter Russell, London, 1952, 34; Iamblichus, *On the Mysteries of the Egyptians, Chaldeans, and Assyrians*, trans. Thomas Taylor, 3d ed., London, 1968; *The Divine Comedy*, tr. A. R. Huse, Rinehart, 1954; *The Inferno*, Italian text and trans. with commentary by Charles Singleton, 2 vols., Bollingen Series, LXXX, Princeton, 1970; Thomas Bullfinch, *Mythology*, New York, 1913; *Plotinus*, Vols. I-VI, Loeb, 1966.

Exegeses

CE, *Ideas*, passim; Dekker, *Cantos*, 7-13; LL, *Motive*, 82-83; Knox, *Pai*, 3-1, 78; JE, *Pai* 8-2.

Glossary Canto XIV

1. **Io venni . . . muto**: I, *Inf.* V, 28: "I came to a place mute of all light." Note rhyme with the darkness of hell in Canto I, and also "there is no darkness but ignorance" [*Twelfth Night*, IV.II.42], a favorite line of Pound's since he conceived that divinity manifested itself through intelligence [cf. preface to *CON*, 20]. In *L*, 191 (to Wyndham Lewis), Pound wrote of the "Hell Cantos": "You will readily see that the 'hell' is a portrait of contemporary England, or at least Eng. as she wuz when I left her." And in *L*, 239 (to John Drummond): "the hell cantos are specifically LONDON, the state of English mind in 1919 and 1920." And in a letter to his father [May 1925]: "I intended Cantos XIV and XV to give an accurate picture of the spiritual state of England in the years 1919 and following. Including Mr. Wilson. They were written before the Harding-Coolidge period, or I shd. have devoted a line or two to the mushiness of the former and the cant of the latter" [YC].

2. **. . . . . .e and . . . . .n**: Lloyd George and Wilson. In *L*, 293 (to John Lackay Brown), Pound wrote: ". . . that *section* of Hell precisely has *not* any dignity. Neither had Dante's fahrting devils. Hell is not amusing. Not a joke. And when you get further along you find individuals, not abstracts. Even the XIV-XV has individuals in it, but *not* worth recording as such. In fact, Bill Bird rather entertained that I had forgotten which rotters were there. In his edtn. he tried to get the number of . . . . . .correct in each case. My 'point' being that not even the first but only last letters of their names had resisted corruption." [For the Lloyd George, Faber has the correct 10 dots while New Directions has only 9.] Thus the name for . . . . . . f in line 22 is Zaharoff, the real name for Metevsky [18:12; 38:2], as Faber has the correct number of dots (7), though N.D. has only 6. Only those censored names that have been identified are glossed.

3. **Profiteers**: Dante puts the usurers with the sodomites at the lowest part of Circle VII, among the violent against God, and treats them as he does all mercenary souls with ultimate contempt: they are not even to be spoken to. Huse (p. 82) summarizes them: "The usurers are still competing, quarreling, rivaling, and envying each other, without honor, courage, good manners, artistic or intellectual distinction." Others in Circle VII include those who are violent against neighbors, fellowmen, and the self (suicides). They crouch at the edge of the deep canyon of Fraud which is Circle VIII. The monster Geryon [51:13, 16] carries Dante and his guide Virgil on his reptilian wings into the lower reaches of Circle VIII (the abode of panders, seducers, flatterers, simonists, soothsayers, barrators, hypocrites, thieves, evil councillors, sowers of discord, falsifiers), a place in Hell called Malebolge [*Luogo è inferno detto Malebolge*].

4. **financiers**: A cue to the scatological content of Pound's hell may be found in this remark: "It is said that Rabelais hid his wisdom in a mass of filth in order that it might be acceptable to his age" [*SR*, 134]. But Dante uses filth imagery at the depths of Malebolge. Although Dante translators are restrained in English, Pound's strong language can be found in such locutions as "The banks were crusted over with a mold. . . . I saw down in the ditch a people plunged in filth that seemed to have come from human privies. . . . I beheld one whose head was so befouled with ordure . . ." [*Inf.* XVIII, 106-120; Singleton trans.].

5. **lashing**: In Circle VIII we meet Dante's first devils who wear horns and ply the condemned with whips: "I saw horned demons with great whips beating the shades fiercely from behind" [Huse, 87].

6. **betrayers of language**: The occupants of Bolgia 10 are the falsifiers, who include impersonators and liars. To use words sloppily or carelessly (the opposite of Chêng Ming [51:20]) is bad enough but, in Pound's ethics, to betray the word with malice afore-

thought is one of the ultimate sins. Pound wrote: "Moral filth is perhaps less poisonous than intellectual filth, when it comes to considering the printed page. Moral filth, in print, poisons the reader; intellectual filth can be toxic to a whole race" [*A Visiting Card*, 34].

7. **howling**: Said Pound: "Hell is the state of man dominated by his passions; who has lost 'the good of the intelligence' " [*SR*, 129].

8. **mysterium**: L, sing. of *mysteria*, "mysteries." Secret rites in divine worship; esp. of the Eleusinian worship of Ceres [Persephone]. Later associated with alchemy.

9. **acid of sulphur**: Used in alchemy. Many literal-minded alchemists discounted the sacred content of the mysteries and were bent on money lust: gold. The process by which the *prima materia* (the mercury of the philosophers) was to be transmuted required the philosopher's stone which came from sulphur: "This sulphur again was not ordinary sulphur, but some principle derived from it, which constituted the philosopher's stone or elixir" [cf. *EB*, "Alchemy"].

10. **jewels**: Although associated with alchemy, here prob. has symbolic content related to works of art which provide "pleasures of the senses" as given in this canto, 10 lines before.

11. **ΕΙΚΩΝ ΓΗΣ**: H, "picture [or image] of the earth."

12. **Pearse**: Patrick Henry P., 1879-1916, Irish author and Sinn Fein leader; commander in chief of the Irish forces in the Easter Rebellion (1916); executed after surrendering his troops.

13. **MacDonagh**: Thomas M., 1878-1916, Irish patriot engaged in the 1916 rebellion in Ireland; executed; member of the Celtic Renaissance movement in literature.

14. **Captain H.**: Captain J. Bowen-Colthurst, British army officer serving in Ireland (1916) who gained notoriety for killing political prisoners in cold blood. Eventually court-martialed and confined to Broadmoor Criminal Asylum.

15. **Verres**: Gaius V., ca. 120-43 B.C., Roman administrator whose corruption astonished even the Romans. He plundered provinces, sold justice, avoided prosecution by selling power and influence, and corrupted and sold art treasures.

16. **Calvin**: John C., 1509-1564, French Protestant theologian who in Pound's view helped destroy the Mysteries of the Church and substituted fear and penance for celebration and rejoicing.

17. **St. Clement of Alexandria**: Titus Flavius Clemens, ?150-220?, Greek theologian of the early Christian church. His writings such as *Protrepticus* show familiarity with Greek mysteries which, after his conversion to Christianity, he rejected in favor of a Pauline, moralistic, and repressive code.

18. **Westminster**: District around Westminster Palace and Houses of Parliament, traditionally associated with the center of government.

19. **pets-de-loup**: F, "university people [scholars]"; lit., wolf farts.

20. **Invidia**: L, "Envy."

21. **corruptio**: L, "corruption."

22 **Episcopus**: L, "Bishop."

Glossary Canto XV

1. **Grasse**: City in France whose main industry, making soaps, perfumes, and the like from fats, created a noxious stench.

2. **middan**: Variant of midden, a dunghill or refuse heap; from ME, "myddung."

3. . . . . . . : Winston Churchill [RO].

4. **USURA**: The beast with a hundred legs is Pound's version of Dante's Geryon as given at the opening of *Inf.* XVII. Pound's own translation of the passage contains these

lines: "Behold the wild brute with sharpened tail. . . . Behold the one that fouleth all the world. . . . And that uncleanly image of fraud came on, . . . the rest was all a serpent's body" [*SR*, 133].

5. **laudatores temporis acti**: L, "admirers of bygone days" [Horace, *Ars Poetica*, 173; the original reads: *laudator temporis acti*].

6. **fabians**: The Fabian Society, a group of socialists, was organized in England in 1884. They espoused slow, evolutionary gradualism and were against Marxian revolution. Citing Major Douglas, Pound called Fabianism "a claim for the complete subjection of the individual to an objective" imposed on him and "a brand of poison" put forward by the intelligentsia as the ideal: "Man as a social unit. German philology with sacrifice of individual intelligence to the Moloch of 'Scholarship' " [*SP*, 207, 210].

7. **et nulla . . . eos**: L, "and no trust among them."

8. **my guide**: Virgil is Dante's guide, but since Pound uses the *Inferno* merely as a metaphor for the London of 1919-20, Virgil will be metamorphosed into Plotinus [cf. 11 below] as the Pythagorean or Neoplatonic philosopher of light who will lead Pound out of the darkness of the contemporary hell. For to both Dante and Pound, hell is a state of mind. Pound called the *Commedia* "Dante's vision of a journey through the realms inhabited by the spirits of men after death" but also "the journey of Dante's intelligence through the states of mind wherein dwell . . . men before death" [*SR*, 127].

9. **bolge**: I, "ditches" as in Circle VIII of *Inf.* From *Malebolge* [14:3]. Pound said it contained "the violent against art, and the usurers," and, in Canto XVII, that "Dante attacks the 'unearned increment.' " Also: " 'Malebolge' is a series of concentric pits, the whole shaped somewhat like a half-opened telescope. Through the *Inferno* there is a biting satire on the aimless turmoil and restlessness of humanity . . . in 'Malebolge,' only at the very root of Hell do we find the end of it, in the still malignity of the traitor's wallow" [*SR*, 133-135].

10. **Andiamo**: I, "Let's go." The rest of Canto XV seems to express a nightmarelike state of struggle: the kind of dream where the hero runs without progress, tries to get out of quicksand with nothing to cling to, tries to follow the directions of someone on the sidelines who cannot really help. The struggle is agonized and the scene is highly dramatic, but the hero survives the nightmare and awakes into sunlight. Yet in the last lines he drops back into an exhausted state of unconsciousness. The passage seems to be an adaptation and amalgam of materials from the Perseus-Gorgon-Medusa myth as found in several oft-used Pound sources: *Inf.* IX (an interlude between Circles V and VI which dramatizes Dante's terror at the gate of Dis); Ovid, *Meta.* IV, 743-765, 934-974; *Meta.* V, passim; the *Enneads* of Plotinus [cf. 11 below] and the Rubáiyát [cf. 16 below]. The technique of so mixing the various scenes and people seems to parallel the technique Pound used to dramatize the delirium state of Niccolò d'Este [cf. 20/90-93] as Pound described it in a letter to his father [*L*, 210]: "Then in the delirium, Nicolo remembers or thinks he is watching death of Roland. . . . The whole reminiscence jumbled or 'candied' in Nicolo's delirium."

11. **Plotinus**: 205-270, most significant of the Neoplatonic light philosophers, and author of the *Enneads*, which were collected by Porphyry and published ca. A.D. 300. The content of the *Enneads* (so-called because the documents were arranged in six groups of nine) is similar in basics to the work of Iamblicus [5:5]. Thus Plotinus, the source of "Iamblichus' light," is an appropriate hope to lead one out of the darkness of hell. But it is also appropriate for Plotinus to be "gone" from hell as given in the last line on page 66.

12. **Medusa**: The worst of the three gorgons, terrifying females who laid waste the land. Bullfinch says: "She was once a beautiful maiden whose hair was her chief glory, but as she dared to vie in beauty with Minerva, the goddess . . . changed her beautiful ringlets into hissing serpents. She became a cruel

monster of so frightful an aspect that no living thing could behold her without being turned into stone" [*Mythology*, 116]. Perseus, the son of Jupiter and Danaë [4:33], was sent to slay the Medusa. Mercury lent Perseus his winged shoes and Minerva lent her shield which he used as a mirror so that he would not have to look upon her directly and be turned to stone. Says Bullfinch: ". . . guided by her image reflected in the bright shield . . . he cut off her head and gave it to Minerva."

13. **souse**: "slop." With Pound's supervision, Mary de Rachewiltz gives "brodaglia" I, "slops." EH, in her trans. into German, gives "den Brei" G, "pap" or "pulp." [JE, *Pai*, 8-2].

14. **rast**: "strip." Mary de R. gives "striscia stretta" I, "narrow strip." EH gives "schmale Joch" G, "narrow strip." [ibid.]

15. **dern**: Scot, "secret," "obscure," "dreadful." Mary de R. gives the phrase "the dern evil" as "il male orrendo." EH gives it as "dem durch unsägliche Greuel," which has the same sense. [ibid.]

16. **Naishapur**: Nishapur, town in NE Iran; birthplace of Omar Khayyám [cf. Rubáiyát, st. 8]. Perhaps in the oblivion of the nightmarish dream, the hero is reminded of this quatrain because of the other lines in it: "Whether the Cup with sweet or bitter run, / The Wine of Life keeps oozing drop by drop, / The Leaves of Life keep falling one by one."

17. **'Héλιον . . .**: H, "The sun, the sun." Homeric form of Attic 'ήλιος.

CANTO XVI

Sources

William Blake, "London," etc.; Peire Cardinal [cf. EP, *SR*, 48, 132]; Cesare de Lollis, *Vita e Poesie di Sordello di Goito* 1896; Dante, *Pur.* VI; Arnaut Daniel [cf. EP, *LE*, 109]; J. G. Frazer, *The Golden Bough*; Virgil, *Aeneid* VI, 136; Bible, Matt. 11: 18; Propertius II, xxvi, 48.

Background

EP, *SR*, 48, 61, 132; *GB*, passim; Michael Howard, *The Franco-Prussian War*, New York, 1961; Lincoln Steffens, *Autobiography*, New York, 1931, 747-756.

Exegeses

LL, *Motive*, 75-76; Dekker, *Cantos*, 167, 169-170; EH, *Approaches*, 142, 172-173, 204, 206; Surette, *Pai*, 3-2, 199; JE, *Pai*, 1-1, 73.

Glossary

1. **hell mouth**: When Dante and Virgil reach the depths of Hell at the center of the earth and the center of gravity, they turn and begin to climb back with difficulty. Just before dawn on Easter Sunday they reach the mouth of Hell and the foot of Purgatory, where Dante saw in the far distance "the beautiful things that heaven bears / and came out to see once more the stars."

2. **Blake**: William B., 1757-1827, English poet and visionary. Seen by Pound as a genuine religious who made heroic efforts to escape from the hell around him in his time; e.g., "The Marriage of Heaven and Hell," "Proverbs of Hell," "A Song of Liberty," "London," and such ideas as "Is the Holy Ghost any other than an intellectual Fountain?" or "What are the Pains of Hell but Ignorance, Bodily Lust, Idleness, and devastation of the things of the Spirit?" ["To the Christians"].

3. **Peire Cardinal**: Provençal troubadour, ca. 1185-ca. 1275, noted for his satiric attacks on evil, especially the Church in the Albigensian period in S France. Said by Pound to be "extremely lucid on the imbecility of belligerents and the makers of wars" [*SR*, 48]. Also, his "invectives against the corruption of the church temporal should be read . . ." [*SR*, 61]. And "Peire Cardinal's fable of the sane man in the city gone mad is a weaker equation for what Dante presents as a living man amongst the dead" [*SR*, 132].

4. **Il Fiorentino**: Dante Alighieri, 1265-1321, who as he left Hell could see Satan, as in a mirror, only backward or "upside down" [*Inf.* 34:103 ff.].

5. **Sordels**: Sordello [2:2; *Pur.* VI-VIII; *SR*, 57-59]. In Dante, Sordello is nowhere shown literally looking at his shield, but his main grief is over the "lack of heart" [courage] in battle of many present-day heads of cities or states. So he proposes that they eat of the heart of the hero, Sir Blancatz, to gain courage to wield their shields. Pound translates: ". . . that they take his heart out, and have it eaten by the Barons who live un-hearted . . ." [*SR*, 58]. Thus Pound continues the metaphor of the hell men continue to create on earth.

6. **Augustine**: Saint A., 354-430. In the *Commedia* Augustine is mentioned twice comparatively and once incidentally [*Par.* 10:120; 12:130; 32:35], but at no point is he pictured "gazing toward the invisible." The line may then summarize the attitude expressed in *The City of God* as well as in Augustine's many other works.

7. **crimen est actio**: L, "crime is action."

8. **Palux Laerna**: L, *Palus Lernae*, the swamp of Lerna where Hercules killed the Hydra, the poisonous snake [cf. Propertius II, xxvi, 48].

9. **aqua morta**: L, "dead water."

10. **Then light air**: The scene from this line to the "one man" who "rose from his fountain / and went off into the plain" is probably based on the vision of the "Earthly Paradise" [Garden of Eden: *Pur.* 28-33]. But it is an impressionistic account in which trees become "saplings"; the two streams and the river across which Dante gazes become the "blue banded lake"; and the ten steps become the "stair of gray stone." The man who went off into the plain may rhyme with Virgil, who leaves Dante at this point since Beatrice has not become his guide. But Pound lists post-Dantean heroes in place of the "founders" Dante encounters here.

11. **patet terra**: L, "the earth lies open."

12. **Sigismundo**: S. Malatesta [8:5]. Since S. is one of the activist heroes of *The Cantos* with a vision of an earthly paradise and with a directed will [*directio voluntatis*: 77/467] rather than a paralyzed will [*abuleia*: 5:44; 54:192], he is shown contemplating his inner vision.

13. **Malatesta Novello**: Domenico Malatesta, 1418-1465, younger brother of Sigismundo,

known popularly as "Novvy"; also a man of vision [10:58].

14. Prone in that grass: After Beatrice upbraids Dante for his sinful and childish life, he is so stung with remorse that he falls down in a faint [*Pur*. 31:85-90]. When he is restored to sense he finds himself in the river up to his throat and he hears the Lady of the Garden [Matilda] saying, "Tiemmi, tiemmi!" ["Cling to me, cling to me!"]. Beatrice has gone for the moment, but Dante is on his way "to the blessed shore" [*Pur*. 31:91-108].

15. et j'entendis des voix: F, "and I heard voices." With these words the scene of the canto switches to the hell and purgatory of contemporary wars: (1) Franco-Prussian; (2) the Silk War of Ragusa; (3) World War I; (4) the Russian Revolution.

16. Strasbourg: French city near the center of action in the Franco-Prussian War of 1870-71. Birthplace of Plarr [cf. 18 below]

17. Galliffet: General Gaston de G. Story of useless courage doomed to defeat, as in "The Charge of the Light Brigade." In the battle for Sedan, the French army, being divided and cut off from retreat, called upon Galliffet's African corps of cavalry to charge the massive German lines at Floing. He made the useless charge "leaving the carcasses of horses and the bodies of their riders lying thick in front of the German lines" [Michael Howard, *The Franco-Prussian War*, 216]. Galliffet rallied the survivors and was asked if he could try again. He said, "As often as you like, *mon général*, so long as there's one of us left." King William, seeing them plunge down the hill a second time to certain destruction, said, "Ah les braves gens!" These words were carved on a memorial erected later. A third charge led to the heaviest bloodshed of all. Legend says that Galliffet and his last followers passed exhausted within a few feet of the enemy line. "The Germans ceased fire; their officers saluted; and the Frenchmen were allowed to ride slowly away, honoured and unharmed" [ibid.].

18. Plarr: Victor Gustave P., 1863-1929, whose family settled in England after the Franco-Prussian War. The M. Verog of *Mauberley*. He told stories of that war including the famous charge of Galliffet ["For two hours he talked of Galliffet," *Mauberley*] against the Prussians and presumably the anecdote about his "Nurse." Pound knew Plarr when he worked as librarian of the Royal College of Surgeons compiling its catalog. [Pound also remarked Plarr's commemoration of the liberation of Strasbourg from the Germans in a poem, "Strasbourg," in the London *Times* of December 18, 1918 (FR)].

19. Brother Percy: Prob. Lord Algernon P., 1792-1865, British naval officer.

20. Ragusa: A port of Dalmatia which was under the control of Venice from 1205 to 1358.

21. Silk War: War between Venice and Ragusa at the beginning of the 15th century. Pandolfo led the Venetians against Ragusa in 1420 but did not capture it.

22. Lord Byron: George Gordon, 1788-1824, the English poet.

23. Franz Josef: 1830-1916, emperor of Austria, whose policies contributed to the outbreak of World War I; he rejected the Serbian note after Sarajevo and declared war on July 28, 1914.

24. Napoléon Barbiche: Charles Louis N. Bonaparte, 1808-1873, Napoleon III, known as Louis N., emperor of the French (1852-1871); called *Barbiche* because of his goatee.

25. Aldington: Richard A., 1892-1962, young associate (1912-1915) of Pound and the Imagists. Married H. D. and lived across the courtyard from Pound in Church Walk. Served as junior officer in British army (1915-1917); saw much action in trench warfare and narrowly escaped death several times. War novels: *Roads to Glory, Death of a Hero*. Poet, novelist, and critic [cf. his autobiography, *Life for Life's Sake*, 1941].

26. Henri Gaudier: 1891-1915, French sculptor who took the name of Gaudier-Brzeska. Joined with Pound, Wyndham Lewis, and others in Vorticist movement. Killed in a charge at Neuville St. Vaast, June 5, 1915. Pound used him as a prime example of the horrible waste of war. With his death a lifetime of sculpture was lost [cf. *GB*, passim, and indexes to any of Pound's volumes of collected prose].

27. T.E.H.: Thomas Ernest Hulme, 1883-1917, English philosopher and poet, killed in World War I. Original member of Imagist group. Leading mind in newly established Poets' Club which Pound joined in April 1909.

28. Kant: Immanuel K., 1724-1804, German idealist philosopher.

29. Wimbledon: Suburb of London.

30. Wyndham Lewis: Percy W. L., 1884-1957, British writer and painter. Original member of Vorticist group. Pound maintained his opinion about the superiority of Lewis's work until the end of his life [cf. 115/794]. Until 1975 edition, Faber uses the pseudonym "Maxy Larmann" in this line.

31. mitrailleuse: F, "machine gun."

32. Windeler: Donald W.

33. Aegaean: The Aegean Sea, which separates Greece from Turkey, the locale of much naval action.

34. Captain Baker: Guy B.; early Faber editions used Captain Corcoran.

35. Fletcher: Erroneously taken to be John Gould F., 1886-1950; American poet whom Pound met in Paris in May 1913. Associated with Imagists but turned against Pound to become "Amygist." In 1915, after World War I broke out, he returned to America, but he came back to England in 1916 to marry Daisy Arbuthnot. Was not involved in war. J. G. F. would have been 28 at outbreak of war. The 19-year-old is unidentified. Faber editions use the name "Bimmy."

36. Ernie Hemingway: Ernest H., 1899-1961, American novelist; Pound knew him well during his Paris years and promoted his work. Early Faber editions used the name Cyril Hammerton.

37. Et ma foi . . . soit bien carré: F, "And really, you know, / all the nervous (or nervy) ones. No, / there is a limit; animals, animals are not / made for that, a horse doesn't amount to much. / The men of 34, on all fours, / who cried 'Mommy.' But the tough guys, / at the end, there at Verdun, there were only those big boys / and they knew exactly what the score was. / What are they worth, the generals, the lieutenant, / they weigh out at a centigramme, / they are nothing but wood. / Our captain, all shut up in himself like / the old military engineer he was, but strong, / a stronghead. There, you know, / everything, everything runs in order, and the thieves, all the vices, but the birds of prey, / there were three in our company, all killed. / They went out to plunder a corpse, for nothing, / they would have gone out for nothing but that. / And the Jerries, you can say anything you want, / militarism, etc. . . etc. . . / All that, but, BUT / the Frenchman, he fights when he has eaten. / But those poor guys / at the end they attacked each other so they could eat, / Without orders, wild animals, they took / prisoners; those who could speak French said: / 'Poo quah? Well, we attacked so we could eat.' / It's the grease, the grease / their supplies came forward at three kilometers an hour, / and they creaked, they grated, could be heard five kilometers away. / (That's what finished the war.) / The official list of dead: 5,000,000 / He tells you, well [yeah, it all smelled of oil. / But, No! I bawled him out / I said to him:] You're a jerk! You missed the war. / O Yeah! all the people with taste, I admit, / all of them in the rear / But a guy like you! / That fellow, a guy like that! / What he couldn't have taken! He was in a factory. / What, burying squad, ditch diggers, with their heads / thrust back, looking like this, / they risked their life for a shovelful of dirt. / Must be nice and square, accurate" [*Index*].

38. Trotzsk: Leon Trotsky, 1879-1940. Leading revolutionist and aide to Lenin who had returned to Russia in 1917. Trotsky was the principal negotiator of Treaty of Brest-Litovsk and accepted humiliating conditions to obtain peace with the Central Powers so that the Bolsheviks would be free to promote the revolution at home.

39. bolsheviki: R, "majority." Group led by Lenin opposed to minority party: Mensheviki. Data about unpremeditated Russian Revolution in March based on lecture given in 1924 by Lincoln Steffens in Paris which Pound attended and was excited by. Steffens incorporated these lecture notes into his *Autobiography*. The "man talking" is Lenin: ". . . when you want a government that will do socialism, then–come to the Bolsheviki" [Steffens, 761].

40. "Pojalouista": R, "if you please." "The Cossacks were summoned . . . they moved carefully, and they used the polite Russian word, 'Pajalista,' which means 'if you please!" [Steffens, 750].

41. lieutenant: Steffens wrote: ". . . out in the great square in front of the Moscow railroad station an infantry officer was trying to command and incite his men to shoot across the open into the quiet mob. They would not. A student standing by jeered at the officer, who, in a rage, thrust the student through. A Cossack . . . saw this . . . charged . . . and drawing his sword . . . cut that officer down. There was a cry: 'The soldiers *are* with us!' and then there was another cry: 'The revolution! The revolution is on!' " [Steffens, 751].

42. Nevsky: Broad avenue that leads into a large square, the scene of the March bread riots. Square is site of station where trains leave for Moscow.

43. Haig: Douglas H., 1861-1928. British marshal, commander in chief of expeditionary forces in France and Flanders, 1915-1919.

CANTO XVII

Sources

Giambattista Pigna, *Historia de Principi di Este*, 1570; Virgil, *Aeneid* VI, 204.

Background

EP, *CON*, 183; E. A. Wallis Budge, "Isis and Osiris," in *Legends of the Gods*, London, 1912; Adrian Stokes, *The Quattro Cento*, London, 1932, *Stones of Rimini*, London, 1934, and *Colour and Form*, London, 1937; Plutarch, *De Iside et Osiride*, ed. and trans. J. Gwyn Griffiths, University of Wales, 1970; Thomas Taylor, *The Eleusinian and Bacchic Mysteries*, 4th ed., 1891; CFT, *Pai*, 2-3, 449-462; 3-1, 92-93.

Exegeses

Quinn, in LL, *Motive*, 92-95; CE, *Ideas*, 139-140; DD, *Sculptor*, 128-129; Surette, *Pai*, 3-2, 200-206.

Glossary

1. **So that**: A new start, in medias res, which echoes the beginning, "And then," and the end, "So that," of Canto I.

2. **the vines burst**: Leaving the Purgatory of Canto 16, we come to the first extended vision of Paradise. In a letter [#745, YC, D. D. Paige transcripts] Pound said of Canto 17 that it was "a sort of paradiso terrestre." The whole scene is charged with vitality from divinity operating in the world. The vines here are "bursting" in contrast with the vinestocks that lie untended, nipped by the north wind in the fading light [cf. 5/18], and the "thin husks," "locust-shells," and "dry pods" in an earlier scene of twilight and lamplight where life seems paralyzed [cf. 7/25-27] by abulia [5:44].

3. **ZAGREUS**: Another name for Dionysus, in late tradition the god of wine, but in Pound the god of "Orgia" [religious ecstasy] and fertility associated with the Eleusinian Mysteries, arcanum, and the rites of spring.

4. **IO**: H, "Hail."

5. **goddess . . . knees**: Artemis [Diana].

6. **palazzi**: I, "palaces." Part of the architectural data derived from impressions of Venice.

7. **The light now**: Neoplatonic, primal light, "not of the sun," associated with Artemis [Diana], where the air is "alight with the goddess" but "not a ray" of sun [4:14]. Dante also uses the light imagery from Plotinus [15:10]: ". . . the divine light so penetrates the universe, in measure of its worthiness that nothing has power to stand against it" [*Par*. XXXI, 22-24]. Pound attributes the same metaphor to the Confucian process: "The celestial and earthly process pervades and is substantial; it is on high and gives light, it comprehends the light and is lucent, it extends without bound, and endures" [*CON*, 183].

8. **Chrysophrase**: Chrysoprase, an apple-green chalcedony, a semiprecious stone used in making jewelry.

9. **Nerea**: Prob. the Nereids, sea sprites who were the daughters of Nereus, Homer's "Old Man" of the sea.

10. **she like a great shell**: Suggests myth of the birth of Venus and Botticelli's *La Nascita*. Thus Venus is pictured as "between them" [the Nerea or sprites] in a "not-of-this-world" scene.

11. **malachite**: A green mineral from which copper is derived.

12. **the light**: The divine Neoplatonic light "not of the sun" [cf. *Pai*, 2-3, 449-462].

13. **panthers**: The hieratic animals throughout the canto are visionary [cf. *Pai*, 3-1, 92-93].

14. **choros nympharum**: L, "chorus of nymphs."

15. **Hermes**: Messenger and herald of the gods; patron of merchants and thieves and god of luck and wealth. But here he is the bearer of the golden wand used by Aeneas to enter the Elysian fields [*Aeneid* VI].

16. **Athene**: Pallas Athena, goddess of wisdom; patron of the arts of peace and of war; guardian of cities, especially of Athens, but here guardian of the visionary city of *paradiso terrestre*.

17. **sylva nympharum**: L, "wood of the nymphs."

18. Memnons: Memnon, son of Tithonus and Eos. A large statue near Thebes, Egypt (supposed to be of Memnon), was reputed to produce a musical sound when struck by the light of dawn.

19. Guiding her . . . evening: For this scene see works of Stokes listed in background material.

20. Borso: B. d'Este, 1413-1471, son of Niccolò d'Este; Lord of Ferrara and patron of learning [10:20]. Here his dedication to the arts, architecture, and the advancement of peace makes him one of the canto characters with a paradisal vision.

21. Carmagnola: Francesco Bussone da C., fl. 1380-1432, Italian militarist serving under Filippo Visconti, Duke of Milan; later he led the forces of Florence and Venice against Visconti. His strange conduct led the Venetians to try him for treason before the Council of Ten, after which he was executed [10:7].

22. i vitrei: I, "makers of glass."

23. In the gloom . . . : Paradisal or "otherworldly" image [cf. 11/51].

24. Zothar: Private reference [EP to FR].

25. sistrum: L, "a sort of rattle used in the worship of Isis."

26. Aletha: Prob. an invention: a sea deity.

27. Koré: H, "daughter"; a reference to Persephone [3:8]. The appearance of Koré occurs with the appearance of the gods and an evocation of the Eleusinian Mysteries, which begins with a descent into the underworld (a repeat of Canto I) where Koré is first encountered. The final 19 lines of the canto are poss. a metaphor for the descent. But as Aeneas with the magic wand of Hermes was led, while in Hell, to a vision of the Elysian fields [the bright meadow], we descend into the darkness of Hell (as the sun descends in the West) and into the mysterious arcanum [cf. Surette, *Pai*, 3-2, 205].

28. brother of Circe: Aeëtes, king of Colchis and father of Medea.

29. Hermes: When on official assignment as a messenger of Zeus, Hermes donned a "splendid" costume, carried the magic wand, and with winged heels sped across the sky [cf. 15 above].

30. Borso: B. d'Este [10:20; 20 above; cf. 10/46]: "And they had a bow-shot at Borso / As he was going down the Grand Canal in his gondola / (the nice kind with 26 barbs on it.)" Just as Dante meets various people long dead in the *Commedia*, we meet several canto characters now dead, including Borso and the two in the glosses below.

31. Carmagnola: [cf. 21 above]. He was "invited to lunch," seized, and executed between the two columns [10:7, 8]. As Yriarte puts it: ". . . that this Count Carmagnola . . . should be decapitated between the two columns of S. Marco, at the accustomed hour after the nones with an iron piece in his mouth and with his hands tied according to the custom followed in the Piazza . . ." [cf. *Analyst* XI, 4].

32. Sigismundo: S. de Malatesta [8:5].

33. Dalmatia: Coastal region of present-day Yugoslavia, for centuries fought over by Croatia and Venice but brought under the control of Venice by 1420.

CANTO XVIII

Sources

Marco Polo, *Il Milione*, Firenze, Successori, Le Monnier, 1916; Louis Antoine Fauvelet de Bourrienne, *Mémoires sur Napoléon*, Paris, 1829.

Background

Richard Lewinsohn, *The Man behind the Scenes: The Career of Sir Basil Zaharoff*, London, 1929; Robert Neumann, *Zaharoff*, New York, 1935; Sir Henry Yule, *The Book of Ser Marco Polo*, Vol. I, 3d ed., rev. by H. Cordier, London, 1921.

Exegeses

EP, "Kublai Khan and His Currency," *New Age*, May 20, 1920, rpt. in *SP*, 204; EP, letter to Homer Pound dated Rapallo, Nov. 29, 1924, Paige collection at Yale ["As to Cantos 18-19, there ain't no key. Simplest parallel I can give is radio where you tell who is talking by the noise they make"] [cf. Nanny, *Pai*, 8-1].

Glossary

1. **Kublai**: K. Khan, 1214-1294. In 1260 he became emperor of the Mongols and in 1280 emperor of all China, giving his dynasty the name Yüan. Kublai led few military expeditions after he became emperor. In 1285 paper money in the form of bank notes was made current. Kublai was often under the influence of his ministers, particularly Ahama and Sang-Ko.

2. **Cambaluc**: Khabalik, Kublai Khan's capital city. The "City of the Great Khan" was built (1264-1267) on the site of the earlier city of Yen by Kublai Khan; site of modern Peking. Kublai's mint was in this city.

3. **hyght**: ME, past participle of *hoten,* "named." ". . . you might say he hath the Secret of Alchemy in perfection" [*SP*, 204].

4. **tornesol:** OF, *tornese,* "of Tours"; a minor coin of base silver or copper, struck in many of the Italian states prior to the unification.

5. **groat**: ME, *grote*, "silver coin worth 4 pence" [Webster].

6. **bezant**: Gold coin issued by the Byzantine emperors, circulating in Europe between 6th and 15th centuries.

7. **Kahn**: Khan [cf. 1 above].

8. **Messire Polo**: Marco P., ?1254-1324?, Venetian traveler, visited Kublai Khan in 1275 and returned to Venice in 1295. In 1296 he was taken prisoner by the Genoese against whom he, with the Venetians, was fighting; he dictated his memoirs while in

prison in Genoa. He brought back information about the khan's currency given above [Yule, I, 423 ff.; *SP*, 204-206].

9. **Genoa**: Seaport in NW Italy.

10. **Constantinople**: Formerly Byzantium, now Istanbul.

11. **Bourrienne**: Louis Antoine Fauvelet de B., 1769-1834, French Diplomat and writer, private secretary to Napoleon (1797-1802). In his *Memoirs of Napoleon Bonaparte*, Hartford, Silas Andrus & Sons, 1856, we read (concerning Napoleon's years at the military school at Brienne): "The temper of the young Corsican was not improved by the railleries of the students, who were fond of ridiculing his name . . . and his country. He has often said to me, 'I will do these French all the mischief in my power' " [p. 17].

12. **Zenos Metevsky**: Sir Basil Zaharoff, 1849?-1933, European munitions magnate. He started selling arms (ca. 1876) for Nordenfeldt & Co. and later joined Maxim, an early competitor; by 1913 both Zaharoff and Maxim had joined Vickers. Zaharoff also had interests in oil, international banks, and newspapers. He had a spotty career, rising from poverty to immense wealth and spending time in prison in England and Greece. But he was able to rebound from all adversity and by extreme cunning (as well as crookedness) defeat his enemies and come out ahead. Zaharoff, who as a boy in Constantinople was kicked by a Britisher and later was imprisoned and tried in England, hated the British secretly all his life [cf. HK, *Era*, 465], a repeat in history of Napoleon's experience with the French.

13. **Biers**: Prob. Hiram Maxim, 1840-1916, inventor of the Maxim machine guns as well as of a smokeless powder, a delayed-action fuse, and a heavier-than-air airplane. He formed an arms company which, through the machinations of Zaharoff, consolidated with Vickers to form Vickers-Armstrong, one of the biggest producers of war materials in Europe.

14. **Metevsky died** . . . : An enemy of Sir B. Zaharoff, one Stephanos Xenos, wrote in his newspaper, *Mikra Ephemeris*: ". . . the convict, Zacharias Basileios Zaharoff, had made a sensational attempt to escape from the old prison in Athens called Garbola. But at the moment when he was trying to get away he was shot by a warden." But it was another prisoner who was shot. Thus, Zaharoff was able to sit in the café and watch what was supposed to be his own funeral. Later, an exhumation of the body enabled Z.'s dentist to say: "This is certainly not Zaharoff!" [Neumann, 58-59].

15. **Yeiner Kafé**: Poss. the Wiener Café.

16. **Humbers**: Pseudonym for Vickers.

17. **Mr. Giddings**: Pseudonym for unidentified salesman of armaments.

18. **La Marquesa . . . Hurbara**: Prob. Madame Maria del Pilar Antonia-Angela-Patrocinio-Simona de Muquiro y Bernete, widow of Villafranca de los Caballeros, whom Sir Basil Zaharoff, then 75 years old, married in 1924. Z. first met her in 1889 on a night train to Spain whither he was going to sell arms. According to one account she was on her honeymoon as the new Duchess of Villafranca; another report said that she literally fell into Z's arms "while flying from her sleeping-car and from the brutality of her just-wedded husband." Neumann [op. cit.] believes that since her husband was cousin to the king of Spain (Alfonso XII) and Z. was on the way to restore a large canceled order for arms, the meeting was not accidental. But the passion between Z. and the duchess became real, transformed his manner of dress and life, and lasted for years. As a devout Catholic she could not get a divorce, so they had to arrange secret meetings. But Z. was quite able to mix passion and business. "According to an entry in the *Internationale Biographische Archiv* of Berlin, the orders Zaharoff got there [Spain] amounted to thirty million pounds sterling two months after his meeting with the Duchess of Villafranca" [Neumann, 86-88].

19. Champs Elysées: Street in Paris inhabited by the very wealthy. Particular source of this anecdote is not known, but it is only one of many such tales circulating in Paris and London in the 1920s.

20. las once: S, "eleven o'clock."

21. Este to Louis Eleventh: Borso d'E. Louis XI, 1423-1483, was king of France from 1461 to 1483 [10:45].

22. Mr. Oige: Unidentified pseudonym.

23. Gethsemane Trebizond Petrol: Prob. a pseudonym for the Anglo-Persian Oil Company, in which Zaharoff had an interest.

24. Manchester Cardiff: Railroad line running from Manchester, England, to Cardiff, Wales.

25. Hamish: Pseudonym for Taffy Fowler, an engineer whose wife conducted a salon for young musicians and poets in Knightsbridge, London, 1908-1909.

26. Melchizedek: A pre-Aaronic and pre-Levitical priest-king to whom Abraham paid tithes; a prototype of the high priest. Zaharoff was the high priest of war and of preparation for war.

27. King Menelik: M. II, 1844-1913, emperor of Ethiopia (1889-1913). In a war with Italy (1896) Menelik freed Ethiopia from Italian control.

28. Qu'est-ce . . .? . . . On don't pense: F, "What do they think? . . . They don't think."

29. "Mais . . . Metevsky?": F, "But, what is thought / of metallurgy in England, what do they / think of Metevsky?"

30. MacGorvish's bank: Poss. either Barclay's or Westminster Bank, London, but the association of banks and promoters of the international arms race is deliberate.

31. Dave: Unidentified. But he and Hamish [Taffy Fowler the engineer] are creative nonusurious developers of technology and wealth as opposed to the usurious and destructive kind represented by Zaharoff [cf. Baldy Bacon and Dos Santos, 12:3 12].

CANTO XIX

Sources

There are no published sources for Canto 19, which is a pastiche of memories of café talk, news-making events, and gossip drawn from pre-World War I years through the early 1920s.

Background

EP, *J/M*, 110; *SP*, 210-223; Lincoln Steffens, *Autobiography*, New York, 1931; Charles Norman, *Ezra Pound: A Biography*, New York, 1969.

Exegeses

Dekker, *Cantos*, 168, 170; Davis, *Vision*, 56-59; CE, *Ideas*, 114-115; Achilles Fang, "Materials for the Study of Pound's Cantos," Ph.D. dissertation, 4 vols., Harvard University, 1958.

Glossary

1. **he**: Identity unknown and unimportant. Point of anecdote is the expected response of any big company to any such challenge by an inventor.

2. **Manhattan**: Island and central borough of New York City, a world financial center.

3. **Hudson**: River in E New York State on whose banks are many old baronial mansions and estates inhabited by predatory usurers and financiers.

4. **Spinder**: Pseudonym for some financial wizard: the type rather than a particular person is important.

5. **Marx**: Karl M., 1818-1883, German political philosopher.

6. **Champz Elyza**: Champs Elysées, broad Parisian avenue leading up to the Arc de Triomphe, favorite haunt of tourists.

7. **Das Kapital**: Major document expounding Marxist doctrine, which conceives of class struggle as the only way to overthrow bourgeois democracy under capitalism to attain a socialist and thence a communist state.

8. **Qui se faisait si beau**: F, "who made himself so handsome."

9. **old kindly professor**: Unidentified, but could be Dr. Douglas Hyde. Fang says Hyde "fits the description [but] does not seem to have been in London about this time" [Fang, II, 105].

10. **stubby little man**: Arthur Griffith, leader of Irish Sinn Fein. In *ABCE* [1933; rpt. in *SP*, 239] Pound wrote: " 'Can't move 'em with a cold thing like economics,' said Mr. Griffiths [sic], the inventor of Sinn Fein." Pound, who met Griffith in Paris in 1924 and tried to convert him to the Douglas plan [Norman, 272], wrote later: ". . . one of the most illuminating hours of my life was spent in conversation with Griffith, the founder of Sinn Fein. We were in his room to avoid the detectives who infested the hotel. It was the time of the armistice when the Irish delegates had been invited to London. . . . Griffith said: 'All you say is true. But I can't move 'em with a cold thing like economics.' "

11. **The Tatler**: British magazine devoted to gossip about the upper class.

12. **the slick guy**: A detective, not reading but watching the scene.

13. **Clio**: Muse of history.

14. **Prishnip**: Prob. Gavrilo Princip who assassinated Archduke Francis Ferdinand at Sarajevo, June 28, 1914.

15. **Vlettmann?**: Unidentified.

16. **Hé Sloveny!**: Serb., *Hej, Sloveni,* "Up the Slavs," an old Pan-Slavic song. In 1945 it was chosen to be the national anthem of Yugoslavia [EH].

17. **Birth of a Nation**: Unidentified, but prob. story about the Russian Revolution.

18. **Boche**: Franco-British slang term for a German.

19. **Naphtha**: Obsolete term for petroleum or gas used as fuel.

20. **Rotterdam**: Trading seaport in the Netherlands connected by waterways to the Ruhr and N Germany. Famous center of transit shipping.

21. Das thust du nicht: G, "Don't you do that?"

22. Albert: Count A. von Mensdorf-Pouilly-Dietrichstein, Austro-Hungarian ambassador to London (1904-1914). Referred to below as "Wurmsdorf" [EH].

23. Nevsky: Broad avenue in St. Petersburg which leads into Alexander Nevsky Square at east end of which is the Nicolai (or Moscow) station. Along the way are "numerous pastry shops (e.g. Andrejew, Filippow, Dominique)" [Fang, II, 319].

24. Governed . . . train . . . lobby: The Mexican Revolution led by Carranza in 1914 who was running the government from traveling trains because he saw that Mexico City governments were corrupted and influenced by "foreigners and Mexican reactionaries." One day the constitutional committee [with Steffens as member] was ordered unexpectedly onto the train very early. Carranza later explained: "You foreigners are very tempting, you know. . . . The train we came on is the only train running these days; so we escaped your lobby . . . till the foreigners could get to Guadalajara on foot or a-horseback" [Steffens, 721, 731-732].

25. oil . . . map: One day the train stopped for lack of fuel . . . and Carranza came up to the constitutional committee in a rage. " 'What do you think of a situation . . . where, in an oil country like Mexico, the government cannot get enough oil to keep its own train moving? What can we do? You ought to be able to tell us that,' he blazed at me." Steffens said: "Maybe I can. Have you a map of the oil regions?" A map was brought and Steffens asked questions about the meaning of the straight lines, the wiggly lines, and so on, to find out what was government property. Then he said: "You could sink wells in them, and they'd be on your property; the oil would be your own government fuel." Carranza agreed and sent off an engine to start drilling for oil. But Steffens stopped him, saying he didn't really have to dig: "The oil men will see what you are up to, and they will offer you all the oil you want if you will stop boring." It worked out that way [Steffens, 730].

26. Tommy Baymont: Thomas Lamont, 1870-1948, American banker, member of firm of J. P. Morgan and Co. He is the junior partner in following passage from Steffens's *Autobiography* [p. 590] concerning an article "Steff" had written for *Everybody's Magazine* (Sept. 1910) in which he charged that J. P. Morgan had absolute power and was "The Boss of all Bosses" [title of article]: "One day soon after my article to this effect was published, I was in the Morgan bank. A junior partner tapped on his glass cage and beckoned me in. He said that he had laid on J. P.'s desk the magazine, open at my article, saw him read it and read it again and then shake his head. . . . The junior partner said that J. P. had no sense of 'absolute power' . . . and he told me an incident to prove it." The incident is the anecdote about the coal mine and the railroad.

27. Jim: James Buchanan Brady, 1856-1917, known as "Diamond Jim Brady" whom J. P. Morgan could not control: "J. P. had discovered that he could not make the New York, New Haven and Hartford Railroad, which he controlled, buy its coal from a coal company he controlled, without the consent of 'Diamond Jim' Brady. He was so enraged that he was going to fight Brady. . . . But he didn't; he accepted him . . . [because] Brady represented a company in which the officers of the New Haven and other railroads held shares" [Steffens, 590].

28. My ole man: Syntax seems to indicate that this man is the uncle of "Wurmsdorf," the ambassador; thus the speaker must be the ambassador's cousin and the scene must be some family gathering just before the outbreak of World War I where all those present reflected on the "good old days." Since Russia was going with the Allies, as the dispatches doubtless showed, these people would thenceforth be divided.

29. Wurmsdorf: [cf. 22 above].

30. Ptierstoff: Aleksander Konstantinovich Beuckendorff, 1849-1917, Russian ambassador to London (1903-1916).

31. Albert: [cf. 22 above].

32. Yash (Jassy): A commercial town in NE Rumania.

33. Healthy but verminous: Although no source is known for the anecdote about the 14 girls, the point of the story seems clear: the actions and attitudes of an Englishman [or of any man] bearing the "white man's burden."

34. Kashmir: Indian state in N India on the Sinkiang and Tibet frontier.

CANTO XX

Sources

Catullus LXI; Homer, *Od*, XII, 183; Bernart de Ventadorn, no. 235 (Appel); Guido Cavalcanti, Sonnet 35; Propertius, *Elegies* II, XX; Arnaut Daniel, "Er Vei Vermeils"; EP, "Cavalcanti," *LE*, 149; Antonio Frizzi, *Memorie per la Storia di Ferrara*, 1791-1796; Giambattista Pigna, *Historia de Principi di Este*, 1570; Virgil, *Aeneid* VI; Homer, *Iliad* III, 153; *Las Almenas de Toro*; Bishop Liutprand, *Pere la Storia de Roma e del Papapo*; Heraclitus, frag. 75; Dante, *Inf. V;* Homer, *Od.* IX; St. Francis, "Cantico Secondo"; Homer, *Od*. IX, X, XII; Ovid, *Meta*. XI; *Pur*. XIV, 109.

Background

EP, *SR*, 22-38, 191-193; Werner L. Gundersheimer, *Ferrara*, Princeton, 1973; Edward Hutton, *Sigismundo Pandolpho Malatesta, Lord of Rimini*, 1906; Anthony Manganaris-Decavalles, *Analyst* XI.

Exegeses

EP, *L*, 210; CE, *Ideas*, 140-141 and passim; DD, *Sculptor*, 133-134; WB, *Rose*, 67-72; HK, *Era*, 114-117; Flory, *Pai*, 6-2, 155-165.

Glossary

1. quasi tinnula: L, "as if ringing." Adaptation of Catullus LXI. Concerned with the "singing-ringing" of wedding bells.

2. Ligur' aoide: H, "Clear, sweet song." *Od*. XII, 183: "[The sirens] raised their clear-toned song" [Loeb, 104, 445].

3. Si no'us . . . val: P, "If I don't see you, Lady for whom I must burn, / Even not seeing you can't match my beautiful thought of you." From Bernart de Ventadorn's poem, "Can par la flors," ll. 23-24 ["When the flower appears"] [Appel, 235].

4. viel: P, "a lutelike stringed instrument."

5. s'adora: I, "She [or he] is adored." Cavalcanti, Sonnet 35 [EP, *T*, 94].

6. Possum . . . tuae!: L, "Can I not remember your nature" [Propertius II, xx, 28]. From address to Cynthia; Loeb [18, 121] translates whole passage: "Many sought thee, but thou has sought me only; can I forget the kindness of thy nature? If I do, may ye, Furies of tragedy, plague me, and thou, Aeacus, pass on me the doom of hell."

7. Qui son . . . : I, "Here are Propertius and Ovid."

8. Freiburg: Freiburg in Breisgau, town in SW Germany.

9. Rennert: Hugo Albert R., 1858-1927, scholar of Romance languages, University of Pennsylvania. One of Pound's favorite professors (1905-06).

10. Provençal: Language of the troubadours in SC France.

11. Lévy: Emil L., 1855-1918, German philologist; author of *Provençal supplement dictionnaire* [8 vols., 1892-1925].

12. Arnaut: A. Daniel, 12th-century Provençal troubadour [cf. *SR*, 22-38].

13. settant . . . Ambrosiana: I, "Seventy-one R [recto] superior Ambrosian." A catalog number in the Ambrosian Library in Milan which locates a manuscript of a Daniel poem in which there is a word [*noigandres*] that prompted Pound to consult Lévy. Seventy-one is the MS number; recto is odd-numbered side.

14. noigandres: P; a word of unknown meaning which has caused much speculation and perplexity. It is known to exist only in one line of Canello's edition of Arnaut Daniel's poetry (1883) which is where Pound found it. The line is the last one of the first verse of Daniel's 13th canzone: "E jois lo grans, e l'olors de noigandres." Kenner suggests the word may not exist at all because "the manuscripts chatter a dissident babel: nuo gaindres, nul grandes, notz grandres" [HK, *Era*, 114-117]. The problem has for years been compounded for Pound scholars until Kenner discovered the actual source (Canello) that Pound used. Suggested meanings of *noigandres* range from "walnuts" to "banishes sadness." Lévy emended the manuscript text to read "d enoi gandres" [cf. 22 below] and came up with "wards off boredom." Pound does not commit himself to any translation but in effect lets the reader devise his own. But in his own translation of the song [*Instigations*], he wrote: "and pain ameises" [HK, *Era*, 114-117].

15. ranunculae: Genus of plants which includes buttercups.

16. Agostino: A. di Duccio, ?1418-1481, Italian sculptor who did the bas-reliefs in Sigismundo Malatesta's Tempio.

17. Jacopo: J. Sellaio, 1422-1493, Florentine painter.

18. Boccata: Giovanni B., ?1435-1480?, Umbrian painter.

19. Sandro: S. Botticelli, 1444-1510, Florentine painter.

20. espalier: A tree or shrub trained to grow in a flat plane against a wall.

21. e l'olors: P, "and the smell."

22. d'enoi ganres: P, "wards off boredom" [cf. 14 above].

23. remir: P, I, "I gaze" [7:30].

24. palla: I, "ball," or poss. "at a horse race"; or misprint or dialectical for *palazzo*, "palace."

25. Parisina: daughter of Carlo Malatesta [26:59] and cousin of Sigismundo Malatesta. She married Niccolò d'Este in a power play by the Malatesta family, although she was much younger than her husband. Later Niccolò discovered she was having an affair with his natural son, Ugo Aldobrandino, and had them both beheaded.

26. **E'l Marchese**: I, "And the Marquise." Niccolò d'Este [8:51]: N. III of Ferrara, 1384-1441, ruler of Ferrara, Modena, Parma, Reggio, Milan; father of Borso [10:20].

27. **Stava per divenir pazzo**: I, "Was about to go crazy." Pound in a letter to his father [*L*, 210] comments at length on Canto XX: "Nicolo . . . in sort of delirium after execution of Parisina and Ugo." His turmoil explains the random associations that follow: "Various things keep cropping up in the poem. The original world of gods; the Trojan War, Helen on the wall of Troy with the old men fed up with the whole show. . . . Rome founded by survivors of Troy."

28. **condit Atesten**: L, "founded Este." Refers to legendary founding of Este family.

29. **Borso**: Third son of Niccolò d'Este III, the most distinguished of the d'Este family rulers of Ferrara, a small city-state surrounded by Mantua, Padua, Verona, and Bologna with Venice and Milan near in the N. Ferrara lacked the manpower to support war and was unlike states that had a surplus of men not needed for farming and public works. "[Niccolò] realized that Ferrara owed its continuing independence to its dominion-like or semi-colonial status in relation to Venice" [Gundersheimer, 74]. Thus his continuing refrain to his sons, especially Borso, to keep the peace [10:20].

30. **Ganelon**: One of the 12 peers in *Song of Roland*; prompted by jealousy, he betrayed the presence of Roland's rear-guard forces to the Moslems. Pound: ". . . in the delirium Nicolo remembers or thinks he is watching death of Roland."

31. **l'olofans**: OF, *olifant*, "elephant." Refers to Roland's horn which was made of ivory. His sword broken, R. used his horn to bash in the head of the Moor who came up to finish him off.

32. **Tan mare fustes**: OF, "You are ill-starred." Pound: ". . . he smashes the moor over the head with his horn . . . and then dies grumbling because he has damaged the ornaments on the horn and broken it. Tan mare fustes, colloquial: You came at a bad moment. Current cabaret song now J'en ai marre: I'm fed up" [*L*, 211].

33. **Toro, las almenas**: S, "The battlements of Toro," a town in Zamora Province, NW Spain. Scenes that follow are based on Lope de Vega's play, *Las Almenas de Toro*, with the characters Elvira, Sancho, Alfonso, and Ancures. Pound: "Elvira on wall or Toro (subject-rhyme with Helen on Wall [of Troy])" [*L*, 210].

34. **Nic Este**: Niccolò d'E. [cf. 29 above].

35. **Epi purgo**: H, "on wall" [*Iliad* III, 153].

36. **peur de la hasle**: MF, "fear of sunburn."

37. **the King said**: Pound writes about *Las Almenas de Toro*: "King Ferdinand had divided his kingdom at his death, leaving the cities Toro and Zamora to his daughters, Urraca and Elvira. The new King, Sancho, is not content. At the opening of the play we find the King, the Cid, and the Conde Ancures before the gates of Toro, which Elvira has closed through fear of her brother. The Cid advises the King to retire and return unarmed. He advises the King to let the sisters keep their cities. The King rejects this counsel, and the Cid is sent forward as ambassador. Elvira comes forth upon the city wall, and replies with delightful irony to the King's proposition that she become a nun. . . . The king sees his sister on the battlements, and, without knowing who she is, falls in love with her. . . . The Cid tells him that it is his sister" [cf. *SR*, 191-193].

38. **telo rigido**: L, "with rigid javelin." The sexual implication is given with typical obliquity.

39. **Ancures**: Companion to King Sancho.

40. **Alf**: Alphonso, brother of King Sancho.

41. **Neestho**: Pound: "translated in text: let her go back" [*L*, 211].

42. arras . . . : Painting of Francesca and Paolo, adulterous lovers also murdered; a subject rhyme with Parisina and Ugo [cf. Peck, *Pai*, 3-1, 60-66].

43. Jungle . . . renewals: As against the destructiveness of mankind, the proliferating energy of nature which continuously produces a new harvest, the true basis of wealth: "basis of renewals, subsistence." But seen in Niccolò's confused mind. Pound: "The whole reminiscence jumbled or 'candied' in Nicolo's delirium. Take that as a sort of bounding surface from which one gives the main subject of the Canto, the lotophagoi: lotus eaters, or respectable dope smokers; and general paradiso. You have had a hell in Canti XIV, XV; purgatorio in XVI etc." [*L*, 210].

44. Zoe: Zoë, d. 1050, a Byzantine empress who poisoned her husband, Romanus III, took the throne, and married Michael the Paphlagonian [cf. Peck, op. cit.].

45. Marozia: D. before 945, wife of Alberic I, prince of Rome; mistress of Pope Sergius III.

46. Zothar: Unidentified; prob. invented name [17:24] Niccolò's guilty wife, Parisina, suggests other guilty women to his wandering mind.

47. HO BIOS: H, "Life."

48. cosi Elena vedi: I, Pound: "(thus I saw Helen, misquote of Dante)" [*L*, 210]. *Inf.* V, 64, concerns Circle Two, Hell-abode of the Carnal. Virgil points to many women guilty of carnal acts, such as Semiramis, Dido, "sense-drugged Cleopatra," and then says, "See Helen there." Pound adds the word *cosi*.

49. Floating: Hallucinatory scene as in mind of one drugged, as were the *lotophagoi*.

50. calyx: Outer protective covering of a flower consisting of a series of leaflike segments called sepals: a funnel shape.

51. olibanum: Frankincense.

52. myrrh: An aromatic gum resin used in perfume and incense.

53. styrax: Resin or gum: storax.

54. Nel fuoco: I, "in the flame." Pound: "The 'nel fuoco' is from St. Francis' 'cantico': 'My new spouse placeth me in the flame of love.' Then the remarks of the opium smoker about the men who sailed under Ulysses" [*L*, 210].

55. Nel fuoco . . . mise: I, "In the flame of love he put me."

56. croceo: I, "saffron-colored."

57. il mio sposo novello: I, "my new spouse."

58. lotophagoi: H, "lotus-eaters" [*Od.* IX, 82-104].

59. spilla: I, "pin, brooch."

60. Voce-profondo: I, "Deep-voiced."

61. Odysseus: Pound: "And then resumé of Odyssey, or rather of the main parts of Ulysses' voyage up to death of all his crew" [*L*, 210].

62. Elpenor: Companion of Odysseus who in drunken stupor fell from roof, died, and was left unburied. The first shade met by Odysseus in Hades [1:12].

63. Spartha: Sparta.

64. ingle: Gaelic, "chimney corner" where Elpenor sat in his drunken stupor.

65. Circe: Enchantress who turned Odysseus's men into swine [1:1].

66. Circe Titania: Circe, daughter of the sun [*Meta*, XIV, 382, 438].

67. Kalüpso: Calypso [*Od.* VII, 234 ff.]. Odysseus says to Queen Arete: "There is an isle, Ogygia, which lies far off in the sea. Therein dwells the fair-tressed daughter of Atlas, guileful Calypso, a dread goddess. . . . There all the rest of my trusty comrades perished, but . . . the gods brought me to the isle . . . where . . . Calypso dwells." Odysseus remained there for 7 years. Calypso offered to make him immortal, but he refused and in the 8th year she sent him on his way bound to a raft.

68. Ear-wax: Pound: "Ear wax, ears plugged so they couldn't hear the sirens" [*L*, 210].

69. Neson amumona: H, "excellent island." Pound: ". . . literally the narrow island: bullfield where Apollo's cattle were kept" [*L*, 210].

70. Ligur' aoide: H, "clear, sweet song" [cf. 2 above].

71. Khan: An unidentified minor khan who must have sent the leopard to Sigismundo M.

72. Salustio: Sallustio Malatesta, 1448-1470. Son of Sigismundo and Isotta [Pound's Ixotta] degli Atti. Sallustio was murdered by his half brother, Roberto [11:9].

73. Ac ferae familiares: L, "And domesticated wild animals."

74. Somnus: The Roman god of sleep [*Meta*. XI, 690 ff., which tells the story of Iris's visit to the House of Sleep and her plea to Somnus to prepare a vision of the Wreck of Ceyx for his wife Alcyone].

75. chiostri: I, "cloisters."

76. le donne e i cavalieri: I, "the ladies and the knights" [*Pur*. XIV, 109, describing past glory of Romany].

77. hennin: OF, a high cone-shaped headdress with a thin veil worn by women in the 15th century.

78. Cramoisi: F, "Crimson cloth."

79. diaspre: I, "jasper."

80. barocco: I, "baroque."

81. Vanoka: Prob. an invented name. But poss. Vannozza Catanei, mistress of Pope Alexander VI and mother of Lucretia Borgia. Pound may have seen a painting of her in the classical mode suggested by the lines.

82. Borso: [cf. 29 above].

CANTO XXI

Sources

Niccolò Machiavelli, *Istorie Fiorentine*, IV, VII, VIII, 1532; Andrew Lipscomb and Albert Bergh, eds., *The Writings of Thomas Jefferson*, IV, Washington, D.C., 1905; Lorenzo de Medici, *Scritti Scelti*, Introduzione e note di Egidio Bellorini, Turin, 1922; C. E. Yriarte, *Un Condottière au XVe siècle*, 1882; *Takasago* (Noh play); Ovid, *Meta*. XIV, 382, 438; Homer, *Od*. XII, 127-132, 140-142.

Background

EP, *L* 269, 273; *J/M*, 33, 79; *PD*, 12-15; J. A. Symonds, *Renaissance in Italy*, 2 vols., Modern Library, 1935; Selwyn Brinton, *The Golden Age of the Medici*, London, 1925; G. F. Young, *The Medici*, 1909 [Modern Library, 1933; documentation in glosses is adjusted to the page numbers of this easily available edition]; Edgcumbe Staley, *The Tragedies of the Medici*, New York, 1908; Maurice Rowdon, *Lorenzo The Magnificent*, Chicago, 1974; *Ovid*, Meta. VIII 621-724, and XI, 90-193; J. E. Cirlot, *A Dictionary of Symbols*, New York, 1962.

Exegeses

EP, *J/M*, 33; CE, *Ideas*, 31-32, 108-109; GD, *Approaches*, 154-155; HK, *Era*, 343.

Glossary

1. **Borso**: [20:29].

2. **"Keep on . . ."**: The credo of Giovanni de'Medici [8:8], who was called "di Bicci," carried on by his son Cosimo. It was through developing their business and commercial interests that the Medici achieved power and not by aspiring to high political office.

3. **res publica**: L, "republic."

4. **"When I was broke . . ."**: Said by Giovanni di Bicci (1360-1429) who left his sons, Cosimo and Lorenzo, a fortune and the beginnings of a great international banking system. [*EB* (1911), Rowdon (1974), and Staley (1908) give the death date of Giovanni di Bicci as 1429, whereas Brinton (1925) and Young (1909) give 1428. Pound's source clearly agreed with the first three.]

5. **cittadini**: I, "citizens."

6. **della gloria**: I, "out of [away from] glory."

7. **di sugello**: I, "with seal," e.g., stamped with a seal to make official or legal.

8. **"with his credit . . .'**: ". . . in the war of 1452, in which Venice and Naples were allied against Florence, one of the chief means by which Cosimo obtained his success was by calling in such immense debts from those countries that they were deprived of resources for continuing the war" [Young, 76].

9. **Cosimo**: C. de' Medici, 1389-1464. Ruled 1434-1464, not as an officeholder but as the real power behind all actions of the state. Patron of the arts and learning. Called "Pater Patriae."

10. **Ficino**: Marsilio F., 1433-1499, son of Cosimo's physician. Cosimo had him educated "for the special purpose of interpreting Greek philosophy." In a letter to Lorenzo de' M., Ficino said: "I owe to Plato much, to Cosimo no less. He realised for me the virtues of which Plato gave me the conception" [Symonds, I, 410]. After the departure of Georgius Gemistus (sometimes called Plethon because of his dedication to Plato [8:31]) to return to the Peloponnesus, Cosimo made Ficino the head of the academy that Gemistus had run.

11. **ells of red cloth**: Cosimo reputedly said: "A few ells of scarlet would fill Florence with citizens" [ibid.]. Purple, because of the rarity and expense of the dye, was for centuries reserved to royalty: hence "royal purple." But any bright dye or color was a sign of wealth.

12. **Col Credito . . . pace**: I, "With his credit . . . Naples and Venice with money / Forced . . . Naples and Venice . . . to that peace."

13. **Piero**: Piero de' M., 1416-1469, eldest son of Cosimo, known as "Il Gottoso" because of the gout from which he suffered all his life. After Cosimo's death in 1464,

Piero carried on in business and affairs of state but relied on his young son Lorenzo, only 15 at the time, to assist him. Not knowing Il Gottoso's real character, the Pitti family formed a conspiracy against him which gathered strength for two years and was supported by forces from Ferrara led by Ercole d'Este.

14. **Diotisalvi**: Dietisalvi Neroni, d. 1482, wealthy Florentine who conspired to overthrow Medici rule after the death of Cosimo (1464). Acting as financial adviser to Piero, Neroni advised him to call in all his debts. This act caused widespread financial disaster, led to Piero's losing much of his popularity, and gave him a reputation for avarice. In 1466 Neroni's plot was uncovered and he was exiled from Florence.

15. **Avignon**: City in SE France; the papal see during the "Babylonian captivity" (1309-1378) and residence of several antipopes during the Great Schism (1378-1417); under papal rule Avignon became an important trading city.

16. **murdered**: In August 1466 the conspirators lay in wait to ambush Piero who was being carried to Florence on a litter. He was saved by the coolness of his 17-year-old son Lorenzo: "Riding on ahead, he [Lorenzo] heard of an armed party who were lying in wait for Piero on the ordinary road; with much adroitness he managed to keep their attention occupied while he sent back word to . . . his father," who took a safe route to Florence and escaped [Young, 111-112].

17. **Lauro**: Lorenzo de' Medici, 1449-1492, son of Piero. He became known as Lorenzo the Magnificent; Florentine statesman, ruler, and patron of arts and letters.

18. **Intestate**: Piero died in 1469 and, despite his largesse and his generous gifts to charities, left to his son Lorenzo one of the largest fortunes in Europe.

19. **In carta di capretto**: I, "On rich parchment."

20. **Nic Uzano**: Niccolò da Uzzano, d. 1432, Florentine statesman and leader with the Albizzi clan of the aristocratic party that opposed the growth of Medici power. But he advised against a contest with the Medici family, which the Albizzi family recognized as a serious threat to their own power. At the death of Giovanni de' Medici in 1429, the Albizzi were restrained from moving against his son Cosimo by Uzzano. But at Uzzano's death in 1432, the young "hotheaded" Rinaldo degli Albizzi threw Cosimo de' Medici into jail. Cosimo fortunately had a friendly jailer, a man named Malavolti, and through him got a bribe to his judge. "The result was seen when . . . his sentence, instead of death, was ten years of banishment at Padua" [Brinton, 11]. On the death of Rinaldo in 1434, the Medici returned to Florence and the power of the Albizzi family was destroyed.

21. **Giuliano**: G. de' Medici, d. 1478, brother to Lorenzo de' M. He was the victim of the Pazzi conspiracy: Lorenzo and Giuliano were attacked during High Mass in the cathedral. Lorenzo escaped with only superficial wounds, but "the bright and justly loved Giuliano, the idol of his family," was immediately killed [Young, 173]. The plot actually greatly increased the Medici power in Florentine politics, for the people came out in emotional support of the Medici when they learned of the murder and took it upon themselves to punish the conspirators: all the Pazzi and Salviati [a family that supported them politically] were proclaimed "enemies," and "they were pursued from house to house, whilst the peasants took up the hue and cry in the *contado*. Bleeding heads and torn limbs were everywhere scattered in the streets; doorposts and curb-stones were dashed with gore; men and women and the children, too, were all relentless avengers of '*Il bel Giulio's*' blood" [Staley, 53]. "The indignation of the people [was] not all . . . on account of the attempt against the Medici, but also on account of the effrontery of such an endeavour to

seize upon their state 'as if a mere spoil of war' " [Young, 173].

22. E difficile . . . in stato: I, "It is difficult / In Florence it is difficult to live like a rich man / Without having any status. / And not having any status, Piccinino / Had to fear whoever was in a high position."

23. Piccinino: Niccolò P., 1375-1444, Italian condottiere [10:17].

24. that man: Thaddeus Coleman Pound, 1832-1914, Pound's paternal grandfather. According to Pound, he built three railroads, less for personal gain than for the public good [cf. "Indiscretions" in *PD*, 12-15; *J/M*, 33].

25. Jefferson: Thomas J., 1743-1826. Letter shows dimensions of mind and character, aspects of a Renaissance man such as Sigismundo or Lorenzo de' Medici. [Complete text of original in *The Writings of Thomas Jefferson*, IV, 41.]

26. affatigandose . . . non: I, "tiring himself, for his pleasure or not" [8:13].

27. Montecello: Monticello. Residence of Thomas Jefferson near Charlottesville, VA.

28. I went up: In July 1469 Lorenzo attended the baptism of the son born to Galeazzo Sforza of Milan. "His gifts on this occasion were magnificent–a gold necklace to the Duchess, and a diamond valued at three thousand ducats–and led Duke Galeazzo to express the wish that he would stand sponsors to all his other children" [Brinton, 107].

29. Duke Galeaz: Galeazzo Maria Sforza, 5th Duke of Milan, son of Francesco Sforza [8:15].

30. the Sultan: Mohammed II. Barnado Bandini, one of the conspirators who murdered Lorenzo's brother, Giuliano, fled to Constantinople. He was captured by the sultan and sent to Lorenzo as a "gift" [cf. 21 above].

31. Soldan of Egypt: Kait Bey (Qa'it Bay), sultan, 1468-1496. Source of line unknown.

32. one pope: Giovanni, second son of Lorenzo, became Pope Leo X.

33. University: In 1472, when only 23, Lorenzo went to Pisa to found the university and stayed there to direct it for some time. In addition to state subsidies, he lavished his own money upon the institution and donated many books to it.

34. Lauro: Lorenzo de' M.

35. made peace . . . in Naples: Because of the failure of the Pazzi conspiracy [cf. 21 above] engineered by Pope Sextus IV, in which Lorenzo's brother Giuliano was murdered, the pope was so enraged that he excommunicated not only the Medici and the citizens of Florence but all Tuscany. Florence for a time was ringed by enemies called upon by the pope to conquer the city. After losing much territory, Lorenzo went alone with great courage to King Ferrante of Naples (putting himself in the power of this ally of the pope) and pursuaded the king of the justice of his cause. The visit resulted in peace and great acclaim for the young Lorenzo, whose power thereafter steadily increased [cf. Young, 182-186]. King Ferrante was the one who "invited to lunch" those he planned to dispose of, as he did with Piccinino [10:17].

36. Gold fades: [cf. 11/51].

37. Placidia's: Tomb of Galla Placidia, ca. 388-450, empress of western Roman Empire; buried in Ravenna, Italy, where her mausoleum adorned with brilliant gold mosaics rivals that of the neighboring Byzantine treasure, the church of San Vitale [cf. HK, *Era*, 343].

38. exarchate: The office of an exarch, a viceroy of a Byzantine emperor.

39. les gradins: F, "the steps" [12:2].

40. palazzo: I, "palace."

41. nel tramonto: I, "in the sunset."

42. **tesserae**: I, small squares used in making mosaic patterns.

43. **Night of the golden tiger . . . borne in the wind**: These 13 lines, which rise to a climax of passion out of which "a thing of beauty is born," present images in action which Pound associates with the Eleusinian Mysteries and the gods Dionysus, Adonis, and Helios as well as the Egyptian solar deities. As the earth turns through sunset, darkness, and into dawn, we encounter the fire of the vision [5:10] as well as the flame and light of passion [cf. *Sacrum, sacrum, inluminatio coitu*, 36/180]. In Egyptian solar myths, lions and tigers are connected with the sun chariot instead of horses, as with the Greek Helios, and they are both associated with the mystery rites [17:27]. Instead of "the lion lift over sand-plain" [17/79], we have here "Night of the golden tiger." Cirlot says that the golden tiger is solar in origin and also that "it is associated with Dionysus" and that "in China the tiger seems to play a rôle comparable with that of the lion in African and Western cultures" [*Dict. of Symbols*, 324]. But Cirlot also says that in Egypt "it used to be believed that the lion presided over the annual floods of the Nile, because they coincided with the entry of the sun into the zodiacal sign of Leo" [ibid., 180]. Here Pound seems to be assigning the functions of both the lion and the tiger to just the golden tiger, anticipating the flooding Nile later on the canto page [cf. 49 below]. The phrase "voices of the procession" evokes the image of women celebrating the death of Dionysus-Tammuz-Adonis by going down to the sea and setting their lamps afloat to go out with the tide [cf. 47/236]. As in Canto II, the "tin flash in the sun-dazzle" announces either the presence or the immediate advent of Dionysus [2/7]. The scene of passion takes place on the beach "between the sea and the mountains" and results in "a petal borne in the wind."

44. **Gignetei kalon**: H, "A beautiful thing is born."

45. **Actium**: Promontory and town, NW Acarnania, Greece; site of the battle (31 B.C.) between Octavian and the forces of Antony and Cleopatra.

46. **Midas**: King Midas recognized a drunk old man to be Silenus, the foster father and teacher of Dionysus. For ten days he took care of Silenus and on the eleventh restored him to the god. When offered a choice of rewards, Midas asked that everything he touched would turn to gold, as thereafter it did, including food and water. But Dionysus rescued him from his fate by telling him where to go to wash away the horrible curse. Thereafter Midas hated wealth and splendor and became a worshiper of Pan, the god of nature, and spent time listening to Pan playing music on his pipes. Thus, "the old man sweeping" suggests Silenus bewailing the bad choice of his benefactor; "Midas without Pan" suggests the coldness and the horror of a life dedicated to gathering up gold if it is not alleviated or balanced by things of the spirit [Ovid, *Meta*. XI, 90-193]. But because of the mention of the Pines of Isé, "the old man sweeping leaves" also suggests the story of Baucis and Philemon [Ovid, *Meta*. VIII, 621-724]. These good old people who served wandering travelers with the best of the food and drink they had without knowing they were gods disguised were also given a reward. Their thatched cottage was changed into a majestic temple of which they became the caretakers. After years of service they were turned into trees [cf. 48 below; 4:22].

47. **Pan**: Greek pastoral god of fertility.

48. **Pines of Ise**: Isé: the two sacred Shinto shrines to the sun-goddess, located at Uji-yamada, S Honshu, Japan [4:23].

49. **Inopos**: A river of Delos said to rise and fall at the same time as the Nile, so that the two rivers were supposedly connected.

50. **Phoibos**: Phoebus Apollo, Olympian god of light, music, prophecy, and pastoral matters.

51. turris eburnea: L, "tower of ivory" [cf. Litany of the Blessed Virgin].

52. hounds: Hieratic paradisal animals [17:13].

53. Pallas: Pallas Athena, goddess of wisdom, patron of the arts of peace and of war, guardian of cities, especially of Athens. Statues of Athena often have an owl carved into the base or otherwise shown with the goddess. Pound wrote: "Poor old Upward [author of *The Divine Mystery* who committed suicide in 1927] had a lot to say about Athene's eyes, connecting them with her owl and with olive trees. The property of the glaux, and olive leaf, to shine and then not to shine, 'glint' rather than shine" [*L*, 269]. Again: "Glaux, owl, totem or symbolic bird (gods connected with the divine animals, as stupid bitch Hera has her bull eyes), glare-eyed, owl-eyed Athena" [*L*, 273].

54. Confusion . . . renewals: [20:43].

55. Titania: Epithet of Circe [1:1; *Meta*. XIV, 382, 438].

56. Athame: Prob. invented as a daughter of the sun, like Phaethusa in the same scene.

57. Phaethusa: Circe tells Odysseus he will come to the isle Thrinacia where fair maidens take care of the flocks of Helios, which are suspended in time. "These bear no young, nor do they ever die, and goddesses are their shepherds, fair-tressed nymphs, Phaethusa" [*Od*. XII, 127-132]. The passage rhymes with the blood drink of Tiresias [1/4] and has a similar content of prophecy. Circe tells Odysseus that if he or his crew harms the goddesses, "late shalt thou come home and in evil case, after losing all the comrades" [*Od*. XII, 140-142].

58. Dis: Roman Pluto, Greek god of the underworld whose rape of Persephone became one basis of the Eleusinian mystery rites.

59. the old man: Like the plowman in Breughel's *Icarus*, the old man is busy and indifferent to the horrendous rape of Persephone [cf. GD, *Approaches*, 154].

60. asphodel: A flower. Supposedly, a climax of the mystery rites is a vision of the paradisal Elysian fields which in classical legend are covered with asphodel.

CANTO XXII

Sources

Pound's personal experiences in 1908 at Gibraltar; Franco Sacchetti, *Le Novelle* (137), Florence, 1724.

Background

EP, *SP*, 189-263; NS, *Life*, 45; G. F. Young, *The Medici*, 1909, I, 43-44 [Modern Library, 1933, 31-32; documentation in glosses is adjusted to the page numbers of this easily available edition].

Exegeses

EP, *J/M*, 33; *LE*, 17-18; Davis, *Vision*, 59-62; CE, *Ideas*, 65, 66, 115-116; EH, *Pai*, 5-3, 413; HK, in *Italian Quarterly*, vol. 16, no. 64, 7; Klink, *Pai*, 5-1, 67.

Glossary

1. **An' that man**: Thaddeus Coleman Pound, Pound's grandfather. In *J/M* (1933) Pound wrote: "I have never believed that my grandfather put a bit of railway across Wisconsin simply or chiefly to make money or even with the illusion that he would make money, or make more money in that way than in some other" [p. 33].

2. **Warenhauser**: Pseudonym for Frederick Weyerhaeuser, 1834-1914, American capitalist known as the "Lumber King"; about 1900 he purchased approximately a million acres of timberland in Washington and Oregon from the Northern Pacific Railroad.

3. **American Curia**: United States Senate.

4. **Northwestern railway**: The Northern Pacific Railroad, running from Duluth and St. Paul, Minnesota, to Seattle, Washington, and Portland, Oregon, was chartered by special act of Congress (1864). Construction began in 1870 and the railway was opened in 1883. Of the land granted by the U.S. government for the construction of the Northern Pacific, more than 2,500,000 undistributed acres were still held by the company in 1948.

5. **he came in**: The "he" (called "Joe" a few lines later) is probably a pseudonym. But the point of the anecdote–the hazards in a profit system based on usury (price of life in the occident)–is clear no matter who "Joe" may be. In other words, Joe's shop is doing such slow and careful work that none of his "chunks" are imperfect: good work costs money. In the assembly-line system, such items must be turned out in mass which means that many of them will be rejected. The anecdote rhymes with the examples in Canto XLV, such as the price of workmanship implied by *Adamo me fecit* [45:14].

6. **C.H.**: Clifford Hugh Douglas, 1879-1952, British engineer and social economist, founder of Social Credit [38:49].

7. **Mr. Bukos**: John Maynard Keynes, 1883-1946, English economist. His early defense of the gold standard and his protest against the Versailles Treaty, expressed in *Economic Consequences of the Peace*, 1919, made him world famous. But he departed from classical free-economy concepts in 1929 and endorsed Lloyd George's programs of public works and government spending by increasing the national debt to increase employment.

8. **H.C.L.**: High cost of living.

9. **Jesu Christo . . . d'Adamo**: I, "Jesus Christ! / Standing in the Earthly Paradise / Thinking as he made himself a companion of Adam," [*standu* is dialect form for *stando*].

10. **Mr. H.B.:** the economist J.A. Hobson [cf. 7 above].

11. **Mac Narpen and Company**: Pseudonym for the Macmillan Company, publishers.

12. **Palgrave's Golden Treasury**: Francis Turner Palgrave, 1824-1897, English poet and critic and professor of poetry at Oxford (1885-1895). He edited the poetry anthology, *The Golden Treasury of the Best Songs and Lyrical Poems in the English Language* [1861, 1897]. See "How to Read," in *LE*, 17-18, for EP's story about "something to replace that doddard Palgrave." The agent he was conferring with replied: "But don't you know that the whole fortune of X & Co is founded on Palgrave's *Golden Treasury*?"

13. Nel paradiso terrestre: I, "In the terrestrial paradise."

14. una compagna . . . fesse: I, "a mate for Adam. How to make her?" Literally *Come si fesse?* means "How did he make himself?"

15. E poi . . . volpe: I (dialect), "And then he saw a vixen."

16. e pensava: I, "and he thought."

17. Corre . . .Della volpe: I (dialect), "She runs, the vixen runs, Christ runs, the vixen runs / Christ runs, and he gave a leap, and he caught the tail / Of the vixen."

18. e di questu . . . una rabbia: I (dialect), "and from this [*questo*] / She was made, / And for this reason / Woman is a fury, / A fury-and-a-rage." Pound overheard an Italian hotelkeeper "teasing his genteel lady cashier" with this anecdote [cf. HK, *Italian Quarterly*, vol. 16, no. 64, 7].

19. Freer: Surname of Pound's great-aunt which Pound apparently used as his own during the summer of 1906.

20. Mohamed Ben Abt el Hjameed: Prob. a merchant in Gibraltar, ca. 1908.

21. Calpe (Lyceo): Mount Calpe is the Rock of Gibraltar; the Calpe Club, Church Street, Gibraltar. [*Lyceo* cannot be Spanish; it may be based on root of French *Lycée*: school or pupil. Here it seems to indicate a café or a social club.]

22. Gibel Tara: Gibraltar.

23. Jeen-jah: Ginger.

24. Mustafa: Prob. a merchant in Gibraltar, ca. 1908.

25. Yusuf: Y. Benamore, a Jewish tourist guide whom Pound met in Gibraltar in 1908 and to whom he felt greatly indebted. He wrote later: "Life saved by Yusuf Benamore." Yusuf took Pound to the synagogue where the scene described later in the canto took place [cf. NS, *Life*, 45].

26. calle: S, "street."

27. Granada: City in S Spain.

28. Edward the Seventh: 1841-1910, king of England (1901-1910), who often visited Gibraltar incognito.

29. e faceva bisbiglio: I, "and whispered [as in gossip]."

30. Down at the court-house: Pound also visited a courthouse. "Case on for rape and black-mail" may have reminded him of the difficulty of enforcing the law in the 14th century, as illustrated in *Le Novelle* (no. 137) of the Florentine writer Franco Sacchetti, source of the following anecdote about the "judge's" trouble.

31. And the judge says: The judge in *Le Novelle* was Messer Amerigo degli Amerighi of Pesaro who tried to enforce the laws prohibiting Florentine ladies from wearing ornaments and furs at the start of the 13th century. The story is retold in Isidoro del Lungo's *Women of Florence* (trans. Mary C. Steegman), London, 1907, 45-52 [EH, *Pai*, 5-3, 413].

32. lattittzo: I (dialect), *lattizo*. Defined in *Vocabulario universale italiano* as "pelle d'animale da latter' [skin of a suckling animal resembling ermine]."

CANTO XXIII

Sources

Michael Constantine Psellos, *De Omnifaria Doctrina*; Porphyry *De Occasionibus, De Abstinentia*; Marsilio Ficino, *Theologia Platonica*, libre XVIII, 1561; Iamblichus, *De Mysteriis Egyptiorum, Chaldaeorum, Assyriorum*; Fritz Schultze, *Georgios Gemisthos Plethon und seine reformatorischen Bestrebungen*, 1874; Marie Curie, *Pierre Curie*, Paris, 1924; Stesichorus, fragment of a lost poem; Franz Cumont, *Textes et Monuments figurés relatifs aux mystères de Mithra*, 1894-1901; Dante, *Inf.* I; Homer, *Od.*; EP, "Provincia Deserta," in *P*; Chabaneau, *Les Biographies des Troubadours en Langue Provençale*; Plutarch, "Why Oracles Are Silent"; Homeric Hymn V, "To Aphrodite"; ΑΘΗΝΑΙΟΥ ΝΑΥΚΡΑΤΙΤΟΥ ΔΕΙΠΝΟΣΟΦΙΣΤΑΙ. *Athenaei Naucratitae Deipnosophistarum libri quindecim. . . .* Argentorati: ex typographia Societatis Bipontinae. Tomus Quartus, Anno XII, 1804, pp. 237-238 (Liber XI.469e, f) [Fang I, 44]; Yriarte, *Un Condottière au XVe siècle*, 1882; *The Greek Bucolic Poets* [Loeb], trans. J. M. Edmonds, 387; Ovid, *Meta*. X.

Background

EP, *GK*, 224-225; *SR*, 101; A. A. Vasiliev, *History of the Byzantine Empire*, Madison, Wisc., 1952; H. F. Tozer, "A Byzantine Reformer," *Journal of Hellenic Studies*, VII, 2, 1886.

Exegeses

S. Libera, "Casting His Gods Back into the NOUS," *Pai*, 2-3, 368-377; J. Peck, "Pound's Lexical Mythography," *Pai*, 1-1, 5-7; J. Peck, "Arras and Painted Arras," *Pai*, 3-1, 63-66; L. Surette, "A Light from Eleusis," *Pai*, 3-2, 195-196; LL, *Motive*; CE, *Ideas*; EH, *Approaches*; DP, *Barb*; WB, *Rose*; HK, *Era*, passim; Fang, I, 41-44; *Pai*, 6-3, 359-361.

Glossary

1. **Et omniformis . . . est**: L, "And every intellect is capable of assuming every shape" [cf. Porphyrios, *De Occasionibus*, chap. 13, "Omnis Intellectus Est Omniformis"; *Pai*, 6-3, 359-361].

2. **Psellos**: Michael Constantine Psellus, 1018-1105?, Byzantine philosopher, politician, writer, and early Neoplatonist. He is one of the several Pound lists as important to the Renaissance humanism derived from Gemistus [*GK*, 224-225].

3. **Gemisto**: Georgius Gemistus, fl. early 15th century; Greek Platonic philosopher, sometimes called Plethon. A significant fig-

ure at the meeting of the Eastern and Western churches held at Ferrara and Florence in 1438 [8:31].

4. **Peloponesus**: Peloponnesus, S part of the mainland of Greece. Home of Gemistus who, to keep out Turkish barbarism and the influence of Eastern Christianity, which had become singularly corrupt, encouraged the emperor, Manuel II, to construct "a wall with numerous towers on the Isthmus of Corinth" [Vasiliev, 637]. Plethon drew up details of a new, pure-Greek society based on reorganization of all society under new laws and social classifications as well as a new religion based on his own ideas of the old polytheism of the early Greeks and Plato. He believed that Christianity made men effeminate and that a new barbarism was issuing from Rome.

5. **Novvy**: Domencio Malatesta, younger brother of Sigismundo, known popularly as Malatesta Novello. When 29, Novvy was lamed in an accident and turned to public works. He endowed Cesena with (1) a library, (2) a hospital for the infirm elderly and for exposed children, and (3) a school for the education of bastard boys and girls [Yriarte, 303]. He also sent an emissary to Greece to find books and manuscripts for the library, but the consignment was lost at sea [10:58, 11:18].

6. **Irol**: Iroline, a French motor fuel.

7. **Houille blanch / Auto-chenille**: F, "water power / caterpillar-tread vehicle."

8. **Invention-d'entités . . . consister**: F, "Invention of more or less abstract entities / in number equal to the things to be explained . . . / Science cannot be composed of it."

9. **J'ai obtenu . . . guérison**: F, "I got a burn . . . from which it took me six months to recover."

10. **M. Curie**: Pierre C., 1859-1906, French chemist and physicist. Marie Curie, his wife, writes in *Pierre Curie*: "In order to test the results announced by F. Giesel, Pierre Curie voluntarily exposed his arm to the action of radium during several hours. This resulted in a lesion resembling a burn, that developed progressively and required several months to heal" [English ed., trans. Charlotte and Vernon Kellogg, Macmillan, 1923, 117].

11. **Tropismes**: F, "tropisms" "responses to stimulus."

12. **῾Αλιος . . .**: H; the Greek and Latin lines here and on the next page are adapted from Johannes Schweighaeuser's bilingual [Greek and Latin] edition of *Athenaeus*, which reads: ῾Αλιος δ᾽ ὑπεριονίδας δέπας ἐσκατέβαινε / χρύσιον ὄφρα δι᾽ ὠκεανοῖο περάσας / ἀφίκηθ᾽ ἱερᾶς ποτὶ βένθεα νυκτὸς ἐρεμνᾶς / ποτὶ ματέρα κουριδίαν τ᾽ ἄλοχον, / παῖδας τε φίλοις. δὸ δ᾽, ἐς ἄδιος ἔβαί / δάφναισι κατάσκιον / ποσσὶ παῖς Διός [Fang I, 41]. Pound has left out a few words, here translated in brackets: "The sun, Hyperion's child, stepped down into his golden bowl and then after crossing the stream of ocean [he reached] the depth of black [and holy] night and joined his mother, his faithful wife, and his dear children. [Meanwhile the son of Zeus] entered [on foot] the laurel-shaded [grove]." The son of Zeus is Heracles on his tenth labor. He is journeying to the West in the sun's boat in search of the cattle of Geryon [for sun's boat, cf. 21:43 and 91/612; for sun's journey, 17/79].

13. **ima vada . . .**: L, "low fords of the dark night." From the Latin version in Schweighaeuser, which reads: Sol vero Hyperionis filius in poculum inscendebat / aureum, ut per oceanum traiiciens / perveniret sacrae ad ima vada noctis obscurae / ad matrem, & Virginalem uxorem, / liberosque caros. Ipse autem in lucum se contulit lauris obumbratum / pedibus filius Iovis [Fang I, 41]. Peck [*Pai*, 1-1, 6] suggests that "The idiot" refers to Odysseus's feigned madness to keep out of the war and the derivation of ῾αλιος to be "fruitless," as Liddell and Scott suggests. But Pound really thinks he has a better etymology for the word, connecting it with

μάταιος, and comes up with the epithet "idiot" [Fang I, 41].

14. ʽήλιος . . . *μάταιος*: ʽήλιος, sun; ʽάλιος (A), of the sea (adj.); ʽάλιος (B), fruitless, idle; *μάταιος*, vain, empty, idle. Pound has just quoted two lines from Stesichorus, in which the Doric form ʽάλιος for ʽήλιος is used. Frederic Peachy shows that Pound looked up ʽάλιος in Liddell and Scott's *Abridged Greek-English Lexicon* and found three definitions: (1) Dor. for ʽήλιος; (2) L, marinus; (3) *μάταιος*: deriv. uncertain [F. Peachy, *Index*, 260; cf. Peck, *Pai*, 1-1, 5-6].

15. **alixantos** . . . : H, "worn by the sea, feeding in the sea [sea-reared], he went down into." Pound is here using Liddell and Scott's *Abridged Greek-English Lexicon* to construe the Stesichorus fragment on the setting sun: *eiskatebaine* is from the fragment. The other words follow immediately [F. Peachy, *Index*, 260; cf. Peck, *Pai*, 1-1, 5-6].

16. **selv' oscura**: I, *selva oscura*, "dark forest" [cf. *Inf*. I, 2].

17. **Phrygian**: Phrygia was an ancient country in WC Asia Minor.

18. **'Yperionides**: H, "son of Hyperion"; Helios. The initial letter should be transliterated as *U*, not as *Y*, and what seems to be a beginning apostrophe should be transliterated from a Greek rough breathing to the letter *H*. Along with Cronos (Saturn) and Ops (Rhea), Hyperion (a child of Heaven and Earth) was one of the Titans and the father of the Sun, the Moon, and Dawn. He is the original sun-god whose functions were later assumed by his son Helios (Apollo). Thus, as the sun's boat appeared in the East, rising from the Phrygian desert, it is imaged as gaining buoyancy for the sky trip by unloading sand.

19. **while I slept**: The "I" may be Niccolò d'Este and the next 22 lines may return to the "arras and painted arras" delirium scene developed earlier [20:42; Peck, *Pai*, 3-1, 64-66].

20. **Capriped**: "goat-footed, a satyr."

21. **Fa Han**: Pseudonym for a female acquaintance of Pound's. Because of her "hair" Pound may associate her with Circe and certain Chinese ladies of the Confucian Odes tradition [cf. Peck, *Pai*, 3-1, 64-66].

22. **Maensac**: Peire de M., a poor knight of Auvergne. Pound invents the story of tossing the coin, but Austors stayed at the castle and Peire became a troubadour and ran away with the wife of Bernart de Tierci, taking her to the castle of Robert, dauphin of Auvergne. When de Tierci tried to regain his wife, the dauphin protected Peire and defeated de Tierci's attack [5:26].

23. **Auvergne:** Center of France, west of the Rhone River. Also Auvergnat [cf. next line and 5/18].

24. **Chaise Dieu**: F, "Seat of God." The Abbey of Chaise Dieu, founded in 1046, in Brioude, near the Languedoc-Auvergne border. Also used in general mythic sense.

25. **Mount Segur**: Montsegur [P, "Secure Mountain"], lofty hill and fort where the last of the Manicheans were besieged and the unrepentant were burned in 1244 during the Albigensian Crusade; now considered a symbol of Provençal glory. Because it was the site of a temple to Apollo, it has been linked to solar-force worship.

26. **Simone**: Simon de Montfort or Simon IV de Montfort l'Amaury, ?1160-1218, Count of Montfort and Earl of Leicester; leader of French forces against Provençals and alleged Manicheans in Albigensian Crusade; killed in battle at Toulouse.

27. **they called us**: Austors is speaking of himself, his brother Peire, and other troubadours and singers of *gai savoir*.

28. **Manicheans**: Followers of the religious system founded by Mani, a system based on the idea of a Good One and an Evil One, both of equal power, existing in the universe. Persecuted indifferently with troubadours during Albigensian Crusade by the

Church and the N French. Long a source of discontent to popes who persecuted them, the Manichaeans who had absorbed Mithraism [a doctrine derived from Mithras, Persian god of light] thrived as "Catharists" or "a pure Christian faith." Innocent III finally sent the crusade against them and destroyed the brilliant Provençal civilization. Pound condemned the mass slaughter in which 200 "Cathari" were burned in one day as well as the hypocritical purpose and result: "The Albigensian crusade, a sordid robbery cloaking itself in religious pretence, had ended the *gai savoir* in southern France" [*SR*, 101; cf. *Pai*, 3-2, 196 ff.].

29. **superbo Ilion**: I, "proud Troy."

30. **they were sailing**: Aeneas, son of Aphrodite and Anchises, en route to the founding of Rome.

31. **Anchises**: Father of Aeneas speaking of the destruction of Troy.

32. **Tethnéké**: H, "He is dead."

33. **Adonis**: A youth loved by Aphrodite; when he was killed by a boar, she caused the anemone to spring from his blood. Adonis is the central figure in a number of fertility rites and myths which celebrate his death and survival; Tammuz is the Babylonian equivalent of Adonis [cf. Bion, *Lament for Adonis*; Ovid, *Meta*. X].

34. **King Otreus**: Legendary king of Phrygia; when Aphrodite took human form to lie with Anchises, she told him that her father was King Otreus, for she wished to keep her identity a secret [cf. Homeric Hymn V, "To Aphrodite"].

35. **Phrygia**: [cf. 17 above].

CANTO XXIV

Sources

Luchino dal Campo, *Viaggio a Gerusalemme di Niccolò da Este*, Turin, 1861; Giambattista Pigna, *Historia de Principi di Este*, 1570; Antonio Frizzi, *Memorie per la Storia di Ferrara*, 5 vols., Ferrara, 1791-1809; Alfonso Lazzari, *Ugo e Parisina nella realtà storica*, 1915, expanded in *Parisina*, Florence, 1949; report of the librarian Cassini; Homeric Hymn IV, "To Hermes."

Background

Werner L. Gundersheimer, *Ferrara*, Princeton, 1973; E. G. Gardner, *Dukes and Poets in Ferrara*, 1904, rpt., New York, 1968.

Exegeses

EP, *SP*, 169; *J/M*, 79; D. J. Hugen, *Pai*, 3-2, 229-238; DP, *Barb*; WB, *Rose*, passim.

Glossary

1. **Zohanne**: Z. Giovanni, servant of Parisina Malatesta [cf. 6 below].

2. **Rimini**: Ancient Ariminum, seaport in Forlì Province, N Italy; seat of the Malatesta family [8:5].

3. **marchesini**: I, *marchisini*, "marks": lire issued by Marquis d'Este.

4. **barbarisci**: I, "wild horses"; associated with Barbary.

5. **Modena . . . San Petronio . . . San Zorzo**: Three races, the second run around a church in Bologna, the third probably around San Giorgio Maggiore in Venice. *Zorzo* is Romagnole dialect form.

6. **Parisina Marchesa**: P. Malatesta, d. 1425, wife of Niccolò d'Este, daughter of Carlo Malatesta. When Niccolò discovered that Parisina was having an affair with his natural son, Ugo, he had them both beheaded [8:51; 20:25].

7. **un libro . . . Tristano**: I, "a French book called Tristan"; Pound uses *franxese* for *francese* (dialect).

8. **Carissimi nostri**: I, "our dearest ones."

9. **palio**: I, "horse race."

10. **madama la marxesana**: I, "Madame the Marchioness," Parisina Malatesta.

11. **Romagna**: Region of Italy which now comprises the provinces of Bologna, Ferrara, Ravenna, and Forlì.

12. **verde colore predeletto**: I, "green color preferred."

13. **ziparello**: I, *zipparèllo*, a decorative, short, sleeveless tunic of the Quattrocento worn over armor. This echoes 11/52, "For a green cloak with silver brocade," which explains its costing as much as 25 ducats. [JE]

14. **Ugo**: Eldest son of Niccolò d'Este and stepson of Parisina Malatesta; he and Parisina were beheaded after Niccolò discovered their adultery.

15. **fiolo del Signore**: I, "son of the Master."

16. **PROCURATIO NOMINE PATRIS**: L, "procuration in the name of the father."

17. **Leonello Este**: Lionello d'E., 1407-1450, second son of Niccolò d'Este, who succeeded as Marquis of Ferrara after death of Niccolò in 1441.

18. **Margarita**: M. d'Este, d. 1452, sister of Lionello d'Este. The "dot" is F. for "dowry."

19. **Roberto Malatesta**: D. 1482, known as the Magnificent. His marriage to Margarita d'Este was arranged by his father Sigismundo M. for political reasons [11:9].

20. **natae . . .Sponsae**: L. "Margaret, daughter of the aforenamed illustrious Lord Niccolò, Marquis of Este, and his wife."

21. **Gualdo**: G. Tadino, town in Perugia Province, C Italy.

22. **Nicolaus Marquis of Este**: Niccolò d'Este, Nicholas III of Ferrara, 1384-1441, ruler of Ferrara, Modena, Parma, Reggio, and Milan; father of Borso, Lionello, and Ercole d'Este; husband of Parisina Malatesta [20:25, 26].

23. **Don Carlo (Malatesta)**: 1368-1429, man of letters and patron of the arts; uncle of Sigismundo [26:59].

24. **Illustrae Dominae Parisinae Marxesana**: L, "Of the illustrious Lady Parisina, Marchioness."

25. **D. Michaeli de Magnabucis**: Notary public of Ferrara (1427).

26. **D. Nicolaeque Guiduccioli**: Prob. represented Carlo Malatesta in making arrangements for the marriage of Carlo's daughter, Parasina Malatesta, to Niccolò d'Este in 1418.

27. **de Arimino**: I, "of Rimini."

28. **Sequit bonorum descriptio**: L, "There follows a description of property."

29. **And he in his young youth . . .** : This passage, concluding in the middle of the next page (112), is based on a scribe's account of Niccolò d'Este's trip to the Holy Land. Pound reduces 45 pages of the "Voyage . . . " in his source for these lines [cf. Hugen, *Pai*, 3-2, 229-238, for full account].

30. **Cithera**: Cythera, epithet of Aphrodite, from the association of the goddess with the island of Cythera, off the SE coast of Laconia.

31. **"dove fu . . . Paris"**: I, "where Helen was kidnapped by Paris."

32. **Pola**: Or Pula, a fortified seaport at S tip of Istrian peninsula.

33. **Naxos**: Largest island of the Cyclades, in the Aegean Sea; center of ancient Dionysus worship; a crossroads tourist stop in Renaissance times [2:14].

34. **Ora vela . . . vespero**: I, "Now with sails, now with oars, on to the hour of evening."

35. **Zefalonia**: Cephalonia, largest of Ionian Islands off Greece.

36. **Corfu**: Island in Ionian Sea.

37. **Rhodos**: Rhodes, island in Aegean Sea; in antiquity a center of trade, and later a major supply stop on route to Holy Land.

38. **Paphos**: Town on SW coast of Cyprus, famous as center for worship of Aphrodite.

39. **backsheesh**: A sort of alms or gift of money asked for by beggars: "Along the way we met streams of beggars and roisterers, some on foot, some on horseback, asking for 'baksheesh' " [Hugen, op. cit., 236].

40. **groat**: Grossi; one paid 7 ducats and 27 Venetian grossi to pass from Joffa to Jerusalem.

41. **Jordan**: River in Palestine.

42. **Pilate**: Pontius P., fl. A.D. 33, procurator of Judea under Emperor Tiberius. Pilate washed his hands as a gesture of innocence at the trial of Christ.

43. **soldi**: *Soldo*; I, "small coins."

44. **Olivet**: Mount of Olives, E of Jerusalem.

45. **Saracens**: Term commonly used in the Middle Ages to designate Arabs and, by extension, Moslems in general, whether Arabs, Moors, or Turks.

46. **Judas's tree**: According to tradition, the tree on which Judas hanged himself after the betrayal and the Crucifixion.

47. **hic . . . mundi**: L, "here is the center of the world."

48. **Ego . . .** : L, "I, the writer of the canto."

49. **Benche niuno cantasse**: I, "Although no one was singing."

50. **Luchino del Campo**: L. dal Campo, companion of Niccolò d'Este on a journey to Jerusalem and author of an account of the trip: *Viaggio a Gerusalemme di Niccolò da Este, descritto da Luchino dal Campo*, ed. G. Ghinassi, 1861.

51. **Aldovrandino**: Friend of Ugo d'Este and Parisina who was executed with them. The *Diario Ferrarese* reported: "1425, in the month of May, a Monday, at the 24th hour, the head of Ugo, son of the illustrious marquess Niccolò d'Este, was cut off, and that of madonna Parisina . . . and this because he had consorted carnally with her. And with them was decapitated one Aldovrandino di Rangoni da Modena, a familiar of the said *signore*, for having been the cause of this evil" [Gundersheimer, 79].

52. **vent 'uno Maggio**: I, "May 21st."

53. **The Marchese**: Niccolò d'Este.

54. **"Signor . . . si"**: I, "Sir . . . yes."

55. **"Fa me hora . . . Ugo"**: I, "Now cut off *my* head, / since you've so soon decapitated my Ugo."

56. **Rodendo . . . mani**: I, "Chewing with his teeth a stick he held in his hands." Trans. of source reads: "All that night the unhappy father and husband paced up and down the

halls and passages of his palace in desperate grief, now gnawing his sceptre with his teeth, now calling passionately upon the name of his dead son or crying out for his own death" [Gardner, 38].

57. **ter pacis** . . . : L, "three times author of the Italian peace." Niccolò, one of the greatest lechers among Italian potentates, practiced seduction rather than rape. He was also known as a peacemaker: witness the recurrent refrain to his son, "Keep the peace, Borso."

58. **Tre cento . . . bombardi**: I, "Three hundred gun salutes . . . bombards." Although Ugo was beheaded, Niccolò ordered an elaborate state funeral; boys pulled the funeral barge from the bank. Niccolò also "sent a written report of the tragedy to all the Courts of Italy, and . . . on receipt of the news the Doge of Venice put off a State tournament" [Gardner, 39].

59. **Florentine baily**: Dieci Della Balia, Council of Ten of the Balia, ruling authority of Florence.

60. **Madonna Laodamia delli Romei**: Gardner [p. 39] writes: "The Marquis is said . . . to have ordered the execution of several noble Ferrarese ladies who were notoriously serving their husbands as Parisina had served him—'in order that his wife should not be the only one to suffer.' . . . One, Laodamia de'Romei, the wife of one of the judges, 'who was known to him,' appears to have been publicly beheaded."

61. **pa della justicia**: I, "palace of justice."

62. **Agnesina**: D. ca. 1430, a matron of Modena who, apparently, had committed adultery and poisoned her husband; under edict she was also beheaded. The point of the edict that resulted in these beheadings is that it came as a result of Niccolò's anguish following the beheading of Parisina.

63. **Monna Ricarda**: Ricciarda di Sallusto, daughter of Marquess Saluzzo. She married Niccolò d'Este in 1431, six years after the execution of his wife, Parisina, and bore him two legitimate sons, Ercole and Sigismundo.

64. **Charles**: Charles VII of France, 1403-1461 (reign 1422-1461).

65. **scavoir faisans . . . Jehan Rabateau**: F, "making known . . . and to come . . . to high / nobility of family and house . . . and great deeds . . . / valor . . . affection . . . our aforesaid cousin . . . / power, royal authority . . . he and his descendants . . . and / as they desire to have henceforth forever in their arms quartering / . . . three golden flower-de-luce . . . on scalloped azure field . . . / enjoy and use. [Dated] 1431, [at] council at Chinon, the King, l'Esne de la Tribouill, Vendoise, [and signed] Jehan Rabateau."

66. **Marchese Saluzzo**: Marquess S., father of Monna Ricciarda [cf. 63 above] and grandfather of Ercole.

67. **Hercules**: Ercole d'Este, 1431-1505, son of Niccolò d'Este and Ricciarda. He became the second ruler of Ferrara after Niccolò and a "Hercules" in advancing music, the arts, and the welfare of the people.

68. **piccolo e putino**: I, "small and boyish."

69. **Polenta**: Ostasio da P. Although he was an ally of the Venetians in 1441, he was deprived by them of Ravenna and exiled to Candia with his family.

70. **E fu** . . . : I, "And he was buried nude." In 1441 Niccolò went to serve as governor of Milan at the request of the ailing duke, Filippo Maria Visconti. He died a month later, aged 58, possibly from poison. His body was returned to Ferrara and at midnight of New Year's Day he was buried in the Church of Santa Maria degli Angeli, "nude, without any pomp, for so he did command in his will" [Gundersheimer, 91].

71. **Ter pacis Italiae**: L, "Three times of the Italian peace" [cf. 57 above].

72. **Bondeno**: Commune in Ferrara Province, N Italy.

73. **Cassini**: Poss. Gherado Casini, Roman publisher.

74. **libraio**: I, "bookseller."

75. **Napoleon**: N. Bonaparte, 1769-1821, emperor of the French (1805-1814).

76. **Via del Po**: I, "Street of the Po [River]."

77. **Piacenza**: Town in the region of Veneto, N Italy.

78. **Marchese Niccolo**: Niccolò d'Este.

79. **Borso**: Third son of Niccolò. The statues of both father and son were erected in the square of Ferrara, prob. in the 15th century.

80. **Piazza**: I, "Square."

81. **Commendatore**: I, "Knight of a chivalric order."

82. **per diletto**: I, "for pleasure" [*Inf.* V, 127], describing activities of the lustful lovers, Paolo and Francesca [cf. *Pai,* 3-2, 229].

83. **Ferrara . . . stomagose**: I, "Ferrara, paradise for clothiers, disgusting festivals."

84. **Apollo**: Phoebus A., Olympian god of light and son of Zeus and Leto whose cattle were stolen by Hermes, son of Zeus and Maia: "Born in the dawn, by midday well he harped, and in the evening stole the cattle of Apollo. . . . When he leaped from the immortal knees of his mother, lay not long in the sacred cradle, but sped forth to seek the cattle of Apollo." Apollo later followed the trail that led to the crib and accused the boy, who said: " . . . great marvel . . . that a new-born child should cross the threshold after kine . . . Yesterday was I born, my feet are tender" [Homeric Hymn IV].

85. **A child of my age**: Hermes.

86. **Albert**: Alberto d'Este, 1347-1393, father of Niccolò d'Este; marchese and vicar of Ferrara. Niccolò is supposedly speaking.

87. **Tura**: Cosimo or Cosmé T., 1430?-1495, Italian painter of murals; a leader of the Ferrarese school and court painter to Borso and Ercole d'Este; one of the Schifanoia muralists.

88. **Julia the Countess**: Prob. member of the Tassoni family of Ferrara, which owned the Schifanoia at one time. Text reference is to the fact that the Schifanoia once was used as a tobacco factory; the Italian verb, *conciare*, means to tan hides, or to cure tobacco, hence the confusion of *tannery* in the text. For recent history of the Schifanoia, see R. Longhi, "Il Palazzo Estense di Schifanoia dal sec. XIV al sec. XX," *Rivista di Ferrara*, July 1935.

CANTO XXV

Sources

Giambattista Lorenzi, *Monumenti per servire alla storia del Palazzo Ducale di Venezia*, Venice, 1868; Tibullus III, 10 (IV, iv), 15, and III, 11 (IV, v), 1; Plato, *Gorgias*; *The Epic of Gilgamesh*; Homeric Hymn V, "To Aphrodite."

Background

William Carew Hazlitt, *The Venetian Republic: Its Rise, Its Growth, and Its Fall, A.D. 409-1797*, London, 1915; Francis

Marion Crawford, *Gleanings from Venetian History*, New York, 1905; Gibbon, *The Decline and Fall of the Roman Empire*, Modern Library, 1932, Vol. II.

Exegeses

Dekker, *Cantos*, 31-35; EH, *Approaches*, 24-25, 30-31; HK, *Era*, 307-308, passim; S. Libera, *Pai* 2-3, 359.

Glossary

1. **Council**: The first two and a half pages and the last page of this canto are taken from various decrees concerning the palace of the doges. The Doge (Duke) of Venice was a nonhereditary officer elected for life by the people. In 1173 a body known as the Great Council or Council Major was set up to control the actions of the duke; it originally consisted of 480 members, but the number of members and the method of election changed frequently. The council gradually became less democratic and was dominated by a smaller body, the Council of Forty [Hazlitt, I, 495-502].

2. **danari**: I, "small coins."

3. **loggia**: I, "open gallery"; Rialto: bridge and quarter of Venice.

4. **soldi**: I, a small coin.

5. **In libro pactorum**: L, "In the book of the agreements (or 'contracts')."

6. **et quod . . .** : L, "and which may be publicly made known."

7. **dicto millessimo**: ML, from I, *millessimo* ("the year or the year and day in a formal date"), "on the said date."

8. **Lord John Soranzo**: Giovanni S., Doge of Venice (1312-1328). Said to be "undeniably one of the most illustrious men elected to the Dogeship in the course of its existence of exactly eleven hundred years" [Crawford, I, 292; Hazlitt, I, 562-566].

9. **Curia**: L, "meeting place of the Senate."

10. **Palace of the Doges**: On the Piazzetta, just off of the SE corner of the Piazza San Marco, Venice.

11. **Castaldio**: The original document has *juxta domus habitationis Gastaldionum* ["next to the habitation of the Administrators"]. *Gastaldo*, a variant spelling of *Castaldo* (I, "bailiff"), was used in Venice for a variety of administrative officers. *Castaldia* means the residence of a bailiff [Hazlitt, I, 594-595].

12. **trabesilis**: The original document has *de trabeselis*; neither word appears in dictionaries of classical or medieval Latin, but the word must be derived from L, *trabs* ["beam" or "timber"], so that the phrase in the document means "of small wooden beams" and Pound's "timbered" is a reasonable translation.

13. **simul commorantes**: L, "living together" [although *commorantes* means "abiding" or "staying," when used with *simul*, the *Index* trans. seems reasonable]. The lion, sacred to St. Mark, is the totem animal of Venice.

14. **Lord King Frederic of Sicily**: Frederick II of Sicily, 1272-1337, King of Sicily (1296-1337).

15. **millessimo**: L, "date" [cf. 7 above].

16. **St. Mark's day**: April 25, the day of the patron saint of Venice; the flag of St. Mark is the Venetian standard.

17. per naturam . . . pilosos: L, "by nature . . . alive and hairy."

18. gyring: "Moving in a spiral," a word often used by Yeats.

19. John Marchesini: Fl. 1328, ducal notary of Venice.

20. St. Nicholas: The Chapel of San Niccolò in the palace of the doges.

21. gross: Pound's translation of *grossorum*, gen. pl. of ML, *grossus* ["small coin" or "groat"].

22. Donna Sorantia Soranzo: Daughter of Giovanni Soranzo, Doge of Venice. Because she was married to Niccolò Querini (d. ca. 1330), a leader of a conspiracy to overthrow the government, she was exiled from Venice in 1320 and permitted to return only to attend her father when he was ill (1327). The next year he died in her arms [cf. Crawford, I, 242-243].

23. Ascension: Ascension Day, 40th day after Easter.

24. ripa del Palazzo: I, "embankment of the Palace."

25. groats: [cf. 21 above].

26. Marc Erizio: Prob. "Erizzo," a member of the Consiglio dei Dieci [Council of Ten], Venice.

27. Nic. Speranzo: Prob. member of the council.

28. Tomasso Grandonico: Prob. Grandenigo, a member of the council.

29. the hall: Hall of the Great Council in the palace of the doges, which was rebuilt between 1309 and 1404.

30. because of the stink: Three councillors were delegated to study the possibility of keeping the prisoners in a place where their odor would be less noticeable to people going up the stairs of the hall of the Great Council.

31. Doge: Michele Steno, Doge of Venice (1400-1413). Money was appropriated to enlarge his private room.

32. vadit pars: L, lit. "a part goes." An authority at the Biblioteca Nazionale Marciana Venezia says that it is a Venetian legal formula meaning "it was decided that."

33. da parte . . . sincere: Original document has *De parte*. I, "on behalf of [i.e., affirmative] / of no [i.e., negative] / . . . not genuine."

34. murazzi: I, "dikes," embankments of the lagoon in Venice. For the same Venetian scene with palace at dawn cf. 21/98 and 17/76.

35. Sulpicia: Fl. 40 B.C. The niece of Messala Corvinus, she was a Roman poet whose six short pieces on her passion for Cerinthus are included in Volume III [13-18] of the works of Tibullus. An unknown author composed five poems (III, 8-12] about her or in her name; Pound is quoting from the third and fourth of these poems.

36. Pone metum Cerinthe: L, "Lay aside fear, Cerinthus." The author tells Cerinthus that his girl (presumably Sulpicia) will get well, since God will not harm lovers.

37. Zephyrus: In Greek mythology the personification of the west wind.

38. deus nec . . . : L, "nor does God harm lovers."

39. Hic mihi . . . : L, "This day a holy one for me." The day is Cerinthus's birthday.

40. Sero, sero: L, "Too late, too late."

41. Pone metum . . . laedit: L, "Lay aside fear, / fear, nor does God harm."

42. bolge: Pound is Anglicizing the I *bolgia*, lit. "a large wallet," Dante's word for the ten ditches in the eighth circle of Inferno [15:9].

43. Civis Romanus: L, "Roman citizen."

44. vanity of Ferrara: The seven lines culminating in *vanity of Ferrara* probably are a comment on the central debate at the council between the Eastern and Western churches convened by Pope Eugenius IV in 1438 at Ferrara. Gibbon summarizes: "Four principal questions had been agitated between the two churches: 1. The use of unleavened bread in the communion of Christ's body. 2. The nature of purgatory. 3. The supremacy of the pope. And, 4. The single or double procession of the Holy Ghost . . . . The procession of the Holy Ghost from the Father alone, or from the Father and the Son, was an article of faith which had sunk much deeper into the minds of men; and in the sessions of Ferrara and Florence the Latin addition of *filioque* was subdividied into two questions, whether it were legal, or whether it were orthodox" [*Decline and Fall*, Modern Library ed., 1286]. And so on. Such rhetorical but dead words leading to dogma are continually contrasted in the *Cantos* with the celebration of the mysterium, the "light from Eleusis," or the "blood rite." That men presume to resolve such questions is a "vanity" [cf. 8:30 and 26:52 for more detail].

45. **Phaethusa**: [21:57].

46. **Phlegethon**: The river of fire in Hades.

47. **pone metum**: L, "lay aside fear" [cf. 36 above].

48. **Napishtim**: Prob. Utnapishtim, a character in the Babylonian epic, *Gilgamesh*. After surviving a universal flood he is granted immortality by the gods; he reveals to Gilgamesh "knowledge depth-hidden," the secret of eternal youth, a flower that was stolen away from him and eaten by a snake [cf. S. Libera, *Pai* 2-3, 359].

49. *νους*: H, "mind." In Neoplatonism the word is used to suggest intelligence as the active principle of deity in the universe [ibid.].

50. **King Otreus**: When Aphrodite appeared in disguise to Anchises, she said she was the daughter of King Otreus [23:34].

51. **Tician**: Titian, Tiziano Vecellio, 1477-1576, Venetian painter.

52. **Tyciano da Cadore**: Titian.

53. **Fondamenta delli Thodeschi**: I, "Embankment [in Venice 'a paved street running along a canal'] of the Germans": the "Fondaco dei Tedeschi," commerical street in Venice.

54. **Ser**: I, "Sir" or "Master," a title once given to notaries and simple priests.

55. **Leonardus Emo**: Leonardo Emo, fl. 1522, Venetian general.

56. **Sapiens Consilij**: L, "Reverend [member] of the Council."

57. **Philippus Capello**: Filippo C., fl. 1522, Venetian nobleman.

58. **Sapiens Terrae Firmae**: L, "Reverend [delegate] from the Mainland."

59. **Zuan Bellin**: Giovanni Bellini, 1430?-1516, leading painter of the Venetian school, noted for his altarpieces and Madonnas.

60. **Canal Grande**: I, "Grand Canal," major canal of Venice.

61. **Sensaria**: Original document has *sansaria*, I *senseria* means "brokerage," as trans. in second line on the canto page.

62. **ducats**: Italian coins of large denomination.

63. **pictor**: L, "painter."

64. **terra . . . carta**: I, "earth . . . document." Original document has *Senato Terra*, which may mean the "Senate of the Mainland" or may use the word "earth" [in a sense not recorded in the dictionary] as "year."

CANTO XXVI

Sources

Fritz Schultze, *Georgios Gemisthos Plethon und seine reformatorischen Bestrebungen*, 1874; Charles Yriarte, *Venice*, trans. F. J. Sitwell, 1896; P. Molmenti, *Carpaccio: son temps et son oeuvre*, 1893; L. A. Ferrai, *Lorenzino de' Medici*, Milan, Hoepli, 1891; L. A. Muratori, *Rerum Italicarum Scriptores*, XXII, 1733; Ludwig Schiedermair, *Die Briefe W. A. Mozarts und seiner Familie*, 5 vols., Munich and Leipzig, 1914, trans. and ed. Emily Anderson, 3 vols., 1938, as *The Letters of Mozart and His Family*.

Background

William Carew Hazlitt, *The Venetian Republic: Its Rise, Its Growth, and Its Fall, A.D. 409-1797*, London, 1915; Jacob Burckhardt, *The Civilization of the Renaissance in Italy*, London and New York, 1890; Patricia H. Labalme, *Bernardo Giustiniani: A Venetian of the Quattrocento*, Rome, 1969; G. F. Young, *The Medici*, 1909; Machiavelli, *History of Florence*, IV, xxix; Philip James Jones, *The Malatesta of Rimini and the Papal State*, Cambridge University Press, 1974; F. C. Hodgson, *The Early History of Venice*, London, 1901; Francis Marion Crawford, *Salve Venetia*, I, New York and London, 1905; Werner L. Gundersheimer, *Ferrara*, Princeton, 1973; Earl Miner, *The Japanese Tradition in British and American Literature*, Princeton, 1958, 121.

Exegeses

EP, *GK*, 45, 133, 115, 224, 241; *J/M*, 79; *ABCR*, 30; CE, *Ideas*, 31-32; HK, *Era*, 420-421; Libera, *Pai*, 2-3, 371; CFT, *Pai*, 6-3, 360.

Glossary

1. **crocodile**: Statue of animal bestridden by St. Theodore atop a marble column in St. Mark's Square in Venice [HK, *Era*, 421, for picture].

2. **barche**: I, "boats" [3:6].

3. **Relaxetur**: L, "Let him be released."

4. **Pasti**: Matteo da Pasti (d. 1468), Veronese sculptor and medalist. He was sent by Sigismundo Malatesta to Candia to paint a portrait of the Turkish emperor, Mohammed II. Because of this commission he was arrested by the Venetians, who suspected him of being in league with the Turks against

them. Pasti was the artist who made the designs in Valturio's *De Re Militari* [10:56; 7 below; Hazlitt, II, 881].

5. **caveat . . .** : L, "let him beware of going to the Turk." The Turk is Mohammed II, Ottoman sultan (reign 1451-1481).

6. **Constantinople**: Capital of the Ottoman Empire, formerly Byzantium, now Istanbul.

7. **Valturio**: Robert de V. (d. 1489). Engineer of Sigismundo's La Rocca and his first secretary. Says Pound: "Malatesta and the late condottieri, their mouths watering over the designs, in Valturio, of war engines, tanks, superior catapults" [*GK*, 115; 9:19]

8. **Nicolo Segundino**: Niccolò Sagundino, spokesman at Rome for the Venetian Senate; charged by the Venetians to try to make peace between Pope Pius II and the Malatesta family.

9. **omnem . . . volve lapidem**: L, "turn every stone."

10. **Pio**: Enea Silvio Piccolomini (1405-1464), Pope Pius II (1458-1464); author, humanist, and patron of writers; in literature he is known as Aeneas Silvius [10:27]. In December 1460, Sigismundo Malatesta and his brother were both excommunicated; by January 1461 Pius II had announced the need for some process, inverting canonization, which would enroll Sigismundo as a citizen of Hell [Jones, 231]. During April 1462, effigies of Sigismundo were burned in Rome. Venice, afraid that too large an increase in the temporal power of the papacy would disturb the complicated balance of power of the city-states, tried to temper the policy of Pius and bring about peace. Much of the "diplomacy" had to be done secretly. But by the end of August 1462, with the help of Frederigo d'Urbino and others, the papal forces totally defeated the Malatestas. "From this reverse Sigismundo was never permitted to recover" [Jones, 232].

11. **Malatesta**: The family of Rimini, prominent from the 13th to the 16th century; in 1462 headed by Sigismundo [8:5].

12. **Borso**: Borso d'Este, who in the politics of the time would be sympathetic toward maintaining the power of Sigismundo as a balance wheel [20:29].

13. **Ferrara**: Capital city of d'Este family.

14. **Bernard Justinian**: Bernardo Giustiniani, 1408-1489. In 1462 he was sent by Venice to Rome to effect an agreement between Pius II and Sigismundo Malatesta, a mission he accomplished the next year. October 28 is the date of his instructions [Labalme, 174-179].

15. **Senato Secreto**: I, "Secret meeting of the Senate."

16. **Hanibal**: Annibale di Constantino Cerboni da Castello, agent of Domenico Malatesta to the Venetians.

17. **Cesena**: Town in Forlì Province, Emilia, Italy; controlled by the Malatestas from 1379 to 1465 [8:55].

18. **flag of St. Mark**: Venetian standard emblazoned with image of the city's patron saint.

19. **Fortinbras**: Carlo Fortebracci, Count of Montone, Venetian condottiere. During the war between Sigismundo and Pius II, Venice could not openly support Malatesta against the pope. But they gave 2,000 ducats to Fortebracci to hire Venetian soldiers and thus supported Sigismundo covertly.

20. **secretissime**: ML, "most secretly."

21. **Henry**: Henry VI of England, 1421-1471; king of England (1422-1461 and 1470-1471).

22. **Inghilterra**: I, "England."

23. **Levant**: The name given to the region extending from Egypt to Turkey along the eastern shores of the Mediterranean.

24. **Corfu**: Island in Ionian Sea. During the Norman expansion (England, 1066) Duke Robert (called Guiscard) led the Norman forces and cause into the Mediterranean with designs of finally conquering Constanti-

nople, at that time under Venetian dominance. Robert occupied Corfu and, if allowed to remain there, could "keep the war ships and merchant men of Venice confined almost to their own lagoons" [Hodgson, 218]. Several battles were fought over it, one (1084) off Corfu and a critical one at sea above Corfu in which Venice, under the leadership of Doge Selvo, was seriously defeated. "The wrath of the Venetians at the ill success of their fleet in the battle led to the immediate deposition of the doge Silvio" [ibid., 222]. The continuous actions against Robert kept him out of Constantinople, at the immense pleasure of leaders of the Eastern Empire. He ameliorated the problem neatly by dying in 1085.

25. **Selvo**: Domenigo Selvo or Silvio, doge (1071-1084). He was married to a Byzantine princess, Theodora, daughter of the Emperor Constantine Ducas XI. She was known for "luxurious extravagance" and was "guilty of many false refinements and fantastic notions," including the use of double-pronged gold forks [Hazlitt, I, 134-142; II, 938, 982].

26. **San Marco**: The Basilica of San Marco, Venice. After being deposed, Selvo "retired into a convent." He "was the first to put up mosaics in the church, and also it was he who required every Venetian ship loading in the East to bring home marbles or fine stones for the basilica" [Hodgson, 227].

27. **Sed aureis furculis**: L, "But with golden forks."

28. **Luxuria**: L, "luxury."

29. **Lorenzo Tiepolo**: Doge of Venice (1268-1275).

30. **Barbers etc.**: Elaborate festivities marked the installation of Tiepolo as doge. Barbers disguised as knights-errant, furriers, smiths, skinners, glassblowers, and many other tradesmen paraded in rich costumes [Hazlitt, I, 417-420]. "The guilds of the arts and trades had been privileged to escort the wife of Lorenzo Tiepolo to the church: . . . first the blacksmiths with flying banner; then the merchants of fur, dressed in their richest garments and most priceless sables . . . ; the weavers next, singing at the top of their voices to the music of trumpets and cymbals, and bearing both silver cups and flagons full of wine. After the weavers the tailors came in the dress of their trade guild, whie robes embroidered with red stars; and the wool-merchants bore olive branches in their hands and had crowns of olive leaves on their heads . . . ; and the sellers of cloth of gold, and the shoemakers, the mercers, . . . the glass-blowers, the jewellers and the barbers, all displaying the rich and fantastic costumes of their guilds in the great procession, a very splendid sight" [Crawford, 298-299]. Pound liked processions and parades of celebration. The first one is noted briefly at 4/16 [cf. also magnificent parade at 43/216-217].

31. **gonfaron . . . de vin**: F, "banner / and their flasks full of wine." The Venetian banner of the Lion of San Marco was called by the Old French name *gonfalon*.

32. **25th April**: In 1435 Niccolò III of Ferrara, 1393-1441, had his son Leonello (reign 1441-1450) married to Margherita Gonzaga (d. 1439), daughter of Francesco Gonzaga of Mantua. Lavish festivities were held at public expense. Probably because of Niccolò's constant concern to maintain good relations with Venice, the wedding party traveled there to continue the celebrations with joustings, horse racing, and the like.

33. **Ugaccion dei Contrarini**: Ugaccione da Contrari, Ferrarese nobleman who was Niccolò's "constant companion, his most trusted general, diplomat, and military adviser, and his closest friend" [Gundersheimer, 84]. He ruled the city during Niccolò's trip to the Holy Land [24:29].

34. **Francesco Gonzaga**: 1st Marchese of Mantua (reign 1407-1444).

35. **pellande**: I, "loose outer garments."

36. **cendato**: I, *cendado*, "silk cloth."

37. **piazza**: I, "square."

38. **Mantua**: Mantova, city in Lombardy.

39. **And that year ('38)**: This line, the next 37, and the last 3 lines on page 124 concern the gathering of the delegates to the council convened by Pope Eugenius IV to explore ways to unite the Eastern and Western branches of the Church. The delegates from the East debarked at Venice, where they remained for several weeks before departing for Ferrara. The pope chose Ferrara because of its long history of peace and the cooperation he received from the Marquis of Ferrara, Niccolò d'Este, as well as for other reasons. But because of an outbreak of the plague the council, at the invitation of Cosimo de'Medici, moved to Florence [8:30; 25:44].

40. **Marquis of Ferrara**: Niccolò d'Este who came to Venice to meet his guests.

41. **Greek Emperor**: Johannes Palaeologus or John VIII, 1392-1448, Byzantine emperor (1425-1448).

42. **Archbishop of Morea Lower**: Eastern Orthodox delegate to the council, as are all those listed in the next four lines. Morea is the ancient Peloponnesus, S Greece.

43. **Lacedaemon**: District of the Peloponnesus in which the city of Sparta is located; in ancient times sometimes used as the name of the city.

44. **Mitylene**: City on island of Lesbos in the Aegean.

45. **Rhodos**: Rhodes.

46. **Modon Brandos**: Prob. Modon (Methoni), town in the SW Peloponnesus.

47. **Corinth**: City in S Greece.

48. **Trebizond**: City and so-called empire on S shore of the Black Sea, which at times included parts of Georgia and the Crimea.

49. **stonolifex**: Defined as "a Greek ecclesiastical official" in Pound's source, Sanuto, *Vitae Ducum Venetorum* [Muratori, *Rerum Italicarum Scriptores*, XXII]. There is no further information [BK].

50. **Cosimo Medici**: Cosimo de' Medici (1389-1464). Although the Albizzi banished Cosimo to Padua [21:20], "he was subsequently permitted to move from Padua to Venice" [Young, 764n]. Machiavelli says: "Wherever he passed, Cosimo was honorably received, visited publicly by the Venetians, and treated by them more like a sovereign than an exile" [*History of Florence*, IV, xxix].

51. **Sigismundo da Rimini**: [8/5].

52. **Trinity**: A central theological point dividing the Eastern and Western churches, derived from a statement adopted at the council of Nicaea (A.D. 325) which said that the Holy Spirit proceeded from both the Father and the Son (*Filioque*); The Eastern Church believed that the Holy Spirit came from the Father only. At the council of 1438 the Western Church tried to support its claim for the Trinity by the age of a particular document which Gemistus proved a forgery [cf. Libera, *Pai*, 2-3, 371; 25:44].

53. **Gemisto**: Georgius Gemistus Plethon [23:3; 8:31]

54. **Te fili . . . anulo**: L, "Thee, my son the Duke, and thy successors / with a golden ring." The annual Venetian ceremony, "Wedding of the Sea," celebrated the domination by Venice over the Adriatic Sea. This domination goes back to the reign of Doge Pietro Orseolo II (991-1008), who conquered several cities on the Dalmatian coast. The most familiar story about the origin of the ceremony is that Pope Alexander III in 1177 gave Doge Sebastiano Ziani a consecrated ring in gratitude for the role of Venice in resolving the pope's quarrel with Emperor Frederick Barbarossa (1152-1190) to the advantage of the papacy. In the ceremony, which continued until the end of the Republic in 1797, the doge threw a ring into the sea, saying that he wedded the sea in token of his dominion over it.

55. Manuel: Manuel I Comnenus, 1120?-1180, emperor of the Eastern Roman Empire (1143-1180); his reign was marked by military victories against Italians, Venetians, Serbs, and Turks, but he was defeated by the Seljuks in Phrygia (1176) with the encouragement of Ziani.

56. Rialto: Legend says that in 809 a wooden bridge on floats, called *soleolo*, was built from the island of Rialto across the Grand Canal because it was the heart of commerce. "In 1180 . . . a permanent bridge [was made] of this temporary one" [Yriarte, 165].

57. Ziani: Sebastiano Z., Doge of Venice (1172-1178). Legend says that Pope Alexander III granted him the privilege of using lead for an official seal instead of sealing wax, an honor reserved to emperors [Hazlitt finds no evidence to support the legend (II, 490)].

58. cendato: I, *cendado*, "silk cloth."

59. Carlo Malatesta: 1368-1429, Lord of Rimini, brother of Pandolfo Malatesta, 1377-1427, and uncle of Sigismundo. Pandolfo was a vigorous general who worked with Carlo to extend the power and influence of the family by forming alliances with the popes and the major city-states, including Venice. In 1411-1412 Carlo and Pandolfo entered Venetian service and succeeded twice in defeating the Hungarians. In the second engagement Carlo "was too severely wounded to continue." In 1413 "Pandolfo and his heirs were awarded Venetian nobility" [Jones, 134; 24:23].

60. Balista: I, *ballista*, a machine like a large bow used to hurl stones.

61. Pandolfo: P. Malatesta [cf. 59 above].

62. Per animarla: I, "to enliven him."

63. San Samuele: Square in Venice where the church of the same name is located.

64. yellow kerchief: Prob. an article of dress to identify prostitutes, who were required by law in Venice to wear a peculiar motley garb [Hazlitt, II, 634].

65. ruffiane: I, "procuresses."

66. Cosimo: [21:9 and 50 above]. While in exile to Padua, Cosimo visited Venice.

67. Luigi Gonzaga: Lodovico Gonzaga, Marchese of Mantua (1444-1478).

68. Casa Giustinian: Lodovico Gonzaga was a friend of Bernardo Giustiniani's [cf. 14 above], but the *casa* ["house"] the Venetian government bought for him in recognition for his services in the war with Milan was not the same as Palazzo Giustiniani at the head of the Grand Canal but the house of another Bernardo called Bernardo della Seta [cf. Labalme, 112n].

69. Bishops of Lampascus and Cyprus: Eastern Orthodox delegates to the Council of Ferrara-Florence [cf. 39-53 above].

70. Lampascus: Lampsacus, city on the Hellespont.

71. Sigismundo: S. Malatesta. His visit to Mantua has not been identified.

72. Albizi: Albizzi, a Florentine family whose members were rivals of the Medici in the late 14th and early 15th centuries. Rinaldo degli Albizzi led the plot that exiled Cosimo de' Medici in 1433-34. The Albizzi were attempting to take over the Medici properties and commercial enterprises, but Cosimo's triumphant return ended their hopes [21:20].

73. Medici bank: Medici Bank in Florence, the foundation of the family's power and influence from the 13th century on.

74. Venetians may stand . . . Constantinople: The source of these seven lines is not known. In context they seem to concern (1) the ascent of Venice during the decline of Florence; and (2) the details of a trade treaty made between Venice and the early Ottoman Empire after the final loss of Eastern Christendom to Islam forces in 1453. Such a treaty was probably signed on April

18 in Constantinople. The significance of 6962 remains a conundrum, but it is probably an early effort to date creation similar to that of Bishop Ussher more than two centuries later.

75. Illmo ac ex^{mo} (eccellentissimo) princeps et d^{no}: L, I, "Most illustrious and most excellent [repeated in I] prince and lord."

76. Sforza: Alessandro S., 1409-1473, Lord of Pesaro and Cotignola [9:13] and brother of Duke Francesco S. Alessandro was the tricky operator who obtained control of Pesaro in 1444 by underhand means.

77. Mr. Pitro: Blacksmith in the service of Alessandro Sforza.

78. Pisanellus: Antonio di Puccio Pisano, 1395?-1455, called Pisanello, Veronese painter and medalist employed by Sigismundo in building the Tempio [8:43] and patronized by Leonello d'Este. He was also known as Vittore Pisano. In this passage he seems to be acting as an agent for Alessandro Sforza, which is possible since in 1453 Sigismundo had alliances with the Sforza family through his marriage in 1442 to Polissena, 1428-1449, daughter of Francesco Sforza, 1401-1466 [9:23]. After her death the relations between the families continued, in spite of rumors that Sigismundo poisoned her. In *ABCR* Pound discusses why Pisanello, as a painter, was a good person to buy horses [p. 30].

79. Vittor Capello: Vittore di Giorgio Capello, 1403-1466, Venetian admiral and in 1456 a member of the Privy Council of Cristoforo Moro, Doge of Venice, 1462-1471 [Hazlitt, I, 979].

80. St. George the Martyr: There has been much dispute about the identity of St. George; if he lived at all, it was before the 6th century, by which time he was recognized as a saint. What was supposed to be his skull was brought as a sacred relic to the Church of San Giorgio Maggiore on the island of the same name.

81. Island of Siesina: Liesina. The island of Lydda, where a huge cathedral was erected in St. George's honor, is the place to which (according to one account) his remains were taken after he was tortured and killed in 303 by order of the Emperor Diocletian [*EB*].

82. San Giorgio Maggiore: I, "Saint George the Greater." One of the islands of Venice; also the church thereon.

83. Cardinal Gonzaga of Mantua: Ercole G., 1527-1563, regent of Mantua during the minority of his nephews, 1540-1556.

84. ultimo febbraio: I, "last of February."

85. Lorenzo de Medicis: The "Lorenzaccio" who assassinated Alessandro [5:33, 39]. After his escape Lorenzo hid in a number of cities and for 11 years eluded murderers set on his trail. But finally, on the date named, he left his house poorly guarded by only "Giovanni Battista Martelli, e da Alessandro Soderini suo zio [his uncle]." The weight of conflicting evidence suggests "che la morte di Lorenzo avvenne a San Toma" ["that Lorenzo's death took place at San Toma"]. The two assassins escaped [cf. Ferrai, 380-390; *Index*, 480, for letter to Gonzaga].

86. de Mendoça: Prob. Diego Hurtado de Mendoza, d. 1575, ambassador of the Holy Roman emperor, Charles V, to Venice.

87. Marquis of Mantova: Francesco Gonzaga, Marchese of Mantua, 1484-1519. [This letter is in Molmenti, 69-70.]

88. Jerusalem: Gonzaga was trying to obtain pictures of various famous cities.

89. berettino: I, "small cap."

90. Lorenzo: Prob. Lorenzo Leonbruno, 1485-1537, a painter who in 1511 was in the service of the ruling house of Mantua.

91. Seignory: The signoria, supreme magistracy of the Republic of Venice.

92. Ancona: Italian city.

93. Victor Carpatio: Vittore Carpaccio, 1455?-1525?, famous Venetian painter, pupil to Lazaro Bastiani and follower of Bellini.

94. **Zuane Zamberti**: Poss. Giovanni Giamberti da Sangallo, 1482-1530, member of a famous family of architects.

95. **aquarelle**: I, *aquarella*, "water color" or "distemper."

96. **Venetijs**: L, "at Venice."

97. **pictore**: I (variant of *pittore*), "painter."

98. **Salzburg**: City in Austria famous as the home of Mozart and the site of the annual Mozart festival. The Prince Archbishop of Salzburg from 1772 to 1812 was Hieronymus Colloredo, b. 1732.

99. **Wolfgang Amadeus**: W. A. Mozart, 1756-1791, Austrian composer.

100. **inter lineas**: L, "between the lines." Pound is reading Mozart's real feelings "between the lines" of the letter which was really written (probably dictated) by his father. The real letter is firm about Mozart's desire to leave but is quite politely worded [*Pai*, 6-3, 360].

101. **Miss Cannabich**: Rosa, elder daughter of Christian Cannabich, 1731-1798, composer and leader of the Mannheim Orchestra. The sonata (KV 309) was composed in 1777. Of this sonata Mozart wrote to his father on December 6, 1777: "ich will es genau nach dem Caractere der Madselle Rose machen . . . wie das andante, so ist sie" ["I want it to match exactly the character of Mlle. Rose . . . she is like the andante"]. Rosa C., Mozart's pupil, was 15 at the time the letter was written [EH].

CANTO XXVII

Sources

Guido Cavalcanti, Ballata 12; Vincenzo di Chiara, "La Spagnuola" [street song popular at turn of century]; "The Wanderer"; Marie Curie, *Pierre Curie*, Paris, 1924; Francis Jammes, *Clara d'Ellébeuse; ou l'histoire d'une ancienne jeune fille*, 1899; Barrett and Davis, *Floradora* (an operetta first performed in 1899); inscription formerly over the altar in Ferrara Cathedral; Carl Appel, *Bernart von Ventadorn,* Halle, 1915; Camille Chabaneau, *Les Biographies des Troubadours en Langue Provençale*; EP, *T*, 124-125.

Background

EP, *SR*, 101; Lincoln Steffens, *Autobiography*, New York, 1931.

Exegeses

Sieburth, *Pai*, 5-2, 280; Mary de Rachewiltz, *Discretions*, 158; EH, *Approaches*, 30.

Glossary

1. **Formando . . . persona**: "Fashioning a new person from desire." [Line 17 from Guido Cavalcanti's Ballata 12: "Quando di morte mi convien trar vita," which Pound translates "If all my life be but some deathly moving" (*T*, 124-125)].

2. **Et quant . . . Pas**: F, "And as to the third / he fell into the / of his wife, [and] won't be seen again."

3. **oth fugol ouitbaer**: OE, "until a bird bore out"; adaptation of line 81 of the anonymous "Wanderer," which reads *sumne fugol othbaer* ["one a bird bore away"]. *Ouit* seems to be from no language, but it recalls the Dutch *uit* ["out"].

4. **Observed . . .** : Prob. a memory of pre-World War I report in which England quickly tried to get its navy in order.

5. **Porta-goose**: Portuguese. Early in 1914 Germany and Britain had reached a contingent agreement on the division of Portuguese colonies. But with Germany's declaration of war against the Triple Entente (Britain, France, and Russia), the British attitude toward all neutral powers changed and they began to woo Portugal as their "oldest ally."

6. **At rests . . .** : Exact source of this quote is unknown, but it is probably from a handbook used in training programs for officers in World War I.

7. **Dr. Spahlinger**: Henry S., 1882-1965, Swiss bacteriologist; inventor of an anti-tuberculosis vaccine.

8. **J'ai obtenu**: F, "I got."

9. **M. Curie**: Pierre Curie [23:10].

10. **Prince des Penseurs**: F, "Prince of Thinkers."

11. **Monsieur Brisset**: Jean-Pierre B., French philologist and writer, among whose works are *La Science de Dieu; ou, La création de l'homme*, 1900, and *Les Origines humaines*, 2d ed., 1913, in which he demonstrated that man is descended from the frog. Pound is parodying such an idea. He also considered the election of Brisset an amusing joke perpetrated by a group of French intellectuals who wanted to mock the pomposity of such an election [*Pai*, 5-2, 280; *Discretions*, 158].

12. **Deputies**: Lower house of the French national assembly.

13. **Messina**: Capital of Messina Province in NE Sicily; in the great earthquake at Messina on December 28, 1908, 90 percent of the city's buildings were destroyed.

14. **Bucentoro/"Stretti!"**: [3:5,6]. . . . "this year, '27" is the year Pound was writing Canto 27.

15. **Milan**: Capital of Milano Province, Lombardy, N Italy.

16. **Clara d'Ellébeuse**: Character in the novel *Clara d'Ellébeuse; ou l'histoire d'une ancienne jeune fille*, 1899, by Francis Jammes; the name is also found in Jammes's *De l'angelus de l'aube à l'angelus du soir, 1888-1897* (1898).

17. **Benette . . . Elfes**: F, "Benette plays the Waltz of the Elves."

18. **salotto**: I, "drawing room": main parlor or lobby.

19. **air de province**: F, "provincial air": manner.

20. **Croat**: The Croats are a south Slavic people.

21. **commercianti**: I, "merchants": commercial people.

22. **Floradora**: English operetta, music by "Leslie Stuart" (Thomas A. Barrett, 1866-1928) and book by "Owen Hall" (James Davis, 1853-1907), first performed in 1899. Published in London by Francis, Day & Hunter, and in New York by T. B. Harms.

23. **Clara d'Ellébeuse**: [cf. 16 above].

24. Sed et . . . populus: L, "And the whole population of the church, too."

25. duomo: I, "cathedral."

26. Glielmo ciptadin: I, "Guglielmo citizen." This inscription in mosaic has now been destroyed; its last two lines were *Fo Nicolao scolptore / E Gliemo fo lo auctore* ["Nicholas was the sculptor, Guglielmo was the author"]. The meaning of the last word is uncertain—perhaps "founder," perhaps "architect." Pound saw the inscription over the altar in the cathedral at Ferrara [cf. *SR*, 101]. It rhymes with the "pride of workmanship" theme in *The Cantos*, as does *Adamo me fecit* [45:14].

27. Brumaire: French Revolutionary month, October 22 to November 20.

28. Fructidor: French Revolutionary month, August 18 to September 16.

29. Petrograd: Leningrad, formerly St. Petersburg, was renamed Petrograd during World War I when the Russian Revolution broke out.

30. Tovarisch: R, "comrade."

31. Xarites: H, *Charites*, "the Graces."

32. Helios: Early Greek sun-god, whose functions were later taken over by Apollo [23:18].

33. Cadmus: Founder of Thebes. A dragon guarding a spring killed the companions of Cadmus, who in turn killed the dragon; by Athena's instruction, he sowed the dragon's teeth, and from them armed warriors sprang up; these were set fighting one another until only five remained: the Sparti (ancestors of many noble families of Thebes) who with Cadmus and his men built the city [4:4]. The great work of Cadmus in creating Thebes is compared here, as in other places [25/118], with the regret over failure.

34. Eblis: Eblis II, Vicomte of Ventadour, 12th-century Provençal nobleman. Bernart de Ventadour, Provençal poet, wrote songs to Eblis's wife. He was banished and she was locked up in a tower [6:29].

35. Ventadour: Former duchy in the department of Corrèze, S central France near Limoges. Pound visited the place in 1919 and prob. found only bees, wild grass in the courtyard, and so on.

36. acanthus: A variety of Mediterranean plant whose ornamental leaves were used as architectural decoration, especially in Corinthian columns. Suggests here the "two-way vegetation of Persephone" [cf. EH, *Approaches*, 30].

CANTO XXVIII

Sources

Current press reports of the Levine-Chamberlin transatlantic flights in, e.g., *Literary Digest*, June 18, 25, 1927, and *Current History*, July 1927; Catullus LXI.

Background

EP, *J/M*, 30; *SR*, 53, 62-63, 65; *LE*, 102-103; *L*, 153; Lincoln Steffens, *Autobiography*, New York, 1931; NS, *Ezra Pound's*

Pennsylvania, Toledo, Ohio, 1976; W. C. Williams, *Autobiography*, New York, 1951; Charles Norman, *Ezra Pound: A Biography*, New York, 1969.

Exegeses

CE, *Ideas*, 32-34, 114-116; DP, *Barb*, 108; John Drummond in Peter Russell, *An Examination of EP*, 1973, 115-116.

Glossary

1. **Boja d'un Dio**: I, "Hangman of a God"; in Romagna dialect an expletive such as "Darn it!"

2. **Romagnolo**: I, *Romagnol*, "an inhabitant of the Romagna," region of Italy now comprising the provinces of Bologna, Ferrara, Ravenna, and Forlì.

3. **Aso iqua me**: I (Romagna dialect), "This is me here."

4. **All Esimo**: I [misprint for *All' Esimio*], "To the Distinguished."

5. **Dottor Aldo Walluschnig**: Prob. an Austrian doctor in Venice, ca. 1925.

6. **Marotti, Virginia**: Venetian woman whose life and that of her son were saved by an operation performed by Dr. Walluschnig in 1925.

7. **Senni**: Seems to be the name of the hospital.

8. **San Giorgio**: Island and church in Venice [26:82].

9. **Mr. Lourpee**: Prob. a pseudonym for an unsuccessful French painter Pound saw at a pension in Madrid in 1906.

10. **Sage of Concord**: Ralph Waldo Emerson.

11. **Mrs. Kreffle**: Pseudonym for a Mrs. Kraft whom Pound knew in Madrid in 1906.

12. **Sevilla**: S, Seville, capital of Seville Province and of Andalusia, SW Spain.

13. **pesetas**: Spanish coins.

14. **West Virginia**: Miss Adah and Miss Ida Mapel, American sisters from West Virginia, were residents of the boardinghouse in Spain where Pound stayed on his trip in 1906 [91/615].

15. **Chiasso**: Town on Italian-Swiss border on the main St. Gotthard railroad line.

16. **year of the strikes**: 1920. One strike occurred in May when Pound was making his way from Como to Paris. At Milan all trains stopped at a certain midnight and he and his wife, Dorothy Shakespear Pound, "came out of Italy on a tram-car" [*L*, 153].

17. **Como**: City on Lake Como in Lombardy, N Italy.

18. **hidalgo**: S, "nobleman."

19. **Trieste**: Seaport on the Adriatic, now in Italy but formerly in Austria.

20. **the Bowery**: Section of lower Manhattan, New York, famous for its bars and its derelicts.

21. **bleeding Kansas**: The name given to the six-year period of border warfare in Kansas following the enactment of the Kansas-Nebraska Bill of 1854.

22. **Clara Leonora**: Graduate student at the University of Pennsylvania, 1906, who was in Professor Hugo Rennert's class with Pound. This line and the 16 lines following concern memories of Clara L. in Professor

Rennert's class. Her claim to authority seems to have rested on the fact that Franz Liszt, on a concert tour, had held her on his knee when she was a child, thus making her opinion about sonnets worth listening to. Pound had doubtless announced his habit of writing a sonnet a day and destroying them at the end of the year [W. C. Williams, *Autobiography*, 53; Norman, *Ezra Pound*, 6].

23. **Rennert**: Hugo Albert R., 1858-1927, scholar in the field of Romance languages at the University of Pennsylvania; Pound was his student, 1905-1906 [*SR*, 67n, 182].

24. **Grillparzer**: Franz G., 1791-1872, Austrian playwright and poet.

25. **il Gran Maestro**: I, "the Great Master."

26. **Mr. Liszt**: Franz von L., 1811-1886, Hungarian composer.

27. **Rio Grande**: River in the SW United States on the Mexican border.

28. **Ceylon**: Island in Indian Ocean; now Sri Lanka.

29. **Loica**: Florence Farr, d. 1917; Mrs. Edward Emery, an actress friend of Yeats who went to teach at Ramanathan College in Ceylon because she was dying of a disfiguring cancer [see Yeats, "All Souls Night"].

30. **Smith**: William Brooke S., a young painter Pound knew in Philadelphia, ca. 1905; Pound dedicated *A Lume Spento*, 1908, to him.

31. **medico's**: I, "doctor's."

32. **gob**: A lump of something; a mouthful of spittle. Prob. here slang for "spittoon."

33. **Byers and Feigenbaum**: Prob. acquaintances of Pound's in Philadelphia, ca. 1908.

34. **Joe Bromley**: Joseph Henry B., University of Pennsylvania class of 1905, who seems to have traveled around the world between graduation and the 1908 scene here depicted [NS, *Ezra Pound's Pennsylvania*, 32].

35. **Comley**: Neighbor who lived two doors away from the Pound house in Jenkintown [*ibid.*, 6].

36. **Jaffa**: City on the coast of Palestine.

37. **Shanghaï**: Shanghai, Chinese city.

38. **Tribune:** The Paris edition of the *Chicago Tribune*, Oct. 14, 1926.

39. **Frank Robert Iriquois:** Frank Robert Cheroka, who claimed "to be a Cherokee Indian of high lineage" was arrested in Paris for peddling drugs; he had already in 1924 been expelled from France for the same offence.

40. **Je suis . . . le poids**: F, "I am / stronger than / the Buddha / . . . I am / stronger than / Christ / . . . / I would have / abolished / weight."

41. **Pyrenees**: Mountain range on French-Spanish border.

42. **Martinique**: French island in West Indies.

43. **sont . . . i-ale**: F, "they are the colonial infantry."

44. **voce tinnula**: [cf. 3:18].

45. **Ce sont . . .** : F, "It's the old Marines."

46. **feitz Marcebrus**: P, "Marcabrun made it."

47. **Marcebrus**: Marcabrun, 12th-century Provençal troubadour; line 2 of his crusade song, "Pax in nomine Domini" ["Peace in the name of God"], ed. Dejeanne, no. 35, says *Fetz M. los motz el son* ["M. made the words and the sounds"]. Pound's interest in Marcabrun started early [cf. *SR*, 53, 62, 65; *LE*, 102-103].

48. **Dr. Wymans**: Prob. a doctor who served in Gallipoli.

49. **Gallipoli**: The Gallipoli campaign, 1915, in which the Allied forces made a futile attempt to capture the Dardanelles.

50. and that man: Thaddeus Coleman Pound, Pound's grandfather. The anecdote is prob. one Pound heard told in his family [22:1].

51. pornoboskos: H [from *πορνοβοσκός*], "a brothelkeeper."

52. Pa Stadtvolk: Unidentified. May be constructed from German as "Pennsylvania city person."

53. Prince Oltrepassimo: Prob. pseudonym for Prince Filippo-Massimiliano Massimo, 1843-1915, created Prince Lancellotti, 1865, by Pius IX; from his half brother, Prince Camillo-Carlo-Alberto Massimo, 1836-1921, he purchased the *Discobolus*.

54. saccone: I, "straw mattress"; also one of the members of an aristocratic order who wore sackcloth and were buried in it.

55. Principe: I, "Prince."

56. Discobolus: Statue of the discus thrower by the Greek sculptor Myron; only copies exist, the best known of which is the Lancelotti *Discobolus*.

57. Pope: Giovanni Maria Mastai-Ferreti, 1792-1878, Pope Pius IX, 1846-1878. In 1870, when the kingdom of Italy took over the city of Rome, Pius refused to recognize this abolition of the temporal power of the papacy and announced that he considered himself thenceforth a prisoner in the Vatican.

58. Second Baronet: Sir John Dean Paul, 1802-1868 [RO].

59. Bayle: Pierre B., 1647-1706, French philosopher and critic. His chief work, *Dictionnaire historique et critique,* 1697, was a major document behind French and German "Enlightenment."

60. Sic loquitur eques: L, "thus speaks the horseman" [or "knight"].

61. Levine: Charles A. L., American millionaire and chairman of the board of Columbia Aircraft Company. He hoped to be the first person to fly the Atlantic nonstop, but before his plane was ready Charles A. Lindbergh (probably the "official pet") flew to Paris. Levine, with Clarence D. Chamberlin as pilot, left Long Island on June 4, 1927, and on June 6 arrived at Eisleben, 110 miles SW of Berlin.

62. Azores: Islands in the Atlantic.

63. Miss Arkansas . . . : Prob. Ruth Elder, a pretty girl from a middle-class Alabama family who on October 11, 1927, at the age of 23, took off from New York with her copilot, George W. Haldeman, to fly the Atlantic by the S route. After flying for two nights and one day and weathering a severe storm, they landed in the ocean and were picked up by a Dutch tanker and taken to the nearest land, the Azores.

64. Peoria: City in NW Illinois. Prob. a reference to the familiar image of Lindbergh as a clean-cut, "all-American" boy from the Midwest.

65. Hinchcliffe: Capt. Walter G. R. Hinchcliffe, who had lost an eye in the war, was hired by Levine to fly his plane, the *Columbia*, back from Europe, but the trip was canceled. On the morning of March 13, 1928, he took off in another plane, the *Endeavour*, from an airport in Lincolnshire and was never heard from.

66. Elsie: E. Mackay, 1894-1928, English stage and screen actress. She was the daughter of James Lyle Mackay, Viscount (and later Earl of) Inchcape (1852-1932), chairman of the Peninsular and Oriental and British India Steam Navigation companies, a partner in many other businesses, and a director of two banks (prob. his claim to being a son of a bitch). Disguised as Capt. Gordon Sinclair, Elsie boarded Hinchcliffe's plane and vanished with it.

67. Dennis: D. Wyndham, English actor, married Elsie in 1917 against violent objections by her father. After their marriage was annulled in 1922 after a sensational trial, she resumed her maiden name.

CANTO XXIX

Sources

EP, *P*, "The Flame;" Giambattista Verci, *Storia degli Ecelini*, 1779; Cesare de Lollis, *Vita e Poesie di Sordello di Goito*, 1896; Dante, *Par.* IX; Psalms 42:8; Dante, *Vita Nuova*; Yeats, *A Vision*, 1925; Dante, *Par.* XXXIII, *Convivio* III; Sordello, "Ailas equem . . .," in Cesare de Lollis, *op. cit.*, 196; T. S. Eliot, recollection; "Nondum orto jubare" from "Alba Bilingalis" in *P*, 1909, and *CEP*, 91.

Background

EP, *GK*, 223; Postscript to trans. of *NPL* by Remy de Gourmont; JW, *The Cruelest Month: Spring, Nature, and Love in Classical and Medieval Lyrics*, Yale, 1965 [identified as *Cruelest* in glosses] ; Drummond, "The Italian Background to the Cantos," in *Ezra Pound*, ed. Peter Russell, 1950.

Exegeses

GK, 107-108; Dekker, *Cantos*, 90-97; DP, *Barb*, 109-113; Earl Miner, *The Japanese Tradition in British and American Literature*, 1958, 149-150; HK, *Era*, 336-337; Nassar, *The Cantos of Ezra Pound: The Lyric Mode*, Baltimore, 1976, 48-49; CB-R, *ZBC*, 134-135.

Glossary

1. **Pearl . . . sunlight**: In Pound's early poem, "The Flame" [*P*, 50] , these phrases are used to evoke a sense of the spiritual sources of passion: "in thy mists . . . thou eternal pearl." The lake is Garda.

2. **Pernella Concubina**: Mistress of Count Aldobrando Orsini, who was the father of Niccolò, the elder son mentioned below. The murdered younger son was named Lodovico.

3. **ainé**: F, "elder."

4. **puiné**: F, "younger."

5. **Siena**: [9:48; 10:1, 2] .

6. **Pitigliano**: Town in S Tuscany ruled after 1410 by counts of the Orsini family.

7. **Nicolo**: Niccolò Orsini, 1442-1510, third Count of Pitigliano, a general in the service of Venice. In 1465 he killed his cousin Penelope Orsini, his father's mistress, and her son because she had had Niccolò's brother poisoned so that her own son could succeed the count in the rule of Pitigliano.

8. **Via Sacra**: L, "Sacred Way." The most famous one is in Rome.

9. **Tritons**: Legendary Greek mermen.

10. hippodrome: Either an arena or a track for horse races.

11. Liberans . . . liberatos: L, "And freeing from every chain those who have been liberated." In Verci [III, 496-497] this passage reads "liberating the men and women who formerly belonged to her father and brothers . . . she sends them away liberated and absolved from every chain" [cf. 14 below].

12. sacerdos: L, "priest."

13. Castra San Zeno: Fortification mentioned in the will of Cunizza. The castle is in the mountains between Bassano and Asolo, NE Italy.

14. Cunizza: C. da Romano, b. 1198, married to Ricciardo di San Bonifazzio, ca. 1222; she was the sixth child of Ezzelino II. Between 1227 and 1229 she had (according to tradition) an intrigue with Sordello, who was staying at Treviso with her brother Ezzelino III of Romano, 1194-1259; at his request Sordello abducted her, primarily for political reasons, though scholars are still not sure what actually happened. In 1265 she executed a deed of manumission, giving freedom to all her slaves but cursing those who had betrayed her brother Alberico [6:35].

15. Alberic: Alberico da Romano, d. 1260, podesta of Treviso and brother of Cunizza and Ezzelino III. He was besieged in his castle of San Zeno by the cities of Verona, Vicenza, Padua, and Mantua; betrayed by his own people, he surrendered and saw his whole family massacred before he himself was tortured to death.

16. Lady Cunizza: Cunizza freed her slaves while she was a guest in Cavalcante's house.

17. Cavalcanti: Cavalcante C., d. ca. 1280, father of Guido C.

18. anno: L, "in the year."

19. Eccelin da Romano: Ezzelino II of Romano, podesta of Treviso, 1191-1192, and of Vicenza, 1211, was the father of Cunizza, Alberico, and Ezzelino III.

20. Richard St. Boniface: Count Ricciardo di San Bonifazzio, podesta of Mantua and husband of Cunizza. When Ricciardo discovered the intrigue between his wife and Sordello, the poet was forced to flee to Provence.

21. Sordello: [2:2, 3].

22. Tarviso: Treviso (L, Tarvisium), city in Treviso Province, N Italy; seat of Lombard duchy in the early Middle Ages; home of Ezzelino III of Romano.

23. Bonius: Bonio, a knight from Treviso, with whom Cunizza had a long affair after Sordello was forced to flee to Provence.

24. nimium . . . : L, "too much enamored of him."

25. "The light of this star . . . ": Trans. of *Par.* IX, 33, where Cunizza says she was controlled by the influence of Venus.

26. Braganza: Capital of Bragança district, NE Portugal, and seat of the house of Bragança, former rulers of Portugal. When Bonio died defending Alberico, Cunizza married Amerio of Bragança. After Amerio's death she married, according to some accounts, a gentleman from Verona.

27. Juventus: L, "Youth."

28. "Passing into the point of the cone . . . ": In Book V of *A Vision*, Yeats divides history roughly into 2,000-year periods, which he symbolizes by the figure of two interlocking cones; at the point of each cone the cycle reverses and is repeated in a kind of mirror image.

29. Jo Tyson: Unidentified.

30. O-hon . . . vi'-a'ge: F, "It is sometimes said in the village." Imitation of colloquial language.

31. ephèbe: F, "handsome young man."

32. djassban: Jazz band.

33. Darwin: Charles Robert D., 1809-1882, English naturalist.

34. Deh! nuvoletta: I, "Alas! little cloud"; like *Deh! Violetta* ["Alas, little Violet"], in Dante's *Lyric Poetry*, ed. Foster and Boyde, no. 23, line 1. Pound's translation of this ballata in *CEP* (p. 151), entitled "La Nuvoletta," begins "Ah little cloud."

35. Wein, Weib, TAN AOIDAN: G, "Wine, Women"; H, "Song." From "Wer nicht liebt Wein, Weib, und Gesang, / Der bleibt ein Narr sein Leben lang" ["Whoever does not love wine, women, and song remains a fool his whole life long"], attributed to Martin Luther.

36. Ailas . . . vuelh: P, "Alas, and what good are my eyes / For they're not seeing what I want." Opening lines and refrain of Sordello poem [ed. De Lollis, 196].

37. "Nel . . . mente mia": I, "Inside your womb or in my mind." A combination of *Par.* XXXIII, 7, to the Virgin Mary, *Nel ventre tuo si raccese l'amore* ["In your womb love was lit again"] and *Convivio* III, Canzone Two, 1, *Amor, che ne la mente mi ragiona* ["Love, which discourses in my mind," quoted in *Pur.* II, 112].

38. Faziamo . . . : I, "Let's do it together."

39. Des valeurs . . . des valeurs: F, "Stocks and bonds, / for God's sake, and / more stocks and bonds."

40. Arnaut: A. Daniel [20:12], here a pseudonym for T. S. Eliot. A wave pattern exists in the stonework of the castle of Excideuil, where Eliot voiced his fear of death; Pound changed his name to Arnaut. The castle is associated with the troubadour Guiraut de Bornelh [HK, *Era*, 336-337].

41. les gradins: F, "the steps" of the arena at Verona [12:1].

42. nondum orto jubare: L, "before sunrise." Add P words, *Phebi claro*, for the complete opening line of an early medieval alba which is translated: "With the clear light of Phoebus not yet risen" [*P*, 1909; *CEP*, 91; JJW, *Cruelest*, 193-194].

43. Phoibos: Apollo.

44. Helios: The sun [23:18].

45. Perugia: City in C Italy, capital of Umbria.

46. San Piero: San Pietro, church and monastery on S edge of Perugia.

47. Brookwater: Used of eyes in "Yeux glauques" [*P*, 192].

48. prore: I, "prows."

CANTO XXX

Sources

Luiz de Camoëns, *Os Lusíadas*, 1572; Chaucer, "Complaint unto Pity"; Giambattista Pigna, *Historia de Principi di Este*, 1570; Antonio Frizzi, *Memorie per la Storia di Ferrara*, 1791-1796; G. Fumagelli, *Dictionnaire géographique d'Italie pour servir a l'histoire de l'imprimerie*, 1905; Hieronymos Soncino, *Petrarca*, 1503.

Background

Simon Harcourt Smith, *The Marriage at Ferrara*, 1952; J. A. Symonds, *Renaissance in Italy*, 2 vols., Modern Library, 1935; Edmund G. Gardner, *Dukes and Poets in Ferrara*, 1904, rpt., New York, 1968.

Exegeses

EP, *SP*, 83; DP, *Barb*, 115-131; GD, "Persephone's Ezra," in EH, *Approaches*, 160-161; Dekker, *Cantos*, 65-70, 170-171; CE, *Ideas*, 120-123; HK, *Pai*, 8-1, "Interview"; CFT, *Pai*, 7-1 & 2, 141-154.

Glossary

1. **Compleynt . . . hearde upon a day**: Poss. variation of Chaucer's "Complaint unto Pity."

2. **Artemis**: Greek name of Diana, goddess of wildlife and the hunt [4:14].

3. **Paphos**: Town on SW coast of Cyprus; famous as site of Aphrodite worship.

4. **Mars**: Roman god of war. He was the lover of Venus [Aphrodite], who was married to the lame smith, Vulcan [Hephaestus], "a doddering fool."

5. **Pedro**: Pedro I, 1320-1367, king of Portugal, succeeded his father, Alfonso IV, in 1357; he was the "husband" of Inés de Castro [3:23].

6. **Lisboa**: Lisbon.

7. **'ΥΛΗ**: H, *hule*, "wood," "material," "slime," "shit." Pound says of *hule*: ". . . the stuff of which a thing is made, matter as a principle of being" [*SP*, 83; 35/175; *Pai*, 7-1 & 2, 141-154].

8. **Madame Hule**: Lucrezia Borgia, 1480-1519, daughter of Rodrigo Borgia, 1431-1503, who became Pope Alexander VI (1492-1503). For political reasons the pope, at the behest of his son Cesare Borgia, 1476-1507, arranged for Lucrezia's marriage to Alfonso d'Este, grandson of Niccolò d'Este and young heir of Ercole I, Duke of Ferrara. Cesare, who as Duke of Valentinois [Valentino] had been extending the power of the Borgia family and the Papal States, first arranged for the assassination of Lucrezia's second husband. In view of Lucrezia's dubious reputation, the d'Este family had no enthusiasm for the match and negotiated long and hard for an excessively large dowry; they demanded it be paid in hard ducats before the ceremony, which was performed by proxy in Rome. Finally, Lucrezia set off for Ferrara with a large entourage on a journey that took more than a month because she was feted by a number of important personages on the way; she arrived at the end of January 1502.

9. **Light of the altar**: With the sanction of her father, the pope.

10. **Honour? Balls . . .** : When the d'Este family found the pope pressuring for the marriage, they said the "honor" of the family required the large dowry. These two lines probably reflect the attitude of Cesare Borgia toward their honor (?) and the dowry.

11. **Messire Alfonso**: Lucrezia's husband, who visited her secretly by night a few days before her arrival. The story goes that he looked at her long and hard and, being a

man of few words, departed. He spoke to no one either coming or going. Although Lucrezia made the last stage of her journey on a large ducal barge, Alfonso came and returned on horseback [Smith, *Marriage at Ferrara*].

12. Caesar's fane: The city of Fano in the province of Pesaro e Urbino. Pound is punning on the original meaning of the Latin word *fanum* ["shrine"]. At that time the city was in the territory of Cesare Borgia. Called *Fano Caesaris* below.

13. Duke of Valent: Another title of Cesare Borgia's [5:32].

14. Aemelia: Emilia, district in N Italy.

15. Fano Caesaris: L, "the Fano of Caesar."

16. Francesco da Bologna: A type designer brought to Fano by Soncino [see 18 below] to found a press to publish books in Hebrew, Greek, Latin, and Italian [cf. Fumagelli].

17. Aldous: Aldus Manutius (Aldo Manuzio, 1449-1515), famous Venetian printer who founded the Aldine press and for whom Francesco cut new typefaces. He is usually credited with inventing italic type.

18. Hieronymous Soncinus: Hieronymos Soncino, ca. 1460-1534, one of a family of Jewish printers, who came to Fano in 1501.

19. the text taken: Petrarch's *Rime* which Soncino printed for Cesare Borgia in 1503.

20. Laurentius: Lorenzo de' Medici [21:17, 33, 35], founder of the Laurentian Library in Florence.

21. Malatesta: Family of Sigismundo [8:5].

22. Pope Alessandro Borgia: [cf. 8 above]. One widely accepted legend about the death of the pope says that he and Cesare, who had invited themselves to dine with the Cardinal Adriano Castellesi of Corneto, sent ahead a gift of poisoned wine intended for the host. But either by accident or by someone else's design, they were hoisted by their own petard and became grievously ill. Some days later, after a long struggle, "Alexander died, a black and swollen mass, hideous to contemplate" [Symonds, I, 215-217]. Some contemporaries say both were stricken, not by poison, but by a malignant fever. Whatever happened, the death of the pope brought the efforts of the Borgias in the advancement of art, the spread of Renaissance culture, and the unification of Italy to a quick and dramatic end. Cesare, stricken by the same disease at the same dinner party, never recovered completely enough to exercise significant influence from then on until his death in 1507.

23. Il Papa mori: I, "The Pope died."

24. Explicit Canto XXX: L, "Canto XXX is ended."

CANTO XXXI

Sources

Andrew Lipscomb and Albert Bergh, eds., *The Writings of Thomas Jefferson*, V, VI, X, XIII, XIV, Washington, D.C., 1905; Philip R. Fendall, ed., *Letters and Other Writings of James Madison*, II, 495-506, Philadelphia, 1865; inscription on tomb of Isotta degli Atti.

Background

EP, "The Jefferson-Adams Letters as a Shrine and a Monument," *SP*, 147-158; *J/M*; "An Introduction to the Economic Nature of the United States," *SP*, 167-185.

Exegeses

Knight, "Thomas Jefferson in Canto XXXI," *Pai*, 5-1, 79-93; DP, *Barb*, 142-151 and passim.

Glossary

1. **Tempus loquendi, Tempus tacendi**: L, "There is a time to speak, there is a time to be silent," the personal motto of Sigismundo Malatesta [Ecclesiastes 3:7] which he had inscribed on the tomb of Isotta degli Atti in Rimini. (It is a reversal of the Vulgate's *Tempus tacendi, et Tempus loquendi*.)

2. **Jefferson**: Thomas J., 1743-1826, 3d president of the United States (1801-1809). Born in Virginia, graduated at William and Mary (1862), and studied law. He became a leader in the House of Burgesses, esp. of the patriot faction, and helped form and served with the Virginia Committee of Correspondence. Served in Continental Congress and wrote Declaration of Independence. While president he espoused agrarian democracy. During the years covered by Canto 31 (1785-1798) he was U.S. minister to France.

3. **modern dress**: Some believed that the statue of Washington should be done in a classical mode. Washington agreed with the recommendation that it be done in modern dress.

4. **Congress**: Continental Congress. The First Continental Congress (September 5-October 26, 1774) met in Philadelphia. The Second Continental Congress met in Philadelphia on May 10, 1775. It issued the Declaration of Independence (July 4, 1776) and carried on the Revolutionary War. Mentioned here is the so-called Congress of the Confederation (1781-1788), succeeded in 1789 by the Congress of the United States.

5. **Annapolis**: Port in Maryland; seat of Congress of the Confederation, 1783-84.

6. **Big Beaver**: River in W Pennsylvania.

7. **Cayohoga**: Cuyahoga River, E Ohio. Jefferson, in his correspondence about a possible canal linking Lake Erie and the Ohio River, spelled it both Cayahoga and Cayohoga.

8. **Lake Erie**: Easternmost of the Great Lakes. Buffalo, at E end of the lake, was W terminus of the Erie Canal, opened in 1825.

9. **T.J.**: Thomas Jefferson.

10. **General Washington**: George W., 1732-1799, 1st president of U.S. (1789-1797). Served with British forces during French and Indian Wars (1752-1758), with rank of colonel; retired (1759) to Mount Vernon, Virginia. Member of Continental Congress (1774-75); elected to command all Continental armies (1775); resigned commission (1783).

11. **Maryland**: Middle Atlantic state whose border with Pennsylvania was the Mason-Dixon line, often used to mark the division between North and South.

12. **Connecticut**: Southernmost of the New England states.

13. **screw**: TJ went to see a ship propelled over water by a blade which he said "operates on the air, as a screw does." Because of "the thinness of the medium," he concluded

that it would work better under water [V, 37; unless otherwise noted, all Jefferson quotes in glosses for this canto are from *The Writings of Thomas Jefferson*].

14. **Bushnell**: David B., ?1742-1824, American inventor noted for invention of a submarine.

15. **Adams**: John A., 1735-1826, 2d president of the U.S. (1797-1801). Delegate to First Continental Congress (1774); served as commissioner to France (1777-1778), minister to United Provinces (1780-1782), envoy to Great Britain (1785-1788). Elected vice-president (1788, 1792), serving under George Washington.

16. **Franklin**: Benjamin F., 1706-1790, American statesman, printer, scientist, and writer; member of committee that drafted Declaration of Independence (1776); appointed sole plenipotentiary to France (1778); negotiated Treaty of Paris (1781-1783) with John Adams and John Jay. In 1785, when Congress sent Jefferson as an additional minister plenipotentiary to Paris, Franklin returned to America.

17. **Paine**: Thomas P., 1737-1809, political philosopher. The letter to Paine is dated March 18, 1801.

18. **Dawson**: John D., 1762-1814, member of House of Representatives (1797-1814) and bearer to Paris of the ratified convention with France (1800).

19. **"English papers . . ."**: Source of quote is TJ letter to James Monroe (Paris, August 2, 1785): "The English papers are so incessantly repeating their lies about the tumults, the anarchy, the bankruptcies and distresses of America, that these ideas prevail very generally in Europe" [V, 99].

20. **"Their tobacco . . ."**: The actual figures in source are only Jefferson's estimate and vary from those used by Pound. The point is that selling the privilege of tax collection to a private monopoly is costly to everyone except those who own the monopoly [V, 68-76].

21. **livres**: F, "pounds," French monetary unit.

22. **Maison Quarée**: Maison Carrée. TJ's proposed model for new Capitol to be built in Richmond, VA. In a letter to Madison dated at Paris, September 20, 1785, he calls it "one of the most beautiful, if not the most beautiful and precious morsel of architecture left us by antiquity" [V, 135].

23. **Nismes**: Nîmes, manufacturing and commercial city, capital of Gard department, S France, noted for its ancient Roman buildings, among them a Corinthian temple (Maison Carrée) restored in 1789 and converted into a museum in 1832.

24. **Madison**: James M., 1751-1836, fourth president of U.S. (1809-1817), member of the Continental Congress (1780-1783) and the Constitutional Convention (1787). As a member of the House of Representatives (1789-1797), Madison led the Democratic-Republican party opposition to Hamilton's financial measures. Secretary of state (1801-1809). Source of Madison note is *Letters and Other Writings of James Madison* [II, 495-506], a memorandum account of Madison's differences with his secretary of state, Robert Smith.

25. **Robert Smith**: 1757-1842, secretary of the navy (1801-1809) and secretary of state (1809-1811). President Madison requested Smith to resign the latter post because of his poor conduct of business at the State Department, "particularly in the foreign correspondence . . . which was almost always so crude and inadequate, that I was in the more important cases generally obliged to write them anew myself." Madison also accused Smith of divulging secrets to political enemies and opposing the whole course of U.S. foreign policy toward Great Britain [ibid., II, 499].

26. **that country**: Holland. Jefferson, believing that Holland would rather have its money in the U.S. than in France, is proposing that Adams borrow enough money from Holland to pay off U.S. debts to France.

27. **This country**: France, the country from which TJ is writing to James Madison, August 2, 1787.

28. **XTZBK . . .** : Source reads: "This country is really supposed on the eve of ****." Pound hit typewriter keys at random. Paul Leicester Ford, in his edition of *The Writings of Thomas Jefferson*, deciphered the letters in the original to mean "a bankruptcy" [*Pai*, 5-1, 86].

29. **Beaumarchais**: Pierre Augustin Caron de B., 1732-1799, French playwright and man of affairs. Line starting "I hear . . ." comes from letter of TJ to John Jay, not to Washington. In the whole letter TJ is recommending that foreign officers should be paid hush money. It seems that B. is among them: "I hear also that Mr. Beaumarchais means to make himself heard, if a memorial which he sends by an agent in the present packet is not attended to, as he thinks it ought to be" [VI, 248-249]. A secret agent of the king, Beaumarchais provided arms, ammunition, and supplies for the American Revolution. Such pains were taken to keep the operation under cover that Beaumarchais never got paid for war supplies he sent, and by 1787 he was threatening to make trouble if he did not receive payment. Although he was paid nothing, years later the Congress finally made some settlement to his heirs [32:2, 10].

30. **Potomac**: River in Virginia. TJ's letter to Washington, dated 1788, reads: "It will infallibly turn through the Potomac all the commerce of Lake Erie" [VI, 447]. Jefferson is arguing for the construction of the Ohio Canal [32:12].

31. **a crowned head**: These three lines ["I can . . . parish"] are preceded in same letter by: "I was much an enemy to monarchies before I came to Europe. I am ten thousand times more so, since I have seen what they are. There is scarcely an evil known in these countries, which may not be traced to their king, as its source" [VI, 454].

32. **Lafayette**: Marie Joseph Paul Yves Roch Gilbert du Motier, Marquis de L., 1757-1834, French statesman and officer; commissioned major general in Continental army (1777); supported American interests in France. Letter from John Adams to TJ is dated at Quincy July 13, 1813 [XIII, 308].

33. **John Quincy Adams**: 1767-1848. In 1784 he was secretary to his father, John Adams.

34. **Cul de Sac**: The cul-de-sac Tête-bout in Paris. TJ leased the town house known as *l'hôtel Tête-bout* from October 16, 1784, to October 17, 1785, when he moved to *l'hôtel du Comte de Langeac*, Grille de Chaillot.

35. **Turgot**: Anne Robert Jacques T., 1727-1781, French economist and disciple of the Physiocrats, who based their theories on the idea that agriculture was the sole source of wealth.

36. **La Rochefoucauld**: François Alexandre Frédéric, Duc de La R., 1747-1827, French politician and philanthropist; member of the States-General (1789).

37. **Condorcet**: Marie Jean Antoine Nicholas de Caritat, Marquis de C., 1743-1794, French philosopher, mathematician, and politician.

38. **Monticello**: TJ's residence near Charlottesville, VA. The correspondence cited in rest of this canto was written during TJ's retirement there.

39. **Barlow**: Joel B., 1754-1812, American writer and diplomat. Appointed U.S. consul to Algiers (1795), he succeeded in releasing American prisoners and negotiating treaties with Algiers. In 1811 he was sent to Europe to negotiate a commercial treaty with Napoleon.

40. **Gallatin**: Abraham Alfonse Albert G., 1761-1849, Swiss-born financier and statesman who came to the U.S. in 1780; member of House of Representatives (1795-1801); member of committee negotiating with England after War of 1812; U.S. minister to France (1816-1823); U.S. minister to Great Britain (1826-1827). In a letter to William Wirt, prompted by Madison's dismissal of

Robert Smith [cf. 25 above], TJ is trying to get Wirt to reconcile William Duane (editor of the influential *Aurora*) and President Madison. TJ knew that one of the causes of Smith's disaffection was his intense rivalry with Gallatin, then secretary of the treasury [*Pai*, 5-1, 89; XIII, 54].

41. **Adair**: James A., 1709?-?1783 18th-century trader in Georgia and the Carolinas; author of *The History of the American Indians* (1775) in which he advanced the theory that the Indians were descendants of the Jews. Interesting as one of numerous examples in the early 1930s of Pound's attitude about anti-semitism: he obviously agreed with TJ that it is "kinky."

42. **Eppes**: John Wayles E., 1773-1823, nephew and son-in-law of TJ and, at time of letter, a member of Congress. TJ is attacking the National Bank proposal then before Congress. The proponents of the bill argued that increasing the public debt would be a good thing for business and would lead to increase of commerce and thus to increase of public revenues. The letter concludes: "That our debt was juggled from forty-three up to eighty millions, and funded at that amount, according to this opinion was a great public blessing, because the evidences of it could be vested in commerce, and thus converted into active capital, and then the more the debt was made to be, the more active capital was created. That is to say, the creditors could now employ in commerce the money due them from the public, and make from it an annual profit of five per cent., or four millions of dollars. But observe, that the public were at the same time paying on it an interest of exactly the same amount of four millions of dollars. Where then is the gain to either party, which makes it a public blessing?" [XIII, 421].

43. **"Man, a rational creature!"**: In his letter John Adams introduces the anecdote by saying that Franklin was "unusually loquacious" the morning in 1775 when he told it.

44. **Gosindi**: Pierre Gassendi, 1592-1655, French philosopher, theologian, and physicist; author of *Syntagma philosophiae Epicuri* (1649). In all his works he staunchly defended experimental science.

45. **Epicurus**: Greek philosopher, ?342-270 B.C. The two lines concerning Gosindi and Epicurus are from TJ letter [not Adams] to Charles Thomson dated January 9, 1816, in which he says he has made "a paridigma of His [Christ's] doctrines" and arranged "them on the pages of a blank book." He adds: "And I wish I could subjoin a translation of Gosindi's Syntagma of the doctrines of Epicurus, which . . . is the most rational system remaining of the philosophy of the ancients" [XIV, 358-386].

46. **Patrick Henry**: American "firebrand orator" and patriot, 1736-1799. In 1773 he was a delegate to the House of Burgesses of Virginia. TJ is talking about the "close of the session" of this house. After the session, the people mentioned agreed that they would propose to their house "the appointment of a committee of correspondence" whose business would be to contact other such houses in the colonies so that they could "promote a harmony of action salutary to all" [XIV, 398-399].

47. **Frank Lee**: Francis Lightfoot L., 1734-1797, American statesman; member of Continential Congress (1775-1779) and signer of Declaration of Independence.

48. **Henry Lee**: Virginian also known as Light-Horse Harry L., 1756-1818. American soldier and statesman best known for his abilities as a cavalry commander in the Revolutionary War when he covered Greene's retreat across North Carolina and Virginia (1781); member of Continental Congress (1785-1788); member of House of Representatives (1799-1801).

49. **D. Carr**: Dabney C., 1773-1837, American jurist; nephew of TJ; justice of the Virginia Supreme Court of Appeals (1824-1837). The five lines from this letter concern the controversy about who proposed the "Committees of Correspondence" as a channel of communication among the colonies

before the Revolution. In the early 1880s renewed interest in the history of the Revolution created controversies. Massachusetts claimed that Adams proposed the committees; TJ is explaining how he remembered the events [XIV, 398-401].

50. St. Peter: St. Peter's Church in Rome. John Adams to TJ, February 2, 1816: "That stupendous monument of human hyprocisy and fanaticism, the church of St. Peter at Rome, which was a century and a half in building, excited the ambition of Leo the Xth, who believed no more of the Christian religion than Diderot, to finish it; and finding St. Peter's pence insufficient, he deluged all Europe with indulgences for sale, and excited Luther to controvert his authority to grant them" [XIV, 423-424].

51. human reason . . . : TJ had asked Adams "How the apostasy from national rectitude of France and England can be accounted for?" In reply, Adams says that he does not know, but, he adds, "human reason, and human conscience, though I believe there are such things, are not a match for human passions, human imaginations, and human enthusiasm" [XIV, 424].

52. A tiel . . . scripture: [Source reads *tiels*] OF, "according to such laws; in old handwriting." In a detailed letter about how far common law agrees with ecclesiastical law, TJ shows that an early "falsification" led to historical error. He then writes: ". . . here then we find *ancien scripture*, ancient writing, translated 'holy scripture.' . . . Thus we find this string of authorities all hanging by one another on a single hook, a mistranslation" [XIV, 73-74].

53. Bonaparte: Napoleon B., 1769-1821, emperor of the French (1805-1814). TJ to John Adams, June 5, 1814: "But *Bonaparte* was a lion in the field only. In civil life, a cold-blooded . . . usurper, without a virtue; no statesman, *knowing nothing of commerce*, political economy, or civil government, and supplying ignorance by bold presumption" [XIV, 145-146].

54. Hic Explicit Cantus: L, "Here the Canto ends."

CANTO XXXII

Sources

Charles Francis Adams, ed., *The Works of John Adams*, X, 182-184, Boston, 1856; Andrew Lipscomb and Albert Bergh, eds., *The Writings of Thomas Jefferson*, XI, XII, XV, XVI, Washington, D. D., 1905; Dante, *Pur.* VI.

Background

Charles J. Stillé, *Beaumarchais and the Lost Million*, Philadelphia, 1887; George L. Clark, *Silas Deane: A Connecticut Leader in the American Revolution*, New York and London, 1913; Elizabeth S. Kite, *Beaumarchais and the War of American Independence*, Boston, 1918; Cynthia Cox, *The Real Figaro*, London, 1962; Alfred Martineau, *Bussy et l'Inde Français, 1720-1785*, Paris, 1935.

Exegeses

There is little exegesis for Canto XXXII in the literature, but passing references may be found in most of the major books on Pound. Consult, for example, indexes in DP, *Barb*; HK, *Era*; and DD, *Sculptor*.

Glossary

1. **Mr. Adams**: In 1815 John Adams, former president, responded to a request for information about the causes and course of the Revolution (to be used in a history of the period) with a letter to Dr. J. Morse which starts: "A history of military operations . . . is not a history of the American Revolution, any more than the Marquis of Quincy's military history of Louis XIV . . . . is a history of the reign of that monarch. The revolution was in the minds and hearts of the people, and in the union of the colonies; both of which were substantially effected before hostilities commenced" [*Works*, X, 182-184].

2. **Amphitrite**: French ship belonging to Beaumarchais [cf. 31:29] which carried supplies to the colonists during the Revolutionary War. Details of its cargo and sailing are from a report of an American agent in France who arranged to buy the materials. Silas Deane, one agent, reported the sailing and arrival of the *Amphitrite* and other ships with details of the cargo. But the exact source of Pound's figures is not known.

3. **Merchants of Morea**: The Morea is in the Peloponnesus, S Greece, but the merchants named and the details given in the next nine lines are from an unidentified source.

4. **et des dettes . . . sur les moyens**: F, "and of the debts of the said Echelles . . . / . . . in the principal decrees of the Council, December [17] 66 / weapons and other implements which can only be for / the government's account . . . M. Saint-Libin / well versed in the languages of the country, known by the Nabobs / . . . to excite him, and to follow hot upon the enemy (to the) English / not very delicate about the means."

5. **Echelles**: The Echelles du Levant, commercial ports of the Near East on the Mediterranean, were long under Turkish control.

6. **Saint-Libin**: Palle-Bot de Saint-Lubin, sent by the French government to India to establish relations with the Mahrattas, who were effectively opposing the British. Haidar Ali [cf. 8 below] had already led the Indian princes to victory earlier and in 1778, while the British were at war with the French, he was opposing the British in India again. In 1780 the French sent a fleet to help him [Martineau, 327-330; BK].

7. **Nababs**: Nabobs. Name first given to governors in India under the Mogul Empire. In 18th or 19th century an Englishman who had acquired a fortune in India was called a nabob.

8. **Hyder Ali**: Haidar Ali, 1722-1782, Indian maharaja of the Hindu state of Mysore. At times he effectively opposed the British by joining forces with their enemies.

9. **Portagoose**: Portuguese. A possible explanation of the line: In 1762 Great Britain assisted King Joseph of Portugal in its war with Spain by sending Brigadier General John Burgoyne at the head of 50,000 troops. Together they defeated the Spanish by 1763. During this time Britain had strong bonds with Portugal. After King Joseph's death in 1777, Pombal (his prime minister who had for 20 years brought about dramatic reforms) was dismissed. Under Queen Maria (who was believed to be insane) the ancien régime and the Jesuits tried to break the bonds with Protestant Britain in favor of Catholic France and Spain.

10. **Beaumarchais**: This famous French dramatist was a natural for secret intrigue as

well as an enthusiast for the cause of the American Revolution. Without his unceasing efforts, the colonies would prob. not have received arms and other war supplies. Using a fake import-export firm, Roderique Hortalez & Co., as a front, Beaumarchais tried to conceal his shipments from the English [31:29].

11. **Burr**: Aaron B., 1756-1836, American Revolutionary officer and political leader; U. S. senator (1791-1797). In 1800, running for the presidency, he received the same number of electoral votes as did Jefferson; the election was thrown into the Congress and Burr withdrew from the race to become vice-president under Jefferson. He was tried for treason and accused of conspiring to seize territory from Spanish America to form a new republic in the SW, but he was acquitted (1807).

12. **Ohio Canal**: George Hay, State's attorney for Virginia, was chief prosecutor of Aaron Burr in the treason trial. In a letter to Hay (June 19, 1807), TJ says that Burr had tried to get a man named Latrobe to employ a number of men supposedly to work on a canal opposite Louisville. A postscript to the letter reads: "Since writing the within I have had a conversation with Latrobe. He says it was five hundred men he was desired to engage. The pretexts were, to work on the Ohio canal, and be paid in Washita lands. Your witnesses will some of them prove that Burr had no interest in the Ohio canal" [XI, 236; unless otherwise noted, all Jefferson quotations in glosses in this canto are from *The Writings of Thomas Jefferson*.] TJ believed that Burr wanted the men to conduct an armed rebellion against the U. S.

13. **coram non judice**: L, "not in the presence of a judge."

14. **as usual . . . solid**: In a letter to Hay (June 20, 1807), TJ outlines what is probably the first declaration of executive privilege by a president: "I did not see till last night the opinion of the Judge on the *subpoena duces tecum* [a requirement to produce certain documents in court] against the President." TJ says that since the document was produced *"coram non judice"* he paid little attention to it, but adds: "Yet I saw readily enough, that, as is usual where an opinion is to be supported, right or wrong, he dwells much on smaller objections, and passes over those which are solid" [XI, 240].

15. **Oryzia mutica**: *Oryza mutica* L, "short-grained rice." TJ mentions what he knows of this upland rice in a letter to Dr. Benjamin Waterhouse. It was of interest because it would grow "without any more water than the common rains" [XII, 204].

16. **Sweden**: In a letter to John Hollis, TJ mentions the seed of both "perennial succory" and the "famous turnip of Sweden": the first was received by General Washington from the Board of Agriculture of London and the second was received by TJ himself from a member of the same board at a later time [XII, 253].

17. **rectus in curia**: L, "right in point of law." In a letter (March 8, 1809) to William Short telling him that the Senate had "negatived your appointment," TJ adds: "I pray you to place me *rectus in curia* in this business with the emperor, and to assure him that I carry into my retirement [from the presidency] the highest veneration of his virtues." Short was TJ's minister plenipotentiary to Russia. It was his nomination for reappointment by President Madison which was "negatived"; "this business" refers to the problem of the appointment [XII, 264-265].

18. **Alexander**: Alexander I, 1777-1825, emperor of Russia (1801-1825). The new American government was at pains to develop good diplomatic and trade relations with Russia but to keep out of continental entanglements and wars.

19. **shepherd dogs**: TJ wanted "the shepherd's dogs" because they would be "a valuable possession to a country now beginning

to pay great attention to the raising [of] sheep" [XII, 260].

20. war: In a letter to President Madison (March 17, 1809) shortly after the latter took office, TJ warns him that war must be avoided: "I know no government which would be so embarrassing in war as ours" because of "the lying and licentious character of our papers" and "the wonderful credulity of the members of Congress in the floating lies of the day" [XII, 267].

21. Ronaldson: James R., 1768-1842, American printer and typographer who established a type foundry in Philadelphia in 1796. He carried a letter from TJ to Spain to obtain "antimony" needed to make type so that the U. S. would not have to obtain its books from England.

22. indians: The following ten lines are adapted from a TJ letter (April 7, 1809) to Governor James Jay concerning the right way to civilize Indians. He recommended the raising of cattle and education so that the Indians could run their own affairs, followed by religious training [XII, 270-271].

23. Creeks: American Indian confederacy in SE United States.

24. Cherokees: Later in 1820 this Indian tribe, the largest and most important in SE United States, formed the Cherokee Nation. The tribe was deported to the Indian Territory (Oklahoma) in 1838 [34:83].

25. and as many . . . : After his retirement to Monticello, TJ heard of a libel suit against a clergyman who had defamed him when he was president. He requested the charges be dropped because, he said, respectable men present would swear on both sides of the question [XII, 288-289].

26. Johnson: William J., 1771-1834, appointed associate justice of the U. S. Supreme Court (1804) by TJ. The 10 lines beginning " . . . deem it necessary," written to Johnson in 1823, concern TJ's analysis of the Monarchist party and its ideas during the early years of the Republic. He traces these ideas of government to Europe and describes the ways in which the party sought to "constrain the brute force of the people." Johnson had asked for the information because he was writing a history of political parties in the U. S. [XV, 440].

27. whether in a stye . . . animals: TJ equates the training of kings with the training of animals: "Now, take any race of animals, confine them in idleness and inaction, whether in a stye, a stable or a state-room, pamper them with high diet, gratify all their sexual appetites . . . they become all body and no mind . . . . Such is the regimen in raising Kings" [XII, 377-378].

28. Cannibals: [cf. 44 below].

29. Marshall: John M., 1755-1835, American jurist; one of the American commissioners to France (1797-1798); member of House of Representatives (1799-1800); secretary of state (1800-1801); chief justice of Supreme Court (1801-1835). Marshall established the basic principles of constitutional interpretation by his decisions, but TJ says that in one particular he was unwise: "This practice of Judge Marshall, of travelling out of his case to prescribe what the law would be in a moot case not before the court, is very irregular and very censurable" [XV, 447].

30. animal . . . thought: In a letter from TJ to John Adams [Pound has it reversed], dated January 8, 1825, he discusses the latest scientific theories about the function of the brain and wonders if an animal deprived of that organ would be entirely without thought [XVI, 91].

31. Louis Sixteenth: 1745-1793, king of France (1774-1792). He and all the monarchs mentioned in next 10 lines are named at the end of the letter to Judge Johnson quoted above. TJ's opinion of monarchs had not been tempered by time. The letter reads: "While in Europe, I often amused myself with contemplating the characters of the then reigning sovereigns of Europe. Louis the XVI. was a fool, of my own knowledge, and in despite of the answers made for him at his trial. The King of Spain was a fool, and of Naples the same. They passed their lives in hunting, and despatched two couriers a week, one thousand miles, to let each other know what game they had killed the preceding days. The King of Sardinia was a fool. All these were Bourbons. The Queen of Portugal [the queen of Portugal is the Maria in 9 above and 36 below], a Braganza,was an idiot by nature. And so was the King of Denmark. Their sons, as regents, exercised the powers of government. The King of Prussia, successor to the great Frederick, was a mere hog in body as well as in mind. Gustavus of Sweden, and Joseph of Austria, were really crazy, and George of England, you know, was in a straight waistcoat. There remained, then, none but old Catharine, who had been too lately picked up to have lost her common sense" [XII, 378-379].

32. **King of Spain**: Charles IV, 1748-1819, king of Spain (1788-1808); subservient to Napoleon; forced to abdicate (1808).

33. **King of Naples**: Ferdinand I of Naples and Sicily, 1751-1825; king of Naples (1759-1806; 1815-1825) as Ferdinand IV; because he remained hostile to Napoleon, he fled to Palermo while the French established the short-lived Parthenopean Republic at Naples (1799); in 1806 Ferdinand fled to Sicily where he ruled as Ferdinand III while Naples was ruled by Joseph Bonaparte and Murat; he was restored to the throne of Naples in 1815 and was made king of the Two Sicilies in 1816 as Ferdinand I.

34. **King of Sardinia**: Victor Amadeus III, 1726-1796; king of Sardinia (1773-1796).

35. **Bourbons**: Royal family of France, branches of which ruled Spain, Sicily, and Parma at various times.

36. **Portuguese Queen**: Maria Francisca, 1734-1816; Maria I, queen of Portugal (1777-1816); she was considered by many to be sickly, weak-minded, or insane, and to be a tool of the Jesuits.

37. **Braganza**: Capital of Bragança district, NE Portugal; seat of the house of Bragança, former rulers of Portugal.

38. **Frederic of Prussia**: Frederick II or Frederick the Great, 1712-1786, king of Prussia (1740-1786).

39. **Gustavus**: Gustavus III of Sweden, 1746-1792; king (1771-1792).

40. **Joseph of Austria**: Joseph II, 1741-1790; king of Germany (1764-1790) and Holy Roman emperor (1765-1790).

41. **George III of England**: 1738-1820; king of England (1760-1820).

42. **Catherine**: Catherine II, 1729-1796; empress of Russia (1762-1796).

43. **a guisa [di] . . . posa**: I, "like a lion . . . when he crouches" [*Pur.* VI, 66, describing Sordello, guard of Vale of Princes (note list of kings and queens preceding)].

44. **Cannibals . . .** : At the end of a letter to John Adams (June 1, 1822), TJ uses this phrase as he turns to "the news of the day." He judges that mankind acts like an animal, devouring his own kind, and in doing so displays a "pugnacious humor [which] seems to be the law of his nature" [XV, 371-373].

CANTO XXXIII

Sources

Charles Francis Adams, ed., *The Works of John Adams*, X, Boston, 1856; Julian P. Boyd, ed., *The Papers of Thomas Jefferson*, II, IV, Princeton, 1950; Karl Marx, *Capital: A Critique of Political Economy*, trans. Samuel Moore and Edward Aveling, 1906, I; Paul Wilstach, ed., *Correspondence of John Adams and Thomas Jefferson, 1812-1826*, Indianapolis, 1925; Grigory Bessedovsky, *Revelations of a Soviet Diplomat*, London, 1931; *Congressional Record, Senate*, February 25, 1931.

Background

EP, *Impact: Essays on Ignorance and the Decline of American Civilization*, 1960; *J/M*; E. C. Mullins, *The Federal Reserve Conspiracy*, Hawthorne, CA, 1971; Arthur Kitson, *A Fraudulent Standard*, London, 1917, *The Bankers' Conspiracy*!, London 1933; John Kenneth Galbraith, *Money, Whence It Came and Where It Went*, Boston, 1975.

Exegeses

William Chace, "The Canto as Cento: A Reading of Canto XXXIII," *Pai*, 1-1, 89-100; Davis, *Vision*, 124-125; CE, *Ideas*, 35, 36, 55-56.

Glossary

1. **Quincey**: Quincy, city in E Massachusetts, eight miles south of Boston; birthplace and home of John Adams and John Quincy Adams. The first nine lines are from the letter of John Adams to TJ on date given.

2. **the gent**: Col. William Finnie, quartermaster of the Albemarle County (VA) prisoner-of-war camp, whose inept administration caused many English and German prisoners to be improperly fed and cared for.

3. **P. Henry**: Patrick H., Revolutionary War patriot from Virginia.

4. **Versailles**: City S of Paris where Louis XIV built the palace known as Versailles. The menagerie was a zoo on the palace grounds. The thrust of the whole letter (JA to TJ, July 13, 1813) is that democracy cannot be based on a population "where only two-percent of the people can read and write."

5. **Napoleon**: N. Bonaparte. The same letter expresses the idea that Napoleon's word, ideology, "is meant to define that particular madness in which a great many men, thinking themselves all equal, practice democracy" [Chace, *Pai*, 1-1, 90].

6. **Theognis**: T. of Megara, aristocratic elegiac poet of the sixth century B.C. His best-known work is *Elegies to Kyrnos*, in

which he considers the values of the aristocratic man in human affairs and cites as exemplum purebred stallions that sire better offspring.

7. **Livingston**: Robert R. L., 1746-1813, American lawyer and statesman; member of Continental Congress (1775-1777; 1779-1781); member of committee that drafted Declaration of Independence; first U. S. secretary of foreign affairs (1781-1783); minister to France (1801-1804).

8. **Humphries**: David Humphreys, 1752-1818, colonel in the American army during the Revolution; aide-de-camp to George Washington; minister to Spain (1794). He was recognized as an expert on raising merino sheep.

9. **Merino**: Breed of sheep, originating in Spain, which was known for its fine, heavy wool. Thrust of argument in letter: If these men can introduce an aristocracy of sheep, can one not arrange some control of the aristocracy of America other than the one based on money lust and land lust?

10. **AGATHOS**: H, "good, wellborn." Applied to Plato's philosophy. Correct date of letter to TJ is September 15, 1813.

11. **kalos k'àgathos**: H, "a perfect gentleman." Lit., "beautiful and wellborn." In Karl Marx, *Capital* (259-260), the passage in which this Greek phrase occurs says that the owner of the means of production lives off surplus labor no matter what he is—Athenian, theocrat, or whatever.

12. **bojar**: R, *boja*, member of the Russian aristocratic order that owned most of the serfs and the land.

13. **difference . . .** : TJ to Giovanni Fabbroni (June 8, 1778), explaining why colonial Revolutionary soldiers suffered fewer casualties than those of England by "about one half." He explains that "this difference is ascribed to our superiority in taking aim when we fire; every soldier in our army having been intimate with his gun from infancy" [Chace, 91].

14. **Grand Duke**: Charles Bellini, a known moneygrubber. After the Declaration of Independence the colonies needed to borrow money abroad to promote the Revolution. In a letter dated August 2, 1777, TJ proposed to John Adams (who was trying to obtain money from almost any source in Europe) that he try Bellini, but that it would be wise to get a letter of introduction from Franklin who was much favored in the courts of Europe.

15. **Condorcet . . . Pharisees**: JA to TJ (June 1815). Condorcet's ideas led Adams to conclude that "philosophers have shown themselves as incapable of governing mankind, as the Bourbons or the Guelphs."

16. **"Outline . . . Human Mind"**: *Esquisse d'un tableau historique des progrès de l'esprit humain* (1801-1804) by Condorcet, in which he traces the human development through nine epochs to the French Revolution and predicts that the tenth epoch will be the ultimate perfection of man. JA reached other conclusions.

17. **Pharisees**: The Jewish religious party that insisted on strict adherence to laws, both written and oral. It was a Christian assumption in the 18th century that in their struggles with the Sadducees, who accepted only the teaching of the Torah, the Pharisees practiced casuistry and the arts of deception to maintain their position.

18. **Lexington**: Town in Massachusetts. Location of opening engagements of the American Revolution, April 19, 1775. Revolution took place in the minds of the people [32:1].

19. **T. J. on provisions**: Part of letter to Patrick Henry [cf. 3 above].

20. **Bonaparte . . . Jefferson**: JA to TJ, August 1815, letter in which Adams mistakenly predicts a similar fate for Wellington.

21. **Cromwell**: Oliver C., 1599-1658, lord protector of England (1653-1658).

22. **Wat Tyler**: Or Walter T., d. 1381, English leader of the Peasants' Revolt (1381)

in protest against the Statute of Laborers and the poll tax.

23. **Jack Cade**: D. 1450, English rebel leader of the Kentish rebellion (May-June 1450) protesting corruption at court.

24. **Wellington**: Arthur Wellesley, 1st Duke of Wellington, 1769-1852, British general and statesman; defeated Napoleon at Waterloo (1815).

25. **Litterae nihil sanantes**: L, "Literature curing nothing." The line is from JA letter to TJ, June 28, 1812. But the "melancholy . . . snow-storm" lines are from JA to TJ letter, November 15, 1813. The phrase "serpents' teeth" refers to Cadmus sowing the dragon's teeth which led to the building of Thebes [27:33].

26. **Whigs**: The Whig party was one of the dominant political parties in the U. S. during the second quarter of the 19th century. Letter from JA to TJ, September 1816, recalls the reaction to the death of Washington.

27. **$75,000** . . . : From letter of TJ to Nathanael Greene, commander of Southern army, about military requisitions and prisoners. Quote may concern plan to reward Revolutionary War veterans with Western land grants.

28. **Das Kapital**: The ten-line quote is based on Vol. I, Part IV, of Marx's *Capital*, entitled "The Production of Relative Surplus-Value." It concerns the horrors of child labor which was the subject of a parliamentary commission report in 1842. One commentator said it was "the most frightful picture of avarice, selfishness and cruelty on the part of masters and of parents, and of juvenile and infantile misery, degradation and destruction ever presented" [Chace, 94].

29. **Rogier**: Charles Latour R., 1800-1885, Belgian statesman; premier of Belgium (1847-1852). The five lines are from a Marx footnote illustrating that even a supposedly advanced labor country such as Belgium had difficulty passing child-labor laws.

30. **Brussels**: City in C Belgium.

31. **Lord H. de Walden**: Charles Augustus Ellis, 6th Baron Howard de Welden, 1799-1868, English diplomat; minister to Stockholm (1832-1833), Lisbon (1833-1846), and Brussels (1846-1868).

32. **Factory Act**: The British act passed in 1825 shortened the hours of child labor; it was amended (1829, 1831) specifically to regulate child employment in cotton mills. The Factory Act of 1848 was resisted by vigorous propaganda. Marx says: "They denounced the Factory Inspectors as a kind of revolutionary commissioners like those of the French National Convention ruthlessly sacrificing the unhappy factory workers to their humanitarian crotchet" [Chace, 95].

33. **Hobhouse**: John Cam H., Baron Broughton de Gyfford, 1786-1869, British administrator, liberal pamphleteer, and sponsor of an act to control child labor. A Marx footnote says about the Hobhouse Act: " . . . it was forbidden to any owner of a cotton-spinning or weaving mill, or the father, son or brother of such owner, to act as Justice of the Peace in any inquiries that concerned the Factory Act" [ibid.].

34. **Leonard Horner**: 1785-1864, English geologist and educational reformer; appointed in 1833 to a commission on child employment and until 1856 was a chief inspector under the Factory Act.

35. **avénement [avènement] . . . (allemand)**: F, "beginning German revolution posed some new problems, / commercial routine to be replaced by the creation of two / funds (of) gold and wheat destined to the victorious (German) proletariat." Source of this quote and the rest of page 163 is *Revelations of a Soviet Diplomat* by Grigory Bessedovsky.

36. **bureaucrat . . . sanguinaire**: F, "a peaceful bureaucrat, Van Tzin Vei showed himself completely incapable of assuming the role of chief of a bloody revolution."

37. **Van Tzin Vei**: Wang Ching-wei, 1885-1944, Chinese statesman; disciple of Sun Yat-sen who, after Sun's death, led the

left wing of the Kuomintang. He later broke with Chiang Kai-shek and the Kuomintang and, in March 1940, became president of the National Government of China at Nanking, a puppet regime under the control of the Japanese government. Bessedovsky [cf. 38, 39 below] said that a personal friend of Stalin's tried to educate Wang but could not because he was "a peaceful bureaucrat, [and] proved himself quite incapable of leading a bloody revolution" [*Revelations*, 165].

38. Bessedovsky: Grigory Zinovevich B., former Soviet diplomat.

39. Midland: Midland Bank in England. Source shows that corrupt Soviet functionaries, by discounting bills in the right places, pocketed the difference and cheated their own government. But worse, Stalin feared that by taking trade advantage of up to 15 million pounds in Midland Bank short-term credits, the Soviets might fall into a trap that would lead "into an economic, and so political, impasse." Bessedovsky, who believed the Soviets should take the loans, negotiate long-term credits, and develop trade, described the opinions of his opponents: "These fears of the Politbureau coincided with interests of certain English companies, and of quite a number of high officials of the U. S. S. R. Soviet bills, in London as elsewhere, were discounted at exorbitant rates of interest, three or four times higher than that fixed by the Midland Bank" [ibid., 232].

40. 150 millions: Bessedovsky complained about the destructive effect of Stalin's economic policies: "Soviet trade was at a standstill, solely because of these exorbitant rates of discount. According to my estimates, we were spending more than 150 million roubles a year merely on usurious discounts" [ibid., 235].

41. he even: The "he" is W. P. G. Harding, governor of Federal Reserve Board.

42. Federal Reserve banks: The U. S. Federal Reserve Bank is a privately owned corporation organized to serve as a bank of reserve and rediscount for member banks (all national banks and many state banks and trust companies). Federal Reserve banks have the power to issue currency even though they are independent of the United States treasury. The U. S. government has no currency other than the few greenbacks issued by Lincoln which are still in circulation.

43. Brookhart: Smith Wildman B., 1869-1950, U. S. senator from Iowa (1928-1932). The remaining lines of the canto, after "to change the subject," are focused on Brookhart's speech to the Senate on February 25, 1931. The message is that a small businessman is injured, to the advantage of giant corporations, through manipulation of government agencies; private information, denied to the general public, allows a few entrepreneurs to make fortunes [Chase, 98-99].

44. Swift amoursinclair: Swift and Armour are American meat-packers. They, along with the Sinclair Oil Company, were privy to the deliberations of the Federal Reserve Board and knew that the depression was coming, but nevertheless they could make huge loans because of anticipated deflation of interest rates.

CANTO XXXIV

Sources

Allan Nevins, ed., *The Diary of John Quincy Adams, 1794-1845: American Political, Social and Intellectual Life from Washington to Polk*, New York, London, Toronto, 1928.

Background

Charles Francis Adams, *The Memoirs of John Quincy Adams*, 12 vols., 1874-1877; Josiah Quincy, *Memoir of the Life of John Quincy Adams*, Boston, 1859; Leonard Falkner, *The President Who Wouldn't Retire*, New York, 1947; George Lipsky, *John Quincy Adams: His Theory and Ideas*, New York, 1950.

Exegeses

CFT, "Canto 34: The Technique of Montage," *Pai*, 6-2, 185-232; DD, *Sculptor* 135-138.

Glossary

1. **Mitchell**: Dr. Samuel Latham M., 1763-1831, author and former professor at Columbia College. The conversation took place at a dinner with President Jefferson on November 3, 1807, which John Quincy Adams [JQA] attended.

2. **black manservant**: On August 5, 1809, JQA left for Russia, with some of his family and a black manservant named Nelson, to serve as minister plenipotentiary for the newly inaugurated President James Madison.

3. **Consistent . . .** : At his first meeting with the Emperor Alexander, JQA assured him that the "political duty of the United States towards the powers of Europe was to forbear interference in their dissensions" and that the U. S. would support the liberal principles of the emperor in all ways "consistent with their peace and their separation from the political system of Europe."

4. **auf dem Wasser**: G, "on the water."

5. **En fait . . . étourdi**: F, "In regard to commerce this [Bonaparte] is a scatterbrain."

6. **Romanzoff**: Count Nicholas Petrovitch R., 1754-1826, minister of foreign affairs for Alexander I. R. assured JQA that Russians had for years been "Anglomanes" but that England's "exclusive maritime pretensions" made it necessary that Russia support a rival commercial state and that the emperor hoped the U. S. would be such a state.

7. **Freedom of . . .** : JQA thought both England and France were impolitic in restricting commerce and that all the U. S. wanted was freedom of the seas and of commerce.

8. **corps diplomatique**: F, "diplomatic corps." The "only members" were "General

Pardo, a Spaniard, and Count Maistre, a Savoyard."

9. **Shakespeare etc.**: JQA talked with Count Romanzoff about literary men until 2 o'clock, when the court was over.

10. **"Monsieur Adams . . . "**: F, "Mr. Adams . . . I haven't seen you for a hundred years." The remark was made when JQA encountered the emperor on his morning walk.

11. **treaty of commerce**: An idea JQA broached to Romanzoff.

12. **ambassador (french)**: Armand Augustin Louis, Marquis de Caulaincourt. He had a bantering conversation with JQA, who said that France would probably make peace between England and the U. S. because the French had promised to repeal the Berlin and Milan decrees which had closed French ports to American trade.

13. **Tilsit**: East Prussian city where, on a raft in the middle of the Neman River, Napoleon and Alexander concluded a peace, July 7-9, 1807. The peace was broken in 1812.

14. **two empresses**: (1) The dowager empress (wife of Alexander's father, Paul I, who had been assassinated), and (2) Alexander's wife.

15. **un peu interessantes**: F, "somewhat interesting." Ironic restraint. Much excitement surrounded Napoleon's new acts of war in 1812. Nevins added a footnote to his text giving approximate number of troops on both sides and commenting: "Alexander could not mobilize more than 200,000 [sic]." He added, however, that Alexander rightly "counted on space and time to win his victories for him." Napoleon, because of his military difficulties, is said to have added to the old list of elements, "earth, air, fire, and water," a fifth element: mud [51/250; 51:2].

16. **Claud Gabriel**: On returning to Russia, Gabriel said "he was obliged to lay aside his superb dress and sabre, which he had been ordered to wear [in America] but which occasioned people to insult and even beat him."

17. **Oranienbaum**: Town near Petrograd, site of an imperial residence, 1727-1914.

18. **Ld. Cathcart**: William Schaw, 1st Earl of Cathcart, 1755-1843; English soldier and diplomat. As ambassador to Russia (1813-1821) he organized and brought Russia into the last coalition against Napoleon (1813).

19. **Madame de Stael**: Anne Louise Germaine Necker, baronne de Staël-Holstein 1766-1817, cosmopolitan French-Swiss woman of letters who always gathered a group of brilliant people around her.

20. **Qu'il fit . . .** : F, "that he committed the folly of Moscow."

21. **Gallatin**: Albert G. and James A. Bayard joined JQA in negotiating with England the end of the War of 1812. The five lines concern details of the negotiations which were concluded in 1815 [31:40].

22. **Tamerlan**: In Paris, after the Treaty of Ghent had been signed, JQA recorded reactions to Napoleon's arrival in the French capital following his escape which opened the Hundred Days. At the Opéra on the night of March 14, 1815 JQA heard *Tamerlan* (with score by P. Winter and libretto by E. Morel De Chéfdeville, based on Voltaire's *Orphelin de la Chine*) and saw the ballet drawn from A. Boieldieu's *Télémaque*.

23. **Auxerre**: Capital of Yonne department, NE central France; it was on Napoleon's route to Paris.

24. **Ney**: Michel N., 1769-1815, marshal of France. Distinguished French commander, a commoner who in the 1805 campaign against Austria attained a brilliant victory at Elchingen and was created Duke of E. by Napoleon. After Napoleon and Murat deserted the army in Russia, Ney worked valiantly to save the remnants. After Napoleon's abdication he swore allegiance to the

Bourbons, and upon Napoleon's return from Elba he was put in command of the king's guard with orders to stop him. Ney intended to do so, but when he saw that the army dramatically preferred Napoleon he considered the Bourbon cause lost and joined Napoleon at Lyons, thus clearing the way to Paris.

25. **King of Rome**: François Charles Joseph Napoleon, 1811-1832, son of N. and Marie Louise, whom N. had made titular king of Rome.

26. **Tuilleries**: Tuileries, Palace in Paris which both N. and Louis XVIII used as chief residence.

27. **Beauvais:** Capital of Oise department, N France.

28. **Seance Royale**: F, "Royal Interview."

29. **Ah, voui, Vive le Roi**: F, "Ah, yeah, Long Live the King."

30. **Bourbon**: [32:31].

31. **Sir James Mackintosh**: On May 25, 1815, JQA reached London with Gallatin and his friends to negotiate a trade treaty with Great Britain. At a dinner held at Holland House on June 2, 1816, Sir James M. (a scholar and a member of Parliament) asked if Dr. Franklin was sincere when "he lamented the revolution." The three lines are JQA's response.

32. **Samuel Adams**: 1722-1803; activist in Revolution; instigator in Boston Tea Party; signer of Declaration of Independence.

33. **Sir James Otis**: 1725-1783; American lawyer and patriot; Revolutionary activist.

34. **Gouverneur Morris**: 1752-1816. When JQA stopped in New York on his way to Washington to serve as James Monroe's secretary of state, Governor De Witt Clinton and Morris attended a dinner at Tammany Hall to honor him.

35. **Mr. Astor**: John Jacob A., 1763-1848, American merchant who made a fortune in fur trading and commerce.

36. **Tammany Hall**: New York City headquarters of the Tammany Society, founded in 1786, a major force in New York politics until 1932.

37. **Mr. Onis**: Don Luis de O., Spanish minister at Washington in 1819. He negotiated treaty with Spain which ceded Florida to the U. S. in 1821 when there was much popular sentiment against Spain.

38. **Mr. Jefferson**: Return to TJ's conversation with Dr. Mitchell [cf. 1 above].

39. **Mr. Bagot**: Sir Charles B., 1781-1843, minister to the U. S. (1815-1820) when he negotiated the Rush-Bagot Convention limiting armaments on the Great Lakes.

40. **De Witt Clinton**: 1769-1828, New York lawyer and politician whose political fortunes ebbed and flowed. U. S. senator (1802-1803); unsuccessful candidate for president in 1812; for two terms governor of New York.

41. **Banks breaking**: On June 10, 1819, JQA recorded: "Crawford told me much of the information which he is receiving with respect to the operations of the Bank, and the gigantic frauds practicing upon the people by means of those institutions. The banks are breaking . . . . "

42. **Colonel Johnson**: Richard Mentor J., 1780-1850, from Kentucky; in House of Representatives (1807-1819), 1829-1837); in Senate (1819-1829); vice-president (1837-1841). Johnson proposed to JQA that the U. S. sell arms to South American countries so that his friend Duane, a journalist, could be a U. S. agent in the deal. Both President Monroe and JQA opposed such chicanery.

43. **Duane**: William D., 1760-1835, for 25 years the editor of the *Aurora* which, according to JQA, was "the most slanderous newspaper in the United States." JQA wrote: "As to sending Duane as an Agent to South America, he [Monroe] had no confidence in him, and believed him to be as unprincipled a fellow as lived" [31:40].

44. moral considerations . . . : These eight lines are JQA's comments on the behind-the-scenes project of selling, secretly, "any number short of twenty thousand stand of arms" to Colombia to extend the South American revolution into Peru and Mexico, despite the U. S. policy of neutrality.

45. secretissime: ML, "most secretly."

46. vice-presidency: In the spring of 1820 President Monroe seemed destined for re-election in the fall. The vice-presidency seemed the only question. A number of men including Henry Clay were jockeying for position. As JQA wrote, "But the Vice-Presidency is, to call things by their proper names, in the market . . . . "

47. Henry Clay: 1777-1852, lawyer and statesman; House of Representatives (1811-1814, 1815-1821, 1823-1825); supported JQA in election of 1824; secretary of state (1825-1829); senator (1849-1852). First half of sentence Pound uses reads: "In politics, as in private life, Clay is essentially a gamester, and, with a vigorous intellect, an ardent spirit, a handsome elocution."

48. Mr. Calhoun: John C., 1782-1850; representative from South Carolina (1811-1817); secretary of war (1817-1825); vice-president (1825-1832); senator (1832-1843); secretary of state (1844-1845); senator (1845-1850); champion of slavery and the Southern cause. JQA: "We conversed upon politics past, present, and future . . . a vague but wide-spread discontent . . . . The primary cause is that which has been the scourge of this country from its Colonial infancy—speculations in paper currency, now appearing in the shape of banks."

49. Mr. Noah: Mordecai N., 1785-1851, American journalist and diplomat; founder and editor of several New York newspapers; surveyor of port of New York (1829-1833). When consul at Tunis he was "recalled for indiscretions" and "published a book of travels against Mr. Madison and Mr. Monroe. He has great projects for colonizing Jews in this country, and wants to be sent as Chargé d'Affaires to Vienna for the promotion of them."

50. George: George Washington Adams, 1801-1828, eldest son of JQA.

51. George Clinton: 1739-1812, New York lawyer and statesman; member of Continental Congress (1775-1776); governor of New York (1777-1795); vice-president (1805-1812). On December 27, 1820 JQA attended a funeral and conversed with Calhoun about the casual way in which the great men of the nation were honored at their deaths.

52. Elbridge Gerry: 1744-1814, American statesman, member of Continental Congress; signer of Declaration of Independence; delegate to Constitutional Convention (1787); member of XYZ mission to France; governor of Massachusetts (1810, 1811); vice-president of U. S. (1813-1814).

53. half-educated: "Clay is an eloquent man, with very popular manners and great political management. He is, like almost all the eminent men of this country, only half educated."

54. Calhoun . . . concerns: The issue was whether the U. S. should follow the lead of Britain and object to the interference of the Holy Alliance on behalf of Spain to get back their South American colonies. JQA's stand that the U. S. act unilaterally led to the Monroe Doctrine.

55. General Lafayette: In October 1824 JQA went to a party attended by Lafayette and his son. Also present were the "two Misses Wright, maiden ladies, who have followed General LaFayette to this country."

56. So that . . . Washington: Anecdote told twice at cabinet meeting by William Crawford, candidate for president along with JQA and Jackson in 1824.

57. They (congress) . . . : JQA's election by the House of Representatives after his failure to gain a majority of the electoral college prevented his programs for education and other matters from being adopted.

58. Black walnut: On May 23, 1828, JQA visited his nursery: "I discovered also several black walnuts, planted the 22d of March; several almond trees . . . . The black walnut, therefore, and the almond, planted in spring, vegetate to the surface in precisely two months." The presidential election took place in the fall of 1828.

59. May 26th: The day was harassing because most of it was devoted to problems of the military and Generals Scott and Macomb. Mr. Mercer, a member of the House, proposed that "at the demand of General Scott, a Court-martial should be assembled, and that General Macomb and General Scott should engage to abide by their decision. This has been a harassing day; but I perceived a tamarind heaving up the earth in the centre of tumbler No. 2; and I planted in tumbler No. I three whole Hautboy strawberries."

60. Interfere . . . : William Wirt, attorney general, had been asked for his professional services by the Baltimore Railway Company against the Ohio Canal Co. and asked JQA if acting in a private case would interfere with his official duties.

61. Evelyn: John E., 1620-1706; English writer and diarist; author of *Sylva*, a book on practical arboriculture.

62. Clay: Henry C. [cf. 47 above]. After Jackson's inauguration Clay, JQA's secretary of state, called on Adams to say good-bye, since both were leaving government service.

63. Shakespeare: Upon reading *Antony and Cleopatra*, a few days after he left the presidency, JQA made these observations [Diary entry of March 17, 1829].

64. lost relish: On September 24, 1829 JQA reflected at length on a lifetime of reading and added: "But of late years I have lost the relish for fiction. I see nothing with sympathy but men, women, and children of flesh and blood."

65. Dec. 13th: Diary dated December 30, 1829. Margaret Eaton, known as Peggy, 1796-1879, daughter of a Washington, D. C., innkeeper; married John B. Timberlake (d. 1828) and then John Henry Eaton in 1829. When Eaton became secretary of war (1829) the wives of the other cabinet members refused to accept Mrs. Eaton socially. Although President Jackson tried to quiet the matter, Eaton was forced to resign in 1832 [37:6].

66. Mrs. Calhoun: Wife of the vice-president. "Mrs. Calhoun, being of the virtuous, and having then declared that rather than endure the contamination of Mrs. Eaton's company she would not come to Washington this winter; and accordingly she remains in the untainted atmosphere of South Carolina."

67. Quarterly Review: Issue of November 1829. One of the two articles was against America and the other, against Russia. "They are both full of rancorous English passions; but I had not time to read them through" [Diary entry of January 27, 1830].

68. Mr. Van Buren: Jackson's secretary of state who approved Jackson's defense of Mrs. Eaton. "Calhoun heads the moral party, Van Buren that of the frail sisterhood; and he is notoriously engaged in canvassing for the Presidency by paying his court to Mrs. Eaton" [Diary entry of February 6, 1830].

69. President Jackson's spittin' box . . . : Part of scene in a political cartoon calling for Jackson's resignation.

70. Nicholas Biddle: 1786-1844; American financier; appointed director of Second National Bank of the U. S. in 1819; became its president in 1822. Biddle was Jackson's chief antagonist in the "bank war" [cf. 88/583].

71. seat Number 203: At the behest of Massachusetts friends, JQA, after leaving the presidency, ran for the House of Representatives in 1830 and was elected. He took seat number 203 in the House.

72. **Mr. Webster**: Daniel W., 1782-1852; American lawyer and statesman; opposed Jackson on the Second National Bank issue.

73. **Miss Martineau**: Harriet M., 1802-1876; English novelist and economist; author of *Illustrations of Political Economy* (1832-1834). JQA visited her and her friends on January 18, 1835 [JQA has the title incorrect].

74. **L'ami de tout le monde**: F, "The friend of all the world."

75. **in the yard**: Demonstration of some hundred laborers in front of the White House to protest against working more than ten hours a day. President Van Buren said he could not parley with them if they presented themselves in that manner.

76. **Queen Victoria**: In 1837, at age 18, she had just ascended the throne.

77. **Legaré**: The speech made in the House was actually given by Francis Pickens of South Carolina, who said that "if the abolitionists of the North would preach insurrection to the Southern slaves, he would retort upon them by preaching insurrection to the laborers against the capitalists of the North."

78. **battling with each other**: On August 2, 1840 JQA reflects that Calvinists and Unitarians have for many years been fighting over religious issues.

79. **Tippecanoe**: The procession at the inauguration of William Henry Harrison in 1841 included "Tippecanoe clubs." Harrison gained fame in wars against the Indians (1811-1812) and was known as "Tip" for his successful battles against the Indians at Tippecanoe.

80. **The world . . . slave trade**: Entry for March 29, 1841.

81. **Adminstration**: Harrison died of pneumonia after exactly one month as president, and Vice-President Tyler assumed office. The line concerns expectations of his term in office.

82. **haec sunt infamiae**: L, "these are the infamies."

83. **Cherokee nation**: Of the Creeks and Cherokees, JQA wrote on June 30, 1841: "Georgia extended her jurisdiction over them, took possession of their lands, houses, cattle, furniture, negroes, and drove them out of their own dwellings. All the Southern States supported Georgia in this utter prostration of faith and justice; and Andrew Jackson, by the simultaneous operation of fraudulent treaties and brutal force, completed the work."

84. **Buchanan**: James B., 1791-1869, president (1857-1861). On April 3, 1843, in commenting on the approaching elections, JQA wrote: " . . . prospects of Henry Clay irretrievably gone . . . . Those of Tyler, Calhoun, Cass, are equally desperate. Buchanan is the shadow of a shade, and General Scott is a daguerreotype likeness of a candidate–all sunshine, through a camera obscura."

85. **Scott**: Winfield S., 1786-1866; American soldier; Whig candidate for president in 1852.

86. **City of Arrarat**: On a trip to the Middle West taken during the summer and autumn of 1843, JQA's party stopped at Grand Island on the way to Buffalo by boat and "inspected the pyramid announcing in Hebrew and in English the city of Ararat, founded by Mordecai M. Noah" [cf. 49 above].

87. **Firemen's . . .** : At most places on JQA's Midwestern trip, the people celebrated by joining a "torchlight procession" run by local firemen.

88. **Morse**: Samuel Finley M., 1791-1872; American artist and inventor. "Electromagnetic" refers to the Morse code.

89. **Constans proposito . . .** : [Source has "Constans Propositi" from Horace, *Odes*,

III, iii, 1]. Julius Pratt & Co. in April 1844 presented to JQA an ivory cane with a gold ring around it on which was engraved: "To John Quincy Adams Justum et Tenacem Proposito Virum." L, "The man tenacious of his purpose in a righteous cause" [Loeb].

90. 信: C, "Integrity" [M2748: The number of the Ideogram in *Mathews' Chinese-English Dictionary*, Harvard Univ. Press, Rev. Ed., 1943; or any of the various reprints through 1972]. Pound sees the two characters together as "Fidelity to the given word. The man here standing by his word" [*CON*, p. 22].

CANTO XXXV

Sources

Il Monte dei Paschi di Siena e le Aziende in Esso Riunite, 9 vols., ed. Narciso Mengozzi, Siena, 1891-1925; personal memories and experiences from the 1920s and early 1930s.

Background

EP, *L*, 246, 268, 326, 343; *GK*, 79; Alfred Perlès, *Le Quatuor en Ré Majeur*, Paris, 1938.

Exegeses

Douglas Stone, "Pound's 'Mr Corles': Canto XXXV," *Pai*, 2-3, 411-414; EH, *Pai*, 5-2, 345-348; *Pai*, 7-3, 620.

[Some details of the glosses identifying the pseudonyms in this canto were supplied by Reno Odlin. Sometime in 1957-58 he asked Pound about some of the names and wrote notes into his text of *The Cantos*. Some of his notes were supplied, not by Pound, but by others who had asked the poet similar questions. Still other notes had other sources. Mr. Odlin is no longer sure what the original source was; he knows only that he would not have written a note without good authority.]

Glossary

1. Mitteleuropa: G, "Central Europe," esp. that part of Europe which the advocates of Pan-Germanism proposed to form into an empire.

2. Mr Corles: Alfred Perlès, Austrian-born writer whom Pound met at a restaurant in 1934. During lunch Perlès told the anecdote about his World War I experience as a line officer [*Pai*, 2-3, 411-414].

3. Mr Fidascz: Tibor Serly, Hungarian musician whom Pound knew in the early 1930s. He assisted in efforts to start a publishing venture in 1933 [cf. *L*, 246, 268, 326, 343]. Pound eventually gave Serly all his music MSS [*Pai*, 7-3, 620].

4. **Nataanovitch**: Leopold Stokowski [RO].

5. **Mattias Passion**: *Passion According to St. Matthew* by Johann Sebastian Bach (1729).

6. **Fraulein Dokter**: Prob. Marie Stiasny, who is referred to as *Fraülein Doktor* in letters at the Yale archive. She was a friend of Mr. S. Schwarzwald, a Viennese banker, and worked at the Wilhelm Braumüller Bookstore in Vienna. She helped Pound find books on Frobenius and others. Pound may have met her during a trip to Vienna in 1928 [M de R].

7. **Tyrol**: Former Austrian, now Italian, province; it includes Bavarian Alps on N border and the Ötztaler Alps in center.

8. **Francois Giuseppe**: I, Franz Josef [16:23].

9. **Tsievitz**: Unidentified.

10. **Mr Lewinesholme**: Richard Lewinsohn, author of several books about munitions makers, including a biography of Sir Basil Zaharoff, *The Man behind the Scenes*, London, 1929. Lewinsohn was financial editor of *Vossische Zeitung* [18:12].

11. **young lady**: Prob. Judith Cohen. RO says there is a Pound letter that starts: "CAN I see Ma Cohen giving him all the choice bits of the chicken and shoving off the neKK and tail on Pa Cohen because I praised their Judith 'si tante' " [S, "so much"]. RO's notes do not tell him anything more about the letter or where it is now.

12. **Mister Axon**: Unidentified.

13. **Dortmund**: A German beer, Dortmunder Aktien Brauerei.

14. **Alexi**: Unidentified.

15. **Murphy**: Unidentified.

16. **Potemkin**: Grigori Aleksandrovich P., 1739-1791, Russian statesman, first the paramour and then the husband of Catherine II. He was not divorced and no biography mentions the death of his grandmother. Prob. the name is used here as pseudonym for a Russian acquaintance of Pound's who was as practiced in lust as the original Potemkin.

17. **Egeria**: Nymph who in Roman legend gave advice to King Numa in the Arician wood [cf. Livy I, xix, 5]; also classical idealization of a mistress. Thus the Potemkin "cover" was probably a painter.

18. **Mr Elias**: Unidentified, but Pound, tracing the name through Ulysses to the Greek Odysseus, speaks of a current Elias as "identified with the prophet" [*GK*, 79]. RO's notes say simply "Abrams Elias."

19. **Hall Caine**: Sir Thomas Henry Hall C., 1853-1931, English novelist, friend of Dante Gabriel Rossetti.

20. **East End of London**: Section of London lying east of the Bank of England, generally occupied by laboring classes.

21. **dixit . . . ?** : L, "thus spoke the happy Elias?"

22. **schnorrer**: Yiddish, "panhandler" or professional beggar; from G, *schnurrer*, "whirr" or "purr," suggesting the musical instruments traveling mendicants used to play.

23. **a peautiful chewisch poy**: A young artist. Pound gave him work space at Rapallo where he produced "a fairly good imitation Gaudier and then went rapidly down hill." RO believes his name was Heinz.

24. **Eljen! Eljen Hatvany!**: Magyar, "Hail! Hail Hatvany!"

25. **Hatvany:** Lajos Hatvany, a Jewish-Hungarian baron of liberal leanings, was disillusioned of his hopes that the Allies would live up to their democratic war propaganda when, in 1919, he went to Belgrade

to meet the French commander and found him as dictatorial as the Prussians.

26. **Comment! . . . bas?**: F, "What! You have fallen so low?"

27. **Franchet de Whatshisname**: Louis Félix Marie, Franchet d'Esperey, 1856-1942, marshal of France; commanded the French 5th Army in battle of the Marne (1914); in 1918 he led the Allies to victory in the Balkans.

28. **Jewish Hungarian baron**: Hatvany [cf. 25 above].

29. **bojar**: Member of Russian aristocracy which owned most of the land and the serfs and formed an advisory council to the czar.

30. **Virtusch**: Uncertain. Perhaps the Italian *Virtu* [used in the sense of "power"] pronounced with a German accent.

31. **fontego**: I, "chamber." This and the next several "Items" [21 lines] concern petitions made to the duke to form the Monte dei Paschi ["Bank of the Pastures"] at Siena, the central subject of Cantos 42-44 [cf. 42:1-10].

32. **scavenzaria**: I, "special sale."

33. **a schavezo**: I, "at special price."

34. **Brescians . . . Resanesi**: People from Brescia, Cremona, Parma, and Resana in N Italy.

35. **inficit umbras**: L, "tinges with a darker shade" [Ovid, *Meta*. X, 596].

36. **Romagnols**: People of Romagna district of N Italy which comprises the present-day provinces of Bologna, Ferrara, Ravenna, and Forlì.

37. **March folk**: People from the Marches, the region in C Italy extending from the E slopes of the Apennines to the Adriatic coast.

38. **una grida**: I, "a proclamation, ban."

39. **stars**: Small flowers of the olive tree, which blooms in late spring and loses its petals in midsummer [49:23].

40. **St. John's eve**: June 23.

41. **Madamę ὕλη**: H, "Matter," the physical as opposed to the spiritual. Epithet applied to Lucrezia Borgia [30:8].

42. **Madame la Porte Parure**: F, "Madame the Wearer of Adornment."

43. **Romancero**: I, neologism of Pound's. May suggest "aura of romance."

44. **luogo di contratto**: I, "place of contract."

45. **the Dominant**: Traditional term applied to Venice: Venezia Dominante.

46. **De Gama**: Vasco da G., ca. 1460-1524, Portuguese navigator [7:24].

47. **omnes de . . .** : L, "all from overseas regions."

48. **Victoria? Where . . .** : Pound saw an unpublished cartoon by Max Beerbohm with this caption.

49. **undersell . . . rags**: Exact source of these data is unknown. But they prob. concern details of a trade treaty made between Venice and one of her overseas trading partners.

50. **Wazir**: Vizier, high executive officer, usually a minister of state, of various Mohammedan countries, esp. the former Turkish Empire.

51. **Mocenigo**: Tommaso M., 1343-1423, doge of Venice (1414-1423).

52. **Tola, octroi . . . decime**: *Tola*: ML, "toll, tribute"; *octroi*: F, "dues, taxes"; *decime*: I, "tithes, imposts."

CANTO XXXVI

Sources

Guido Cavalcanti, "Donna mi priegha," 5th ed., 1527; rpt. *LE*, 163-167; Cesare de Lollis, *Vita e Poesie di Sordello di Goito*, 1896.

Background

EP, "Cavalcanti," *LE*, 149-200; *GK*, 304-341.

Exegeses

CE, *Ideas*, 14-15, 185-186; Dekker, *Cantos*, 125-128; DP, *Barb*, 154-159; HK, *Era*, 451; CB-R, *ZBC*, 236-237 and passim; JW, *Epic*, 59-85; Bradford Morrow, "De Lollis' *Sordello* and Sordello: *Canto 36*," *Pai*, 4-1, 93-98.; William Tay, *Pai*, 4-1, 37-54.

Glossary

1. **A Lady asks . . . no will to make company**: Complete trans. of Cavalcanti's canzone, "Donna mi priegha" a project Pound had in process for some 25 years [cf. *LE*, 149-200].

2. **virtu**: I, "power." Perhaps "latent power" is a more accurate trans. of this difficult medieval word. Although present-day English "virtue" [meaning sexual chastity] comes from same root, the canzone word has a different meaning. It is distinguished from *potenza* ["force"] in the same line.

3. **Where memory liveth**: Trans. of *dove sta memoria* which Pound uses as a sort of leitmotif elsewhere in *The Cantos* [63:54; 76/452, 457].

4. **diafan**: I, "diaphanous substance," translucent. Albertus Magnus writes in *De Anima*: "For we see light not by itself but in a certain subject, and this is the diafane" [cf. JW, *Epic*, 78].

5. **Mars**: Roman god of war, but here a metaphor for the male principle in love and in contradistinction to Venus [Aphrodite] as a metaphor for the female principle. Pound said concerning the Italian *Da Marte*: "I suppose as 'impulse.' At any rate there is a Neoplatonic gradation of the assumption of faculties as the mind descends into matter through the seven spheres, *via* the gate of Cancer: in Saturn, reason: in Jupiter, practical and moral; in Mars, the 'spirited'; in Venus, the sensuous" [*LE*, 184].

6. **name sensate**: An attempt to render Cavalcanti's hard surface [*e a sensato / nome*]. Said Pound: "Unless a term is left meaning one particular thing, and unless all attempt to unify different things . . . is clearly abandoned, all metaphysical thought degenerates into a soup. A soft terminology is merely an endless series of indefinite middles" [*LE*, 185].

7. **He is not vertu but . . .** : Love [He] flows from virtu just as in the epigraph to Canto 90 [90:1] love is said to flow from the soul. Thus, perhaps, virtu can be called an attribute or function of the soul.

8. "Called thrones . . . ": A pastiche from *The Divine Comedy* prefiguring the attainment of Paradise. The Thrones (to be used as the title for Cantos 96-109) are the angels in control of the seventh sphere (*voi dicete Troni* ["which are called Thrones"], *Par.* IX, 61), the reference to whom is shortly followed (69) by a passage mentioning the ruby (*balasso*, mod. I, *balascio*). Later, and again in connection with the Thrones, Dante refers to rubies (*rubin, Par.* XXX, 66), following ten lines later with a description of the surrounding brilliance of gleaming water and light (*Il fiume, e li topazii ch'entrano ed esconso* [" . . . and the topazes that plunge in and leap forth"]) [JE].

9. Eriugina: John Scotus Erigena, ca. 800-ca. 877, medieval philosopher, theologian, and early Greek scholar. His works on the Eucharist (calling it only a symbol) and on "predestination" marked him as unorthodox [see *EB* for excellent account]. Pound, in *SP* [p. 61], attributes to Scotus the line, "authority comes from right reason," and sees him as an important link in Neoplatonic light philosophy. It was not Scotus whom they dug for, but a disciple of his, Amaury de Bène [cf. HK, *Era*, 451; 74/429; 83/528; *Pai*, 4-1, 49 ff.].

10. Manicheans: Christian sect considered heretical [23:28].

11. Aquinas: St. Thomas A., 1225-1274, scholastic philosopher; author of *Summa Theologica*. Since he seemed to rely on logic, rhetoric, and rationalized dogma and to neglect the *mysterium*, Pound sees him as getting things backward, "head down," and to have no means of support and thus to be "in a vacuum."

12. Aristotle: Cf. *GK*, 304-341, for EP's analysis of the *Nichomachean Ethics* and his suspicions about "Arry's" logic.

13. Sacrum . . . coitu: L, "Sacred, sacred, the illumination in coitus." Scotus Erigena and Cavalcanti saw sex as revelatory, as an expression of the sacred mystery.

14. Lo Sordels . . . : P, "Sordello is from Mantua" [2:3].

15. Goito: Name of castle and town (10 miles from Mantua) where Sordello was born.

16. Five castles: Gift to Sordello from Charles I, king of Naples and Sicily, for service in the battles at Benevento and Tagliacozzi.

17. dye-works: Later Sordello found himself possessed of another village, Palena, "famous well into the 19th century for its fabrics and dyes" [Morrow, *Pai*, 4-1, 98]. When S. found himself responsible for a major industry, his reaction was "what the hell!"

18. His Holiness: In 1266 Pope Clement IV wrote a letter to King Charles reprimanding him for his cruel and "inhuman" treatment of his subjects, even of soldiers who had served him faithfully, including Sordello: "And now your soldier Sordello . . . at least should be redeemed in keeping with his worth." Maybe the pope's letter worked, but not rapidly: three years later, in 1269, Charles began to distribute awards and fiefs, including the five castles, to Sordello [ibid., 94-95].

19. Dilectis . . . Thetis: *Dilectus* . . . L, "Most beloved and familiar soldier . . . the fort of Monte Odorisio / Monte San Silvestro with Pagliete and Pila . . . / In the region of Thetis." Pound's *pallete et pile* are the names of castles in the source as indicated by capitals [ibid., 97].

20. Thetis: Locality in the Abruzzi, Italy.

21. land incult etc.: Paraphrased from same decree as above.

22. pratis nemoribus pascius: L, "meadows, woodlands, pastures."

23. sold the damn lot: [For details of Sordello's transactions, cf. ibid. and De Lollis, op. cit.].

24. Quan . . .pensamen: P, "When I think deep in my rich thought" [line 17, Canso 21, of Sordello; De Lollis, 180].

CANTO XXXVII

Sources

George Bancroft, *Martin Van Buren to the End of His Public Career*, New York, 1889; Edward M. Shepard, *Martin Van Buren*, American Statesmen Series, Boston and New York, 1899; *The Autobiography of Martin Van Buren* (Annual Report of the American Historical Association for the Year 1918, in two volumes; Vol. II, *The Autobiography*, ed. John C. Fitzpatrick); Allan Nevins, ed., *The Diary of John Quincy Adams, 1794-1845*, New York, London, Toronto, 1928; review in Boston *Herald* entitled "Peggy Eaton's Own Story," March 30, 1932.

Background

The Autobiography of Peggy Eaton, with preface by Charles F. Deems, New York, 1932; Arthur Schlesinger, Jr., *The Age of Jackson*, Boston, 1946.

Exegeses

No exegesis has been published for this canto, but most of the major works on Pound have passing references to it. See also LL, *Motive*, 67-68; CE, *Ideas*, 35, 37; Dekker, *Cantos*, 168, 171; Davis, *Vision*, 90-91, 126-127.

Glossary

1. **Martin Van Buren**: 1782-1862, 8th president of the U.S. (1837-1841). A practicing lawyer who early in life became an active Democrat in state politics. MVB is one of the Odyssean, *directio voluntatis*, heroes of *The Cantos* because he supported Andrew Jackson in his war against the banks and he defended Petty Eaton [34:68, 8 below], and also because he fought for the welfare and liberty of the common man and maintained a vigorous antislavery position. After Vice-President Calhoun's faction had paralyzed Jackson's government for two years because of the Peggy Eaton affair, Van Buren resigned as secretary of state; his action led the way for the rest of the cabinet, including Major Eaton, Jackson's secretary of war, to resign, thus making it possible for Jackson to appoint a new cabinet and get the government operating. Jackson responded to these good offices by supporting Van Buren for president in the 1836 election. His enemies accused him of playing politics in these moves; Pound believes Van Buren's actions were morally based.

2. **debt**: As a New York state senator, MVB was faithful to his campaign promise and in 1813 introduced a "Bill for the Relief of Small Debtors." In 1818 he reported a "Bill to Abolish Imprisonment for Debt, and to Punish Frauds," which was adopted by a 21-5 vote [Bancroft, 54; cf. 44/223].

3. **immigrant**: During a brief term (Jan. to

March 12, 1829) as governor of New York, MVB sponsored a safety fund to protect people against bank failures. It was an insurance scheme requiring banks to contribute to the fund. In his inaugural address MVB cited many examples of the need for such a fund, including instances of monetary injustice to the poor and powerless as well as that of the immigrant made penniless [Bancroft, 160; Shepard, 168 ff.].

4. rich patroon: In colonial times governors had issued numerous royal patents which ceded to individuals "hundreds of thousands of acres" in New York with loosely defined boundaries. Those who fell heir to the patents interpreted them as broadly as possible and in MVB's time were "encroaching on a humble class of freeholders" and driving them off their land. "In defending their rights against encroachments, Van Buren stood alone . . . having the ablest of his seniors at the bar arrayed against him" [Bancroft, 8-9]. Under old Dutch law, a patroon was a holder of entailed estates and had certain manorial rights.

5. High judges: As a U.S. senator, MVB opposed extension of the powers of the Supreme Court into the jurisdiction of states. In 1826 he said: "I believe the judges of the Supreme Court (great and good men as I cheerfully concede them to be) are subject to the same infirmities, influenced by the same passions, and operated upon by the same causes that good and great men are in other situations. I believe they have as much of the *esprit de corps* as other men" [Bancroft, 133].

6. The Calhouns: Mrs. Calhoun let it be known that she would not associate with Peggy Eaton because Mrs. Eaton lacked the virtue one should expect in the wife of a cabinet member. As the wife of the vice-president, Mrs. Calhoun rallied most Washington wives to the "standard of feminine virtue" [34:65, 66].

7. Mr. Adams: John Quincy A., defeated for reelection by Jackson in 1828, recorded [*Diary*, Dec. 30, 1830] his understanding of the Eaton affair: "This question has occasioned a schism in the party. . . . Mrs. Calhoun . . . declared that rather than endure the contamination of Mrs. Eaton's company she would not come to Washington this winter."

8. Peggy Eaton: After retiring from public life some 45 years later, Mrs. Eaton left a manuscript for posterity telling her side of the story. Scribner's published it in 1932 under the title: *The Autobiography of Peggy Eaton*. An unsigned review of the book in the Boston *Herald* of March 30, 1932, says: "All the trouble, in the judgment of Mrs. Eaton, was due to 'the Calhounites.' [Calhoun] . . . was Vice-President in the early part of Jackson's first term, as he had been in the term of Jackson's predecessor, John Quincy Adams, and expected to follow Jackson in the presidency. In the cabinet were two or three men whom Calhoun could not control, especially Eaton. The Calhoun men, therefore, must break down Peggy's husband, and the way to do it was to attack Peggy's character. Says Mrs. Eaton: 'I was the victim of these political machinations.' The results were the disruption of the cabinet and the blocking of the political ambitions of Calhoun. Jackson saw to it that Martin Van Buren and not Calhoun should be his successor." The reviewer concludes: "It is hard to believe that Mrs. Eaton did not write the truth in this apologia."

9. muncipal government: Source unidentified.

10. Ambrose: A. Spencer, 1765-1848, significant political figure in Governor De Witt Clinton's Republican party in New York. He opposed all efforts of MVB to extend the franchise at a time when only half the population were entitled to vote. "Ambrose Spencer . . . would not extend the franchise to 'those who work in factories, and are employed by wealthy individuals in the capacity of laborers' " [Bancroft, 78].

11. Van Renselaer: Stephen Van Rensselaer, 1764-1839, New York Republican. As "one of the committee on the elective franchise . . . [he desired] to confine the suffrage to tax-payers who had been longer resident in the state" [ibid.].

12. State Convention: In 1821, as leader of the Democratic party, MVB called a convention for the express purpose of extending the franchise from "freeholders and actual tenants" [ibid., 62-63] to as many citizens as possible.

13. dixit Spencer: L, "said Spencer." To give the vote to those who worked for the wealthy might "in reality give it to their employers. The man who feeds, clothes, and lodges another has a real and absolute control over his will" [ibid., 80].

14. Kent: James K., 1763-1847, judge of New York State Court of Chancery (1814-1823). He said: "I wish to preserve our Senate as the representative of the landed interest." He warned that if the Senate was not so preserved, "our posterity will have reason to deplore in sackcloth and ashes the delusion of the day. . . . The tendency of universal suffrage is to jeopard the rights of property and the principles of liberty" [ibid., 81-82].

15. Tompkins: Daniel D. T., 1774-1825, governor of New York (1807-1817); vice-president (1817-1825). He said: "Property, when compared with our other essential rights, is insignificant and trifling. Life, liberty, and the pursuit of happiness, not of property, are set forth in the Declaration of Independence. . . . How was the late war sustained? Who filled the ranks of your armies? Not the priesthood, not the men of wealth, not the speculators. The former were preaching sedition, and the latter decrying the credit of the Government to fatten on its spoil" [ibid., 83-84].

16. Two words: Said MVB: "There are two words which came into common use with our Revolutionary struggle. . . . They are, taxation and representation" [ibid., 88].

17. Spencer: At the end of a long speech MVB turned to Chief Justice Spencer (whose argument that workers would be influenced by employers put him in a dilemma) and said: "If they are so influenced, they will be enlisted on the side of property which you propose to promote; if they are independent of their employers, they will be safe depositaries of the right" [ibid., 94-95].

18. turnpike: As U.S. senator, MVB opposed federal funding of highways and canals on the grounds that it was an unconstitutional intrusion into the jurisdiction of the states, would extend federal power, and would lead to abuses: ". . . but when the turnpike before the farmer's door depends on Congress or the Cabinet at Washington, the opportunity of local supervision is lost" [ibid., 115].

19. foreign associations: As U.S. senator, MVB vigorously opposed the slave trade, but he rejected the right of England [also opposed to the slave trade] to seize and search U.S. ships. "He opposed every attempt to surrender the 'control of our conduct in the support of our rights, or the discharge of our duties to foreign associations' " [ibid., 144].

20. working . . . stock: In 1836, as vice-president during Jackson's second term and a candidate for president himself, MVB strongly opposed the chartering of the national bank and argued for specie as a circulating medium: "Gold and silver should constitute a much greater proportion of the circulating medium of the country than they now do. To protect the working-classes (who . . . have no control over a paper currency, and derive no profit from bank stock) against losses arising from depreciation . . . should be our 'first object,' as it is our 'imperative duty' " [ibid., 189-190].

21. merchants: In June 1836 a federal surplus resulting from high tariffs was distributed by the Congress among the states, thus exhausting the Treasury. By the time of MVB's inauguration, "every financial evil at once gathered round" his administration. Debts of merchants to Great Britain and the speculation of banks led to massive deflation: "The whole community was involved in the great disaster. The merchants of New

York, unwilling to confess over-trading; the speculators, refusing to condemn themselves for yielding to the bad counsels of eager cupidity . . . all sent their committees to the General Government for relief" [ibid., 199-200].

22. **revenue**: To deal with the disaster, MVB called a special session of the Congress in September 1837 and set forth a new principle in the use of public funds: "The system was a strict recurrence to the principles of the Constitution and to the general laws that regulate commerce. He advised to collect only revenue enough for the wants of the Government; to collect that revenue not in uncertain promises, but in real money, and to keep such revenue under public responsibilities for public purposes" [ibid., 205-206].

23. **banks of deposit**: Part of MVB's plan was to establish an "independent treasury," which would separate the government from all involvement in the credit system of banks and businesses. The act of 1840 "tended to make the flow of credit steady; not adding, in seasons of ardent speculation, new fuel to the flame by throwing the national revenue into banks of deposit to be loaned out for the gain of the banks" [ibid., 211, 220].

24. **patronage**: "By forbidding loans of public money, it diminished the patronage of the General Government, which no longer could select from among eight hundred banks its few favored ones" [ibid., 221].

25. **sailor**: "The evils of arbitrary power in the navy . . . were alleviated and circumscribed; . . . by an order [of MVB] in March, 1839, the sailor before the mast was protected against the lash, except as a punishment ordered by a court" [ibid., 226-227].

26. **land . . . Mr. Clay**: MVB proposed to deed public land to settlers. Henry Clay opposed the plan: "The men for whose benefit it was designed he characterized as a lawless rabble of intruders, as a class entitled to no consideration" [ibid., 227].

27. **Mr. Eaton**: Before the death of Peggy E.'s first husband, her "father had become deeply involved . . . [with well-known merchants] in a contract to furnish the government with pork." By the merchants' chicanery, the estate of Peggy's father was threatened. John Eaton stepped in, assumed all debts, bought the estate at auction in his own name, and then secured the property back to Peggy's father and mother. Said Peggy: "God bless his memory! for God knows that John H. Eaton had no other reason for his munificence towards my dear father and mother than the promptings of his own generous heart" [*Autobiography*, 59]. Washington society thought otherwise. They chose to believe that Peggy's continual munificence to Eaton in her husband's absence had much to do with the promptings of his heart [cf. 8 above].

28. **loose morals . . . uncivil**: JQA wrote [*Diary*, 483]: "There are many features in the character of Mr. Van Buren strongly resembling that of Mr. Madison—his calmness, his gentleness of manner, his discretion, his easy and conciliatory temper. But Madison had none of his obsequiousness, his sycophancy, his profound dissimulation and duplicity. In the last of these he much more resembles Jefferson, though with very little of his genius. The most disgusting part of his character, his fawning servility, belonged neither to Jefferson nor to Madison."

29. **"No where . . . "**: In his second annual message to the Congress, Jackson said that "the resources of the nation beyond those required for the immediate and necessary purposes of government can nowhere be so well deposited as in the pockets of the people" [Shepard, 204-205].

30. **union five years**: Source unknown.

31. **Bank . . . currency**: Recalling that the charter of the Bank of the United States would come up for renewal in 1836, Jackson said in his first annual message to the Congress: "Both the constitutionality and the expediency of the law creating this bank are well questioned . . . ; and it must be admitted by all that it has failed in the great

end of establishing a uniform and sound currency" [ibid., 203].

32. import grain: Within two months after the inauguration of MVB as president, the greatest commercial disaster ever to hit the country occurred. The Panic of 1837 was caused in part by an "explosion" of commercial paper and notes issued by banks. MVB called the Congress into special session and met it "with a message which marks the zenith of his political wisdom" [ibid., 326]. Among the many causes of the panic, he cited "the diversion to other pursuits of labor that should have gone to agriculture, so that this first of agricultural countries had imported two millions of dollars worth of grain in the first six months of 1837" [ibid., 328].

33. Bank of England: During the crisis MVB faced many demands to reestablish the national bank. He said such an act would do nothing: "... the same motives would operate on the administrators of a national [bank] as on those of state banks, ... the Bank of the United States had not prevented former and similar embarrassments, and ... the Bank of England had but lately failed in its own land to prevent serious abuses of credit" [ibid., 328-329].

34. Mr. Webster: Standing against Jackson and MVB and, in Pound's mind, for the forces of usury, Daniel Webster was one of the most vocal defenders of banking interests. But it was Henry Clay who actually spoke the lines attributed to Webster. In a speech to the Senate [Sept. 25, 1837], Clay said he saw no remedy for the panic which did "not comprehend a national bank as an essential part of it." He further asserted that in banking corporations, indeed, "the interests of the rich and poor are happily blended" [ibid., 337].

35. Maccoboy: In 1832-33 Jackson gradually removed $10 million in government deposits from the chartered Bank of the United States for deposit in different state banks, an act that caused an uproar among the bank's supporters. In a Senate speech Clay implored Vice-President Van Buren to go to President Jackson "and tell him without exaggeration, but in the language of truth and sincerity, the actual condition of this bleeding country, ... of the tears of helpless widows no longer able to earn their bread, and of unclad and unfed orphans." Van Buren's response at the end of the harangue was a rebuff: he "went up to the eloquent and languishing Kentuckian, asked him for a pinch of his fine maccoboy snuff, and walked away" [ibid., 253].

36. In Europe: Part of MVB's argument in refusing to support a national bank was that it was not necessary: "Throughout Europe domestic as well as foreign exchanges were carried on by private houses, and often ... without the assistance of banks" [ibid., 329].

37. Relief: In the continual financial crises caused by bad banking practices and speculation, MVB stood firm against those who advised him to solve the problem by increasing the public debt. "We must not turn for relief to gigantic banks .... Relief was to be sought, not by the increase, but by the diminution of debt ... let it be indelibly engraved on our minds, that relief is not to be found in expedients. Indebtedness cannot be lessened by borrowing more money, or by changing the form of the debt" [ibid., 373-374].

38. Justice Marshall: A reference to Jefferson's judgment that John Marshall erred when he sought to make legal distinctions on "for instances" that were outside the case he had in hand [32:29]. The suggestion is that MVB, in citing European practice and the Bank of England, lost contact with the people and consequently was defeated in the 1840 election.

39. Tip an' Tyler: General Benjamin Harrison (with John Tyler for vice-president) ran as the Whig candidate against MVB in 1840. Harrison was elected because of his fame as an Indian fighter in the battle of Tippecanoe. A campaign slogan was "Tippecanoe and Tyler too." A campaign song ran: "Farewell, dear Van, / You're not our man; / To guard the ship, / We'll try old Tip. / With Tip and Tyler / We'll burst Van's biler" [Shepard, 389].

40. luxuria . . . furculis: L, "luxury but with golden forks" [26:25, 27]. This "vice" was attributed to MVB as opposed to Harrison, who provided for his followers a barrel of cider and told his soldiers that his door would never be shut. "Van Buren meantime, with an aristocratic sneer upon his face, was seated in an English carriage, after feeding himself from the famous gold spoons bought for the White House" [ibid., 388].

41. Mr. Lee: MVB did not approve of ostentation. He wrote later: "As far back as . . . Mr. Monroe's administration, a quantity of very extravagant French furniture was purchased for the Presidential mansion, through the agency of Consul Lee, himself an ostentatious man; and among the rest, a parcel of spoons, which were alleged to be of pure gold" [*Autobiography*, 769].

42. doughface: In 1835 a bill was introduced in the Senate forbidding postmasters to deliver antislavery material. MVB's political enemies skillfully contrived to achieve a tie so that MVB would have to cast the deciding vote. If he voted for the bill, they believed he would lose some of his Southern support. Recognizing the nature of the plot against him as political, MVB cast a "political" vote for the bill. Shepard says: "Van Buren never deserved to be called a 'Northern with Southern principles' " [278]. "Doughface" was an epithet for Southern whites who defended slavery. Shepard's index refers to the vote by the phrase: "Not a 'doughface,' 278" [Shepard, 494].

43. Authorized: Anticipating the possible veto by President Jackson of any congressional act extending the charter of the Bank of the United States, Nicholas Biddle [34:70], president of the bank, began, in the last half of Jackson's first term, to build a political campaign in the press. The idea was to prevent Jackson's reelection if he exercised his veto power. MVB wrote: "The exercise of that power was the obstacle most feared by the bank. . . . Authorization of its President to employ the funds of the institution at his discretion to influence the Press . . . had been provided for" [*Autobiography*, 620].

44. veto power: MVB wrote: "The possession of majorities in both branches of the national Legislature enabled the bank to drive the Executive to resort to the extreme power [of the veto] . . . . This power . . . had been used with marked hesitation and reserve by his predecessors and was nowhere favorably received" [ibid.].

45. charter existing: Nicholas Biddle had intimations of Jackson's attitude from remarks made in his first two annual messages: "These intimations and declarations went no further than to announce objections to the bank under its existing charter" [ibid., 619].

46. Friendly feeling . . . November: The editor of MVB's *Autobiography* wrote: "It is well-nigh impossible for natures like Andrew Jackson and Nicholas Biddle to understand each other and that Biddle misunderstood the situation does not seem to have occurred to Van Buren even as a remote possibility" [ibid., 619n]. But Biddle did misunderstand, as shown by letters he wrote after a meeting with Jackson: "I found with great pleasure a friendly feeling towards the Bank in the minds of the President & his particular friends" [letter to Robert Lennox, 1759-1839, New York merchant and president of the New York Chamber of Commerce, 1827-1839]; "The rumor to which you allude, I have not heard . . . & I believe it is entirely without foundation . . . . I had much conversation of a very full & frank character with the President. . . . [He] spoke in terms the most kind & gratifying towards the institution—expressed his thanks for the services it had rendered" [letter to Aexander Hamilton; for Hamilton cf. 56 below and 62:134].

47. Victoria: Source of the line about Jackson's autograph to the future queen of England has not been identified.

48. line of discounts: One of Biddle's ploys to prevent a Jackson veto was to increase the bank's credit line, especially in the Midwest, so much that financial disaster would ensue if the charter was not renewed: "Forty millions had been for years the average amount of the loans of the bank. In October 1830 they stood at $40,527,523. Between January 1831 and May 1832 they were increased to $70,428,007: the highest figure ever reached" [MVB, *Autobiography*, 621].

49. Sorrento . . . : In 1854, at the age of 71, MVB retired to the Italian coast to rest and write his memoirs. In the first chapter he wrote: "With these scanty preparations, but under the stimulus imparted by high health, the exhilaration of this beautiful situation and salubrious climate in the mountains of Sorrento, and the thought-stirring vicinage of Vesuvius . . . the island of Capri, and the exhumed cities of Pompeii and Herculaneum, I have once more determined . . . [to write the autobiography]." He worked from many documents and from memory [ibid., 9].

50. Dan Webster . . . : No one supported the bank more vigorously than Webster. MVB, though granting Webster "consummate ability" in oratory, shows that the materials he used came directly from Biddle and his henchmen. The bill to renew the charter of the bank passed both branches of Congress, but Jackson "interposed his *veto*, and the Bill failed for want of a two-thirds vote." To get that two-thirds vote, Webster had pulled out all his stops. MVB commented: "Thirty millions of the capital of the bank (said he) are now on loan and discount in States on the Mississippi. These will all have to be called in within three years and nine months if the charter is not extended . . . . 'I hesitate not to say,' he continued, 'that as this *Veto* travels to the West it will depreciate the value of every man's property from the Atlantic to the Capital of Missouri. Its effects will be found in the price of land, the great and leading article of Western property, in the price of crops, in the produce of labor, in the repression of enterprise and in embarrassments of every kind of business and occupation' " [ibid., 622-623].

51. de mortuis: L, "about the dead." In avowing to tell the whole truth about the fight over the bank charter, MVB saw that he would have to tell about acts less than good done by people now dead: "The aphorism *'de mortuis nil nisi bonum'* [about the dead nothing except good] is doubtless founded in the most humane principles . . . ; it does not however apply to a case of this character" [ibid., 629].

52. 4 to 5 . . . secret service: MVB cites figures to show the enormous monetary power wielded by the president of the bank, compared with the limited control of the president of the country over federal funds; then he shows how the bank deliberately used its power to cause financial chaos and panic: "The balance of the National Treasury, at the commencement of the 'panic session' was between four and five millions, the receipts from all sources for the year between 31 and 32 millions and the estimate of the accruing revenue for the year, from which it did not vary much, amounted to between 32 and 33 millions, whilst the annual operations of the bank in discounts and foreign and domestic exchanges and according to its own published statements, at the same period amounted to three hundred and forty one millions of dollars, and it had on deposit a yearly average in its vaults of six millions of dollars belonging to the Federal Government, besides the deposits of individuals. The revenue of the United States was in due time appropriated by law to specific purposes, but whether this was or was not done the President could not use a cent of it, until after the passage of the law authorising him to do so, without exposing himself to the penalties of impeachment; and of the national legislature, by which alone such an act could be passed, it is not too much to say that a majority in one of its branches—the Senate—were the devoted partisans of the bank. The public money subject to the individual control of the President was that portion constituting the secret service fund, which was limited to fifteen or twenty thousand dollars" [ibid., 633].

53. **employing . . .** : It was MVB's opinion that after Jackson's veto the bank and its defenders deliberately devised a plan to create panic and financial distress, so that the Congress would submit the Act of Renewal again and Jackson would be forced to sign it: "Hence the origin of the plan which was carried out with such unrelenting vigor,–that of employing the vast means at the disposal of the bank in deranging the credits of the Country and of embarrassing business concerns to an extent sufficient to create wide spread distress and to infuse intense alarm for the safety of its every interest into all the ramifications of a great community–to excite public indignation against the Executive branch of the Government by imputing these disastrous occurrences to the interposition of the President's *Veto* and to the necessity he had wantonly imposed on the bank of preparing to wind up its affairs" [ibid., 639-640].

54. **Bank's directors**: One of Biddle's acts was to appoint a special committee with power to supersede the actions of the authorized board of directors: "most important . . . was . . . the 'Exchange Committee,' composed of only five directors, of whom the President of the bank was one and the other four were selected by him, and the bestowment of all but unlimited power on this Committee, whose doings were confidential and from whose councils the Government directors were invariably excluded" [ibid., 641].

55. **Bank president–thirties**: These phrases may be found in random order in the source [ibid., 648-649].

56. **Mr. Hamilton**: MVB does not impute to Biddle any design "to feather his own nest." Biddle was as innocent of acting for his own monetary gain as was Alexander Hamilton; he, like "Hamilton, who never hesitated to jeopard the general for the support and encouragement of special interests . . . would never have countenanced the application of the public money in direct bribery and would not have . . . permitted a dollar of it to reach his own pocket unworthily" [ibid., 650].

57. **Bank curtailed**: As part of its program of creating panic, the bank managed a "total reduction in thirteen months, including that which took place before the first of December, $17,100,851 upon a discount line of sixty four millions" [ibid., 654].

58. **Mr. Taney . . .1834**: Roger P. T., secretary of the treasury, was praised by Churchill C. Cambreleng, a representative from New York: "Armed with these millions in Western drafts, with balances steadily accumulating, the branch at New York would have drawn from our city banks their last dollar and would have broken every bank in the Union had not the Secretary of the Treasury . . . prevented that branch from collecting $8,760,000–had he not armed our city institutions with near nine millions to defend the whole Country in this war upon its trade and currency. (*Extra*-Globe, 1834, page 181.)" [ibid., 656].

59. **Peggy Eaton**: [cf. 8 above].

60. **Marietta**: Unidentified.

61. **Dolores**: Unidentified.

62. **Placuit oculis**: L, "She pleased the eyes."

63. **Irritable . . . life**: Source unknown.

64. **Sorrento**: MVB stayed at an inn named Villa Falangola at Sorrento while writing his memoirs [cf. 49 above].

65. **Judge Yeats**: Joseph C. Yates was a jurist MVB knew during his years in state politics. Yates was elected governor of New York after De Witt Clinton retired and just before MVB took his seat in the U.S. Senate. Upon his transfer to federal service, MVB found he could still be held responsible for state affairs, an "inconvenience . . . very disagreeably illustrated by bringing me very early into disfavour with the new Governor whose

nomination I had preferred and aided in effecting. Judge Yates was an honest man, possessed of a good understanding, who always designed to do what he thought was right. He warded off too strict a scrutiny into his mental capacities by a dignified and prudent reserve—a policy that long practice had made a second nature" [*Autobiography*, 113].

66. **Alex Hamilton**: When a man named Reynolds intimated that he possessed information that would inculpate Hamilton's administration of the Treasury Department, Hamilton revealed to an investigating committee a full exhibition of documents showing that "his connection with Reynolds grew out of a criminal intercourse between himself and Mrs. Reynolds" [ibid., 119]. Eventually Hamilton published the full documents, but his friends were at great pains to have the book destroyed. MVB read it early in life "with great interest, and could not but be strongly and favorably impressed by the readiness with which Gen. Hamilton exposed his moral character to just censure . . . while vindicating his official conduct from unmerited reproach" [ibid., 120-121].

67. **Marshall, said Roane**: MVB took a trip to Richmond, VA to visit Spencer Roane [1762-1822, American jurist and political writer] and found him on a sickbed from which he never rose, but he also found Roane to be "a root and branch Democrat, clear headed, honest hearted, and always able and ready to defend the right regardless of personal consequences." The two men talked for several hours: "Mr. Roane referred . . . to the course of the Supreme Court, under the lead of Chief Justice Marshall, in undermining some of the most valuable clauses of the Constitution to support the pretensions of the Bank of the United States" [ibid., 126].

68. **Tom Jefferson**: As MVB was leaving, he referred to the way Roane had arranged the busts of Jefferson, Madison, and Monroe in the room, and said that "if there had been anything of the courtier in his character he would have placed Mr. Monroe, he being the actual President, at the head instead of the foot. He replied with emphasis, 'No! No! No man ranks before Tom Jefferson in my house!' " [ibid., 126-127].

69. **wool-buyers** . . . : A number of New York woolgrowers had succeeded in having a "Woollens Bill" introduced into Congress as a protectionist measure. Since MVB was a fervent free-trade Democrat, a number of his opponents sought to humiliate him publicly by passing a vote of censure against him for his course of action in regard to the bill. At a public meeting at the Capitol arranged for this purpose, MVB listened to all that anyone else had to say and then "addressed the meeting for nearly two hours." His friend Benjamin Knower was in the audience; and the meeting ended without taking up the question of censure. MVB thought the speech one of his best speeches, though admitting a defect: "Mr. Knower came to me in the evening and told me that, on his way home from the Capitol, Mr. Wood, one of his wool buyers and a sensible man, said to him—'Mr. Knower! that was a very able speech!' 'Yes, very able!' he answered. 'Mr. Knower!' again said Mr. Wood, after a considerable pause,—'on which side of the Tariff question was it?' 'That is the very point I was thinking about when you first spoke to me, Mr. Wood!' replied Knower.

"I have frequently been told and have always believed that I rendered much service to the cause of truth by that speech, but this conversation between two intelligent and interested men would seem to indicate that directness on all points had not been its most prominent feature" [ibid., 170-171].

70. **James Jones . . . compromise**: Because of a series of contretemps caused by several well-intentioned but inept politicians, MVB's party was in a shambles: "I left Albany for Washington as completely broken down a politician as my bitterest enemies could desire. On board of the small steamer that took us to the larger one that waited for her passengers below the *overslaugh* it was my

luck to meet Mrs. Clinton (the Governor's wife) and her brother James Jones. The latter said to me whilst we were seated at the breakfast table, 'Now is the time admirably fitted for a settlement of all difficulties between Mr. Clinton and yourself.' I thanked him for his friendly suggestion—the sincerity of which I did not in the least doubt—But replied that my fortunes were at too low an ebb to be made the subject of a compromise, and that when they improved a little I would remember his generous offer" [ibid., 149].

71. **John Adams**: MVB reflects in several pages on "Mr. Adams's subsequent failure in public life" and concludes that it "was, in no [in]considerable degree, owing to an overweening self esteem and consequent impatience under honors conferred on his contemporaries." He adds: "These well known circumstances, in connection with his after expressed admiration of the English system, always excepting its corruptions, gave rise to the imputation, undoubtedly unjust, that his resistance to the Crown did not arise so much from opposition to Monarchy in the abstract as to a natural preference for the House of Braintree over that of Hanover" [ibid., 189-190].

72. **his son**: John Quincy Adams, sixth president [34:passim], was seen by MVB to be burdened by the unpopularity of his father as well as by an insensitivity to political realities. To make his point, MVB quoted from JQA's first annual message in ironical tone to show the fantastic nature of his program, which "embraced among several other specified objects a University and Astronomical Observatories, describing the latter as 'light houses of the skies!' " He implied that JQA had a deficient sense of the meaning of the democratic process by citing the end of his first annual message: it "closed with an admonition as to the consequences of attempting to excuse our failure in duty by proclaiming to the world that we had allowed ourselves 'to be paralized by the will of our Constituents' " [ibid., 195].

73. **publicly answered**: MVB tells an anecdote illustrating the effect political labels had on his reputation. He was accused of not taking clear-cut stands on controversial issues. When asked about the content of a letter, a colonel said to a general: "Upon that point his letter is quite *Van Buren-ish* and leaves us altogether in the dark!" MVB denied the validity of the label, saying: "I publicly answered . . . " [ibid., 196-197].

74. **Mr. Webster**: MVB says that perhaps Webster's enthusiastic support of the bank was really disinterested, but if so his "superiority to the influence of money in the discharge of public functions" was not supported by the facts: " . . . his eagerness to borrow and the recklessness with which his loans were made were very generally known and his being largely in debt to the bank and . . . within its power, was undoubted" [ibid., 661].

75. **Damned** . . . : In 1826 Henry Clay accused someone of accepting bribes in issues involving Spanish claims. Clay said: "I think we can pay these people with land." Mr. Buchanan dissented. Then Clay said: "that yellow rascal is to have $70,000 of the money." When asked if he meant Webster, Clay said that he did [ibid., 662].

76. **Taney**: Roger T., secretary of the treasury [cf. 58 above], ordered that government deposits be withdrawn from branches of the Bank of the United States and placed in state banks. For months the adherents of the bank challenged Taney's power to do so just to keep the issue alive, but they never proposed any legislation: "It was, in fact, debated *de die in diem* three months and a day, a duration unprecedented in this or, I believe, any Country and that without the introduction . . . of a solitary proposition which . . . would have reversed the action of the Secretary of the Treasury or have afforded redress to the bank or have relieved the distress of any one" [ibid., 716-717].

77. **HIC . . . LIBERATOR**: L, "Here / Lies / the Liberator of the Treasury."

CANTO XXXVIII

Sources

Dante, *Par.* XIX, 118; EP, articles in *New English Weekly* [*NEW*], 1932-33; Richard Lewinsohn, *The Man behind the Scenes: The Career of Sir Basil Zaharoff*, London, 1929; Dexter Kimball, *Industrial Economics*, New York, 1929; Cary T. Grayson, *Woodrow Wilson: An Intimate Memoir* [*Wilson*], New York, 1960; J. Q. Adams, *Diary*, ed. Allan Nevins, New York, 1928; Charles W. Beebe, *Beneath Tropic Seas*, New York, 1928; Leo Frobenius, *Erlebte Erdteile*, V. Frankfurt, 1925-1929; Lucien Lévy-Bruhl, *How Natives Think*, London, 1926; Lorin Blodgett, *The Textile Industries of Philadelphia*, 1880; Clifford Hugh Douglas, "Credit Power and Democracy," serial in *New Age*, beginning in 1920, and published as a book, *Social Credit*, 1924; Robert Pinot, *Le Comité des Forges de France au service de la nation*, 1919; Franco Sacchetti, *Le Novelle* (181), Florence, 1724; Fenner Brockway, *The Bloody Traffic*, London, 1933.

Background

Leo Frobenius, 1873-1973, ed. Erik Haberland, Wiesbaden, 1973.

Exegeses

GD, "Pound and Frobenius," *Motive*, 33-59; EH, *Pai*, 1-1; CE, *Ideas*, 81-82, *passim*; EH, *Pai*, 5-2, "Answers to Queries"; HK, *Era*, 113-114, 306-307; Witemeyer, in *Occident*, 7-1 (1973), 51-53, rpt. in *Pai*, 8-1.

Glossary

1. **il duol . . . la moneta**: I, "the woe brought upon the Seine [Paris] / by falsifying the coinage [*Par.* XIX, 118]. Outcry against false manipulation of currency which Dante attributes to Philip the Fair, of France, who debased the coinage to a third of its value to finance his Flemish campaigns in 1302.

2. **Metevsky**: Sir Basil Zaharoff, Greek-born arms salesman for Vickers, British armaments and shipbuilding firm, and later one of its directors; he owned shares, also, in Schneider-Creusot [cf. 57 below] and several other armaments firms. "That year" seems to have been 1894, and the two South American belligerents, mentioned in lines 1, 11, 13, 19-23, are Bolivia and Paraguay [18:12].

3. **the Pope**: Achille Ratti, Pius XI. Pound met him when he was subprefect at the Vatican library (1911-1918).

4. **Mr. Joyce**: James J., Irish novelist.

5. **Marconi**: Marchese Guglielmo M., Italian engineer who perfected wireless telegraphy.

6. **Jimmy Walker**: Irish Catholic mayor of New York (1925-1932), involved in Tammany Hall scandals and accused of all kinds of political and religious hypocrisy.

7. **Lucrezia**: L. Borgia, sister of Cesare Borgia and daughter of Pope Alexander VI, who married Alfonso d'Este, heir to the Duke of Ferrara. Possibly she wanted the rabbit's foot as a charm against conception since she had "three children, five abortions, and died of the last" [30:8].

8. **(thus cigar-makers . . . Kimball 1929)**: Dexter Kimball, op. cit., 79-80, verbatim; the context defends the routine manual task imposed by the division of labor on the ground that it leaves the mind free for thought.

9. **Don't buy . . . etc.**: Sales ploy used by Zaharoff to governments of nations: he sold happily to both sides and liked war because it was good for business.

10. **Akers**: Fictional name for Vickers.

11. **gentle reader . . . before**: Not in *The Cantos*; perhaps the "reader" is that of *NEW*, in which Pound first published Canto 38 and to which he had been contributing articles and letters during the year before the poem appeared.

12. **Mr. Whitney**: Richard W., New York banker and stockbroker.

13. **short sellin'**: Selling shares or commodities not yet owned in anticipation of a fall in price.

14. **two Afghans**: Five Afghans went to Europe in 1921 and signed a treaty with Soviet Russia; later that year a peace treaty signed with Great Britain restored the right of Afghanistan to import munitions through India. Committee work on the Geneva disarmament conference began in 1920, under the aegis of the League of Nations; preparation for the conference took 12 years; the conference itself ran from 1932 to 1934 and was never formally concluded.

15. **secretary of something . . .**: Prob. Albert B. Fall, secretary of the interior, who in 1929 was found guilty of accepting bribes in 1922 to transfer government oil fields from the Navy Department to private oil companies. The action led to a Senate investigation and the resulting Teapot Dome scandal.

16. **In the name . . . this date**: In 1901 William Knox d'Arcy, an Australian oil explorer, obtained from the shah of Persia the sole right to most of the Persian oil fields for 60 years; he founded the Anglo-Persian Oil Company, in which both Zaharoff and the British government later took an interest and which Zaharoff used to help penetrate the French oil market.

17. **Mr. Mellon**: Andrew M., American banker who was secretary of the treasury at the time of the Wall Street crisis (1929); in 1932 President Hoover (1928-1932) made him ambassador to Great Britain to provide him a graceful exit from the treasury, but his term expired with Hoover's.

18. **Mr. Wilson . . . prostatitis**: Admiral Grayson, Wilson's personal doctor, who lived at the White House and attended Wilson until his death, has a chapter in his book (*Wilson*) on the president's medical history. Minor diseases such as measles and hemorrhoids are mentioned as well as major ones such as neuritis and phlebitis. Prostatitis is not.

19. **new Messiah**: A label applied to President Wilson who was received with great acclaim in both England and France for his visionary stands in the conferences following World War I which led to the Treaty of Versailles.

20. **Her Ladyship**: Emerald Cunard, 1872-1948, née Maud Burke, usually referred to as

"Her Ladyship" by her daughter, Nancy Cunard.

21. **Jenny**: Pseudonym for Nancy Cunard, 1896-1965, contemporary American poet and patron of the arts.

22. **Ipswich, Agot**: Prob. Margot Asquith, 1864-1945, second wife of Herbert Henry A., 1st Earl of Oxford and Asquith, British statesman; prime minister, 1908-1916. The countess was a celebrated London wit whose autobiography became such a *succès de scandale* in 1920-1922 that she went on to write a novel and several volumes of reminiscences, including *Places and Persons* (1925) and *More Memories* (1933).

23. **And that year**: 1914, when World War I began.

24. **louse in Berlin**: Kaiser Wilhelm II of Germany.

25. **François Giuseppe**: Franz-Josef, emperor of Austria.

26. **Will there . . . May 1914**: An anecdote prob. relating to Violet Hunt, English novelist who lived with, and later married, Ford Madox Ford. Pound saw them frequently when he lived in London before and during the war.

27. **Mr. Gandhi**: Mohandas Karamchand G., 1869-1948, Indian religious and political leader and architect of his country's independence from the British (1947).

28. **if we don't buy . . .** : I.e., armaments and cotton cloth from the British. Gandhi's idea was that the money so saved could be spent on food and the cause of peace.

29. **Monsieur Untel**: F, "Mr. So-and-so."

30. **Jockey Club**: A smart social club in Paris; cf. Pound, "By All Means Be Patriotic," *NEW*, I, 25 (Oct. 6, 1932), 589: "When somebody, for purely social reasons, hunts up Mr Whatshisname, the French toy-maker, and doesn't find him in the Jockey Club, but does ultimately locate him in Japan, some weeks before the Manchurian shindy, this either is, or ought to be, news."

31. **Mitsui**: Japanese holding company whose interests include shipping and armaments; one Mitsui company was a subsidiary of Vickers; also the name of a (related) central bank in Japan.

32. **"The wood . . . gunstocks"**: J. Q. Adams experimented with black walnut seedlings [*Diary*, 374-375, 551]; he also recorded a visit to the Springfield, MA, armory, where "we saw the various processes of making the gun-barrels and the black walnut gun-stocks" [ibid., 552; 34:58].

33. **Muscou**: Moscow (cf. F, Moscou).

34. **Italian marshes**: The Pontine Marshes, drained and reclaimed by the Fascists, one of the projects that inclined Pound to favor Fascist social programs.

35. **Tiberius**: T. Claudius Nero Caesar, 42 B.C. to A.D. 37, 2d Roman emperor. He was adopted as the heir of Emperor Augustus and succeeded him without difficulty in A.D. 14. Pound sees him as an intellectual: "And there are Italian intellectuals, and from the time of Tiberius the Italian intelligentzia has been *talking* about draining the swamps" [*J/M*, 23].

36. **Beebe**: Charles William B., American zoologist who dived to a record depth in a bathysphere in 1934; his book, *Beneath Tropic Seas*, is a beautifully written description of tropical fish.

37. **Rivera**: Miguel Primo de R. y Orbaneja, Marqués de Estella; his dictatorship (1923-1930) of Spain, based on the Italian model, was supported by the king.

38. **Infante**: Prob. eldest son of last king of Spain, Alfonso XIII, who supported Rivera's revolution.

39. **gothic type . . . type**: Cf. Pound, "Orientation and New Sense," *NEW*, II, 12 (Jan. 5, 1933), 273-274: "Vienna is tragi-

comic. . . . Herr Baur [Otto Bauer, Austrian Social Democrat and advocate of the Anschluss, the political merger of Austria and Germany] is (or was a few months ago) still printing his 'advance guard' journal in Gothic type. And they explained to me at the party headquarters . . . that they kept this type because the old people were used to it. Every shop sign in Vienna that is intended to be read, to convey information to the by-passer that something in particular is for sale, is printed in Roman or block letters."

40. **Schlossmann**: Unidentified, but prob. a U.S. correspondent Pound met in Vienna in 1928. The Anschluss refers to Hitler's success in forming a political union with Austria even though a majority of Austrians was against the union.

41. **Baluba**: Should read Biembe; refers to an incident between an African tribe and the German anthropologist Leo Frobenius, whom Pound was reading and admiring in the early thirties; the tribe threatened to attack Frobenius's party, but were deterred by a thunderstorm; next morning Frobenius's interpreters heard the tribe refer, in a drum signal, to the "white man who made the thunderstorm in Biemba"; but Frobenius [op. cit., V, 53] says: "Der Weisse, der in Biembe das Gewitter gemacht hat" [cf. EH, *Pai*, 1-1, 85].

42. **The country**: Presumably Austria; this and the "Schlossmann" episode appear to be private reminiscences. The "hungarian nobleman" is prob. Bernhard Deutsch [35:25].

43. **Kosouth**: Ferenc Kossuth, 1841-1914, leader of Hungarian Independence Party.

44. **losing the Tyrol**: The Austrians lost the Tyrol to Italy in the peace settlement following World War I.

45. **Frobenius**: Leo F., 1873-1938, German cultural anthropologist whom Pound met in 1927. F. spent some 17 years doing fieldwork all over Africa and knew Africans from the Mediterranean to the far reaches of the south. Pound preferred Frobenius's work to Frazer's. In a letter to T. S. Eliot, 1940, he said: "However, for yr. enlightenment, Frazer worked largely from documents. Frob. went to *things*, memories still in the spoken tradition, etc." [*L*, 336]. Frobenius became even more important to the Africans. Leopold Senghor, African poet and first president of Senegal (from 1960), said: "For no one did more than Frobenius to reveal Africa to the world and the Africans to themselves" [*Leo Frobenius*, ed. Erik Haberland, VI].

46. **Bruhl**: Lucien Lévy-B., professor of philosophy at the Sorbonne (1899-1927), took an interest in the "prelogical mentality" of primitive peoples and paid close attention to the details of their languages. Pound's summary may be a paraphrase of Lévy-Bruhl [op. cit., 125-127], but Pound "improves" the thesis to fit his aesthetic theory more closely; Lévy-Bruhl argues, not that natives are incapable of generalization, but that they generalize according to different criteria from those of modern Europeans, including traditional anthropologists like Sir James Frazer.

47. **Romeo and Juliet**: Pseudonyms given to cover a contemporary death and suicide case Pound knew about. Newspaper (or other) cutting unknown.

48. **Mr. Blodgett**: Prob. Lorin B., American economist; his prediction may appear in his book, *The Textile Industries of Phildelphia*.

49. **Douglas**: Clifford Hugh D., 1879-1952, British engineer and economist who founded Social Credit, an economic system championed by Pound, published in *NEW* a five-part essay answering some of his academic critics. "The New and Old Economics" ran in *NEW*, II, nos. 6-10; Pound's "I have of course . . . prices at large" is drawn from the first installment of the essay [Nov. 24, 1932, 126-127]. Douglas wrote: "I have, of course, never said that the cash

(by which in Great Britain is meant not merely 'till' money, but deposits of the Joint Stock Banks with the Bank of England) is constant in amount no matter what may be the amount of deposits which the banks acquire as the result of creating loans. The ratio of cash to loans . . . is simply a result of an actuarial estimate of the percentage of 'till' money in a given country which is required to meet the ordinary habits of the population. On August 4, 1914, as a result of a panic, the population of Great Britain suddenly demanded cash for an unusual proportion of its deposits, with the result that, in the ordinary meaning of the word, all the banks became bankrupt simultaneously. When the depositors had drawn out all the *cash*, about eight hundred millions of *deposits* remained, which were only satisfied by printing Treasury notes."

50. **A factory . . . large**: These 19 lines, taken from Douglas's paraphrase of his A & B theorem in "Credit Power and Democracy" [21-23], form his central critique of the capitalist system of distribution.

51. **per forza**: I, "by force."

52. **and the light . . . bewildered**: [*Par.* XXVIII, 16-19]: "Un punto vidi che raggiava lume / Acuto sì, che'l viso ch'egli affuoca / Chiuder conviensi per lo forte acume" ["I saw a point of light so sharp that I had to close the eyes it burned, so strong was it"].

53. **Herr Krupp**: Alfred K., 1812-1887, who took over his father's small Prussian foundry and turned it into one of the largest steel and armaments firms in the world; Krupp started making musket barrels and breastplates in 1843 and produced his first cannon four years later.

54. **1847 orders . . . Crimea**: Krupp built his first cannon in 1847 [cf. above] and in 1855 took a larger version of it to the Paris Exhibition; Emperor Napoleon III ["Barbiche"] made Krupp a knight of the Legion of Honor, but no one bought his cannon until 1857, when the viceroy of Egypt ordered 36. By that time Krupp had already sold gun bores to France and later supplied guns to both Britain and Russia for the Crimean War, 1854-1856 [Brockway, 53-55].

55. **Pietro il Grande**: I, Peter the Great (1672-1725); czar of the Russians (1682-1725). An honor and decoration bestowed upon Herr Krupp by the Russian government was the Order of Peter the Great.

56. **Command . . . Honour**: At another Paris world's fair, 1867, Krupp was made an officer of the Legion of Honor.

57. **Creusot**: Schneider-Creusot, French steel and armaments firm.

58. **Sadowa**: Battle of Sadowa, also called Königgrätz, between the Austrian and Prussian forces in 1866.

59. **The Emperor . . . Schneider**: In 1868 Krupp sent Napoleon III a catalogue "exhibiting steel cannon which I have supplied to *several powerful European Governments*" [his italics]; the reply, which Pound summarizes, came from General Leboeuf, a relative of the Schneider family; despite the gracious tone, the sale was not made [Brockway, 56-57].

60. **Leboeuf**: Edmond Leboeuf (1809-1888), French statesman, minister of war (1869-1870), marshal of France (1870); disgraced in Franco-Prussian War.

61. **Schneider**: Joseph Eugène S., 1805-1875.

62. **operai**: I, "workers."

63. **53 . . . country**: The figures are from Brockway [58].

64. **Bohlem und Halbach**: Gustav Krupp von Bohlen und Halbach (Alfred Krupp's son-in-law) took the family name and directed the firm during World War I.

65. **Herr Schneider**: Charles-Prosper-Eugène S., grandson of Joseph Eugène Schneider, directed Schneider-Creusot during World

War I when the firm dominated French armaments production.

66. **Eugene, Adolf**: Joseph Eugène and Adolphe Schneider, brothers who established the Schneider company in 1836.

67. **Alfred**: A. Pierrot Deseilligny, 1828-1875, son-in-law of Joseph Eugène Schneider and comanager of the iron works with Henri Schneider, son of Joseph Eugène.

68. **Soane et Loire**: I.e., he was a member for Saône-et-Loire, the region in France in which the city of Le Creusot is situated.

69. **always . . . a conservative**: Charles-Prosper-Eugène Schneider was also a conservative deputy for Saône-et-Loire.

70. **Schools . . . children**: Established by the Schneiders for their workers at Le Creusot; Krupp's, too, built housing, schools, bars, public baths, a church, and a cemetery for their workers; even Zaharoff financed homes for soldiers and sailors in France.

71. **Herr Henri**: Prob. H. de Wendel, director, with his brother Robert, of an old French steel company that cooperated with the Schneiders in 1880 to build a steel mill capable of processing the phosphorus-heavy iron ore of Lorraine.

72. **Chantiers de la Gironde**: Shipyard in Bordeaux partly owned by the Schneiders.

73. **Bank of the Paris Union**: Partly owned by the Schneiders; Eugène was its director. Zaharoff, too, owned shares in it.

74. **franco-japanese bank**: Eugène Schneider was on its board.

75. **François de Wendel**: Son of Henri, president of the Comité des Forges, the powerful French industrialists' union, of which the Schneiders' company was the most important member.

76. **Rober Protot:** R. Pinot, secretary-general of the Comité des Forges in World War I, serving under the presidency of François de Wendel; author of *Le Comité des Forges de France au service de la nation (Août, 1914–Novembre, 1918)*.

77. **'And God . . . Hawkwood**: Sir John de H., 14th-century English mercenary captain who finally settled in Florence. An Italian story tells of two mendicant friars greeting Hawkwood with their customary "Monsignor, God give you peace," to which he answered, "and God take your living from you, too"; when questioned about his rebuff to their benevolence, he replied: "How can you believe you wish me well when you come to me and say, may God make you die of hunger? Don't you know that I live by war, and that peace would undo me?" [cf. Sacchetti, *Le Novelle*, 181; *SR*, 70];

78. **Journal des Débats**: French nationalist newspaper in which François de Wendel had a controlling interest.

79. **Le Temps**: French popular newspaper in which François de Wendel had a controlling interest.

80. **Echo de Paris**: French newspaper that campaigned vigorously against disarmament after World War I; Brockway claims [159] the paper received several large "gifts" from armaments firms to finance the campaign: In "Orientation and New Sense" [*NEW*, II, 12, 273-274] Pound says that the *La Stampa* articles "explain why the 'Comité des Forges' can afford to pay out subsidies measured by the million in francs to the 'Temps,' 'Journal des Debats,' "Echo de Paris,' 'Ordre,' etc."

81. **Polloks**: Unidentified.

82. **Mitsui**: [cf. 31 above].

83. **"faire passer . . . la nation"**: F, "to put these matters before those of the nation."

CANTO XXXIX

Sources

Homer, *Od.* X; *Pervigilium Veneris* [Loeb]; Ovid, *Meta.* XIII, XIV; Dante, *Par.* XXIII, 129, XXX, 62; Catullus XXXIV; Virgil, *Aeneid* VI; *Lyra Graeca* [Loeb], 11, 84; 14th-century lyric, "Alisoun"; *Odyssey*, Latin trans. by Clark and Ernestus, 1804.

Background

EP, "Translators of Greek: Early Translators of Homer," *LE*, 249-275.

Exegeses

EP, *SP*, 53; FR, "A Man of No Fortune," in *Motive*; DP, *Barb*, 161-164 and passim; Dekker, *Cantos*, 171-172 and passim; Surette, *Pai*, 3-2, 204, 211.

Glossary

1. **the cat:** Conflation of many memories including the sound of the looms on the hill path leading up from Rapallo, E.P.'s many years of feeding hungry cats, and, most important, the sound of Circe's loom overheard by Odysseus's men as they approached her house of "polished stone" [*Od.* X, 211].

2. **song**: "They heard Circe singing with sweet voice, as she went to and fro before a great imperishable web" [*Od.* X, 221-223].

3. **ingle**: Gaelic, "chimney corner." The "I" is taken to refer to Elpenor [1:12].

4. **Circe**: Elpenor seems to be remembering scenes in Circe's house after Odysseus and his men had fallen into her snares. Thus we have a flashback to events that took place before the exodus dramatized in Canto I.

5. **panthers etc.**: *Od.* lists "mountain wolves and lions."

6. **tisane**: F, "a decoction of herbs."

7. **Kaka . . . edóken**: H, "She gave them evil drugs" [*Od.* X, 213].

8. **lukoi . . . leontes**: H, "mountain wolves and lions" [*Od.* X, 212].

9. **Helios**: H, Apollo, god of light, father of Circe.

10. **Perseis**: H, Perse, mother of Circe and Pasiphaë [*Od.* X, 138-140].

11. **Pasiphae**: Pasiphaë, sister of Circe who became wife of Minos, king of Crete, and mother of the Minotaur.

12. **Venter . . . cultrix**: L, "Belly beautiful, cunny tender."

13. **Ver . . . novum**: L, "New spring singing, new spring." From *Pervigilium Veneris* [Loeb, 348].

14. **KALON AOIDIAEI**: H, "She sings beautifully." So Polites describes Circe's voice [*Od.* X, 227].

15. e theos . . . thasson: H, "either a goddess or a woman . . . let us quickly call to her" [*Od.* X, 228]. Last line of Polites' speech.

16. honey . . . acorns: Details of what Circe fed the men before and after she administered the "evil drugs" [*Od.* X, 233-243].

17. illa . . . vocem: L, "She hushed with grief, and her voice likewise." Hecuba's reaction to the death of her last child, Polydorus, whose corpse is washed ashore [*Meta.* XIII, 538 ff.].

18. 'Αλλ' . . . Περσεφόνεια: H, "But first you must complete another journey, and come to the house of Hades and dread Persephone, to seek soothsaying of the Theban Teiresias, the blind seer, whose mind abides steadfast. To him even in death Persephone has granted reason, that he alone should have understanding" [*Od.* X, 490-494]. Pound does not give the last line he indicated in margin.

19. Hathor: Egyptian fertility goddess, usually imaged as either a cow or a cow and woman combined.

20. Mava: Unidentified.

21. Che mai . . . diletto: I, "So that never will the delight part from me" [*Par.* XXIII, 129, where past tense ("did part") is used in talking of heavenly bliss].

22. Fulvida di folgore: I, "dark [or reddish yellow] in its splendor [lightning]" [*Par.* XXX, 62]; *fulvido* describes the light (*lume*) shaped like a river in a spring setting.

23. Glaucus: G. of Anthedon. Made immortal by a magic herb, he jumped into the sea and became a sea-god famous for gift of prophecy.

24. nec ivi . . . sum: L, "Nor went I to the pigsty / Nor into the pigsty did I enter." Since Eurylochus did not enter the house of Circe, as did the rest of his men, he was free to report back to Odysseus [*Od.* X, 255-260]. Pound uses *harum* rather than *haram* for "pigsty" because the word occurs thus in his source: Clark and Ernestus Latin version, 1st printing, 1804 [cf. *LE*, 249 ff.].

25. Euné . . . Kirkh: H, "Making love in bed, said Circe." Pound elides *Od.* X, 335-336, and transliterates the Greek *eta* as *h* in Circe's name.

26. es thalamon: H, "into the bedroom" [*Od.* X, 340].

27. Eurilochus: Odysseus's lieutenant who led first party of men to explore Circe's island [1:4].

28. Macer: Prob. Macareus, a companion of Eurylochus's [*Meta.* XIV, 223 ff.].

29. Kirke: H, Circe.

30. "I think . . .": What Circe says when her evil drug and wand did not work on Odysseus [*Od.* X, 330].

31. feel better . . . past: [*Od.* X, 460-465].

32. Ad Orcum . . . pervenit: L, "Has anyone ever been to hell in a black ship?" [*Od.* X, 502].

33. Sumus . . . sub nocte: L, "We have the protection / and girls, let us sing / beneath the night" [cf. Catullus XXXIV, 1-4, for two lines and *Aeneid* VI, 268, for the last line]. These lines start a celebration of the "rites of spring" or the rebirth of the god in the vegetation rites.

34. Flora: Roman goddess of fertility and flowers.

35. ERI . . . KUDONIAI: H, "In the spring the quinces," first words of a fragment by Ibycus [*Lyra Graeca*, II, fr. 1, 84; *OBGV*, no. 164]. The line is used as epigraph to "The Spring" [*P*, 87].

36. Betuene . . . . Merche: From 14th-century lyric "Alisoun": "Bytuene Marsh and Averil / When spray beginneth to spring."

37. Goddess: Aphrodite.

38. Circeo: A mountain near Terracina which forms N arm of a bay on W coast of Italy.

39. Terracina: Seaport in C Latium, SE of Pontine Marshes (some 5 miles S of Circeo), where the ruins of a temple to Jupiter still stand. In "Credo" Pound wrote: "Given the material means I would replace the statue of Venus on the cliffs of Terracina" [*SP*, 53].

40. "Fac deum! . . . Est Factus": L, "Make god! . . .He is made."

41. Ver novum!: L, "new Spring!" [cf. 13 above].

42. A traverso le foglie: I, "through the leaves."

43. sic . . . nupta: L, "So the bride speaks / So the bride sings."

CANTO XL

Sources

Lewis Corey, *The House of Morgan* [*Morgan*], New York, 1930; *The Periplus of Hanno*, trans. Wilfred A. Schoff, 1912.

Background

Davis R. Dewey, *Financial History of the United States*, New York, 1922; EP, "Civilization, Money and History," *SP*, 187-355; *GK*, 227.

Exegeses

CFT, *Pai*, 1-2, 223 ff.; WB, *Rose*; Davis, *Vision*, 62-67, 128-130; DP, *Barb*, 165-166.

Glossary

1. Smith, Adam: Adam S., 1723-1790, Scottish economist; author of *Inquiry into the Nature and Causes of the Wealth of Nations* (1776). Pound discusses this oft-quoted squib from Smith in several places; e.g., "The Trade Unions are naïve seekers of plunder offering no solution, but presenting rather an extended demonstration of Adam Smith's basis of 'Economics' to the effect that 'Men of the same trade . . .' " [*SP*, 209].

2. Independent use . . . : The general thesis of those who were against the Bank of the United States [37:33], as well as the theses of those who founded the Sienese bank [42:9].

3. De banchis . . . : ML, "From the exchange mart" [the word should be *banchiis*].

4. Venice 1361: The event in Venice for the year referred to here is not known.

5. **Toward producing**: The vision of seigneurial splendor which motivated the robber barons who desired to create a financial "royalty" with all the trappings; "undsoweiter": G, "and so forth."

6. **Peabody**: George P., 1795-1869, a shrewd yankee who made a fortune in commercial ventures but finally went into banking and international finance with headquarters in London. In 1854 Junius Spencer Morgan became a partner in the firm, Peabody and Co., which, upon George Peabody's retirement in 1863, became J. S. Morgan and Co., the origin of the house of Morgan. Peabody and Co. were several times racked by the severe financial panics that occurred every few years in the U.S., and were almost wrecked by the panic of 1857. During that year money could be secured only through the Bank of England. "Junius Morgan . . . negotiated with the Bank for a loan of £800,000 and was crushed by the answer: The Bank would make the loan providing Peabody & Co., agreed to cease business in London after 1858. But George Peabody was a fighter; he dared the Bank to cause his failure, mobilized powerful British support, received the loan and survived the crisis" [*Morgan*, cf. 21 below].

7. **D'Arcy**: William Knox d'A. [38:16].

8. **'62 report** . . . : During the Civil War a "committee of the House of Representatives in 1862 reported large frauds in the purchase of ordnance. . . . J. Pierpont Morgan appeared in a case as financing the sale to the government of the government's own arms at an extortionate profit. The facts are in the Congressional Reports, 'Case No. 97' " [*Morgan*, 58-59].

9. **Morgan**: John Pierpont M., 1837-1913, built the family fortune into a vast network of holding companies and demonstrated the supremacy of finance over industry and commerce as well as over the U.S. government. He developed vast interlocking directorates which reached across the whole industrial world. Pound's source [*Morgan*, passim] demonstrates that Morgan's operations, though often crooked or downright corrupt, sometimes gave him the power to assist the nation during financial crises, but they were crises that the house of Morgan had helped to create.

10. **forcing up gold**: "The price of gold was intimately affected by military events" [*Morgan*, 65]. Gold speculation, however, was considered unpatriotic; it was practiced in a place called the Coal Hole, "a dark, repulsive basement" [ibid]. Morgan with all his foreign connections was in an excellent spot: "In one spectacular coup forcing up the price of gold, Morgan and an accomplice reaped a profit of $160,000–" [*Morgan*, 66].

11. **After Gettysburg**: With "unscrupulous" partners, Morgan took advantage of the Civil War emergency to reap vast profits in gold speculation. If the South seemed to be winning, the price of gold would rise: "Early in 1863 gold was selling at 163. A series of Union victories produced considerable price declines. The Gettysburg victory sent the price down five points in one day" [*Morgan*, 66-67].

12. **Bulls** . . . : The New York *Times* ascribed "the enormous and unprincipled speculation in gold" to "a knot of unscrupulous gamblers who care nothing for the credit of the country." It was urged that "Congress at once order the erection of scaffolds for hanging" them. But Morgan and his henchmen had it both ways. Concludes Corey: "The speculators were bulls on gold and bears on the Union" [*Morgan*, 69].

13. **Business** . . . : Congress attempted to curb or control the speculation and passed the Gold Bill in 1864. But the bankers screamed that the bill was "only one more instance of the utter lawlessness of Congress" [*Morgan*, 70]. The bill did not work, for the money-making facts of life were clear to many big businessmen: If business prospered because of war failures, then war failures would have to go on [*Morgan* 66-73].

14. **If a nation**: A sort of summary statement of Pound's money pamphlets [cf. *SP*, 187-355].

15. Boutwell: George S. B., 1818-1905, of Massachusetts; secretary of the treasury (1869-1873). Boutwell's policy was to refinance the government debt, created during the Civil War at high interest rates, by a new issue of bonds, some as low as 4 percent [cf. Dewey, *Financial History*, 352 ff.]. Boutwell would have liked the treasury to sell directly to the public. "The Ways and Means Committee of the House of Representatives held meetings on the new loan, there being considerable sentiment in Congress for the direct sale of bonds by the Treasury." But the bankers won. "Levi Morton, appearing for the Morton syndicate . . ., [said] 'I do not know of any other method of negotiating a government loan except by bankers' " [*Morgan*, 119-120].

16. Republican party: Some big financiers gave large sums to the Republican party in the hope that by "sweetening up" politicians they would get government business, but they discovered that politicians were "as unreliable as their principles." Morgan made no such mistake; he was "contemptuous of politics and politicians," though he kept on "contributing generously to the Republican party" [*Morgan*, 119].

17. Beecher: Henry Ward B., 1813-1887, Congregational minister who achieved national fame by using his pulpit in Brooklyn as a political platform from which to discuss important questions of the day. He was an abolitionist, preached woman suffrage, and was converted to the theory of evolution. Later on, however, he became the tool of reactionaries. Says Corey: "Henry Ward Beecher, himself the recipient of $20,000 a year and whose church had been organized as a profit-making enterprise by real-estate speculators, sermonized against labor amid the applause of Plymouth's congregation." Said Beecher: " 'Is the great working class oppressed? Yes, undoubtedly it is. God had intended the great to be great and the little to be little. . . The trade union, originated under the European system, destroys liberty. . . . I do not say that a dollar a day is enough to support a working-man. But it is enough to support a man! Not enough to support a man and five children if a man insist on smoking and drinking beer. . . . But the man who cannot live on bread and water is not fit to live' " [*Morgan* 123-124].

18. Belmont: August B., 1816-1890, head of one of the largest financial houses, August Belmont and Co. He dealt in international money markets and often represented in the U.S. the house of Rothschild, Morgan's competitor in international money markets. In 1876 Morgan's company organized a syndicate to secure "a government issue of $5,883,000 5% bonds against the competition of August Belmont representing the Rothschilds." Morgan won [*Morgan*, 124].

19. specie payment: The banking community after the Civil War made a great killing by defeating the Greenback party, which wanted to pay the national debt in greenbacks rather than to resume the redemption of Civil War Bonds in gold. "As after the Revolution redemption of the worthless paper currency enriched a clique of speculators . . ., so the resumption of specie payments enriched a small group of bondholders—while depression oppressed the people" [*Morgan*, 125].

20. stock subscription: Stock manipulation, "watering," in the financing of railroads was dominated by banking buccaneers: "The buccaneers plundered investors as much as they plundered business and the public. . . . In 1876, railroad bonds in default represented 39 percent of the total" [*Morgan*, 145].

21. Corey: Lewis C., pseudonym for Louis C. Fraina, 1894-1953, political scientist and author of numerous books, including *The House of Morgan*, 1930. The central institution in London is the Bank of England.

22. Pujo: Arsène Paulin P., 1861-1939, American lawyer and legislator, chairman of the House Committee on Banking and Currency (1911-1913) and head of the money-trust investigations that led to the formation of the Federal Reserve Bank.

23. **Mr. Morgan**: Samuel Untermeyer directed the investigation of the money trust for the Pujo committee. He asked J. P. Morgan, who appeared before the committee, " 'Do you approve of short selling?' Morgan: 'I never did it in my life, that I know of' " [*Morgan*, 405]. Earlier Corey writes: "J. P. Morgan & Co. were in shipshape condition to meet the crisis [1907 panic] having learned from the experience of 1903-4 to maintain a high degree of liquidity in their resources" [*Morgan*, 342].

24. **Mr. Baker**: George Fisher B., 1840-1931, one of the founders of the First National Bank of New York and closely associated with the house of Morgan. " . . .Baker . . .unquestioningly accepted Morgan's authority" [in measures taken to meet the 1907 panic]. Morgan told his son later: " 'Of course, you see, it could not have been done without Mr. Baker; he is always ready to do his share—and more' " [*Morgan*, 343].

25. **government's arms**: Pound cites this anecdote in his economic writings: "The great Morgan, during the Civil War, bought on credit a certain quantity of damaged rifles from the War Department in Washington, and sold them to a Military Command in Texas, and was paid by the latter before he had to pay the former" [*SP*, 171; cf. 8 above].

26. **Ionides**: Prob. Luke Ionides. Pound wrote: "Note, when I got to London the men who were old *enough* were all right. Col. Jackson, Luke Ionides represented something hearty, pre-Victorian, they had something that Palmerston might have recognized as appertaining to men" [*GK*, 227].

27. **Palladio**: Andrea P., 1518-1580, Italian architect who adapted the principles of Roman architecture to the requirements of the Renaissance. These eight lines are a reprise of the motivation of the great robber barons and a list of the trivial things they used their money to buy. These items of conspicuous consumption imply a cultural wasteland. The list is as significant for what it does not include as for what it does [note echoes of the 2d baronet, 28/139].

28. **AGALMA**: H, ἄγαλμα, "ornament" or "statue" or any beautiful object.

29. **ormoulu**: F, *or moulu*, "ormolo," brass made to imitate gold.

30. **brocatelli**: I, "types of brocade."

31. **HANNO**: Ca. 470 B.C. The Carthaginian navigator who led an expedition through the Strait of Gibraltar and founded seven towns on the Atlantic shore of Morocco. The account of his voyage is *The Periplus of Hanno*. Although Hanno was a common name in Carthage at the time, a consensus says that this Hanno was either the father or the son of the Hamilcar who led the expedition to Sicily ca. 470 B.C. All but the last six of the remaining lines of Canto 40 are adapted from *The Voyage of Hanno, King of the Carthaginians*, trans. Schoff [CFT, *Pai*, 1-2, 223 ff.].

32. **pillars of Herakles**: Strait of Gibraltar.

33. **60 ships . . . provision**: The source reads: "And he set forth with sixty ships of fifty oars, and a multitude of men and women, to the number of thirty thousand, and with wheat and other provisions" [cf. ibid. for this quote and all those below for Canto 40]. Pound gets the idea of Phoenician cities from his source: "It pleased the Carthaginians that Hanno should voyage outside the Pillars of Hercules, and found cities of the Libyphoenicians."

34. **Gibel Tara**: Gibraltar.

35. **Thumiatehyon**: The first city Hanno founded, identified as "Mehedia at mouth of Sbou River."

36. **Solois**: Prob. Cape Cantin.

37. **Entha hieron P.**: H, "there a temple of Poseidon."

38. Karikon, etc.: The Phoenician cities founded by Hanno.

39. Lixos: The river at which Hanno stopped and also the town, the modern Larache.

40. High Libya: Roughly present-day Algeria.

41. lixitae: Name of the nomadic people who lived on the banks of the river.

42. aethiopians etc.: Source reads: "Above these folk lived unfriendly Aethiopians, dwelling in a land full of wild beasts, and shut off by great mountains, from which they say the Lixus flows, and on the mountains live men of various shapes, cave-dwellers, who, as the Lixitae say, are fleeter of foot than horses."

43. Cyrne: Island of Cerne, or Herne, in the mouth of the Rio de Oro.

44. Xrestes: The modern St. Jean River.

45. West Horn: The modern Bay of Bissau, chief port of Portugese Guinea.

46. fires etc.: Source reads: " . . . we came to a great bay. . . . In it there was a large island, and within the island a lake of the sea, in which there was another island. Landing there during the day, we saw nothing but forests, but by night many burning fires, and we heard the sound of pipes and cymbals, and the noise of drums and a great uproar. The fear possessed us, and the soothsayers commanded us to leave the island."

47. One pillar etc.: Source reads: "After a journey of four days, we saw the land at night covered with flames. And in the midst there was one lofty fire, greater than the rest which seemed to touch the stars. By day this was seen to be a very high mountain, called Chariot of the Gods."

48. carroch: I, *carroccio*, "flag car of an army" or "chariot."

49. Gorillas etc.: Source reads: ". . . the interpreters called them *Gorillae*. When we pursued them we were unable to take any of the men; for they all escaped, by climbing the steep places and defending themselves with stones; but we took three of the women, who bit and scratched their leaders, and would not follow us. So we killed them and flayed them, and brought their skins to Carthage. For we did not voyage further, provisions failing us." Thus ends the last section of *The Voyage of Hanno.*

50. baily: Bail, the outer walls of a feudal castle or the court thereby enclosed.

51. NOUS: H, *νους*, "mind, intellect, spirit."

52. Karxèdonión . . . : H, "the King of the Carthaginians."

CANTO XLI

Sources

EP, *J/M*; EP, *GK*; Wilhelm Baur, *Geschichts-und Lebensbilder aus der Erneuerung des religiösen Lebens in den deutschen Befreiungskriegen*, 2 vols., Hamburg, 1864; Andrew Lipscomb and Albert Bergh, eds., *The Writings of Thomas Jefferson*, V, IX, Washington, D.C., 1905; George Seldes, *Iron, Blood, and Profits*, New York and London, 1934.

Background

EP, *A Visiting Card*, 15; *SP*, 314, 325; NS, *Life*, 306.

Exegeses

Davis, *Vision*, 130-131; DP, *Barb*, 140-141; WB, *Rose*, 88, 141; Knight, *Pai*, 5-1, 83.

Glossary

1. **Ma questo . . . è divertente**: I [Romagnol dial.], "But this is amusing."

2. **Boss**: Benito Mussolini, 1883-1945, Italian founder of fascism and head of government (1922-1945). Pound met M. on January 30, 1933, at the Palazzo Venezia. While leafing through *A Draft of XXX Cantos*, M. made the above remark. Pound probably took politeness to indicate quick comprehension by a genius [NS, *Life*, 306].

3. **Vada**: Village in Livorno Province, Tuscany, C Italy. Its nearby swamps were drained by M. and planted to crops. Pound wrote: ". . . from the time of Tiberius the Italian intelligentsia has been *talking* about draining the swamps" [*J/M*, 23]. Hence the line: "Waited 2000 years . . ." [38:35].

4. **Circeo**: Town near Vada.

5. **vani**: I, "rooms." Accomplishments of M.'s leadership: increased housing and the water supply.

6. **XI of our era**: The 11th year of the Fascist state, 1933.

7. **mezzo-yit**: I, Yiddish, "half (or rotten) Jew." *Mezzo* can mean either "half" or "rotten." The anecdote seems to show that the person telling it is partly of M.'s [and Pound's] opinion that such "consortiums" formed by "hoggers of harvest" are not for the public good. In time a "yit" in Pound comes to mean one guilty of "usurious" practices. In 1933 it seems to have had another meaning.

8. **confine:** Error in spelling by pubishers. Pound has correct spelling in his several manuscripts as well as original edition of *XI New Cantos* in 1934. Perhaps "confino" was intended. Around 1933, he wrote: "Get it into your head that Italy was, even in 1900, immeasurably ahead of England in so far as land laws and the rights of the man who works on the soil are concerned. Some of the follies and cruelties of great English owners would not now be permitted in Italy. Certain kinds of domestic enemy would be shipped to the *confino*" [*J/M*, 70]. The context here suggests a prison or concentration camp.

9. **Noi ci facciam sgannar . . .** : I, "We would let ourselves be butchered [*scannar*] for Mussolini." It was a hotelkeeper in Rimini who made this remark to Pound "years ago, thinking I knew nothing about the revolution and wanting to get it into my head." The hotelkeeper was also the *commandante della piazza*. He cut through red tape to help Pound see a manuscript he had come to Romagna to look at [*J/M*, 26].

10. **commandante della piazza**: I, "commander of the square." Title of a local official in Italian government.

11. **"Popolo . . . ignorante!"**: I, "The people . . . ignorant!" Pound wrote: "Gigi aged two used to stand up on his chair after lunch and say 'Popolo ignorante!' as a sort of benediction, one day he added the personal note 'And the worst of all is my *nurse* [*donna*]' " [*J/M*, 53].

12. **Messire Uzzano**: Niccolò da U., d. 1432,

Florentine statesman, "a truly disinterested man" [21:20].

13. Orbe: Town in Vaud Canton, W Switzerland, on Orbe River.

14. Eleven hours . . . : Working hours and wages in pre-Fascist Italy, apparently when "the boss" [Mussolini] was young.

15. documento: I, "document."

16. Geschichte und Lebensbilder: G, "history and pictures of life."

17. Erneuerung des Religiosen Lebens: G, "revival of religious life."

18. In den Deutschen Befreiungskriegen: G, "In the German wars of liberation."

19. Wilhelm Baur: 1826-1897. Author of *Geschichts- und Lebensbilder aus der Erneuerung des religiösen Lebens in den deutschen Befreiungskriegen*, Hamburg, 1864.

20. Uhlan officer: Fritz von Unruh, 1885-1970, German playwright, poet, and novelist; officer in World War I.

21. Augusta Victoria: Augusta Viktoria von Schleswig-Holstein, 1858-1921, wife of last German emperor, Wilhelm II.

22. ordine, contrordine e disordine: I, "order, counterorder, and disorder."

23. una pace qualunque: I, "some kind of peace or other."

24. San Casciano: Hospital [?] in Val di Peas, town in Firenze Province, near Florence in C Italy.

25. Corriere di Domenica: I, *Sunday Courier*, a newspaper.

26. Hindenburg: Paul von H., 1847-1934; German general in command on E front early in World War I; president of Weimar Republic (1925-1934).

27. Fritz' father: Fritz's father was Karl von Unruh, German military officer [cf. 20 above].

28. Herr Nvon so Forth: Karl von Unruh.

29. Battle of Waffenschlag: Invented battle; G. *Waffen* = "weapon," and *schlag* = "strike."

30. Udine: City in NE Italy used in World War I as a military base for Italian operations against Austria; occupied by Austrian troops in October 1917.

31. Hun: Slang for "German."

32. french vacation: French leave, or AWOL: absent without leave.

33. Winston's mama: Jennie Jerome, [1854?-1951] who married Lord Randolph Henry Spencer Churchill in 1874 and became mother of Winston Churchill.

34. his cousin: Of Shane Leslie (1885-1971) Pound wrote: "Shane Leslie was greatly bedazzled by his stout cousin Winston. He wrote a book to tell it to dh' woild. Winston once said to Leslie apropos of thinking and having ideas (in the sense of making ideas for oneself): 'Don't waste your time making munitions, be a GUN and shoot off other people's munitions.' Leslie, as a journalist, of sorts, was overwhelmed by this brilliance. Both cousins are half-breed Americans, determined to succeed, just like the cheapest of Mr. Lorimer's heroes" [*J/M*, 64].

35. M. Crevel: René C., 1900-1935, French author who wrote *Les Pieds dans le Plat* (1933). Speaking of Crevel's work as a novelist and the work of poets such as Cros, Vlaminck, and Bunting, Pound wrote: " . . . it may be said that they are better than the foreign crap currently displayed [1941] on the bookstalls" [*SP*, 325].

36. Esperanza...: Esperanza (Duchess of Monte Putina), Lady Primrose (Marquise of Sussex), and Augusta (an Austrian archduchess) are the three principal characters in Crevel's *Les Pieds dans le Plat*.

37. Bill Yeats: William Butler Y.

38. Pig and Piffle: Prob. English journal *Sport and Country*.

39. Times: Refers to *Town and Country*.

40. censorship: Pound wrote: "As the Duce has pithily remarked: 'Where the Press is "*free*" it merely serves special interests' " [*J/M*, 41].

41. Cosimo First: C. de'Medici [21:9].

42. Monte dei Paschi: I, "the mountain of the pastures": Sienese bank founded in 1624 and still running. It was established by a grant from Ferdinand II of Tuscany and its credit was based upon the Sienese public lands: the pastures of Maremma. Pound refers to it by a number of names: Bank, Monte, Monte Nuovo, Monte Paschale, Mount, New Monte, New Mount, and New Mountain [42:7].

43. CH: C. H. Douglas [38:49].

44. Woergl: Wörgl, small town in Austrian Tyrol which in the early 1930s issued the form of stamp scrip proposed by Silvio Gesell and created a miniboom in the midst of the depression that surrounded it [cf. *A Visiting Card*, 15; *SP*, 314].

45. Vergennes: Charles Gravier, comte de V., 1717-1787, French statesman; minister of foreign affairs under Louis XVI (1774-1787) and during the years when Thomas Jefferson was U. S. ambassador to France. The anecdote is repeated from Canto 33 [cf. 33/154; Knight, *Pai*, 5-1, 83].

46. Mrs. Trist: Eliza House, friend of Jefferson who cared for his daughter while he was in Europe. In a letter to her from Paris, August 18, 1785, Jefferson wrote: "Indeed, it is difficult to conceive how so good a people . . . should be rendered so ineffectual . . . by one single curse,—that of a bad form of government. . . . Of twenty millions of people supposed to be in France, I am of opinion there are nineteen millions more wretched, more accursed in every circumstance of human existence than the most conspicuously wretched individual of the whole United States" [Jefferson, *Writings*, V, 81].

47. Public debt . . . Colonel Monroe: These 12 lines are excerpted from Jefferson's letter to Colonel James Monroe, the future president, who was U.S. ambassador to France in 1796 when Jefferson wrote: "Congress have risen. . . .I had always conjectured, from such facts as I could get hold of, that our public debt was increasing about a million of dollars a year. You will see by Gallatin's speeches that the thing is proved. You will see further, that we are completely saddled and bridled, and that the bank is so firmly mounted on us that we must go where they will guide. They openly publish a resolution, that the national property being increased in value, they must by an increase of circulating medium furnish an adequate representation of it. . . . All the imported commodities are raised about fifty per cent. By the depreciation of the money. . . . Lands had risen within the vortex of the paper, and as far out as that can influence. . . . Mechanics here get from a dollar to a dollar and a half a day, yet are much worse off than at the old prices" [ibid., IX, 337-338].

48. Gallatin: At time of letter (TJ to Col. James Monroe, June 12, 1796), Gallatin was a member of House of Representatives [31:40].

49. 120 million german fuses . . . : The Krupp armaments firm in Germany sold its patented fuses to Germany, England, or to any country that would buy, during the years when it and other great companies such as Vickers in England and Schneider-Creusot in France, armed Europe for World War I. "After the war, Krupps, with cynical effrontery, sued the British firm for 123,000,000 shillings, one shilling royalty for each Krupp patent fuze (Kpz 96/94) used on the British hand grenades to kill German soldiers" [Seldes, *Iron, Blood, and Profits*, 69].

50. Jena: City in Thuringia, Germany.

51. Schneider Creusot: [38:57, 59].

52. Hatfield: Sir Robert Hadfield of Hadfield, Ltd.

53. ad interim: L, "in the meantime" or "for the time being."

CANTOS XLII-XLV

Sources

Il Monte dei Paschi di Siena e le Aziende in Esso Riunite, 9 vols., ed. Narciso Mengozzi, Siena, 1891-1925; Herbert C. F. Bell, *Lord Palmerston*, London, 1936; Antonio Zobi, *Storia civile della Toscana dal MDCCXXXVII al MDCCCXLVIII*, 5 vols., Firenze, 1850-1852; MSS inedit. concerning Il Monte dei Paschi preserved in the Archivio di Stato, Palazzo Piccolomini, Siena [referred to as Archivio-Piccolomini].

Background

EP, *GK*; *Social Credit: An Impact*, London, 1935, 112, 115; *SP*, 61; *America, Roosevelt, and the Causes of the Present War*, London, 1951; "Civilization, Money and History," *SP*, 187-355; HK, *Era*.

Exegeses

John Drummond, "The Italian Background to *The Cantos*," in *Ezra Pound*, ed. Peter Russell, London, 1950; Giuseppe Galigani, "Montis Pascuorum," *Yale Literary Magazine*, 127 (1958), 18-23; JE, *Pai*, 4-3, 547; Witemeyer, *Pai*, 4-1, 85-88.

[Most of the glosses for Cantos 42, 43, and 44 (the Leopoldine Cantos) were written by Ben Kimpel and T. C. Duncan Eaves and were based on their detailed study of the sources published in *Pai*, 6-3; 7-1 & 2; 8-3].

Glossary Canto XLII

1. **Palmerston**: In 1863 the British prime minister, Lord Palmerston (1784-1865), wrote to the foreign minister, Lord John Russell (1792-1878), that though he was going to detain ironclads ordered by the Confederate States on the insistence of the American minister, Charles Francis Adams (1807-1886; "H" should read "F," as in the older Faber edition), he considered that the American demands should be resisted.

2. **H.G.**: The novelist Herbert George Wells (1866-1946) delighted Pound by asking why the monument of Queen Victoria was still allowed to stand in front of Buckingham Palace.

3. **Lex salica**: L, "the Salic law," a law in France that prevented women from succeeding to the throne. The Germanic law [*lex Germanica*], in England and other countries, permitted women to reign.

4. **Antoninus**: Antoninus Pius, Roman emperor, 137-161; Antoninus confirmed the fact that at sea the customary law of

Rhodes, designed by commercial interests, rather than Roman law, should be followed.

5. **nell' anima**: I, "in the mind or soul."

6. **Illustrious College**: the ruling magistracy of the Tuscan city of Siena, the Collegio de Balìa. Later in this canto Pound translates Balìa as "Bailey."

7. **Monte**: I, literally "mountain"; here a "fund of money" or a "bank."

8. **banco di giro**: I, "a bank for transfer of credits."

9. **With paternal affection . . .**: Like most of this canto and a good deal of the next two cantos, what follows is translated from *Il Monte dei Paschi di Siena e le Aziende in Esso Riunite*, 9 vols., Siena, 1891-1925. The document quoted in this passage is a report of the decisions of the General Council of Siena, March 4, 1622-23, in reference to the foundation of a new bank, Il Monte dei Paschi ["Mountain of the Pastures"], whose funding was guaranteed by the income from grasslands south of Siena.

10. **S.A.**: I, *Sua Altezza*, "Your Highness."

11. **dei ministri**: I, "of the administrators."

12. **scudo**: I, coin, usually translated as "crown."

13. **id est, piú [piu] utilmente**: L, I, "that is, most usefully."

14. **contrade**: I, "the divisions of a city."

15. **Loco Signi**: L, "Place of the Sign." The original reads *Loco Sigilli*, "Place of the Seal."

16. **cross**: The source actually has a cross for the seal in the margin.

17. **benché [benchè]**: I, "however."

18. **idem**: L, "the same."

19. **Consules, Iudices**: L, "Consuls, Judges."

20. **pro serenissimo**: I, "for the most serene" [the Most Serene Grand Duke of Tuscany, Ferdinando II, 1610-1670].

21. **Mount of Pity**: Pound's translation of *Monte de Pietà* [I, "pawnshop"]. What follows is from another document, a report of the Florentine Council to the grand duke about the request of the Sienese Balìa to erect a new bank, December 29, 1622.

22. **AA VV**: I, *Altezze Vostre*, "Your Highnesses." The plural refers to the Grand Duke and his two guardians or regents, his mother, the Grand Duchess Maria Maddalena, 1591-1631, and his grandmother, the Grand Duchess Christina, 1565-1636.

23. **Universities . . .**: In the source, *Universita* is probably used to include all the people of a given region [that is, the congregations of the region]. But Pound uses it in a modern sense [Kimpel, *Pai*, 6-3, 336]. *Luoghi* literally means "places." But Pound gives his interpretation as "companies . . ." etc.

24. **Mallevadoria**: I, "Security."

25. **'The Abundance'**: I, *L'Abondanza*, a magistracy charged with provision of grain.

26. **fruit**: I, *frutto*, means also "interest on money."

27. **Xember**: December. Siena was still on the old calendar (Julian), under which December was the tenth month of the year, which began at the spring equinox (March 23).

28. **Nicolo de Antille**: Misprint for Niccolò Dell'Antella.

29. **Horatio Gionfiglioli**: Misprint for Horatio Gianfigliazzi.

30. **Tutrice**: I, "female guardian."

31. **Hor^{o} della Rena**: Horatio della Rena, secretary of the grand ducal government.

32. Fabbizio bollo vedo: Misprint for *Fabrizio Colloredo*, member of the Tuscan council of four who were to act as advisers to the regents during the minority of the grand duke.

33. Governatore: I, "Governor."

34. Cenzio Grcolini: Misprint for Orazio Ercolani.

35. ACTUM SENIS: L, "transacted at Siena," from a third document (Nov. 2, 1624), the formal instrument founding Il Monte dei Paschi.

36. Parish of San Joannij: Parish of San Giovanni (or John).

37. Marquis: The two marchesi are Giovanni Cristoforo de Malaspinis, son of Antonio Maria, and Giovanni de Binis, son of Andrea.

38. Ego . . . filius: L, "I . . . son of."

39. Pavia . . . Adige: Pavia and Vicenza are cities in NE Italy; San Zeno Maggiore in Verona on the Adige River is one of Pound's favorite Romanesque churches. He is probably referring to the triptych in that church painted by Andrea Mantegna, which shows three medieval Italian cities.

40. I Nicolaus . . . Senensus: I, "I Nicholas Ulivis [misprint for Ulixis (Ulisse or Ulysses)] of Cagnascis [misprint for Magnanis] citizen of Pistoja, a Florentine notary of public countersigning [for the] Senate and people of Siena." Kimpel and Eaves say of the passage starting "ACTUM SENIS": "Pound is partly joking about the names, partly giving the impression of reading a crabbed legal document, and perhaps partly puzzled" [Kimpel, *Pai*, 6-3, 358].

41. OB PECUNIAE SCARCITATEM: L, "because of the scarcity of money."

42. Monte non vacabilis: L, "a bank whose shares do not expire but have an unlimited duration"; *publico* goes with the following Latin phrase in the document, *publico eorum commodo* ["for the public convenience"].

43. cauteles: L, "guarantees."

44. die decima ottava: I, "on the eighteenth day."

45. Don Ferdinandus Secundus Dux Magnus: L, "Lord Ferdinando II, Grand Duke."

46. Chigi: The four members of the Balìa designated to sign the agreement were Agostino Chigi; Alessandro de Sozzini; Marcello de Augustini [*Illuri* is perhaps a deliberate misreading of the original's "Ill$^{\text{m.i}}$," an abbreviation for Latin "Most Illustrious," which modifies the name of his father], Lord of Caldana; and Cesare de Marescotti, Lord of Mont'Albano.

47. Loca Montis: L, "Shares of the Mountain."

48. ex certe scientia et: L, "from certain knowledge and."

49. de libris septeno: The original reads *de Libris septem*, Latin for "of seven pounds."

Glossary Canto XLIII

1. serenissimo . . . Domino: L, "most serene Lord." Pound continues to quote from the third document [42:35].

2. et omnia alia juva: L [the original reads jura], "and all other rights."; "juva" means "aid" (imperative of *juvo*) [See Kimpel, *Pai*, 8-3, 514 for the confusion of *r* and *v* in the Sienese documents.]

3. Pawn Shop (Mount of Pity): [42:21].

4. eiusdem civitatis Senén: L, "of the same city of Siena."

5. Most Serene M Dux and serenest (feminine) tutrices: The Grand Duke Ferdinando II, the Grand Duchess Maria Maddalena, and the Grand Duchess Christina [42:22].

6. **Bailey**: Collegio de Balìa [42:6].

7. **videlicet alligati**: L, "evidently under obligation," or ML, "evidently leagued together."

8. **Tuscanissimo Nostro Signore**: I, "Our Most Tuscan Lord," This superlative for Tuscan is doubtless a Poundian joke about the grandiose honorary titles in Italian. The word is not in the source. Pound was also puzzled by the word *Inditione* in the source. It means "indication" or a fiscal cycle. Thus the translated source would read: "In the Name of Omnipotent God and of the Glorious Virgin Mary Our Advocate, and to the honor and exaltation of the Most Serene Grand Duke of Tuscany our Lord. The year of the Lord 1622, Sixth Fiscal Period, Saturday the 4th day of March" [Kimpel, *Pai*, 6-3, 343].

9. **dilettissimo**: I, "most beloved."

10. **siano soddisfatti**: I, "that they be satisfied."

11. **Ob pecuniae scarsitatem**: L, "Because of the scarcity of money."

12. **S.P. SENEN**^sis^ ... **civitatis**: L, "The Senate and the People of Siena and in its behalf the Most Illustrious College of the Balìa to whose watchfulness over all the state" [*amplissim* is an abbreviation for *amplissimum*, and *civices* is used instead of the original *cujus* ("whose"); *civices* seems to be a cross between the Latin *civicus* ("civic") and *cives* ("citizens")].

13. **Urban VIIIth**: Pope, 1623-1644.

14. **Ferd. I**: In both instances this should be *Ferd. II*: Ferdinand II, 1578-1637, the Holy Roman emperor–elect, and *mag duce d^o n^o* ["Our Lord the Grand Duke"], Ferdinando II of Tuscany [42:20]. The Latin words *felcitatem dominante et* mean "ruling happiness and," but the source reads: *feliciter dominante*, "happily ruling."

15. **1251 ... arabic**: Mengozzi's Volume III contains the notary's copies of the three documents concerning the founding of Il Monte dei Paschi. On the spine is printed: "Stanza Prima. Scaffale No. XII Lettera F N°. 4." Pound renders this information in these two lines.

16. **To the end**: The next 17 lines mostly concern a parade and a celebration by the people, who after so many years finally got their bank; Pound enjoys all the sense impressions (sound, sight, color) as well as the pomp and ceremony with the animals and triumphant chariot: *carroccio*. St. George and the Unicorn and prob. others were pictured on flags or banners carried by different craft guilds in the parade. *Hokey-pokey* means ice-cream stands and by extension any hucksters who appear at carnivals and fairs or on feast days to sell their wares. *Nicchio* is not a particular person, but the voice of some mother whose young son is doubtless lost in the crowd. The *one box* is doubtless a box of candles and *200 lire* is prob. the price, for traditionally parades ended at a cathedral where candles were used as votive offerings.

17. **contrade**: I, "divisions of a city."

18. **kallipygous**: H, "with beautiful buttocks."

19. **salite**: I, "hill paths."

20. **'laudate pueri'**: L, "praise, boys."

21. **palio**: Sienese horse race held annually on July 2 and August 16. Pound is presumably describing his own memories of this famous festival.

22. **Duomo**: I, "Cathedral."

23. **quocunque aliunde**: L, "from anywhere else."

24. **obligatio**: L, "obligation."

25. **scudi**: I, coins, usually translated as "crowns."

26. **Maister Augustino Chisio equites ... holy)**: The original Latin reads *Domino Augustino Chisio, equiti Sacrae III.^{mae} Religionis Divi Stephani papae et martiris* ["Lord Agostino Chigi, Knight of the Sacred

and Most Illustrious Order of St. Stephen pope and martyr"] [for Chigi, see 42:46].

27. **ducatorum? no. ducentorum**: L, "of ducats? no. of two hundred thousand."

28. **parish of San Giovanni (Joannis)**: Parish in Siena. L, *Joannis*, "of Giovanni or John."

29. **libris septem**: L, "seven pounds" [lire].

30. **summam, scutorum**: L, "the sum, of scudi [crowns]."

31. **Out of Syracuse**: Pound is referring to Demosthenes' oration "Against Zenothemes," prosecuting an attempt to defraud creditors by trying to sink a ship supposed to be loaded with borrowed money.

32. **S.O.**: The older Faber edition reads "Standard Oil." Presumably this passage describes a modern instance of commercial chicanery similar to the ancient Greek one.

33. **Loca Montis**: L, "Shares (literally 'Places') of the Mountain."

34. **Il Banditore**: I, "The Town Crier."

35. **Ill^us Balìa eseguisca in tutto**: I, "The Illustrious Balìa executes in everything."

36. **ACTUM SENIS in Parochia [Parocchia] S. Giovannis [Joannis]**: L, "transacted at Siena in the Parish of San Giovanni."

37. **hoc die decim' octavo**: L, "on this eighteenth day."

38. **Celso**: Celso Cittadini, 1555-1627. Before the founding of Il Monte dei Paschi Cittadini had proposed increasing the cultivation of grain and hemp.

39. **stati fatti Signoria**: I, "was made a Lordship." Paris Bolgarini was the first supervisor of Il Monte dei Paschi.

40. **cancellarius**: ML, "chancellor."

41. **Luoghi**: [42:23].

42. **fondo**: I, "fund," "base," "deep."

43. **'entrate'**: I, literally "entrances"; here "incomes." Such incomes are given in the next lines. "M" equals 1,000–thus 150 to 200 thousand scudi (a unit of currency]. But the source indicates the incomes are the costs of management. Kimpel and Eaves translate thus: "And to this end it is reported that the administration and management of this Mountain will not, it is believed, turn out to be more than one-hundred-and-fifty to two-hundred thousand crowns (scudi). And therefore it is enough to assign it a certain and sure income of eight to ten thousand crowns yearly on the incomes of the Excise Taxes [gabelle] or Customs [dogana] or other safe organ of that city [gabelle]" [Kimpel, *Pai*, 6-3, 336].

44. **Epifany**: Epiphany, the feast celebrated on January 6 commemorating the coming of the Magi.

45. **Off^o de Paschi**: I, "Office of the Pastures" [42:9].

46. **Donna Orsola**: An official prostitute. The documents are unclear about the heinous crime that deprived her of her official sanctions. The source has a blank space (probably an erasure) which accounts for Pound's words "of wherever" [cf. Kimpel, *Pai*, 8-3, 515]. The "book" becomes the "register" where Mrs. Gallo's (next canto page) crime of thievery is made crystal clear.

47. **black money**: Defined as lead money [bottom of next canto page]. The source shows the Balìa instructing customs officers to be more diligent because "of the introduction into this state of so much foreign black money with injury to the public." The reader should note the content of *hilaritas* and outright comedy in the admixture of business, ranging from the sacred through the profane to the brilliant trivia that come before this high council and are somberly recorded by the secretary and given legal sanction by the notary. One of the points obviously is to show that human nature changes but little. The comic point can be nothing but devastatingly clear to professors who have served on high academic councils. In 1626 the Sienese Balìa kept getting into more of a "stew" [cf. next canto page] about the black money. Finally on May 19,

1626, a prohibition against *quattrini neri* ["black pennies"] was promulgated [Kimpel, *Pai*, 8-1, 516].

48. **Monte de Firenze**: I, "Bank of Florence."

49. **vacabile**: I, "the shares of which do expire." The Bank of Florence was so eager to get money that it announced that even bandits could contribute.

50. **Pietro de Medici**: Pietro de' Medici, 1554-1604, youngest son of Cosimo I. This member of the grand ducal house had a reputation for profligacy, and the government refused to allow his bastards to be recognized, but it was arranged that they would be recognized as the bastards of the secretary, Orazio della Rena. [For della Rena, see 42:31].

51. **Orbem . . . implevit**: L, "Urban VIII filled the world with wars, the city with taxes."

52. **Monte Nuovo**: I, "New Bank" (literally "New Mountain").

53. **Xbre**: I, *dicembre*, "December."

54. **Monte Paschale, fatto Signoria**: I, "Mountain of the Pastures, made a Lordship."

55. **Grosseto**: A city in the Maremma, S of Siena.

56. **1676 ambassadors to Firenze**: Ambassadors from Siena to the government in Florence are protesting the devaluation of Spanish pieces of eight.

57. **non intendeva di quella materia**: I, "did not understand that matter."

58. **Buonuomini**: I, literally "Good Men," a Florentine tribunal.

59. **Tolomei**: Celso Tolomei had left money to found a college to which Il Monte dei Paschi made a loan in 1678.

60. **fruitage**: I, *frutto* means both "fruit" and "interest."

61. **LL AA**: I, *Lora Altezze*, "Their Highnesses" [42:28, 29].

62. **prestare**: I, "lend."

63. **Paschi di detta Città**: I, "Pastures of the said City." They were located in the Maremma [cf. 55 above].

64. **cautele**: I, "guarantees."

65. **Hor° della Rena**: [cf. 50 above].

66. **Orazio Grcolini**: Misprint for Orazio Ercolani.

67. **Stile senese**: I, "in Sienese style," i.e., according to the old calendar [42:27].

68. **S. Gionni, in palatio**: I, "San Giovanni, in the palace."

69. **Firenze 1749 . . . 12,000**: This is one of several examples of useful public works financed by Il Monte dei Paschi.

70. **the end of the Medici**: The grand ducal house of Medici became extinct in 1743.

71. **lire pre-war**: Value of the lire in pre–World War I currency [cf. 50/246 on debt; 50:4].

Glossary Canto XLIV

1. **Pietro Leopoldo**: 1747-1792; member of the Austrian house of Hapsburg-Lorraine, became Leopoldo I, Grand Duke of Tuscany, 1765-1790, and Leopold II, Holy Roman emperor, 1790-1792. The lines above his name are one of the various decrees with which his government tried to alleviate the economic hardships of Tuscany [note rhyme with 37/181].

2. **Heavy grain crop unsold**: Under the Medici there were many restrictions on free trade, and in 1721 and 1723, when the harvests were unusually rich, the government

prohibited the importation of grain ("shut down on grain imports").

3. never had the Mount . . . investments: Very often an excess of capital forced Il Monte dei Paschi to cut down the interest rate. The date of the first reduction mentioned was 1680; the other dates are correct.

4. that trade . . . impediments: The government of Pietro Leopoldo was strongly in favor of free trade; this decree was issued in 1781.

5. motu proprio: I, *motuproprio*, "voluntary decree."

6. Ferdinando EVVIVA!!: I, "Long live Ferdinando!!" Ferdinando III, 1769-1824, the second son of Pietro Leopoldo, was grand duke of Tuscany from 1790 to 1799 and again from 1814 until his death.

7. Flags trumpets horns drums . . .: This and the following lines describe a celebration at Siena in 1792 in honor of Ferdinando III's restrictions on the exportation of grain and his regulation of small hucksters.

8. the chapel of Alexander: The Capella di Alessandro VII in the Cathedral of Siena.

9. St. Catherine's chapel in S. Domenico: The Capella di Santa Caterina in the Church of San Domenico in Siena. Saint Catherine is the patron saint of Italy.

10. Fonte Giusta: Fontegiusta, a church in Siena.

11. contrade: I, districts of the city.

12. Palace of the Seignors: The Palazzo Pubblico or town hall of Siena, located in the Piazza del Campo.

13. the tower in the piazza: The Torre del Mangia, which rises from the Palazzo Pubblico.

14. procession: Pound loved a parade [43:16].

15. e di tutte le qualità: I, "and of all kinds."

16. mortaretti: I, "little mortars."

17. chapel of the Piazza: The Capella di Piazza, at the foot of the Torre del Mangia.

18. Evviva Ferdinando il Terzo: I, "Long live Ferdinando the Third."

19. Piazza del Duomo: I, "Cathedral Square."

20. Dovizia annonaria: I, "abundance of provision," specifically a reference to the annual income in natural products, mostly corn or grain, and the body of restrictive laws shaped to provide Florentine industry with cheap food in order to undercut the prices of Florence's competitors. Enforced by the office of the Abbondanza [I, "abundance"], these laws exploited and ruined the peasantry by fixing the prices of commodities, prohibiting the import and export of food, and disallowing all free exchange. Offenders were prosecuted as common criminals.

21. Frumentorum . . . conservit: L, "freedom of grains restrained of provision reduced for the good of poor and of rich preserves (or retains)." This quotation is not only altered from the original, but makes no sense as it stands: among other things, none of the nouns can be the object of the final verb, which has an impossible ending. The original refers to Ferdinando and asks the people to pray for him "quod / frumentariorum licentia coercita / Re annonaria laxata / Pauperum aeque ac divitum bono / consylverit" ["because when the freedom of grain dealers was restrained and the supply of provisions expanded, he had consideration for the good of the poor and equally of the rich"].

22. refused . . . nation: When driven out by the French armies in 1799 [Pound's date is wrong], Ferdinando did not take valuable and easily portable treasures.

23. il più galantuomo del paese: I, "the most honest man in the country."

24. Fr Lenzini: Under the French occupation the Sienese clergy, among them the archbishop, who like everyone in Revolutionary France was called simply "citizen," took part in the ceremony of erecting a tree of liberty. *Fr* stands for "Francesco." Abram was the French commissioner.

25. from 750 . . . April: This rise of prices took place in 1799, soon after the beginning of the French occupation.

26. and on June 28th . . . little powder: An uprising that began in the city of Arezzo drove the French out of Tuscany for a while; when the liberators took Siena, they let the French escape to the fortress and turned their attention to burning Jews. Traitors tried to ruin the cartridges of the liberators from Arezzo. The Roman Gate [Porta Romana] was the gate one used when journeying to Rome.

27. semolina: I, "coarse meal."

28. Respectons les prêtres: F, "Let us respect the priests." It was actually Napoleon who wrote to his foreign minister, Charles Maurice de Talleyrand-Périgord, 1754-1838, that the only way to live at peace with the peasants of Italy was to respect the priests.

29. Premier Brumaire: F, the first day of the French Revolutionary month, October 22 to November 20.

30. Vous voudrez citoyen: F, "You will, citizen." This order was delivered by the French forces to Il Monte dei Paschi.

31. fraternité: F, "brotherhood."

32. Delort: Jacques-Antoine-Adrien, Baron Delort, 1773-1846, French officer, later general.

33. Dupont: Pierre D., Later Comte Dupont de L'Etang, 1765-1840.

34. Louis King of Etruria, Primus: Luigi, Duke of Parma, 1773-1803, was in 1801 made Louis I of Etruria, a new kingdom formed by Napoleon which included Tuscany.

35. Gen. Clarke: Henri Jacques Guillaume Clarke, 1765-1818, had been a general under Napoleon, and when he made this sarcastic remark about the taxes of the king of Etruria at the time of his death, he was French ambassador to that state.

36. Ministro degli [Affari] Esteri: I, "Foreign Minister."

37. Whereas . . . expenses: This low percentage was the difference between the rate of interest paid to shareholders and the rate of interest paid by borrowers.

38. Madame ma soeur et cousine: F, "Madame my sister and cousin." This letter, down through the signature "NAPOLEON," was written to Maria Luisa, 1782-1824, infanta of Spain and widow of Louis I of Etruria. On the death of her husband she became regent for their infant son, Louis II, but in 1807 she was informed that Napoleon had made a treaty with Spain under which Tuscany was to become an integral part of France and that she had to leave the country. She appealed to Napoleon and this letter was his answer. The French original sometimes addresses her in the second person and sometimes in the third; a footnote points out that it was probably written by a secretary.

39. General Reile: Honoré Charles Michel Joseph Reille, 1775-1860. He was at this time a general in the French army and later became a marshal of France.

40. Lisbon: The original has *Livourne* (Livorno or Leghorn); "that capital" in the next line is Lisbon.

41. And those men . . . prepared: In 1809 Napoleon granted the grand duchy of Tuscany to his sister Maria Anna Elisa Bonaparte (Mme Felice Bacciocchi), 1777-1820, princess of Lucca and of Piombino. The diarist Bandini reports that when she entered Siena men took the horses from her carriage and pulled it themselves, but that he was sure their action was not based on genuine enthusiasm.

42. "Artists . . . Napoleon: Napoleon believed that Tuscany under his sister was favorable to the arts and that artists of high rank were the only aristocrats not overturned by the recent events.

43. **'Semiramis'**: Semiramis was the queen of Assyria who was renowned in legend as the builder of Babylon. Elisa was called "Semiramis of Lucca." She was forced to leave Florence in January 1814.

44. **her brother's law code**: The writer of *Il Monte dei Paschi* [42:9] praises several results of the French administration, especially the Code Napoléon, which he called a *monumento di civile sapienza* ["monument of civil wisdom"]. He quotes another writer who remarked that Napoleon was one of those men whom we must take pride in and admire, but it is the grace of God that he sends such men very rarely.

45. **And before him . . . Habsburg Lorraine**: The writer of *Il Monte dei Paschi*, by way of contrast with the very mixed blessing of Napoleon, lists for three pages the reforms of Pietro Leopoldo. Pound has brought his effort to abolish the state debt from the middle of the list to the beginning.

46. **gabelle**: I, "excise taxes."

47. **Val di Chiana**: I, "Valley of Chiana." The Chiana is a river in Tuscany which rises in the Apennines and used to flow for some 60 miles to the Tiber. In the Middle Ages the valley was swampland, but in the late 18th century Count Fossombroni moved the watershed some 25 miles south so that the Chiana now flows partly into the Arno and partly into the Tiber. This engineering feat made it possible for the third Ferdinand to improve tillage of the now arable land; note rhyme with Mussolini's drainage of the Pontine marshes [41:3] and the Emperor Yü's controlling of the Yellow River [53:15].

48. **porto franco**: I, "free port." On his restoration Ferdinando III protected the interests of the free port of Livorno in addition to accomplishing several other reforms, but Pound has exaggerated the size of his tax cuts.

49. **Letizia**: Maria Letizia Ramolino Bonaparte, 1750-1836, mother of Napoleon.

50. **Niccolò Piccolomini, Provveditore**: Piccolomini called himself the *provveditore* ["supervisor"] of *Il Monte dei Paschi*. The book does emphasize the effort to combat usury.

Glossary Canto XLV

1. **Usura**: L, I, "Usury." Pound defines the way he uses the word at the end of this canto. Usury functions in *The Cantos* to dramatize the forces at work in human nature which prevent the human race from creating a paradise on earth—or realizing the vision first announced in Canto V. The man without a paradisal vision will have no "painted paradise on his church wall."

2. **harpes et luz**: OF [*luthes*], "harps and lutes"; part of line 896 from Villon's *Testament* in the ballad for his mother, where she speaks of seeking paradise painted.

3. **virgin receiveth**: Prob. a reference to various paintings entitled *The Annunciation.*

4. **Gonzaga:** Refers to a fresco by Mantegna, part of the point being that a fresco is an integral part of the building, the sort of thing you don't do on a bank's money. A house built via usura is an anonymous shell that can be repossessed and sold [HK].

5. **thy bread**: First protest against the adulteration of bread which since Pound's time has become a continuously louder clamor [cf. 74/428 where "white bread" is so bad even birds won't eat it, and 80/493 where it is said Spanish bread used to be "made out of grain"].

6. **line grows thick**: Pound wrote: "I suggest that finer and future critics of art will be

able to tell from the quality of a painting the degree of tolerance or intolerance of usury extant in the age and milieu that produced it" [*GK*, 27].

7. **Pietro Lombardo**: 1435-1515, Italian architect and sculptor. His most famous work is Dante's tomb at Ravenna.

8. **Duccio**: D. di Buoninsegna, 1278-1319, Italian painter and leader of the Sienese school.

9. **Francesca**: Piero della Francesca, 1420?-1492, Italian painter from Umbrian region who is famous for his portraits and altarpieces [8:11].

10. **Zuan Bellin'**: Giovanni Bellini, 1430?-1516, Venetian painter known for his altarpieces and Madonnas [25:59].

11. **'La Calunnia'**: I, "The Slander." Title of painting by Sandro Botticelli, 1444?-1510, now in Uffizi Gallery, Florence.

12. **Angelico**: Fra [Brother] A. Known also as Giovanni da Fiesole, 1387-1455; Italian painter from Florence.

13. **Ambrogio**: A. de Predis, 1455?-1508, Italian portrait and miniature painter from Milan.

14. **Adamo me fecit**: L, "Adam made me." Inscription on pillar in Church of San Zeno, Verona. Pound makes much of this column, which the artist was proud enough of to sign, and contrasts it with columns turned out by the hundreds in modern times [cf. HK, *Era*, 324, who gives a picture of the column; the full inscription reads: ADAMINUS DESCO GEORGIO ME FECIT; see also *Pai*, 4-1, 85-88].

15. **St. Trophime**: Beautiful church in Arles, France, noted for its cloistered courtyard with sculpted columns [cf. HK, *Era*, 328-329].

16. **Saint Hilaire**: Church in Poitiers, France [cf. ibid., 327].

17. **cramoisi**: F, "crimson cloth."

18. **Memling**: Hans M., 1430?-1495, religious painter and portraitist of Flemish school.

19. **CONTRA NATURAM**: L, "against nature."

20. **Eleusis**: Town in Attica where the Eleusinian Mysteries were celebrated. One of the major poles of *The Cantos*: "Between Kung [an ethical system] and Eleusis [celebration of the mysteries]." Thus usury debauches what is most sacred: "the love of money is the root of all evil" [cf. 52/258].

CANTO XLVI

Sources

Personal experiences and memories of Pound; Christopher Hollis, *The Two Nations*, London, 1935; Dante, *Inf.* XVII.

Background

EP, *GK*, 184, 35-36; *A Visiting Card*, Peter Russell, London, 1952; *SP*, 311, 272-273, 57, 280, 437-439.

Glossary

1. **Eliot**: Thomas Stearns E., 1888-1971, poet and critic and lifelong friend of Pound's. Called "Reverend" because in 1927 he became a devout Anglo-Catholic churchman. Also before and during the time when Pound was writing Canto 46, Eliot was writing on religious subjects.

2. **natural language**: A language close to nature and therefore mythic or "paideumatic." Eliot's language in *The Waste Land* drew on primitive myth via Christianity. Pound sought to infuse his language with the European myths of Eleusis.

3. **hell**: Because Pound sees hell as the locus of greed, Geryon, and usury as the dominating thrust of Western civilization, he does not believe anyone will traverse it quickly: "Abomination of desolation . . . lasting on into our time in the infamy which controls English and U.S. finances and has made printing a midden, a filth, a mere smear, bolted down by the bank racket. . . . The first step toward a new Paideuma is a clearance of every prelate or minister who blocks, by diseased will or sodden inertia, a cleaning of the monetary system. There is no mediaeval description of hell which exceeds the inner filth of these mentalities" [*GK*, 184].

4. **Zoagli**: Town on the Ligurian coast, NW Italy, a few miles S of Rapallo.

5. **Seventeen . . . nineteen . . . ninety**: Writing in "a.d. 1935" [cf. 46/235], Pound is recalling the formal beginning of his economic struggle when he met and listened to Major Douglas in *The New Age* offices in 1918 or 1916. "Ninety" prob. refers more generally to the *bellum perenne* against Geryon and Usura.

6. **the fuzzy bloke**: Pound referring to himself ironically as he listened and responded to Major Douglas.

7. **The major**: C. H. Douglas, the Social Credit economist. Social Credit proposed a national dividend as one instrument to keep purchasing power equal to the goods and services being marketed.

8. **Decennio**: Tenth anniversary celebration of Italian fascism (1932).

9. **Il Popolo**: *Popolo d'Italia*, newspaper started by Mussolini in 1914.

10. **Mills bomb**: Mills hand grenade, invented by Sir William Mills and used by British and Allies in World War I.

11. **the teapot**: Poss. Pound talking so that the *ours* refers to the celebration of 1932, which had no such record to contend with as the Teapot Dome Scandal of the late 1920s. But the lines, *Waal . . . brown one*, may refer to the first meeting with Major Douglas in Orage's office. Pound's obituary for Orage [*New English Weekly*, Nov. 15, 1934; rpt. *SP*, 437-439] discusses the number of years Orage fought for the truth about the monetary system [cf. 38/190; 38:49]. If so, the *teapot* may have been a real pot sitting next to a Mills bomb on some table, all part of the scene.

12. **5 millions**: "Liste officielle des morts 5,000,000," i.e., in World War I [cf. 16/73].

13. **Debts . . . New York**: Source reads: "Owing to the tariff, the whole South was going into debt. We must never forget the important statistic which Horace Greeley . . . gave at the outbreak of the Civil War, that southern debtors owed at least $200,000,000 to money-lenders in New York City alone" [Hollis, 208]. Thus the Civil War was more over money than over slavery.

14. **Max's drawings**: The drawings of Max Beerbohm, who caricatured the Victorian, Edwardian, and Georgian eras.

15. **Balfour**: Arthur James B., 1848-1930, British statesman; foreign minister (1916-1919); author of the Balfour Declaration which pledged British support to the founding of a Jewish state in Palestine as part of the solution to Middle East problems.

16. Johnny Bull: Nickname for Great Britain.

17. Orage: Alfred Richard O., 1873-1934, English journalist; editor of *The New Age.*

18. G.B.S.: George Bernard Shaw, 1856-1950, Irish playwright.

19. Mr. Xtertn: Gilbert Keith Chesterton, 1874-1936, English journalist, writer, and defender of Catholicism; a brilliant representative of Edwardian England.

20. Mr. Wells: [42:2].

21. John Marmaduke: Marmaduke William Pickthall, 1875-1936, English novelist living in the Near East and, like Pound, a writer for *The New Age*, was converted to Mohammedanism. His racial slurs against the Greeks were prob. meant to document his ignorance, because Pound's own opinions about the Greeks, including their art and religion, were quite different. The more Marmaduke talks the more he shows his true character.

22. Abdul Baha: Sir A. B. Bahai, 1844-1921, leader of the religion known as Bahaism, founded by his father Baha Ullah. Bahaists believe in the unity of all religions, universal education, world peace, and equality of the sexes.

23. Camel driver said: Presumably Pound heard this anecdote directly from Pickthall.

24. Uberton, Gubberton: Prob. refers to Surbiton, a town on the Thames, in Surrey.

25. Mohammedans: Followers of the prophet Mohammed.

26. Paterson: William P., 1658-1719, British financier, chief founder of the Bank of England (1694). Source reads: "As Disraeli put it, 'the principle of the system was to mortgage industry in order to protect property,' or, as Paterson, the originator of the Bank [of England], himself explained with charming simplicity, 'The bank hath benefit of the interest on all moneys which it creates out of nothing' " [Hollis, 30].

27. Mr. Rothschild: Prob. Junius R. or John Pierpont R., Sr. In *A Visiting Card*, Pound says: "It was a Rothschild who wrote: 'Those few who can understand the (usurocratic) system will be . . . busy getting profits, . . . while the general public . . . will probably never suspect that the system is absolutely against their interests,' (From a letter of Rothschild Bros., quoting John Sherman, addressed to the firm of Ikleheimer, Morton and Van der Gould, dated 25 June 1863)" [*SP*, 311].

28. anno domini: L, "in the year of the Lord."

29. Foundation of Regius Professors: Royal endowment of professorships at Oxford and Cambridge universities. Leading 18th century Whigs became alarmed at the "unpopularity of the debt-system among the gentry who had to pay the taxes to meet its charges." Therefore a "Whig" history was written [*History of Our Own Times*] and a deliberate campaign to subvert the faculties of Oxford and Cambridge was undertaken: 12 fellows from each university were invited to preach a sermon and receive a £ 30 emolument. None could hope to receive a share of this bounty "but they who are staunch Whigs and openly declare themselves to be so." The sermons worked so well that Townshend [a famous Whig leader], thinking they should be permanently endowed, proposed to George I that a regius professorship be established at both Oxford and Cambridge. The professors' real business would be to propagandize Whig political and economic views. So that there would be no mistake, wrote Townshend, "George himself [meaning the Whig prime minister] is to put in the professors" [Hollis, 35-52].

30. Whiggery: Prob. the doctrines of laissez-faire economics.

31. Macmillan Commission: MacMillan Committee, a British committee on finance and industry (1929) under the chairmanship of Lord MacMillan. Since the committee placed major blame for the depression not on the maintenance of the gold standard itself, but upon the shortsighted handling of it by major nations and upon the gold-hoarding policies of the U.S. and France, it agreed that the gold standard should be replaced. Pound's source adds: "That policy [return to stable price level] had already been recommended by the MacMillan Report which said: 'The ultimate aim should be the stability of the international price-level, meaning by this the composite price at wholesale of the principle foodstuffs and raw materials entering into international trade as measured by the best known wholesale index numbers' " [Hollis, 243].

32. **ex nihil**: L, "from nothing." Refers to the statement attributed to William Paterson [cf. 26 above; *A Visiting Card*, 9].

33. **Mr. Marx, Karl**: Pound wrote: "Marx and La Tour du Pin were equally deaf, dumb and blind to money. . . . And the amazing history of the 19th century is summed up in: 'Marx found nothing to criticize in money' " [*SP*, 272-273]. Pound seems to be using the L *monumental* (which means lit. "a memorial" or "a monument") in the sense of "enormous" or "monumental."

34. **St. Peter's**: [31:50].

35. **Manchester**: Manufacturing city, Lancashire, NW England.

36. **Si requieres Monumentum?**: L, "If you require a memorial?"

37. **Hic est hyper-usura**: L, "This is hyper-usury."

38. **Mr. Jefferson:** From Jefferson, XIII, 297. The prohibition epitomizes Jefferson's economic thought.

39. **Replevin**: In law, the return to, or recovery by, a person of goods or chattels wrongfully taken or detained, upon giving security to try the matter in court and return the goods if defeated in the action.

40. **estopple**: Estoppel. In law, a bar to alleging or denying a fact because of one's own previous action by which the contrary has been admitted, implied, or determined.

41. **VanBuren**: Martin V. B. That the lender must have the money to lend was a recurrent theme in Van Buren's and Jackson's long fight against the renewal of the charter of the Bank of the United States in the mid-1830s [37:passim].

42. **Antoninus**: [42:4]. A. Pius, Roman emperor (137-161), famous for early work on maritime law. Significant because Pound associates the beginnings of usury in the Occident with events in his reign: "The archeologist and serendipidist can . . . find the known beginnings of usury entangled with those of marine insurance, sea lawyers, the law of Rhodes; the disputed text of Antoninus Pius on the limits of his jurisdiction. Even then the dealers in metal appeared to be privileged over other merchants, and the insurance risk mainly paid by the takers of greater risk" [*SP*, 272-273].

43. **lex Rhodi**: L, "the law of Rhodes."

44. **usura**: L, I, "usury." Concerning usury, Pound wrote: "The 'Church' declined and fell on this issue. Historians have left the politics of Luther and of Calvin in the blurr of great ignorance . . . . The Church slumped into a toleration of usury. Protestantism as factive and organised, may have sprung from nothing but pro-usury politics" [*SP*, 273].

45. **Athens**: As opposed to Sparta, where "the true nature of money was comprehended," Pound sees Athens as the home of monetary fraud: ". . . you might make out a fairly good case against Athens as the mother of rascality, did one not see her as the grand-daughter of a long line of markets and mediterranean trading posts. Every form of fraud flourished there in perfection, nothing is added in ingenuity. . . . There sat the scoundrel . . . lending out his shilling a day. . . . Further along a bloke with a table performing the next grade of usury" [*GK*, 35-36].

46. **Luther**: Martin L., 1483-1546. Pound wrote: "I take it that the Catholic Church broke from the top, as Paganism had pos-

sibly broken. I mean to say that the Church was no longer interested in theology, it no longer believed or even knew what it meant. Leo X was interested in administration, in culture, in building St. Peter's. It simply never occurred to him that anyone would take Luther seriously. No one in his set did take Luther seriously, I mean as a writer or thinker. He was merely a barbarian bore. Protestantism has no theology. By which I mean it has nothing that a well grounded theologian can possibly consider salonfahig" [*SP*, 57].

47. 1527: . . . art thickened: Pound wrote before 1931: "Certainly the metamorphosis into carnal tissue becomes frequent and general somewhere about 1527. The people are corpus, corpuscular, but not in the strict sense 'animate,' it is no longer the body of air clothed in the body of fire; it no longer radiates, light no longer moves from the eye, there is a great deal of meat, shock absorbing, perhaps–at any rate absorbent. It has not even Greek marmoreal plastic to restrain it. The dinner scene is more frequently introduced, we have the characters in definite act of absorption; later they will be but stuffing for expensive upholsteries." [*LE*, 153].

48. 'Hic nefas' . . . 'commune sepulchrum': L, "Here is infamy . . . the common sepulcher."

49. Aurum est . . .: L, "Gold is a common sepulcher. Usury, a common sepulcher."

50. helandros . . . helarxe: H, "destroyer of men, and destroyer of cities, and destroyer of governments" [2:8; 7:2].

51. Hic Geryon . . .: L, "Here is Geryon. Here hyperusury." Geryon was (1) a three-headed or three-bodied monster living on the island of Erythia, killed by Heracles; (2) the symbol of fraud and guardian of the eighth circle of hell in the *Inferno*; (3) sometimes a symbol of usury and violence against nature and art [*Inf.* XVII, passim].

52. FIVE million . . .: The state of the U.S. economic system as reported variously in the press in 1935. Pound's thesis is that an economic system that produces such results is sadly deficient.

53. F. Roosevelt, signed F. Delano: Franklin Delano R., 1882-1945, president of the U.S. (1933-1945). Pound wrote: "In contrast to the idiotic accumulation of debt by Roosevelt, observe that *if* such government expenditure be necessary or advisable, the direct payment of workers, etc., in stamp scrip would in eight years consume itself, and leave the next decade *free* of all debt. The Roosevelt system is either a fraud or a selling of the nation's children into slavery without the ghost of excuse" [*SP*, 280].

54. Eunited: Pun on "United," with Greek prefix *eu*-, meaning "done well."

55. foetor: L, "stench."

56. Mr. Cummings: Homer Stillé C., 1870-1956, American lawyer and politician; attorney general (1933-1939).

57. Farley: James Aloysius F., 1888-1976, American politician, who was rewarded by being made postmaster general. The irony of the headline under the conditions of the economy is obvious.

CANTO XLVII

Sources

Od. X, 250 ff., XI, 1-150, XII, 80-100; Frazer, *The Golden Bough*, 1890 and many later editions [references in the glosses are paged to the easily available Gaster abridgment of 1959, 286-296] ; Bion, "The Lament for Adonis" [Loeb, 387-395] ; Hesiod, *Works and Days* [Loeb, 31-45] .

Background

EP, *GK*, 146; Ovid, *Meta*. III.

Exegeses

Dekker, *Cantos*, 36-46 and passim; DP, *Barb*, 172-192; EH, *Approaches*, 167-168, 198-199; Rosenthal, *Pai*, 6-3.

Glossary

1. **Who . . . entire**: Tiresias. [*Od.* X, 493; 1:7] . Pound believed that the Greeks thought intelligence in man manifested divinity in man. Zeus said of Odysseus, "A chap with a mind like THAT! The fellow is one of us." Pound follows this free translation from the *Odyssey* with the remark: "I hope that elsewhere I have underscored and driven in the greek honour of human intelligence 'Who even dead yet hath his mind entire' [*GK*, 146] .

2. **First. . . end**: Circe gave directions to Odysseus in the dark: "But when the sun set and darkness came on . . . I went up to the beautiful bed of Circe" [*Od.* X, 480] . He asked that she let him and his men go home. In consenting, Circe said: "Odysseus . . . abide ye now no longer in my house against your will; but you must first complete another journey, and come to the house of Hades and dread Persephone, to seek soothsaying of the spirit of Theban Teiresias, the blind seer, whose mind abides steadfast" [*Od.* X, 488-494; 39:18] .

3. **Ceres**: Latin name of Demeter, goddess of the harvest and central figure in the Eleusinian Mysteries.

4. **Tiresias**: Greek seer who was struck blind by Hera, wife of Zeus. Since Zeus could not undo the act of the goddess, he compensated for the loss of sight by giving Tiresias the power of prophecy [Ovid, *Meta*. III] .

5. **beefy men**: Men in the flesh, before death.

6. **phtheggometha thasson**: H, "let us raise our voices without delay." Transliteration of the Greek words in next line [cf. 39/193; 39:15] .

7. **The small lamps**: During the July festival of Montallegre Madonna, Pound could see at Rapallo local women set votive lights adrift in the Golfo Tigullio. He relates the cere-

mony to early vegetation rites held to celebrate the death of "Tammuz-Adonis."

8. **Neptunus**: L, Neptune. Roman god of the sea.

9. **Tamuz**: Tammuz, Babylonian name of Adonis.

10. **By this gate**: Janus ruled the two gates, one into life and the other into death. Here it is the gate into the underworld, rhyming with the Persephone- Adonis myth. See repetition of line below followed by "Thy day is between a door and a door" [cf. also "And that all gates are holy," 94/634].

11. **Scilla**: Scylla, according to Greek myth, was a sea monster who lived in a cave opposite Charybdis. She had six heads, each with a triple row of teeth, and barked like a dog [cf. *Od*. XII, 80-100].

12. **TU DIONA**: H, "You Dione." Aphrodite. In myth, she fell in love with Adonis who after his death spent part of the year with Persephone in Hades and returned to earth (with spring) to be with Aphrodite for the rest of the year.

13. ***Kai* MOIRAI' ADONIN**: H, "And the fates . . . Adonis." From Bion's "Lament for Adonis." The complete line reads: "The fates cry over Adonis."

14. **The sea is streaked red**: Spring freshets used to bring red-stained water from the mountains into the sea. Eastern Mediterranean people related the color to the blood of Adonis, the yearly slain [*Golden Bough*, 286-296].

15. **Wheat shoots rise**: Reference to "Gardens of Adonis" in which pots were filled with earth and the seed of "wheat, barley, lettuces, fennel. . . . Fostered by the sun's heat, the plants shot up rapidly . . . and at the end of eight days were carried out with the images of the dead Adonis, and flung with them into the sea" [*Golden Bough*, 293].

16. **Two span**: Source unknown.

17. **Moth . . . bull**: Answering blind sexual call through odors in the air.

18. **naturans**: L, "obeying its nature." Creative nature was called *natura naturans* by Johannes Scotus Erigena.

19. **Odysseus**: Called to the "lair" of Circe [*Od*. X, 300 ff.].

20. **Molü**: Herb given to Odysseus by Hermes to resist the evil potion of Circe [ibid.; 39:7].

21. **Begin thy plowing . . . time**: Most of this 14-line passage is adapted from Hesiod's *Works and Days*: "When the Pleiades . . . are rising begin your harvest, and your ploughing when they are going to set. Forty nights and days they are hidden and appear again. . . This is the law of the plains, and of those who live near the sea. . . . Get two oxen, bulls of nine years; for their strength is unspent . . .they are best for work. . . . Mark when you hear the voice of the crane who cries . . . above for she gives the signal for ploughing" [Hesiod, 31 ff.].

22. **Pleiades**: The seven daughters of Atlas who became a cluster of stars in the constellation Taurus.

23. **small stars**: Olive-tree blossoms are shaped like small stars, but they do not fall at the time of spring plowing. Perhaps the stars of the Pleiades going "down to their rest" are to be seen through the olive-tree branches. But the falling stars may be phosphorescent insects [48:53].

24. **Tellus**: Roman goddess of the earth.

25. **Scylla**: [cf. 11 above].

26. **cunnus**: L, "female sex organ."

27. **Io**: H, "Hail."

28. **Zephyrus**: West wind.

29. **Apeliota**: East wind.

30. **Adonis falleth**: At the harvest or in the waning year when the god of the vegetation myths dies.

31. **KAI MOIRAI' etc.**: [cf. 13 above].

32. **almond bough . . . flame**: Rebirth of Adonis in the vegetation myths. The coming of spring makes the sap run and the almond "flame" with flower.

33. **Tu Diona**: [cf. 12 above].

34. **power over wild beasts**: Attribute of the god Dionysus-Adonis-Tammuz [cf. 2/8]. A power also attributed in myth to special humans, as to Apollonius of Tyana in *The Cantos* [91/616; 93/623].

CANTO XLVIII

Sources

Personal experiences and memories of Pound; Remy de Gourmont, *The Natural Philosophy of Love*, New York, Boni and Liveright, 1922; rpt., New York, Collier Books, 1972, 39-40.

Background

Mary de Rachewiltz, *Discretions*, Boston and Toronto, 1971, 72-73; EP, *J/M*, 18.

Exegeses

HK, *Pai*, 2-1, 41; DG, *Pai*, 4-2, 3, 225 ff.; CE, *Ideas*, 38, 39, 114, 116; WB, *Rose*, 60.

Glossary

1. **money be rented**: Exact source unidentified, but the four lines are a Poundian paraphrase of Jackson's and Van Buren's ideas in their fight in the mid-1830s against renewal of the charter of the Bank of the United States [37:passim].

2. **Mahomet VIth Yahid Eddin Han**: Mohammed VI, 1861-1926, last Ottoman sultan (1918-1922); deposed in 1922 when Turkey became a republic.

3. **San Remo**: Seaport in Imperia Province, NW Italy, on Ligurian Sea, a resort where the exiled sultan died.

4. **Abdul Mejid**: 1823-1861, Ottoman sultan (1839-1861), father of Mohammed VI.

5. **At beatification**: The Paris edition of the *Herald Tribune*, June 12, 1930, contained an item about the electric illumination in St. Peter's for the beatification of Paula Frasinetti, 1809-1882, founder of the Sisters of St. Dorothy, a religious teaching order for poor children. The last line of the

Tribune story reads: "For the beatification ceremony 80 loudspeakers were used" [HK, *Pai*, 2-1, 41]. A rhyme with other items concerning growth of scientific inventions [cf. "Electro-magnetic" at 34/171, and "Marconi . . . electric shakes" at 38/187].

6. **Turkish war**: When Kara Mustafa came to the Turkish throne, he wanted to memorialize his regime by some "great exploit." Thus, in a quite unjustifiable war, he marched a vast Turkish army (more than 200,000) to the walls of Vienna from which the emperor and his court fled. Because of the fantastic ineptness and military stupidity of Mustafa, John Sobieski, king of Poland, put the entire Turkish army to flight with a force of 20,000 men and saved the cause of Christianity. In Austrian history, the siege of Vienna in 1683 looms as large as the battle of Waterloo does in the West.

7. **Mr. Kolschitzky**: Georges François Koltschitzky de Szombor, fl. 1683, interpreter for a commercial company of the East who was employed to spy on Turkish forces during the siege of Vienna (1683). As payment he was granted a patent to open the first coffeehouse in Vienna and was given a quantity of coffee found in the Turkish camp.

8. **(de Banchiis cambi tenendi)**: L, "concerning banks for carrying on exchange" [40:3].

9. **Von Unruh**: Fritz von U., 1885-1970, German playwright, poet, and novelist; officer in World War I [41:20].

10. **Kaiser**: Wilhelm II, 1859-1941, German emperor and king of Prussia (1888-1918).

11. **Verdun**: Scene of the longest and bloodiest battle of World War I; 2 million men were engaged and 1 million were killed.

12. **Mr. Charles Francis Adams**: 1807-1886, American statesman, minister to Great Britain (1861-1868). Traveled widely in Europe, graduated Harvard in 1825, studied law with Daniel Webster. Became famous writer and editor of his grandfather's letters, diaries, and papers [62:29]. Where Charles Francis A. made this remark is unknown, but the thought rhymes with similar statements made by his father, John Quincy Adams, who complained that only the "corps diplomatique" had any interest in conversation [cf. 34/165].

13. **Browning**: Robert B., 1812-1889. In addition to his "hearty" opinions, it was the vigor and cacophony in his verse which at first made Browning seem un-English to the English.

14. **Van Buren**: Martin V. B. Pound came to believe that Van Buren's *Autobiography*, written in 1854 but not published until 1918, was deliberately suppressed ("kept in the cellarage").

15. **J. Adams**: John A. Source of the words he supposedly said is unknown.

16. **Marx**: In his discussions of the ill effects of child labor, Karl Marx was concerned not only with the horrors the children suffered at the moment but also with lasting ill effects, since some of them would grow up to "become fathers of the next generation" [cf. 33:28, 32, 33].

17. **Bismarck**: Otto von B., 1815-1898, German soldier and statesman. Source of line is unknown.

18. **Rothschild**: Source of line is unknown.

19. **Disraeli**: Benjamin D., 1804-1881, 1st Earl of Beaconsfield, British statesman and author; prime minister (1874-1880).

20. **DIGONOS**: H, [Δίγονος], "twice-born." Associated with Dionysus who was twice-born, once from his mother, Semele, and then from the thigh of his father, Zeus [74/425]. Leopards and all animals in the cat family are sacred to Dionysus [2: passim].

21. **Your Highness**: Prob. Queen Victoria. Neither the writer nor the source of the letter is known.

22. Cawdor: Prob. Cawdor Castle, Nairnshire, N Scotland.

23. Dhu Achil: Gaelic, "Black Achilles," prob. a dog.

24. Mr. Rhumby: Pseudonym for Bainbridge Colby, secretary of state under Wilson (1920-1921). The juxtaposition of the lines in parentheses makes an ironic contrast: British royalty choosing a pedigreed dog with an American president choosing a secretary of state.

25. Mr. McLocherty: Doubtless a Scottish friend of the royal agent who is writing the letter.

26. Galileo: G. Galilei, 1564-1642, Italian mathematician and astronomer.

27. 'Garry Yeo': Galileo.

28. err' un' . . . mondo: I, "he was an imbecile; and he has made imbecile / . . . the world." Prob. official attitude of Church toward theories of Galileo.

29. Salem: City in Massachusetts, once an important center of fishing, shipping, and shipbuilding. Similar ironic comment on the reasonable requirements for a trustee of the Salem Museum as opposed to politicians making appointments in the smoke-filled backroom: ". . . three senators: four bottles of whiskey."

30. Good Hope: The cape at tip of S Africa.

31. The Horn: Cape Horn at the tip of S America.

32. Bithynia: Bythnia, ancient country of NW Asia Minor; it became a Roman province in 74 B.C. when Nicomedes IV willed his kingdom to Rome.

33. theign: OE, one of a class of free attendants on a lord; later, a baron.

34. Athelstan: D. 940; king of the English (924-940) who introduced guilds. Pound considers him to be one of the wisest of early English kings. The ironic contrast continues.

35. 'A little more stock': In the early days of uncontrolled stock speculation, the so-called robber barons could (and did) print any amount of stock and sell it without regard to the assets of the company.

36. Norse engineer: Unidentified. But Pound is prob. using a story told him about "this amazing navigational feat."

37. 'while she bought . . . Sunday shoes?': The first four lines in this 24-line passage are based on a letter to Pound from Olga Rudge who [according to Pound's daughter, Mary de Rachewiltz] at the time was in Paris where she had escorted a lady of means on a shopping expedition. The 20 following lines are based on a letter written by Mary herself from her foster parents' home in the Italian Tyrol [*Discretions*, 72-73]. Thinking about such celebrations as the ones depicted, she wrote later: "But time was never grudged for Church activities and we had grand processions and parades when the Bishop came for the confirmation ceremony or when one of the village boys came to officiate at his first Mass. No greater blessing or honor could have befallen the village; the grown-ups rejoiced and we children were wildly excited. . . . The new pair of shoes I needed when the Bishop came and I had to recite a poem."

38. una nuova . . . festa: I, "a new mass / (12th year of the Fascist era) / beautiful ceremony."

39. full of fires: Apparently an annual celebration of the founding of fascism included religious observances, parades, fireworks in the mountain villages, music, etc. Rhymes with mountain fires in *The Periplus of Hanno* [40:31, 46].

40. in giro . . .: I, "around the countryside."

41. carrozze: I, "carriages."

42. orchis: H, "a testicle." Prob. a metaphor for "chrysalis" as a step in the process of metamorphosis into the *farfalla* ["butterfly"], a creature of wings. The metaphor is much elaborated in the Pisan cantos [cf. 83/532]. It appears as a leitmotiv in later cantos, such as "the king-wings in migration" [cf. 106/754] and "the kings meet in their island, / where no food is after flight from the pole" [cf. Drafts/802; for insect themes in summary cf. DG, *Pai*, 4-2 & 3, 225 ff.].

43. Mt. Segur: The last stronghold of the Catharists and Albigensians which, when they were persecuted by Innocent III, became their graveyard [23:25].

44. Val Cabrere: Valcabrère, village in S France on road to Mt. Segur.

45. San Bertrand: A village in S France, once a large Roman city.

46. Terminus: An altar, in Provence, to the great god Terminus, the sacred boundary stone that stood in the great temple of the Capitoline Jupiter in Rome.

47. Savairic: Savaric de Mauleon, whose native town is near Mt. Segur [5:20].

48. Gaubertz: G. de Poicebot, who traveled by Mt. Segur on his way to Spain [5:21].

49. Paris: The Church in N France, coached by Innocent III, insisted that the Christians in Provence (S France) come under its jurisdiction and help wipe out heretical sects such as the Manicheans. But the Manicheans, insisting they were the true Christians, would not accept the authority of Paris.

50. Falling Mars: Poss. a metaphor [derived from Gourmont] for a male insect armed for sexual consummation: "Everyone knows the flying-stag . . . which flies through the summer evening buzzing like a top. . . . He is the male, his war-gear pure ornament . . . females are devoid of warlike apparatus. . . . The glow-worm is a real worm. . . . The male of this female is a perfect insect, provided with wings which he uses to seek in the darkness' [Gourmont, 39-40]. Here Pound also associates "direction of the will" with "instinct" and sees them, acting in concert, to be superior to conventionalized intellect. He wrote: "The flying ant or wasp or whatever it was that I saw cut up a spider at Excideuil may have been acting by instinct, but it was not acting by reason of the stupidity of instinct" ["Directio Voluntatis," in *J/M*, 18]. The whole amalgam of images here becomes a mosaic of one of the most important themes in *The Cantos*: the way that divinity manifests itself as intelligence in process, the kind of intelligence that makes the cherrystone become a cherry tree [51:8; 113/788].

51. ox . . . spire-top: Poss. details of place where Pound saw and was struck by the mating of a certain flying insect which dramatically illustrated precise descriptions by Remy de Gourmont.

52. jet avenger . . .: Another insect, prob. a flying wasp, gets its prey while, nearby, the ants get theirs.

53. Mars in the air . . .: The conclusion. Many an insect in Gourmont exists for a brief moment to be used (for generation) and then dies; it becomes a "was": "There is a kind of lamprey of which both sexes are equally phosphorescent, one in the air, the male, the other on the ground where she awaits him. After coupling they fade as lamps when extinguished. . . . When the female sees the small flying star descend toward her, she gathers . . . exults in fear, trembles in joy. The fading light is symbolic of the destiny of nearly all insects . . . coupling accomplished . . . life vanishes from them" [Gourmont, 40; cf. 47:23].

54. Lido: Town at N end of the island, outside the Lagoon of Venice, which has a famous beach.

55. an old man . . . placed a stone: I.e., on beach cloths to keep them from blowing away. His sexual potency gone, he has become in the universal process (or "the way") a kind of death-in-life [cf. "the old man sweeping leaves," etc., 21/99-100].

CANTO XLIX

Sources

A manuscript of *Sho-Sho Hakkei* [eight paintings of scenes along the Sho-Sho River] in Pound's possession; notes [inedit.] Pound took from verbal translations and comments on the Chinese poems; Fenollosa Notebooks (inedit.), University of Virginia Library; Sasaki Genryu, *Poems in Chinese and Japanese on the Eight Famous Scenes by Genryu*, 1683; H. A. Giles, *A History of Chinese Literature*, London and New York, 1901.

Background

Ichisada Miyazaki, *Prosperity of the Empire of Shin*, Tokyo, 1967; Shigeki Kaizuka, *A History of China*, 3 vols., Tokyo, 1971.

Exegeses

Sanehide Kodama, "The Eight Scenes of Sho-Sho," *Pai*, 6-2, 131-145; Angela Jung Palandri, "The 'Seven Lakes Canto' Revisited," *Pai*, 3-1, 51-54; HK, "More on the Seven Lakes Canto," *Pai*, 2-1, 43-46; DP, *Barb*, App. B; Dekker, *Cantos*, 179-181; Fang, Ph.D. dissertation, Harvard University, I, 77.

Glossary

1. **seven lakes**: Because of this first line, Canto 49 has come to be known as "The Seven Lakes Canto." Kenner says it "consists of (1) [eight] anonymous poems much rearranged; (2) the Emperor's poem; (3) a folk song; (4) a terminal Poundian distich and four interpolated Poundian lines" [HK, *Pai*, 2-1, 46]. Kodama identifies the source of the poems as eight famous paintings of scenes along a river in C China which pours into Lake Dotei. Ezra Pound's parents owned an old Japanese manuscript book which contained the eight Chinese and eight Japanese poems illustrated by the paintings. The book is entitled *Sho-Sho* [the river] *Hakkei* [Kodama, *Pai*, 6-2, 131-145; unless otherwise noted, quotations in the following glosses are from this article]. "Sho-Sho" is Japanese for Chinese "Hsiao-Hsiang" (M2622-M2565); the river Hsiao flows into the Hsiang, a major tributary of the Yangtze, at Lingling in S Hunan province. "Hakkei" is Japanese for Chinese "pa ching" (M4845-M1129), traditionally defined as the "eight classes of scenery."

2. **Rain . . . weeping**: These five lines are based on a poem for Scene 6, entitled "Night Rain in Sho-Sho." The poem concerns events after the legendary emperor Yü Shun died, causing his wives such grief that their tears dyed the bamboo leaves purple; dappled purple bamboos still grow in the area. "Later [the wives] killed themselves,

and their shrine is said to be near the River. The narrator of the poem is on his way to the shrine, and is filled with sorrow."

3. **Autumn ... reeds**: These six lines are based on a poem for Scene 5, entitled "Autumn Moon on Lake Dotei." "Lake Dotei" is the Chinese "Tung-t'ing Hu" (M6609-M6405, M2168), long anglicized as "Tungting Lake", a large shallow body of water in N Hunan province. The Hsiang, after being joined by the Hsiao, drains E Hunan, flowing north into this natural reservoir of the Yangtze.

4. **Behind ... wind**: From Scene 7: "Evening Bell of a Misty Temple." Kodama writes in a footnote: "According to one interpretation, the poem refers to the ruin of a Buddhist temple on top of Mt. Kyugi in the Sho-Sho area, and the bell the narrator hears is from a nearby temple." "Kyugi" is prob. "Chiu-chi" in Hunan province.

5. **Boat fades ... river**: Based on Scene 2: "Sailboats Returning to Far-off Shores," which evokes a feeling of loneliness and yearning.

6. **Where wine flag ... light**: Based on Scene 3: "Mist over a Mountain Town." Kodama renders some of the lines as "A wine flag on the pole is in the slanting sun / Some houses are in the mist."

7. **Comes ... cold**: Based on Scene 4: "Evening Snowfall over the River." Key words and phrases in original are "colorless clouds," "low sky," "jewel dust flying," "small leaflike boat."

8. **San Yin**: Pound's notes show this originally transcribed as "Sai Yin." The two Chinese characters "shan yin" (M5630, M7444)—"san yin" in the dialects of C China—form a phrase meaning "the north side of the mountain"; but Pound turned them into a place name. [See Kodama, *Pai*, 6-2, 136, n. 6 for another view].

9. **Wild geese ... autumn**: Scene 1: "Wild Geese Plummeting to the Flat Sands,"

10. **Rooks ... sky line**: Scene 8: "Sunset Glow over a Fishing Village." Some phrases are "Twilight bewilders the crows," "clamors of fish and shrimps," "the waves are colored in the track of the setting sun."

11. **Tsing**: Ch'ing, name of the 22d dynasty, 1616-1912. It was prob. K'ang-hsi, the 2d Ch'ing emperor (1662-1722), who visited the hill lakes. Kodama says that he seems to have visited the Seven Lakes area with the empress in 1699. His reign is the subject of Cantos 58-61; the *Sacred Edict* of K'ang-hsi is the main subject of Cantos 98-99.

12. **State ... debt?**: Attitude of Presidents Thomas Jefferson, Andrew Jackson, and Martin Van Buren [cf. 37/183: "Relief is got not by increase / but by diminution of debt"].

13. **Geryon**: [46:5].

14. **TenShi**: Prob. a village to which Yodai's canal went.

15. **old king**: Yodai [Yang-ti], 605-618, a king who found that building canals gave pleasure to himself and to his people; the canals became economically useful.

16. **KEI ... KAI**: These four lines are a transliteration of Japanese pronunciation of a classical Chinese poem Pound found in the Fenollosa Notebooks. Translations are many and varied. Kodama gives: "The auspicious clouds bright and colorful / Twist and spread. / The sun and the moon shed their rays / Morning after morning."

17. **sun up ... what is it?**: These five lines are based on the translation of an ancient Chinese poem to be found in a Fenollosa Notebook as well as several other places. The intent or tone of the poem is controversial. Fang calls it the well-known "Clod-Beaters Song" [Chi-jang-ko] "supposedly sung by contented peasantry of the time of Shun's predecessor Yao" [53:14]. Others have translated it as "a coolies' song": the lazy king does nothing and lives off the sweat of the laboring man. A Fenollosa note says of it:

"This is called an earth beating song, because old folk beat the ground (for music) in singing this song." Kodama believes Pound achieves "the simplicity of a folk poem" by consulting Fenollosa [*Pai*, 6-2, 144].

18. **The fourth . . . beasts**: Pound told a visitor that in Canto 49 he intended to present "a glimpse of Paradiso" [Palandri, *Pai*, 3-1, 51]. The paradisal thrust of the lines is suggested by stillness ["the still point of the turning world" in Eliot] as well as the Dionysian power over wild beasts [cf. 2/8]. Note also rhyme with Apollonius [94/635].

CANTO L

Sources

Antonio Zobi, *Storia civile della Toscana dal MDCCXXXVII al MDCCCXLVIII*, 5 vols., Firenze, 1850-1852; Christopher Hollis, *The Two Nations*, London, 1935; Charles Francis Adams, ed., *The Works of John Adams*, X, Boston, 1856; Andrew Lipscomb and Albert Bergh, eds., *The Writings of Thomas Jefferson*, XIV, Washington, D.C., 1905; *Il Monte dei Paschi di Siena e le Aziende in Esso Riunite*, 9 vols., ed. Narciso Mengozzi, Siena, 1891-1925.

Background

Fang, Ph.D. dissertation, Harvard University, I, 80; any of the standard biographies of Napoleon, Wellington, and Metternich.

Exegeses

Kimpel and Eaves, *Pai*, 8-1.

Glossary

1. **Revolution' said Mr. Adams**: John Adams in a letter about the history of the Revolution [32:1].

2. **Peter Leopold**: Pietro Leopoldo, Duke of Tuscany, who worked hard to improve conditions in his land. A rhyme with what the early Revolutionists were doing in New England [44:1].

3. **Count Orso . . . place**: The source shows that on December 23, 1624, Count Orso and "suoi figli et descendenti maschi legittimi et naturali ["his sons and male descendants legitimate and natural"] were enfiefed with the territory of Monte Pescali and entrusted by the Grand Duke of Tuscany with the . . . administration of Civil and Criminal Justice in the said Place" [Kimpel and Eaves, *Pai*,

8-1]. According to Kimpel, the lines are "almost certainly" meant to describe the situation under the old rulers of Tuscany, the Medici, who became extinct in 1737.

4. **debt when the Medici**: [43:70]. The debt of the Medici recorded from Il Monte dei Paschi in the last lines of Canto 43/222 Pound found also in Zobi, who noted: "When the Medici came to the throne, the debt of the Republic calculated all together did not exceed five million ducats; and at the time of their extinction the Tuscan debt has grown to fourteen million scudi, the interest on which absorbed the best incomes of the State" [Zobi, I, 118; trans. Kimpel, *Pai*, 8-1].

5. **the first folly** . . . : Zobi says [I, 120] that the germ of the decay of the commercial prosperity of Tuscany was the avidity of Florentine merchants, which caused them to establish wool factories in Flanders, England, and elsewhere in order to save the cost of transportation of raw materials; the English, who produced the raw wool, soon prohibited its export.

6. **the arts** . . . : Zobi [I, 153-163, esp. 160] laments the decay of letters and the graphic arts in Tuscany.

7. **and Leopoldo** . . . : [cf. 2 above]. Pound had stressed the wise reforms of the Grand Duke Pietro Leopoldo of Tuscany toward the end of Canto 44. Here he adds, from Zobi, the abolition of many taxes [II, 99, 182, 269-270], the refinancing and reduction of the national debt [II, 104-107, 441-446], the expulsion of the Jesuit order [II, 133], and the abolition of the Catholic Inquisition [II, 305].

8. **'Un' abbondanza che affamava'**: I, "An abundance which famishes," a play on the name of the Abbondanza ["Abundance," the office in charge of relief works]. Zobi reports [I, 403] that before Pietro Leopoldo's reign it had no funds and was called "l'affamatrice Abbondanza." Pietro Leopoldo created a new office to replace the old Abbondanza, "che facevano l'ufficio d'*affamare*" ["whose office it was *to starve*"]. Thus, Leopold becomes one of the minor heroes of *The Cantos*, a man, *directio voluntatis*, who gets things done [II, 60].

9. **Mr. Locke's / essay on interest**: Pietro Leopoldo entrusted the direction of finance to Angelo Tavanti, one of the very few Italians who had studied French and English writers on politics and economics; he collaborated on a translation of *Several Papers Relating to Money, Interest and Trade, . . . Writ upon Several Occasions and Published at Different Times*, by John Locke (1632-1704), the famous philosopher and political theorist [Zobi, II, 267-268n].

10. **but Genoa took our trade** . . . : Because of the close connection between the grand duke and the royal family of Austria, the trade of the Tuscan port of Livorno (Leghorn) suffered when Austria got involved in a war with Turkey, and its old rival the independent city of Genoa took advantage of the situation; similarly, the grand duke refused to have relations with the American Colonies while they were at war with England, and when they became independent they preferred to trade with Genoa, which had had early commercial ties with them, so that trade from Livorno had to pass through Genoa [Zobi, II, 388-389].

11. **Te, admirabile, O VashinnnTTonn! . . . Voi, popoli transatlantici admirabili!**: I, "You, Oh admirable Washington! . . . You, admirable people across the Atlantic." Zobi seizes the occasion described in the above note for a digression [II, 389-390], which he hopes his readers will pardon, on the virtues of the Americans and their leader. He calls America the daughter of Italy and contrasts her independence and hopeful future with the servile state of Italy after the failure of the revolutions of 1848.

12. **two thirds of state debt**: The public debt in 1788 was 12,330,000 crowns; Pietro Leopoldo, who wanted to abolish the whole

debt, had arranged for the cancellation of 8,256,343 crowns [Zobi, II, 444n].

13. **they sent him off . . . and Paris exploded**: [44:1]. When he became Holy Roman emperor on the death of Josef II in 1790 (just as the French Revolution was starting), Pietro Leopoldo necessarily went to Vienna [Zobi, II, 509]. Pound had expressed his dislike of the Austrian Empire and especially of Franz Josef, 1830-1916, who became emperor in 1848, in Cantos 16 and 35 [16:23; 35:8]. In 1790 Franz Josef was not yet born, and Klemens Wenzel Nepomuk Lothar, Prince von Metternich, 1773-1859, the dominating figure of the reactionary period following the fall of Napoleon, did not become chancellor until 1809, but Pound is looking ahead. Pietro Leopoldo's son, the Grand Duke Ferdinando III, prevented the union [Anschluss] of the crowns of Austria and Tuscany, which were declared to be absolutely separated [Zobi, II, 554-555]. The Austro-Hungarian Empire, which succeeded the Holy Roman Empire, prided itself on its multinational nature ("embastardized cross-breeds"); *merdery* is a coinage from the French word for excrement. The explosion was the French Revolution.

14. **'certain practices called religious'** . . . : In discussing the reasons for the success of the American Republic and the failure of the Roman Republic set up at the time of the French Revolution, Zobi mentions [III, 230] that the Italians were too much given to such practices "by scoundrels," which served only to weaken mind and body "and in short make man less than man." He also mentions the Italian ignorance of economics.

15. **Pius sixth**: Giovanni Angelo Braschi, 1717-1799, elected pope in 1775. He followed an ultrareactionary policy even before the French Revolution; Zobi gives [III, 39] several examples of his unwise actions, such as his "excessive imprudence" in writing a letter to Louis XVI congratulating him on his escape from France before Louis had in fact got out of the country (he was caught and brought back). The letter was intercepted by the National Assembly and helped induce France to persecute the Gallican church and to invade Italy. The French took Rome in 1798, a republic was set up there, and the pope died a prisoner.

16. **MARENGO . . . a.d. 1800**: Marengo, near Alessandria in Piedmont, NW Italy, was the site of Napoleon's great victory over the Austrians on June 14, 1800, which gave him effective control of Italy. Napoleon had been in control of France, as first consul, since his coup d'etat of 18 "Brumale" or Brumaire [Nov. 9, but Zobi says Nov. 10], 1799. Zobi remarks [III, 406] that Napoleon thereby disposed the national representatives, so "1791" may be a misprint for 1799; or Pound may be thinking of the short-lived Constitution of 1791, which ended the power of the king and replaced the Constituent Assembly with a legislative assembly. The latter, a little more than a year later, was dominated by the radical Jacobin party, as the first step toward the end of representative government. "I left peace . . . to yr enemies" is from a speech, quoted by Zobi, which Napoleon made to his soldiers in Paris after his return from Marengo; Zobi says the speech was most truthful (as to the state of France) and most seditious (in giving Napoleon a reason to increase his power).

17. **interest at 24** . . . : Zobi reports [III, 440-441] the scarcity of money caused by the impositions of this war period, with the resulting rise in interest rates and decline of commerce.

18. **1801 the triumvirs** . . . : The three men governing Tuscany tried to restore some of the reforms of Pietro Leopoldo but were overthrown by a French army under Murat [Zobi, III, 461-463].

19. **A thousand . . . English frigate descended**: In 1814 Napoleon, forced by the allied armies to abdicate, was made king of the small island of Elba, off the Tuscan coast, the capital of which is Portoferraio.

On May 3 a British frigate landed him on Elba, where he was soon joined by a thousand men of his old guard. Pound states the income the allies granted him. Napoleon claimed to have chosen the island because of "the sweetness of their [the inhabitants'] customs and the goodness of their climate" [Zobi, III, 757-759].

20. **Ferdinando Habsburg**: Ferdinando III [44:6, 18; Zobi, III, 762] makes the remark about the state of his finances when he was restored as Grand Duke of Tuscany after the fall of Napoleon.

21. **England and Austria . . . bloody oppression**: A brief summary of the peace terms imposed by England and Austria, along with Russia and Prussia, in the Treaty of Vienna after the fall of Napoleon [the treaty is printed in Zobi, IV, 40-78]. The powers attempted to restore the pre-Revolutionary status, but went even further in extinguishing three old Italian republics: Venice went to Austria, Genoa to Sardegna (Sardinia), and Lucca to Maria Luisa, former queen of Etruria [44:38].

22. **Rospigliosi**: In 1814, before Ferdinando III could take charge of Tuscany, the state was temporarily administered by Prince Rospigliosi, who issued to the independence-loving Tuscans a proclamation containing "the enormous indecency that the Grand Duchy was the patrimony of foreign lords, as if states could be an allodial property and their inhabitants serfs" [Zobi, IV, 24].

23. **throne of England**: In 1814-1815 the English king, George III, had been insane for a number of years and his son, the future George IV, was regent.

24. **Austrian sofa**: The Austro-Hungarian emperor was Franz I, 1768-1835.

25. **four Georges**: The first four Georges ruled England from 1714 to 1830.

26. **Spain**: In 1814 the Bourbons were restored to Spain in the person of Fernando VII, 1784-1833.

27. **Wellington**: Arthur Wellesley, Duke of Wellington, 1769-1852, the victor of Waterloo. The conferees at the Congress of Vienna [including Wellington] are regarded by Hollis [*Two Nations*, 134-136] as not seeing the facts as they were. Pius the VI and the monarchs were persuaded that the old order had been restored. "Metternich and Stadion . . . were the rulers of Austria [they thought] because they were called the rulers of Austria. . . . The papacy [cf. 15 above] saw Metternich and Stadion in their seats of office. They did not see Stadion pocketing the loans of the Rothschilds and Metternich creeping down into the Frankfort ghetto to learn their latest will" [Hollis gives as sources *Rise of the House of Rothschild* (1928) and *Reign of the House of Rothschild* (1928) by C. E. Corti and *Metternich* (1933) by Algernon Cecil]. In the mid-thirties Pound saw Wellington as one of many willing victims of the usurers: "For fifty years after Waterloo Papal policy was directed by pious and simple men. They preached sincerely the Church's doctrine against usury . . . because in their innocence of the world they did not know they were usurers." It is important to note that in this canto Pound distinguishes "Jew" and the Jewish God from "jew" as "Rothschild usurer," saying that no Jew God would be foolish enough to keep a man like Pius VI in office [cf. 15 above]. But by the early 1950s he began to see other sides of Wellington's character [cf. "Wellington's peace after Vaterloo," 85/543].

28. **'Leave the Duke, Go for gold!'**: As evidence that a few bankers could plunge England into chaos, Hollis writes that when Earl Grey resigned as prime minister in 1832 because the king refused to create enough new peers to pass the first reform bill, the Duke of Wellington made an effort to form a Tory government. The watchword among the reformers was, "To stop the Duke, go for gold," that is, corner gold and thus create a run on the banks. Because of this threat the Whigs regained power [Hollis, 106].

29. Metternich: [13, 27, above].

30. 'From the brigantine Incostante' . . . into Flanders: A description of the Hundred Days during which Napoleon tried to recover his empire. Zobi tells [IV, 62] how Napoleon left Elba on the brigantine *Incostante* and landed at Cannes, in S France, on March 1, 1815. France quickly rallied behind him and his armies advanced into Flanders, but there, at the battle of Waterloo, on June 18, he was finally defeated, partly because Marshal Michel Ney, Prince de La Moskova, 1769-1815, was thrown from his horse and Emmanuel, Marquis de Grouchy, 1766-1847, did not bring up his troops in time [IV, 89].

31. Bentinck's word . . . Sardegna: In 1814 Lord William Cavendish Bentinck, 1774-1839, commander of the British forces in Sicily, led an expedition against Genoa and declared the republic there restored [Zobi, IV, 10, 102-103]. But the republic did not remain restored.

32. 'Not' / said Napoleon . . . : Zobi quotes [IV, 223n-224n] Earl Grey as reporting a statement made by Napoleon (after his final imprisonment on the island of St. Helena) that he "had fallen not because of the league formed against him but because he contradicted the spirit of the century."

33. Zeitgeist!: G, "Spirit of the times!"

34. OBIT, aetatis 57: L, "He died, aged 57." Napoleon died in 1821, and Dante Alighieri in 1321; but Napoleon was born in 1769 and died at the age of 51.

35. il sesso femminile: I, "the female sex." Zobi [IV, 273], describing the death of Napoleon's second wife, Maria Luisa of Parma, 1791-1847, is of the opinion that she was "certainly not distinguished for that which most embellishes the female sex and makes it estimable."

36. Italy ever doomed: Zobi, describing the enthusiasm for Pius IX [37 below] before 1848 but writing just after the failure of the revolutions of 1848, which attempted to unify the peninsula and cast out the Austrians who dominated much of it, laments [IV, 618] the fall of "this poor Italy, always destined to be ruined by pursuing brilliant abstractions and deceptive purposes."

37. Mastai, Pio Nono: Giovanni Maria Mastai-Ferretti, 1792-1878, became Pope Pius IX ("Pio Nono") in 1846. After giving early hopes of a more liberal policy [Zobi, V, 21], he was forced to flee from Rome in 1848, and on his return in 1850 he became steadily more conservative [for a later stage of his career, cf. 28:57].

38. D'Azeglio: Massimo, Marchese d'Azeglio, 1798-1866, was one of the leaders of the Italian nationalist revival and fought against Austria in 1848. Zobi reports [V, 27] that he was exiled from Tuscany in 1847 because of his liberal sentiments.

39. Lord Minto: Gilbert Elliot, 2d Earl of Minto, 1782-1859, lord privy seal, was sent by the British government to Sardinia, Tuscany, and Rome in the autumn of 1847 to encourage a policy of reform and to report on the state of Italy. Zobi describes [V, 236-237n] his enthusiastic reception on October 30 in Arezzo (on the road from Florence to Rome) as representing the friends of Italian liberation and of a customs union. He responded with a salute to Leopoldo II [cf. 42 below] and to Italian independence, which gave unjustified encouragement, since the British government favored a policy of slow but sure, not revolutionary, reform.

40. Bowring had preceded: Sir John B., 1792-1872, English writer and traveler, visited Italy in the autumn of 1836 and the next year reported to Lord Palmerston's government on the state of trade in Tuscany as well as in other regions [Zobi, V, 36-37].

41. EVVIVA . . . INDIPENDENZA: I, "Long live . . . independence."

42. Leopoldo: Leopoldo II, 1797-1870, succeeded his father, Ferdinando III, as Grand Duke of Tuscany in 1824 and abdicated in

1855. The old Leopoldo is of course Pietro Leopoldo, Leopoldo I [cf. 2 above].

43. Lalage ... Dirce: Classical names of women, prob. not used with reference to any specific personages. Lalage was a common name for a courtesan; Dirce was the wife of Lycus, king of Thebes, but Pound is probably thinking of the beautiful Dirce in one of his favorite poems, Landor's "Stand close around, ye Stygian set."

CANTO LI

Sources

Guido Guinicelli, "Al cor gentil repara sempre amore"; Charles Bowlker, *The Art of Angling, Greatly Enlarged and Improved* ..., Ludlow, 1829; Dante, *Inf*. VII, 97-98.

Background

EP, *LE*, 186, 211; *SR*, 101-117; *T*, 441; Francesco De Sanctis, *History of Italian Literature*, trans. Joan Redfern, New York, 1931; John Hill, *A History of Fly Fishing for Trout*, New York, 1921; Charles Fox, *Rising Trout*, 1967.

Exegeses

EP, *GK*, 172; HK, *Era*, 431; Robert Demott, "Ezra Pound and Charles Bowlker: Note on Canto LI," *Pai*, 1-2, 189-198; DP, *Barb*, 216-220.

Glossary

1. Shines ... eye: Trans. of part of stanza 4 of "Al cor gentil repara sempre amore" ["Love always repairs to the noble heart"] by Guido Guinicelli, ca. 1230-1276; it is an important Neoplatonic poem which links the poet's lady with angels and also serves as a model for Dante's school. As the first image in this canto which, at the time it was written (ca. 1936), Pound considered central to his design of probably 100 cantos, these lines are most significant: they emphasize light as the major Neoplatonic symbol of divine intelligence operating in the created universe as opposed to the darkness of ignorance which Pound associates with hell as in Cantos I, XIV, and XV.

2. Fifth element ... Napoleon: The same Guinicelli canzone (1 above) has a stanza that starts, "Fère lo sol lo fango tutto 'l giorno: / vile riman, né il Sol perde calore. / Dice uom altier:–Gentile per schiatta torno:– / lui sembra il fango, e 'l Sol gentile valore," which Redfern translates as "The Sun shines on the mud the whole day long: the mud remains vile and the Sun keeps its heat. When a proud man says, 'I am noble because of my race,' he is like the mud, the true nobility is like the Sun" [De Sanctis, 32]. The word "mud" is thus carried from the Guinicelli context into a Napoleonic one, repeating a motif stated earlier [34/116]. "Mud" for Pound seems to be a metaphor for the basic stuff of the universe through which mind can operate. He wrote: "mud does not account for mind" [*GK*, 172]. The significance of the fifth element is controversial. Some believe that because of his experience in military campaigns, Napoleon added to the classical list (earth, water, fire, and air) the combination that caused him the most trouble: "mud."

3. **usura**: L, I, "usury" [for this and the remaining names on p. 250, see 45:1 ff.].

4. **looms are hushed**: "Japan's quest for foreign markets hushed all the looms in those hills" around Rapallo [HK, *Era*, 431].

5. **Blue dun**: One of the two most popular fly patterns dressed by experts for use in fishing. Although "Number 2" in Pound's source [Bowlker, *The Art of Angling*] refers to the number of an illustration, he uses it accurately enough as the size of a hook. The first eight lines contain data on making the fly and suggest the best and only times to use it. The next ten lines contain similar data on another popular fly, the Granham [Demott, *Pai*, 1-2, 189 ff.].

6. **Hen pheasant's . . . Granham**: Bowlker's heading is "Granam, or Green-tail. No. 6" Pound has selected his data from this passage: "It derives the name of Green-Tail from a bunch of eggs, of a green colour, which it deposits in the water while floating on the surface. The wings lie flat on the body, and are made of a shaded feather from the wing of a partridge, or hen pheasant; the body of the dark fur of a hare's ear, and a yellowish grizzled cock's hackle for legs; a small quantity of bright green wax (or green harl from the eye of a peacock's tail) about the size of a pin's head." One of the amazing things revealed in *The Art of Angling* is the precision of nature in process. Trout will rise for a dressed fly only if it duplicates exactly a natural fly that can be expected not only that season of the year but also the right time of day. Any variation from nature and the fish will not take the bait: "As long as the brown continues, no fish will take Granham."

7. **light of the doer . . .** : The juxtaposition of the fly-fishing sequence and usury is not casual; since fly-fishing is an art that depends on nature's increase as well as profits from it, it has none of the destructive effects of usury, which is CONTRA NATURAM [45:19].

8. **Deo . . . adeptus**: L, "Godlike in a way this intellect that has grasped." Adapted from Albertus Magnus [cf. *LE*, 186]. "Light" in the doer is divinity manifested through the intelligence of man and nature: central Neoplatonic concept of *The Cantos*. Other metaphors of the idea are "the kind of intelligence that makes the cherrystone become the cherry tree" [48:50] or "the weasel eat rue, / and the swallows nip celandine" [cf. 92/618].

9. **Grass**: Like "the brown marsh fly" which after eleven "comes on," grass is nature's increase and is "nowhere out of place."

10. **Königsberg**: Rudolf Hess, Hitler's deputy and Reichsminister, used the following German and Latin phrases in a radio message broadcast from Königsberg in East Prussia, July 8, 1934 [EH].

11. **Zwischen . . . wird**: G, "Between the [two] peoples a modus vivendi is achieved."

12. **modus vivendi**: L, "way of life."

13. **circling etc.**: Dante and Virgil climb on the back of Geryon [14:3] who circles down with them into the depths of fraud. Virgil said: "Geryon, move now; fly in big

circles and descend slowly" [*Inf.* XVII, 97-98]. After he set them down "he darted off like an arrow from the bow." As opposed to art, where "Slowness is beauty" [cf. 87/572], usurers are in a hurry: "Time is money!"

14. the 12: Unidentified.

15. the regents: Pound told Daniel Pearlman that the regents are "bankers" [DP, *Barb*, 218n].

16. Geryone: Geryon, the Dantean personification of usury [46:51]. Says Pound: "We . . . see more clearly the grading of Dante's values, and especially how the whole hell reeks with money. The usurers are there as against nature, against the natural increase of agriculture or of any productive work. Deep hell is reached via Geryon (fraud) of the marvellous patterned hide, and for ten cantos thereafter the damned are all of them damned for money" [*LE*, 211].

17. help . . . aged . . . peace: Prob. satirical note on the international gnomes and usurers who say their stock supports widows and orphans and who promote wars and arms sales in order to obtain "universal peace," as witness Zaharoff, the house of Morgan, etc. The international gang speaks in many languages.

18. eel-fishers basket: This obscure phrase occurs also in Fragments/799. Perhaps the eel is the tail of Geryon. Someone told me that on the Mediterranean they fish for eels by dragging a basketlike instrument as if it were a net. But this possibility has not been documented. [CT]

19. League of Cambrai: A brief (1508-1510) alliance of states, led by Maximilian and Louis XII, which tried to crush Venice. The league, joined by England and Spain, succeeded briefly, but Venice recovered [DP, *Barb*, 220].

20. Ideograms: Chêng^4 [M351]: "right"; Ming^2 [M4524]: "name."

CANTO LII

Sources

S. Couvreur, *Li Ki, ou mémoires sur Les Bienséances et les Cérémonies. Texte Chinois avec une Double Traduction en Français et en Latin*, Ho Kien Fou, 1913.

Background

S. Wells Williams, *The Middle Kingdom*, 2 vols., New York, 1883; EP, *SP*, 84, 87, 300n, 159; *GK*, 181; *L*, 250; M. Beer, *An Inquiry into Physiocracy*, London, 1939.

Exegeses

John Drummond, "The Italian Background to *The Cantos*," in *Ezra Pound*, ed. Peter Russell, London, 1950, 100-102; CE, *Ideas*, 40-41; Davis, *Vision*, 98-99, 135-136; DP, *Barb*, 222-223; HK, *Era*, 171, 426, 465.

Glossary

1. **Duke Leopold**: Leopold II, 1747-1792, Holy Roman emperor (1790-1792). As Leopold I of Tuscany, he carried out many reforms in administration, taxation, punishment for crime [44:1, 4].

2. **abundance etc.**: Pound's central thesis, deriving with additions and modifications from the Physiocrats, a French economic group that developed in reaction to "mercantilism": "They generalized their views in the economic doctrine that agriculture was the only source of riches or the only productive occupation, while manufacture and traffic were sterile. . . . The inordinate fostering of 'sterile' manufacture at the expense of productive tillage; the striving for a monetary balance of trade; the restrictive regulations imposed on trade and commerce, and, finally, the agelong restrictions on the marketing and exportation of grain, formed . . . the source of the misery of the French people, and were the cause of all social distempers and devastating wars between nations. They believed that those policies and restrictions . . . were in conflict with the moral basis of economic life, that is, with equality of exchanges, just prices, or commucative justice" [Beer, 14]. The Physiocrats' theories developed and flowered during the century before the French Revolution and may be seen in Jeffersonian agrarianism. Physiocratic theories also formed the basis of Duke Leopold's activities in Siena. As were the Physiocrats, Pound would be opposed to such characteristics of mercantilism as: "(i) Conception of money (coin, and bullion or treasure) as the essence of wealth. . . . (ii) Regulating foreign trade with a view to bringing in money by the balance of trade," etc. [ibid., 13n].

3. **Schacht**: Horace Greeley Hjalmar S., 1877-1970, German financier who became president of the Reichsbank under Hitler and presided over the financial operations of the Nazi state.

4. **anno seidici**: I, *anno sedici*, "year sixteen." Refers to 1938, the sixteenth year of the Fascist era.

5. **commerciabili beni**: I, "goods for commerce."

6. **neschek**: Heb., "usury." The serpent: Geryon [51:16].

7. **Vivante**: Leone V., 1887- , Italian writer and critic, author of *English Poetry* (1950) (issued with a preface by T. S. Eliot), lived in a villa on a hill near Siena. Author of *Note sopra la originalità del pensiero*. Pound mentions him twice in "Mang Tsze," *The Criterion*, 1938 [*SP*, 84, 87; *GK*, 181].

8. **yitt**: From German *Jude*, slang for "Jew." Usually applied to poor Jews as opposed to financial operators such as the Rothschilds.

9. **goyim**: Heb., "gentiles." Pound's apparent intent is to deplore the way anti-Semites in the 1930s blamed all Jews, including poor ones, for the destructive financial practices of a very few. At least, in a letter to T. C. Wilson in 1934 [*L*, 250], Pound wrote: "Don't be an anti-Semite." And later, on November 21, 1935, he said: "Usurers have no race. How long the whole Jewish people is to be a sacrificial goat for the usurer, I know not" [*SP*, 300n].

10. **Miss Bell**: Gertrude M. L. B., 1868-1926, British authority on the Near East, where she served as military intelligence agent and political secretary.

11. **Stalin**: Joseph [Iosif] Vissarionovich Dzhugashvili, 1879-1953, seized power over the Soviets after Lenin's death.

12. **Litvinof**: Maksim Maksimovich Litvinov, 1876-1951, Russian revolutionary who in various roles became a powerful figure in Stalin's government during the 1930s.

13. **entrefaites**: F, "events."

14. **Johnnie Adams**: Adams said: "All the perplexities, confusion, and distress in Amer-

ica arise, not from defects in their constitution or confederation, not from want of honour and virtue, so much as from downright ignorance of the nature of coin, credit, and circulation" [cf. *SP*, 159; 31:15].

15. **Ben**: Benjamin Franklin. The document on which this line was based has been exposed as a forgery; Franklin never said anything of the kind.

16. **chazims**: Yiddish, *chaseirim*, "pigs."

17. **Black lines**: To avoid possible libel suits, the publishers wanted to delete six lines of names from the text; Pound would not consent but said they could be blacked out to show the censorship. Both New Directions and Faber made the same deletions.

18. **KUNG**: Kung Fu-tse [Confucius; see 13:1]. Two major ingredients of *The Cantos* are the ethical system of Kung and the sacred mysteries represented by Eleusis: everything takes place between these poles [45:20].

19. **Golden Roof**: Church of La Daurade, Toulouse, France.

20. **la Dorata**: I, "the Golden One," the French *La Daurade*. The church was visited by Guido Cavalcanti.

21. **baldacchino**: I, "canopy."

22. **Riccio**: Guido R., Sienese hero at the siege of Montemassi; a fresco of him on horseback (1328) is in the Palazzo Pubblico in Siena.

23. **Montepulciano**: Erroneous for Montemassi, a town in C Italy SW of Siena.

24. **groggy church**: A thesis of *The Cantos* is that the Church, which used to forbid usury [*neschek*], began to decline when it changed this policy and joined the money-makers.

25. **Burgos**: Capital of Burgos Province, N Spain, in Old Castile, the home and burial place of El Cid [3:16]. The firm song is *The Epic of the Cid*.

26. **Cortona**: Town in Tuscany, C Italy.

27. **Gregory**: Pope Gorgory I, who initiated the Gregorian chant.

28. **Know then**: The remainder of the canto is based on *Li Ki* [*Book of Rites*], one of the five Chinese classics. *Li Ki* is held in special esteem because people believe it contains Confucius's views on government and manners. *Li*, usually translated as "rites" or "ceremonies," cannot be conveyed in English by one word, for the Chinese idea of *li* includes "not only the external conduct, but involves the right principles from which all true etiquette and politeness spring. The state religion, the government of a family, and the rules of society are all founded on the true *li*, or relations of things" [S. Wells Williams, I, 645]. *Li* is both the spirit and the substance of Confucianism.

29. **Hyades**: A cluster of stars in the constellation Taurus. When they rose with the sun, it was supposed to rain.

30. **Lord of the Fire**: A spirit in the religion of ancient China.

31. **Son of Heaven**: Title of Chinese emperor.

32. **Gemini**: The third zodiacal constellation represented by the twins, Castor and Pollux. The sun enters Gemini about May 21.

33. **Virgo**: The Virgin: the constellation (due S of the handle of the Dipper) represented as a woman holding a spike of grain in her hand.

34. **Hydra**: A southern constellation having the form of a serpent.

35. **Antares**: The brightest star in Scorpio (called Scorpio's Heart), a southern constellation.

36. **Andromeda**: A northern constellation, between Pegasus and Perseus, represented as a chained woman.

37. **Ming T'ang**: The "Temple of Light" (or "Wisdom") where the imperial family of China worshiped its ancestors.

38. **manes**: L, "spirits of the dead."

39. Lords of the Mountains: Spirits in ancient Chinese religion.

40. Sagittarius: The southern constellation represented as a centaur shooting an arrow.

41. Orion: The constellation on the celestial equator represented as a hunter.

42. Houai: Hwai River in S Honan and NW Anhwei provinces in E China flows into the Hwang Ho, or Yellow River, above Hungtze Hu.

43. Heaven's Son: The emperor.

44. archer's shoulder: Prob. the archer is the constellation Orion.

45. Spirit of Mountains: Spirit of the ancient Chinese religion.

46. Lord Palmerston: One of the minor *directio voluntatis* people celebrated in *The Cantos*, who worked for the people and got things done [cf. 42:1].

47. Sligo: Seaport of county Sligo in N Eire on Sligo Bay. When Palmerston was prime minister, he promoted such public works as are listed for Sligo and London.

48. chih³: M939, "to stop."

CANTOS LIII-LXI

THE CHINESE CANTOS

Sources

J. A. M. de Moyriac de Mailla, *Histoire Générale de la Chine*, 13 vols., Paris, 1777-1785; A. de Lacharme, *Confucii Chi-King*, ed. Julius Mohl, Stuttgart and Tübingen, 1830, XI-XII; Homer, *Od.* X, 305; I, 3; Robert Grosseteste, "De Luce seu de inchoatione formarum," in L. Baur, *Die philosophischen Werke des Robert Grosseteste*, Münster, 1912.

Background

Henri Cordier, *Histoire Générale de la Chine et de ses Relations avec les Pays Étrangers*, 4 vols., Paris, 1920; Homer H. Dubs, *The History of the Former Han Dynasty*, 3 vols., London, 1938-1955; Burton Watson, *The Records of the Grand Historian of China*, 2 vols., New York, 1961; René Grousset, *The Empire of the Steppes*, New Brunswick, NJ, 1970; H. A. Giles, *A History of Chinese Literature*, London and New York, 1901; H. G. Creel, *What Is Tao-ism?* Chicago, 1970; EP, "Mang Tsze," *SP*, 81; EP, *CON*, 83; EP, *LE*, 161; EP, *GK*, 215, 249.

Exegeses

DG, "The Sources of Canto LIII," *Pai*, 5-1; Tay, "Between Kung and Eleusis," *Pai*, 4-1; JW, "Two Heavens of Light and Love," *Pai*, 2-2; JN, "The Sources for Canto LIV," *Pai*, 5-3, 6-1; JN, "The Sources for Canto LV," *Pai*, 7-1 & 2; JN, "The Sources for Canto LVI," *Pai*, 8-2, 3; HK, *Era*, 468, 435.

Pound's adaptation of Mailla's French transliterations as they appear in *The Cantos* is used for all items glossed and indexed; this form is followed by the Standard Wade System according with Karlgren's tables. For Mongolian or Turkic words which have no established form, Pound's usage is followed without a list of variants. B.C. is given for dates before the common era. To save space A.D. is used through the 1st century only.

Glossary Canto LIII

1. **Yeou**: Yu Tsao-chi, mythical king of China. He followed the reign of the great trinity of powers (the three august ones) who ruled 18,000 years each. Yu is said to have taught men to build houses, and his name means "nest having." Source says that Yu stopped vagabondage and showed the people how to make bird's-nest huts with branches [DG, *Pai* 5-1, 123; all references in the glosses to this article in *Pai* are by volume and page numbers.]

2. **Seu Gin**: Sui Jen-chi, mythical king of China who followed the reign of Yu. He is said to have introduced the use of fire and wood; accounting, by tying knots in string; and the beginnings of trade. His name means "producer of fire and wood."

3. **Fou Hi**: Fü Hsi, reigned 2852-2737 B.C., first of the five emperors of the legendary period of China. He is said to have taught his people to hunt, fish, and keep flocks. He invented a calendar, formed musical instruments, developed marriage contracts, invented writing, and taught people to cook flesh. His name means "to be humble, to hide."

4. **ante Christum**: L, "before Christ."

5. **Chin Nong**: Shên Nung, reigned 2737-2698 B.C., second of the five emperors of legendary China. He introduced a system of barter. He taught the art of agriculture and was known as the "Prince of Cereals." Through his glass-covered stomach he could watch his own digestive processes and thus studied the properties and effects of herbs. His name means "divine agriculturalist."

6. **gros blé**: F, "coarse wheat."

7. **Kio-feou-hien**: Chüeh-fou-hsien, near city of Yen-chou-fu in Shantung Province.

8. **Souan yen**: Hsuan Yen, fl. 2722 B.C., one of the favorite governors serving under Emperor Shên Nung.

9. **Hoang Ti**: Huang Ti, reigned 2697-2597 B.C., the "Yellow Emperor" from whom all later kings and princes of China claimed descent. A practical and beneficent ruler, he fought successfully against barbarians. He started official historiography, invented bricks, introduced calendar reform, invented carts and musical instruments, and devised the "well-field" method of dividing up a plot of land into a "latticework" system, with the outer sections tilled by individual families and the center by all in common.

10. **Syrinx**: Nymph pursued by Pan; when she changed into a tuft of reeds, Pan fashioned the reeds into pipes, the pipes of Pan.

11. **Kiao-Chan**: Chiao-shan, mountain in the district of Chung-pu, in Shensi Province.

12. **Ti Ko**: Ti Ku, reigned 2436-2366 B.C., was noted for administering justice to and evincing interest in his people. He attained fame by being the first emperor to have more than one wife. His name means "imperial communication."

13. **Tung Kieou**: Tung-chiu, a place near the department of Ta-ming-fu in Chihli (or Hopei) Province, NE China.

14. **Yao**: Son of Ti Ku, reigned 2357-2259 B.C.. He was so benevolent a ruler that even the weather was favorable toward him. He commanded the royal astronomers to create an agricultural calendar. Like Shun, Yao was one of the ideal emperors of China against whom all emperors were measured; at his death there were three years of mourning before Shun took the throne. On the eve of his death Yao passed over his own incompetent son and named Shun as his successor.

15. **Yu**: Ta Yü or Great Yü, reigned 2205-2197 B.C.; founder and first emperor of Hsia dynasty. It was Shun who first brought Yü to the attention of Emperor Yao, and Yü was assigned the task of controlling the floodwaters of the Yellow River. He was so successful that Shun had him serve as his vice-regent and offered him the throne in place of his own son. Like Yao and Shun, Yü is one of the standards by which all Chinese emperors are measured.

16. **Shantung**: Province in NE China; one of the Five Northern Provinces.

17. **Ammassi**: I, "grain pools," for careful collection with an eye to the future; the plan was backed by Mussolini.

18. **Siu-tcheou**: Siu-ch'ou, department in the province of Kiang-Nan, E China.

19. **Yu-chan**: Yü-shan, mountain in the province of Kiang-Nan.

20. **Se-choui**: Se-shui, river in Kiang-Nan which joins the Yangtze.

21. **Tsing-mo'**: *Tsing-mao*, a Chinese herb.

22. **molü**: H, the magic herb Hermes gave Odysseus to counteract the drugs of Circe [cf. *Od.* X, 305].

23. **Chun**: Shun, reigned 2255-2205 B.C.. After serving a 28-year apprenticeship Shun was selected to follow Yao as emperor. He was noted as a governor, an astronomer, and as one who regulated the order and ceremony of religious service.

24. **Chang Ti**: Shang Ti, Supreme Ancestor or Ruler of Heaven: the active divine force as opposed to T'ien, the passive divine force. Shang Ti, a personalized deity, is associated with an abode of or "haven" for departed spirits.

25. **que . . . conforme**: F, "that your verses express your intentions and that the music conform."

26. **Yao**: Ideogram across from name [M7295]: "Eminent" [cf. 14 above].

27. **Chun**: Ideogram across from name [M5936]: "Wise" [cf. 23 above].

28. **Yu**: Ideogram across from name [M7620; name of founder of Hsia dynasty [cf. 15 above].

29. **Kao-Yao**: Ideograms across from name [M3285, M6156]: "Bless" + "Kiln." A famous minister under Emperor Yü of Hsia, Kao-Yao, who died in 2204 B.C., was said to have been the first to introduce laws for the repression of crime.

30. **Empress**: Min, wife of Emperor Ti-hsiang. When he was killed by the usurper, Han-tsuo, she fled and gave birth to Shao Kang, who grew up during the interregnum.

31. **Chao Kang**: Shao Kang, reigned 2079-2055 B.C. This emperor, Min's son, came to the throne after the interregnum of forty years, which began when Han-tsuo, the usurper, was deposed by the people. Shao Kang quelled disorder in the empire and gave the state of Hsia its first prominence.

32. Fou-hi: [cf. 3 above].

33. Chin-nong: [cf. 5 above].

34. Hoang Ti: [cf. 9 above].

35. Chan: Chao. Prob. a reference to Shao-Hao [M5675 + M2072]: "little-vast." Fourth of the legendary five emperors; son of and successor to Huang Ti. His reign was weakened by poor judgment and neglect.

36. Tchuen: Tchuen-hio, Chuan Hsü, reigned 2513-2436 B.C. The grandson of Huang Ti, he was the fifth of the legendary emperors of China.

37. Chun: [cf. 23 above].

38. Yu: [cf. 15 above].

39. Chang Ti: [cf. 24 above].

40. Tching Tang: Ch'êng T'ang, who reigned 1766-1753 B.C., founded the Shang dynasty (1766-1122). He was a model king who subordinated every passion and feeling to the good of his people. In time of drought he coined money so the people could buy grain, but there was no grain to buy until his sacrifices were accepted by Heaven and rain fell. On his washbasin he inscribed the admonition, "Make it new."

41. der . . . hat: "[The white man] who made the tempest in Baluba." Just as "magic" was attributed by the Biembe to Frobenius, so here Tching's "magic" [prayer] brought rain [38:41].

42. hsin[1]: [M2737], "new."

43. jih[4]: [M3124], "sun." The four characters mean: "make new, day by day, make new." This "spirit" of Emperor Ch'êng T'ang describes the regenerative and ethical metamorphoses effected by the Shang dynasty and functions at all neo-Confucian periods in the dynastic cantos [cf. *Pai*, 5-1, 130; 4-1, 45; 2-2, 188; Pound, "Mang Tsze," *SP* 81].

44. Hia: Hsia [M2521]: "Summer" [cf. ideogram in middle of canto page]. With the fall of Hsia, the first dynasty of China, 2205-1766 B.C., the Middle Kingdom was ruled by the Shang-Yin Dynasty, 1766-1122, which is the first historically verifiable state. The dynastic title was changed to Yin by Pan Keng in 1041.

45. Chang Ti: [cf. 24 above].

46. Tang: [cf. 40 above].

47. Yu: [cf. 15 above].

48. Yin: The Shang dynasty (1766-1122); the name of the dynasty was changed to Yin ca. 1401 B.C.

49. Wen Wang: Wên Wang [M7129 + M7037]: "Elephant king," 1231-1135 B.C. Wên Wang ruled the principality of Chou in the W reaches of the Shang Empire. Called "Chief of the West," he was glorified by historians as an ideal administrator. Because the Shang rulers degenerated into love of pleasure and cruel treatment of the people, Wên Wang tried to overthrow their last king, Chou Hsin. He was captured and imprisoned but was released on payment of a fine. Although he failed to overthrow the Shang-Yin dynasty [a feat eventually achieved by his son, Wu Wang], he is celebrated as the father of the Chou dynasty and was later honored by Confucius as a model for good kings. The entire *Shih Ching* [*Book of Odes*] is a four-part tribute to his greatness as founder of the Chou dynasty.

50. Uncle Ki: Chi Tzŭ, fl. 1153 B.C., was the uncle of Chou Hsin, the depraved emperor of Yin. Because he bravely criticized his nephew, saying, "You drink only out of jeweled vases and eat bear's paw and leopard's blood," Chi was degraded and imprisoned [cf. *Pai*, 5-1, 131].

51. Lou Tai: Lü-t'ai, the "Stag Tower" built by the last Shang emperor, Chou Hsin, as a palace for his mistress, T'a Chi. It was the scene of torture, sexual orgies, and crime.

52. Tan Ki: T'a Chi, d. 1122 B.C., concubine of Emperor Chou Hsin, was an evil woman. After Wu Wang's victory at Mou Ye, she was executed, "to the delight of nearly everyone who knew her."

53. Kieou's daughter: Chiu Hou, ca. 1147 B.C., was a noble who served Emperor Chou Hsin. His daughter disapproved of the evil emperor and his concubine, T'a Chi, so they had her killed, quartered, cooked, and served up to her father for dinner. Repeat in history [4:8].

54. Y-king: *I Ching,* [*Book of Changes*], one of the five classics, was written by Wên Wang while in prison at Yu-li.

55. Mou Ye: Battlefield in N Honan, in the country of K'i, where the forces of Wu Wang and Chou Hsin met (1122 B.C.). Chou Hsin was defeated and the Shang dynasty brought to an end [cf. *Classic Anthology*, ode 236].

56. Cheou-sin: Chou Hsin, who reigned 1154-1122 B.C., was the last emperor of the Shang (or Yin) dynasty. His career was marked by extravagance, lust, and cruelty. The *Odes* say that when he went to battle, his hosts "were as a forest on route." After his defeat Chou Hsin set fire to his own palace and perished in the flames.

57. Wu Wang: 1169-1115 B.C., son of Wên Wang, continued his father's battles against Emperor Chou Hsin. Wu Wang assembled a huge army and defeated the emperor at Mou Ye, in Honan, ending the Shang (or Yin) dynasty. Upon entering the city Wu Wang ordered that all grain be given to the people and the immense riches in the treasury be given to the army [cf. *Pai*, 5-1, 133].

58. Nine vases of Yu: "When Wu Wang was preparing to return to the capitol . . . after conquering Shang, he took with him the nine vases that the Emperor Yu had cast in bronze which displayed the geographic description of each of the nine provinces of the empire" [ibid.].

59. Hoa-chan: Hoa-shan, mountain in Shensi Province.

60. South Chariot: More commonly called the "south-pointing chariot." The ancestor of the mariner's compass, the chariot is said to have been invented by Chou Kung, the Duke of Chou. It was not a magnetic compass, as Mailla supposes, but rather a system of gear wheels which would keep an original pointing. Chou Kung presented the chariot to the court as it prepared to move to Loyang.

61. Lo Yang: Loyang, city in N Honan Province, E central China. Founded in 1108 B.C., it served as capital through several dynasties.

62. Middle Kingdom: One of the many names for the Chinese Empire. Others are "Flowery Kingdom" and "Celestial Empire."

63. Tcheou Kong: Chou kung, d. 1106 B.C. Duke of Chou, adviser to his brother Wu Wang and regent for his nephew Chêng Wang. His activities, devoted wholly to the welfare of the state, aided greatly in establishing the Chou dynasty. Credited with inventing the south-pointing chariot, Chou Kung is one of the measuring sticks for the greatness of any ruler.

64. eleven o six ante Christum: 1106 B.C., the year in which the Duke of Chou died.

65. Tching-ouang: Chêng Wang, son of Wu Wang, reigned 1115-1078 B.C. as the second ruler of the Chou dynasty. He fostered cultivation and reclamation, brought good men into government, and regulated the measure of money and cloth.

66. tchu: Chu, 1/24 of a tael.

67. tchang: Chang, a unit of measurement equal to 141 inches.

68. Chao Kong: Shao Kung, d. 1053 B.C., the Duke of Shao, kinsman to Wu Wang. He was a counselor famous for dispensing justice from his seat under a wild pear tree. The next 23 lines give details of the celebration Shao arranged for the coronation of K'ang Wang, son of Wu Wang.

69. Tching-ouang: [cf. 65 above].

70. Hong-pi: *Hung-pi*, a precious stone.

71. Yuen-yen: *Yuan-yen*, a precious stone, perhaps jade.

72. Mt. Hoa-chan: [cf. 59 above].

73. Chun: [cf. 23 above].

74. In: Yin, name given to the Shang dynasty [85/543].

75. Ouen Ouang: Wên Wang [cf. 49 above].

76. Kang: K'ang Wang, third Chou ruler, 1078-1052 B.C. Though apparently weak, he was supported by strong ministers.

77. Tcheou: Chou, the third dynasty (1122-255 B.C.).

78. Confucius: K'ung Ch'iu or K'ung Fu-tse, or K'ung, ca. 551-479 B.C., Chinese philosopher and statesman. Confucianism is an organized series of precepts dealing with morals, the family system, social reforms, statecraft, and ceremonials. It considers action, directed by right thinking, to be the highest good. It postulates the innate virtue of man. It opposes the passivity of Buddhism and the mysticism of Taoism. A philosophy of reason, it influenced the thought of the French Enlightenment [52:18].

79. Chao-Kong: Shao Kung, the great minister who served both Wu Wang and K'ang Wang. Next several lines list his activities.

80. Yao and Chun: Great kings of the Hsia dynasty [cf. 14, 23, above].

81. Chou: [M1293]: "To encircle." Ideogram for the Chou dynasty.

82. Kang Ouang: [cf. 76 above]. In the 16th year of his reign he lost his most valuable minister, Pe Chin.

83. Pé-kin: Pe Chin, d. 1063 B.C. Ruler of the principality of Lü (Lou). Son of Shao Kung, the Duke of Shao, he succeeded his father as chief minister to K'ang Wang.

84. Prince of Lou: Pe Chin.

85. Kang Ouang: K'ang Wang. In the 26th year of his reign . . . .

86. Kang Wang: He died the same year as Shao Kung, his great minister.

87. Tchao-ouang: Chao Wang, fourth Chou ruler, reigned 1052-1001 B.C. He allowed the government to become weak and the prosperity of the country to decline. He was drowned while crossing the river Han, prob. the victim of a plot.

88. Mou-Ouang: Mu Wang (1001-946 B.C.), fifth ruler of Chou dynasty, was famous for his military campaigns. He decreed that punishments might be redeemed by money payments, and some 3,000 offenses were made expiable by this method.

89. Chun: [cf. 23 above].

90. Law of Mou: [cf. 88 above].

91. Lin hing: *Lü-Hsing*. Sec. 21, Chap. XXVII of *Shu Ching*, the history classic, records the foregoing idea about "Riches. . . ."

92. Chu King: *Shu Ching* [*Book of History*], supposedly collected and edited by Confucius.

93. governor's daughters: The three beautiful daughters of the provincial governor of Mie during the reign of Kung Wang, who became enraptured over them.

94. King-Ho: King or Ching, river of China rising in NE Kansu Province, N central China, and flowing to the Wei River in C Shensi.

95. Kong: Kung Wang, sixth ruler of Chou dynasty, reigned 946-934 B.C. Enthralled by Mi's daughters, Kung waited for them for a year (*un an entier*) and then, being denied, destroyed the town, an act he came to regret.

96. Y-wang: I Wang, son of Kung Wang and seventh ruler of Chou dynasty (934-909 B.C.). During his reign barbarian tribes frequently invaded China.

97. Hiao wang: Hsiao Wang, eighth Chou ruler (909-894 B.C.) known as "The Filial," brother of I Wang. He was a weak ruler whose reign was marked only by the appearance of Fei Tzŭ, whose descendants were later to overthrow the Chou dynasty.

98. **Han-kiang**: Han River, which flows through Shensi and Hupeh provinces and into the Yangtze River at Hankow [*kiang*, "river"].

99. **Fei-tsei**: Fei Tzŭ, fl. 900 B.C., ancestor of Yih, an official in the government of the great Shun. Fei Tzŭ was given charge of Hsiao Wang's studs. His appointment as head of his clan was followed by a heavy hailstorm in Shensi; many oxen and horses died and the Han River was frozen. These omens seemed to be unlucky for the Chou dynasty. Fei Tzŭ, given a small portion of land in Kansu Province, whose chief town was Ch'in, became the Prince of Ch'in.

100. **Pe-y**: Pe I, ancestral house of Fei Tzŭ, who became Prince of Ch'in and founder of the house that was to become the Ch'in dynasty.

101. **Li Wang**: Tenth Chou ruler (878-841 B.C.), known as the "Stern One." Remorseless in his treatment of those who opposed him, he was avaricious in seeking money to carry out his cruel plans. When his people finally rose in rebellion, Li Wang fled to Shensi.

102. **à ce que l'argent circule**: F, "that money circulate."

103. **Heou-Tsie**: Hou Chi, fl. 2357 B.C., chief minister of agriculture and animal husbandry under Emperor Yao.

104. **Youi-leang-fou**: Yü Liang-fu, fl. 860 B.C., was one of the first officers of the empire under Emperor Li Wang.

105. **Chao-kong**: Shao Kung, Duke of Shao during the reign of Li Wang (878-841 B.C.); not to be confused with the earlier Duke of Shao. He is said to have advised Li Wang that to suppress the feelings and the speech of his people would lead only to disaster.

106. **Lord to the four seas of China**: Prob. refers to the Chou ruler, Li Wang.

107. **Interregnum of Cong-ho**: *Kung-ho*, historical name for the interregnum (841-827 B.C.) between the reigns of Li Wang and Hsüan Wang, his son.

108. **west tarters**: A western tribe of barbarians, the Ch'iang, lived to the W of Kansu. They defeated the forces of Hsüan Wang in the battle of "The Thousand Acres" (788 B.C.).

109. **Siuen-ouang**: Hsüan Wang (827-781 B.C.), eleventh ruler of Chou dynasty. He was a good ruler who chose trustworthy counselors. Although the kingdom was bothered by attacks from barbarians, Hsüan managed for some time to repel them with royal troops.

110. **contra barbaros / legat belli ducem**: L, "against the barbarians / he appoints a leader in war" [cf. Lacharme, 308].

111. **Chaoumoukong**: Shao Mu-king, fl. 826 B.C. The name, which means "Mu, Prince of Shao," was given to Shao Hu after his death. He was a general in the service of Hsüan Wang.

112. **Hoailand**: Hwai, territory roughly identical with the old province of Kiang-nan. It is a rich agricultural area watered by the Hwai Ho, S Honan and NW Anhwei provinces of modern E China.

113. **Hoai river**: Hwai Ho, river in S Honan and NW Anhwei provinces in E China which flows into the Hwang Ho above Hungtze Hu.

114. **Tchang wine**: Chang, river that rises in Shensi Province and flows NE, parallel to the Hwang Ho, joining it on the Great Plains.

115. **Juxta . . . mora**: L, "By the river Hwai the battle line is drawn up without delay" [cf. Lacharme, III, 3, ode 9, st. 4; *Classic Anthology*, p. 192].

116. **Yangtse**: Yangtze, principal river of China.

117. **agit considerate**: L, "he leads with deliberation" [Lacharme, III, 3, ode 9, st. 3].

118. Han: Han Hu, fl. 800 B.C., military officer during the time of Hsüan Wang. For his services in battle Han Hu was given the districts of Yüeh and Me, which he developed into important principalities.

119. Yuei: Yüeh or Yü-yüeh, kingdom or principality in S China.

120. Siuen: Hsüan Wang [cf. 109 above]. He began his reign with so successful a defense against the attacks of the Tartars that he was praised in the *Shih Ching.* In praising Hsüan, Pound conflates Lacharme's translation and notes for odes 262 and 263 [cf. *Pai*, 5-1, 141].

121. Sié: Sie, town in the principality of Chin, in Shansi Province, NE China.

122. RITE is: The Chinese rites of spring, a rhyme with the vegetation rites of Dionysus [47:7], include the ceremonial duties of the emperor recorded in the next several lines. Since Hsüang did not observe the rite [*so did not Siuen*], famine ensued.

123. hac . . . alluit: L, *haec loca* . . . : "these places the river washes."

124. Campestribus locis: L, "in country places."

125. Lady Pao Sse: Pao Ssŭ, ca. 8th century B.C., concubine of Chou ruler, Yu Wang. Earthquakes preceded her coming to the throne and the great eclipse of the sun on August 29, 775, followed it. She enslaved the emperor and incited him to the wildest acts of folly: "[She] usurped the queen's throne and led the emperor a reckless dance to his ruin. . . . Rivers trembled and boiled; Mt. Ki-shan, the cradle of the emperor's family, split apart; eclipses (ode 193), comets, and frozen rivers appeared" [cf. *Pai*, 5-1, 143].

126. Tcheou: Chou, the third dynasty (1122-255 B.C.). Surrounded by barbarians, Yu Wang was overwhelmed in 771 B.C., his palace was destroyed, and he and his concubine, Pao Ssŭ, were killed, thus bringing the western Chou dynasty to an end.

127. Mount Ki-chan: Chi-shan, mountain in China destroyed by the earthquakes that appeared as evil omens during the reign of Yu Wang.

128. Yeou Ouang: Yu Wang (781-771 B.C.), a thoroughly bad and unprincipled ruler who was under the influence of Pao Ssŭ. Before Yu's death many of his feudal chiefs, outraged by his wickedness, refused to obey his orders and began to act as independent lords. After Yu and the end of the western state, the whole Chou dynasty began to decline.

129. Tçin: Ch'in. "A prince of Tçin [Weng Kung] dreamed of imperial aspirations and broke away from the declining Chou empire in 749 B.C." [ibid. This Ch'in is not to be confused with the later Ch'in dynasty 255-206 B.C.].

130. Tartar: Tartars, Tatars, northern barbarians, were nomadic tribes on the borders of Chihli, Shansi, and Kansu provinces. When they began to demand the empire in payment for their services, the Prince of Ch'in helped drive them out.

131. tombs fallen: The fall of Chou could be seen in spreading neglect, including that of dynastic temples and tombs. In 745 B.C. each prince asserted independence and the nine original states of the Chou empire were split into 21 parts. This fragmentation began the "Spring and Autumn" period of unrighteous wars described by Confucius as "a rain of stars," because "9 Tcheou wd / not stand together."

132. Siang: Hsiang, territory in central Hunan Province, SE central China, watered by the Hsiang River.

133. Ouen Kong: Wên Kung, d. 609 B.C., Prince of Lü, was a benevolent and capable ruler who distributed grain to the people in time of famine.

134. Sung: Important Chinese state that occupied (1113-285 B.C.) the lower part of the valley of the Hwai River. Confucius's ancestors are said to be of the royal house of Sung.

135. Siang: Tchao- Kung, brother of Wên Kung, spurned the people, which caused the Princess of Hsiang to have him murdered on a hunting trip.

136. Ouen: [cf. 133 above] But Wên died early so that the "states of Lou were still unfortunate" [*Pai*, 5-1, 144].

137. States of Lou: Lü, a state established by Tan, the Duke of Chou, in 1122 B.C. His son established his capital at Chieh-fu (in Shantung Province, NE China) about 1115 and was called Duke Lü. Lü was the birthplace of Confucius.

138. Their Richards: Like Richard III of England who murdered the princes in the Tower, the followers of Wên Kung's second wife [Hsüan-kung] hatched a plot to murder the two sons of his first wife.

139. Ling Kong: Ling Kung (d. 608 B.C.) was a depraved and homicidal Prince of Ch'in whose only pleasure lay in shooting people and eating bears' paws. He died in his own snare at a banquet when he was trying to murder someone. "Without virtue, without sense, his heart turned naturally to evil" [*Pai*, 5-1, 145].

140. Nine Urns of Yu: The nine vases that Emperor Yu had cast in bronze and engraved with geographical descriptions of the nine provinces of the empire. The vases were to be found in the capital of Chou, the principality.

141. King Kong: Ching Kung (d. 578 B.C.), Prince of Ch'in, was a powerful warrior who became the leader of the other princes. In 584 B.C., hearing a prisoner play the dynastic music of Chou, he was so affected that he sent the prisoner home loaded with gifts, an act that led to a peace pact.

142. Cheou-lang: K'ung Shu Liang-ho (d. 548 B.C.), father of Confucius, was chief magistrate of Tsu in Shantung Province. He was remarkable for his gigantic stature and great strength. After fathering nine daughters by his first wife, he remarried at seventy and his second wife, Cheng Tsai, bore him Confucius in 551 B.C.. A year before Confucius's birth there were two eclipses of the sun.

143. portcullis: Refers to an episode ca. 562 B.C. when Confucius's father saved his troops by holding up a portcullis that had trapped them during the siege of a city.

144. hillock: It is said that Confucius's father was given the name Ch'iu ("hillock") because of a "protubérance qu'il avait sur la tête" [Cordier, I, 146; cf. Mailla, II, 81].

145. Man of Sung: Refers to Confucius's father, Shu Liang-ho, whose ancestors may have come from the ancient state of Sung.

146. Lou land: Land of the state of Lü, where Confucius was born.

147. Kung-fu-tseu: K'ung Fu-tse: Confucius.

148. Chung Ni: [M1505 + M4654], Confucius's cognomen. It literally means "second in order of birth."

149. Taught and the not: Prob. Pound is pointing out that in both the Confucian and the Greek patterns virtue must be learned and is part of a process of initiation.

150. Eleusis: Town in Attica where the Eleusinian Mysteries of Demeter were held. Originally an agrarian festival, the mysteries came to be concerned with underworld deities, the descent into Hades, and mystic visions of future life. In *The Cantos*, the phrase "Between Kung and Eleusis" names the two most important poles between which human value systems must be established: "the ethical life and the sacred mysteries" [52:18].

151. catechumen: The word *alone* is placed ambiguously; perhaps it is used in the sense of "only": only the student can hope to achieve the Confucian ethic or the knowledge of the mysteries.

152. Kung was poor: When he was only 19 years old, Kung had a great reputation in the kingdom of Lü although he was very poor. Thus Chao Kung "le fit intendant des vivres" ["made him supervisor of victuals"], a job of little importance which paid enough [Mailla, II, 190; all references to this source are referred to hereafter by volume and page numbers only].

153. Pien's report: In 552 B.C., when 18 or 19, K'ung married Pien-kuan-chi, a woman of Sung. He did his job with so much wisdom that he was promoted to be "l'intendance des bestiaux" [ibid.].

154. Scorpio: In the winter of 525 B.C. a great comet in "le coeur du *scorpion* ou *antares*" spread across the west as far as the Milky Way [II, 193].

155. Kiang: Yangtze River on which, in 525 B.C., a terrible battle was fought between the forces of the princes of Chou and Wu which lasted without interruption for a whole day and night [ibid.].

156. King Wang: Ching Wang, in 524 B.C., thinking he could make a big profit by changing the base of the currency, did so even though warned by his council that it would ruin commerce and impoverish the people [cf. *Pai*, 5-1, 147].

157. *μεταθεμένων* . . . : H, "of change of moneys." An act in opposition to all the principles of Confucius.

158. Fen-yang: Fên Yang, fl. 520 B.C., general and adviser to Ching Wang. He was honored because he refused to carry out orders to murder an innocent prince [ibid.].

159. King Kong: Ching Kung, a feudal prince of Tsi [Chi]. He asked Confucius how a king could be a good ruler and was told "by being a ruler acting like a ruler." Later Kung said the advice was good but that he was too old to start following it.

160. Kungfutseu: In 497 B.C., Confucius, aged 54, was promoted to the rank of minister of state.

161. C. T. Mao: Shao Ching-mao, who, because he was causing serious disorder, was arrested and put to death on Confucius's order. When the latter's disciples asked about his severity, he replied that "Mao's five kinds of deceit and improbity in government made him more criminal than a thug" [ibid.].

162. LOU rose: Lü. Because of the morality Confucius brought to the state in 497 B.C., the state's significance increased.

163. Tsi sent girls: The Prince of Chi, jealous of Lü's success, tried to corrupt its prince by sending him beautiful singing girls.

164. Kungfutseu: The Prince of Lü was corrupted by the singing girls (he did not leave his palace for three days); hence Confucius left Lü and went to the state of Wei.

165. Tching: Ching, feudal state in E central China. When Confucius was strolling near the East Gate of the city, someone saw him and told the king that a man, wandering about like a lost dog, had the forehead of Yao [cf. 14 above], the neck of Kao-Yao [cf. 29 above], the shoulders of Tsé Chin, and the height of Yü [cf. 15 above; II, 211].

166. Confucius: K'ung denied his similarity to great emperors but admitted to the lost-dog description [ibid.].

167. Tchin: Chin, feudal principality in NE China.

168. Yng P: Ying Pi, illegitimate son of Ling Kung, who wanted to make Ying his heir. "But Yng refused the honor because it would have sullied their ancestors" [*Pai*, 5-1, 148].

169. Tsai: Feudal state in Honan Province, E central China. When Confucius was on his way to the Prince of Chu in 489 B.C., "he was intercepted and driven into an arid and rocky desert by the princes of Tchin and Tsai who feared his wisdom" [*Pai*, 5-1, 149]. There he went without food for seven days. Most of his disciples were sick with hunger, but K'ung, seeming not to be sad, sang the odes and played music more than before [II, 214].

170. Tcheou: Chu, feudal state in NE China whose prince sent troops to rescue Confucius and then received him with great honor.

171. Tsao: A small state created in 1122 B.C. which lasted until 501 B.C.. It was finally lost by its prince, Yang Kung, because he followed the advice of an extravagant minister.

172. odes: Because the princes of the states would not follow his advice, K'ung in 493 B.C. retired to work on the odes.

173. Yng star ... Sin: The stars Mailla names *Yng* and *Sin* have not been identified with certainty.

174. King Ouang: Ching Wang, 25th ruler of Chou dynasty [not to be confused with the Ching Wang who changed the currency (cf. 156 above)]. Since he ruled from 519 to 475 B.C., 479 was the 40th year of his reign. In that year K'ung, aged 73, died.

175. Min Kong: Min Kung, d. 478 B.C., created great disorder in the land.

176. Fan-li: Fan Li, fl. 474 B.C., a minister who connived to reduce the power of rival princes. Afterward he withdrew secretly to the five lakes.

177. Snow ... Apricots ...: Strange portents in nature are seen to signal the decline of the Chou dynasty: eclipses, comets, snow in summer, fruit in winter, etc. "In the sweltering summer of 435 B.C. snow fell, and in mid-winter of 428 apricots bore fruit" [*Pai*, 5-1, 150].

178. Tai-hia: *Tai Hsia* high mountains.

179. Hoang-ho: Hwang Ho, the Yellow River, second largest in China. About 387 B.C. Wu Chi said that rivers and mountains were not impregnable barriers: "a state's power is its humanity. Neither high cliffs nor torrents will defend an inhumane ruler" [ibid.].

180. douanes: F, "customhouses" or "custom duties."

181. Kong-sung-yang: Kung Sung-yang, d. 338 B.C., chief prince or noble. Also known as Wei Yang or Shang Yang, he became minister of the state of Ch'in in the middle of the 4th century B.C. Under his direction, Ch'in's laws and administration were reorganized and the foundations were laid for the eventual victory of Ch'in over its rivals and the founding of the first Chinese Empire. Note that the Faber edition reads "280 died Hao tse." The "280" refers to the page number in Mailla, II. "Hao tse" may be Pound's abbreviation of "hao Han tzu" ["tse" in Mailla], meaning "a true Chinese man," literally "a good son of Han"; or he may have intended "good prince," Mailla using "tse" frequently in this sense.

182. Sou-tsin: Su Ch'in, d. 317 B.C., Taoist philosopher who was for a time minister of the state of Ch'in. He was one of the wandering scholar-diplomats of the time. Mocked by a prince of Ch'in, Su turned [as a Taoist in Mailla would] to revenge, intrigue, warmongering, etc. Finally dishonoring himself by having an affair with the "dowager queen," he was murdered in 317 B.C.

183. Tchan-y: Chang I, d. 309 B.C., Chinese condottiere who served the states of Wei, Ch'in, and Chou during the feudal wars near the end of the Chou dynasty.

184. Tsin: Ch'in [*Sou-tsin* in text].

185. POLLON IDEN: H, *Pollon d'anthropon iden*, "And of many men he saw" [*Od.* I, 3].

186. Tchao Siang: Chao Hsiang, who fl. 288 B.C. King Chao Hsiang of the state of Ch'in, in his many wars with contending states, did much to bring the Chou dynasty to its final demise and prepare the way for the Ch'in empire. In 288 B.C. Chao Hsiang assumed for himself the title of emperor of the West. He gave to the Prince of Chi the title of emperor of the East.

187. Sou Tsi: Su Chi, fl. 288 B.C., was a general in the court of Chao Hsiang. He carried the message about the new emperor titles to the Prince of Chi. It was the prince, not Su Chi, who called the title "un simple badinage."

188. Yo-Y: Yo I, fl. 285 B.C., minister of the feudal state of Yen, which lasted from 1122 to 265 B.C., near Peking.

189. corvées: F, "forced labors."

190. Hillock: [cf. 144 above].

191. Chou: The dynasty K'ung said he was for [cf. 81 above].

Glossary Canto LIV

1. Tien-tan: T'ien Tan, fl. 279 B.C., a soldier and later a commander of the forces of Chi.

2. dragons . . . : These first nine lines describe a battle ploy practiced by T'ien: he let loose 1,000 oxen with daggers attached to their horns and torches burning on their tails and drove them into the camp of Ch'i Chieh whose men fled into the night [JN, *Pai*, 5-3, 421; further references to this article give *Pai* with volume and page numbers].

3. Ki-kié: Ch'i Chieh, fl. 279 B.C., commander of the forces of the Prince of Yen. He was killed in the battle of the thousand oxen, his army was dispersed, and the inhabitants of Chieh-me were set free.

4. Tsié-mé: Chieh-me, town in Shantung Province.

5. For three hundred years . . . : During the last 300 or 400 years of the Chou dynasty, intermittent warfare was carried on by the various states of feudal China; thus the period came to be known as the time of the warring states.

6. Wall: Great Wall of China. Begun at various places by rulers of several frontier states, the wall was finally put together as a unit by the first Ch'in emperor, Shih Huang Ti. It extends for approximately 1,250 miles from Mongolia to the Yellow Sea.

7. Tsin Chi: Ch'in Shih Huang Ti, reigned 246-209 B.C. Fourth ruler of the state of Ch'in, he subdued all his enemies and established himself as the first emperor of a unified Chinese empire. His name means "First Emperor of the Ch'in."

8. Tcheou: Chou, third dynasty (1122-255 B.C.).

9. Tsin: Ch'in, fourth dynasty which lasted only until the death of Erh Shih Huang Ti in 206 B.C.

10. China: During the centuries prior to Shih Huang Ti's time, rulers of the Chinese states had the title of Wang ["king"]. Shih Huang himself was known as King Cheng. But after he unified all China, he assumed the title of Huang Ti ["sovereign emperor"], indicating that he now held sway over all the Chinese states, each ruled by a lesser prince. But to warn the princes not to take too much pride in their rank, "when he spoke of himself, he made a point of using Tchin, which means the surplus, as you might say the surplus in the empire" [*Pai*, 5-3, 423].

11. Li-ssé: Li Ssŭ, d. 208 B.C., prime minister under Emperor Shih Huang Ti. Li Ssŭ convinced the emperor that all the unrest in the kingdom was the result of scholarly research and writing. He also suggested that it might be useful to destroy all history so that Shih Huang Ti could be recorded as the "first emperor" of China. All existing literature, except for works on agriculture, medicine, and divination, was ordered destroyed.

12. Han: Fifth dynasty, or Earlier Han dynasty, from 206 B.C. to A.D. 25.

13. some fishin' . . . : Unidentified.

14. some cook . . . : Dorothy Pound made a marital stipulation that she not be required to cook, a condition about which she was adamant, as Pound came to see.

15. Tse-Yng: Tzŭ Ying, who reigned 206 B.C., was the grandson of the Ch'in Shih Huang Ti, nephew of Erh Shih Huang Ti, the last emperor of the Ch'in dynasty. After holding the throne for only 29 days, he was seized by a rebellious prince, who eventually had him decapitated.

16. Siao-ho: Hsiao Ho, d. 193 B.C., adviser to Liu Pang, Prince of Han. Much of Liu Pang's success in founding the Han dynasty was owing to the efforts of Hsiao Ho, who kept the army supplied, provided accurate maps, and helped to create a new penal code and a stronger administration. The first Han emperor named Hsiao Ho chancellor of state, and so great was the respect for him that the title was not used again during the Han dynasty.

17. Lieou-pang: Liu Pang, 247-195 B.C., one of the two leaders of a revolt against the Ch'in dynasty. The two had agreed that the first to reach the capital would gain the principality of Ch'in; Liu Pang arrived first and Emperor Tzu-Ying surrendered. The second general, Hsiang Yü, now not satisfied with the bargain he had made, fought Liu Pang from 206 to 202. In 202 Liu Pang defeated Hsiang Yü and became emperor, founding the Han dynasty and taking the title of Kao Huang Ti, or Han Kao-Tse, the "Exalted One."

18. Eulh: Erh Shih Huang Ti, who reigned 209-206 B.C., was extremely inept as emperor. He was controlled by the eunuch Chao Kao, who finally contrived a plot that, according to modern scholars, led to Erh Shih's suicide. Mailla says both Erh Shih and Chao Kao were murdered [*Pai*, 5-3, 425].

19. Hiang-yu: Hsiang Yü, 233-202 B.C., a general who at first fought with Liu Pang against the Ch'in dynasty and then turned against his ally after the dynasty was overthrown. Hsiang Yü's forces were crushed in 202 and their leader was killed [cf. 17 above].

20. bloody rhooshun: This epithet is not in the *Histoire* which has the other details of the passage including: "He showed no less repugnance when they tried to teach him fencing which placed (one) in the position to resist only one man; but it was altogether different for the art which teaches one person to defeat ten thousand, an art in which he made very great progress" [*Pai*, 5-3, 426].

21. Kao: Kao Huang Ti, also known as Han Kao-Tse, who reigned 202-195 B.C., was founder and first emperor of the Han dynasty. Known formerly as Liu Pang, he was an able emperor who had many wise ministers to whom he listened most of the time. He established a firm foundation for the Han dynasty.

22. "when the quarry . . . ": Said by a loyal general who was plotted against.

23. "It appears . . . : The response of Kao when asked how he was able to gain the empire: "[Because] . . . of using everyone according to his talents" [*Pai*, 5-3, 428].

24. Lou-kia: Lü Chia, fl. ca. 200 B.C., adviser to and confidant of Emperor Kao Huang Ti, was sent by the emperor as his envoy to Ch'ao T'o, ruler of the state of Nan Yüeh in SE China (modern Kwangtung), in an effort to gain Ch'ao's allegiance. After Lü Chia's return he was scolded by the emperor for referring to the Chinese classics. The emperor said: "I got the empire on horseback, why should I bother with the Book of Odes or the Book of History?" To which Lü Chia replied: "You got it on horseback, but can you rule it from horseback?" Lü Chia left a treatise on government called *New Discourses* [Dubs, I, 21].

25. Nan-hai: The name often used for the state of Nan Yüeh in SE China.

26. Chu king: *Shu Ching* [*Book of History*], supposedly collected and edited by Confucius but probably pieced together both before and after his time.

27. Chi king: *Shih Ching* [*Book of Odes*], supposedly collected and edited by Confucius but probably pieced together both before and after his time.

28. **Lou**: [see 24 above].

29. **"The New Discourse" (Sin-yu)**: Hsin Yu. The Han emperor commissioned his adviser Lü Chia to write a treatise on good government. Lü "accordingly set out to describe, in a work with twelve sections, the keys to political survival and defeat. As each section was presented to the throne, the emperor never failed to express his delight and approval, while all those about him cried 'Bravo!' " The book was given the title *New Discourses* [cf. 24 above].

30. **Kung fu tseu**: Confucius.

31. **videlicet**: L, literally *videre licet*, "it is permitted to see," "namely," "that is."

32. **Fan-kouai**: Fan Kuai, d. 189 B.C., a dog butcher of P'ei (in modern Kiangsu) who early attached himself to Liu Pang and joined his group of advisers when Liu became emperor. After the last battle against the Ch'in, Liu Pang (Kao Huang Ti) entered the royal Ch'in palace, where he found treasure and waiting women. Fan Kuai, however, admonished him and urged him to return to the field with his troops, which he did. The anecdote is a flashback to days following the collapse of the Ch'in dynasty [cf. 17 above].

33. **Hien-yang**: Hsien-yang, capital city of the Ch'in dynasty, where Kao Huang Ti finally defeated the last Ch'in emperor. Today it is Sian, capital of Shansi Province in NE central China.

34. **Siao-ho**: Hsiao Ho, the most respected chancellor of state of the first Han emperor [cf. 16 above].

35. **Au douce . . . pascor**: OF, P, "In the sweet season of spring." Echo of troubadour verse, esp. Bertrans de Born's "B'em platz lo gais temps de pascor" ["How I Like the Gay Time of Spring"].

36. **Tchang-tsong**: Chang Ts'ang, fl. 202-195 B.C., a member of the court of Emperor Kao Huang Ti who studied the theory of music.

37. **Sun-tong**: Shu Sun-t'ung, fl. 202-195 B.C., member of the court of Emperor Kao Huang Ti, whose task it was to write on the ceremonies and usages of the rites. Upon the urging of the emperor he devised a set of protocol rules which were much more simple and less ostentatious than those of the Ch'in. As the emperor said: "But make it easy to learn! Keep in mind that it must be the sort of thing that I can perform" [Watson, I, 293].

38. **Imperial Seal**: The seal of the emperor of China during the Earlier Han dynasty.

39. **Hiao Hoei Ti**: Hsiao Hui Ti, who reigned 194-187 B.C., was the second son of Kao Huang Ti. He was a kindhearted, but rather feeble-minded, youth who was completely controlled by his mother, the Empress Lü. His name means "Beneficial Rule."

40. **Y-yang**: I-yang-hsien, town and region near the modern city of Loyang in Honan Province, E central China. It is recorded that in April, 191 B.C., Hui Ti, the emperor-to-be was "capped" (came of age) and "in Y-yang it rained blood." It is also recorded that in late 190 B.C. "peach and plum trees flowered" [Dubs, I, 103].

41. **Liu-heou**: Lü Hou, wife of Kao Huang Ti. She dominated her son during his reign and after his death she continued to rule the empire by placing puppet rulers on the throne. She was an adept murderess but an able ruler.

42. **Hiao Ouen**: Hsiao Wên Ti, who reigned 179-156 B.C., was famous for his generosity, humanity, and economy. He decreed that a man's family should not suffer for his crimes. He established the unit of money in the empire and reserved to the government the sole right to coin money. For the punishment of mutilation he substituted flogging and made beheading the only severe penalty. He also ordered that the classical books be hunted out again and that scholars start studying them. His name means the "Literary Ruler." The eldest son of Kao Huang Ti and prince of the state of Tai, he

succeeded the ineffectual Emperor Hui Ti after some intricate maneuvers following Empress Lü's death.

43. **Chief of the Southern Barbarians**: The southern barbarians were the tribes of the region of Yüeh, a state in SE China.

44. **Nan-yuei**: Nan Yüeh, state in SE China and part of Annam. The ruler of Nan Yüeh, Ch'ao T'o, had been enfeoffed by Kao Huang Ti, but during the days of Empress Lü he had reason to believe that the Han court had reneged on its promises. He thereupon assumed the title of Emperor Wu of Nan Yüeh. The Emperor Wên Ti, however, was able to mend this fence on his S frontier. Ch'ao T'o gave up the title of emperor and Nan Yüeh continued as before in a tributary status.

45. **Kia-Y**: Chia I, fl. 178 B.C., member of the court of Emperor Hsiao Wên Ti and head of office of tax collection.

46. **Hiao Ouen Ti**: [cf. 42 above].

47. **Chang Ti**: Shang Ti, Supreme Ancestor or Ruler of Heaven, was involved in the controversy between Chinese and Jesuits about the name of God. One question was: could the "God" in the Mass be equated with Shang Ti as Ruler of Heaven? [53:24].

48. **Tchao-tso**: Ch'ao T'so, fl. 170 B.C., minister at the court of Emperor Hsiao Wên Ti.

49. **Li-kouang**: Li Kuang, fl. 144 B.C., commander of forces on NW frontier of China whose task it was to guard against Tartar tribes, or Hsiung-Nu. In one battle Li Kuang fooled them into thinking his small band was really the vanguard of a larger force. The Hsiung-Nu withdrew and Li Kuang and his small force escaped.

50. **Hiong-nou**: Hsiung Nu, one of the nomadic tribes on China's NW frontier which posed a continuous threat to the security of the empire. They were prob. related to the Huns who burst into Europe in the fifth century A.D.

51. **Yu**: Ta Yü or Great Yü [53:15].

52. **Chun**: Shun [53:23].

53. **Yao**: [53:14].

54. **Hiao King**: Hsiao Ching Ti, reigned 156-140 B.C. In his second year as emperor the feudal lords rebelled but said they would disband their forces if the emperor would execute his chief counselor, Ch'ao Tsu, who had urged the emperor to abolish all feudal dependencies. The peace terms were met, but the feudal lords attacked again and were not defeated until later. The emperor's name means "Luminous Ruler."

55. **Ideogram**: [M2737] "new."

56. **Sin/jih/jih/sin**: Hsin Jih Jih Hsin: "make new, day by day, make new" [53:43].

57. **Hia**: Hsia [53:44].

58. **Han Ou**: Han Wu Ti, who reigned 140-86 B.C., was perhaps the greatest of the earlier Han emperors; the dynasty reached the peak of its power under his rule. The half century of his reign is noted both for extensive foreign conquests and for significant developments in internal administration. Above all he was instrumental in establishing Confucianism as the basis for Chinese government. His name means "Martial Ruler."

59. **Prince of Hoai-nan**: Lieou-ngan or Liu An, Prince of Huai-nan, was fond of reading books and playing the lute. He seems to have spent most of the rest of his time plotting revolts against the Han emperor.

60. **Hoai-nan**: Huai-nan, princely state south of the Hwai River.

61. **Prince of Ho-kien**: Lieou-te or Liu Te, d. 130 B.C., was Prince of Ho-chien and son of Emperor Hsiao Ching. The prince spent much money and effort to recover and restore the Chinese classics.

62. **Ho-Kien**: Ho-chien, state in the province of Hopeh.

63. **Chu King**: *Shu Ching, Book of History* [53-92].

64. Tcheou-li: *Chou-li, Rites of the Chou Dynasty.*

65. Li-ki: *Li Chi, Book of Rites* compiled by the Elder and Younger Tai (fl. second and first centuries B.C.) from documents said to have come from Confucius and his disciples. The text, frequently revised, was not completed until the second century B.C.

66. Mencius (Mong-tsé): Méng-tzu or Mêng K'o, 372-289 B.C., Chinese philosopher who was a follower of Confucius; he was author of the second of the Chinese classics, the *Book of Mencius*.

67. Chi-King or Odes of Mao-chi: *Shih Ching* [cf. 27 above].

68. Tchun-tsiou: *Ch'un Ch'iu [Spring and Autumn Annals]*, the last of the five classics, is a chronological record of the chief events in the state of Lü between 722 and 484 B.C. It is generally regarded as the work of Confucius, whose native state was Lü.

69. Tso-kieou-min: Tso Chiu-min, fl. fifth century B.C., was a disciple of Confucius. He wrote a commentary on the *Spring and Autumn Annals [Ch'un Ch'iu]* of Confucius. Tso has been canonized as the "Father of Prose," for he expanded the brief entries of Confucius into dramatic episodes. His commentary is known as *Tso Chuan*.

70. Li-yo: *Li Yu*, Chinese treatise on ceremonies and music.

71. Han Tchao Ti: Han Chao Ti, reigned 86-73 B.C. In the second year of his reign he remitted the land tax in impoverished areas. When crops failed in 80 B.C. the emperor's ministers said he should "pay more attention to the good government of the people." The people said they wanted taxes on salt, iron, spirits, and property abolished. Han Chao Ti compromised and abolished taxes on spirits and property. His name means "Illuminating Ruler." Emperor Chao came to the throne at the tender age of eight. During the first ten years of his reign affairs of state were handled by the regent, Ho Kuang. Most of the economic reforms noted were undertaken on Ho Kuang's initiative.

72. Han Sieun (or Siun): Han Hsüan Ti, reigned 73-48 B.C., was an able emperor who in 65 sent out Kung-Su to deal with the many men who had become brigands during a famine. Kung-Su said that every man with a hoe on his shoulder would be treated as an honest man. Every poor man was invited to present his case to the emperor, and farmers without seed were assisted. One of the most able and compassionate of the Han emperors, Hsüan Ti did much to ease the burdens of his people. During his reign the Hsiung Nu (Tartars) were a continuing problem. But in 60 B.C. an internal struggle for power prompted the Hsiung Nu king to come to the Han capital in Ch'ang-an in search of help. He was well received, was treated as a guest, and became a loyal vassal to the Han emperor. His name means "Proclaiming Emperor."

73. Tchang-ngan: Ch'ang-An, the modern city of Sian in Shensi Province, NE China. It was the capital of the empire under the Han dynasty.

74. Mandarins: Members of the mandarinate, the scholar ruling class, or civil service, of China which came into being about 600 B.C. The mandarins were disliked, but respected, by the people of China. Trained in the Confucian classics, by Emperor Hsüan Ti's time they had become the core of the Chinese administrative system.

75. Ouan-soui!: *Wan-sui*, "Ten thousand years!" A traditional Chinese phrase for "a long time!"

76. Tchen-yu: Shan yu, title the Tartars gave their kings.

77. Prince of Hiong-nou: The Tartar prince who because of all the celebrations in his honor "came into the empire."

78. Si-yu: Hsi-yu, large region in W China outside the limits of Shensi Province. Once the territory of the Tartar tribes, it is now modern Sinkiang Province.

79. Tchang-ngan: [cf. 73 above].

80. Bay of Naples: An exhibition of submarine warfare was put on by Mussolini for Hitler in the Bay of Naples in 1938, year 16 of the Fascist state [HK, *Era*, 435].

81. **Ngan**: Chang-an. The assumption here is that since the Hsiung Nu (Tartars) were now vassals of the Chinese emperor, the emperor controlled everything from the Han capital, Ch'ang-an, to the Caspian Sea. The assumption, of course, was not true.

82. **Fong-chi**: Fêng Shih, fl. 6 B.C., concubine of Emperor Han Yüan Ti. During the reign of his grandson, Han Ai Ti, she emerged as the grand empress dowager née Wang.

83. **Fou-chi**: Fü Shih, fl. 6 B.C. Another concubine of Han Yüan Ti, she may have been the mother of Emperor Han Cheng Ti and the grandmother of Emperor Han Ai Ti. She was known as the empress dowager née Fu.

84. **Han Yuen**: Han Yüan Ti, emperor 48-32 B.C., started his reign by cutting taxes and forcing the court to be economical, but he later came under the control of the eunuch Shih Hsien who "seduced the emperor into immoral habits." His name means "Foremost Emperor."

85. **Fong faced him**: The bear escaped while the emperor was walking with his wives, all of whom fled except Fêng. The emperor asked why such courage. She said her life was worth nothing, but "the days of your majesty are precious to the state, and there was no reason for me to hesitate" [*Pai* 5-3, 445].

86. **bhuddists**: Buddhists. The neo-Confucian bias against Buddhism is recorded faithfully in Mailla's *Histoire*. But Mailla, a good Jesuit, deplores Buddhism: "It is at this time that the sect of *Foe* came to infect China with its pernicious doctrines" [*Pai*, 5-3, 445].

87. **Han Ping**: *Han Ping Ti*, emperor A.D. 1-6. Since he was only nine when he came to the throne, the empire was ruled by Wang Mang, a scheming minister who usurped all power and may have murdered Han Ping Ti. His name means "Peaceful Emperor."

88. **tael**: Chinese coin. The scheming Wang Mang served the people well. At a time of drought he won their favor by suggesting to the empress "that she decrease her expenses and wear simpler clothes. . . . Only the most common foods were to be served at his table. . . . He ordered up to one million taels to be distributed to the poor" [*Pai*, 5-3, 446].

89. **Tseou-kou**: Ch'ou Ku, fl. A.D. 73. He and Tchong [Ching Ch'ang] were generals during the reign of Emperor Han Ming Ti.

90. **Prince of Ou-yen**: Wu Yen, fl. A.D. 73, was a Tartar chief during the reign of Emperor Han Ming Ti. Mailla's *Histoire* says "they met the Prince of Ou-yen, whom they defeated, killing him and more than a thousand soldiers. . . . They went on to capture Y-ou, and after having placed a strong garrison there, they employed the rest of their troops in cultivating the land" [*Pai*, 5-3, 445].

91. **Kouang Ou**: Kuang Wu Ti, reigned 25-58, first emperor of the Later Han dynasty. His reign was marked by a series of wars, as rebellions arose within the empire and Tartars attacked from without. Kuang Wu Ti was a successful warrior and also had sympathy for scholars and literary men. His name means "Luminous Martial Emperor."

92. **Han Ming**: Han Ming Ti, reigned 58-76, is known for having introduced Buddhism, and consequently idolatry, into China. Having dreamed that there was a holy man in the West named Foé, he sent ambassadors to discover his teachings and bring back books of his doctrines. His name means "Brilliant Emperor."

93. **Yang Tchong**: Yang Chung, fl. A.D. 76, was a member of the privy council of Emperor Han Chang Ti (76-89).

94. **Tartar war**: Wars between the Chinese Empire and the Tartars during the first century A.D.

95. Empress Ma Chi: Ma Shih, fl. A.D. 77, mother of Emperor Han Chang Ti (76-89). Her wisdom and virtue aided the young emperor when he took the throne at the age of 18.

96. Empresses' relatives: In A.D. 77 Empress Ma Shih advised her son the emperor that only trouble could ensue should relatives of empresses be elevated to high positions.

97. Ouang Chi: Wang Shih, fl. A.D. 15. She was a scheming empress during the time of Wang Mang who arranged that her five brothers be raised to high office.

98. Han Ho Ti: Emperor 89-106; during his reign the military fame of China was higher than ever before. At this time eunuchs were raised to the rank of mandarin, thus setting a precedent that led to many seditions and intrigues in later years of the empire.

99. Han Ngan: Han An Ti, reigned 107-126, was a very just emperor. Unfortunately he elevated women to the rank of court officials, and from that time on there was widespread corruption, justice was perverted, and honest men were driven from the government. His name means "Peaceful Emperor."

100. Empress: Wifę of Emperor Han An Ti.

101. Teng-tchi: Têng Chê, fl. A.D. 107. He refused to be made a prince, but later returned to the court to aid the government of Emperor Han An Ti.

102. Yang-tchin: Yang Chên, fl. 107, was a philosopher of Shensi Province who came to be known as the "Confucius of the West." At the age of 50, yielding to repeated requests to come out of retirement, he became a governor in Shantung. His old friend Huang-mi came, bringing the usual present of money to a superior, but Yang Chên refused.

103. Léang-ki: Liang Chi, d. 159. Uncle of Emperor Han Chung Ti (145-146); Liang Chi and the queen dowager, Liang, became great powers in the empire. Liang Chi served as prime minister under Han Huan Ti; he sent poisoned cakes to those who insulted him and was not very well liked. Finally Han Huan Ti sent 3,000 men to put Liang Chi to death. Liang Chi, realizing what was happening, ate one of his own cakes. All the members of his house were slain and his treasure became the emperor's.

104. Huon: Han Huan Ti, reigned 147-168. In 158 he did away with his corrupt prime minister, Liang Chi, and confiscated his estate, which amounted to 300 million taels. Because he had so much money, Han Huan Ti remitted the land tax for a year. He also built a temple to honor Lao-tzŭ. Unfortunately Huan Ti had to rely on the palace eunuchs in his successful plot to destroy the Liang family, a policy simply perpetuating the political instability that led to the downfall of the dynasty.

105. Taoists: Followers of Lao-tzŭ.

106. Téou-Chi: T'ou Shih, fl. 168. As queen dowager she was appointed regent over Emperor Han Ling Ti.

107. Han Ling: Han Ling Ti, emperor 168-189. His reign was distinguished while T'ou Shih was regent and her father Tou Wu (d. 167) was prime minister. But the chief eunuch persuaded the emperor that Tou Wu was dangerous, so Han Ling Ti executed him and banished the queen dowager. In 184 an outbreak in the northern provinces started the series of calamities that brought the downfall of the Han dynasty in 221.

108. Han: The Later Han dynasty (25-221).

109. three kingdoms: The fall of Han was followed by the period of the Three Kingdoms (221-263), when China was divided into three parts: Wei (north), Wu (south), and Shu-Han (west). It was during this period that certain Taoists who called themselves the "Seven Wise Men of the Bamboo Forest" said happiness came from wine and that everything came from the void [*Pai*, 6-1, 46].

110. Lieou-Tchin: Liu Chin, fl. 263, son of the Minor Han emperor, Han Hou-chu (223-264). The Minor Han was also called the Shu-Han, from its base in Szechwan Province.

111. Tçin: Chin, seventh dynasty (265-420), was divided into the Western Chin (265-317) and the Eastern Chin (317-420).

112. Tou-yu: Tu Yu, fl. 247, an officer serving Emperor Chin Wu Ti who proposed to build a bridge over the Hwang Ho [Yellow River]. He also led an attack against the kingdom of Wu.

113. Tçin Ou Ti: Chin Wu Ti, emperor 265-290, also known as Ssu-Ma Yen, founded Western Chin dynasty. His most important act was to overthrow the kingdom of Wu, one of the Three Kingdoms.

114. Yang-Hou: Yang Hu, d. 278, was an important general serving Emperor Chin Wu Ti. Since the emperor needed to take the kingdom of Wu in order to control all China, Yang Hu was directed to plan the campaign, but he died before accomplishing his task.

115. Ouang-siun: Wang Hsün, fl. 280, was a general serving Emperor Chin Wu Ti. He engaged in campaigns against the kingdom of Wu.

116. San-chan: San-shan, mountain in the province of Kiang-nan.

117. Kiang: Chiang, a general term for "river," but here meaning the Yangtze.

118. Sun-hao: Sun Hao, d. 283, was ruler of the kingdom of Wu, which controlled the territory south of the Yangtze. Emperor Chin Wu Ti spent many years trying to bring the kingdom under his rule, finally succeeding in 280. Sun Hao was a cruel king, and his people finally revolted to join the emperor.

119. Tçin Ou: Chin Wu Ti [cf. 113 above].

120. Ou: Wu, one of the Three Kingdoms; it controlled the territory south of the Yangtze. After its conquest by Chin Wu Ti, taxes were remitted for those who would submit to the new ruler.

121. Emperor: Chin Wu Ti.

122. Quindicennio: I, Fifteenth anniversary celebration of rule.

123. Lieou-Y: Liu I, fl. 289, was a highly respected adviser to Emperor Chin Wu Ti, who had begun his reign well but had let the government decline in favor of dancing girls. When asked by the emperor what former rulers he should be compared with, Liu I said Huan [cf. 104 above] and Ling Ti [cf. 107 above], with one difference. They sold offices as Chin did but they put the money into the public coffers while Chin put the money into his own pocket.

124. Yang Siun: Yang Hsün, fl. 289, father-in-law of Emperor Chin Wu Ti. When the emperor became occupied with the entertainments of the court, which had originally belonged to Sun Hao, he told Yang Hsün to govern the kingdom.

125. Tchang: Wang Chang, fl. 290, was a Tartar chieftian who refused to accept a high post from the infamous Yang Hsün.

126. prince Imperial: Refers to the heir apparent during the reign of Chin Hui Ti, second emperor of the Chin dynasty who reigned 290-307. While amusing himself, the prince went in for moneymaking and "operated taverns where he collected the profits from selling wines" [*Pai*, 6-1, 52].

127. Lao Tse: Lao-tzŭ, ca. 604-531 B.C., one of China's most famous teachers, popularly regarded as the founder of Taoism. His teachings centered on the need to become one with *tao*, "the way." He professed to have found the clue to all things human and divine. Central to his teaching is the doctrine of inaction which states: "Do nothing, and all things will be done." Later, pure Taoism became mixed with magic, astrology, alchemy, and the search for an elixir of life.

128. Hoai Ti: Chin Huai Ti, reigned 307-313, was a very intelligent emperor who was versed in the arts of government, but he had no success in war with the prince of the Eastern Sea (who was to bring the Eastern

Chin into prominence). Because the emperor was so poor a commander in battle, he was eventually deposed.

129. Min Ti: Chin Min Ti, emperor 313-317. His reign was disturbed by attacks of Tartars who in 317 captured the capital and made the emperor a prisoner.

130. Lieou-Tsong: Liu Tsung, fl. 317, was the son of the Tartar prince Liu Yuan, who had invaded N China about 308. Liu Tsung launched an attack against the Chin capital at Loyong, conquered the city, and made the Chin emperor his prisoner. Liu Tsung considered himself the heir to the Han dynasty, and all China N of the Yangtze came under Tartar control.

131. Tçin Tching: Chin Ch'eng Ti, emperor 326-343, was not himself a bad man, but he came to the throne at the age of five and had incompetent and cruel advisers.

132. Tçin Ngan: Chin Ai Ti, emperor 362-366. "His health had been ruined by the potions which the followers of Lao-tse . . . had given him." He died in the fourth year of his reign [*Pai*, 6-1, 53].

133. Tçin Hiao: Chin Hsiao Wu Ti, emperor 373-397. His reign was plagued with civil wars, for Chin was declining in power and the Liu Sung dynasty was about to appear. This emperor is noted for his poor knowledge of female psychology. He told one of his wives that as she was nearing 30 she should think of retiring so that he could replace her with a younger girl. He was making a joke, but the wife didn't think it was funny. She got him drunk and then strangled him [*Pai*, 6-1, 53].

134. piquée de ce badinage: F, "stung by this banter."

135. Sung: Liu Sung, eighth dynasty (420-479).

136. Lieou-yu: Liu Yü, 356-423, founder of Liu Sung dynasty. In 399 he enlisted in the imperial army and was given a command of 70 men. So able was he that by 416 he was made commander in chief and Duke of Sung. In 419 he caused Emperor Chin Ai Ti to be strangled and set up the latter's brother, Chin Kung Ti, as emperor. After sixteen months Chin Kung Ti abdicated and Liu Yü took the throne with the title Kao Tsu.

137. Kao-Tsou: Kao Tsu Wu Ti, reigned 420-423, formerly Liu Yü, known generally as Wu Ti, founder of the Liu Sung dynasty. He proved to be a good emperor but he did not live long enough to be effective.

138. Li-Chan: Liu-shan, mountain in Kiangsi Province near Lake Po-yang. It was the residence of the scholar Lei Tzu-tsung who refused to leave his mountain once he had seen to the courses of study at the academies founded by Wen Ti in 438.

139. Et les Indiens disent que Boudha: F, "And the Indians say that Buddha." Refers to a folktale which says that Buddha was the result of the miraculous union of a chaste queen and a white elephant.

140. Queen Nana: In the legends that gathered about the historical Buddha, Nana is said to have been a virgin who miraculously gave birth to Buddha after the figure of the Supreme Being appeared to her in the form of a white elephant.

141. Prince of Ouei: Toba Tao, d. 452, prince of the kingdom of Wei. An important and powerful ruler, he paid much attention to education in his domain. Because he once entered a Buddhist monastery and found the priests all drinking whiskey and the monastery full of women, he banished Buddhists from his kingdom.

142. hochangs: *Ho-shang*, Buddhists.

143. shamen: Shamans, those who practice shamanism, here meaning Buddhists.

144. Taotssé: Taoist, a believer in Taoism, supposedly founded by Lao-tzŭ [cf. 127 above].

145. Ouen Ti: Wên Ti, reigned 424-454 as ruler of the Liu Sung state. In spite of the opposition of the state of Wei, he extended the power of the emperor over a large territory. As he was fond of literature and the arts and interested in education, he established national colleges. He was eventually killed by his own son.

146. To-pa-tao: Prince of Wei [141 above].

147. placet: F, "petition." Derived from L, *placet*, "it pleases."

148. Yupingtchi: Yü Ping-chih, fl. 448, president of the judicial tribunal under Emperor Wen Ti. He sought after justice so ardently and with such severity that he ruined multitudes of poor people. The emperor finally had to remove him from office.

149. Oueï land: Wei, principality in the general region of the modern Sian, a city in Shensi Province, NE central China, on the Wei River where it joins the Hwang Ho.

150. à la Valturio: F, "in the manner of Valturio" [9:19].

151. Ou Ti: Wu Ti, ruler (483-494) of the state of Ch'i, which replaced the Liu Sung. He paid attention to the laws of the kingdom and cut down the number of retainers at court. While worrying about rebellion within the empire, however, he forgot to consider the threat of the powerful kingdom of Wei to the north.

152. Yen Yen: Yen Yen-chih, d. 456, although of peasant stock, rose to be prime minister of the empire under Emperor Wu Ti. He was a model of modesty, frugality, and disinterestedness.

153. Oueï prince: The Wei Tartars attacked, but since Sung reacted strongly "the Wei forces withdrew" [*Pai*, 6-1, 60].

154. Tien: *T'ien*, "heaven." It was an old tradition that in the "spring rites" the emperor should plough a furrow to ask heaven for a good harvest; and that the empress set a good example by the ceremony of feeding silkworms.

155. Ou: Hsiao Wu Ti, emperor 454-465. Little happened during his reign, and he had no able minister to spur him to activity. The emperor was very frivolous, giving people of the court nicknames and having his servants chase mandarins with a stick. Thus, no respect was paid Hsiao Wu Ti, and he became known as the "Discarded."

156. Kao: Kao Ti, first emperor (479-483) of the Ch'i dynasty (479-502). He is said to have been deficient in heroic qualities.

157. Siao: Hsiao Tzŭ-liang, son of Emperor Wu Ti, 483-494, ruled less than a year after his father died. He collected antique vases.

158. Topas: The people of Topa, of Turkic origin, who founded the kingdom of Wei (386-534).

159. Tan Tchin: Fan Chên, fl. 484, Chinese scholar, one of a group that gathered about Hsiao Tsu-liang, son of Emperor Wu Ti. The prince was a Buddhist, but Fan Chên took it upon himself to discourse on the methods Buddhist monks (bonzes) used to deceive the people.

160. Ou Ti: Wu Ti, reigned 502-549, overthrew the Ch'i dynasty and founded the Liang dynasty. A good emperor who helped his people during the famine and purged the court of corruption, he became a Buddhist and imported 3,000 Buddhist priests. During his reign more than 13,000 Buddhist temples were built in the empire. In 527 Wu Ti became a Buddhist monk. So seriously did he adhere to his Buddhist vows that he became an ineffectual statesman and was overwhelmed by a rebellious general.

161. Ping Tching: P'ing-ch'êng, capital of the kingdom of Wei (386-534).

162. Crown Prince: The son and heir apparent of Emperor Wu Ti.

163. Topa Hong: To Pa Hung, ruler of the kingdom of Wei from 466 to 471, also known as Hsien Wen Ti, became a Buddhist. In 471 he abdicated in favor of his son, who, while adhering to many Buddhist teachings, also gave support to Confucian precepts and required his officials to use the Chinese language and wear Chinese dress.

164. Yuen: Yüan. In 496 To Pa Hung, ruler of Wei, changed the name of his family from To Pa to Yüan. The northern Wei was also known as the Yüan Wei.

165. Kung-fu-tseu: Confucius.

166. Ou Ti: Wu Ti, first ruler of the Liang dynasty [cf. 160 above].

167. 46 tablets: "The Stone Classics," a basic Confucian document. In 517, when Hu Hsi was empress, they were torn down and used to build a Buddhist temple.

168. Yo Lang: Lo Yang. In 494 the ruler of the northern Wei (the son of To Pa Hung) moved his capital from P'ing-ch'êng to the ancient Chinese capital of Lo Yang [53:61].

169. Foé: Fu, the name of Buddha and more commonly the name given to Buddhist priests [*foés, foéist*, in French transliteration] and to Buddhism.

170. Hou-chi: Hu Hsi, the dowager queen who ruled the kingdom of Wei from 515 to 528. An unscrupulous but able woman, she perpetrated the most horrible crimes but also, as a devout Buddhist, did much to further the Buddhist cause in N China.

171. Ou Ti: Wu Ti, founder of the Liang dynasty, finally became a Buddhist monk [cf. 160 above] and left the kingdom to its fate.

172. Ouen Ti: Prob. Shang Ti, "Spirit of Heaven" [53:24].

173. Yang-kien: Yang Ch'ien, emperor 589-605, reunited China, founded the Sui dynasty, and became one of the greatest Chinese emperors. He ruled under the name of Sui Wên Ti until 604, when he was assassinated, apparently by his son.

174. Soui: Sui, a minor state that later became a dynasty.

175. Sou-ouei: Su Wei, fl. 580, adviser to Yang Ch'ien.

176. Heou: Hou Chu, reigned 583-589, was the last of the rulers of the small state of Ch'en. Not heeding the signs that his rule was at its end, this prince pursued a course of extravagance and debauchery. He built three huge buildings [the three Towers] for his favorite concubines. When he was told that Yang Ch'ien was about to overthrow his dynasty, he told his ministers not to worry because the rebellion would probably be unsuccessful; but it wasn't.

177. Soui: Sui, twelfth dynasty (589-618).

178. Yang-Kien: Yang Ch'ien, personal name of Sui Emperor Wên Ti.

179. Mt. Taï Chan: T'ai Shan, sacred mountain of China in W Shantung Province, 32 miles S of Tsinan. There are many shrines on the road to the top where temples were built.

180. Gin Cheou: Name of palace built by Sui Emperor Wên Ti in 593.

181. Touli-Kahn: Tuli Kohan, fl. 593, leader of Kohan, of the Tu-chüei, a Turkic tribe that had established its power in what is now Mongolia. He was given a daughter by the first Sui emperor, Wên Ti [Yang Ch'ien], which eventually led to Sui domination over this border territory.

182. Ouen: Wên Ti, reigned 589-605, known as Yang Ch'ien, was the first emperor of the Sui dynasty (589-618). He concerned himself with agriculture, but was unable to control his scheming brothers.

183. Yang (kouang) Ti: Yang Ti or Yang Kuang, reigned 605-618, son of Wên Ti. He moved the imperial capital to Lo Yang and began building palaces, gardens, and canals, employing, it is said, 2 million men. His canals in the provinces of Hupeh, Shantung, and Honan were designed primarily to facilitate state progress, and they greatly improved commerce in the N. But Yang Ti's methods were harsh, leading to a rebellion; he was soon overthrown and the Sui dynasty came to an end.

184. Kou-choui: Ku-shui, river in Shantung Province which was part of Yang Ti's canal system.

185. Hoang Ho: Yellow River.

186. Wall: Great Wall of China: Chang-chêng. A defensive wall extending 1,250 miles from Mongolia to the Yellow Sea. It was started in the third century B.C. and finished during the reign of the Chin emperor, Shih Huang Ti. In the early seventh century Yang Ti repaired the section between Yü-lin and Tzü-ho.

187. Yu-lin: Yü-lin, city in N China on N border of Shensi Province.

188. Tsé-ho: Tzü-ho, city on N border of Shensi Province.

189. Pei-kiu: Pei Chü, fl. 607, was sent by Emperor Yang Ti to be governor in Hsi-yu and turned his journey to good account by mapping the country.

190. Si-yu: Hsi-yu, large region in W China outside the limits of Shensi Province in the territory of the Tartars.

191. Kong: Kung Ti, who reigned 618-619 as the last emperor of the Sui dynasty, was one of the two puppets who were set up as emperors after the death of Yang Ti. Both were killed within the year.

192. abuleia: L, "paralysis of the will." One of two poles in *The Cantos* [the other: *directio voluntatis*] used to describe the "paideuma" of persons or periods. Thus the Sui dynasty died out because it no longer could put "ideas into action" [5:44].

193. Tang: T'ang, thirteenth dynasty (618-907).

194. Kao Tseu: Kao Tsu, reigned 618-626, known as Li Yüan, was the first emperor of the T'ang dynasty. As the Count of T'ang he had served as governor of a military district in Shansi. A rather timid man and a dedicated Confucianist, he was extremely reluctant to participate in the revolt against the corrupt Sui dynasty. It was his son, Li Shih-min, who actually led the revolt and succeeded in overthrowing the Sui. By a bit of clever intrigue Li Shih-min brought his father into the revolt so that the latter would become the first T'ang emperor.

195. Li-Chi: Li Shih, d. 623, daughter of Emperor Kao Tsu. In 617 she raised an army and came to the aid of her father and brother in their struggles to gain the empire.

196. Tou-kou-hoen: Tu-Yü Hun, Tartar tribe that occupied the territory around Lake Koko Nor in Tsinghai Province, W central China.

197. Fou: Fü I, fl. 626, served as minister under Emperor Kao Tsu. He petitioned that all Buddhist establishments be abolished and that all Buddhist monks and nuns be sent to their homes because, he argued, Buddhism demoralized the empire by de-emphasizing the proper relationships between ruler and people, between parents and children.

198. foé: Fu, Buddhists.

199. Taï Tsong: T'ai Tsung, reigned 626-649. T'ai Tsung was the title adopted by Li Shih-min when he replaced his father on the T'ang throne. He was one of China's most remarkable emperors. A disciple of Confucius, he noted that emperors who embraced Taoism or Buddhism brought about the downfall of their dynasties: "Just as wings are necessary for the birds and water for the fishes, so I put my trust in the teachings of the sages of our country." He cut government costs, reduced taxes, built libraries, aided scholars, and saw that his people had more than enough for their daily needs. He greatly expanded the empire to the west. In 645 he invaded Korea but could not bring it completely into the empire. In 649 he composed *Notes on Conduct*.

200. Fou-Y: [cf. 197 above].

201. Kung: Confucius.

202. Oueï-Tching: Wei Chêng, d. 643, was an astute minister who served Emperor T'ai Tsung. He was noted for the frankness with which he criticized the emperor.

203. Tchang-sun Chi: Chang Sun-shih, d.

636, empress of T'ai Tsung, was one of the great queens of China. Like her husband she was a foe of Taoism and Buddhism. At her death she asked the emperor not to build her an elaborate tomb because it would cost the people too much. She, like Wei Chêng, was not loath to criticize her husband.

204. "Notes for Princesses": Work by Empress Chang Sun-shih on the lives of the princesses of the Chinese Empire before her time.

205. denar: Coin. From L, *denarius*; variant of I, *denaro*, or F, *dener* or *denier*.

206. palatio: L, "palace." Rhyme with the various intrigues and plots in the palaces of the Italian city-states.

207. Corea: Korea. Only in Korea was T'ai Tsung's foreign policy unsuccessful.

208. Caspian: Caspian Sea.

209. Koulihan: Ku-li-kan, nation NW of China and N of Caspian Sea. It was said they lived so far north that "the days are very long and the nights very short." They sent an embassy to China in 647.

210. Kieï-kou: Chieh-ku, barbarian tribe, obviously European, living W of China. These people had red hair and blue eyes. They were tall and had a martial air. "The such like had never been seen in China before." They sent an embassy to China in 648.

211. Atchen (Atkins) Chélisa: Shih Pu-chü Atchen, fl. 647, first officer of Che-li-sa [Shih-li-sa] of the Chieh-ku. As ambassador to the court of Emperor T'ai Tsung, he demanded that the emperor give him the title of grand mandarin. Since titles cost nothing, the emperor made him grand general of the army as well.

212. "Notes on Conduct": Treatise with twelve sections on "How a king should conduct himself," written by Emperor T'ai Tsung for his son.

213. Hempire: Chinese Empire.

214. Empress Ou-heou: Wu Hou, 625-705, one of the concubines of Emperor T'ai Tsung. In 656, after his death, she became the empress consort of Kao-Tsung and for the next forty years was one of the most important figures in Chinese political history. Cruel and unscrupulous, she controlled two emperors and became virtual ruler of the empire. She forced her husband to make her coruler (they were know as "The Two Holy Ones") and finally took over all his power. During the years 684-705 her son Chung Tsung was nominally the emperor, but the period is often known as the reign of Empress Wu Hou.

215. Contraption: The administrative machinery set up by T'ai Tsung was run by good people he brought into government. Because it worked in spite of Wu Hou, the empire was at peace for several years.

216. Tching-gintai: Chêng Jen-t'ai, fl. 662, was a general of the imperial troops serving Emperor Kao Tsung (650-684). He was sent to deal with the Tartar tribes that had been attacking the borders of the empire. His campaign was a success, but on the return journey snow raised havoc: ". . . almost the entire army died of misery and fatigue, so that barely eight hundred men were able to reach the Chinese frontier" [*Pai*, 6-1, 86].

217. hochang: Buddhists. During the T'ang period their power and influence increased. One of their leaders gave the empress a book in which they pretended to prove that she was the daughter of Buddha and that she should succeed to the T'ang dynasty.

218. Tartars: A Tartar chief refused to give his daughter in marriage to a nephew of Wu Hou and threatened to invade China and restore the house of T'ai Tsung.

219. Tchong: Chung Tsung, reigned 684-710, was a weak emperor who was controlled by women. His mother, Wu Hou, ruled the empire until 705; from 705 to 710 the emperor was dominated by his wife, Wei, who wanted to be a second Wu Hou. Wei was murdered in 710.

220. **Hieun**: Hsüan Tsung, reigned 713-756, was one of the most celebrated emperors in Chinese history. He paid strict attention to governing his people and made sumptuary laws for the court in order to cut down state expenses. In 740 he ordered that Confucius be elevated to the rank of prince. But his reign ended in rebellion and palace politics, and Hsüan Tsung resigned in favor of his son, Su Tsung. Hsüan forbade display at court: "He ordered the precious stones and the clothes embroidered with gold and silver to be burned" [*Pai*, 6-1, 88].

221. **Lang-tchéou**: Lang-ch'ou, city in Honan Province, was one of the places where mathematicians implemented Hsüan Tsung's orders to make accurate astronomical observations. Pound gives the results in the text.

222. **Tsiun-y**: Chün-i, village in Honan Province, N of Lang-ch'ou.

223. **Lou-tchéou**: Lu Chou, home village of Hsüan Tsung who traveled there in 723 and exempted it from taxes for five years "to let it be known that he did not forget his home country" [*Pai*, 6-1, 89].

224. **Chépoutching**: Shih-pu-chêng, city in N China.

225. **Ngan-yong**: An-Yang, city in N China and ancient capital of Shang dynasty.

226. **Tou-san**: T'u-fan. Prob. refers to the T'u-fan people of Tibetan stock. The Chinese lost two cities to the T'u-fan but later recaptured them.

227. **taozer**: In 741 a Taoist named Chang-ko came to court claiming to have the secret of immortality. The emperor seemed convinced until the "Taozer" suddenly died.

228. **Koué-fei**: Yang Kuei-fei, d. 756, was the favorite concubine of Emperor Hsüan Tsung and second in importance to the empress. During the An Lu-shan rebellion in 756 the soldiers demanded her death because of her political intrigues. The emperor finally consented and she was strangled. When her body was shown to the soldiers, they promptly returned to their posts. But because she was innocent and the victim of a plot, the emperor became so sad that he resigned the throne that same year.

229. **Tchang-siun**: Chang Hsün, fl. 756, was a commander of imperial troops serving Emperor Su Tsung. He is best known for his defense of Yung-Chiu during a siege. It was he who devised the arrows ploy that resulted in defeat for the Tartars.

230. **Sou Tsong**: Su Tsung, reigned 756-763. At the start of his reign the barbarians held both the E and W capitals of the empire. His reign was one of continual wars, but he was served by able generals.

231. **Yong-kieu**: Yung-chiu, city in Honan Province.

232. **Li-yen**: Li Yen, fl. 779, was a mandarin serving in the government of Emperor Te Tsung.

233. **Té Tsong**: Te Tsung, reigned 780-805, was a weak but amiable emperor. His ministers urged him to obtain revenue by imposing new taxes and to abolish the three existing taxes: land tax, compulsory labor, and payment in kind. The new tax was an annual collection in money. Once the emperor became aware of the condition of the peasants, he gave special attention to making their lot easier, but his ministers prevented him from accomplishing many of his aims. He was a poet and wrote his imperial decrees in verse.

234. **Nestorians**: Members of the Nestorian church, originally the ancient church of Persia. It is related to Catholicism but is not part of the Catholic communion. Its period of greatest expansion was from the seventh to the tenth century, when missions were sent to India and China. In 631 the Nestorians brought Christianity into China. The famous Nestorian tablet (in Sian, Shensi Province) is a record, in Chinese and Syriac, of the progress of Christianity in China from 631 to 781, when the tablet was erected.

235. Kouo-tsé-y: Kuo Tsu-i, 697-781, was one of the most famous Chinese generals. He served four emperors: Hsüan Tsun, Su Tsung, Taï Tsung, and Te Tsung. His campaigns against the rebel An Lu-shan and the Tartars were successful. He proved an able governor of various cities and provinces. His loyalty to the empire, unlike that of most officials, was never questioned. His name is mentioned in the famous Nestorian tablet.

236. Li-ching: Li Shêng, fl. 787, was a captain in the imperial troops who enjoyed great success against the Tartars. It was he who said that war with them was better than peace. In 787, when it was discovered that he was having an affiar with a daughter of Emperor Su Tsung, the latter became so angry that he exiled Li Shêng to Kwangtung.

237. Sintien: Hsin-tien, prob. a town close to Ch'ang-an, capital of the T'ang dynasty, in Shensi Province. The rest of the canto concerns an anecdote that Pound neatly summarizes from the *Histoire*, VI [*Pai*, 6-1, 96].

239. bé: F, "well!"

240. corvée: F, "labor required by the state." Te Tsung did nothing about taxes in general, but he relieved the peasants he visited from required labor.

Glossary Canto LV

1. **Orbem bellis, urbem gabellis / implevit**: L, "Filled the world with wars, the city with taxes." Said of Pope Urban VIII.

2. **Tchun**: Shun Tsung, reigned 805, a mild and good man, was ill with an incurable disease when he came to the throne. After eight months he abdicated in favor of his son, who ruled under the name of Hsien Tsung.

3. **Li-Chun**: Hsien Tsung, reigned 806-821, son of Emperor Shun Tsung whom he succeeded.

4. **Ouie-Kao**: Wei Kao, d. 805, was a general of the imperial troops who won significant victories over Tartars and Tibetans. As governor of Szechwan Province for 21 years he gained more fame, for during that time the people of his province paid exactly the tax demanded by the emperor from the province–and no more.

5. **Lin-Yun**: Lin Yün, fl. 806, was a military officer serving under the rebel Liu Pi. When he objected to the rebellion Liu Pi ordered him beheaded, but Lin Yün was so brave that he was given his freedom.

6. **Lieou Pi**: Liu Pi, d. 806, succeeded the illustrious Wei Kao as governor of Szechwan Province. He raised a rebellion because the territory he ruled was not expanded. Defeated in his first major battle against imperial troops, Liu Pi, with all his family, was sent to the capital and executed.

7. **Liki**: Li Chi, fl. 807, was governor of a department in the province of Kiang-nan who accumulated and hoarded the treasure of six departments. The emperor ordered that the money be put back into circulation to stimulate commerce. Li Chi launched a revolt, was defeated, sent to the court, and executed.

8. **Hien-Tsong**: Hsien Tsung, reigned 806-821. He started his reign by regulating the revenue of the empire, ending the practice of giving presents, forbidding slavery, and remitting taxes. In a series of wars (814-819) he reestablished imperial control over the provincial governors. The emperor, however, was controlled by the court eunuchs, who often opposed his reforms. Toward the end of his reign he became a Buddhist and died suddenly after taking some pills that were supposed to ensure his immortality.

9. **Ideograms**: From top to bottom, right column first, the 13 characters read: *Jên*

[M3099]: "Humane"; *chê* [M263]: "who"; *i* [M293]: "take"; *ts'ai* [M6662]: "wealth"; *fâ* [M1768]: "to develop"; *shên* [M5718]: "themselves"; *Pu* [M5379]: "Negative." The rest of the characters are repeated in different order: *Jên*, *chê*, *i*, *shên*, *fâ*, *ts'ai*. The literal sense of this Confucian saying is: "Humane men use wealth to develop themselves; inhumane men use themselves to develop wealth." Pound translates it: "The humane man uses his wealth as a means to distinction, the inhumane becomes a mere harness, an accessory to his takings" [*CON*, 83].

10. **eunuchs**: Usually placed in charge of the royal harem, they were able to observe, and perhaps influence, the sexual activities of the royal family. From this unique position they found it possible to bring tremendous influence to bear upon royal decisions. In times of weak emperors, such influence was usually malevolent and had disastrous consequences for the dynasty.

11. **tao-tse**: Taoists [54:105, 127].

12. **hochangs**: Buddhists [54:217].

13. **Hien**: [cf. 8 above].

14. **Hoai**: Hwai [53:112].

15. **Li Kiang**: Li Chiang, fl. 812, was a minister serving Emperor Hsien Tsung.

16. **Tien Hing**: T'ien-Hsing, fl. 812, a minister serving Emperor Hsien Tsung.

17. **Tching-Ouang**: Chêng Wang [53:65].

18. **Kang**: K'ang Wang [53:76].

19. **Han-Ouen**: Hsiao Wên Ti [54:42].

20. **Han King Ti**: Hsiao Ching Ti [54:54].

21. **Tou-san**: Tu-fan [54:226].

22. **Mou-Tsong**: Mu Tsung, reigned 821-825. He thought it likely that his father had been poisoned, but he didn't make a big thing over it: he had the Taoist who promised his father immortality put to death and banished the rest of the Taoists [VI, 430].

23. **Ouen-Tsong**: Wên Tsung, reigned 827-841. He began his reign by cutting government expenditures, dismissing 3,000 women from the royal harem, and giving audiences to his ministers every other day. But he lacked firmness of purpose, and soon the power of the court was usurped by the eunuchs. The latter thus became a national danger, but all efforts to get rid of them failed.

24. **Ou-Tsong**: Wu Tsung, reigned 841-847. His one important decree was that all Buddhist priests and nuns in the empire should return to their homes and stop living in idleness and immorality. He also proscribed the Christian cult of Manicheism.

25. **bonzes**: Buddhist monks.

26. **Tsaï-gin**: Wang Tsai-jen, d. 847, was the favorite concubine of Emperor Wu Tsung. She hanged herself as soon as Wu died.

27. **Siuen**: Hsüan Tsung, reigned 847-860. An emperor of intelligence and decision, he became known as the "little" T'ai Tsong.

28. **'Gold Mirror'**: *Chin-ching*, or *The Mirror of Gold*, a work by Emperor T'ai Tsung. This work may be the same as T'ai Tsung's *Notes on Conduct*.

29. **Tai Tsong**: T'ai Tsung [54:199].

30. **Hien**: Hsien Tsung [cf. 8 above].

31. **Y Tsong**: I Tsung, reigned 860-874, was an emperor with little common sense; he preferred his own pleasures to the responsibility of governing his people. During his reign there were rebellions and barbarian invasions.

32. **Hi-Tsong**: Hsi Tsung, reigned 874-889. He left the government to eunuchs while he devoted himself to sport, music, and mathematics. During his reign the most serious rebellions of the T'ang dynasty occurred; they devastated much of China and led to the ruin of the dynasty.

33. **Sun Te**: Sun Tê-chao, fl. 901, was first general of the empire during the reign of

Emperor Chao Tsung (889-905). He freed the emperor from the control by the eunuchs and had several of them executed. In gratitude, the emperor made his family an affiliate of the royal house and gave him the honorary name of Li Chi-chao.

34. **Prince of TçIN**: Li K'o-yung, d. 908. Of Turkic origin, he became a distinguished commander of the imperial troops. His campaigns against the T'u-fan invaders (barbarian tribe in the province of Sinkiang, W China) were so successful that Emperor Chao Tsung (889-905) made him Prince of Chin in 895.

35. **TçIN**: Chin, principality in the province of Shansi.

36. **Li-ké-Yong**: Li K'o-yung [cf. 34 above].

37. **Tchu**: T'ai-tsu, reigned 906-913. Known as Chou Wên, he was first emperor of the Later Liang Dynasty (907-923). When the last emperor of the T'ang dynasty made him Prince of Liang, T'ai-tsu assumed much of the emperor's power and assassinated him in 907. Tai-tsu's reign was troubled by rebellions and invansions of the Ch'i-tan Tartars.

38. **Hiu**: Li Ts'un-hsü, d. 926, son of Li K'o-yung, overthrew the Later Liang dynasty and in 923 set himself up as the first emperor of the Later T'ang dynasty, ruling under the name Chuang Tsung (923-926). He waged successful wars against the Ch'i-tan Tartars, regaining the province of Szechwan for the empire. Finally he gave himself up to sensuality and was assassinated by an actor.

39. **douanes**: F, "custom duties."

40. **chançons de gestes**: F, *chansons de geste*, "songs of heroic deeds."

41. **Khitans**: Ch'i-tans, Mongol tribe N of China, near Korea. By 907 they had become very strong under the chieftain Yeh-lü A-pao-chi, who proclaimed himself emperor of an independent kingdom with the dynastic title of Liao ["iron"]. The Ch'i-tans encroached on the empire until China was divided at the Yellow River. Kai Feng became the capital of the empire, and Peking became for the first time a metropolis and the Ch'i-tan capital.

42. **Yeliou Apaoki**: Yeh-lü A-pao-chi, d. 926, chieftain of the Ch'i-tan Tartars.

43. **Chuliu**: Shulu, d. ca. 953. Also known as Empress Ying T'ien, she was queen of the Ch'i-tan chieftain, Yeh-lü A-pao-chi. She was a woman of great beauty and wisdom, and her husband often depended on her advice in matters of state and military operations.

44. **Tching-tcheou**: Poss. city of Ting-ch'ou in Hopeh Province, N China.

45. **Prince Tçin**: Chin [cf. 35 above].

46. **Ouang Yeou**: Wang Yu, fl. 921, was a rebel commander of the troops of Li Ts'un-hsü, Prince of Chin. He invited the Ch'i-tan Tartars to attack some cities in China, which they did.

47. **Khitan of Apaoki**: Ch'i-tan, Tartars.

48. **TçIN**: Chin [cf. 35 above].

49. **Tang**: T'ang: The Later T'ang, the fifteenth dynasty (923-936). Founded by Li Ts'un-hsü, Prince of Chin.

50. **Chou**: A principality in the province of Szechwan, S central China.

51. **Prince . . . but no Emperor**: Son of the Later T'ang Emperor Chuang Tsung who died in 926 and was replaced by Tartar general Li Ssu-yuan [VII, 251-254].

52. **Tartar Yuen**: Li Ssu-yuan, 866-934, adopted son of Li K'o-yung. Like his father, he was a brilliant general and did much to preserve the Later T'ang dynasty. After the death of his half brother, Li Ts'un-hsü, he was proclaimed emperor by the army. He ruled under the name Ming Tsung.

53. **Ming Tsong**: Ming Tsung, reigned 926-934, proclaimed emperor by the army but refused for a time to function as anything but regent. By 932 the art of printing had

been invented and the nine classics were printed by imperial orders from wooden blocks and sold to the public.

54. **Li Tsongkou**: Li Ts'ung-k'o, 892-936, commanding general of the imperial guards who in 934 came to the throne as the fourth emperor of the Later T'ang dynasty, ruling under the name Liu Wang (934-936). His dynasty fell to the Ch'i-tan Tartars.

55. **Kungfutseu**: Confucius.

56. **Chéking-Tang**: Shih Ching-t'ang, 892-944, general and governor of Shantung Province under the Later T'ang. He bribed the Ch'i-tan Tartars with a promise of half of Chihli and Shansi to help him to the throne. In 936 he proclaimed himself emperor, ruling under the name of Kao Tsu (936-944). He was the founder of the Later Tsin [Chin] dynasty.

57. **Apaoki son of Chuliu**: Yeh-lü-Tê-kuang, d. 947, second son of Ye-Lü-A-pao-chi. In 927 he succeeded to the throne of the Ch'i-tan Tartars (the Liao dynasty) as Emperor T'ai Tsung and in 936 he agreed to help Shih Ching-t'ang gain the empire in return for territory in Chihli and Shansi provices. The revolt was successful, and Yeh-lü-Tê-kuang, the "Father-Emperor," received a yearly tribute from Shih Ching-t'ang, the "Child Emperor" of the Later Chin.

58. **Chuliu**: [cf. 43 above].

59. **Te Kouang**: [cf. 57 above].

60. **Ouan soui!!**: [54:75].

61. **evviva, evviva**: I, "hurrah!"

62. **Lieou-Tchi-Yuen**: Liu Chih-yüan, d. 948, was a distinguished general and governor of Shansi Province under Emperor Chi Wang of the Later Chin (943-947). When the emperor ordered his troops to attack the Ch'i-tan Tartars, Liu Chih-yüan refused, knowing the imperial troops could not withstand the barbarians. After the Tartars withdrew from Kaifeng, the imperial capital, Liu Chih-yüan was proclaimed emperor by his army. He ruled under the name Kao Tsu (947-948) and founded the Later Han dynasty.

63. **Turk . . . of Chato**: Prob. refers to Liu Chih-yüan whose family was of Sha T'o Tartar descent and thus of Turkic origin.

64. **Caïfon fou**: K'ai Feng, city in Honan Province, E central China. It served as the capital of various Chinese states during the period of the Five Dynasties (907-960).

65. **Sung**: Nineteenth dynasty (960-1280). It is divided into two parts: the Sung (960-1127), sometimes called the Northern Sung, and the Southern Sung (1127-1280).

66. **Teoui-tchéou**: Ts'ui Ch'ou-tu, fl. 952, was an officer of the imperial troops, serving Emperor T'ai Tsu of the Later Chou dynasty.

67. **Taï-Tsou**: T'ai Tsu, reigned 951-954, founder and first emperor of the Later Chou dynasty. Although his reign was disturbed by the rebellious Prince of Han, T'ai Tsu proved to be an able administrator and leader. He was a patron of literature and honored the memory of Confucius by saying, "Confucius is the master of a hundred generations of emperors."

68. **Kung**: Confucius.

69. **Ou-tchao**: Wu Chao-i, fl. 953. Wishing to start a college, he requested permission of the Prince of Chou to have *Shu Ching* [*Book of History*] and *Shih Ching* [*Books of Odes*] printed (953). The permission was granted.

70. **Chi-Tsong**: Shih Tsung, reigned 954-959, was a benevolent and generous emperor of the Later Chou. He waged successful wars against the Ch'i-tans and the Northern Han and enlarged the empire. When there was a scarcity of money, he ordered all copper utensils given up for imperial uses. He also seized all the bronze images of Buddha and converted them into coin, remarking that Buddha, who had given so much to mankind, was not likely to object.

71. **Tçé-tchéou**: Tz'u-ch'ou, city near Liuchow in Kwangsi Province, SE China. In 954

the Northern Han attacked Liuchow and Emperor Shih Tsung engaged the Han troops near Tz'u-ch'ou.

72. **Han**: Later Han dynasty.

73. **Chi**: Shih Tsung [cf. 70 above].

74. **hochang**: Buddhists.

75. **bonzes and bonzesses**: Buddhist monks and nuns.

76. **Chou**: Later Chou dynasty (951-960).

77. **Tang**: T'ang. The southern T'ang, a principality in the province of Kiangsu, E China. Formerly this region was the principality of Wu, but in 937 the princes of Wu changed their name to T'ang.

78. **Hoaï-ho**: Hwai Ho, river in S Honan and NW Anhwei provinces in E China. It was on the Hwai River that a naval battle was fought between the armies of Emperor Shih Tsung and those of the ruler of the Later T'ang [cf. Cordier, II, 52].

79. **Kiang**: Yangtze River.

80. **Hoaï-nan**: City on the Hwai River.

81. **devast**: F, "ravaged."

82. **Ouang-po**: Wang Po, d. 959, was statesman, mathematician, and personal counselor to Emperor Shih Tsung.

83. **pourvou que ça doure**: F, "provided that it lasts."

84. **Han**: Prob. Later Han dynasty (947-951); Yin Ti, the last emperor of the Later Han, was 18 when he came to the throne.

85. **Tchao Kouang**: Chao K'uang-yin, founder of the Sung dynasty (960-1127) who ruled as Emperor T'ai Tsu [cf. 90 below].

86. **South Han**: Nan-han, roughly the area of the provinces of Kwangsi and Kwangtung in SE China; this principality lasted from 905 to 971.

87. **douanes**: F, "custom duties."

88. **Tsiuenpiu**: Wang Ch'uan-pin, fl. 965, was a general serving Sung Emperor T'ai Tsu. He was in charge of the expedition that overcame the remnants of the Later Chou dynasty.

89. **Chou**: Hou Chou, Later Chou dynasty (951-960).

90. **emperor**: T'ai Tsu, reigned 960-976, founded Sung dynasty. He was serving as a general under Emperor Shih Tsung when his troops invested him with the yellow robe of emperor. His greatest accomplishment was the restoration of the empire. He reclaimed the lands of Southern Han, the Later Chou, Szechwan, and other provinces for the throne, and only Northern Han resisted his attacks. He encouraged the study of literature, revised the law courts, improved the criminal code, and stabilized the economy.

91. **this general**: Wang Ch'uan-pin. He received the emperor's robe with tears of happiness. The emperor sent a message with the robe saying he wished he was able to send one to all his generals. Because of such acts the troops loved the emperor and for him rapidly conquered the states of Chou.

92. **Koué**: C, *Kue*, the constellation Andromeda.

93. **Tai Tsong**: T'ai Tsung, reigned 977-998, was a mild but decisive emperor who governed with economy. His first important act was to suppress the state of Northern Han (979), a task his brother, T'ai Tsu, had not completed. But T'ai Tsung was unable to check the Ch'i-tan Tartars or to stop a dangerous alliance between the Ch'i-tan and Nüchên Tartars. He was a student of history, honored Confucius, and studied the classics.

94. **true BOOKS**: Prob. refers to a multivolume work, *T'ai-Ping Yu Lan*, prepared under the direction of Emperor T'ai Tsung.

95. **Ssétchuen**: Szechwan, province in W central China.

96. **Ouang Siaopo**: Wang Hsiao-po, fl. 993, was a man of the people who roused Szech-

wan province to revolt against its governor in 993. There was little money in the province because the conquering Sung troops had carried it away a few years before. The mandarins were fleecing the people. The rich were buying up small farms and depriving the poor of land and food. Imperial troops soon put down the rebellion, and Emperor T'ai Tsung appointed a governor who improved the condition of the poor.

97. **Tsing-chin**: Ch'ing-shên, city in Szechwan Province, later known as Koan-hsien.

98. **Pongchan**: Peng-shan, district and city in the province of Szechwan.

99. **Jelly Hugo**: Yeh-lü Hsiu-ko, d. 998, was governor of the region of Yen, which surrounds the city of Peking (once called Yen as well). He was a general of the Ch'i-tan Tartars and is known for his humanity and his just and liberal administration.

100. **Ghengis**: Genghis Khan, 1162-1227, Mongol emperor. His personal name was Temujin or Temuchin and his imperial title was Tai-Tsou [T'ai-Tsu]. He proclaimed himself emperor of the Mongols in 1206. By 1214, through a series of wars with various Tartar tribes (mainly Ch'i-tan and Nü-chên), he became master of all the territory north of the Hwang Ho, except for Peking, capital of the Chin dynasty of the Nü-chên. He conquered Korea, and by 1221 he controlled much of C Asia. During his career of conquest he established the power of the Mongols in a large part of Asia.

101. **Tchin-Song**: Chên Tsung, reigned 998-1023, was a capable emperor but a devout Taoist, whose superstition led him to disgrace. K'ou Chun, a brilliant general and statesman, forced the emperor to fight the Ch'i-tan Tartars and to make peace with them by promising an annual tribute of 100 ounces of silver and 200 pieces of silk. When court intrigues led to the ouster of K'ou Chun, the emperor fell into the hands of ministers who used his superstition to their advantage. Three books, reputed to be from heaven, were presented to the emperor, who was so impressed by this supposed honor that he ordered a huge temple built; the project took seven years to complete and cost so much that some historians date the decline of the Sung dynasty from this extravagance. By 1020 the emperor was insane and his power had passed to eunuchs.

102. **marte zibbeline**: F, *martre zibeline* "sable."

103. **Tchin-Tsong**: Chên Tsung.

104. **King of Khitan**: Yeh-lü-Lung-hsü, d. 1031, was king of the Ch'i-tan Tartars. After leading his troops into the empire and taking over a large area in 1004, he was met by imperial troops and after several battles was persuaded to make a peace that was honorable both for himself and for Emperor Chên Tsung.

105. **Tchongking**: Chung-ching-fu, modern city of Chungking in Szechwan Province.

106. **Tchin**: Chên Tsung. "Going mumbo" suggests the ravings of his insanity [cf. 101 above].

107. **Gin Tsong**: Jen Tsung, reigned 1023-1064. Internal rebellions and invasions weakened the empire, and in 1042 Jen Tsung was forced to make a humiliating peace with the Ch'i-tan Tartars to keep them quiet. As a patron of literature he encouraged a golden age of Chinese literature in which many of China's most noted poets, historians, and scholars emerged.

108. **Fou-Pié**: Fü Pi, d. 1085, was a scholar and diplomat serving Emperor Jen Tsung. In 1042 the Ch'i-tan Tartars demanded ten counties of the empire and threatened war if the emperor refused. Fü Pi was sent to negotiate, and the resulting treaty enjoined the Ch'i-tan to keep peace and promised them an annual tribute of 100,000 ounces of silver and 100,000 pieces of silk in addition to the tribute promised in 1006 by Emperor Chên Tsung. Fü Pi's treaty, though humiliating to the empire, was a masterpiece of diplomacy.

109. **Chin-Tsong**: Shên Tsung, reigned 1068-1086, was an able administrator, am-

bitious for his empire, his people, and himself. His chief ally was the minister, Wang An-shih.

110. Ngan: Wang An-shih, 1021-1086, became Emperor Shên Tsung's confidential adviser and minister of state in 1069. He and the emperor instituted reforms based on Wang's new and "more correct" interpretations of the classics: state administration of commerce, state support for farmers, compulsory military service, a state system of barter, a new land tax system. In the face of strong opposition, the emperor put Wang's reforms into practice, but Wang tried to move too rapidly and lived to see all his reforms abolished. After his death he was disgraced and his tablet was removed from the Confucian temple.

111. Tcheou emperors: Chou [cf. 53: passim].

112. douanes: F, "custom duties."

113. Yao: [53:14].

114. Koen: Kun, fl. 2297 B.C., Earl of Ch'ung and father of the Great Yu. He was minister of works under Emperor Yao and was appointed to drain the empire after the disastrous overflow of the Hwang Ho in 2295. In 2286, after he had worked for nine years but had accomplished little, his son was given the task. After another nine years, Yu succeeded.

115. confino: I, "in exile."

116. Liu-hoei: Liu Hui-ching, 1031-1111, a minister serving Emperor Shên Tsung who originally opposed the reforms of Wang Anshih.

117. Ngan: Wang An-shih. The word "twister" comes from the idea of a soul that seemed simple and open on the outside but was full of detours on the inside.

118. Hoei: Liu Hui-ching [cf. 116 above].

119. Tengtcheou: Têng-ch'ou, city on the N coast of Shantung Peninsula in Shantung Province, NE China.

120. denar: Coin [54:205].

121. Fan-chungin: Fan Chun-jen, fl. 1069, was the minister sent by Emperor Shên Tsung to inspect the progress of Wang Anshih's reforms in the province of Shensi. Fan Chun-jen complained of the new regime because it did away with the traditional form of government in China.

122. Heoi-king: Liu Hui-ching [cf. 116 above].

123. Ssé-ma: Ssŭ-ma Kuang, 1019-1086, was a distinguished statesman, historian, and scholar. He was minister of state under Emperor Jen Tsung (1023-1064) and an important minister under his successor, Emperor Shên Tsung. Ssŭ-ma Kuang zealously opposed the reforms of Wang An-shih and, when Shên Tsung refused to part with the latter, retired to private life. In 1085 he returned to the government, but died a few months later. His greatest work was *Tzu Chih T'ung Ch'ien* [*A Comprehensive Mirror for the Aid of Government*] which was finished in 1084 after more than 20 years of work. Ssŭ-ma Kuang also wrote a history of 35 centuries of Chinese culture, a dictionary, and a number of miscellaneous papers.

124. Tsong of Tang: T'ai Tsung [54:199].

125. Chin: Shên Tsung [cf. 109 above].

126. Ngan: Wang An-shih [cf. 110 above].

127. Ssé-ma Kouang: Ssŭ-ma Kuang [cf. 123 above].

128. Fan Tsuyu: Fan Tsu-yu, fl. 1084, was a historian at the court of Emperor Shên Tsung. He was one of those who helped Ssuma Kuang compile *Tzu Chih T'ung Ch'ien.*

129. Lieou Ju: Liu Ju, fl. 1084, was a historian at the court of Emperor Shên Tsung. He helped Ssu-ma Kuang compile *Tzu Chih T'ung Ch'ien.*

130. Tsé-tchi tong kien hang mou: *Tzu Chih T'ung Ch'ien,* commonly called *T'ung Ch'ien* or *Mirror of History*, is a history of China from the fifth century B.C. to the beginning of the Sung dynasty, A.D. 960. Ssŭ-ma Kuang was editor and chief author. The work, begun before 1064, was completed in 1084 and presented to Emperor Shên Tsung. Later abridged and cast in a new form, it was given the title *Tzŭ-chih t'ung-ch'ien kang-mu* or *Kang-mu.*

131. **Tso kieou ming**: Tso Chiu-min [54:69].

132. **Oueï-Lie**: Wei-Lieh Wang, reigned 425-401 B.C. The reign was uneventful except that the tripods of Yu began to make noises, thus signaling that the end of the Chou dynasty was near.

133. **Tcheou dynasty**: Chou [53:77]

134. **Chin-Tsong**: Shên Tsung [cf. 109 above].

135. **Lux . . . partem**: L. "For light of herself into every region" [Grosseteste, *De Luce seu de inchoatione formarum*, ed. Baur, 51; cf. *LE*, 160-163].

136. **Tcheou Tun-y**: Chou Tun-i, 1017-1073, scholar and philosopher, held small posts in the government. His chief works are elucidations of the mysteries of the *Book of Changes*, or *I Ching*, which is ascribed to Wên Wang. Chou Tun-i is considered one of the forerunners of the neo-Confucian movement led by Chu Hsi.

137. **seipsum . . . diffundit**: L, "itself, it diffuses itself."

138. **risplende**: I, "it gleams," key verb from line 26 of Cavalcanti's "Donna mi priegha," trans. in 36/177 as "shineth out," describing the action of loving is here related to Chinese views of reason and the Latin of Grosseteste [cf. *LE*, 161].

139. **et effectu**: L, "and in effect."

140. **Yao**: [53:14].

141. **Chun**: [53:23].

142. **Nenuphar**: F, "water lily." Refers to Chou Tun-i who, because he lived by a stream full of water lilies, was called "Master of the Water Lily" [*Pai*, 7-1, 2, 235].

143. **Caïfong**: K'ai Feng [cf. 64 above].

144. **Ssé-kouang**: Ssŭ-ma Kuang [cf. 123 above].

145. **anti-tao, anti-bhud, anti-Ngan**: Refers to the anti-Taoist, anti-Buddhist, anti-Wang An-shih thought of Ssŭ-ma Kuang.

146. **Kung**: Confucius.

147. **Tsaï King**: Ts'ai Ching, 1046-1126, partisan of Wang An-shih. In 1107 he became lord high chamberlain under Emperor Hui Tsung and gained control of the administration. He filled all posts with his own men, made oppressive changes in the salt tax and the coinage, and led the empire into expensive wars. He was several times degraded but always managed to work his way back to power. Ts'ai Ching is known in Chinese history as "Chief of the Six Traitors."

148. **Ngan**: Wang An-shih [cf. 110 above].

149. **Hoeï**: Hui Tsung, reigned 1101-1126, was a clever artist and collector of antiques, but not much of an emperor. He was dominated by his minister, Ts'ai Ching, who led him into Taoism. Unable to resist the Chin Tartars, the emperor abdicated and surrendered himself to the invaders. They gave him the title of "Besotted Duke."

150. **Tsaï**: Ts'ai Ching [147 above].

151. **Akouta**: Akuta, 1069-1123, was chieftain of the Chin Tartars. In 1114 he rebelled against the Liao dynasty of the Ch'i-tan Tartars and entered into an agreement with Emperor Hui Tsung. He attacked the Liao and then invaded the empire, forcing Hui Tsung off the throne. The Chin withdrew to Peking and made it their capital.

152. **Kin**: Chin, Tartar tribe formerly known as Nü-chên. In 1114 Akuta, chieftain of the Nü-chên, proclaimed himself an emperor and gave the name of Chin ("gold") to his dynasty, which lasted from 1115 to 1234.

153. Hoang-ho: Hwang Ho, or Yellow River.

154. old Turk's country: Refers to tribes of Turkic origin which controlled the territory N and W of China during the last years of the T'ang dynasty.

155. Leao: Liao, dynasty of the Ch'i-tan Tartars which lasted from 907 to 1125 and controlled much of N China from their capital at Peking. After the capture of Peking by the Chin Tartars, the house of Liao was diminished to a minor dynasty known as the Western Liao (1125-1168).

156. Nutché: Nü-chên, Tartar tribe formerly of N Korea near the headwaters of the Yalu River. It was long dominated by the Ch'i-tan Tartars, but in A.D. 1114 it defeated them. The tribe's chieftain, Akuta, proclaimed the Chin dynasty of the Nü-chên Tartars.

157. Corea: Korea.

158. Ghengiz: Genghis Khan [cf. 100 above].

159. Tai-Tsou: T'ai Tsŭ, imperial title of Genghis Khan.

160. Témouginn: Temuchin, personal name of Genghis Khan.

161. Chi-Tsou: Shih Tsu, name taken by Kublai Khan when he began his reign over China (1280).

162. Koublai: Kublai Khan [18/80].

163. Hoang ho: Hwang Ho, or Yellow River.

164. Sung: [cf. 65 above].

165. shagreen: Rough skin of the shark; shagreen leather.

166. Oulo: Shih Tsung, also known as Wanyen P'ou, fifth emperor of the Chin dynasty of the Nü-chên Tartars. During his reign (1161-1190) the Chin gained much territory in China, mainly in Honan Province. An exceptional man, wise and benevolent, he was sometimes called "Little Yao and Shun."

167. Hia: Hsia, minor kingdom or principality (fl. ca. 1150) near the Ordos Desert, a territory bordered on one side by the Hwang Ho [Yellow River] and on the south by the Great Wall. The territory is on N border of Shensi and was occupied by Tartars.

168. Ghingiz: Genghis Khan [cf. 100 above].

169. Tchinkis: Genghis Khan. It is said that *Tchinkis* is an imitation of the cry of a celestial bird which no one has ever seen but which will herald great happiness when it does appear.

170. mores: L, "customs."

171. fumée maligne: F, "evil smoke."

172. Yéliu Tchutsaï: Yeh-lü Ch'u-ts'ai, 1190-1244, a Ch'i-tan Tartar, served as adviser to Genghis Khan and to Ogotai Khan. Yeh-lü was largely responsible for the establishment of a regular administration among the Mongols, for a system of taxation, and for a code of criminal law. When paper money was issued in 1236 it was owing to Yeh-lü's advice that the issue was limited to 100,000 ounces of silver. As a patron of literature and a student of Confucius, he did much to civilize the Mongols. Some of his contemporaries suspected that he had grown rich in government service, but when his house was searched after his death, all that could be found were musical instruments, pictures, and several thousand books.

173. Sung: [cf. 65 above].

174. Antzar: Antsar, fl. 1231, was a Mongolian general who served under Emperor Ogotai Khan during the great Mongol campaigns against the Chin Tartars in Honan Province.

175. Tang and Teng: T'ang and Têng are villages in the province of Honan, near the modern city of Nanyang.

Glossary Canto LVI

1. **Billets, biglietti**: F, I, "paper currency."

2. **Ou-Kiai**: Wu Ch'ieh, fl. 1135, captain of the imperial troops who served Southern Sung Emperor Kao Tsung (1127-1163), had some success against the Tartars.

3. **tartars**: Here the Chin Tartars.

4. **Yu-Tchong**: Yü Chung, fl. 1081, governor of Ching Ch'ou, department in Shensi Province.

5. **Kingtcheou**: Ching Ch'ou, capital and seventh department of Shensi Province.

6. **Chensi**: Shensi Province, NE central China, one of the Five Northern Provinces.

7. **Sung**: Nineteenth dynasty [55:65].

8. **Hoei**: Hui Tsung [55:149].

9. **Tchinkis**: Genghis Khan.

10. **Tartary**: Indefinite region in Asia and Europe extending from Sea of Japan to Dnieper River, controlled at different times by various Tartar tribes. The Tartars who invaded China occupied the area beyond N boundaries of Shensi, Shansi, and Hopeh provinces.

11. **Yeliu-Tchutsai**: Yeh-lü Ch'u-ts'ai [55:172].

12. **Yeliou apaoki**: Yeh-lü A-pao-chi [55:42].

13. **Ouanyen**: Wan-yen, family name of rulers of Chin Tartars.

14. **akouta**: Akuta [55:151], a chief of the Chin Tartars [Grousset, 134], succeeded in the early 12th century in uniting all China N of the Yangtze River [ibid., 516].

15. **Kin**: Chin Tartar tribe formerly known as the Nü-chên [55:152].

16. **Khitan**: Ch'i-tan, Tartar tribe [55:41].

17. **Genghis**: Genghis Khan.

18. **Yuen**: Yüan, twentieth dynasty (1206-1368). This dynasty of Mongol emperors was proclaimed in 1206 by Genghis Khan. By 1280, under Kublai Khan, the Yüan had extended its control over the entire Chinese Empire.

19. **Ogotai**: Ogotai Khan, 1185-1241, second khan of the Mongols, succeeding Genghis Khan in 1228. With the help of his minister, Yeh-lü Ch'u-ts'ai, he gave to the Mongols and the people they conquered a stable administration, taxation, and criminal jurisprudence. In 1236 he issued paper money and started a system of government examinations. He campaigned in Korea, China, and C Asia and managed to extinguish the Chin Tartars in 1234.

20. **Bojars**: R, *bojas*, members of a Russian aristocratic order favored with certain exclusive privileges [33:12].

21. **Hoang Ho**: Hwang Ho, or Yellow River.

22. **Mt Kuai**: Mt. Kuei-ki. Japanese pronunciation of Kuei-Chi [Fang, I, 136].

23. **Taozers**: Taoists, followers of Lao-tzŭ. Their idea of an "elixir of internal life" was anathema to neo-Confucians [54:127].

24. **li Sao**: *Li Sao* ["Falling into Trouble" is a collection of poems by Ch'ü Yüan, 343-290 B.C. [cf. Giles, 50-53].

25. **Mt Tai . . . carpet**: Three lines from a poem by Li Po.

26. **Mongols**: Nomadic barbarian tribes that occupied a vast territory N of China [55:41]. A royal prince of Chin, submitted to barbaric torture, suffered it all with a constancy that astonished the barbarians. "Plusieurs versèrent à terre du sang de cavalle, & prièrent qu'un si brave homme renaquit parmi les *mongous*" [Mailla, IX, 156].

27. **Ouen yan Tchin hochang**: Wan-yen Chen Ho-shang, d. 1232, prince royal of the Chin dynasty and an officer leading Chin troops in the battles between the Chin and

the Mongols. He suffered the torture noted in 26 above.

28. **Yao, Chun, Yu**: The ideograms are for these emperors [53:14, 23, 15].

29. **Han**: Prob. Later Han dynasty, 947-951 [55:84].

30. **Sung**: Nineteenth dynasty [55:65].

31. **mogul**: Mongol.

32. **mus ingens . . . comedere**: L, "huge, huge mouse, don't eat my grain" [cf. Lacharme, Pt. I, Bk. 9, ode 7, p. 47; *GK*, p. 215; in *Classic Anthology*, Pound translates it: "RATS, big rats, lay off our wheat" (113, p. 54)].

33. **Kin Lusiang**: Chin Li-hsiang, 1232-1303, scholar at the court of the Sung. After the fall of the Southern Sung dynasty in 1280, he retired to Mt. Jen where he attracted many disciples. He wrote a history of early China and many commentaries on the classics.

34. **Pa Yang**: Pan-yang, poss. P'ing-yang, city in Shansi Province. Mailla says that 2,410,070 mulberry trees perished there in the frigid spring weather [IX, 485].

35. **I-Tching-tcheou**: Ching-ch'ou, village near city of Kai Feng Fu.

36. **Ogotai**: [cf. 19 above].

37. **Nik-ia-su**: Nin-chia-ssu, reigned 1225-1234 as last emperor of Chin dynasty. His reign was marked by almost continuous war with the Mongols of Ogotai Khan.

38. **Ozin (Wodin) Youriak:** Emperor Ojin [c. 270-310] and Yuryaku [456-479]. Wodin the Germanic God.

39. **Ghenso**: Genghis Khan.

40. **chi**: C, "winnowing basket," used as measuring device.

41. **denar**: Coin [54:205].

42. **ZinKwa:** Japanese Emperor Senkwa [536-539].

43. **Ten Bou**: Prob. Wu Tu Pu, reigned 1213-1224, emperor of Chin dynasty. His reign was marked by almost continuous war with Genghis Khan's Mongols.

44. **Yeliu Tchutsai**: Yeh-lü Ch'u-ts'ai [55:172].

45. **Meng Kong**: Meng Kung, d. 1246, was an officer of imperial troops serving Sung Emperor Li Tsung (1225-1265). Meng Kung was the leader of several imperial campaigns against the Mongols.

46. **Han**: Han-ch'ou, large town in Szechwan Province.

47. **Lang**: Lang-ch'ou, modern city of Langchung [formerly Paoning], Szechwan Province.

48. **Ouen**: Wen-chiang-hsien, district in Szechwan Province.

49. **Kong**: Chiung-ch'ou, large town in Szechwan Province.

50. **Mie**: Mei-ch'ou, large town in Szechwan Province.

51. **Kien**: Ch'ien-ch'ou, large town in Szechwan Province.

52. **Tchong, King Fou**: Chung-ching-fu, modern Chungking [55:105, 54 below]. The comma after *Tchong* is an error.

53. **Pong**: Pêng-shui-hsien, district in Szechwan Province.

54. **Chun King**: Chung-ching-fu, modern city of Chungking in Szechwan Province.

55. **Vendome**: Vendôme, town in Loir-et-Cher department, N central France.

56. **Beaugency**: Town in Loire department, on Loire River, France. An old French song runs: "Orleans, Beaugency! /Notre Dame de Cléry! / Vendôme, Vendôme / Quel chagrin, quel ennui / De compter toute la nuit / Les Heures–les heures!"

57. **Notre Dame de Clery**: Church of Our Lady in Cléry, town in Loire department, SW of Orléans.

58. Kujak: Kuyuk, reigned 1246-1248, son of Ogotai Khan, was a Mongol king who held a magnificent court in Tartary. A footnote in Mailla [IX, 245] says that Kuyuk raised two armies to fight Hungary and Poland and declared his intention to send another one against Livonia and Prussia. The first armies were to depart for E Europe in March 1247, but the premature death of Kuyuk halted the preparations.

59. Mengko: Mangu Khan, 1251-1259, Mongol emperor who put down all feudal opposition to his rule, reduced the tax burden, and curbed the power of the nobles. In 1259 he invaded Szechwan Province and besieged Ho-Chou (60 miles N of Chungking). The city resisted, plague broke out in the Mongol ranks, and Emperor Mangu died of the disease [Grousset, 284].

60. Caï Fong: K'ai Feng, city in Honan Province which at times served as the Chinese capital [55:64].

61. ammassi: I, "grain pools" to be available in times of bad harvest [53:17].

62. Yao, Shun, Yu: Early emperors [53:14, 23, 15].

63. Kung: Confucius.

64. Tchin Ouang: Chêng Wang, second ruler of Chou dynasty [53:65].

65. Ouen: Wên Wang, the elegant king called "Chief of the West" [53:49].

66. Ghengiz Khan: Genghis Khan.

67. Bagdad: Baghdad, city in Iraq, on Tigris River. The brother of Mangu Khan, Hulugu, was ordered to attack Baghdad in 1254 [cf. Grousset, 282].

68. Kukano: Koko Nor, large lake in W China in what is now known as Chinghai Province.

69. Ho-tcheou: Ho-ch'ou, city on Kialing River, 60 miles N of Chungking, where Mangu Khan died in 1259.

70. Ogotai: [cf. 19 above].

71. Kublai: Kublai Khan [18:1]. As a great general serving his brother Mangu, he consolidated the victories over the Sung and extended the power of the empire not only to the S into Tibet and the Na-khi territories but also into the NW. When Mangu died in 1259, Kublai ascended the throne and led the empire into its most illustrious and powerful period. By 1280 the last of the Sung emperors, Ti Ping, drowned himself and Kublai's power was no longer resisted. He built a new capital, Khanbalik "City of the Khan", known in European chronicles as Cambaluc and later as Peking. All Mongol princes became his vassals and paid him tribute. Marco Polo visited Kublai Kahn during his reign [18:8]. Although he ruled discreetly and munificently, relieving the distress of the poor, undertaking public works, and patronizing art and literature, the Chinese never forgot that he was both an alien and a barbarian. Few regretted his death in 1294 when his grandson, Timur, succeeded him with the title of Yüan-chêng.

72. Mt Hianglou: Hsiang-lu, prob. a mountain near the Yangtze River, in Honan Province.

73. Kiang: Yangtze River.

74. Sung: The Southern Sung, second part of nineteenth dynasty (1127-1280).

75. Li Tsong: Li Tsung, reigned 1225-1265, fifth emperor of Southern Sung dynasty. He broke his treaty with the Mongols and attacked them in 1234. Thereafter his reign was marked by almost continuous warfare with the Mongols.

76. Kiassé: Chia Ssu-tao, fl. 1273, minister and military officer serving Sung Emperor Li Tsung. He made a secret treaty with Kublai Khan in 1259, representing the emperor as willing to pay a tribute to the Mongols to ensure peace. Kublai accepted the treaty and turned his troops north, but Chia Ssu-tao attacked the rear of the Mongol troops. For this treachery, Kublai vowed to ruin the Sung dynasty. Chia Ssu-tao was minister to two other emperors: Tu Tsung (1265-1275) and K'ung Ti (1275-1276). His attempts to deal with the Mongols, either by diplomacy or by armed force, never seemed to do the Sung much good. He died disgraced.

77. **Pasepa**: Phags-pa, Tibetan lama who provided the Mongols with an alphabet [cf. Cordier, II, 337-338]. Kublai Khan raised him to a princely title [Grousset, 298].

78. **Yai**: Yai-shan, small island in a bay 30 miles SW of Canton, Kwangtung Province, which served as the last stronghold of the Southern Sung dynasty. In 1279 the Mongol fleet attacked the island, defeating the Sung fleet and prompting Emperor Ti Ping (1271-1279) to drown himself. Thus ended the Southern Sung. Kublai Khan became ruler of all China.

79. **Yuen**: Dynastic name adopted by the Mongols [cf. 18 above].

80. **Hoang-ho**: Hwang Ho, or Yellow River.

81. **Ouang tchi**: Wang Chu, d. 1282, chief officer of city of Peking. He led the conspiracy to assassinate Ahmed, the corrupt financial minister under Kublai Khan. Wang Chu lured Ahmed to the palace late at night and killed him with an iron mace. Kublai had Wang Chu executed [cf. Cordier, II, 315], a deed he later regretted.

82. **Ahama**: Ahmed Fenaketi, d. 1282, Kublai Khan's finance minister who used his power to enrich himself. Alarmed at his excesses, several members of the court, led by Wang Chu, formed a conspiracy and assassinated him [cf. Grousset, 297].

83. **Ouen Tiensiang**: Wên T'ien-hsiang, 1236-1283, one of the most patriotic men in Chinese history. He served the last five emperors of the Southern Sung dynasty as minister and general. All his efforts to stem Mongol invasions failed, and when the dynasty fell he was taken prisoner (1279). Unlike most others he refused to pledge his loyalty to the Mongols. The general who captured him did not want to execute a man so loyal to his own country, but he was pressured into doing so by courtiers.

84. **Lou-chi**: Lü Shih-chung, d. 1285, was so dishonest a minister that he was known as the "second Ahmed." He made so many enemies by his intrigues that he was finally condemned to death and butchered; his body was thrown into the street.

85. **Tchin-kin**: Chên Chin, d. 1286, son of Kublai Khan and prince royal of the empire. He was a model of all virtues and manners, learned in the humanities and the arts of war and ruling. His early death was a serious loss to his father and to the empire.

86. **L Sieuen**: Liu Hsuan, fl. 1286, was the minister who persuaded Kublai Khan to give up his plans to conquer Japan and Annam.

87. **Annam**: Part of present-day Vietnam.

88. **Yeliu**: Yeh-lü Yiu-shang, fl. 1287, was a scholar who received permission from Kublai Khan to reopen the Imperial College, which had not been in operation since the time of Ogotai Khan.

89. **Sangko**: Sang Ko, d. 1291, served as finance minister to Kublai Khan (1288-1291). A villain who was clever and apt at flattery, he sacrificed the honor of the empire to his own interests. He was executed in 1291 [cf. Grousset, 297].

90. **Ouantse**: Wan Tzŭ, fl. 1291, one of Kublai Khan's ministers of state. One of Kublai's great accomplishments was the creation of an effective administrative system and the introduction of a systematic code of law, projects in which Wan Tzŭ played a part.

91. **Timour**: Timur Khan, reigned 1294-1308, was the grandson of Kublai Khan, whom he succeeded on the throne. He ruled as Emperor Ch'eng Tsung. Timur was an honest ruler who tried to promote the welfare of his people. He improved the administration, reformed the system of selecting officials, curbed the power of the nobility, expelled dishonest officials, and cut down bribery. When mandarins wanted to move strongly against thieves and brigands in many provinces, and Timur found that the

latter stole because they were hungry and not to gain wealth, he ordered that they be fed instead of being hunted down and killed. In 1303 he was confined to his bed and the government was run by palace ladies and corrupt officials.

92. Sung: The last Sung emperor was Ti Ping, who drowned himself [cf. 78 above].

93. Ghengiz: Genghis Khan.

94. Hia: Hsia, first dynasty [53:44].

95. Chang: Shang, ancient Chinese dynasty (ca. 1766-1121 B.C.) which preceded the great Chou dynasty.

96. Tcheou: Chou, third dynasty [53:77].

97. Kungfutseu: Confucius.

98. Han: Former Han dynasty, 206 B.C. to A.D. 25 [54:12].

99. Tcin: Chin, Western Chin dynasty, A.D. 265-317 [54:111].

100. Tang: T'ang, thirteenth dynasty [54: 193].

101. Sung: Nineteenth dynasty [55:65].

102. Yuen: Yüan, twentieth dynasty [cf. 18 above].

103. Isle of Yai: Yai-shan, island where the last Sung was defeated [cf. 78 above].

104. Ming: Twenty-first dynasty (1368-1644).

105. (Cambuskin): Cambyuskan or Cambiuskan, the Tartar king in Chaucer's "The Squire's Tale" (line 12) and usually identified as either Genghis Khan or Kublai Khan.

106. Tchin Tiaouen: Chên Tiao-yen, fl. 1297, was a brigand in S China who gathered a large band of vagabonds. He attacked the city of Chang-chou and killed Kang Wên-hsing, its commander.

107. Tchang tcheou: Chang-chou, city in Fukien Province, SE China.

108. Ouang Chi: Wang Shih, d. 1297, was the wife of Kang Wên-hsing, commander of Chang-chou. Rather than become the wife of Chên Tiao-yen, murderer of her husband, Wang Shih threw herself onto her husband's funeral pyre. Emperor Timur, deeply impressed by the deed, built a memorial to her.

109. Kanouen: Kan Wên-hsing, d. 1297, Wang Shih's husband.

110. corvée: F, "forced labor."

111. Gin Tsong: Jen Tsung or Ayuli Palpata, reigned 1312-1321 as eighth emperor of the Yuan dynasty; he was also known as Buyantu (Ayur paribhadra) [Grousset, 321]. An able administrator, well read in Confucius and Buddha and averse to war, he tried to improve the government by abolishing abuses brought to his notice, but the practice of giving the highest government posts to Mongols was not effective and the people were oppressed. He enacted sumptuary laws and established regular examinations for officials.

112. Miao Haokien: Miao Hao-chien, fl. 1318, wrote a treatise on cultivation of mulberry trees and silk production. Emperor Jen Tsung had copies of the work circulated in the provinces.

113. Aiulipata: Ayuli Palpata, personal name of Emperor Jen Tsung, who was also known as Aiyulipalipata.

114. Algiaptou khan: Prob. Aiyulipalipata, Emperor Jen Tsung. In 1313 he restored the ceremonies instituted to honor Confucius.

115. Tiemoutier: Tiehmutiehr or Temudar, d. 1322, minister of state under Emperor Jen Tsung and prime minister under his son Emperor Ying Tsung (1321-1323). Tiehmutiehr was an unscrupulous minister who grew rich through official robberies. After his death, Ying Tsung abrogated all his honors and started to put his followers to death; some of them plotted to assassinate the emperor and succeeded in 1323.

116. lamas: Tibetan priests. Pound links them with anti-Confucians and with Buddhists [*foés*] and Taoists.

117. Jason: Pound's name for Yesun-Temour: like the Greek Jason, he killed assassins.

118. Chunti: Shun Ti, reigned 1333-1368, was also known as Timur, last Mongol emperor of the Yüan dynasty. Weak and pleasure loving, he was incapable of action and his reign was marked by continual rebellion of the Chinese as well as by famine among the people. Among the wonders that augured the end of the dynasty was "une pluie de sang qui teignit les habits de tous ceux qui l'essuyèrent." At the third moon there fell "des filamens de couleur verte qui ressembloient à des cheveux" [Mailla, IX, 563].

119. Hanjong: Han Jung, fl. 1347, imperial inspector serving Emperor Sung Ti. When Han Jung found temples on land needed for cultivation, he had them destroyed. When he found young people who wanted to learn, he had schools established.

120. Kung's epigon: Poss. "Confucius descendant" [ibid., 575].

121. Pleiades: In 1350 a star as large as the moon exploded in the "constellation des sept étoiles" with a noise like thunder [ibid., 590].

122. Hoang-ho: Hwang Ho, or Yellow River.

123. Milé Buddha: Mille (or Maitrêya) Buddha, the goddess of mercy, a reincarnation of Buddha. The reign of Emperor Shun Ti was marked by unrest, famines, earthquakes, and heavenly disturbances. When the emperor started work on the diversion of the Hwang Ho, there was a surge of popular resentment, and it was rumored that Buddha was soon to descend to save China from the Mongol dynasty. This rumor was used for political purposes by the White Lotus Society.

124. pseudo-Sung: White Lotus Society, a secret society that arose in China (1351) in opposition to the Mongol dynasty. Ostensibly the society was organized to worship the Mille Buddha, or goddess of mercy, who was to free China from the Mongols, but actually it was used to raise a rebellion against Emperor Shun Ti. The leader of the White Lotus pretended to be a descendant of the Sung dynasty, and at a large meeting he sacrificed a white horse and a black cow and had all those who would follow his standard wear a red cap.

125. Tienouan: T'ien-wan, name of the dynasty that Hsü Chou-hui attempted to found (1351-1357). His revolt against Shun Ti was successful for a time, but he was captured and killed (ca. 1357). The name of the general who "beat the rebels" was Tung Pu-hsiao.

126. Taipou: T'ai Pu-hoa, d. 1352, scholar and military officer serving Emperor Shun Ti. He successfully encountered the rebels on several occasions but finally died in battle.

127. Singki: Hsing Chi, d. 1352, commander of imperial troops serving Emperor Shun Ti. His sudden death from a wound gave the rebels an unexpected victory in Kiangsi Province.

128. Tang dance: Called T'ang because the dancers wore headdresses like those used by the T'ang dynasty.

129. Kongpei: Kung Pe-sui, fl. 1353, officer in imperial troops under Emperor Shun Ti.

130. Toto: T'o-t'o, 1313-1355, minister of state under Emperor Shun Ti, was one of the latter's few honest ministers. T'o-t'o attempted to quell the rebellions of the rising Ming, but court intrigue hindered his efforts. His campaign against the rebels was stopped by a decree stripping him of all honors and sending him into exile. In 1355 he was poisoned, but by 1363 his reputation was again being honored. He is also known for his historical studies, particularly for his history of the Chin Tartars.

131. Red Caps: The Red Turban Society which raised the standard of revolt in 1356. Its leader proclaimed himself Emperor Ming Wang [Cordier, II, 355].

132. Ming Ouan: Ming Wang, dynastic title assumed by Han Lin-êrh, d. 1367. In 1355, when the Red Turban Society proclaimed him emperor of a new Sung dynasty, he set up his capital at Po-chou in Honan Province. This new Sung dynasty, created in opposition to Emperor Shun Ti of the Yüan dynasty, was one of many such ventures during the reign of this last Mongol emperor. As a symbol of revolt, Han Lin-êrh's dynasty was effective, but it was not permanent.

133. Yuentchang: Chu Yüan-chang, 1328-1399, founded the Ming dynasty. He was a Buddhist novice, but when the Buddhists were forced to abandon some monasteries, Chu Yüan-chang offered his services to Kuo Tzŭ-hsing (d. 1355), a rebel leader. He later parted from Kuo Tzŭ-hsing and proclaimed himself Prince of Wu (1364). After that he led the major force seeking the overthrow of Emperor Shun Ti and the Mongol dynasty. In 1367 he proclaimed himself emperor of China, founded the Ming dynasty, and called himself Hung Wu.

134. Ito Yen: Poss. Ho Yen, town in what is now Anhwei Province. It was taken by Chu Yüan-chang forces in 1355 without suffering pillage.

135. Kiang river: Yangtze River.

136. Taiping: Poss. a city on the right bank of the Yangtze River in present-day Anhwei Province. It was taken by Chu Yüan-chang without plunder.

137. Tchang star: Chang, Chinese name for the constellation Hydra.

138. Tai Ming: Geographical region, poss. in C China.

139. South Country: Prob. the area comprised by the modern province of Anhwei which was the birthplace of Chu Yüan-chang, founder of the Ming dynasty.

140. Yukiou: Yu Chiu, d. 1358, commander of the city of Ngan-king (Anking) in Anhwei Province. He was killed while defending the city against the rebels fighting Emperor Shun Ti.

141. Chang-tou: Shangtuho, city in Mongolia not far N of China border. The city that Coleridge called Xanadu, it was the famous summer residence of Kublai Khan and other Mongol emperors, from 1260.

142. Kouetchin: Fang Kuei-chên, fl. 1358, Chinese pirate during the reign of Shun Ti. He operated a fleet of junks off the S China coast and added his bit to the general rebellion that ended the Mongol dynasty.

143. Corea: Korea.

144. Peyen: P'eyen Temur, d. 1362, king of the Koreans.

145. lake Peyan: Poyang Hu, lake in N Kiangsi Province, SE China; it is China's second-largest lake, into which flows the Han River.

146. Hoang Ho: Hwang Ho, or Yellow River.

147. Yeougin: Ch'ên Yu-jen, fl. 1363, brother of Ch'ên Yu-liang, took part in the battle of Lake Poyang (1363) in which his brother was defeated by Chu Yüan-chang, founder of the Ming dynasty.

148. Tching brothers: Ch'ên Yu-jen and Ch'ên Yu-liang. Ch'ên Yu-liang (d. 1363) was commander of an independent rebel force during the general uprisings against Shun Ti. In 1358 he proclaimed himself Prince of Han and styled himself emperor of a "Han" dynasty. By 1363 his power in China was second only to that of Chu Yüang-chang, the great rebel leader who founded the Ming dynasty. In 1363 the two forces met in a battle at Lake Poyang, and Ch'ên Yu-liang was killed by a stray arrow and his army was routed. His two brothers, Ch'ên Yu-jen and Ch'ên Yu-kuei, were associated with him in his career.

149. Leou Lean: Ch'ên Yu-liang, leader of the brothers.

150. Tchin-li: Ch'ên Li, fl. 1363, second son of Ch'ên Yu-liang. After his father was defeated in battle at Lake Poyang, Ch'ên Li was allowed by Chu Yüan-chang to retain the family estates.

151. **KianKing**: Prob. error for Nanking.

152. **Timour**: Timur Khan [cf. 91 above].

153. **Yuen**: Yüan, twentieth dynasty: the Mongols.

154. **Yuentchang**: Chu Yüan-chang, founder of Ming dynasty [cf. 133 above].

155. **suis fils d'un pauvre laboureur**: F, "I am the son of a poor workingman." He was, in fact, from a poor family.

156. **Ssetcheou**: Ssŭ-ch'ou, town near modern city of Feng-yang in Anhwei Province.

157. **Kiangnan**: Chiang-nan, an old province, roughly the area of the present provinces of Anhwei and Kiangsu.

158. **Tsehing**: Kuo Tzu-hsing, d. 1355, was one of the more successful rebels in the reign of Emperor Shun Ti. He captured Anhwei Province and proclaimed himself generalissimo. His nephew, Chu Yüan-chang, served under his flag for a time but later left to raise an independent rebellion of his own; thereby he became the founder of Ming.

159. **Schicksal**: G, "destiny."

160. **Li**: Li Hsiang-kuei, fl. 1355, fighting companion of Chu Yüan-chang's.

161. **Su**: Su Hsiang-kuei, fighting companion of Chu Yüan-chang's.

162. **Tong**: Tung Ping-chang, fighting companion of Chu Yüan-chang's.

163. **Chantong**: Shantung, one of the Five Northern Provinces.

164. **Pekin**: Peking, in Hopeh Province, NE China, was the capital of China during the Yüan and subsequent dynasties.

165. **Su Ta**: Hsu Ta, d. 1385, was a lieutenant serving under Chu Yüan-chang during his struggles to found the Ming dynasty. When Chu became emperor (using the name Hung Wu), Hsu Ta became his adviser.

166. **Chang Shang**: Chou, Han, important early dynasties.

167. **Chung Ni (Confucius)**: [cf. 53:148].

168. **Yuen**: Yüan, twentieth dynasty.

169. **Tai Tsong**: T'ai Tsung [54:99].

170. **Kao Tsue**: Kao Tsu Wu Ti [54:137].

171. **Tai Tsou**: T'ai Tsu, reigned 960-976, founder of the Sung dynasty. While he was serving as a general under Emperor Shih Tsun, of the Later Chou, his troops invested him with the yellow robe of emperor. His greatest accomplishment was the restoration of the empire. He encouraged the study of literature, revised the law courts, changed the criminal code, and stabilized the economy.

172. **Hong Vou**: Hung Wu, reigned 1368-1399, founder of the Ming dynasty. He started his career as a rebel against Emperor Shun Ti. In 1368 he overthrew the Yüan dynasty, took the throne, and adopted the reign title of Hung Wu. Once emperor, he showed himself an able administrator. He reformed the law code and the system of taxation, reestablished government coinage on a sound basis, prohibited eunuchs from holding office, and patronized literature and education [cf. 133 above].

173. **Ideograms**: Yao, Shun, Chou [53:26, 27, 81]; Han [M2039].

174. **Ninghia**: Ninghsia, province in far NW China.

175. **Yé-ouang**: Yeh Wang, fl. 1375, admiral serving Emperor Hung Wu. He won several victories over the Mongols.

176. **Yuen**: Yuän, Mongols or Tartars.

177. **Coreans**: Koreans.

178. **Emperor**: Ai Yu Shih Litala, d. 1378, king of the Mongols. He succeeded Emperor Shun Ti.

179. **Li-ouen**: Li Wen-chung, d. 1384, one of the best military officers serving Emperor Hung Wu.

180. Su Ta: Hsu Ta [cf. 165 above].

181. Et / En l'an . . . funérailles: F, "And / In the thirty-first year of his Rule / the year sixty of his age / Hong Vou, seeing his strength weaken / said: May virtue inspire you, Tchu-ouen, / you faithful mandarins, cultivated people, soldiers / Help my grandson sustain / the dignity of this power, the weight of his office / And just as for Prince Ouen Ti of Han in former times, / make the obsequies for me" [Mailla, X, 104].

Glossary Canto LVII

1. **Kien Ouen**: Ch'ien Wên Ti, reigned 1399-1403, second emperor of Ming dynasty and grandson of Hung Wu. A weak emperor, he was unable to deal with rebellions led by his uncle, the Prince of Yen, fourth son of Hung Wu. In 1403 the prince took Nanking, the capital, and assumed the throne as Emperor Yung Lo. Ch'ien Wên Ti was about to kill himself, when he was told of a chest that Hung Wu had left to be opened in such an emergency. In the chest were the dress of a Buddhist priest, a diploma, a razor, and money. So, dressed as a Buddhist monk, Ch'ien Wên Ti escaped to a monastery in Yunnan. After wandering for 35 years he was discovered during the reign of Ying Tsung (1436-1450).

2. **Tcheou-kong**: Chou Kung [53:63].

3. **Tching-ouang**: Chêng Wang [53:65].

4. **Hong Vou**: Hung Wu, founder of Ming dynasty and grandfather of Ch'ien Wên Ti [56:172].

5. **Kouémen**: Kuei-men, gate of Nanking, or perhaps the underground passage through which Emperor Ch'ien Wên Ti escaped from the city in 1403.

6. **Chin Lo-koan**: Shen-lo-Kuan, Buddhist temple outside Nanking.

7. **Ouangchin**: Wang Shên, Buddhist priest serving in the temple of Shen-lo-Kuan, outside Nanking.

8. **Ouan Soui**: C, *wan-sui*, "Ten thousand years". A cheer in honor of an emperor or king.

9. **Yang-long**: Yang Ying-lung, member of the court of Emperor Ch'ien Wên Ti, one of the nine who helped the emperor escape from Nanking.

10. **Yé Hihien**: Yeh Hsi-hsien, member of the court who also helped the emperor to escape.

11. **Kien Ti**: Ch'ien Wên Ti, the young emperor.

12. **Yng-tsong**: Ying Tsung, reigned 1437-1450, 1457-1465. He came to the throne at the age of eight and, although his mother tried to provide a responsible guardian, the young emperor was much influenced by the eunuch Wang Chin. In 1449 Wang Chin precipitated a war with the Mongols, who invaded Shansi, defeated the troops commanded by Wang Chin, and captured the emperor. Ching Ti was made emperor in his brother's place, but in 1457 Ying Tsung returned to the throne and executed many who had served his brother.

13. **Yong Lo**: Yung Lo, reigned 1403-1425. As the Prince of Yen, he dethroned his nephew, Ch'ien Wên Ti, in 1403 and took the throne himself. He repopulated areas devastated by war, drew up a penal code, and sent missions to Java, Sumatra, Siam, and Ceylon. A patron of literature, he compiled a gigantic encyclopedia, known as *Yung Lo Ta Tien*, which included many commentaries on the classics.

14. **Bengal**: State on NE coast of India. A tribute mission from Bengal arrived at the Ming court in 1415.

15. **Malacca**: Roughly, the area of the Malay Peninsula. A tribute mission from Malacca arrived at the Ming court in 1409.

16. Yang Lo: Yung Lo [cf. 13 above].

17. summa: L, "the whole," a treatise covering the whole of a field. Here it refers to the encyclopedia *Yung Lo Ta Tien* commissioned by Emperor Yung Lo.

18. Mahamou: Mahamu, d. 1418, chief of the Oirat Mongol tribe. In 1416 he sent a tribute gift of horses to Emperor Yung Lo.

19. Gin Tsong: Jen Tsung, reigned 1425-1426, came to the throne at the age of 47 and ruled only a little more than nine months.

20. Yng Tsong: [cf. 12 above].

21. Hong Vou: Hung Wu, founder of Ming dynasty.

22. Yukien: Yü Ch'ien, 1398-1457, minister serving Emperor Ching Ti, was the only person who kept his head when Emperor Ying Tsung was captured by Mongols in 1450. He defended Peking, the capital, against the invaders and succeeded in driving them beyond the Great Wall. On the death of Ching Ti in 1457, Ying Tsung returned to the throne and had Yü Ch'ien executed for supporting Ching Ti. This act was an injustice, for Yü Ch'ien had done great service for the empire and had made Ying Tsung's return from captivity possible. The execution of Yü Ch'ien was engineered by Shih Hêng [cf. 27 below].

23. King Ti: Ching Ti, reigned 1450-1457, came to the throne after his brother, Ying Tsung, was captured by Mongol invaders. Ching Ti regarded his position as a permanent one and did not wish to give it up when his brother was rescued by General Yü Ch'ien. But before he could establish the succession on his son, Ching Ti died and Ying Tsung returned to the throne.

24. Fan-kuang: Fan Kuang, fl. 1450, commander of imperial troops defending Peking from Mongol warriors.

25. Yésien: Yeh Hsien, d. 1454, commander of Mongol forces that invaded the empire in 1449. He captured Emperor Ying Tsung and attacked Peking in 1450. In 1453 he seized supreme power over the Mongols but was killed in a battle with a rival.

26. Péyen: P'eyen T'iehmur, fl. 1450, Mongol general who took charge of the captured Emperor Ying Tsung. He also participated in the Mongol attack on Peking in 1450.

27. Che-heng: Shih Hêng, d. 1460, one of the generals serving Emperor Ching Ti who defended Peking against the Mongols in 1450. He later plotted against the empire and died of poison.

28. Honan: Province in E central China.

29. Shantung: Province in NE China.

30. carroch: I, *carroccio*, "army flag car" or "triumphal car."

31. vide Valturio: Roberto de Valturio [9:19].

32. li: C, measure of length, ca. one-third of a mile.

33. Hien Tsong: Hsien Tsung, reigned 1465-1488, a weak emperor, was ruled by his concubine and by eunuchs. Despite rebellions in the northern provinces, he did repair the Great Wall, improve the Grand Canal, and restore the reputation of Yü Ch'ien with posthumous honors.

34. Kungfutseu: Confucius.

35. Hoai-ngan: Huai An, fl. 1487, palace eunuch who became president of the tribunal of mandarins and then minister of state under Emperor Hsiao Tsung.

36. Ideogram: P'ien [M5245], "Metamorphosis," a subject rhyme with alchemy in the West.

37. Hoai of Sung: Hui Tsung. He and Hsien Tsung of T'ang were earlier emperors done in by Taoists [55:8, 149].

38. Ou Ti of Léang: Wu Ti [54:151] economized and advanced the rule of law.

39. Hoei-Tsong: Hui Tsung [55:149].

40. Laoist: Follower of Lao-tzŭ, founder of Taoism.

41. foéist: Follower of Buddha.

42. Yao and Shun: Early great emperors [53:14, 23].

43. Tcheou Kong: Chou Kung [53:63].

44. Hiao Tsong: Hsiao Tsung, reigned 1488-1505, had able ministers and instituted several administrative reforms, stopped internal rebellions, dealt with Mongol invasions, and curtailed the power of eunuchs.

45. Lieu: Liu Chin, d. 1510. He and seven other palace eunuchs conspired to gain control over the young Emperor Wu Tsung by pandering to his tastes and enjoyments. So successful was the scheme that in 1508 the emperor decreed that all petitions had to pass through the hands of Liu Chin. Then the emperor's uncle raised a rebellion and demanded Liu Chin's death as the price of peace. The emperor consented to imprison the eunuch, but when large amounts of treasure were found in the latter's house, the emperor ordered his execution.

46. Hong Vou: Hung Wu, founded Ming dynasty [56:172].

47. Ou Tsong: Wu Tsung, reigned 1506-1521, a weak and childish emperor who was persuaded to execute the eunuch Liu Chin [cf. 45 above]. He then chose Chiang Ping, a military adventurer, as his chief adviser. Wu Tsung came to the throne as a minor, but as he grew older he did not grow wiser. He devoted himself to leisure and frivolity and left no heir.

48. Manchu: Tartar tribe originally descended from the Nü-chên Tartars. The Manchu power was established in present-day Manchuria in 1587 by Nurhachi. In 1644 the Manchu brought about the fall of the Ming dynasty and established the Ch'ing dynasty (1644-1912).

49. Lieou-kin: Liu Chin [cf. 45 above].

50. Chi-tsong: Shih Tsung, reigned 1522-1566. Like many other Ming emperors, Shih Tsung consistently picked peer advisers and refused to listen to the most able men in his kingdom.

51. Hien Tsong: Hsien Tsung [cf. 33 above].

52. Tchang Chi: Chang Shih, fl. 1521, empress dowager, mother of Emperor Wu Tsung. At the death of her son, who left no heir, she called a council to name the next emperor. Shih Tsung, grandson of Emperor Hsien Tsung, was chosen.

53. Kiang-ping: Chiang Ping, d. 1521, military adventurer who became the favorite of Emperor Wu Tsung. He corrupted the emperor by providing him with pleasures and, in 1520, attempted to murder him. After Wu Tsung's death Chiang Ping was ambushed and killed by order of Emperor Shih Tsung. His entire family was also killed and his property was confiscated. Chiang Ping, like Liu Chin before him, had amassed a huge fortune.

54. Mansour: Mang Su Erh, fl. 1522, prince of the Tartar tribes that occupied the area of Turfan, in Sinkiang Province, W China.

55. regnicoles: F, "inhabitants of a kingdom."

56. Yng-che: C, *Ying-shih*, "the Five Sisters."

57. Mt. Tien-cheou: T'ien-shou, range of hills NW of Peiping where the tombs of the Ming emperors were located.

58. Hai men: Hai Men, department of what is now Kiangsu Province.

59. Oua-chi: Wa Shih, fl. 1559, princess in Kwangsi Province who led Chinese troops against Japanese pirates attacking SE coast of China.

60. wolves of our Lady: The troops led by Princess Wa Shih were called *Lang Ping*, "Loups soldat" [Cordier, III, 60].

61. Fou-kien: Fukien, province in SE China.

Glossary Canto LVIII

1. **Sinbu**: Jimmu Tenno, first of the legendary emperors of Japan, reigned 660-585 B.C. Jimmu is regarded as a direct descendant of the sun-goddess and as the founder of the Japanese imperial dynasty, which has remained unbroken since his accession to the throne. The Japanese Era is dated from the beginning of his reign (Feb. 11, 660 B.C.).

2. **Sun land**: Japan.

3. **Nippon**: Japan.

4. **Dai**: J, "great." The term is used to refer to the Dairi dynasty of Japan and, by extension, to Japanese emperors.

5. **Shogun**: Japanese title of commander in chief or generalissimo. The title originated in the eighth century during the wars against the Ainu. Shoguns became military dictators who held the real civil and military power in Japan, while the imperial dynasty was theoretically and ceremoniously supreme.

6. **Joritomo**: Or Yoritomo, 1146-1199, who assumed power in 1185, was the first true shogun in Japanese history. A great statesman, he inaugurated a system of military government which ran the affairs of Japan until the dissolution of the shogunate in 1868.

7. **reges sacrificioli**: L, "priests with kingly functions."

8. **Miaco**: Present city of Kyoto. It was established as the capital of Japan in A.D. 784 and remained the official capital until 1869, when the imperial government was moved to Tokyo.

9. **Ten Seo Daisin**: Tensio Dai Sin or, in Japanese, *Amaterasu-o-mi-kami*, Japanese sun-goddess and chief goddess of the Shinto religion. Her descendants became the emperors of Japan.

10. **jeu de paume**: F, "court tennis."

11. **escrime**: F, "fencing."

12. **Messire Undertree**: Hideyoshi Toyotomi, d. 1598. In Japanese his name means "the man found under a tree." He was known to the Chinese as Ping Hsiu-chi. Born of poor parents, he rose through his military exploits to be the greatest power in Japan. In 1586 he was named *kwam paku* ["regent"] and became far more powerful than the emperor. He is noted for his toleration of Christianity, but in 1587 he expelled the Portuguese Jesuits from Japan because he thought they might make his country a vassal of Portugal. In 1592 he declared war on Korea, hoping to destroy Korean control of the sea and to reopen trade with China, but he was unable to subdue Korea completely.

13. **Sa Mo**: Satsuma, feudal fiefdom on Kyushu Island, Japan.

14. **Portagoose prelates**: Portuguese Jesuit missionaries in Japan.

15. **Xtians**: Christians.

16. **Ouan Li**: Wan Li, title used by Emperor Shên Tsung, whose long reign (1573-1620) brought about the end of the Ming dynasty [cf. 38 below].

17. **Lord Lipan**: Li Pan, d. 1618, king of the Koreans.

18. **Pinyang**: Pyongyang, ancient capital of Korea.

19. **Ku ching**: Chang Chü-chêng, scholar and statesman who was tutor to Emperor Mu Tsung (1567-1572) and regent for Emperor Shên Tsung (1573-1620). He centralized the government, promoted peace and order in the empire, and tried to balance the budget. Often accused of taking bribes, he was deprived of his titles and property in 1584.

20. **Chin Song**: Shên Tsung [cf. 38 below].

21. **Nutché**: Nü-chên, Tartar tribe from which came the Chin dynasty [55:156].

22. **Kaiyuen**: Kai-yüan, city in S Manchuria.

23. **Pe**: P'ei-k'ou, the North Pass, which is N of Nan-kuan. The work may also refer to the Nü-chên Tartar tribe which takes its name from the region of the pass.

24. **Nan-koan**: Nan-kuan, the South Pass, a few miles N of Nankow, Hopeh Province, in NE China. The word may also refer to Nü-chên Tartar tribe which takes its name from the region of the pass.

25. **Ming**: Twenty-first dynasty.

26. **martes zibbeline**: F, *martre zibeline*, "sable."

27. **Nankoen**: Nan-kuan [cf. 24 above].

28. **Suen Te**: Hsüan Teh, 1426-1436, fifth emperor of Ming dynasty.

29. **ginseng**: Herb prevalent in Manchuria and Korea which, when dried, was thought to have medicinal properties.

30. **Père Ricci**: Mathieu or Matteo Ricci, 1552-1610, founder of the Jesuit Catholic missions in China, arrived at Macao in 1582. He tried to show that Christian doctrines were not antithetical to the teachings of the Confucian classics. Ricci died in Peking in 1610, having made a considerable impact on many of the scholar-officials at the Chinese capital.

31. **Emperor**: Shên Tsung [cf. 38 below].

32. **Ku Tchang**: Chang Chü-chêng, scholar and statesman, regent for Shên Tsung [cf. 19 above].

33. **cabal**: "Secret plot." Princesses of the palace and many others joined in the plot against Chang Chü-chêng, and finally the emperor was forced to dishonor him and exile his family. His eldest son hanged himself from grief rather than finish his days in ignominy.

34. **Tientsin**: City of E Hopeh Province in NE China, at junction of Pei River and Grand Canal.

35. **Père Mathieu**: Mathieu Ricci [cf. 30 above].

36. **Rites**: A tribunal of rites was set up by Emperor Shên Tsung in 1601, after the Jesuit mission had been in China almost 20 years, to consider the merits of Christianity. The tribunal, particularly offended by the idea of relics, rejected Christianity. Although its members recommended that Ricci be sent back to his own country, the emperor allowed him to remain at court. The report of the tribunal was made by the eunuch Ma Tang, who said that on a similar occasion Han Yü had reported the ruin brought to the empire by Buddhists [cf. next gloss]. Pound has confused Ma Tang with Han Yü [Mailla, X, 390].

37. **Han Yu**: Han Yü, 768-824, investigated Buddhism in the empire during the reign of T'ang Emperor Hsien Tsung. In a memorial to the emperor, Han Yü said that the Buddhists had been the ruin of many dynasties, that they had perverted the old ways of the Chinese, that they exercised a pernicious influence in the empire, and that they and their temples should be stamped out.

38. **Chin Tsong**: Shên Tsung, reigned 1573-1620. Under the title of Wan Li, his long reign ushered in the ruin of the Ming dynasty. After the death of Chang Chü-chêng, the regent, Shên Tsung abandoned himself to sensuality and extravagance. From 1585 to 1610 no one except the court eunuchs saw the emperor. High taxes ruined the people, Manchu hordes raided from the N, and Japanese attacked from the SE. The damage wrought by floods, droughts, and famines was not alleviated by the corrupt officials.

39. **ghazel**: Arabic, *ghazila*, a form of Persian love poetry in couplets rhyming on the same sound: *aa*, *ba*, *ca*, etc.

40. **hoang miao**: *Hung-mao*, "redheads," was the term used by the Chinese to designate European barbarians, especially British and Dutch.

41. **TO KALON**: H, "the beautiful."

42. Ti Koen: Pound has incorrectly taken Tien-ki [T'ien Ch'i], the reign title of Emperor Hsi Tsung, as a person. Mailla wrote: "Au commencement de l'an 1622, deuxième de *Tien-ki*, on entendit des cris effroyables du Côté de cette forêt." He gets the phrase "bull tanks" from *grandes machines* [X, 423].

43. Tchu-yé: Chu Yeh-yuan, fl. 1622, was commander of imperial forces in Shantung serving Emperor Hsi Tsung (1621-1627). His clever ruse of throwing *petards*, "firecrackers," *sur les boeufs* led to the defeat of the rebel forces in 1622 [X, 423].

44. Hoai Tsong: Huai Tsung, reigned 1628-1644, last true emperor of the Ming dynasty. He tried to rule well, but heavy taxes and poor harvests drove the NW to revolt. The emperor managed to keep peace with the Manchus, but Chinese rebels, led by Li Tzŭ-ch'eng, captured the province of Honan and by 1642 had advanced into Shensi. When Peking fell in 1644, the emperor killed himself.

45. ly: C, *li*, about a third of a mile.

46. Tsunhoa: Tsun-hua, fortified city in the province of Hopeh, fell to the Manchu forces in 1629 during their march on Peking.

47. Tai Tsong: T'ai Tsung or T'ien Ts'ung, 1591-1643, reigned 1625-1643, son of T'ai Tsu (1559- 1625) who founded Manchu power. In 1635 T'ai Tsung proclaimed himself emperor of China, although the Ming dynasty still held Peking. In 1636 he established the Manchu rule as the Ch'ing dynasty, conquered Mongolia, and gained control over much of the empire. He modeled his government after that of the Chinese, especially in the matter of holding public examinations, but offended the Chinese by abolishing some of their customs. T'ai Tsung's Manchu name was Abahai. His father, T'ai Tsu, was known as Nurhachi.

48. Manchu: T'ai Tsung not only continued Chinese law for the Chinese, but he also established it for the Manchu who were forbidden to marry "leur belle mère, leur belle-soeur ou leur nièce." The Manchu were not accustomed to marrying their sisters. Pound's source covers only mother-in-law, stepmother, sister-in-law, stepsister, and niece [X, 449].

49. Li koen: Li-chiu-chêng, fl. 1631, was not a viceroy but an officer in command of Ming troops during the Manchu invasion. He stole the money the viceroy, Sun Yuan-hua, gave him to pay the soldiers; the unpaid troops mutinied and the general turned traitor and highway robber [X, 455].

50. Suen fou: Hsuan-hua-fu, city near Peking, in province of Hopeh.

51. Spirit of Heaven: Shang Ti [53:24].

52. Kong Yeou: Kung Yu-teh, fl. 1633, rebelled against Ming dynasty and joined forces with the Manchu leader T'ai Tsung.

53. hetman: Headman, chieftain.

54. Aba tchan, Maen tchan, Tihali tchan: Manchu general officer ranks.

55. Berlitz: School of language studies founded by Maximilian Delphinus Berlitz (1852-1921). T'ai Tsung started such a language school [X, 462].

56. Kourbang tourha: Kur-bang-turha, town in Inner Mongolia.

57. Mongrels: Mongols. As T'ai Tsung established his dynasty, many tribal chieftains came to pledge allegiance.

58. Ho-che: Hoshih Te-kelei, fl. 1643, a Mongol prince who allied himself with T'ai Tsung during one of the many raids on Shansi Province, was ordered "pénétrer par la gorge de Tou-ché-kéou" [X, 463].

59. Ton: Tu-shih-k'ou, gorge N of Shansi Province, leading from Inner Mongolia into China.

60. Tai chen: T'ai Shên, fl. 1634, another Mongol prince who allied himself with T'ai Tsung, was ordered to get to Sou-Tcheou by "passant à l'ouest de Tai-Tong" [X, 463].

61. **Taitong**: Tai-tung, city in Shansi Province, just inside N border between China and Inner Mongolia.

62. **Chensi**: Shensi [56:6].

63. **Tai Tsou**: T'ai Tsu or Nurhachi (1559-1624), reigned 1616-1625, was the real founder of Manchu power. He consolidated the tribes of Inner Mongolia and brought most of the territory NE of the Great Wall under his control. In 1625 he established the Manchu capital at Mukden.

64. **Mougden**: Mukden, city in S Manchuria which controls the N-S trade there. It became the Manchu capital in 1625 and later (1644) served as the base for the Manchu invasion of China.

65. **Yao, Shun . . . Yu**: Early great emperors [53:14, 23, 19].

66. **Kungfutseu**: Confucius.

67. **Tartary**: Land of the Mongols.

68. **Suen-hoa-fou**: Hsuan Fu, city near Peking in province of Hopeh.

69. **Tengyun**: Lü Tên-yün, fl. 1635, officer in the imperial army serving Ming Emperor Huai Tsung. He fought engagements against the Manchu forces then invading China. According to Mailla, a dispatch he wrote to the emperor fell into the hands of T'ai Tsung, who was outraged by the lies it contained. In reality, the lying general was Ts'ao Wen-chao, and it was not to him but to another general, Chang Tsung-heng, that T'ai Tsung addressed his challenge [Fang, I, 155].

70. **Princes of Manchu**: Princes of Manchu tribes who owed their loyalty to T'ai Tsung.

71. **Hong Vou**: Hung Wu [56:172].

72. **Kin**: Chin dynasty, 1115-1234 [55: 152].

73. **Yuen**: Yüan, twentieth dynasty, 1206-1368 [56:18].

74. **Princes Mogul**: Princes of the Mongolian tribes that formed a confederation in 1635 under the hegemony of T'ai Tsung, the Manchu leader.

75. **Ming**: Twenty-first dynasty (1368-1644), now coming to an end because of misrule and corruption.

76. **(gallice Chantong)**: L, "in French, Shantung."

77. **Kiangnan**: Chiang-nan [56:157].

78. **Ousan**: Wu San-kuei, d. 1678, commander of imperial forces during last years of Ming dynasty. In 1643 Wu San-kuei received news that Peking had fallen to the rebel Li Tzŭ-ch'eng and that the emperor had committed suicide. After stipulating conditions for the treatment of the Chinese, Wu San-kuei gave his allegiance to the Manchus. As a result the Manchus captured Peking and established their dynasty in China.

79. **Kai fong**: Kaifeng, capital of Honan Province. In a footnote Mailla gives details of a terrible famine, worse than that caused by the siege of Jerusalem: "On vendoit publiquement de la chair humaine, & on croyoit faire un acte de piété en jettant dans les rues les corps morts, pour servir de nourriture à ceux qu'un même sort attendoit" [X, 477].

80. **Litse**: Li Tzŭ-ch'eng, 1606-1645, rebelled against the Ming dynasty. Leading an army of brigands, he overran parts of Hupeh and Honan provinces (1640) and captured Shensi Province (1642). In 1644 he proclaimed himself first emperor of the Great Shun dynasty and marched on Peking. The city fell and Ming Emperor Huai Tsung killed himself. But Wu San-kuei enlisted the aid of the Manchus and drove Li Tzŭ-ch'eng out of Peking. When Li was slain in battle, the Manchus, left in control of China, established the Ch'ing dynasty (1644-1912).

81. **Li Sao**: [56:24].

82. **Kientsong**: Chang Hsien-chung, fl. 1643, rebel chieftain with a reputation for extreme cruelty, tortured and killed all the residents of villages he captured [X, 479].

83. **HOEI**: Huai Tsung, last Ming emperor [cf. 44 above].

84. **Likoue**: Li Kuei-cheng, fl. 1644, commander of Peking. After the death of Emperor Huai Tsung, Li Kuei-cheng was forced to surrender the city to Li Tzŭ-ch'eng, but he first demanded permission to give the emperor and the empress a full imperial funeral.

85. **Atrox MING, atrox finis**: L, "frightful Ming, frightful end."

86. **Ousan**: Wu San-kuei [cf. 78 above].

87. **OUAN SOUI**: C, *wan-sui*, "ten thousand years."

88. **A NOI**: I, "ours."

89. **eijen**: Unidentified. Poss. misspelling of *Eljen* (Magyar), "Hail!"

90. **Litse**: Li Tzŭ-ch'eng [cf. 80 above].

91. *τάδ' ὧδ' ἔχει*: H, "that's how it is" [*Agamemnon*, 1413]. From Clytemnestra's line: "This is Agamemnon, my husband, dead by my right hand, and a good job. That's how it is."

Glossary Canto LIX

1. **De libro . . . censeo**: "Concerning the book, *Shih Ching*, I think thus" [Lacharme, XI-XII; the other Latin phrases on 324 are from the same place; cf. *GK*, 249].

2. **Chi-King**: *Shih Ching*, *Book of Odes*.

3. **Chun Tchi**: Shun Chih [cf. 20 below].

4. **Ut animum . . . rationis**: L, "To purge our minds, Confucius says, / and guide [them] to the light of reason."

5. **perpetuale effecto**: I, "perpetual effect." Part of line 26 of Cavalcanti's "Donna mi priegha" [36:1] describing the action of love, or perhaps of "love in action" [meaning process]. Here associated with reason as intelligence in process [cf. *LE*, 161].

6. **Chi King . . . servat**: L, "the *Shih Ching* shows and exhorts. But the just man and the one free from lust so serve their masters" [source: *domino*].

7. **obsequatur . . . deflectat**: L, "obeys his parents / never turns aside" [source: *obsequitur parentibus*].

8. **igitur . . . enconomiis**: L, "therefore, in my praises."

9. **anno undecesimo**: I, "eleventh year" [source: *undesimo* and *1654*; Lacharme's date is wrong]. The year in the reign of Shun Chih, the first Manchu emperor (1644-1661) [cf. 20 below].

10. **periplum**: H, "circumnavigation." Used by Pound in objective case as a coastal voyage.

11. **tarters**: Mongols N of Great Wall [53:130].

12. **sojers with lanthorns**: Soldiers with lanterns.

13. **Nanking**: City in Kiangsu Province, E China, on S bank of Yangtze. It served as the Ming capital from 1368 to 1403. The name means "Southern Capital."

14. **Tchinkiang**: Chinkiang, city and port of Kiangsu Province, E China.

15. **Kouei**: Kuei or Kuei Wang, d. 1662, was the last person to be proclaimed emperor of the Ming dynasty. About 1648 he set up a government in the S provinces. The Manchus, however, were determined to destroy all Ming power, and Kuei Wang was soon overthrown. In 1651 he fled to Burma, and in 1663 the Burmese returned him to the Chinese authorities. The Manchu Emperor K'ang Hsi had him strangled.

16. **utilité publique, motif trop élevé**: F, "public usefulness, too elevated a motive" [source has *rélevé* (X, 511)].

17. **Young Manchu**: Shun Chih, the young emperor, only 14 years old in 1649, was controlled by his uncles. They arranged his marriage for reasons of state [XI, 9].

18. **hong-mao**: C, *hung-mao*, "redheads," term designating certain European barbarians.

19. **Macao**: Portuguese colony on a peninsula W of mouth of Pearl River in Kwangtung Province, S of Canton.

20. **Chun Tchi**: Shun Chih, reigned 1644-1661, first emperor of the Manchu dynasty to rule over China. He consolidated Manchu power by crushing what remained of the Ming dynasty. In 1645 Manchu troops took Nanking, a stronghold of Ming power, and in 1651 the "last" emperor of the Ming dynasty, Kuei Wang, was defeated. A wise and generous ruler, Shun Chih eliminated eunuchs from the court, set up a civil administration, and treated Catholic missionaries with favor.

21. **Kang Hi**: K'ang Hsi, reigned 1662-1723, second emperor of Manchu dynasty to rule over China. In 1675 the Manchu dynasty was threatened by the revolt of the three feudatories (one of them was Wu San-kuei), but by 1681 K'ang Hsi had reestablished a firm rule over all China and, two years later, over Formosa. He extended the empire to the borders of Kokand and Badakhshan and into Tibet. He was a patron of the Jesuits, whom he employed (especially Verbiest) to survey the empire, study astronomy, and cast cannon. Later, fearing the Jesuits' propaganda and the possible influence of the pope on the government of China, he restricted missionary activities. A great patron of literature and scholarship, the emperor directed the writing of the *Imperial Dictionary* and the great *Concordance* of all literature. K'ang Hsi was an emperor in the tradition of Yao, Shun, and Yu.

22. **Johnnie Bach**: Johann Sebastian Bach, 1685-1750, German organist and composer.

23. **portagoose**: Portuguese.

24. **frog**: Reference to French people.

25. **Pereira**: Thomas Pereyra, d. 1708, Jesuit missionary in China, served with the French Jesuit Gerbillon on the Manchu-Chinese Commission to negotiate the Treaty of Nerchinsk between China and Russia (1689).

26. **Gerbillon**: Jean-François G., 1654-1707, Jesuit missionary to China, was a skilled linguist and mathematician. He arrived in Peking in 1688 and his talents at once impressed Emperor K'ang Hsi. He served with Pereyra on the commission to negotiate a border treaty between China and Russia in 1689, the Treaty of Nerchinsk. He wrote an account of his journeys in Tartary.

27. **Mt. Paucity**: Desolate mountain range in Manchuria called the "Mountains of Poverty" by the Chinese.

28. **ho fo**: C, *huo-fu*, "living Buddha."

29. **assez mal propre**: F, "rather slovenly."

30. **Hans of Kalkas**: Kings of the Khalkhas, Mongol tribe to the NW of China. Khalka chiefs were known as khans.

31. **Eleutes**: Or Eleuthes, Mongol tribe to the N and NW of China. The period of their greatest power was 1680-1696, when they were led by Galdan.

32. **Oros**: Russians.

33. **Selinga**: Selenginsk, town on the border between Russia and China, SE of Lake Baikal.

34. **Nipchou**: Nerchinsk, town on the upper Amur River, on the Chinese-Russian frontier, where the treaty between China and Russia was signed in 1869. The treaty, requiring Russia to withdraw from the Amur Valley, served for a while to check Russian colonization in that area.

35. **Cha houkoen**: Shan Hai Kuan Pass, near the place where the Great Wall reaches the Yellow Sea.

36. **Kang**: K'ang Hsi.

37. **ly**: [cf. 58:45; source says 200 *li*].

38. **Amur**: River in NE Asia forming boundary between Manchuria and the Chita Region and Khabarovsk Territory of Russia.

Glossary Canto LX

1. **Jesuits**: Members of the Society of Jesus, founded by St. Ignatius Loyola in 1534. Jesuit missionaries established the modern Roman Catholic missions in China. First to arrive was Matteo Ricci (1582), followed by Johann Adam Schall von Bell (1619). The period of most intensive missionary effort began in 1688 when Gerbillon and Verbiest gained the favor of Emperor K'ang Hsi (1662-1722).

2. **Galileo**: Galileo Galilei, 1564-1642, Italian mathematician and astronomer. No works of Galileo were specifically listed in the *Index Librorum Prohibitorum*, but many of his thoughts were considered heretical and he was subjected to enormous pressure by the Church.

3. **Grimaldi**: Philippe G., fl. 1691, Jesuit missionary to China, aided the Manchu in calendar reform.

4. **Intorcetta**: Fl. 1691, Italian Jesuit missionary to China.

5. **Verbiest**: Ferdinand V., 1623-1688, Jesuit missionary to China, arrived in Peking in 1660 and introduced the Chinese to the astronomical systems of Copernicus and Galileo. He was also employed by Emperor K'ang Hsi as a mathematician and a cannon founder. Verbiest's plea that Chinese priests be ordained, that they be allowed to say a vernacular Mass, and that ancestor worship be tolerated was not granted by Rome. The disagreement led to the famous rites controversy of the 18th century [cf. 59/327].

6. **Koupelin**: Philippe Couplet, fl. 1680, Jesuit missionary to China, arrived in Peking with Verbiest (1660) and served as procurator of the China missions. In 1682 he returned to Rome, carrying Verbiest's plea for ordination of Chinese priests and a vernacular Mass.

7. **Orosians**: Russians.

8. **lama**: Tibetan priest.

9. **hochang**: C, *ho-shang*, Buddhist priests.

10. **taotsé**: Taoists: followers of Lao-tzŭ.

11. **Kang Hi**: K'ang Hsi [59:21].

12. **Emperor**: K'ang Hsi. Thus, the year 1691.

13. **Gerbillon**: Jean-François G. [59:26].

14. **Fourtères**: Jean de Fontaney, Jesuit missionary to China.

15. **Bournat**: Joachim Bouvet, Jesuit missionary to China. With Gerbillon and four other Jesuits, he arrived in Peking in 1688. Bouvet and Gerbillon were made professors of mathematics by K'ang Hsi and translated several Tartar works on mathematics into Chinese. Bouvet also served as surveyor and cartographer in the Chinese provinces.

16. **Hoang Tchang**: Huang-chêng, region within the walls of the imperial palace at Peking. In 1693 the first permanent church and residence of the Jesuits in China was established there at the expense of Emperor K'ang Hsi.

17. **Feyenkopf**: Fei Yang-ku, d. 1701, Chinese general in the service of Emperor K'ang Hsi. His greatest military feat was the part he played in the campaigns against Galdan, chief of the Eleuthes. In 1696 he pursued Galdan's forces through the Gobi desert and defeated them at Chao-modo, S of Urga. In 1697 Galdan died and his followers submitted to the emperor all the country E of the Ordos.

18. **Kaldan**: Galdan, d. 1697. Chief of the Eleuthes, a nomadic tribe NW of China. In 1680 Galdan became khan of his people and invaded the territory of the Kalkas. When Emperor K'ang Hsi declared himself on the side of the Kalkas, Galdan, daring the emperor's power, invaded China in 1691. He was beaten but not crushed. When he invaded China again (1695), his forces were destroyed by the imperial troops, who used cannon.

19. **Eleutes**: Eleuthes, Mongol tribe led by Galdan [59:31].

20. **Mohamedans**: Mohammedans, tribes that were making incursions on the SW borders of the empire.

21. **de suite**: F, "consecutively."

22. **Crown Prince**: Prob. the future Emperor Yung Ch'eng.

23. **Kalkas**: Mongol tribe that traced itself back to Genghis Khan.

24. **Hoang Ho**: Hwang Ho, or Yellow River.

25. **Ortes**: Ordos, Tartar tribe occupying the territory of Ordos, a desert region S of the Hwang Ho in Suiyuan Province, C Inner Mongolia.

26. **Taouen**: Ta-wan, principality in Shensi Province. According to legend, the horses of Ta-wan were celestial (*Tien ma*) and their sweat was the color of blood. "Blood sweating" probably came from small lesions caused by parasites [Creel, 176].

27. **Tien ma**: C, *T'ien-ma* "Heavenly horse." A term dating back at least to Han times [ibid.].

28. **Tchaomed**: Chao-modo, town N of the Gobi desert, where Fei Yang-ku defeated Galdan, leader of the Eleuthes.

29. **Tipa**: Or "Dezi," title of the viceroy who governs Tibet for the Grand Lama. After some years of patient listening to the protests of the Tipa about peace and allegiance to the emperor, K'ang Hsi finally concluded that all the lamas were liars and traitors [XI, 272].

30. **the sun . . .** : K'ang Hsi was an amateur astronomer. These figures were added to the letter [Mailla says in a note (XI, 273): "one degree twenty minutes less"].

31. **Paichen**: Hsin-a-pai-cheng, prob. modern city of Sining (or Hsining) in Tsinghai Province, N central China.

32. **Kalda**: Galdan [cf. 18 above].

33. **Samarkand**: City in Soviet Central Asia.

34. **Bokara**: Bukhara city in W Uzbek Republic, USSR, once a center of Moslem worship.

35. **Grimaldi**: [cf. 3 above].

36. **Pereira**: Thomas Pereyra [59:25].

37. **Tony Thomas**: Antoine T., fl. 1691, Jesuit missionary to China.

38. **Gerbillon**: [59:26].

39. **placet sic**: L, "it is agreed, thus." Formula phrase used on the petition sent in.

40. **Kung-fu-tseu**: Confucius.

41. **Material Heaven**: Prob. refers to the Christian concept of a physical heaven. The Jesuit missionaries wanted to adapt Chinese religious ritual into Christianity. A big bone of contention was the noise one made when he said "God." Could a different sound in a different language mean the same thing? In a footnote, Mailla says that the four Jesuits wanted to know what the Chinese intended by the words "T'ien" and "Shang Ti." Did they intend "le ciel matériel ou le Seigneur du ciel"? Although such questions mightily perplexed the Jesuits, the Chinese seemed not to understand why they should. A part of the rites controversy.

42. **Changti**: Shang Ti. An all-pervasive force which the Christians tried to equate with their God [53:24].

43. **manes**: L, "spirits of the dead."

44. **cartouche**: Scroll or tablet in ornamental form.

45. **wallahs**: Slang expression for VIPs.

46. **archbish of Antioch**: Charles-Thomas Maillard de Tournon, 1668-1710, titular patriarch of Antioch who, in 1704, was sent to China by Pope Clement XI with the title of papal legate and charged with the task of studying the merits of the rites controversy [59/327]. He arrived in Canton in 1705 and had an interview with Emperor K'ang Hsi in Peking. After making a complete fool of

himself, he returned to Canton; he was arrested and imprisoned, upon the emperor's orders, by the Portuguese in Macao. He died there in 1710.

47. **Canton**: City and port in Kwangtung Province, SE China.

48. **Monseigneur Maillard de Tournon**: Patriarch of Antioch [cf. 46 above].

49. **Clemens**: Clement XI; 1649-1721, pope (1700-1721). He condemned the custom of Chinese ancestor worship and denied the Jesuit petition that the Mass might be said in Chinese, or that the Chinese could be ordained as priests.

50. **papa**: I, "pope."

51. **Kiao Hoang**: C, *chiao-hua huang*, "the sovereign pontiff of the prosperous religion." Chinese term for the pope.

52. **Portagoose king**: John V, 1689-1750, king of Portugal (1706-1750).

53. **Kang Hi**: K'ang Hsi. In 1709 the emperor contracted an illness that grew worse each day. It reached a point where no hope could be expected from Chinese doctors. Then Europeans, asked for help, brewed up an "Alchemical Confection" which they gave to the emperor with wine from the Canary Islands. It worked; and little by little his strength returned [XI, 320].

54. **Batavia**: City on NW coast of Java. In 1716 the emperor was told that moneymakers were shipping large quantities of rice out of the country by liaisons with Chinese established in Batavia. K'ang Hsi stopped the exporting.

55. **Tommy Juffusun**: Thomas Jefferson. In 1716 Jefferson was yet to be born [21:25; 31 passim].

56. **tsong-ping**: C, *tsung-ping*, "brigadier general."

57. **Tching mao**: Ch'en Mao, mandarin of the second rank, held a military command in Kwangtung and served as viceroy of Canton. In 1717 he memorialized Emperor K'ang Hsi, recommending that Christian missionaries be expelled from the empire and European merchants from Macao. The emperor, insulted by the actions of Clement XI, proclaimed that no missionaries could stay in China unless they agreed to follow the "Rites of Ricci." Those who did not were to be expelled.

58. **Ming**: The struggles toward the end of the Ming dynasty [56:104].

59. **Siam**: Country in SE Asia, modern Thailand.

60. **Tonkin**: Tongking, region in N French Indo-China, once a part of China; now N Vietnam.

61. **Hong-mao**: C, *hung-mao*, "redheads" [58:40].

62. **Yenkeli**: C, prob. Pidgin English for Englishmen in China.

63. **Yntsa**: C, prob. Indians, or Eastern Indians, though Pound takes it to refer to the French.

64. **froggies**: Slang reference to French people.

65. **Holans**: C, "the Dutch."

66. **Manilla**: City of Manila on SW Luzon, Philippine Islands.

67. **Tching Mao**: Ch'en Mao, mandarin who signed the petition to the emperor [cf. 57 above].

68. **edict of '69**: The emperor gave the petition about dealing with European barbarians to his tribunal with orders to report on it. On April 16, 1717, the chiefs of the tribunals "united in general assembly" adopted a resolution and sent it to the emperor. It was based on an edict of 1669. There is no mention of a sea captain in Mailla [XI, 325].

69. **Verbiest**: One of the earlier Jesuit missionaries [cf. 5 above]. He and his colleagues had been permitted to practice their religion. Since that time the Christians had continued to spread and build churches all over China.

70. Peter of Russia: Peter I, or Peter the Great, 1672-1725, emperor of Russia (1682-1725), founder of the modern Russian state. The embassy referred to is that of L. V. Izmailoff.

71. Kiao-hoang: *chiao-hua huang*, Chinese name for the pope.

72. Haitse: Hai-tzŭ, game preserve near Peking where Emperor Kang Hsi "caught a cold" while hunting in 1722.

73. Yong Tching: Yung Chêng, reigned 1723-1735, fourth son of Emperor K'ang Hsi. His first act was to degrade and confine his brothers in order to reduce contention for the succession. He then turned against the Christian missionaries, some of whom had supported other candidates for the throne, and confined them to either Peking or Macao. In 1732 he tried to expel all Christians, but finding that they taught filial obedience (a central doctrine of Confucius) he left them alone, stipulating, however, that no more missionaries should enter the country. He was concerned with the people's welfare and avoided wars, although he did expand the empire to the Laos border.

74. Tartary: Area N of the Great Wall inhabited by Mongols.

75. Verbiest: [cf. 5 above].

76. Pereira: [59:25].

77. Gerbillon: [59:26].

78. Bouvet: Joachim B., Jesuit mathematician [cf. 15 above].

79. mémoires . . . Paris: F, "memoirs of the Academies / of Sciences of Paris" [XI, 364].

80. qu'ils veillèrent . . . termes propres: F, "that they looked to the purity of the language / and that one should use only suitable terms" [XI, 365].

81. Ch'ing ming: C, *chêng-ming*, "to regulate the names"; "to define the correct term"; a precise definition.

82. Ideograms: Chêng, M351: "right"; Ming, M4524: "name."

83. En son Palais divers ateliers: F, "in his Palace various workrooms."

Glossary Canto LXI

1. Yong Tching: [Yung Chêng], fourth son of K'ang Hsi [60:73].

2. hochang: ho-shang, Buddhists.

3. sic in lege: L, "thus in the law."

4. Gerbillon: Jean-Francois G., Jesuit missionary [59:26].

5. Kung: Confucius.

6. Tientsing: Tientsin [58:34].

7. Lieu-yu-y: Liu Yü-i, fl. 1725, imperial examiner for the province of Shansi. He dealt successfully with a famine in his province and gained the approval of Emperor Yung Chêng.

8. magazines: F, *magazins*, "stores."

9. Chan-si: Shansi Province in NE China; one of the Five Northern Provinces.

10. fontego: I, "chamber," used by Pound as a place that lends money [35:31].

11. AMMASSI: I, "grain pools" [53:17].

12. 8th degree button: The Chinese civil service was divided into nine ranks, each having two grades. The highest was 1a and the lowest, 9b. Each rank carried with it the right to wear special insignia, or "buttons" [XI, 426].

13. One . . . painter: "Un seul d'entre-eux, qui passoit pour un excellent peintre, étoit employé au palais; les autres n'y avoient aucun accès . . . ." (Only one among them [the Europeans allowed to reside in Peking], who had the reputation of being an excellent painter, was employed in the palace; the others had no access to it . . . [XI, 428-429].

14. **Pope's envoys**: Envoys of Pope Benedict XIII (1724-1730). At the end of their audience in the imperial palace each envoy was given a melon by the eunuchs. The emperor sent bolts of silk, some gold-brocaded, and gin-seng root to the pope [XI, 431-432].

15. **Lon Coto**: Lung Kodo, fl. 1725, cousin of Emperor Yung Chêng and a prince of the empire. In 1725 he was accused of conspiring against the emperor and sentenced to exile in Ninghsia, in the remote NW. In 1727 he was recalled by the Tribunal of Criminal Affairs and sentenced to death. The sentence was later commuted to life imprisonment [XI, 481-483].

16. **confino**: I, "in exile."

17. **Kang Hi**: K'ang Hsi [59:21]. It was the emperor who said he couldn't resign.

18. **Victor Emanuel**: V. Emmanuel II, 1820-1878, king of Italy (1861-1878).

19. **Count Cavour**: Camillo Benso di C., 1810-1861, Italian statesman, premier (1852-1859). In 1851, shortly after Charles Albert, king of Piedmont, abdicated in favor of his son, Victor Emmanuel II, Cavour got into an argument with the president of the chamber which prompted his resignation. Since Cavour was technically only a minister, the new king was bound to accept the resignation. Cavour used the brief period to travel to the major courts of Europe, including those of England and France. A new crisis in Piedmont resulted in his appointment as prime minister, a position he maintained with two short interruptions until his death.

20. **Old Worker's Hill**: Shen Nung Tan, "Altar dedicated to Shen Nung," the mythical emperor of China who invented the plow. Commonly known as the Temple of Agriculture, situated in Peking directly across from the T'ien Tan, or "Altar of Heaven." In 1726 Emperor Yung Chêng revived the ancient rites connected with the Altar of Agriculture [XI, 442-443].

21. **Li Ki**: *Li Chi*, or *Book of Rites* [52:28].

22. **Christers**: Christians.

23. **Dom Metello**: Alexandre Metello-Souza-y-Menezes, fl. 1726, Portuguese emissary to Emperor Yung Chêng. Metello and the Jesuit Antoine Magalhaens reached Peking in 1727 and tried to negotiate a treaty that would provide for more lenient treatment of missionaries. The emperor assumed, however, that the two had merely come to pay tribute to him, and the talks had no result.

24. **Portagoose boss**: John V of Portugal [60:52].

25. **Sounou**: Sunu or Sourniama, 1648-1725, a prince of royal blood descended from Nurhachi and from an older branch of the Manchu princes than was Emperor Yung Chêng. Sunu was regarded as a threat to the throne and at the age of 77 he was banished to exile in Shansi. Several of Sunu's sons were Christians, and he, too, may have been baptized before his death.

26. **Yun-nan**: Yunnan, province in SW China.

27. **button 8th class**: [cf. 12 above].

28. **arpens**: F, "acres."

29. **cramoisi**: F, "crimson cloth."

30. **Governor**: Viceroy of Honan Province in 1728.

31. **Chiyeou**: Shih Yu, fl. 1727, a poor laborer of Shensi Province who found a purse and gave it back to its owner without accepting a reward. Emperor Yung Chêng was so impressed when he heard of this that he rewarded the man with 100 ounces of silver and used the honesty of Shih Yu as the text of a long letter to his people, urging them to reform their morals.

32. **muggin' up**: British slang for "cramming," as for an exam.

33. Kien: Ch'ien Lung, reigned 1736-1795, fourth son of Emperor Yung Chêng. He was an excellent administrator and is often compared with his grandfather, K'ang Hsi. After ten years spent in reorganizing the government, Ch'ien Lung put down a revolt of the aborigines in W China, forced Burma and Nepal to pay tribute, established Chinese supremacy over Tibet, and maintained friendly relations with Western nations. The emperor was an indefatigable poet and published a total of 33,950 pieces. His work is very correct, but rather mediocre. Under his patronage, historical works, encyclopedias, and library catalogues were printed. His reign began 40 years before the American Revolution of 1776.

34. canaglia: I, "rascals."

35. FU: C, *fu*, "happiness, prosperity" [M1978].

36. Coupetai: Gubadai, d. 1709, was a Manchu general and president of the Tribunal of Rites. He had been picked by K'ang Hsi to tutor Yung Chêng.

37. Cai Tsong Hien Hoang Ti: Shih Tsung Hsien Huang Ti, dynastic title of Emperor Yung Chêng.

38. Kien Long: Ch'ien Lung [cf. 33 above].

39. Adamses: The Adams family in the U.S. John Adams was born in 1735, during the last year of Yung Chêng's reign.

40. haskai: Hashar, a petty court in the khanate of Bukhara region, C Asia.

41. yerqui: Yerquen, a petty court in the khanate of Bukhara region, C Asia.

42. hotien: Khotan, town in C Asia on far W border of China. It was important as a caravan junction.

43. teuke: Piece of money used by Russians in W Asia.

44. tael: Chinese coin containing about one and a third ounces of silver.

45. Tchao-hou: Chao Hui, 1708-1764, a general serving Emperor Ch'ien Lung, was responsible for the success of the campaigns to put down the Eleuthes. Under the leadership of Amursana they revolted against the empire and attempted to take the district of Ili in Sinkiang Province in 1757.

46. Kasgar: Kashgar, city in W Sinkiang Province, W China, which became a part of China in 1759. It was the chief city of Chinese Turkistan, now known as Sinkiang.

47. Boucaria: Bukhara, city in W Uzbek Republic, USSR, formerly Chinese Turkistan.

48. EMPRESS Hiao Ching Hien Hoang Heou: Hsiao-shêng, Hsien-huang-hou, 1693-1777, empress dowager, mother of Emperor Ch'ien Lung. After her death she was accorded great honors by her son.

49. Beauties of Mougden: "The Eulogy on Mukden," a poem written by Emperor Ch'ien Lung in 1743 after a visit there to honor the tomb of his ancestors.

50. Ming histories: *Ming Shih Kang Mu*, a history of the Ming dynasty. This work, finished in 1742, did not receive imperial approval, and *T'ung Chien Kang Mu San Pien* was substituted for it in 1775. Emperor Ch'ien Lung's redaction of the Ming histories was published under the title *Yu Chih Kang Chien.*

CANTO LXII

Sources

Charles Francis Adams, ed., *The Works of John Adams*, I, Boston, 1850 (citations from this basic source are given simply by volume and page numbers); Frederick K. Sanders, *John Adams Speaking*, Orono, Maine, 1975, pp. 50-107.

Background

L. H. Butterfield, ed., *Diary and Autobiography of John Adams*, 4 vols., Cambridge, Mass., 1961; Catherine Drinker Bowen, *John Adams and the American Revolution*, Boston, 1950; Page Smith, *John Adams*, 2 vols., Garden City, N.Y., 1962; Clinton Rossiter, "The Legacy of John Adams," *Yale Review*, 46 (1957), 528-550; Peter Shaw, *The Character of John Adams*, Chapel Hill, N.C., 1974; EP, "The Jefferson-Adams Letters as a Shrine and a Monument," *Impact*, 166-183; EP, "Civilisation, Money, and History," passim, in *SP*.

Exegeses

Vasse, "American History and the Cantos," *Pound Newsletter*, no. 5, 13-19; EP, *L*, 319, 322; EP, *GK*, passim; CB-R, *ZBC*, passim; DD, *Sculptor*, passim; Dekker, *Sailing*, passim; CE, *Ideas*, passim; Fraser, *Ezra Pound*, 70; HK, *Poetry*, passim, *Era*, passim; DP, *Barb*, passim; NS, *Exile*, passim; NS, *Reading*, passim.

[Little exegesis has been done for the Adams cantos. Most Pound scholars mention them in passing or with only a generalized comment. Thus under the exegeses heading for these cantos, the major authors who comment are listed with page numbers for readers who would like to know typical attitudes or changes of opinion over the years, though no extended comment should be expected.]

Glossary

1. **'Acquit . . . Europe'**: In the summer of 1829, after leaving the presidency, John Quincy Adams started a biography of his father, John Adams, later taken up by Charles Francis Adams. Aware of the inherent difficulties, CFA knew the account would contain errors, but he hoped that he might be "acquitted of evil intention" and he promised to "correct any errors with cheerfulness." He was particularly concerned over judgments about motives which were subject to interpretation [preface, vi-vii].

2. **To The Governor And The Companie**: In these words ["planting . . . ruling," etc.] Charles I granted land to the Massachusetts

Bay Company in a charter dated "the 4th of March, 1629" [not 1628].

3. **Thomas Adams**: One of the grantees of the charter.

4. **18th assistant**: At a meeting on October 20, 1629, John Winthrop was elected governor; 18 assistants to the governor were also elected "of whom Thomas Adams was the last" [I, 4].

5. **Merry Mount**: By 1627, the new name of Mount Wollaston.

6. **Braintree**: Town in Massachusetts (now Quincy), home of the Adams family; incorporated 1640.

7. **Weston**: Thomas W., ?1575-1644?, English merchant and adventurer; organized the expedition of colonists who settled an area near Mount Wollaston in Massachusetts (1625). Perhaps ancestor of Pound's maternal grandfather.

8. **Capn Wollanston**: Wollaston, English adventurer and colonist who settled an area within the limits of what is now Quincy, Massachusetts, and gave it the name of Mount Wollaston (1625); neither his dates nor his Christian name survives.

9. **ten head . . .**: The records of Boston read: "24th day, 12th month, 1640. Granted to Henry Adams, for ten heads [members of a family], forty acres, upon the same covenant of three shillings per acre" [I, 5 n. 4].

10. **brewing**: Henry's son, Joseph, ran the brewery business as his life's work and "after a lapse of more than forty years, left the malting establishment to his youngest son" [I, 11].

11. **Henry**: H. Adams, founder of Adams family in America [cf. 9 above]. During the six years before his death, Henry Adams may have started the brewing business.

12. **Joseph Adams**: ?1626-1694, youngest son of Henry Adams, great-grandfather of John Adams and Samuel Adams.

13. **old style . . . new style**: In 1752 England adopted, by act of Parliament, the Gregorian (New Style) calendar to replace the Julian (Old Style) calendar which did not accurately measure the length of the solar year. Eleven days were dropped from the 1752 calendar (September 2, Wednesday, was followed by Thursday, September 14) and the beginning of the new year was changed from March 25 to January 1.

14. **John Adams**: 1735-1826; graduated from Harvard at age 19. Charles Francis Adams [CFA] says: "His condition, as the teacher of a school . . . could not be permanent . . . . Its emoluments gave but a bare and scanty subsistence" [I, 22; 31:15].

15. **Calvinism**: JA considered and rejected "the study of theology, and the pursuit of it as a profession," for reasons Pound gives [I, 42].

16. **order than liberty**: JA believed that "Parliament could not lawfully tax the colonies. His whole soul was in the cause. But to him it was not less the cause of order and of justice than of liberty" [I, 80].

17. **Burke**: Edmund B., 1729-1797, British statesman and writer; prominent Whig under George III; favored liberal treatment of American colonies. CFA says of him and Gibbon: "Such a beautifier of imperfect figures is the illusive mirror of national pride!" [I, 92].

18. **Gibbon**: Edward G., 1737-1794, British historian.

19. **tcha**: *ch'a* [M101], "tea." The character is given in the margin.

20. **Lord North**: 1732-1792, 2d Earl of Guilford, English statesman. As prime minister under George III (1770-1782), North made himself the agent of the king's plans to control the American colonies; he supported the Stamp Act and the tax on tea. JQA assigns him, next to the king, the heaviest responsibility for the Revolution and says he followed "the same middle path, the perpetual resource of second-rate statesmen" [I, 94]. During the French

and Indian Wars, British troops were welcome protectors of the colonists. North's policies changed their attitudes toward the redcoats [British soldiers, so-called because they wore red uniforms].

21. **Rapallo**: Town of Liguria, NW Italy, on Gulf of Rapallo; residence of Pound, 1924-1945.

22. **Lard Narf**: Lord North. Spelling (as in other instances) is an effort to reproduce the Boston accent. Source says: "At about nine o'clock of the night on which Lord North declared himself impassible to menace, a single sentry was slowly pacing his walk . . . in King Street . . . . It was moonlight, and a light coating of fresh snow had just been added to the surface of the ground" [I, 97].

23. **King St.**: Street at Boston's commercial center.

24. **Styschire**: Invented by Pound as a pun on the naming of British regiments by counties, such as Wiltshire and Hampshire. It seems to imply that soldiers were pigs living in a sty. Both the 14th and 29th regiments were stationed in Boston at the time.

25. **Brattle St**: Street in Boston on which John and Abigail Adams lived (1768) and on which Murray's barracks were located.

26. **Murray's barracks**: Barracks on Brattle Street where British soldiers were quartered (1770) at timc of Boston Massacre.

27. **barber's boy**: Source reads: "In this case, it was a barber's boy whose thoughtless impertinence [in tormenting the lone sentry] opened the floodgates of passion in the town. The resentment of the sentinel and the complaints of the boy drew the attention of stragglers . . . to the soldier's isolated condition, which soon brought his fears to the point of calling upon his comrades for support" [I, 98].

28. **Capn Preston**: Thomas P., captain of the British troops involved in the Boston Massacre (March 5, 1770). Source says: "A corporal and six men of the guard, under the direction of Captain Preston, came to his releif . . . . The movement could not take place without exciting observation, the effect of which was the collection around them [the sentinel and other men] of forty or fifty of the lower order of town's people, who had been roving the streets armed with billets of wood" [ibid.].

29. **Chawles Fwancis**: Charles Francis Adams, 1807-1886, son of John Quincy Adams and editor of *The Works of John Adams*. Spent much of his youth in European capitals, graduated from Harvard in 1825, and studied law under Daniel Webster. He became a leader of the Whigs. In 1848 he was the Free-Soil party candidate for vice-president; during the Civil War he was minister to Great Britain. In writing about the Boston Massacre and the 40 rowdies who gathered around the sentinel, "scarcely averse to . . . a quarrel," he said it "was the first protest against the application of force to the settlement of a question of right" [ibid.].

30. **Louses of Parleymoot**: Houses of Parliament.

31. **sojers aiming?**: The 40 or 50 men who had gathered began to throw snowballs and rocks at the nine members of the guard, who became frightened and fired their muskets. Although they apparently intended to fire over the heads of the crowd, some of the bullets miscarried. But CFA writes: "So fatal a precision of aim, indicating not a little malignity, . . . is one of the most singular circumstances attending the affray" [I, 99].

32. **Gent . . . five deaders**: Source reads: "Five men fell mortally wounded, two of them receiving two balls each. Six more were wounded, one of whom, a gentleman, standing at his own door, observing the scene, received two balls in his arm" [ibid.].

33. **'never Cadmus'**: Source continues: "The drops of blood then shed in Boston were like the dragon's teeth of ancient

fable—the seeds, from which sprung up the multitudes who would recognize no arbitration but the deadly one of the battle-field" [ibid.]. After slaying the dragon, Cadmus was told to scatter its teeth over the ground. From each tooth a fully dressed warrior sprang out of the earth. They fought one another to the death until only five were left. Then they declared a truce and founded with Cadmus the city of Thebes [27:33].

34. **legal advisor**: Source says: "It was not as a politician, but as a lawyer, that John Adams was first drawn into public life. The patriotic party stood in need of a legal adviser at all times, but never more than now . . . . John Adams was looked to as a guide in those measures in which questions involving professional knowledge were to be discussed with the authorities representing the crown" [I, 107].

35. **Blaydon**: Colonel Bladen, member of the Board of Trade and Plantations, objected, around 1740, to the enacting form used for provincial laws. The wording, "Be it enacted by the Governor, Council, and House of Representatives *in General Court assembled, and by authority of the same*," he believed implied an authority outside that of the king. So he arranged to have the standing instructions of the governor of Massachusetts include a prohibition against the use of the objectionable words, and they had not been used for thirty years when, in JA's time, the House reinstated them. In the ensuing debate between the House and Governor Hutchinson about the reintroduction of the former wording, JA played an influential role in shaping the argument for the House [I, 108].

36. **Encourage arts**: A committee with JA as a member "was directed to mature a plan for the encouragement of arts, agriculture, manufactures and commerce" [I, 109].

37. **not suggest . . . 1770, Bastun**: These 22 lines concern JA's defense of Captain Preston and the British soldiers, an exceedingly unpopular job he undertook in the name of justice. Feelings were running high in the colony, and Adams was seen by some to be no less than a traitor. Most people wanted the British soldiers hanged. But reason prevailed. JA said that until abandoned by the administration of England, "we must try causes . . . by the law of the land." Since the very small guard had been attacked by all kinds of missiles thrown by an angry mob which was gathering force, JA argued that in human nature they were entitled to defend themselves: "If an assault was made to endanger their lives, the law is clear; they had a right to kill in their own defence. If it was not so severe as to endanger their lives, yet if they were assaulted at all, struck and abused by blows of any sort, by snowballs, oyster-shells, cinders, clubs, or sticks of any kind, this was a provocation, for which the law reduces the offence of killing down to manslaughter, in consideration of those passions in our nature which cannot be eradicated" [I, 113].

38. **brand 'em in hand**: Two of the soldiers, found guilty of manslaughter, prayed for benefit of clergy (an old form of English law) which was granted. They were publicly "burnt in the hand" and then were "suffered to depart" [I, 114].

39. **mens sine affectu**: L, "a mind without feeling [passion]" a phrase JA quoted from a work by Algernon Sidney. It is a favorite quotation in defense of the "rule of law" instead of the "rule of men," who are likely to be controlled by their feelings [ibid.].

40. **Burke**: [cf. 17 above]. He said: "Bad laws are the worst sort of tyranny. In such a country as this, they are of all bad things the worst." It was not Burke but an unknown person who "disputed the right . . . of seizing the lands occupied by the heathen, by virtue of authority vested in the head of the Catholic Church, and granting them to any Christian monarch whose subjects might be the first to discover them" [I, 120; 121-122].

41. **feudatory**: JA wrote: "If our govern-

ment be . . . merely feudatory, we are subject to the king's absolute will, and there is no authority of Parliament, as the sovereign authority of the British empire" [I, 126]. And later: " 'Every subject is presumed by law to be sworn to the king, which is to his natural person,' says Lord Coke. 'The allegiance is due to his natural body;' and he says: 'In the reign of Edward the Second, the Spencers, the father and the son, to cover the treason hatched in their hearts, invented this damnable and damned opinion, that homage and oath of allegiance was more by reason of the king's crown, that is, of his political capacity, than by reason of the person of the king; upon which opinion, they inferred execrable and detestable consequents' " [I, 127].

42. **'The Spensers'**: Hugh le Despenser, 1262-1326, Earl of Winchester, and his son supported Edward II and were beheaded as traitors.

43 **Coke**: Sir Edward C., 1552-1634, English jurist, best known for his four *Institutes* (1628-1644), the first of which is called *Coke upon Littleton*.

44. **Mercantile** . . . : CFA said: "The mercantile and manufacturing temper of Great Britain regarded the people of the colonies not as friends and brethren, but as strangers who might be made tributaries" [I, 132].

45. **Oliver**: Peter O., 1713-1791, Massachusetts loyalist. When, as chief justice of Massachusetts colony (1771-1776) Oliver agreed to accept special monetary grants from the English Crown to the Massachusetts judiciary, the legislature tried to impeach him. JA drafted the articles of impeachment, but Governor Thomas Hutchinson blocked the proceedings. In 1774, after Adams's articles of impeachment had appeared in the newspapers, several Massachusetts grand juries refused to serve under Oliver. The Oliver case was critical. The Crown had offered to assume the payment of the salaries to judges. Most judges seemed willing to accept the "steady patronage of the crown" in lieu of the possible acts of "an uncertain and capricious legislative assembly." JA's idea was that if the Crown paid the judges, the Crown would own them [I, 135 ff.].

46. **wigs**: Massachusetts judges who, in the English manner, wore wigs when presiding in court.

47. **Governor**: Thomas Hutchinson, 1711-1780, American colonial administrator; member of Massachusetts governor's council (1749-1766); accepted legality of the Stamp Act (1765); royal governor of Massachusetts (1771-1774). Hutchinson was a firm believer in British authority, and his policies in Massachusetts did much to hasten the American Revolution.

48. **Abigail**: A. Adams, 1744-1810, wife of John Adams. On May 12, 1774, when she was at Braintree, JA wrote to her from Boston expressing despair over his trials and the trials of the colony: "The town of Boston, for aught I can see, must suffer martyrdom. It must expire." He also spoke of his money troubles: "It is expensive keeping a family here, and there is no prospect of any business in my way in this town this whole summer. I don't receive a shilling a week [not month]." But he ended the letter on a spirited note: "Don't imagine, from all this, that I am in the dumps" [I, 143].

49. **June 7th**: On June 17 [not 7th], 1774, a town meeting was held at Faneuil Hall with JA acting as moderator. It voted not to pay for the tea thrown into the sea at the Boston Tea Party the preceding December. Later that day the House of Representatives, meeting in Salem, adopted a motion that a "General Congress of deputies meet at Philadelphia to consult together upon the present state of the Colonies." This action, taken in the greatest secrecy, was critical in the history of the Revolution. After the motion was adopted, "five delegates from Mass. were named and agreed on" [Bowen, op. cit., 444].

50. Bowdoin: James B., 1726-1790, American statesman. He was nominated to the Continental Congress in 1774 but was too ill to serve. Later he became a leading figure in the Massachusetts councils during the American Revolution and became governor of the state in 1785.

51. Cushing: Thomas C., 1725-1788, American political leader; member of Boston Committee of Correspondence (1773) and of Continental Congress (1774-1776).

52. Sam Adams: Samuel A., 1722-1803, 2d cousin of John Adams, was one of the most active of the Revolutionaries. As colonial resistance to the Crown stiffened, Sam Adams took a lead in expressing the case of the discontented. He helped organize the Sons of Liberty and assisted the cause by his writings. He signed the Declaration of Independence.

53. Paine: Robert P., 1731-1814, American jurist; member of Continental Congress (1774-1778) and signer of Declaration of Independence; judge of Massachusetts Supreme Court (1790-1804).

54. mope . . . : Phrases JA confided to his diary, along with the reflection: "I am often in reveries and brown studies. The objects before me are too grand and multifarious for my comprehension. We have not men fit for the times" [I, 148].

55. le / personnel manque: F, "the personnel is lacking." A phrase Pound adds to the text. Because the colonies do not have men competent to meet the needs of the time, JA sees only bad times ahead. Thus he exhorts Abigail to watch the money and cut down on expenses in every way [I, 150].

56. non importation . . . : The Congress at Philadelphia believed the colonies could force England into bankruptcy by cutting off all trade of any kind with the motherland. JA believed that such an act would not work, but he went along with it, looking to better action in the future. His caveat was reinforced by examples from the orient. CFA said that inconvenience might result from a total embargo, but not bankruptcy of a whole community: "The history of countries like China and Japan proves clearly enough that it is by no means essential to national existence that they should trade with outside nations at all" [I, 163].

57. Boston Gazette: Newspaper, published 1719-1798, which strongly favored the American Revolution.

58. Lexington: Here, on April 19, 1775, the first shot was fired in the Revolution. Thereafter, JA stopped writing for the *Boston Gazette*.

59. Novanglus: JA used the pen name Novanglus ["New Englander"] to sign a series of articles (*Boston Gazette*, 1774-75) in which he sought to demonstrate that the laws of England could not be made to apply to the American colonies; the articles were an answer to a series of loyalist papers by Daniel Leonard (*Massachusetts Gazette and Post Boy*, 1774-75), who signed himself "Massachusettensis."

60. Taking a side: CFA, analyzing the situation, said that in all civil convulsions a certain group will wait to see who is likely to win before taking sides: "This naturally leads them [such fence-sitters] to oppose, with all their might, any and every measure likely to precipitate their decision. Already, at the first congress, both the Adamses had been marked by these persons as partisans of extreme, if not treasonable opinions" [I, 171].

61. bills of credit: Among the exertions CFA attributes to JA were "the selection of . . . general officers, . . . maturing the form of commission and the instructions for the commander-in-chief; and, lastly, in superintending the preparation of the continental bills of credit which were to serve the purposes of money during the earlier stages of the struggle" [I, 178].

62. navee . . . ridicule: JA strongly believed that the colonies should "procure the establishment of a fleet . . . . This naked proposition was at once met with a storm of ridicule" [I, 187].

63. Guided pubk mind: JA created public support by such pamphlets as "Thoughts on Government" and other writings not formally published: "In this way his sentiments were so extensively diffused as materially to guide the public mind in the construction of many of the State constitutions. The immediate effect was particularly visible in those adopted by New York and North Carolina, the last of which remained unchanged for sixty years" [I, 209].

64. retain . . . despotism: These five lines give the gist of CFA's analysis of JA's temperament and education: ". . . he [JA] applied his mind to the task of saving whatever experience had proved to be valuable in the British constitutional forms, and cutting off only those portions which were not adapted to the feelings, manners, habits, and principles of a young nation oppressed by no burdens transmitted from a ruder age." JA believed in "the States as nations wholly independent of each other, and needing no bond of union stronger than a single federal assembly of representatives fairly apportioned, with authority sacredly confined to cases of war, trade, disputes between the States, the post-office, and the common territories." CFA avers, however, that JA needed to do more thinking so that he could see that "republican jealousy which seeks to cut off all power from fear of abuses, sometimes does quite as much harm as if it created a despotism" [I, 210-211].

65. 9th Feb.: . . . Nation: CFA makes a judgment: "It is probable that the period embraced between the 9th of February, the day of his return to Philadelphia, and the end of this year [1776], was the most laborious and exciting of Mr. Adams's long life. . . . He felt, not that three millions of men were to declare their own emancipation, but that a nation was to come into being for a life of centuries" [I, 213].

66. Birth of a Nation: Pound's comment, emphasizing the role of JA in the Continental Congress of 1776 in bringing about the creation of a new, independent nation. Poss. refers to D. W. Griffith's 1914 film of the same name, a story of the Civil War and Reconstruction. The Poundian view thus challenges a popular 20th-century view that regards the Civil War as the real crucible in which the nation was formed and regards Abraham Lincoln as the true founding father; instead Pound asserts that the story of the nation's founding must begin at the beginning, and it is especially important that at the beginning were Jefferson and JA [cf. "The Jefferson-Adams Letters as a Shrine and a Monument"].

67. privateers . . . : JA wrote to Abigail on April 12, 1776: "The ports are opened wide enough at last, and privateers are allowed to prey upon British trade. This is not independency, you know. What is? Why, *government in every colony, a confederation among them all, and treaties with foreign nations* to acknowledge us a sovereign State, and all that" [I, 213].

68. Brit. majesty: JA helped draft the preamble of a resolution which began: "Whereas his Britannic Majesty, in conjunction with the lords and commons of Great Britain, has, by a late act of parliament, excluded the inhabitants of these United Colonies from the protection of his crown . . ." [I, 218].

69. May 12th: Source states. "The committee reported a draft [of the resolution] on the 13th, which was debated and passed on the 15th [of May 1776]." Perhaps Pound assumed it was written on May 12 [I,218].

70. 12 months ago: On May 16 Adams wrote to a friend about the resolution: "Yesterday the Gordian knot was cut. If such a resolution had been passed twelve months ago, as it ought to have been, . . . how different would have been our situation!" [ibid.].

71. June 7th: Congress finally agreed to a formal discussion of independence. CFA states: "The movement took place, accordingly, on the 7th of June." Since treason was an idea in the air, caution was necessary; thus CFA adds about the motion: "It appears on the journal, recorded with the customary caution, as follows:–'Certain resolutions respecting independency being moved and seconded,–. . ." [I, 221].

72. **spies . . . punished.** JA was a member of a group called in his journal the "Committee on Spies." It reported resolutions on June 17 which were adopted in part a week later. In part, the resolution reads: "Resolved, that it be recommended to the several legislatures of the United Colonies to pass laws for punishing, in such manner as they shall think fit, persons who shall counterfeit, or aid or abet in counterfeiting, the continental bills of credit, or who shall pass any such bill in payment, knowing the same to be counterfeit" [I, 225].

73. **orationem . . . elegantissimam**: L, "oration . . . most elegant." [10:35]

74. **Routledge**: Edward Rutledge, 1739-1800, American lawyer; member of Continental Congress (1774-1777) and signer of Declaration of Independence; member of South Carolina legislature (1782-1796) and governor of South Carolina (1798-1800); brother of John Rutledge. Patrick Henry described him "as the most elegant speaker in the first congress" [I, 228].

75. **hackneyed**: The debates in the Congress on the Declaration of Independence may have impressed others, but in a letter to Samuel Chase, JA said: ". . . nothing had been said which had not been hackneyed in that room for six months before" [I, 229].

76. **Chase**: Samuel C., 1741-1811, American patriot; signer of Declaration of Independence; delegate to First and Second Continental Congresses; appointed associate justice of Supreme Court (1796).

77. **Schicksal, sagt der Führer**: G, "Destiny, says the Führer [leader]."

78. **(sero)**: L, "too late."

79. **Cavalier**: Virginian, from CFA's passage comparing the New England and Virginian attitudes concerning loyalty to the Crown of England and finding citizens of both colonies, though having origins in different social classes in England, committed to the "spirit of personal independence" [I, 243].

80. **Impassible**: "The army, although at heart patriotic, was all the time filled with personal jealousies and discontents, which nothing kept within reasonable bounds but the impassible moderation of Washington" [I, 265].

81. **Clearest head**: An unidentified member of Congress wrote about JA: "In a word, I deliver to you the opinion of every man in the House, when I add that he possesses the clearest head and firmest heart of any man in the congress" [I, 273].

82. **Thumon**: H, "Soul, life, strength, courage, mind."

83. **Bordeaux**: JA was appointed a member of the commission to arrange the purchase of war materials from France and solicit the favor of the French toward the American cause. He reached Bordeaux safely, "was received with honors, and immediately passed on to Paris, where he arrived on the 8th of April, 1778" [I, 277].

84. **Franklin**: Benjamin F. [31:16]. JA did not think much of BF's ethics, which seemed to allow him to enjoy advantages "obtained at the expense of others." In defense of his expression of opinion about Franklin, JA wrote: "Yet if rigid moral analysis be not the purpose of historical writing, there is no more value in it than in the fictions of mythological antiquity" [I, 319].

85. **Leyden Gazette**: Dutch newspaper published in 1782 by John Luzac, with whom JA had established permanent relations when he was in Holland trying to negotiate a loan from the Dutch government.

86. Magazine Politique Hollandais: Dutch magazine established ca. 1782 by a man named Cerisier. JA wrote out the answers to many questions the Dutch had about America. His responses, published in this magazine and in the *Leyden Gazette*, counteracted information previously published in Holland which came only from English sources.

87. Calkoen: Hendrik C., 1742-1818, Amsterdam lawyer; instrumental in swaying Dutch opinion in favor of the American colonies during the Revolution. At his request JA wrote "Twenty-six Letters upon interesting subjects respecting the Revolution of America," and Calkoen arranged to have them published in the Dutch press in October 1780.

88. Amsterdam: Dutch city where JA served as American minister to the Netherlands (1780). While there, Adams cultivated as many of the most reliable bankers as he could because they would be a factor in his efforts to negotiate loans for the newly established and independent United States.

89. Cornwallis: Charles C., 1738-1805, British general who surrendered to the Americans and French at Yorktown, Virginia, in 1781. His defeat bolstered the cause of the colonies in Europe and helped make it possible to borrow money to carry on as well as to persuade the Dutch to acknowledge "the independence of the United States" [I, 346].

90. De Ruyter: Michel Adriaanszoon de R., 1607-1676, Dutch admiral and naval hero; active in cause for Dutch freedom.

91. doivent . . . de la France: F, "they ought always to cry Liberty–friends of France." Source reads: "Les amis de la France devaient toujours *crier* la liberté." In referring to this description of French policy under Louis XV, CFA [I, 345n] remarks: "From that quarter it was a cry and nothing else, as well in Holland as in America."

92. Flassans: Jean Baptiste Gáetan de Raxiš de Flassan, 1760-1845, French diplomat and historian; author of *Histoire Générale et Raisonée de la Diplomatie Française* (1808).

93. Van Capellen: Joan Derk, Baron van der Capellen tot dem Pol, Dutch statesman; friend of American interests during late 18th century.

94. der Haag: The Hague, capital of the Netherlands. JA undertook the bold policy of insisting that the U.S. be recognized as an independent nation. Thus he began (on Jan. 8, 1782) "a series of formal visits, in person, to the chief officers . . . at the Hague, in which he respectfully reminded them of the memorial he had addressed to them, asking for the recognition of his country . . . . He then stated the object of his visit to be to demand a CATEGORICAL ANSWER" [I, 347].

95. Leyden: Industrial town in South Holland, SW Netherlands.

96. Harlem: Haarlem, city in North Holland, W Netherlands, near Amsterdam.

97. Zwol: Zwolle, city in Overijssel Province, E Netherlands, on Ijssel River.

98. Zeland: Zeeland, province, SW Netherlands, composed of several small islands. Source reads "Zealand."

99. Overyssel: Overijssel [cf. 97 above].

100. Gronye: Groningen, province in NE Netherlands.

101. Utrecht: Province in C Netherlands and its capital city.

102. Guilderland: Gelderland, province in E Netherlands. In many Dutch towns and provinces "petitions were gotten up, setting forth . . . reasons why the provincial States . . . should be instructed early to declare in favor of granting Mr. Adams's demand" [I, 347].

103. U.S.N.A.: United States of North America.

104. Birth of a Nation: [66 above]. JA received a favorable categorical answer and was "acknowledged in quality of envoy of the United States of North America" and "as the accredited minister of the new nation." Later JA was presented to the ministers of other European states "as a new and recognized member of the *corps diplomatique* at the Hague" [I, 348-349].

105. corps diplomatique: F, "diplomatic corps."

106. Dumas: Charles William Fredrick D., d. 1796, Swiss man of letters whom Franklin employed as an agent to promote American affairs in Holland (1775), he acted as JA's secretary in Holland (1780-1782) and remained there as American chargé d'affaires, though he never officially held that title. Adams found him completely trustworthy.

107. Willink: Wilhem and Jan W., directors of Dutch banking house bearing their name (ca. 1780).

108. van Staphorst: Nicholas and Jacob van S., fl. 1780, directors of Dutch banking house bearing their name.

109. Fynje: De la Lande and Fynje, Dutch banking house (ca. 1780).

110. guilders: Amount of the first loan JA negotiated with Dutch bankers. From that time until he returned to America in 1788, he kept up relations with the bankers of Amsterdam and through them received successive advances [I, 351].

111. Adam Street: Street in C London. On October 20 JA set out, for reasons of health, with his son [the young JQA who was acting as his secretary] and one servant for London. On his arrival a postboy told him he was being carried to the best inn in London. JA wrote: "Whether it was the boy's cunning, or whether it was mere chance, I know not, but I found myself in a street which was marked John's Street. The postilion turned a corner, and I was in Adam's Street. He turned another corner, and I was in John Adam's Street! I thought, surely we are arrived in Fairy land. How can all this be?" [I, 403].

112. Adelphi: Adelphi Hotel on the Strand, London, where JA stayed in 1783.

113. Hired!: A bookseller told JA: "Sir, the men of learning are all stark mad. There are in this city at least one hundred men of the best education, the best classical students . . . any one of whom I can hire for one guinea a day to go into my closet and write for me whatever I please, for or against any man or any cause. It is indifferent to them whether they write *pro* or *con*" [I, 404].

114. Ice, broken ice . . . : JA's return trip from England to Holland was the worst experience he ever had. He gives comparative details of bad trips, such as "once, in 1777, in the dead of winter, from Braintree to Baltimore, five hundred miles, upon a trotting horse," and in 1778 "in a furious hurricane . . . which struck down our men upon deck, and cracked our mainmast"; he concludes that he never suffered "so much . . . as in that jaunt from Bath to Amsterdam" [I, 412].

115. fundamentals: JA went to England as a visitor for his health. As a guest auditor in Parliament, he heard George III confess that "he had thrown away an empire." The king, far from dishonoring the name of his American auditor, said that the Adams "name was henceforth to go out indelibly graven by his act upon the list of those who, by upholding fundamental principles at critical moments, originate the beneficial movements of the world!" [I, 413].

116. literature . . . : Mrs. Adams joined JA in Paris in the summer of 1784. JA wrote that the place had changed. "Literature and philosophy had become the rage even in fashionable circles" [I, 415].

117. Frederick: Frederick II (the Great) of Prussia adopted a trade treaty with the U.S. which was different from any such treaty yet made: "Free trade, freedom of neutrals, respect for individual property of enemies at sea, the abolition of privateering, and the limitation over the power to confiscate contraband of war, were new and bold steps in the progress of international civilization" [I, 416].

118. philanthropy: Since the treaty would protect the U.S. from British sea power, JA was bound to add: "Hence their [the Americans'] philanthropy was not wholly free from suspicion of incidental benefit to ensue to themselves" [I, 417].

119. The Duke: John Frederick Sackville, 1745-1799, Duke of Dorset; English ambassador extraordinary and plenipotentiary to France (1783-1789). In February 1785 the Congress made JA the envoy to the Court of St. James's. The duke remarked to him in Paris that "he would be stared at a great deal" [I, 418].

120. to make gain . . .: JA wrote: "The pamphlet of Lord Sheffield [which in 1783 got the U.S. excluded from trade with other British colonies] had its effect upon the formation and adoption of the federal constitution of 1788. Thus it often happens with nations that think to make a gain out of the embarrassments and miseries of their neighbors . . . . Lord Sheffield's interference must be classed among the secondary misfortunes which befell Great Britain in the disastrous record of the American war" I, 423].

121. Euclid. Greek mathematician, 3d century B.C. JA said that the "infallible truth" of the doctrines of the Constitution was as clear as any demonstration in Euclid.

122. taste and elegance: In order to defend the Constitution to New Englanders and others, JA published *A Defence of the Constitution of the United States of America against the attack of M. Turgot*. He wrote the treatise hastily because it had to be published immediately to do any good, and people complained that it lacked "taste and elegance." JA said that such things would have to come after "substance."

123. Libertatem Amicitiam Fidem: L,"Liberty, Friendship, Loyalty" [*Tacitus* I.XV (Loeb, no. 111, p. 28)]. The sentence from which these words are taken reads: "Fidem, libertatem, amicitiam, praecipua humani animi bona, tu quidem eadem constantia retinebis." ["Honour, liberty, friendship, the chief blessings of the human mind, you will guard with the same constancy as before" (Loeb trans.).] CFA writes: ". . . the passage from Tacitus . . . became such a favorite with Mr. Adams that he selected the first three words and the governing verb *retinebis*, as a motto for himself, which he caused to be engraved in various forms for his private use" [I, 433].

124. a new power: In talking about national prosperity, JA wrote: "The commercial and moneyed interests, which were the first to feel it, at once rallied around Mr. Hamilton [Washington's secretary of the treasury] as their benefactor, and they never deserted him afterwards. A new power arose, that of the fundholders, the rapid increase of which inspired Mr. Jefferson with alarm and a determination to resist it" [I, 452].

125. rotation: In a letter to his wife [Jan. 2, 1794], JA wrote: "Our anti-federal scribblers are so fond of rotation, that they seem disposed to remove their abuse from me to the President" [I, 460].

126. To be punctual . . . unmercantile: In a letter to Abigail [Feb. 8, 1794], JA wrote of his boredom after presiding over the Senate for two months: "I . . . am wearied to death with *ennui*. Obliged to be punctual by my habits, confined to my seat, as in a prison, to see nothing done, hear nothing said, and to say and do nothing." And later: "Borrowing of banks for a trading capital is very unmercantile" [I,465-466].

127. war: In a letter dated March 27, 1794, JA wrote: "I have one comfort; that in thought, word, or deed I have never encouraged a war" [I, 469].

128. horror: In an April 19 letter JA wrote: "You cannot imagine what horror some persons are in, lest peace should continue" [I, 471].

129. DEBT: In a letter of May 5, JA wrote: "While I confess the necessity of it . . . I lament the introduction of taxes and expenses which will accumulate a perpetual debt and lead to future revolutions" [I, 473].

130. Adet: Pierre-August A., 1763-1834, French envoy to U.S. (1795) with rank of minister plenipotentiary. He represented the Directory whose short-lived regime began after the execution of Robespierre.

131. Jay: John J., 1745-1829, American jurist and statesman; member of Continental Congress (1774-1777, 1778, 1779); aided in peace negotiations with Great Britain (1782-83); chief justice of Supreme Court (1789-1795); negotiated Jay's Treaty with Great Britain (1794-95). That Jay was elected governor of New York before the treaty was published JA thought a happy circumstance, "for the parties against him would have quarrelled with the treaty, right or wrong, that they might give a color to their animosity against him" [I, 479].

132. J.Q.A.: John Quincy Adams [34: passim].

133. nominatim: L, "by name."

134. King: Rufus K., 1755-1827, American statesman, member of Continental Congress (1784-1787) and of U.S. Senate (1789-1796, 1813-1825); minister to Great Britain (1796-1804). He was a strong supporter of Alexander Hamilton. He, and the others named, refused to be secretary of state after the resignation of Edmund Randolph, who had been compromised by revealing a secret correspondence with the French envoy. The comments about "good men and true" are taken from letter to Abigail [Jan. 7, 1796; not 1795]. [I, 483].

135. Henry: Patrick H. refused to accept office of secretary of state [31:46].

136. Cotsworth: Charles Cotesworth Pinckney, 1746-1825, American statesman. He was sent to France on a special mission (1796) but when the French refused to recognize his status he went to Amsterdam, where he was approached by members of the French government who offered terms under which negotiations might start (the main point was Jay's Treaty); this incident became the famous XYZ Affair [70:16].

137. War Office: U.S. Department of War.

138. expenses etc.: In a letter to Abigail [Jan. 7, 1796], JA spoke of the difficulty of filling the cabinet: "The expenses of living at the seat of government are so exorbitant, so far beyond all proportion to the salaries, and the sure reward of integrity in the discharge of public functions is such obloquy, contempt, and insult, that no man of any feeling is willing to renounce his home, forsake his property and profession for the sake of removing to Philadelphia, where he is almost sure of disgrace and ruin. Where these things will end, I know not. In perfect secrecy between you and me, I must tell you that now I believe the President will retire." JA believed that he should not serve as vice-president under a new president whose sentiments might differ from his own or be "so opposite . . . as to endanger the peace of the nation. It will be a dangerous crisis in public affairs, if the President and Vice-President should be in opposite boxes" [I, 483-484].

139. Philadelphy: Philadelphia was the meeting place of the First Continental Congress (1774), of the Second Continental Congress (1775-76, 1777, 1778-1789) and of the Constitutional Convention (1787). It also served as the capital of the U.S. (1790-1800).

140. hate speeches: In a letter to Abigail [March 1, 1796], JA listed the things he hated about government. In addition to those Pound lists, he said: "I hate to speak to a thousand people to whom I have nothing to say. Yet all this I can do" [I, 487].

141. Amphion: A musician, so excellent that he drew stones after him with the music of his lyre. JA wrote: "Alas! I am not Amphion. I have been thirty years singing and whistling among my rocks, and not one would ever move without money. . . . I cannot sing nor play. If I had eloquence, or humor, or irony, or satire, or the harp or lyre of Amphion, how much good I could do to the world" [I, 488].

142. House: House of Representatives. JA wrote: "If Mr. Jefferson should be President, I believe I must put up as a candidate for the House. . . . I declare, however, if I were in that House, I would drive out of it some demons that haunt it" [I, 489].

143. Washington's: Washington declined to run for a third term in the election of 1796, a decision that created violent partisan politics. CFA wrote: "The retirement of President Washington removed the last check upon the fury of parties. . . . The individual whom the opposition would sustain, with marked unanimity, was Thomas Jefferson. . . . The federalists . . . enjoyed no such advantage. A portion of them . . . reposed implicit confidence in Alexander Hamilton. But they were . . . compelled to admit that that confidence was not shared by the people at large, and that an attempt to oppose him to Mr. Jefferson would be futile" [I, 490-491].

144. Mr. Hamilton: Alexander H., 1755-1804, American statesman, member of Continental Congress (1782, 1783, 1787, 1788) and first U.S. secretary of the treasury (1789-1795). The proponent of a strong federal government, he was instrumental in securing the ratification of the Constitution, especially in New York. In Washington's administration Hamilton established a national fiscal system and placed public credit on a sound basis. But from Pound's point of view, his decision to model the U.S. banking system on the Bank of England has had destructive effects ever since. Pound also pillories him for the "scandal of the assumption" [*SP*, 169] and for being anti-John Adams, anti-Jefferson, and anti-Andrew Jackson in their struggles for the people versus financial interests [*SP*, 338]. Here Hamilton quarreled with JA primarily because he was a threat to Hamilton's control of Federalist party policies. Knowing that in the controversies of partisan politics Adams would not necessarily be a strict party man, Hamilton [69:67] sought to diminish Adams's influence by working behind the scenes to deny him party support. In the presidential campaign of 1796, Hamilton encouraged Federalist electors to vote unanimously for Thomas Pinckney for vice-president, hoping that Pinckney would receive enough additional electoral votes to become president, with Adams as vice-president. But Adams was elected president and, partly as a result of Hamilton's maneuverings, Thomas Jefferson of the opposition Republican party was elected vice-president. During Adams's presidency Hamilton contrived to have Secretary of State Timothy Pickering, Secretary of the Treasury Oliver Wolcott, and Secretary of War James McHenry report to him behind Adams's back the confidential business transacted at cabinet meetings. In May 1800, when Adams finally recognized the intrigues against him, he dismissed Pickering and McHenry and reorganized his cabinet. Hamilton made a treacherous attack on JA in the presidential campaign of 1800 by writing a pamphlet entitled *Letter from Alexander Hamilton, concerning the Public Conduct and Character of John Adams, Esq., President of the United States*, which contributed to Adams's defeat in his bid for a second term [71:60]. Ironically, Hamilton, who approved of Adams's politics much more than he did those of Jefferson, ended up throwing his support to Jefferson in the 1800 election, seeing him as a lesser evil than Aaron Burr, who, in July 1804, was to kill Hamilton in their famous duel [37:56, 66].

145. '96 till 1854: Pennsylvania deserted New England and voted for Jefferson. Adams received 71 electoral votes, only one more than necessary. But in all subsequent elections until 1854, Pennsylvania voted for the nominee who was elected.

146. Giles: William Branch G., 1762-1830, American statesman, member of House of Representatives (1790-1798); member of Senate (1804-1815). Giles opposed the founding of the first Bank of the United States and brought charges of corruption against Hamilton (1793), which were dismissed. After the election of 1796, JA reported to Abigail what Giles had said: " 'The point is settled. The V.P. will be President. He is undoubtedly chosen. The old man will make a good President, too. . . . But we shall have to *check* him a little now and then.' . . . There have been manoeuvres and combinations in this election that would surprise you" [I, 495-496].

147. Constitution: JA's inaugural address emphasized ideas whose time had not come. He referred in part to "a love of science and letters, and a wish to patronize every rational effort to encourage schools, colleges, universities, academies, and every institution for propagating knowledge, virtue, and religion among all classes of people, not only for their benign influence on the happiness of life in all its stages and classes, and of society in all its forms, but as the only means of preserving our constitution from its natural enemies" [I, 505].

148. Elleswood: Oliver Ellsworth, 1745-1807, American statesman and jurist, delegate to Continental Congress (1777-1784); chief justice of Supreme Court (1796-1799). Ellsworth was appointed to the second peace mission to France by John Adams and, with William Vans Murray and William Davie, concluded the convention with France at Mortefontaine (1800). He "administered the oath of office to JA with great energy."

149. Napoleon: Napoleon I [31:53]. Napoleon made a separate peace with Sardinia in May 1796; entered Milan on May 14; laid siege to Mantua in July; and negotiated favorable armistices with the king of Naples and the pope. Victories at Arcole, Rivoli, and Mantua followed, after which Napoleon crossed the Alps toward Vienna and soon became the idol of Europe.

150. Miranda: Francisco de M., 1750-1816, Venezuelan revolutionist and leader of the Venezuelan struggle for liberty; in 1806 he sought foreign aid and led an expedition to the Venezuelan coast, but the military venture was a failure; he was a commander of the forces during the revolution of 1810 and was dictator for a short time. During JA's term in office, Alexander Hamilton became involved with Miranda in South America in the hopes of conquering the American [South and North] possessions of Spain. Secretary of War McHenry reported sub rosa to Hamilton on actions by Adams's cabinet. CFA says: "Mr. Hamilton had become a party to a grand project of revolution in South America, conceived years before in the fertile brain of Francisco de Miranda" [I, 523].

151. Talleyrand: Charles Maurice de Talleyrand-Périgord, 1754-1838, French statesman; minister of foreign affairs (1797-1807). Implicated in the XYZ Affair [70:16]. The Hamilton party was all for war with France; it was JA's policy to follow any lead to prevent war. Thus a dispatch of Talleyrand's which indicated a hope of "a good understanding with America" was picked up by Adams, who had to undertake the most delicate kind of political maneuvering to get a new envoy sent to France. JA's success in preventing a war with France was the most important accomplishment of his term in office. But the war-mongering press, led by Hamilton's Federalists, saw America's backing down from open conflict as a weakness; thus Adams's cause was not popular in the nation at large.

152. Murray: William Vans M., 1760-1803, minister to The Hague (1798) replacing John Quincy Adams. Murray was instrumental in preparing the way for recognition of an American minister to France; in

February 1799 JA appointed him envoy to France on the second peace mission. Adams later added Oliver Ellsworth and Patrick Henry to the mission but Henry, who was unable to go, was replaced by William Davie. Murray had been the person through whom Talleyrand's dispatch was transmitted to the U.S. government. Hence he was JA's nominee to be the special envoy to France.

153. **vindictive**: In a letter to Abigail [Feb. 22, 1799], JA said: "I do not remember that I was ever vindictive in my life, though I have often been very wroth. . . . [Murray's] mission came across the views of many, and stirred the passions of more. This I knew was unavoidable" [I, 545]. CFA commented on the problem with France: "He roused the country to war, solely as a measure of defence, and to deter France from further persevering in her aggressions" [I, 541]. "Ready for war, if France continued faithless, he was not less ready for peace the moment she showed signs of returning reason" [I, 550].

154. **Fries**: John F., ?1750-1818, American insurgent who, opposed to a federal property tax, led a force of Pennsylvania Germans against assessors and collectors in 1799; Fries was arrested by government troops, tried, and found guilty of treason under the Sedition Act; JA pardoned him in 1800. CFA says about the case: ". . . the cabinet could not complain that they had not been consulted at every step. But that seems to have made no difference in the feeling with which at least one of the disaffected viewed the direction of the President . . . that a pardon should be made out for all the offenders" [I, 573].

155. **Snot**: James McHenry, 1753-1816, American politician; aide to General Washington and to Lafayette during the Revolution; member of Continental Congress (1783-1786); delegate to Constitutional Convention (1787); secretary of war (1796-1800). While secretary of war in JA's cabinet, McHenry remained loyal to the interests of Alexander Hamilton.

156. **Bott**: Prob. Timothy Pickering, 1745-1829, American general and statesman; during the Revolution member of the Board of War (1777) and quartermaster general (1780-1785); postmaster general (1791-1795); secretary of war (1795); secretary of state (1795-1800). JA dismissed Pickering from his last office because his anti-French attitude was not in line with Adams's foreign policy and because of his intrigues on behalf of Alexander Hamilton. JA's foreign policy was to maintain neutrality in all European conflicts. The Federalists wanted to align the U.S. with Britain against France.

157. **Cott**: Prob. Oliver Wolcott, 1760-1833, American lawyer and politician. He succeeded Alexander Hamilton as secretary of the treasury in Adams's cabinet (1795-1800) and during that time cooperated with Hamilton in his efforts to control and manipulate Adams's policies. Fang [I, 176] believes that Snot, Bott, Cott refer to Cabot [69:68] and Wolcott.

158. **ego scriptor** . . . : L, "I, writer of the canto."

159. **pater patriae**: L, "father of his country."

160. **arriba**: S, "hail!"

CANTO LXIII

Sources

Charles Francis Adams, ed., *The Works of John Adams*, I, II; Frederick K. Sanders, *John Adams Speaking*, Orono, Maine, 1975, 108-127; Guido Cavalcanti, "Donna mi priegha," 5th ed., 1527; rpt. *LE*, 163-167.

Background

L. H. Butterfield, ed., *Diary and Autobiography of John Adams*, I, Cambridge, Mass., 1961; Catherine Drinker Bowen, *John Adams and the American Revolution*, Boston, 1950; Gilbert Chinard, *Honest John Adams*, Boston, 1964 (first publ. 1933); Peter Shaw, *The Character of John Adams*, Chapel Hill, N.C., 1974; Page Smith, *John Adams*, 2 vols., Garden City, N.Y., 1962.

Exegeses

CE, *Ideas*, 43; Dekker, *Cantos*, 179, 186-187; DP, *Barb*, 233; CB-R, *ZBC*, 240.

Glossary

1. **Ellsworth . . . Fries**: [62:148, 152, 154]. JA, in sending Oliver Ellsworth to join William Vans Murray on a second peace mission to France (1799) and in pardoning John Fries, charged with treason under the Sedition Act and sentenced to death for leading a tax rebellion, had acted contrary to the wishes of Alexander Hamilton and his followers. Hamilton, in his *Letter . . . concerning the Public Conduct and Character of John Adams* (1800), referred to both incidents in his efforts to discredit JA's influence in the Federalist party, despite JA's 25 years of public service.

2. **General Pinckney**: Charles Cotesworth P. [62:136, 144]. Alexander Hamilton wanted to use General Pinckney to challenge the leadership of JA in the Federalist party as the election of 1800 approached, but Pinckney, when he realized what Hamilton was doing, insisted that he would participate only on a ticket that included JA.

3. **Mr Hamilton**: [62:144]. CFA's opinion about Hamilton's morals was based on Hamilton's reaction to being blackmailed by a Mr. Reynolds with whose wife he had had an affair. Rather than be thought guilty of mishandling the nation's finances, Hamilton wrote out a complete statement of his marital infidelity and faced the ensuing scandal bravely. CFA thinks he would have done better to remain silent.

4. **they effect . . . flourish**: Words from JA's last speech to the Congress [Nov. 22, 1800], delivered at the new Capitol in Washington.

5. **Washington 4th March 1801**: On this day Thomas Jefferson was inaugurated president, at the first inauguration held in Washington.

6. in ardour . . . good deed: Pound's source reads "a great deal" for the last phrase [I, 607]. The reference is to the election of 1802 in which J. Q. Adams [JQA] was nominated, despite the hostility of certain Massachusetts Federalists, to run for a seat in the House of Representatives. JQA lost this election.

7. Pickering: [cf. 62:156]. The reference here is to the election of 1803 to fill two vacancies in the U.S. Senate. After an unsuccessful attempt to elect Timothy Pickering to one of the vacant seats, support swung to JQA; after he was elected the way was clear for Pickering to take the other seat.

8. J. Adams: John Quincy Adams, elected to the Senate (1803) in an election that saw Timothy Pickering, his father's former antagonist, win the other Massachusetts seat.

9. rights . . . treaty of peace: From a resolution in which the Massachusetts Convention paid tribute to JA for revising the state constitution (1820-21) which JA had been so influential in drafting forty years earlier; JA, then 86, declined the honor of serving as presiding officer at this convention.

10. Chas Holt: Editor of the *Bee*, Republican newspaper in Connecticut, who was imprisoned under the Sedition Act (1798) for his attacks on the administration of JA. In a letter of March 4, 1825, Holt congratulated JA on the election of his son JQA as sixth president.

11. John Quincy Adams: Upon being elected president by the House of Representatives in February 1825, JQA wrote to JA a note that began: "My dear and honored father" [I, 632].

12. Scott's fictions . . . Ld / Byron: JA enjoyed having the writings of Scott and Byron read to him, in his 90th year, by members of his family.

13. property: CFA wrote: "In Mr. Adams's vocabulary, the word *property* meant land. He had no confidence in the permanence of any thing else" [I, 639].

14. From Fancy's dreams: These lines are inscribed on the tomb of John and Abigail Adams: "From lives thus spent thy earthly duties learn; / From fancy's dreams to active virtue turn: / Let Freedom, Friendship, Faith, thy soul engage, / And serve, like them, thy country and thy age." [I, 644].

15. cats: Catholics.

16. Franklin: [31:16]. JA, writing in the *Boston Patriot*, May 15, 1811, of Benjamin Franklin's attitude of "unlimited toleration in matters of religion" [I, 661].

17. Eripuit caelo fulmen: L, "He snatched the lightning from the sky." Turgot's epigram on Franklin reads: *Eripuit coelo fulmen; mox sceptra tyrannis* ("He snatched the lightning from the sky; next the sceptres from the tyrants"). JA, in the *Boston Patriot*, May 15, 1811, recalled that the compliment paid to Franklin in the motto *Eripuit coelo fulmen sceptrumque tyrannis* ("He snatched the lightning from the sky and the sceptre from the tyrant") acknowledged Franklin's experiments with electricity and his opposition to Great Britain's oppression of the colonies; but when Turgot changed the second part of the motto, the implication was that "Mr. Franklin was soon to destroy or at least to dethrone all kings and abolish all monarchical governments" [I, 662].

18. and all that: A reference to Franklin's efforts, in 1780, with the encouragement of the French foreign minister, Vergennes, to discredit JA as commissioner to France and to have his role substantially reduced. A good account of the quarrel between JA and Franklin, and of the question of the devaluation of American paper money which precipitated it, is found in Shaw, chap. vi.

19. No books . . . : JA writing in his diary, April 24, 1756, at age 20.

20. even bagpipe: JA heard the bagpipers in

the army of Sir Geoffrey Amherst when it passed through Worcester, Mass., after the capture of Fort Louisburg, Nova Scotia, in 1758.

21. **Mrs Savil**: Wife of Dr. Elisha Savil, a friend of JA's in Worcester; JA occasionally read Ovid's *Art of Love* to Mrs. Savil [JA's diary, Oct. 5, 1758].

22. **Ars Amandi**: L, for *Ars Amatoria*, "The Art of Love," by Ovid.

23. **half after three**: Pound's source reads "half after ten" [II, 45].

24. **Court House**: On October 24, 1758, JA traveled from Braintree to Boston to visit the courthouse to be sworn in as a member of the bar.

25. **Saml Quincy**: Samuel Q., 1735-1789, American lawyer and JA's friend; became solicitor general of Massachusetts under the Crown; a loyalist, he left the country in 1776. Quincy went to Boston with JA to be sworn.

26. **Dr Gordon**: Sylvester Gardiner, 1708-1786, American physician; he was a loyalist and fled America when the Revolution started.

27. **Gridley**: Jeremiah G., 1702-1767, American lawyer and attorney general of Massachusetts Bay Province; in 1761 he defended the legality of the Writs of Assistance. JA visited him in October 1758 to ask his advice about studying law. The advice Gridley gave had a permanent effect on JA, which is summarized in the next 10 lines of the canto. JA asked Gridley if he should study Greek. Gridley replied, "It is a matter of mere curiosity" [II, 47].

28. **Reeve**: Sir Thomas R., d. 1737, English jurist; author of *Lord Chief Justice Reeve's Instructions to his Nephew concerning the study of law.*

29. **Judge Leighton**: Robert Lightfoot, 1716-1794, loyalist of Rhode Island; judge of the British Court of Vice-Admiralty for the southern district of North America.

30. **Institutes**: *Institutes of the Laws of England* (London, 1628-1644), a work containing Sir Thomas Littleton's *Tenures* with commentary by Sir Edward Coke, "long the standard authority on real property in England and America" [Butterfield, I, 56 n. 3].

31. **Coke**: [62:43].

32. **Littleton**: Sir Thomas L., ?1407-1481, English jurist and writer on law. His *Tenures* is the earliest printed treatise on English law; the text is the basis of Coke's commentary known as *Coke upon Littleton* [major source of Cantos 107-109].

33. **Mr Thatcher**: Oxenbridge Thacher, 1720-1765, American lawyer and member of the Massachusetts General Court; associated with James Otis and Stephen Sewall in the controversy over the Boston Writs of Assistance (1761). On October 25, 1758, when JA visited Thacher to ask if he would concur in sponsoring JA before the bar, Thacher talked about many subjects before finally coming around to the subject most on JA's mind.

34. **country**: Pound's source reads "county" [II, 47]. Meaning full of lawyers.

35. **Van Myden**: Van Muyden's *Short Treatise on the Institutions of Justinian*, which Jeremiah Gridley lent JA in a Latin edition [JA's diary, Oct. 26, 1758].

36. **editio terza**: I, "third edition."

37. **Ideogram**: Chêng [M351], "upright, true."

38. **of technical terms**: JA's comment on Hoppius's *Commentaries on Justinian*: "The design of this book is to explain the technical terms, and to settle the divisions and distributions of the civil law. By the way, this is the first thing a student ought to aim at, namely, distinct ideas under the terms, and a clear apprehension of the divisions and distributions of the science. This is one of the principal excellencies of Hawkins's Pleas of the Crown, and it is the very end of

this book of Van Muyden" [II, 48]. Pound underlines the Confucian concern for terminology here expressed by JA, by including the ideogram.

39. **Hawkins**: William H., 1673-1746, English lawyer, author of *Treatise of the Pleas of the Crown* (1716).

40. **Bracton**: Henry de B. (or Bratton), d. 1268, English jurist; author of the first systematic treatise of law in England, *De legibus et consuetudinibus Angliae.*

41. **Britten**: John le Britton (or Breton), d. 1275, bishop of Hereford; author of *Britton*, a treatise on English law.

42. **Fleta**: Name of a Latin textbook on English law: *Fleta, seu Commentarius Iuris Anglicani* (ca. 1290); believed to have been written in Fleet prison by one of the corrupt judges imprisoned by Edward I.

43. **Glanville**: Ranulf de G., d. 1190, English statesman and jurist; adviser to Henry II of England.

44. **Fleta on Glanville**: Pound's source reads "Fleta and Glanville" [II, 50 n. 2].

45. **must dig . . .** : JA's comment on the difficulties of starting a law practice [*Diary*, Dec. 18, 1758].

46. **Tully**: Marcus Tullius Cicero, also known as Tully, 106-43 B.C., Roman orator and philosopher. JA noted the value of reading Cicero aloud [*Diary*, Dec. 21, 1758].

47. **Cataline**: Lucius Sergius Catilina, ?108-62 B.C., Roman politician. In 63 he entered into a conspiracy to assassinate the consuls and plunder Rome, but his plot was stopped by Cicero.

48. **Ruggles**: Timothy R., 1711-1798, prominent loyalist. The reference is to JA's assessment, in April 1759, of Ruggles as a lawyer.

49. **practising law**: Biographical note on Ruggles quoted from *Sabine's American Loyalists* [II, 67n].

50. **Sandwich**: Town in SE Massachusetts.

51. **Novascotia**: Nova Scotia, province in E Canada.

52. **1788**: Pound's source reads "1798" [II, 67n].

53. **tory**: Member of the loyalist party in America during the Revolution.

54. **in quella . . . memora**: I, "in that part / where memory is" [Cavalcanti, "Donna mi priegha"; cf. 36:3].

55. **Colonel Chandler**: Leader of Boston pre-Revolutionary troops with which JA sometimes served.

56. **Mr Quincy**: Edmund Q., 1703-1788, friend of JA's; father-in-law of John Hancock and Jonathan Sewall [II, 81].

57. **Franklin . . .** : Benjamin F. The episode mentioned in these nine lines is found in JA's diary, May 26, 1760; it is a very complimentary account of Franklin's kindness in response to Edmund Quincy's expression of interest in viniculture for his province [II, 81-82].

58. **Timon of Athens**: JA read this Shakespeare play on a rainy day, June 6, 1760.

59. **Ira**: L, "Anger." JA noted in his diary on June 10, 1760, that "the mind must be agitated with some passion, either love, fear, hope, &c., before she will do her best" [II, 87-88].

60. **la qual manda fuoco**: I, "which sends fire." In *LE*, 157, Pound translates this phrase from "Donna mi priegha" as "that breaketh into flame" and, in Canto 36 [p. 178], as "rouseth the flame."

61. **Braintree**: [62:6]. JA, disturbed at the excessive number of lawsuits in his town, wrote in his diary (June 19, 1760): "The town is become infamous for them throughout the country" [II, 90].

62. **fraud . . . into system**: JA's opinion of an institute of the canon law, which he borrowed from Jeremiah Gridley and read

at Gridley's recommendation. He said that he was glad he read it for it would "explain many things in ecclesiastical history, and open that system of fraud, bigotry, nonsense, impudence, and superstition, on which the papal usurpations are founded" [II, 116].

63. 'Our constitution'... laugh: A quotation from an anonymous newspaper article JA recorded in his diary on March 21, 1761. The year 1760 mentioned by Pound may be an error.

64. hoarse laugh: Pound's source reads "horse laugh" [II, 121].

65. Cockle: James C., customs officer in Salem, Mass., who petitioned the court to grant him Writs of Assistance to let him search for prohibited merchandise. James Otis and Oxenbridge Thacher represented the protesting Boston merchants; Jeremiah Gridley appeared for Cockle in support of the writs. Cockle won his case (1761) but Otis's speech against the writs crystalized for JA the nature of the conflict to come [see II, App. A, 521-525, for an abstract of the arguments presented at the trial and for a version of Otis's speech].

66. Writ(s) of Assistance: Writs of Assistance, authorized by the statute of 12 Charles II (1672), were issued to officials to aid them in the search for smuggled or uncustomed goods; in practice, a writ was a general search warrant. Writs of Assistance were issued in Boston (1760) to allow English port agents to discover smuggled goods; they were not very effective and served to stir up discontent against the British [71:9].

67. Mr Sewall: Stephen S., 1702-1760, American jurist; judge of the Supreme Court of Massachusetts in 1739 and chief justice from 1752; he opposed the British Writs of Assistance.

68. Oxenbridge Thayer: O. Thacher [cf. 33 above].

69. Otis: James O. [34:33].

CANTO LXIV

Sources

Charles Frances Adams, ed., *The Works of John Adams*, II; Frederick K. Sanders, *John Adams Speaking*, Orono, Maine, 1975, 128-173; EP, *SP*, 21.

Background

L. H. Butterfield, ed., *Diary and Autobiography of John Adams*, I, II, Cambridge, Mass., 1961; Catherine Drinker Bowen, *John Adams and the American Revolution*, Boston, 1950; Peter Shaw, *The Character of John Adams*, Chapel Hill, N.C., 1974; Page Smith, *John Adams*, 2 vols., Garden City, N.Y., 1962; Bernard Bailyn, *The Ordeal of Thomas Hutchinson*, Cambridge, Mass., 1974.

Exegeses

CE, *Ideas*, 43; DD, *Sculptor*, 163-164, Davis, *Vision*, 139; DP, *Barb*, 233.

Glossary

1. **John's bro, the sheriff**: Peter Boylston Adams, 1738-1823, who, as a result of JA's efforts, was appointed deputy sheriff of Suffolk County in the summer of 1761 as part of JA's campaign against pettifoggers, amateurs who dabbled in legal affairs. Of his brother, JA wrote in his *Autobiography*: "He was young, loved riding, and discharged his duties with skill and fidelity; but his disposition was so tender, that he often assisted his debtors with his own purse and credit, and upon the whole, to say the least, was nothing the richer for his office" [II, 129n].

2. **Cromwell**: Oliver C. [33:21]. This judgment was expressed to JA by the Reverend Anthony Wibird, Congregational minister at Braintree, September 10, 1761.

3. **Prayer . . . crown**: JA's reflections on the application to his own situation of the following passage from Pope's "Fourth Satire of Dr. John Donne, Dean of St. Paul's, Versifyed": "Bear me, some god! Oh! quickly bear me hence, / To wholesome solitude, the nurse of sense, / Where contemplation prunes her ruffled wings, / And the free soul looks down to pity kings" [II, 132].

4. **George**: George III of England [32:41].

5. **Louis**: Louis XV, 1710-1774, king of France (1715-1774).

6. **Frederick**: Frederick II of Prussia [32:38].

7. **Palmer**: Joseph P., 1718-1788, American soldier. As a colonel in the colonial militia Palmer helped defend the coast near Boston; in 1777 he was appointed brigadier general and given command of the Massachusetts militia defending Rhode Island. JA visited him in October 1762 at his home in Germantown, Massachusetts, and took a particular interest in his husbandry.

8. **1752**: Prob. 1762, the year JA visited Deacon Palmer.

9. **Gridley of Abingdon**: Pound's source reads "Greenleaf of Abington" [II, 137].

10. **ramshorn of straw**: Pound's source reads "ram's-horn or straw" [II, 137].

11. **sub conditione fidelitatis:** L, "under condition of faith" or "on trust" [cf. II, 149, where the phrase is quoted from a work of Strykius]. Source reads "*Sub conditione . . . fidelitatis*." This quotation came up at a meeting of a sodality of lawyer friends informally organized by Jeremiah Gridley to improve their familiarity with the law. JA hosted, at Blodget's in Boston, on this occasion [*Diary*, Feb. 21, 1765].

12. **Oliver**: Andrew O., 1706-1774, secretary of the province of Massachusetts and later lieutenant governor. On August 14, 1765, in response to reports that Secretary Oliver would distribute stamps when the Stamp Act went into effect, a Boston mob hanged him in effigy. Later that day the mob burned Oliver's office building, burned him in effigy, and vandalized his house and garden. When Lieutenant Governor Hutchinson tried to restore order, the mob drove him and the sheriff away. In his diary [Aug. 15, 1765] JA condemned the behavior of the mob: "But to be carried through the town in such insolent triumph, and burned on a hill, to have his garden torn in pieces, his house broken open, his furniture destroyed, and his whole family thrown into confusion and terror, is a very atrocious violation of the peace, and of dangerous

tendency and consequence." But JA also believed that the people had a measure of provocation because of the powerful offices controlled by Lieutenant Governor Hutchinson: Andrew Oliver was Thomas Hutchinson's brother-in-law and Andrew's brother, Peter Oliver, was chief justice of the superior court of the colony.

13. **Lieutenant Governor**: Thomas Hutchinson [62:47].

14. **By 40 towns**: In 1765 JA drafted the "Braintree Instructions," a document directing Braintree's representative to the provincial assembly, the General Court, to give the stated reasons for Braintree's refusal to accept the terms of the Stamp Act. JA's document was printed in Draper's *Massachusetts Gazette and Boston News Letter* (Oct. 10, 1765) and was subsequently adopted by 40 other towns as instructions to their representatives.

15. **instrument**: Pound's source reads "instructions" [II, 153].

16. **Sam Adams**: [34:32]. Chosen by the town of Boston to prepare instructions for its representatives, Samuel Adams, upon reading what JA had written for Braintree, incorporated some parts of the "Braintree Instructions" into his own document.

17. **Stamp Act**: A revenue law passed by Parliament (1765) which extended the British stamp tax to America and required all publications and legal documents issued in the colonies to bear a stamp. The violent opposition throughout the colonies culminated in the Stamp Act Congress, which met on October 7, 1765, in New York City and petitioned the king and Parliament to remove the tax. Fearing loss of trade with the colonies, the British repealed the act in 1766.

18. **Stamp Act . . . America's**: JA's description of the effects of resistance to the Stamp Act [*Diary*, Dec. 18, 1765].

19. **To renounce under tree**: JA noted that Andrew Oliver had been compelled "to renounce his office of distributer of stamps, by a declaration under his hand and under his oath, taken before Justice Dana in Hanover Square, under the very tree of liberty, nay, under the very limb where he had been hanged in effigy, August 14th, 1765" [*Diary*, Dec. 19, 1765].

20. **Gridley**: [63:27]. On December 18, 1765, Gridley, Otis, and JA were chosen counsel for Boston to argue before the governor of the province, Francis Bernard, that the courts, closed since November 1, when the Stamp Act had gone into effect, be reopened. Since legal documents had to carry stamps indicating payment of the tax, and since the citizens of Massachusetts refused to accept the validity of the Stamp Act, no legal business could be conducted.

21. **Jas Otis**: James O., one of JA's senior mentors in the law [34:33; 71:89, 91].

22. **Lord Bacon**: Sir Francis B., 1st Baron Verulam, 1561-1626, English philosopher and statesman. JA's reflections on the events of December 18 "call to mind my Lord Bacon's observation about secret, invisible laws of nature, and communications and influences between places that are not discoverable by sense" [*Diary*, Dec. 19, 1765].

23. **Coke**: Lord C. To Pound's mind one of the greatest writers on the law for all time [62:43]. His Institutes are the source of Cantos 107-109/756-774.

24. **3rd Inst.**: Pound's source reads "2 Inst." [II, 159]. JA wrote: "The law is the subject's best birthright." Coke wrote: "It is called, right, because it is the best birthright the subject hath" [*Magna Charta*, cap. 29, sec. 11, sub. 3, p. 56].

25. **actus . . . injuriam**: L, "an act of law does harm to none" [II, 159].

26. **Governor in council**: On December 20, 1765, JA, Gridley, and Otis appeared before Governor Bernard to argue that the law courts should be reopened without imposition of the stamp tax, JA saying that the act

was invalid, "it not being in any sense our act, having never consented to it," and that in any event the dispute over the act should not justify a failure to make justice available to citizens through the courts. Governor Bernard, evading the issue, responded that his office had no power to act on the request to open the courts and that the petitioners should therefore approach the judges directly so that they could decide the question for themselves. When asked his opinion of the best response to Governor Bernard's decision, JA suggested that the petitioners follow the governor's advice and first call upon the governor-in-council, as the supreme court of probate; then ask the judges of the superior court their opinion on the question of opening the courts for business without stamps; then consult with the judges of the inferior courts; and if there is still no satisfactory response to the petition, then request that the governor convene the two houses of the colonial legislature and, if he refuses, attempt to convene the two houses themselves [II, 158, 162].

27. **by more . . . plague**: JA's opinion of office seekers who desired appointment from the Crown [*Diary*, Dec. 25, 1765].

28. **tendency of the act**: Stamp Act.

29. **Ipswich Instructions**: The instructions given by the people of Ipswich to Dr. John Calef, their representative in the Stamp Act Congress (1765), argued that the colony would be bound to the laws of England under three conditions: that the emigration of the original colonists be a national act; that the original emigrating be at national expense; and that the place settled be land already belonging to the Crown. JA thought the questions raised were debatable [II, 171-172].

30. **waddled**: "A great storm of snow last night; weather tempestuous all day. Waddled through the snow driving my cattle to water at Doctor Savil's;–a fine piece of glowing exercise" [*Diary*, Jan. 2, 1776; II, 173].

31. **Shutting courts**: James Otis, using the pseudonym Hampden, wrote a newspaper essay answering Pym (pseudonym of an English writer who supported the Crown) with arguments from Grotius and other writers, that "shutting up the courts is an abdication of the throne, a discharge of the subjects from their allegiance, and a total dissolution of government and reduction of all men to a state of nature" [II, 174].

32. **Louisburg**: Port city of E Nova Scotia. On January 13, 1766, the day the inferior Court of Common Pleas reopened at Boston, JA took a case involving rum stolen from a vessel in Louisburg.

33. **Pitt**: William, "the Elder Pitt," 1708-1778, English statesman who opposed the Stamp Act and British taxation of the American colonies. In March 1766 JA learned that Pitt had appeared before the House of Commons to argue that "the House granted taxes in their representative capacity, not in their legislative, and, therefore, that the Parliament had not the right to tax the colonies" because they were not represented in the House of Commons [II, 190-191].

34. **Grenville**: George G., 1712-1770, prime minister under George III (1763-1765). His most famous act was writing the Stamp Act (1765); he was also responsible for the Quartering Act of 1765 which required colonists to furnish lodging for British troops if barracks were not available.

35. **Thatcher**: Thacher [63:33].

36. **Goffe**: Edmund Trowbridge, 1709-1793, Massachusetts jurist who used the surname of his guardian, Edmund Goffe, during most of his early life. He presided at the Boston Massacre trial in 1770 and in 1774 renounced the royal salary grant. During the Revolution he remained neutral.

37. **Eaton**: Joseph E., Massachusetts laywer of doubtful character. JA wrote: "This Eaton, Goffe set up, as Pynchon tells me, to be a justice, but Thacher got him indicted

in the county of Essex for a barrator, which defeated the scheme of Goffe, and he came near conviction. Goffe grew warm, and said that Eaton's character was as good as any man's at the bar." The same entry in the diary [Nov. 5, 1766] continues: "Spent the evening at Mr. Pynchon's . . . very agreeably. Punch, wine, bread and cheese, apples, pipes and tobacco" [II, 201].

38. Martin's: An inn between Salem and Boston. The money in specie (i.e., silver dollars) JA sees going to England is a "luminous detail" [*SP*, 21]. Taxes due England had to be paid in metal, so that over a period of time most metal would be drained from the colonies. If they were not allowed to print paper money, they would be left with no means of transacting business.

39. Salem: [48:29].

40. lopping . . . : "Went up to my common pasture to give directions about trimming the trees." About the misshapen pines JA said: "These I fell without mercy, to open the prospect and let in the sun and air" [II, 201].

41. case between negro . . . : [cf. 48 below].

42. Hutchinson: [62:47].

43. Dr Tuft: Cotton Tufts, 1732-1815, American physician; friend of JA, whose affairs he administered while JA was in London. JA dined with him on April 8, 1767.

44. White House: The first house of John and Abigail Adams in Boston, to which they moved in April 1768.

45. office lucrative: In 1768 Governor Bernard arranged to have JA's friend Jonathan Sewell offer JA the office of advocate general in the Court of the Admiralty, a position that promised prosperity, royal favor, and promotion, but JA refused the offer "on account of the unsettled state of the country and my scruples about laying myself under any restraints or obligations of gratitude to the government for any of their favors" [II, 211].

46. new statutes: The Townshend Acts, passed by Parliament in June 1767, placed a tax upon glass, lead, tea, and paper.

47. J.Q.A.: John Quincy Adams. JA wrote in his *Autobiography*: "The year before this, that is, in 1767, my son John Quincy Adams was born, on the eleventh day of July, at Braintree; and at the request of his grandmother Smith, christened by the name of John Quincy, on the day of the death of his great grandfather, John Quincy of Mount Wollaston" [II, 210].

48. between negro . . . : While attending the 1768 session of the superior court at Springfield, JA was engaged "in a cause between a negro and his master." He says he argued it "in such a manner as engaged the attention of Major Hawley, and introduced an acquaintance which was soon after strengthened into a friendship that continued till his death" [II, 213].

49. Mr Hawley: Joseph H., 1723-1788, American political leader who was associated with James Otis, Samuel Adams, and JA. He was one of the first to urge a declaration of independence and unified colonial administration.

50. 100 towns: A convention was proposed at a regular town meeting in Boston and, with only one week's notice, a hundred towns sent representatives. This show of support for the colonists' cause probably influenced General Gage's decision to quarter the majority of his troops in Boston rather than at the castle in Boston harbor.

51. 10 o'clock: Pound's source reads "one o'clock at noon" [II, 213 n. 2].

52. Byles: Mather B., 1707-1788, American Congregational clergyman and writer of light verse. On his return from the legal circuit JA said: "I found the town full of troops [British redcoats], and, as Dr. Byles, of punning memory, expressed it, our grievances red-dressed. Through the whole succeeding Fall and Winter, a regiment was exercised by Major Small, in Brattle Square, directly in front of my house. The spirit-stirring drum and the ear-piercing fife aroused me and my family early enough every morning, and the indignation they excited, though somewhat soothed, was not allayed by the sweet songs, violins and flutes, of the serenading Sons of Liberty under my windows in the evening" [II, 213].

53. **Sons of Liberty**: Groups organized throughout the American colonies to resist enforcement of the Stamp Act (1765); Samuel Adams was a prominent leader.

54. **Boston Gazette**: [62:57]. JA was chosen in 1768 and 1769 to draft the "Instructions" for the Boston representatives [III, 501-510, where these "Instructions" are reprinted].

55. **Madeira**: Largest island of the group W of Morocco, N Africa.

56. **Mr Hancock**: John H., 1737-1793, American merchant and statesman; member of Continental Congress (1775-1780; 1785, 1786); first signer of Declaration of Independence; governor of Massachusetts (1780-1785; 1787-1793). On June 10, 1768, John Hancock's sloop *Liberty* was seized in Boston harbor for carrying a cargo (wine) not listed on its loading permit. The *Liberty* was sold, and Hancock was subsequently charged with an earlier offense of smuggling wine: i.e., not paying British customs duty. The case dragged on for months, but JA finally won for his client what is generally regarded as a masterful courtroom victory. The 12 lines following "a cargo of wines" are from JA's reflections upon the case [II, 215].

57. **Battle of Lexington**: [33:18]. JA's long struggle in the courts stopped when the Revolution began, for, he said, the "battle of Lexington . . . put an end, forever, to all such prosecutions" [II, 216].

58. **Mt Wollanston**: Wollaston [62:8].

59. **East chamber**: The view from the home of Norton Quincy, uncle of Abigail Adams, whom JA visited on August 13, 1769.

60. **Liberty Tree**: An elm that stood on Washington Street in Boston, on which unpopular persons were hung in effigy during the Stamp Act agitation. The "buttonwood" tree is from JA, II, 194. Bowen (op. cit., 270) says it was an elm.

61. **Brackett's**: Bracket's Tavern, the Cromwell Head Inn, Boston.

62. **Case of a whale**: JA represented Joseph Doane in a suit versus Lot Gage tried in the Court of Vice-Admiralty: "Doane had sunk the first iron, but Gage had taken the whale. The question was whether Doane had been 'fast' when Gage struck; if so, Doane was entitled to a one-eighth share of the value of the whale" [Butterfield, I, 344].

63. **British Statutes**: Prob. *State Trials and Statutes at Large*, ed. John Selden, from which JA cited a law (6 Anne, chap. 37, sec. 9) prohibiting impressment of seamen in America. In 1769 JA defended four sailors accused of killing Lieutenant Panton of the British frigate *Rose* while he was attempting to impress them. When Governor Hutchinson saw that JA had the statute before him, he refused to allow the public trial to continue; a verdict of self-defense was given, and the statute was subsequently repealed.

64. **1769**: Refers not to the repeal of the statute prohibiting impressment but to the occasion of JA's thoughts about the case.

65. **9 o'clock**: March 5, 1770, the evening of the Boston Massacre, in which British soldiers, shooting into a crowd, killed five Boston citizens [62:31, 32]. Source reads "barber's boy" [62:27].

66. **Mr Forest**: James Forrest, Boston merchant and loyalist, born in Ireland, who asked JA to defend Captain Preston and the British soldiers involved in the Boston Massacre.

67. **Captain Preston**: [62:28].

68. **Mr Quincy**: Josiah Q., Jr., 1744-1775, American lawyer, younger brother of Samuel Quincy, the loyalist. He is known

for his political pamphlets written in support of the Revolution. With JA, he served as counsel for Captain Preston in the Boston Massacre affair of 1770; he doubtless was willing to defend the British soldier because of his loyalist sympathies. JA defended the British because of his firm belief in the principles of law and justice.

69. **Mr Auchmuty**: Robert A., d. 1788, colonial jurist and loyalist; appointed judge of the Court of Vice-Admiralty for Massachusetts and New Hampshire. With JA, he was counsel for Captain Preston in the Boston Massacre case (1770). He returned to England in 1776.

70. **But he must . . . accepted**: These five lines express part of JA's response to Mr. Forrest when he said he would take the Preston case and Mr. Forrest's response of giving him a retaining fee.

71. **Hutchinson**: [62:47]. CFA in an editorial note wrote: "Hutchinson, who in his third volume has done much to embody, in a permanent form, these floating insinuations of the day, . . . alludes to this affair [JA's defense of Capt. Preston] in the following insidious manner: 'Captain Preston had been well advised to retain two gentlemen of the law, who were strongly attached to the cause of liberty, *and to stick at no reasonable fees for that purpose.*' " The passage implies that JA made a great deal of money on the defense. JA himself wrote: "Forrest [the man who persuaded him to take the case] offered me a single guinea as a retaining fee, and I readily accepted it. From first to last I never said a word about fees . . . and I should have said nothing about them here, if calumnies and insinuations had not been propagated that I was tempted by great fees and enormous sums of money" [II, 230-231].

72. **ego . . .** : L, "I, writer of the Cantos." "Scrofulous," meaning "morally degenerate," is Pound's judgment of Hutchinson.

73. **10 guineas . . . and 8**: Total fees JA received for his defense of the British, but he said he did not ask any fee and would have handled the case for nothing.

74. **But where the devil**: Words attributed to Governor Shirley, former governor of Massachusetts province, while he was living in retirement in Roxbury [II, 233].

75. **Oxenbridge Thatcher**: Pound's source reads "Thacher." The reference is to CFA's note that by the time of the Boston Massacre (1770) JA had superseded Thacher and James Otis as legal adviser for the patriot cause [II, 233n].

76. **Beccaria**: Cesare, Marchese di B., ?1735-1794?, Italian economist and jurist; author of *Tratto dei Delitti e delle Pene* [*Essay on Crimes and Punishments*]. In his defense of Captain Preston JA began with the following quotation from Beccaria: "If, by supporting the rights of mankind, and of invincible truth, I shall contribute to save from the agonies of death one unfortunate victim of tyranny, or of ignorance equally fatal, his blessing and tears of transport will be a sufficient consolation to me for the contempt of all mankind" [II, 238].

77. **He went out**: Reference to an anonymous citizen JA met on June 28, 1770.

78. **nihil humanum alienum**: L, "nothing human is alien." Refers to a man charged with rape whom JA defended; acquitted, the man was promptly held on a charge of assault with intent to ravish. "This was a worthless fellow," in JA's opinion, but "nihil humanum, alienum." The phrase is from "The Self-Tormentor" by Terence, l. 77.

79. **When he came away**: Pound's source reads: ". . . when I came away, took a view of the comet . . ." [II, 243].

80. **to roll and cool**: "Rode to Patten's, of Arundel, and Mr. Winthrop and I turned our horses into a little close to roll . . ." [II, 244].

81. **Subillam . . . apothanein**: L, "Sibyl / at Cumae I with my own eyes. . . ." H, "What

do you want?" L, "She replied." H, "To die." [cf. Petronius, *Satiricon* XLVIII, 8. Pound alludes to this passage in reference to a lady named Poke, said to be 110 or 115 years old, whom JA visited on July 2, 1770. Cf. also the epigraph to Eliot's *The Waste Land*, based on the same source.] With several others JA walked a quarter of a mile to see Mrs. Poke: "We looked in at the window and saw an object of horror." When told who had come, she said: "Gentlemen . . . I am glad to see them; I want them to pray for me; . . . I have been praying so long for deliverance" [II, 244-245].

82. Nantasket: A point on Beacon Island, where Boston Light stands, opposite Nantasket; JA visited the island on August 19, 1770.

83. non vi sed saepe legendo: L, "not by violence, but by frequent reading" [II, 248]. JA relates a story about how he and some friends were trying to recollect an old Latin distich. They remembered the first line, 'Gutta cavat lapidem, non vi, sed saepe cadendo" ["The drop wears away the stone, not by force, but by constant dripping"], but couldn't remember the second; but JA recollects it and records it later: "Sic homo fit doctus, non vi, sed saepe legendo" ["So man becomes learned, not by violence, but by constant reading"].

84. Severn Ayres: S. Ayers, member of the Virginia House of Burgesses in 1770, visited Cambridge with JA on August 22, 1770.

85. Mr Bull: William B., 1710-1791, colonial lieutenant governor of South Carolina, visited Cambridge with JA on August 22, 1770.

86. Mr Trapier: An acquaintance who visited Cambridge with JA on August 22, 1770.

87. Chas Second's time: Reference to a tax, dating from the reign of Charles II. JA says Ayers told him about it: ". . . two shillings a hogshead upon all tobacco exported from the Colony, to his Majesty forever. This duty amounts now to a revenue of five thousand pounds sterling a year, which is given, part to the Governor, part to the Judges, &c. to the amount of about four thousand pounds, and what becomes of the other one thousand is unknown. The consequence of this is, that the Governor calls an Assembly when he pleases, and that is only once in two years" [II, 249-250]. The reference to *Carolina* may be a misprint for *Virginia*, the home colony of Colonel Severn Ayers.

88. which wd / render: JA's reaction to stories about new policies regarding law in the colonies [II, 252].

89. green tea: Served at a dinner JA attended at John Hancock's home on February 14, 1771. JA: ". . . and spent the whole afternoon, and drank green tea, from Holland, I hope, but don't know" [II, 255].

90. recovered at Braintree: JA's reference to fatigue from his journey from Northborough to Boston to Braintree on May 1, 1771.

91. Stood by . . .: A diary entry for May 2, 1771: "I have very cheerfully sacrificed my interest, and my health, and ease and pleasure, in the service of the people. I have stood by their friends longer than they would stand by them. I have stood by the people" [II, 260].

92. 1771 make potash: JA's reference to commerce in Connecticut.

93. Hartford and Middletown: JA's diary (June 8, 1771) contains a detailed account of these two Connecticut towns which he visited.

94. just as we got there: At Bissell's in Windsor, Connecticut, JA on his journey home June 10, 1771.

95. One party . . . 13th, Thursday: JA is concerned about implications of reports in that day's paper on new harmony between Governor Hutchinson and the leadership of the patriots. He feels that everyone else has returned to "confidence and affection" for the governor except himself, and so he feels "quite left alone in the world" [II, 279].

96. landlady: At Treadwell's in Ipswich, where JA boarded June 22, 1771, he found preoccupation with Puritan emphasis on sin.

97. Governor Endicott: John E., ?1589-1665, one of six persons who bought the patent from Plymouth Council in England for territory on Massachusetts Bay; acted as first governor of the colony (1628) until Winthrop took charge (1630); served as assistant governor, deputy governor, and governor at various times (1630-1664).

98. Indian preacher: JA recorded this anecdote after an unremarkable day in court: "The Indian preacher cried, Good God! that ever Adam and Eve should eat that apple, when they knew in their own souls it would make good cider" [II, 289].

99. Mrs Rops: Pound's source reads "Mrs. Ropes." JA had tea at Judge Ropes's on November 9, 1771.

100. Tells old stories: Refers to a Colonel Pickman with whom JA spent the evening of November 9, 1771.

101. Always convinced that the liberties: JA's reflections on Governor Shirley's remarks about the "brace of Adams." John and Samuel Adams believed Hutchinson was most dangerous because they had direct knowledge of "his character, his unbounded ambition, and his unbounded popularity" [II, 295].

102. 'Is mere impertinence a contempt?': James Otis's explanation of the question he would raise in court concerning the proposal that "your Honors are to be paid your salaries, for the future, by the Crown out of a revenue raised from us without our consent" [II, 298-299, 300]. The controversy over the independence of the judges was to occupy JA's attention in 1773-74 and would lead him to draw up articles of impeachment against Chief Justice Peter Oliver for his refusal to renounce the salary grants from the Crown [62:45].

103. Hutchinson: In the three years after 1770, the year of the Boston Massacre and the repeal of the Townshend Acts (in which duties on all items except tea were eliminated), Massachusetts province had enjoyed a measure of tranquility, and Governor Hutchinson, thinking that the patriot movement was fading, addressed the General Court in January 1773, declaring that "the Parliament of Great Britain had an authority supreme, sovereign, absolute, and uncontrollable over the Colonies, in all cases whatsoever," and especially in matters of taxation. To JA the presumption of such a speech clearly exhibited Hutchinson's "plenitude" of "vanity and self-sufficiency" [II, 311].

104. Moore: Sir Francis M., 1558-1621, English law reporter; his most important work, often called "Moore's Reports," is *Cases Collect and Report* (1663). When JA was consulted to help frame a reply to Governor Hutchinson's speech of January 1773, he contributed passages "from a law authority which no man in Massachusetts, at that time, had ever read. Hutchinson and all his law counsels were in fault; they could catch no scent. They dared not deny it, lest the book should be produced to their confusion. . . . The book was Moore's Reports. The owner of it, for alas! master, it was borrowed, was a buyer, but not a reader, of books. It had been Mr. Gridley's" [II, 313].

105. Mr Gridley: Jeremiah G., 1702-1767 [63:27]. Gridley had been JA's legal patron.

106. N/Y state has done: In early 1773 JA began publishing in the *Boston Gazette* a series of eight letters, arguing the necessity of the independence of the judges, in response to a General Brattle, who approved of salary grants from the Crown for the judges. Some of the principles JA espoused in these letters were later incorporated in the New York state constitution, in the Massachusetts state constitution, and in the federal constitution of 1787.

107. Hutchinson's letters: On December 2, 1772, Benjamin Franklin, then London agent of the Massachusetts House of Representatives, sent a letter to the speaker of the House, Thomas Cushing, and included with it seventeen letters from the years 1767-1769 written by Hutchinson, Andrew Oliver, Moffat, Paxton, and Rome. How Franklin secured the correspondence was not revealed, but after the letters had been made public Franklin lost his position as postmaster general; in England Sir John Temple, the person suspected of delivering the letters to Franklin, fought a duel with Thomas Whately, to whom the letters were originally sent; and the Massachusetts House of Representatives petitioned for the removal of Hutchinson and Andrew Oliver from their offices. Hutchinson's letter of January 20, 1769, contained the passages most offensive to the colonists, including the statement, "There must be an abridgement of what are called English liberties" [a detailed account of this episode is in Butterfield, II, 80 n. 1].

108. Oliver: Andrew O. Oliver was secretary and lieutenant governor of Massachusetts and stamp officer to enforce the Stamp Act in Massachusetts. He advocated the dispatch of British troops to America and the prosecution of Samuel Adams for his political agitation [cf. 12 above].

109. Moffat: Thomas Moffatt, d. after 1779, loyalist of Rhode Island; comptroller of the customs at New London (ca. 1770). He left America in 1775.

110. Paxton: Charles P., 1704-1788, British commissioner of customs at Boston and head of the Board of Commissioners. He left America in 1776.

111. Rome: George R., d. after 1788, loyalist merchant of Newport, Rhode Island; during the Revolution he served as a contractor for the royal forces.

112. Sir John Temple: According to CFA, Sir John Temple was responsible for delivering the purloined letters to Benjamin Franklin; Temple fought a duel with Thomas Whately in England over this allegation [II, 319 n. 1].

113. Col. Haworth: Colonel Howarth. On August 30, 1773, JA dined at the home of his wife's uncle; an inconspicuous guest on this occasion was a Colonel Howarth.

114. Bohea: A kind of tea, a reference to the Boston Tea Party of December 16, 1773.

115. House: The Massachusetts colonial legislature consisted of a lower house, the House of Representatives, and an upper house, the Council.

116. Gridley: Benjamin G., b. 1732, d. before 1800; nephew of Jeremiah Gridley [63:27], a loyalist who went to England in 1776. The reference here is to the winter of 1773-74 when JA was assisting Major Hawley and other members of a committee to draft articles of impeachment against Chief Justice Peter Oliver for his refusal to renounce salary grants from the Crown.

CANTO LXV

Sources

Charles Francis Adams, ed., *The Works of John Adams*, II, III; Frederick K. Sanders, *John Adams Speaking*, Orono, Maine, 1975, 174-264; EP, *SR*, 42.

Background

L. H. Butterfield, ed., *Diary and Autobiography of John Adams*, II, III; Cambridge, Mass., 1961; Samuel Flagg Bemis, *A Diplomatic History of the United States*, New York, 1936; Richard B. Morris, *The Peacemakers: The Great Powers and American Independence*, New York, 1965; Peter Shaw, *The Character of John Adams*, Chapel Hill, N.C., 1974; Page Smith, *John Adams*, 2 vols., Garden City, N.Y., 1962; Carl Van Doren, *Secret History of the American Revolution*, New York, 1941.

Exegeses

CE, *Ideas*, 43, 176, 177; Dekker, *Cantos*, 185-186; Davis, *Vision*, 122, 139-140; DP, *Barb*, 232.

Glossary

1. **Chief Justice**: Peter Oliver. JA, in his *Autobiography*, refers to jurors in Massachusetts who refused to serve under Chief Justice Oliver while he faced articles of impeachment drawn by JA in 1774 [62:45].

2. **Moses Gill**: Lieutenant governor of Massachusetts (1794-1800), here mentioned by JA's friend, Justice Samuel Pemberton, as another example of how justices can be controlled by money [JA's diary, March 13, 1774].

3. **(His Majesty)**: George III of England. JA's diary [Aug. 20, 1774] included a description of this statue and other sights observed on a tour of New York City made by JA when he stopped there on his journey to the First Continental Congress in Philadelphia.

4. **the Province**: Royal province of New York, established 1685-1717; area of the present state of New York.

5. **Hakluyt**: Richard H., ?1552-1616, English historian and geographer.

6. **J. Cabot**: John C. Pound's source, JA's diary [Aug. 23, 1774], refers to "the Voyage of Sebastian Cabot." Sebastian Cabot, ?1476-1557, was the son of John Cabot, 1450-1498, erroneously mentioned by Pound. JA recommended this account to Ebenezer Hazard, a New York bookseller who was seeking advice about documents concerning early American history. Hazard eventually published a collection of such documents under the title *Historical Collections; Consisting of State Papers . . . Intended as Materials for an History of the United States*, Philadelphia, 1792-1794.

7. **Hudibras tavern**: Tavern near Nassau Hall College in Princeton, New Jersey, where JA stopped on August 27, 1774. The president of the College of New Jersey, John Witherspoon, D.D., later to sign the Declaration of Independence for New Jersey, suggested to JA the employment of writers favorable to the cause of the colonists in English newspapers.

8. **Washington**: In Philadelphia, JA heard from Thomas Lynch, Sr., of South Carolina the widely reported story (now regarded as apocryphal) of George Washington's offer, in a speech at the Virginia Convention, to help Boston.

9. **Patrick Henry**: Pound begins his redaction of JA's notes of the debates of the First Continental Congress with Patrick Henry's

declaration of a new national identity (Sept. 6, 1774).

10. in capite: Refers to the holding of land under direct grant of the lord or king; lit., "in chief" [cf. 11 below].

11. Galloway: Joseph G., ?1729-1803, American lawyer and loyalist; member of Pennsylvania colonial legislature (1756-1764; 1765-1775); member of Continental Congress (1774-75). Galloway's first remarks, in JA's notes on the debates, argued that the English Constitution was founded on the ancient principle that landholders, tenants in capite, had a right to vote. Thus the ancestors of the present colonists, when they came to America, would have been bound by laws made before they left England but not by laws subsequently passed by Parliament since they, the landholders in the New World, tenants in capite, had had no vote on those laws. According to JA's notes [Sept. 8, 1774], Galloway said: "I have ever thought we might reduce our rights to one–an exemption from all laws made by British Parliament since the emigration of our ancestors." But although Galloway recognized that these sentiments identified him with the independence movement, he was a loyalist who believed the solution to the current grievances was a "British American legislature" under the Crown, as his Galloway Plan proposed (Sept. 28, 1774).

12. Bill of Rights: A reference to the committee selected by the Congress "to prepare a bill of rights or a declaration of the rights of the Colonies." JA was appointed to the committee.

13. Mr Rutledge: John R., 1739-1800, American statesman; member of Continental Congress (1774-1776; 1782-83); governor of South Carolina (1779-1782); associate justice of U.S. Supreme Court (1789-1791); appointed chief justice (1795) but appointment not confirmed [II, 373-375].

14. Turtle . . . : JA dined at Mr. Willing's. "A most splendid feast, again–turtle and every thing else." Afterward he went to the Moravian evening lecture [*Diary*, Sept. 11, 1774] where the audience heard "soft, sweet music, and a Dutchified English prayer and preachment."

15. 17th of September: On this day in 1774 the Continental Congress endorsed the "Suffolk Resolves" of Suffolk County, Massachusetts. Parliament, during the summer of 1774, had passed the so-called Intolerable Acts, whose most important provision was that the port of Boston should be closed until the tea destroyed the preceding December had been paid for. The "Suffolk Resolves" declared the Intolerable Acts null and void. JA was happy with sentiments expressed: "This day convinced me that America will support the Massachusetts or perish with her" [II, 380].

16. American legislature: The preceding quotation refers to Patrick Henry's criticism of the Galloway Plan which proposed the creation of an American legislature under the British Crown. Henry believed the Crown would try to bribe any assembly under its authority.

17. Domenica: Dominica, island and British colony in British West Indies, mentioned in a committee resolution concerning a nonimportation policy.

18. Philadelphy: The First Continental Congress adjourned on October 26, 1774, and two days later JA left Philadelphia to return home.

19. 2nd petition: The second petition to the king, the "olive branch petition" proposed by John Dickinson in an effort at reconciliation to head off independence. JA saw it as a delaying tactic and was extremely disappointed when Congress approved it in July 1775 and sent it to the king.

20. Mr Hancock: When the Second Continental Congress convened in May 1775, JA recognized that, in addition to factional disputes over independence or loyalty to

England, there was a strong sectional division between representatives of the northern and southern colonies. To get unified support in the Congress for the army before Boston, JA decided that a Southerner should be appointed its commander. He nominated George Washington, Samuel Adams seconded, and the Congress voted its approval. But John Hancock, who was presiding officer of the Congress at the time, wanted the position of commander-in-chief for himself and was bitterly disappointed when he realized that JA had turned his back on a fellow citizen of Massachusetts.

21. **Dickenson**: John Dickinson, 1732-1808, American statesman; member of Continental Congress (1774, 1775, 1779) and delegate from Delaware to federal Constitutional Convention. In 1767 Dickinson had begun publishing *Letters from a Farmer in Pennsylvania to the Inhabitants of the British Colonies* to protest the Townshend Acts passed in the summer of 1767. But at the Continental Congress Dickinson worked tirelessly for reconciliation with England, proposed the second petition (the "olive branch petition"), and resisted independence until he saw his position decisively defeated in July 1776.

22. **alum**: JA, on January 28, 1776, noted in his diary how alum could be extracted from a certain stone found in Brookfield, Massachusetts, according to his host, Mr. Upham.

23. **yr/ladyship**: Abigail Adams, as JA addressed her in his letter of October 11, 1776, explaining that he had obtained leave from the Continental Congress to return home.

24. **Red Lion**: An inn between Philadelphia and Bristol, Pennsylvania, where JA stopped on October 13, 1776, on his way home.

25. **Bethelehem**: Bethlehem, town in Pennsylvania. Almost a year had elapsed since JA stopped at the Red Lion [cf. 24 above]. On September 19, 1777, JA and other members of the Continental Congress left Philadelphia, fearing that the city would fall to the British army commanded by Sir William Howe. During his absence JA visited the Moravian community at Bethlehem where he saw the mills and works described [II, 440].

26. **sharing house**: Pound's source reads "shearer's house."

27. **no account of the powder**: Pound's source reads "produced an account of the powder" [II, 448 n. 2].

28. **Cushing**: [62:51]. Cushing said: "I . . . winter." R. R. Livingston [33.7] said: "Ammunition cannot be had, unless we open our ports. I am for doing away our non-exportation agreement entirely." Chase [62:76] said: "We can't support the war and our taxes without trade. . . . We must trade with foreign nations . . . export our tobacco to France, Spain or any other foreign nation" [II, 453-455].

29. **Rutledge**: Edward R. [62:74]. He said: "Take . . . precarious," [II, 455]. Livingston said: "The Americans are their own carriers now, chiefly."

30. **Mr Zubly**: John Joachim Z., 1725-1781, clergyman, delegate to Continental Congress from Georgia (1775), although he was more a loyalist in sentiment than a Revolutionary. He published several political pamphlets: *The Stamp Act Repealed* (1766) and *The Law of Liberty* (1775). He said: "The navy can stop our harbors and distress our trade; therefore it is impracticable to open our ports" [II, 457]. Pound has changed the word "impracticable" to "imperative" which reverses the meaning of the line in the source.

31. **Spain**: Lee said: "Suppose provisions should be sold in Spain for money, and cash sent to England for powder." Prob. Richard Henry Lee, 1732-1794, delegate from Virginia to Continental Congress and signer of Declaration of Independence [II, 461; cf. 53 below].

32. **Livingston**: Robert R. L., member of Continental Congress [33:7]. He said: "We

are between hawk and buzzard; we puzzle ourselves between the commercial and warlike opposition" [II, 461].

33. pleased that: CFA has a headnote saying that on October 10, 1775, the Congress adopted a resolution recommending that the Convention of New Jersey raise two battalions, composed as stated in the four canto lines.

34. Who to appoint . . .: JA posed the question of appointment.

35. Personal friends: Chase [62:76] said: "In my Province, we want officers. Gentlemen have recommended persons, from personal friendships, who were not suitable" [II, 467]. Ward [Samuel W., Rhode Island delegate] said: "I would rather take the opinion of General Washington [about the appointment of officers] than of any convention" [II, 468].

36. Trade . . . houses: These seven lines are Pound's summary of the issues raised and commented on by JA in "Notes/Debates" (Oct. 10, 1775) in the Continental Congress.

37. Mr Zubly: [cf. 30 above]. The 17 lines from "Everything we want" through "*in terrorem*" [L, literally "in terror"; in law, "as a warning"] are a précis of Zubly's speech on October 12, 1775 [II, 469-470].

38. (commerciabili?): I, "for trade."

39. Deane: Silas D., 1737-1789, member of Connecticut legislature and later of Continental Congress (1774-1776); served as one of American commissioners in Paris. Charged with profiteering during this mission (1778), he was unable to clear himself and spent the rest of his life in exile. In 1842 Congress granted restitution to his heirs. As Deane's successor in Paris, JA found his records as commissioner very confusing. On October 20, 1775, Deane said: "I would have traders prohibited from importing unnecessary articles, and from exporting live stock, except horses." Chase [62:76] said: "We have letters from Guadaloupe, Martinique, and the Havana, that they will supply us with powder for tobacco."

40. Guadaloupe: Guadeloupe, name applied to two islands in French West Indies, Basse-Terre and Grande Terre; separated by a narrow channel.

41. Martinique: [28:42].

42. Jay: [62:131]. The four lines give the sense of what Jay said.

43. Wythe: George W., 1726-1806, American jurist and statesman; member of Continental Congress from Virginia (1775-76); signer of Declaration of Independence. His speech, summarized in the two lines, led to the formation of a committee which brought in a resolution: "That two more vessels be fitted out with all expedition" [II, 484n].

44. 6th April: CFA comments: "This discussion was continued from time to time until the sixth of April [1777], when the Congress came in to sundry resolutions taking off the restrictions on trade" [II, 485].

45. oblige Britain: It was JA's idea that an American navy would "oblige Britain to keep a navy on foot, the expense of which will be double to what they will take from us."

46. FAECE . . . republica!: L, "in the dung of Romulus, not in Plato's republic!" [cf. Cicero, *Epp. ad Atticum* II, i, 8]. Wythe [cf. 43 above] used the Cicero quotation and gave the substance of the next five lines, except that he said: "By inviting foreign powers [not "powders"] to make treaties of commerce with us" [II, 486].

47. Bristol: Port city, Gloucestershire, England.

48. Liverpool: Port city, Lancashire, England.

49. Resolved . . . sail cloth: The Continental Congress adopted four different resolutions embodying the sense of these seven lines.

50. France: From JA's notes for a speech given on March 1, 1776. He adds to the question Pound uses in the canto line: ". . . to join with Britain, or to join with the Colonies? Is it not her interest to dismember the British empire?" [II, 488].

51. Resentment . . . without it: From JA's notes for a speech given on March 4, 1776.

52. Hooper: William H., 1742-1790, member of Continental Congress (1774-1777) and signer of Declaration of Independence.

53. Lee: Richard Henry L., 1732-1794, American statesman; with Patrick Henry and Thomas Jefferson he initiated the intercolonial Committees of Correspondence (1773); delegate from Virginia to Continental Congress (1774-1780) where he supported JA's proposal to negotiate a treaty with France; signer of Declaration of Independence; again a member of Congress (1784-1789); member of Senate (1789-1792).

54. Sherman: Roger S., 1721-1793, American jurist and statesman; judge of Connecticut superior court (1766-1767; 1773-1788); member of Continental Congress (1774-1782; 1784) where he supported JA's proposal to negotiate a treaty with France; signer of Declaration of Independence; member of House of Representatives (1789-1791) and of Senate (1791-1793).

55. Gadsden: Christopher G., 1724-1805, American Revolutionary leader; delegate from South Carolina to Continental Congress (1774-1776) where he supported JA's proposal to negotiate a treaty with France; served as brigadier general in Continental Army (1776-1778).

56. Rush: Benjamin R., ?1745-1813, American physician and political leader; member of Continental Congress from Pennsylvania (1776-77) and signer of Declaration of Independence; surgeon in Continental Army (1777-78); member of Pennsylvania Constitutional Ratification Convention (1787); treasurer of U.S. mint (1797-1813). JA, in a letter dated August 6, 1822, is relating his memory of events leading up to the Declaration of Independence. He wrote that he and some friends met Rush and the others listed with him here on a trip from Massachusetts to Philadelphia. During that meeting Rush told him of the rumors being spread that the Sons of Liberty in Boston were being represented "as four desperate adventurers" [II, 512-515n].

57. Franklin: Pound's addition; Benjamin Franklin is not mentioned as being present in the source [II, 512n]. Pound appears to have transcribed *Frankfort*, the place where Dr. Rush, Mr. Mifflin, and Mr. Bayard met the Massachusetts delegation, as *Franklin*.

58. Bayard: John Bukenheim B., 1738-1807, Philadelphia merchant; colonel in Philadelphia Volunteers during Revolution; member of Continental Congress (1785-86).

59. Mifflin: Thomas M., 1744-1800, American Revolutionary officer and statesman; member of Continental Congress from Pennsylvania (1774-1776; 1782-1784) and its president (1783); aide-de-camp to General Washington (1775) and later major general; member of Constitutional Convention (1787).

60. Mr Jefferson . . . slavery: These six lines are from JA's recollections, in a letter written to Timothy Pickering on August 6, 1822, of how the Declaration of Independence came to be written by Thomas Jefferson and approved in its present form by the Continental Congress.

61. Board of War: Special committee selected by the Continental Congress and headed by JA in the summer and fall of 1776 to act as intermediary between Congress and the military. It was activated by a resolution adopted on September 18, 1775. JA said it kept him "in continual employment . . . from the 12th of June, 1776, till the 11th of November, 1777, when I left Congress forever." The board was charged specifically to do the things listed, beginning with "To contract . . ." [III, 3, 6].

62. had conversed . . . plundah': Letters from London prompted the Congress, on October 5, 1775, to appoint a committee of three "to prepare a plan for intercepting two vessels . . . on their way to Canada, laden with arms and powder." JA says that his experience talking with the fishermen in New England convinced him that "if they were once let loose upon the ocean, they would contribute greatly to the relief of our wants, as well as to the distress of the enemy." JA was all for such action. Those who opposed the idea used the argument that its implementation would have a bad effect on the words and characters of the seamen [II, 6, 7].

63. Lord Howe: Richard H., 1726-1799, 4th Viscount and 1st Earl; British naval officer who fought in American Revolution (1776-1778). JA made this remark to Lord Howe at the Staten Island Conference held September 11, 1776, to which JA, Benjamin Franklin, and Edward Rutledge had been sent by the Congress. Nothing came of the conference.

64. 88 battalions: The numerous resolutions recorded in the journal "contain the whole plan of an army of eighty-eight battalions, to be enlisted as soon as possible, to serve during the war" [III, 82n; CFA's editorial note].

65. dash: John Langdon, 1741-1819; member of Continental Congress from New Hampshire (1775-76; 1786-87). Langdon enjoyed profitable business connections as long as Silas Deane was commissioner in Paris, so he regretted the decision of Congress to recall Deane and send JA in his place.

66. Ray de Chaumont: Donatien le Ray de C., who in 1778 donated his house at Passy to the American legation in Paris. He was influential and friendly toward the American Revolution and contributed supplies to American forces, but in his relationship with Silas Deane he encouraged private profiteering.

67. (1804): The year JA wrote his *Autobiography*, from which Pound has taken the lines referring to JA's visit to Lord Howe and the affairs of Langdon, Deane, and Ray de Chaumont [III, 91-92].

68. Capn Sam Tucker: Samuel T., 1747-1833, American naval officer; as captain of the *Franklin* and the *Hancock* he preyed on British shipping during the Revolution; he was commander of the frigate *Boston* which carried JA to his post as commissioner to France (1778).

69. W. Vernon: William V., 1719-1806, American merchant; in 1777 appointed chairman of the Navy Board of the Eastern Department.

70. J. Warren: James W., 1726-1808, Massachusetts political leader; paymaster general of Continental Army (1775-76); member of Navy Board (1776-1781); member of Massachusetts governor's council (1792-1794). His wife was Mercy Warren. He and Vernon signed the orders to Captain Tucker about the treatment of JA.

71. Navy Board: Navy Board of the Eastern Department, the American Continental Navy Board of Direction, established in Boston (1777) upon the recommendation of JA.

72. Sunday 15th: Date in February 1778 on which the *Boston* set sail. On the 19th Captain Tucker saw three large ships "bearing east, standing to the northward." He changed his course to see if they were chasing him. They were.

73. Smoke . . . : JA's comment about "mal de mer."

74. in calm . . . etcetera: Captain Tucker prepared to fight. JA notes: "[He] said his orders were to carry me to France, and to take any prizes that might fall in his way; he thought it his duty . . . to avoid fighting, especially with an unequal force, if he could, but if he could not avoid an engagement, he would give them something that should make them remember him." The *Boston* lost sight of the enemy who did not seem "very ardent to overtake" the Americans. "But the wind increased to a hurricane" [III, 99]. The next 17 lines concern the effects of the hurricane. Pound interpolates the line "ane blasterend . . . ding" taken from the *Aeneid*, trans. Gavin Douglas.

75. Mr Johnnie: John Quincy Adams. JA took his eldest son, then 11, with him on his first journey to Europe in 1778, where he would act as his father's secretary, making copies of letters and duplicates of dispatches.

76. inexpressible . . . noise: These 11 lines are from JA's diary which contains a detailed criticism of the ship and its management. In fact, JA gave Captain Tucker a number of memos about how to run a ship and the captain followed them [III, 101-105].

77. What . . . army?: JA resolved that when he arrived "at any port in Europe" he would inquire first about the enemy: ". . . what is the state of the British nation? . . . what the state of finances and of stocks?" [III, 105-106].

78. So that . . . head: On Tuesday, March 9, Captain Tucker "spied a sail." He asked JA for permission to give chase "which was immediately granted." In his diary JA wrote: ". . . we soon came up with her; but as we had borne directly down upon her, she had not seen our broadside, and knew not our force. She was a letter of marque, with fourteen guns, eight nines, and six sixes. She fired upon us. . . . I happened to be upon the quarter deck . . . so that the ball went directly over my head. We, upon this, turned our broadside, which the instant she saw, she struck" [III, 108-109].

79. Tucker: CFA has a footnote about the story Captain Tucker told years later, a story that had doubtless "improved" with age. When he started to give chase to the enemy ship Tucker stipulated that JA would have to stay below in a safe place. "But no sooner had the battle commenced, than he was seen on deck, with a musket in his hands, fighting as a common marine." Ordered below again, JA still would not behave. When the captain's back was turned, he resumed firing until finally Tucker said: "Why are you here, sir? I am commanded by the Continental Congress to carry you in safety to Europe, and I will do it" [III, 109n].

80. The Martha: English merchant ship, commanded by Captain McIntosh, which was captured (1778) by the *Boston*. It was loaded with a valuable cargo. Thus it was that the captain and four of his men were taken prisoners on the *Boston*, and the *Martha* was dispatched to Boston as a war prize with the consent of JA, who said in his diary: "The Captain is very much of a gentleman" [III, 109].

81. Oleron: Île d'Oléron, island in Bay of Biscay at mouth of Charente River in France; noted for its Laws of Oléron, a medieval code of maritime laws which forms the basis of modern maritime law. JA wrote of his landfall in Europe: "We have been becalmed all day in sight of Oléron" [*Diary*, March 29, 1778].

82. Bordeaux, at Blaye: Major port city on Gironde estuary; Blaye-et-Sainte-Luce is a village N of Bordeaux on the Gironde. JA wrote in his diary: "My first inquiry should be, who is Agent for the United States of America at Bordeaux, at Blaye, &c" [III, 116].

83. de lonh: P, "far-off." From a song by Jaufre Rudel [cf. *SR*, 42].

84. First dish . . . coops: These seven lines concern a dinner JA was invited to by the captain of a French ship in port bound for St. Domingue [III, 117].

85. the King: Louis XVI of France.

86. 4 sorts: Someone told JA that of "the first growths of wines in the Province of Guienne there are four sorts," and Pound lists them [III, 118].

87. fish and bean salad . . . : Source reads: . . . we had fish and bread, and salad. . . ." JA was invited to dine with a Mr. McCreery "in the fashion of the country." After dinner they went to the opera [III, 118].

88. Trompette: Chateau near Bordeaux visited by JA on April 2, 1778.

89. Vauban: Sébastien Le Prestre, Marquis de V., 1633-1707, French military engineer; commissary general of fortifications (1678); marshal of France (1703).

90. Louis XV: [64:5].

91. Malesherbes: Chrétien Guillaume de Lamoignon de M., 1721-1794, French statesman and writer on politics and law; banished by Louis XV but recalled (1774) by Louis XVI; minister of the interior (1775-76). Here the premier-president of the Parliament of Bordeaux has told JA that he sympathizes with all who suffer in the cause of liberty, since he himself had been banished because of his cooperation with Malesherbes in the reign of Louis XV [III, 119].

92. 'Les deux avares': A play by Fenouillot de Falbaire de Quingey (1770), which JA saw on April 2, 1778, while in Bordeaux.

93. Lights in the garden . . . : The people of Bordeaux gave a garden party to honor JA before his departure. It was "beautifully illuminated." The source reads: "God save the Congress, Liberty and Adams." The caps and curve are Pound's idea.

94. Their eagerness . . . : As JA passed through Châtellerault on his way to Paris, his carriage stopped for a change of horses and was immediately surrounded by young women selling knives and scissors [III, 121].

95. Rue Richelieu: Rue de Richelieu, street in Paris, runs past the Bibliothèque Nationale and the Palais Royal to the Louvre.

96. Hôtel de Valois: Hotel in Paris on the Rue de Richelieu where JA stayed upon his arrival in Paris.

97. Basse Cour: The house in Passy, formerly the Hôtel de Valentinois, donated to the American ministers (1778) by Donatien le Ray de Chaumont. Benjamin Franklin lived there, and JA, aware of the reputation of Silas Deane, observed: "Although Mr. Deane, in addition to these [apartments and furniture], had a house, furniture, and equipage, in Paris, I determined to put my country to no further expense on my account, but to take my lodgings under the same roof with Dr. Franklin, and to use no other equipage than his, if I could avoid it" [III, 123].

98. Mr Schweighauser: John Daniel S., U.S. commercial agent at Nantes. JA found the records and affairs of the commissioners charged with making military and other supplies in total disarray; there were few if any financial records. One of his first projects was to bring order out of chaos and establish legitimate business records. Thus he wrote a series of letters to people who demanded money and put them off unless they could produce documents.

99. Lee: Arthur L., 1740-1792, American diplomat; appointed in 1776 by the Continental Congress as one of the three commissioners to negotiate a treaty with France; becoming suspicious of his associates, Benjamin Franklin and Silas Deane, Lee circulated charges against them. After the treaty was signed (1778) Deane was recalled; he charged in return that Lee did not have the confidence of the French foreign minister. Lee was then recalled in 1779. Lee served in the Continental Congress (1781-1785), was a member of the Treasury Board (1784-1789), and opposed the adoption of the Constitution. But since JA and he agreed about settling accounts, Franklin joined in signing the letters.

100. J. Williams: Jonathan W., 1750-1815, American diplomat and army officer; lived abroad from 1776 to 1785 and acted at times as a purchasing agent for the colonies; superintendent of West Point (1805-1812). He was the grandnephew of Benjamin Franklin. This and the preceding reference reflect JA's concern that the financial records of the American commissioners, in some disarray as a result of the dealings of Silas Deane and, JA thought, the carelessness of Benjamin Franklin, be put in order as promptly as possible.

101. Mr Beaumarchais: [31:29].

102. Madame Helvetius: Anne Catherine H., 1719-1800, Countess of Ligniville d'Autricourt; wife of Claude Adrien Helvétius, French philospher.

103. Long Champ: Longchamp, racecourse in Bois de Boulogne, Paris, which JA visited on April 17, 1778. An annual parade of carriages took place there on Good Friday; the practice started because the theaters were closed for the week before Easter and fashionable people became "*si ennuyés* "so bored" that they cannot live" [III, 133].

104. descent: Pound's source reads "decent" [III, 136]. The word is used to describe the family of Mr. Ferdinand Grand, a Protestant from Switzerland who lived near JA at Passy and who, JA discovered, had "obtained the reputation and emolument of being the banker to the American ministers" [III, 136].

105. M. Condorcet: [31:37]. On April 20, 1778, JA dined at the home of the Duchesse d'Enville, whose guests included nobles, abbots, and M Condorcet. JA supposed his whiteness came from hard study.

106. Bancroft: Edward B., 1744-1821, American scientist and secret agent. During the American Revolution he served as a secret agent for the American commissioners in Paris and as a double agent for the British. In view of what is now known about Bancroft, JA's fear of spies in Paris proves to have been well founded [Van Doren, op. cit.].

107. the Lees: The brothers Arthur Lee, American diplomat, and William Lee (1739-1795), American merchant and diplomat. William Lee was appointed U.S. commercial agent in France (1777); negotiated a commercial treaty, never ratified, with Holland (1778); recalled by Congress (1779).

108. Voltaire: Assumed name of François Marie Arouet (1694-1778), French philosopher. On April 27, 1778, JA attended a performance of Voltaire's *Alzire* and found himself seated near Voltaire.

109. Mme la Duchesse d'Agen: Henriette-Anne-Louise d'Aguesseau de Fresne, Duchesse d'Ayen, wife of Jean François Paul de Noailles. F, "Madame the Duchess d'Agen has five or six children contrary to the custom of the country." Source reads: "Mme la Duchesse d'Ayen a cinq ou six enfans, contre la coutume de ce pays çi" [III, 149].

110. des Noailles: Distinguished French family; head of the family during the time JA was in France was Philippe de Noailles, duc de Mouchy, 1715-1794, marshal of France; he was guillotined in 1794. The Marquis de Lafayette represented this family in the American Revolution, serving under General Washington. For faithful service to the Crown of France the Noailles family received "eighteen millions of livres [pounds, not louis d'or] annually from the crown" [III, 149].

111. The King's bed chamber: JA's first audience with Louis XVI of France, May 8, 1778, at Versailles.

112. Mr Deane: Silas D., 1737-1789, American diplomat and commercial representative in France in 1776 [cf. 39 above].

113. Many other qualities: JA's characterization of the French people: "There was a sort of morality. There was a great deal of humanity, and what appeared to me real benevolence. Even their politeness was benevolence. There was a great deal of charity and tenderness for the poor. There were many other qualities that I could not distinguish from virtues" [III, 171].

114. His Majesty: Louis XVI of France.

115. Offer to make 200 peers: Refers to a letter delivered anonymously to the American commissioners in Paris, interpreted as expressing sentiments of King George III of England, recommending that America be governed by a congress of American peers appointed by the king.

116. Mme du Barry: Marie Jeanne Bécu, 1743-1793, Comtesse Du Barry, mistress of Louis XV of France. On July 17, 1778, JA strolled to the house of Madame Du Barry but did not visit her because of the late hour.

117. Turgot: [31:35]. On November 26, 1778, after dining with the abbés Chalut and Arnous, JA returned to Passy to find Turgot, Condillac, and Mme. Helvétius present.

118. Condillac: Étienne Bonnot de C., 1715-1780, French philosopher.

119. Mme Helvetius: [102 above].

120. M. Genet: Edmé-Jacques Genêt, 1715-1781, head of Bureau of Correspondence of French Department of Foreign Affairs (1762). He was a close friend when JA was in France, and he supported American independence, editing, with help from Benjamin Franklin and, later, from JA, *Affaires de l'Angleterre et de l'Amerique* (1776-1779). His son, Edmond Charles Genêt (1763-1834), succeeded his father in the French foreign office; but when Edmond came to the U.S. as first minister of the French Republic (1793), calling himself "Citizen Genêt," he behaved so intemperately that the Washington administration demanded his recall to France.

121. Barbier de Séville: Play by Beaumarchais, first presented in 1775, which JA saw performed on April 14, 1779, in Nantes, where he had stopped on his way home.

122. Comédie: Theater in Nantes.

123. electrical eel: While at Nantes waiting to sail for home, JA enjoyed dinner talk: "At dinner, much conversation about the electrical eel, which gives a shock to a ring of persons, like the touch of a bottle or conductor. What is the name of this fish?" [III,199].

124. P. Jones: John Paul J., 1747-1792, naval officer serving America during the Revolution. JA met him at Nantes in May 1779. Between the line about Jones's voice and the next canto line much happened. JA returned to the U.S. on the French frigate, the *Sensible*, arriving at Boston on August 2, 1779. On the 9th JA was chosen to represent Braintree at the convention called to frame a constitution for Massachusetts. After he served at the convention, he sailed again on the *Sensible* for Europe on November 13. The ship, leaking badly from damage in heavy weather, reached El Ferrol (near Corunna) in Galicia, Spain, on December 8 [III, 229, headnote; 229-231].

125. Visigoths: West Goths; founded kingdom in Spain, S France, and N Africa.

126. Justinian: J. I, 483-565, Byzantine emperor (527-565). His greatest accomplishment, codification of Roman law, called *Corpus Juris Civilis*, was done under his direction by Tribonian. This code and the "Laws of the Visigoths" were mentioned to JA by the French consul from Corunna, M Detournelles, who had come to El Ferrol to welcome JA and who extended to him and his party, including his sons John Quincy and Charles, many kindnesses during their stay in Corunna.

127. Galicia: Region and ancient kingdom in NW Spain.

128. Corunna: Seaport-commune of La Coruña Province in NW Spain from which JA began his overland journey to Paris on December 26, 1779. The canto lines from here to the middle of page 375 are JA's notes and reflections, recorded in his diary, on people, places, and things seen on this trip, which lasted ca. six weeks.

129. Chief Justice: President of the Sovereign Court of Galicia at Corunna whom JA visited on December 19.

130. la Belle Poule: French frigate anchored at Corunna; JA dined aboard on Christmas Eve [III, 240].

131. Galicia: JA's description of the house he stayed at in Castillano on December 27, early on his journey through N Spain.

132. O'Brien: Lewis O'B., an Irishman

whom JA met in Lugo, Spain, on December 30.

133. St James Campostella: St. James Compostela, church in Galicia where there is a shrine to St. James, a famous objective of pilgrims during the Middle Ages. JA gave an account of St. James in his diary entry for December 28 and wrote of meeting the Irishman O'Brien near the Lugo cathedral on the 30th, but he nowhere mentions Compostela. Pound added the word to complete the identification. Since the shrine was supposed to be the sepulcher of St. James, Pound may have visited it during the brief period he was acting as a tourist guide in Spain in 1906.

134. Frontenac: Prob. Frontignac, a French muscatel of the Pyrenees region.

135. Leon: Region in NW Spain comprising modern provinces of Léon, Salamanca, and Zamora. On New Year's Eve, 1779, JA wrote in his diary: "We are now on the highest ground of all, and within gun-shot of the line between Galice and Leon" [III, 245].

136. Valcaire: Valcarce, river in Léon Province, Spain, which JA described in his diary on January 1, 1780.

137. Astorga: Town in Léon Province, NW Spain, which JA reached on January 3, 1780.

138. Mauregato: Town near Astorga, Spain.

139. Hoy mismo . . . tomaron: S, "Today have arrived at this square the knight / John Adams member / etc. / the Englishmen evacuating Rhode Island / the Americans took over" [III, 247].

140. Gazette de Madrid: While in Astorga JA was shown a copy of this newspaper containing the preceding passage.

141. Asturias: Mountainous region, NW Spain, described by JA in his diary on January 5.

142. Burgos: [3:16]. JA arrived here on January 11.

143. French consul: Detournelles, French consul at Corunna who took care of JA's party in December 1779.

144. Charent: Charente River, W France, which flows into the Bay of Biscay. JA noted that this river runs by the town of Angoulême, France, which his party passed by on February 4, 1780.

145. Vergennes: [41:45]. When JA arrived in Paris in February 1780, he carried with him two commissions from the Congress, one to negotiate a peace and the other to make a treaty of commerce with England. JA consulted Comte de Vergennes about making the commissions public, and Vergennes advised him to announce the peace commission but to keep the commerce commission secret. JA accepted the suggestion but refused to honor Vergennes's request that JA show him his instructions from Congress. JA believed that both commissions should be made known to the British and that Vergennes wanted to keep the U.S. "embroiled with England as much, and as long as possible," and to make the U.S. as dependent on France as possible. Only with the signing of the controversial Jay's Treaty with England (1794) was there to be normalization of trade with England, in JA's opinion. Vergennes's success in frustrating JA's efforts to be recognized in his full capacity as commissioner led JA to journey to Holland on his own initiative in the summer of 1780 in an effort to achieve an alliance there that would make the U.S. less dependent upon France. [III, 265].

146. John . . . Baastun: Pound's comment about the effect of JA's success in extending US territorial rights to include the Atlantic fishing grounds.

147. Those who wish to investigate: JA thought that the members of the Continental Congress who had decided that American negotiation of a commerce treaty with England should be guided by the will of the French should be identified.

148. Amsterdam: [62:88]. On July 27,

1780, JA, with his sons John Quincy and Charles, set off for Amsterdam. At this time JA did not know that on June 20 Congress had commissioned him to seek a loan in the Netherlands.

149. **rye, barley etc.**: These five lines are from JA's account of what he saw while traveling to Brussels.

150. **Italian style**: On a visit to the cathedral in Brussels JA saw a picture in a tapestry "of a number of Jews stabbing the wafer, the *bon Dieu*, and blood gushing in streams from the bread. This insufferable piece of pious villany [sic] shocked me beyond measure; but thousands were before it, on their knees, adoring" [III, 268].

151. **excellent character**: Prince Charles, brother of the empress queen; uncle of the emperor and the queen of France. "He was extremely beloved by the people, and has left an excellent character. The Emperor did not like him, it is said" [III, 268].

152. **Van der Capellen tot de Pol**: [62:93]. In his diary [Jan. 14, 1781] JA noted Van der Capellen's view that those with English funds might try to protect their holdings by making a dishonorable peace.

153. **Van Berckel**: Engelbert Francois V. B., 1726-1796, pensioner of Amsterdam and friend of the American cause against England, took part in the first negotiations for a trade treaty between America and the Netherlands (1779).

154. **Don Joas Tholomeno**: D. J. Theolomico de Almeida, envoy extraordinary of Portugal at Paris Peace Conference (1782).

155. **Mirabel**: Comte Montagnini M., minister plenipotentiary of Victor Amadeus III, king of Sardinia, who asked JA why the British were reluctant to accept the fact of American independence [*Diary*, Sept. 14, 1782; III, 273].

156. **aetat 46**: JA was 46 years of age in 1782 when the treaties he had negotiated with the Dutch were prepared for signature.

157. **Rheingrave**: Rhinegrave de Salm, one of negotiators of Treaty of Paris (1783). JA dined with him September 14, 1782, at a formal dinner at court in Holland.

158. **Colonel Bentinck**: Berent Henrik B., 1753-1830, one of Dutch negotiators of Treaty of Paris. JA attended a formal dinner at court with him on September 14, 1782.

159. **Prussian minister**: Baron de Thulemeyer, minister from Prussia at the Paris Peace Conference (1783), whom JA met in Holland.

160. **Verjaring ... Natie**: Source reads "van" for "dan" and "op" for "of." D, from passage in *Rotterdamche Courant* copied by JA into his diary [Oct. 5, 1782]. The complete passage translates as follows: "It is remarkable that the States General have recognized the independence of the United States on exactly the 19th of April of this year, this day being the seventh anniversary of the battle at Lexington, and what makes the matter still more remarkable is that Mr. Adams' First Memorial, which has made such a deep impression on the Dutch nation, is dated 19 April 1781" [Butterfield, III, 14 and n. 2].

161. **Deputies of Holland and Zeeland**: Baron de Lynden de Blitterswyk and Baron Van den Santheuvel, who met JA at the State House for the signing of the treaty with the Dutch (Oct. 8, 1782). The source says "Zealand," largest of the Danish isles. Pound corrected the source to "Zeeland," a province in SW Netherlands.

162. **firmness heaven has given you**: Spoken by the French minister in Amsterdam, the Duke de la Vauguyon, to JA, upon learning that JA had been commissioned to go to Paris for peace negotiations with England [*Diary*, Oct. 1782]. Vauguyon, under instructions from Vergennes, had earlier tried to obstruct JA's mission in Holland.

163. **Bruge**: Bruges, capital of W Flanders, NW Belgium, once a great trading city.

164. Ostend: Port city of W Flanders Province, N Belgium.

165. vingt à . . . nourri: F, "twenty to twenty-five ships in the basin / . . . warehouses [or armories] of the city are filled / a man's day (is worth) 15 sous, / including food" [source reads "16 sous." Extract from the journal of Count Sarsfield for June 5, 1782; III, 283].

166. Count Sarsfield: Guy Claude, Comte de S., 1718-1789, French military officer and amateur philosopher who sought out JA's friendship during JA's stay in Holland.

167. Œuvre . . . de Vauguyon: F, "the work of the Duke of Vauguyon." Pound's source reads "ouvrage" [III, 285].

168. 16,000 times: JA's diary [Oct. 11, 1782] reads: "Spent most of the day in signing obligations for the United States. It is hard work to sign one's name sixteen hundred [sic] times after dinner" [III, 288-289].

169. Mr Vischer: Visscher, a pensioner of the Hague, with whom JA conversed on October 15, 1782.

170. the Stadtholder: William V, 1748-1806, Prince of Orange, stadtholder of the Netherlands (1751-1795).

171. le plus . . . une: F, "the biggest t . . . of this country / stubborn as a . . ." [III, 291]. [Butterfield, III, 28 n. 1, suggests the first phrase might read *le plus grand trouble* or *le plus grand tyran*].

172. Valenciennes: City in Nord department, N France, where JA, on his journey back to Paris for peace negotiations, was forced to stop (Oct. 23, 1782) because the axletree on his carriage had broken.

173. Mlle de Bourbon: Louise Adelaide de Bourbon-Conde, 1757-1824.

174. la mode: F, "fashion." Pound's source reads: ". . . to preserve . . . national influence over the *mode*" [III, 298]. JA is complaining that upon arrival in Paris one must "send for a tailor, peruke-maker, and shoemaker . . . neither clothes, wigs, nor shoes, made in any other place, will do."

175. des Petits Augustins: Rue des Petits Augustins, Paris; the Hôtel d'Orléans, where John Jay, the third peace negotiator (with JA and Benjamin Franklin), stopped, was on this street.

176. Franklin: In his diary [Oct. 27, 1782] JA speculated on what he would find in the conduct of his two fellow negotiators, Franklin and Jay. It was Jay whom JA quoted as saying, "I will make a good peace or no peace." ". . . he will make a good peace or none" [III, 300].

177. Gulf of St. Lawrence: Gulf off E coast of Canada.

178. Nova Scotia: [63:51].

179. Cape Sable: Cape Sable Island off S tip of Nova Scotia. This and the preceding two references appear in JA's draft of a fishing rights agreement presented to the British negotiators, Richard Oswald and Henry Strachey, on November 4, 1782.

180. Tartary: In conversation with Caleb Whitefoord, secretary to Richard Oswald, British negotiator, JA discussed the possibility that winds from Tartary might carry influenza to France. He went on to explain his view of the problems the U.S. would face in foreign policy. JA subsequently presented the same ideas to Mr. Oswald [III, 307-308].

181. FISHERIES . . . you have been: These 13 lines dwell on JA's anger and frustration with France whose policy was to pressure the U.S. to give up its right to the fisheries; to attain this goal French ministers had intrigued to keep JA from carrying out his commission to negotiate a treaty of commerce with England [III, 319-320]. Interspersed are other attitudes about the French, who JA finds have traits common with certain other men: ". . . such are the objects which men pursue,–titles, ribbons, stars, garters, crosses, keys, are the important springs that move the ambition of men in high life" [III, 326]. Speculating about the tensions between France and England over the fisheries, JA wrote in his diary: ". . . had England rather France should supply the markets of Lisbon and Cadiz with fish, and take the gold and silver, than we? France would never spend any of that money in London; we should spend it all very nearly" [III, 328-329]. Note that Pound changed the word "spend" in the source to "send" in the canto line. JA also recorded in his diary a conversation with Oswald [cf. 182 below]: " 'If I have not been mistaken in the policy of France, from my first observation of it to this hour, they have been as averse to other powers acknowledging our independence as you have been.' Mr. Jay joined me in the same declaration. 'God!' says he, 'I understand it now; there is a gentleman going to London this day,–I will go home and write upon the subject by him' " [III, 347]. Perhaps the words "and send it" are intended before the words "by him." The source shows that it was Jay and not Oswald who said "God . . ." etc.

182. Oswald: Richard Oswald, English statesman. In 1782 the Shelburne ministry authorized him to conduct the final peace negotiations.

183. To exempt fishermen: From an article proposed by Franklin for inclusion in the final draft of the peace treaty.

184. The King: Gustavus III of Sweden. JA, shown a miniature of the Swedish king on a snuffbox, made this observation of a likeness between John Hancock and the king.

185. Lady Lucan: Margaret Smyth Bingham, Countess of Lucan, d. 1814; famous for her paintings; celebrated by Horace Walpole. JA copied some of her verses on England's exploitation of Ireland in his diary [Dec. 25, 1782; III, 351].

186. Connecticut constitution: Connecticut Charter, granted (1662) to John Winthrop. JA in his diary gives neither the passages that were obscure to the Duc de la Rochefoucauld nor his explanation [III, 352].

187. Mr Eliot: Eliot is not mentioned in Pound's sources. It may be that the four lines in parentheses on this canto page are cut into the canto text and concern T. S. Eliot's visit to Pound while he was writing this canto. Eliot may have listened to Pound read Lady Lucan's verses on Ireland, made no comment, but got up and left, which may have seemed to Pound a "fairly English" gesture.

188. Mr Vaughn: Benjamin Vaughan, 1751-1835, British diplomat; a friend of Franklin's, he sided with the colonists during the Revolution and unofficially promoted conciliation in the Anglo-American negotiations of 1782. He settled in America in 1796. The reference here is to whether or not England should accept the principle of liberty of navigation claimed by the "confederated neutral powers" and the Dutch. JA had argued that England should accept and Vaughan agreed, though saying that England had to try to get some advantage by holding out [III, 353].

189. Billy Franklin: William Temple F., 1762-1823, grandson of Benjamin Franklin; served as secretary to his grandfather in Paris; published editions of Franklin's works (1816-1819). Reference is to a letter Benjamin Franklin wrote recommending his grandson to Congress as a possible future candidate for ministerial appointment [III, 355].

190. Mlle Bourbon: Elizabeth B.; JA's observation after his visit to Versailles on January 21, 1783, to pay his respects to Louis XVI.

191. Chatham: William Pitt, 1st Earl of C., 1708-1778, English statesman known as "the Elder Pitt" and later as the "Great Commoner." Here Mr. Oswald's secretary,

Mr. Whitefoord, has explained to JA how a policy of Chatham's had had a bad effect on England's ally, Sardinia [III, 359].

192. Sardegna: A reference to Victor Amadeus III.

193. congress has double XX'd me: JA's reference to instructions passed by Congress and sent to the commissioners in Paris saying that they were "ultimately to govern themselves by the advice and opinion of the French Ministry" in the peace negotiations. JA defied these instructions [III, 300n, 359].

194. M. Malesherbes: Chrétien Guillaume de Lamoignou de Malesherbes: "the famous first president of the Court of Aids, uncle of the Chevalier de la Luzerne, and son of the Chancelier de Lamoignon" [III, 360].

195. Luzerne: Anne César Chevalier de la L., 1741-1791, French diplomat; ambassador to America (1779-1783); played major role in Paris Peace Conference; ambassador to England (1788-1791).

196. tiers état: F, "third estate": the people, commons.

197. Passy: In the 18th century a village NW of Paris where the American delegation to France stayed; now a fashionable section of Paris.

198. S'il . . . savoir: F, "If a false knowledge reigns" [III, 362]. JA quotes from the *Mercure de France* (Feb. 1783): ". . . s'il y regne un faux savoir, pire que l'ignorance."

199. Livingston: [33:7]. Livingston, when secretary for foreign affairs, in a letter to Franklin dated January 7, 1782, set forth details to be followed in the peace negotiations. Franklin neglected to mention the letter to JA. Only by accident over a year later, after the negotiations were completed, did JA learn about the letter. JA often expressed frustration with Franklin's cavalier way of conducting affairs.

200. Englishman Duke: George Montagu, 1737-1788, 4th Duke of Manchester, English ambassador sent to France to treat for peace (1783).

201. Hartley: David H., 1732-1813, English diplomat who, with Benjamin Franklin, drafted and signed the peace treaty between the U.S. and Great Britain in 1783. In a struggle in Holland between the Republicans (who were fighting for the liberties of the people) and the stadtholder (who was trying to maintain and broaden the powers of the elite class), England and Prussia had taken the side of the stadtholder. JA told Hartley that they were wrong and that they ought to remain neutral, for if Holland "should be annexed to the Empire or to France, it would be fatal to Great Britain." JA said the kings of England and Prussia would do well to consider that, if they supported the stadtholder, "France and the Emperor would not assist the republicans, and thus throw all Europe into a flame" [III, 369].

202. Emperor: Frederick II of Prussia [32:38].

203. commerce: JA drafted a statement recommending to the Continental Congress that a trade treaty be negotiated between England and the U.S. [III, 374].

204. Gt Britain: JA wrote in his diary [May 22, 1783]: "It was observed last evening, that all the laws of Great Britain for the regulation of the plantation trade, were contrived solely for the benefit of Great Britain" [III, 374].

205. Dutch vessels: Pound's source reads "Danish vessels." Baron de Waltersdorf, chamberlain of the king of Denmark, told JA this as evidence of the potential growth of trade between Europe and the U.S. [III, 376].

206. Sardinian ambassador: This remark, made by Comte Montagnini Mirabel to JA at Versailles on June 17, 1783, emphasizes the illogicality of some commercial arrangements: furs from Hudson Bay end up in

Siberia, a short 150 leagues from where they started, but first they twice travel halfway around the world, to London and back. Thus the canto closes by calling attention to a major aspect of JA's role in the treaty negotiations: his bitter contest with the French ministry to speak directly for his country's interests in a commerce agreement along with his tireless insistence on an agreement that would bring reasonable and appropriate benefits to both England and the U.S. [III, 380].

CANTO LXVI

Sources

Charles Francis Adams, ed., *The Works of John Adams*, III; Frederick K. Sanders, *John Adams Speaking*, Orono, Maine, 1975, 265-301.

Background

Catherine Drinker Bowen, *John Adams and the American Revolution*, Boston, 1950; Peter Shaw, *The Character of John Adams*, Chapel Hill, N.C., 1974; Page Smith, *John Adams*, 2 vols., Garden City, N.Y., 1962; Marie (Goebel) Kimball, *Jefferson: The Scene of Europe, 1784 to 1789*, New York, 1950, chap. vii; L.H. Butterfield, ed., *Diary and Autobiography of John Adams*, III, Cambridge, Mass., 1961.

Exegeses

CE, *Ideas*, 43, 176-177; EH, *Approaches*, 14; CB-R, *ZBC*, 240.

Glossary

1. Could not . . . seamen: In a conversation with the duc de la Vauguyon on June 18, 1783, JA continued to explore future trade relations between the U.S. and the countries of Europe. The duke's response here is to JA's question about whether the French will permit American ships to carry goods from French islands in the West Indies and the Atlantic to Europe [III, 381]. Source does not mention Spanish seamen.

2. (Bois de Boulogne): In September 1783 JA moved into Thomas Barclay's home at Auteuil, just outside Paris. Nearby was the Bois de Boulogne, a large park containing the Longchamp racetrack. From his bedchamber at Auteuil JA could see the village of Issy and the chateau of Meudon, built by Louis XIV, surrounded by the Forêt de Meudon [III, 383].

3. **Amiens**: Manufacturing city in Somme department, N France, where JA dined on his journey to London with JQA in October 1783.

4. **Abbeville**: Commune in Somme department, N France, where JA and JQA stayed the night of October 21 on their journey to London.

5. **Dover**: On October 24 JA reached Dover and climbed up the cliffs, noting the nature of the soil. Once at the top he looked down and saw "the whole town and harbor of Dover" [III, 386].

6. **Mr Johnson**: Joshua J., 1742-1802, American merchant who settled in England before the Revolution. During the Revolution he lived for a time in Nantes where he undertook commissions for the Congress; he returned to London after the Revolution, where he served as the first U.S. consul (1790-1797). He was the father of Louisa Catherine, who married John Quincy Adams in 1797.

7. **Gt Tower Hill**: Joshua Johnson, after he returned from Nantes, took up residence in Cooper's Row, Great Tower Hill. JA used Johnson's residence as his mailing address during his visit to London in late 1783.

8. **Messrs Willin(c)k(s)**: [62:107].

9. **Hague**: The Hague, Netherlands. In January 1784 JA made a perilous journey from London to Holland to save American credit by negotiating a second loan with the Dutch. He remained in the Netherlands through the summer of 1784 while Congress debated his future service in Europe. At length Congress took the side of JA's supporters rather than that of Benjamin Franklin and Thomas Jefferson, allowing him to negotiate treaties of amity and commerce with 23 foreign governments. JA's diary for June 22, 1784, concludes with the mention of treaties previously negotiated with France (Feb. 6, 1778), Holland (Oct. 7, 1782), Great Britain (Sept. 3, 1783), and Sweden (ca. April 3, 1783).

10. **Ambassador**: A foreign ambassador at Versailles, upon learning that JA would be the first U.S. ambassador to England, asked him on May 3, 1785, if he was of English extraction. JA replied that since no member of his family had lived in England for 150 years, he had "not one drop of blood in my veins but what is American." The ambassador answered, "Ay, we have seen proof enough of that," an answer that flattered JA [III, 392].

11. **Sends to Morocco**: In a conversation with JA at Versailles on March 20, 1785, the Comte de Vergennes made this observation about France's trading policy with Morocco (III, 391]. Butterfield suggests that *glaces* should be *glasses* (looking glasses) [III, 175 n.2].

12. **Lord Carmathen . . . often**: Words spoken to JA by the Duke of Dorset, British ambassador in Paris, on May 3, 1785, in a conversation about JA's new assignment as minister to the Court of St. James.

13. **Lord Carmathen**: Carmarthen Francis Osborne, 1751-1799, 5th Duke of Leeds, known until 1789 as Marquis of Carmarthen. As foreign secretary under Pitt (1783-1791), he introduced JA to King George III of England.

14. **Mr Pitt**: William, "the Younger Pitt," 1759-1806, English statesman; prime minister (1783-1801, 1804-1806).

15. **Presq' isle**: Presque Isle, once a military fort in N Maine controlled by the British in Canada. Source reads "Presqu' Isle."

16. **Sandusky**: Once a military fort on Sandusky Bay in N Ohio controlled by the British.

17. **Detroit Michilimakinac**: Two installations, one at Detroit and the other on the Straits of Mackinac in the far N of Michigan.

18. St Joseph: Military fort on the Great Lakes once controlled by the British.

19. St Mary's: Military fort on the Great Lakes. The names of these forts (Presq' isle . . . St. Mary's) appear on a memorandum JA wrote in his diary on May 9 or 16, 1785. They were forts in American territory which the British continued to occupy in violation of the 1783 Treaty of Paris. The question of British occupation of the forts was not finally resolved until the signing of Jay's Treaty in 1794.

20. daughter married: On March 26, 1786, JA dined with Jonathan Shipley, bishop of Saint Asaph's, who was a friend of Benjamin Franklin's and of the colonial cause many years earlier. Mrs. Shipley made the remark about her daughter on this occasion.

21. Mr Hamilton: William H., 1745-1813, wealthy Pennsylvanian whose house near Philadelphia JA would later occupy when the federal government established itself at Philadelphia in 1790. JA presented him to the queen "at the drawing-room" on March 30, 1786 [III, 393].

22. the Queen: Charlotte Sophia, 1744-1818, wife of George III of England.

23. Mr Jefferson: In March 1786 Thomas Jefferson, who had succeeded Benjamin Franklin as minister to Versailles a year earlier, joined JA in London to conclude treaties of commerce with Portugal, Tripoli, and Great Britain. Early in April 1786, while in England, Jefferson joined JA on a tour of the famous estates and gardens on the Thames and its tributaries W of London.

24. Woburn Farm: Estate near Weybridge, Surrey, belonging at the time to Lord Peters, visited by JA and Jefferson on their second day out of London. Jefferson was later to incorporate certain characteristics of the gardens at Woburn Farm in his plans for Monticello.

25. Stowe: Estate belonging to the Marquis of Buckingham, in Buckinghamshire, whose gardens were widely known in Georgian England; JA and Jefferson visited Stowe on April 6, 1786.

26. Stratford: Stratford on Avon, Warwickshire, England, birthplace of William Shakespeare; visited by JA and Jefferson on April 6.

27. Stourbridge: Lord Lyttelton's seat at Hagley was near Stourbridge, Worcester; JA and Jefferson visited Hagley on April 8.

28. Woodstock: Municipal borough in Oxfordshire; Blenheim Palace, which JA and Jefferson visited on April 9, is near Woodstock.

29. High Wycombe: Municipal borough in Buckinghamshire, SE central England, visited by JA and Jefferson on their return journey to London.

30. Grosvenor Sq.: Fashionable square in London; residence of JA when he was in London as minister to the Court of St. James's.

31. Pope: On the first day of their tour JA and Jefferson visited Twickenham, Alexander Pope's famous residence and garden on the Thames.

32. Thompson: James Thomson, 1700-1748, Scottish poet, author of *The Seasons* (1726-1730).

33. Shenstone: William S., 1714-1763, English poet who developed Leasowes, one of the earliest landscape gardens in England; JA and Jefferson visited Leasowes in April 1786.

34. Lexington: [33:18].

35. Child: A descendant of Samuel Child, son of Sir Francis Child, 1642-1713, banker and lord mayor of London. The Child family seat at Osterly Park, Heston, Middlesex, was visited by JA and his family, accompanied by Jefferson, on April 20, 1786. The interior of the house was a famous example of the work of the brothers Adam.

36. Dr. Grey: Edward Whitaker G., botanist and keeper of natural history collections and antiquities at the British Museum, which JA visited on April 24, 1786 [Butterfield, III, 191 n.1].

37. **Buffon**: Georges Louis Leclerc, Comte de B., 1707-1788, French naturalist.

38. **Mr H.**: Thomas Brand-Hollis, 1719-1804, English friend of JA's and a sympathizer with republican forms of government. He inherited the property of Thomas Hollis, benefactor of Harvard College, and added his benefactor's name to his own. JA and his family visited Brand-Hollis's country seat, the Hyde, in Essex, on July 24, 1786.

39. **Palladio**: [40:27].

40. **July 18th**: Pound's source reads "Quincy July 12." The year is 1796. Ten years have elapsed between this line and the preceding one. JA returned from Europe in 1788 and was elected vice-president for two terms with Washington. Although he was quite interested in the election in November 1788, most of his diary entries concern details of farm management at Quincy to which he had returned from Philadelphia in mid-May. Source reads: "mowed all the grass" [III, 416].

41. **Stony Hill**: Stony-field Hill, part of Stony Acres, JA's property in Braintree, Mass.

42. **this day**: July 13, 1796. This line, the preceding one, and the twelve that follow refer to the summer of 1796, before the election that was to bring JA the presidency and after the controversy in Congress concerning Jay's Treaty.

43. **T.**: Prob. Thomas Trask, one of JA's farmhands at Braintree.

44. **Otis**: Samuel Allyne O., 1740-1814, American statesman; member of Constitutional Convention; secretary of U.S. Senate (1789-1814). Otis dined with JA on July 16, 1796, and reported the maneuverings of both Federalists and Republicans to secure the successor to George Washington [III, 417].

45. **Henry**: Patrick H. He, with Jefferson and Aaron Burr, was interested in the coming election, all three jockeying for power and position [31:46].

46. **leaves of white oaks**: Pound's source reads "leaves only the white oaks" [III, 419].

47. **To barley**: JA's inspection of his farm on July 23, 1796.

48. **Rhode Island**: On August 10-11, 1796, David Howell from Rhode Island, former member of the Continental Congress, visited JA to discuss his commission to settle the boundary dispute between the U.S. and Canada called for by Jay's Treaty; while at Braintree he reported the latest gossip about the coming election.

49. **Hamilton**: [62:144]. David Howell told JA the "funding system" would make Rhode Islanders unanimous in choosing President Washington's successor. He also said that "they wanted Hamilton for Vice-President." JA adds: "I was wholly silent" [III, 423].

50. **Wheretoward . . .** : This and the following six lines come from the concluding pages of JA's *Dissertation on the Canon and the Feudal Law* (1765), in which he attacked the Stamp Act as a contemporary example of "feudal" oppression [III, 460-464].

51. **Runing Mede**: Runnymede, meadow on S bank of Thames in Surrey, S England, where King John signed the Magna Charta in 1215.

52. **Prince of Orange**: King William III, 1650-1702, king of England (1689-1702). JA refers to the Glorious Revolution of 1688 in which the Parliament deposed James II and made William of Orange king to protect the rights of the people from Stuart authoritarianism.

53. **James Second**: 1633-1701, king of Great Britain and Scotland (1685-1688); deposed in the Glorious Revolution.

54. **Thos. Hollis**: Thomas H., 1720-1774,

English student of political philosophy and an ardent supporter of republican principles. In 1765 he arranged for the publication of JA's *Dissertation on the Canon and the Feudal Law* in England, erroneously attributing the work to Jeremiah Gridley, as many citizens of Massachusetts had done on its first appearance. When he discovered the true author of the work, Hollis publicly corrected his error.

55. Ob Pecuniae Scars[c]itatem: L, "On account of the scarcity of money" [42:41]. In his "Braintree Instructions," written to explain the objections of the town of Braintree to the Stamp Act and printed in the *Boston Gazette* [Oct. 14, 1765], JA used an English form of this phrase: "considering the present scarcity of money" [III, 465]. Since England required that taxes be paid in specie [metal], one of the colonies' chief concerns was the effect on commerce, because in time they would have no money to do business with: " . . . for a short space of time would drain the country of its cash, strip multitudes of all their property, and reduce them to absolute beggary" [III, 465-466].

56. Stamp Act: [64:17].

57. yr / humanity . . . the subject: These 24 lines are all taken from JA's Clarendon letters; the Chinese ideogram is Pound's interpolation [cf. glosses below].

58. Earl [of] Clarendon: Pseudonym used by JA in a series of three letters sent to the *Boston Gazette* in January 1766 in answer to an article published in the *London Evening Post* [Aug. 20, 1765] and signed with the name Pym. Pym's essential argument was expressed in these words: " 'Let me inform my fellow-subjects in America, that a resolution of the British Parliament can at any time set aside all the charters that have ever been granted by our monarchs' " [III, 469].

59. Baastun Gazette: *Boston Gazette* [62:57].

60. Jan 17th 1768: Pound's source reads "13 January, 1766" [III, 469 n. 1].

61. Danegeld: OE, annual tax paid by the Britons to the Danes; continued later as a land tax. In the first of his Clarendon letters, JA found the Stamp Act similar to the Danegeld in its effects.

62. what are powers: Anticipating that the local courts might not prosecute violations of the Stamp Act, Parliament had made the penalties " 'recoverable in any court of record or in any court of admiralty in the Colony, where the offence should be committed, or in any court of vice-admiralty, which might be appointed over all America, at the election of the informer or prosecutor' " [CFA quoting from *Minot's History of Massachusetts*, II, 167-168; III, 471 n. 1].

63. per pares . . . : L, "by peers and the law of the land." A phrase used by Sir Edward Coke which JA quoted to Pym, asking by what procedure and authority the admiralty courts would decide violations of the Stamp Act. Coke had used this phrase in speaking of an act of Parliament passed in the reign of Henry VII which stated "that justices of assize, as well as justices of peace, without any finding or presentment of twelve men, upon a bare information for the king, should have full power and authority to hear and determine, by their discretions, all offences against the form, ordinance, and effect of certain penal statutes" [III, 471]. Sir Richard Empson and Edmund Dudley, made justices under the act, committed many offenses against justice until the first year of Henry VIII's reign, when Parliament declared the act unconstitutional and void; Empson and Dudley, found guilty of treason, were executed.

64. petit: JA asked Pym whether, with the new powers enjoyed by the courts of admiralty, petit juries would be needed any longer to try the facts in any Stamp Act violations and thus to determine guilt or innocence [III, 471].

65. per legem terrae: L, "by the law of the land."

66. Institutes Digest Roman: Source does not have this title but reads: "the institutes, digests, and codes and novels of the Roman law" [III, 472].

67. Become . . . just observation: JA's description to Pym of the colonists' reaction to the Stamp Act and to the nature of their liberties guaranteed by the English constitution.

68. ching ming: Chêng [M351]: "right"; Ming [M4524]: "name."

69. Jury answers . . . : In the conclusion of his third letter to Pym, JA, as Clarendon, explained the meaning of trial by jury under English law: "But by the British Constitution, *ad quæstionem facti respondent juratores*,—the jurors answer to the question of fact. In this manner, the subject is guarded in the execution of the laws. The people choose a grand jury, to make inquiry and presentment of crimes. Twelve of these must agree in finding the bill. And the petit jury must try the same fact over again, and find the person guilty, before he can be punished. Innocence, therefore, is so well protected in this wise constitution, that no man can be punished till twenty-four of his neighbors have said upon oath that he is guilty. So it is also in the trial of causes between party and party. No man's property or liberty can be taken from him till twelve men in his neighborhood have said upon oath, that by laws of his own making it ought to be taken away, that is, that the facts are such as to fall within such laws" [III, 481].

70. pompous rituals . . . as he please: These ten lines are taken from letters written by "Governor Winthrop to Governor Bradford" in January and February 1767 in response to Philanthropos (Jonathan Sewall) in a debate over (1) the value of the Puritan religion, which does not have "pompous rituals . . . to terrify," and (2) the question of whether a ruler acting through chancery should decide the legality of elections, rather than the Commons. [III, 487].

71. Elizabeth: E. I, 1533-1603, queen of England (1558-1603). JA refers to an occasion when Queen Elizabeth tried to interfere in an election.

72. James First: 1566-1625, king of Great Britain and Scotland (1603-1625).

73. Goodwin: Sir Francis G., principal of the Goodwin case (1604) in which the House of Commons asserted its right to be the sole judge of the returns in elections of its members.

74. (London Chronicle): Not the London paper established in 1757; prob. refers to the parliamentary debates and court decisions during the reign of James I.

75. Stamp Act: This and the following 20 lines are taken from the "Boston Instructions" written by JA and adopted June 17, 1768, to protest the seizure of John Hancock's sloop *Liberty* and the impressment of American seamen in violation of a law (6 Anne chap. 37, sec. 9) dated February 14, 1707 [III, 501-504; cf. 64:56].

76. Braintree: Pound's source reads "Boston" [III, 501].

77. Anne: 1665-1714, queen of England (1702-1714).

78. Her Majesty: Queen Anne.

79. St Valentine's day: February 14.

80. Governor Hutchinson: In the spring of 1769, when a number of British troops were stationed in Boston, the main guard was assigned a house across from the courthouse door and, according to Governor Hutchinson, some small cannon outside the guardhouse "*happened* to point to the door of the court house" [III, 505]. But the implied intimidation provoked the Boston town meeting to call for instructions to protest the appearance of intimidation. JA drafted the "Boston Instructions" which were adopted May 15, 1769.

81. To the Hnbl . . . recommended you: This 17-line passage is taken from JA's

"Boston Instructions" of May 15, 1769 [III, 505-510].

82. James Otis et al: Representatives of Boston in Massachusetts legislature, 1769.

83. 41st section: JA is concerned here with the jurisdiction of the courts of admiralty which he sees developing "by degrees into a system that is to overturn our constitution and to deprive us entirely of our best inheritance, the laws of the land." He adds later: " . . . in the forty-first section of the statute of the fourth [year] of George III. chap. XV. we find that 'all the forfeitures and penalties inflicted by this or any other act of parliament, relating to the trade . . . may be prosecuted, sued for, and recovered in any court of admiralty.' " Judgment was thus put into the hands of a single judge [III, 507-508].

84. Magna Charta: Not the original document now known as "The Charter of Runnymede" which the English barons forced King John to sign on June 15, 1215, at Runnymede, but a much later document Sir Edward Coke used as the basis of his work, *The Second Part of the Institutes of the Laws of England*. The later document, entitled *Magna Charta, Edita Anno Nono H. III*, is dated 1225, the ninth year of the reign of Henry III [107-109/756-774].

85. the 29th chapter: JA quotes the English translation of *Magna Charta* (1225) as given by Coke: "No freeman shall be taken or imprisoned, or disseised of his freehold or liberties or free customs or outlawed or exiled or any otherwise destroyed, nor will we pass upon him nor condemn him, but by lawful judgment of his peers or the law of the land" [III, 509]. The whole statute in *Magna Charta* has another sentence: "We will sell to no man, we will not deny or defer to any man either justice or right" [*Magna Charta*, cap. xxix; Coke's rendition, p. 45].

86. Lord Coke: [62:43]. As in his Clarendon letters to Pym the year before, JA in the "Boston Instructions" attacked the extension of the authority of the admiralty courts by quoting Edward Coke on *Magna Charta*.

87. Empson: Sir Richard E. [cf. 63 above], d. 1510; judge during the reign of Henry VII of England. Coke, in his commentary on cap. xxix of *Magna Charta*, used Empson and Dudley as examples of what can happen when judges condemn people on premises that are in defiance of the law of the land. In 11 Henry VII, Coke found an act of parliament which negated the guarantees of trial by a jury of one's peers given in *Magna Charta*. About that act, which was in force until Henry VII died, Coke said: "By colour of which act, shaking this fundamentall law, it is not credible what horrible oppressions, and exactions, to the undoing of infinite numbers of people, were committed by Sir Richard Empson knight, and Edm. Dudley." But in 1 Henry VIII, Parliament voided the act because it was against *Magna Charta*. Empson and Dudley were tried for treason, found guilty, and beheaded. Says Coke: " . . . the ill successe hereof, and the fearfull ends of these two oppressors, should deterre others from committing the like, and should admonish parliaments, that in stead of this ordinary, and pretious [precious] triall *per legem terrae*, they bring not in absolute, and partiall trialls by discretion" [*Magna Charta*, 51]. Pound's *direction* is doubtless an error for "discretion," which is found in his source [III, 509] as well as in JA's source, *Magna Charta* itself [cf. 63 above].

88. Dudley: Edmund D., ca. 1462-1510, a brilliant young man who, after studying at Oxford and Gray's Inn, was noticed by Henry VII and is said to have become a privy councillor when only 23. He and Empson assisted the king in controlling "the lawlessness of the barons" [*EB*] but in the process practiced extortion until they both amassed great wealth and became very unpopular. The two were tried for "constructive treason." In spite of Coke's interpretation, they were not found guilty on the legal issues of the charter, but on the quite different grounds of being *fiscales judices* or, in

Pound's terms, "hoggers of harvest, the curse of the people."

89. Natural tendency . . . : The lines from here to the end of the canto concern the question as to whether or not judges should receive salary grants from the Crown. The first item concerns the decision of the Cambridge, Massachusetts, town meeting on December 21, 1772, to challenge the Crown grants. The meeting adopted a motion that the Cambridge representative to the legislature should protest the policy of paying Crown salary grants to judges without the consent of the citizens of Massachusetts.

90. Andrew Boardman: Town clerk of Cambridge in 1772.

91. Judges salaries: William Brattle argued that judges should be independent of both king and people by virtue of being appointed for life.

92. common lay: Pound's source reads "common law" [III, 518].

93. Wm/Brattle: William B., 1702-1776, brigadier general in Massachusetts militia. In 1773 JA and General Brattle engaged in a debate published in the Boston newspapers; their remarks were collected under the title, *The Independence of the Judiciary*. A loyalist, Brattle went to England during the Revolution.

94. It is the wish . . . : From JA's essay in the *Boston Gazette* (Jan. 11, 1773).

95. Edward First: 1239-1307, king of England (1272-1307).

96. beneplacitu nostro: L, "in accordance with our [royal] good pleasure." Source reads "beneplacito" [III, 521].

97. Ad regis . . . : L, "To endure at the king's command." This and the following 19 lines are taken from JA's essay in the *Boston Gazette* (Jan. 18, 1773).

98. Fortescue: Sir John F., ?1394-1476?, English jurist and one of England's first constitutional lawyers.

99. custos rotolorum: L, "keeper of the rolls." Source reads "rotulorum" [III, 527].

100. King: James I, 1566-1625. In November 1616, persuaded after a lengthy campaign by Francis Bacon, James dismissed Coke as lord chief justice of England.

101. timid jurors . . . Crown: JA here quotes from Hume's *History of England*: "The people had entertained such violent prepossessions against the use which James [James II] here made of his prerogative, that he was obliged, before he brought on Hales's cause, to displace four of the judges" [III, 529].

102. James Second: 1633-1701, king of Great Britain and Scotland (1685-1688).

103. Hales: Sir Edward H., fl. 1686. Principal in a law case by which James II attempted to establish the Crown's dispensing power in regard to the Test Act; having failed to gain support for such power from Parliament, James tried to secure it by verdict of the judiciary (1686).

104. Jones: Sir Thomas J., d. 1692, English jurist, chief justice of Common Pleas, dismissed in 1686 by James II for refusing to rule in favor of the Crown's dispensing power in the Hales case. The king met the judges in secret to learn their opinions. He turned them all out saying that he'd have twelve judges of his own opinion. ". . . one of them, Jones, had the fortitude and integrity to tell the king to his face, that he might possibly make twelve judges, but *he would scarcely find twelve lawyers of his opinion*" [III, 530].

105. Charter: Charter of province of Massachusetts.

106. William III: King of England (1689-1702).

107. Edward IV: 1442-1483, king of England (1461-1470, 1471-1483).

108. Beauchamps: Richard de Beauchamp, ?1430-1481, bishop of Hereford and Salisbury, Chancellor of the Order of the Garter. JA quotes a letter patent granted by Edward IV: " 'We will and ordain that Richard Beauchampe, &c., should have it (that is, the office of the chancellor of the garter) for his life, and after his decease, that his successors should have it forever'; and 'it was resolved unanimously that this grant was void; for that a new office was erected, and it was not defined what jurisdiction or authority the officer should have; and, therefore, for the uncertainty, it was void' " [III, 538].

109. Wales: Part of the United Kingdom of Great Britain and Northern Ireland; made an English principality (1284); incorporated with England in reign of Henry VIII. The reference is to the conclusion of JA's *Boston Gazette* letter of January 25, 1773, in which JA quoted the statute of 27 Henry VIII chap. 24 to the effect that the king alone had the power to make judges, "by letters-patent [commissions], under the king's great seal," in all dominions of the realm [III, 539]. General Brattle had claimed that "by the charter and common law of England, there is no necessity of [the judges'] having any commission at all; a nomination and appointment recorded is enough" [III, 536]. But JA, quoting Matthew Bacon's *Abridgment*, argued that "all judges must derive their authority from the crown by some commission warranted by law," since a commission defined the limits of the judge's authority, something "a nomination and appointment" did not do.

CANTO LXVII

Sources

Charles Francis Adams, ed., *The Works of John Adams*, III, IV, V, VI; Frederick K. Sanders, *John Adams Speaking*, Orono, Maine, 1975, 302-355; Guido Cavalcanti, "Donna mi priegha," 5th ed., 1527.

Background

Hannah Arendt, *On Revolution*, New York, 1965; Zoltán Haraszti, *John Adams and the Prophets of Progress*, Cambridge, Mass., 1952; Clinton Rossiter, "The Legacy of John Adams," *Yale Review*, 46 (1957), 528-550; Peter Shaw, *The Character of John Adams*, Chapel Hill, N.C., 1974; Page Smith, *John Adams*, 2 vols., Garden City, N.Y., 1962; H. Blair, *An Introduction to Anglo-Saxon England*, Cambridge, 1970; L. H. Butterfield, ed., *Diary and Autobiography of John Adams*, II, Cambridge, Mass., 1961.

Exegeses

CE, *Ideas*, 43; Davis, *Vision*, 140-141.

Glossary

1. **Whereof memory . . . his power**: These 30 lines opening the canto continue JA's arguments for the independence of the judiciary in reply to General William Brattle's article in the *Massachusetts Gazette* (Jan. 4, 1773); the first 20 lines are taken from JA's essay in the *Boston Gazette* (Feb. 1, 1773) [III, 540-550].

2. **Dome Book**: Not the famous Domesday Book authorized by William the Conquerer, for the reference is to JA's description of the digest of laws collected by Edward the Confessor as "no more than a fresh promulgation of Alfred's code, or Dome Book, with such improvements as the experience of a century and a half had suggested." General Brattle had claimed [III, 518] that according to English common law judges had appointments for life, and JA undertook to refute this idea by examining what the term "common law" meant by tracing its roots back to Anglo-Saxon law.

3. **Ina**: 688-726, king of the West Saxons. He issued a code of laws which was later appended to a law code drawn up by King Alfred the Great.

4. **Offa**: 757-796, ruler of Mercia, one of the best and most powerful of the Anglo-Saxon kings. King Alfred the Great was familiar with the laws of Offa.

5. **Aethelbert**: Died A.D. 616; became king of Kent in 560, the first Christian English king. He issued, between 597 and 616, a code of laws based on Roman law, the "earliest surviving Anglo-Saxon document written in the vernacular" [cf. Blair, 329].

6. **folcright**: OE, *folcriht*, "the people's rights." They were expressed in the common law.

7. **Gamaliel**: Great teacher of Jewish law who died A.D. 88; the name is applied to any great teacher, especially of law.

8. **Mr Read**: George R., 1733-1798, American constitutional lawyer from Delaware. Daniel Leonard, JA's opponent in the Novanglus correspondence, studied law with Read.

9. **single dictum**: Source reads "simple dictum" [III, 542].

10. **arguendo**: L, "in arguing or reasoning."

11. **latterly'**: Source reads "lately" [III, 542]. JA quoted these words of General Brattle's to object to his tactic of claiming a point proven by past authorities without offering any proof himself.

12. **Aula regum**: L, "King's court." Source reads "aula regis" [III, 544], the single great court in Norman England. Near the end of the Norman period it was divided into four parts (High Court of Chancery, Queen's Bench, Exchequer, and Court of Common Pleas) in order to break the power and authority concentrated in the hands of thc *summus justiciarius*, or chief justice, presiding officer of the great court.

13. **summus justiciarius**: L, "chief justice."

14. **Capet**: Hugh C., ?940-996, son of Hugh the Great; Duke of France (956-996); king of France (987-996); founder of Capetian line of French kings.

15. **Regalia principis**: L, "The rights royal of a prince." JA pointed out that "the creation and annihilation of judges was an important branch" of these rights [III, 545].

16. **judiciary**: Source reads "justiciary" (i.e., justice or judge). JA's point is that in those times the authority of the justice "ceased entirely in the king's presence" [III, 545].

17. **cum delegans revocarit**: L, "when one who sends a delegate calls him back" [cf. Bracton, *De Legibus* III, 10, where text reads: *Item cum delegans revocaverit jurisdictionem*; III, 546].

18. **(Bracton)**: [63:40].

19. **Ching**: Chêng [M351]: "right."

20. (Brattle): [66:93].

21. Fortescue: [66:98].

22. Coke: [62:43].

23. Foster: Sir Michael F., 1689-1763, English jurist.

24. Hume: David H., 1711-1776, Scottish philosopher whose *History of Great Britain* JA used as a source for his arguments for the independence of the judiciary.

25. Rapin: Paul de R. de Thoyras, 1661-1725, French historian; author of *Histoire d'Angleterre* (8 vols., 1723) covering English history up to the accession of William and Mary.

26. Rushworth: John R., ?1612-1690, English historian; author of *Historical Collections* (8 vols., 1659-1701), covering the period 1618-1648.

27. de Burgh: Hubert de B., d. 1243, Earl of Kent; chief justice of England under Henry III (1216). JA mentioned him as an example of a chief justice who was said to have had an appointment for life; but knowing of no document to support the story, JA said it was without foundation.

28. Mr Shirley in 1754: This line begins a 109-line redaction of passages from JA's *Novanglus*, which first appeared as a series of articles in the *Boston Gazette*, starting in January 1775. The articles JA signed "Novanglus" were written in answer to articles by Daniel Leonard signed "Massachusettensis" and contained JA's view of the constitutional arguments justifying the patriot cause.

29. Mr Shirley: William S., 1694-1771, English lawyer and governor of Massachusetts colony (1741-1749, 1753-1756). In 1756 he was recalled to England to answer charges of financial mismanagement and poor military organization.

30. Dr. Franklin: JA wrote of Benjamin Franklin: "This sagacious gentleman, this eminent philosopher and distinguished patriot, to his lasting honor, sent the Governor an answer in writing." Franklin wrote such things as these: "That the people always bear the burden best, when they have, or think they have, some *share* in the direction. That when public measures are generally distasteful to the people, the wheels of government must move more heavily.... That natives of America would be as likely to consult wisely and faithfully for the safety of their native country, as the governors sent from Britain, whose object is generally to make fortunes, and then return home" [IV, 19].

31. Shirley: [cf. 29 above]. JA is referring to the replacement of Governor Shirley by Thomas Pownall, a man friendly to the constitutional rights of the colonists; with Governor Pownall in office, the plan of Parliament to tax the colonies was not pursued. Pound added the word "skunk."

32. Pownall: Thomas P., 1722-1805, colonial governor of Massachusetts (1757-1760). An able governor, Thomas Pownall made enemies of the supporters of former Governor Shirley and of Thomas Hutchinson; faced with factional opposition in his province, according to JA, Pownall requested permission to return to England.

33. Bernard: [64:20, 26]. Sir Francis Bernard, governor of New Jersey, replaced Pownall as governor of Massachusetts in 1760.

34. and thus the total government: JA's description of the purpose of the revenue act, which was to have the Crown, rather than the citizens, pay salary grants to the governor, lieutenant governor, and judges so that both the executive and the judicial branches of the government would be independent of the people.

35. Novanglus: JA's pseudonym [cf. 28 above].

36. Mr. Grenville: [64:34]. While chancellor of the exchequer, Grenville was responsible for the Sugar Act (1764), the Stamp

Act (1765), and the Quartering Act (1765). The preposterous "improvement" he suggested was taxing the colonies and using the revenue to pay salaries to officials and to support the army in the colonies.

37. Obsta principiis: L, "Resist the beginnings." JA used this phrase to emphasize the necessity of firm protest at the first manifestations of oppression: "*Obsta principiis*, nip the shoots of arbitrary power in the bud, is the only maxim which can ever preserve the liberties of any people" [IV, 43].

38. the army: Said JA [as Novanglus]: "Besides, every farthing of expense which has been incurred on pretence of protecting . . . America . . . has been worse than thrown away. . . . Keeping an army in America has been nothing but a public nuisance."

39. Massachusetts: Source reads "Massachusettensis" (i.e., author of the articles JA answered in *Novanglus*) [IV, 57].

40. Irritat . . . implet: L, "Annoys, soothes, and fills with false fears." Cf. Horace, *Epistles* II, i, 212, which JA quoted [IV, 99] to describe what Massachusettensis wanted to accomplish in writing his newspaper articles. Source has "Irritat, mulcet, falsis terroribus implet."

41. casus omissus: L, "omitted case." JA's argument was that nothing in English common law stated that colonies beyond the British Isles should be governed "by authority of parliament" [IV, 121].

42. Hen. VIIIth: Henry, 1491-1547, king of England (1509-1547). After he declared himself head of the English church, Henry assumed authority over Englishmen in whatever country and by act of Parliament invested in himself what had been the supremacy of the pope.

43. Cardinal Pole: Reginald P., 1500-1558, created cardinal by Pope Paul III in 1536; opposed the divorce and the religious reforms of Henry VIII.

44. Most fanatical: Source reads "most. . . fantastical" [IV, 125], the most fantastical idea being that "a king of England had a right to all the land his subjects could find, not possessed by any Christian state or prince, though possessed by heathen or infidel nations." But even if that were so, it would not, according to JA, mean that Parliament possessed authority "over the new countries conquered or discovered" [IV, 125].

45. right of contract: I.e., the king did have the right to grant charters to his subjects which would confer upon them the rights and liberties of Englishmen in colonies established under such charters. For this context the source reads: ". . . for an English king had no right to be absolute over Englishmen out of the realm, any more than in it" [IV, 126].

46. the oily writer: Pound's characterization of Massachusettensis in summarizing JA's repudiation of various of his claims.

47. Parliament: JA asserted that the citizens of Massachusetts wanted nothing new, but rather continuation of privileges enjoyed for 150 years, during which they had governed their own internal affairs and Parliament had governed their trade.

48. Wales: JA explained that Wales and the American colonies had analagous situations in that Wales was held by the Crown of England and so the English monarch had a right to homage from the Prince of Wales. "But yet Wales was not parcel of the realm or kingdom, nor bound by the laws of England" [IV, 133].

49. Edwardus . . . dominium: L, "Edward by the Grace of God [King] of England, / Lord of Ireland, and Duke of Aquitaine (holding) the land of Wales together with its inhabitants / in possession of our private ownership." Source has "Dei" for "Deo," "Rex Angliæ" for "Angliae." Pound also leaves out a number of phrases and clauses found in the source and alters the word order [IV, 134].

50. now partly to divert . . . Hibernia habet parliamentum: These 23 lines come from a long passage in *Novanglus* in which JA recounted how Ireland came to be under English dominion [IV, 151-165].

51. Becket: Thomas à B., 1117-1170, archbishop of Canterbury (1162-1170); murdered by agents of Henry II.

52. Adrian: A. IV, d. 1159, first and only English pope (1154-1159).

53. power of pence of Peter. Source reads "prospect of Peter's pence": an annual tax, originally one penny, levied on each householder in England by the papacy [IV, 152].

54. Henry's demand: Source reads "design" [IV, 152]; Henry II [6:17].

55. Eire: Ireland.

56. Macmorral: Dermot MacMurrough, ?1110-1171, king of Leinster, one of "five distinct sovereignties in Ireland." JA called him "a licentious scoundrel . . . who had been driven from his kingdom . . . by his own subjects" [IV, 152]. Source reads "Macmorrogh."

57. Rourke: Tiernan O'R., d. 1172, king of Breifne and ruler of part of Meath (1144). In 1152 his wife was carried off by Dermot MacMurrough. Henry II was able to use the greed of MacMurrough and O'Rourke to divide the Irish and make their subjugation easier. JA said that just as Henry II played different kings of Ireland against one another, so the government of England tried to play the colonies against one another, except that "the American colonies. . . have more sense than to be divided" [IV, 152]. Source has "Ororic."

58. our junto: Crown officers in Massachusetts, primarily Governor Bernard, Thomas Hutchinson, and the Oliver brothers.

59. Henry V: 1387-1422, king of England (1413-1422). JA quoted a statute of Henry V which stipulated that all Irishmen not belonging to certain categories ("graduates, sergeants") had to depart the realm of England [IV, 155].

60. "shall put in surety": This quotation comes from a statute of Henry VI which established specific conditions for any Irishmen entering England.

61. Poyning's law: Named for Sir Edward Poynings, 1459-1521, English soldier and diplomat. As governor of Ireland, he summoned the Drogheda Parliament (1494) which enacted Poynings' Law, providing that no bill could be introduced into the Irish Parliament unless it had first received the sanction of the English Privy Council and that all former laws of England would subsequently be binding in Ireland. JA's argument was that the American colonies had never agreed to or passed a "Poynings' law." Source has "Poyning."

62. Edgardus . . . parliamentum: L, "Edgar, King of the English, / emperor and ruler of the isles of the ocean, I thank / almighty God who so enlarged and extended my kingdom beyond the kingdom of my fathers, / granted the good offices of divinity . . . / Ireland has a parliament." JA here quoted Sir Edward Coke (*Reports*, 7, 22b) on the question of who first conquered Ireland for England. Coke had quoted the Latin of a charter made by Edgar, king of England (944-975), and then had acknowledged that the conquest of Ireland was customarily attributed to the later reign of Henry II [IV, 161]. Source reads "Edgarus" for "Edgardus," "gratias" for "gratium," "exaltavit" for "explicavit." Pound also omits words and phrases found in the source.

63. Sir J. Pilkington: Sir John P., fl. 1454. The case of Sir John Pilkington (32 Henry VI chap. 25) substantiated the fact that Ireland was a dominion separate and divided from England [Coke, *Reports*, 7, 22b].

64. majesty near the seventy: A reference to George II, 1683-1760, king of England (1727-1760). This and the following five lines come from the reaction of Lord Mansfield, as JA imagined it, as the reign of George II approached its end.

65. amiable successor: George III, who ascended the throne of England in 1760 at the age of 22.

66. militant spirit: Source reads "martial spirit" [IV, 167]. JA's characterization of Lord Mansfield's belief that, although the English would certainly defeat the French in the Seven Years War [French and Indian War in America], the English nation would be left with an immense debt. Thus the war should be brought to a close for "we have not the martial spirit and abilities of the great commoner" [the Elder Pitt].

67. How shall we manage it?: I.e., raise revenue to pay the war debt.

68. Lord Mansfield: William Murray, 1705-1793, 1st Earl of Mansfield; English jurist and parliamentary debater.

69. Hutchinson: [62:47]. As JA described it, the solution to the debt problem, according to Lord Mansfield and Thomas Hutchinson, lay in "annexing" North America to "the realm of England" [IV, 166].

70. regalia: L, *regalia principis*, "the rights royal of a prince" [cf. 15 above].

71. a little knowledge: Massachusettensis had written that Jersey and Guernsey "are no part of the realm of England, nor are they represented in parliament, but are subject to its authority" [IV, 169]; JA undertook to provide a better understanding of this subject.

72. Chester: City in NW England; also a palatine county, one that came under special jurisdiction of the prince. But Parliament passed laws preventing the citizens of Chester from committing crimes outside the county, or citizens outside from seeking legal refuge in the county. JA's point is that America could be included in no such acts of Parliament.

73. jure regalia: L, *jura regalia*, "royal rights."

74. 3 knights: Source reads "two knights." Earlier Chester "'had been excluded from parliament, to have any knights and burgesses there' [i.e., representing it in Parliament].... For remedy whereof, two knights of the shire and two burgesses for the city are established" [IV, 172].

75. Durham: Palatine county in N England.

76. Queen's writ: Refers to 31 Elizabeth chap. 9.

77. 25 Charles II: JA used Chester and Durham as examples because, since they were counties palatine, their lords enjoyed "royal rights," although they did acknowledge the rights of the English king to his crown. The laws of Parliament and the judicial authority of the king did not extend into counties palatine, but when the two counties, previously exempt from Parliament's authority, asked permission to have representation in Parliament, it was quickly granted. "America, on the contrary, is not in the realm; never was subject to the authority of parliament by any principle of law; is so far from Great Britain that she never can be represented; yet, she is to be bound in all cases whatsoever!" [IV, 170-172]. 25 Charles II was the statute enabling Durham to send representatives to Parliament.

78. our oily opponent: Pound's characterization of Massachusettensis.

79. more zeal than knowing: JA on the claim of Massachusettensis that the terms of the first charter of Massachusetts made it a part of the British Empire and bound the original settlers to the laws of England.

80. Nation . . . into our charter: JA refers to the fact that at the time the first charter for settling Massachusetts was granted, the British Empire did not exist.

81. King: Charles I, 1600-1649, king of England (1625-1649); granted its first charter to colony of Massachusetts (March 4, 1629). Massachusettensis had claimed that the original charter had made the province subject to England's protection, but JA replied that no money had ever been provided to the first settlers for that purpose.

82. **Style royal?**: To the claim of Massachusettensis that the precedent for submission to Parliament was implicit in the "royal style" of the original charter, JA replied: "The style is this: 'Charles, by the grace of God, King of England, Scotland, France, and Ireland, Defender of the Faith,' &c. Now, in which capacity did he grant that charter; as King of France, or Ireland, or Scotland, or England? He governed England by one parliament, Scotland by another. Which parliament were we to be governed by?" [IV, 174].

83. **homage, fealty**: JA explains that in feudal language homage and fealty were due a lord in his natural person; one did not pay homage to "the body politic, the political capacity, which is not corporated, but only a frame in the mind, an idea" [IV, 176-177]. Since the king held lands in his natural person and not in his political capacity, Massachusettensis was wrong, according to JA, to declare that he was due the homage of political loyalty.

84. **the king might have commanded**: That the king did not command the original settlers of the province to return was tacit acknowledgment that they were out of his realm and therefore out of the legal jurisdiction of Parliament.

85. **Lexington**: The Novanglus papers are subtitled "A History of the Dispute with America, from its origin, in 1754, to the present time; written in 1774, by John Adams." They were collected and published together in 1819. CFA includes the whole edition in Volume IV of *WJA* along with a note that reads: "Hostilities at Lexington, between Great Britain and her colonies, commenced on the nineteenth of April, two days succeeding the publication of this last essay" [IV, 177].

86. **Plan of Government**: "The Plan," the first of three sections into which CFA divided JA's major writings dealing with the form of American government; the other sections are titled "The Model" and "The Defence" [IV, 185-VI, 220].

87. **Philadelphy**: A letter JA sent from Philadelphia to Richard Henry Lee (Nov. 15, 1775) appears to be the earliest expression of JA's plan of government.

88. **R. H. Lee**: [65:53].

89. **on sudden emergency**: The imminent likelihood of independence from England would necessitate the creation of new governments for the colonies.

90. **legislative, executive and judicial**: JA's political philosophy had always centered on a division of powers that would encourage checks and balances in government, as was evident in his early letter to R. H. Lee.

91. **Printer John Dunlap**: 1747-1812, printer in Philadelphia who published the first edition of JA's *Thoughts on Government* (1776).

92. **Mr Wythe**: [65:43]. In January 1776 George Wythe had asked JA what plan he would recommend "in order to get out of the old government and into a new one" [IV, 191]. JA's answer was *Thoughts on Government*.

93. **some forms . . .** : This and the following 25 lines (except the Italian at the eighth line, which is Pound's interpolation) are all taken from *Thoughts on Government.*

94. **Kung**: K'ung [13:1]. JA used the more familiar form "Confucius" [IV, 193].

95. **Zoroaster**: Religious teacher of ancient Persia, fl. 5th century B.C. He founded Zoroastrianism, originally a kind of fertility religion which later developed a more complex cosmogony and eschatology, deriving from the struggle of the Zoroastrian supernatural spirits.

96. **Mahomet**: Mohammed, 570-632, Arabian prophet. JA says that these sages have agreed "that the happiness of man, as well as his dignity, consists in virtue" [IV, 193].

97. in some principle: Source reads "is some principle" [IV, 194].

98. ma che si sente dicho: I, "but that is felt, I say," from "Donna mi priegha" [36:1].

99. Locke: [50:9]. All those mentioned in this line preached the concept of government by law, not by men [IV, 194].

100. Milton: John M., 1608-1674, English poet.

101. Nedham: Marchamont N., 1620-1678, English political writer; author of *The Case of the Commonwealth of England Stated* (1650).

102. Neville: Henry N., 1620-1694, English political writer; author of *Discourses Concerning Government* (1698).

103. Burnet: Sir Thomas B., ?1694-1753, English judge and political writer.

104. Hoadly: Benjamin H., 1676-1761, bishop of Bangor and Hereford; author of religious and political treatises, among them *An Essay on the Origin of Civil Government.*

105. of learning . . . : JA's description of qualities needed by judges.

106. Pat Henry: [31:46]. The following 12 lines come from a letter Patrick Henry sent to JA from Williamsburg on May 20, 1776 [IV, 201-202].

107. Declaration: Patrick Henry's reference to a resolution approved by the Continental Congress on May 10, 1776, which recommended that the colonies adopt new governments of their own design to meet their needs in dealing with the current crisis. The preamble, written by JA, and adopted on May 15, called for the virtual abolition of all British authority in the colonies [Butterfield, II, 240-241 n. 2, gives details about this episode].

108. Colonel Nelson: Thomas N., 1738-1789, American Revolutionary patriot; colonel in 2d Regiment of Virginia; member of Continental Congress (1775-1777); signer of Declaration of Independence; governor of Virginia (1781).

109. Paris: Patrick Henry believed it very important that the colonies get their representatives to the French court ahead of the British and that they quickly make a public declaration of independence so that they could seek alliances in Europe.

110. Bracton: Source has "Braxton" [IV, 202]. Carter Braxton, Virginia delegate to the Continental Congress, had written a pamphlet in answer to JA's *Thoughts on Government* [cf. 86 above].

111. Sam Adams: Also S.A., four lines later [cf. 34:32].

112. John Taylor: 1753-1824, printer and political writer from Caroline County, Va. In his *Inquiry into Principles and Policy of the Government of the United States* (1814) he printed a letter JA had written to John Penn in 1776.

113. John Penn: ?1741-1788, American Revolutionary leader; member of Continental Congress from North Carolina (1775-1780) and signer of Declaration of Independence. JA wrote Penn in answer to a request from the North Carolina delegation that he, JA, suggest the form of government best suited to replace the administration of the Crown should that become necessary. The following six lines are taken from JA's letter to Penn. JA kept no copy, so the letter was not printed until 1814 [IV, 203].

114. Jonathan Sergeant: J. Dickinson S., 1746-1798, American lawyer; New Jersey delegate to First Continental Congress (1774). JA wrote him a letter similar to the one he wrote to Penn, "but no copy has been found" [IV, 209n].

115. Fixed laws . . . : These eight lines are from a resolution passed by the Massachusetts convention on September 3, 1779, which led to the drafting of a new constitution for Massachusetts.

116. I was apprehensive: In his draft of the

constitution of Massachusetts, JA had recommended, in section ii, the encouragement of literature, the sciences, and a natural history of the province, as well as such personal qualities as charity, honesty, and good humor.

117. Chawles Fwancis: Charles Francis Adams (1807-1886), editor of *WJA* (1850).

118. who have since been erected: The source reads "who have since been elevated" [IV, 261n]; the reference is to officials elected to the highest public offices.

119. and no public man: This and the following five lines come from CFA's preface to JA's *Defence of the Constitutions of Government of the United States of America, Against the Attack of M. Turgot, in His Letter to Dr. Price, Dated the Twenty-Second Day of March, 1778* [IV, 276-277]. In it CFA, noting the controversies provoked by the appearance of the work (1787-88), remarks that although by the time he is writing his preface (1850) government by democratic majority rule is so widely admired that no public official would risk criticizing its limitations, that was not true in the last decades of the 18th century when JA wrote about his theories of government and when the viability of the modern democratic republic remained unproven. JA had written *Defence* in response to Turgot's letter arguing the superiority of a unicameral assembly and also in response to the tax revolt in western Massachusetts known as Shay's Rebellion (1786). The three-volume work was a defense of state constitutions, not of the federal constitution, which did not exist at that time. Although JA was still in Europe when the Constitutional Convention of 1787 met, the first volume of *Defence* did influence the convention.

120. 'Either content . . . at large': Observing that theorizing about forms of government had gone out of fashion in the U.S., CFA speculated that the reason might be the awareness of dangers attendant upon thinking unpopular thoughts about democratic rule which might lead to ruined reputations; the reception of JA's *Defence* would be a case in point.

121. representatives of the people: This and the following 26 lines are taken from JA's preface to *Defence* [IV, 283-298]. Source reads "representations."

122. Thucydides: ?471-400, Greek historian. Refers to Thucydides' account of the consequences of unrestrained factionalism in Greece which, in JA's opinion, could have been prevented by a balance of powers in government.

123. Mr Hume: [cf. 24 above].

124. D. Siculus: Diodorus S., Greek historian of 1st century B.C.; author of *Biblioteca Historica* (40 vols.).

125. Ephesus: One of the principal Ionian cities on coast of Asia Manor.

126. Cyrenians: People of the ancient city of Cyrene in part of Africa known as Cyrenaica [modern Bardia in NE Libya].

127. Phaebidas: Phoebidas, Spartan commander who seized stronghold of Thebes in Boetia in 382 B.C. [IV, 286].

128. Philiasia: Phliasia, territory of Phlius, town in NE Peloponnesus.

129. Aegesta: Segesta, town on NW coast of Sicily [near modern Alcamo], said to have been founded by the Trojans; called Egesta or Aegesta by the Greeks. Of these brutalities (at Ephesus and Segesta) JA wrote: "Such were the fashionable outrages of unbalanced parties. In the name of human and divine benevolence, is such a system as this to be recommended to Americans, in this age of the world?" [IV, 287].

130. No interviews . . . this service: I.e., the service of designing the forms of American governments (state and federal).

131. Grosvenor Sq.: [66:30]. JA's residence at the time he wrote his preface (dated Jan. 1, 1787).

132. Vitruvius: Marcus V. Pollio, fl. 1st century B.C., Roman architect whose work served as one of the models for Renaissance architecture.

133. Palladio: [40:27]. Like architects called upon to design new buildings, who consult such masters as Vitruvius and Palladio, American patriots such as JA, called upon "to erect new systems of laws for their future government," consulted the wisest political philosophers on government [IV, 293].

134. the young gents of literature: Source has "younger gentlemen of letters" [IV, 294].

135. Tacitus: Publius Cornelius T., 55-120?, Roman historian. He praised the idea of a republic ruled by a governor, a senate, and a house of representatives, although he doubted the "practicability" or "duration" of such a division [IV, 294].

136. facilius . . . potest esse: L, "it is more easily praised than discovered / or not lasting / excellently blended in moderation . . . / is nevertheless brought about in unison . . . a state by agreement / where there is no justice, there can be no law." (For sources of these fragments see Tacitus, *Annales* IV, xxxiii, 20, where the test reads: . . . *laudari facilius quam evenire, vel si evenit, haud diaturna esse potest*; Cicero, *De Re Publica* II, xxiii, 41, where the text reads: *statu esse optimo . . . confusa modice*; Cicero, *De Re Publica* II, xlii, 69, and III, *Fragmenta*, where the text reads: *Ubi justitia vera non est, nec jus potest esse*, a quotation from St. Augustine, *De Civitate Dei* XIX, 21.) [IV, 294-296].

137. San Marino: Republic on Italian peninsula, cited by JA as an example of a government of "checks and limitations" which had lasted for "thirteen hundred years, while all the other states of Italy have several times changed masters and forms of government" [IV, 308, 304].

138. Dalmatia: [17:33].

139. their own rights: Source says "their own privileges" [IV, 345]; JA's comment on Geneva's history after the 16th century.

140. nobles . . . manufacturies: JA refers to Genoa where the nobles themselves were often prosperous merchants and thus not separated from a competing merchant class in a way that generated factionalism.

141. Venice: The 12 lines that follow deal with JA's account of Venetian history [IV, 347-356].

142. Anafeste: Paul Luc A., died A.D. 717, early tribune of Venice and first doge; reputed to have been a just magistrate.

143. 5 massacred . . . 5 abdications: JA's summary of fates of doges during one period of Venetian history. The doge was the chief magistrate of Venice.

144. before they thought . . . government: JA refers to Venetian government down to the 12th century.

145. cunning: "The aristocracy is always more sagacious than an assembly of the people. . . . It is always more cunning, too . . . " [IV, 354-355].

146. whereon nobles depend from: Source reads "dependent on" [IV, 355].

147. stadtholder: Chief of state in Holland; JA refers to the hereditary ruler of Holland.

148. Lolme: John Louis de L., 1740-1806, Swiss lawyer. Author of *The Constitution of England* (1771), said by JA to be "the best defence of the political balance of three powers that ever was written" [IV, 358].

149. Ukraine: JA quotes from the writings of King Stanislaus of Poland, who lamented the despair of the inhabitants of the Ukraine after their unsuccessful insurrection to assert their rights. JA's point is that a balance of powers in government would protect the people from such suppressions by king or nobles.

150. Neuchâtel: Swiss canton in Jura

Mountains. JA observes that the constitution of Neuchâtel divided the government into three branches, and that it was "the only constitution in which the citizens can truly be said to be in that happy condition of freedom and discipline, sovereignty and subordination, which the Greeks express so concisely by their 'αρχειν και 'αρχεσθαι" [IV, 377].

151. *'αρχειν και 'αρχεσθαι*: H, "to rule and to be ruled." The words constitute a theme in Greek political thought, going back as far as Solon and reappearing in Aristotle's *Politics*: "Ruling and being ruled . . . not only belongs to the category of things necessary, but also to that of things expedient" (Barker's translation). Barker summarizes the chapter (I.v) thus: "There is a principle of rule and subordination in nature at large: it appears especially in the realm of animate creation. By virtue of that principle, the soul rules the body; and by virtue of it the master, who possesses the rational faculty of the soul, rules the slave, who possesses only bodily powers and the faculty of understanding the directions given by another's reason" [*Politics* 1277b, 15; III.iv].

152. Rhodes: [24:37]. JA believed that the constitution of ancient Rhodes was probably very similar to the constitution of Neuchâtel.

153. jura ordo . . . æquitas leges: L, "rights order . . . equity laws" [Livy, *Annals* III, 63]. In JA's opinion these are the characteristics of a government in which powers are divided and balanced. Source reads "æquatas" [IV, 377].

154. stadtholder: [cf. 147 above].

155. avoyer: F, chief magistrate of a free city or a canton in French Switzerland.

156. alcalde: S, "chief administrator."

157. capitaneo: I, an administrative official. In his "Recapitulation" at the end of Volume I, chapter 3 of *Defence*, JA observes that all republics in past history seem to have had some kind of chief magistrate, however different the titles given him in different countries.

158. Turgot: [31:35; 119 above]. JA's criticism of Turgot was that if Turgot had known of any examples of a successful country that did not have a chief officer, he would have revealed his knowledge to the world; but since he had not done so, there must be no such examples. Therefore, the Americans should not be censured for creating the office of "governor" for their states [IV, 379].

159. orders of officers: Source reads "orders of offices" [IV, 380]. In contrasting the American system with traditional European governments, JA observes: "In America, there are different orders of *offices*, but none of *men*. Out of office, all men are of the same species, and of one blood; there is neither a greater nor a lesser nobility" [IV, 380].

CANTO LXVIII

Sources

Charles Francis Adams, ed., *The Works of John Adams,* IV, V, VI, VII; Frederick K. Sanders, *John Adams Speaking*, Orono, Maine, 1975, 356-399.

Background

Peter Shaw, *The Character of John Adams*, Chapel Hill, N. C., 1974; Page Smith, *John Adams*, 2 vols., Garden City, N. Y., 1962; Samuel Flagg Bemis, *The Diplomacy of the American Revolutionn*, Bloomington, Indiana, 1957; L. H. Butterfield, ed., *Diary and Autobiography of John Adams*, II, Cambridge, Mass., 1961.

Exegeses

CE, *Ideas*, 43, 176, 177; Davis, *Vision*, 141-142; CB-R, *ZBC*, 121.

Glossary

1. **Regis optimatium populique**: L, "Of the king, of the aristocrats, of the people" [cf. Polybius, Fragments, VI, quoted by Jonathan Swift, *A Discourse of the Contests and Dissensions between the Nobles and Commons of Athens and Rome*; quoted in *WJA*, IV, 383]. The first 12 lines of this canto, which come from the chapter in JA's *Defence* [cf. 11 below] titled "Opinions of Philosophers," continue his major theme that the best form of government is one of divided powers with checks on one another.

2. **Lycurgus**: Spartan lawgiver, 9th century B.C.

3. **Spartha**: Sparta.

4. **reges, seniores, et populus**: L, "kings, elders, and people." Recognizing that people in each of these categories were subject to corruption, Lycurgus had proposed a government combining all three.

5. **both greeks and italians**: JA refers to "the most ancient and inherent principle" of limited and divided powers in government, recognized by both Greeks and Italians [IV, 384].

6. **archons**: Chief magistrates of Athens.

7. **suffestes**: L, *sufes* (*-fetis*): suffetes. A suffete was one of the two highest magistrates in Carthage. Source has "suffetes."

8. **consuls**: Joint magistrates of the Roman Republic. From JA's quotation of Jonathan Swift's remark about the similarities between Greek monarchies and Italian republics, that the Greek kings at Troy held a power comparable to that of the Athenian archons, the Carthaginian suffetes, and the Roman consuls.

9. **Athenians . . . Achaians**: Achaeans. Greek peoples that at one time or another tried to achieve a "universal monarchy" for Greece [IV, 387].

10. **using the people . . . not in maintaining**: JA quotes Swift's criticism of popular assemblies, that a people who think they rule are often manipulated into accepting a tyrant and that popular opinion can be more easily set to tearing down than to preserving what is valuable in government. [IV, 388]

11. **Turgot**: Anne Robert Jacques T., 1727-1781, wrote a letter that JA conceived to be an attack upon the U. S. system of government. JA's response, *A Defence of the Constitutions of Government of the United States of America, Against the Attack of M. Turgot, in His letter to Dr. Price, Dated the Twenty-Second Day of March, 1778*, appeared in three volumes in 1787, all of them included in *WJA* Volumes IV-VI. [This work is referred to elsewhere as

Defence, but the citations are to *WJA*, as here: IV, 405.]

12. **How shall the plow**: JA quotes Lord Bacon's observation that if the nobility grow too populous, commoners will tend to lose their independence and become little more than hired laborers, thus weakening the balance among monarch, aristocrats, and commoners [IV, 428]. Source has "plough."

13. **Lycurgus**: Reference to why Lycurgus wanted to balance the powers of three branches of government against one another [IV, 443].

14. **Plato**: After several pages of analysis of Plato's *Republic*, Book IV in particular, JA concludes with the lines Pound quotes and associates Plato's ten ideas with parts of Sir Thomas More's *Utopia* [IV, 461-463].

15. **Sir Thos More**: Sir Thomas M., 1478-1535, English statesman, humanist, and author of works on political philosophy which JA finds to be more than "Utopian."

16. **Bedlam**: Bethlehem Royal Hospital in London, where the insane were incarcerated.

17. **Milton**: Pound's summary of JA's criticism of Milton as a political philosopher. JA quotes a statement Milton made in *Ready and Easy Way to Establish a Free Commonwealth*: "I doubt not but all ingenuous and knowing men will easily agree with me, that a free commonwealth, without single person or house of lords, is by far the best government, if it can be had," but Milton goes on to elaborate this premise in such a way that JA concludes: "Can one read, without shuddering, this wild reverie of the divine, immortal Milton?" [IV, 464-465].

18. **Lowered interest**: Refers to Solon's policy, in ancient Greece, of reconciling the rich with the poor: "... this he accomplished by lowering the interest without annulling the debt, and by taking from the creditor the exorbitant powers over the person and family of the debtor" [IV, 477]—a principle of fiscal justice which Pound along with JA endorses.

19. **in this transaction**: Source reads "in this translation" [IV, 568], i.e., Pope's translation of the *Odyssey*.

20. **Mr Pope**: Alexander P., 1688-1744. Of Pope's translation of part of Alcinoüs's speech to Odysseus, "Twelve princes in our realm dominion share / O'er whom supreme imperial power I bear" [*Od*. VIII, 390-391], JA said: "Mr. Pope, indeed, in this translation, has given him the air of a sovereign; but there is nothing like it in the original. There, Alcinoüs, with all possible simplicity and modesty, only says,—'Twelve illustrious kings, or archons, rule over the people, and I myself am the thirteenth' " [IV, 568].

21. **Tacitus**: [67:135]. Source reads: "Through the whole of Tacitus and Homer, the three orders are visible both in Germany and Greece ... [Troubles] arose entirely from the want of having the prerogatives and privileges of those orders defined, from the want of independence in each of them, and a balance between them" [IV, 578].

22. **and mankind ... Constitutions**: At the end of Volume III of *Defence* (more than 800 pages later than preceding note), JA concludes that such a work will not be much encouraged because "mankind, in general, dare not as yet read or think upon CONSTITUTIONS" [VI, 217].

23. **'No man**: I.e., no one who interpreted JA's *Discourses on Davila* (1790) as a pro-monarchy tract accepted his opinions on the dangers of the popular egalitarian dogmas of the French Revolution [VI, 227].

24. **Davila**: Enrico Caterino D., 1576-1631, author of *Istoria delle Guerre Civili di Francia* [*History of French Civil Wars*], 1630. While vice-president JA wrote *Discourses on Davila* (1790), partly in response to certain currents of thought stirred by the French Revolution and partly as a sequel to *Defence*, reminding his countrymen once

again of the importance of a division of governmental powers for political stability. JA's defense of titles such as king and duke in this work led to attacks from Anti-Federalists who claimed that JA wanted to introduce hereditary offices into the U. S. government.

25. Be bubbled out . . . : JA said "Americans . . . are too enlightened to be bubbled out of their liberties." [JA, IV, 466].

26. Hume: [67:24]. JA's criticism (in *Defence*) of Hume for criticizing such writers as Locke, Sidney, and Hoadley for being inappropriately reputed to be the equals of the ancient philosophers.

27. Franks: Group of Germanic tribes. JA called it the "great misfortune" of the Franks that they never decided whether their national assembly or their king had sovereignty [VI, 228].

28. J.A.: John Adams began writing *Davila* in his first year as vice-president. In a footnote CFA cites JA's remark about reactions to the work. Of one reviewer he said: "The writer was 'a young man; a forward young man' " [VI, 229].

29. Pharamond: Legendary king of Salian Franks, ca. 5th century B.C. He supposedly published the Salic code, which included penal and civil laws.

30. Sala: River in the Netherlands, the modern Ijssel River, the N mouth of the Rhine. Sala, its ancient name, is applied to the inhabitants along its banks, the Salian Franks.

31. here . . . jargon: JA refers to the idea of a single central authority with the unresolved question of whether that authority lies in the States General or in the king, a dominant problem in French history.

32. Miseria . . . vagum: Source says "misera." L, "Slavery is a misery, where rights are undefined" [VI, 230n]. JA added this phrase in 1804 as a marginal comment on a passage in *Davila* about the calamities that had befallen the French because of their uncertainty over the claims of sovereignty in the different branches of government.

33. predilections: Source says "propensities" [VI, 232].

34. commended: Source says "considered" [VI, 232].

35. Mr Hillhouse: James A. H., 1754-1832, American lawyer, member of House of Representatives (1791-1808). In 1808 Hillhouse submitted to the Senate a pamphlet entitled "Propositions for Amending the Constitution of the United States." This and the following four lines are taken from JA's analysis of Hillhouse's propositions [VI, 525-550]. Hillhouse wrote that the U. S. Constitution had been modeled on that of England which, combining monarchy, aristocracy, and democracy, was an inappropriate model because the first two branches were hereditary. JA's answer was that a more accurate model was to be found in the colonial constitutions, in which offices were not hereditary.

36. Emissaries: Hillhouse had recommended annual elections for federal officials as a way to weaken the influence of party caucuses; JA replied that caucuses would continue in any event and that anyone seeking to influence policy, whether foreigner or American, would still do so if elections were held annually.

37. Commission to France: From a letter of Henry Laurens, president of Continental Congress, to JA, dated December 3, 1777, notifying JA of his appointment to replace Silas Deane [65:39] as commissioner to France [VII, 5].

38. Lafayette: In his letter to JA [cf. 37 above], Laurens mentioned a skirmish at Gloucester, N. J., in November 1777, in which Lafayette, leading a group of Morgan's Rifles, had bested a superior force of British and Hessians.

39. Morgan: Daniel M., 1736-1802, American Revolutionary soldier. He and his sharpshooters played a decisive role in the battles of Saratoga, New York, and Cowpens, South Carolina.

40. Henry Laurens: 1724-1792, American Revolutionary statesman from Charleston, South Carolina; member of Second Continental Congress and its president (1777-78). Sent to the Netherlands in 1780 as U. S. commissioner, he was captured en route by the British and imprisoned in the Tower of London; he was exchanged for Cornwallis in 1781. With Laurens was captured a copy of the proposed United States-Netherlands treaty, called the "Amsterdam treaty" by JA, which had been accepted by William Lee for the U. S. and by Jean de Neufville for the regency of Amsterdam in 1778 at Aix-la-Chapelle. The British used the discovery of this treaty as a pretext for war against the Netherlands [cf. Butterfield, II, 452-453 n. 1, for concise account].

41. Mons. le Comte de Broglie: Victor François, duc de B., 1718-1804, marshal of France (1759); minister of war (1789). Upon learning that JA had been appointed commissioner to France, Baron de Kalb [cf. 42 below] offered to provide JA letters of introduction to certain parties in France, including the duc de Broglie [VII, 9].

42. De Klab: Johann Kalb, 1721-1780, known as Baron de Kalb; German army officer commissioned major general in Continental Army (1777-1780); killed at battle of Camden, South Carolina.

43. Lafayette: Hearing that JA was going to France, Lafayette asked him to take a letter to friends reporting his experience in the "noble cause" of the fight for American independence [VII, 10-11].

44. novelty of the scene: From a letter JA wrote the Committee of Commerce of the Congress (May 24, 1778) reporting the disorder he found in American financial affairs when he reached France, its possible cause, and what he planned to do to correct it.

45. some facilities: Source reads "same facilities" [VII, 23].

46. De Sartine: Antoine Raymond Jean Gualbet Gabriel de S., comte d'Aloy, 1729-1801, French statesman; minister of marine (1774-1780). On July 29, 1778, de Sartine wrote to the U. S. commissioners in France that the formal alliance with France signed in February 1778 should make it easier for American privateers to dispose of their prizes in French ports, and that, in reciprocation, he expected French privateers to receive similar opportunities in American ports [VII, 23].

47. B.Fr. A.Lee J.A. . . . : Benjamin Franklin, Arthur Lee, and John Adams to the comte de Vergennes. The preceding six lines come from a letter the U. S. commissioners wrote to Vergennes on August 28, 1778, requesting an additional 750,000-livre loan from the French government to allow the U. S. to pay interest due on paper money which had been borrowed in large quantities [VII, 25-27].

48. Vergennes: [45:45].

49. (Beaumarchais): [31:29]. Refers to a letter from the American commissioners to Beaumarchais dated September 10, 1778. The commissioners were trying to settle a dispute involving the French merchant ship *Theresa* as part of an effort to get American financial accounts in order. Beaumarchais claimed that the *Theresa* belonged to his firm, Roderique Hortalez & Co.

50. M. Monthieu: John Joseph de M., business partner of Beaumarchais also connected with Roderique Hortalez & Co. Monthieu arranged the sale and rental of armed vessels to America during the Revolution.

51. John Baptiste Lazarus: J. B. L. de Theveneau de Francy, commercial agent for Beaumarchais.

52. Roderique Hortalez: R. H. & Co., a

mock company set up secretly by Beaumarchais to sell military supplies to the American colonies during the Revolution. The reference here is to a letter from the Committee of Commerce of the Continental Congress to the American commissioners in France, who communicated it to Vergennes on September 10, 1778, stating that the Committee of Commerce had entered into a contract with the firm of Roderique Hortalez & Co. through agent Lazarus [cf. 51 above].

53. Ray de Chaumont: [65:66]. As part of his undertaking to straighten out American accounts in Europe, JA had inquired about rent due on the house at Passy where he and Franklin stayed. The preceding four lines come from Le Ray de Chaumont's letter to JA (Sept. 18, 1778), explaining that he refuses rent for this house as part of his support of the American struggle for independence [VII, 32-33].

54. Bersolle: Fl. 1778; Frenchman engaged in the repair of ships.

55. the Drake: English ship captured by John Paul Jones in 1778.

56. Jones's: John Paul J. [65:124].

57. supplies or slops: Source says "supplies of slops" [VII, 65]. The U. S. commissioners were saying that by act of Congress "the whole of all vessels of war taken by our frigates belong to the officers and men." Thus they, and not Congress, must pay for repairs.

58. the Ranger: Ship commanded by John Paul Jones in 1777-78.

59. the Chatham: This English ship, captured by the *Ranger* during the American Revolution, created a special problem: "As the Lord Chatham belongs, half to the public and half to the captors, all necessary expenses on her account should be paid; a moiety out of the captors' half, and the other moiety out of the half which belongs to the United States" [VII, 65].

60. Schweighauser: [65:98]. The preceding ten lines come from a letter the American commissioners wrote to Schweighauser (Nov. 4, 1778) explaining which expenses of John Paul Jones should be paid with government funds and which expenses should come out of the bounty he and his men received from the prizes they captured.

61. de Sartine: [cf. 46 above]. The preceding six lines come from a letter the American commissioners sent to de Sartine (Nov. 12, 1778) requesting that supplies for winter warfare be included in the cargo of French warships sailing to America [VII, 68-69].

62. It is certain . . . wanted: From a letter JA wrote to Lafayette (Feb. 21, 1779) concerning the need of a loan to support the value of the paper currency issued by the Continental Congress [VII, 84].

63. Master Johnnie: Source reads "master Johnny": John Quincy Adams, mentioned in Franklin's letter of April 3, 1779, to JA. The letter exhibited the formal courtesies maintained by the two men despite their frequent disagreements about the conduct of the American mission in France [VII, 90].

64. Leghorn: Livorno, Italian seaport S of Pisa. In a letter of August 4, 1779, to John Jay, president of the Congress, JA pointed out that although the fortunes of Italy were in general decline, the U. S. after independence might find the privileges of the port of Leghorn useful if an American minister were accepted at the court of Vienna [VII, 109].

65. Huntington: Samuel H., 1731-1796, member of Continental Congress (1776-1783) and its president (1779-1781); signer of Declaration of Independence. Refers to Huntington's letter (Oct. 20, 1779) informing JA that he had been appointed minister plenipotentiary to negotiate treaties of peace and commerce with Great Britain and telling him what his salary would be [VII, 119].

66. My Dear General: Salutation of JA's letter to Lafayette (Feb. 18, 1780) concerning England's propaganda and other activities, such as making "new contracts with other petty princes in Germany" [VII, 123].

67. **Petersburg**: JA told Lafayette that the English "claimed to have concluded a treaty with the Court of Petersburg, by which Russia is to furnish them with twelve ships of the line and twenty thousand men" [VII, 123].

68. **(. . . and to Genet)**: JA sent a similar letter to Genêt [65:120] containing essentially the same information about British war propaganda intended to discourage other European powers from supporting the American war of independence [VII, 124-125].

69. **19th (next day)**: This and the following line come from Lafayette's reply to JA's letter in which he discounted the effectiveness of British rumors.

70. **Mr Burke**: [62:17, 71 below].

71. **Mr Fox**: Charles James F., 1749-1806, English statesman who sided with Burke against Lord North's policies toward the American colonies. This and the preceding line come from JA's letter of March 24, 1780, to President Huntington of the Congress, in which he mentioned a bill proposed by Edmund Burke doing away with the policies that had made British authority odious to the colonies, and Mr. Fox's charge that Thomas Hutchinson [62:47] had been, as JA put it, the "firebrand that lighted up all the fire between the two countries" [VII, 136].

72. **Bolingbroke**: Henry St. John, Viscount B., 1678-1751, English statesman and orator; author of *Idea of a Patriot King* (1749). The lines "the precise point . . . / prejudice" come from JA's letter to Genêt (April 29, 1780) recommending that Genêt print Bolingbroke's observation that the turning point in the shift of political power, like the point of the solstice, is often imperceptible and unrecognized.

73. **Elbridge Gerry**: [34:52]. The lines "For the calling . . . / . . . by warrants" come from Gerry's letter to JA (May 5, 1780) reporting the steps Congress had taken to prop up the value of American currency [VII, 188-190].

74. **$40 to 1 in specie**: The rate of depreciation of American paper money adopted March 18, 1780, by resolution of Congress. Vergennes called JA's attention to this decision in a letter of June 21, 1780, protesting the loss such a policy would mean to the French. The 20 lines that follow deal with the depreciation controversy, the cause of a bitter quarrel between JA and Vergennes as well as between JA and Franklin. JA expected Franklin to support him in defending the depreciation policy; Vergennes wanted Franklin to back the French objections with the Congress. Franklin chose not to take sides, but in a letter to Congress declared that JA was an obstruction to the alliance with France. Vergennes attempted to have JA recalled; through the efforts of his agent in Philadelphia, the Chevalier de la Luzerne, Franklin did succeed in having JA's commerce commission withdrawn and JA's role in the peace negotiations diminished by having that commission enlarged to include (in addition to Franklin) Jefferson, Henry Laurens, and John Jay [cf. Shaw, chap. vi, for an account of this episode].

75. **Chevalier de Luzerne**: [65:195]. Vergennes, in his letter of June 21, 1780, to JA said that Luzerne had already received instructions to make strong objections to the Congress; in his reply (June 22, 1780) JA, suspecting that maneuvering had been going on behind his back, asked Vergennes whether the orders had been sent "so long ago as to have reached the hand of the Chevalier da la Luzerne" or had just recently been decided and sent [VII, 193].

76. **Mazzei**: Philip M., 1730-1816, Italian physician who came to Virginia in 1773. He strongly supported the American Revolution and served as an American agent in Italy (1779-1783). This and the three following lines come from a letter JA sent to Thomas

Jefferson (June 29, 1780) reporting a meeting with Mazzei.

77. Value . . . de Vergennes: Knowing he had a degree of sympathy from Franklin and from certain members of Congress for his objections to the depreciation policy, Vergennes sent JA a letter (June 30, 1780) chastising him for not recognizing the justice of the French objections. These seven lines are from that letter [VII, 213].

78. Rush: [65:56]. From a letter dated April 28, 1780, JA received from Rush, who reported on conditions at home.

79. If the french fleet: In a letter to Vergennes (July 13, 1780), JA detailed his analysis of the military situation and the role the French fleet could play. The context of the JA line suggests that "that coast" means the whole E coast of North America. Earlier in the same letter JA wrote: "The appearance of a French fleet upon our coasts has repeatedly compelled, and ever must compel, the English to call off from their cruises all their frigates and other ships, and to assemble them at New York for their security, and the defence of that place" [VII, 223].

80. Vergennes: On July 17, 1780, JA wrote Vergennes that he was unable to see any reasons for having had to conceal his authority to negotiate a commerce treaty with the British, as Vergennes had asked him to do in a letter of February 24, 1780.

81. Amsterdam: [62:88]. On July 23, 1780, JA wrote Huntington, president of the Congress, that he had informed Vergennes of his decision to go to Amsterdam [65:148].

82. Europe: JA remarked in a letter to Franklin (Aug. 17, 1780) that only when their countrymen demonstrate their ability to win the war by themselves can they expect European nations to extend them support.

83. to show U. S.: In another letter to Huntington (Sept. 5, 1780), JA wrote that because the Athenians and Romans had left eloquent records of their achievements, they had been models down through the centuries, convincing reasons why the U. S., in its literature, should want to leave posterity a worthy record of achievements.

84. Ching Ming: Chêng Ming, "Right name" [51:20].

85. Mr Bicker . . . Neufville: The advice, as JA recalled it in his *Letters to the Boston Patriot* (1809), of Henrick Bicker, 1722-1783, an Amsterdam merchant who in 1780 recommended to JA the best way to go about securing a loan from the Dutch.

86. Neufville: Jean de N. & Sons, Dutch banking house through which JA tried to arrange an American loan; his effort failed, although the firm did what it could to support JA's request.

87. provision . . . 3 million guilders: Terms of a loan to the U. S. as explained in a letter to JA (Sept. 29, 1780) [VII, 262].

88. I answered . . . to be known: From JA's explanation of how he came to write "Twenty-Six Letters upon Interesting Subjects respecting the Revolution of America," newspaper articles by which "just sentiments of American affairs began to spread, and prevail over the continual misrepresentations of English and Stadtholderian gazettes" [VII, 265-266].

89. Mr. Calkoen: [62:87].

90. wd / be burdensome . . . on the contrary: Comments from JA's "Twenty-Six Letters."

91. Charleston: City in South Carolina captured May 12, 1780, by Sir Henry Clinton and held by British forces until December 14, 1782.

92. when England . . . regular ministers: From a letter JA wrote to Franklin (Oct. 14, 1780) in which he mentioned the difficulties of securing a loan and the need for the U. S. to send ministers to all European courts in an effort to win recognition of U. S. independence.

93. Laurens: [cf. 40 above].

94. dont la fâcheuse . . . Congrès: F, "whose regrettable catastrophe makes me most unhappy . . . / a relative indicates to me that he is inclined to invest twenty thousand Dutch florins in it / Ven der Kemp can be very useful to the Congress" [VII, 317-318]. These lines come from a letter to JA from Joan Derk, Baron van der Capellen tot den Pol [62:93; 65:152], a leader of the Patriot party in the Netherlands friendly to the U. S.

95. King of Spain . . . (meaning placing one): These nine lines are taken from a letter Franklin wrote JA concerning another possibility for a loan to the U. S.

96. Monsieur Necker: Jacques N., 1732-1804, French statesman; minister of finance (1776-1781); director general of finance (1788-1790).

97. depuis qu'il . . . à la Tour: F, "since he . . . has been locked up in the Tower" [VII, 323]. In a letter to JA (Nov. 1, 1780), L. M. Dumas made this inquiry about the condition of Henry Laurens, held captive in England.

98. towYer of London: Tower of L., ancient fortress, prison, and royal residence.

99. America is willing: JA's observation to Henrick Bicker in a letter (Nov. 6, 1780) about conditions for a loan.

100. Mortier and Meerkemaer: Dutch brokers employed by banking house of Van Staphorst.

101. Mssrs Staphorst: [62:108].

102. Mr Blomberg: Banker in Amsterdam. This and the preceding line come from a letter Bicker sent to JA (Nov. 7, 1780). Blomberg's illness made it necessary for JA to deal with another broker.

103. Tenkate: The Messrs. Tenkate, Amsterdam brokers; this and the following line reflect Bicker's opinion.

104. Mr Van Vloten: Van Vlooten, Dutch broker, recommended by Bicker with some reservations in a letter to JA (Nov. 11, 1780) as another possible source for a loan.

105. H. Bicker: [cf. 85 above]. The preceding three lines come from Bicker's letter to JA (Nov. 11, 1780) [VII, 327-328].

106. but have never . . . J.A.: JA's comment on the failure of his efforts up to that time to secure a loan, written in a letter to Alexander Gillon of South Carolina, who was in Amsterdam to negotiate a loan for South Carolina and had submitted a request for money to JA [VII, 328].

107. Sir Jo. Yorke: Joseph Y., Baron Dover, 1724-1792, English diplomat; ambassador to The Hague (1751-1780). In a letter to Huntington, president of the Congress (Nov. 16, 1780), JA corrected an erroneous description of the government of the Netherlands presented by Sir Joseph Yorke in a memorial to the States General (Nov. 10, 1780), which contained British protests against the proposed "Amsterdam treaty" between the U.S. and the Dutch and demanded punishment of the regents who had supported it.

108. England: In a letter to Huntington (Nov. 17, 1780), JA explained that one difficulty hindering his efforts to secure a loan was the long-established habit the Dutch had of thinking of England as their natural ally and of France as their natural enemy. Taking advantage of their past relationship, George III was demanding that the Dutch repudiate the proposed Amsterdam treaty and punish the Amsterdam regents participating in its negotiation. When the Dutch did not submit to British demands, war broke out. In time JA succeeded in negotiating loans with the Dutch.

109. la persécution . . . d'Holland: F, "the persecution against M. Van Berckel / and his associates / . . . not to rush your departure / business . . . crisis . . . time could / object of the English beyond that of amusing the Republic of Holland" [VII, 334-336]. This passage comes from a letter Van der

Capellen sent JA (Nov. 28, 1780) in response to the controversy resulting from the British protest against the Amsterdam treaty. E. F. Van Berckel had been singled out for particular criticism because he had sponsored the treaty. Source reads "pourroit" for "pourrait."

110. loss of Charleston . . . neutrality: JA's letter (Dec. 14, 1780) to Huntington contained these observations as to why the Dutch were not eager to provide political or monetary help to the U.S. [cf. 92 above].

111. tout crédit . . . de faire face: F, "all credit whether of a people or an individual / . . . of two things / the opinion as to the good faith / and as to the chances of his meeting." These lines come from a letter Van der Capellen sent to JA (Dec. 24, 1780) reminding him of the conditions conducive to winning the support he was seeking [VII, 344].

112. Affaires . . . upon 'change: Lines taken from JA's letter to Huntington (Dec. 25, 1780). Source reads "holydays" [VII, 346].

113. 'What they . . . years later: Taken from *Letters to the Boston Patriot* (1809) in which JA again spoke of the need for checks and balances in governmental authority. Thus Pound returns to the theme that opened the canto: "There is nothing so instructive to aristocracy and democracy as the history of Holland . . . nothing which ought so forcibly to admonish them to shake hands and mutually agree to choose an arbitrator between . . ." [VII, 348n].

CANTO LXIX

Sources

Charles Francis Adams, ed., *The Works of John Adams,* VII, VIII; Frederick K. Sanders, *John Adams Speaking,* Orono, Maine, 1975, 400-427; Claude G. Bowers, *Jefferson and Hamilton,* New York, 1925; Dante, *Inferno,* passim.

Background

Broadus Mitchell, *Alexander Hamilton*, New York, 2 vols., 1957-1962; L. H. Butterfield, ed., *Diary and Autobiography of John Adams,* II, Cambridge, Mass. 1961; Samuel Flagg Bemis, *The Diplomacy of the American Revolution,* Bloomington, Indiana, 1957.

Exegeses

CE, *Ideas,* 43; Dekker, *Cantos,* 186; Davis, *Vision,* 142; WB, *Rose,* 46; CB-R, *ZBC,* 240.

Glossary

1. **Congress**: Still concerned with his problems in Amsterdam, JA wrote to the president of Congress that in the event that Holland aligned itself with France, Spain, and America, a permanent minister from Congress to Holland would be useful. He added: "In case the armed neutrality take it up, a minister authorized to represent the United States to all the neutral courts, might be of use" [VII, 348].

2. **Huntington**: Samuel H., 1731-1796, president of Continental Congress (1779-1781), sent JA a commission as minister plenipotentiary to the Low Countries.

3. **Madame . . . Schorn**: F, "Madame the widow of Henry Schorn." JA in a letter to Francis Dana revealed a secret address given him by the widow. The line in Dutch means: "up near the Agsterburg Wall in the Hoogstraat" [VII, 353].

4. **depreciation . . . only six**: These 18 lines summarize most of a letter from JA to Baron van der Capellen (Jan. 21, 1781) [62:93]. The letter of several pages includes: "England has spent sixty millions in this war. America six. Which people then are the ablest to pay? Yet England has credit, America not. Is this from reasoning or prejudice?" [VII, 357-360].

5. **a british minister**: A letter (March 17, 1781) from JA to Charles Dumas [cf. 21 below] asks a rhetorical question: "When will mankind cease to be the dupes of the insidious artifices of a British minister and stockjobber?" [VII, 379]. The minister referred to, not in source, is prob. Shelbourne [cf. 17 below].

6. **Vergennes**: French minister of foreign affairs [65:145]. JA, writing 28 years later (1809) to the *Boston Patriot* about a proposed congress of Vienna, protests that his many letters have been received in silence. He reports that he is happy because the plot of England to use such a congress to cheat the U.S. out of its liberty was defeated by his letters to Vergennes and with the help of two emperors, Alexander I of Russia and Joseph II of Austria. The congress, which did not take place, should not be confused with the Congress of Vienna of 1814-15.

7. **La Cour de Londres . . . Etats Unis**: F, "The Court of London will avoid as long as it can / the admission direct / or indirect of the independence of the United States." From letter of France to courts of Petersburg and Vienna about the proposed congress at Vienna [VII, 667]. Source has ". . . et aussi long-temps, qu'elle le pourra, l'aveu direct et indirect . . ."

8. **Cornwallis**: A return to the events of 1781. This line comes from JA's letter to the president of Congress saying that the defeat of Cornwallis has resulted in the "appearances of a growing interest" among Hollanders for "an alliance with France and America" [VII, 488].

9. **J'ai honte d'être Hollandais**: F, "I am ashamed of being Dutch." Said in letter to JA by Joan Derk, Baron van der Capellen, Dutch statesman and friend to America [62:93; 68:94], whose plan to lend 12,000 florins was circumvented. Source reads "Hollandois" [VII, 501].

10. **burgomasters**: To get a loan, JA went next to the "house of Haerlem" where he was met by the described people [VII, 505] who, he concluded in a letter to Franklin, were paid to refuse him [VII, 508-509].

11. **schepens**: D, "sheriffs."

12. **Friesland**: Province in N Netherlands to whose government JA made advances and by whom he was officially received.

13. **M. Berdsma**: Bergsma, fl. 1780, official of province of Friesland.

14. **Province House**: Official building of province of Friesland.

15. hanseatic: In another letter, JA said he had not been authorized to deal with the Hanseatic cities, but he believed it was in the nature of the situation that trade between them and America would flourish.

16. old gentleman: Henry Laurens [68: 40]. He was on parole from London for his health. JA talked with Laurens and reported to Franklin his opinions about the English government in 1782.

17. Shelbourne: Sir William Petty, 1737-1805, 2d Earl of Shelburne, 1st Marquis of Lansdowne; English statesman; secretary of state under Pitt (1766-1768) when he attempted conciliation of American colonies. But as first lord of the treasury and prime minister (1782-1783) Shelburne's attitude seemed ambiguous, although he eventually conceded American independence. Source has "Shelburne."

18. Fiseaux . . . etc.: Dutch banking houses and moneyed men. JA planned to obtain from them jointly a loan of 5 million. Source reads "Fizeaux" [VII, 575].

19. Le corps . . . Schiedam: F, "The businessmen of this city / wishing to add their acclamations to those of the whole nation / J. Nollet, Schiedam." From letter of Jacob Nolet to JA (April 19, 1782) expressing enthusiasm for the independence of the United States.

20. 'On m'a dit . . . de Rotterdam': F, "I have been told that these gentlemen of Schiedam / are giving this repast for a hundred people / and that there will be many people from Rotterdam." Source reads "donneront un repas" [VII, 576].

21. Dumas: From letter from Dumas to JA (April 30, 1782). Charles William Frederick D., Swiss man of letters employed by Franklin as an agent to promote American interests in Holland. He acted as secretary to JA while he was there and stayed in Holland as American chargé d'affaires after JA left.

22. remedium: L, "remedy." From letter of May 11, 1782. Pound dates it 1780 [VII, 583].

23. Willinck . . . : The bankers who made the loan of 5 million to JA.

24. piddling: JA in letter to Francis Dana (May 13, 1782). He added: "I shall be plagued with piddling politicians as long as I live" [VII, 584].

25. Van Vloten: Van Vlooten, Dutch broker who helped negotiate loan. From letter of JA to Willinck and other bankers [VII, 585].

26. The minister of the Emperor: Source says: "I come now to the most difficult task of all, the description of the foreign ministers. The minister of the Emperor is ninety years of age, and never appears at court, or anywhere else" [VII, 623]. The foreign minister and chancellor under Emperor Joseph II from 1753 to 1792 was Wenzel Anton, Fürst von Kaunitz, who was born in 1711. In 1782, therefore, he would have been only 71. JA's remark must have been based on rumor.

27. Oswald: Richard O., 1705-1784, English statesman. In 1782 he was authorized to make peace with the U.S. at the Paris peace negotiations. From letter of John Jay to JA (Sept. 28, 1782) [VII, 641-642].

28. statuum quorum: L, "of the condition of which."

29. (Lafayette): In a letter to Lafeyette, JA tells how much money in loans he has got and says he hopes France will make up the rest that is needed [VII, 642].

30. J. A. to Jefferson: Source says this letter of October 7, 1782, is from JA to John Jay, not Jefferson [VII, 645].

31. France: In a letter to JA, Francis Dana analyzes France's efforts to convince Russia to sell to her during the war. Source reads "same from America" [VII, 650].

32. King's loans: JA wrote from Paris:

"There are great complaints of scarcity of money here, and what there is is shut up. The King's loans do not fill. The war has lasted so long, and money has been scattered with so much profusion, that it is now very scarce in France, Spain, and England, as well as Holland" [VII, 664].

33. Vergennes: JA believed that he and John Jay were deliberately given bad advice in protocol which, had they followed it, would have resulted in embarrassment to the U.S., and any European statesman would have known the advice was bad. Vergennes recommended that they deal with the English and Spaniards before they "were put upon the equal footing that our rank demanded." JA believed that if he and Jay "had yielded the punctilio of rank" they would have "sunk in the minds of the English, French, Spaniards, Dutch, and all the neutral powers." Since any European statesman would have known this, JA could only conclude that Vergennes meant to keep them down: ". . . to keep his hand under our chin to prevent us from drowning, but not to lift our heads out of the water?" [VIII, 4].

34. avoid . . . : JA is protesting that since 1775 he has advanced the principle that the U.S. should not become too dependent on any one European power [VIII, 35].

35. Nous sommes . . . la Société Bourgeoise: F, "Meanwhile we are delighted to see / that the states of the other provinces and consequently the / entire republic have, following the example of the States of Friesland / recognized . . . / (signed) the members of the Société Bourgeoise" [VIII, 56]. The sentence is completed by "the liberty and independence of America."

36. de Leeuwarde: Leeuwarden, commercial and industrial town, Friesland Province, N Netherlands.

37. W. Wopkins V. Cats: Officials of Friesland Province; members of the Société Bourgeoise established at Leeuwarden. Source has "Wopkens."

38. S. P. Q. Amst . . . juncta: L, "Senate and People of Amsterdam—in most fortunate union joined" [Vol. VIII of *WJA* has picture of the medal as a frontispiece].

39. factions etc.: In a letter to Robert Morris (May 21, 1783), JA says that many slanders and falsehoods are told him in the belief that he will relay them, and thus mislead, the Congress and the secretary of state. He adds: "I think it necessary, therefore, to employ a little discretion in such cases" [VIII, 59].

40. his Majesty: In his letter of May 27 JA says: "His Lordship then said, that . . . after the levee, I should be presented to his Majesty [Geo. III], in his closet, and there deliver my letter of credence" [VIII, 251-252].

41. To T. J / : JA asks Jefferson in letter of July 18, 1785: "Can it be a secret understanding between St. James's and Versailles? The design of ruining, if they can, our carrying trade, and annihilating all our navigation and seamen, is too apparent" [VIII, 279; the editor at top of page: *"The rest in Cipher, and kept secret"*].

42. St James: The Court of St. James's, London.

43. Act of navigation: JA in letter to John Jay (Aug. 8, 1785) opposes a law that would require all goods shipped to the U.S. to come in American ships navigated by American masters, with three-fourths of the seamen American [VIII, 297].

44. bubbles . . . : In a letter to Jay, JA says: "We have hitherto been the bubbles of our own philosophical and equitable liberality; and . . . both France and England have shown a constant disposition to take a selfish and partial advantage of us because of them." He hopes that "we shall be the dupes no longer than we must." Source dates this letter August 10, 1785 [VIII, 299].

45. Jay: John J., 1745-1829, American statesman who assisted in peace and trade negotiations with Great Britain.

46. Barbary: Barbary States, N Africa. JA wrote to Jefferson (Aug. 18, 1785): "He [the emissary from the Barbary States] should be instructed further, to make diligent inquiry concerning the productions of those countries which would answer in America, and those of the United States which might find a market in Barbary" [VIII, 301].

47. both governments: France and England. To Jefferson, JA says that, if these governments have been opening his mail, "much good may those contents do them. They both know they have deserved them. I hope they will convince them of their error, and induce them to adopt more liberal principles towards us" [VIII, 301].

48. Mr Pitt: William P. the Younger, 1759-1778 [66:14]. In a letter to Jay (Aug. 25, 1785), JA explains his explanation to Pitt, who had said the English got their interest on debts straight through wars. JA says that American lawyers believed that interest and principal, as well as all laws, were negated upon a declaration of war.

49. spermaceti: JA reporting to John Jay on a sales pitch he made (1785) to the British to persuade them to buy U.S. whale oil. He wrote that he had said (after the lines in the canto): ". . . we are all surprised that you prefer darkness, and consequent robberies, burglaries, and murders in your streets, to the receiving, as a remittance, our spermaceti oil. The lamps . . . in Downing Street . . . are dim by midnight, and extinguished by two o'clock; whereas our oil would burn bright till nine o'clock in the morning, and chase away, before the watchmen, all the villains, and save you the trouble and danger of introducing a new police into the city" [VIII, 308-309].

50. Portugal . . . better: JA protests the Methuen treaty which restricted trade. Port is a wine from Portugal [VIII, 324].

51. Lisbon: A sweet, light-colored wine produced in Estremadura and shipped from Lisbon, Portugal.

52. Madeira: Wine made on the island of Madeira; Malmsey, Sercial, and Bual are the best-known varieties.

53. His Lordship: Lord Carmarthen. JA wished there would be "nothing of greater difficulty and more danger between the two countries" [VIII, 325].

54. Holland: JA sent to John Jay an English translation of a contract for a new loan from Holland [letter of June 16, 1787; VIII, 441-442].

55. Lafayette: Letter to JA describes Lafayette's hopes for a French constitution. He says they will have the best, but one. "May *that one* . . . be forever the happy lot of the sons of America!" [VIII, 456].

56. T. Jefferson: JA says: "We agree . . . that the many should have a full, fair, and perfect representation. You are apprehensive of monarchy, I, of aristocracy" [VIII, 464].

57. In this matter of redeeming certificates . . . : This line and the remainder of the canto concern what is to Pound a major turning point in the economic direction of the nation. Pound's immediate source for the lines is Bowers, chapters iii and iv (pp. 43-91), which contains a discussion of the strategy and step-by-step maneuvering Hamilton employed to implement his elaborate plan for controlling the states and getting them into the power of the federal government: "With the startling effect of a magician at his tricks he created the machinery of his complicated department . . . outlined his plans for revenue immediately required, and sat down with joy to the preparation of his 'Report on the Public Credit,' which was to proclaim the public faith and establish the Nation's credit" [p. 43]. Part of Hamilton's plan was the so-called Assumption Bill, a mechanism by which the federal government would assume the debts of the states and redeem at full value certificates issued to pay soldiers and buy war materials–certificates that had sunk to a fraction of their face value. JA approved the plan as a necessary and honest measure to establish the credit of the nation. So did Madison at first. But it soon became known that Hamilton in secret meetings had leaked information to a number of friends and financial operators who were buying up the certificates at almost no cost in order to make a financial killing: "The greater part of the certificates were in the hands of the prosperous who had taken advantage of the necessities of the orignal holders–Revolutionary soldiers, small farmers, hard-pressed country merchants. The funding system would tax all the people to pay to the rich a hundred cents on the dollar for evidence of debts that had cost them fifteen or twenty. With the people taxed to pay the interest–it was proposed to perpetuate the debt. Thus, for generations . . . the Government would operate for the enrichment of the few already rich, and the masses would pay the piper" [p. 45].

58. in margine: L, "in the margin."

59. King . . . Sedgwick: Part of Hamilton's plan was a national bank, not conceived as part of the treasury but modeled upon the Bank of England. It was designed as a private institution from which the government as well as other banks, institutions, or individuals might borrow. In spite of a bitter fight which some say created the split between the Hamiltonians and the Jeffersonians and resulted in a two-party system, the first Bank of the United States was chartered in the summer of 1791. Bowers writes: "Then came the election of Bank directors in the fall, and indignation flamed when the prizes went to leaders in the Congress that had created the Bank–to Rufus King, Samuel Johnson of North Carolina, William Smith of South Carolina, Jeremiah Wadsworth of the 'fast sailing vessels,' John Laurance of New York, William Bingham of Philadelphia, Charles Carroll of Carrollton, George Cabot, Fisher Ames, and Thomas Willing, the partner of Robert Morris" [p. 90].

60. King: Rufus K., 1755-1827, American statesman, graduated Harvard, 1777; served in Revolution; practiced law in Massachusetts; delegate to Continental Congress (1784-1787); moved to New York and was elected to first U.S. Senate. A strong advocate of Federalist doctrines, he supported Hamilton's programs, defended Jay's Treaty, and was defeated at various times as a candidate for vice-president and president.

61. Sam Johnson: William Samuel J., 1727-1819, American jurist and educator; member of Continental Congress (1784-1787) and U.S. Senate (1789-1791); president of Columbia College (1787-1800).

62. Smith (W.): William Loughton S., ?1758-1812, American statesman; member of House of Representatives (1789-1797); minister to Portugal (1797-1801). He supported Hamilton's financial policies and was a heavy speculator in government paper.

63. Wadsworth (Jeremiah: J. W., 1743-1804, American soldier and politician; commissary general of Continental Army (1778-1779); member of House of Representatives from Connecticut (1789-1795). When he was assured the Assumption Bill would pass, he sent two fast-sailing vessels to the South to buy up certificates cheap. In the debate on the bill he responded to a speaker who said soldiers were being victimized: "Poor Soldiers! . . . I am tired of hearing about the poor soldiers" [Bowers, 55].

64. J. Lawrence: John Laurance, 1750-1810, Revolutionary soldier and statesman; member of House of Representatives (1789-1793); U.S. senator (1796-1800); active supporter of Hamilton's monetary policies.

65. Bingham: William B., 1752-1804, American politician from Philadelphia; founder of Bank of North America (1781); U.S. senator (1795-1801); elected director of first Bank of the United States.

66. Carrol of Carrolton: Charles Carroll of Carrollton, 1737-1832, Revolutionary leader from Maryland; member of Continental Congress (1776-1778); signer of

Declaration of Independence; member of U.S. Senate (1789-1792).

67. **Hamilton**: Alexander H., 1757-1804, American statesman, born in Nevis, West Indies, whence he came as a brilliant student to Columbia College in 1774. He wrote articles espousing the patriot cause so well that they were thought to be by John Jay [62:131]. As a captain of artillery in the war, he attracted the attention of Washington, who made him aide-de-camp and private secretary, in which offices he provided invaluable services. But in 1781 he left Washington's staff for more active field duty and performed brilliantly at Yorktown. Through marriage he connected himself with the old and powerful financial circles of New York, where he practiced law and became a member of the Continental Congress. Always the proponent of a strong federal authority, he was a delegate to the Annapolis Convention and to the federal Constitutional Convention. He helped get the Constitution ratified by a series of articles in *The Federalist Papers.* Washington made him the first secretary of the treasury, from which office he was able to promote his ideas for fiscal management of the young republic, which involved several premises: (1) the government should be run as a sound business venture; (2) the federal government should assume all debts of the states and pay them in full; (3) income to pay the debts should be derived from excise taxes, tariffs, and the like. Thus Hamilton [AH] tied the operation of government to the money interests. He himself founded the Bank of New York and knew the international banking and financial operations of Europe. Though Washington wanted to avoid political parties, AH's programs and his methods of getting them adopted resulted almost immediately in the formation of two political forces: the Federalists, led by AH and JA, and the Anti-Federalists who organized under the banner of Jefferson. Although AH never used his office to make money himself (on the contrary, he died without significant wealth), many of his followers did use secret information and the AH program to make huge fortunes. Since part of his program involved using the bank to lend the government money, a procedure that has kept the U.S. in debt for most of its history, Pound deems AH responsible for starting the country on the wrong road to eventual economic disaster; Pound's tone thus is that of an outraged moralist, and AH is the "pink-haired snot" and a traitor, and those who stood against him [Jefferson, Madison, and James Jackson] are the heroes.

68. **Cabot**: George C., 1752-1823, American businessman and politician; senator from Massachusetts (1791-1796).

69. **Fisher Ames**: 1758-1808, member of House of Representatives (1789-1797), where he was the eloquent defender of AH's financial program.

70. **Thomas Willing**: 1731-1821, American banker and statesman; member of Continental Congress (1775-1776); president of first Bank of the United States (1791-1807); supporter of Hamilton's financial policies; business partner of Robert Morris [cf. 71 below].

71. **Robt Morris**: Robert M., 1734-1806, American financier and statesman; member of Continental Congress (1776-1778); signer of Declaration of Independence; member of U.S. Senate (1789-1795). Morris was AH's chief legislative agent in the Senate [Bowers, 47]. During the debate on the Assumption Bill, "Sinister stories were finding their way into print" which involved Morris: if the bill was passed, "Robert Morris would benefit $18,000,000, Jeremiah Wadsworth [cf. 63 above] would profit $9,000,000" [Bowers, 50].

72. **Sedgwick**: Theodore S., 1746-1813, American jurist and statesman; member of Continental Congress (1785-1788), of House of Representatives (1789-1796, 1799-1801), and of Senate (1796-1799).

73. natural burella: I, "natural dungeon" [*Inf.* XXXIV, 98]. Implying that the followers of AH belong in the lowest depth of Hell.

74. Arnold: Benedict A., 1741-1801, American army officer and traitor, received rank of brigadier general in Continental Army. In 1779 he began correspondence with the British forces and in 1780, while he was commander of West Point, he arranged for the surrender of the fort to the British. The plot was discovered and Arnold fled to British protection.

75. Bancroft: Edward B., 1744-1821, b. Westfield, Mass., spy during the Revolution. While in London he became a friend of Ben Franklin's and began to serve as a secret agent, sending reports to the commissioners in France. But he was a double agent and reported movements of the Americans to the British. In 1778 he gave advance information about the Franco-American alliance to the British, thus clearly establishing himself as a traitor to the American cause.

76. per l'argine sinistra dienno volta: I, "by the bank to the left they wheeled around" [*Inf.* XXI, 136, "Per l'argine sinistro volta dienno"]. Dante is describing comic movements of devils guarding the grafters in the 5th ditch of the 8th circle of Hell. The tone of much of Bowers's account is one of hilarity; his first chapter is entitled "Days of Comedy." He wrote: "On the opening of the debate one champion of Assumption let the cat out of the bag with the statement that 'if the general Government has the payment of all the debts, it must of course have all the revenue, and if it possesses the whole revenue, it is equal, in other words, to the whole power.' 'Yes' cried the irrepressible Jackson [cf. 84 below] in stentorian tones, 'if it lulls the Shays of the North it will rouse the Sullivans of the South'–and the fight was on . . . . Very soon, Maclay [cf. 83 below], watching the proceedings in the House with ferret eyes, thought he observed 'the rendezvousing of the crew of the Hamilton galley.' He found that 'all hands are piped to quarters'" [Bowers, 60-61]. In fact, opposition became heated and vocal enough to cause AH's supporters concern. They delayed a vote until Vining of Delaware could arrive. Wild rumor had it that AH was prepared to give him, says Bowers, "a thousand guineas for his vote. 'A thousand guineas,' snorted Maclay, . . .' they could get him for a tenth that sum'" [Bowers, 61].

77. Mr Schuyler (Filippo): Philip John S., 1733-1804, American statesman; member of Senate (1789-1791); AH's father-in-law. By using the Italian form of his name, Pound links him with Filippo Argenti, famous denizen among the wrathful [*Inf.* VIII, 61]. Schuyler is one of those who became overwrought and nervous as the debate over assumption increased in violence. Says Bowers: "The debate was becoming bitter. The able, bitter-tongued Edanus Burke of South Carolina made a ferocious attack on Hamilton, and the lobbies, coffee-houses, streets, buzzed with talk of a duel. . . . King [cf. 60 above] 'looked like a boy who had been whipped.' And the hair on Schuyler, a heavy speculator and father-in-law of Hamilton, 'stood on end as if the Indians had fired at him'" [Bowers, 62].

78. sifilides: I, "ones with syphilis" [*Inf.* VIII, 51: *orribili dispregi!* "horrible diseases"; Pound probably supplies the word as an example].

79. in their progeny: The offspring of the latest generation of all those who in the beginning and for personal gain put the country on the wrong economic and financial basis. Pound's polemic tone comes from his conviction that even today they show no repentance.

80. quindi . . . membruto: I, "thus Cocytus, Cassius the big-membered" [amalgam of lines 52, 67, *Inf.* XXXIV, joining the lake of ice at the pit of Hell with the Roman devoured in one of Satan's three mouths].

81. **Mr Madison**: James M., 1751-1836, 4th president of the U.S. (1809-1817). With JA, Washington, and others he opposed British colonial measures and helped generate the patriot cause. As a graduate of the College of New Jersey (now Princeton) he became an early expert in constitutional law. His knowledge increased with time and experience until he was deferred to by almost everybody as the single most authoritative and dispassionate interpreter of constitutional problems. In 1776 he helped to draft a constitution for Virginia and later served in the Continental Congress (1780-1783, 1787-1788). He saw the weakness of the Articles of Confederation and succeeded in having the federal Constitutional Convention convened in 1787. He was a contributor to *The Federalist Papers* and the chief hand in the actual drafting of the Constitution. He was also a strong advocate of the Bill of Rights. Although some consider him responsible for the conservative nature of the Constitution, he was opposed to the measures of AH and became a supporter of Thomas Jefferson. His loyalties became increasingly clear with his reactions to AH's specific bills in the first Congress.

82. **not speculators**: AH's "Report on the Public Credit" involved several pieces of legislation; one was the Assumption Bill and another was a funding measure that would provide the money to pay the debts assumed. Bowers says: "All men of honor sympathized with the purpose of discharging the debt. . . . Few at the moment found fault with the funding system, though some would have preferred a speedy liquidation through the sale of the public lands. Then–sudddenly–a low murmur of protest, followed by acrimonious attacks" [Bowers, 44-45]. Madison listened to the debate for a number of days without comment. Finally, deciding that justice was to be found on both sides, he offered a substitute measure which included a formula for payment to original holders of the certificates rather than providing exorbitant profits to speculators. His last comment in the debate on his measure was that only when "he had parted with his self-respect 'could he admit that America ought to erect the monuments of her gratitude, not to those who saved her liberties, but to those who had enriched themselves on her funds.'" Several days later "Madison's plan was voted down. It was found long afterward that of the sixty-four members of the House, twenty-nine were security-holders" [Bowers, 56].

83. **Maclay**: William M., 1734-1804, American statesman; as a member of the Senate (1789-1791) he strongly opposed Hamilton's financial measures. Bowers wrote: "The astonishing thing is that the comparatively crude Maclay from the wilds of Pennsylvania and the leather-lunged James Jackson [cf. 84 below] from sparsely settled Georgia should have caught the full significance of it all [the Assumption Bill] before it dawned on Jefferson and Madison" [pp. 45-46]. As more and more congressmen got into the business of buying up certificates cheap, Maclay wrote: "I really fear the members of Congress are deeper in this business than any others" [p. 47].

84. **Jim Jackson**: James J., 1757-1806, American statesman, member of House of Representatives (1789-1791); governor of Georgia (1798-1801). Born in Devonshire, he came during boyhood to the Georgia frontier where he early became known for violence. Gallatin called him a "pugnacious animal." Said Mitchell: "He fought through the revolution . . . later held the rank of brigadier in the state militia pressing back the Indians. He liked single combat too, whether eye gouging or with pistols in his many duels; he killed the lieutenant governor in an 'interview' without seconds in 1780. . . . In politics he was irregularly Republican, but always violent" [Mitchell, II, 45-46].

85. **Tom**: Thomas Jefferson. Of Madison's

relationship with Jefferson, Bowers says: "Jefferson loved him as a son. . . . Through many years they constantly interchanged visits, corresponded regularly, and traveled together whenever possible." But after a page of comment on the closeness of the two men, Bowers adds: "But when Madison rose that cold February day to make his first attack on Hamilton's programme, he acted on his own volition and without consultation with the man who was to be his chief," meaning Tom Jefferson [Bowers, 53].

CANTO LXX

Sources

Charles Francis Adams, ed., *The Works of John Adams*, VIII, IX; Frederick K. Sanders, *John Adams Speaking*, Orono, Maine, 1975, 428-458; Guido Cavalcanti, "Donna mi priegha," 5th ed., 1527.

Background

L. H. Butterfield, ed., *Diary and Autobiography of John Adams*, II, Cambridge, Mass., 1961; Broadus Mitchell, *Alexander Hamilton*, New York, 1962; Catherine Drinker Bowen, *John Adams and the American Revolution*, Boston, 1950.

Exegeses

Sanders, "The French Theme of Canto 70," *Pai*, 2-3, 379-389; CE, *Ideas*, 43, 116, 176-177; Davis, *Vision*, 95, 143; DP, *Barb*, 7, 233; CB-R, *ZBC*, 240.

Glossary

1. **J.A.**: John Adams expressed this sentiment about being vice-president in a letter to John Trumbull [Jan. 23, 1791). He added : '. . . I wish myself again at the bar, old as I am" [IX, 573].

2. **Mr. Pinckney**: Charles C. P., 1746-1825, sent by Washington, near the end of his presidency, on a special peace mission to France (1796-97). Because the French refused to recognize his status, Pinckney was forced to go to Amsterdam, where members of the French government told him of Talleyrand's monetary requirements. The incident became the famous XYZ Affair [cf. 16 below]. In a memo

(dated April 14, 1797) to the secretary of state, JA, who had been president only a month, asked: "Whether the refusal to receive Mr. Pinckney, and the rude orders to quit Paris and the territory of the republic . . . are bars to all further measures of negotiation" [VIII, 540].

3. **Mr. Adams**: A number of people seemed to be possessed with the idea of "leading" Mr. Adams. In a note CFA says "Fortunate would it have been for all the parties, if the idea of *leading* Mr. Adams had not been always uppermost in their minds!" VIII, 547n].

4. **Blount**: William B., 1749-1800, American political leader; U.S. senator from Tennessee (1796-97). Blount was expelled from the Senate on the charge of plotting to aid the British to get control of Spanish Florida and Louisiana. President Adams became suspicious of his money speculations abroad.

5. **Gerry**: Elbridge G., 1744-1814, American statesman, member of the XYZ mission to France [cf. 16 below]. In a letter (July 8, 1797) JA instructs Gerry to check into the general conduct of Americans abroad, including Blount. He adds: ". . . I fear these speculators have done this country no good. . . . Decorum must be observed. You will be surrounded with projectors and swindlers. You will not be deceived by them" [VIII, 548].

6. **Marshall**: John M., 1755-1835, American jurist who later became one of the great chief justices of the Supreme Court [32:29]. In 1797 he was one of the commissioners Adams sent to France in his efforts to prevent a war between that country and the U.S. JA wrote: "I sincerely wish peace and friendship with the French [frogs]; but, while they countenance none but enemies of our Constitution and administration . . . , self-defence, as well as fidelity to the public, will compel me to have a care what appointments I make" [VIII, 549].

7. **St Jago de Cuba**: S, Santiago de Cuba, seaport and capital of Oriente Province in E Cuba. French privateers cast numbers of American sailors ashore on Cuba, a place where no trading ships stopped. To get off the island the sailors had to take service on privateers, on which they were mistreated. In response to this problem and others JA wrote: "[There] will be no relief to our commerce . . . until our vessels arm in their own defence. This is my opinion" [Oct. 14, 1797; VIII, 553-554].

8. **Secretary**: Secretary of the treasury. A bill before the Congress (engineered by Hamilton behind the scenes) set that office up, "premeditatedly," to rival that of the president. JA wrote: ". . . and that policy will be pursued, if we are not on our guard, till we have a quintuple or a centuple executive directory, with all the Babylonish dialect which modern pedants most affect" [VIII, 555].

9. **Vervennes**: Charles Gravier, comte de Vergennes, French minister of foreign affairs [65:145]. In a letter to JA, Timothy Pickering [62:156], secretary of state, made a remark to which JA referred in a return letter to Pickering. CFA excerpted from Pickering's letter the passage involved and includes it in a footnote which has the sentence: "The friends of Vergennes . . . do not like the facts laid to his charge. M. Marbois would have wished Colonel P. had not so deeply pressed that matter" [VIII, 556n]. The situation was extremely delicate. The note is of interest because it is one of JA's earliest official reactions as president to a problem that in the next four years grew to violent confrontation and increased the polarity between Congress and the public; it finally resulted in JA's defeat for a second term. The Hamilton-led forces were pro-British and increasingly called for war with France. The Jefferson forces were pro-French and antiwar. JA's efforts to ameliorate the differences, maintain the dignity of the new nation, and keep out of war satisfied extremists on neither side. As the situation developed, the extremist forces grew in numbers and in stridency.

10. Hamilton: As the clamor for war with France increased in the Hamilton-guided press, the possibility of such a war also increased; it therefore became JA's policy to "prepare for war and negotiate for peace." Although personally he was all for developing the navy, being certain that a war with France would be conducted mostly at sea, he finally nominated Washington to be "commander-in-chief of all the armies raised or to be raised in the United States." The question then was who should be second-in-command. Washington anguished over three people: Knox, Pinckney, and Hamilton. Hamilton's followers intrigued with Washington to get him appointed, but Washington couldn't decide. JA wanted no command for Hamilton. In a letter to James McHenry, secretary of war, he wrote (Aug. 29, 1798) that a procedure he outlined would result in Hamilton's being commissioned with the others but that Hamilton would not be in command. He added: "There has been too much intrigue in this business with General Washington and me" [VIII, 588].

11. McHenry: James M. [62:155]. Washington, late in his second term, had made McHenry secretary of war (1796). JA kept him on in his cabinet, but when he discovered that McHenry was serving Hamilton better than himself, he got rid of him.

12. We shd / have frigates: Sentiments of JA, who believed that merchant vessels should be armed and that the American merchant marine should be protected at sea.

13. expedient . . . Pickering: From a letter JA wrote from Quincy (Oct. 20, 1798), anticipating the opening of Congress. Some of the questions he raised are those of the canto lines [VIII, 609-610].

14. Pickering: Timothy P., 1745-1829; b. Salem, Mass.; graduated Harvard, 1763. He was active in the American cause both before and during the Revolution. He entered the colonial army as a colonel and rose to become adjutant general, member of the Board of War (1777), and quartermaster general (1780-1785). Pickering held other offices in which he so distinguished himself that Washington made him secretary of state in 1795. JA continued him in that office until his pro-Hamilton intriguing and his prowar stance became too blatant; JA finally dismissed him in 1800.

15. Talleyrand: [44:28]. Although Talleyrand supported the French Revolution, he was a firm believer in constitutional monarchy. After the fall of the monarchy he fled to England (1793); a year later he took refuge in the U.S., where he lived in poverty until the Directory was established in 1795. He then returned to France and in 1797 was made minister of foreign affairs and associated himself with the rising star of Napoleon. His involvement in the XYZ Affair (1797-98) [cf. 16 below] and his endorsement of Napoleon's plan to seize Egypt led to his resignation from office in July 1799. Later that year he was reappointed to the same office.

16. X, Y, Z: XYZ Affair, an incident in the diplomatic relations between America and France (1797-98). Members of the American commission to France, Charles Cotesworth Pinckney, John Marshall, and Elbridge Gerry, accused agents X, Y, and Z of suggesting that a bribe of £50,000 in the form of a loan to France would be welcomed by the Directory and particularly by Talleyrand. The uproar created by the incident in the United States aided those who wished to destroy Franco-American relations and to be more friendly toward England, the reverse of John Adams's foreign policy. The wave of frenzy was led by the Hamiltonian faction of the Federalists. Pinckney supposedly replied to the request for money: "Millions for defense, sir, but not one cent for tribute."

17. Mr. Gerry: [cf. 5 above].

18. Hague: The Hague, seat of government of the Netherlands, 30 miles SW of Amsterdam. Vans Murray dated his letter to JA from The Hague [cf. 19 below].

19. Vans M: William Vans Murray, 1760-1803, appointed in 1798 by JA as minister to The Hague to replace John Quincy Adams. Murray helped prepare the way for recognition of an American minister to France. The canto line, "peculators . . .," comes from a letter Murray wrote in cipher to JA. The second man in the moderate party told Murray in confidence that in certain circumstances "they meant to overturn the present men, whom he represented as peculators, and as men who exhausted every thing in enormous bribes, to arrange their internal affairs, and the first moment in their power to drive out the French" [VIII, 678]. The desire of the moderate party was to join with the U.S. against France and thus get out from under complete French domination.

20. Talleyrand: JA in a letter to Washington says he intended "to nominate Mr. Murray to be minister plenipotentiary to the French republic." He planned to do so on the strength of a letter from Talleyrand, who said that any such minister would be received with honor. JA adds: "As there may be some reserves for chicane, however, Murray is not to remove from his station at the Hague until . . ." He reflects, too: "There is not much sincerity in the cant about peace; those who snivel for it now, were hot for war against Britain a few months ago, and would be now, if they saw a chance. In elective governments, peace or war are alike embraced by parties, when they think they can employ either for electioneering purposes" [VIII, 624-626].

21. My appointment: The Murray appointment finally signaled to the Hamiltonian faction that their hopes for a war against France were doomed. In a letter to his attorney general, JA said his appointment of Murray "has shown to every observing and thinking man the real strength or weakness of the Constitution. . . . To me, it has laid open characters" [VIII, 629].

22. Tim Pickering: Beginning with the secret messages from Murray and special letters from Gerry, Adams began to gather information that Pickering as secretary of state had concealed from him in order to implement Hamilton's hopes for war with France. JA did not act hastily, but when the crisis with France had diminished he fired Pickering. The letter was formal and brief: "Sir,—Divers causes and considerations, essential to the administration of the government, in my judgment, requiring a change in the department of State, you are hereby discharged from any further service as Secretary of State/JOHN ADAMS/ *President of the United States*" [IX, 55].

23. John Marshall: [cf. 6 above]. JA directed the secretary of war "to execute the office of Secretary of State so far as to affix the seal of the United States to the inclosed commission to the present Secretary of State, John Marshall, of Virginia, to be Chief Justice of the United States, and to certify in your own name on the commission as executing the office of the Secretary of State *pro hâc vice*" [IX, 95-96].

24. pro hâc vice: L, "in return."

25. Hamilton's . . . : After the death of Washington (Dec. 14, 1799), Hamilton became angry because JA would not entrust to him the command of the army. That plus "the avowed disinclination of Mr. Adams further to pursue the war policy with France" [IX, 239], along with other more ancient animosities, led Hamilton to try to prevent JA's reelection. To this end he composed a pamphlet—"The public conduct and character of John Adams, Esquire, President of the United States"—and issued it surreptitiously so that as president JA could "take no notice of it without materially compromising the dignity of his position." But after his term expired on March 15, 1801, JA answered Hamilton's allegations: "Mr. Hamilton, in his pamphlet, speaking of Talleyrand's despatches, says, 'overtures so circuitous and informal . . . were a very inadequate basis for the institution of a new mission.' . . . Here again, Mr. Hamilton's total ignorance or oblivion of the practice of our own government, as well as the constant usage of other nations in diplomatic proceedings, appears in all its lustre" [IX, 273].

26. eternal neutrality: One of Hamilton's complaints concerned the way JA went about sending a new mission to France. AH implied that JA acted through unorthodox channels and without principle. JA later wrote: "The institution of an embassy to France, in 1779, was made upon principle, and in conformity to a system of foreign affairs, formed upon long deliberation . . . and supported in Congress,–that is, a system of eternal neutrality, if possible, in all the wars of Europe" [IX, 242]. The principle is significant as JA passed on his firm convictions about it to his son, JQA, who, as secretary of state under President Monroe, used it to counter widespread opposition in laying the foundation for the Monroe Doctrine [34:54].

27. Dec. 28th 1800: Date of a letter JA wrote after he was defeated for reelection: "Before this reaches you, the news will be familiar to you, that after the 3d of March I am to be a private citizen and your brother farmer. I shall leave the State with its coffers full, and the fair prospects of a peace with all the world smiling in its face" [IX, 577].

28. 73 for Jefferson: Hamilton based his efforts to have JA defeated in the election of 1800 on promoting Aaron Burr behind the scenes. His campaign split the vote between two Federalists, JA and Burr, and resulted in the election of Jefferson, who was anti-Federalist, anti-Burr, and anti-Hamilton. JA wrote ironically to Gerry: "How mighty a power is the spirit of party! How decisive and unanimous it is! Seventy-three for Mr. Jefferson and seventy-three for Mr. Burr" [IX, 577].

29. a few foreign . . . : In a letter to a friend (March 31, 1801), JA expressed concern about the nature of the electorate: "A group of foreign liars, encouraged by a few ambitious native gentlemen, have discomfited the education, the talents, the virtues, and the property of the country. The reason is, we have no Americans in America. The federalists have been no more Americans than the anties" [IX, 582].

30. formato loco: I, "formed space." The phrase occurs in "Donna mi priegha" as *formato locho* which, at 36/178, Pound translates as "formèd trace." In LE (187-188) he discusses the term in detail: "The 'formato locho' is the trait or locus marked out in the 'possible intelletto.' . . . I do not think the Egidio is sound in thinking the 'formato locho' is a single image. Determined locus or habitat would be nearer the mark." The memory image, from the same source, Pound translates at 36/177 as "where memory liveth." The line is not in *WJA*.

31. My compliments . . . Sirens: These four lines and the rest of the canto return to events in JA's life from 1773 to his first years as vice-president. The four lines are from a letter to James Warren (Dec. 22, 1773) which recommends in a spirit of jest a project to tell the story of the Boston Tea Party (Dec. 16, 1773) in mythological dress. JA was most elated about the "tea party" and wrote in this tone: "Make my compliments to Mrs. Warren, and tell her that I want a poetical genius to describe a late frolic among the sea-nymphs and goddesses" [IX, 335]. Hyson, Congo, and Bohea are kinds of tea.

32. Tories . . . : In a letter to J. Warren (April 9, 1774), JA estimates political attitudes: "The tories were never, since I was born, in such a state of humiliation as at this moment." He traces their affability to plain fear, but adds that "there is not spirit enough on either side to bring the question to a complete decision, and . . . we shall oscillate like a pendulum, and fluctuate like the ocean" [IX, 336-337].

33. slow starvation: JA's perception of a part of England's plan to subjugate Boston.

JA's own words are "slow torments and lingering degrees" [IX, 338].

34. conclave . . . statesmen: Some of JA's thoughts after he was selected as a delegate to the first Congress at Philadelphia. He wrote to J. Warren on June 25, 1774: I view the assembly, that is to be there, as I do the court of Aeropagus, the council of the Amphictyons, a conclave, a sanhedrim, a divan, I know not what. I suppose you sent me there to school. . . . It is to be a school of political prophets, I suppose, a nursery of American Statesmen" [IX, 338-339].

35. treasons . . . : In a letter (July 25, 1774) Joseph Hawley told JA he wanted Southern gentlemen to be deeply impressed by the fact that all acts of British legislation are "absolutely repugnant to liberty." For the future he expected "nothing but new treasons, new felonies, new misprisions, new præmunires and, not to say the Lord, the devil knows what" [IX, 345].

36. Virginia: A happy note on the cooperation of Virginia in reducing trade with Britain. By sowing wheat instead of tobacco, "so many of her planters have desisted from exporting the old crop, that the vessels cannot get freight. Their men are ready to march" [IX, 355].

37. never happy . . .: Adams said this of himself when weary of the social life of Philadelphia.

38. Quincy's knowledge: From letter to Josiah Quincy (July 29, 1775) in which JA said: "I have a great opinion of your knowledge and judgment . . . concerning the channels and islands in Boston harbor" [IX, 361].

39. 2 million: Sum that a committee of the whole house unanimously agreed should be issued in "bills of credit" [IX, 357].

40. old to bind . . . franchise: From a long speculation on majority and minority rights in government by the consent of the people: "Shall we say that every individual of the community, old and young, male and female, as well as rich and poor, must consent . . . to every act of legislation? . . . Whence arises the right of the men to govern the women, without their consent? Whence the right of the old to bind the young . . . ? But why exclude women?" And later in the same letter: ". . . power always follows property. . . . Nay, I believe we may advance one step farther, and affirm that the balance of power in a society, accompanies the balance of property in land" [IX, 375-376].

41. been months here . . . : Complaint in a letter of May 29, 1776, that JA had been required to neglect his health and forgo exercise [IX, 380].

42. Justinian . . . Taylor: In a letter to Jonathan Mason (Aug. 21, 1776), JA considers the "beauties" of the law. He includes Bracton in one list and then goes on to consider civil law: "You will find it so interspersed with history, oratory, law, politics, and war and commerce, that you will find advantages in it every day. Wood, Domat, Ayliffe, Taylor, ought to be read. But these should not suffice. You should go to the fountain-head, and drink deep of the Pierian spring. Justinian's Institutes, and all the commentators upon them that you can find, you ought to read" [IX, 433].

43. Justinian: [65:126].

44. Bracton: Henry de Bracton [63:40].

45. Domat: Jean D. [or Daumat], 1625-1696, French jurist; author of *Les Loix civiles dans leur ordre naturel*, "Civil Laws in Their Natural Order" (3 vols.; 1689-1694).

46. Ayliffe: John A., 1676-1732, English jurist and legal authority.

47. Taylor: John T., 1703-1766, English jurist and scholar; author of *Elements of Civil Law* (1755).

48. from 61: Source unidentified.

49. Aversion to paper . . . : From letter to Elbridge Gerry dated at Braintree (Dec. 6, 1777). The extreme inflation in the paper money issued by the colonies caused serious difficulties, and JA found "a general inclination among the people to barter" [IX, 469-470].

50. Rush: In a letter to Benjamin Rush (Feb. 8, 1778), JA expresses a sentiment he stated many times about a subject little understood: ". . . I mean money, is least understood of any. I fear the regulation of prices will produce ruin sooner than safety. It will starve the army and the country, or I am ignorant or every principle of commerce, coin, and society" [IX, 472].

51. English reports . . . devil knows that: These seven lines concern the kinds of lies the English were spreading all over Europe, "everyone of which," wrote JA, "I know to be false. They still, however, find stock-jobbers and other persons to believe them." The English were spreading the lies to create the impression that there were serious dissensions between the Americans and the French and among Americans themselves. The five lines in quotation marks are almost verbatim from the source [IX, 474].

52. 40,000 Russians: Source unidentified, but in a letter of February 18, 1780, JA mentioned British rumors about "20,000 Russians" ready for war [68:67].

53. solicitation: In a letter to E. Gerry (Nov. 4, 1779), JA wrote: "I am more solicitious about the means of procuring the salary you mention than the sum of it. I can make it do, if I can get it" [IX, 506].

54. quails, partridges . . . Europe: These 11 lines are from two different letters. One, to James Warren (June 17, 1782) at The Hague, contains a reminiscence about the country around Braintree: "I love every tree and every rock upon all those mountains. Roving among these, and the quails, partridges, squirrels, &c, that inhabit them, shall be the amusement of my declining years. God willing, I will not go to Vermont [where his wife had bought some land]. I must be within the scent of the sea" [IX, 512-513]. The lines in parentheses, the third of which should be closed after the word "Europe," come from a letter to Jonathan Jackson, dated at Paris (Nov. 17, 1782), and are concerned with French policy: "In substance it has been this; in assistance afforded us in naval force and in money, to keep us from succumbing, and nothing more; . . . to prevent us from obtaining consideration in Europe" [IX, 515].

55. Holland: Letter from The Hague (Sept. 6, 1782) says: "One thing, thank God, is certain. I have planted the American standard at the Hague. . . . I shall look down upon the flagstaff with pleasure from the other world" [IX, 513].

56. populariser . . . : F, "popularize, depopularize." These three lines are from a letter written almost 15 years later (March 30, 1797), while JA was president. It confirms the same judgment about French policy he had made during his 1782 mission. Since Jefferson was pro-French and Washington was identified to some extent with the Hamiltonians, it was French policy to promote in the late 1790s the cause of Jefferson and to undermine the positions of the Federalists. In 1797 JA wrote about the French: "Their apparent respect and real contempt for all men and all nations but Frenchmen, are proverbial among themselves. They think it is in their power to give characters and destroy characters as they please, and they have no other rule but to give reputation to their tools, and to destroy the reputation of all who will not be their tools. Their efforts to '*populariser*' Jefferson, and to '*dépopulariser*' Washington, are all upon this principle" [VIII, 536].

57. our interest: These lines return to JA at The Hague. In a letter of April 12, 1783, he wrote: "French politics are now incessantly at work in England, and we may depend upon it they labor less for our good than their own. If our interests were the same with theirs, we might better trust them; yet not entirely, for they do not understand their own interests so well as we do ours" [IX, 518].

58. Dutch interest: Source reads: "I have hitherto paid the interest in Holland out of the principal." Letter to Arthur Lee (Sept. 6, 1785) [IX, 537].

59. Court as putrid: Source reads: "Perhaps you will say that the air of a Court is as putrid as that of Amsterdam. In a moral and political sense, perhaps"; but, he adds, "Politics are the divine science, after all" [IX, 512].

60. Sale of six million: This line occurs in a letter written five years after the preceding one by R. H. Lee to JA (Sept. 3, 1787). Lee says that the Congress had "lately contracted for the sale of six millions of acres, on the north-western side of Ohio, in the ceded territory, for lessening the domestic debt" [IX, 554].

61. the society . . . : Back in Braintree, JA reflects on what he missed in his years abroad: "I regret the loss of the book-shops, and the society of the few men of letters that I knew in London; in all other respects I am much better accommodated here. Shall I hope to hear from you as you have leisure? A letter left at the New England Coffee House will be brought me by some of our Boston captains." Pound adds the word "London" to make clear the place [IX, 558].

62. Hollis Brook: Earlier in the same letter [61 above], JA wrote to Thomas Brand-Hollis about the beautiful prospects from spots on his farm, but adds: "I wish . . . that Mr. Brand-Hollis would come and build a Hyde near us." Then JA lists a number of places he would rename Hollis, such as a mead and a hill, and continues: "There is a fine brook, through a meadow, by my house; shall I call it Hollis Brook?" [IX, 557]. "Hyde" means a park such as Hyde Park in London.

63. Hollis: Thomas Brand-Hollis [66:38].

64. After generous . . . : Source says: "After a generous contest for liberty, of twenty years' continuance, Americans forgot wherein liberty consisted" [letter of Aug. 18, 1789, which contains the following Latin quotation; IX, 560].

65. meminisse juvebit: L, "it will be pleasing to recall." Source reads "juvabit," [IX, 561].

66. seeks information: Source reads: "No man, I believe, has influence with the President [Washington]. He seeks information from all quarters, and judges more independently than any man I ever knew" [IX, 561].

67. fisheries . . . absence: In 1781 JA had been commissioned to act with Franklin, Jefferson, John Jay, and Henry Laurens to negotiate a peace treaty with Great Britain, a treaty finally confirmed in 1783. From this time on, as with all subsequent commercial treaties he was involved in, JA maintained the American rights to offshore fisheries, a concept he advanced in the face of strong European opposition and American indifference [71:51]. The source of the five lines reads: "The fisheries are so essential to the commerce and naval power of this nation, that it is astonishing that any one citizen should ever have been found indifferent about them. . . . But . . . when . . . more than one foreign nation would endeavor to deprive us of them, there were many Americans indifferent, and not a few even disposed to give them away. A knowledge of this was the first and strongest motive with me to embark for Europe a first and a second time. . . . The present of four boxes of fish has been received . . . and is in every point of view very acceptable to me" [from Braintree, Nov. 7, 1789; IX, 562-563].

68. Their constitution: Source reads: "The Constitution [of France] is but an experiment, and must and will be altered. I know it to be impossible that France should be long governed by it. If the sovereignty is to reside in one assembly, the king, princes of the blood, and principal quality, will govern it at their pleasure as long as they can agree; when they differ, they will go to war." JA added: "I thank you, Sir, for your kind compliment. As it has been the great aim of my life to be useful, if I had any reason to think I was so . . . it would make me happy. . . . It is incredible how small is the number, in any nation, of those who comprehend any system of constitution or administration, and those few it is wholly impossible to unite" [IX, 564].

69. **Price**: Richard P., 1723-1791, Welsh moral and political philosopher; author of *Observations on Civil Liberty and War with America* (1776), an attack on British policy during the Revolution. He was a friend of JA's and Franklin's.

70. **Americans . . . balance**: Source (letter to B. Rush, April 18, 1790] reads: "I own that awful experience has concurred with reading and reflection, to convince me that Americans are more rapidly disposed to corruption in elections that [sic] I thought they were fourteen years ago [thus, 1776, not 1774]. My friend Dr. Rush will excuse me, if I caution him against a fraudulent use of the words *monarchy* and *republic*. I am a mortal and irreconcilable enemy to monarchy. . . . I am for a balance between the legislative and executive powers [IX, 566].

71. **Ideogram**: Chung [M1504]: "the middle." Part of the title to one of the Stone classics, *Chung Yung*, which Pound translates as "The Unwobbling Pivot." "[It] contains," he said, "what is usually supposed not to exist, namely the Confucian metaphysics. It is divided into three parts: the axis; the process; and sincerity, the perfect word, or the precise word" [*CON*, 95]. The ideogram underlines Pound's conviction that JA was an American exemplum of Confucian ideals.

72. **An aversion**: Source reads: "I know not how it is, but mankind have an aversion to the study of the science of government. . . . To me, no romance is more entertaining" [letter of June 1, 1790; IX, 567].

73. **Thames . . .** : Line from letter to Thomas Brand-Hollis [66:38].

74. **73 . . . 73**: [cf. 28 above].

75. **Dum Spiro**: L, "While I breathe"; *Dum Spiro Amo*: "While I breathe I love" [letter of June 1, 1790 to Brand-Hollis; IX, 569]. Pound added *Amo*.

76. **nec lupo . . .** : L, "nor entrust a lamb to a wolf," which JA tells Brand-Hollis (June 11, 1790) is his "fundamental maxim of government" [IX, 571].

78. **rational theory**: Source, which concerns JA's reflections on government, reads: "But . . . the feelings of mankind are so much against any rational theory, that I find my labor has all been in vain" [IX, 573].

CANTO LXXI

Sources

Charles Francis Adams, ed., *The Works of John Adams*, IX, X; Frederick K. Sanders, *John Adams Speaking*, 459-506, Orono, Maine, 1975.

Background

L. H. Butterfield, ed., *Diary and Autobiography of John Adams*, II, Cambridge, Mass., 1961; Saul Padover, *The Complete Jefferson*, New York, 1943; Broadus Mitchell, *Alexander Hamilton*, New York, 1962.

Exegeses

LL, *Motive*, 96, 114; CE, *Ideas*, 43; Dekker, *Cantos*, 139; DD, *Sculptor*, 163; Davis, *Vision*, 87, 143, 148-149; DP, *Barb*, 233; WB, *Rose*, 123-124; HK, *Era*, 319.

Glossary

1. **St. Paul**: Most of Canto 71 is taken from letters written between 1804 and 1819 at Quincy, where JA had retired after his defeat for reelection in 1800. The first three lines are from a letter (March 3, 1804) to F. A. Vanderkemp, who inquired about a manuscript he had sent to an academy JA belonged to. In his reply JA wrote: "A German ambassador once told me, 'he could not bear St. Paul, he was so severe against fornication.' On the same principle these philosophers cannot bear a God, because he is just" [IX, 588].

2. **Dismissed . . . parties**: Source [JA to Vanderkemp, Feb. 5, 1805] reads: "At the close of the 18th century, I was dismissed, to the joy of both parties, to a retirement in which I was never more to see any thing but my plough between me and the grave" [IX, 589-590].

3. **curse the day**: Source [JA to B. Rush, May 1, 1807] reads: "Now, Sir, to be serious, I do not curse the day when I engaged in public affairs" [IX, 593].

4. **Now in . . . constitution**: These nine lines are from a letter to Rush [May 21, 1807] which contains JA's lengthy reminiscence about the idea of the Revolution being in the minds of the people before it was in the minds of the leaders. In 1774 JA, on circuit court, stopped at a tavern in Shrewsbury and overheard the conversation which Pound summarizes by key phrases. Source has "half a dozen, or half a score . . . yeomen" [IX, 597].

5. **build frigates**: JA had urged that the U.S. build "fast-sailing frigates" from pre-Revolutionary days on, particularly at times when American shipping was being attacked at sea [70:7]. In 1808 [letter of Dec. 26] he was still at it: "In the mean time apply all our resources to build frigates, some in every principal seaport. . . . I never was fond of the plan of building line of battle ships. Our policy is not to fight squadrons at sea, but to have fast-sailing frigates to scour the seas and make impression on the enemy's commerce; . . . I conclude with acknowledging that we have received greater injuries from England than from France, abominable as both have been" [IX 607-608].

6. **I am for fighting**: Source reads: "If either of the belligerent powers [England or France] forces us all into a war, I am for fighting that power, whichever it may be" [March 13, 1809; IX, 615].

7. **swindling banks**: Source [letter of Feb. 16, 1809] reads: "Our medium is depreciated by the multitude of swindling banks, which have emitted bank bills to an immense amount beyond the deposits of gold and silver in their vaults, by which means the price of labor and land and merchandise and produce is doubled, tripled, and quadrupled. . . . Every dollar of a bank bill that is issued beyond the quantity of gold and silver in the vaults, represents nothing, and is therefore a cheat upon somebody" [IX, 610].

8. **Cape Breton . . . 89-'09**: These ten lines are based on an impassioned reminiscence by JA [letter of March 11, 1809] which reads in part: "From my earliest infancy I had listened with eagerness to his [my father's] conversation with his friends during the whole expedition to Cape Breton, in 1745, and I had received very grievous impressions of the injustice and ingratitude

of Great Britain towards New England in that whole transaction, as well as many others before and after it, during the years 1754, 1755, 1756, and 1757. The conduct of Generals Shirley, Braddock, Abercrombie, Webb, and above all Lord Loudon . . . gave me . . . a disgust of the British government. . . . In 1758 and 1759, Mr. Pitt coming into power, sent Wolfe, and Amherst, whom I saw with his army, . . . and these conquered Cape Breton and Quebec. I then rejoiced that I was an Englishman. . . . But, alas! how short was my triumph in British wisdom and justice! In February, 1761, I heard the argument . . . upon writs of assistance, and there saw that Britain was determined to let nothing divert me from my fidelity to my country." [By the Peace of Utrecht (1713) the French lost Nova Scotia and Newfoundland but retained Cape Breton and were allowed to fortify the island. In 1745 a volunteer force from New England led by Sir William Pepperell captured Cape Breton with the aid of the British fleet under Commodore Warren. JA, ten years old at the time, was excited by stories of the campaign.] At this time [32:1] JA was being consulted about the history of the Revolution. In this letter he is answering 20 specific questions asked by Skelton Jones about his life and career. Jones's seventh question was when and why JA had retired from public affairs. JA's answer: "The 4th of March, 1801 [date of Jeffersons's inauguration]. The causes of my retirement are to be found in the writings of Freneau [he lists eight more causes] and many others, but more specifically in the circular letters of members of Congress from the southern and middle States. Without a complete collection of all these libels, no faithful history of the last twenty years can ever be written, nor any adequate account given of the causes of my retirement from public life" [IX, 611-612]. Pound added "89-'09".

9. Shirley: William S., 1694-1771 [67:29]. Shirley started the issuing of Writs of Assistance in Boston in 1761; they were supposed to aid in the search for smuggled goods, but they caused discontent without being very effective [63:66].

10. Braddock: Edward B., 1695-1775, commander in chief of British forces in America (1754).

11. Abercrombie: Sir Robert A., 1740-1827, British general in the French and Indian Wars and in the American Revolution.

12. Webb: Daniel W., English soldier who commanded the British forces in America until succeeded by Abercrombie after 1756.

13. Lord Loudon: John Campbell, 4th Earl of Loudoun, 1705-1782, commander of British forces in the French and Indian Wars. He distressed the people of Boston by quartering his troops on them.

14. Pitt: William P. [64:33]. JA was happy because the Elder Pitt opposed the Stamp Act.

15. Wolf: James Wolfe, 1727-1759, British major general who commanded the expedition against Montcalm at Quebec.

16. Amherst: Lord Jeffrey A., 1717-1797, English general who commanded the British force that captured Cape Breton from the French (1758); took Ticonderoga (1759); and was made commander in chief of British forces in America (1759).

17. totis viribus: L, "with all my strength." Source [letter of March 13, 1809] reads: "I am *totis viribus* against any division of the Union, by the North River, or by Delaware River, or by the Potomac, or any other river, or by any chain of mountains. I am for maintaining the independence of the nation at all events" [IX, 615].

18. Independence . . .: In the source [letter of April 20, 1809] JA speaks of his lifelong fight for independence from both Britain and France. He adds: "The federal papers for the last year or two, assisted by English hirelings, have been employed in varnishing over the conduct of Great Britain . . . till they appear to have obtained a temporary majority in New England. I greatly respect the public opinion of New England, when it is truly informed. In the present instance, with infinite grief I fear it is not" [IX, 621].

19. Vergennes: [70:9] Source reads: "... the Comte de Vergennes, once said to me, 'Mr. Adams, the newspapers govern the world!' ... Let me ask you ... if the world is governed by ungovernable newspapers, whether it does not follow ... that the world is ungovernable" [letter of June 19, 1809; IX, 622].

20. Took Matlock . . . : Source [same as 19 above] reads: "A Convention in Pennsylvania had adopted a government in one representative assembly, and Dr. Franklin was the President of that Convention. The Doctor, when he went to France in 1776, carried with him the printed copy of that Constitution, and it was immediately propagated through France that this was the plan of government of Mr. Franklin. In truth it was not Franklin, but Timothy Matlack, James Cannon, Thomas Young, and Thomas Paine, who were the authors of it. Mr. Turgot, the Duke de la Rochefoucauld, Mr. Condorcet, and many others, became enamored with the Constitution of Mr. Franklin. And in my opinion, the two last owed their final and fatal catastrophe to this blind love." JA does not mention Beaumarchais [IX, 622-623].

21. Matlock: Timothy Matlack, d. 1829; assistant secretary to Continental Congress (1775); member of Pennsylvania Constitutional convention (1776) and of committee that drafted the instrument.

22. James Cannon: Member of committee to draft the constitution of Pennsylvania (1776).

23. Thomas Young: ?1731-1777, American Revolutionary patriot and physician; member of Pennsylvania Constitutional Convention (1776) and of committee that drafted the instrument.

24. Thomas Paine: [31:17].

25. Beaumarchais: [31:29; 32:10].

26. Condorcet: [31:37].

27. English Constitution: Source [same as 19 above] reads: "I have represented the British Constitution as the most perfect model that has as yet been discovered . . . for the government of the great nations of Europe. It is a masterpiece. . . . Our own Constitutions I have represented as the best for us in our peculiar situation, and while we preserve ourselves independent and unallied to any of the great powers of Europe. An alliance with either France or England would, in my humble opinion, put an end to our fine system of liberty" [IX, 622].

28. Their inexperience: Source [same as 19 above] concerns Turgot, Rochefoucauld, and Condorcet, whom JA knew during his 1780 mission to France. JA wrote: "They were as amiable, as learned, and as honest men as any in France. But such was their inexperience in all that relates to free government, so superficial their reading in the science of government, and so obstinate their confidence in their own great characters for science and literature, that I should trust the most ignorant of our honest town meeting orators to make a Constitution sooner than any or all of them" [IX, 624].

29. Merchants wd/ say: JA is answering a question asked by a friend concerning the best means by which the "military and commercial spirit" might be made most helpful to a free nation. He wrote: "Nine tenths of our nation would say the militia, the other tenth a standing army. The merchants would all say, 'let commerce alone—merchants do as they please;' others would say, 'protect trade with a navy'" [IX, 625].

30. without Louisiana . . . intentions: These five lines express JA's ideas about the Louisiana Purchase and the congressional interpretation of the Constitution which justified the purchase. The source [JA to

Josiah Quincy, Feb. 9, 1811] is adequately summarized by Pound [IX, 631].

31. **oligarchy**: Source [JA to Josiah Quincy, Feb. 18, 1811] concerns Americans who are jealous of European nobility: "This jealousy is often actuated by the purest spirit of patriotism, . . . but . . . it never has ceased to encroach, until it has made the executive a mere head of wood, and drawn all the power and resources of the nation into the insatiable gulf, the irresistible vortex, of an aristocracy or an oligarchy" [IX, 634].

32. **church-going . . . Hamilton**: These three lines come from a letter to B. Rush [Aug. 28, 1811] which emphasizes JA's belief that "religion and virtue are the only foundations" of any government. But JA did not feel free to say much about his belief: ". . . if I should inculcate this doctrine in my will, I should be charged with hypocrisy . . . and for being a church-going animal." He adds: "If I should inculcate 'fidelity to the marriage bed,' it would be said that it proceeded from resentment to General Hamilton, and a malicious desire to hold up to posterity his libertinism" [IX, 636-637].

33. **forgot . . . himself**: These three lines are a footnote JA added to the letter [32 above] three days later [Aug. 31]: "I had forgot the story of the four English girls whom General Pinckney was employed to hire in England, two for me and two for himself" [IX, 637].

34. **The number . . . year**: These six lines [source as in 32] are from a lengthy disquisition on JA's lifelong and zealous but losing fight against the public's use of alcohol: "Fifty-three years ago I was fired with a zeal . . . against ardent spirits, the multiplication of taverns . . . dram-shops, and tippling houses. Grieved to the heart . . . I applied to the Court of Sessions . . . [and] reduced the number of licensed houses." But JA was called a "hypocrite" and a "demagogue." "The number of licensed houses was soon reinstated; drams, grog, and sotting were not diminished, and remain to this day as deplorable as ever. You may as well preach to the Indians against rum as to our people. Little Turtle petitioned me to prohibit rum to be sold to his nation, for a very good reason; because he said I had lost three thousand of my Indian children in his nation in one year by it" [IX, 637-638].

35. **Funds . . . crazy**: These nine lines express convictions of JA which Pound responded to strongly, frequently quoting them as well as similar passages: "Funds and banks I never approved, or was satisfied with our funding system; it was founded in no consistent principle; it was contrived to enrich particular individuals at the public expense. Our whole banking system I ever abhorred, I continue to abhor, and shall die abhorring. But I am not an enemy to funding systems. They are absolutely and indispensably necessary in the present state of the world. An attempt to annihilate or prevent them would be as romantic an adventure as any in Don Quixote or in Oberon. A national bank of deposit I believe to be wise, just, prudent, economical, and necessary. But every bank of discount, every bank by which interest is to be paid or profit of any kind made by the deponent, is downright corruption. It is taxing the public for the benefit and profit of individuals; it is worse than old tenor, continental currency, or any other paper money. Now, Sir, if I should talk in this strain, after I am dead, you know the people of America would pronounce that I had died mad" [source same as 32 above].

36. **Wigwams . . . left there**: These six lines continue JA's pleasurable memories of local Indians. Source [JA to TJ, June 28, 1812] says: "There was a numerous family in this town, whose wigwam was within a mile of this house. This family were frequently at my father's house, and I, in my boyish rambles, used to call at their wigwam, where I never failed to be treated with whortleberries, blackberries, strawberries, or apples, plums, peaches, &, for

they had planted a variety of fruit trees about them; but the girls went out to service and the boys to sea, till not a soul is left" [X, 20].

37. and so . . . England: These three lines are from a letter [Nov. 25, 1812] concerned with party forces which paralyze the nation: "When I was exerting every nerve to vindicate the honor, and demand a redress of the wrongs of the nation against the tyranny of France, the arm of the nation was palsied by one party. Now Mr. Madison is acting the same part . . . against Great Britain, the arm of the nation is palsied by the opposite party. And so it will always be while we feel like colonists, dependent for protection on France or England" [X, 23].

38. With wood . . . please: The two lines are from an anecdote JA tells to show the amazement of Europeans that America never used its vast natural resources to become a first-rate sea power. Source [letter of Jan. 5, 1813] tells the story of a conversation JA had in 1779 with an admiral, "or, as the French call him, *Général* or *Chef d'Escadre,"* who said, "Your Congress will soon become one of the great maritime powers." JA replies that it will not be soon. The admiral wanted to know why not: "No nation has such nurseries for seaman so near it. You have the best timber for the hulks of ships, and best masts and spars . . . [he lists much more]. What is wanting?" To JA's response, "The will . . . may be wanting and nothing else," the admiral continued: "We have a maxim among us mariners, that with wood, hemp, and iron, a nation may do what it pleases" [X, 26].

39. Taxes laid . . . : Source [letter of March 28, 1813] gives JA's frank opinion about the War of 1812: "The taxes must be laid, and the war supported" [X, 36].

40. Histories . . . : Source [letter to TJ, July 9, 1813] concerns the difficulties of making improvements or preserving historical truth under any form of government: "I say, parties and factions will not suffer improvements to be made. As soon as one man hints at an improvement, his rival opposes it. No sooner has one party discovered or invented any amelioration of the condition of man . . . than the opposite party belies it, misconstrues it, misrepresents it, ridicules it, insults it, and persecutes it. Records are destroyed. Histories are annihilated or interpolated or prohibited; sometimes by Popes, sometimes by Emperors, sometimes by aristocratical, and sometimes by democratical assemblies, and sometimes by mobs" [X, 50].

41. our 'pure . . . : Source [letter to TJ, Sept. 2, 1813] asks Jefferson's opinion about JA's translation from Greek of a poem by Theognis and wonders whether anyone else had ever caught the idea better: "Tell me, also, whether poet, orator, historian, or philosopher, can paint the picture of every city, county, or State, in our pure, uncorrupted, unadulterated, uncontaminated federal republic . . . in more precise lines or colors?" [X, 64].

42. Sir Wm. Keith: Sir William K., 1680-1749. British colonial governor of Pennsylvania and Delaware (1714-1726). Source [Thomas McKean to JA, Sept. 28, 1813] contains memories about ways the British devised for raising revenues in America, one of which was to appoint congresses: "In 1739, Sir William Keith, a Scotch gentleman, who had been a lieutenant-governor of Pennsylvania, proposed such an assembly to the ministry. He also proposed the extension of the British stamp-duties to the colonies. He was then, I believe, in the Fleet prison. The hints he gave were embraced, the first in 1754, the second in 1764. It has been long a matter of surprise to me, that no gentleman of talents and character has undertaken to write a history of the former British colonies . . . at least from 1756 to 1806, a period of fifty very important years. . . . On reflection, I cannot refer to a single instance of . . . friendship of Great Britain towards this country during the period you mention" [X, 74-75].

43. Thos. McKean: Thomas M., 1734-1814, member of Continental Congress (1774-1783) and its president in 1781; signer of Declaration of Independence; governor of Pennsylvania (1799-1808).

44. (1600-1813): JA had written to McKean [Aug. 31, 1813] asking for information McKean supplied [cf. 42 above]. In his letter JA said: "Were I a man of fortune, I would offer a gold medal to the man who should produce the most instances of the friendship of Great Britain toward this country from 1600 to 1813" [X, 62].

45. THEMIS CONDITOR: H, "Themis." L, "the founder." Source [JA to TJ, Oct. 4, 1813] has Θέμιϛ [another name for Hera or Juno] but Pound adds the Latin. JA wrote: "Θέμιϛ was the goddess of honesty, justice, decency, and right. . . . She presided over all oracles, deliberations, and councils. She commanded all mortals to pray to Jupiter for all lawful benefits and blessings. Now, is not this (so far forth) the essence of Christian devotion?" [X, 75].

46. In the Congress . . . third: These five lines are from two sources [JA to TJ, Nov. 12, 1813; JA to James Lloyd, Jan. 1815]. The first says: "In the Congress of 1774, there was not one member, except Patrick Henry, who appeared to me sensible of the precipice . . . on which he stood, and had candor and courage enough to acknowledge it. America is in total ignorance, or under infinite deception, concerning that assembly; . . . one third tories, another whigs, and the rest mongrels" [X, 78-79]. And the second source, on divisions of the people, says: " . . . I should say that full one third were averse to the revolution. . . . An opposite third conceived a hatred of the English, and gave themselves up to an enthusiastic gratitude to France. The middle third . . . yeomanry, the soundest part of the nation . . . were rather lukewarm both to England and France" [X, 110].

47. Persons . . . cease: Source [T. McKean to JA, Nov. 15, 1813] reads: "The Society in London 'for propagating the gospel in foreign parts,' . . . foresaw, that if America became an independent state or nation, their salaries [i.e., of the society's ministers in the colonies] would necessarily cease. It was their interest . . . to oppose the revolution, and they did oppose it, though with as much secrecy as practicable" [X, 81].

48. Laws of Charondas . . . fury: These five lines continue JA's polemic against the destructiveness of party spirit. Source [JA to TJ, Dec. 25, 1813] suggests some of JA's Christmas Day reading at the age of 78: "Zaleucus, the legislator of Locris, and Charondas of Sybaris, were disciples of Pythagoras, and both celebrated to immortality for the wisdom of their laws, five hundred years before Christ. Why are those laws lost? I say, the spirit of party has destroyed them; civil, political, and ecclesiastical bigotry. Despotical, monarchical, aristocratical, and democratical fury, have all been employed in this work of destruction of every thing that could give us true light, and a clear insight of antiquity. For every one of these parties, when possessed of power, or when they have been undermost, and struggling to get uppermost, has been equally prone to every species of fraud and violence and usurpation" [X, 84-85].

49. adopted by Moses: JA is here quoting from Priestley an idea, with which he does not concur, about the Fall of man and the Mosaic law: ". . . this history [in Genesis] is either an allegory, or founded on uncertain tradition, . . . a hypothesis to account for the origin of evil, adopted by Moses, which, by no means, accounts for the facts." JA says, a few lines later: "I shall never be a disciple of Priestley." At another place in this letter to TJ, which was written at intervals [Feb.-March 1814], JA says: "There is a work which I wish I possessed. It has never crossed the Atlantic . . . Acta Sanctorum, in forty-seven volumes in folio" [X, 93].

50. Acta Sanctorum: L, "Acts of the Saints." Source continues to speculate on this book and adds: "What would I give to possess, in one immense map, . . . all the legends, true, doubtful, and false?" He lists several legends he would like to know the truth about and concludes with these: ". . . whether the face of Jesus Christ was painted on the handkerchief of St. Veronique; and whether the prepuce of the Savior of the world, which was shown in the church at Antwerp, could be proved to be genuine" [X, 94].

51. many a kept . . . ocean: These seven lines concern the nature of heroism, the fisheries, and naval power. Source [JA to Richard Rush, May 30, 1814] starts with listing heroes such as Alexander, Caesar, "and millions of others" who come to bad ends: "Read the history of our missionary societies. Is there not the same enthusiasm, the same heroism? I scarcely dare to say what I know, that many a kept mistress has dared for her lover as great hazards and sufferings." The letter later turns to the Tories, who say such things as "Mr. Adams saved the fisheries once I hope his son will save them a second time. We have no confidence in Gallatin, Clay, Russell, or even Bayard; we believe they would all sacrifice the fisheries for Canada or even for peace." But JA was not one to be taken in by Tory ploys and give them ammunition which they could use to interfere with the delicate negotiations his son JQA and the others named were engaged in at the time in London. He said his invariable answer was that "you deceive yourself with imaginary fears. You know that the men Bayard, Russell, Clay and even Gallatin would cede the fee simple of the United States, as soon as they would the fisheries." He goes on to comment on the idea that America should command the Great Lakes: "The lakes, the lakes, the lakes! shocking, indeed, that we have not the command of the lakes! But I could convince you that it is still more shocking that we have not the command of the ocean, or at least an independent power upon the ocean" [X, 97-98].

52. Clay, Gallatin, Russell: [34:47; 34:21; 31:40].

53. J. Bull: Source [JA to Mrs. Mercy Warren, July 15, 1814] reads: "France is humbled and Napoleon is banished; but the tyrant, the tyrant of tyrants is not fallen. John Bull still paws, and bellows terrible menaces and defiances" [X, 100].

54. I wish France: Source [JA to TJ, July 16, 1814] says: "He [Bonaparte] could no longer roar or struggle, growl or paw, he could only gasp his grin of death; I wish that France may not still regret him" [X, 102].

55. our treaty: Source [JA to President Madison, Nov. 28, 1814] is specific about the War of 1812: "All I can say is, that I would continue this war forever, rather than surrender one acre of our territory, one iota of the fisheries, as established by the third article of the treaty of 1783, or one sailor impressed from any merchant ship" [X, 106].

56. No part . . . navy: Source [letter written sometime in Jan. 1815] dwells upon JA's attempts while president to build up the navy, to build ships, to purchase navy yards, to select officers: "And what was the effect? No part of my administration was so unpopular, not only in the western, the southern, and middle States, but in all New England, and, strange to tell, even in Marblehead." Later in same letter JA defended his missions to France as "the most disinterested and meritorious actions" of his life: "I reflect upon them with so much satisfaction, that I desire no other inscription over my gravestone than: 'Here lies John Adams, who took upon himself the responsibility of the peace with France in the year 1800'" [X, 111,113].

57. No printer . . . Sanctorum: Source of these five lines, a letter to James [not L.] Lloyd [Feb. 11, 1815], expresses great frustration about parties and churches reading only their own newspapers, circulars, ets., and condemning anyone else's writings as heresy. Thus any party reads only "its own libels." JA goes on: "With us, the press is under a virtual imprimatur, to such a degree, that I do not believe I could get these letters to you printed in a newspaper in Boston." JA continues to describe the continuous spate of circular letters from members of Congress to their constituents, filled with lies, many of them against JA, which began in 1789 and continued to 1801. These letters "swelled, raged, foamed in all the fury of a tempest at sea against me. A collection of those circular letters would make many volumes, and contain more lies . . . than the *Acta Sanctorum*" [cf. 49, 50 above; X, 117-119].

58. **Mihites**: Unknown term. Perhaps a mistranscription of L, *Milites*, for soldiers, or poss. a play on L, *mihi*, thus "egoists"; or perhaps a garbled version of a nickname for the Irish, such as *Mickies*.

59. **they believed . . .** : Source [JA to J. Lloyd, Feb. 14, 1815] reads: . . . the English, Scotch, and Irish Presbyterians [plus four other sects] with Dr. Preistley at their head . . . had been carried away with the French revolution, and firmly believed that Bonaparte was the instrument of Providence to destroy the Pope and introduce the millennium. . . . Mr. Jefferson knew them all. These parties had all been making their court to him for fifteen years" [X, 120].

60. **My answer . . . delegates)**: Source of these five lines [JA to J. Lloyd, Feb. 17, 1815] concerns Hamilton's intrigue to prevent JA's reelection in 1800. While AH was in New England trying to get voters there to "sacrifice Adams," JA, about the same time, on a walk in Philadelphia, met Colonel Joseph Lyman of Springfield who, seeing the president, crossed the street to tell him he had some news. JA said he hoped his news was good. Lyman said: "Hamilton has divided the federalists, and proposed to them to give you the go-by and bring in Pinckney. By this step he has divided the federalists and given great offence to the honestest part of them. I am glad of it, for it will be the ruin of his faction." JA saw in the plot also the ruin of his own faction, which led to his defeat. So he said: "Colonel Lyman, it will be, as you say, the ruin of his faction; but it will also be the ruin of honester men than any of them." During the intrigue, a list of mediocre men Hamilton was promoting as candidates in New York was brought to Aaron Burr by a friend: "Burr . . . read it over, with great gravity folded it up, put it in his pocket; and, without uttering another word said 'Now I have him all hollow.'" Burr went about making a list of his own and getting Hamilton's men defeated, but Burr's men elected electors who went unanimously for Jefferson "though New York in all antecedent elections voted unanimously for Adams" [X, 124-125].

61. **Walcott**: Oliver Wolcott [62:157], JA's secretary of the treasury. In seeking loans to support the army, Wolcott maintained that proposals should be announced for 8 percent interest. JA in "consultation after consultation," insisted that 8 percent was too much and that the money could be had for 6 percent. JA finally lost patience and gave in [X, 129-130].

62. **South Americans**: In the source [JA to J. Lloyd, March 26, 1815], JA expressed his amazement that Pitt and the British cabinet could believe that South America could be revolutionized: "Did they believe the South Americans capable of a free government, or a combination of free federative republics?" [X, 141].

63. **lucid interval**: Source [JA to Lloyd, March 29, 1815] says: "Very fortunately for me and for this nation, the French Directory had a lucid interval [70:19-21] and gave me a fair opportunity to institute that mission to France" [X, 147].

64. **No people**: Source [JA to J. Lloyd,

March 30, 1815] expresses an old, growing, and frustrating conviction of JA's: "The truth is, there is not one people of Europe that knows or cares any thing about constitutions. There is not one nation in Europe that understands or is capable of understanding any constitution whatever. . . . If there is a colorable exception, it is England" [X, 149-150].

65. God forbid . . . : And in a letter to Lloyd the next day [March 31] JA wrote about another primary concern: "God forbid that American naval power should ever be such a scourge to the human race as that of Great Britain has been!" And in the same paragraph, speaking of his "most earnest, sedulous, and . . . expensive exertions to preserve peace with the Indians" all the time he was president, he concludes: "I had the inexpressible satisfaction of complete success. Not a hatchet was lifted in my time" [X, 153].

66. Nor has . . . Mississippi: In the source of these five lines [JA to R. Rush, April 5, 1815], JA restates his adamant convictions about the fisheries controversy: "Neither nature nor art has partitioned the sea into empires, kingdoms, republics, or states. There are no dukedoms, earldoms, baronies, or knight's fees, no freeholds, pleasure grounds, ornamented or unornamented farms, gardens, parks, groves . . . as there are upon land. . . . We have a stronger and clearer right to all these fisheries . . . than any Britons or Europeans ever had or could have." The Treaty of Ghent, the document agreed upon between the U.S. and Great Britain in ending the War of 1812, resolved few differences and left many questions unanswered. But JQA stuck to his father's guns and agreed only to British rights of navigation on the Mississippi in return for concessions to the U.S. on the fisheries. The treaty, finally ratified on February 17, 1815, did not end controvery in the U.S. So JA kept up his clamor to most people he wrote to: "Former treaties not formally repeated in a new treaty, are presumed to be received and acknowledged. The fisheries are therefore ours, and the navigation of the Mississippi theirs, that is the British, as much as ever" [X, 160-161].

67. Money or no money: Source [JA to T. McKean, July 6, 1815] says, as a third point among six proven by the Madison administration: "That money or no money, government or no government, Great Britain can never conquer this country or any considerable part of it" [X, 168].

68. They will print . . . unopened: Source [JA to TJ, Aug. 24, 1815] says: "That our correspondence has been observed, is no wonder. . . . No printer has asked me for copies, but it is no surprise that you have been requested. These gentry will print whatever will sell; and our correspondence is thought such an oddity by both parties, that they imagine an edition would soon go off, and yield them profits. There has, however, been no tampering with your letters to me. They have all arrived in good order" [X, 173].

69. Price: Richard P., Welsh friend of JA's [70:69]. A book JA received, *Memoirs of the Life of Dr. Price,* by William Morgan, is the source of the four lines [JA to TJ, Nov. 13, 1815]. JA quotes some things Morgan said concerning Dr. Price's disappointment that his [Price's] views about the success of and his hopes for the French Revolution were not embraced by Adams. In his letter JA quotes from Morgan: "'In a long letter . . . he [JA] expresses himself in terms of contempt in regard to the French revolution; and after asking . . . what good was to be expected from a nation of atheists, he concludes with foretelling the destruction of a million of human beings, as the probable consequence of it. These harsh censures and gloomy predictions were particularly ungrateful to Dr. Price.'" After the quotation JA says he does not know what to think of one who 25 years later finds private correspondence and produces it before the world. He adds: "Mr. Morgan has been more discreet and complaisant to you than to me. He has mentioned respectfully your letters from Paris to Dr. Price, but has given us none of them. As I would give more for those letters than for all the rest of the book, I am more angry with him" [X, 175-176].

70. speeches . . . Spain: Source [T. McKean to JA, Nov. 20, 1815] contains thoughts that show JA's gloomy predictions 25 years earlier to Dr. Price [cf. 69 above] to have been correct: "I do not recollect any *formal* speeches . . . to have been made in the revolutionary Congress . . . We had no time to hear . . . speeches . . . ; action was the order of the day." And later: "What changes in Europe have occurred . . . ! Louis XVIII, is again on the throne of France; the great Napoleon at the bottom of the wheel, never to rise more, a prisoner for life. The French nation miserable; Spain has reëstablished the tribunal of the Inquisition" [X, 177-178].

71. black, white . . . : Source [JA to T. McKean, Nov. 26, 1815] says: "General Wilkinson may have written the military history of the war that followed the Revolution; that was an effect of it, and was supported by the American citizens in defence of it against an invasion of it by the government of Great Britain and Ireland, and all her allies, black, white, and pied; but this will by no means be a history of the American Revolution" [X, 180].

72. fleet to protect: In a long letter to Dr. J. Morse [Jan. 1, 1816] JA reviews the growing spirit behind the Revolution and focuses on events of the mid-1760s. After "a new act of tyrannical taxation rekindled all the fires of opposition and resistance on this side the water," the colonies rebelled so strongly that the British ministry "thought it necessary to send a fleet and army to protect Temple, Hallowell, Paxton, Birch, and Robinson, their adherents and followers" [X, 199].

73. Paxton: Charles P. [64:110]. British customs commissioner.

74. Birch, Temple: Minor English agents operating in Boston in 1766.

75. Otis: James O. [34:33]. Lawyer and Revolutionary leader who opposed the Stamp Act and organized the Stamp Congress in 1765.

76. Poor soldiers: Source [same as 72 above] summarizes attitudes toward British soldiers, whose officers "put themselves and their men upon the compassionate list. 'The poor soldiers were innocent. They knew not why they were sent here'" [X,199].

77. North called 'em: [62:20]. In the source [as in 72 above] JA outlines growing discontent which climaxed in the Boston Massacre (March 5, 1771) and celebrates Samuel Adams for his "caution, his discretion, his ingenuity" [and four more such attributes], which received applause from both parties and had a good result: "The troops were ordered to the Castle, and Lord North called them from this time 'Sam Adams's two regiments'" [X, 200].

78. Hutchinson: Thomas H., chief justice and later royal governor of Massachusetts [62:47]. JA comments on Hutchinson's style of dress: "I pass over that scenery, which he introduced, so showy and so shallow, so theatrical and so ecclesiastical, of scarlet and sable robes . . . and enormous tie wigs, more resembling fleeces of painted meriono wool than any thing natural to man" [X, 233].

79. State Trials: [64:63].

80. At State House . . . Paddock: Of the crisis in Boston after massacre [62:26-38], source [JA to W. Tudor, April 15, 1817] says: "The whole militia of the city" was called up. And "I had the honor to be summoned, in my turn, and attended at the State House with my musket and bayonet, my broadsword and cartridge-box, under the command of the famous Paddock." Now nearing 82, JA looks back to his early exploits with more and more relish [X, 251].

81. Paddock: Adino P., Boston coachmaker and captain of militia, was called up for the "civilian night watch" after the Boston Massacre on March 5, 1770.

82. Jesuits . . . : Source [JA to TJ, April 19, 1817] concerns JA's denial of total human depravity: "The most abandoned scoundrel that ever existed, never yet wholly extinguished his conscience, and, while conscience remains, there is some religion. Popes, Jesuists [sic], and Sorbonnists, and Inquisitors, have some conscience and some religion. So had Marius and Sylla" [X, 254].

83. Sylla: Lucius Cornelius Sulla, 138-78 B.C., Roman general who served with Marius in Africa, led a bloody sack of Athens, made himself dictator of Rome in 82 B.C., and began a systematic butchery of his enemies. His name and that of Marius became synonymous with cruelty.

84. Marius: Caius M., ca. 155-86 B.C., Roman general, tribune, and praetor. He became a rival of Sulla, lost, and fled Rome. But, allied with the consul Cinna, he returned home and butchered his opponents.

85. Hancock: John H. [64:56]. Source of next eight lines [JA to W. Tudor, June 1, 1817] is a paean to Hancock: "If he had vanity and caprice, so had I. And if his vanity and caprice made sometimes sputter, . . . mine . . . had often a similar effect upon him. . . . His uncle, the most opulent merchant in Boston, . . . adopted him, . . . educated him at Harvard college, and then took him into his store. And what a school was this! Four large ships constantly plying between Boston and London. . . . This was in 1755. He became an example to all the young men of the town. . . . His uncle sent him to London, from whence . . . he returned to his store . . . unaltered in manners or deportment, and pursued his employments with the same punctuality and assiduity, till the death of his uncle, who left him his business. . . . No alteration appeared in Mr. Hancock either from his travels in England, or from his accession to the fortune of his uncle. . . . Your honored father told me, at that time, that not less than a thousand families were . . . dependent on [him]." JA one day met Sam Adams on a walk. They came upon Hancock's house, whereupon Sam said that the town had done a wise thing that day. To JA's question as to what the wise thing was, Sam replied that the town had that day "chosen Mr. Hancock into the legislature of the province" [X, 259-260].

86. Joseph Hawley: [64:49]. Although Hawley was one of the first to urge a declaration of independence, no source includes him with the others. Source [JA to W. Tudor, June 5, 1817] says about the most important men in starting the Revolution: "James Otis, Samuel Adams, and John Hancock were the three most essential characters; and Great Britain knew it, though America does not" [X, 263].

87. Jay: John J. [62:131].

88. Magis . . . fabulis: L, "more suitable to poetic myths." From the preface to Livy's histories: *Ab Urbe Condita* ["From the Founding of the City"], Book I (Loeb, p. 4). The phrase is taken from this sentence: "Quae ante conditam condendamve urbem poeticis magis decora fabulis quam incorruptis rerum gestarum monumemtis traduntur, ea nec adfirmare nec refellere in animo est." [Loeb trans.: "Such traditions as belong to the time before the city was founded, or rather was presently to be founded, and are rather adorned with poetic legends than based upon trustworthy historical proofs, I purpose neither to affirm nor to refute."] JA used parts of the Livy sentence in his letter to W. Tudor [see 86 above].

89. Otis: Source of lines here from two letters that deal with the education, talents, and skills of Otis, who wrote Latin and Greek prosodies: ". . . I asked his daughter whether she had found that work [on Greek prosody] among her father's manuscripts. She answered . . . that she 'had not a line from her father's pen; that he had spent much time, and taken great pains, to collect together all his letters and other papers, and, in one of his unhappy moments, committed them all to the flames'" [X, 265].

90. may be . . . neutrality: Source or significance of these two lines is unknown; perhaps the "swat on the pow" refers to the beating by the "coffee house bandits" [cf. 91 below]. If Otis survived the beating for a time before his death, he may have burned his papers during that period.

91. the greek prosody: JA borrowed Otis's work on Greek prosody. Source of six lines [JA to H. Niles, Jan. 14, 1818] says: "When I returned it, I begged him to print it. He said there were no Greek types in the country, or, if there were, there was no printer who knew how to use them." In the same letter JA continues to amass facts to show that Otis was a great patriot: "Mr. Otis resigned his commission from the crown, as Advocate-General, an office very lucrative at that time, and a sure road to the highest favors of government in America, and engaged in the cause of his country without fee or reward." And later, in consequence of this act, which both JA and Pound saw as patriotic, "Otis was basely assassinated in a coffee-house, in the night, by a well-dressed banditti, with a commissioner of the customs at their head" [X, 275-278].

92. Otis . . . writs: Writs of Assistance [cf. 9 above].

93. JA . . . judiciary: Against the judicial system of the Crown as it was developing in Boston.

94. Defended Preston: Captain Preston, the British officer whom JA defended [62:37].

95. Fisheries . . . 1800: List of some of the greatest ideas and accomplishments of JA [65:20].

96. Gold . . . lumber: Expression of one of JA's and Pound's profound conceptions concerning the nature of money. Source [JA to J. Taylor, March 12, 1819] says: "Silver and gold are but commodities, as much as wheat and lumber." JA then refers to a work by Count Destutt de Tracy which TJ had translated from the French and sent to him: "His chapter 'of money' contains the sentiments that I have entertained all my lifetime. . . . 'It is to be desired, that coins had never borne other names than those of their weight, and that the arbitrary denominations . . . had never been used'" [X, 375-376].

97. Keep out of Europe: JA's Lifelong refrain about keeping America neutral and not getting entangled in the affairs of any one nation or group of nations [18, 27 above].

98. Charlie Mordecai: Unknown person and unknown source. The *Index* suggests that the name might refer to Karl Marx. But since most of the remaining lines in this canto derive from statutes of William III which refer to acts of Parliament in "the reign of the late King Charles II" and "in the 22nd and 23rd years of his said late Majesties reign" [X, 339], I am satisfied to believe that "Charlie Mordecai" means "Charles, the dead," or, closer to the Latin root, "Charles of the teeth."

99. Not free 'em . . . 1818: These 17 lines show JA's outrage at British laws deliberately intended to subjugate people, particularly seamen, women, and Negroes. Source [JA to W. Tudor, Aug. 6, 1818] says: "Mr. Otis had reasoned like a philosopher upon the navigation acts, and all the tyrannical acts of Charles II.; but when he came to the revenue laws, the orator blazed out." JA goes on to say that, while it may be tedious to read those old statutes; "yet it behoves our young and old yeomen, mechanics and laborers, philosophers, politicians, legislators, and merchants to read them. However tedious and painful it may be for you to read, or me to transcribe any part of these dull statutes, we must endure the task, or we shall never understand the American Revolution." These lines must be either an ironic suggestion or a come-on, for the statutes, which are full of blood, are anything but dull. JA then transcribes the preamble to one statute which has as its intent no less than the enslavement of "all the colonies in Europe, Asia, and America, and, indeed, all nations, to the omnipotence of the British Parliament and its royal navy! . . . Recollect and listen to the preamble of this statute, of the 7th and 8th of William III, Chapter 22d." JA then goes on to show the effect of such statutes on British colonial landowners: "Will you be so good, Sir, as to pause a moment on this preamble? To what will you liken it? Does it resemble a great, rich, powerful West India planter, Alderman Beckford, for example, preparing and calculating and writing instructions for his overseers?" JA quotes such instructions: "You are to have no regard to the health, strength, comfort, natural affections, or moral feelings, or intellectual endowments of my negroes. You are only to consider what subsistence [not "substance"] to allow them, and what labor to exact [not "extract"] of them will subserve my interest. According to the most accurate calculation I can make, the proportion of subsistence and labor, which will work them up, in six years upon an average, is the most profitable to the planter. And this allowance, surely, is very humane; for we estimate here the lives of our coal-heavers upon an average at only two years, and our fifty thousand girls of the town at three years at most. And our soldiers and seamen no matter what." After exploding this (dull?) bombshell, JA has a question for his correspondent: "Is there, Mr. Tudor, in this preamble, or in any statute of Great Britain . . . the smallest consideration of the health, the comfort, the happiness, the wealth, the growth, the population, the agriculture, the manufactures, the commerce, the fisheries of the American people?" The question was rhetorical, but JA gives an answer and a warning: "All these things are to be sacrificed to British wealth, British commerce, British domination, and the British navy, as the great engine and instrument to accomplish all" [X, 338-340].

100. Hobhouse: John Cam H. [33:33]. Pound is implying that many of Hobhouse's liberal ideas about the emancipation of people from all kinds of slavery can be found in JA, as shown in the letters he wrote in 1818. In 1842 (24 years later), Hobhouse was fighting for child labor laws in England.

101. Ignorance . . . circulation: An Adams concept to which Pound often referred was the first item in his "Introductory Textbook" on economics. JA wrote: "All the perplexities, confusion, and distress in America arise, not from defects in their constitution or confederation, not from want of honour and virtue, so much as from downright ignorance of the nature of coin, credit, and circulation" [*SP*, 159].

102. *κύδιστ' . . . κυβερνῶν*: H, "Most honored of the immortals, worshipped under many names, all powerful forever, Zeus, founder of the natural order, who rules over all things by law." Pound has rearranged the opening two lines of Cleanthes' *Hymn to Zeus* [*OBGV*, no. 483] to suit his own metrical fancy. He gives his own free rendition of the lines as a note to the table of contents for Cantos LII-LXXI (p. 256): "Glorious, deathless of many names, Zeus aye ruling all things, founder of the inborn qualities of nature, by laws piloting all things."

CANTO LXXIV

Sources

Leo Frobenius and Douglas Fox, *African Genesis*, 1937, reissued by Benjamin Blom, New York, 1966; James Legge, *The Four Books*, Shanghai, 1923 [Legge] ; the Bible; M. E. Speare, *The Pocket Book of Verse*, 1940; *Time*, European edition; *Stars and Stripes*, editions of Paris and Mediterranean Theatre, May-October; Homer, *Od*. IX, II, XII, XI; Dante, *Pur*. X, *Inf*. XXVII, XXXII, XXXIII; Virgil, *Aeneid* I; Aristotle, *Nicomachean* [*Ethics*] ; *Lyra Graeca* I; *Oxford Book of Greek Verse* [*OBGV*] .

Background

EP, *SP*, 320, 338-339, 314, 284; *LE*, 166; *SR*, 91, 101; *GK*, 58-59, 34, 81-83, 229; *CNTJ*, 98-104; *PE*, 125-126; *T*, 427; *PD*, 42-50, 3-10; *ABCR*, 43-44; F. C. Burkitt, *The Religion of the Manichees*, Cambridge, 1925; Frances Frenaye, *The Fall of Mussolini, His Own Story by Benito Mussolini*, New York, 1945, a trans. of *Una "Cicogna" sul gran Sasso* by Ed. Mondadori, Milan, 1945; Sir Montagu Webb, *India's Plight*, Daily Gazette Press, Karachi, 1914; Douglas C. Fox, "Warkalemada Kolingi Yaoburrda," *Townsman*, vol. 2, no. 7, August, 1939; Michael King, "Ezra Pound at Pisa: An Interview with John L. Steele," *Texas Quarterly*, vol. XXI, no. 4, Winter, 1978; Achilles Fang, Ph.D. dissertation, Harvard Univ., II, III, IV; Erich Maria Remarque, *All Quiet on the Western Front*, 1929; E. Gilson, *La Philosophie du Moyen Age*, Paris, 1925; George Anthiel, *Bad Boy of Music*, New York, 1945; Villon, *Testament*; CFT, *Basil Bunting: Man and Poet* [Bunting] ; Ford Madox Ford, *Mightier than the Sword*, London, 1938.

Exegeses

HK, *Era*, 458; DP, *Pai*, 9-2, 313-317; DG, *Pai*, 6-1, 42; CFT, *Pai*, 3-1, 98-100, 93-94; HK, *Pai*, 1-1, 83; Tay, *Pai*, 4-1, 53; Michaels, *Pai*, 1-1, 37-54; CFT, *Pai*, 2-3, 458, 451; Hunting, *Pai*, 6-2, 179; Surrette, *Pai*, 3-2, 204; Shuldiner, *Pai*, 4-1, 73, 81; Moody, *Pai*, 4-1, 6-57; Knox, *Pai*, 3-1, 71-83; EH, *Pai*, 2-2, 336; Hankins, *Pai*, 2-2, 337; Martin, *Pai*, 6-2, 167-173; Nasser, *Pai*, 1-2, 207-211; GD, *Pai*, 8-2, 335-336; D'Epiro, *Pai*, 10-2, 297-301; Elliot, *Pai*, 8-1, 59; BK, *Pai*, 10-2, 307; DD, *Ezra Pound*, 78.

[It is known that Pound had very few books at Pisa: the Bible, *The Four Books* he had with him when arrested, *The Pocket Book of Verse* he found in the camp, a few copies of *Time* magazine that were passed around, perhaps a random newspaper at times, and a small number of unidentified books available in a collection in the quarters of the DTC cadre. Where Pound has used materials from memory (Homer, Dante, Virgil, etc.), these works have been listed as sources even though he did not have them physically at hand. The books listed under "Background" might be increased to dozens. Since credit has been given in individual glosses, the list under "Exegeses" has been similarly restrained.]

Glossary

1. **tragedy . . . dream**: Significant, as it reveals one social good Pound thought Fascism would accomplish. The dream may refer to Mussolini's promise in 1934 that every Italian peasant would have a house of his own in 80 years. Pound wrote, "I don't the least think he expects to take 80 years at it, but he is not given to overstatement" [*J/M*, ix].

2. **Manes**: ?216-276; Persian sage; founder of the Manicheans [23:28]; for his teaching he was condemned and crucified. "Mani's corpse, or his flayed skin stuffed with hay, was set up over one of the gates of the royal city" [Burkitt, 5; Fang, III, 90].

3. **Ben**: Benito Mussolini [41:2].

4. **la Clara a Milano**: I, "and Clara at Milan." Mussolini and his mistress, Claretta Petacci, after being summarily tried and shot with 16 others in a nearby village, were brought to Milan and at 3 A.M. April 27, 1945 were dumped in the Piazzàle Loreto. A few hours later, the bodies of Mussolini and Claretta were hung by the feet from a scaffold. The execution occurred before Pound surrendered himself and asked the partisans to take him to the nearest American headquarters.

5. **maggots**: Contemptuous label for "the Partisans," an anti-Mussolini political group. On April 30, the Committee of Liberation in N Italy took responsibility for the execution. Mussolini is seen as the dead bullock sacrificed.

6. **Digonos**: H, "twice-born" [48:20]. In mythology, Dionysus was born twice. But there is no record of one who was "twice-crucified," which Pound implies happened to M, who was first shot and then hanged.

7. **Possum**: T. S. Eliot. "The Hollow Men" begins, "We are the hollow men / We are the stuffed men" [cf. 2 above] and ends, "This is the way the world ends / Not with a bang but a whimper."

8. **Dioce**: [Deïoces]. The first great ruler of the Medes, who built the city of Ecbatana [4:32]. By being a fair judge, he won the hearts of the people who made him king, after which he built his visionary city. Pound likens Deïoces' aspiration to create a paradisal city with what he perceived to be Mussolini's intentions.

9. **process**: The Taoist way, in which all life should blend and flow with the flow of nature [HK, *Era*, 458]. Pound associates a number of names and concepts here in a cluster similar to one in Canto 4 [4:30, 31, 32, 33].

10. **Kiang**: C, "river," the Yangtze [53:98].

11. **Han**: The Han River, which flows through Shensi and Hupeh provinces and into the Yangtze River at Hankow. After Confucius's death some of his disciples wanted to render to Yu Jo (who resembled the Master) the same observances they had rendered to Confucius. But one of the disciples, Tseng, said: "This may not be done. What has been washed in the waters of Këang and Han, and bleached in the autumn sun:—how glistening is it! Nothing can be added to it" [Legge, 635].

12. **"the great periplum"**: Pound said that the geography of the *Odyssey* "is correct

geography; not as you would find it if you had a geography book and a map, but as it would be in 'periplum,' that is, as a coasting sailor would find it" [*ABCR*, 43-44]. Here, the great periplum is the voyage of Helios.

13. Herakles: The pillars of Herakles [Hercules] denote the cliffs on either side of the Strait of Gibraltar.

14. Lucifer: The planet Venus when it is the morning star. In its periplum it might appear from Pisa to be descending in the west over North Carolina. But, more important, Lucifer has serious occult significance to the group close to G. R. S. Mead that Pound knew in his early London years. Mead coedited, with Helene Blavatsky, a journal called *Lucifer*, which had an article on Plotinus [vol. 16, April 15, 1895] which may well have introduced Pound to the works of Thomas Taylor and reinforced his interest in all the Neoplatonic light philosophers [documents provided by WF]. Identification has been controversial, however [cf. *Pai*, 9-2, 313; *Pai*, 8-2, 335-336; *Pai*, 10-2, 297-301].

15. N. Carolina: Line probably refers to a shower of meteorites that, according to a dramatic article in the *Saturday Evening Post* [Sept. 9, 1944, p. 12], fell on a band of states including NC [Pearlman, *Pai*, 9-2, 313-317]. Pauthier in *L'Universe* had written [as translated by David Gordon]: "All the meteors and phenomena which occur in the sky, like rain, wind, thunder; all the elements which are attached to the earth like water, and fire, all these things concur with the volition of the sage or of the prince who has proposed to govern men in order to render all happy" [DG, *Pai*, 6-1, 42].

16. scirocco: I, a hot, southeast, Mediterranean wind.

17. ΟΥ̇ ΤΙΣ: H, "No Man." The name for himself that Odysseus uses to trick the Cyclops [*Od.* IX, 366].

18. wind: The Taoist way [cf. 9 above; also, CFT, *Pai*, 3-1, 98-100].

19. sorella la luna: I, "sister moon": reminiscence of St. Francis of Assisi's *Canticle of the Creatures*, line 11 [JW]. The moon is also part of the ideogram 明 [M 4534], which Pound renders as: "The sun and moon, the total life process, the radiation, reception and reflection of light; hence the intelligence" [*CON*, 20].

20. precise definition: Major element of the Confucian ethic. In "Terminology" Pound describes 誠 [M 381] as "Sincerity" or "the precise definition of the word" [*CON*, 20].

21. Sigismundo: S. Pandolfo Malatesta, 1417-1468, soldier and patron of the arts [8:5].

22. Duccio: Agostino di D., 1418-c.1481, Florentine sculptor who executed most of the marble ornaments of the chapels in the Tempio [20:16]. To be distinguished from the painter Duccio Di Buoninsegna [45:8].

23. Zuan Bellin: Giovanni Bellini [25:59], Italian painter who, like Duccio, transmitted a tradition by precise definition in his art.

24. trastevere: I, "Trans-Tiber," a district in Rome across the river from the main city.

25. La Sposa: I, "the Bride" [the church].

26. Sponsa Cristi: L, "the Bride of Christ."

27. in mosaic: In *A Visiting Card* [Rome, 1942, in Italian] Pound wrote: "And the mosaics in Santa Maria in Trastevere recall a wisdom lost by scholasticism, an understanding denied to Aquinas" [*SP*, 320].

28. snotty barbarian: Pound used this pungent phrase to refer to F. D. Roosevelt.

29. T'ang: The 13th Dynasty, 618-907. Pound wrote: "From the day when the T'ang Emperors began to issue their state notes . . . the use of gold in the manufacture of money was no longer necessary . . ." [*SP*, 316].

30. Charlie Sung: Tzu-wen Sung or T. V. Soong became premier of China in 1945. Member of the prominent Soong family. His father, Charles Jones Soong, was a Methodist missionary in Shanghai and made his fortune as a Bible manufacturer and salesman. Chiang Kai-shek resigned his post as premier and appointed Soong, his brother-in-law, in his place. *Time* [June 11, 1945, p. 34] said: "The appointment of U.S. educated T. V. Soong, who more than any other Chinese has in the past showed a grasp of Western methods, men and purposes, could scarcely fail to please the U.S. and simplify the task of Chiang's U.S. advisers . . . ." Pound's reference may be either to the father or the son, one of whom he must have heard, perhaps during his 1939 visit to the U.S., was trying to negotiate a loan.

31. **anonimo**: I, "anonymous."

32. **India . . . gold standard**: As chancellor of the exchequer, Churchill returned to the gold standard in 1925 and created a severe depression not only at home but throughout the empire, particularly in India. The phrase "18 per hundred" concerns the relation of the Indian rupee to the English shilling. The government had set the rate at 1s. 6d. (18 d.) which depressed the currency in India. A number of economists protested. Sir Montague Webb [*India's Plight*, passim] proposed "that the rupee be derated to some figure less than 18d. (1s. 6d.) and India revert to silver" [Fang, III, 38]. Webb also wrote [p. 8]: "The gross distortion of the purchasing price of the rupee . . . compels the agriculturalist to give to the Tax Collector, the local money lender, and other creditors *twice as much of the produce of his fields* as he gave five years ago to meet exactly the same amount of Land Revenue, Interest, and other demands!" In *Gold and Work* Pound wrote: "For every debt incurred when a bushel of grain is worth a certain sum of money, repayment is demanded when it requires five bushels or more to raise the same sum . . . . By returning to gold, Mr. Churchill forced the Indian peasant to pay two bushels of grain in taxes and interest which a short time before he had been able to pay with only one . . . . C. H. Douglas, Arthur Kitson, Sir Montague Webb give the details" [*SP*, 338-339].

33. **Oh my England . . .**: Restatement of recurrent theme: "Free speech without freedom of radio is a mere goldfish in a bowl" [*Townsman*, vol. III, no. 11, June 1940].

34. **Stalin**: Joseph Vissarionovich Dzhugashvili, 1879-1953, Russian statesman and Communist leader. Primary tenet of Marx-Leninism is that "the workers should own the means of production." Pound thought that if he could talk to Stalin for 20 minutes, he could explain that all he had to do was control the money and he would solve the problems.

35. **R. C.**: Roman Catholic. A sixteen-page, cheaply printed summary of major elements of the Catholic missal used during mass. It was prepared by the Paulist fathers and distributed to all Catholic soldiers who showed up for religious services. Pound kept his copy and drew in the margin next to some of the Latin phrases Chinese characters taken from Legge which were evoked by the missal. The "field book" line reflects the traditional injunction against work on Sunday. The line derives from the "preparation before confession." A copy of the chaplain's handbook, one of the few books Pound found at the DTC, was examined at Brunnenburg by Hugh Kenner, the source of these details.

36. **im Westen nichts neues**: G, "Nothing new in the west": title of novel by Erich Maria Remarque translated into English as *All Quiet on the Western Front*, 1929.

37. **"of sapphire . . . sleep"**: Dante's idea of this gem is given in a Pound translation: "The sweet color of oriental sapphire which was gathering on the serene aspect of the pure air even to the first circle, / to mine eyes restored delight" [*SR*, 137; Nassar, *Pai*, 1-2, 207-211]. In later lines Dante evokes the idea of a paradisal blue in the sky into which he will rise to come as near as possible to the vision of Beatrice. In "The Flame" he saw in "Sapphire Benacus" (Lake Garda) "Nature herself's turned metaphysical, / Who can look on that blue and not believe?" [*P*, 64]. In "Phanopoeia" he connected

"bedposts" and sexual imagery to this gem: "The swirling sphere has opened / and you are caught up to the skies, / You are englobed in my sapphire" [*P*, 179]. The stonesleep theme derives from Prester John [76:145].

38. **words . . . earth**: Pound's paraphrase of *Analects* IV, X where Legge has the Master say: "The superior man, in the world, does not set his mind either for anything, or against anything; what is right he will follow" [Legge, 42]. The words "bird-hearted," "timber," and "earth" come from visual aspects of the characters and, according to Fang, "cannot be reconciled with the Chinese language" [Fang, IV, 133]. But Pound's intent is probably to evoke the intelligence of nature in process. Neither birds nor trees think: they express themselves naturally and the right follows. Pound's own translation of *Analects* IV, X is, "He said: a proper man is not absolutely bent on, or absolutely averse from anything in particular, he will be just" [*CON*, 207].

39. **Rouse**: William Henry Denham R., 1863-1950, a classical scholar who translated Homer as well as East Indian literature. In several letters Pound commented on his translations of *The Odyssey*. Said Pound: "W. H. D. Rouse went to the right place for his Homer—namely, to the Aegean in a sail boat, where they are still telling the same yarns even if they tell them about prophet Elias . . ." [*PE*, 125-126].

40. **Elias**: Elijah, the Hebrew prophet.

41. ΟΫ ΤΙΣ: H, "No Man." [cf. 17 above].

42. **Wanjina . . . things**: Wondjina. In Australian folklore W., the son of a god (the rainbow snake Ungur), created the world by saying the names of things. But W. created so many objects that his father closed his mouth so that he could not speak. Fox [mentioned in *GK* twice, 91, 133] says of a story told him in Australia: "As one old man explained, if Ungar had not very wisely done as he did, then the blackfellow would have been burdened with all the glittering claptrap of the white man's culture and would not have been able to devote himself properly to the important things of life: conversation, dancing, hunting and warfare" [*Townsman*, vol. 2, no. 7, August, 1939].

43. **Ouan Jin**: C, Wen-Jen [M 7129, 3097], "Man of Letters; Writer."

44. **Frobenius**: Leo F. [38:45]. F. died at Biganzolo, Lago Maggiore, 9 August 1938, but his students carried on his work [Fang, IV, 32].

45. **in principio . . . sinceritas**: L, "In the beginning was the Word / the Holy Ghost or the perfect Word: sincerity" [John 1.1].

46. **Mt. Taishan**: [Tai or T'ai Shan]. A sacred mountain of China in W Shantung Province, 32 miles S of Tsinan; there are many shrines on the road to the top, on which stand the temples. A mountain Pound could see from the DTC reminded him of Taishan.

47. **Pisa**: Tuscan city in Italy noted for its towers. Location of the DTC.

48. **Fujiyama**: Sacred mountain in Honshu, Japan.

49. **Gardone**: Gardone Riviera, a town on Lake Garda in Brescia Province, N Italy, where Mussolini set up the Salò Republic after the fall of his government in Rome.

50. **Villa Catullo**: The villa on Lake Garda, Italy, where Catullus lived for a time; it was here that he wrote his salutation to the promontory of Sirmio.

51. **poluphloisboios**: H, "loud-roarings." Pound said that this often used Homeric kenning has "the magnificent onomatopeia, as of the rush of the waves on the sea-beach and their recession . . ." [*LE*, 250]. A subject rhyme of *Iliad* priest walking by sea and Pound walking by Lake Garda [HK].

52. **Nicoletti**: Giachino N., prefect at Gardone. Nicoletti was the go-between of M and the socialists when he was trying to give Fascism a socialist coloring during the time of the Salò Republic.

53. "La Donna": I, "the woman." Prob. knowing Pound was a poet, Nicoletti recited a sonnet he had written, with the kind of impassioned cadence in these repeated words that only an Italian could give—thus making the moment and measure memorable. [MSB's note says only: Reciting to E. P. an early sonnet of his]. The idea of the lady may have evoked the memory of several famous ones, Claretta Petacci above, Bianca below, as well as others.

54. "Cosa . . . ginnocchion": I, "Why must it go on? If I fall . . . / I will not fall on my knees." [Pound supplied MSB with a line that preceded this: "I am married to Capello"; and a note: Defiance when they were trying to crush free spirit in Vienna].

55. Bianca Capello: ?1542-1587, mistress of Francesco de' Medici, Duke of Tuscany, who married her in 1579 and proclaimed her Grand Duchess of Tuscany four months later. She was said to have been poisoned by Francesco's brother, Ferdinand. The situation of Clara Petacci may have reminded Pound of this response.

56. the key: The notebooks for Canto 74 at Yale reveal that the key lists Chinese books, the *Analects, Mencius,* and *Chung Yung,* as well as a few Western authors (Cocteau, Wyndham Lewis, Frobenius), and books on specific subjects: economics, history, and monetary theory [for details see *Pai*, 12-1].

57. Lute of Gassir: The introductory song to the legend collection the *Dausi*. Gassire, son of Nganamba Fasa, was king of the Fasa tribe. The story of Gassire's envy and its consequences [cf. 134 below] is told in the legend collection, which deals with the history of Wagadu. A summary is given by Frobenius in *Erlebte Erdteile* [cf. GD, "Pound and Frobenius," LL, *Motive*, 33-59].

58. Hooo: Af. dial. "Hail!" [cf. 134 below]

59. Fasa: A tribe of heroes in N Africa.

60. lion-coloured pup: Prob. a dog running loose in the DTC.

61. les six potences . . . absoudre: F, "the six gallows / Absolve, may you absolve us all" [Villon, *Epitaphe de Villon: Mais Priez Dieu que tous nous vueille absouldre*].

62. Barabbas: The bandit held in jail at the time of the arrest of Christ.

63. Hemingway: Ernest H., 1898-1961, the American novelist Pound knew during his Paris years.

64. Antheil: George A., 1900-1959, American composer and pianist who was sponsored with several other modern musicians by Pound during the 20s. Pound wrote about him in *Antheil and the Treatise on Harmony*.

65. Thos. Wilson: A Negro "trainee" at the DTC [cf. 257 below].

66. Mr K.: DTC trainee.

67. Lane: DTC trainee.

68. Butterflies, mint: Paradisal cues [48:42, 50; 79/487; Frags.:38]. Even in hell or purgatory, the paradise-oriented man is conscious of his divine end. Pound takes the metaphor from Dante: "O proud Christians . . . do You not know that we are worms, born to form the angelic butterfly" [*Pur.* X, 121-125].

69. Lesbia's sparrows: Clodia, wife of the consul Mettelus Celer, was a notorious profligate celebrated by Catullus, who referred to her as Lesbia. Catullus 2, lines 1-4 may be translated: "Sparrow, thing of delight to her I love / Often she plays with you and holds you in her lap, / Offering her fingertip to your eager beak, / Asking for your darting nip".

70. voiceless . . . roosts: Prob. reference to the Wagadu legend; Pound relates the four gates of the legend to the four corner guard towers at the DTC [cf. 57 above; 96 below]. The "voiceless" may be the drum message about the tempest in Baluba [38:41].

71. el triste . . . rivolge: I, "the sad thought turns / toward Ussel. To Ventadour / goes the thought, the time turns back." Pound's own poetry based in part on Bernart de Ventadorn's *Lo tems vai e ven e vire* ["Time goes and comes and turns"]. Also echo of Dante's *era gia' lora che volge il disio* ["It was now the hour that turns back the longing"] [*Pur.* VIII, 1].

72. Ussel: Town in Corrèze Department, S central France, near Ventadour. Pound had fond memories of it and its 15th- and 16th-century houses. The Hôtel des Ducs de Ventadour has on its facade an inscription honoring the last troubadours.

73. Ventadour: Former duchy in the department of Corrèze, S central France, near Limousin.

74. Limoges: Manufacturing and commercial city of Haute-Vienne Department, W central France, not far from Ventadour. Perhaps the polite salesman is the same one celebrated by T. S. Eliot in "Gerontion" as Mr. Silvero. Pound said that all the troubadours who knew letters or music had been taught "at the abbeys of Limoges" [*SR*, 91].

75. which city: Fang identifies the forgotten city as Les Eyzies, a small town near which "are numerous sites of pre-historic Europeans" [II, 223].

76. Urochs: *Aurochs*, the European bison [cf. 152 below].

77. Mme Pujol: A landlady in Provence. Excideuil, between Limoges and Perigueux, was the place where Mme. Pujol or Poujol kept an inn. Pound told HK that Madame would be dead but the inn would still be there.

78. white bread: Observation on the adulteration of food by additives. Cf. "is thy bread ever more of stale rags / " [45/229].

79. Mt Taishan: [cf. 46 above].

80. Carrara: The city in Tuscany, Italy. The marble used in building the leaning tower of Pisa came from its quarries.

81. Kuanon: Kuan-yin (J: Kuanon). The Chinese goddess of Mercy; the compassionate bodhisattva [90:29].

82. Linus: St. Linus, pope ?67-76. His name appears first in all lists of the bishops of Rome. Earlier glosses [cf. 35, 45 above] and several of those following this one indicate that Pound was attending mass.

83. Cletus: St. Cletus (or Anacletus), pope ?76-88.

84. Clement: St. Clement I, pope ?88-97?. Also known as Clement of Rome. The names of the first three bishops of Rome appear after the names of some of the apostles as the beginning of a list of early church fathers in Canon I of the Mass.

85. the great scarab: Egyptian symbol of fertility and rebirth which was usually carved on basalt or green stone [Hastings, *Ency. of Rel. & Ethics*, vol. 11, 223-227]. Also conceived as one form of the sun god [Tay, *Pai*, 4-1, 53]. The design on the back of the priest's chasuble at mass suggested the idea of the scarab [M de R].

86. plowed . . . early: At the first conjunction of the sun and moon in spring, the emperor, the Son of Heaven, had to plough the field of God with his own hands, and at late spring, "The empress offers cocoons to the Son of Heaven" [52/258].

87. virtù: I, "creative power" [36:2].

88. Ideogram: Hsien [M2692]: "display, be illustrious." Pound uses as "tensile light descending" and relates it to the Ming ideogram [M4534]: "The sun and moon, the total light process . . . hence, the intelligence. . . . Refer to Scotus Erigena, Grosseteste and the notes on light in my *Cavalcanti*" [*CON*, 20; Michaels, *Pai*, 1-1, 37-54; CFT, *Pai*, 2-3, 458].

89. "sunt lumina": L, "are lights." From "Omnia, quae sunt, lumina sunt" [trans. on line 22, p. 429 of the text as "all things that are are lights"]. Passage derives from Erigena as quoted by Gilson [*La Philosophie du Moyen Age*, 2d ed., 1944, p. 214; cf. *LE*, 160].

90. Erigena: Johannes Scotus Erigena [36:9], medieval philosopher and theologian. His book, *De Divisione Naturae*, was condemned in 1225 by Pope Honorius III [80:90].

91. Shun: One of the legendary emperors, reigned 2255-2205 B.C. Pound sometimes calls him Chun [53:14, 23]. We read in *Chung Yung*: "Kung said: Shun was a son in the great pattern . . . he offered the sacrifices in the ancestral temple and his descendants offered them there to him [*CON*, 133]. For "precision" see 20 above.

92. Mt Taishan: [cf. 46 above]. *The Four Books* nowhere say Shun was at Taishan, but the visit is recorded in *Shu Ching* [I, ii, 8; Fang, IV, 110].

93. paraclete: In John 14.26, Christ speaks of Paracletus as the intercessor or comforter. Capitalized, the Paraclete is the third person of the Trinity. Here it is "the divine spirit," which Pound believes is the same at all times and all places, East and West.

94. Yao: Legendary early ruler [53:14].

95. Yu: [53:15].

96. 4 giants . . . bones: DTC scene with a guard in a tower at each corner of the camp. Some of the "trainees" became fond of Pound and, although not allowed to speak to him, performed helpful services.

97. Zion: Part of Jerusalem called the city of David. The name is symbolic of the promised land and of the messianic hopes of Israel.

98. David rex: L, "King David," king of the Hebrews, who died ca. 972 B.C.

99. Isaiah: Late Hebrew prophet who flourished in 8th century B.C. The Lord told him He'd "had enough of burnt offerings and . . . the blood of bulls." Instead, He said, "Zion shall be redeemed by justice, and those in her who repent, by righteousness" [Isaiah 1:11, 27].

100. Light tensile . . .: *Chung Yung* [XXVI, 10] quotes *Shi King* and comments on the quote. Pound translates the passage in part thus: "As silky light, King Wen's virtue / Coming down with the sunlight, / what purity! . . . Here the sense is: In this way was Wen perfect. The *unmixed* functions [in time and in space] without bourne. The unmixed is the tensile light, the Immaculata. There is no end to its action" [*CON*, 187].

101. "sunt lumina": [cf. 89 above].

102. Oirishman: Erigena [cf. 90 above].

103. King Carolus: Charles II, called "the Bald," 823-877, Roman emperor and king of the West Franks, grandson of Charlemagne, inherited with his half-brothers the kingdom of Emperor Louis the Pious. After the death of Louis in 840, his sons and heirs began a protracted struggle to gain control of each other's parts of the kingdom. His later success in dealing with enemies was helped by the bishops and Pope John VIII [83:10].

104. dug him up: No record exists that Erigena was exhumed. Perhaps Pound means the 13th-century heretic Amalric (or Amaury) de Bene, whose pantheistic theories derive from E. Amalric (d ca. 1204-1207); he was dug up in 1209 [80:90] and burned, along with 10 of his still living followers, before the gates of Paris [*EB*].

105. soi disantly: F, "supposedly."

106. Manichaeans: [23:28].

107. Les Albigeois: F, "The Albigensians." Like the Manichaeans, they derived part of their thought from Mithras, the Persian god of light. They were destroyed by a crusade mounted against them by Innocent III [cf. 2 above].

108. problem of history: Since the Inquisition "ruthlessly extirpated the sect and its books," the only historical evidence left is what the church would endorse [Fang, II, 232]. That evidence is grossly slanted. Pound related the spirit of the movement to *gai savoir* and called the Albigensian crusade "a sordid robbery cloaking itself in religious pretence" which "ended the *gai savoir* in southern France" [*SR*, 101].

109. Salamis: Island off Piraeus, in the gulf of which the Greeks defeated the Persians in 480 B.C.

110. money . . . state: Themistocles won the battle of Salamis in ships built by money made from the state-owned silver mines at Laurion, which the state loaned to the shipwrights. A recurrent refrain in the Pisan and later cantos [cf. 155, 344 below and 77:63, 79:55]. Pound uses the incident to illustrate a major thesis of Social Credit, that the extension of credit should be the prerogative not of private banks but of the state, which should benefit from the interest: "The state can lend. The fleet that was victorious at Salamis was built with money advanced to the shipbuilders by the State of Athens" [*SP*, 314, 342].

111. Tempus . . . loquendi: L, "A time to speak, a time to be silent" [31:1].

112. dixit: L, "said."

113. Lenin: Nikolai L. Vladimir Ilich Ulyanov, 1870-1924, Soviet statesman and Marxist theoretician. Lenin is quoted again at 80/497 [80:81].

114. Pisa: Location of DTC.

115. 23 year: Since the formation of the Mussolini government in 1922.

116. Till: Louis T., American soldier, DTC, Pisa, who was executed July 24, 1945. Ironically, Mr. Till's son Emmet, from Chicago, was murdered by two white citizens (Roy Bryant and John Milan) of Money, Miss., where he was visiting at age 14.

117. Cholkis: Colchis, the kingdom of Aeëtes, son of Helios, where Jason and the Argonauts sought the golden fleece.

118. Zeus ram: In the myth, the ram with the golden fleece was sacred to Zeus.

119. Snag . . . : Snatch of GI dialog overheard at DTC. Snag may have been a nickname for Till.

120. Ideogram . . .: Mo [M4557], "A negative; not; no."

121. ΟΥ̇ ΤΙΣ: H, "No Man" [cf. 17 above].

122. a man . . . down: Metaphor often applied to Odyssean hero in time of trouble: to Odysseus in the power of Circe or the Cyclops and prob. by extension to Pound himself who, like Till, faced possible death at the DTC.

123. the ewe: Remark probably made by Till. The incongruity of such sentiment from one hung for murder and rape is suggested.

124. Hagoromo: Classical, one-act, Noh play [*CNTJ*, 98-104]. The "hagoromo" is a "feather-mantle" or magical cloak of a "Tennin," or nymph, who leaves it hanging on a bough where it is found by a priest. Pound calls the tennin "an aerial spirit or celestial dancer." She wants her magic cloak back and the priest finally promises to return it, "if she will teach him her dance." Pound goes on: "She accepts the offer. The chorus explains that the dance symbolizes the daily changes of the moon. . . . In the finale, the tennin is supposed to disappear like a mountain slowly hidden in mist" [ibid., 98]. The *Hagoromo*, mentioned in Ur-Canto 1 [*Poetry* 10 (1917), 117], is evoked several times in the Pisan and later cantos [79/485, 80/500].

125. Taishan: [cf. 46 above].

126. tovarish: R, "comrades" [27:30]. Here Pound prob. refers to himself as the one who, at the DTC, blessed all creation and "wept in the rain ditch."

127. Sunt lumina: L, "are lights" [cf. 89 above].

128. stone . . . form: A favorite idea of Pound's which informed his perception of sculptors as discoverers or unveilers of form [*GB*, passim].

129. sia . . . Miracoli: I, "either Cythera [Aphrodite] or Isotta [Malatesta, 9:59], or Saint Mary of the Miracles" [church in Venice].

130. Pietro Romano: Pietro Lombardo, 1435-1515, Italian architect and sculptor who did Dante's tomb at Ravenna as well as work listed in gloss above.

131. **ΟΥ ΤΙΣ . . . . down**: [cf. 121 and 122 above].

132. **diamond die**: A metaphor to suggest that although civilization has been overwhelmed by the avalanche of the war, things of real and permanent value in man's aspirations will, like the diamond, prevail in the end, untarnished.

133. **first must destroy . . .** : Mencius: "A man must first despise himself, and then others will despise him. A family must first destroy itself, and then others will destroy it. A kingdom must first smite itself and then others will smite it" [Legge, 704]. This Confucian idea is illustrated by the story of Wagadu in "Gassire's Lute."

134. **4 times . . . Fasa**: "Gassire's Lute," the Soninke legend, starts with these words: "Four times Wagadu stood there in all her splendor. Four times Wagadu disappeared and was lost to human sight: once through vanity, once through falsehood, once through greed and once through dissension. Four times Wagadu changed her name. First she was called Dierra, then Agada, then Ganna, then Silla. Four times she turned her face. Once to the north, once to the west, once to the east and once to the south. For Wagadu, whenever men have seen her, has always had four gates: one to the north, one to the west, one to the east and one to the south. Those are the directions whence the strength of Wagadu comes, the strength in which she endures no matter whether she be built of stone, wood and earth or lives but as a shadow in the mind and longing of her children. For really, Wagadu is not of stone, not of wood, not of earth. Wagadu is the strength which lives in the hearts of men and is sometimes visible because eyes see her and ears hear the clash of swords and ring of shields, and is sometimes invisible because the indomitability of men has overtired her, so that she sleeps. Sleep came to Wagadu for the first time through vanity, for the second time through falsehood, for the third time through greed and for the fourth time through dissension. Should Wagadu ever be found for the fourth time, then she will live so forcefully in the minds of men that she will never be lost again. . . . Hooh! Dierra, Agada, Ganna, Silla! Hooh! Fasa!" The rest of the legend (12 pages) gives a number of stories of how Wagadu was lost, each section ending with the refrain "Hooh! . . . " repeated 10 times. The legend illustrates a Confucian doctrine central to Pound's thinking: If a king (or chief) lacks order in himself that leads to lack of order in the family, which leads to lack of order in the state, which thus becomes lost [cf. "Chêng Ming: A New Paideuma," inside front cover of *Pai*; 57 above].

135. **dell' Italia tradita**: I, "of betrayed Italy." Pound is stating that Italy was betrayed by the king and Pietro Bodoglio, who replaced M as head of the government. This act derived from a lack of order as expressed by the Confucian *Chêng Ming* ("right name") or lack of "a new paideuma," which Pound associates with Frobenius [*SP*, 284; *GK*, 58-59].

136. **a terrace . . .** : [cf. 8 above].

137. **la luna**: I, "the moon."

138. **Demeter**: Greek goddess of fertility.

139. **contrappunto**: I, "counterpoint."

140. **ch'intenerisce**: I, "that softens." Dante [*Pur.* VIII, 2] describes thus the twilight hour softening the hearts of the homeward bound.

141. **a sinistra la Torre**: I, "to the left of the Tower."

142. **Che . . . cader**: P, The 3d line of Bernart de Ventadour's "Lark" poem: "che s'oblia es laissa chazer," "who forgets and lets himself fall" [*T*, 427].

143. **NEKUIA**: Book XI of the *Odyssey* [1: Sources]. Odysseus, before and after the Nekuia, saw the spirits of Tyro and Alcmene in Hades [*Od.* II, 120; XI, 235, 266].

144. Alcmene: Amphitryon's wife. She was visited by Zeus, in the form of her husband, and bore his son, Heracles.

145. Tyro: [2:12].

146. Charybdis: The whirlpool opposite Scylla, off the coast of Sicily, by which Odysseus had to pass [*Od*. XII, 104-106].

147. femina . . . : L, "woman."

148. hamadryas: L, hamadryad, "tree nymph."

149. Vai soli: A misspelling of L, *vae soli*, "woe to (one who is) alone"; the biblical sentence "Vae soli, quia cum ceciderit, non habet sublevantem se" ("Woe to him who is alone when he falls for he has no one to help him up"). Pound got the phrase from Laforgue who got it from the Bible [Ecclesiastes 4.10]. Pound used it for a translation he called "Pierrots" [*T*, 247].

150. 'HΛION . . . : H, "the sun around the sun."

151. Lucina: Minor Roman diety, an aspect of Juno, the goddess of childbirth. Also Diana Lucina, lunar aspect of tidal and menstrual periodicity.

152. urochs: "Aurochs," European bison.

153. Bunting: Basil B., 1900- , English poet who followed in the Whitman-Pound tradition. He visited Pound and lived for several years (at different times) at Rapallo. Pound dedicated *GK* to Bunting and Zukofsky. In 1918, after WWI was over, Bunting refused induction into the British army as a conscientious objector on the principle that if there were a war he wouldn't go, so if there weren't he couldn't enlist. After 6 months in jail he went on a hunger strike. The guards put a roast chicken in his cell every day, but Bunting held out and after 11 days they let him go [*B. B.: Man and Poet*, 29].

154. "Red . . . Met . . .": Misprint for *Redimiculum Matellarum* (L, "A garland of chamberpots"), a collection of Bunting's poetry published in 1930.

155. Salamis [cf. 109 above].

156. Joe Gould: Joseph Ferdinand G., 1889-1957, Greenwich Village bohemian. Cummings painted his portrait and referred to him twice in his work [*Eimi*, 315; *CP*, 1938, no. 261]. Gould, Harvard 1911, started as a police reporter but after 1917 supposedly spent his life writing *An Oral History of Our Times*, scribbled in hundreds of nickle notebooks (left in cellars and closets), a few bits of which were printed by Pound [*Exile* 2, 1927, 112-116] and Richard John [*Pagany* II, 2, Spring 1931]. After his death it transpired that very little of the history was actually written [HK]. Since both Bunting and Cummings were imprisoned because of WWI, Pound may have thought Gould was also; but the record does not reveal this.

157. cummings: edward estlin c., 1894-1962; American poet, author of *Eimi* and *The Enormous Room*, an account of his imprisonment by the French army at the end of WWI, during the early years of which he served as a volunteer ambulance driver.

158. black . . . translucent: The black panther in the Roman zoo [HK].

159. Est . . . Ite: L, "It is finished, Go." Formula used at end of Catholic Mass, derived from Christ's final words on the cross.

160. Tangier . . . flame: The seaport of NW Morocco; Pound visited it with his Aunt Frank and doubtless saw the fakir recalled here.

161. Rais Uli: Ahmed ibn-Muhammed *Raisuli*, 1875-1925, Moroccan brigand who kidnapped Ion Perdicaris and his nephew, Cromwell Varley, around 1910 and collected $80,000 ransom from the U.S. But the sultan of Morocco paid back the $80,000 to avoid war with the U.S. and England [Fang, II, 48-49]. Pound wrote an imaginary interview called "The Rais Uli Myth . . . being Tangier in Dry Point" and sent it to his father with an idea that *McClure's* would publish it.

162. Elson: A missionary Pound visited in Gibraltar in 1906 and 1908. Pound wrote to Homer Pound: "Elson is about the most livest thing in Tangiers. Had a bully good gallop over hills to his home—next to the Perdicari's place which we inspected" [unpub. letter in Yale collection].

163. villa of Perdicaris: Perdicaris's house was situated on a hill on the road running from Tangiers to Cape Spartel. After he was kidnapped, the villa "never saw its master again; the fine view out to sea, the delightful gardens, the comfortable house, remained deserted" [Fang, II, 49].

164. color di luce: I, "color of light."

165. Fordie: Ford Madox [Hueffer] Ford, 1873-1939, the English novelist, critic, poet, and editor. "Riesenberg," a brief prose piece he wrote, concerns two giants who lie helplessly bound in a valley of the Upper Silesian mountains.

166. William: W. Butler Yeats. His whole work, early and late, is so filled with dreams that assigning a specific source can only be idle speculation.

167. Jim the comedian: James Joyce, 1882-1941, the Irish novelist, who sometimes clowned around as a singer.

168. Plarr: Victor Gustave P., 1863-1929, librarian of the Royal College of Surgeons of England, author of *In the Dorian Mood* (1896) and other works. His father, Gustave, was a mathematician.

169. Jepson: Edgar J., 1863-1938, English novelist. Iris Barrie wrote in *The Bookman*, Oct. 1931: "Pound and his close friend Edmond Dulac . . . were both passionately fond of jade, and Jepson collected it. He used to pass pieces of it about the table: Pound would finger each piece long and lovingly" [Fang, II, 116].

170. Maurie: Maurice Henry Hewlett, 1861-1923, English essayist, novelist, and poet. Author of *The Queen's Quair*, based on the life of Mary Queen of Scots [80 / 515].

171. Newbolt: Sir Henry John N., 1862-1938, the English poet.

172. Kokka: Colonel Goleyevsky, military attaché to Beckendorff, tsarist ambassador to the court of St. James and, ca. 1913, to Baron Stalevesky, tsarist ambassador to Washington. An acquaintance of the Pounds during their Paris years. Referred to anonymously in *GK*, 34, 81-83, 229: "[Kokka] . . . remarked that if you are covered with brass chains, a sword, etc.; if your sartorial sheath is rigid and every time you move something jangles you naturally do not loll, you sit still and upright" [p. 83].

173. old Marchesa: Pound wrote of her: "Countess M. (an Italian title) counted her high water mark a wedding at the court in St. Petersburg" [*GK*, 83].

174. Spain: When asked if any "good society" remained, Kokka "meditated and finally thought there was some left in Spain." When asked, " 'Is it a society in which you wd. care to spend much of your time?' " the general said, " 'Good GOD, No!!' " [ibid.].

175. Sirdar: A restaurant on the Champs-Elysées in Paris.

176. Bouiller: The Bal Bullier, a dance hall on the boulevard Saint-Michel, Paris. Now demolished but in the 20s noted as a resort of students and frequented occasionally by some of the staff of Ford's *Transatlantic Review* [MSB note: "Respectable landmarks in Paris. Bouiller was an open air dance place now gone."].

177. Les Lilas: Closerie des Lilas, restaurant in Paris, at the corner of Boulevard Saint-Michel and Boulevard Montparnasse, facing the Bal Bullier.

178. Dieudonné London: A restaurant in London named for the famous chef, Dieudonet. Located at 11 Ryder Street, St. James. First number of *Blast* was celebrated there on July 15, 1914. There also (2 days later) Amy Lowell gave an Imagiste dinner which Richard Aldington called her "Boston Tea Party for Ezra" [Fang, II, 301].

179. Voisin's: A restaurant in Paris at 261, rue St. Honoré and 16, rue Cambon. Recorded in *Baedeker* as a restaurant of "the highest class" [Fang, II, 309].

180. Uncle George: George Holden Tinkham, 1870-1956, member of the House of Representatives from Massachusetts (1915-43); a conservative and isolationist whom Pound knew in Venice.

181. ῬΕΙ ΠΑΝΤΑ: H, "all things flow." Inversion of Heraclitus πάντα ῥεῖ. Seems to imply that while everyone else flowed on the path of least resistance, Uncle George stood firm as a rock.

182. fills up . . . : When asked what Kung found in water to praise, Mencius said: "There is a spring of water; how it gushes out! . . . It fills up every hole, and then advances, flowing up to the four seas" [83/530; *CON* 217].

183. Nevsky: The Nevsky Prospekt is the major avenue of St. Petersburg, similar to the Champs-Elysées in Paris.

184. Schöners: The Schöner Restaurant at 19 Siebensterngasse, Vienna. Prob. the place where Pound encountered Antheil and his wife in 1928 [cf. Antheil, *Bad Boy of Music*, 215; Fang, II, 313].

185. der Greif at Bolsano: A hotel with a restaurant at 9 Walterplatz, Bolzano, in the Tyrol, Italy.

186. Mouquin's: A famous French restaurant in New York, ca. 1900, which was closed in 1925. Pound, in *Letters* and other writings, associates it with W. C. Williams. See "Dr. William's Position" [*Dial*, 1928, reprinted, *PE*, 70] : "All of which belongs to an American yesterday and is as gone as les caves de Mouquin" [Fang, II, 321].

187. Robert's: A restaurant at 33 West 55th St. In 1939 Pound visited it with E. E. Cummings.

188. La Marquise de Pierre: A friend of Remy de Gourmont who became a friend of Pound [RO].

189. Huddy: William Henry Hudson, 1841-1922. Born in Argentina of American parents, he came to England in 1870. Ford wrote of Hudson: "An immensely long form would be leaning in the doorway that separated the upper rooms of the Mont Blanc. . . . After a pause of almost breathlessness we would all of us exclaim 'Hud . . . son' . . . all except Mr. Edward Garnett, who, as his discoverer, permitted himself to say 'Huddie!' " [*Mightier than the Sword*, 60]. Hudson was a naturalist and novelist. Pound acclaimed his *Green Mansions*.

190. où sont les heurs: OF, "where are the good times" [variation of Villon: "Où sont les neiges d'antan."].

191. Mr. James: Henry J., 1843-1916, the American novelist.

192. Mrs. Hawkesby: Henry James's housekeeper at Rye.

193. Mr. Adams: Henry Brooks A., 1838-1918, son of Charles Francis Adams; American historian, taught medieval history at Harvard (1870-77); author of *The Education of Henry Adams*, which contains the seed of this anecdote [Chap. XIX, "Chaos"]. Pound got the story from Santayana [*L*, 338].

194. the monument: Santayana [RO].

195. Haec sunt fastae: L, *haec sunt fasti* (?): "these are the festivals (?)."

196. quatorze Juillet: F, "14 July" (Bastille Day, 1945).

197. Amber Rives: Amélie Rives, 1864-1945, *Time*, June 25, 1945, obit.: "Died . . . Amélie Rives . . . 81, who . . . scandalized readers . . . with her popular novel, *The Quick or the Dead. . . .*" Pound played tennis with her in London at the South Lodge home of Ford Madox Ford [Fang, II, 99-100; MSB note reads: 2nd rate British novelist].

198. Mr. Graham: R. B. Cunninghame G., 1852-1936, Scottish essayist, biographer, and world traveler, noted for his journey by horse through South America. Honored in

Blast, I. Sir John Lavery did a portrait of Graham on horseback, his left ear and black beard accented. A picture in the *Time* mentioned above prob. reminded Pound of Graham's portrait. In a letter to Harriet Monroe about what artists, poets, and sculptors did at the outbreak of WWI in 1914, Pound wrote: "Cunninghame Graham volunteered, after having lived a pacific socialist. He is to be sent off to buy re-mounts, as he is overage and knows more about horses than anyone else except Blunt" [*L*, 46; MSB note: Mr. Graham. Heir to Scottish throne; would not claim the title; getting himself photographed].

199. Farben works: The I. G. Farben (*Interessensgemeinschaft Farbenindustrie Aktiengesellschaft*) works, German chemical and dye cartel, officially organized as a monopoly in 1925 at Frankfurt-on-Main. The same issue of *Time* [p. 21] reports: "the great I. G. Farben plant in Leverkusen has already asked the military government for permission to make a long list of chemicals out of raw material on hand. . . . Germany the practitioner of total war, most certainly did not suffer total defeat" [MSB note: The fine things have been destroyed; Farben survived].

200. Lilibullero: Lillibullero, a song mocking the Irish Catholics, popular in England during the revolution of 1688. It was used as a signature theme by the BBC during WWII and was sung by both British and American soldiers [Hunting, *Pai*, 6-2, 179].

201. Adelphi: Old hotel on the Strand [62:112] which was damaged [?] during the war [MSB note: One of the last bits of decent architecture. Comes in Adams' canto]

202. Mr. Edwards: Henry Hudson E., black soldier who made out of a packing box a table Pound could write on. DTC rules did not allow Pound to speak or to be spoken to by other prisoners. But many soldiers had the "charity" and found the means to ignore the rule.

203. Baluba: Pound's name for tribe in SW Belgian Congo [38:41; MSB note: hooking up with Frobenius].

204. nient' altro: I, "nothing else."

205. XIX Leviticus: "Ye shall do no unrighteousness in judgment, in meteyard, in weight, or in measure" [19.35].

206. First Thessalonians: The verse cited says: "And that ye study to be quiet, and to do your own business, and to work with your own hands, as we commanded you" [4.11].

207. Dioce: [cf. 8 above].

208. Terracina: Seaport on the west coast of Italy [39:39]. The several lines evoke (1) the birth of Aphrodite from the sea foam, and (2) the restoration of the goddess to her pedestal there, a lifelong wish of Pound [Surette, *Pai*, 3-2, 204].

209. Anchises: Father of Aeneas who was approached by Aphrodite in human disguise. As Virgil put it [*Aeneid* I, 404-405], he knew her by her walk [23:31, 34].

210. wind . . . rain . . . process: [cf. 9 above].

211. Pleiades: A cluster of stars in the constellation of Taurus (the seven daughters of Atlas). "Her mirror" is the sky and "she" is the recumbent earth [HK].

212. Kuanon: [cf. 81 above].

213. this stone: The spiritual peace evoked by the stone statue of Kuanon is similar to the peace evoked by the sapphires of Dante and Prester John [cf. 37 above; 76:145].

214. χθόνια . . . : H, "Nether earth, Mother."

215 herbs . . . : Hieratic herbs associated with paradisal vision [CFT, *Pai*, 3-1, 93-94].

216. katydid: Large green insect of grasshopper family which Pound prob. saw near his tent; unable to fly because it was minus its right wing.

217. ΤΙΘΩΝΩΙ: H, Tithonus. In the myth

T. was given immortality without freedom from process of aging. He pleaded for death but could not die. He was loved by the goddess Eos, who turned him into a grasshopper, the most musical of insects, so that she might hear her lover's voice sounding forever in her ears.

218. in coitu . . . : L, "in coition the light shines." The "lumen," or divine light, is expressed sexually [36:13].

219. Manet: Édouard M., 1832-1883, French impressionist painter. He painted a picture of the bar at the Folies-Bergère, 32, rue Richter.

220. La Cigale: A dance hall and restaurant near Place Pigalle, Montmartre, at 120, boulevard de Rochechouart.

221. Les Folies: F, "The Folies" (Bergère).

222. she did her hair . . . : Olga Rudge, who for a time dyed her hair red in honor of Vivaldi, who was known in his time as the Red Priest because of his flaming hair.

223. Drecol or Lanvin: Famous Parisian dress designers.

224. Aeneas: When he first met his mother (Aphrodite) in *The Aeneid*, he knew her at once.

225. la France . . . : F, "Nineteenth-century France."

226. Degas: Edgar D., 1834-1917, French impressionist painter who significantly influenced followers such as Picasso.

227. Guys: Constantin G., 1802-1892, newspaper illustrator who did drawings for the *London News* during the Crimean War. He settled in Paris (ca. 1885) and sketched the life and manners of the Second Empire during the period when impressionism, as well as all the arts, flourished.

228. Vanderpyl: Fritz-René V., 1876- ; a Dutch writer Pound knew during his Paris years [7:22].

229. Vlaminck: Maurice V., 1876-1905, French painter, printmaker, and writer.

230. this stone: [cf. 213 above].

231. staria . . . scosse: I, "it would rest without further tossing." Guido da Montefeltro says these words [*Inf.* XXVII, 63] about respite from the tossing flames that encase him in the hell of evil counsellors [cf. epigraph to Eliot's "Prufrock"; MSB note: Dante and the Possum: if I thought I was talking to anyone returning to the world, flame would not keep speaking].

232. eucalyptus: On the way to Lavagna, Pound picked up a eucalpytus pip and kept it with him thereafter [M de R; 80:9].

233. mare Tirreno: I, "the Tyrrhenian Sea."

234. Malmaison: A chateau near Paris; residence (1809-1814) of the Empress Josephine, and later of Maria Christina of Spain and of the Empress Eugénie.

235. Sirdar: [cf. 175 above].

236. Armenonville: Pavillon d'Armenonville, fashionable restaurant in the Bois de Boulogne, Paris: "between the Porte Maillot and the Jardin d'Acclimatation" [Fang, II, 309].

237. Ventadour: Town near Egletons, SW of Ussel. A ruined castle of a famous ducal family is located there [cf. 72, 73 above].

238. Ussel: [cf. 72 above].

239. la bella Torre: I, "the beautiful tower." The Leaning Tower of Pisa.

240. Ugolino: Ugolino della Gheradesca, ?1212-1289, Ugolino da Pisa. He conspired to seize power in Pisa but was imprisoned and his wealth confiscated (1276). After other treasons against Pisa, he, his two sons, and two grandsons were imprisoned in the tower of Gualandi (since called Torre Della Fame) and starved to death [*Inf.* XXXIII]. Dante [*Inf.* XXXII] pictures U. eating his son's head.

241. H.: Adolf Hitler.

242. M.: Benito Mussolini.

243. Frobenius: Leo F. [38:45; cf. 44 above].

244. der Geheimrat: G, "the privy councillor."

245. der . . . hat: G, "the [white] man who in Baluba made the thunder storm" [38:41].

246. Monsieur Jean: J. Cocteau, 1891-1963, French poet, playwright, and man of letters, whose creative powers Pound regarded most highly during the 20s and 30s: "Yet Greek drama exists. Cocteau by sheer genius has resurrected it" [*GK*, 93]; "Gaudier had and Cocteau has genius" [*GK*, 105].

247. Possum: Pound endowed T. S. Eliot with this nickname because, like the possum, he was good at playing dead.

248. pouvrette . . . lus: F, "poor and old never did I read a letter" [Villon, *Testament*, "Ballade Pour Prier Nostre Dame"]. Pound was impressed with this Villon ballad early on and discusses it in a chapter entitled, "Montcorbier, *alias* Villon" [*SR*, 166-178].

249. magna NUX animae: L, "great nut of the soul." Some scholars believe this phrase should really be "great night of the soul," to evoke mystics who talk about "the dark night of the soul" [Shuldiner, *Pai*, 4-1, 73]. But Pound probably means what he says, "nut," to evoke the Pythagorean theme of "the body is in the soul" [CFT, *Pai*, 2-3, 451] and establish the motif that will climax as "the great acorn of light" [116:8].

250. Barabbas: Thief released from prison in place of Christ who was then crucified with two other thieves [cf. 62 above].

251. Mr. Edwards: [cf. 202 above].

252. Hudson: [cf. 189 above].

253. comes miseriae: L, "companion of misery."

254. Comites: L, "Companions."

255. Kernes: Trainee at DTC.

256. Green: Trainee at DTC who was in a "security cage" near Pound [77:158].

257. Tom Wilson: Black trainee at DTC [77:91].

258. Whiteside: The black turnkey at DTC, used by Provost Section to handle the solitary cells and "security cages."

259. bag o'Dukes: Dukes Mixture, a brand of roll-your-own tobacco used at the DTC [Williams, *Poetry*, 1949, 218].

260. ac ego in harum: L, "and I too in the pig-sty" [39:24].

261. Circe: [1:1].

262. ivi . . . animae: L, "I went into the pig-sty and saw soul-corpses" [39:24].

263. Carrol (of Carrolton): Charles Carroll of Carrollton, 1737-1832, Revolutionary leader [69:66]. A number of the trainees, particularly blacks from the south, had names of former presidents and even of famous men who did not get as far, such as Carroll.

264. Crawford: Carrol C., inmate at DTC.

265. ΘΕΑΛΓΕΙΝ: H, (infinitive of Θέλγω): "to enchant, bewitch," which is what Circe did; also, in Homer, to cheat, cozen.

266. nec benecomata: L, "nor fair-tressed" [cf. Andreas Divus, trans., *Od*. XI].

267. Kirkê: H, "Circe."

268. *κακὰ . . . ἔδωκεν*: "she had given them dreadful drugs" [39:7]. Circe bewitched the "mountain wolves and lions" with her potions.

269. veleno: I, "poison."

270. Predappio: Town in NE Italy where Mussolini was born, the son of a blacksmith. The several lines ending here concern usury as a disease that infects the whole social fabric. Said Pound: "When a given hormone defects, it will defect throughout the whole system" [*GK*, 60].

271. Upward . . . bank: [cf. 275 below]. In a poem entitled "The Discarded Imagist" [*The Egotist*, June 1, 1915; rpt. *Poetry*,

Vol. 6, no. 6, 1915], Upward wrote: "I withstood the savages of the Niger with a revolver: / I withstood the savages of the Thames with a printingpress" [EP, *GB*, 118]. In 1901 as British Resident in Nigeria he stood on "the blood-stained stone of Somarika, with a revolver in his hand, and three human skulls at his feet" and faced "an ogre, whose boast it is that he never had to strike more than one blow to cut off a human head." [*Some Personalities*, London, 1912.] Later he started a publishing venture in London which became "The Wisdom of the East" series.

272. Sitalkas: The Delphian Apollo [Σιτάλκας], "Prohibitor of Corn-Growing." Upward bought at Corfu an ancient Greek gem that seemed to represent John Barleycorn with a seed basket on his arm and three spikes rising from his cap. Upward seems to have had a seal ring made out of the gem: "a sardonyx or blood-stone, green with red spots." An impression of the seal is used on the cover of Upward's book *The Divine Mystery* [Moody, *Pai*, 4-1, 56-57; 78/479].

273. Niger: River in W Africa.

274. Thomas bank: The Thames River bank.

275. Upward . . . shot himself: Allen U., 1863-1926, cultural anthropologist, student of primitive religions, world traveler and friend of many people around Pound (1911-21), including G. R. S. Mead and A. R. Orage. Pound's idea of the Eleusinian mysteries were seen through such books as Upward's *The Divine Mystery*, 1910 [Knox, *Pai*, 3-1, 71-83]. Upward committed suicide in 1926.

276. Matteo: M. da Pasti, d. 1468, Veronese sculptor and medalist. Made intaglio medallions of Sigismundo Malatesta, Isotta, etc. [26:4].

277. Pisanello: Antonio Pisano, ?1397-1455, Veronese painter and medalist. Made medals of Sigismundo, his brother Novello, etc. [26:78].

278. Babylon: Prob. the owner of Babylon, suggesting the confusion of voices from which the work of Matteo and Pisanello rescued the 15th century.

279. nox animae magna: L, "great night of the soul" [cf. "Dark Night of the Soul," St. John of the Cross; cf. variant "nux" in 249 above].

280. Taishan: [cf. 46 above].

281. To study . . . untrumpeted: Pound translates the opening lines of the *Analects* thus: "1. He said: Study with the seasons winging past, is not this pleasant? 2. To have friends coming in from far quarters, not a delight? 3. Unruffled by men's ingnoring him, also indicative of high breed" [*CON*, 195].

282. filial . . . process: Pound renders *Analects* I, II, 2 thus: "2. The real gentleman goes for the root, when the root is solid the (beneficent) process starts growing, filiality and brotherliness are the root of manhood, increasing with it" [ibid.].

283. nor . . . alacrity: *Analects* I, III: "He said: Elaborate phrasing about correct appearances seldom means manhood" [ibid.].

284. employ . . . harvest: *Analects* I, V: "He said: . . . respect what you do and keep your word . . . be friendly to others, employ the people in season. [*Prob. meaning public works are not to interfere with agricultural production.*]" Pound's brackets and italics [ibid.].

285. E al Triedro . . . la Luna: I, "And at the trihedral corner, Cunizza/and the other woman: 'I am the moon' " [6:34].

286. Cunizza: Cunizza da Romano [6:34]. Here the image of the compassionate woman.

287. Nύξ animae: H, "night," animae: L, "of the soul."

288. San Juan . . . ad posteros: L, "St. John . . . to posterity." The Spanish mystic Juan de Yepis y Alvarez, 1542-1591, known as St. John of the Cross. He wrote of "the Dark Night of the Soul" as a stage in the mystic way.

289. Ugolino: [cf. 240 above].

290. la vieille de Candide: F, "Candide's old woman" [Voltaire, *Candide*, XI-XII].

291. Corporal Casey: Soldier in cadre of the DTC.

292. Le Paradis . . . : F, "Paradise is not artificial" [cf. Baudelaire, *Les Paradis Artificiels*].

293. spezzato: I, "broken."

294. mint: One of the hieratic herbs related to the vision of paradise.

295. Ladro: I, "thief, rogue." Reference to a cat in the DTC [M de R].

296. Nemi: Lake Nemi, a small crater lake in the Alban Hills of Latium, Italy; here were the sacred grove and the temple of Diana, guarded by a priest who held the post until he was killed by another who sought the office [Frazer, *The Golden Bough*, 3].

297. Zarathustra: Zoroaster, fl. 5th century B.C., a religious teacher of ancient Persia; founder of Zoroastrianism, originally a kind of fertility religion which later developed a more complex cosmogony and eschatology deriving from the struggle of the Zoroastrian supernatural spirits.

298. desuete: F, "obsolete, out of date."

299. Jupiter . . . Hermes: Major deities in the train of thought evoked by the idea of paradise as not artificial.

300. castellaro: [Poss. *castello*] : I, "castle." Prob. here "small castle." A place near Sant Ambrogio, near Rapallo [EH].

301. saeculorum Athenae: L, "immemorial of Athena."

302. γλαύξ, γλαυκῶπις: H, "little owl, with gleaming eyes." Note in context that the olive is sacred to Athena, who created it, and that γλαυκὸς, like γλαυκὸ, is used to describe the sheen of the olive [79:60].

303. olivi: I, "olive trees."

304. Boreas Apeliota libeccio: Seriatim: "North Wind, East Wind, South Wind."

305. "C'è il babao": [*babau*]. I, "there's the bugbear."

306. il Pozzetto/al Tigullio: I, "the Little Well/at Tigullio." The beach on the Bay of Tigullio, near Rapallo, where Pound lived in 1930s.

307. Oedipus: Greek hero who inadvertently murdered his father and married his mother [Sophocles, *Oedipus Rex*].

308. nepotes Remi magnanimi: L, "grandsons (descendants) of the great-souled Remus."

309. Mr. Bullington: Prob. inmate at DTC.

310. Lady be good: Popular song of the 30s.

311. in harum . . . : [*haram*]: L, "into a pig-sty I too have gone" [cf. 260 above].

312. three months . . . : Pound translates *Analects* VII, XIII: "In Ch'i he heard the 'Shao' sung, and for three months did not know the taste of meat; said: didn't figure the performance of music had attained to that summit" [*CON*, 220].

313. song . . . radiance: Pound's visual reaction to the ideogram for "the name of the music of the legendary Emperor *Shun*." Shao [M5691]. In the left component he sees the sun under an image of rays. (Note that no Chinese philologist sees anything of the kind [Fang IV, 74].)

314. Chi: [Ch'i], principality in Shensi Province; ruled by Wen Wang.

315. Shun: Legendary Chinese ruler [M5936]. Pound calls him Chun [53:23].

316. λιγύρ': H, "clear, shrill."

317. tanka: The Japanese verse form of five lines; the first and third have five syllables, the others seven. Memory of "A Shadow," tanka by Katue Kitasono. Pound once asked him, "Did you see the *Hawk's Well*—is it any use in Japan?" "Hawk's eye," above, and "hawk's wing" in next line prob. recalled the Yeats play.

318. babao: I, "bugbear" [cf. 305 above].

319. no fortune . . . : [1/4].

320. J. Adams: [31:15] Pound several times refers to the statement Adams often made: "every bank of discount . . . is downright corruption" [71:35; 76:113].

321. at 35 . . . 21.65: Roosevelt's change of the value of gold.

322. Byzantium: Ancient city on the Bosphorus; site of modern Istanbul.

323. Meyer Anselm: Mayer Amschel Rothschild, 1743-1812, usually considered to be the founder of the House of Rothschild.

324. old H.: Henry Morgenthau, Sr. [DG/RO].

325. young H/: Henry Morgenthau, Jr. [DG/RO].

326. Sieff: Israel Moses S., British merchant; reputed anonymous owner of the London tabloid the *Daily Mirror* during the late 1930s.

327. a rrromance: Idea that money, "high finance," and international money operations were "a great romance" was current during the 1930s.

328. yidd: [yitt, yit]: Yiddish dialect, "Jew." G, *Jude*. A term of approbrium first applied by wealthy German Jews to low-class "ghetto" Jews from central European countries when they began migrating west. Pound associated "the blond bastards" with *The Magnificat* based on Luke 1.52: "He hath put down the mighty from their seats, and exalted them of low degree" [DG/RO].

329. goyim: Yiddish, "gentiles." A term used by Jews for non-Jews. In context, it can be pejorative or not.

330. versalzen: G, "to oversalt; to spoil." Derived from Christ's remarks at the end of the Sermon on the Mount [Matthew 5.13]: "Ye are the salt of the earth." Pound said Christ was addressing the Jews (not the gentiles) and refers at them as "oversalted" [HK].

331. With justice: "Redeem Zion with justice" [cf. 99 above].

332. Yu: [53:15] Emperor after Shun. The laws of Jehovah on money and control of usury are better than those of the early Chinese emperors.

333. sha-o: The succession dance, which mimed the peaceful accession of Emperor Chun [Shun]. *Analects* III, XXV [*CON*, 205].

334. XIXth Leviticus: Verse 35: "Ye shall do no unrighteousness in judgment, in meteyard, in weight, or in measure."

335. Jeremiah: Major Hebrew prophet: "the son of Hilkiah, of the priests that were in Anathoth in the land of Benjamin" [*Jer.* 1.1].

336. tower of Hananel: In the north corner of Jerusalem on the wall. The data concerns directions for building the city [*Jer.* 31.38-40].

337. Goah: Goath: "And the measuring line shall yet go forth . . . and shall compass about to Goath" [ibid.].

338. Anatoth: A city of Benjamin where Jeremiah was born. The value of its currency was slightly different from that of Jerusalem: one-half of 17 shekels was $8.50 there: "And I bought the field of Hanameel my uncle's son, that was in Anathoth, and weighed him the money, even seventeen shekels of silver" [*Jer.* 32.6-10].

339. Benjamin: The plateau of E central Palestine, near the Jordan River, between Jerusalem and Bethel.

340. Chocorua: Mount Chocorua, E New Hampshire, in the Sandwich Range of the White Mountains.

341. meteyard and measure: [cf. 334 above].

342. comman': Sound of "corps man," for soldiers from the medical corps.

343. METATHEMENON . . . : H, "if those who use a currency give it up in favour of another." From Aristotle, *Politics* 1275b, 16 [53:157; 77:67; 97:77].

344. Salamis fleet: [cf. 110 above].

345. Wörgl: (Woergl), a small town in the Austrian Tyrol which in the early 1930s issued its own money, a form of the stamp script [41:44]. The new money created prosperity: "The town had been bankrupt: the citizens had not been able to pay their rates . . . etc. But in less than two years everything had been put right. . . . All went well until an ill-starred Wörgl note was presented at the counter of an Innsbruck bank. . . . The burgomaster was deprived of his office, but the ideological war had been won" [*SP*, 314].

346. Gedichte: G, "Poems."

347. Heine: Heinrich H., 1797-1856, German lyric poet and critic.

348. Tyrol: I.e., N Tyrol, Austria.

349. Innsbruck: Capitol of N Tyrol, W Austria.

350. N.E.P.: "New Economic Policy." The Bolshevik Revolution of 1917 left the country in an economic doldrums that it could not get out of. Marx had provided an analysis of the workings and functions of "capital," but he provided no economic program for a socialist state. The country continued in a state of shock while the people suffered terribly. Lenin finally created the N.E.P. as a temporary five-year plan. It was a capitalist economic device that was criticized by a number of Marxist purists, but Lenin conceived it to be a temporary transitional economic device between the former bourgeois system of exploitation and the dictatorship of the proletariat, in whicl an economic paradise would be created. Pound's theory here is that all Lenin needed to have done was issue certificates to the workers for work done, which could have been used as money and thus have created the kind of prosperity had by Wörgl. Instead, the N.E.P. was started by borrowing money at high interest rates, which kept the people enslaved in the same old way [103:6].

351. canal work: The Soviets used forced labor (nearly 300,000 prisoners from labor camps) to build the White Sea-Baltic Canal, begun in 1931 and completed in 1933-34. David J. Dallin, in his book *The Real Soviet Russia* [Yale University Press, 1947], quotes "a French engineer . . . sentenced to forced labor," who "managed to escape across the Finnish border": "More than 50,000 [prisoners] died during a period of a year and a half" [p. 242].

352. dumping: Placing large quantities of a basic commodity on the market at a price less than the cost of producing it. Pound wrote: "The Roman Empire was ruined by the dumping of cheap grain from Egypt, which sold at an unjustly low price. And usury corrodes" [*SP*, 316]. Similar devices were employed by Roosevelt's New Deal to restore the market economy.

353. each . . . god: One of the several paraphrases Pound makes of a biblical line: "For all people will walk every one in the name of his god, and we will walk in the name of the LORD our God for ever and ever" [Micah 4.5].

354. Aristotle: *The Nicomachean Ethics*, 1095a, has such a statement. Pound analyzes the *Ethics* with a conclusion as premise: "As ethics, Arry is not fit to clean the boots of Confucius" [*GK*, 326].

355. Katholou: H, "generalities."

356. hekasta: H, "particulars."

357. Yaou: Yao [cf. 94 above].

358. Shun: Pound ends the passage about Shun [Chun; cf. 315 above] from *Chung Yung* in these words: "Shun was a son in the great pattern . . . he perforce came to the throne, perforce had these high honors, perforce this enduring fame, and longevity" [*CON*, 133]. And, "He liked to ask questions of people, and to listen to their simple answers. He passed over the malice and winnowed out the good. He observed their discordant motives and followed the middle line" [*CON*, 107]. And, "He said: lofty as the spirits of the hills and the grain mother, Shun and Yu held the empire, as if not in a mortar with it" [*CON*, 227].

359. wd/. . . seacoast: In a discussion of what Shun as emperor would have done had his father been guilty of murder. Seeing that he could not order that his father not be arrested as the law justly required, he said: "Shun would have regarded abandoning the empire as throwing away a worn-out sandal. He would privately have taken ***his father*** on his back, and retired into concealment, living somewhere along the seacoast" [Legge, 965; Pound's source was Pauthier, 443]. An analog to Aeneas carrying his father, Anchises, to safety on his back.

360. son père: F, "his father." Both Legge and Pauthier italicize the phrase.

361. Dai Nippon Banzai: J, "Hail to Great Japan."

362. Kagekiyo: A one-act play [*CNTJ*, 105-112]. The story of an old blind man whose daughter goes to extremes to find him, but in the end they part. Near the end of the play the chorus says: "The vizard broke and remained in his hand and Miyonoya still fled afar, and afar, and he looked back crying in terror, 'How terrible, how heavy your arm!' And Kagekiyo called at him, 'How tough the shaft of your neck is!' And they both laughed out over the battle, and went off each his own way" [*CNTJ*, 111].

363. Kumasaka: A play in two acts [*CNTJ*, 39-45]. The ghost of the hero, Kumasaka, "comes back to praise the bravery of the young man who had killed him in single combat" [*CNTJ*, 39].

364. quia . . . est: L, "because it is impossible." From Tertullian: "Credo qui impossible"; i.e., "in these domains only faith will sustain me" [HK].

365. Gassir: [cf. 134 above].

366. KOPH . . . : H, "Daughter, the blind man's shining." Persephone and Tiresias are evoked [1:7, 11], also Kagekiyo's daughter [cf. 362 above].

367. Wemyss: Rosslyn Erskine W., 1864-1933, became admiral of the fleet and was created Baron Wester Wemyss in 1919. With Foch, he signed the WWI armistice on behalf of the Allies. He and Lady Wemyss spent part of each year at Cannes, where Pound may have seen the mishap which he describes of the monocled (glass-eyed) admiral.

368. Gesell: Silvio G., 1862-1930. Finance minister in First (independent Socialist) Munich Councils Republik, which lasted from April 7 to 16, 1919. He was subsequently tried for high treason but was acquitted; thereafter, he wrote numerous books and pamphlets on anarchist and monetary theories.

369. Lindhauer government: Gustave Landhauer, 1870-1919, German literary scholar. An independent Socialist he was appointed minister of education to the First Munich Councils Republik in 1919, which resigned after ten days in office. Following the violent overthrow of the Second Munich Councils Republik (600 civilians killed in the streets by the military acting under the orders from the Social Democratic Government in Berlin), of which he was not a member, Landhauer was arrested and taken to Stadelheim Prison, where he was shot dead on arrival by an army officer [EH].

370. il danaro c'è: I, "the money is there." Statement made by Pellegrini [cf. 371 below] on November 27, 1943. P. told M he would allot 125,000 lira per month to him as "il capo dello stato." M refused, saying that 4000 lira for his family of four would be enough. P.'s response was that M should take it because "the money is there." M agreed for a while, but on December 27, 1944 he had further payment stopped [Fang, III, 88]. But M thought it strange [78/479].

371. Pellegrini: Gianpietro Domenico P., undersecretary in the Italian Ministry of

Finance (1943) in the government of the Salo Republic; official in the Consigli Nazionale and the Corporazione della Providenza e del Credito.

372. **circs**: Circumstances.

373. **musketeers . . .**: A term EP used to refer to his inner circle. "Rather more" in English idiom suggests several years more. Thus, 20 years plus several after Landhauer's death would be the time of the Salò Republic.

374. **Περσεφόνεια**: H, "Persephone."

375. **Che pende**: I, "that leans."

376. **Pontius**: Prob. Pontius Pilate.

377. **Von Tirpitz**: Alfred von T., 1849-1930, German admiral, who developed submarine and torpedo warfare against Allied commerce in WWI. "Beware of their charm" refers to the English [DG; 77:2].

378. **ΣΕΙΡΗΝΕΣ**: H, "Sirens." The Sirens who charmed sailors are suggested by the Von Tirpitz warning to his daughter.

379. **this cross**: The grammate cross adopted by Nazi Germany. The swastika with arms directed to the right was thought to represent the vernal progress of the sun [Shuldiner, *Pai*, 4-1, 81].

380. **faute de**: F, "in lieu of."

381. **ΧΑΡΙΤΕΣ**: H, "the Graces."

382. **Kuanon**: [cf. 81 above].

383. **a la marina**: I, "to the coast, ashore."

384. **nautilis biancastra**: I, *nautilo biancastro*: "a white-colored shell," as in Botticelli's painting of Venus.

385. **Dantescan rising**: In *The Divine Comedy*, Virgil leads Dante through Hell and up Mt. Purgatory in a systematic, ordered way. At the summit of the Mt. in the Earthly Paradise, Beatrice appears and leads him in an equally orderly way through the various spheres until they approach the Empyrean.

386. **tira libeccio**: I, "the southwest wind blows."

387. **Genji**: Central character in Lady Murasaki's *Tale of Genji*. A play translated by Pound is entitled *Suma Genji* [*CNTJ*, 22-36]. In speaking of the qualities of the Noh, Pound notes "the blue-grey waves and wave pattern in Suma Genji" [p. 27].

388. **Suma**: Village on Oska Bay, near Kobe, Japan. Here Genji lived in exile from the court [*CNTJ*, 22].

389. **Tiro, Alcmene**: [cf. 143 above]. People Odysseus sees in Hell.

390. **Europa . . . Pasiphaë**: L, "Europa nor chaste Pasiphaë." Europa, the daughter of Agenor, king of Tyre, was courted and captured by Zeus in the form of a bull. Pasiphaë was the wife of King Minos of Crete, the sister of Circe, and the mother of the minotaur.

391. **Eurus**: The East or Southeast Wind.

392. **Apeliota**: The East Wind.

393. **Io son la luna**: [cf. 285 above].

394. **Cunizza**: [cf. 286 above].

395. **Rupe Tarpeia**: L, "the Tarpeian Cliff," a place in Rome where criminals and traitors were hurled to their death. Perhaps a restaurant had this name.

396. **Castelli**: Among the most common wines in Rome.

397. **"Spiritus veni"/adveni**: L, " 'come spirit,'/come."

398. **schema**: L, "figure, form."

399. **Arry**: Aristotle, who in *Nicomachean Ethics*, 1, 3, 5-7 (1095a), says political science is not for the young because "they have not experience of life and conduct . . . and they are led by their feelings" [cf. 354 above].

400. **stagirite**: A native of Stagira, here Aristotle.

401. **Apeliota**: The East Wind.

402. **Time . . . evil**: [30/147].

403. *βροδοδάκτυλος*: *ροδοδάκτυλος*, "rosy-fingered," is the Homeric epithet of Ηως,

"Dawn." βροδοδάκτυλος is the Aeolic form, found in Sappho as the epithet of σελάννα, Doric of σελήνη, "the moon": *Lyra Graeca* I, fr. 86, 246 [*OBGV*, no. 145].

404. le contre-jour: F, "against the light."

405. Achaia: Achaea, region of ancient Greece, N Peloponnesus, on Gulf of Corinth; later the Roman province Achaia, founded by Augustus.

406. Venere: I, "Venus."

407. Cytherea: L, "Cythera."

408. aut Rhodon: L, "or Rhodes."

409. vento ligure, veni: I, "Come Ligurian wind."

410. Mr. Beardsley: Aubrey Vincent B., 1872-1898, English illustrator and writer, associated with the symbolist movement and contributor to *The Yellow Book*.

411. Mr. Kettlewell: Prob. John Kettelwell, a student at St. John's College, Oxford, in 1913, when Edward, Prince of Wales, was in his first year at Magdalen.

412. pseudo-Beardsley: An unfinished drawing of the Prince of Wales on a bicycle done in the manner of Beardsley by W. Lawrence.

413. W. Lawrence: William George L., 1889-1915, younger brother of T. E. Lawrence; Will Lawrence invited Pound to St. John's College to speak on poetry. Pound read a paper on Cavalcanti at Oxford in February 1913 and while there seems to have witnessed Kettlewell telling W. L., who had run his bicycle into the Prince of Wales, that it was a pity he hadn't run into him hard enough to kill him.

414. W. L.: William George Lawrence.

415. Edvardus: Future King Edward VIII and Duke of Windsor. Here a student at Oxford.

416. a.d. 1910: It would have to be 1913 to have all the people of the passage present in the circumstances indicated.

417. Berlin to Bagdad: [or Baghdad]. A German initiated project to build a railroad linking western Europe, Istanbul, Mesopotamia and the Persian Gulf. England opposed the plan, thinking it would jeopardize British control of the sea route between Europe and India. Construction started in 1888 and was mostly completed by 1904. The project became a symbol of German imperialism [EH, *Pai*, 2-2, 336; Hankins, ibid., 337; Martin, *Pai*, 6-2, 167-173].

418. Arabia Petra: Arabia Petraea, an ancient cliff city, "a rose-red city half as old as time" [Hankins, *Pai*, 2-2, 337]; but T. E. Lawrence described the stones there as "red and black and grey with streaks of green and blue." Lowell Thomas wrote of them as "great rainbows of stone flashing out white, vermilion, saffron, orange, pink, and crimson." Lawrence was a photographer and probably had his own pictures of Petra.

419. LL.G.: Lloyd George, English prime minister at WWI peace conference at Versailles.

420. frogbassador: Georges Clemenceau, chairman of Versailles peace conference. In *J/M* Pound wrote: "I saw Arabian Lawrence in London one evening after he had been with Lloyd George and, I think, Clemenceau or at any rate one of the other big pots of the congeries. He wouldn't talk about Arabia, and quite naturally he wouldn't talk about what happened in the afternoon" [p. 33]. Fang writes: "From January to October 1919 T. E. Lawrence was at the Peace Conference with the Arab delegation; he was disgusted with the power politics played by Clemenceau and Lloyd George." And Fang quotes Vyvyan Richards, *Portrait of T. E. Lawrence*, p. 176: "At Versailles, though, however sympathetically Lloyd George understood Lawrence's concern for Feisal, and however much he would have liked to fulfill the promises made to the Arabs, the French proved immovable. So they got Damascus in the end, and with it endless trouble and expense" [II, 181].

421. Talk modern art: T. E. Lawrence was reluctant to talk of his personal experiences, which is what people wanted to hear about. He preferred to talk about the arts [cf. *T. E. Lawrence and His Friends*, passim, which mentions often his passion to set up a printing press].

422. T. L.: T. E. Lawrence. Will Lawrence probably showed Pound some of his brother's photographs of the rock temples in Arabia Petra which were probably taken during his second stay at Carchemish (spring 1912-spring 1914). During that time T. E. L. had an unpleasant encounter with Germans constructing the Constantinople-Bagdad line of the 3B (Berlin-Belgrade-Bagdad) railway.

423. Snow: Thomas Collins S., M.A. Oxford 1874, lecturer in English language and literature at Jesus College in 1913. He was among those who took part in the discussion after Pound had read his paper on Cavalcanti, in which he probably asserted that in some ways Cavalcanti could compare with Sappho.

424. *φαίνε-τ-τ-τ-τττ-αί μοι*: H, *φαίνεται μοι*: "He seems to me." Sappho's poem "To Anactoria", *Lyra Graeca* I, fr. 2, p. 186 [*OBGV*, no. 141], begins with the words: *φαίνεταί μοι κῆνις ἴσος* ("A very god he seems to me"). The very aged Snow cited this line as evidence that Sappho was better than Cavalcanti.

425. l'aer tremare: I, "the air to tremble"; part of 2d line of Cavalcanti's sonnet 7 [*T*, 38].

426. Magdalen: A college of Oxford University.

427. "The Hound of Heaven": Poem by Francis Thompson, 1859-1907, which appeared in his *Poems* (1893).

428. burn and freeze: Traditional hallmark of Sappho because of an Ambrose Philips translation (1711) of her "Hymn to Aphrodite" ["To Anactoria" in 424 above], in which he interpolated two lines: "Though now to freeze, he soon shall burn / And be thy victim in his turn."

429. Siki: "Battling" Siki, a light-heavyweight boxing champion of the 1920s, a Senegalese of brutish strength. But Pound remembered Siki for his deftness not his brutality [HK].

430. Burr: Prob. prisoner at DTC.

431. Corporal Casey: Member of cadre at DTC.

432. le bonhomme Staline: F, "simple Stalin."

433. Koba: R, "the bear." Nickname of Stalin as a boy in Georgia [52:11].

434. Rhys: Ernest R., 1859-1946. One of the few English editors Pound knew from his earliest years in England and could praise.

435. "A'hv joost........Tommy Luff": Prob. a comic anecdote Pound heard Rhys tell. The carefully counted dots prob. replace "buggered."

436. Clio: The muse of history.

437. Terpsichore: The muse of the dance.

438. Granville: Prob. Harley Granville-Barker, 1877-1946, English actor, manager, and playwright.

439. three ladies: Perhaps the "Tre donne Intorno" [78:133], or the three Graces, or both.

440. *εσσομένοισι*: H (aspirate *ἐσσομένοισι*), "for generations to come" [Elpenor's line: 1:12; *Od.* XI, 76].

441. aram vult nemus: L, "the grove needs an altar" [first statement of recurrent theme: 78:91; 79:126; 90/607].

442. Madame Lucrezia: Lucrezia Borgia [30:8, 11].

443. Cesena: Town in Forli Province, Emilia, Italy; controlled by the Malatestas from 1385 to 1465. Site of the Biblioteca Malatestiana, where Pound deposited a copy of *A Draft of XVI. Cantos* in 1926.

444. joli . . . Malatestiana: F, "pleasant quarter-hour." I, "in the Biblioteca Malatestiana." Fang says now there are no initials on the back of the door [II, 269].

445. Torquato where art thou?: Manlio Torquato Dazzi, in 1926 director of the Malatestiana. "There will be a public copy of the XVI in the Malatestiana at Cesena, if Dazzi consents to house it for me" [*L*, 190].

446. Tevere: I, "Tiber." Evokes assassination of Duke of Gandia at 5/18 ("Click of hooves on the cobbles") [5:32, 46].

447. la Stuarda: I, "the Stuart." Mary Queen of Scots [80:423].

448. Mead: George Robert Stow M., 1863-1933, editor of a quarterly review called *The Quest* (London 1909-1930), which was devoted to occult and/or mystic subjects such as reincarnation. Pound wrote about him as having a sense of humor and gave lines from Mead to illustrate: " 'I know so many people who were Mary Queen of Scots. And when I consider what wonderful people they used to be in their earlier incarnations, I ask WHAT they can have been at in the interim to have arrived where they are' " [*GK*, 226].

449. metempsychosis at . . . . ? : Reincarnation.

450. Fortean Society: A society, organized in 1931, directed by Tiffany Thayer, devoted to the study of the works of Charles Fort (1874-1932), an American journalist who was interested in researching and documenting unusual and unexplained natural phenomena. The Fortean Society's magazine was called *Doubt*.

451. bambooiform: Neologism to suggest shape of grass.

452. "La Nascita": I, "the birth." *The Birth of Venus* by Botticelli. The child is prob. Mary, Pound's daughter, and the eyes are those of her mother Olga Rudge.

453. Capoquadri: Name of the house in Siena where Pound used to stay during visits [83:36].

454. Helios: The sun. The "form beached" is Aphrodite in *La Nascita*.

455. funge la purezza: I, "the tensile light pours down" [HK, *Pai*, 1-1, 83; 4:20; 85:214; cf. 88 above].

456. formato locho: I, "in a prepared place" [*LE*, 166, from "Donna mi prega"; 36/178].

457. Arachne: The girl who challenged Athena to a weaving contest; because the girl dared to contest the gods, Athena changed her into a spider so she could weave forever; hence, "a spider."

458. mi porta fortuna: I, "brings me good luck."

459. ΕΙΚΟΝΕΣ: H, "pictures, images."

460. Trastevere: [cf. 24 above]. Pound wrote in *A Visiting Card*: "And the mosaics in Santa Maria in Trastevere recall a wisdom lost by scholasticism. . . . In his *After Strange Gods* Eliot loses all the threads of Arachne" [*SP*, 320].

461. black Jim: A servant, during the 1890s, at the Hotel "Easton," the boardinghouse at 24 E. 47th St., New York, run by the Weston branch of Pound's family, where he spent time as a youth ["Indiscretions," *PD*, 42-50].

462. . . . Ritz-Carlton: Famous luxury hotel, now the office building at 380 Madison Ave., which replaced the Westons' boardinghouse at 24 E. 47th St., New York [JW].

463. Monsieur Fouquet: John D. F., an architect with an office in Grand Central Depot who lived at the boardinghouse during the early 1890s. He had once been Uncle Ezra's partner in a hotel they ran at Nyack. Their lively arguments impressed young Pound, who described Fouquet as having a "shrill, high, normal tone . . . ascending to pure Punch and Judy or drooping to a false double-bass . . . I adored both him and my great-uncle" [*PD*, 34; JW, *Pai*, 12-1, 55-75]. Uncle Ezra is named Amos in "Indiscretions."

464. Napoleon 3rd: Charles Louis N. Bonaparte, 1808-1873, known as Louis Napoleon; emperor of the French (1852-1871); called Barbiche because of his goatee.

465. barbiche: F, "goatee."

466. Mr. Quackenbos, or Quackenbush: Abraham Quackenbush, a real estate man who in 1906 had an office at 236 E. 87th St. He was an old bore who lived at the boardinghouse and was always put at the head of "the other long table" so that he would not interfere with Uncle Ezra's heated conversations with M. Fouquet [ibid.].

467. Mrs. Chittenden's . . . : Poss, Kate Sara C., 1856-1959, American organist, composer, and lecturer, who may have been a transient resident at the boardinghouse, which, along with Ezra Weston's hotel in Nyack, preserved the elegance of "the old South" observed by Weston when he was caught in the American South during the Civil War.

468. Mouquin's: New York French restaurant Pound referred to in letter to WCW [*L*, 159].

469. Train: George Francis T., 1829-1904, American merchant and writer. Founded Train & Co., which sent clipper-ships to California, and made a fortune backing the Union Pacific Railroad. As an independent candidate for U.S. President in 1872, Train made famous inflammatory speeches against politicians, for which he was castigated. He traveled around the world in 67 days and delivered speeches on the downfall of Napoleon III which were hailed by the French people. Before his death Train often sat on the street outside Mills Hotel in Greenwich Village; earlier he was called the "Sage of Madison Square" because he fed birds and spoke to people openly in the park. Train spent many of his later years in silence, writing messages. He died a pauper [JW]. In "Indiscretions" Pound wrote: "Francis Train still sat white-headed, or with, I think, a stiff straw hat on the back of his head, in a plain wooden hemicycular chair on the pavement before some hotel . . . I was told that he was Francis Train . . . and I read that . . . he had been jailed" [*PD*, 10].

470. fellow throwing a knife: "Indiscretions" gives: "a man throwing a large jackknife some fifty feet after a fleeing male figure" [*PD*, 10].

471. Towers of Pisa . . . : First in a long list of bric-a-brac brought back from Europe and North Africa by Aunt Frances (Frank) Weston. She took the young Pound with her in 1892 and 1898. Also mentioned are family memorabilia from Massachusetts, the home state of the Westons [*PD*, 3-10].

472. 1806 Barre Mass'chusetts: Barre, Mass. Town in central Massachusetts, NW of Worcester.

473. Charter Oak: In writing of his ancestry Pound said: "hence Joseph Wadsworth, who stole the Connecticut charter and hid it in Charter Oak, to the embarrassment of legitimist tyranny" [*PD*, 6].

474. Torwaldsen lion: Bertel Thorwaldsen, 1770-1844, the Danish sculptor; one of his best known works is the statue of a lion at Lucerne, Switzerland.

475. Paolo Uccello: Paolo di Dono U., ca. 1396-1475, Florentine painter; one of the "realists" of the 15th century. "I liked Quattrocento paintin'. P. Uccello. First freshman theme, I wrote was on Paulo Uccello, picture in Louvre I reckon" [*Speaking*, 138].

476. Al Hambra: The famous group of buildings of Granada, Spain.

477. el mirador . . . Lindaraja: S, "the gallery of Queen Lindaraja"; prob. *Lindaraxa*, the Zegri princess in Gines Perez de Hita's *Guerras Civiles de Granada*.

478. Perdicaris/Rais Uli: [cf. 161, 163 above].

479. Mr. Joyce . . . Hercules: From Victor Bérard's works on the *Odyssey*, especially *Calypso et la Mer de L'Atlantide* [Armand Colin, Paris, 1927-1929]. Joyce got the idea that Calypso's island was near Gibraltar, which he conceived to be the "Pillars of Hercules." Leopold Bloom's train of thought, as he prepares Molly's breakfast and lurks outside her bedroom door (*Ulysses*, Chap. II, p. 56], associates a gift, also from the

Tangiers area, with Gibraltar: "He heard then a warm heavy sigh . . . and the loose brass quoits of the bedstead jingles . . . All the way from Gibraltar" [DG].

480. Mrs. Jevons' hotel: Prob. an inn Pound stayed at in Gibraltar.

481. veder Nap'oiiiii: [vedere . . .]: I, "to see Naples." Part of Italian proverb: "See Naples and die"; i.e. you will then have seen everything [HK].

482. Pavia the romanesque: Capital of Pavia, province of Lombardy, N Italy. Its Church of San Michele is an excellent example of 12th-century Lombard Romanesque architecture.

483. San Zeno: San Zeno Maggiore, a Romanesque church in Verona. Contains the column signed *Adamo me fecit* [45:14].

484. S. Pietro: San Pietro Martire (formerly San Giorgetto dei Domeniconi), on right bank of Adige in Verona. Contains fresco by Giovanni Maria Falconetto: "The Coronation of the Virgin," with kneeling Teutonic knights [Fang, II, 260].

485. madonna in Ortolo: L, *Madonna in the Garden*, painting by Stefano da Verona [4:45].

486. e "fa . . . tremare": I, "and 'make the air tremble with clarity' " [cf. 425 above].

487. Trattoria . . . : I, "Inn of the Apostles (twelve)." Small restaurant in Verona where Pound and Manlio Torquato Dazzi ate in 1912 when they visited the Biblioteca Capitolare to consult the Cavalcanti MSS [Fang, II, 316].

488. "Ecco il tè": I, " 'Here is the tea.' "

489. piccolo: I, "young boy"; here the first stage in the multistaged career of a waiter.

490. Assisi: Town in Umbria, central Italy; birthplace of St. Francis of Assisi. Above the saint's tomb, two Gothic churches were built, both decorated with frescoes by Cimabue, Giotto, and others [for decline of coffee see Kimpel, *Pai*, 10-2, 307].

491. Orleans: Town in Loiret Department, N central France.

492. Mr. Carver: George Washington C., ?1864-1943, American agricultural chemist who discovered many new uses for products of the South. He got farmers to give up soil-exhausting cotton for crop rotation of peanuts and sweet potatoes. "From the peanut he made cheese, milk, coffee, flour, ink, dyes, soap, wood stains and insulating board" [*EB*].

493. arachidi: I, "peanuts." As food shortages developed during the war, Pound tried to persuade a number of bureaucrats that Italy should start cultivating peanuts. In *A Visiting Card* he wrote: "Peanuts could bring self-sufficiency in food to Italy or, rather to the empire, for these 'monkey nuts' would grow better in Cyrenaica" [*SP*, 319].

494. wops: Italian immigrants who attempted to enter the U.S. without permission had a form given to them at Ellis Island stamped WOPS—"without papers." Thus, the term came to refer to Italians in general. Pound does not use it in a pejorative sense.

495. Ragusa: A port of Dalmatia; from 1205 to 1358 under the control of Venice.

496. Herr Bacher's father: Heinrich B.'s father, Michael, was a woodcarver who resided near Brunico, in the Italian Tyrol [EH].

497. Salustio's . . . : S. Malatesta, 1448-1470, son of Sigismundo Malatesta and Isotta [Ixotta] degli Atti. The "itaglios" refer to the seals of Salustio cut by Pisanello: see specimen in frontispiece of *GK*.

498. crystal jet: Recurrent image of divinity manifest. The progression from water in early cantos to crystal, jade, and other forms—such as the great acorn of light in the later, paradisal cantos—becomes ever clearer.

499. Verlaine: Paul V., 1844-1896. "The one word 'Verlaine' assembles 'crystal' and 'jet' and sculptor under the sign of his 'Clair de Lune' which closes with great ecstatic fountains among statues ('les grands jets d'eau sveltes parmi les marbres')" [HK, *Era*, 482-483].

500. Zephyrus/Apeliota: West and East winds: "Wind also is of the process."

501. nec accidens est: L, "and is not an attribute."

502. est agens: L, "it is an agent."

503. rose in the steel dust: A pattern formed under magnetic influence. A graphic image of divine order operating in the material world—a miracle which can be seen occasionally in such a thing as the "down" on a swan. Allen Upward had written: "He who has watched the iron crumbs drawn into patterns by the magnet; or who in the frostwork on the window pane has apprehended the unknown beauty of the crystal's law, seems to me to have an idea more wholesome to our frail imaginings of the meaning of the Mystery of Life" [Upward, *The New Word*, 222; cited by Knox, *Pai*, 3-1, 81].

504. Swansdown: In "Her Triumph," by Ben Jonson, we read: "Ha' you felt the wool of beaver / Or swan's down ever? / Or have smelt o' the bud o' the briar? / Or the nard in the fire?" [from *A Celebration of Charis: in Ten Lyric Pieces* (1624)]. All are examples of miracles of creation [DD, *Ezra Pound*, 78].

505. Lethe: The river of forgetfulness in Hades.

CANTO LXXV

Sources

Virgil, *Aeneid* VI; EP, *GK*, 203, 151-152, *ABCR*, 54.

Background

EP, *Townsman*, 1 (Jan. 1938), p. 18; R. Murray Schafer, *Ezra Pound and Music*, New Directions, New York, 1977, 348-399 and passim.

Exegesis

EH, *Pai*, 10-2, 295-296; WB, *Pai*, 10-3, 594; Stephen J. Adams, "The Soundscope of *The Cantos*," *Humanities Assoc. Review*, 28 (Spring 1977), 167-188.

Glossary

1. Phlegethon: The river of fire in Hades [25:46]. The flaming river flows around the walls of a mighty city, from which the groans and screams of the inhabitants are heard by Aeneas [*Aeneid* VI]. Horror-stricken, he asks the Sibyl (his guide) what they are. She says that they come from the judgment hall of Rhadamanthus, who brings to light crimes done in life. In the depths under the city, guarded by the Hydra, are the Titans and such condemned men as Salmoneus, Sisyphus, Tantalus, and Ixion.

The Sibyl then leads the hero toward the Elysian Fields, where the inhabitants are dancing and singing and where "Orpheus struck the chords of his lyre, and called forth ravishing sounds.". Pound said the Allied fire-bombing of Dresden suggested "the flaming river" [HK].

2. **Gerhart**: G. Münch, German (Dresden) pianist, composer, and arranger who during the 1930s spent a lot of time in Rapallo, where he played concerts with Olga Rudge. He arranged Janequin's *Le Chant des Oiseaux*, along with other old music that appealed to Pound [*GK*, 151-153]. Along with Antheil [74:64], Pound considered Münch in the vanguard of the moderns.

3. **Buxtehude**: Dietrich B., 1637-1707, German composer and organist who influenced the work of Bach.

4. **Klages**: Ludwig K., 1872-1956, German anthropologist to whom Münch addressed a number of letters. Klage's major work in five volumes, *Der Geist als Widersacher der Seele* [The intellect as adversary of the soul], had an influence upon Münch's work. His name and ideas came to Pound via Münch [EH, *Pai*, 10-2, 295-296]. Not to be confused with Charles Klages a 19th-century French composer and guitarist.

5. **Ständebuch**: G, "collection" [*GK*, 203]. The word, not to be found in most German dictionaries, occurs in the title of a book of Jost Amman's illustrations to the songs of Hans Sachs [WB, *Pai*, 10-3, 594].

6. **–not of one . . .** : Pound wrote of the Janequin piece: "The gist, the pith, the unbreakable fact is there in the two pages of violin part . . . [heard] not one bird but a lot of birds as our violinist said on first playing it" [*Townsman*, 1 (Jan. 1938), p. 18; Adams, 182].

7. **The handwritten words say: (Sidelights from Salassi: La canzone da li ucelli** (I, "the song of the birds"). **Fatto del Violino** (I, "made for the violin"). **Francesco da Milina (5 cento)** ([F. da Milano] I, "Francesco of Milano (15th-century)" [cf. 8 below]). **Gerhart Münch (g canto)** [cf. 2 above]. **[per metamorfosi]** (I, "by metamorphosis").

8. **Milano**: Francesco da M., 1497-ca. 1543, Italian lutist and composer known as "Il divinio" to his devotees. His version of Janequin's "Song of the Birds" became the basis for Münch's [cf. 2 above] version for violin and piano, which became a favorite item for the Rapallo concerts. The violin line by Münch, the basis of the canto, became for Pound a prime example of the mutual support song and music could give each other: "Clement Janequin wrote a chorus, with words for the singers of the different parts of the chorus. These words would have no literary or poetic value if you took the music away but when Francesco da Milano reduced it for the lute the birds were still in the music. And when Münch transcribed it for modern instruments the birds were still there. They ARE still there in the violin parts" [*ABCR*, 54]. Pound connects the dynamic form in Janequin to "swansdown" and "the rose in the steel dust," which ended Canto 74: "If F. Di Milano . . . chiselled down Dowland's and Janequin's choral words . . . I have a perfect right to HEAR Janequin's intervals, his melodic conjunctions from the violin solo. . . . The *forma*, the immortal *concetto*, the concept, the dynamic form which is like the rose pattern driven into the dead iron-filings by the magnet, not by material contact. . . . Cut off by the layer of glass, the dust and filings rise and spring into order. . . . Thus the *forma*, the concept rises from the death. . . . Janequin's concept takes a third life in our time. . . . And its ancestry I think goes back to Arnaut Daniel and to god knows what 'hidden antiquity' " [*GK*, 151-152]. The reader should pause for thought: Canto 75 is an exemplum of the *forma* or the dynamic form of *The Cantos* as a whole as well as a transitional move out of hell [cf. 1 above] toward *paradiso terrestre*.

9. [illegible] : Prob. early bone inscription form for 亲斤 [53:42, 43]: "make it new" [DG].

CANTO LXXVI

Sources

Cavalcanti, "Donna mi prega," *LE*, 163-167; Dante, *La Vita Nuova*, XXIV; EP, *CON*, 20, 29, 239; Micah 4.5; Leviticus 19.35-36; EP, "Three Cantos," *Poetry*, June 1917; Homer, *Od.* I, 4; Dante, *Par.* VIII, 37; *Time*, June 4, 1945, 36 and June 11, 1945, 50; Herodotus I, 98, Loeb, I; *Lyra Graeca* I, fr. 1, 184; *OBGV*, No. 140; Goethe, *Faust*, pt. 2, Act II, 11. 6819-7004; Ralph Cheever Dunning, *The Four Winds*, London, 1931; Herman Suchier, *Aucassin und Nicolette*, Paderburn, F. Schöningh, 1889; Paracelsus, *De generationibus rerum naturalium*, Passage, 238; Ford Madox Ford, *Provence*, London, George Allen & Unwin, 1938.

Background

EP, *GK*, 111, 17, 109, 328, 259, 159; *SP*, 454, 433, 322; *Townsman*, April 1939; *SR*, 84, 121; *MIN*, 390; *L*, 254, 249, 147, 282; Henry James Warner, *The Albigensian Heresy*, New York, Russell, 1967; Gianfranco Ivancich, *Ezra Pound's Italy*, New York, Rizzoli, 1978; Aristotle, *Politics*; *Nichomachean Ethics*; Marion K. Sanders, *Dorothy Thompson, A Legend in Her Time*, Boston, Houghton-Mifflin, 1973; Kenneth Quinn, *Catullus, An Interpretation*, New York, Barnes & Noble, 1973.

Exegeses

Achilles Fang, "Materials for the Study of Pound's Cantos," Ph.D. dissertation, Harvard University, 1958, II, III, IV [Fang]; Stuart Gilbert, *Letters of James Joyce*, New York, Viking, 1957; M de R, *Discretions*, 221; HK, *Era*, 469; NS, *Life*, 47; EP, *Pai*, 10-3, 605-618; Shuldiner, *Pai*, 4-1, 72-73; Bowers, *Pai*, 2-1, 53-66, BK & TCDE, *The Explicator*, 40 (1981), 43.

Glossary

1. **the sun**: Apollo, Helios, source of the tensile light descending; metaphor for the divine presence in the world which is somewhat obscured to those in the Pisan hell.

2. **dove sta memora**: I, "where memory liveth" [36:3]. Pound's translation from the *Donna mi prega*.

3. **Signora Agresti**: Signora Olivia Rossetti Agresti, daughter of William Michael Rossetti. Living in Rome, Signora Agresti for years wrote on 20th-century economic problems [Fang, III, 116].

4. **Alcmene**: The wife of Amphitryon [74:144].

5. **Dryas**: Dryad [3:11]; a tree nymph that lived only as long as the particular tree it was associated with.

6. Hamadryas ac Heliades: L, "Hamadryad and Heliads." The hamadryad [74:148] was a tree nymph. The Heliads were daughters of Helios. They were changed into poplar trees as they mourned for their brother, Phaethon, who was struck dead by a thunderbolt of Zeus to prevent him from setting the world on fire after he turned out to be too weak to manage the sun chariot of his father, Helios, for one day.

7. Dirce: The wife of Lycus, early mythological king of the Greek city that later became Thebes. They treated Antiope, the mother of the twins Amphion and Zethus, with such cruelty that she plotted revenge. She, the twins, and a band of herdsmen slew Lycus and tied Dirce by the hair of her head to a bull. The bull dragged her over the ground until she was dead. Pound's immediate source was Landor's "With Dirce in one bark conveyed." The three ladies, Dirce, Ixotta, Guido's donna, are "in the timeless air" because placed there by three poets [HK].

8. et Ixotta: L, "and Isotta." Isotta degli Atti [9:59].

9. e che fu . . . : I, "and she who was called Primavera [Spring]"; the lady of Guido Cavalcanti [Dante, *La Vita Nuova*, XXIV, 20-23], to whom he addressed a number of ballate.

10. nel clivo ed . . . : I, "on the slope and at the trihedral corner": a place where three roads cross. Pound traversed such a crossroad daily on his way from Rapallo up to Sant' Ambrogio.

11. periplum: H, "circumnavigation" [59:10].

12. sotto le . . . : I, "under our cliffs."

13. Sigismundo: S. Malatesta [8:5].

14. Aurelia to Genova: L, "The Aurelian [way]," the highway that runs along the coast from Rome to Pisa and thence to Genoa.

15. la vecchia . . . : I, "old woman." Here, the old road under St. Pantaleo at St. Ambrogio [M de R].

16. Cunizza: C. da Romano [6:34]. In 1265, at age 67, she freed a number of slaves, an act of piety that led Dante to place her in Paradise [74:286].

17. qua . . . scalza: I, "here at the corner and the barefoot girl."

18. she who said . . . mould: Caterina Sforza Riàrio (1463-1509), daughter of Galeazzo Maria Sforza and wife of both Girolomo Riàrio and Giovanni de' Medici. As Countess of Forlì she was noted for her ruthlessness and celebrated by Machiavelli [*Discourses*, III, 6] for foiling the Orsi conspiracy. Leaving her small children as hostages, she entered Ravaldino promising to hand over the fortress. Mounting the walls, she exposed her genitalia and announced that she still had "the mould for casting more children" [Richard Taylor, letter, 19 April 1983].

19. Ussel: Town near Ventadour in S central France, described in standard handbooks as one of the wettest regions of France and the source of many rivers. It is the district of Provence Pound walked through in 1911 [*GK*, 111].

20. cette . . . venggg: [ce mauvais vent] : F, "that rotten wind" (in Provençal accent?).

21. Tolosa: L, "Toulouse," city on the Garonne. It was earlier called Tolosa, "a beautiful old city, built entirely of red brick" [Fang, II, 224].

22. Mt Segur: [23:25] Site of a castle in Provence, the last stronghold of the Albigensians, who were finally destroyed in the crusade of the 1240s.

23. Mithras: [Mithra] : Ancient Persian god of light and therefore associated with Helios and other sun gods in the Middle East. By the 2d century the worship of Mithra had spread throughout the Roman Empire, as it was popular with the Roman legions. Mithraism was based on an ethic of loyalty, a cult of mystery, rituals of blood baptism, and a sacred banquet. Christianity was its mortal enemy and forced the adherents of Mithra to seek refuge in Manichaeism [23:28], a label that "suited well the purpose of the Church, because the name 'Manichaen' had had for centuries sinister associations, aroused the utter detestation of the orthodox and brought down upon those accused of it the severest penalties of Church and State" [Warner, *The Albigensian Heresey*, 9].

24. **il triedro**: I, "the juncture of three roads."

25. **Castellaro**: [74:300].

26. **Scirocco**: I, a hot southeast wind off the Mediterranean.

27. **la scalza**: I, "the barefooted girl."

28. **Io son' la luna**: I, "I am the moon" [74:137; 80/500].

29. **the huntress**: Prob. a statue of Diana which Pound remembers.

30. **tempora . . . mores**: L, "time [ages], time . . . customs" [NB: Cicero, "O Tempora! O Mores!"].

31. **Babylonian wall**: The subject of a poem by Dunning [see essay by Pound on Dunning with a selection of his poetry in *Pai*, 10-3, 605-618].

32. **memorat Cheever**: L, "Cheever remembers." Refers to Ralph Cheever Dunning, ca. 1865-1930, American poet born in Detroit who lived his last 25 years in Paris. His output was small but *Poetry* published whatever he sent. Pound praised his work and published it in *Exile*. He appeared also in *transatlantic review* and *transition*. His *The Four Winds*, 1925, received the Levinson Prize. H. Monroe wrote a short eulogy in *Poetry*, January 1931. The title poem of *The Four Winds* has this stanza: "My garden hath a wall as high / As any wall of Babylon, / And only things with wings shall spy / The fruit therein or feed thereon."

33. **very confidentially**: From popular song of 1930s prob. heard over loud speaker: "Ain't she sweet? See her coming down the street / I ask you very confidentially / Ain't she sweet?"

34. **Dieudonné**: Dieudonet, a famous London chef. His restaurant, called "Dieudonné," in the St. James district of London, was frequented by Pound and other literary figures, 1910-20 [74:178; 77:78].

35. **Mouquin**: A New York restaurant famous at the turn of the century [74:186].

36. **Voisin**: A famous restaurant in Paris at 261 Rue St. Honoré and 16 Rue Cambon.

37. **Nevsky**: The Nevsky Prospect is a long, fashionable avenue along which there used to be numerous pastry shops, such as Andrejew, Filippow, and Dominique.

38. **The Greif**: A hotel with restaurant and café (called Grifone in Italian) at Bolzano in the Italian Tyrol.

39. **Schöners**: [Schöner]: A restaurant at 19 Siebensterngasse, Vienna [74:184].

40. **Taverna**: Poss. the Taverna Romolo Remo at 5, IV Resselgasse, Vienna.

41. **Robert's**: A New York restaurant at 33 West 55th St. which Pound visited with e e cummings in 1939 [Fang, II, 321].

42. **La Rupe**: Prob. the Rupe Tarpeia [74:395] in the garden of the Casa Tarpeia on the southern hill called Monte Caprino in Rome. Fang says: "As it is not certain that there was a restaurant or café on the Tarpeian Rock, it is possible that there was one [elsewhere] named after it" [II, 319].

43. **finito**: I, "finished."

44. **Pré Catalan**: [Pré-Catelan]: Restaurant du Pré-Catelan, an eating place "of the highest class" on the right bank of the Bois de Boulogne [Fang, II, 309].

45. **Armenonville**: Pavillon d'A. A high class restaurant in Paris located between the Porte Maillot and the Jardin d'Acclimation.

46. **Bullier**: The Bal Bullier at 33, avenue de l'Observatoire in the Latin Quarter of Paris. It was noted as a student resort [cf. Bouiller at 74:176].

47. Willy: Henri Gauthier-Villars [78:70].

48. Teofile's: Pierre Jules Théophile Gautier handed on to his daughter, Judith Gautier, certain bric-a-brac [80:213] which was seen by literary people who visited her apartment, where she lived "with her monkeys, her bibelots (Chinese, Hindu, and prehistoric) and her cats" [Fang, II, 193].

49. Cocteau's: Jean Cocteau, 1891-1963, French poet, playwright, and man of letters considered by Pound to be a 20th-century genius [74:246; NB: "Cocteau in his fumoir with his discs and his radio," *SP*, 454]. And, "The livest thing in Paris 1933 was Jean Cocteau. A dark inner room, no clatter of outside Paris" [*SP*, 433].

50. Eileen: Eileen Agar, an artist from London Mayfair society living in Europe. She took up with Josef Bard, the husband of Dorothy Thompson. After assignations with her, Josef divorced Dorothy (who went on to marry Sinclair Lewis) and married Eileen. The "trick sunlight" is an effect she obtained by placing light behind yellow curtains [M de R].

51. b . . . . h: The line mimics the rhythm of 30/148 [30:10].

52. la pigrizia: I, "sloth."

53. ground and the dew: May refer to sleeping conditions Pound endured in the "cage" at Pisa. The forced inactivity may have induced lethargy or "sloth."

54. Chung: [M1504]. "Middle." So trans. by Pound in explication [77/476]. With **yung**, he trans. "unwobbling pivot." In *Townsman* [April 1939, 12] he applied the word to money as "pivot: . . . the moment in fact that there is a common denominator of exchange, that moment the denominator, the measure, i.e. money becomes the PIVOT of all social action. Only a race of slaves and idiots will be inattentive thereafter to the said pivot."

55. three weeks: *Chung Yung*, III, says: "Center oneself in the invariable: some have managed to do this, they have hit the true center, and then? Very few have been able to stay there" [*CON*, 105]. Even for 3 weeks is implied.

56. government . . . it: Fang says this line coming in conjunction with *chung* must refer to Shun [Chun], who "took hold of their two extremes, *determined* the Mean, and employed it in *his government of* other people" [IV, 103].

57. Ideogram: Ch'eng [M381]. Pound gives the sense of this character as "Sincerity" and adds: "The precise definition of the word, pictorially the sun's lance coming to rest on the precise spot verbally. The righthand half of this compound means: to perfect, bring to focus" [*CON*, 20].

58. Kung fu Tseu: "K'ung" [M3720]: Confucius. The "fu Tseu" means "Master" [13:1; 53:78].

59. Chung Ni: A courtesy name for K'ung [53:148], whom Pound reveres for his work on the histories of China, especially the Chou dynasty, and for his work in recovering and making a collection of the best odes.

60. each one . . . god: From a conflation of the biblical "in nomine Dei sui" [Micah 4.5] and Gavin Douglas's trans. of Virgil's *inferretque deos Latio*: "the lateyn peopil taken has their name / bringing his gods into Latium / saving the bricabrac." Pound gives seven different versions of Micah's words: "each one in his god's name" [74/435]; "each in the name of its god" [74/441]; "in the name of its god" [74/443]; and at 78/479, 79/487, and 84/540 [Fang, III, 76].

61. Gibraltar: The scenario of Pound's visit to the synagogue is given at 22/104-105.

62. @$8.50 . . . : Half of 17 shekels [74:338].

63. meteyard: AS, *metgeard*. A yard or rod used as measure.

64. Leviticus: Third book of the Pentateuch or so-called Law of Moses [74:205].

65. chapter XIX: Lev. 19.35-36 [King James] reads: "Ye shall do no unrighteousness in judgment, in meteyard, in weight, or in measure. / Just balances, just weights, a just ēphäh, and a just hin, shall ye have."

66. **Zion**: The hilltop site of the temple and the royal residence of King David and his successors. The Jews regard Zion as the symbolic center of Jewish national culture, government, and religion [74:97].

67. **Don Fulano**: S, used as is "John Doe" in English.

68. **Caio e Tizio**: I, like Don Fulano: "John Doe and Richard Roe."

69. **Why not rebuild it**: Pound's interpretation of a passage from the *Analects*. He wrote: "The inhabitants of Lou wished to put up a new public granary." Someone asked "Isn't the old one still good enough? Is there any need of a new one which will cost much sweat to the people?" Kung endorsed this man's idea [*GK*, 17]. Pound's own translation of the passage [*CON*, 239] has the man say: "What about repairing the old one? Why change and build?" Thus, "rebuild" suggests "repair the old one" rather than "build anew."

70. **Snag**: Nickname of one of the prisoners at the DTC [74:119].

71. **ante mortem no scortum**: L, "before death no prostitute." Prob. the black murderer was under sentence of death and demonstrated his knowledge of Latin by this ironic statement.

72. **progress**: Note repetition of this line.

73. **Burnes**: A prisoner named Jones. Said Pound: "I did an unfair ballad about Jones and destroyed it" [RO].

74. **Cahors**: Chief town in department of Lot, south of Périgueux and about halfway between it and Toulouse. It possesses one of the "finest ancient bridges in the world" [Fang, II, 224].

75. **Chalus**: A village a little S of Limoges which has two 12th-century castles, one outside the walls. It was while besieging this one in 1119 that Richard Coeur-de-Lion was mortally wounded. The inn, doubtless visited by Pound on his 1911 walking trip, must have been on the banks of the Tardoire [cf. "Provincia Deserta"].

76. **Aubeterre**: A town in Perigord with "two Romanesque churches: St. Jean, hollowed in the rock and containing a two-storied monument, with mutilated statues (added later) of Marshal de Lussan (d.c. 1620) and his wife; and St. Jacques, with a richly-carved 11th century facade" [Muirhead, *Guide to Southern France*, 1926, 338; quoted by Fang, II, 225].

77. **Poitiers**: [formerly spelled Poictiers]: Chief town in department of Vienne, W central France, where are found two of Pound's favorite buildings. He wrote: "For European architecture a development occurs in St. Hilaire (Poitiers) and the Hall of Justice of Poitiers. Here the architect has invented. The cunning contrivance of lighting and the building of chimneys is, at least for the layman, something there invented, something that has no known fatherhood" [*GK*, 109].

78. **Sergeant Beaucher**: Prob. an NCO at the DTC.

79. **Santa Marta**: A Romanesque church from which one could see a castle on a distant hill which Ford Madox Ford called "the White Tower that you see from Tarascon" [Ford, *Provence*; Fang, II, 227].

80. **Tarascon**: A town of Bouches-du Rhône department in SE France.

81. **"in heaven . . . women**: From chap. 6 of *Aucassin and Nicolette*: "En paradis qu'ai jë a faire. . . ." Pound praised Andrew Lang's version by saying he "was born in order that he might translate it perfectly" [*SR*, 84]. Aucassin protests to a religious person who wants him to prepare for paradise: "In Paradise what have I to win? Therein I seek not to enter, but only to have Nicolete, my sweet lady." He lists a lot of people bound for paradise: clerics, the halt, lame, blind, pious relics, and kill-joys. "These be they that go into Paradise, with them have I

naught to make." Aucassin prefers hell, where go "goodly knights" and "stout men at arms" and "all men noble." Also, all the courteous and fair ladies. "With these I would gladly go, let me but have with me Nicolete, my sweetest lady" [Fang, II, 228].

82. **vair**: A fur worn by the nobility of the 14th century.

83. **Memling**: Hans M., ?1430-1495, a painter of the early Flemish school known for his religious subjects.

84. **Elskamp**: Mac E., 1862-1931, a Belgian symbolist poet who wrote on religious subjects. Thus the nonreligious tradition of Aucassin is contrasted with the religious tradition in art.

85. **Danzig**: City in N Poland; after WWI, an international free city and seaport.

86. **Galla**: G. Placidia, 388-450, Roman empress. Her mausoleum is the Church of St. Nazario Celso in Ravenna. Pound seems to be saying that the "rest" (sleep) of Galla was destroyed during WWII along with a great many works of art. Galla wasn't destroyed, although rumor may have said so. Pound endorses a friend's opinion, which he translates: "every self-respecting Ravennese is procreated, or at least receives spirit or breath of life, in the Mausoleum of Galla Placidia" [*SP*, 322].

87. **Crawford**: This same list of U.S. presidents with Crawford is given at 74/436 [cf. 74:264].

88. **Tout . . . fortune**: F, "Everyone says that fortune does not last."

89. **Joyce et fils**: F, "Joyce and son." James Joyce with his son, Giorgio, came to meet Pound for the first time at the town of Desenzano on the southwestern bay of Lake Garda. He came in spite of a bad storm. Joyce wrote: "Mr. Pound wrote to me so urgently from Sirmione (lake of Garda) that in spite of my dread of thunderstorms and detestations of travelling I went there bringing my son with me to act as lightning conductor" [*Letters of James Joyce*, 142].

90. **Catullus**: Gaius Valerius C., ?84-54 B.C. Roman lyric poet whose work Pound much admired. He associates C. with Sirmio on Lake Garda because Catullus regarded Sirmio and environs as his favorite place, as Poem 31 makes clear. Says Quinn [*Catullus, An Interpretation*, 158]: "Clearly, arrival at Sirmio meant arriving home."

91. **Gardasee**: Lake Garda.

92. **Miss Norton**: Sara N., daughter of Charles Eliot Norton and editor of her father's letters. Pound met her in Venice in 1908.

93. **Tout dit**: [cf. 88 above].

94. **Canal Grande**: The Grand Canal of Venice [Ivancich].

95. **Florian's**: A famous café on the south side of the Piazza San Marco, Venice. Named in the earliest version of Canto I: "True it was Venice, / And at Florian's and under the North arcade / I have seen other faces, and had my rolls for breakfast . . ." ["Three Cantos," *Poetry*, June 1917].

96. **La Figlia di Jorio**: I, "Jorio's Daughter," A 1904 play by D'Annunzio.

97. **Oedipus of the Lagunes**: I, "O, of the Lagoons." Prob. a play that mocked the sentimental melodramatic characters in *La Figlia di Jorio*.

98. **D'Annunzio**: Gabriele D., 1863-1938, Italian novelist and playwright [93:134].

99. **l'ara sul rostro**: I, "the altar on the rostrum."

100. **20 years**: Perhaps a reference to the dream of the great society of justice and help for people which Pound believed Mussolini was going to build [74:1].

101. **young Mozart**: [41/204]. On Oct. 16-17, 1777, M. wrote to his father describing the son of a local magistrate, an arrogant patrician who had been insulting him by making fun of an award M. had been given while at the same time offering him a pinch of snuff. M. got increasingly enraged and

in his turn offered the son a pinch of snuff along with a more pointed insult. This little scene went on through many a pinch and sniff. M. told his father he had decided that the whole company of patricians could get a better sniff by licking his arse. Say BK and TCDE, "Pound is surely remembering the incident as a little battle in the long war between the artist and the patronizing bourgeoisie" [*The Explicator*, 40 (1981), 43].

102. **prise**: F, "pinch of snuff."

103. **Ponce**: Juan Ponce de Léon, ?1460-1521, Spanish governor of Puerto Rico and discoverer of Florida, which he found while looking for the Fountain of Youth.

104. **alla fuente florida**: I, "to the" S, "flowery fountain."

105. **Anchises**: The father of Aeneas, to whom Aphrodite appeared as a beautiful woman, posing as the daughter of King Otreus [23:34].

106. **Cythera potens**: L, "powerful Cythera," an epithet for Aphrodite [24:30].

107. **Κύθηρα δεινά**: H, "dread [of fearful] Cythera."

108. **the crystal body**: Major metaphor for final manifestation of divinity in the universe [74:498], as "the great ball of crystal" [116/795] and "pure Light, we beseech thee / Crystal, we beseech thee" [Fragments/799], etc.

109. **Κόρη, Δελιά δεινά**: H, "daughter [Persephone], dread Delia [Δηλιά]"; or Artemis, so-called because she was the virgin goddess of the isle of Delos.

110. **et libidinis expers**: L, "to whom passion is unknown."

111. **πολλά παθεῖν**: H, "to suffer much" [*Od*. I, 4: "and his heart experienced many sufferings upon the sea"].

112. **dove sta memoria**: I, "where memory lives" [36:3].

113. **J. Adams**: John A. said, "But every bank of discount . . . is downright corruption" [71:35]. A major economic statement Pound recalls often in the Pisan and later cantos.

114. **Sergeant XL**: Poss. Sgt. Lauterback, disciplinary NCO at the DTC, whose nickname was "the Ripper."

115. **ac ferae familiares**: L, "and domesticated wild animals" [20:73].

116. **a destra**: I, "to the right."

117. **atasal**: Prob. transliteration from Arabic, meaning "union with the divine." Pound in discussing the deficiencies of Aristotelian ethics as set forth in the *Nichomachean Ethics* sets certain precepts against "R. St Victor's gradation of processes: (1) the aimless flitting of the mind, (2) the systematic circling of the attention around the object, (3) contemplation, the identification of the consciousness WITH the object" [*GK*, 328]. The third stage here he then relates to "remarks on arabic ideas about *atasal*, union with the divine." Fang [IV, 31] suggests the Pound "atasal" comes from *ittisale* in Jalaluddin Rumi's couplet: "Ittisale bi-taquaiyuf bi giyas / Hast baina 'nasa wa Rabb 'annas" [Union exists beyond all thought and speech between great Allah and the soul of each]. Eva Hesse believes the word derives from Avicenna, the Mohammedan physician and philosopher, as Pound suggests in *MIN*, 390.

118. **nec personae**: L, "nor people" (individuals in the flesh).

119. **hypostasis**: Pound uses the word not in the theological sense (the separate personal subsistence in one divine substance of each entity of the Trinity) but in the philosophical sense, "an entity conceived as a self-subsisting object" different from spirit, as in the line "whether of spirit or hypostasis" [81/520].

120. **Dione**: Consort of Zeus, mother of Aphrodite, derived from ancient earth-mother or sky-goddess deity. Thus, "her

planet" would be Venus. Bion's *Lament for Adonis* uses Dione as a name for Aphrodite herself [47:12].

121. **Helia**: Misprint for Delia [cf. 109 above].

122. *κύπρις*: H, "Cypris," i.e., the home of the Cyprian goddess Aphrodite.

123. **"both eyes . . . his cow"**: Pound's daughter, while working in a German military hospital as the war in Italy came to an end, wrote her father about a young man of 23 sent home from the hospital blind. He disapproved "of his father letting the old cows get so thin he could count their ribs with his fingers" [M de R, *Discretions*, 221].

124. **Carrara**: A city in Tuscany.

125. **un terzo cielo**: I, "a third heaven" [*Par*. VIII, 37].

126. **Prefetto**: I, "prefect." Gioacchino Nicoletti was a local officer at Gardone near Salò on Lake Garda, where "a powerless Mussolini was . . . administering a Republic of Italy. . . . Pound made his way there more than once, talked to the Minister of Foreign Affairs, hoped to bring fiscal enlightenment into the dream, sat at nearby Gardone with the Prefect . . . where in sight of a mountain that looked like Fujiyama a quiet cat stalked a railing and quiet water moved southward" [HK, *Era*, 469; 74:49].

127. **La Donna**: Prob. Clara Petacci, the mistress of Mussolini, who followed him to Gardone and caused public concern [74:53].

128. **Bracken . . . to lie**: These five lines were prompted by *Time* articles in 1945 [June 4, 36 and June 11, 50]. Churchill (the "squeak-doll") resigned as premier at noon on May 23, 1945, but at 4 p.m. the same day he returned to Buckingham Palace to accept the invitation of King George to form a new government. Brendan Bracken was thus "out" only two days. He had been boss of the British Ministry of Information, which controlled wartime censorship of the BBC. Pound's perception of Bracken is not the same as that of *Time*. *Time* reported that before Bracken ran the M.O.I. it "was sneered at as the Ministry of Misinformation. . . . He saw to it that censors blue-penciled only military information" [*Time*, ibid.].

129. **ego scriptor**: L, "I, the writer."

130. **Lucca**: Capital of Lucca Province, Tuscany, central Italy.

131. **Forti dei Marmi**: [Forte dei Marmi]: A small town in Lucca Province.

132. **Berchthold**: Unidentified. But if "after the other one" is construed as after WWI, the name may be a misspelling for Leopold Graf von Berchtold (1863-1942), Austro-Hungarian foreign minister, whose reckless policy made the war inevitable [87:8]. After the war, he was out of the government completely and retired to his private estate. Perhaps the parallel with Churchill suggested his name to Pound.

133. **Thetis**: A nereid, wife of Peleus and mother of Achilles. Her appearance here and 6 lines later associated with crystal, colors, and "tangibility" suggests some kind of visionary experience.

134. **spiriti questi**: I, "are these spirits."

135. **personae**: L, "people."

136. **atasal**: [cf. 117 above].

137. **Maya**: Poss. the Hindu earth-mother personified as a maiden: the real world is conceived in Hindu philosophy as only illusion. Or poss. Maia, daughter of Atlas and Pleione and mother of Hermes. Maia is the oldest and most beautiful of the Pleiades [74:211].

138. *Ἀφροδίτη*: H, "Aphrodite" [1:26].

139. **Zoagli**: A town a few miles S of Rapallo [46:4].

140. *οἱ βάρβαροι*: H, "the barbarians."

141. **Sigismundo's Temple**: The Tempio built by S. Malatesta [8:43].

142. Divae Ixottae: I [Variant], "Divine Isotta." Mistress and then third wife of Sigismundo who built the Tempio in her honor [9:59]. A marble bust of Isotta was installed on the N side of the burial ground, Campo Santo, at Pisa: hence, "her effigy" [Fang, II, 248].

143. Ladder at swing: Poss. a reference to a fresco in the Campo Santo at Pisa destroyed during WWII [M de R]. Or poss. memory of medieval Christian icons and paintings entitled "descent from the cross." This interpretation supposes the "he" ("the wing'd fish") of the phrase (7 lines before) "he comes out into the air" is a metaphor for Christ the "living arrow" [M. Shuldiner, *Pai*, 4-1, 73].

144. La Cara: **amo**: I, "the loved one"; L, "I love."

145. Her bed . . . sapphire: The notebooks [Yale, 11] contain a note which says: "Prester John, 1476= Throne of gold set with gems, 7 tiers, gold, ivory, crystal,–to the rubys, for this stone giveth sleep." The legend of Prester John derives from a letter, widely circulated in 16th-century Europe, in which he told of a Christian utopia he had founded. Among other great luxuries he listed his bed: "the bed I sleep on is entirely covered with sapphires, by virtue of which I maintain my chastity. I have many beautiful women, but I only sleep with them three months of the year . . . and then only for purposes of procreation" [Shuldiner, *Pai*, 4-1, 72]. Pound appears to use this stone as a metaphor for spiritual repose [74/426, 435; 74:37]. But the idea of 7 tiers is significant: it rhymes with the seven walls of Ecbatan [4:32], which according to Herodotus were built seriatim up the side of a great hill. Each one was of a different color of ascending value; the next to the top was made of silver, and the last on the crest (within which was the king's treasury and home) was made of gold [Herodotus I, 98, Loeb, I].

146. hoi barbaroi: [cf. 140 above].

147. pervenche: F, "periwinkle."

148. et sequelae: L, "and the consequences."

149. Le Paradis . . .: F, "Paradise is not artificial" [74:292].

150. *δακρύων*: H, "weeping" if pres. part. nom. masc. sing; if gen. pl., "of tears."

151. L. P.: Laval, Petain [RO].

152. gli onesti: I, "the honest ones" [7:14].

153. J'ai . . . assez: F, "I had pity for others, probably not enough."

154. l'enfer non plus: F, "hell isn't either."

155. Eurus: An east or southeast wind.

156. la pastorella . . . : I, "the little herdess of the swine."

157. benecomata dea: L, "the fair-tressed goddess." Circe [1:1].

158. San Vio: The Campo (field) San Vio, which runs to the Grand Canal of Venice, where the Church of San Vio is located [Ivancich]

159. Salviati: A glass shop where they still blow glass [M de R].

160. Don Carlos: The Bourbon Don Carlos, Duke of Madrid (1848-1909), who in 1908 was living at the Palazzo Loredan, Campo San Vio, Venice.

161. le bozze: I, "proofsheets."

162. "A Lume Spento": I, "With tapers [lights] quenched," The title of Pound's first book of verse published in 1908. The 8 lines ending with "or wait 24 hours," concern a dramatic moment in Pound's life as well as a turning point. According to his own account, he sat on the bank of the Grand Canal trying to decide whether he should throw the proofsheets of his book into the water and give up poetry, or shift to the other side of the canal and walk "by the column of Todero" on the way to deliver the proofsheets to the printer (presumably) or do neither, but wait for 24 hours before deciding [NS, *Life*, 47].

163. Todero: [Todaro]: "Theodore." The

column in the Piazza di San Marco where the statue of St. Theodore stands on a crocodile [26:1].

164. the Era: The Fascist era during which a number of public works which Pound approved of were completed. After WWI, a wooden bridge, *Ponte dell'Accademia*, replaced the iron bridge of 1854 [Ivancich].

165. Vendramin: Palazzo Vendramin-Calergi, on the right bank of the Grand Canal, famous as the place where Richard Wagner died in 1883.

166. Contrarini: [Contarini]: Several grand buildings on the canal have Contarini as part of their names. Also, Pound stayed at the Palazzo Contarini at San Trovaso during Christmas, 1939 [M de R].

167. Fonda, Fondecho: Poss. "Fonda," which means nothing, is an abbreviation of *fondamenta* ("foundation") or an attempt to spell the Venetian sound of *fondaco* ("warehouse"), which is "fontego." Two buildings on the canal have such a designation.

168. Tullio Romano: T. Lombardo, ?1455-1532, Italian architect and sculptor who did the Vendramini tomb in Venice [cf. 165 above]. The sirenes are the four marble figures in Santa Maria Dei Miracoli also in Venice [Ivancich].

169. custode: I, "guard."

170. Santa . . . Miracoli: Famous Venetian church: "the jewel box" [Fang, II, 276].

171. Dei Greci, San Giorgio: The Church of St. George of the Greeks.

172. Carpaccio: Vittore C., ?1455-1525?, Italian painter [26:93].

173. San Marco: I, "St. Mark." The cathedral on the square.

174. Arachne: I, "spider." Arachne was the name of the girl who challenged Athena to a weaving contest. Because of her effrontery, the goddess changed her into a spider and thus condemned her to lifelong weaving [74:457].

175. che mi porta fortuna: I, "who brings me good luck."

176. Unkle George: [74:180] George Holden Tinkham, congressman from Massachusetts whom Pound met at the Hotel Excelsior in Venice in 1936 and again at the Lido in Washington in 1939. Pound corresponded with him over a number of years [M de R].

177. Brassitalo: Italian painter, Italico Brass, 1870-1943, who signed some of his work this way [Fang, II, 288].

178. abbazia: I, "abbey."

179. voi . . . via: I, "you who pass by this way." Perhaps a paraphrase, in part, of Dante's "O voi, che per la via d'Amor passate," from the second sonnet of *Vita Nuova* [Pound quotes the line in *SR*, 121].

180. D'Annunzio: Gabriele D. [cf. 98 above; 93:134]. He did live at the Casetta Rossa on the Grand Canal in 1920 while he wrote of his war experiences as an aviator in a book entitled *Notturno*. Thus Katherine Heyman and Pound may have visited him, or tried to, in that year [Ivancich].

181. K.H.: Katherine Ruth Heyman, a concert pianist for whom Pound acted as an impresario in 1908 [Bowers, *Pai*, 2-1, 53-66].

182. Veneziana: I, "Venetian woman."

183. Non combaattere: I, "Don't fight."

184. Giovanna: Poss. the name of the "Veneziana." Or the name of a servant in a Venetian house where Pound used to stay.

185. Arachne: [cf. 174 above].

186. Athene: From Sappho's "Hymn to Aphrodite."

187. *τίς ἀδικεῖ*: H, "Who wrongs [you]?" Reminiscent of Aphrodite's question to Sappho: *τίς τ', ὦ Ψάπφ', ἀδικήει* ("Who is it Sappho that does them wrong?") [*Lyra Graeca* I, fr. 1, 184, *OBGV*, No. 140].

188. butterfly: Along with other flying insects, the butterfly is a wide-ranging metaphor for the soul in flight from the body, as well as for spiritual aspirations or feelings [cf. 48:42, 50, 53].

189. smoke hole: Old army pyramidal tents had a smoke hole through which the pipe of a crude, funnel-shaped stove could be fitted in the winter. The literal smoke hole of the tent may have evoked the thought of the smoke hole in Faust's laboratory later in the canto [cf. 217 below].

190. Unkle George: [cf. 176 above].

191. Ct/Volpe: Count Giuseppe Volpi, 1877-1947, was finance minister under Mussolini, who created him Conte di Misurata: "He was supposedly responsible for the rural electrification of the Adriatic Coast and for the development of the port of Venice, where he was born" [Fang, III, 88].

192. Lido: Resort town on the N end of the island outside the Lagoon of Venice.

193. "Rutherford Hayes: The 19th president (1877-1881) of the U.S. Besides the 3 times on this page, Tinkham is mentioned a number of other times in the Pisan Cantos, always with a Venetian setting [74:180; 80/509]. Either Pound himself said that Tinkham looked like some statue of Hayes, or he overheard the phrase in quotes.

194. princess: Prob. Princess Winnaretta Eugenia (1870-1943), widow of Prince Edmond Melchior de Polignac (1834-1901), whom she married in 1893 after a previous marriage was annulled by the Holy See, Feb. 1, 1892. She was the daughter of Isaac Merritt Singer, the wealthy inventor of the Singer sewing machine. She helped Pound obtain the Janequin music of Canto 75, for which he thanked her in a letter from Rapallo [*L*, 254]. He mentioned her in another letter [*L*, 249].

195. Dafne's Sandro: Sandro Botticelli's painting of Daphne, who while being chased by Apollo was turned into a laurel tree. Such a word inversion is a type of metonymy ("misnamer").

196. Trovaso, Gregorio, Vio: The Church of San Trovaso, the Abbazia San Gregorio, and the Church of San Vio are all on the canal—Rio de San Trovaso—which is named after the church [Ivancich].

197. Dottore: I, "doctor." Alexander Robertson, D.D. Cavaliere of the Order of St. Maurice and St. Lazarus, Italy, was the bearded minister of the Scotch Presbyterian Church in Venice. Pound once told an anecdote in broad dialect about him [*GK*, 259]. He also mentioned him in a letter to Marianne Moore, dated Feb. 1, 1919: "I have seen/Savanarola still swinging a crucifix,/down from Salò for the week-end of exhorting/the back-sliders of Venice; and the Reverend Cavaliere Dottore Alessandro/ Robertson denouncing the Babylonian woman/and the Rrrroman releegion/with fervour::::" (the first half of the letter is cast in verse [*L*, 147[).

198. Babylonian intrigue: From 1309 to 1378, the popes, all French and supported by France, resided at Avignon, rather than Rome, a period known as the Babylonian Captivity because of its parallel with the 586-536 captivity of the Jews after the fall of the Temple. Before, during, and after this period intrigue of both the Italian and French factions in the dispute became pandemic.

199. Squero: I, "shipyard."

200. Ogni Santi: A canal in Venice. In 1908 Pound lived near the conjunction of the San Trovaso and Ogni Santi canals [Ivancich].

201. ends and beginnings: Based on Pound's interpretation of a Confucian text in *The Great Digest*: "Things have roots and branches; affairs have scopes and beginnings. To know what precedes and follows, is nearly as good as having a head and feet" [*CON*, 29]. The theme recurs at 77/465 and other places in the later cantos.

202. cassoni: I, "treasure chests." Here, bas-relief panels at Rimini.

203. the hidden nest: A large abstract painting done for Pound by Tamijuro

Koumé [Michio Ito: 77:86], which Pound called "Tami's dream." In a letter to Katue Kitasono [May 24, 1936], Pound said: "I had all Fenollosa's notes and the results of what he learned.... But since Tami Koumé was killed in that earthquake [1923] I have had no one to explain the obscure passages or fill up the enormous gaps of my ignorance" [*L*, 282]. When Pound vacated his Paris studio, he sent the painting to a friend in Auteuil. In 1931 it was brought to Venice, but it was sequestered as alien enemy property during WWII and disappeared as did "the great Ovid" [Ivancich].

204. the great Ovid: Ovid's *Fasti*, printed by a successor of Bodoni, which Pound bought from Sig. Cassini, seller of rare books, and had bound in wooden covers.

205. bas relief of Ixotta: Yriarte attributes a bas-relief of Ixotta [9:59] (now with Olga Rudge) to Agostini di Duccio [9:78]. A picture of the bas-relief with a picture of Ixotta's tomb in the Tempio Malatestiano was published in 1761 [Fang, II, 250].

206. Olim de Malatestis: L, "Once of the Malatestas."

207. Fano: A city near Rimini once under control of the Malatestas [9:3].

208. 64 countries . . . sargent: Prob. a remark of one of the DTC cadre overheard by Pound, who may be estimating the number of countries involved in WWII. He also mentions his prewar occupation, the illegal nature of which strikes an ironic note.

209. vino rosso: I, "red wine."

210. mountain oysters: A locution sometimes used to label a dish made from sheep testicles.

211. lisciate con lagrime: I, "smoothed with tears."

212. politis lachrymis: L, "elegant [or polished] tears."

213. ΔΑΚΡΥΩΝ: H, "tears."

214. ex nihil: L, "out of nothing." Prob. meant to evoke phrase from scholastic dichotomy concerning the creation of the universe. One side said, "ex nihilo, nihil fit" ("out of nothing, nothing is made"); the other, "ex nihil ens creatum" ("out of nothing, being is created").

215. la concha: S, "conch."

216. ΠΟΙΚΙΛΟΘΡΟΝ' . . . : H, "richly enthroned, immortal." Opening words of Sappho's hymn to Aphrodite [*Lyra Graeca*, 182; *OBGV*, No. 140].

217. that butterfly . . . smoke hole: [cf. 188 above]. The source for the smoke hole here and the German quote 7 lines later is the laboratory scene [ll. 6819-7004], Part Two, Act II of Goethe's *Faust*. In that scene, Mephistopheles and Wagner, amidst fantastic medieval alchemical apparatus, are busy making a human being. According to the notes that Passage, the translator, derived from Witkowski's edition of the German text, to create a human being was the "supreme objective of the alchemists." For a few years (1768 and in the late 1790s), Goethe was a passionate student of the history of alchemy, particularly the work of the previous three centuries. Passage translates lines from the opening of the scene thus: "In the retort a fire dot grows, / And like a living coal it glows." He has a note that says: "To the alchemists, 'living coals' took fire from their own inner spark." What for the alchemists may have been scientific fact becomes for Pound a metaphorical rhyme with all the other fire and light images in *The Cantos*. Wagner continues: "Yes, like a splendid ruby's spark / It flashes lightnings through the dark. / A clear white light begins to brighten!" With a loud rattling of the door, Mephisto comes in and asks: "What are you making there?" Wagner says: "A human being!" Mephisto: "A human being? And what loving pair / Have you got hidden in the smoke hole there?" ("Habt ihr in's Rauchloch eingeschloffen," [l. 6837]). Wagner says, "none," and keeps on with his work in a scene evocative of Frankenstein movies. Within a few minutes he has completed a nine months' process and created a homunculus, following somewhat the recipe of Paracelsus's work *De generationibus rerum naturalium*, Book I. A note by Passage says in part: "Allow male sperm to putrefy for forty days in a covered jar until it visibly stirs with new life and somewhat resembles a man's form . . . ; keep warm for weeks (9 months) and feed daily with *arcano sanguinis humani* . . . after which time it will become a . . . homunculus" [Passage, 238]. Shortly, Wagner has spirited one up out of the retort and free of the smoke hole. The homunculus then talks to him and Mephisto.

218. **saeva**: L, "cruel."

219. **Leonello**: Prob. Lionello d'Este [24:17].

220. **Petrus Pisani pinxit**: L, "Peter Pisano painted [it]." Poss. Antonio Pisano [26:78], a painter employed by Sigismundo and patronized by Lionello d'Este. He was also known as Vittore Pisano.

221. **cameo should remain**: Focuses Pound's interest in seals, cameos, and fragments [*GK*, 159].

222. **Arezzo**: City in central Italy [44:26].

223. **Cortona**: Town in Tuscany where churches have paintings by Fra Angelico [45:12].

224. **po'eri di'aoli**: I, "poor devils." RO's text has a marginalium (presumably given by Pound) which says "Favai," but this word, unless it is slang, means nothing in Italian. *Fava*, ("bean") is used in slang expressions such as "not worth a bean." Perhaps, "beans," in this sense, is intended.

225. **Knecht [e] gegen Knecht [e]**: G, "Slave against slave." From *Faust* [cf. 217 above]. Continuing the *Faust* scene, Wagner, Mephisto, and the homunculus come to talk about such things as destiny, pleasure, struggle, and fate, until Mephisto says, "Spare me / That clash of servitude with tyranny! . . . The struggle is, they say, for freedom's rights, / Look closer, and it's *slave with slave* that fights" [ll. 6962-6963].

226. **METAΘEMENΩN. . . .** : H, "changing." Key word of quote from Aristotle's *Politics* concerning the results of changing one currency from another [74:343].

227. **NHΣON'AMYMONA**: H, "a noble island." From lines in which Odysseus is telling of his approach to the island where his companions killed the cattle of the sun [20:69].

CANTO LXXVII

Sources

EP, *CON*, 277, 29, 233, 264, 173, 20, 87-89, 201; *CNTJ*, 113-121; *SR*, 160; Horace, *Odes* III, *Satires* II; Dante, *De Vulgari Eloquentia* II, *Inf.* X; Marcus Aurelius, *Meditations* IV; G. R. S. Mead, "Ceremonial Game-Playing and Dancing in Mediaeval Churches," *Quest*, vol. 4, no. 1, Oct. 1912, 91-123; De Mailla, *Histoire générale* . . . , Paris, 1777-1785, X, 23; Pauthier, *Chine ou Description historique, geographique et littéraire* . . . , Paris, 1853 [*Chine*]; *The Wanderer*, line 81.

Background

EP, *GK*, 188, 79, 93, 89, 127; *SP*, 172, 339, 96, 408, 230-231, 179, 341, 448; *GB*, 17; *PD*, 115; *LE*, 288; *PE*, 129; Voltaire, *Le siècle de Louis XIV*, 1751; *New Age*, Oct. 16, 1913, 728; *Dial*, Dec. and Oct. 1920; W. B. Yeats, *Plays and Controversies*, London, Macmillan, 1923 [*Plays*]; J. E. Cirlot, *A Dictionary of Symbols*, New York, Philosophical Library, 1962 [Cirlot]; Sisley Huddleston, *Paris Salons, Cafés, Studios*, Philadelphia and London, 1928, [SH, *Paris*]; James Wilhelm, *Dante and Pound*, Orono, 1974; James Legge, *The Four Books*, Shanghai, 1923 [Legge]; Francis Trevelyan Miller, *History of World War II*, Philadelphia and Toronto, 1945; Helen Caldwell, *Michio Ito: The Dancer and His Dances*, Berkeley, Los Angeles, and London, University of California Press, 1977; T. S. Eliot, "Whispers of Immortality"; Achilles Fang, "Materials for the Study of Pound's Cantos," Ph.D. dissertation, Harvard University, 1958, II, III, IV; James G. Fraser, *The New Golden Bough*, ed. Theodor H. Gaster, New York, 1959; CFT, *Basil Bunting: Man & Poet*, Orono, 1980; M de R, *Discretions*, 35-37, 194-196, 44, [M de R]; Lord Byron, *Works*, ed. Rowland E. Prothero, London, I, 173; Leonard Doob, ed., *Ezra Pound Speaking*, Connecticut, Greenwood Press, 1978 [Doob, *Speaking*].

Exegeses

Sieburth, *Pai*, 6-3, 382; Anderson, *Pai*, 6-2, 235-250; Nassar, *Pai*, 1-2, 211; Riccardo M. degli Uberti, "Ezra Pound and Ubaldo degli Uberti: History of a Friendship," *Italian Quarterly*, XVI, 64, Spring 1973, 95-107.

Glossary

1. **Abner . . . action**: Prisoner at the DTC who apparently had little enthusiasm for manual labor.

2. **Von Tirpitz**: German admiral [74:377].

3. **Maukch**: Gothardt Maukshk, an Italian bookdealer, still living, who worked for Sansoni, a publisher in Florence. Pound visited him there with Riccardo degli Uberti in 1959 [M de R].

4. **Katin**: Katyn. A Russian village west of Smolensk occupied by the Germans in WWII. It is the location of the mass grave of about 10,000 Polish soldiers whom the Russians and Germans have ever since accused each other of killing. The Soviets refused to allow an international investigation, but Pound had reliable inside information that told him that the Russians directed and carried out the massacre [M de R].

5. **le beau monde gouverne**: F, "society governs."

6. **toujours**: F, "always."

7. **Chung**: [M1504] "the middle" [76:54].

8. **"and having got 'em . . ."**: "He said: How can one serve a prince along with these village-sized (kinky) minds? Until they get on they worry about nothing else, and, when they have, they. worry about losing the advantages. When they are afraid of losing

(advantages, privileges) there is nothing, absolutely nothing they will not do to retain (them) (no length they won't go to)" [*CON*, 277].

9. **Kungfutseu**: Confucius [13:1].

10. **Bros Watson's . . . scope**: These 12 lines seem to record a memory of Pound's of a scene he observed at the age of 19 when he was attending Hamilton College in Clinton, New York, 1903-1905. The Watson Drug Co. (located on the north side of College St., about a mile east of Hamilton) was founded by Col. James T. Watson in 1904. It dispensed drugs and sundries and had a telegraph office and chess tables in the rear [V. Mondolfo, letter, March 13, 1979].

11. **(a.d. 1904 . . .** : The missing closing parenthesis should prob. be after "1904."

12. **Ideogram**: Hsien [M2702]: "first, foremost." Pound explicates the characters at end of the canto, p. 476. They are taken from *The Great Digest* (*TA HIO*). The lines around the characters paraphrase Pound's trans. of the Confucian text: "Things have roots and branches; affairs have scopes and beginnings. To know what precedes and what follows is nearly as good as having a head and feet" [*CON*, 29].

13. **Ideogram**: Hou [M2143]: "afterwards; to follow."

14. **process**: Pound's sense of an ideogram not given: "Tao" [M6136]: "the way; the truth" [74:9].

15. **vide**: L, "see."

16. **Epictetus**: Stoic philosopher (fl. 55-135) who wrote *Lectures*, on the value of endurance. "He taught that the universe is the work of God, and that Divine Providence manifests itself in its unity and order" [*OCD*].

17. **Syrus**: Publius S., a writer of Latin mimes and maxims in the first century B.C.

18. **Arcturus**: Major star in the constellation Boötes.

19. **bloke . . . open**: Source unknown.

20. **camion**: A military truck (derives from F).

21. **Awoi**: The Lady Awoi in the Noh play *Awoi no uye* which Pound translated from Fenollosa's notes [*CNTJ*, 113-121]. Awoi, the first wife of Genji, is consumed with jealousy of his later wives [110:43].

22. **hennia**: Hannya. An evil spirit in Noh plays. In *Awoi no uye* the hannya appears "Clothed in a scarlet hakama" and joins "the great dance climax of the play," during which she is exorcised [*CNTJ*, 120-121].

23. **der im Baluba**: [38:41].

24. **Faasa . . . 4 times**: Also Agada, Ganna, Silla [74:134].

25. **Il Scirocco . . .** : [lo Scirocco]: I, "the South Wind is jealous."

26. **χΘόνος**: H, "of the earth." Gen. sing. of *χΘών*.

27. **Mt Taishan**: [74:46].

28. **Ideogram**: Ho [M2109], "how."

29. **Ideogram**: Yüan [M7734], "far."

30. **"How . . . it"**: From the fragment of a poem on which Confucius commented: "1. The flowers of the prunus japonica deflect and turn, do I not think of you dwelling afar? 2. He said: It is not the thought, how can there be distance in that" [*CON*, 233].

31. **Boreas**: H, "the North Wind."

32. **kylin**: [ch'i-lin]: C, "A fabulous animal which has the body of a deer, the tail of an ox, the hooves of a horse, one fleshy horn, parti-colored hair on its back, and a yellow belly" [EH].

33. **Ideogram**: Tan [M6037], "dawn." Since *tan* is pronounced "dahn," it's almost a homophone of *dawn*.

34. **Scudder's Falls**: On the Schuykill River, N of Philadelphia.

35. **Ideogram**: K'ou [M3434], "mouth, hole, opening."

36. Regent's canal: A canal along the N edge of Regent's Park in London.

37. Theodora: Private reference to a lady not to be named.

38. Daimio's: Tami Koumé [76:203]. "The Tailor's bill was $100" [RO].

39. Grishkin: The last half of Eliot's "Whispers of Immortality" concerns the feline promise of Grishkin, whose "friendly bust / Gives promise of pneumatic bliss." The photo still exists (at Hamilton in 1980).

40. Mr Eliot: T. S. Eliot.

41. dance . . . medium: The several references to the dance here, on the next page, and elsewhere in the Pisan Cantos [78/477; 79/491; 81/518] derive from Pound's memory of an article by Mead [74:448] in *Quest* entitled, "Ceremonial Game-Playing and Dancing in Mediaeval Churches" [vol. 4, no. 1, Oct. 1912, 91-123], especially the sections on "The Pelota of Auxerre": "one of the choir-boys used to bring to church a whipping-top. . . . When the moment came in the service . . . the boy, whip in hand, scourged the top down the pavement of the church and out of doors" [Fang, IV, 25].

42. native mountain: "a well-known Sino-Japanese term meaning one's place of birth" [Fang, IV, 153].

43. Ψυχάριον ὰι . . . : [the ὰι should be έι] : H, "You are a tiny soul supporting a corpse." Saying attributed to Epictetus in the *Meditations* of Marcus Aurelius [IV, 41].

44. Justinian: Byzantine emperor [65:126]. Pound seems to believe that the emperor included religious dancing in his great codification of the law [94:45].

45. Padre José: José Maria de Elizondo, the Spanish priest who helped Pound get a photostat of the Cavalcanti MS in the Escorial, Madrid [*GK*, 158].

46. sumne . . . othbaer: OE, "The ship [or bird] carried one of them away." *The Wanderer*, line 81 [27:3].

47. Corpus: I, (Corpus Domini), or L, (Corpus Christi): A feast day honoring the institution of Eucharist.

48. Auxerre: Capital of Yonne department, NE central France [cf. 41 above].

49. καλλιπλόκαμα: H, "with beautiful locks [hair]."

50. Ida: The mountain where Aphrodite and Anchises were married and where the Judgment of Paris took place. Also, at the end of every eight years King Minos of Crete "retired for a season to commune with his divine father Zeus on Mount Ida" [Fraser, *The New Golden Bough*, 234].

51. Nemi: In the opening chapter of *The Golden Bough*, the King of the Wood is seen prowling the sacred grove on the shore of Lake Nemi defending the tree of the golden bough. The priest-king will keep his office until his successor succeeds in plucking the golden bough and then murdering him and becoming priest in his stead: "In his hand he carried a drawn sword, and he kept peering warily about him as if at every instant he expected to be set upon." So it went on from day to day until his murderer arrived [ibid., p. 3].

52. liars . . . Siracusa: Syracuse, the port in Sicily, where sailors still tell "yarns from the *Odyssey*" [*GK*, 79]. A recurrent theme [74:39; 80:363].

53. dum . . . scandet: L, "As long as he goes up the Capitol hill" [Horace, *Odes* 3, 30]. The seven words are the Latin quote plus "the rest is explodable," a reference to the atomic bomb.

54. Shun: Chun [74:91].

55. King Wan: Wen Wang [53:49].

56. two halves of a seal: The 13 lines around this recurrent theme of the halves of a tally stick derive from a passage of Mencius: "Shun was born in Choo-fung . . . a man near the wild tribes of the east. King Wan was born in Chow by Mount K'e . . . a man near the wild tribes on the west. . . . Those regions were distant from one another more than a thousand li [97:243], and the age of the one *sage* was posterior to that of the other more than a thousand years. But when they got their wish, and carried their principles into practice throughout the Middle Kingdom, it was like uniting the two halves of a seal. When we examine the sages,–both the earlier and the later,–their principles are found to be the same." Legge's notes say one of the characters "should be called a tally or token, perhaps, rather than 'a seal'. Anciently, the emperor delivered, as the token of investiture, one half of a tally of wood or some precious stone, reserving the other half in his own keeping. It was cut right through a line of characters, indicating the commission, and their halves fitting each other when occasion required, was the test of truth and identity" [Legge, 730-731].

57. **directio voluntatis**: L, "direction of the will" [Dante, *De Vulgari Eloquentia* II, 2]. A recurrent theme, the opposite of "abuleia" [5:44; 54:192], "paralysis of the will."

58. **Ideograms**: The 8 characters from top to bottom are translated at the end of the canto, p. 476. Their English sounds and Matthews numbers are Fei [M1819], Ch'i [M525], Kuei [M3634], Erh [M1756], Chi [M465], Chih [M935], Ch'an [M174], Yeh [M7312], Chih [M971]. The two characters on the next page are Fu [M1922], and Chieh [M795].

59. **Lord Byron**: Pound got the idea from Pauthier, who said, "Quel malheur que Confucius n'ait pas rédigé en Vers ses admirables préceptes de morale!" [*Chine*, 172]. At least, after reading this Pound wrote: "Byron regretted that Kung hadn't committed his maxims to *Verse*" [*GK*, 127]. Byron also said, "In morals, I prefer Confucius to the Ten Commandments, and Socrates to St. Paul" [Byron, *Works*, vol. 1, p. 173]. With this Pound would agree with enthusiasm.

60. **Voltaire**: Francois Marie Arouet de V., 1694-1778, French philosopher and historian.

61. **Louis Quatorze**: *Le Siècle de Louis XIV*, 1751, by Voltaire. The last chapter of this book deals with Chinese rites and Christian practices and asks whether they are compatible. He compares the tolerance of the Emperor K'ang Hsi [59:21] with the violent repression of both Protestants and Jansenists by the bigot King Louis [Sieburth, *Pai*, 6-3, 382].

62. **1766 ante Christum**: L, "... before Christ." In 1766 B.C. the emperor Ch'eng T'ang opened a copper mine and made money which he gave to the people to buy grain [53:40].

63. **Salamis**: [74:109, 110].

64. **Thales**: Fl. 6th century B.C. One of the Seven Sages, said by Aristotle to be the founder of physical science. Pound relates a story from Aristotle about Thales "wishing to show that a philosopher could easily 'make money' if he had nothing better to do." He foresaw a bumper crop of olives so he "hired by paying a small deposit, all the olive presses on the islands of Miletus and Chios. When the abundant harvest arrived, everybody went to see Thales" [*SP*, 172].

65. **Siena**: In *Gold and Work* Pound wrote; "The true basis of credit was already known to the founders of the Monte dei Paschi of Siena at the beginning of the seventeenth century" [*SP*, 339].

66. **interest ... nothing**: A recurrent theme in *The Cantos* and in many of Pound's economic writings [46:26].

67. **METATHEMENON**: [74:343; 97:77].

68. **Le Paradis ...**: [74:292].

69. **Κύθηρα**: H, "Cythera"; Aphrodite.

70. *ὑπὸ χθονὸs*: H, "under the earth" [cf. 26 above].

71. *γέα*: H, "earth." Reference to men rising out of the earth in full battle-gear in the Cadmus myth. They turned and fought each other until all but five were killed. These assisted Cadmus in building Thebes.

72. **"like an arrow ..."**: From *Analects*

XV, 6: "He said: Straight, and how! the historian Yu. Country properly governed, he was like an arrow; country in chaos he was like an arrow" [*CON*, 264.].

73. **"Missing . . . himself"**: Said Pound in "Mang Tsze": "The ethic of Confucius and Mencius is a Nordic ethic. . . . It is concentrated in the Mencian parable: 'An Archer having missed the bullseye does NOT turn round and blame someone else. He seeks the cause in himself' " [*SP*, 96].

74. **total sincerity**: In *Chung Yung* Pound said: "Only the most absolute sincerity under heaven can bring the inborn talent to the full and empty the chalice of nature" [*CON*, 173]. And in "Terminology," for the word "Sincerity," he said: "The precise definition of the word, pictorially the sun's lance coming to rest on the precise spot verbally" [*CON*, 20].

75. **Tellus**: Roman goddess of the earth; the Greek Rhea.

76. **Pirandello**: Luigi P., 1867-1936. Most significant of the modernist Italian dramatists [Freud, 91:55]. Pound wrote: "Pirandello was worried at the news that Cocteau was trying an Oedipus; for a moment he 'feared' or 'had feared' that M. Jean wd. fall into psychoanalysis, and caught himself the next moment with 'No, he won't fall into that mess. It est trop bon poète' " [*GK*, 93].

77. **Campari**: Cafe C. at Galleria Vittorio Emanuele, Milan. Perhaps Pirandello told the story of Cocteau there.

78. **Dieudonné**: [74:178].

79. **Voisin**: [74:179].

80. **Gaudier**: G-Brzeska, 1892-1915, Vorticist sculptor killed in WWI, and celebrated by Pound: "Among many good artists . . . there was this one sculptor already great in achievement at the age of twenty-three, incalculably great in promise and in the hopes of his friends" [*GB*, 17].

81. **Miss Lowell**: Amy L., 1874-1925, an American poet and critic who went to London in 1914 to become involved in imagism. With her money, dynamic energy, and mass (some 250 lbs.), she drew many into her circle and transformed the movement into "amygism." She held a formal dinner at Dieudonné 17 July 1914 to celebrate the first imagist anthology. Miss L. had 12 guests, including Ezra and Dorothy Pound, Allen Upward, and Gaudier-Brzeska, who seems to have measured the planes and angles of her massive breasts (see "two teats of Tellus" above) with–amazement? G-B whispered to Pound as Amy stood up to speak, "God! I'd like to see her naked." MSB says, "Pound really stressed the GAWD when he told me this anecdote."

82. **Upward**: [74:275]. Pound wrote: "Of course, it is very irritating: if you suggest to Mr. Upward that his mind is as clear as Bacon's, he will agree with you. If you suggest to Mr. Upward that his middles are less indefinite than Plato's, he will agree with you" [*SP*, 408].

83. **Haff . . . basshunts?**: "Have you no political passions?" in a Russo-German accent.

84. **Demokritoos, Heragleitos**: Democritus, Heraclitus.

85. **Doktor Slonimsky**: Henry S., 1884-1970. Born in Minsk, he was a classmate of Pound's at U. of Penn. 1902-1903. In 1912, he received a Ph.D. degree from the University of Marburg with a dissertation entitled *Heraklit und Parmenides*. Pound speaks of him as "A Russian, who had taken degrees . . . on prehistoric Greek philosophers . . . who, . . . said he was going 'to convert England to philosophy' " [*PD*, 115]. Also, he wrote, "Slovinsky [sic] looked at me in 1912: '. . . Boundt haff you gno bolidigal basshuntz?' Whatever economic passions I now have, began *ab initio* from having crimes against living art thrust under my perceptions" [*SP*, 230-231].

86. **Miscio**: Michio Ito (ca. 1892-1961), a Japanese dancer from a samurai family who

trained in Japan, in Paris (with Nijinsky and the Ballet Russe), and at a school of eurhythmics in Germany. When WWI broke out he fled to London and was reduced to poverty. He lived in a rooming house run by an Irish woman. After pawning about all he had including neckties, he finally went for three days without any hot water or light. "Out of the sixpence he realized from his neckwear he put two pennies into the gasometer and went out to buy some bread with the remainder of his fortune." That night a painter took him to a party at Lady Ottoline Morrell's where Lady Cunard invited him to dinner the next day. He began dancing at parties, thereafter, for literary and artistic audiences. Once, after he had danced before an audience of 100, a distinguished gentleman asked him about Japanese art. Ito could not speak English but said that if he might speak German he could answer. The gentleman, no less than Prime Minister Asquith, concurred and they spoke quite easily in German [Caldwell, *Michio*, 40-41].

87. **Ainley**: Henry A., an actor who played the part of Cuchulain in *At the Hawk's Well*, by Yeats. Allan Wade played the Old Man and Michio Ito the Guardian of the Well. The line in quotes is probably a remark made by Ito during a rehearsal. The play was performed on the afternoon of April 2, 1916 in Lady Cunard's drawing room. Yeats said later of these days: "I shall not soon forget the rehearsal of *The Hawk's Well*, when Mr. Ezra Pound, who had never acted on any stage, in the absence of one chief player rehearsed for half an hour" [*Plays*, 214].

88. **Mrs Tinkey**: Prob. the Irish landlady of Ito.

89. **"Jap'nese . . .** : This remark of Ito certainly impressed Pound. In a letter to Katue Kitasono, 22 Jan. 1940, he said: "Ito's first remark to me in 1914 or '15 [was] 'Jap'nese dance all time overcoat' " [*L*, 335].

90. **Jack Dempsey**: William Harrison D., 1895-1983, American heavyweight boxing champion, 1919-1926.

91. **Mr Wilson**: Tom Wilson, DTC trainee [74:257]. A popular song sung by Mr. Wilson had these lines: "My girl's got great big tits / Just like Jack Dempsey's mitts" [DG].

92. **old Dublin pilot**: In a piece entitled "John Synge and the Habits of Criticism" [*The Egoist*, Feb. 2, 1914], Pound said: "'She was so fine and she was so healthy that you could have cracked a flea on either of her breasts,' said the old sea captain bragging about the loves of his youth. It seems a shame that the only man who could have made any real use of that glorious phrase in literature is dead."

93. **precise definition**: [cf. 74 above].

94. **bel seno**: I, "beautiful bosom." *in rimas escarsas*: P, "in rare rhymes." *vide sopra*: L, "see above."

95. **Arno**: River in central Italy. The 2 mountains so divided make an enormous, if not beautiful, bosom.

96. Δημήτηρ: H, "Demeter." Goddess of harvest [47:3].

97. **copulatrix**: L, "one who copulates."

98. **Ciano**: Conte Galeazzo Ciano di Cortelazzo, 1903-44, Italian statesman, secretary of state of press and propaganda (1935), minister of foreign affairs (1936-43), ambassador to the Holy See (1943). He was the son-in-law of Mussolini, and according to many, a treacherous stuffed-shirt type guilty of corruption and profiteering [Anderson, *Pai*, 6-2, 244].

99. **the admiral**: Ubaldo degli Uberti, 1881-1945, a longtime Italian naval officer who retired in 1931 but returned to service during WWII, at which time he was promoted to admiral. Since early 1934 Uberti and his family had been friends of Pound. They had similar political and literary sympathies, and Uberti assisted in translating Pound and getting his work published. Pound saw Uberti often during his last months in Rome. His son Riccardo provided the ski shoes he wore on his walk (after the fall of the government) north to join his

daughter. The "he" in the line is Mussolini. The Italian fleet was surrendered to the Allies 8-10 Sept. 1943. Admiral Uberti was ambushed and shot by a platoon of Russian-German soldiers who thought his car belonged to partisans. He died in hospital 28 April 1945, a few days before Pound arrived at the DTC [Uberti, "History of a Friendship," 105].

100. Chilanti: Felice C., 1914-1982, a journalist and novelist Pound knew and visited often in the early 1940s. He was a member of a group of dissident Fascists Pound listened to but didn't agree with. In 1972 he wrote "Ezra Pound among the Seditious in the 1940s" [Anderson, *Pai*, 6-2, 235-250].

101. 12 . . . daughter: Tati C. During Pound's many visits to Chilanti's group, she used to listen avidly to all the talk and sometimes "sat on his knees while he cast about for answers which would satisfy him" [ibid., 240].

102. Sold . . . Gais: The village in the Tyrol where Mary, the daughter of Pound and Olga Rudge, was brought up and about which Mary de Rachewiltz (M de R) writes so memorably in *Discretions*: "All that is gone now. In its place there is a new school, a post office, a hotel and a cement factory near the river" [for the quote and the cattle bedding see *Discretions*, 35-37].

103. Chung Ni: Confucius [53:148]. Reprise of "Mongols are fallen / from losing the law of Chung Ni" [56/308], which derives from De Mailla, *Histoire*, X, 23.

104. alpino's statue: "The monument to the *Alpini* in the Piazza in Bruneck has always been one of the Tyrolean Targets for anti-Italian manifestations. In September 1943 they placed beside it an empty valise, to remind Italians it was time to pack up and leave" [M de R, 194].

105. Brunik: [Bruneck]: A town in the Italian Tyrol.

106. Dalmatia: Territory on the east shore of the Adriatic Sea which became Yugoslavia and Albania; its indigenous people had no enthusiasm for Italian encroachments.

107. treasure of honesty . . . : A recurrent theme in Confucian writings: "A state does not profit by profits. Honesty is the treasure of states" [*CON*, 87-89].

108. dog-damn . . . labour: These several lines concern the conviction of many of Mussolini's followers (prob. including Pound) that his government fell not because of his shortcomings (or the difficulty of Fascism as an ideology) but because of fraud and corruption in the bureaucracy. By September 23, 1943 M had formed La Repubblica de Salò. Although the 20 years' labour of the old had been ruined, M's new program would work. Pound seemed to hope and dream so. Jactancy (ostentatious public boasting) would be replaced by work [M de R, 194-196].

109. Petano: Since there is no town in Italy of this name, it is prob. an error for Adano. John Hersey's novel *A Bell for Adano* (1945) may have evoked the line. Mary de Rachewiltz remembers that her father read the book around 1945.

110. Alice and Edmée: Edmée refers to Edmund Dulac, 1882-1953, a French artist, who married Alice May de Marini in 1903. He had done colored illustrations for *The Arabian Nights* (1907), *The Tempest* (1908), and *The Rubáiyat of Omar Kháyyam* (1909). Although born in Toulouse, he settled in London in 1905 and became a British citizen in 1912. Pound knew him when they were both on the faculty of "The College of Arts" in 1914, an outfit organized to serve students during the difficult years of WWI. Pound mentions him in a number of letters in this connection [*L*, 42n, 47, 93, 95, 104]. Maybe Ed and Alice had a multicolored mutt named Arlechino.

111. Arlechino: I, "Harlequin." Central character in the Commedia del Arte who usually appears in a bright, multicolored costume. Perhaps a multicolored mutt at the DTC was so named by Pound.

112. *καὶ 'Ἴδα, θέα*: H, "and Ida goddess" [cf. 50 above].

113. Apollo: Helios, the sun.

114. E la Miranda: I, "and the Miranda." Isa Miranda (Ines Isabella Sampietro, b. 1909), famous Italian actress who did stage work in Italy, France, the U.K., and the U.S.A., as well as films for famous directors in all these countries. Her first film role, *La Signora di tutti* (1934), established her reputation. She had done 10 major films before 1945, including one in Hollywood opposite Ray Milland: *Hotel Imperial* (1939).

115. Romano Ramona: Prob. a guard in the DTC cadre.

116. ὕλη: H, "shit."

117. Margherita: An abandoned child brought up by the same family Mary was housed with. Everyone called her Margit. On a visit once Pound brought little Mary "a diapason" (tuning fork) as a gift: "He said it served to set the right tone when singing or playing an instrument. I said Margherita could give the right tone by ear and if we sang at two voices she first started out on my note and then found hers" [M de R, 44].

118. O . . . griefs: Reminiscence of Hopkins, "Spring and Fall: To a young child," a 15-line lyric which starts, "Márgarét, are you grieving." [MSB note: "Margaret Cravens committed suicide back in 1912."]

119. Lanier: Sidney L., 1842-1881, American poet and musician who wrote *The Symphony*, a long epic poem in which he discusses the interaction of trade and ethics [89:123].

120. Jeff Davis: Jefferson D., 1808-1889, president of the Confederate States of America (1861-1865).

121. Atreus: King of Mycenae. Son of Pelops, who brought a curse on his house. Thyestes, Atreus's brother, seduced Atreus's wife; Atreus murdered three of the four sons of Thyestes and served them to their father. Thyestes laid a curse on the house of Atreus which descended upon his sons, Agamemnon and Menelaus: hence, the doom which seemed to haunt the South as a similar curse.

122. Mercury: The Roman equivalent of the god Hermes; the caduceus of Mercury, the insignia of the medical branch of the U.S. Army, is a wing-topped staff with two snakes winding about it.

123. Buddha: The past participle of the verb *budon* ("to enlighten"). Thus Gautama Siddhatha became "the Enlightened One" and the central prophet of certain branches of Hindu-Sino-Japanese religions. Pound's anti-Buddhist bias [98: 65-67] makes the phrase "Born with B's eye" pejorative.

124. Mason and Dixon: The imaginary line that separated slave states in the South from nonslave states in the North. From the English astronomers Charles Mason and Jeremiah Dixon, who surveyed the line between Pennsylvania and Maryland.

125. Ils . . . existence: F, "They don't exist, their surroundings confer an existence upon them."

126. Emanuel Swedenborg: 1688-1772, the Swedish scientist and inventor who after 1747 became a visionary and religious writer because of what he took to be divine revelation. His theosophic system as set forth in *Divine Love and Wisdom* rhymes with Pound's light / intelligence metaphors for divinity manifest in the universe. In ES a divine sphere, which emanates from God, appears in the spiritual world as a sun from which flows the sun of the natural world: "The spiritual sun is the source of love and intelligence, or life, and the natural sun the source of nature or the receptacles of life." There are three spheres all deriving from God incarnate as the Word in Scripture: "This word is an eternal incarnation, with its threefold sense—natural, spiritual, celestial." It is in the celestial sphere that one should not argue.

127. the lotus: In Oriental religions, the lotus rhymes somewhat with the "multifoliate rose" of the West. Pound may conceive it as above the "celestial sphere" because it stands finally for the source of all spheres: "The lotus flower growing out of the navel of Vishnu symbolizes the universe growing out of the central sun—the central point or the 'unmoved mover'. . . . In lotus symbolism, the idea of emanation and of realization predominated over that of the hidden Centre, which is a Western accretion" [Cirlot, 185].

128. **nenuphar**: The European water lily or lotus.

129. **Kuanon**: [74:81].

130. **Lethe**: [74:505].

131. **Barzun**: Henri-Martin B. (b. 1881), a French poet and critic who advocated *simultanéisme*, an idea Pound discussed in "The Approach to Paris, VII": "Barzun has an idea that we should write poems like orchestral scores with a dozen voices at once . . . I suppose one could learn to read five or ten at once. . . . Of course, there are any number of objections" [*New Age*, Oct. 16, 1913, 728]. But in a letter to John Quinn in 1918, Pound refers to Barzun as among the lunatics with the Lowells and Lindsays [*L*, 134].

132. **anno domini**: L, "year of the Lord."

133. **raison**: F, "argument" or "proof." Pound valued Barzun's maxim "Pourquoi doubler l'image?" and may well be referring to this idea rather than *simultanéism* [cf. 131 above] [HK].

134. **old André**: A. Spire, 1868-1966, French poet and strong advocate of Zionism. Said Pound: "(I have not counted the successes in Spire's new volume *Le Secret*, but it contains abundant proof that André Spire is a poet, however much time he may spend in being a Zionist, or in the bonds of necessity" [*Dial*, LXIX, 4 Oct. 1920, p. 407]. Also, "Allowing for personal difference, I should say that Spire and Arcos write 'more or less as I do myself' " [*LE*, 288]. Again in "Retrospect: Interlude": "There was in those days still a Parisian research for technique. Spire wrangled as if *vers libre* were a political doctrine. De Souza had what the old Abbé called *une oreille tres fine*, but he, the Abbé, wrapped up De Souza's poems and asked me to do likewise in returning them lest his *servante* should see what I was carrying" [*PE*, 129].

135. **Rousselot**: Abbé Jean Pierre R., 1846-1924, French pioneer in experimental phonetics and in the study of dialect as related to geography and genealogy; author of *Précis de Prononciation Française* (1902). Said Pound: "M. Rousselot . . . had made a machine for measuring the duration of verbal components" [ibid.]. Pound wrote in 1920: "M. l'Abbé made such handy little discoveries for . . . the locating of submarines, . . . the cannon is just a large beast that roars, and the submarine is someone walking who cannot absolutly muffle the sounds of his footsteps" [*Dial*, Dec. 1920].

136. **De Sousa**: Robert de Souza, 1865-1946, a minor French symbolist poet [cf. 134 above].

137. **fin oreille**: [fine oreille]: F, "a good ear."

138. **"Un curé . . . déguisé**: F, "A disguised priest . . . Looks to me like a disguised priest." At the door / "Don't know, Sir, he looks like a disguised priest."

139. **Cocteau**: [74:246].

140. **Maritain**: Jacques M., 1882-1973, French neo-Thomist theologian and philosopher.

141. **men of letters**: Cocteau is disguised as "Z" here: " 'I thought I was among men of letters,' said Z. 'and suddenly saw they were garage assistants' " [*GK*, 89].

142. **Daudet**: Leon D., 1867-1942, son of Alphonse Daudet, was a leader of the Royalist *Action Française* and one of the ten members of the Goncourt Academy who held an annual meeting in the Restaurant Drouant [SH, *Paris*, 343]. An arch conservative, he would be unlikely to help elect Cocteau as a member.

143. **Académie Goncourt**: F, "the Goncourt Academy," founded in the will of Edmond G. to encourage letters. The Academy elects meritorious writers as members and makes

an annual award for fiction known as the Goncourt Prize.

144. **La Comtesse . . .** : Nadajda de la Rousselière-Clouard, who married in 1901 Guillaume-Joseph-Marie, Comte de Rohan-Chabot. Her salon is mentioned by Huddleston [ibid., 156].

145. **Mr Martin**: The Comtesse de Rohan lived in Paris at 39 av. Henri-Martin. Pound may have recalled the address, which suggested another Martin, Joseph William M., 1884-1968, Republican representative from Mass. (from 1925) who became a powerful leader during WWII. His wrong was to be against Uncle George Tinkham [76:176].

146. **"30,000 . . . "**: Pound said he had heard that someone's manager spent $30,000 "gettin' the nomination" when he could have had it for $6,000, which showed the "temporary debility of a so-called great party" [EP, *Speaking*, 208]. Prob. Alf Landon is the nominee [BK].

147. **Landon**: Alfred Mossman L. (b. 1887), American businessman, governor of Kansas (1933-1937), and Republican nominee for president in 1936.

148. **Wendell Willkie**: Wendell Lewis W., 1892-1944, Republican nominee for president in 1940. Pound mentioned him 10 times in the broadcasts in unflattering terms as another weak victim of the international monetary conspiracy; e.g., "And when you have got six hundred billion in debt . . . then will come Wee Willie Willkie or some other trump card . . . and quadrupple the burden, by putting you back onto a solid dollar, worth five or ten the one wherein you got indebted" [Doob, *Speaking*, 328].

149. **Roi . . . daigne**: F, "I am not the king; I do not condescend to be the prince." This is one of the several variants of the motto of the House of Rohan. Pound's version seems to derive from a reported reply of Mussolini to the king's offer to make him a noble. M said: "No . . . a title of that kind would make me ridiculous. . . . I shan't be so vain as to say: Roi ne puis, prince ne daigne, Rohan je suis, but I beg of you not to insist" [Fang, II, 189].

150. **Citizen . . . ginocchion'**: Mussolini had been made an honorary citizen of Florence, June 12, 1923, a fact which recalls Farinata degli Uberti of the *Commedia*, about whom Mussolini had written: "he who, after the battle of Arbia, had saved the city of Florence from destruction at the hands of the Ghibelline Council, after their victory. Here he says: 'But I was the sole one there who, when all consented to destroy Florence, defended her with open face' " [Fang, II, 190].

151. **Arbia**: River near Siena.

152. **"in gran dispitto"**: I, "with great disdain" [*Inf.* X, 36]; description of Uberti. Continuing the quote [150 above], we have: "Scornful, as if he held hell in great disdain . . . he rises from his torture to a battle of wits with his political enemy." The passage is a favorite with Pound: "It is part of Dante's aristocracy that he conceded nothing to the world, or to opinion–like Farinata, he met his reverses, 'as if he held hell in great disdain'" [*SR*, 160; 78:79].

153. **King**: Victor Emanuel. These lines concern Mussolini's henchmen, including Ciano [cf. 98 above], who used to obey orders, but who in the Fascist Grand Council meeting held during the night of July 24-25, 1943, divested M of his power. The king had to (and did) sign the decrees which also authorized Italy's surrender to the Allied Forces [78:1].

154. **se casco . . .** : I, "If I fall, I do not fall on my knees." Bianca Capello, a Medici duchess of Florence, made this proud statement which Pound seems to think reflects the attitude of Mussolini, who did not surrender but went north to establish the Salò Republic.

155. **Schifanoja**: Schifanoia. The palace built by Alberto d'Este in Ferrara in 1391, and extended by Borso d'Este [10:20], which is famous for the frescoes of Cosimo Tura and Francesco del Cossa.

156. (del Cossa): Francesco del C., fl. 1435-1477, Italian painter who did the Glorification of March, April, and May frescoes in the Schifanoia Palace.

157. St. Louis Till: [74:116].

158. Green: [74:256].

159. Hobo Williams: DTC trainee.

160. Crawford: DTC trainee. The fragments in quotes here and elsewhere in the Pisan Cantos are meant to characterize the quality or nature of the repartee floating to Pound's ears as he sat typing in the medical tent. He said that you can tell who is talking by the noises they make.

161. Roma . . . terras: L, "Fleeing to Rome from the land of the Sabines," variant spelling of Horace line [*Satires* II, 6; 78:34].

162. Sligo: County in Ireland Yeats was fond of.

163. uncle William: W. B. Yeats. He lived at Rapallo (about one-half of each year from 1928 to 1934), which is situated on the Gulf of Tigullio. He seems to have remarked once that the misty scene evoked a kind of paradisal Sligo.

164. Mr Joyce: James J., the Irish novelist Pound spent years promoting.

165. Kitson: Arthur K., 1860-1937, British author who wrote a number of works on money and monetary systems which Pound publicized, such as *The Money Problem, Trade Fallacies*, and *A Fraudulent Standard*. Pound mentions him often among the truth-tellers about money [*SP*, 179, 339, 341, 448].

166. Vetta: I, "summit." Name given to the Portofino Promontory, a public park near Rapallo.

167. Tellus-Helena: [cf. 75, 81 above].

168. Arno: [cf. 95 above].

169. "How is it . . . ": [cf. 30 above].

170. Basil: B. Bunting [74:153], English poet who knew Pound in Paris and visited him for lengthy periods in the late 20s and early 30s in Rapallo. Pound dedicated *Guide to Kulchur* to Bunting and Zukofsky. Bunting learned classical Persian in order to translate parts of the *Shah Namah* for Ezra and Dorothy Pound. By this means, he became overwhelmed by the musical nature of Persian poetry [CFT, *Bunting*, 53-55; 81:19].

171. Shah Nameh: or *Shah Namah* [The book of kings], the great Persian epic composed during the years around A.D. 1000.

172. Firdush': Firdausi, ca. 940-1020, the nom de plume of Abul Kasim Mansur, author of the *Shah Namah*. The characters are his name in Persian.

173. Kabir: One of the 12 disciples of Ramananda and a notable reformer who flourished in northern India 1400-1450. Myth has it that he was exposed as an infant and found on a lotus in a pond near Benares. His teaching aimed at the fusion of Hinduism and Islam and he was famous for speaking in the tongue of the people, a quality that may have endeared him to Pound, who, with Kali Mohan Ghose, translated some of his poetry: "Certain Poems of Kabir" appeared in *The Modern Review* (Calcutta), vol. 13, no. 6, Jan. 1913, 611-613 [Fang, IV, 30]. The refrain "Thus said Kabir" occurs often in the poems.

174. Rabindranath: R. Tagore, 1861-1941, the Bengali poet who was awarded the Nobel Prize for Literature in 1931. Pound knew him over the years and admired and promoted his work. He also (with Evelyn Underhill) translated Kabir (*Songs of Kabir*, 1915).

175. Sir Montagu: Sir Montague de Pomeroy Webb [74:32]. The "every peasant" concerns Indian farmers who ought not be politically inactive no matter how hot the day or how many flies are around.

176. bunya: [banya]: Hindu, "money-lender."

177. hypostasis: [81:55].

178. Hancock's wharf: [71/414].

179. Kohinoor: The most famous Indian diamond now among the British crown jewels.

180. Tom: A DTC trainee. The "tin disc" prob. refers to dog tags, the identification tag all service men are required to wear around the neck. It gives name and serial number.

181. Wanjina: [74:42].

182. obstruct future wars: A theme developed at length in later cantos [88/passim; 89/passim].

183. Frascati: Town in Roma Province, central Italy. After Italy signed an armistice on Sept. 8, 1943, but before Eisenhower announced her unconditional surrender at 5:30 P.M. that day, "Flying Fortresses bombed the Roman suburb of Frascati, destroying German headquarters" [Miller, *History*, 702].

184. Das Bankgeschäft: G, "The banking business."

185. Wabash: Fragment of popular American song heard over DTC sound system: "The Wabash Cannonball."

186. Ferrarese: Around Ferrara [8:30].

187. Taishan: [74:46].

188. Del Cossa: [cf. 156 above].

189. Schifanoja: [cf. 155 above]. The constellations Ram and Bull are shown in the Cossa paintings used as end papers in *Dante and Pound*, by J. Wilhelm.

190. house-boats . . . : [19:33; 19/88].

191. plenum: L, "full."

192. Cassandra: Trojan prophetess who was considered mad. Apollo gave her the gift of true prophecy but later ordained she should never be believed.

193. Sorella . . . zecchin': I, "Sister, my sister / who danced on a golden sequin [coin]." Perhaps, an Italian popular song heard on the DTC loudspeaker [78:3]. It connects with the "Io son la Luna" theme [Nassar, *Pai*, 1-2, 211].

194. Ch'êng: [M379] "to perfect." The right component of [M381] is also "Ch'eng," which Pound uses for sincerity: "The precise definition of the word . . . " etc [76:57].

195. Zagreus: One of the various names of Dionysus [17:3].

196. Explication: *Analects*, Two, XXIV: "1. He said: To sacrifice to a spirit not one's own is flattery. 2. To see justice and not act upon it is cowardice" [*CON*, 201].

CANTO LXXVIII

Sources

The Bible, Micah 4.5; EP, *CON*, 247, 248; Homer, *Od*. VI, XXIV, I; James Legge, "The Works of Mencius," *The Four Books*, Shanghai, 1923 [Legge]; Virgil, *Aeneid*, trans. Bishop Gawin Davis.

Background

EP, *SP*, 313, 272, 261, 306, 311, 89, 274-282, 87; *LE*, 245, 265; *P*, 252; *ABCE*, 119; *PE*, 101, 126; *Exile*, no. 4, Autumn 1928, 5, and no. 2, 1927, 117; *MIN*, 232; *SR*, 120, 160; *CON*, 247, 248; *GK*, 247, 166, 246; Michael King, "Ezra Pound at Pisa: An Interview with John L. Steele," *Texas Quarterly*, Vol. XXI, no. 4, Winter 1978, 49-61 [King, "Steele"]; Ivancich, *Ezra Pound in Italy*, New York; Rizzoli, 1978; *Thomas Taylor, the Platonist: Selected Writings*, eds. Kathleen Raine and George Mills Harper, Princeton, 1969; Achilles Fang, "Materials for the Study of Pound's Cantos," Ph.D. dissertation, Harvard University, 1958, Vols. II, III, IV; H. Finer, *Mussolini's Italy*, New York, 1935; M. I. Rostovtzeff, *History of the Ancient World*, 1924-26, *Social and Economic History of the Hellenistic World*, 1941; Lady Anne Blunt, *The Celebrated Romance of the Stealing of the Mare*, 1892; NS, *Life*, 243; Odon Por, *Finanzia nuova* (*Italy's Policy of Social Economics, 1939-1940*), Bergamo; Instituto d'Arte Grafiche, 1941; Harriet Wilson, *Memoirs*, 1825 (ed. J. Laver, 1929).

Exegeses

Peck, *Pai*, 1-1, 3-37; Anderson, *Pai*, 6-2, 244, *Pai*, 5-1, 47; M de R, *Discretions*, 190; Riccardo M. degli Uberti, "Ezra Pound and Ubaldo degli Uberti: History of a Friendship," *Italian Quarterly*, XVI, 64, Spring 1973, 95-107; Flory, *Pai*, 5-1, 45-52.

Glossary

1. **Ida**: [77:50] Perhaps a scene at the DTC with a number of people arguing (or gabbling like geese) reminded Pound of the Judgment of Paris which was made on Mt. Ida and resulted in the abduction of Helen, the Trojan War, the enslavement of Cassandra, and so on. Or maybe an ironic reference to the peace treaty signed by King Emmanuel with the Allies [77:153].

2. **pax mundi**: L, "peace of the world."

3. **Sobr'un zecchin'**: [77:193]. Italian equivalent of "on a saxpence" [HK].

4. **Cassandra**: [77:192]. The image of eyes becomes more pronounced from here on in the Pisan Cantos [Peck, *Pai*, 1-1, 3-37].

5. **war . . . come to an end**: The bankers and munitions makers who promote and maintain wars in order to sell guns and ammunition. A recurrent theme early and late in the poem.

6. **del Cossa**: [77:156].

7. **ter flebiliter**: **Ityn**: L, "thrice mournfully: Itys" [4:8, 9].

8. **Janus**: The god who was guardian of the gate, usually represented as having two faces, looking both before and behind. The closing of the *Janus geminus* ("twin") in the Roman forum signified peace.

9. **bifronte**: I, "two-faced." The "Janus bifronte," because of its sound, may suggest Ciano, Mussolini's son-in-law, because Janus in Italian is Giano and the phrase is quite common for "traitor" [Anderson, *Pai*, 6-2, 244]. Pound certainly thought Ciano "was a two-faced bastard" for betraying M and signing the fall of his government [77:153].

10. **Napoleon . . . Mussolini**: [104:100]. In *A Visiting Card* Pound recounts overhearing these lisping words: "Let them erect a commemorative urinal to Mond, whose

brother said in the year of the Sanctions: 'Napoleon wath a goodth man . . . ,' adding as an afterthought, 'and the economic war has begun.' I know that drawing-room; that sofa where sat the brother of Imperial Chemicals. I know it. It is not something I read in some newspaper or other; I know it by direct account. Fortunately these messes have no sense of proportion, or the world would already be entirely under their racial domination" [*SP*, 313]. By "their" Pound means Jewish money barons such as the Rothschilds and Monds.

11. **via Balbo**: A street in Rome.

12. **Avignon**: [21/96; 21:8]. Cosimo's red notebook contained details of debts to be called in.

13. **pax Medicea**: L, "the peace of the Medici."

14. **Naples**: Concerns Lorenzo's heroic mission to King Ferrante of Naples to obtain peace [21:35].

15. **inoltre**: I, "also." As did Sigismundo and other Renaissance men, Lorenzo wrote poems.

16. **"alla . . . abbandonata"**: I, "to the abandoned earth" [cf. 17, 18 below].

17. **Metastasio**: Pietro M., 1698-1782, adopted name of P. Bonaventura Trapassi, Italian poet and dramatist, who became the court poet in Vienna from 1729. He wrote the lyrics and librettos of a number of operas, including *Didone Abbandonata* (1724).

18. **"alla" non "della"**: I, " 'to the' not 'of the' " [86:63]. MSB's note says, "The rights *to* property not the rights *of* property. Pound's admiration of M is here centered in his use of the precise word."

19. **il . . . Verona**: I, "the Program of Verona." The manifesto written by Mussolini and adopted in November as the principles of action of his new republic at Salò.

20. **Sirmio**: [74:50]. On Lake Garda.

21. **Foresteria**: I, the part of a monastery where visitors are housed.

22. **Salò, Gardone**: Place where Mussolini lingered to dream the Republic. In establishing the "Repubblica Sociale" at Salò, M said that Fascism had made a romantic mistake in not doing away with the monarchy in 1922: "The Fascist Revolution stopped short of the throne. . . . As things have turned out, the Crown has expiated with its fall the dagger it stuck in the back of the Fascist regime and the unpardonable crime it perpetrated upon the nation. But the nation can come to life again only under the auspices of a republic" [Fang, III, 70].

23. **San Sepolchro**: Town in Arezzo Province, central Italy, but also the name of the square in Milan (Piazza San Sepolcro) where M launched his Fascist career.

24. **four bishops . . . altar**: On his long walk north from Rome [77:99], Pound stopped in Milan and saw the results of bombing attacks.

25. **la fede**: I, "the faith." An important slogan of Fascism.

26. **Goedel**: Carl G., member of the English section concerned with radio broadcasting, 1942-1943, and later with the propaganda agencies of the Salò Republic.

27. **Naxos**: [2:14]. Naxos was the island Dionysus stopped at on his way home. Before that, Theseus had stopped there on his return home from slaying the minotaur in Crete. Pound thus sees himself, as did both Dionysus and Theseus, on his way home. The 15 lines concern his walk from Rome to Gais [M de R, 190].

28. **Fara Sabina**: A locality a little north of Rome. The lines following in quotes are scraps of phrases people said to him on his walk.

29. **minestra**: I, "soup."

30. **il zaino**: I, "the knapsack." Pound said this.

31. branda: I, "folding bed" or "camp bed."

32. Bologna: City he walked through on his way north.

33. Gruss Gott . . . gekommen: G, "God bless us," "The Master!" "Daddy has come!" South German dialect [EH]. The first half was a greeting to Pound when he arrived at Gais and the last half was said by his daughter Mary.

34. Roma . . . terras: [77:161].

35. and . . . Latium: These 4 lines are quoted from the *Aeneid*, translated by the Scottish Bishop Gawin Douglas. In 1917 Pound quoted from the same passage about the trials of Aeneas: "Grete payne in battelles, suffered he also / On he his goddis, brocht in Latio / And belt the ciete, fra quham of nobil fame / The Latyne peopil, taken has thare name" [*LE*, 245].

36. bricabrac: Pound said: "Literature that tries to avoid the consideration of causes remains silly bric-a-brac" [*SP*, 272].

37. "each one . . . ": [74:353; 76:60]. A quote from Micah 4.5.

38. Gaudier: [77:80].

39. Hulme: [16:27].

40. Wyndham: Percy W. Lewis, 1882-1957, a British writer and painter Pound defended and promoted for a lifetime. Lewis joined with Gaudier-Brzeska and Pound to establish Vorticism and publish *Blast*. His birth-date is often given as 1884 because he made himself two years younger to enhance his precocity [HK].

41. Mana aboda: Title of a poem by T. E. Hulme [*P*, 252].

42. Steele . . . : Lt. Col. John Steele, commanding officer of the DTC. Col. Steele later "could understand" the accusation of sadism. The record seems to show that he went quite a way beyond express orders to allow Pound privileges [King, "Steele," 50].

43. Blood: Probably the name of a DTC "trainee" all of whom had their names stencilled on their prison garb. Steele says he "could have been 'the cheerful reflective nigger' in the latrine" [*Pai*, 12-2 & 3, 297].

44. Slaughter: Colonel Steele remembers him as "a black soldier" [ibid].

45. Pallas: Athena [21:53].

46. Δίκη: H, "justice." This epithet is used because of Athena's function at the end of the *Oresteia*, where the chorus acts as a jury and the goddess casts the determining ballot and finds Orestes innocent in the name of justice.

47. "definition . . . ": A camera may record a scene but not define meaning.

48. front name . . . : A recurrent axiom of Fascist thought which Pound repeats often in his prose: "We are tired of a government in which there is no responsible person having a front name, a hind name and an address" [*Exile*, no. 4, Autumn 1928, 5; see also *PE*, 101; *Exile*, no. 2, 1927, 117; *ABCE*, 119; *SP*, 261].

49. "not a right . . . ": A Mussolini statement, "La libertà non è un diritto: è un dovere" (Liberty is not a right but a duty), was a part of the Fascist credo Pound endorsed; he had it printed on his stationery. He used *Libertà un Dovere* as the epigraph for *Carta da Visita* [*SP*, 306].

50. "Presente!": I, "Present." A significant word at Fascist gatherings: "It [Fascism] even has the mystery of Transubstantiation. For members who have died in great exploits. . . . When the roll is called, and the unbreathing lips remain silent, his circle of Fascist comrades reply, 'Presente!' " The prayer of the Fascist militia says in part: "Oh, God, who lights every flame and strengthens every heart, renew my passion for Italy in me day by day! Make me worthier of our dead, so that they themselves—ever strongly—shall answer to the living, 'Presente! . . . Amen' " [Finer, *M's*

Italy, 360; quoted Fang, III, 83]. M de R objected to this as a gross overstatement.

51. **merrda . . . swine**: Presumed accomplishments of Mussolini Pound mentions often [41/202].

52. **Sitalkas . . . Upward**: [74:272].

53. **Pellegrini**: Giampietro P. (b. 1899), finance minister of Salò Republic. On November 27, 1943 he told M he would allot 125,000 lira a month to him as chief of state. M refused the money, saying that "4000 lira for his family of four would be more than ample." But Pellegrini insisted and M "agreed to the sum, but on December 27, 1944 he had the further payment of the money stopped." M seemed suspicious that that much money should honestly be there [Fang, III, 87-88].

54. **Justinian**: [65.126, 77:44; 94:45].

55. **Titus**: T. Flavius Vespasianus, A.D. 9-79, Roman emperor (69-79) noted for administrative and financial reforms that salvaged the empire from the critical state it was left in by Nero. "He was industrious, and the simplicity of his life was taken as a model. . . . He cultivated a bluff manner, characteristic of the humble origins he liked to recall. His initial appointments . . . reflect his astuteness in building a powerful party, of which the core was his own family" [*OCD*, 1116]. Prob. Pound believed M was a 20th-century Vespasian [94:118].

56. **Antoninus**: A. Pius, 86-161, Roman emperor; adopted son of Hadrian, whom he succeeded in 138. He was followed by Marcus Aurelius, whom Hadrian persuaded him to adopt. The reign of Antoninus was marked by reason, restraint, fiscal wisdom, and vastly improved administrative techniques. "The general tone of harmony and well-being under Antoninus is well expressed by Aristides . . . [who] pictures the Empire as a congery of happy, peaceful, and prosperous city-states under the aegis of Rome's beneficent hegemony and protection. . . . Deified by universal accord, he received all the usual honours, including a commemorative column in the Campus Martius" [*OCD*, 76]. Pound mentions A. often in his prose: "[One] can . . . find the known beginnings of usury entangled with those of marine insurance, sea lawyers, the law of Rhodes, the disputed text of Antoninus Pius on the limits of his jurisdiction" [*SP*, 272; cf. 58 below].

57. **lex Rhodi**: L, "the law of Rhodes" [42:4].

58. **private misfortune**: Said Pound: "the cultural tradition with regard to money . . . may be traced . . . from the indignation of Antoninus Pius, that people should attempt to exploit other people's misfortunes (e.g., shipwrecks . . .)" [*SP*, 311].

59. **Rostovseff**: Michael Ivanovich Rostovtzeff, 1870-1952, American historian; professor of classical philology and ancient history at St. Petersburg, Fla. (1901-18), professor of ancient history at U. of Wisconsin (1920-25) and at Yale (1925-39); author of *History of the Ancient World* (1924-26) and *Social and Economic History of the Hellenistic World* (1941).

60. **Mencius . . . verse 7**: In quoting from the passage indicated, Pound said in "Mang Tsze" [Mencius]: " 'Nothing is worse than a fixed tax.' A fixed tax on grain is in bad years a tyranny, a tithe proper, no tyranny" [*SP*, 89].

61. **T'ang Wan Kung**: C, "Duke Wan of T'ang": title of Book III of *The Works of Mencius.*

62. **grillo**: I, "cricket."

63. **quattrocento**: I, "fifteenth century."

64. **o-hon . . . tout**: F, imitation of colloquial language: "It is sometimes said in the village / that a helmet has no use / none at all / It is only good to give courage / to those who don't have any at all" [29:30].

65. **Salzburg**: Austrian city famous for its annual Mozart festival.

66. **Qui . . . gamba**: I, "Here sings Wolfgang the cricket / Piano (softly), the bass viol."

67. **Wolfgang**: W. Amadeus Mozart.

68. **Lake Garda**: [76:90].

69. **Tailhade**: Laurent T., 1854-1919, French poet.

70. **"Willy"**: Henri Gauthier-Villars, 1859-1931, a French novelist, essayist, and biographer, nicknamed "Willy."

71. **Mockel**: Albert Henri Louis M., 1866-1945, Belgian-French poet and critic, the founder (1886) and editor of *La Wallonie*, a magazine of the Belgian symbolists. His strange aesthetic came to a climax in *The Immortal Flame* (1924).

72. **en casque . . .** : F, "in pink crystal helmets the mountebanks," from *Ballet*, by Stuart Merrill [cf. "Essay on French Poets," *MIN*, 232], a poem first published in *La Wallonie.*

73. **cakeshops . . . Nevsky**: [16:42; 74:183].

74. **Sirdar**: [74:175].

75. **Armenonville**: [74:236].

76. **Kashmiri**: I, "of Kashmir." [19:34].

77. **Mozart's house**: Not the house in which he was born but the Mozart-Haus in the Schwarz-Strasse (Salzburg), "built in 1912-14 by the international 'Stiftung mozarteum' . . . with two concert-rooms, an academy of music, and archives" [*Baedeker's Austria*, 1929, 251; Fang, III, 118].

78. **San Zeno**: [74:483]. A romanesque church in Verona which Pound visited with Edgar Williams (W. C. Williams's brother), which had a signed column [45:14]. In his "Paris Letter" [*Dial*, vol. 74, 1923, 89], Pound ends his tale of the visit with: "Williams looked at the two simple spirals of red marble cut in one block, and burst out, 'How the hell do you expect us to get any buildings when we have to order our columns by the gross?' "

79. **Farinata**: F. degli Uberti. The great Ghibelline leader of Florence. He was born in Florence at the beginning of the 13th century and saw the development of the Guelph-Ghibelline factions. When he became the head of his house in 1239, he became the leading Ghibelline and in 1248 took part in the expulsion of the Guelphs. The Guelphs returned and in 1258 expelled the Ghibellines. But with the help of the Sienese, Farinata led his men to the battle of Montaperti (1260) and crushed the Guelphs. At the council at Empoli afterwards, it was proposed that Florence be completely destroyed and reduced to the status of a village. According to Villani, "When this proposal was made, the valiant and wise knight, Messer Farinata degli Uberti, arose and opposed it . . . saying . . . that such talk was madness. . . . So long as there was life in his body, he said, he would defend the city with sword in hand." He prevailed. But because he was posthumously condemned as a heretic, Dante places him in the 6th circle of Hell. When F. rises up out of his tomb in Hell to speak with Dante, his arrogance is described by his attitude: "Com' avesse l' inferno a gran dispitto" ("As if he had a great scorn of Hell"). The lines here prob. refer to a statue of Farinata in the courtyard ("cortile") at San Zeno. "Ubaldo" refers to Pound's friend, a descendant of the Farinata, Ubaldo degli Uberti, an admiral in the Italian Navy [cf. "Ezra Pound and Ubaldo degli Uberti: History of a Friendship," by Riccardo M. degli Uberti (his son), *Italian Quarterly*, XVI, 64, Spring 1973, 95-107]. Pound refers to him occasionally in his prose [*SR*, 120, 160].

80. **cortile**: I, "court, patio."Prob. a statue of Farinata kneeling which Pound remembered in a church at San Zeno, Verona.

81. **Ubaldo**: [77:99].

82. **Can Grande**: C. G. della Scala, 1291-1329, lord of Verona and greatest member of the Ghibelline family that ruled Verona from 1277-1387. He was a friend and protector of Dante. The face on an equestrian statue surmounting his tomb outside the Church of Santa Maria Antica in Verona is striking because of a broad grin [Ivancich, *Ezra Pound in Italy*, has picture].

83. Tommy Cochran: Said Pound: "just a nice kid I knew in Wyncote" [ibid.].

84. "E fa . . . tremare": I, "And makes the air tremble with light" [74:425].

85. we sat there: The "we" included Pound, T. S. Eliot, and D. M. G. Adams [RO; DG]. The visit took place in the early 20s [*Pai*, 5-1, 47].

86. Thiy: Bride Scratton. Pound called her Thiy after an early Egyptian queen [NS, *Life*, 243].

87. il decaduto: I, "the decadent one." T. S. Eliot [EH].

88. Rochefoucauld: La R. Perhaps a memory of the Eliot poem that ends, "I mount the steps and ring the bell, turning / Wearily, as one would turn to nod good-bye to Rochefoucauld / If the street were time and he at the end of the street, / And I say, 'Cousin Harriet, here is the Boston Evening Transcript.' "

89. Cafe Dante: A cafe in Verona. Pound recalls with fondness the great literary plans they made there by the arena, even though they came to naught.

90. Griffith: [19:10].

91. Aram vult nemus: [74:441].

92. under . . . (confusions): *Analects* XXI, 1: "Fan Ch'ih walking with him below the rain altars . . . said: Venture to ask how to lift one's conscience in action; to correct the hidden tare, and separate one's errors?" [*CON*, 247].

93. "Chose . . . off": *Analects* XXII, 3-6: "He said: Promote the straight, and grind the crooked. . . . Shun had the Empire, picked out Kao-Yao [53:29] from the multitude, promoted him, and wrong 'uns departed. T'ang . . . picked out I Yin [85:5] from all the hordes, promoted him, and the wrong 'uns departed" [*CON*, 248].

94. One hell of a fight . . . : The next dozen lines concern U.S. Senate fights over the League of Nations and the 18th amendment. Pound turned against the League because it voted sanctions against Italy for invading Ethiopia: "America (the U.S.) has not paid its debt even in thought to the men who kept the U.S. OUT of the league at Geneva. If we have Susan B. Anthony . . . shoved onto our postage stamps, we shd. think up something better . . . for Lodge, Knox, Borah, and George Holden Tinkham for having kept our fatherland out of at least one stinking imbroglio. The League of Two Measures" [*GK*, 247].

95. Lodge: Henry Cabot L., 1850-1924, American legislator; member of the House of Representatives (1887-93), and of the Senate (1893-1924); as chairman of the foreign affairs committee of the Senate, he was opposed to the peace treaty and the League of Nations (1919).

96. Knox: Philander Chase K., 1853-1921, American political leader, member of the U.S. Senate (1904-09; 1917-21); against entry of the U.S. into the League of Nations.

97. Bacchus: Dionysus. Here as a god of wine.

98. Number XVIII: The 18th amendment to the Constitution of the United States, prohibiting the manufacture and sale of intoxicating liquors; ratified in 1919, repealed in 1933.

99. Mr Tinkham: [74:180].

100. Odon: O. Por (b. 1883). One of Pound's favorite Italian writers on social and economic problems. "In six weeks Por had two articles out" [*GK*, 166]; "Odon Por has kept a level head, being in Rome and keeping tab on international knowledge" [*GK*, 246]. The volume referred to here is probably *Finanzia nuova*, which Pound translated: *Italy's Policy of Social Economics, 1939-1940*, Bergamo, Instituto d'Arte Grafiche, 1941, in the Library of Congress.

101. METATHEMENON: [74:343; 77:67; 97:77].

102. Churchill: [41:33].

103. return to Midas: As chancellor of the exchequer in 1925, Churchill restored the gold standard. The act created a devastating depression at home and great suffering in other places in the empire [74:32].

104. taxes: A major premise of social credit is that if the government controls the extension of credit and receives interest for extending it, the people of a nation will collect dividends rather than pay taxes.

105. cancelled: A premise of Gesell [74:368], who recommended that hoarding of money could be avoided and its velocity maintained by fixing stamps that had to be purchased: the cost of the stamps cancelled a proportion of the face value of a bank note [*SP*, 274-282].

106. Ideogram: Tao [M6136], "the process," or "the Taoist Way."

107. à la Wörgl: F, "in the manner of W" [41:44; 74:345].

108. Sd/ . . . efficiently: Pound tried to persuade Mussolini to adopt the Gesellite economy as Wörgl had. M said he'd have to think about it.

109. "For a pig . . . ": Ref. to M's death [74:4].

110. Jepson: Edgar J., 1863-1938, English novelist.

111. The Stealing . . . : *The Celebrated Romance of the Stealing of the Mare*, translated from the original Arabic by Lady Anne Blunt, done into verse by Wilfred Scawen Blunt, 1892. A medieval romance popular in Egypt and N Africa for over 800 years. It tells how Emir Abu Zeyd stole a treasured mare from the stable of the Agheyli Jaber with the help of Jaber's daughter, Princess Alia, whose life he once saved. The act was a cause of war but none took place.

112. casûs bellorum: L, "cause of wars."

113. "mits": A popular song popular with Mr. Wilson had these lines: "My girl's got great big tits / Just like Jack Dempsey's mitts" [77:91].

114. Mr Wilson: [74:65].

115. Harriet: Harriette Wilson, 1789-1846, her *Memoirs* (1825; ed. J. Laver, 1929) have a discussion between Wellington and her concerning the propriety of a man having sex with his boots on. The story Pound's text seems to refer to is usually associated with the duke and duchess of Marlborough.

116. Wellington: [33:24].

117. mannirs: "Manners." Early variant spelling as in Gawin Douglas, whose translation of the *Aeneid* Pound liked [*LE*, 245].

118. videt et urbes: L, "he saw and cities." [cf. trans. *Odyssey* I, 2: *qui mores hominum multorum vidit et urbes, LE*, 265].

119. *πολύμητις*: *Polumetis* [9:38].

120. ce rusé personnage: F, "this shrewd character." Said Pound: "Dr. Rouse has at last translated 'polumetis.' Salel in 1543 found a living phrase when he called Ulysses 'ce rusé personnage' " [*PE*, 126].

121. Otis: James O., 1725-1783, American lawyer and patriot who resigned as advocate general of Boston in protest against the issuing of writs of assistance. He was head of the State Committee of Correspondence, opposed the Stamp Act, and did scholarly work on Latin and Greek prosody [71:89].

122. Nausikaa: Nausicaa, daughter of the Phaecian king Alcinous [*Od.* VI]; Odysseus approached her as she was playing ball on the beach, just after she had finished washing the household linen.

123. Bagni Romagna: Bagno di Romagna is a commune in Forli Province, N Italy.

124. Cassandra: [77:192]. At 23/109 we have the waves of the sea "a glitter of crystal. . . . No light reaching through them" [cf. 4 above].

125. the asphodel: Homer said: "But they passed beyond the flowing waters of ocean, and the rock Leucas, and the gates of the sun, and the people of dreams; and they immediately came into meadows of asphodel, where souls the images of the dead reside" [*Od.* XXIV, 10-14]. Pound may have made Neoplatonic connections from Thomas Taylor's translation of Porphyry's *De Antro Nympharum* [Concerning the Cave of the Nymphs]: "Now these *meadows of Asphodel* form the supreme part of Pluto's dominions: for, according to Pythagoras . . . the empire of Pluto commences downward from the Milky Way; so that these meadows are most probably situated in *the Lion*, the constellation into which souls first fall, after they leave the tropic of Cancer" [*Thomas Taylor the Platonist: Selected Writings*, Bollingen Series LXXXVIII, Princeton University Press, 1969, p. 316n].

126. **Lope de Vega**: Felix L. de V., 1562-1635. Most prolific of the Spanish playwrights. Pound's teacher Hugo Rennert was an authority on L. de V., a fact which resulted in Pound's intention at one time to do a doctoral dissertation on his work. He received a fellowship to visit Spain to do the research, but when the fellowship was not renewed he gave it up.

127. **No hay . . . celos**: S, "There is no love without jealousy."

128. **Sin . . . amor**: S, "Without secrecy there is no love." The title of a play by Lope de Vega which was edited by Hugo Rennert and published by the MLA, 1894.

129. **Dona Juana**: 1479-1555, daughter of Ferdinand of Aragon and Isabella of Castile and mother of Emperor Charles V. She was driven mad by the death of her husband Philip. But during his later years her passionate jealousy, for which she had "just cause, led to deplorable scenes."

130. **la loca**: S, "the mad woman." According to Rennert, "La loca was an actress by the name of Lucia de Salcedo who was at one time a sweetheart of Lope de Vega" [Fang, III, 141].

131. **Cunizza**: [6:34; 29:14].

132. **al triedro**: I, "in the corner" [76:24].

133. **Tre . . . mente**: I, "three ladies around in my mind." Paraphrase of Dante's "Tre donne intorno al cor son venute" [Three ladies have come around my heart], an allegorical poem presenting a vision of Justice, Generosity, and Temperance reduced to beggars by the evil society around them. Most critics believe that Pound has three particular ladies in mind but disagree about who they are. Dorothy Pound and Olga Rudge are in most lists; there are several candidates for third place [Flory, *Pai*, 5-1, 45-52; Fang, III, 114]. The "Tre donne" may be anticipated by "and the three ladies all waited" [74:439].

134. **that roman**: Unidentified.

135. **Olivia's stairs**: Prob. Olivia Rossetti Agresti [76:3].

136. **Dr Williams**: William Carlos Williams, 1883-1963, American poet and friend of Pound from their student days together at the University of Pennsylvania.

137. **put in the cart**: A major tenet of Williams's poetic theory was "no ideas except in things," which became a tenet also of *The Objectivists*. The cart is suggested by the much-anthologized red wheelbarrow.

138. **Lucca**: [76:130].

139. **"The Spring and Autumn"**: *Spring and Autumn Annals*, the *Ch'un Ch'iu*. This, the last of the Five Classics, is a chronological record of the chief events in the state of Lou (Lu) between 722 and 484; it is generally regarded as the work of Confucius, whose native state was Lou. Pound mentions it in "Mang Tsze" [*SP*, 87]. In Mencius VII, ii, 2, 1-11, we read: "Mencius said, 'In the *Spring and Autumn* there are no righteous wars. Instances indeed there are of one war better than another' " [*Legge*, 977].

CANTO LXXIX

Sources

Time, Aug. 27, 1945, Aug. 6, 1945; Homer, *Od* IX, X, XII; EP, *CON*, 269, 207; Dante, *Inf.* XIV.

Background

EP, *Odes*, 143; *SP*, 119-120, 407; *GK*, 182, 82; *SR*, 62, 101; Ivancich, *Ezra Pound in Italy*, New York, Rizzoli, 1978; *The Oxford Companion to Music*, 2d ed., 1938 [*OCM*]; Raymond Post, *That Devil Wilkes*, New York, 1929, 204.

Exegeses

Achilles Fang, "Materials for the Study of Pound's Cantos," Ph.D. dissertation, Harvard University, 1958, Vols. III, IV; HK, *Era*, 8-10, 13; JW, *Medieval Song*, 197-203; Hughes, *Pai*, 2-1, 39; CFT, *Pai*, 3-1, 93-94; CE, *Ideas*, 145-147; DP, *Barb*, 268-274; WB, *Rose*, 136-138.

Glossary

1. **battistero**: I, "baptistery." A two-page spread in Ivancich shows a church at Pisa with baptistery and leaning tower, all in whiteness, in the background.

2. **Del Cossa**: [77:156].

3. **you wd / gain**: The "you" is prob. Dorothy Pound or Olga Rudge.

4. **I had not . . . womankind**: Paraphrase from "To Althea From Prison," by Lovelace, in which the last line of the quatrain is "Loved I not honor more."

5. **Salzburg**: [78:65]. *Time* [Aug. 27, 1945] said: "Last week the Salzburg Festival was on again. . . . Inside the Festspielhaus some 50 hand-picked Austrians . . . were carefully segregated from U.S. soldiers who filled two-thirds of the auditorium."

6. **Amari-li**: A famous solo song composed by Giulio Caccini, who with Jacopo Peri invented opera around 1600. "Amarili mia bella" was published at Florence in 1602 [Hughes, *Pai*, 2-1, 39].

7. **her hair . . . thirty**: Poss. Constanze Weber, Mozart's wife (a younger sister of his real love), whom he married Aug. 16, 1782 when he was 26 years old. M. died Dec. 5, 1791 when not quite 36 years old, and Constanze was "not yet 30."

8. **Spielhaus**: G, "theater."

9. **Astafieva**: Serafima A., 1876-1934, a Russian dancer and teacher. She was a member of the corps de ballet of the Maryinsky Theatre (1895–1905) and of the Diaghilev Company (1909-1911). She opened a ballet school in London.

10. **Wigmore**: Wigmore Gallery, Marylebone, London.

11. **wd / . . . cart**: W. C. W. would have [78:137].

12. G. Scott: A trainee at the DTC.

13. Lili Marlene: Most popular German war song during WWII.

14. Goedel: [78:26].

15. in memoriam: L, "in memory."

16. G. P.: Giorgio Paresce, Italian Fascist whom Pound knew.

17. Où sont?: F, "Where are?" First half of "Where are the snows of yesteryear?" Context suggests, Where are all of Mussolini's former followers, and which ones will adapt and survive?

18. Pétain: [80:34]: Henri Philippe P., 1856-1951, marshal of France. He was convicted of "intelligence with the enemy" (1945) and sentenced to life imprisonment [*Time*, Aug. 6, 1945]. The vote not to execute was close: 14 to 13.

19. Scott & Whiteside: [74:258]. Black prisoners at DTC.

20. 8 birds . . . : Janequin's bird song of Canto 75 receives graphic visual illustration all through 78. Birds sitting on the barbed wires that Pound could see from his tent seemed to form a musical score. As the birds took off and landed, a different tune seemed to be carved in the air.

21. Mr Allingham: A trainee at the DTC.

22. Bechstein: A make of piano.

23. quattrocento: I, "15th century."

24. a cavallo: I, "on horseback."

25. Cosimo Tura: [24:87].

26. Del Cossa: [77:156]. One of the Schifanoia muralists at the palace in Ferrara.

27. Beethoven: Ludwig von B., 1770-1827, the German composer whose piano works are considered by many to be his crowning achievement.

28. Piazza S. Marco: I, "St. Mark's Square," a famous location in Venice.

29. papal major: Ironic question suggested by something Pound sees outside his tent.

30. castrum romanum: L, "Roman fort."

31. "went . . . quarters": Paraphrase of the line that ends Book I of Caesar's *Gallic Wars*.

32. Janequin: [75:8].

33. per esempio: I, "for example."

34. Orazio Vechii: O. Vecchi, ?1550-1605, Italian composer known mainly for his *L'Amfiparnasso: Commedia Armonica.*

35. Bronzino: Il Bronzino (Agnolo di Cosimo), 1502-1572, Florentine painter at the court of Cosimo I.

36. Hagoromo: Japanese Noh play [74:124].

37. Kumasaka: A Noh play [74:363].

38. Troas: The Troad, the territory surrounding the ancient city of Troy.

39. Ismarus . . . : Odysseus attacked Ismarus soon after he left Troy, but after an initial defeat, the Ciconians rallied and drove the Greeks back to their ships [*Od.* IX, 39ff.]. An example of the "Greek rascality" just mentioned, which justified the gods' 10-year delay of his nostus [80:364].

40. e poi basta: I, "and then nothing else." In *Analects* XV, 40, Pound says: "He said: Problem of style? Get the meaning across then STOP" [*CON*, 269].

41. Ideogram 1: Tz'u [M6984], "words, speech, message."

42. Ideogram 2: Ta [M5956], "intelligent . . . to apprehend." As drawn, one component in the right of the character is missing. Pound said to Kenner: "What Confucius has to say about style is contained in two characters. The first says 'Get the meaning across,' and the second says 'Stop.' " When Kenner asked what he saw in the first character, he said, with protestations and a Jamesian pause: "lead the sheep out to pasture" [HK, *Era*, 13].

43. what's his name: Attempt to recall the name of Guido d' Arezzo, fl. 1000-1050, who devised the system of Hexachords which lasted about 500 years: "he improved the notation, developing the two-line staff into the present one of five lines" [*OCM*, 866]. Pound recalls "the name of that bastard" a page later [cf. 62 below].

44. aulentissima . . . : I, "most odorous, fresh rose." Inverted order of the beginning words of a poem by the Sicilian poet Ciullo d' Alcamo, fl. 1230-1250 [cf. JW, *Medieval Song*, 197-203; *SR*, 62, 101]. A recurrent musical phrase [98:107; 100/719; 107:1].

45. Assisi: [74:490].

46. Goncourt: [77:143].

47. "paak . . . ": [74/442]. The voice of the Japanese sentry telling arriving dignitaries where to park is heard several more times as background in Canto 79.

48. bacon-rind banner: A military flag seen flying with the Ugolino palace as background.

49. Ugolino: [74:240].

50. San . . . Cavalieri: A church in Pisa richly hung with Turkish and Arabian banners, trophies of the victories of the Knights of San Stephano.

51. Attlee: Clement Richard A., 1883-1967, British statesman and leader of the Labour party who took over from Churchill July 26, 1945 [*Time*, Aug. 6, 1945]. Since Attlee's program included the nationalization of the Bank of England, Pound doubtless had some hope for him [80:406], that is, if he didn't do "a Ramsey."

52. Ramsey: James Ramsey MacDonald, 1866-1937, the British statesman and leader of the Labour party who several times became prime minister briefly. Perhaps because he gave support to the abortive labor strike of 1926, or, later, joined with Conservatives in the economic crises of 1931, Pound sees him (as did many others) betraying his cause to the money barons.

53. "Leave the Duke . . . ": [50:28].

54. "in less . . . epoch": H. L. Mencken wrote a letter to Pound in 1937 which he quotes with approval. Saying first that because a politician messes something up doesn't prove it's wrong, H. L. M adds: "Nevertheless, I believe that all schemes of monetary reform collide inevitably with the nature of man in the mass. He can't be convinced in anything less than a geological epoch." Pound comments: "Above statement does not invalidate geological process" [*GK*, 182].

55. Fleet . . . Salamis: [74:109].

56. Wilkes: John W., 1727-1797, onetime lord mayor of London. A book by Raymond Postgate entitled *That Devil Wilkes* [New York, 1929] said: "His chief power to tip the balance in favor of the poor lay in his authority to fix the price of bread—or rather since the loaf was fixed at a penny, to fix the size of the loaf" [p. 204]. In 1775, Wilkes did it [Fang, III, 22].

57. ἦθος: H, "moral bent" or "cultural force," or prob. both.

58. Athene: [17:16] In speaking of the Greek panetheon of women [*Patria Mia*], Pound talks of "Ceres, the mother" type; then, "Juno, the British matron" type, "propriety and social position to be maintained, no one's comfort considered. Women of this type have been always, and, thank God, always will be, deceived by their husbands. Aphrodite—enough said. Pallas Athene, the much pitied intellectual" [*SP*, 119-120].

59. caesia oculi: L, "gray eyes."

60. γλαύξ: H, "the owl . . . so called from its *glaring* eyes" [*L & S*]. Pound quotes from Allen Upward thus: "How hard the old cloistered scholarship . . . has toiled to understand the word glaukopis given to the goddess Athene. Did it mean blue-eyed or grey-eyed, or—by the aid of Sanskrit—merely glare-eyed? And all the time they had not only the word glaux staring them in the face, but they had the owl itself cut at the foot of every statue of Athene and stamped on every coin of Athens, to tell them that she was the owl-eyed goddess, the lightning that blinks like an owl. For what is characteristic of the owl's eyes is not that they glare, but that they suddenly leave off glaring like lighthouses whose light is shut off" [*SP*, 407; 74:302].

61. **mah?**: I, "but then?"

62. **D'Arezzo**: [cf. 43 above].

63. **chiacchierona**: I, chiachierona, "cackler."

64. **Ideogram 1**: Huang [M2297], "yellow."

65. **Ideogram 2**: Niao [M4688], "bird."

66. **Ideogram 3**: Chih [M939], "rests." Pound translates the refrain of Ode 230 in the *Book of Poetry* thus: "the silky warble runs in the yellow throat, bird comes to rest on angle of the hill" [EP, *Odes*, 143]. The three characters are taken from this ode.

67. **auctor**: L, "author."

68. **Tellus**: [77:75].

69. **si come . . . dispitto**: I, "as if he held Hell in great disdain" [77:152; 78:79].

70. **Capanaeus**: Capaneus. One of the seven against Thebes who defied the divine command of Zeus by attempting to scale the wall. Zeus zapped him with a thunderbolt and Dante placed him among the blasphemers in Hell [*Inf.* XIV, 43ff.].

71. **γέα feconda**: H, "earth"; I, "fruitful." For Helen's breast see 106/752 [106:9].

72. **"each one . . . "**: Recurrent phrase from the Bible [74:353].

73. **mint, thyme and basilicum**: Plants associated with paradise [CFT, *Pai*, 3-1, 93-94].

74. **"half dead . . . "**: From "Blood and the Moon," by W. B. Yeats: "In mockery I have set / A powerful emblem up / . . . In mockery of a time / Half dead at the top."

75. **goyim**: Yiddish epithet for non-Jews.

76. **Yu-en-mi**: The Youanmi Gold Mines. Ltd., promoted by Herbert Hoover in 1912.

77. **Mr Keith**: Poss. William Keith, 1838-1911, an American painter.

78. **Donatello**: Donato di Niccolo di Betto Bardi, ?1386-1466, Italian sculptor.

79. **O Lynx**: One of the feline animals sacred to Dionysus. The lyric refrains and appeals to the lynx in the rest of the canto may be conceived as a generalized prayer to the god of sex and wine, but as imagining a particular woman. Scholars debate whether Pound had Dorothy Pound or Olga Rudge or Bride Scratton or even someone else in mind. One might note that, as far as the poetry is concerned (here and in a number of other identifications), it doesn't matter.

80. **Manitou**: The Algonquin Indian name for the natural power that permeates all things.

81. **Khardas**: Poss. Persian Khärbät, the lead donkey in the *Shah Nameh* [77:171] of Firdausi [EH].

82. **"Prepare . . . "**: [*Od.* X, 450].

83. **How is it far . . .** : Recurrent leit-motif [77:30].

84. **Lidya**: Lydia Yavorska, 1874-1921, a Russian-born actress (and erstwhile wife of Prince Vladimir Bariatinsky) who acted in London, 1910-1921. She prob. told Pound the story of the executioner. Pound may have seen her accost Henry James: "Men of my time have witnessed 'parties' in London gardens where . . . everyone else (male) wore grey 'toppers.' As I remember it even Henry James wore one, and unless memory blends two occasions he wore also an enormous checked weskit" [*GK*, 82].

85. **Mr. James**: [7:13, 74:191].

86. **"Cher maître"**: F, "Dear Master."

87. **fish-tails**: The Sirens.

88. ἐνὶ Τροίῃ: H, "in Troy." From the song of the Sirens to Odysseus [*Od.* XII, 189-190].

89. **Eos nor Hesperus**: The Morning and Evening stars here [80:110].

90. **Silenus**: A satyr, sometimes called the son of Hermes or Pan, who was a companion of Dionysus.

91. **Casey**: Corporal at the DTC.

92. **bassarids**: Thracian maenads.

93. **Maelids**: Tree nymphs [3:12].

94. **cossak**: [cf. 84 above]. He executes because he likes to.

95. **Salazar . . .** : Trainees at DTC. Presumably many of the trainees, especially black soldiers, had names of early presidents of the United States and even of famous non-presidents such as Calhoun.

96. **Calhoun**: [34:48]. The "Retaliate" theme, developed in detail in Cantos 87-89, is first sounded here.

97. **Priapus**: God of fertility, son of Dionysus and Aphrodite.

98. Ἴακχος, Io! . . . : H, "Hail Iacchos [another name for Dionysus], Hail Cythera [Aphrodite]."

99. **having root . . .** : Perhaps the idea of *Analects* IV, 16: "The proper man understands equity, the small man, profits" [*CON*, 207].

100. **Io!**: A Greek salute usually translated, "Hail!"

101. **you can make . . . converts**: The China missionary heard here may be the one at 28/136.

102. **Sweetland**: Prob. one of the trainees at the DTC.

103. ἐλέησον: H, "have mercy."

104. **Kyrie eleison**: H, "Lord, have mercy." Phrase from Orthodox liturgy and Roman Mass.

105. **Astafieva**: [cf. 9 above].

106. **Byzance**: Byzantium.

107. "Ἴακχε . . . : H, "Iacchos, Rejoice!"

108. **"Eat if it not . . . error**: Because Kore ate the pomegranate seeds that Dis gave her, Zeus condemned her to return to Hades for four months each year.

109. **AOI**: MF(?), occurs 172 times in ms. of *La Chanson de Roland*: meaning unknown. Perhaps it means "Hail" as in "Io."

110. Κόρη: H, "Daughter." Persephone, the daughter of Demeter.

111. **Pomona**: Ancient Italian goddess of fruit trees.

112. **fire . . . flame**: The potent sexuality all nature is alive with, particularly fruit, in which the seed is concentrated.

113. **Melagrana**: I, "Pomegranate."

114. **Heliads**: [76:6].

115. **crotale**: I, "the rattlesnake's rattle."

116. γλαυκῶπις: H, "with gleaming eyes." Epithet for Aphrodite, Cythera [Kuthera] [cf. 60 above].

117. **crotales**: I, "castanets." Made from the rattle of the rattlesnake and used in the dances of the bassarids.

118. ἰχώρ: H, "ichor." The juice that flows in the veins of the gods. It was conceived to be different from blood, but came to be blood.

119. **kalicanthus**: The calycanthus flower.

120. 'ΑφροδίΤην: H, "Aphrodite."

121. Ἥλιος: H, "Helios." The sun at dawn. The "red glow in the pine spikes" anticipates the Na-Khi flora and ambience in *Thrones* and Cantos 110, 112 [102:49].

122. δεινὰ . . . : H, "You are fearful, Cythera."

123. Κόρη . . . : H, "Daughter [Persephone],

and Delia [Artemis/Diana], and Maia [mother of Hermes]."

124. Κύπρις . . . : "Cyprus Aphrodite."

125. Κύθηρα: H, "Cythera [Aphrodite]."

126. aram . . . vult: L, "The grove needs an altar." Recurrent theme which climaxes at 90/607 when, in a visionary passage, the grove gets its altar [74:441].

127. Cimbica: Writing about the work of W. H. Hudson, Pound said: "He would lead us to South America . . . for the sake of meeting a puma, Chimbica, friend of man, the most loyal of wildcats" [*SP*, 431]. A rhyme with other animals of the cat family who have significance as manifestations of the divine presence in nature.

CANTO LXXX

Sources

Time, Aug. 13, Aug. 6, Jul. 2, 1945; Homer, *Od.* X, V; Horace, *Odes* I; James Legge, *The Four Books*, Shanghai, 1923 [Legge]; Thomas Lovell Beddoes, *Death's Jest-Book*; T. S. Eliot, *The Waste Land*, *Ash Wednesday*; Horace, *Ars Poetica*; Dante, *Inf.* V. IX; Shakespeare, *Twelfth Night* IV, *Julius Caeser* III, sc. 2; Samuel Johnson, *The Plays of William Shakespeare*, 1765; Pierre de Ronsard, *Sonnets pour Hélène*, II; Wyndham Lewis, *Blasting and Bombardiering*, London, 1937 [*Blasting*]; Enrico Pea, *Moscardino*, trans. Ezra Pound, New York, New Directions, 1955; EP, *CON*, 218, 257, 229, 99, 247, 145; *P*, 271, 257, 39, 192, 28; Morris Speare, *The Pocket Book of Verse*, 1940 [Spear].

Background

EP, *L*, 21, 95, 131, 331, 333, 338, 341, 179, 52, 228; *GK*, 199, 88-89, 200, 80-81, 309-310, 179, 185, 189, 110, 180-181, 227, 31, 79, 146; *PE*, 23, 29, 205, 11; *NEW*, 163; *SP*, 414, 378-383, 24, 115-117, 124, 418; *ABCR*, 43, 79-80; *LE*, 431-440, 276; *SR*, 161, 84, 208; Michael Holroyd, *Augustus John*, New York, 1974 [Holroyd, *John*]; *Dictionary of Literary Biography*, vol. 4; *American Writers in Paris, 1920-1939*, by George Wickes, Detroit, 1980; John Gould Fletcher, *Life is My Song*, New York, 1937; George Santayana, *Persons and Places*, vols. 1, 2, New York, 1944-45; Ford Madox Ford, *Portraits from Life*, New York, 1937; *Poetry*, March 1918; Julian Franklin, *Heraldry*, London, ARCO, 1965.

Exegeses

Chilanti, *Pai*, 6-2, 245; Shuldiner, *Pai*, 4-1, 73-78; Nassar, *Pai*, 1-2, 210; Davie, *Pai*, 6-1, 102; Kimpel, *Pai*, 10-2, 308; CFT, *Pai*, 3-1,

94-100; Peck, *Pai*, 1-1, 9; Flory, *Pai*, 5-1, 45-46; HK, *Pai*, 2-3, 492; CFT, *Pai*, 5-1, 69-76; Surette, *Pai*, 6-1, 111-13; BK, *Pai*, 5-2, 350; JW, *Pai*, 12-1, 55-75; DP, *Barb*, 274-284; WB, *Rose*, passim; HK, *Era*, 72-74, 113-114, 476-481, 488-489, passim; Achilles Fang, "Materials for the Study of Pound's Cantos," Ph.D. dissertation, Harvard University, 1958, Vols. II, III, IV; Michael King, "Ezra Pound at Pisa: An Interview with John L. Steele," *Texas Quarterly*, XXI,4, Winter 1978, 49-61 [King, "Steele"]. NS, *Life*, 45, 322; R. Sieburth, *Instigations*, Cambridge, Harvard University Press, 1978, 15; Charles Norman, *Ezra Pound*, New York, Macmillan, 1960 [CN, *Pound*]; CB-R, *ZBC*, 106.

Glossary

1. **Ain' committed** . . . : Opinion of why he's in the DTC expressed by Mr. A. Little—or one of the trainees.

2. **Θέμις**: H, "law (not as fixed by statute, but) as established by custom: justice, right" [*L&S*]. The vagaries of justice come from murderers and rapists receiving sentences similar to ones received by those guilty of minor transgressions.

3. **Amo ergo sum**: L, "I love; therefore I am." Rephrasing of the Cartesian *cogito*. A musical figure often used by Pound.

4. **Margot**: M. Asquith [38:22]. *Time* [Aug. 6, 1945] carried her obituary: "Died. Margot Asquith, 81, The Countess of Oxford and Asquith, witty widow of British Prime Minister (1908-16) Herbert H. Asquith, longtime society *enfant terrible*. . . . Her lifetime of audacities included writing a note in pencil to Queen Victoria, declining to stay at a dinner party despite King Edward's request." Pound was fond of her. She ordered copies of *Blast* in advance [Fletcher, *Life is My Song*, 137] and had her portrait sketched by Gaudier-Brzeska [Fang, II, 82].

5. **Walter**: W. Morse Rummel, 1887-1953, German pianist and composer who was much interested in 12th- and 13th-century French songs. Pound lived with him for months at a time in Paris and mentions him often [*L*, 21, 95, 131; *GK*, 199]. Like Michio Ito [77:86], he seems to have lacked a coin for the gas meter at times.

6. **Finlandia**: A tone poem by the Finnish composer Sibelius.

7. **Debussy**: Claude D., 1862-1918. French composer.

8. **pains au lait**: F, "milk rolls"

9. **eucalyptus**: On the day Pound was arrested by the Partisans, he picked up a seed of the eucalyptus tree on the salita and carried it as a good luck charm.

10. **"Come pan, niño!"**: S, "Eat bread, boy."

11. **Spanish bread**: Before adulteration [45:5].

12. **senesco sed amo**: L, "I age, but I love."

13. **Madri'** . . . : Spanish cities Pound remembered from his younger days as a guide there.

14. **Gervais**: Brand name of a French dairy company.

15. **Las Meniñas**: A painting by Velasquez of "the page girls" of the queen, which Pound saw at the Prado Museum along with several others he lists here.

16. **Philip** . . . : Portraits of Philip III on horseback, ca. 1635: Philip IV on horseback, ca. 1635; Philip IV hunting wild boar, ca. 1638; Philip IV in hunting suit but not on horseback, etc.

17. the dwarfs: Portrait of the dwarf Sebastian de Morra, ca. 1643-1649; portrait of the dwarf El Primo, 1644.

18. Don Juan: Painting so named.

19. Breda: *Las Lanzas*, or *The Surrender of Breda*, a painting in which lances are prominently displayed; done ca. 1635.

20. the Virgin: *The Virgin Delivering the Chasuble to St. Ildefonso*, ca 1618-1620.

21. Los Boracchos: *The Drinkers*, 1629.

22. Las Hilanderas: *The Carpet Weavers* (female), painted ca. 1655-1660.

23. the Prado: The National Museum of Painting and Sculpture in Madrid.

24. "Las Américas": Bazaar in Madrid.

25. Symons: Arthur S., 1865-1945, British poet and critic important in the development of symbolism in the 1890s. He may have told the story Ernest Rhys [74:434] reported in *Everyman Remembers*. "One droll impression connects Symons with Paul Verlaine. It was at a Paris party given by Verlaine in his tiny bedroom. He had been ill. . . . But Verlaine was a humorous host. He produced . . . a ten-franc note, and said . . . 'I have money: I will have pleasure. Go, Jean–and buy a bottle of rum.' When the rum arrived, as there was only one tumbler, they all drank from it in turn" [pp. 111-112]. Symons or Rhys probably told this or a similar anecdote at the Tabarin.

26. Tabarin: The Bal Tabarin was a Montmartre nightclub at 58 rue Pigalle, on the Right Bank.

27. Hennique: Léon H., 1851-1935, French dramatist and novelist. Speaking of literary lights in France, Pound said: "A few more than middle aged gents had reminiscences. Hennique remembered Flaubert and Maupassant. Men distinctly of the second line conserved this, that, or the other" [*GK*, 88-89].

28. Flaubert: Gustave F., 1821-1880, French novelist.

29. Turgenev: Ivan T., 1818-1883, Russian novelist who was much influenced by his many years of friendship with Flaubert. The sentiment about death comes from his *Une Nicheé de Gentilshommes*, which Pound frequently cited [*PE*, 23; *GK*, 200; *SP*, 414].

30. Tiresias: [1:7]. Prob. invoked here in the capacity of seer and prophet.

31. ἀγλαὸς . . . : H, the 4 words do not construe. Pound is trying to recall a line from Homer [*Od*. X, 490-495] which says, "Bright Persephone has granted reason to the blind man" [Tiresias; 74:366]. MSB's note reads: the blind see to whom Persephone still provides intelligence."

32. Still hath: Recurrent epithet for Tireseas [39:18; 47:1].

33. X———y: Quisling [RO].

34. Pétain: [79:18].

35. Verdun: [16:37].

36. Blum: Léon B., 1872-1950, French socialist, statesman, and writer. After he became premier in 1936, he reorganized the Banque de France into the Banque de la France. Prob. Pound meant "bank" by "bidet." Writing about books one should have in an Oriental series, he said in 1938: "We need the economics volume of the Chinese encyclopedia among other now unavailable works. Probably contains a bit more dynamite to blow up Blum, and the Banque with him" [*NEW*, Dec. 15, 163; Fang, III, 79].

37. bidet: F, "sitz-bath."

38. To communicate . . . : [79:40].

39. simplex . . . : L, "plain in her neatness" [Horace, *Odes* I, 5].

40. Legge: James L., 1815-1897, Scottish missionary and sinologist; editor of *The Chinese Classics*, a translation with critical and exegetical notes, prolegomena, and copious indexes, in 7 vols. (London: 1861-86), of which Vol. I contains the *Confucian*

Analects, the *Great Learning*, and the *Doctrine of the Mean*. These plus *Mencius* make up the *Four Books*.

41. **Tsu Tsze**: Tzu Hsi, empress dowager of China and actual ruler, 1898-1908. Pound tells an anecdote from Katherine Carl's book, *With the Empress Dowager*: "Under the insistence of the Empress she turned out . . . an excellent work of art, in the course of producing which she observed the Dowager charming birds, definitely luring at least one down from a tree. . . . Mrs. Carl also describes the old lady painting or writing the ideograms, writing them large and with great and delicate perfection" [*GK*, 80-81].

42. **Confucius**: *Analects* VI, 26: "He went to see (the duchess) Nan-tze. Tse-Lu was displeased. The big man said: Well, I'll be damned, if there's anything wrong about this, heaven chuck me" [*CON*, 218].

43. **Nancy**: N. Cunard, 1896-1965, contemporary American poet and patron of the arts. Nan-tze in the *Analects* above suggests this Nancy who had a violent love affair with Henry Crowder, an American Jazz musician [84:9], which scandalized the expatriates in Paris during the late 20s.

44. **Hartmann**: Sadakichi Hartmann, 1867-1944, American poet, playwright, and art critic whom Pound thought highly of. He wrote: "Sadakichi Hartmann sends me a sort of helter-skelter table . . . and Aristotle is among the 'near great' on his list. I mention this because Sadakichi has lived. Has so lived that if one hadn't been oneself it wd. have been worth while to have been Sadakichi. This is a tribute I can pay to few men (even to those listed in his table of glories:" [*GK*, 309-310].

45. **Manhattan**: Hartmann noted on the title page of his *A Tragedy in a New York Flat* that it was "written in a New York flat, '95-'96, on nothing a week" [Fang, II, 56].

46. **Hovey**: Richard H., 1864-1900, American poet.

47. **Stickney**: Trumbull S., 1874-1904, American poet.

48. **Loring**: Frederic Wadsworth L., 1848-1871, American poet and journalist.

49. **Santayana**: George S., 1863-1952, b. Madrid, Spain, but moved with his family to the U.S. in 1872. He graduated from Harvard in 1886 and taught philosophy there from 1889 to 1912, except for a year at Cambridge and the Sorbonne. After 1912 he became an expatriate recluse and lived mostly in Italy. His early works, *The Sense of Beauty*, 1896, and *The Life of Reason*, 5 vols., 1905-1906, were traditional. But he developed new theories in the 1920s and 30s in such works as *The Realms of Being*, 4 vols.; *The Realm of Truth*, 1937; and *The Realm of Spirit*, 1940. He appears to have been an avowed materialist, but his doctrines about faith and the "essences" are difficult to fit into so restricted a mold. He was also a poet whose prose style was called poetic. A novel, *The Last Puritan* (1935), was a best-seller among the literate. Pound met Santayana in Venice late in 1939 and was much taken with his honesty and corresponded with him thereafter [*L*, 331, 333, 338]. Pound prob. read the MS of his memoirs, *Persons and Places* (Vols. I-II, 1944-1945), sometime in 1940 [81:37, 40].

50. **Carman**. Bliss C., 1861-1929, Canadian poet and journalist. He spent much time on the open road in the U.S., singing his poems for food and a place in the barn to sleep.

51. **Whitman**: In his book *Conversations with Walt Whitman*, Hartmann mentions "a can of lobster" they ate together. In a letter to H., Pound said: "On the strength of the oysters to Walt (who died before the body emerged from the--------------of time) you might git a sandwich" [*L*, 341]. Pound is telling H. that, because of his meeting with and book about Whitman, he might receive some kind of grant from the American Academy of Arts and Sciences he has just been elected to. He confused the lobster with oysters.

52. **Nenni . . .** : Pietro N., 1891-1980, head

of the Italian Socialist party, who took an important role in Italian governments after the fall of Mussolini in 1943 [*Pai*, 6-2, 245]. *Time* [July 2, 1945] carried a note about the government of Feruccio Parri: "Most restive was Vice Premier Nenni, who had hoped to be Premier himself. But liberal philosopher Benedetto Croce had voiced a general opinion: 'Nenni, you cannot be Premier. First, because you are Nenni, second, because you have no idea of administration' " [pp. 34-35].

53. **Tseng**: Tzu Kung, disciple of Confucius who was important in diplomacy. He asked, "What shall we add . . . " [74:11].

54. **Benito**: B. Mussolini [41:2; 74:3]. The next 20 lines contain Pound's perception of Mussolini in relation to the people around him who Pound thinks helped destroy a great and idealistic humanitarian.

55. **Billyum**: W. B. Yeats, who for a while served as senator in the Irish Free State, and flirted, briefly, with the Fascist movement there.

56. **O woman . . .** : First line of a Padraic Colum poem: "O woman, shapely as the swan, / On your account I shall not die."

57. **Padraic Colum**: 1881-1972, an Irish poet Pound much admired.

58. **Ulster**: Northernmost province of Ireland, which, being mainly Protestant, did not join the Irish Free State during the revolution.

59. **If a man . . .** : Yeats wrote in "A Packet for Ezra Pound" [1929]: "My dear Ezra, Do not be elected to the Senate of your country. . . ." This is Pound's response.

60. **Palio**: I, "horserace" [20:24]. Annual event in Siena.

61. **"Torre! . . . "**: I, "Tower! Tower! Owl!" cries at the horserace. But the words are also names of the districts of the town [M de R].

62. **giribizzi**: I, "fancies."

63. **dove . . .** : I, "where is Barilli?"

64. **Barilli**: Bruno B., 1880-1952, Italian music critic and composer.

65. **calvario**: I, "calvary."

66. **prete**: I, "priest."

67. **carrocchio**: I, "flag car of an army." Here, the lead float in the parade, in which each city ward has its symbols or flags [JW]

68. **contrade**: I, "districts"

69. **"non è una . . . "**: I (Sienese dialect), "it's not a district, it's a complex." Siena is divided into 17 *contrade* [JW].

70. **arti**: I, "guilds."

71. **hamomila de hampo**: I (Sienese dialect), "camomile of the fields."

72. **Osservanza**: I, the Church of the Observants outside Siena, containing many art works from the Della Robbia family. Some were destroyed in WWII.

73. **de la Robbia**: [Della Robbia], the Florentine family of sculptors and ceramicists. Their terra cotta enamels bear the name "Della Robbia ware."

74. **busted**: The church had a Coronation of the Virgin by Andrea della Robbia at the second altar on the left. A postwar report stated: "Direct bomb-hits caused the complete collapse of the roof, the vaulting of the nave, the aisles, the Chapels, and the Sacristy. . . . Fragments of the reliefs by Della Robbia and Cozzarelli have been recovered" [Fang, II, 256]. The Della Robbia has since been so finely restored that the lay eye can detect no damage [HK].

75. **Li Saou**: Li Sao [56:24]. Since Pound has confused certain characters, Fang says: "The enigmatic phrase 'and near what? Li Saou' probably means the same as 'near what pine trees?' [80/512]. If so, it may refer to 'The pine at Takasago / grows with the pines of Ise' (4/15) and 'Grow with the Pines of Ise' (21/99)" [IV, 151-152]. Lacking any other cue at all, perhaps so.

76. Tempio, Rimini: [8:43]. The facade was damaged in WWII.

77. Mutholini: Said by Sir Robert Mond [78:10].

78. 35 via Balbo: I, "35 Balbo Street." It appears that Pound met Mond in the drawingroom of 35 via Balbo in Rome in 1935.

79. Waterloo: The battle of 12 June 1815 in which Napoleon was defeated by Wellington.

80. Leave the Duke . . . : [50:28; 79:53].

81. "Will never be used . . . ": Remark of Lenin [74:113].

82. Mosqu: Attempt to get Slavic sound of the name Moscow.

83. Andy Jackson: Andrew J., 1767-1845, seventh president of the U.S. He was a member of the House of Representatives (1796-1797) and of the U.S. Senate (1797-1798). He defended New Orleans against the British in 1814, was a two-term president (1828-1836), and led the struggle against the Bank of the United States [37:passim; 88, 89:passim; 103:76].

84. Napoleon: [31:53].

85. a partial resurrection: These several lines through *luz* may concern medieval conceptions of the Resurrection at the Last Judgment as reflected in paintings, theology, and pious belief [cf. Shuldiner, *Pai*, 4-1, 73-75].

86. Cairo: The city in Egypt. Beddoes's song in *Death's Jest-Book* [see 90 below] entitled "The Song that Wolfram Heard in Hell" has two lines: "Old Adam, the carrion crow, / The old crow of Cairo. . . " [reprinted in *The New Book of English Verse*, p. 683; Fang, IV, 47].

87. Sadducees: A sect of Jews at the time of Christ. Urban and aristocratic, the Sadducees were firm upholders of the prescriptions of the law and were religiously conservative, denying immortality and resurrection.

88. Mr. Eliot: T. S. Eliot [46:1].

89. Beddoes: Thomas Lovell B., 1803-1849, English poet whom Pound believes is greater than anyone else believes he is ["Beddoes and Chronology," *SP*, 378-383].

90. luz: Beddoes wrote that, like a seed which can raise up a green herb again, "So is there in such a man, a seed-shaped bone, / Aldabaron, called by the Hebrews Luz, / Which, being laid into the ground, will bear / After three thousand years the grass of flesh, / The bloody, soul-possessed weed called man" [*Death's Jest-Book*, Act III, sc. 3, ll. 447-454]. According to rabbinical teaching, the "os coccygis" is the only bone in the human body which resists decomposition after death. The bone has the shape of a hazelnut (H, *kókkos*). The idea that if you could find and destroy the bone Luz, you could condemn a person to perpetual hell, was the reason Amalric [74:104], or in Pound's mind, Erigena, was dug up out of sepulture.

91. Mr Eliot: Prob. a reference to Eliot's question in *Ash Wednesday*: "And God said / Shall these bones live? Shall these / Bones live?"

92. (T.L.): Thomas Lovell Beddoes, whose major subject was death.

93. (and pearls): Evokes "Those are pearls that were his eyes," of *The Waste Land*.

94. croce . . . sol: I, "Cross of Malta, figure like the sun." Pound considered his eucalyptus pip a sort of magic talisman because the markings on it suggested a cat face, a maltese cross, and/or the sun with rays [74:232].

95. Ideograms: [77:28, 29]: "How is it far."

96. "Hot . . . cat": Sound of drill sergeant counting cadence.

97. Prowling night-puss . . . : The remainder of this page and some of the next is a comic interlude addressed to a wandering cat, Pound's favorite animal. The hungry cat climbs into a box that bacon came in, which has its contract number (W-110090) stamped on it, etc. This passage is just one of many human/comic notes all through the poem and especially the Pisan Cantos. They are important as they connect with the paradisal theme of "hilaritas," perhaps most specifically underlined in the Bible with the recurrent refrain "Be glad and rejoice for the Lord is with thee." But since it's rather officious to keep saying "that's a joke man," I'll take this one liberty and henceforth practice faith and silence.

98. **Confucius**: One of the three books Pound had at Pisa.

99. **kitten on the keys**: A popular piano composition of the 20s by Zez Confrey.

100. **Calliope**: The muse of eloquence and epic poetry, but here, ironically, a steam organ, a musical instrument made up of steam whistles played on a keyboard. Prob. as with other music or songs referred to in the passage, the lines are prompted by things played over the loudspeaker.

101. **Battle Hymn . . .** : Pound used this and the phrase "mi-hine eyes hev" as examples in explaining his technique to the DTC censors, who in passing the manuscripts began to suspect (because of his reputation as a spy and traitor) that they contained coded messages for the enemy [King,"Steele,"59].

102. **crooning**: In 1945 Rudy Vallee's "crooning" was still pandemic.

103. **temporis acti**: L, "bygone days" [Horace, *Ars Poetica*, 173].

104. **ΟΥΤΙΣ**: H, "No Man" [74:17].

105. **ἄχρονος**: H, "without time."

106. **p.c.**: Postcard

107. **Bingen**: A city located on the Rhine above a whirlpool known as the Bingerloch.

108. **Perkeo**. A fool in the court of Karl Philip; Perkeo's tub is the Great Vat of Heidelberg, which according to Scheffel's song was emptied by Perkeo alone; a wooden figure of Perkeo stands on the wall of the vat room.

109. **Ideogram**: Ch'üan [M1650], "dog." Here Canis Major or Sirius the dogstar.

110. **Eos**: Dawn or Venus at Dawn [cf. *Pai*, 5-1, 45].

111. **Jones**: The lieutenant who was the provost officer at the DTC.

112. **man and dog**: Prob. the constellation Orion and the dogstar, Sirius, the brightest in the sky.

113. **bloke in the . . .** : The ideogram should be placed after "the" as object of the preposition "in".

114. **Kuan Chung**: *Analects* XIV, 18, 2: "He said: Kwan Chung . . . aided Duke Hwan as prime minister. . . . But for Kwan Chung we'd be wearing our hair loose and buttoning our coats to the left" [*CON*, 257]. Legge has a note interpreting this passage: "The sentiment of Confucius is, that but for Kwan Chung, his countrymen would have sunk to the state of the rude tribes about them" [Legge, 202].

115. **ma/cosi . . . maligno**: I, "But thus I descended through the malignant air" [*Inf.* V, 1].

116. **on doit . . . vient**: F, "One must take the weather as it comes" [*Inf.* V, 86].

117. **take the sheep out . . .** : [79:42]; "g.r." is "gentle reader."

118. **leaving America**: He landed in Gibralter, after a trip on a cattleboat, with $80 and (so he said in notes written to L. Untermeyer) "lived on the interest for some time" [NS, *Life*, 45].

119. **Thomas Hardy**: 1840-1928, English poet and novelist to whom Pound in 1908 sent a copy of *A Lume Spento*. The letter he took from England contained Hardy's objection to Pound's title: "Homage to Sextus Propertius." He would have preferred something like "Propertius Soliloquizes." Note the diminuendo: $80 → letter → pip. Or is it a crescendo? [HK].

120. **"a S. . . . sembianza**: I, With a couple

of changed endings we can read: "At St. Bartholomew's I saw myself with the little boy, / Who was nailed to the ground with his arms spread apart / in the form of a cross. He groaned and said, 'I am the moon.' With his feet on a silver scythe / he seemed to me to have a pitiful look" [cf. *Pai*, 1-2, 210].

121. S. Bartolomeo: The church in the town of S.B. in Galdo, S Italy.

122. the young Dumas . . . : When asked if by young Dumas he meant himself, Pound said that he didn't: he meant young Dumas [King, "Steele, " 59]. Says HK: "He told me it was Dumas the younger, who said, 'Je pleure parce que j'ai des larmes.' "

123. semina motuum: L, "seeds of motion." A recurrent leitmotif that will occur frequently in later cantos [90:24].

124. hagoromo: Several lines around this word involve the plot of the Noh play by the same name [74:124]. Nautili are seashells.

125. At Ephesus: She (Diana) was the patron of silversmiths, who made silver shrines in her honor. But the zeal of St. Paul affected their livelihood. Acts 19.24-28 tells the story of how the silversmiths rebelled and cried out, saying, "Great is Diana of the Ephesians."

126. paraclete: [74:93].

127. Monte Gioiosa: Prob. town on N coast of Sicily named Giojosa: "Mount Joy."

128. Allegre: [Frags./802]. Mont'allegre, above Rapallo, now reached by a funicular. Pound once saw a whole field of larks rise there [HK].

129. Cythera egoista: L, "Aphrodite"; I, "selfish."

130. Actaeon: He received the wrath of Diana [4:12].

131. Fano Caesaris: [9:3] Roman colony built at an ancient Etruscan site by Caesar Augustus and named after an ancient *Fanum Fortunae* ("Temple of Fortune") there. The Malatestas possessed it for a while but it was later annexed by the Pope. Cesare Borgia founded there a printing press, which did books in Greek, Hebrew, Latin, and Italian [30:12].

132. olim de: L, "Formerly of" [9:3].

133. wan: Wên [M7129]. In *Analects* IX, 5, 2; Pound translates as "the precise knowledge" [*CON*, 229].

134. caritas: L, "love, esteem."

135. ΧΑΡΙΤΕΣ: H, "the Graces."

136. like an arrow: Pound gives *Analects* XV, 6.1 as: "He said: Straight, and how! the historian Yu. Country properly governed, he was like an arrow; country in chaos he was like an arrow" [*CON*, 264; CB-R, *ZBC*, 106].

137. Ade du: A pun: G, *Ade du* and F, *Adieu*, "farewell." From British war song "Tipperary".

138. Piccadilly: Famous square in London.

139. Lesterplatz: German for Leicester Square in London.

140. Bellotti: Owner of Bellotti's Ristorante Italiano, 12 Old Compton Street, London, where Pound and friends congregated, 1910-1920.

141. "There is no darkness . . . ": A quotation from *Twelfth Night* IV, ii, 45-47 engraved on the sculpture of Shakespeare in Leicester Square. The bard is leaning on a pile of books and pointing to the quote on the pedestal. In the play the clown says: "Madman, thou errest: I say, there is no darkness but ignorance; in which thou are more puzzled than the Egyptians in their fog." The reader should ponder the line carefully as it is at the heart of Pound's monism and light-philosophy. Divinity manifests as the light descending and reveals itself as intelligence in man [*CON*, 20]. Darkness is not different from light but the absence of light.

142. Lady de X: Lady Grey [RO], apparently one of the many lady friends of Edward while he was the Prince of Wales. The "he" of "he sd" is old Bellotti telling of incidents at his restaurant.

143. Caressor's: The Prince who is about to become Edward VII.

144. 3 penny bits: An ironically small gratuity.

145. Rothschild: Since it's a memory of Bellotti covering many years, it might have been any one of several English Rothschilds in a moment of distraction. Most of the time all, except for the early Nathan R., gave very large gratuities.

146. DeLara: Prob. Isidore de Lara, 1858-1935, the English composer.

147. risotto: I, Milanese rice dish requiring saffron.

148. Sam Johnson's: Dr. Johnson's *The Plays of William Shakespeare*, 1765, and subsequent English editions based on his work do not have the lines of the clown [cf. 141 above].

149. Julius Caesar: Act III, sc. ii.

150. Rubicon: Caesar crossed the Rubicon (present day Urgone) in 49 B.C. Sigismundo M. of Rimini erected a stone pedestal in honor of the event in an old forum now named Piozza Giulio Cesare. Nearby is the Arco d' Augusto (Arch of Augustus).

151. Rimini: [24:2].

152. Augustus: First Roman emperor, who ruled 27 B.C.-A.D. 14.

153. H. Cole: Horace de Vere C., 1874-1935, "the country's most eminent practical joker, who claimed descent from Old King Cole" [Holroyd, *John*, 406], friend of the painter Augustus John. The dialogue is one Cole reported took place between him and John, the "he" of "thought he wd / ." Holroyd wrote of Cole: "He was a commanding figure, with needle blue eyes, a mane of classic white hair, bristling upswept moustaches and the carriage of a regimental sergeant-major. . . . What John liked about Cole was his way of repunctuating life with absurdity. . . . When John learnt how Cole, dressed as 'the Anglican Bishop of Madras,' had confirmed a body of Etonians, he laughed out loud. But when Cole took some of John's drawings, sat in the street with them all day in front of the National Gallery, and having collected a few coppers, came back with the explanation that this was their value on the open market, John was less amused" [ibid., 536]. Pound's memories of several practical jokes played by Cole are the substance of the next 15 lines.

154. Innes: George Inness, 1825-1894, American landscape painter and member of the Hudson River School, or his son George, 1854-1926, also a painter.

155. Zanzibar: The then British protectorate of Tanganyika, E Africa. Holroyd said: "A young friend . . . Horace de Vere Cole, who, in the guise of Sultan of Zanzibar had ceremonially inspected Cambridge, now . . . recommended a castle in Spain. 'I met the Sultan of Zanzibar in Bond Street yesterday,' Augustus reported . . . " [ibid., 286].

156. Kardomah: A chain. There are dozens of Kardomah tea rooms in London.

157. Soho: A district in West End, London, famous as the haunt of bohemians in the manner of Greenwich Village in New York or the Left Bank in Paris.

158. Italy's entry: Italy declared war on Germany and Austria on May 23, 1915.

159. Napper . . . Gaddy: Pound used the old Remington typewriter in the medical tent. These trainees pass him on the way tc sick call.

160. belladonna: A medicine prescribed for control of acid conditions and stomach ulcers.

161. Achilles: Achille Ratti, 1857-1939, who became Pope Pius XI. Pound's prose references to him were favorable [*GK*, 179, 185, 189]. Pound knew him when he was librarian of the Ambrosiana in Milan [HK, *Era*, 114].

162. **Hannibal**: Carthaginian general [9:72].

163. **Hamilcar**: H. Barca, 270-228 B.C. Carthaginian general [40:31] who commanded in Sicily, 247-241, and in Spain, 237-228; the father of Hannibal [cf. 162 above].

164. **"Jolly woman"**: The landlady is still, and happily forever, unidentified.

165. **old Kait**: Prob. the heroine of the Alfred Venison (pen name used by Pound in mid-30s) poem "Ole Kate," the charwoman who "died on the job" and "Fell plump into her pail" [*P*, 271].

166. **Gt Tichfield**: Venison was called "the Post of Titchfield Street" [*P*, 257].

167. **sacerdos**: L, "priest."

168. **Ixion**: A man from Thessaly who courted Hera, the wife of Zeus; for his effrontery he was condemned to eternal torment on a wheel in hell.

169. **Trinacrian**: Davie wrote: " 'Trinacria,' the ancient Greek name for Sicily, is related to the legend of how Vulcan . . . solved the problem of perpetual motion by a wheel with three dog-leg spokes: its never ceasing to roll recalling the wheel that was the hellish and interminable torment of Ixion. (The same three-spoked wheel is the heraldic emblem of the Isle of Man.)"

170. **manxman**: A native of the Isle of Man.

171. **Sauter**: George S., 1866-1937, a Bavarian portrait painter who lived in London, 1895-1915. He was one of the sponsors of the International Society of Sculptors, Painters and Gravers founded in 1898. Whistler was its first president and Sauter acted as its honorary secretary for some time. He lived in Kensington near Pound [Fang, III, 133].

172. **Bismark**: Otto von B. [48:17].

173. **Von Moltke**: Helmuth Karl Bernard, Graf von Moltke, 1800-1891, Prussian field marshal. He was responsible for the successes of the Prussian army in the Danish War (1864) and the Austro-Prussian War (1866) and the Franco-Prussian War (1870-71).

174. **Boer war**: British war against the Boers of South Africa, 1899-1902.

175. **Whistler**: James Abbott McNeill W., 1834-1903, the American painter who became a sort of lion in London toward the end of the century. His work was much honored by Pound [*GK*, 110, 180-181; *SP*, 24, 115-117, 124, 418].

176. **Sarasate**: Pablo Martin Meliton Sarasate y Navascues, 1844-1908, a Spanish violinist whose portrait was done by Whistler. The protrait entitled *Arrangement in Black: Señor Pablo Sarasate* (now in Carnegie Institute, Pittsburgh) centers on the violin, and according to Whistler "all is balanced by the bow."

177. **Ysaÿe**: Eugene Y., 1858-1931, a violin virtuoso from Belgium. It was he who, on seeing the painting, said, "What a fiddle!" [Fang, III, 134].

178. **Homer**: Said Pound: "The sheer literary qualities in Homer are such that a physician has written a book to prove that Homer must have been an army doctor" [*ABCR*, 43].

179. **Holland Park**: The site of Holland House on Kensington Road in London.

180. **Mr Leber**: Prob. Albert Leber, a confectioner of Notting Hill in Kensington, London, 1915. The name of the shop, mentioned again [80/504] is not known. He was apparently a harmless German victimized by wartime hysteria.

181. **Dulac**: Edmund D., 1882-1953, French artist and illustrator who was disgusted with the senseless beatings.

182. **navvy**: British term for construction worker or longshoreman: brawn without brains is often implied.

183. **Church St.**: A street in the Royal

Borough of Kensington, London, in a court off which Pound lived (1909-1914).

184. ne povans desraciner: OF, "not being able to uproot."

185. Tosch: Like "Spot," a common name for a dog.

186. Tolosa: [76:21]. But Pound may mean Toulouse, a city in France which he visited in April 1919.

187. "Willy": Henri Gauthier-Villars, 1859-1931, French novelist, essayist, and biographer, known to his friends as "Willy" [78:70].

188. papa Dulac: The father of Edmund D. [181 above]. Concerning a postcard sent from Toulouse, April 24, 1919, Dorothy Pound wrote in 1970: "Papa Dulac found us a room and gave us many meals. . . . We stayed many weeks and took walks from this center" [HK].

189. Leber's: [cf. 180 above].

190. Colonel Jackson: Joseph Jackson. Said Pound: "Note, when I got to London the men who were old *enough* were all right. Col. Jackson . . . represented something hearty . . . something that Palmerston might have recognized as appertaining to men" [*GK*, 227]. A John Wayne type.

191. Gaudier: G-Brzeska [16:26].

192. "mes compliments": F, "my compliments."

193. la Patrie: F, "the Fatherland" (Gaudier was French).

194. Ulster: [cf. 58 above].

195. "la bonne . . . soldat": F, "good soup makes a good soldier."

196. Yeats: [74:166].

197. Dolmetsch: Arnold D., 1858-1940, French musician and instrument maker, especially of early stringed and key instruments, whom Pound honored for years. See "Arnold Dolmetsch" [*LE*, 431-436] and "Vers Libre and Arnold Dolmetsch" [ibid., 437-440]. [81:48].

198. "Il est . . . pain": F, "It is good as bread." Proverbial: "It is as good as gold.".

199. Mockel: Editor of *La Wallonie* [78:71].

200. Willy: [cf. 187 above].

201. Gauthier: "Willy."

202. Dial: American literary magazine, 1880-1929. Pound recalls Mockel wanting to get "Willy" to contribute to it.

203. Gluck: Christoph Willibald G., 1714-1787, best known for his operas such as *Iphigénie en Tauride*.

204. Les moeurs . . . reste: F, "Customs go and pain remains."

205. "En casque . . . ": F, "In pink crystal helmets the mountebanks" [78:72].

206. Mallarmé: Stéphane M., 1842-1898, French symbolist poet.

207. Whistler: [see 175 above].

208. Charles Condor: C. Conder, 1868-1909, English decorative painter, described as "a wistful, tentative, ailing man, his hair luxuriant but lifelessly hanging, a brown lock perpetually over one malicious blue eye, who admitted, in a voice exhausted to the point of inaudibility, to being a little 'gone at the knees' " [Holroyd, *John*, 92]. This year he was 31.

209. Degas: [74:226].

210. Follies: [74:221].

211. Manet: [74:219].

212. 'La Concorde': Place de la Concorde, central square of the Tuilleries, Paris.

213. Judith: J. Gautier, 1850-1917, French poet and novelist, the daughter of Théophile Gautier. Her junk shop was her apartment located at 30 rue Washington. She was the only woman member of the Académie Goncourt [77:143]. She lived "with her monkeys, her bibelots (Chinese, Hindu, and prehistoric) and her cats" [Fang, II, 193]. The junk shop and bricabrac are mentioned earlier [76:48].

214. Ca s'appelle . . . : F, "That is called an attic."

215. Rue Jacob: Street on the Left Bank in Paris where for 60 years the house of Natalie Barney at number 20 was a landmark.

216. à l'Amitié: F, "to friendship." Refers to "Temple à l'Amitié," a small Doric gazebo in the garden of Natalie's elegant Parisian townhouse [Sieburth, *Instigations*, 15].

217. M. Jean: J. Cocteau [74:246].

218. École Militaire: F, "Military School." The building on the Champ-de-Mars, Paris, used as the French General Staff College.

219. "Il me paraît . . .": Repeat of anecdote about Maritain [77:138].

220. Natalie: N. Clifford Barney, 1876-1972, one of the most famous of the American expatriate writers, whose salon was a center of literary activity, especially during the 20s and 30s. She was known as "the Amazon," a sobriquet which inspired Rémy de Gourmont's *Lettres à L'Amazone*. Pound knew her first in pre-WWI visits to Paris, and since she was a close friend of Gourmont, he tried to arrange publications of his work in English as early as 1913. Since she was possessed of some wealth, Pound persuaded her to support some of his causes and authors such as "Bel Esprit," Valéry, George Antheil, etc.

221. apache . . . : The male apache of a bistro (nightclub) dance team who was purported to treat his partner violently, throwing her about the stage with sadistic intent. They were, and still are, popular tourist attractions. Since Miss Barney never went out to cafés, she may have imported such a team to entertain at her salon one evening.

222. vous êtes . . . : F, "You are very badly brought up." Implying it is "ill-mannered" to treat a lady in such a way.

223. Tiens . . . : F, "Look, she's telling you."

224. jambe-de-bois: F, "wooden leg," meaning "The man with. . . ."

225. "Entrez . . . monde": F, "Enter, then, go on in / it is everybody's house." Prob. Natalie's welcome to arriving guests.

226. H. Liveright: Horace Brisbin L., 1886-1933, American publisher and theatrical producer who, with Albert Boni, founded the firm of Boni and Liveright in 1918.

227. vers le Noël: F, "around Christmas." This visit was prob. after WWI.

228. three small boys . . . : The anecdote of the smacked young fanny (the incident occurred in Pound's presence according to M de R) was a story Natalie told of her early days in Paris. Her salon was known as a place liberated in talk and morals. She was famous as a writer: "But her reputation is due even more to the emancipated ideas by which she lived and to the personal magnetism which she exercised in her many love affairs. She was unquestionably the most candid, the most daring, and the most famous lesbian of her time . . . if they [younger people] listened, they might be surprised by her witty and unconventional remarks" [Wickes, *American Writers in Paris*, 23, 24].

229. ce sont les . . . : F, "These are the morals of Lutèce." *Lutetia Parisiorum* was the ancient name for Paris.

230. Le Musée de Cluny: The Cluny Museum. A 14th-15th-century Gothic and Renaissance structure in the Left Bank, Saint-Germain des Prés district, on the Boulevard St.-Michel. Built by the abbot of Cluny, it houses medieval and Renaissance art objects and curios.

231. teatro romano: I, "Roman theater."

232. Uncle William: W. B. Yeats [77:163].

233. **Ronsard**: Pierre de R., 1524-1585, a French poet and leader of the Pléiade. Earlier, Yeats had done his "When you are old . . . " on one of Ronsard's *Sonnets pour Hélène*.

234. **the ink's heir**: Eugene Ullman, 1877-1953 (whose father manufactured ink for printers), did a portrait of Pound around 1912 which was used as a frontispiece in Donald Davie's *Poet as Sculptor* [OP].

235. **Monsieur C.**: Cocteau [cf. 217 above].

236. **La Falange**: Prob. *La Phalange*, the Parisian literary magazine. Or possibly money paid to the Spanish Falangists [M de R].

237. **Arnold Bennett**: Enoch A. B., 1867-1931, English novelist.

238. **old Carolus**: Charles Auguste Emile Carolus-Duran, ?1837-1917, French portrait and genre painter.

239. **"vous . . . toile?"**: F, "Are you going to shave a canvas?" In a 1955 letter about the female nude in painting Pound described an event of 1912 in Paris. The authorities felt that three paintings of Carrière needed retouching because they were *too* nude. So he "putt on a few dabs of pastel." While he was doing it, Durand passed by and said, "Ah Monsieur, vous allez raser une toile?!" [Kimpel, *Pai*, 10-2, 308].

240. **Puvis**: Pierre Puvis de Chavannes, 1824-1898, French muralist. Some of his best work is in the Sorbonne and the Panthéon.

241. **Carrière**: Eugène C., 1849-1906, French painter and lithographer; known for his portrait of Verlaine and for decorations in the Sorbonne.

242. **o-hon dit quelque fois au vi'age**: Recurrent phrase [29:30; 78:64]: "It is sometimes said in the village."

243. **Brisset**: Anecdote repeated [27:10, 11].

244. **Romains**: Jules R., pseudonym of Louis Farigoule, 1885-1972, French poet and novelist who invented unanimism.

245. **Vildrac**: Charles V., pseudonym of Charles Messager, 1882-1971, French essayist, critic, poet, dramatist, and author of children's books.

246. **Chennevière**: Georges C., 1884-1927, French poet.

247. **Quand . . . vieille**: F, "When you are very old." A line from *Sonnets pour Hélène* [II, 42] which inspired Yeats poem that starts, "When you are old and grey and full of sleep."

248. **mia pargoletta**: I, "my little girl." The phrase may be addressed to Pound's daughter, Mary. The manuscripts of the Pisan Cantos were sent directly to her to make clean copies for the publisher.

249. **Jugoslavian**: Yugoslavian.

250. **Schlag**: G, a Viennese idiom, "with whipped cream." Used to garnish Vienna coffee.

251. **that café**: The Vienna Café [cf. 255 below].

252. **Mr Lewis**: Percy Wyndham L. [78:40].

253. **Mr Binyon**: Laurence B., 1869-1943, English poet, keeper of the prints and drawings, British Museum, authority on Oriental art, and translator of Dante. His *Flight of the Dragon* [1911] made a big impression on Pound [*Pai*, 3-1, 94-100].

254. **Penthesilea**: Binyon's narrative poem in two parts ("The Coming of the Amazons" and "The Battle"), which concerns the battle between the queen of the Amazons (Penthesilia) and Achilles and dramatizes her defeat by the Greek hero. Pound heard the story from one of Binyon's three daughters (prodigies) and was prompted to hunt the story up at the British Museum. He wrote "demme if I remember anything but a word, one name, Penthesilia, and that not from reading it, but from hearing it spoken

by a precocious Binyonian offspring" [*PE*, 29].

255. WIENER CAFÉ: The Vienna Café at the corner of Oxford and Hart streets. Wyndham Lewis wrote: "When the Belgian fortresses fell to the 'Hun,' the Vienna Café tottered and fell, too. For it was staffed and owned entirely by Germans, or Austrians, 'Alien enemies.' It would not have survived under all-British management. So it became a Bank" [Lewis, *Blasting*, 280]. Lewis first met Pound there ca. 1910.

256. Jozefff: Prob. a waiter at the Vienna Café who returned to Austria to follow Emperor Franz Joseph.

257. Neptune: Name for Sturge Moore [HK].

258. Laomedon: Thomas Sturge Moore's *The Rout* (Pound recalls *Defeat*) *of the Amazons* (1903) opens with these lines: "*Faun*: Ahi, ahi, ahi, Laomedon! / *Laomedon*: It is the faun: He is in sore dismay: / That shrewd 'ah ee' denoteth grief or pain." The sonority of the lines so impressed Pound that he refers to them in an early article on Dante [*SR*, 161; rpt. *PE*, 205].

259. Mr Newbolt: Sir Henry John N. [12:5, 74:171]. His "A Ballad of John Nicholson" contained inversions Pound couldn't endure: "the captains passed in silence forth / And stood the door behind." He indicates profane thoughts about the line in a piece on Harold Monro: "*But* . . . (blanks left for profanity) . . . it, Hewlett, look at the line: 'He stood the door behind.' " [*PE*, 11].

260. cummings: e. e. cummings [74:157].

261. meum . . . in tabernam: L, "it is my intention . . . [to die, *mori*] in a tavern." First 2 lines of stanza 12 of the Goliardic confession poem *Estuans intrinsecus* (Burning up inside) attributed to the so-called Archpoet of the Middle Ages, included in the *Carmina Burana* [JW].

262. Chinese food . . . débacle: This seeming nonsequitur has a Poundian logic about it: Any country so backward and uncivilized as not to have a Chinese restaurant is due for disaster.

263. Mr Bridges: Robert B., 1844-1930, English poet who became laureate in 1913. Pound said: "Anecdote: years ago when I was just trying to find and use modern speech, old Bridges carefully went through *Personae* and *Exultations* and commended every archaism (to my horror), exclaiming 'We'll git em all back; we'll git em *all* back' " [*L*., 179].

264. Furnivall: Frederick James F., 1825-1910, English scholar and philologist who edited the *Oxford English Dictionary* in the beginning (1861), founded the Early English Text Society, the Chaucer Society, etc.

265. Dr. Weir Mitchell: Dr. Silas W. M., 1829-1914, a noted neurologist and man of letters from Philadelphia. Pound prob. met him when young and approved some of his cultural projects, such as a Chaucer dictionary and the Franklin Inn Club, of which he was the guiding spirit and president from its foundation in 1902 until his death. He invented the "phantom limb" concept to describe the sense people have of an amputated limb still being there.

266. old William: W. B. Yeats [74:166]. His poem "Upon a House Shaken by the Land Agitation" contains the contention.

267. Gesell: [74:368].

268. Mabel: Mabel Beardsley, 1872-1913, sister of Aubrey B.

269. Sligo in Heaven: [77:162]. Sligo was one of Yeats's favorite places.

270. old "da": John Butler Yeats, 1839-1922, Irish artist, father of W. B. Yeats, who spent many years in New York. Pound said in a letter of 1915 to John Quinn: "I have still a very clear recollection of Yeats père on an elephant (at Coney Island), smiling like Elijah in the beatific vision, and of you plugging away in the shooting gallery" [*L*, 52].

271. **Mr John Quinn**: [12:18; 103:54].

272. **"Liquids and fluids!"**: The Cuala Press in May, 1917, published a 60-page book: *Passages from the Letters of John Butler Yeats, Selected by Ezra Pound*. Norman says, "old J. B. Yeats, who used to worry that his son would run off with a ballet dancer, had begun to worry that he would never run off with anyone. He began to frequent fortune tellers to learn, if possible, what his chances were of becoming a grandfather . . . " [CN, *Pound*, 203]. Conversation between the palmist and J. B. Yeats was prob. reported in one of these letters.

273. **Warren Dahler**: A painter Pound knew during his 1910-1911 months in New York, when he visited J. B. Yeats often. Dahler is seen as the discoverer of Patchin Place, where Cummings lived at no. 4 for many years after WWI. Pound wrote to Cummings in 1930: "Does a venerable figure called Dahler still live at No. 7 Pat. Pl?" [*L*, 228].

274. **Hier wohnt**: G, "Here lives."

275. **Whitman**: Just as the tradition lived on in Camden, N.J. while Walt Whitman lived there.

276. **596 Lexington**: Address of a rooming house, the home of Pound's maternal grandmother Mary Weston from about 1887-1892. Pound was shown many family relics there, including pictures [*PD*, 6-8, 12, 18-19; JW, *Pai*, 12-1, 55-87].

277. **24 E. 47th**: Address of boardinghouse in New York that belonged to Pound's great uncle Ezra B. Weston and his wife Frances Amelia (Aunt Frank) Weston. Pound lived there as a boy [JW, *Pai* 12-1, 55-87].

278. **Jim**: [74:461].

279. **Aunt F.**: Aunt Frank. The Windsor Hotel, on Fifth Avenue between 46th and 47th streets, burned down March 7, 1899. Hence the time of her remark to Jim, the black servant boy, and prob. Pound, aged 13 [ibid.].

280. **Regents Park**: Regent's Park, London.

281. **Alma-Tadema**: Sir Lawrence Alma-Tadema, 1836-1912, English painter who lived at no. 34 Grove End Road on the west of Regent's Park. The "maison" was beautified "with a series of panels by eminent artists, and many other works of art" [Fang, II, 92].

282. **Leighton House**: The residence of Frederick, Lord Leighton, 1830-1896, at 12 Holland Park Road: "The beautiful Arab Hall, in the centre of which is a fountain, is decorated with Saracenic and Persian tiles, mainly of the 16th cent." [ibid., 93].

283. **Selsey**: The town, near the tip of Selsey Bill, S coast of England, where Ford Madox Ford and Violet Hunt lived and Pound used to visit. But after the Ford-Hunt separation, she packed the memorabilia away.

284. **Swinburne**: The story as told by Ford is that a cabby appeared and said to a housemaid, "I've got your master very drunk in my keb." Finally she said, "That's Mr. Swinburne. Help me carry him upstairs and put him in the bath" [*Portraits from Life*, New York, 1937, 186-187]. Pound refers to the story more obliquely in "Swinburne Versus Biographers" [*Poetry*, March 1918].

285. **Tennyson**: Pound said about him: "When he began to write for Viccy's [Victoria's] ignorant ear, he immediately ceased to be the 'Tennyson so muzzy that he tried to go out through the fireplace' " [*LE*, 276].

286. **Miss Braddon**: Mary Elizabeth B., 1837-1915, a prolific writer of sensational novels. She was admired by Thackeray and Stevenson. Fordie is Ford M. Ford who, being poor, marvelled at scenes of wealth.

287. **Richmond**: A suburb of London inhabited by people of wealth.

288. **Périgueux**: Capital of Dordogne department, SW France. The Cathédrale St-Front there [cf. "Provincia Deserta"]

may have reminded Pound of New York skyscrapers.

289. si com' ad Arli: I, "just as at Arles." So Dante describes the high walls of the "City of Dis" [*Inf.* IX, 112].

290. sarascen: The walls of Dis enclosed a vast cemetery. Arles, France, is the site of the famous Aliscans (Alyschamps; Elysian Fields) cemetery for warriors against the Saracens.

291. "Surrender of Breda": [cf. 19 above].

292. Velásquez: [cf. 15 above].

293. Avignon: The seat of popes from 1309 to 1377 and, after them, two antipopes. In the porch of the cathedral Notre-Dame des Doms at A., there are "dilapidated frescoes by Simone Martini" [Fang, II, 320].

294. y cavals armatz: P, "and horses all armed" [7:10].

295. "Me Hercule!": L, "By Hercules!"

296. c'est nôtre comune: F, "It's our bailiwick."

297. "Borr": Dialect pronunciation of Born, ancestral town in French Périgord of troubadour Bertran de Born, whose family moved to the castle of Altafort (Hautefort) when his brother married into the Delastours family [JW].

298. Ventadour: [6:29; 27:35; 74:73].

299. Aubeterre: [76:76]. Visited on the 1911 walking tour.

300. Unkle George: G. Holden Tinkham [74:180]. Pound visited Monte Grappa near the Piave with him [M de R].

301. sul Piave: I, "on the Piave." A river in NE Italy.

302. Volpe: Giuseppe Volpi [76:191].

303. Lido Excelsior: Excelsior Palace Hotel on the island Lido off Venice [76:192].

304. Florian's: Café on the south side of St. Mark's square in Venice [76:95].

305. Sir Ronald: R. Storrs, 1881-1955, British administrator and historian.

306. the Negus: Title of Haile Selassie, the sovereign of Ethiopia.

307. Menelik: [18:27]. For the gold bars in the palace, see "Sammy's nevvy" [104:24].

308. Alessandria: Alexandria. Pound's memories of his 1898 visit to Tangiers with his Aunt Frank evoke memories of data in Pea's novel.

309. Pea: Enrico P., 1881-1952, Pound translated his novel *Moscardino* and said: "the only time in my life that I have ever wanted to translate a novel" [*SP*, 318]. Pea tells about his talks with Pound while they worked together: "I was able to tell him how I made iron-bound wooden chests for the Ottoman Bank, for the shipment of gold sovereigns overseas; and, when the Anglo-Egyptian Bank sumptuously renewed its premises . . . how I had supplied the desks of red mahogany at a price of £60 each" [Pea, *Moscardino*, New Directions, 1955, 5].

310. Whitcomb Riley: James W. R., 1849-1916, an American poet whose dialectical sounds appealed to Pound from his earliest school days: some of his own juvenilia was written in the manner of Riley.

311. Nancy: N. Cunard, 1896-1965, poetess and wealthy patron of the arts visible in all the expected places in the 20s and 30s. In 1934, Pound contributed a piece on Frobenius to a book she edited called *Negro Anthology* [NS, *Life*, 322]. Both she and her money were valuable to many a struggling artist and poet. Her Hours Press was the first publisher of *A Draft of XXX Cantos* [HK].

312. Whither . . . cisclatons: Based on the passage from chapter 6 of *Aucassin and Nicolette,* which Pound likes in Andrew Lang's version. The lover says he doesn't want to join the "priests and halt old men" in paradise but rather he'll head toward hell where goodly knights and ladies go and where "goes the gold, and the silver, and cloth of vair, and cloth of gris" ("et s'i va li ors et li argens et li vairs et li gris"). Pound said Lang was born to translate the book [*SR*, 84]. The opening of "Blandula, Tenella, Vagula" comes from the Lang version [*P*, 39].

313. **vair**: P, "varicolored furs."

314. **cisclatons**: P, "rich silk gowns."

315. **Excideuil**: Town in SW France [29:40].

316. **Mt Segur**: [23:25].

317. **Dioce**: [74:8].

318. **Que . . . lune**: F, "that every month we have a new moon."

319. **Herbiet**: Georges H., French poet who, in 1921 under the name of "Christian," translated Pound's "Moeurs Contemporaines" for the Dadaist journal *391* [105/746].

320. **Fritz**: F. Vanderpyl [7:22].

321. **treize . . . Lussac**: F, "13, Gay-Lussac Street." On the left bank. A circular stone bas-relief of Fritz is still visible on the balcony [HK].

322. **Orage**: Alfred Richard O. [46:17].

323. **Fordie**: Ford Madox Ford [74:165].

324. **Crevel**: René C. [41:35].

325. **de . . . vengan**: S, "out of my solitude let them come." From poem by Lope de Vega [cf. *SR*, 208].

326. **Rossetti**: Dante Gabriel R., 1828-1882, English painter and poet who was the founder and leader of the Pre-Raphaelite school. He found remaindered copies of Fitzgerald's *Rubàiyat* in a secondhand book shop. Pound mentions the discovery in several places: "Yeux Glauques" [*P*, 192; *ABCR*, 79-80].

327. **Cythera**: Here the planet Venus [Peck, *Pai*, 1-1, 9]. When Pound was at Pisa, the planet was bright in the autumn sky. Here he sees it with a crescent moon [Flory, *Pai*, 5-1, 46].

328. **Münch**: Gerhardt M. [75:2]. The anecdote suggests the Kommandant was a German in Italy because of the pronunciation of Puccini as "Spewcini."

329. **man seht**: G, "one sees."

330. **Les hommes . . . beauté**: F, "Men have I don't know what strange fear / . . .of beauty."

331. **Beardsley**: [74:410].

332. **Yeats**: W. B. Yeats [74:166]. Yeats tells the anecdote about beauty. "I said to him once, 'you have never done anything to equal your Salome with the head of John the Baptist.' I think that for the moment he was sincere when he replied, 'Yes, yes; but beauty is so difficult' " [*The Autobiography*, Anchor A142, p. 223].

333. **Burne-Jones**: Sir Edward B.-J., 1833-1898, English painter and decorator, strongly influenced by the Rossettis and an exponent of Pre-Raphaelite principles.

334. **Arthur**: A. Symons, 1865-1945, British poet and critic, author of *The Symbolist Movement in Literature*. His poem "Modern Beauty" has lines Pound always liked: "I am the torch, she saith, and what to me / If the moth die of me? I am the flame / of Beauty, and I burn that all may see."

335. *βροδοδάκτυλος* *'Ηώς*: H, "rosy-fingered dawn" [74:403].

336. *Κύθηρα δεινὰ*: H, "Fearful Cythera." Aphrodite, or here the planet Venus, which on this Pisan dawn appeared to be in the arms of the crescent moon [cf. 327 above].

337. **Sandro**: S. Botticelli [20:19].

338. **Jacopo**: J. Sellaio [20:17].

339. **Velásquez**: [cf. 15 above].

340. **Rembrandt**: R. Harmenszoon van Rijn, 1606-1669, Dutch painter.

341. **Rubens**: Peter Paul R., 1577-1640, Flemish painter.

342. Jordaens: Jacob J., 1593-1678, Flemish painter. All the names in this passage denote painters of Venus [HK, *Era*, 363-365]. For painters of our time [cf. 349 below] we have Cocteau (a hermaphrodite), a prepubescent girl, and 3 fat ladies [HK].

343. "This alone . . . the all: Chu Hsi comments on the opening lines of *Chung Yung* and says, among other things: "The main thing is to illumine the root of process. . . . The components, the bones of things, the materials are implicit" [*CON*, 99]. Fang is at a loss to see how Pound could derive leather from the characters but proposes a possibility: "it may . . . be conjectured that he either interpreted the lower part of *ku* as 'flesh' . . . or the lower part of *li* as 'bean' . . . which is conspicuous by the shell (i.e., leather)" [Fang, IV, 118].

344. *τὸ πᾶν*: H, "the whole, the all."

345. Chu Hsi: (rhymes with "juicy"), 1130-1200, Chinese philosopher and most important of the neo-Confucians of the southern Sung dynasty.

346. luz: [cf. 90 above]. This bone was considered the seed from which at the last judgment the whole physical body could be made to spring: a sort of medieval, eschatological cloning.

347. Sigismundo: Invokes Platina and the usual subject of conversation among intelligent men [11:26, 29].

348. Cocteau: [cf. 217 above].

349. Marie Laurencin: 1885-1956, French painter and illustrator. She did the 6 color plates for *Alice in Wonderland* [Black Sun Press, 1930]. The painting of Cocteau is mentioned by Nina Hammet [*Laughing Torso*, London, 1932], who saw it at the salon of Cocteau's mother [p. 190].

350. Whistler: [cf. 175 above].

351. Miss Alexander: Miss Cecily Henrietta A. In 1872 Whistler did a full-length standing portrait of her and entitled it *Arrangement in Grey Green: Miss Alexander* [Fang, III, 144].

352. Sargent: John Singer S., 1856-1925, an American painter who did a number of paintings of three ladies together, with an occasional fat one—but none in which all the ladies can be called fat.

353. Rodenbach: Georges R., 1855-1898, Belgian poet of the symbolist group. The painting was done by Levy-Dhurmer [HK, *Era*, 479].

354. L'Ile St Louis: F, "St. Louis Island." One of the islands in the Seine at Paris.

355. Abélard: Peter A., 1079-1142, French philosopher and teacher who was such a favorite that "to hear him, his pupils crossed the Petit Pont by thousands." The Rodenbach self-portrait indicated places the poet at the center: "its background consists of a bridge, several gabled houses, two spires, but not trees" [Fang, III, 135]. But the bridge may have reminded Pound of the Petit Pont, which may be called Abélard's bridge.

356. Elysium: In Greek mythology, the Islands of the Blessed.

357. *πάντα ῥεῖ*: H, "Everything flows." As the sage Heraclitus says [*GK*, 31, 79, etc.]. Pound associates the Greek aphorism with the Confucian process [96:168].

358. rain altars . . . parapets: *Analects* XII, 21, 1 says: "Fan Ch'ih walking with him below the rain altars . . . said: 'Venture to ask how to lift one's conscience in action' " [*CON*, 247].

359. Aliscans: [cf. 290 above].

360. Mt Segur: [cf. 316 above].

361. Spencer: H. Spencer, Pound's instructor at the Cheltenham Military Academy. Pound said: "A fellow named Spenser [sic] recited a long passage of *Iliad* to me, after tennis. That was worth more than grammar when one was 13 years old" [*GK*, 145].

362. **Bill Shepard**: William Pierce Shepard, 1870-1948, professor of romance languages at Hamilton College who was Pound's teacher 1903-1905.

363. **Siracusa**: [77:52].

364. *ὑπὲρ μόρον*: H, "beyond what is destined." A recurrent phrase in Homer. Perhaps here because of the word γλαυκῶπις used several times in the Pisan and earlier cantos; it come from *Od.* V, 536-537. The island attacked may be Ismarus of the Cicones [79:39].

365. **with a mind**: Speaking of savoir-faire in translating, Pound said about "polumetis" [9:38, 78:119]: "And as Zeus said: 'A chap with a mind like THAT! The fellow is one of us. One of US' " [*GK*, 146].

366. **Favonus, . . . benigno**: L, "west wind." I, "with kindly breeze."

367. **Je suis . . . forces**: F, "I am at the end of my tether." According to Wyndham Lewis, an expression frequently uttered by the owner of the Golden Calf Nightclub in London [EH].

368. **gates of death**: Pound means the gates of the DTC, but he adapts lines from the Bible taken from Speare's *Pocket Book*: "Have the gates of death been opened unto thee? Or hast thou seen the doors of the shadow of death" [Job 38.17].

369. **Whitman**: Walt W., 1819-1892, represented in Speare by 5 selections: "When Lilacs . . . ," "O Captain . . . ," "Mannahatta," "When I heard the Learn'd Astronomer" (8 lines), and "Out of the Cradle . . . " (complete).

370. **Lovelace**: Richard L., 1618-1658, represented in Speare by "To Althea, from Prison" and "To Lucasta, Going to the Wars."

371. **jo-house**: Latrine.

372. **Professor Speare**: Morris Speare, erstwhile editor of *The Pocket Book Of Verse*, New York, first published in 1940 but followed by many reprintings.

373. **the raft broke**: [*Od.* V, 365-369; 95:75].

374. **Immaculata, Introibo**: L, "Immaculate, I shall enter" (from preparation of the Roman Catholic Mass).

375. **Perpetua**: Saint Perpetua, d. 203, a Carthaginian martyr.

376. **Agatha**: Saint Agatha, 3d-century Sicilian virgin, martyred by Decius.

377. **Anastasia**: Saint Anastasia, 4th-century Roman noblewoman martyred under Diocletian. All 3 of these saints are recalled in the Mass.

378. **saeculorum**: L, "of the ages."

379. **repos donnez à**: F, "give rest to" (from Villon, "Grand Testament").

380. **cils**: OF, "those."

381. **senza termine funge**: I, "acts without end," from the end of Pound's Italian translation of *Chung Yung*. The passage reads: "The *unmixed* functions [in time and in space] without bourne. This unmixed is the tensile light, the Immaculata. There is no end to its action" [*CON*, 187]. The reader should note well. Here Pound states his perception of "the process" as the divine mystery in action.

382. **Immaculata Regina**: L, "Immaculate Queen" (from Roman Catholic Mass; the Virgin Mary).

383. **Les larmes . . . Tristesse**: F, "The tears that I created flood me / Late very late have I known your sadness" (from rondo after stanza 165 in "Grand Testament" of Villon)[cf. *SR*, 171-178].

384. **(Nadasky . . .)**: Soldiers whose names are called out to do KP duty or who line up for sick call.

385. **hieri**: I, *ieri*, "yesterday."

386. **no fortune**: A musical figure [1/4; 74:319].

387. **Bankers**: A corporal in the provost section, DTC.

388. Seitz: A captain in the provost section.

389. Hildebrand: Major in charge of post utilities.

390. Cornelison: Sergeant in provost section. Following names, unless identified, prob. soldiers at the DTC.

391. K.P.: Kitchen patrol.

392. gratia: L, "with thanks to." Pound seems to want to give thanks to these particular people at the DTC who helped make his imprisonment tolerable.

393. Bedell: Lieutenant in provost section.

394. africanus: L, "from Africa."

395. souterrain: F, "underground."

396. Carleton: Mark Alfred C., 1886-1925, agricultural scientist and cerealist who introduced hardy wheat strains from Russia and developed and introduced hardy and more productive groups of oat and barley seed, vastly increasing the yield per acre of these and other cereal grains. Internationally known expert in control of plant diseases. His work led to vast increases in the world food supply. In 1901 the French government recognized his service by creating him Chevalier du Merite Agricole. An inverse rhyme with usurers and "hoggers of harvest" [*SP*, 278-281; WB, *Pai*, 11-3, 442].

397. celebrate Christ: The lines may concern a mass with eucharist in memory of Carleton.

398. Demeter: Ceres [47:3] goddess of grain.

399. (Zupp, Bufford, and Bohon): Trainees at the DTC.

400. men of no fortune: [cf. 386 above].

401. Elpenor: [1:12].

402. Zoagli: [76:139].

403. Pepitone: Trainee.

404. o. t. a.: Of the army.

405. Oh . . . out: Paraphrase of the rhythms of Browning's "Home-Thoughts from Abroad" [Speare, 227].

406. Winston: W. Churchill [41:33]. *Time* reported the defeat of Churchill in 1945 as "the biggest electoral upset in British history" [Aug. 6, p. 38]. The Labor party of Clement Attlee was expected to nationalize the Bank of England.

407. the bank: The Bank of England. *Time* [Aug. 13, 1945] carried a note which encapsulated its history from 1694 to the moment: "But last week many an Englishman hearing Labor's Harold Laski demand the immediate nationalization of the Bank of England wondered how long it would stay what it has been for over two centuries—the world's most powerful private bank" [p. 82].

408. the tower: A tower at Lacock Abbey in Salisbury Plain which Ezra and Dorothy once visited. Dorothy said about the visit: "My aunt took me there a couple of times, and once Ezra and I crawled over the roof to a turret to see a copy of the Magna Charta, kept there in a glass case" [HK, *Pai*, 2-3, 492].

409. the old charter: The copy of the Magna Charta once at Lacock. It is technically an "Exemplification of Henry III's reissue of Magna Carta, 1225" [CFT, *Pai*, 5-1, 69-76].

410. John's first one: A document presented to King John by the nobility who wanted confirmation of their rights—as expressed by the so-called Coronation Charter of Henry I, of 1100—was called "The Articles of the Barons." With changes and emendments, the document the king signed became known as "The Charter of Runnymede" [ibid., 70].

411. and still there: So far as Pound knew; but ironically, in the year he was writing the Pisan Cantos (1945) the Charter was presented by Miss Matilda Talbot to the British Museum, where it is now.

412. Chesterton: [46:19] The lines seem to imply a crossroads. The new government *could* make money "free again" and return to the old England owned by right-wingers such as Chesterton [Surette, *Pai*, 6-1, 111-113].

413. Talbot: Charles Talbot was of the Shakespear family and a cousin of Dorothy Pound. It was he who inherited Lacock Abbey and left it to his niece, who, in order to pay the death duties, had to sell treasures such as paintings and the Magna Charta. "Dorothy's father had and Omar now has a beautiful gold seal of the Talbots: their dog emblem both as handle and in imprint" [HK, *Pai*, 2-3, 492].

414. Let backe . . . : The rhythms of this passage are based on a variety of 15th-century lyrics Pound saw in Speare, such as "Jolly good ale and old." "Back and side go bare, go bare, / Both foot and hand go cold; / But, belly, God send thee good ale enough, / Whether it be new or old."

415. boneen: Irish, *baneen* or *bainin*, a litter of pigs.

416. Claridge's: A most posh and fashionable hotel on Brook Street in West End, London.

417. Hewlett's: [74:170]. Hewlett lived at the Old Rectory, Broad Chalke, Salisbury. Pound wrote to his mother on Dec. 24, 1911 saying he was at Salisbury and expected to "motor over to see Henry Newbolt sometime or other" [BK, *Pai*, 5-2, 350].

418. Southampton: City on southwestern coast of England.

419. the green holly: "Heigh-ho! unto the green holly: / Most friendship is feigning, most loving mere folly," from *As You Like It* [Speare, 70].

420. Salisbury plain: In SW England, NW of Salisbury, an undulating chalk plateau noted for a number of ancient monuments, especially Stonehenge.

421. the Lady Anne: Lady Anne Blunt, wife of W. S. Blunt [81:61], who was born Lady Anne Isabella King-Noel, a descendant of Lord Byron. The Noel may have provided the link in the chain of associations.

422. Le Portel: [82:9] French fishing port which Pound, erroneously, associates with Swinburne, who dramatized the assassination of Queen Mary Stuart's secretary, David Rizzio.

423. La Stuarda: Mary Stewart. Maurice Hewlett wrote a novel about her life (*The Queen's Quair*, 1903) as well as a play in 1912, which deals dramatically with the murder of Rizzio. In a small cabinet or boudoir, Mary was having supper with a small party. Darnley, her husband, and others came in to get Rizzio. "Suspecting their purpose, Rizzio threw himself behind the queen and caught hold of her dress, but was stabbed by George Douglas" [*Pai*, 5-1, 74].

424. Si tuit li dolh . . . : P, "If all the griefs, and the laments, and the pain." Imperfectly remembered 1st line from Bertran de Born's lament at the death of Henry the young king [84:1].

425. leopards: The struggle for power in the House of Plantagenet between Eleanor of Aquitaine and her husband Henry II was carried on by alliances among their children. Henry's eldest son, called the young king, was actually crowned in 1170 to rule with his father. Richard the Lion-hearted, the youngest son, at one time declared war against his brother. "The Leopard," as we recall from "Sestina: Altaforte," was "the device of Richard Coeur de Lion" [*P*, 28]. But later on during the War of the Roses, the heads of leopards became identified mainly with the House of York.

426. broom plants: The heraldic devices of the Lancasters had a plantagenet (sprig of broom).

427. Tudor: The royal family that ruled England beginning with Henry VII in 1485 to the death of Elizabeth in 1603. The stanzaic and rhythmic pattern of the three verses derives from the part of the *Rubàiyat* in Speare's *Pocket Book*.

428. Blood-red, blanch-white: The War of the Roses between the House of York (White) and the House of Lancaster (Red). When the duke of Richmond (Lancaster) became Henry VII and married Elizabeth of York and started the House of Tudor, the heraldic devices showed both roses: "The rose, either red or white, survived in sweet simplicity till Tudor times, when the one, of a small diameter, was superimposed upon the other, as a symbol that the Yorkists and Lancastrians were united" [Julian Franklin, *Heraldry*, 68].

429. Howard: Catherine H., ?1521-1542, queen of England, fifth wife of Henry VIII; she was accused of immoral conduct before her marriage and was beheaded.

430. Boleyn: Anne B., ?1507-1536, second wife of Henry VIII and mother of Queen Elizabeth I; she was beheaded.

431. York: The English royal house of York, one branch of the Plantagenets, which came into prominence with Richard Plantagenet, 3d duke of York (1411-60); Yorkist kings of England were Edward IV (1461-70; 1471-83), Edward V (1483), Richard III (1483-85).

432. Lancaster: The House of Lancaster; the English royal house derived from John of Gaunt, who was created duke of Lancaster in 1362; Lancastrian kings were Henry IV, Henry V and Henry VI.

433. Serpentine: A curved pond in Hyde Park near Kensington and Church Walk, where Pound lived for a time.

434. couturier: A male dress designer. A grand one designs expensive costumes for royalty and the very wealthy. The Mediterranean sunset in which the roses glow at the top of this page has now transformed the whole landscape in spectacular fashion.

CANTO LXXXI

Sources

Loeb, *The Greek Bucolic Poets*, 26; George Santayana, *Persons and Places*, vols. 1, 2, New York, 1944-45; Morris Speare, *The Pocket Book of Verse*, 1940 [Speare]; *Poetry*, vol. 3, no. 4, Mar. 1914, 220-223.

Background

EP, *GK*, 53, 182, 155, 71, 248, 151; *J/M*, 47; *PE*, 79; *L*, 331, 333, 34; *LE*, 431-440; NS, *Life*, 352; George Orwell, *Homage to Catalonia*, Boston, Beacon Press, 1962; John Espey, *Ezra Pound's Mauberley*, Berkeley, 1974, 98; Claude Gernade Bowers, *Beveridge and the Progressive Party*, Cambridge, Mass., 1932, 112; Edith Finch, *Wilfred Scawen Blunt*, London, 1938; John Burnet, *Early Greek Philosophy*, 1892 [Burnet]; Augustin Cabanes, *The Erotikon*, trans. from French by Robert Meadows, New York, Anthropological Press, 1933.

Exegeses

LL, *Motive*, 121-123; CE, *Ideas*, 148-149; DD, *Sculptor*, 171-172; EH, *Approaches*, 340-347, 376-377; HK, *Era*, 132-133, 155-156, 489-492; Peck, *Pai*, 1-1, 3-36; Achilles Fang, "Materials for the Study of Pound's Cantos," Ph.D. dissertation, Harvard University, 1958, Vols. II, III.

Glossary

1. **Zeus . . . bosom**: Divine power abides in nature and manifests itself through the green world of Ceres (Demeter), the goddess of corn, the harvest, and fruitfulness.

2. **Taishan**: [74:46].

3. **Cythera**: Aphrodite, the planet Venus.

4. **Hay . . . desaparacen**: S, "Here is much Catholicism / . . . and very little religion / . . . I believe that kings disappear."

5. **Padre José**: [77:45].

6. **Dolores**: [37:61]. Perhaps the girl who told the young Pound to eat bread in 1907.

7. **Come pan . . .** : S, "eat bread, boy." A recurrent phrase [80:10].

8. **Sargent**: [80:352]. Perhaps the girl in Sargent's 1891 painting "La Carmencita" is Dolores [Fang, III, 136].

9. **Velázquez**: [80:292].

10. **Museo del Prado**: The Spanish National Museum [80:15].

11. **peseta**: Spanish monetary unit, similar to Italian lira.

12. **Bowers**: Claude Gernade B., 1879-1958, American historian and diplomat, ambassador to Spain, 1933-1939. Pound praised his historical study *Jefferson and Hamilton* in a number of places and wrote to him in 1938. Bowers's letter in reply, dated May 10, 1938, mentions "the atmosphere of incredible hate" in Spain [NS, *Life*, 352].

13. **London reds**: During the time of the Spanish Civil War, Moscow considered the collective security of the Allied nations to be more important than any other issue. They wanted Britain, France, the U.S., and the Soviets to stand firm against the Nazi-Fascist threat. To that end, it was official policy not to upset the Western democracies by sponsoring worldwide revolution. Thus, at the time of the people's revolution against Franco and the Falangists in Spain, there were several Red or Communist groups. Some joined the fight against Franco, but because of the Moscow line, some were actually fighting on the side of Franco. The two groups were represented among the Marxists in London and the U.S. Some English units left for Spain to join the battle, as did the Abraham Lincoln Battalion from the United States. But some, following the Moscow line meticulously, would not expose the agents of Franco working in London [George Orwell, *Homage to Catalonia*, Boston, Beacon Press, 1962].

14. **Franco**: Francisco F., 1892-1975, Spanish general and dictator who was victorious with the help of Germany and Italy in the Spanish Civil War.

15. **Alcázar**: Alcazar de San Juan, town in central Spain which Pound visited in 1906. He lists it as one of the Islamic monuments that gave "a sense of man and of human dignity yet unobliterated" [*GK*, 53]. Ironically, it was the bloody siege of Alcazar that Franco said won the war for him.

16. **Eso es . . . muerto**: S, "that is mourning, Ha! / my husband is dead."

17. **locanda**: I, "inn."

18. **Cabranez**: Prob. Dr. Augustin Cabanès, 1862-1928, author of some 60 volumes, in-

cluding *Les Indiscretions de l' histoire*, 6 vols., Paris, 1903-1909, which is in Pound's library at Brunnenburg. A. C. was most famous for his research in sexual behavior, as reported in his last book *The Erotikon: Being an Illustrated Treasury of Scientific Marvels of Human Sexuality*, trans. by Robert Meadows and privately issued by the Anthropological Press, New York, 1933. An introductory note to the book says, "Dr. Cabanès, actuated by the spirit of the real scientist, has brought to light strange data which make vital contributions to our knowledge of the forces controlling the intimate life of men and women." Cabanès's work would thus interest Pound as a continuation of Remy de Gourmont's work on the sexuality of other species in *The Natural Philosophy of Love*. The meaning of the egg in his pocket is not known, though a weird theory has been suggested [*Pai*, 11-3, 451-453].

19. **Basil . . . Canaries**: B. Bunting, born in the Tyne Valley area of England, and still (in 1982) going strong. [For the story of his life and work see *Pai*, 9-1, Spring 1980, devoted to him and his Pound connections]. During the three days between the Crucifixion and the Resurrection, when Christ was supposed to have been harrowing Hell, the villagers—man, woman and child—were supposed to beat drums day and night nourished by little except wine. They did this until the hands of many became a bloody mess and hundreds were groaning with pain. They called the annual event a simple village fiesta. "As for life in the Canaries," says Bunting, "I suppose Ezra is thinking of my description of the sexual mores of the islands in those days, so very unlike those of New York and Philadelphia in his time, perhaps even a bit alarming to his fundamentally puritan soul" [Bunting, *Pai*, 10-3, 619-621].

20. **Possum**: T. S. Eliot.

21. **portagoose**: Portuguese.

22. **Cole**: [80:153]. Reprise of the demonstration Cole mounted at Italy's entrance into WWI.

23. **André Spire**: [77:134]. Pound wrote: "Old Spire who had sat on a Credit Agricole board said: 'Yes, very nice, communal credit, but when you get your board, every man on that board has a brother-in-law' " [*J/M*, 47]. The agricultural credit board was a device to extend credit to farmers for seed, fertilizer, etc. Since community credit for development is at the heart of Social Credit economics, note that Pound was aware of one of the most serious flaws in it as a program: influence and favoritism, which, being impossible to prevent, posed serious problems even with reasonable control.

24. **John Adams**: [31:15; 69:56]. JA said that TJ feared monarchy but that he (JA) feared an aristocracy.

25. **Mr Jefferson**: [31:2].

26. **To break . . . heave**: To bring poetry back to the speech of the people, it was necessary to get rid of artificially imposed rhythms: a first premise of Pound's revolution in poetry.

27. **Jo Bard**: Josef B., 1882-1975, Hungarian writer Pound knew in the late 20s and early 30s. Bard wrote essays for the *Dial*, the *New English Weekly*, etc. Pound mentions him in a review of W. C. Williams's *A Voyage to Pagany*. A book by Bard, *Shipwreck in Europe*, shows Americans not speaking: "I think the continental author mentions as a general and known post-war quantity: the American or Americans who comes or come to Vienna to find out why they can't enjoy life even after getting a great deal of money" [*PE*, 79]. Bard married Eileen Agar of the "trick sunlight" [76:50]. Pound visited them and saw the effect of the light when he went to London in 1938 for the funeral of Olivia Shakespear. It was Bard who introduced Pound to Frobenius [HK].

28. **La Rouchefoucauld**: La Rochefoucauld [31:36]. A sophisticated French stylist.

29. **de Maintenon**: Françoise d'Aubigné, Marquise de M., 1635-1719, first the mistress and later the second wife of Louis XIV of France. A woman of wit and wisdom.

Pound's criticism, agreeing with Bard, was that in novels and poetry ordinary people such as bakers and innkeepers were made to sound like people of wit and wisdom.

30. Te cavero . . . a te: I, "I'll cut your guts out / [and I] yours" [10:21]. Highly idiomatic and strong talk in the language of the people.

31. Mencken: H. L. M., 1880-1956, American editor, author, critic, and philologist with whom Pound corresponded for years. Pound was much impressed with a remark of his and mentions it often: "Nevertheless, I believe that all schemes of monetary reform collide inevitably with the nature of man in the mass. He can't be convinced in anything less than a geological epoch" [*GK*, 182].

32. Some cook . . . : [54:14].

33. Ἰυγξ . . . ἄνδρα: H, "Little wheel . . . . . man to my house." The first word should be ἶυγξ and the accent on ποτί should be grave. The line occurs in Theocritus, "Idyll 2" [Loeb, *The Greek Bucolic Poets*, 26]. The complete line is a refrain repeated 10 times as a magic spell worked by a young maid to draw her lover, who has taken up with another, back to her.

34. Benin: The city and river in S Nigeria, whence Frobenius collected masks and artifacts.

35. Frankfurt: The German city in which the Frobenius Institute is located and where many cultural objects from Africa were housed. Pound's indirect way of saying that the black soldier who made his table was as handsome as any his race ever produced.

36. Kuanon: [90:29].

37. And at first . . . : The next several lines derive from Santayana's *Persons and Places*, which Pound prob. read in manuscript sometime in 1940 [*L*, 331, 333]. Santayana was born in Spain and tells of his first impressions of Boston, where he arrived at age 9: "my eye . . . was caught by symbols of Yankee ingenuity and Yankee haste. . . . I was fascinated by the play of those skeleton wheels . . . and I was disgusted by such a dirty ramshackle pier for a great steamship line" [Santayana, *Persons and Places*, I, 134].

38. Santayana: [80:49].

39. Muss: Mussolini. He affected a populist image by cultivating localisms of the province he came from.

40. the grief . . . climax: Santayana wrote about his aunt's grief at the death of her daughter, that it "was violent, but violent only by fits, as when each new visitor came to condole with her, and she had to repeat the whole story, with appropriate floods of tears, sobs, and lamentations" [ibid., 127]. [These passages from Santayana were identified by Carol H. Cantrell in a MS submitted to *Paideuma*.]

41. George Horace: G. H. Lorimer, 1868-1937, American journalist and editor-in-chief of the *Saturday Evening Post* (1899-1936), and a neighbor of the Pounds at Wyncote.

42. Beveridge: Albert Jeremiah B., 1862-1927, U.S. senator (1899-1911), a supporter of Theodore Roosevelt and an organizer of the Progessive party in 1912. He made an inspection trip to the Philippines in 1899. He refused to discuss or write about the trip because "he was saving his observations for the speech he planned to make as his initial bow to the Senate" [Bowers, *Beveridge and the Progressive Party*, 112]. All others failed to get an interview with the senator but Lorimer went to Washington and succeeded by persistence: "The spring and summer of 1900 found Beveridge feverishly at work. He had agreed with George H. Lorimer . . . to write six articles in the imperialistic vein, on his experiences in the Philippines" [ibid., 131]. Thus, to be accurate Pound's "three articles" should read "six" [Fang, II, 68].

43. AOI!: [79:109]. A noise perhaps of lamentation, picking up from the idea of grief in preceding lines: *Aoi* occurs 172 times in the Oxford manuscript of *Chanson de Ro-*

land, generally following the last lines of a *laisse*.

44. Althea: Intended to evoke the Lovelace poem, "To Althea from Prison," which says "And my divine Althea comes / To whisper at the grates." Pound has no such visitor.

45. libretto: Just as Canto 75 is the musical score of Janequin, so the climactic pages of Canto 81 are given a musical label to underscore the extraordinary musical cadences deliberately evoked in one of the major climactic statements of the poem.

46. Lawes: Henry L., 1596-1662, the English musician and composer noted for his masques and airs for voice. But he did not write for the crowd, as Pound knew: "Lawes and Campion will not gather 10,000 groundlings. Not in our time" [*GK*, 155]. Lawes set Waller's "Go, Lovely Rose" to music [Espey, *Mauberley*, 98].

47. Jenkyns: John Jenkins, 1592-1678, English composer and musician to Charles I and II. He composed many fancies for viol and organ.

48. Dolmetsch: [80:197]. Arnold D. The Dolmetsch foundation (1928) was founded to encourage interest in old music. Pound celebrates his work often [*GK*, 71, 248; *LE*, 431-440].

49. Hast 'ou . . . shade: The 4 lines derive from the 3d stanza of Ben Jonson's "The Triumph of Charis," which goes: "Have you seen but a bright lily grow, / Before rude hands have touched it? / Ha' you marked but the fall o' the snow / Before the soil hath smutched it? / Ha' you felt the wool o' the beaver? Or swan's down ever?" [74:504].

50. Waller: Edmund W., 1606-1687, the English poet who wrote: "Go, lovely Rose." Pound glances at this poem in his "Envoy" to *Mauberley*.

51. Dowland: John D., 1563-1626, Irish composer and lutanist. Pound mentions his lute compositions [*GK*, 151].

52. Your eyen . . . susteyne: From *Merciles Beaute*, attributed to Chaucer.

53. Ed ascoltando . . . : I, "and listening to the gentle murmur." Pound told HK: "Not a quotation, merely author using handy language."

54. new . . . eyes: Image of reflected divinity, with sexual overtones as the sacred vision (inluminatio coitu [36:13]) becomes more urgent and pervasive here and in many later cantos [Peck, *Pai*, 1-1].

55. hypostasis: Here divinity of the object as object in itself, not as container for a spirit that might come or go.

56. Ειδὼς: H, "knowing" or "seeing." Part of a verb which in context and some of its forms may mean either "know" or "see." Pound's source is debatable, because the word is pandemic. Since Pound was a devotee of the Pre-Socratics (in particular the Pythagoreans) and kept John Burnet's *Greek Philosophy* at hand, he may have noticed the extended discussion Burnet gives to 'Εἴδος and Ἐίδη as "figures" (in the sense of "forms") deriving from the "boundless" or unformed. Earlier thinkers had thought of air as a sort of "mist." But Pythagoras was the first to conceive of abstract space in which forms had to exist to be seen and known. This line of thought led to the conclusion that all things that are are numbers. "The early Pythagoreans represented numbers and explained their properties by means of dots arranged in certain 'figures or patterns' " [Burnet, 52]. The most famous figure is the tetraktys. It, as are all other figures or patterns, is an εἶδος. Ειδὼς, as participle substantive, would give us "shape, figure, or being apprehensible to the eyes and mind (seeing or knowing)."

57. Learn of the green world: Or in other words: "See the lilies of the field, they toil not neither do they spin; yet I say unto you Solomon in all his glory is not arrayed like one of these."

58. Paquin: A Parisian couturier [80:434; WB, *Pai*, 11-3, 444].

59. The green casque: The "bottle" from which Madam La Vespa is born [83:72].

60. "Master thyself . . . ": Paraphrase of the rhythm of Chaucer's "Subdue thyself, and others thee shall hear" from the "Ballade of Good Counsel" [Speare, 1].

61. Blunt: Wilfred Scawen B., 1840-1922, poet, diplomat, politician, world traveler, and defender of home rule for India, Egypt, and even Ireland, for which he became the first Englishman to go to prison. In the London years, Pound thought highly of Blunt and sent some of his poetry to Harriet Monroe, saying, "the Blunt stuff, glory of the name etc. ought to build up our position . . . " [*L*, 34]. On Jan. 18, 1914, a committee of poets including Yeats, Masefield, Pound, and several others "presented to Wilfred Scawen Blunt 'in token of homage' a reliquary carved . . . by the brilliant young sculptor, Gaudier-Brzeska. . . ." So Pound wrote in *Poetry* [vol. 3, no. 4., March 1914, 220-223]. Edith Finch [*Wilfred Scawen Blunt*], reporting on a visit made to Blunt by Pound and Aldington says that Pound said: "I am trying to persuade them both into some kind of sanity. . . . Where there is neither decency nor art . . . verse is a mere outrage" [p. 338]. In "Homage to Wilfred Blunt" Pound wrote about Blunt's double sonnet, "With Esther": "Mr Blunt is about the last man who has been able to use the old-fashioned Elizabethan 'grand style' effectively" [*Poetry*, vol. 3, no. 4, 220-223]. These impressions flooded back over 30 years later. Blunt was a man of action who with a fine old eye helped create "a live tradition."

CANTO LXXXII

Sources

EP, *CON*, 22; Aeschylus, *Agamemnon*; Morris Speare, *The Pocket Book of Verse*, 1940 [Speare]; Petrarch, *Sonetti e Canzoni*, Fano, 1503.

Background

EP, "Salve O Pontifex;" *ALS*, 63; *SP*, 227; *L*, 7, 55, 62, 65, 80-83; *LE*, 269-270, 274-275; *ABCR*, 48; *The Cambridge History of English Literature*, Vol. XII [CHEL]; Edmund Gosse, *The Life of A. C. Swinburne*, London, 1917 [Gosse, *Swinburne*]; Dafne Fielding, *Those Remarkable Cunards*, New York, Atheneum, 1958 [DF, *Cunards*]; *Dial*, vol. 71, Aug. 1921; Rudolph Hirsch, *Printing, Selling, and Reading, 1450-1550*, Wiesbaden, 1967; H. Price, *Fifty Years of Psychical Research*, New York, Arno Press, reprinted 1975.

Exegeses

Knox, *Pai*, 3-1, 77-78, LL, *Motive*, 118-120; EH, *Approaches*, 338-350, WB, *Rose*, 95-156; HK, *Era*, 486-488; Achilles Fang, "Materials for the Study of Pound's Cantos," Ph.D. dissertation, Harvard University, 1958, Vol. II [Fang].

Glossary

1. **hunting dog**: [80:112]. Prob. Orion and Sirius, the dog-star.

2. **"Guten . . . "**: G, "Good morning, sir."

3. **Jeffers et al**: Trainees at the DTC.

4. **Swinburne**: Algernon Charles S., 1837-1909. The English poet whose richness of pattern, cadence, and sound impressed Pound early and late. He was still living when Pound arrived in England, but he missed seeing him and always regretted it. Pound's "Salve O Pontifex" is dedicated to Swinburne [*ALS*, 63].

5. **Landor**: Walter Savage L., 1775-1864, English poet and essayist. Swinburne visited the 90-year-old Landor twice in the year of his death. Gosse says about the first visit that "the unknown little poet, with his great aureole of fluffed red hair," merely confused the old man. But Landor called him "dear friend" and was charmed into giving him "a Correggio in commemoration of the occasion" [Gosse, *Swinburne*, 101-104].

6. **old Mathews**: Elkin M., 1851-1921, London publisher who did several of Pound's early works. Pound mentions him quite often in his early letters [*L*, 7, 55, 62, 65, etc.; *SP*, 227]. Pound prob. heard the anecdote from Mathews himself, perhaps at the time of Swinburne's death in 1909.

7. **Watts Dunton**: Theodore Walter Watts-Dunton, 1832-1914, English poet, novelist, and critic; the friend and caretaker of Swinburne who lived with him from 1879 until his death in 1909.

8. **Dirce's shade**: [cf. 39 below].

9. **Le Portel**: Swinburne told Gosse the story of the rescue at sea and Gosse wrote it down soon afterwards. It seems that around 10 o'clock on an early October morning in 1869, Swinburne went alone to Porte d'Amont near Étretat, where he was staying with a friend named Powell. He jumped into the sea and was shortly carried away by the tide. While people stood helpless on the beach, the captain of a fishing boat fished the poet out of the water and let him ashore at Yport (not Le Portel), a little north of Étretat. As soon as he was picked up, Swinburne began preaching to the captain and his men. He told Gosse that they surrounded him "in rapturous approval." So, being a man violently in favor of democracy, he preached to them "the doctrines of the Republic [of France], and then he recited to them 'by the hour together,' the poems of Victor Hugo" [Gosse, *Swinburne*, 178-179]. Pound's memory played him false with Aeschylus.

10. **"On the Atreides'** . . . : The watchman at the opening of *Agamemnon* says: "I ask the gods some respite . . . of this watch time measured by years I lie awake . . . upon the Atreides roof dogwise to mark the grand processionals of all the stars at night" (trans. by Richmond Lattimore). One of Pound's main preoccupations during his Pisa captivity was to mark the grand processional of all the stars and planets.

11. **ΕΜΟΣ** . . . : H, "my husband . . . hand." Clytemnestra [*Agamemnon*, 1404-1406] says: "This is Agamemnon, my husband, dead by my right hand, and a good job" [cf. *LE*, 269-270].

12. **hac dextera mortus**: [dextra mortuus]: L, "dead by this right hand." Pound, in comparing the Thomas Stanley Greek and Latin editions of the play, cites these lines.

13. **Lytton**: It was not Lytton but Lady Gregory's husband, Sir William Gregory, who first saw Blunt in the bullring. In 1862, at a bullfight in Madrid, Sir William was "struck by the extraordinary good looks of the young matador . . . and asking who he was, heard that he was an attaché from the English Embassy, Wilfred Blunt" [Lady Gregory's preface to Blunt's diaries, cited by Fang, II, 163].

14. **Packard**: Frank Lucius P., 1877-1942, Canadian author of such books as *Greater*

Love Hath No Man (1913), *The Beloved Traitor* (1915), *Doors of The Night* (1922), *The Devil's Mantle* (1927), and a dozen others.

15. **Percy**: Percy B. Shelley [MSB].

16. **Basinio**: [9:7]. On the argument about the merits of Greek poetry vs. Latin poetry, Pound said [*ABCR*, 48] some snobs preferred any Greek over any Latin. Then, "Basinio of Parma, proclaimed a very different thesis: he held that you couldn't write Latin poetry really well unless you knew Greek. . . . In the margins of his Latin narrative you can still see the tags of Homer that he was using to keep his melodic sense active." "Mould" is used instead of "model" to accent the sense of shape and form in the melodic line.

17. **Otis**: James O. [71:89, 91]. Said Pound: "Otis wrote a Greek Grammar which he destroyed, or which was lost for the lack of a competent printer" [*SP*, 174].

18. **Soncino**: [30:16-19]. The spread of learning, activated by the art of printing, increased dramatically at the end of the 16th century. Demand for paper resulted in improved technology for producing paper. An increase in the number of printers increased competition. Competition created demand for ways to decrease costs. Says Rudolph Hirsch [*Printing, Selling, and Reading, 1450-1550*, 70], "the general trend was the reduction of prices for printed books . . . Aldo Manuzio [30:17] proceeded on this plan, when he started his octavo series . . . in 1501. . . . He kept expenses low by introducing an italic type, designed for him by Francesco Griffo da Bologna, which permitted him to place more text on one page." Hieronymous Soncinus "pointed out with some venom" that Franceso and not Aldo was the designer. In a dedication to Cesare Borgia, which appeared in Petrarch's *Sonetti e Canzoni* [Fano, 1503], Soncinus wrote: "Francesco da Bologna . . . ha escogitato una nova forma de littere dicta cursiva, o vero cancelleresca, de la quale non Aldo Romano . . . ma esso M. Francesco e stato primo inventore et designatore" ("Francesco of Bologna has devised a new form of handwriting called cursive, or rather chancery writing, whose first inventor and designer was not Aldo Romano but this M. Franceso"). The implication in the context suggests that Soncinus and Francesco are memorialized in thousands of books and, like other great printers and designers, did much to spread knowledge and civilization, while many supposedly great men carved in statues in public squares are only "marble men." The classic books will reappear in ever new editions; the statues will slowly wither away.

19. **Mr Clowes**: A member of William Clowes and Sons, Ltd., a firm of English printers, which did Pound's *Lustra* and *Gaudier-Brzeska* in 1916. The story involved concerns 25 poems the printer objected to as obscene and the publisher agreed should be left out of the volume. Negotiations cut down the number to 17. Yeats was called in but didn't manage to help, so Pound issued a private "unexpurgated" edition. The story is told in various letters [*L*, 80-88] and mentioned in "Murder by Capital" [*SP*, 227].

20. **Mr Birrell**: Augustine B., 1850-1933, English essayist.

21. **Tom Moore**: Thomas M., 1779-1852, Irish poet whose "Little" poems were supposedly shocking, but which Saintsbury says "were never very shocking" and "the poems have been purged . . . [of all improprieties] for more than a century" [*CHEL*, Vol. XII, 103].

22. **Rogers**: Samuel R., 1763-1855, a minor English poet whose verse also was subject to censorship and / or bowdlerization.

23. **her Ladyship YX**: Unidentified. Perhaps Lady Emerald Cunard, 1872-1948 (the mother of Nancy [80:311]), whose restlessness might well have led to the acts indicated. She was a good friend of Lady Churchill [cf. 24 below] and, like her, was born an American and married into an English titled family [DF, *Cunards*, 31-32].

24. **Ladyship Z**: Lady Churchill (Jennie Jerome), the American wife of Lord Randolph Churchill, 1849-1895, whom she married in 1874 [RO].

25. **Mabel Beardsley**: [80:268].

26. **Mr Masefield**: John M., 1878-1967, English poet (laureate from 1930 on). *The Everlasting Mercy* (1911) and other long poems caused a scandal. "The combination of profanity and ecstasy, sordid melodrama and spiritual elevation created a sensation; they overwhelmed the critics as well as ordinary readers" [L. Untermeyer, *Modern British Poetry*, 1950, 219]. A subject rhyme with Rogers, Moore, and Clowes above.

27. **Old Neptune**: [80:257].

28. **Flaubert**: [80:28].

29. **Miss Tomczyk**: Stanislawa T. (Mrs. Everard Fielding), a Polish medium who could "produce telekinetic movements to order, in the laboratory" [H. Price, *Fifty Years of Psychical Research*, 28]. One of the many occultists from Madam Blavatsky on whom Yeats became involved with.

30. **society . . . research**: Punning(?) reference to the Society of Psychical Research founded in 1882.

31. **18 Woburn Buildings**: The London residence of W. B. Yeats. In 1896 Yeats moved from Fountain Court to 18 Woburn Buildings (now no. 5, Woburn Walk), where he lived when in London for 24 years. Not to be confused with Woburn Place, also in the British Museum area off Russell Square.

32. **Mr. Tancred**: Francis W. T., one of the imagist poets published in the first vol. of *Poetry*. Pound makes a mental connection with Tancred, the Norman king of Sicily, who died in 1194 leaving the kingdom to his four-year-old son Frederick, later to become famous for his book on falcons [25:14; 98/689]. Early drafts of Canto 6 quote letters between another Tancred (who became famous in the first crusade) and King Richard. This Tancred reached Jerusalem [*Dial*, vol. 71, August 1921; *Poems* 1918-1921; Fang, II, 142].

33. **Dickens**: Charles D., 1812-1870, English novelist. Pound seems to be saying that Tancred was a second Dickens, but on what grounds only random speculation could be contrived.

34. **Ford**: Ford M. F., 1873-1939, English novelist [74:165].

35. **res non verba**: L, "objects not words."

36. **William**: W. B. Yeats.

37. **Ideo**: Jen [M3099], "humanitas" or "humaneness." The left component, 亻, is the character for man, 人, when used as one element among others in an ideogram. The top stroke is "heaven," the bottom one "earth." Thus, the man who lives out heaven's process on earth is the perfect man [*CON*, 22].

38. **Cythera**: Aphrodite and/or Venus.

39. **Dirce**: In a poem called "Dirce," Landor wrote: "Stand close around, ye Stygian set, / With Dirce in one boat conveyed! / Or Charon, seeing may forget / That he is old and she a shade" [50:43].

40. **Be glad poor beaste . . .** : Prob. variation on rhythm of Burns's lines from "To a Mouse" [Speare, 94-96].

41. **Terreus!**: Tereus. Legendary king of Thrace. In the Philomela legend three people were turned into birds [4:8].

42. **Spring and . . .** : [78:139].

43. **Cnidos**: The ancient town at Cape Krio, SW Asia Minor. The victory or defeat at Troy was to be communicated by a series of lights on the Greek Islands. The watchman on the roof at the opening of the *Agamemnon* is waiting for the signal. Pound deals with the scene in "Early Translators of Homer" [*LE*, 274-275].

44. **Mitylene**: The island of Lesbos in the Aegean.

45. **Reithmuller**: Richard Henri Riethmuel-

ler, 1881-1942(?), instructor in German at the University of Pennsylvania, 1905-1907; author of *Walt Whitman and the Germans*, 1906.

46. **Tdaenmarck**: Presumably the sound of a German saying "Denmark" and "even the peasants know him," but this instructor appears to have a bad cold.

47. **Whitman**: [80:51].

48. **Camden**: [80:275]. In 1906, Whitman lived about 10 miles from Philadelphia at 328 Mickle Street, in Camden.

49. **"O troubled . . . "**: Quotes from "Out of the Cradle Endlessly Rocking" [Speare, 249-256].

50. **O GEA TERRA**: H, "Earth"; L, "Earth." These 10 lines are an intense lyrical evocation of the Dionysian-Ceres / Isis-Osiris metamorphosis theme of death and regeneration, with paradisal overtones indicated by the herbs and reinforced by the chthonic choral a few lines later [Knox, *Pai*, 3-1, 77-78].

51. **Ferrara**: [8:30].

52. **fu Nicolo . . . Po**: I, "was Niccolo [d'Este] / and here beyond the Po" [24:22, 70].

53. *'εμὸν τὸν ἄνδρα*: [81:33].

54. **Kipling**: Rudyard K., 1865-1936, English poet and novelist. What he suspected is not known.

55. **two halves . . . tally**: [77:56].

56. **connubium . . . mysterium**: L, "the marriage of the earth . . . mystery."

57. *ἔφατὰ . . . ἐμός*: H, "she said my husband" [*Agamemnon*, 1404; *LE*, 269-270; cf. 11 above].

58. ΧΘΟΝΙΟΣ: H, "earth-born" (adjective, masc. nom. sing.).

59. ΧΘΟΝΟΣ: H, "of the earth" (noun, gen. sing.).

60. 'ΙΧΩΡ: H, "Ichor," the fluid that flows in the veins of the gods.

61. *δακρύων*: H, "weeping" or "of tears."

62. *ἐντεῦθεν*: H, "thereupon."

CANTO LXXXIII

Sources

Dante, *Pur.* XXVI; James Legge, *The Four Books*, Shanghai, 1923 [Legge]; Horace, *Odes* III; EP, *CON*, 217, 247.

Background

EP, *L*, 25; *GK*, 267; Erigena, *De Divisione naturae*, ed. C. B. Schlüter; Robert Grosseteste, "De Luce seu de inchoatione formarum," in L. Baur, *Die Philosophischen Werke des Robert Grossetesta*, Munster, 1912; *Poetry*, May 1914; *Letters of W. B. Yeats*, New York, Macmillan, 1955, 590.

Exegeses

Achilles Fang, "Materials for the Study of Pound's Cantos," Ph.D. dissertation, Harvard University, 1958, Vol. II; NS, *Life*, 3; G. Ivancich, *Ezra Pound in Italy*, Rizzoli, 1978 [Ivancich]; Libera, *Pai*, 2-3, 374; Schuldiner, *Pai*, 4-1, 78-79; CFT, *Pai*, 2-3, 451-454; Flory, *Pai*, 5-1, 52.

Glossary

1. ὕδωρ: H, "water."

2. **et Pax**: L, "and peace."

3. **Gemisto**: [8:31]. In his philosophical studies he made Neptune (Poseidon) the greatest of the gods, from whom all flows. In the Neoplatonic sense, that means especially mind or intelligence (*νοῦς*).

4. **Rimini**: Sigismundo had Gemisto's ashes removed to Rimini [8:31]. The bas reliefs that feature the muses and signs of the zodiac are the subject of Adrian Stokes in *Stones of Rimini*. The figures in the carvings "have the appearance of marble limbs seen in water" [Libera, *Pai*, 2-3, 374].

5. **Mr Yeats**: [74:166]. His opinion given here is reflected in a similar one of Erigena below. It was Erigena's "hilarity and the things which he said so cleverly and wittily [which] pleased the king" [ibid.].

6. **lux . . . accidens**: L, "for light / is an attribute of fire."

7. **prete**: L, "priest." The priest is C. B. Schlüter, who edited Erigena's, *De Divisione Naturae*, 1818.

8. **Scotus**: Johannes S. Erigena [36:9; 74:90].

9. **hilaritas**: L, "joyousness." Schlüter in his preface speaks of Erigena's "piety and cheerfulness" (*hilaritas*) and discerns at its root a "sublime joy of wonder and intellectual love." However, this intellectual love "will often appear to the outside observer as little less than hilarious" [Shuldiner, *Pai*, 4-1, 78].

10. **King Carolus**: Charles the Bald [74:103]. He is the king who was pleased by Erigena's hilarity [cf. 5 above].

11. **the queen**: Ermentrude, d. 869, first wife of Charles the Bald. She was noted for her ornamental needlework. Erigena compared her with Athena.

12. **"toujours Pari"**: F, "always Paris."

13. **Charles le Chauve**: Charles the Bald, King Carolus above.

14. **pyx**: A casket or box made of precious metal in which the Host is preserved.

15. **Omnia . . . sunt**: L, "Every thing that exists is light" [74:89].

16. **they dug up his bones**: Because Erigena's Neoplatonic ideas bordered on pantheism and his theories were exploited by the Albigensian heretics, he was condemned as a heretic by Pope Honorius III in 1225. It was not Erigena but Amalric who was dug up [74:104].

17. **De Montfort**: Simon IV de Montfort l'Amaury [23:26].

18. **Le Paradis . . .** : [74:292].

19. **Uncle William**: W. B. Yeats

20. **Notre Dame**: The cathedral in Paris.

21. **Notre Dame**: F, "Our lady." A statue of the Virgin over the door of the cathedral.

22. **St Etienne**: The basilica of St. Etienne, a 12th-century church in Périgueux.

23. **Dei Miracoli**: Santa Maria Dei M. in Rome [74:129; 76:170].

24. **Mermaids, that carving**: The sirenes carved by Tullio in Santa Maria Dei Maracoli in Venice [76:168].

25. **Zoagli**: [46:4]. A town near Rapallo.

26. **pax** ὕδωρ . . . ῞ΥΔΩΡ: [see 1, 2 above].

27. **The sage** . . . : *Analects* VI, 21: "He said: the wise delight in water, the human delight in the hills. The knowing are active; the humane, tranquil; the knowing get the pleasure, and the humane get long life" [*CON*, 217].

28. **Uncle William**: Yeats wrote in "Down by the Sally Gardens": "She bid me take life easy, as the grass grows on the weirs; / But I was young and foolish, and now am full of tears."

29. **consiros**: P, "with grief" or "longing." Arnaut Daniel uses the word to describe his condition [*Pur.* XXVI, 144].

30. **St What's his name**: San Giorgio, a cathedral in Pantaneto, Siena. The traditional procession which carries the wax offerings to the Madonna takes place the day before the August Palio [Ivancich].

31. **Cane e Gatto**: I, "Dog and Cat." The name of the place where two streets meet near San Giorgio.

32. **soll . . . sein**: G, "is to be your love."

33. **Palio**: Semiannual horserace held in Siena: July 2, Festival of Our Lady's Visitation and August 15, Festival of Our Lady's Assumption [80:60].

34. **level the windows**: The Palazzo Capoquadri Salimbene has windows that overlook the procession: "the first floor windows from which Pound watched are about level with the church roof" [Ivancich].

35. **Olim de** . . . : L, "Formerly of the Malatestas."

36. **Maria's face**: The face in a panel painting over one of the doors of the large hall at Palazzo Capoquadri Salimbene reminded Pound of his daughter's face [Ivancich reproduces the picture].

37. **Montino**: "The same 'child's face' is alluded to in Canto LXXIV [74/446] as is 'Montino's,' the young son of Prince di San Faustino, whose resemblance to one of his family, in a painting, 'the family group 1820,' brought to Pound's mind Hardy's poem 'The family face' " [Ivancich].

38. **Hardy**: Thomas H., 1840-1928, English poet and novelist much admired by Pound. There is a lushness about the multifigured fresco which is indeed not wholly Hardy's material.

39. πάντα ῥεῖ: H, "Everything flows" [80:357; 96:168].

40. **below the altars**: *Analects* XII, 21 [78:92; *CON*, 247].

41. **"When . . . forward"**: [74:182].

42. Δρυάς: H, "Dryad," a tree nymph [3:11].

43. **Taishan**: [74:46].

44. **the hidden city**: Paradisal motif with hieratic animals [17/passim], with the seeds in motion anticipating Canto 90 et seq.

45. **Chocorua**: A peak in E New Hampshire in the Sandwich range of the White Mountains. MSB note: Running all mountains together. Brancusi getting all forms to one form.

46. **Plura diafana**: L, "more things diaphanous." From Grosseteste's *De Luce*. A recurrent phrase [100/722] that relates to Erigena's "lux enim" [CFT, *Pai*, 2-3, 451-454].

47. **Heliads**: The daughters of Helios who were changed into poplar trees as they mourned for their brother Phaethon [76:6].

48. **brightness of 'udor** . . . : The opening dawn scene in Canto 83 replays the mystic symbolism in Neoplatonic thought, where everything that is (in this world) is a reflection of the divine order: thus images relected in water become a graphic way of evoking manifestations of the divine process.

49. **this breath . . . inanition**: These 14 lines precis Pound's idea of a Mencius passage in

which Mencius says it is difficult to describe what he means by his "vast, flowing passion nature." Then he says: "This is the passion nature:–It is exceedingly great, and exceedingly strong. Being nourished by rectitude, and sustaining no injury, it fills up all between heaven and earth. . . . It is the mate and assistant of righteousness and reason. Without it *man* is in a state of starvation. It is produced by the accumulation of righteous deeds; it is not to be obtained by incidental acts of righteousness. If the mind does not feel complacency in the conduct, *the nature* becomes starved" [Legge, 529-530].

50. **debt . . . Clower**: Prob. Clowes, the printer [82:19]. The question of "who wd / pay for the composition" may have resulted in an unpaid debt. That the line should be here is a sort of comic double take.

51. **move with the seed's breath**: The *semina motuum* theme [80:123].

52. **Non combaattere**: I, "Don't fight."

53. **Giovanna**: A servant in a Venetian family Pound knew [76:184].

54. **Ideogram**: Wu [M7208], "not"

55. **Ideogram**: Chu [M1370], "help."

56. **Ideogram**: Ch'ang [M213], "grow"

57. **Kung-Sun Chow**: Book II of Mencius, which tells the anecdote of a man of Sung who was grieved because he pulled on his corn to make it longer and pulled it up by the roots. He went home looking stupid and said, "I have been helping the corn to grow long" [Legge, 531]. This story is told in the next section after the passage quoted in 49 above as an illustration of the way most people deal with their passion nature: "There are few in the world *who do not deal with their passion nature, as if* they were assisting the corn to grow long" [ibid., 531-532].

58. **San Gregorio**: Church in Venice [76:196].

59. **San Trovaso**: Church in Venice [76:196].

60. **Old Ziovan**: Prob. a Venetian named Giovanni whom Pound knew in Venice.

61. **Adriatic**: The Adriatic Sea, which seemed to Pound to have a particular blue, to which he relates eyes [*Pai*, 5-1, 52]. "I recall the Adriatic as a grey-blue, not unlike EP's own eyes" [HK].

62. **San Vio**: Church in Venice [76:196]. Related to the color of the eyes at 97/676.

63. **Redentore**: I, "Redeemer." Church on the island of Giudecca, Venice, which was the scene of an annual festival involving a bridge of boats and a votive offering to stop the plague. It was colorful and featured colored lights at night [Fang II, 292].

64. **Giudecca**: Island and canal in Venice.

65. **Ca'**: I, "house" (in Venetian dialect).

66. **Ca' Foscari**: A Venetian palace, on the Grand Canal.

67. **Ca' Giustinian**: A palace of justice, of which there are three on the Grand Canal.

68. **Desdemona**: The Palazzo Contarini–Fasan on the Grand Canal was sometimes called this.

69. **le Zattere**: I, "the rafts." Name of a long embankment on N edge of Giudecca Canal in Venice.

70. **Sensaria**: I, "Brokerage House"–in Venice.

71. **DAKRUŌN . . . :** H, "weeping . . . weeping."

72. **La vespa**: I, "the wasp."

73. **Bracelonde**: Prob. Braceliande, the enchanted forest of Arthurian romance, as in Crétien de Troyes's *Yvain*, l. 189 [BK].

74. **Perugia**: City in central Italy with an excellent 14th-century cathedral and a fountain with sculptures by Niccolo and Giovanni Pisano.

75. **Bulagaio's**: Prob. an acquaintance of Pound in Venice.

76. **Mr. Walls**: Prob. trainee at DTC.

77. **signorinas**: I, "young ladies."

78. **Jones**: Lieutenant and provost officer at DTC [80:111]. MSB note: "Jones rodents: The inmates who had to pull up grass."

79. **Tellus**: Roman divinity of the earth [47:24]. Here just the earth [77/468].

80. **XTHONOS**: H, "of the earth" [77:26; 82:59].

81. ΟΙ ΧΘΟΝΙΟΙ: H, "the ones of the earth" (nom. plural).

82. *εἰς χθονιους*: H, "to the ones under the earth" (acc. pl. after prep. implying motion).

83. Περσεφόνεια: H, "Persephone" [1:11; 74:374].

84. **Tiresias**: The blind sage of Thebes [1:7].

85. **Cristo Re, Dio Sole**: I, "Christ the King, God the Sun."

86. **Kakemono**: J, "a painted scroll."

87. **Uncle William**: W. B. Yeats. Pound acted nominally as his secretary during the winters of 1913, 1914, 1915, at a cottage in Sussex: Yeats worked downstairs and Pound worked upstairs.

88. **Peeeeacock**: The Peacock poem was published in *Poetry*, May 1914. It may have been based on the peacock luncheon W. S. Blunt gave the committee of poets who visited him to pay homage on January 18, 1914 (Yeats, Moore, Manning, Masefield, Plarr, Flint, Aldington, and Pound), memorialized by a photo [see NS *Life*, 239]. Pound attempts to give the impression both of Yeats's Irish brogue and his highly mannered way of reading. See HK, *A Colder Eye* [p. 55], for connection with Pennell's *Life of Whistler* [pp. 301, 306] for the reading which includes a proposal for "a great peacock ten feet high."

89. **aere perennius**: L, "more enduring than bronze" [Horace, *Odes* III, 30].

90. **Stone Cottage**: Coleman's Hatch, Ashdown Forest, in Sussex, where the events reflected in these anecdotes took place—a kind of hilaritas [*Pai*, 4-1, 79]? Pound's early idea of it was not promising: "My stay in Stone Cottage will not be the least profitable. I detest the country. Yeats will amuse me part of the time and bore me to death with psychical research the rest. I regard the visit as a duty to posterity" [*L*, 25]. But he ended up liking it.

91. **Wordsworth**: Part of Pound's secretarial duties included reading to Yeats, whose eyes were very weak. Yeats wrote to his father: "I have just started to read through the whole seven volumes of Wordsworth" [*The Letters of W. B. Yeats*, 590]. But Pound did the reading.

92. **Ennemosor on Witches**: *The History of Magic*, by Joseph Ennemoser, trans. from German by William Howitt, 1854. The book had an appendix by Mary Howitt which contained "the most remarkable and best authenticated stories of apparitions, dreams, second sight, . . . divinations, etc.": in a word, the kind of stuff Yeats, in those years, would have liked best.

93. **Doughty**: Charles Montagu D., 1843-1926, English traveler and writer; author of *Arabia Deserta* (1888) and an epic poem, *The Dawn in Britain* (1906). Pound said of *Arabia Deserta*: "Doughty's volume is a bore, but one ought to read it" [*GK*, 267].

94. **Summons . . .** : During WWI a summons, later withdrawn, was served on both Dorothy and Pound for being aliens in a prohibited area. Stone Cottage was on the coast.

95. **The eyes . . . sea**: Reprise of eyes-*eidos*-sea lyric at 81/520.

96. **und . . . Greis**: G, "and the ladies say to me you are an old man." Pound's version of one of the *Anacreontea*, which usually goes: "Oft am I by the women told, Poor Anacreon, thou grow'st old" [Cowley].

97. **Anacreon**: Greek lyric poet, fl. 525 B.C.

98. **novecento**: I, "of the 20th century."

99. quattrocento: I, "of the fifteenth century."

100. Tirol: The Tyrol. Herr Bacher's father is the 20th-century sculptor of Madonnas [74:496].

101. "Das heis' . . . : G, "That is called Walter Square." A place in Bozen, a German-speaking town in the Tyrol, named after Walther von der Vogelweide. It was called Bolzano after it was ceded to Italy in 1919.

102. Senate: Pound's mother once visited the United States Senate to listen to the proceedings [NS, *Life*, 3].

103. Westminister: Here, the House of Parliament.

104. Senator Edwards: Ninian E., 1775-1833, U.S. Senator from Illinois. He was first appointed governor of the Illinois Territory (1809) and then served as one of its first senators when it became a state. His memorable tropes have not yet been identified.

CANTO LXXXIV

Sources

Time, Oct. 1, Oct. 8, July 30, Aug. 27, 1945; *The Republic*, Armed Services edition (P-29), 425; Dante, *Pur* XXVI; the Bible, Micah 4.5; EP *CON*, 279, 20.

Background

EP, *SP*, 300; H. A. Giles, *A History of Chinese Literature*, London and New York, 1901; *Dial*, LXXI, 4, Oct. 1921; Daphne Fielding, *Those Remarkable Cunards*, Atheneum, 1968; Anne Chisholm, *Nancy Cunard*, New York, Knopf, 1979 [AC, *Nancy*].

Exegeses

Achilles Fang, "Material for the Study of Pound's Cantos," Ph.D. dissertation, Harvard University, 1958, Vols. III, IV; Tay, *Pai*, 4-2 & 3, 549; Bosha, *Pai*, 4-1, 99; Peck, *Pai*, 1-1, 7-9; Bosha *Pai*, 11-2, 284-286; DP, *Barb*, 291-292; CF, *Ideas*, 151-153; LL, *Motive*, 79-80.

Glossary

1. Si tuit . . . : P, "If all the grief and the tears /. . . . Recurrent refrain [80:424].

2. Angold: J. P. A., 1909-1943, British poet who died in action as a pilot in the RAF in 1943. The *London Times* carried his necrology January 14, 1944, MSB note: Got word Angold had been shot down. E.P. working on Angold's economics. Angold had contributed in the early 30s to the *New English Weekly* on economic matters.

3. τέθνηκε: H, "He is dead."

4. tuit . . . bes: P, "all the worth, all the good" [80:424].

5. Bankhead: John Hollis B., 1872-1946,

U.S. Senator from Alabama (1930-1946). Pound thought highly of him because he was a believer in the efficacy of a stamp scrip and proposed it in a Senate bill [*SP*, 300]. Pound heard the remarks on his 1939 visit. The mule is likely Roosevelt.

6. **Borah**: William Edgar B., 1865-1940, U.S. Senator from Idaho (1907-1940). A leading spokesman on foreign affairs. Pound's offer to do what he could to help keep the U.S. out of the war elicited this response [Bosha, *Pai*, 11-2, 284-286].

7. **ye spotted lambe . . . delight**: Source unknown.

8. **Roy Richardson**: Captain in charge of prisoner training, DTC, Pisa.

9. **Demattia . . . Crowder**: Presumably both "blacke and white" trainees at the DTC, the white ones named first and the "(dark)" ones later. One of the black soldiers prob. looked like Henry Crowder, a black jazz musician with whom Nancy Cunard [80:43] had a violent and scandalous love affair (1928-1935). Nancy's mother and many others disowned her because of it, but Pound defended both her and Crowder [AC, *Nancy*, 118-171, 176-182, passim]

10. **Slaughter**: A major in the cadre at Pisa [78:44].

11. **Mr. Coxey**: Jacob Sechler C., 1854-1951, American reformer. *Time* [Oct. 1, 1945] reported about him: " 'General' of the famed tatterdemalion army of unemployed that marched from Ohio on Washington in 1894, still full of fight at 91, gave a Chicago isolationist gathering something to wrestle with: 'The Government takes 20% out of your salary to pay you interest on the 10% you have deducted from your salary to buy bonds. . . . Then they have to tax the people so the Government can pay interest to the banks, so the banks will support Government bonds upon which money is issued' " [p. 46].

12. **Sinc**: Sinclair Lewis, 1885-1953, American novelist. *Time* [Oct. 8, 1945, 100] carried a review of his *Cass Timberlane* which dealt with Lewis's whole work.

13. **Bartók**: Bela B., 1881-1945, Hungarian composer, pianist, and collector of folk music. *Time* carried an obit [ibid., 74].

14. **Mr. Beard**: Charles Austin B., 1874-1948, American historian. The line in question here occurred in the Armed Services edition (P-29) of *The Republic:* "Beard: But all the democracies have new deals or managed economies of one kind or another. If any government keeps control over its own currency, it will in practice, more or less manage its economy" [p. 425].

15. **Mr John Adams**: During the controversies when some politicians and the press wanted war with France, Adams's foreign policy was to keep talking and keep out of war, a quite unpopular stance that helped defeat him in his bid for a second term [70:9, 10]. The idea is also (in Adams letter to B. Rush August 28, 1811) against banks of discount [71:35; 94:10].

16. **Carrara**: Source of marble near Pisa [74:80]. MSB note: "Brancusi went down to buy marble. Found it all monopolized by some company. He noticed how they had destroyed the mountains."

17. **Garonne**: River [4:41].

18. **Spagna**: I, "Spain."

19. **T'ao Ch'ien**: A.D. 365-427, called T'ao Yuan-ming when young, he was the most famous Middle Kingdom poet of his time. He left official life, for which he was unfitted, to return to his home, children, and gardens. His "Peach-blossom fountain" is an allegory that tells of how a fisherman lost his way and came into a beautiful land "of fine houses, of rich fields, of fine pools . . . [where] young and old alike appeared to be contented and happy" [Giles, *Chinese Literature*, 130-131]. The beautiful land is the land of his youth now lost forever, or the Old Dynasty.

20. **Ho Ci'u**: Prob. the town named Sié on a river in Shansi Province [53:121]. The Chi-

nese word for river is Ho. David Gordon has a note saying this town in old China is known only because of the event described: where it is described is not known.

21. **Κύθηρα δεινά**: H, "Fearful Cythera." A recurrent musical figure [76:106; 80:129].

22. **Carson**: Prob. E. G. Carson, a miner whom the Pound family knew ca. 1910.

23. **My old great aunt**: Aunt Frank, who owned the Hotel "Easton" at 24 E 47th street and managed it after the death of "Amos" but did not have much financial success at it [74:461].

24. **Tangiers**: [74:160].

25. **Natalie**: N. C. Barney [80:220]. In remarks about her *Pensées d'une amazone*, Pound wrote: "[They] contain possibly several things not to be found in the famous *Lettres* addressed to that allegory, and at least one sublime sentence running I think 'Having got out of life, oh having got out of it perhaps more than it contained' " [*Dial*, LXXI, 4, Oct. 1921, 458].

26. **cielo di Pisa**: I, "sky of Pisa."

27. **Wei**: (Wei Tzu), 12th century B.C., viscount of the principality of Wei. He was the stepbrother of Cheou-sin, last sovereign of the Yin dynasty [53:56]; Wei became so disgusted with the cruelty of his kinsman that he retired from the court and left the kingdom.

28. **Chi**: (Chi Tzu). Viscount of the principality of Chi, 12th century B.C. Uncle of Cheou-sin, last sovereign of the Yin dynasty. Because he protested against the practices of the emperor, Chi was put into prison.

29. **Pi-kan**: (Pi Kan) 12th century B.C., uncle of Cheou-sin, last emperor of the Yin dynasty. When Pi-kan objected to the excesses of Cheou-sin, the emperor had him disembowelled on the spot. *Analects* XVII, 16: "The Viscount of Wei retired. The Viscount of Chi became a slave. Pikan protested and died . . . Kung-Tze said: Yin had three men (with a capital M)" [*CON*, 279].

30. **Yin**: [53:48].

31. **humanitas**: L, "humaneness."

32. **jên**[2]: C, [82:37], "humaneness."

33. **Xaire**: H, "Hail!"

34. **Alessandro**: A. Pavolini, secretary of the Fascist Republican party of the government established at Salò in 1943 [Tay, *Pai*, 4-2 & 3, 549].

35. **Fernando**: F. Mezzasoma, minister of popular culture of the Salò Republic. After Mussolini was executed, Mezzasoma and Pavolini were shot along with 13 others. They were later hanged head down, with Mussolini, in Milan [ibid.].

36. **e il Capo**: I, "and the leader." Mussolini.

37. **Pierre**: P. Laval, 1883-1945, premier of Vichy France [1942-1945].

38. **Vidkun**: V. Quisling, 1887-1945, Norwegian politician who collaborated in the German conquest of Norway (1940) and became head of the government under the German conquest of Norway (1940) and became head of the government under the German occupation.

39. **Henriot**: Philippe H., French Fascist journalist and radio propagandist who was appointed to a ministerial post in the Vichy government during the German occupation of France in WWII. Shot by French Resistance on 28 June 1944 [Bosha, *Pai*, 4-1, 99].

40. **Imperial Chemicals**: The British chemical combine. The one who went out of industrials was Wm. C. Bullitt, 1891-1967 [RO]. He became an assistant to Cordell Hull and served as ambassador to the USSR and then to France, 1936-1941. After this he enlisted in the French army and served as a major during 1944-1945. The implication seems to be that, as an inside wealthy Yale man, he knew the depression was coming and sold all his stocks. He is contrasted with Dorothy Pound, who sold her stocks in a munitions company not to save money but so as not to be mixed up with the killing.

MSB note: She inherited the stock. Refused to have blood money.

41. **quand . . . escalina**: P, "when you come to the top of the stair" [*Pur.* XXVI, 146]. Part of the appeal of Arnaut Daniel. It is followed up: "In the time to come remember my pain. Then he dived back into the fire that refines them." Eliot used the verse in the notes to *The Waste Land*.

42. **ἦθos**: H, "custom, usage, character" [Peck, *Pai*, 1-1, 7-9; DP, *Barb*, 291-292]. MSB note: EP translates as gradations.

43. **ming²**: C, [M4534]. Defined by Pound as the light descending from both sun and moon, thus intelligence [74:88; *CON*, 20]. MSB note: Distinctions in clarity means "degrees of decency in action."

44. **John Adams**: [31:15].

45. **Brothers Adam**: Prob. Samuel Adams and John Adams, commonly known as "the brace of Adamses," as at 64/360 [EH].

46. **Chung¹**: C, [M1504], "center, balance" as in Chung Yung.

47. **Micah**: Hebrew prophet who flourished ca. 700 B.C. Micah 4.5: "Everyone in the name of his god." A passage Pound quotes in various ways: 74/435; 74/441; 74/443; 76/454; 78/479; 79/487.

48. **Kumrad Koba**: Joseph Stalin [74:34]. Koba, "the bear," and/or "the indomitable," [*Pai*, 11-2, 285] was his boyhood nickname. "Kumrad" is borrowed from e. e. cummings's book *No Thanks. Time* [Aug. 27, 1945], in a note about Potsdam, says Stalin disliked Churchill and his long-winded speeches. Once when Churchill was complaining about "Russian plundering in southeastern Europe, Stalin merely grunted; his interpreter said that he had no comment. Truman sprang up, said that he had investigated the British charges and was prepared to substantiate them. Stalin twinkled pointedly and replied: "I will believe the Americans' " [p. 30].

49. **Winston, P.M.**: *Time* [July 30, 1945]. Since Churchill was defeated in the election of July 26, a photograph showing him leaving Hitler's chancellery in this issue may have evoked the words "last appearance."

50. **e poi . . . uguale**: I, "and then I asked the sister / of the little shepherdess of the hogs / and these Americans? / do they behave well? / and she: not very well / not very well at all / and I: worse than the Germans? / and she: the same."

51. **Lincoln Steffens**: Joseph Lincoln S., 1866-1939, an American journalist whose political speeches and writings appealed to Pound in the late 20s [19:24, 25].

52. **Vandenberg**: Arthur Hendrick V., 1884-1952, member of the U.S. Senate from Michigan (1928-52); he was leader of the Senate "isolationist bloc" before WWII, but later served as a U.S. delegate to the United Nations conference in San Francisco (1945).

CANTO LXXXV

Sources

David M. Dewitt, *The Judicial Murder of Mary E. Surratt*, Baltimore, 1895; Guy W. Moore, *The Case of Mrs. Surratt*, Univ. of Oklahoma, 1954; Séraphin Couvreur, *Chou King*, Paris, Cathasia, 1950 [Couvreur]; Russell Grenfell, *Unconditional Hatred*, Devin-Adair, 1953 [*UH*]; *CON*, 27-29, 232, 21, 20, 77; James Legge, *The Four Books*, Shanghai, 1923 [Legge]; Sophocles, *Electra*, line 351; *WT*, 50; Dante, *Par.* X, *Conv.* 4, *Pur.* XXIV; Aristotle, *Politics* VII, 4; Otto Eisenschiml, *Why Was Lincoln Murdered?*, Little, Brown, 1937; James Legge, *The Shoo King*, in *The Chinese Classics*, vol. III, 1865 (rpt. Hong Kong University Press, 1960).

Background

EP, *SP*, 322, 71, 323; *GK*, 77, 84, 105; *P*, 152; *SR*, 48; Otto Eisenschiml, *In the Shadow of Lincoln's Death*, New York, Wilfred Funk, 1940; Eustace Mullins, *This Difficult Individual, Ezra Pound*, New York, 1961, [EM, *Difficult*]; I. Kirkpatrick, *Mussolini: A Study of a Demagogue*, London, 1964.

Exegeses

Thomas Grieve, "Annotations to the Chinese in *Section: Rock-Drill*," *Pai*, 4-2 & 3, 362-509 (unless otherwise documented, the Chinese materials in the glosses for *Rock-Drill* are based on this study). HK, *Era*, 528; Neault, *Pai*, 3-2, 219-27; JW, *Seven Troubadours*, 156-57; Mondolfo, *Pai*, 3-2, 286; HK, *Pai*, 1-1, 83; Richard Jesse Freidenheim, "Ezra Pound: Canto 85," Ph.D. dissertation, Univ. of California, Berkeley, 1977.

Glossary

1. **Ideogram**: Ling[2] [M4071]. Combines "heaven" over "cloud" over "3 raindrops" over "ritual." Pound translates as "sensibility."

2. **Our dynasty**: The Shang dynasty (1753-1121 B.C.). The line is Pound's version of a line in Couvreur's *Chou King*, P. IV, Chap. XIV: "Now our Chou King grandly and excellently has taken over God's affairs" [p. 295]. This chap., entitled "The Numerous Officers," is an announcement to the remaining officers of the Shang dynasty made by the duke of Chou after he had helped King Wu conquer Shang and move to the new city, Lo. The message of Chou is that Cheou, the last king of Shang, lost his sovereignty to King Wu because of his moral disorder [53:56].

3. **Ideogram**: I [M2936], "he, she, it, that one."

4. **Ideogram**: Yin [M7439], "ruler," thus "I yin" means "the one who rules."

5. **I Yin**: Chief minister of Ch'êng T'ang, 1766-1753 B.C., first emperor of the Shang dynasty. After the death of T'ang, I Yin became a sort of regent and mentor to the young king and taught him the principles of virtuous government. His teachings are the substance of P. III, Chaps. IV, V, and VI [pp. 113-132] of *Chou King*.

6. **roots**: "The word 'roots' is emphatic . . . ; a dynasty grows massively when a great sensibility roots it" [HK, *Era*, 528]. Note rhyme with the tree Yggdrasil of Norse Mythology [cf. 38 below; 90:3].

7. **Galileo . . . 1616**: In 1616 no works of Galileo were specifically listed in the *Index Librorum Prohibitorum* established in 1564; but the essential principles of his thought as found in Copernicus were cited. Pound's source is *Unconditional Hatred* by Captain Russell Grenfell [87:21]. This book is also the source of "Wellington's peace." Grenfell examines the accusation that Germany was the sole cause of two world wars and rejects

it as unscientific and biased. But war propaganda in England made it impossible to talk about: "It became as dangerous from 1940 to 1945 to suggest this accusation was not in accordance with the evidence as it had been for Galileo to question the belief . . . supported by the Papacy . . . that the sun went around the earth. Galileo's published theory was put on the Index . . . in 1616. . . . In like fashion, any objection to the official propaganda . . . that the Germans were the wicked people of the world was liable to get the objector into trouble" [pp. 186-187].

8. **Wellington's peace**: Grenfell (*UH*) contrasts the unreasonableness of the Churchill-Roosevelt war objectives (the total destruction of Germany as a European power following "unconditional surrender") with the wisdom of Wellington, whose guidelines after Waterloo prevented either Germany or France getting territory which might lead to future wars [87:21].

9. **Ideogram**: Chih [M939], "come to rest." This character, used 8 times in *The Cantos*, has a pivotal function: as in the *Ta Hsio, chih* is the ground whence virtuous action springs. Pound translates: "The Great Learning . . . is rooted in coming to rest, being at ease in perfect equity. Know the point of rest and then have an orderly mode of procedure" [*CON* 27-29]. To the *Analects* Pound adds a note: "There is no more important technical term in the Confucian philosophy than this chih (3) the hitching post, position, place one is in, and works from" [*CON*, 232]. Pound based a number of his visual reactions to Chinese characters on the etymologies of Morrison [87:87], which are now supposed to be unscientific and inaccurate. As did Morrison, Pound saw a base horizontal stroke, —, as "earth," a top horizontal stroke, —, as "heaven," and a middle horizontal stroke, , as "man," who lives between heaven and earth. Thus, the ideogram for the fully humane man who lives according to the process of heaven and earth is the character for man used in combination with the horizontal strokes for heaven and earth 仁. Since this gloss is a cue to Pound's continuous perception about hundreds of other characters, the reader is urged to get the idea firmly in mind. The character for *ling*, above, has the strong base line for earth and the strong stroke for heaven over all. Here *chih*[3] pictures the hitching post based firmly on the earth. If we add a horizontal stroke at the top for heaven, we get the character for "right." Put the sun, 日, over the earth, —, and we have "dawn." The ideogram for "earth, soil, land" shows an element of the character for "tree" standing on the earth: 土. The character for "king," 王, has a vertical line showing the king's function as a man translating heaven's will to the people. The character for *p'i* [cf. 179 below] adds a perception of Pound not shared by many others: the 3 strokes between heaven and earth become an arrow pointing toward heaven. And the same character minus the horizontal base stroke becomes a negative, "with no ground beneath it." At 98/685, this perception is applied to "the lot of 'em, Yeats, Possum and Wyndham." And so on with numerous characters in the text [John Cayley, *Pai*, 13-1].

10. **gnomon**: (a) a sundial; (b) a column or shaft erected perpendicular to the horizon. Shadows define the position of the sun and the time of day. Also a Neoplatonic light metaphor: shadows are defined as light (lux, lumen) pours. *Chou King* contains records of astronomers watching their gnomons and fixing the seasons.

11. **Queen Bess**: Elizabeth I [66:71]. Pound was impressed with her scholarship and the Confucian qualities she demonstrated as a magnanimous ruler [107:126].

12. **Ovid**: [4/15; 7/24; 76/462]. Elizabeth was famous for her learning. The record shows that at a visit to Cambridge she was asked to say a few words, "just three would do," in Latin. She finally rose and delivered a 600 word oration in impeccable Latin. The record does not show exactly what of Ovid she translated.

13. **Cleopatra**: Realizing as she did that control of the currency and of coinage was a

central responsibility and function of the state, she was a Western ruler, one who, like Elizabeth, can be identified with the Confucian idea of order.

14. Versus . . . (turbae): L, "Opposed to . . . disorderly crowd." Couvreur: " 'Quae despiciebant probos prudentesque viros et adhaerebant potentibus, vere plurimae erant turbae' " (" 'Many were the unruly men who scorned virtue and ability and aligned themselves with might' ") [Pt. III, Chap. II, sec. 4]. Tchoung Houei, one of the principal ministers of Ch'êng T'ang is describing the rabble (*turbae*) who, disdaining men of worth (*hsien*), followed instead the dissolute and slothful Chieh and thus jumped to what they believed to be "the winning side." Ch'êng T'ang, with the assistance of his minister I Yin, successfully opposed Chieh and established the Shang dynasty. Pound extends the example to all civilization: the consequence of condemning virtue and ability is social disorder.

15. Ideogram: Hsien [M2671], "virtuous, worthy, good."

16. II.9: Chap. II, sec. 9 (the announcement of Chung Hui) in Pt. III of *Chou King*. "Tchoung" and "Cheu" appear in that chapter: "he who would take care of his *end* must be attentive to his beginning."

17. Tchōung: Chung [M1500], "end-death."

18. chèu: Shih [M5772], "beginning."

19. Ideogram: Jen [M3099], "perfect virtue; humaneness."

20. Ideogram: Chih [M933], "wisdom; prudence."

21. i-li: I [M2932], "by, with"; li [M3886], "politeness."

22. 衷: Chung [M1508], "heart, rectitude." Note that the phrase "(1508, Mathews)" in the right margin should be next to this character.

23. 好 : Hao [M2062], "good, excellent."

24. 甲 : Chia [M610], "armour, scaly."

25. epitome . . . : A "gist" or "pith" summarizing the passages from *Chou King* with emphasis on the characters.

26. The sun: In the character for *chih*^{4} [cf. 20 above], we have three components: 智. The top two carry the sense of prudence; the bottom one, 日, is the sun radical and indicates "process" or the idea of "through time."

27. Justice . . . prudence: F, "justice of civility, of wisdom." An explanatory note of Couvreur says that heaven gave man ("put into his heart") these principles.

28. wei heou: French transcription of *wei* [M7066], "only," and *hou* [M2144], "ruler," which together mean "sovereign."

29. Σθφία: H, "wisdom."

30. chueh: [M1680]. A personal pronoun: "his, their." What Pound sees in the character 厥 is not what philologists see. The first component, 厂, he sees as a shelter; under this, 屰, "grass"; and to the right, 欠, a radical which means "lacking," which may imply hopes. When these three things cohere we have a rhyme with "what SPLENDOUR' IT ALL COHERES" [109:17; 116/797].

31. Not led . . . contriving: Pound's idea of a Couvreur passage concerning the motivation of a good sovereign.

32. eccellenza: I, "excellence."

33. THE FOUR TUAN: The four principles of Confucianism–love, duty, propriety, and wisdom.

34. Ideo: Tuan [M6541], "principles, foundations."

35. Hulled rice . . . easter: Pound sees in the character for *i* [M3001], 彝 (not in canto), components for hulled rice, 米, and silk, 糸. The character refers to cups or vases used in libations in a religions context: thus, the idea of Easter.

36. bachi: I, from *bachicoltore*, "silk worm breeder," meaning "cocoon." Italian peasant women brought *bachi* to mass concealed in their aprons, an old pagan tradition persisting into the present.

37. **T'ang**: [53:40]. He inscribed on his bathtub, "Make it New."

38. **Ygdrasail**: Yggdrasil. In Norse mythology the great tree whose branches extend throughout the universe. In Western terms a subject rhyme with "the process" or "the way."

39. **poi**: I, "then."

40. **Ideogram**: Shih [M5780], "a period of time."

41. **Ideogram**: Ch'ên [M331], "sincere, trustworthy."

42. **Ideogram**: Ch'ên. Another form. Together, *shih ch'en*, meaning "to be sincere," comes from a Couvreur passage that Legge translates: "Oh! let us attain *to be sincere* in these things and so we shall likewise have a happy consummation."

43. **"Birds . . . excess"**: Legge translates: "The earlier sovereigns of Hea cultivated earnestly their virtue, and then there were no calamities from Heaven. The spirits . . . were all in tranquillity; and the birds and beasts, the fishes and tortoises, all realized the happiness of their nature." Flood and flame are calamities from heaven.

44. **Hia**: Hsia. The first dynasty [53:44].

45. **i moua pou gning**: I [M3021], mo [M4557], pu [M5379], ning [M4725]. Couvreur's French transcription: "likewise all were in tranquility."

46. **Perspicax . . .** : L, "He who cultivates himself is keen." The line does not occur exactly in this form in Couvreur's Latin, but the idea does.

47. **This "leader" . . . pole**: The ideas in these lines with the gouged pumpkin are not clearly in the relevant sections of Couvreur or Legge. Thus they probably derive from a Poundian nonphilological examination of some characters. The young king [cf. 55 below] was named T'ai Chia. The second component in his name [cf. 24 above] may have suggested a gouged pumpkin hoisted on a pole. As recorded in the "T'ai Chia", I Yin sent the young king into seclusion by the tomb of his grandfather because he did not follow I Yin's advice.

48. **Ideogram**: Tê [M6162], "virtue." Pound's idea of the character: "the action resultant from this straight gaze into the heart. The 'know thyself' carried into action" [*CON*, 21].

49. **Τέχνη**: H, "skill in making things." A 1952 addenda to *GK* [p. 351] says that before Aristotle was "cold in his grave, the compilers of the so-called 'Magna Moralia' had already omitted TEXNE from the list of mental faculties given in the Nicomachean Ethics."

50. *σεαυτόν*: H, "oneself."

51. **Dante**: [74:385].

52. **St Victor**: Richard, ?-1173, said to be from Scotland, was a celebrated scholastic philosopher and the most important 12th-century mystic; his system, both visionary and down-to-earth, made him significant for both Dante and Pound. Dante wrote: "Richard / Who in contemplation was more than a man" [*Par.* X, 131-132]. Richard's *De Contemplatione* [*Benjamin Major*] is mentioned by Dante in his letter to Can Grande [*Epistula* XIII, 80]. Pound mentions Richard often in his prose works. Richard's distinctions between cogitatio, meditatio, and contemplatio are, in the design of *The Cantos*, as important (in my opinion more) as Dante's Hell-Purgatory-Paradise design in *The Divine Comedy*. Said Pound: "I would say that every book of value contains a bibliography declared or implied. The *De Vulgari Eloqui* refers us to Richard of St Victor, Sordello, Bertran de Born, and Arnaut Daniel. Dante was my Baedeker in Provence" [*SP*, 322]. In fact, Pound expresses his own convictions about the way divinity manifests in the world as much by quotations from Richard as any other way. In 1956 he documented a

piece entitled "Deus est Amor," published in 1940, by "Quotations from Richard St Victor" [*SP*, 71]. The people who inhabit *The Cantos*, early and late, may be judged as types belonging to Hell, Purgatory, or Paradise on the basis of several criteria. One of the most important of these is their mode of thought. Said Pound: "Richard St Victor had hold of something: sic: There are three modes of thought, cogitation, meditation and contemplation. In the first the mind flits aimlessly about the object [Hell], in the second it circles about in a methodical manner [Purgatory], in the third it is unified with the object [Paradise]" [*GK*, 77]. Richard will come up by name and citations from his thoughts with increasing frequency in the later cantos [87/570, 576, 90/607]. Richard's three modes of thought come to be expressed graphically by other clusters of threes: earth, cocoon, wasp; earth, crysalis, butterfly (the kings in their islands); light, crystal, jade; and so on [Neault, *Pai*, 3-2, 219-227].

53. **Erigena**: [36:9; 83:8]. To entertain the king (Charles the Bald) he brightened up his style with classical quotes, he being about the only person around in the 9th century who could do so [83:10].

54. **Y Yin**: [cf. 5 above].

55. **young king**: T'ai Chia [cf. 47 above].

56. **CONTEMPLATIO**: It is what Pound calls "chinks," "sophists," and "hindoo immaturities" which are out to destroy Richard of St Victor's state.

57. **T'oung loco palatium"**: L, "T'ung the place of palaces." According to I Yin, the young king was not learning to be a virtuous sovereign but rather he was being stubborn, with a self-centered mind of his own ("squirrel-headed"), a state of mind which I Yin was not about to encourage by pampering. So I Yin said of the young king, "failure to change his course. This is real unrighteousness, and is becoming by practice a second nature. I cannot bear to be near such a disobedient fellow. I will build a place in the palace at T'ung, where he can be quietly near the remains of the former king."

58. **fish-traps**: The character for "deceive" is used in a metaphor that translates, "a fish-trap of wicker," suggesting something weak and temporary. If the young king were to go on in his old ways, he would, when ruler, "bitch" the generation he ruled by weak, unprincipled expedients (in a word, Confucian disorder) and not build on solid virtue and humanitas.

59. **k'o . . .** : K'e [M3320], "competent"; chung [M1500], "end"; yun [M7759], "sincere"; te [M6162], "virtue" [cf. 48 above]. Or, "In the end he [the young king] became sincerely virtuous."

60. **elbow-grease**: Pound's rendition of, "What achievement can be made without earnest effort?"

61. **Szu**: [M5592]. "To sacrifice." Couvreur's "seu," "year." From the "T'ai Chia" "on the first day of the 12th month of the 3rd year, I Yin took the imperial cap and robes, and escorted the young king back to Po" [Legge, IV, V, ii].

62. **vain . . . done**: From, "When the sovereign will not with disputatious words throw the old rules of government into confusion, and the minister will not for favour and gain continue in an office whose work is done;–then the country will lastingly and surely enjoy happiness" [Legge, IV, V, III].

63. **i jênn iuên**: I [M3016], "one"; jen [M3097], "man"; yuan [M7707], "good." Together, "let the one man be good." If the emperor be good, order will flow from him.

64. **Ideogram**: I [M2932], "whereby."

65. **Ideogram**: Chen [M346], "virtue."

66. **reddidit . . .** : L, "he restored the government to the emperor." Couvreur's Latin. The context of these words informs the rest of this canto page. I Yin, "having returned the government into the hands of his sovereign, and being about to announce his retire-

ment, set forth admonitions on the subject of virtue."

67. **Ideogram**: Ch'en [M339], "present."

68. **Ideogram**: Chiai [M627], "admonitions."

69. **pivot**: NB: "Chung Yung," or "the Unwobbling Pivot." The emperor will become such a pivot from which all goods will flow if he follows the precepts of Yin.

70. **quam . . . Imperatoris**: L, "how simple [pure] is the soul of the emperor."

71. **III. 6 xi**: Couvreur III, VI, 9, 11, pp. 130-131 has the Latin and French for the following, but Pound inserts the characters (in his own order) for the expostulation from Legge IV, VI, iv, 9, 11, pp. 218-219.

72. **Ideogram**: Huo [M2412], "to seize" (1st character, right-hand column).

73. **Ideogram**: Tzu [M6960], "self."

74. **Ideogram**: Chin [M1082], "all."

75. **Ideogram**: P'i [M5170], "an ordinary person."

76. **Ideogram**: Fu [M1908], "husband" (1st character, left-hand column).

77. **Ideogram**: P'i [M5170], "one of a pair; a mate."

78. **Ideogram**: Fu [M1963], "wife."

79. **Bill of Rights**: In the seven characters, Pound has left out a negative in his source. Legge, with the negative condition, gives: "If ordinary men and women do not find the opportunity to give full development to their virtue." The sentence ends: "the people's lord will be without the proper aids to complete his merit."

80. **P'an**: The name of the reign of the 17th emperor of the Chang dynasty: P'an Keng. Legge says that more than 3 centuries were left blank in the histories between the young king, T'ai Chia, and P'an Keng.

81. **Ideogram**: P'an Keng [M4903], emperor, 1401-1373. He moved the capital to Yin and changed the name of the dynasty to Yin. After the move, he exhorted the people to care for the young and helpless and to make the best of their new home. The following 5 characters are a part of that exhortation: "Seek every one long continuance in your new abode."

82. **Ideogram**: Ko [M3368], "each, all."

83. **Ideogram**: Ch'ang [M213], "long, of space or time."

84. **Ideogram**: Yu [M7592], "to proceed."

85. **Ideogram**: Chueh [M1680], personal pronoun: "he, she, it, etc."

86. **Ideogram**: Chu [M1535], "to dwell."

87. **Baros . . .** : P, "barons put up as pawns." In *Near Perigord* Pound translates the phrase of Bertrans de Born by, "Pawn your castles, lords!" [*P*, 152]. The idea was to mortgage to the hilt before a battle so that, if you lost, the mortgage would fall on the man you lost to [*SR*, 48]. For a detailed and different reading see JW, *Seven Troubadours*, pp. 156-157.

88. **Alexander**: A. the Great, 356-323 B.C., king of Macedon. His act of largesse to his troops becomes a recurrent musical figure in the later cantos. Pound believes the fall of the Macedonian empire was as great a loss to Western civilization as was the later fall of Rome [*GK*, *SP*, indexes]. Dante placed him among the world's foremost bestowers of largesse [*Conv.* 4.11.14], which contrasts him with Bertrans de Born [89:230].

89. **Ideogram**: Te [cf. 48 above]: "virtue."

90. **The pusillanimous . . . as core**: These 16 lines derive from Grenfell's *Unconditonal Hatred* [cf. 7 above]. Grenfell says Dexter White was the author of the plan to crush Germany. Roosevelt approved, but the plan to reduce Germany to an agrarian state was never put into action [*UH*, 207]. In the 1860s Napoleon III made one claim after another for pieces of Germany, but Grenfell shows that Bismarck agreed to none of them [*UH*, 50-53].

91. **Mr. Roosevelt**: [46:53].

92. **Dexter White**: Harry D. W. After the U.S. joined with the USSR in 1941, he became a privileged right-hand man, with the status of assistant secretary, to Morganthau, secretary of the treasury, 1934-1945. A 1955 Senate investigation produced documents that implied that Communists, with the aid of White, were infiltrating the higher branches of the government. According to Eustace Mullins, Old Lampman [97:60], who had worked in the Treasury Department during the 1930s said: "Men who had been in the Treasury Department all their lives were suddenly shunted aside and stripped of their power. We were told to clear everything with new officials, such as Harry Dexter White" [EM, *Difficult*, 315-316].

93. **Nap III**: Napoleon [16:24; 38:59; 74:464].

94. **Proclamation**: Louis Napoleon III, elected as president of the French Republic in 1848, made plans and arrangements to outfox his enemies and successfully became by proclamation, Dec. 1, 1852, emperor of the French. He cultivated different groups in different ways and only a few knew what he was up to before faced with the fait accompli. This thought leads to a reflection about U.S. university education, by which students are kept off the labor market and never learn anything about the economic conspiracy being practiced against them.

95. **prezzo giusto**: I, "just price." A major concept in Poundian economics in which an important document is *Il Giusto prezzo nel Medio Aveo* by Sac. L. P. Cairoli [*SP*,323].

96. **UBI JUS VAGUM**: L, "Where law is uncertain." Prob. a variant on the adage, *Ubi jus incertum, ibi jus nullum* ("Where law is uncertain, there is no law"), as well as on Aristotle's maxim, "Good law means good order" [*Politics* VII, 4] [DJN].

97. **Alexander**: [cf. 88 above].

98. **T'ang**: [53:40; 74:29] The "Make it New" emperor.

99. **Ideogram**: Kao [M3290], "noble"

100. **Ideogram**: Tsung [M6896], "ancestor." The emperor Woo-Ting of the Chang dynasty was known posthumously as Kao Tsung. He ruled from 1324-1265, a total of 59 years, as the text says. He was a good emperor who wanted to restore the values of the dynasty's founder, Ch'eng T'ang.

101. **Whetstone . . . clouds**: Upon appointing Yueh as prime minister, Kao Tsung outlined the ways a good minister would serve his emperor, and the way he would make use of his minister: "Suppose me a weapon of steel;–I will use you for a whetstone. Suppose me crossing a great stream;–I will use you for a boat with its oars. Suppose me in a year of great drought;–I will use you as a copious rain."

102. **jòu tso li**: French transliteration of *ju* [M3142] *tso* [M6780] *li* [M3909]: "Use you as a whetstone."

103. **cymba et remis**: L, "boat and oar." The character for *lin*^{2} [M4026], 霖, which means "long-continued rain," has several components: the lower ones mean "trees"; the upper one means "rain." Pound sees "trees prop up clouds."

104. **Praecognita . . . moveas**: L, "Know (beforehand) the good so that you may move yourself." Part of Kao Tsung's advice to his minister. The sentence is followed by another which translates, "And act only if the time is right."

105. **Ideogram**: French "liú," lu [M4292], "consider." *Ideo:* French "cheu," shih [M5780], "time."

106. **"Fatigare . . . revereri"**: L, "Immoderate sacrifice is called irreverence." Advice of Prime Minister Yueh to the emperor. He added: "Ceremonies when burdensome lead to disorder. To serve the spirits properly is difficult." These ideas are repeated in Apollonius of Tyana as a subject rhyme [94:42].

107. **Fou iue**: French form of Fu Yueh, the name of Kao Tsung's prime minister.

108. III. viii, 11.: Location of the Latin quote in Couvreur.

109. Ideogram: French "tchoung," chung [76:54].

110. in rites not flame-headed: The character for "burdensome" [106 above] is *fan*: 煩: the left component is "fire"; the right component is "head." Hence, Pound's "Flame-headed."

111. "Up to then . . . : The emperor, Kao-Tsung, said to his minister Yueh: "Come, O Yue. I, the little one, first learned with Kan Pwan. Afterwards, I lived concealed in the rude country . . . and the result has been that I am unenlightened."

112. chung . . . : Chung [M1500], "the end result"; wang [M7045], "in vain"; hsien [M2692], "seems." "The result seems to have been in vain."

113. Imperator . . . mustum: L, "The emperor. Just as wine and must" [see 115 below].

114. directio: L, "direction." Evokes "direction of the will," a major theme of the poem. The word does not occur in Couvreur's Latin. Instead of combining it with "voluntatis," as he usually does [77:57], Pound combines it here with a Chinese word for will: "tchéu," or chih [M971], "determination; will."

115. fermentum . . . : L, "fermentation and fruit [seeds/grain]." These words, along with the Latin in 113 above, are fragments of a whole sentence of Kao Tsung to Yueh which says: "Be to me as the yeast and the malt in making sweet spirits; as the salt and the prunes in making agreeable soup."

116. study . . . hawk: More of Yueh's advice to the emperor.

117. taó tsi: French translation for *tao* [M6136], "truth" and *chi* [M500], "store up."

118. Τέχνη: H [context of 49 above], "skill in an art."

119. Tch'eng T'ang: Ch'êng T'ang [cf. 5 above].

120. Ideogram: Chen [M346], "direction."

121. You will go . . . : Yueh answers Kao's appeal for advice on how to be a good emperor by defining the proper subjects of study. Pound summarizes by the 1/2-research-1/2-observation-etc. device, adding to this the practices of T'ang, the founder of the dynasty. He says if Kao Tsong will do these things he will not slip or slop over in his rule.

122. Nisi . . . regit: L, "Unless he does not rule with the wise." Kao responds to Yueh's advice and says in effect, "an emperor must rule through ministers who are wise."

123. "Best you retire: Pound jumps 200 years to the end of the Shang dynasty. The grand tutor, viscount of Ki, tells Wei, son of the emperor Shou, to retire from the court before ruin comes.

124. nunquam ego: L, "not I." Ki said: "You go but not I."

125. Ideogram: Wang [M7045], "not."

126. Ideogram:Pou, p'u [M5401],"servant."

127. Ki: The grand tutor to Prince Wei.

128. Corea: Korea.

129. "abire decere": L, "it is best to go." The passage that ties these lines together is Ki's advice to the prince: "Calamity now befalls the house of Shang. I will arise and share in its ruin; for when Shang has fallen, I will not be servant or minister to another dynasty. I recommend, that for you, the emperor's son, it is best to go away. . . . If the emperor's son does not leave, we [the house of Shang] will perish." Wei did leave and Ki remained to be imprisoned for a while; but because of his virtue and wisdom he was eventually freed and sent to Corea to govern. Another story has it that he feigned madness and was released by King Wu of the new Chou dynasty and then fled to Corea.

130. Meng-ford: From the phrase that follows ("tá houéi Méng tsin"), which means "greatly assembled at Meng Ford." It is part of the first line of the Great Declaration, which consists of three speeches King Wu gave to his officers and people after his conquest of the Shang dynasty [Pt. IV, Chap. I, Couvreur's *Chou King*].

131. Heou Tsi . . . Tàn Fóu: A summary of a Couvreur historical note that traces the history of the royal family of the Chou dynasty, showing the results of the watchword "our dynasty came in because of a great sensibility," a reprise of the opening of the canto [cf. 2 above]. Grieve has a note that gives much in little: "Tan Fou . . . was the great-grandfather of Wu Wang, the king who, continuing the rebellion of his father, Wen Wang, defeated the tyrant emperor Chou Hsin [last of the Shang dynasty] and in 1122 B.C. founded the Chou dynasty. It was Tan Fou who first established the Chou state at the foot of Mount Ki in 1326 B.C. King Wan . . . passed on the Chou hereditary dominions to his son . . . Wu Wang."

132. Les moeurs . . . fleurit: F, "The morals had been reformed; virtue flourished."

133. Ideogram: Ling [cf. 1 above]. We return to the ideogram that opened this canto. While Pound uses several other characters to stand for the virtue, humanity, and sensitiveness of the individual, he uses this one to tie together the processes of heaven with the processes of nature and the Confucian ideals of order in man. Just as the transcendant order of Neoplatonic thought is imaged by the heavens and clouds being reflected in water, so here the sky-cloud components on the top of this character, with the rain in the center and the earth-ceremonies of the bottom components, imply in parallel fashion the harmony that results when the processes of heaven's will are reflected in the actions of the emperor who has the good of the people at heart. Note too the way the three components of *ling* articulate with the three panels of Cosimo Tura [79:25].

134. Ad Meng vadum: L, "At the ford of Meng."

135. Huang Ho: "Yellow River."

136. ch' e' ditta dentro: I, "which he dictates within me" [*Pur.* XXIV, 54]. Bonagiunta of Lucca asks Dante if he is the one "who brought forth new rhymes, beginning: Ladies that have understanding of love?" Dante answers him, "I am one who, when Love inspires me, takes note, and goes setting it forth after the fashion which he dictates within me" [Singleton].

137. Cheóu . . . aerumnas: L, "Chou inflicts calamities." This Chou is the last emperor of the Shang dynasty. In the spring at the ford of Meng, Wu Wang spoke to his officers and people: "Heaven and earth are the parents of all things; and of all things, man alone has reason. He who is most intelligent and perspicacious becomes the supreme sovereign; and the supreme sovereign becomes the parents of the people. Now Chou [Cheóu], the emperor of Shang, does not stand in awe of heaven above and inflicts calamities on the people below."

138. Ideogram: Ts'oung, ts'ung [M6916], "astute."

139. Ideogram: Tàn [M6048],"sincere."

140. Ideogram: Ming [M4534], "intelligent." This character is central to Pound's idea of divinity manifesting itself through the intelligence of man [*CON*, 20].

141. tso iuên heóu: French for tso [M6780], "to make"; yüan [M7707], "chief, great"; hou [M2144], "king." "To be a great sovereign."

142. "Gentlemen . . . : King Wu (chief ruler of the West) went on to tell his people (from the western states) more reasons why heaven desired him to overthrow the emperor and become ruler of all the Middle Kingdom. Legge translates: "Oh! my valiant men of the West, Heaven has enjoined the illustrious courses of duty, of which the several characters are quite plain."

143. Ideogram: Hsien [M2692], "manifest." Legge translates as "quite plain"; Pound says "perfectly clear."

144. Ideogram: Wu [M7195], "warlike; fierce." The title of the first ruler of the Chou dynasty. One day Wu came to the borders of Shang and addressed his army: "In his left had he carried a battle-axe, yellow with gold, and in his right he held a white ensign, which he brandished, saying, 'Far are ye come; ye men of the Western regions.' "

145. "e canta la gallina": I, "and the hen crows." Couvreur's Latin gives "Gallinae matutinus cantus est domus exinanitio." In French, "Le chant de la poule le matin annonce la ruine de la famille" ("The crowing of a hen in the morning indicates the ruin of the family"). King Wu [in the speech in 144 above] is showing that Emperor Chou ("Cheou" in the canto) erred in following the counsel of his women rather than attempting to follow the will of heaven. Pound may have put it in Italian because the phrase recalled an old "skipping rope song": "treneta, quaranta / la gallina canta / e canta nel pollaio, / e cana nel cortile" [Mondolfo, *Pai*, 3-2, 286].

146. ganged up: Wu accuses Chou of having for ministers and officers men "who are only the vagabonds of the empire, loaded with crimes . . . making them great officers and nobles."

147. "6 steps . . . fugitives": Wu's speech to the army continues with instructions on how to fight: "In today's business, do not advance more than six blows, or seven blows; and then stop and adjust your ranks. . . . Do not rush on those who fly to us in submission."

148. Ideogram: French "chèu," chih [M939], "stop". Ideogram: T'si, Ch'i [M560], "adjust."

149. nài tcheù t'si: "And then stop and adjust [your ranks]."

150. Cheóu's host . . . jo lin: These lines concern the decisive battle at which King Wu defeated the forces of Cheou: "[Cheou] led forward his hosts like a forest, and assembled them in the wilderness of Muh."

151. quasi silvam convenit: L, "like a forest assembled."

152. jo lin: Jo [M3126], "like." Ideogram: lin [M4022], "forest." "Like a forest."

153. "Liking . . . no man.": The sources do not provide this precise sentence, which may be Pound's summary judgment of the actions of Wu.

154. The 4th part: Refers to Book IV, Part IV of Couvreur's *Chou King*, which is called "The Great Plan." The chapter concerns details, "marginalia," about the duties of government.

155. Liu dogs . . . : Couvreur Book IV, Part V is entitled "Le Chien de Liu" [Legge, "The Hounds of Liu"]. In it, the grand counselor Cheu advises King Wu not to accept the hounds as a gift from tribes under his rule.

156. T'oung . . . chenn: Ideogram: t'ung [M6618], "pain"; Ideogram: kuan [M3560], "cause distress"; Ideogram: nai [M4612], "however"; Ideogram: shen [M5718], "the body." King Wu is giving advice to his younger brother, Fung: "Oh! Fung . . . it is as if some disease were in your person. . . . Where you go, employ all your heart."

157. ôu iu chouèi: French for wu [M7180], "not"; yu [M7643], "in"; shui [M5922], "water."

158. Ideogram: Transcription error for 民, min [M4508], "mankind" or "the people."

159. Ideogram: Kien, chien [M839], "oversee."

160. 10.12: Chap. X, sec. 12, of Part IV, Couvreur.

161. . . . thy mirrour . . . : Wu tells Fung that the Ancients have said: "Let not men look only into water; let them look into the glass of other people." And then asks: "Ought we not to look much to it as our glass, and learn how to secure the repose of our time."

162. Ideogram: T'u [M6532], "land"; Ideogram: chung [M1504], "center." These two characters begin a break in the text from Chap. X to Chap. XII of Couvreur. The duke of Chou is telling the king to bring his government to the city of Lo, "the center of the land." In the text these characters are separated from the following ones, which are "gists" and do not form a sentence.

163. Ideogram: Tan [M6037], "dawn." Here the name of the duke of Chou. Ideogram: Yueh [M7694], "said". "Tan said."

164. Ideogram: P'ei [M5019], "worthy"; Ideogram: huang [M2283], "sovereign." These characters do not occur together in the Chinese text of Couvreur. Pound may want them construed as "mate of heaven." Legge gives: "Tan said, 'Now that this great city has been built, from henceforth he [the king] may be the mate of great heaven.' "

165. XIII, 9: Couvreur, Chap. XIII, sec. 9 of Book IV.

166. k'i p'eng: Ideogram: ch'i [M525], "his"; Ideogram: p'eng [M5054], "companion"; 火 : huo [M2395], "fire"; cho (灼) [M1256], "burn." The duke of Chou is giving advice to his young son and says he should have friends and companions but not have favorites or be partial or indulgent: "If you do so, the consequences hereafter will be like a fire, which . . . blazes up, and by and by cannot be extinguished."

167. Ideogram: Ching [M1138], "reverence." The duke tells his son if he will "Go and be reverent," one of his rewards will be "to know the sincere."

168. Tch'eng T'ang: Ch'êng T'ang [53:40], with the gold engraved bathtub, who was the founder of the Shang dynasty.

169. 戈: ko [M3358], "spear." This character does not appear alone in the Couvreur text but as a component in the next character, 成: ch'eng [M379], "to perfect." 湯: t'ang [M6101], "hot water." The founder of the Shang dynasty. Thus Pound put together some elements that say: "With his spear, Tch'eng T'ang overthrew Hia."

170. Hia: The Hsia dynasty, 2205-1766.

171. Praestantissimos . . . : L, "most outstanding men to rule." The Latin and Chinese tags in this and the next several lines are from a speech by the duke of Chou, who, in an address to the remaining officers of the house of Shang, enumerates those characteristics of the deposed Shang dynasty upon which the new Chou dynasty (founded by Wu Wang) has been established: (1) an original charge from heaven, (2) rule only by the best-qualified men, (3) the emperor's desire to make virtue illustrious throughout the empire, (4) attention to the sacrifices and to the favor of god, and (5) a sincere attempt by the emperor always to manifest a goodness corresponding to that of heaven. The ultimate object is the welfare (tranquillity) of the people. Pound incorporates all these characteristics into the *sensibility* (*ling*^{2}), which he subsequently defines as "the feel of the people" [86/560].

172. Ideogram: Tien [M6350], "to rule."

173. Ti I: Penultimate emperor of the Shang dynasty, 1191-1154.

174. nullus . . . sociavit: L, "Everyone made it [virtue] illustrious. Everyone allied himself [with the will of heaven]."

175. ut benefaceret: L, "so that he might benefit."

176. k'i tche: French for ch'i [M525], "his"; che [M277], "benefit."

177. Tcheou: Usually Pound gives Couvreur's "Cheou" for this last Shang emperor, Chou Hsin. Do not be confused. The 3d dynasty, the one that followed the Shang, is known as the Chou dynasty. Its first king was Wu Wang, who was honored and served by the duke of Chou. These people are not to be confused with this Chou, who is the last, weak emperor of Shang, Chou Hsin.

178. Ling^2: [cf. 1 and 133 above].

179. Ideogram: P'i [M5137], "great." This goes with the ideogram for *ling* on the previous page: "great sensibility" [cf. 9 above].

180. The arrow . . . points: A thematic statement for *The Cantos* as a whole, and the point of 85 in particular. The *Chou King* (or *Book of History*) is made up of a number of odes. Said Pound: "The Master Kung collected the Odes and the historical documents of the ancient kings, which he considered instruments worthy of preservation.

"We find two forces in history: one that divides, shatters, and kills, and one that contemplates the unity of the mystery. 'The arrow hath not two points.' There is the force that falsifies, the force that destroys every clearly delineated symbol, dragging man into a maze of abstract arguments, destroying not one but every religion" [*A Visiting Card*, 1942; *SP*, 306]. Legge gives the king's remark as: "We have followed no double aims." Maybe "have not gone in two directions" would be closer.

181. pou éul cheu: French for pu [M5379], "not"; Ideogram: erh [M1752], "double"; shih [M5822], "go." "Two directions."

182. "O numbreux officiers: F, "O numerous officers." The title of a chapter in Couvreur and a phrase used often by the duke of Chou as he addresses the officers of the conquered Shang dynasty.

183. Imperator ait: L, "The emperor affirms."

184. Ideogram: I [M3037], "city." Here the new capital of Lo.

185. Iterum dico: L, "I say again."

186. T'AI MEOU: Posthumous title of Tcheou Koung (Chung–Tsung), 7th emperor of the Shang dynasty, who ruled 1637-1562. T'ai [M6020], a term of respect in titles; Ideogram: Meou Wu [M7197], "Heavenly Stem."

187. OU TING: Posthumous title of Kao Tsoung (Kaou-tsung), 20th emperor of the Shang, who ruled 1324-1265. Just as with "T'ai Meou" above, the characters to the left are his name: Ideogram: Wu [M7195]; Ideogram: Ting [M6381].

188. cognovit aerumnas: L, "He has known hardships." The phrase does not come from the relevant Latin of Couvreur, but it applies to both the ancient emperors just cited as well as to Tsou Kia, to come. In their early years they "toiled away . . . from the court" and "lived among the inferior people" and, indeed, knew hardships. These experiences later made them compassionate rulers.

189. TSOU KIA: Legge gives us: "In the case of Tsoo-Këa, he . . . was at first one of the inferior people. When he came to the throne, he understood the law of the support of the inferior people, and was able to exercise a protecting kindness towards their masses. . . . Thus it was that Tsoo-Këa enjoyed the throne for thirty years."

190. Ideogram: Wei [M7066], "only"; Ideogram: Chêng [M351], "right"; Ideogram: chih [M935], personal pronoun; Ideogram: kung [M3710], "contribution." From a statement about King Wan: "from the various states he received only the right amount of contribution." "Contribution" is a word for taxes. King Wan taxed justly and "enjoyed the throne for fifty years."

191. invicem docentes: L, "teaching and learning in turn."

192. Ideogram: Siu, hsü [M2835], "all, together."

193. Ideogram: Chiao, kiaó [M719], "teach, instruct." This character has particular implications. Pound uses it along with "Sagetrieb," the German word he created to mean "pass on the tradition." The word and phrase have moral and social implications. It is the moral duty of this generation to pass on the wisdom received from the previous generation to the young of the next. That was what Confucius did. He gathered the best of all the odes and history and music from the old generation and organized it into new forms so that it could be passed on to the new. Pound conceives one of the functions of *The Cantos* as to pass on the tradition—the great tradition. But in this case it is the tradition of the East that he would pass on to the West. As he stated it at 13/60: "The blossoms of the apricot / blow from the east to the west, / And I have tried to keep them from falling" [13:32].

194. Sagetrieb: G, a Pound-invented word that has had a number of interpretations. David Gordon, having had the benefit of hearing Pound talk about it in the context of writing both *Rock-Drill* and *Thrones*, says it means "Pass on the tradition."

195. Ideogram: Chêu, shih [M5780], "depends"; Ideogram: ngo [M4778], "I, me, we, us." "It depends on us."

196. XVI.4: Chap. XVI, sec. 4, Couvreur, where we read: "O! you said, O Prince, 'It depends on ourselves.' I also do not dare to rest in the favour of God."

197. We flop . . . : Pound's rendition of Legge's sentence continued from above: "The favour of Heaven is not easily preserved. Heaven is hard to be depended on. Men lose its favouring appointment because they cannot pursue and carry out the reverence and brilliant virtue of their forefathers."

198. Diuturna . . . : L, "Think of the future." Sec. 10 Couvreur, goes on: "Think of the distant future, and we shall have the decree in favour of Chou made sure."

199. respect . . . men: Legge: "If you can but reverently cultivate your virtue, and bring to light our men of eminence, then you will resign to some successor in a time of established security."

200. Ideogram: Ming [M4534], here "train"; ngo [cf. 195 above], "our"; Ideogram: tsiun (chun) [M1727], "superior," or "fit." Couvreur has the character for "men" [M4508] in this group.

201. Ideogram: This character, *ming*[4] [M4537], should not be confused with *ming*[2] [M4534] in 200 above. This one means "will of God" or "life-destiny." Pound believes that divinity manifests in the intelligence of all men great and small. The duke of Chou is explaining why the Hsia dynasty fell: "God sent down correction on Hea, but the sovereign only increased his luxury and sloth, and would not speak kindly to the people. . . . He kept reckoning on the decree of God in his favour, and would not promote the means of the people's support."

202. subsidia: L, "support."

203. "And don't pester . . . fights": Legge gives us, politely: "Do not err in regard to the litigations and precautionary measures;—let the proper officers regulate them." The numbers in the margins refer to the appropriate chapters and sections of Couvreur.

204. Hio Kòu jou kouàn: Legge says: "Study antiquity in order to enter on your offices." Pound likes his "mot juste" line better.

205. Ideogram: Touan, tuan, [M6547]: "stop" or "cut off." In the *Ta Hsio* ("Ta Seu"), Pound translates this character as "cut the cackle" because he sees the right component as an ax and the left components as the archives tied up with silk [*CON*, 77].

206. Awareness . . . fatiguing: Legge says, "Practise them [reverence and economy] . . . and your minds will be at ease. . . . Practise them in hypocrisy, and your minds will be toiled."

207. nor laws . . . : Legge says: "Do not rely on your power to exercise oppression; do not rely on the laws to practise extortion."

208. Not all things . . . : Legge: "Be not passionate with the obstinate, and dislike them. Seek not every quality in one individual."

209. Ideogram: Pei[4] [M4997], "prepare." This character appears in the passage from which 208 is cited.

210. Ideogram: Yung² [M7560], "forbearance." This character is the *ioung* in the next gloss, which "is, in some cases, charity."

211. iou ioung te nai ta: Legge gives: "Have forbearance and your virtue will be great."

212. Ideogram: Chong, sheng [M5738], "to beget, be born." Ideogram: heou: hou [M2147], "virtuous, good." Legge: "The people are born good, and are changed by external things."

213. The 5 laws . . . : The 5 laws are the laws of relationships: (1) king and official; (2) father and son; (3) husband and wife; (4) brother and brother; (5) friend and friend. This line is formative for this canto and *The Cantos* as a whole. All human relations derive from a deep awareness of how divinity manifests in the minds and hearts of men, how intelligence and love in the tensile light descending derive from divinity and are in fact the divine in process–the motivating force of the process.

214. che funge: I, "which is continually in action." *Funge* is an Italian neologism Pound created for a particular use [74:455]. M de R believes that it derives from Latin *fungor*, and she points out that in the Italian rendition of his *Unwobbling Pivot* he translates "La purezza funge" as "the unmixed function" and adds: "The unmixed is the tensile light, the Immaculata. There is no end to its action" [HK, *Pai*, 1-1, 83]. The tensile light, the light descending, the intelligence that informs awareness, is thus at the root of human motivation to exemplify the 5 laws. All of the precepts that Pound has culled from Couvreur in Canto 85 concern how the will of heaven should be exemplified in the ruler as well as in the life of every man.

215. Brancusi: Constantin B., 1876-1957, the Rumanian sculptor who settled in Paris in 1904 and became a leader of the modernist movement toward abstraction. Pound knew him in the 20s and 30s. He is mentioned dozens of times in his prose writings and Pound remembered "a few evenings in Brancusi's old studio, wherein quiet was established" [*GK*, 84]. Also, "Brancusi in some dimensions a saint" [*GK*, 105]. Under the heading "Values" Pound wrote: "I would put up a dozen brass tablets to one phrase of Constantin Brancusi's [he sets the phrase in caps]: One of those days when I would not have given up fifteen minutes of my time for anything under heaven" [*SP* 283].

216. Piazzale Loreto: The public square in Milan where the corpses of Mussolini, Clara Pitacci, and four others from the Salò government "were hung, head downwards" by a group of partisans [Kirkpatrick, *Mussolini*, 671].

217. Holohan: John H., a witness who could have given evidence of the innocence of Mary Surratt, who was executed as a conspirator in the assissination of President Lincoln. As was Mussolini, she was tried by a military court and did not have benefit of a jury. A book by David De Witt available to Pound was entitled *The Judicial Murder of Mary E. Surratt* [*Pai*, 12-2 & 3].

218. Jury . . . Athens: [87:40].

219. *οὐ δελίαν*: H, "Shall we to all our ills add cowardice?" Sophocles, *Electra*, 351 [Loeb, 151]. Pound uses this line as an illustration at the end of his *Women of Trachis* [*WT*, 50], as a note to "IT ALL COHERES" [109/772; 116/797]: "This is the key phrase for which the play exists, as in the *Electra*: 'Need we add cowardice to all the rest of these ills?' " [DG].

220. King Owen . . . Cheng: Ou-Ouang (Wen Wang). Legge: "King Wan was able to . . . unite . . . the great empire" because he had "such ministers as his brother of Kih, Hwang Yaou [Houng Ieo], San E-sang [San I Cheng]."

221. Ideogram: "Sagetrieb" [see 194 above].

222. Ideogram: Ping [M5291], "grasp." Morrison [8603] analyses the components of this character as "from a hand grasping grain." This prob. caught Pound's eye because the basic Fascist symbol is a hand holding together many spears of wheat.

223. Ideogram: Mao [M4373], "to go forward with eyes covered," or "to rush upon." Mathews uses several phrasal examples of *mao*, such as "to throw out sparks" and "to smoke–as a chimney." Hence the line "Risked the smoke. . . ."

224. aperiens . . . : L, "opened up his soul to you." The duke said to the officers: "King Wen . . . opened up his soul to you." He implored them to follow Wen's example and carry out his decrees. Pound uses phrases from this same speech to open Canto 86. As with the end of Canto 1, the colon indicates a motion forward into the next canto, tying the end of the one to the beginning of the other.

CANTO LXXXVI

Sources

Séraphin Couvreur, *Chou King*, Paris, Cathasia, 1950; James Legge, *The Four Books*, Shanghai, 1923; Lewis A. Maverick, *China A Model for Europe*, San Antonio, Texas, 1946.

Background

EP, *SP*, 43, 160, 326, 328, 169; *GK*, 260; Virginia Cowles, *The Rothschilds: A Family of Fortune*, New York, Knopf, 1973; M de R, *Discretions,* 195; Christopher Hollis, *Two Nations,* London, 1935; William E. Woodward, *A New American History*, 1936; Cicero, *De Officiis* II, 89; Eustace Mullins, *This Difficult Individual, Exra Pound*, New York, 1961 [EM, *Difficult*].

Exegeses

Grieve, *Pai*, 4-2 & 3, 362-508; EH, *Pai*, 2-3, 497-498; HK, *Pai*, 2-1, 41; BK and TE, *Pai*, 9-3, 432; Walkiewicz and Witemeyer, *Pai*, 9-3, 441-459; Cookson, *Pai,* 8-2, 361.

Glossary

1. Ideogram: Hsu [M2862], "sympathy," or "solicitude." The duke continues his speech [85:224]. Where Couvreur gives the phrase "une sollicitude sans limite," Legge gives "boundless anxieties": "Think of the virtue of King Wan and enter greatly into his boundless anxieties." The Roman numerals in the text identify the part, chapter, and section in Couvreur.

2. Turbationem: L, "confusion, disorder": The Latin passage in Couvreur says: "The Duke said: . . . Guardian Shih, you will be able, I hope, to profit from my advice, to consider the great ruin and disorder of the house of Yin."

3. Bismarck: Otto von B., 1815-1898 [48:17; 80:172]. Cited by Pound as an exemplum of balance and order: "Having become really conversant with the activities of either of these men [Bismarck, Gladstone], would not almost any document of the period fall, if we read it, into some sort of orderly arrangement?" [*SP*, 43]. It was Bismarck's opinion that the Franco-Prussian War, 1870-71, would be the last European war.

4. **Dummheit, nicht Bosheit**: G, "stupidity not malice." Old M's opinion about how Germany got into WWI [cf. 9 below].

5. **Old Margherita**: Queen mother of King Victor Emmanuel II of Italy [EH, *Pai*, 2-3, 497].

6. **Elenor? dowager**: May suggest Margherita compares in some way to Queen Eleanor of Aquitaine.

7. **"Sono . . . Cattivi"**: I, "They are all heretics, Holy Father, but they are not wicked." Statement about the Germans, prob. made by Queen Margherita to the pope.

8. **Ballin**: Albert Reeder B., 1857-1918, a director of the Hamburg-Amerika [Steamship] Co., a familiar of the Kaiser's, and a friend of Chancellor von Bülow. The remark prob. concerns the Allied blockade against Germany. If he'd known it was going to happen, Ballin was one of the few people who could have "stuffed all Hamburg with grain."

9. **Bülow**: Bernhard von B., 1849-1929, German statesman and diplomat who became foreign minister in 1897 and chancellor in 1900. It was his intransigence in dealing with France, England, and Russia which helped increase German isolation and strengthen the Triple Entente. In his memoirs Bülow tells of a conversation between his wife, Maria, and Queen Margherita, who asked her bluntly: "Tell me frankly, Maria, you wanted the war, didn't you?" Maria said "She was prepared to swear by the Virgin Mary and all that was sacred that neither the Kaiser nor the German people had wanted the war." Queen Margherita replied: "Then the German diplomatists and ministers in office in 1914 must be the greatest asses the world has ever seen" [EH, *Pai*, 2-3, 498].

10. **Talleyrand**: [44:28; 62:151]. French statesman who helped restore the Bourbons after the fall of Napoleon. In pursuing a "balance of power" policy he created, in the Quadruple Alliance (1834), buffer states and the Bourbon dynasty [103:22]. Earlier, as grand chamberlain under Napoleon, he had set up a first dynasty. In WWI, the existence of Belgium on the side of France ("Frogland") was one of the factors that saved France. "Svizzera" (Switzerland) remaining neutral may have been another.

11. **only two of us**: Couvreur IV, XVI, 20 continues the Duke's speech [cf. 1, above]. Legge translates: "I simply say, 'The establishment of our dynasty rests with us two.' Do you agree with me? Then you also will say, 'It rests with us two' . . . ."

12. **Brancusi**: [85:215]. Pound often quotes this remark made by the sculptor.

13. **je peux . . . finiiir**: F, "I can start something every day, but finish!"

14. **Ideogram**: Hsiang [M2579], "to judge."

15. **Ideogram**: [85:1]: By not having *ling*, the Hsia emperor "lost the feel of the people."

16. **Ideogram**: Tien [M6347], "to be in charge of."

17. **Ideogram**: Sagetrieb [85:194].

18. **Ideogram**: Chien [M837], "documents" or "to appoint." These three characters do not appear together as a sentence in the source. The context in which they occur suggests that some officers of the state did "take charge of the good of the people," did try "to instruct and pass on the tradition," and did "appoint" good officers to serve the prople. By putting them together, Pound may be suggesting something like: "Sensibility will come by passing on the tradition as contained in the documents."

19. **way . . . loveless**: Legge: "The paths which you tread are continually those of

disquietude;–have you in your hearts no love for yourselves?"

20. Get men . . . : The sense of the Couvreur passage is that if you get real men, "brave as bears," to serve, the empire will grow in glory.

21. milites instar ursorum: L, "warriors like bears."

22. Not in two minds: Legge translates the phrase: "[ministers] of no double heart." N.B. "The arrow has not two points" [85:180].

23. Ideogram: Tuan [M6541], "principles."

24. jóung: French for yung [M7567], "use," or "act on." Hence, "Act on principles."

25. Edictorum: L, "proclamations."

26. Ideogram: T'i [M6246], "the essential" or "complete."

27. Ideogram: Iao, yao [M7300], "the important." Legge gives the phrase that ties these characters together as: "in proclamations a combination of completeness and brevity are valuable."

28. ta seu: Ta hsüeh; *The Great Digest.*

29. ta hiún: Ta hsun; "great counsel."

30. te i: "Awareness of morality."

31. Quis . . . documenta: L, "What man teaches without documents [lessons]."

32. even barbarians . . . : The sense of the duke's speech here is that righteousness and good government will have such an influence on the people that "the wild tribes, with their coats buttoning on the left, will all seek their dependence on them."

33. Non periturum: L, "imperishable."

34. Ideogram: Kiue; chi [M453], "to finish." Pound's "kiue sin" is a transcription of Couvreur's "ki kiuĕ sĭn" for Mathew's *chi, chueh, hsin.*

35. Ideogram: Sin; hsin [M2735], "heart, mind."

36. Mencius: [54:66; 78:60, 139]. The context suggests that the characters are the basis of Legge's "exert your mind to the utmost." That will lead to "Mou Wang" below.

37. MOU WANG: King Mu, the 5th emperor of the Chou dynasty (reigned 1001-946 B.C.). Couvreur and Legge view him as a lightweight who wandered around aimlessly, talking great but doing little. Ideogram: Mu [M4601]; "majestic"; Ideogram: wang [M7037]; "king."

38. Ideogram: Tou; tu [M6514], "true"; Ideogram: tchoung; chung [M1506], "loyal"; Ideogram: tchen; chen [M346], "virtuous." King Wang, speaking to his ministers, attributes these qualities to ministers of an earlier time.

39. Kiun Ia: "Keun-ya." Legge: "The king spoke thus: "Keun-ya, do you take for your rule the lessons afforded by the former courses of your excellent fathers." Pound gives the essence of his speech in: "live up to your line."

40. T'ai Tch'âng: The imperial banner. In his words to Keun-ya, King Mu said that Keun-ya's father and grandfather had served the royal house so well that they "accomplished a merit which was recorded on the grand banner." Ideogram: ch'ang [M221], "principle."

41. ice and tigers: Now king Mu says, as he starts his rule "the trembling anxiety of my mind makes me feel as if I were treading on a tiger's tail, or walking upon spring ice."

42. Ideogram: Hsien [M2697], "law, regulations, constitution." Legge: "The king said, . . . 'Ever help your sovereign to follow the regular laws [constitution].' " This character ends Chap. XXVI of Couvreur.

43. Ideogram: Lü [M4280]. The name of the duke of Leu, who according to tradition was King Mu's minister for crime. This character opens Chap. XXVII of Couvreur.

44. etiam . . . inspiciendus: L, "even appearance must be examined." Legge gives the whole sentence: "When you have examined, and many things are clear, yet form a judgment from studying the appearance of the parties."

45. Ideogram: Mao [M4368], "appearances" [Chap. XXVII]. The next 4 characters [from Chap. XXX] go together.

46. Ideogram: i [M3021], "moreover"; Ideogram: shang [M5670]; "still"; Ideogram: i [M3016], "one"; Ideogram: jen [M3097], "man." Legge give the whole sentence: "The glory and tranquillity of a State also may perhaps arise from the excellence of one man."

47. Edwardus: Edward, Prince of Wales, later Edward VIII and duke of Windsor [cf. 89/601; 95:39]. According to Von Hoesch, the telephone conversation he had delayed the start of WWII by three years [109:40].

48. von Hoesch: Leopold von H., German ambassador to England in the mid-thirties.

49. Eva's pa: Fritz Hesse, ca. 1900-1980, the father of Eva Hesse. Eva is a scholar, critic, historian and official translator of *The Cantos* as well as numerous critical works into German. A senior editor of *Paideuma*, she is a great resource to all. Her father was press attaché at the German embassy in London in the mid-1930s and told the story of overhearing the conversation between King Edward VIII and the ambassador. The king called von Hoesch "Leo" and referred to himself familiarly, "hier spricht David" [HK, *Pai*, 2-1, 41].

50. Bismarck: [cf. 3 above]. His idea was no wars after 1870.

51. Ideogram: i [M3002], "righteousness."

52. "Nicht . . . cattivi": [cf. 4 & 7 above].

53. Hamburg: [cf. 8 above].

54. Miss Wi'let: Prob. Violet Hunt. Answer to the question, "Will there be war?" [38/188]. Answer the same [38:26].

55. 20 years . . . Bonaparte: Echo of repeated anecdote [78:10].

56. gold . . . Spain: During England's effort to assist Spain against the armies of Napoleon, the British government had a hard time in providing Arthur Wellesley (later duke of Wellington) money to pay his troops. Everyone insisted upon being paid in gold. All A. W. could do was issue drafts on British treasury bills, which were bought only at massive discounts by "a mob of Maltese and Sicilian financiers" [Cowles, *The Rothschilds*, 42]. The drafts finally arrived in England (after going through a chain of speculators), where Nathan Rothschild bought them up very cheap. Knowing this procedure could not go on for long without great harm to England, he and his brothers in France and Germany began buying all the gold they could get. Finally the government went to Nathan Rothschild for help. He was prepared. Gold shipped by sea was often sunk, so getting it to A. W. in Spain was a difficult and treacherous business. Says Cowles: "Nathan's scheme [to do it] . . . was comparable to burglary in broad daylight" [43]. With the help of his family in France, he let it be known that England was trying to prevent the flow of gold and silver to France. Napoleon had relaxed his blockade in order to help the French consumer, so that at a place near Dunkirk 'legal smuggling' was permitted. Once N got the idea the English didn't want to lose gold, he helped the Rothschilds with what he thought was their plan "to drain away Britain's reserves." What they were really doing was helping the English and undermining the Bank of France. James Rothschild hoodwinked Napoleon and his finance minister, Molliens: "So the French Government allowed the Rothschilds to establish an artery of gold, running the length and breadth of France, to the heart of enemy resistance: Wellington's headquarters in Spain" [ibid.]. Karl Rothschild crossed the Pyrenees, as if an innocent traveler, and eventually emerged "with . . . Wellington's receipts in his hand" [ibid., 44].

57. Geschäft: G, "employment" or "business."

58. Buchanan: [34:84]. Buchanan said to

Pierce, in a letter of 1852 (*not* 1850): "The Rothschilds, the Barings, and other large capitalists now control, to a great extent, the monarchies of continental Europe" [BK & TE, *Pai*, 9-3, 432].

59. **Pierce**: Franklin P., 1804-1869, 14th president of the U.S., 1853-1857, who made a reputation in the House (1833-1837) and Senate (1837-1842) while very young and, after retiring from politics, as a brigadier general during the Mexican War. As an anti-slavery candidate in the convention of 1852, he was nominated on the 49th ballot as a compromise candidate, was elected, and served one term. A kindly, courteous person, Pierce was weak, unstable, and vacillating as president.

60. **question?**: Wasn't England owned by the banks in the 1850's? Pound's answer is: Not at that time. England was not wholly owned by the banks until 20 years later, after the Suez deal.

61. **Suez**: In November 1857, Disraeli discovered that the Khedive of Egypt, "a notorious spendthrift who was drowning in debt," was trying to sell his shares in the Suez to the French government. Disraeli was fearful that the French might snap them up and thus control what he thought was a vital British interest. But if the French knew the British wanted the shares, they'd doubtless buy at once. Speed and secrecy were necessary. D found out from Lionel Rothschild beforehand the price England would have to pay. Then he had to convince the cabinet, which was not easy; but they finally agreed that they should buy the shares if they could borrow the money. The story is that D poked his head out of the door of the cabinet room and said "Yes" to his secretary, who sped to the Rothschilds and said that D needed £4 million. " 'When?' asked Lionel... 'Tomorrow' [said the secretary] ... 'What is your security?' [said Rothschild ...] 'The British Government' [said the secretary]. 'You shall have it' [said Rothschild]." D wrote to Queen Victoria: "There was only one firm that could do it–Rothschilds. They behaved admirably: advanced the money at a low rate, and the entire interest of the Khedive is now yours, Madam" [Cowles, 162]. The facts do not support Pound's opinion. Disraeli could not have asked Parliament, because of the need for speed and secrecy. Says Cowles: "The purchase turned out to be one of the best investments ever made by the government. In 1898, the market value of the shares was £24 million; in 1914 £40 million; in 1935 £95 million. And for nearly twenty-five years earnings were at a rate of fifty-six percent on the original investment" [ibid., 163].

62. **Ideogram**: Hsin [M2748], "trust."

63. **"Alla non della"**: I, "*to*, not *of*." A much repeated recollection of Mussolini's precision in language in drawing up his Program of Verona for the Republic of Salò, est. Sept. 23, 1943. "It is a right *to* property not a right *of* property," is the sense of Pound's source. M de R [*Discretions* 195] cites the quote with the explanation, "work is not the object but the subject of economy" [108:3].

64. *οὐ ταῦτα . . . κακοῖσι*: H, "not all ... ills." Part of *Electra* phrase [85:219].

65. **Alexander**: Alexander the Great [85:88].

66. **OBIT apud Babylonios**: L, "He [Alexander] died among the Babylonians."

67. **Arrian**: Flavius Arrianus, 2d C. A.D., pupil of Epictetus. His chief book, *Anabasis*, is a history of Alexander; the book's main source was Ptolemy.

68. **Hamurabi**: Hammurabi. Babylonian king, fl. 2100 B.C. His code of laws carved on a diorite column in 3600 lines of cuneiform is one of the greatest and most humanitarian of all ancient codes.

69. **Regius Professorships**: See gloss to "Chris Hollis" below.

70. **apud**: L, "from the writing of."

71. **Chris Hollis**: Christopher Hollis, author of *Two Nations*, a study of the development of power based on money and banking in

England, which Pound cites often in his prose works on money [*SP*, 160, 326, 328]. In that book Hollis cites the seminal statement about Paterson and the founding of the Bank of England: "the bank hath benefit of the interest on all moneys which it creates out of nothing" [*Two Nations*, 30]. In a chapter entitled "The Origin of the Progressive Legend," Hollis traces the careful plans made by the Whig government to see to it that the history of England was properly understood by the people, which meant being understood from their highly sectarian vangtage point. Several steps were involved. First they sponsored a Whig history, *The History of our Own Times*, "calculated to impose the debt system on the gentry in return for freedom from enslavement." The next step was to get the book read. That was more difficult because both Oxford and Cambridge were hotbeds of Toryism: "In those seats of education instead of being formed to love their country and constitution, the laws and liberties of it, they are rather disposed to love arbitrary government and to become slaves to absolute monarchy" [ibid., 37-38]. Right away it was perceived that "the important task was to capture the educational machine." This they did. In 1724 it was arranged for 24 persons, "'Fellowsof Colleges in the two Universities, 12 from Oxford and 12 from Cambridge' to preach a sermon each year at Whitehall." As money men, they understood that money would do the trick; they paid £30 for each sermon, an enormous sum at the time. But no one could receive the sum except those who were "staunch Whigs and openly declare themselves to be so." The number of enthusiastic Whigs who had been secretly hiding out at these universities was a suprise to some but not to those behind the conspiracy. This program finally became firmly entrenched by the establishment of a Regius Professorship in the name of King George for the teaching of history and modern languages. People were selected to fill the positions only if they avowedly adopted and promulgated the new Whig theory of history. Thus, says Hollis, the entire nation was bemused with a curriculum of half-truths, and this result was achieved intentionally and with malice aforethought [ibid., 37-52].

72. **Bowers**: [81:12].

73. **La Spagnuola**: I, "The Spanish Woman."

74. **scripsit**: L, "wrote."

75. **Woodward**: William E. Woodward, author of *A New American History*, which Pound quoted from [*SP*, 169], and an economist whose writings on money Pound liked. Pound corresponded with him and, since he was an adviser to the Roosevelt administration, Pound "occasionally suggested items that he might pass on to the President" [EM, *Difficult*, 258]. The lines are W.E.W.'s response.

76. **HE**: Franklin D. Roosevelt.

77. **Cato speaking**: In Cicero's *De Officiis* we have a discussion of things that have great value in life, such as strength, health, glory, wealth, and so on. Then we read of an anecdote told of Cato. When asked about the most profitable feature of an estate, he said it was raising cattle. When asked the next most profitable, he said it was raising crops. After several such questions he was asked, "What about money-lending?" and he answered, "What about murder?" [Bk. II, 89;96/664].

78. **some Habsburg**: Joseph II [cf. 81 below], an elightened despot, was strongly influenced by his mother Maria Theresa of Austria. During the 18th century there was a vogue in Europe for Chinese customs. France, following the physiocrats, wanted to use China as a model for economic and agrarian reform. The frontispiece of a book by Mirabeau, *Philosophie Ruräl* (1764), showed a Chinese emperor plowing an imperial furrow to hearten his subjects and to carry on an age-old ritual [53:122]. Hence the young Dauphin was required to hold a toy plow in his delicate hands to show princely sympathy with the French peasants. In 1769 Joseph went the whole way: he took a real plow and plowed some real land

to show he meant business. Pound's interest was sparked by a particular book that contains these data: *China A Model for Europe*, 1946 [DG, *Pai*, 5-3, 394].

79. **old Theresa**: Prob. not Maria Theresa of Austria, but suggested by association.

80. **Cleopatra**: [85:13].

81. **Joseph two**: Emperor of Austria, 1741-1790, who came to the throne in 1765 and continued the reforms begun by his mother, including the 1786 reform of the code of civil law.

82. **Tuscany**: Province in central Italy which includes Pisa, Siena, Florence, etc., an area subjected to punishment in many wars, in particular the latter part of WWII.

83. **Konody**: Paul K., an art critic from Austria who settled in London; Pound "saw a good deal of him from 1909 or even 1908" [letter to Patricia Hutchins, 16 Nov., 1957, MS in British Library (BK)]. He is mentioned among the blessed in *BLAST* 1.

84. **"We fight . . ."**: Perhaps conversation overheard during the years of the mitteleurope cantos 35 and 38.

85. **Schwartz**: Repeat of a similar conversation overheard during WWII. Point: As always, the little, innocent people are the ones led to slaughter in Bellum perenne [cf. 108 below].

86. **"Mai . . . chic homme"**: F, "But the Prussian! The Prussian is a natty man."

87. **femme de ménage**: F, "lady of the establishment" or "madam."

88. **"Vous . . . rosse"**: F, "You would like to roll [slang for sex act] me, but you do not roll me because I am too decrepit."

89. **litigantium dona**: L, "gifts of litigation." Return to Couvreur. The whole sentence in Legge is: "Gain got by the decision of cases [litigation] is no precious acquisition."

90. **Ideogram**: Fei [M1819], "not."

91. **Ideogram**: Pao [M4956], "precious."

92. **non coelum . . . medio**: L, "not heaven not neutral." Legge: "It is not Heaven that does not deal impartially with men, but men ruin themselves."

93. **Fortuna**: L, "destiny." Pound is saying that the words "but man is under Fortuna" is a forced translation of the Latin line before it, as indeed it is. A recurrent theme [96/656; 97/676].

94. **La Donna . . .** : I, "The lady who turns." From "Io son la [I am the] donna che volga," the opening line of Cavalcanti's "Canzone to Fortune," where Dame Fortune (of Fortune's Wheel) is speaking [Anderson, *Pai*, 12-1, 41-46].

95. **Ideogram**: Chên [M315], "terrify." The sequence of lines in Cavalcanti's poem says that fortune's wheel, in its turning (not from heaven's will), is terrifying.

96. **Iou Wang**: Yu Wang, Chou ruler, 781-770, whose bad administration contributed to the decay of the Chou dynasty. Ideogram: yu [M7505], "dark"; Ideogram: wang [M7037], "king."

97. **King Jou**: Legge's transcription. He says, "King Jou was a recipient of divine justice." Thus he was "A Man under Fortune." As proof of a fateful destiny we read: "In the sixth year of his reign . . . occurred an eclipse of the sun. It is commemorated in the Chou King . . . as 'an announcement of evils by the sun and moon.' " Couvreur has a note that says Yu Wang was killed by barbarians from the West ("barbares occidentaux") in the 770th year before our era.

98. **Ideogram**: I [M3002], "right conduct"; Ideogram: ho [M2115], "harmony." The name of an uncle of King Ping Wang, who was a valuable aid to his administration.

99. **in angustiis . . .** : L, "You have defended me in my difficulties." The quote is transposed from Couvreur's Latin: "defendisti me in angustiis." From a speech of Ping Wang, who said, according to Legge: "Uncle E-ho . . . you have done much to repair my

losses and defend me in my difficulties. . . . I reward you with a jar of spirits, made from the black millet, mixed with odoriferous herbs; with one red bow and a hundred red arrows; with one black bow, and a hundred black arrows."

100. ne inutile quiescas: L, "be not uselessly at ease." The speech made by Ping Wang, known as "the Tranquillizer" (reigned 770-719), ends with these words. He was the last emperor of the Chou dynasty recorded in *Chou King*.

101. Ideogram: Pe [M4977], "uncle" or "elder"; Ideogram: k'in, ch'in [M1100], "birds" or "animals." Here the name of "the prince of Loo under the reign of Ch'eng Wang." Pound returns to the next to last chapter of *Chou King* for more data concerning the disintegration of the Chou dynasty. Legge gives us for Pe K'in's speech: "We must now largely let the oxen and horses loose . . . shut up your traps, and fill up your pitfalls, and do not presume to injure any of the animals let loose. . . . When your followers . . . abscond, presume not to leave the ranks to pursue them. . . . And let none of your people presume to rob or detain vagrant animals or followers, or to jump over enclosures and walls to steal away horses or oxen . . . . On the day Keă-shu I will punish the tribes of Seu;—prepare roasted grain and other provisions."

102. Ideogram: Tch'eng, ch'eng [M379], "to perfect"; Ideogram: wang [M7037], "king." Ch'eng Wang (reigned 1115-1078) was the son of Wu Wang and the second and last great Chou emperor. His name and reign are evoked here as a contrast to the present disorder.

103. HE: [cf. 76 above].

104. Woodward: [cf. 75 above].

105. Dwight L. Morrow: Dwight Whitney M., 1873-1931, American banker and diplomat who was a civilian aide to Gen. John J. Pershing in WWI. In 1927 he was ambassador to Mexico, where he started a new era of understanding and cooperation. He served in the U.S. Senate 1930-1931. His daughter, Anne Morrow, married Charles Lindbergh. Pound tells a story of how he asked the late Senator Cutting in a letter, "How many literate senators are there?" Said Pound: "He sent nine names, ending 'and I suppose Dwight L. Morrow' " [*GK*, 260].

106. Br . . . C . . . .g: Prob. Bronson Cutting, although the dots in the name are not exact as in Pound's usual practice. [E. P. Walkiewicz and H. Witemeyer, *Pai*, 9-3, 441-459]. It was not 1932 but earlier, since Morrow died in 1931.

107. "hysteric presiding . . . ": A controversial reference. The context convinces me that Roosevelt is intended. Based on notebooks Pound gave him, W. Cookson believes the "hysteric" is Hitler [*Pai*, 8-2, 361]. The " '39" appears to go with this line.

108. Bellum cano perenne: L, "I sing of war everlasting." A musical figure that occurs often in the poem [88:21; 87:2].

CANTO LXXXVII

Sources

EP, *WT*, 8, 50, 54; Dante, *Vita Nuova*, 12.4 [*VN*].; Sophocles, *Electra*, line 351; EP, *CON*, 22, 27, 232; Séraphin Couvreur, *Chou King*, Paris, Cathasia, 1950 [Couvreur]; James Legge, *The Four Books*, Shanghai, 1923 [Legge].

Background

EP, *America, Roosevelt and the Causes of the Present War*, London, Peter Russell, 1951 [*ARCPW*], *GK*, 46, 105, 58, 324, 357, 77, 109, 278-279, 225, 57, 182, 15; *SP*, 323, 272-273, 311, 65, 29, 53, 240, 436; *L*, 255, 348, 173-176; *NPL*, 149-158; Francis Steegmuller, ed., *The Letters of Gustave Flaubert, 1830-1857*, Harvard Univ. Press, 1980 [Steegmuller]; Aeschylus, *Eumenides*, line 752; William Cabell Bruce, *John Randolph of Roanoke*, New York and London, G. P. Putnam's Sons, 1922, Vol. II, 232; Philip Spencer, *Flaubert, A Biography*, New York, Grove Press, 1952; G. Legman, *The Guilt of the Templars*, New York, Basic Books, 1966 [*Guilt*]; Jessie L. Weston, *From Ritual to Romance*, Cambridge, 1920; M de R, *Discretions*, 196; Charles Norman, *Ezra Pound*, Macmillan, 1960 [Norman]; Ford Madox Ford, *Portraits from Life*, 1937 (later published as *Mightier than the Sword*, London, Allen & Unwin, 1938); D'Arcy W. Thompson, *On Growth and Form*, Cambridge, 1916, rpts. MacMillan, 1942-1948; Sir Arthur Evans, *The Palace of Minos at Knossos*, Vol. III, Biblo and Tannen, New York, 1964.

Exegeses

CE, *Ideas*, 47-56; Achilles Fang, Ph.D. dissertation, Harvard, Vol. III; EH, *Pai*, 2-1, 141; CFT, *Pai*, 2-2, 223 ff.; Grieve, *Pai*, 4-2 & 3, 481; HK, *Era*, 331, 335 ff.; FR, *Pai*, 7-2 & 3, 29 ff.; WB, *Approaches*, 303-318; L. Surette, *A Light From Eleusis*, Oxford University Press, 1979, 263-267; HK, *Pai*, 4-2 & 3, 381.

Glossary

1. **between the usurer**: [45:1]. This recurrent theme is further developed in many of Pound's writings on economics [*GK*, 46; cf. also CE, *Ideas*, 47-57], e.g., "To repeat: an expert, looking at a painting . . . should be able to determine the degree of the tolerance of usury in the society in which it was painted" [*SP*, 323].

2. **perenne**: L, "continued, perennial." Part of recurrent tag: "bellum perenne." For, usury is the cause: "Wars are provoked in succession, deliberately, by the great usurers, in order to create debts, to create scarcity, so that they can extort the interest on these debts, so that they can raise the price of money . . . altering the prices of the various monetary units when it suits them . . . completely indifferent to the human victim" [*ARCPW*, 8].

3. **without . . . credit**: Partial definition of usury [45/230].

4. **perché . . . mettere**: I, "why do you wish to put." In 1932 Mussolini asked this question. Pound gives the question and his answer, "Pel mio poema" ("For my poem"), later [93:75], thereby showing insistence on a Confucian order in his own mind [*GK*, 105].

5. **Grock**: The stage name of Charles Wettach (1880-1959), circus performer, acrobat, and comic musician with violin and piano.

Originator of routine developed later by Jack Benny, Victor Borge, and others. Grock made a London appearance in 1911, where Pound may have first seen him: "He perfected those adventures of a simpleton among musical instruments . . . wonder as to where the strings had gone when he held his fiddle the wrong side up and at his labours to sit nearer the piano by pushing it toward the stool." The French dialog is typical of the nonsequiturs he used with his straightman partner, a clown he teamed up with named "Brick." Grock's autobiography appeared in 1956 [*Die Memoiren des Königs der Clowns*].

6. **Où ca?**: F, "How's that?"

7. **J'ai une idée**: F, "I have an idea."

8. **Berchtold**: Leopold, Graf von B., 1863-1942, Austro-Hungarian foreign minister who, after the assassination of Archduke Ferdinand at Sarajevo, followed a harsh, reckless policy that contributed to the start of WWI. Although he was outwardly calm, the effect of the assassination on him was dynamite. The lines suggest that Pound met Berchtold, perhaps during his visit to Vienna in 1928 [35:6; 76:132].

9. **Varchi**: Italian historian who made no judgment as he did not have enough facts [5:33, 58].

10. **Of Roanoke**: John Randolph, 1773-1833, American statesman called "of Roanoke." During the years 1799-1829, he served a total of 24 years in the U.S. House of Representatives and 2 years in the Senate (for 4 of those years he was out of office). He became a powerful force as well as a flamboyant orator. The more he was against something, the more dramatic and biting his oratory became. His violent excoriations of Henry Clay and JQA led to the famous duel [88:passim]. Because of his opposition to Jefferson on the acquisition of Florida, he lost his leadership in the House temporarily. He also opposed James Madison and the Northern Democrats, the War of 1812, the second Bank of the United States, the tariff measures, and the Missouri compromise. He is a continuous, if at times shadowy, presence in Cantos 87-89.

11. **"Nation silly . . . "**: A recurrent theme cited in all of Pound's writings on the economic history of the United States, and a major theme of *R-D* [88:passim]. In a letter to Benton [88:80], Dec. 12, 1829, Randolph said: "It is obvious that the discounting of private paper has no connection with the transfer of public monies, or a sound paper currency. My plan was to make the great custom-houses branches of our great national bank of deposit—a sort of loan office, if you will . . . . This would give one description of paper, bottomed upon substantial capital, and whensoever Government might stand in need of a few millions, instead of borrowing their own money from a knot of brokers on the credit of said brokers, it might, under proper restriction, issue its own paper in anticipation of future revenues on taxes to be laid; such notes to be cancelled within a given time" [Bruce, *Randolph*, Vol. II, 232]. N.B.: Herein is the heart of the social credit idea as well as Pound's basic attitude about debt-free money.

12. **Polk**: James K. P., 1795-1849, 11th U.S. president (1845-1849), lawyer and statesman from Tennessee; supporter of President Jackson, especially in the war against the bank. Thus, he deserves to be among those honored for fighting the "usurocracy."

13. **Tyler**: John T., 1790-1862, 10th U.S. president (1841-1845). He stood between the great parties and was opposed to most of the policies of Jackson and Van Buren, except for a brief period while senator from Virginia [34:81; 37:39].

14. **paideuma**: A word taken from Frobenius [38:45] which Pound defines not as the Zeitgeist but as "the gristly roots of ideas that are in action" during a period of time [*GK*, 58].

15. **Buchanan**: James B., 1791-1868. As

president (1847-1861) he was not a rigorous henchman of the money interests [34:84].

16. **Infantilism**: An epithet Pound applies to those who continue to have puerile or simpleminded ideas about economics, who emphasize the idea of "circulation" and neglect the importance of the source of money and/or credit.

17. **the problem of issue**: A central question of *Economic Democracy* [C. H. Douglas, 1920] and the social credit movement: who should issue the money and how should the issue be tied to production.

18. **Nakae Toji**: 1608-1648, Japanese philosopher known as "the Sage of Omi." He expounded the neo-Confucian philosophy of Wang Yang-ming. Pound got the name and the association from Carson Chang, who visited him at St. Elizabeths [Fang, III, 96].

19. **Wai' Ya'**: Wang Yang-ming, 1472-1528, the Ming dynasty neo-Confucian. In Carson Chang's Kiangsu dialect, "Wai' Ya' " approximates the sound for the name. "Min's lamp" is Wang's enlightened philosophy [ibid.].

20. **Nippon**: Japan.

21. **Grenfell**: Russell Grenfell, 1892-1954, author of *Unconditional Hatred*, which purports to prove that the Roosevelt-Morgenthau-Churchill program of unconditional surrender and the reduction of Germany after WWII to a powerless agrarian state showed less wisdom than the program of Wellington at the Congress of Vienna to build a lasting balance of power in Europe. This theme is developed at length in Cantos 100-105 [85:7].

22. **Antoninus**: A. Pius, A.D. 86-161, the Roman emperor (137-161) Pound often cites for his knowledge and promotion of wise maritime laws [42:4; 46:42; 78:56].

23. **"state shd / . . . benefit"**: Concept Pound attributes to Antoninus, who fought against widespread piracy and supported maritime insurance. Antoninus was indignant that people should exploit the misfortunes (e.g., shipwrecks) of others [*SP*, 272, 311].

24. **Salmasius**: Claudius S., 1588-1653, latinized name of Claude Saumaise, author of *De Modo Usurarum*, which Pound says, "appears not to have been reprinted since 1639 to 40" [*SP*, 323, 65, 272-273, 311].

25. **Χρεία**: H, "use, service, need." Pound said the word, as used in Aristotle, should be translated as "demand" and not "value." In his opinion the lack of precision in translating such a key word as this does damage to correct thinking through the ages [*GK*, 324, 357].

26. **Ari**: Aristotle.

27. **"Cogitatio . . . "**: L, Pound translates as "cogitation, meditation, and contemplation." He further illustrates: "In the first the mind flits aimlessly about the object, in the second it circles about it in a methodical manner, in the third it is unified with the object" [*GK*, 77; *Pai*, 2-2, 182].

28. **Richardus**: Richard St. Victor [85:52].

29. **Centrum circuli**: I, "center of a circle." In the *Vita Nuova*, Amor (Love) says to Dante: "I am the center of a circle, which possesseth all parts of its circumference equally but thou not so" [12.4]. Pound first quoted it in the *New Age* 1912 [*SP*, 29].

30. **Remove the mythologies**: An ironic recommendation. Pound believes the myths as retold by Ovid (for one) express the interaction of the human and the divine. Hence, when asked what he believed, Pound said he "answered such questions by telling the enquirer to read Confucius and Ovid" [*SP*, 53].

31. **Picabia**: Francis P., 1879-1953, a French painter who advanced the cause and practices of the cubists, dadaists, and surrealists. He was part of the Parisian group of artists, including Man Ray and Cocteau, whose creativity Pound respected most.

32. **Alsace-Lorraine**: An area along the Rhine bank between France and Germany

control of which has been contested from the time of the Roman occupation of Gaul. Since the Treaty of Verdun (843) it has passed back and forth between Germany and France a number of times.

33. **Vlaminck**: Maurice de V., 1876-1958, was one of the fauvist painters influenced by Van Gogh, a group that included Derain and Matisse. Pound knew them in his Paris years. Perhaps the "Art is local" is a response to W. C. Williams's attribution of the idea to John Dewey. In the "Author's Note" to *Paterson*, WCW said that Dewey said: "The local is the only universal, upon that all art builds."

34. **Wops**: Italian immigrants at Ellis Island who were "without papers" were identified with these initials. Not a pejorative label: just the language of the people.

35. *διάβορον* . . . : H, a fusion of words from lines 676-677 of Sophocles' *Trachiniae* (*διάβορον πρὸς οὐδενὸς/τῶν ἔνδον, ἀλλ' ἐδεστὸν ἐξ αὐτοῦ φθίνει*] and line 351 of *Electra* (*οὐ ταῦτα πρὸς κακοῖσ δειλίαν ἔχει;*). Thus: "Destroyed by nothing within, but eaten by itself, it wastes away; and in addition to our woes, shall we add cowardice?" A Sophoclean rhyme with the previous 2 lines: "The pusillanimous . . . dishonesty" [86:64] [DG].

36. **quia . . . est**: L, "which is impossible."

37. **Ver novum**: L, "Fresh spring" [39:13].

38. **hic est medium**: L, "here is the center."

39. **chih**: [M939]. "Rest in."

40. **Ἀθάνα**: H [Ἀθηνᾶ.], "Athena." At the end of the *Oresteia*, Athena broke the tie of the jury [*Eumenides*, 752; Loeb, 344: "this man stands acquitted on the charge of murder. The number of the casts [ballots] are equal"]. The play provides the first evidence of trial-by-jury in Judeo-Hellenic-Christian civilization.

41. **Shang**: [M5673]. Second dynasty: 1766-1121 B.C.

42. **Y Yin**: A minister of the Shang dynasty. His dedication to the concept of justice rhymes with the act of Athena [85:5].

43. **Ocellus**: Or Occelus. A 5th-century-B.C. Pythagorean philosopher from Lucanus who may have been a pupil of Pythagoras. An Ionic treatise attributed to him, entitled *On the Nature of the Universe* (quite certainly spurious), dates not earlier than the 1st century B.C. "It maintains the doctrine that the universe is uncreated and eternal; that to its three great divisions correspond the three kinds of beings—gods, men and daemons; and finally that the human race with all its institutions . . . must be eternal. It advocates an ascetic mode of life, with a view to the perfect reproduction of the race and its training in all that is noble and beautiful" [*EB*]. Since Ocellus is listed by Iamblicus [5:5] as a Pythagorean, Pound associates him with the important philosophers of light, and attributes to him the phrase "to build light" [94:172]. Ocellus was translated by Thomas Taylor in 1831.

44. **Erigena**: [36:9; 74:90]. Because Pound associates Erigena with light-philosophers, he attributes to him the phrase from Grosseteste, "All things are lights," as a way of suggesting his agreement with Grosseteste.

45. **Greek tags**: His dates, about 800 to about 877, make him one of the earliest philosophers to know Greek and thus one of the most complete scholars of his time.

46. **Alexander**: A. the Great, 356-323 B.C. In the spring of 323, A moved to Babylon to undertake great new developments, including a plan to open up maritime routes from Babylon to Egypt around Arabia: "under his supervision was prepared . . . an immense fleet, a great basin dug out to contain 1000 ships.'' But on June 15 and 16 of that year, at the beginning of a great enterprize, he "caroused deep into the night at the house of the favourite Medius. On the 17th he developed fever; . . . on the 27th his speech was gone . . . on the 28th Alexander died" [*EB*]. "In him the soul wore out the breast, and he died, in his thirty-third year, of a fever which might well have spared him

had he ever known how to spare himself" [*OCD*]. Pound may have got the idea that he was "bumped off" from Goleyevsky [cf. 47 below]. But his death did put a stop to a lot of planned development in the civilized world of his time.

47. **Gollievski**: Goleyevsky, a Russian general with an English wife whom the Pounds knew in Paris in the early 20s. Pound mentions him anonymously [*GK*, 229]: "To recapitulate, I take it from my ex-Russian ex-General that the fall of Alexander's empire was a disaster" [EH, *Pai*, 2-1, 141].

48. **Greece** . . . : Goleyevsky had another idea: "Most European history saw the fall of Rome, but failed to calculate the possible greater loss to knowledge, learning, civilization implied in the fall of the Macedonian empire" [ibid.].

49. **Justinian's codes**: J. the Great, 527-565, inherited the corpus of Roman law called *Codex Theodosianus*, issued in 438, which by his time needed up-dating [65:126]. He promoted a new *Codex*, which in time had to be redone under Basil and Leo the Wise [CFT, *Pai*, 2-2, 223 ff.; 94:45].

50. **"abbiamo** . . . ": I, "we have made a heap."

51. **Mus. viva voce**: I, "Mussolini orally" [with live voice]: Implies M tried to get parties to avoid the haystack of laws by settling out of court.

52. **Ocellus**: [cf. 43 above].

53. **jih**: [M3124]. "The sun, a day" [53:43].

54. **hsin**: [M2737]. "New."

55. **The play**: Sophocles' *Trachiniae.*

56. *φλογιξόμενον*: H, "in a blaze of light." Pound translates, "as is the lightning blaze" [*WT*, 8].

57. **gospoda**: Transliteration from Russian: "citizen."

58. *Δηάνειρα*: H, "Daianeira." Wife of Hercules, who was tricked into sending him as a gift the "Nessus shirt" which, after he put it on, became such a painful "shirt of fire" that he persuaded his son Hyllos to build a pyre and have him consumed by flames to end the terrible pain. Hercules is associated in tradition with "solar vitality."

59. *λαμπρὰ συμβαίνει*: H, "What splendour. It all coheres." Or so Pound translates [*WT* 50] and adds in a note: "This is the key phrase, for which the play exists" [109/772].

60. **dawn blaze** . . . : *The Women of Trachis* opens at dawn, and the pyre that consumes Hercules burns at sunset at the end of the play. Hercules' attitude is that under the law of the gods, "What has been, should have been," while his young son who must start the blaze believes, "And for me a great tolerance / matching the gods' great unreason" [*WT*, 54].

61. **Destutt**: Antoine Louis Claude Destutt de Tracy, Comte, 1754-1836, a French philosopher who became a deputy to the Constituent Assembly in 1789. His major works include *Elements d'ideoligie* and *Commentaire sur l'esprit des lois* [71:96].

62. **"Pity to stamp** . . . ": If a gold or other coin is stamped for a value less than its value by weight of metal, it will be melted down and disappear from the marketplace. Pound calls people who do such things "gold-bugs": they are a drag on any monetary system.

63. **Ari**: [Aristotle]: A saw "money as a measure," which is "called NOMISMA because it exists not by nature but by custom *and can therefore be altered or rendered useless at will* [Pound's italics]. If we put this 'be rendered comparatively useless' we shall have got the juice out of 'altered and rendered' [which], . . . is now part of the bank wheeze" [*GK*, 278-279]. "Wheeze" has an informal meaning of "trickery."

64. **chih**[4]: [M971]. "Aim, intention." Pound defines this: "The will, the direction of the will, *directio voluntatis*, the officer standing over the heart" [*CON*, 22].

65. directio voluntatis: L, "direction of the will" [77:57]: "The science of economics will not get very far until it grants the existence of will as a component; i.e. will toward order, will toward 'justice' or fairness, desire for civilization, amenities included. The intensity of that will is definitely a component in any solution" [*SP*, 240].

66. "An instrument . . . ": Major theme of *Economic Democracy* (1920).

67. Douglas: [38:49]. A criticism he often made: economic disaster resulted because money was used not as a just measure but for political ends.

68. Jean C: J. Cocteau [74:246]. Pound regarded him as one of the greatest and most perceptive of French poets and playwrights.

69. "gros légumes": F, "large vegetables." Slang sense: "fat cats." A pejorative epithet Cocteau applied to bankers. Pound quotes: "Alors, si l'idée de fantôme te fait sauter en l'air, c'est que tout le monde, riche ou pauvre à Thebes, sauf quelques gros légumes qui profitent de tout . . . " [*SP*,436]. The sentence comes from *L'Infernal Machina*, a play about Oedipus.

70. in pochi: I, "in a few." From Machiavelli: "Gli uomini vivono in pochi . . . " ("mankind lives in a few . . . "). Pound used the quote as an epigraph to *GB* in 1918.

71. causa motuum: L, "cause of motion [or emotion]."

72. pine seed . . . : The power in nature by which the seed realizes itself: a leitmotif of the hidden city [83/530], restated often, as in "the clover enduring" [94:19] and "bois dormant" [93:128].

73. BinBin: Laurence Binyon, 1869-1943. British poet, orientalist, and translator. Pound recalled in a 1934 letter to him [*L*, 255] that he used to say, "Slowness is beauty."

74. San: [M5415]. "Three."

75. Ku: [M3470]. "Solitary." The "San Ku" was a sort of secret-society council of three Pound found in Couvreur [IV, XX, 5-6, 333-334; Legge, 527-528]. They were part of the San Kung: "I appoint the Grand Tutor, the Grand Assistant, and the Grand Guardian. These are the three Kung." These were assisted by juniors called the San Ku: "I appoint the Junior Tutor, the Junior Assistant, and the Junior Guardian. These are called the three Koo [Ku]. They assist the Kung to diffuse widely all transforming influences; they with reverence display brightly the powers of heaven and earth:—assisting me, the one man" [Grieve, *Pai* 4-2 & 3, 481]. Stock called it "a sort of masonic council" [90:8].

76. Poictiers: Poitiers [76:77]. A town in W central France, ancient capital of Poitou. It dates from pre-Roman times; early on it became a center of Christian orthodoxy and an episcopal see, with St. Hilaire as bishop in the 4th century. The tower of the Hall of Justice was built here in the 12th century and has a room where on bright days the light is suffused indirectly so that no shadow is cast [HK, *Era*, 331, picture]. Pound listed this building as one where the architect invented something: "The cunning contrivance of lighting and the building of chimneys is . . . something that has no known fatherhood" [*GK*, 109].

77. Jacques de Molay: 1250?-1314. The last grand master of the Knights Templars. He was burned at the stake as a lapsed heretic on March 19, 1314 by order of King Philip IV of France. Pound seems to believe that the Templars were destroyed because they undermined the money powers by lending money at nonusorious interest rates. Latest scholarship shows that they were indeed the major money dealers of the time, but that they charged excessive fees for their capital and were destroyed so that their enormous wealth could be expropriated by the king and his reluctant henchman, Clement V (the first French pope), whom the king moved to Avignon. Their headquarters in Paris, called the Temple, was the money center of the Western world: "The Temple lent money to kings and merchants and collected its interest under the guise of rent . . . though the Church never ceased to denounce the Jew [*sic*] moneylenders" [*Guilt*, 28]. "*Usury* was the principal guilt of the Templars, and the secret of their enormous wealth" [ibid., 22]. The Italian banking system grew enormously through the Renaissance because it filled the gap left by the destruction of the Templars [90:11].

78. **"Section"**: The Golden Section of Pythagoras, a numerical process which seemed to involve mystical relationships representing proportions in nature. The proportion is expressed as a/b + b/c = c/d . . . = $1/\theta$ where θ is greater than 1. Here, the architecture of the tower is seen as expressing proportions that relate it harmoniously with the cosmos [FR, *Pai*, 7-2 & 3, 29 ff.].

79. **false . . . barocco**: Expresses Pound's belief that "usury" or money lust fosters bad art.

80. **Mencius**: [54:66; 78:60]: "Mencius said, 'All who speak about the nature of things, have in fact only their phenomena to reason from, and the value of a phenomenon is in its being natural.' "

81. **monumenta**: L, "memorials, monuments, statuary." Pound, following Heydon, distinguishes "monumenta" (plastic arts), "documenta" (verbal arts), and "phenomena" (art of nature). The oak endlessly bears a precise pattern of the oak leaf, directed by an intelligence in nature, without the aid of man [92/622].

82. **John Heydon**: English astrologer and alchemist, 1629-?, author of *The Holy Guide*, 1662, and other books in the hermetic tradition. In the first version of Canto 3, Pound devoted 23 lines to him, calling him a "worker of miracles," a visionary, and a "servant of God and secretary of nature." Pound saw in Heydon's "doctrine of signatures" an idea he related to a chain of Neoplatonic thought involving Trismegistus, Psellus, and Porphyry [*GK*, 225] and the kind of intelligence in nature that makes an acorn produce only an oak tree. Heydon [91:96] is mentioned several times in *Rock-Drill* with occult writers such as Apollonius [91:9, 25] and Ocellus [91:12, 26] and in contexts of intelligence as light descending [WB, *Approaches*, 303-318; Surette, *Eleusis*, 263-267].

83. **Σελλοί**: H, "the Selli." Original inhabitants of Dodona, among whom was the oracle of Jove. Jessie L. Weston [*Ritual*] connects the Templars with pagan priests known as "Salii." Pound prob. rhymes the "secret society" ambience of the Selli with other secret societies, such as the San Ku [cf. 75 above; 109:48]

84. **old Jarge**: George Santayana [80:49]. Although G. S. maintained he was a materialist and a mechanist, his four-volume work on "essences" (*The Realms of Spirit*) accepted the historical facts that religious faiths and traditions assumed much more than a materialist theory of knowledge could allow [Marginalia in DP's copy of *The Cantos*. Note provided by OP].

85. **houris**: For all faithful men who died for Allah, the Islamic paradise contained an endless line of couches, each occupied by a houri, a nymph created from musk and spices and endowed with eternal youth and perfect beauty.

86. **hsin**: [M2735]. "Heart, mind."

87. **Morrison**: Robert M., 1782-1834, first Protestant missionary to China, whose dictionary in 6 quarto volumes was published between 1815 and 1822. He also promoted cultural interchange, education, and medicine.

88. **Remy**: R. de Gourmont, 1858-1915, French writer, thinker, and stylist celebrated by Pound for many years for his *Natural Philosophy of Love*, which celebrates sensuality as a natural process in the universe which makes the cosmos continue [cf. *NPL*, 149-158].

89. **Sant' Ambrogio**: Small town at the end of the *salita* leading up from Rapallo, where at one time during the war Pound, Dorothy, and Olga Rudge lived together. They were

joined there toward the end of WWII by Mary de Rachewiltz. The area escaped serious harm, although the Ligurian coast nearby was heavily damaged.

90. **Baccin**: An elderly friend from Rapallo, who, in the spring of 1944, helped Pound carry "the accumulation of twenty years of books and papers, letters, manuscripts, drawings" up the hill to casa 60, Sant' Ambrogio [M de R, *Discretions*, 196].

91. **ulivi**: I, "olive trees."

92. **Monsieur F.**: Prob. Gustave Flaubert (1821-1880), who had visionary experiences that were prob. a bizarre form of epilepsy. They were always cued and accompanied by brilliant light and "a million thoughts, images . . . crowding at once into his brain like blazing rockets in a flood of fireworks" [Steegmuller, 22]. Flaubert spoke of his visions as combinations of "Santa Theresa, Hoffman, and Edgar Poe."

93. **Windeler**: B. Cyril Windeler, author of *Elimus*, a story with 12 designs by Dorothy Shakespear, one of the 6 books published by Three Mountains Press, Paris, ca. 1923. This press, run by William Bird, also published Pound's *Indiscretions* and Hemingway's *In Our Time*.

94. **Windeler's vision**: Pound wrote: "and you have Mr. W., a wool-broker in London, who suddenly at 3 A.M. visualizes the whole of his letter-file, three hundred folios; he sees and reads particularly the letter at folder 171, but he sees simultaneously the entire contents of the file, the whole thing about the size of two lumps of domino sugar laid flat side to flat side" [*NPL*, 155].

95. **Santa Teresa**: Or Theresa (1515-1582). Spanish visionary and mystic who had visionary trances that "recurred frequently . . . and grew more and more vivid. The cross of her rosary was snatched from her hand one day, and when returned it was made of jewels more brilliant than diamonds, visible, however, to her alone" [EB]. Pound said, "You have the visualizing sense, the 'stretch' of imagination, the mystics . . . Santa Theresa who 'saw' the microcosmos, hell, heaven, purgatory complete, 'the size of a walnut' " [*NPL*, 155],

96. **Butchers**: Pound divided primitive men into four categories: (1) hunters, (2) killers of bulls, (3) killers of lesser cattle, and (4) agriculturists. "Ethics begins with agriculture, i.e. enough honesty to let him who plants reap. Plenty of religion in hunters, magic, etc. with reverent apology to ancestor of beasts killed" [letter from Pound to William Cookson].

97. **Fell between horns**: Prob. an actual occurrence of a bullfighter attempting a ring maneuver such as "salta sin barra." Says HK: "DP told me that EP saw bullfights at Arles. Ez wanted to join the fighters in the ring but DP's hand on his coattails held him back. 'With his eyesight!', she said."

98. **"salta sin barra"**: S, "[he] leaps without pole." Goya, in a series of etchings called *La Tauromaquia* (*The Art of Bullfighting*), shows a bullfighter vaulting over a bull on a pole grounded between the attacking horns. One might describe the movement as a "leap with pole" [Goya, *Complete Etchings*, plate 20]. In *The Palace of Minos*, by Sir Arthur Evans, a number of illustrations show a maneuver, performed by both women and men, in which the "Taureador" seized a bull by the horns and executed various acrobatic feats, sometimes landing on the bull's back before springing in another somersault to the ground, in effect a "salta sin barra." [Vol III, 203-232; see CFT, *Pai* 13-2].

99. **Mr. Paige**: Douglas Duncan P., editor of *The Letters of Ezra Pound*. He prob. described Ligurian butchery in an unpublished and unlocated letter to Pound.

100. **Ligurian**: Of an area in NW Italy reaching from the French border to Le Apezia. It includes the Ligurian Alps in the west and the Ligurian Apennines in the east; the coastal strip forms the Italian Riviera; Genoa is the capital.

101. **Mont Ségur**: F, "Segur Mountain." From Latin "Mons Securus," indicating a

stronghold. Site of Provence castle / temple of the Catharists [23:25,28]. Pound believed "a light from Eleusis" persisted in this area until the temple was destroyed by the Albigensian Crusade. Studies of the ruins indicate elaborate sun-worship rituals [HK, *Era*, 335 ff.].

102. San Bertrand: A French town on the Garonne near Montsegur where the Albigenses defended their citadel until they were all massacred. It was on the road to this town that Poicebot had a visionary experience [5:24] and suffered a sea change, suggesting a "delightful psychic experience" [*SR*, 92] akin to the experiences of Flaubert, Santa Teresa et al.

103. Frobenius: Leo F. [38:45; 74:44]. The quote from *Frobenius* [*GK*, 57] is one of Pound's favorites [*SP*, passim], since it expresses a cultural coherence—"gristly roots of ideas that are in action" [*GK*, 58].

104. oak cats: Poundian for "squirrels."

105. Indians say: Paraphrased: "High weeds precede a hard winter."

106. water-bug: An image Pound had in mind for years. It seems to relate to Pythagorean light imagery: just as light through air shadows forth creation, so does light through the denser medium water produce a pattern of beauty on stone, a pattern that rhymes, in turn, with the "rose in the steel dust" [74:503]. Pound said in letter to Katue Kitasono: "I wonder if it is clear that I mean the shadow of the 'mittens'? and can you ideograph it; very like petals of blossom" [*L*, 348; 91:105]. "The interaction between heaven, prince, and people paralleled by that between the descent of light, the refractive processes of dented water, and the substantiality of the water-bug, which results in . . . the special flower on the stone" can be seen as a "metaphysical image" that effects "a blending of the moral ambience of the tê ideogram" [HK, *Pai*, 4-2 & 3, 381].

107. nel botro: I, "in the pool."

108. Ideogram: Tê [M6162], "awareness." Pound says: "the process of looking straight into ones own heart and acting on the results" [*CON*, 27]. The ideogram introduces again the idea of process in nature [74:9].

109. "Bomb him down . . . : Prob. a memory from the Pisan confinement.

110. "Und . . . Shinbones!: Pound's idea that one can tell who is talking by the noises he makes is partly true. Here, one can tell the kind of person (which matters) but not his name (which doesn't). The scene of ecstasy relates to the discovery of another example of how divine intelligence works in the world. Just as the branches of a plant are spaced with mathematical precision so that they can spread their leaves to absorb the maximum amount of energy from the sun, so skeletal structures express optimal economy of weight, size, and shape for the load to be carried. A rhyme with other processes in nature, such as the cherrystone producing only the cherry tree [113/788]. Or phyllotaxis [104:87; 109:49]. For detailed account of the mathematical precision of nature, see Thompson, *On Growth and Form* in particular Chap. IX on Spicular Skeletons and Chap. XIV, "On Leaf-Arrangement, or Phyllotaxis."

111. ottocento: I, "19th century."

112. Mencken: Henry L. M. [81:31]. Recurrent theme [*GK*, 182].

113. Mencius: Meng-tzu [78:60]. The lines are a compressed statement on taxing or sharing (tithing) which occurs in Mencius III, I, iii, 6 [cf. Legge, 612-613].

114. T'ang Wan Kung: C, "The duke Wan of T'ang." Title of Bk. III, Pt. I of *The Works of Mencius* [ibid.].

115. Ideogram: Shang [M5669], "supreme, top, first."

116. pu erh: Pu [M5379], "not"; erh [M1752], "double." Here, "no dichotomy."

117. Ideogram: Li [M3867], "profit." The "grain cut" is the annual renewable product of nature, which is distinguished from usury: to harvest acorns brings legitimate profit; to cut down the oak tree for profit is usury. In Legge [Mencius I, I, 1, 125-127], King Hui of Liang says to Mencius that, having traveled a thousand *li* [57:32], he must have come with counsels "to profit my kingdom." Said Mencius "Why must your majesty use that word 'profit'?" He said he offered only "counsels to benevolence and righteousness."

118. Ideogram: Chih [M933], "wisdom" [85:9]. The sun (lower) element of the ideogram suggests "the light descending," in Pound's recurrent religious metaphor.

119. Religion: A deficiency of contemporary Christianity, which has no ritualistic dances in celebration of the mystery. Without such rites, Pound implies by tone, no creed can be effective or affective as a religion.

120. Cytharistriae: Followers of Cythera [24:30; 79/492]. To be seen here as dancing girls used in ritual.

121. Vide: L, "See."

122. Neruda: Pablo N., pseudonym of Neftali Ricardo Reyes, 1904-1973, a surrealist poet from Chile. His work is distinguished by his use of bold metaphors and the common tongue. He made sensuous verse out of grief and despair and had wide influence in Hispanic America in both social and literary thought. Many of his poems contain Cytharistriae.

123. "Stink" Saunders: A. P. Saunders, dean of Hamilton College. Pound saw him during his 1939 visit to the college [Norman, 367]. "An independence" equaled enough money for an artist to live on so that he could devote his time to his art. The idea was behind Pound's efforts with "Bel Esprit" to create an independence for artists. He tried to start with a fund for Eliot [*L*, 173-176].

124. nomignolo: I, "nickname." Saunders was called "Stink" because of the odors created in the chemistry lab.

125. Henry's: Henry James [7:13]. In a letter to Wyndham Lewis, undated, Pound wrote: "[re] member that touching passage in H.J.'s [a] bout the dissolving view?" [Xerox of letter at Cornell provided by T. Materer]. The "dissolving view" is illustrated on the next page [cf. 127 below]. In this context the idea seems to be that a body of coherent thought reaches dissolution by slow attrition or seepage because it is not hitched solidly to "the one principle," as expressed by the ideogram. Sse's response in the *Analects* is, "I have reduced it all to one principle" [*GK* 15]. Just as Mencius preserved the name of Confucius, from whom coherent thought came, so should we preserve such principles by monuments to the founding fathers, such as John Adams—a spirit and a solid block to build on, or become hitched to.

126. Ideogram: Chih [M939], "the hitching post, position, place one is in, and works from" [*CON*, 232; 85:9].

127. Henry again: Henry James. A passage from Ford M. Ford is indicated: "How often . . . haven't I heard him say whilst dictating the finish of a phrase: 'No, no, Dash . . . that is not clear . . . Insert before "we are all" . . . Let me see . . . yes, insert "Not so much locally, though to be sure we're here; but temperamentally in a manner of speaking.' " . . so that the phrase, blindingly clear to him by that time, when completed would run: 'So that here, not so much locally, though to be sure we're here, but at least temperamentally in a mannner of speaking, we all are' " [Ford, *Portraits from Life*, 25]. An example of a "disolving view."

128. De Molay: [cf. 77 above].

129. Church councils: Whereas early church councils were clearly against usury, they began "bumbling" the issue during the early Renaissance.

130. Justice: Anticipates one of the central themes of *Thrones* [96:headnote].

131. directio voluntatis: L, "direction of the will" [77:57]. Recurrent leitmotif.

132. Richardus: Richard St. Victor [85:52].

133. Benjamin Major: Companion work to Benjamin Minor.

134. Old crocks: Three of those "to die in a bug-house" seem to be listed after the colon. For Gallagher, MSB has a note: "did a book on America's aims, Asia's aspirations." But there is no information about either the "old colonel" or "T. F." Pound commonly referred to St Elizabeths as "the bug-house."

135. Sikandar: The Indian name for Alexander the Great. MSB has two notes: "legend [tigers?] go out and howl at full moon over tomb of Alexander the Great" / "Erigena who said God himself didn't know who he was." The point is the mutual empathy of the great cats with the sage, mystic, or charismatic leader, a leitmotif repeated with Apollonius of Tyana [94:42, 43] and others. The last of the mythic kings in *Shah Nameh* [77:171].

CANTO LXXXVIII

Sources

Thomas Hart Benton, *Thirty Years' View; or, A History of the Working of The American Government for Thirty Years, from 1820 to 1850*, Vols. I, II, New York, Appleton, 1854 [*TYV*]; Christopher Hollis, *The Two Nations*, London, 1935; Willis A. Overholser, *A Short Review and Analysis of the History of Money in the United States*, Libertyville, Illinois, Progress Publishing Concern, 1936; Sophocles, *Antigone*, II, 337-338; EP, *CON*, 112, 269, 27-33, 193; Dante, *Inf.* XI, 46-66; George Tucker, ed., *Blackstone's Commentaries: with Notes of Reference, to the Constitution and Laws, of the Federal Government of the United States; and of the Commonwealth of Virginia*, 1803 [Tucker]; Homer, *Iliad* IX, 63; James Legge, *The Four Books*, Shanghai, 1923 [Legge].

Background

EP, *GK*, 354, 45, 47, 43, 249, 243; *IMP*, 65, 33, 252, 196; *SP*, 295, 172, 265, 313, 176; *LE*, 86; *P*, 139-140; e. e. Cummings, *Collected Poems*, 1954; Anatole France, *L'Ile des Pengouins*, 1908; Brooks Adams, *The New Empire*, New York and London, Macmillan, 1902; Alexis de Tocqueville, *Democracy in America*, 4 vols., 1835-40; Davis R. Dewey, *Financial History of the United States*, 1902; Benito Mussolini, *My Autobiography*, New York, C. Scribner's & Sons, 1928 [Auto].

Exegeses

HK, *Era*, 13; EH, *Pai*, 2-1, 143.

[Although the bulk of the source identifications for Cantos 88 and 89 were completed before 1975, many of the most elusive ones come from a dissertation by Charles Watts, which is in the process of being published under the title of *The Duel of Giants: The People vs. the Bank.*]

Glossary

1. **It . . . relation**: The opening lines of chap. 26, entitled "Duel Between Mr. Clay and Mr. Randolph." of Thomas Hart Benton's *TYV* [Vol. I, 70], except that after the word "session," the source has some added detail: "that Mr. Randolph came to my room at Brown's Hotel, and (without explaining the reason of the question) asked me if I was a blood relation of Mrs. Clay?" Senator Benton said that he was. His response told Randolph that he would be unable to ask him to act as his second in a duel to which he had just been challenged by Mr. Clay, and that he must apply instead to Colonel Tattnall.

2. **Clay's right**: Clay issued the challenge because of news reports that Randolph had made incriminating remarks about some of Clay's actions as secretary of state. Randolph insisted Clay had no right to hold him accountable for anything he said in the Senate, but as a private person he would answer for any injury Clay believed he had received. For this reason Randolph confided in Benton that he would not return Clay's fire. Benton summarizes the nuances: "As senator he had a constitutional immunity, given for a wise purpose, and which he would neither surrender nor compromise; as individual he was ready to give satisfaction for what was deemed as injury. He would receive, but not return a fire. It was as much as to say: Mr. Clay may fire at me for what has offended him; I will not, by returning the fire, admit his right to do so" [*TYV*, I, 71].

3. **Brown's**: A Washington hotel frequented by members of the government.

4. **Col. Tatnall**: Edward F. Tattnall, 1788-1832, of Savannah, Georgia; state solicitor general, 1816-1817; member of state legislature, 1818-1819; member of Congress, 1821-1827. Not to be confused with Josiah Tattnall (1795-1871), a naval officer from Georgia who served in the War of 1812 and the Mexican War but was not promoted to captain until 1850. (Pound's incorrect spelling comes from Benton.)

5. **Defiance of Adams**: John Quincy Adams [34:passim]. The challenge to duel derived from deep-rooted antipathies between the Federalists and "the party of the people" which came to a climax in the election of 1824. The electoral college, bound by its constituents, could not provide a majority (131 out of 260) for any of the four candidates, so "the election devolved upon the House of Representatives" [*TYV*, I, 44-45]. Jackson [37:passim], with 99 votes, had the highest count (Adams, 84; Crawford 41; Clay 37). Before the House voted Henry Clay [34:47] visited JQA. No one else was present at the meeting. Despite denials that a bargain was made between the two men, the facts suggested otherwise, for when the House voted, Clay switched his allegiance to JQA, who won the election and soon after made Clay secretary of state. Long before Clay's visit to JQA, he told Benton that he planned to support Adams even though they had been political adversaries. Clay, with others, said he preferred JQA's intelligence and experience to that of a military chieftan [ibid., 47]. JQA said he made Clay secretary

of state not because of any bargain struck before the election but because he was the best qualified for the job. But appearances were against them. According to Benton, the people bided their time and in 1828 elected Jackson over JQA with a margin of over 2 to 1 and thus made up for what they considered "a violation of the demos krateo principle" [ibid.]. John Randolph, senator from Virginia and a fiery orator, was implacably opposed to many of JQA's foreign policy initiatives, including the president's proposed Panama mission, which engendered fierce debate in the Senate and became the precipitating cause for Clay's challenge [*TYV*, I, 65-69]. Randolph's intemperate remarks were in defiance of JQA's policy rather than Clay's pursuit of it.

6. **Jessup**: Thomas S. Jesup, 1788-1860, a soldier from Va. who rose through the ranks to become a major general and in 1836 assumed command of the army in the Creek nation.

7. **waive privilege**: Randolph's willingness to waive his privilege as a senator became a delicate point of negotiation between the seconds. Randolph's stand was that he would answer in his person for any offense given, but not for his actions in the Senate.

8. **Salazar's letter**: It was reported that Randolph said "that a letter from General Salazar, the Mexican minister at Washington, submitted by the Executive to the Senate, bore the ear-mark of having been manufactured or forged by the Secretary of State, and denounced the administration as a corrupt coalition between the puritan and blackleg; and added, at the same time, that he (Mr. Randolph) held himself personally responsible for all that he had said." Benton comments: "This was the report to Mr. Clay, and upon which he gave the absolute challenge, and received the absolute acceptance" [ibid., 73]. "The puritan" was supposed to refer to JQA and "blackleg" to Clay.

9. **"forgery"**: Jesup wrote to Tattnall: "The injury of which Mr. Clay complains consists in this, that Mr. Randolph has charged him with having forged or manufactured a paper connected with the Panama mission; also, that he has applied to him in debate the epithet of blackleg." Jesup wanted Randolph to declare that he did not intend to charge Clay "with forging or falsifying any paper . . . and also that the term blackleg was not intended to apply to him" [ibid.].

10. **Charlotte jury**: Tattnall replied that Randolph said he used these words in debate: "that I thought it would be in my power to show evidence sufficiently presumptive to satisfy a Charlotte (county) jury that this invitation was manufactured here-that Salazar's letter struck me as bearing a strong likeness in point of style to the other papers. I did not undertake to prove this, but expressed my suspicion that the fact was so. I applied to the administration the epithet, puritanic-diplomatic-black-legged administration." Benton says these words ameliorated the harsh words "forging and falsifying" attributed to Randolph and adds: "The speech was a bitter philippic, and intended to be so, taking for its point the alleged coalition between Mr. Clay and Mr. Adams with respect to the election, and their efforts to get up a popular question contrary to our policy of non-entanglement with foreign nations" [ibid.]. Benton believed that if Clay had been present at the speech he would not have shown resentment at it, but he could not prevent the duel from taking place.

11. **Right bank . . . that**: These six lines are taken from the source: "The afternoon of Saturday, the 8th of April, was fixed upon for the time,: the right bank of the Potomac, within the state of Virginia, above the Little Falls bridge, was the place,—pistols the weapons,—distance ten paces. . . . There was a statute of the State against duelling within her limits; but, as he merely went out to receive a fire without returning it, he deemed that no fighting, and consequently no breach of her statute. This reason for choosing Virginia could only be explained to me, as I alone was the depository of his secret" [ibid., 73-74].

12. I went to Clay's . . . : Benton visited Clay on Friday night and Randolph on Saturday noon, April 8th, the day of the duel. Pound chooses phrases from the source to give a sense of the people and the scene.

13. Georgetown: A section of NW Washington one passed through "to cross the Potomac into Virginia at the Little Falls bridge" [ibid., 74].

14. Could not . . . value: Benton could not ask Randolph directly if he had changed his mind about not firing, as that would have been to doubt his previous word. So he decided to get at the point indirectly by mentioning his visit, the tranquillity of Mrs. Clay and the sleeping child, "and added, I could not help reflecting how different all that might be the next night. He understood me perfectly, and immediately said, with a quietude of look and expression which seemed to rebuke an unworthy doubt, '*I shall do nothing to disturb the sleep of the child or the repose of the mother*,' and went on with his employment . . . which was, making codicils to his will, all in the way of remembrance to friends; the bequests slight in value, but invaluable in tenderness of feeling and beauty of expression" [ibid.].

15. Macon: Nathaniel M., 1758-1837, American statesman who served in the Revolution and became a political leader in N.C., a champion of states' rights, an ardent Jeffersonian, and an opponent of the reestablishment of the Bank of the United States. Macon, Ga., bears his name, as does Randolph-Macon College, along with that of his good friend John Randolph.

16. Young Bryan: John Randolph Bryan, his namesake, "then at school in Baltimore . . . had been sent for to see him, but sent off before the hour for going out, to save the boy from a possible shock at seeing him brought back" [ibid.].

17. Johnny: Randolph's "faithful man," a black manservant.

18. Branch bank: The anecdote that Pound summarizes from his source [ibid., 74-75] points up the struggle against the bank which is the main theme of Cantos 88 and 89. The bank's lies about its gold holdings, its desire to substitute its own notes in payment, and its readiness to back down when challenged by a powerful politician, represents in miniature the war that Benton, Randolph, Macon, Jackson, Van Buren and many others conducted against the bank throughout the Jackson era. They deplored the fact that a private company was authorized to issue bank notes so that the "power to issue" money was transferred from the public to a private agency.

19. His (R's) stepfather: St. George Tucker, 1752-1827, revolutionary soldier, constitutional delegate, lawyer, and judge. The book was entitled *Blackstone's Commentaries: with Notes of Reference, to the Constitution and Laws, of the Federal Government of the United States; and of the Commonwealth of Virginia*, 1803.

20. The place . . . : A description of the spot where the duel took place. Benton uses the phrase "depression or basin," rather than "basis." Pound leaves the duelists here. Two shots were fired but neither Clay nor Randolph was injured. Clay insisted on the second shot, which ripped Randolph's coat. The duelists shook hands and Randolph said, "You owe me a coat, Mr. Clay." Clay promptly replied, "I am glad the debt is no greater" [ibid., 74]. This minor fracas was merely a symptom of the continuous war between the antibank forces represented by Randolph and the probank forces represented by Clay.

21. Bellum perenne: L, "everlasting war" [86/568; 87/569].

22. 1694: The year William Paterson and others founded the Bank of England with the deliberate intention of creating great profit out of nothing [46:26].

23. 1750: In 1751 Parliament passed an act that forbade the issue of paper money in the colonies. The act caused great misery as England required payment for goods in metal specie, which drained the colonies of so much of it that too little was left to carry on trade. Another act in 1763, even more stringent, became a primary cause of the Revolution [Overholser, *History of Money*, 21-29].

24. Lexington: A reference to a letter of John Adams to Thomas Jefferson which Pound often quotes [33:18; 50:1]: "The Revolution was in the Minds of the people . . . 15 years before a drop of blood was drawn at Lexington." Adams made the point elsewhere in his correspondence [32:1].

25. '64 "greatest blessing": Lincoln, in a letter to Col. Edmund Taylor, Dec. 1864, wrote about the greenbacks the government issued to help pay the Civil War debt: "Chase thought it a hazardous thing, but we finally accomplished it and gave to the people of this Republic THE GREATEST BLESSING THEY EVER HAD–THEIR OWN PAPER TO PAY THEIR OWN DEBTS" [Overholser, *History of Money*, 44; *GK*, 354; *SP*, 159].

26. 1878: Pound discovered in 1928 that his grandfather, Thaddeus Coleman Pound, "had already in 1878 been writing about, or urging among his fellow Congressmen, the same essential of monetary and statal economics" that he was for in the 1920s" [*IMP*, 65]. Elsewhere Pound wrote: "In 1878 a Congressman expressed or explained his position by saying that he wanted to keep at least part of the non-interest bearing national debt in circulation as currency" [*IMP*, 33].

27. sangue, fatica: I, "blood, fatigue." In describing war Pound wrote: "Sangue, merda e fatica, was the definition given me by an officer in the last European war. Blood, dung and fatigue" [*IMP*, 252].

28. blood . . . surveillance: Exact source unknown, but the idea is everywhere present in Pound's writings about money and banking (usury) as causes of war: "A financial system wherein it is more profitable to sell guns than to sell farm machinery, textiles or food stuff is fundamentally vicious" [*IMP*, 252].

29. peerage: . . . P. C. 377: These 12 lines are taken from Tucker's edition of *Blackstone's Commentaries*, Chap. V, entitled "Public Wrongs." Peers of the realm were once allowed to plea benefit of clergy, which resulted in lesser sentences. The distinction was abolished for a time but was "virtually restored by statute I Edward. VI, c. 12 [Book VI, caput (or chapter) 12 of the laws enacted during the reign of King Edward the First] which statute also enacts that lords of parliament and peers of the realm . . . etc" [Tucker, 365-368].

30. The books . . . villein: In Tucker's edition Blackstone has a note that quotes Lord Coke [107:3]: "contenement signifieth his countenance, as the armour of a soldier in his countenance, and the like," and adds, "the *wainagium* [Anglo-Latin source of *wainage*] is the countenance of the villein, and it was great reason to save his wainage, for otherwise the miserable creature was to carry the burden on his back" [Tucker, 379].

31. the Histories: The next six lines list a number of occasions in history when kings, emperors, or other rulers understood the distributive function of money and tried to use public credit for the public good.

32. T'ang: Pound wrote of T'ang [53:40]: "The emperor opened a copper mine and issued round coins with square holes and gave them to the poor. . . . That story is 3000 years old, but it helps one to understand what money is and what it can do. For the purpose of good government it is a ticket for the orderly distribution of WHAT IS AVAILABLE" ["What is Money For," 1939; reprinted, *SP*, 295].

33. the chuntze: C, chün tzu [M1715-18], "the princely man." A gentleman, the wise man, a man of complete virtue, the beau ideal of Confucianism." Pound wrote that such a man "stands firm in the middle of what whirls without leaning on anything either to one side or the other" [*CON*, 113].

34. monopoly: Pound wrote, "The usual

frauds of bookkeeping, monopoly, etc., have been known since the beginning of history. . . . Aristotle . . . relates how Thales, wishing to show that a philospher could easily 'make money' if he had nothing better to do, foreseeing a bumper crop of olives, hired by paying a small deposit, all the olive presses on the islands of Miletus and Chios. When the abundant harvest arrived, everybody went to see Thales. Aristotle remarks that this is a common business practice" [92:74; *SP*, 172].

35. **Thales**: One of the seven sages. Aristotle called him the founder of physical science and attributed to him the view that everything comes from and returns to water, which is thus both eternal and divine. Said Thales: "All things are full of gods."

36. **Antoninus**: A. Pius, Roman emperor A.D. 137-161, b. A.D. 86 near Rome. Adopted by Hadrian, he became his successor. During his moderate reign he cut taxes, decreased the public debt, left a surplus in the treasury [42:4; 46:42], and lowered interest rates [78:56].

37. **"Trying", he said**: The "he" is Thaddeus Coleman Pound, who said this in 1878 [cf. 26 above]. But Pound suggests Antoninus had similar policies.

38. **Mencius**: [87:80]. Tithing every year so that the good years would prepare for the bad years was better than taxing, according to Mencius.

39. **Perenne . . .** : L, "Everlastingly. I sing everlastingly."

40. **Dai Gaku**: J, "The Great Digest." Japanese name for the Confucian text *Ta Hsio*. In "Date Line" Pound said: "as to what I believe: I believe the *Ta Hio*" [*LE*, 86].

41. **Belascio**: I, "balascio." A kind of ruby [36:8]. A leitmotif linking the paradisal theme of love in Canto 36 and the major theme of thrones as justice in Cantos 96-109 [104:116].

42. **Erigena**: Johannes Scotus Erigena, or Eriugina, 815?-877?, medieval theologian [36:9].

43. **Carolus Calvus**: Charles the Bald, 823-877, holy Roman emperor, who died the same year believed to be the year of Erigena's death [74:103].

44. **"Captans . . . sit!"**: L, "Hoggers of harvest, cursed among the people." So Pound translates the phrase of St. Ambrose [*GK*, 45, 47]. He associates him with the age-old fight against usury and monopoly.

45. **Ambrose**: St. A. (340?-397), bishop of Milan, doctor of the church, popular with the people, known for his eloquent preaching. Said Pound: "St Ambrose didn't rise suddenly and without forebears. A transition from self-centered lust after eternal salvation into a sense of public order occurred somewhere and sometime" [*GK*, 43]. Pound sees St. Ambrose as one of a number of great leaders from Antoninus Pius [cf. 36 above] on who were concerned with justice, the just price, and the welfare of the people.

46. **Delcroix**: Carlo D. A veteran, blinded in the Fascist revolution, who was admired by Mussolini. Describing a time of violence in 1925, Mussolini wrote: "Finally on June 6th Delcroix with his lyric speech, full of life and passion, broke that storm-charged tension" [*Auto*, 228]. Later Delcroix became president of the Association of War Wounded and Invalids [92:49; 95:12; 98/690]. Pound said that Delcroix thought poets should be concerned with "credit, the nature of money, monetary issue etc." [*GK*, 249]. The problem, from Antoninus Pius to the present, is thus "always the same."

47. **Get . . . quit**: In Pound's translation of the *Analects*, we read: "He [Confucius] said: Problems of style? Get the meaning across and then STOP" [*CON*, 269]. [79:40; HK, *Era*, 13].

48. **Baccin**: [87:90].

49. **Under the olives . . .** : Pound wrote: "Happy the man born to rich acres, a saecular vine bearing good grapes, olive trees spreading with years" [*GK*, 243]. Such a man's wealth is based (as with the grasslands of the Sienese Bank [42, 43:passim]) on a

continuous, renewable resource, which is different from nonproductive gold.

50. saecular: Derived from L, saeculum, "long period of time." Thus, "going on from age to age."

51. ad majorem: L, "to the greater."

52. Dum . . . scandet: L, "Now to Ambrosia [Ambrose?] he ascends." Perhaps Pound is recalling Baccin walking up the *salita* ("hillside") to Sant' Ambrogio, the place above Rapallo where Pound lived with Dorothy, Olga Rudge, and his daughter Mary during the last part of WWII.

53. sacro nemori: L, "to the sacred grove."

54. altro che tacita: I, "another who quiets."

55. ἀφρήτωρ . . . : H, "Without brotherhood, lawless, hearthless." A luminous detail of Homer's "Out of all brotherhood, outlawed, homeless shall be that man who longs for all the horror of fighting among his own people" [*Iliad* IX, 63].

56. To . . . Emperor: The end of the passage Pound often cited from the *Great Digest* reads: "From the Emperor, Son of Heaven, down to the common man, singly and all together, this self-discipline is the root" [*CON*, 27-33].

57. Antoninus: [cf. 36 above]. In his own time Antoninus was a model for humane and reasoned action.

58. slavery and . . . bhoogery: Antoninus's actions were counterbalanced in his time by inhumane and destructive practices: "By great wisdom sodomy and usury were seen coupled together" [*SP*, 265]. [14:3; *Inf.* XI, 46-66].

59. Estlin: Edward Estlin Cummings, 1894-1963. His poem 14 of "1 x 1" has these lines: "pity this busy monster, manunkind, / not. Progress is a comfortable disease: . . . " [*Collected Poems*, 397].

60. ching . . . : [M1138]. "To reverence; to respect; to honour." In the *Analects* Pound defines *ching*[4] as "respect for the kind of intelligence that enables grass seed to grow grass; the cherry-stone to make cherries" [*CON*, 193]. Hence "respect the vegetal powers" [85:167].

61. Hindoustani: The Hindu practice of nurturing all living things, including vermin as well as the sacred cows.

62. Make . . . springs": Early Chinese religious rites for the burial of the dead involved making figures of straw to place with the corpse. In the Chou dynasty, the straw figures were replaced by more and more sophisticated humanoid figures, a practice Kung was against for good reason. In *Mencius* I, 1, iv, 6, we read that Chung-ne said: "Was he not without posterity who first made wooden images *to bury with the dead*?" Legge's note reads in part: "In ancient times bundles of straw were made to represent men imperfectly . . . and carried to the grave, and buried with the dead, as attendants upon them. In middle antiquity . . . for those bundles of straw, wooden figures of men were used, having springs in them, by which they could move. . . . By and by, came the practice of burying living persons with the dead, which Confucius thought was an effect of this invention, and therefore he branded the inventor as in the text" [Legge, 442]. (During the time this canto was being written, Pound was working with David Gordon on a translation of B. I of *Mencius*. This item provoked lively discussion at St. Elizabeths. DG's work was copyright Harvard in 1954 and published in a limited edition copyright David Gordon in 1964.)

63. Ideogram: A composite character invented by Pound from elements of *shih*, 尸 [M5756], and *yin*, 尹 [M7439]. In a discussion of whether more reverence is due to a near relation or to someone who is "personating a dead ancestor," a conflict of rules developed. Thus, some disciples went to Mencius for the answer; he said, in effect, although more respect is ordinarily given to the elder, it would be given to one younger, or even a villager, during the season in which he is personating the dead [*Mencius* VI, 1, v, 4]. Legge has a note: "In sacrificing to the departed, some one–a certain one of the descendants, if possible,—was made the 尸, or 'corpse,' into whose body the spirit of the other was supposed to descend to receive the worship" [Legge, 858].

64. Père Henri Jacques: A Jesuit missionary [4:35].

65. Sennin: J, "genies or spirits" [4:36]. ["Sennin Poem," *P*, 139-140].

66. Rokku: J, "a mountain" [4:37]. Not a translation but a phonetic transcription.

67. Mr Tcheou: An Oriental Pound once knew. In "A Visiting Card" he wrote: "The Counsellor Tchou said to me 'These peoples (the Chinese and Japanese) should be like brothers. They read the same books" [*SP*, 313].

68. Marse Adams: President John Adams [31:15].

69. The Major: C. H. Douglas, the author of *Economic Democracy* (1920) and *Social Credit* (1932) [38:49].

70. First Folio (Shx): Prob. Shakespeare. Perhaps Major Douglas had such a valuable item, but no evidence of it has been found.

71. "Every . . . corruption": JA wrote to Benjamin Rush [65:56], "every bank of discount, every bank by which interest is to be paid or profit of any kind made by the deponent, is downright corruption" [*SP*, 313].

72. Waal . . . Europe: America had natural abundance that could replenish itself; but predatory exploitation wasted it. They got their capital from Europe and bled the land to pay it off. "The American tragedy is a continuous history of waste—waste of the natural abundance first, then waste of the new abundance offered by the machine, and then by machines. . . . The usurers now called financiers, plotted against abundance" [*SP*, 176; see also Hollis, *The Two Nations*, 213-216].

73. Anatole: A. France, 1844-1924. A satirical portrait of industrial nations controlled by financial syndicates was the subject of his *L'Île des Pengouins* in which Professor Obnubile is amazed to find that prosperous nations do not promote peace. After listening to a parliamentary debate about wars that had been promoted, he asked, "Have I heard aright? . . . you an industrial people engaged in all these wars!" His interpreter explained that they were industrial wars: "Peoples who have neither commerce nor industry are not obliged to make war, but a business people is forced to adopt a policy of conquest. The number of wars necessarily increases with our productive activity" [*Penguin Island*, 145-149; See Pound's comment, *IMP*, 196]. For rhyming refrains, "done tol' 'em," see e. e. Cummings, poem 13 of "1 x 1," *Collected Poems*, 396.

74. Perry: Matthew C. Perry, 1794-1858, who as a naval captain "opened" Japan. His squadron entered Yeddo Bay July 8, 1853: "Terror reigned on shore. The people of Yeddo prepared for defense." Eventually, "the Shogun fell. . . . The immediate effect was war" [Brooks Adams, *The New Empire*, 186-189]. Adams shows in his early chapters that the need to export to new markets led to this result.

75. foreign coin: Benton, in describing the efforts to create a U. S. coinage, traces the history of attempts to exclude foreign coinage [89:68]. He wrote: "which brought the period for the actual and final cessation of the circulation of foreign coins, to the month of November, 1819. . . . An exception was continued . . . in favor of Spanish milled dollars" [*TYV*, 446].

76. every dealer . . . : The effect of the laws was to reduce the value of the Spanish coinage below its value as metal. Thus, "Every money dealer is employed in buying, selling, and exporting them" [ibid.].

77. exclusion: "At the head of these injuries he was bound to place the violation of the constitution . . . . He denounced this exclusion of foreign coins as fraud" [ibid.].

78. intrinsic values: The states in giving power over the coinage to Congress clearly implied that currency in foreign coins was to be kept in use. "Yet that currency is suppressed; a currency of intrinsic value, for which they paid interest to nobody, is suppressed; and a currency without intrinsic value, a currency of paper subject to every fluctuation, and for the supply of which corporate bodies receive interest, is substituted in its place" [ibid.].

79. **this country**: "Since that law took effect, the United States had only been a thoroughfare for foreign coins to pass through" [ibid.].

80. **Benton**: Thomas Hart B., 1782-1858, American statesman who entered the U.S. Senate from Missouri in 1821, where he served five terms to 1851. He became a powerful force in the Jackson-Van Buren war against the Bank of the United States. His *Thirty Years' View*, written 1854-1856, is one of the major historical documents of the period.

81. **OBEUNT** . . . : L, "They die." Benton wrote: "This gives me a right to head a chapter with the names of Mr. John Adams and Mr. Jefferson . . . who, entering public life together, died on the same day,–July 4th, 1826–exactly fifty years after they had both put their hands to that Declaration of Independence" [*TYV*, I, 87].

82. **Not battlements**: Benton long protested the sale of lands to settlers and preferred that the land be given. In one oration he waxed lyrical and even seemed to break out into verse: "What constitutes a State? / Not high-rais'd battlements, nor labored mound, / Thick wall, nor moated gate," etc., for 9 lines [*TYV*, I, 104; 89:11].

83. **Tariff**: Benton often derides Tocqueville [cf. 84 below] for his inaccuracies. T believed the tariff was essential to America's continued existence.

84. **Monsieur de Tocqueville**: Alexis de T., 1805-1859, French liberal politician and writer who visited the U.S. to study the penal system. His work, which appeared in France in 1835, and in the U.S. as *Democracy in America*, 4 vols., 1835-1840, showed he studied the penal system a little but everything else a lot more.

85. **Macon**: [cf. 15 above]. In a description of Nathaniel Macon's heroism in the army and his further service in the General Assembly, Benton shows how Cornwallis was finally turned back by Greene at the battle of Guilford [*TYV*, I, 115].

86. **Renewal**: President Jackson in talking about the renewal of the bank charter said that it had failed to achieve its proper end: "a uniform and sound currency" [*TYV*, I, 123-124].

87. **salt tax**: In his efforts to defeat a salt tax proposed for the U.S., Benton said that in England, "the salt tax has been overthrown by the labors of plain men" [*TYV*, I, 144].

88. **Andy vetoed**: Henry Clay sponsored a bill to give funds to the Maysville Turnpike Company, which meant public money would go to a privately owned commercial toll road. President Jackson vetoed it on constitutional grounds.

89. **unconvertable paper**: A central issue in the question of whether or not to renew the charter of the Bank of the United States was that it would be entitled to issue paper money that could not be converted to its value in gold or silver. Benton, in arguing against renewal, praised France when it stuck to precious metals, but "England, with her overgrown bank, was a prey to all the evils of uncovertible paper" [*TYV*, I, 187].

90. **mines**: "The United States possess gold mines, now yielding half a million per annum, with every prospect of equalling those of Peru. . . . We have what is superior to mines, namely, the exports which command the money of the world; that is to say, the food which sustains life, and the raw materials which sustain manufactures" [ibid]. Note that this concept is a central premise of Social Credit.

91. **Geryon**: The loathsome creature in Dante's Hell which Pound uses as the image of fraud, financial corruption, and the fount

of usury [46:51; 51:16]. The phrase "prize pup" is not in Benton, but a description of the bank as monster is: "the great monster, in going down, had carried many others along with her; and . . . slew more in her death than in her life. Vast was her field of destruction–extending all over the United States and reaching to Europe" [*TYV*, II, 365].

92. **Nicholas Biddle**: President Jackson's prime opponent in fighting for renewal of the charter of the Bank of the United States [34:70].

93. **An amendment . . . murdered indigo**: These 21 lines are all taken from a chapter entitled "Revision of the Tariff": "Mr. Benton then proposed an amendment, to impose a duty of 25 cents per pound on imported indigo. . . . He stated his object to be twofold . . . first, to place the American System beyond the reach of its enemies, by procuring a home supply of an article indispensable to its existence; and next, to benefit the South by reviving the cultivation of one of its ancient and valuable staples. Indigo was first planted in the Carolinas and Georgia about the year 1740. . . . An act was passed for the encouragement of its production . . . in the reign of George the Second. . . . At the breaking out of the Revolution [the export of] it amounted to 1,100,000 lbs. . . . After the Revolution . . . the British . . . looked to India. . . . The export of American indigo rapidly declined. In 1800 it had fallen to 400,000 lbs.; in 1814 to 40,000 lbs.; and in the last few years to 6 or 8,000 lbs. In the meantime our manufactories were growing up; and having no supply of indigo at home, they had to import from abroad. . . . Our manufacturers now paid a high price for fine indigo, no less than $2.50 per pound." What's more, "it had to be paid for almost entirely in ready money." Bad federal legislation had drained money from the South to the North, "and this in the midst of the fact that the South, in four staples alone, in cotton, tobacco, rice and indigo . . . had exported produce since the Revolution, to the value of eight hundred millions of dollars, and the North had exported comparatively nothing. This sum was prodigious; it was nearly equal to half the coinage of the mint of Mexico since the conquest by Cortez . . . The Tariff of 1816 contributed to destroy the cultivation of indigo; sunk the duty on the foreign article, from twenty-five to fifteen cents per pound" [*TYV*, I, 19-99].

94. **Sardegna**: Prob. a press release of 1954 suggested a parallel, but it has not been identified.

95. **Freemen . . .** : The tariff on indigo did not prevail. A spokesman for the South deplored the fact that the Congress controlled by the North would not pass legislation that would enable them, not to look for bounty, but to rely on themselves: "He is not in fact a freeman, who habitually looks to the government for pecuniary bounties. . . . An idea more fatal to liberty could not be inculcated" [*TYV*, I, 100].

96. **Freeholds . . . 1823**: From Benton's arguments that land should be given to settlers [cf. 82 above], in which he quotes from a proclamation published in Europe: "Mirza Mahomet Saul, Ambassador to England, in the name, and by the authority of Abbas Mirza, King of Persia, offers to those who shall emigrate to Persia, gratuitous grants of land, good for the production of wheat, barley, rice, cotton, and fruits, free from taxes or contributions of any kind, and with the free enjoyment of their religion . . . London, July 8th, 1823" [*TYV*, I, 106].

97. **Jackson . . .** : In the election of 1828 Jackson received 178 (not 183) electoral votes and John Quincy Adams received 83. Benton remarks about the election, "there was no jealousy, or hostile, or aggressive spirit in the North at that time against the South!" [*TYV*, I,111].

98. **Stay laws . . . tongue**: These 7 lines are from Benton's defense of President Jackson against the critical remarks of Tocqueville, who said he was "a man of violent temper and mediocre talents. . . . He was raised to the Presidency . . . soley by the recollection of a victory which he gained twenty years

ago, under the walls of New Orleans. . . ." Benton lists many of Jackson's accomplishments (of which Pound notes a few) and tells Tocqueville that his writings may pass for American history in Europe but not in the U.S. [*TYV*, I, 112].

99. Guilford: A key battle in the revolutionary war [cf. 85 above]. It was Benton's concern to show that this battle prepared the way for the victory of Yorktown.

100. Yorktown: A town on the Chesapeake Bay where in 1781 the final battles of the American Revolution were fought. Washington captured Cornwallis here.

101. Used plough and hoe: In his encomium on the life of Nathaniel Macon [cf. 15 above], Benton emphasizes his patrician stateliness as well as his life close to the soil. "He was not rich, but rich enough to dispense hospitality and charity, to receive all guests in his house, from the President to the day laborer" [*TYV*, I, 115-117].

102. Γᾶν ἄφθιτον: H, "He furrows the imperishable, inexhaustible earth" [*Antigone,* II, 337-338].

103. Drew a knife . . . : Continuing his praise of Macon, Benton celebrates his steadfastness to friends. He "would stake himself for a friend, but would violate no point of public duty to please or oblige him. Of this his relations with Mr. Randolph gave a signal instance. He drew a knife to defend him in the theatre at Philadelphia" [*TYV*, I, 117].

104. DEBT: Benton quotes from Jackson's first inaugural address: "The observance of a strict and faithful economy . . . will facilitate the extinguishment of the national debt—the unnecessary duration of which is incompatible with real independence . . . it will counteract that tendency to public and private profligacy which a profuse expenditure of money by the government is but too apt to engender" [*TYV*, I, 119].

105. Martin Van Buren: [37:1]. He was confirmed as President Jackson's secretary of state.

106. Jas Hamilton: James H., 1786-1857. The source says: "Mr. James A. Hamilton, of New York, son of the late General Hamilton, being charged with the duties of the office until Mr. Van Buren could enter upon them" [ibid.].

107. Ingham: Samuel D. I., 1779-1860. He became secretary of the treasury in 1829.

108. Berrien: John M. B., 1781-1856, attorney general of the U.S., 1829-1831.

109. Barry: William T. B., 1785-1835, was made postmaster general in 1829.

110. defence: In describing Jackson's "First Annual Message" to the Congress, Benton mentions his sentiments about the navy: "it was, a navy for DEFENCE, isntead of CONQUEST; and limited to the protection of our coasts and commerce" [*TYV*, I, 122].

111. West Indies: The recovery of trade with the West Indies, lost following the American Revolution, became a part of Jackson's program [*TYV*, I, 124].

112. Nathan Dane: 1752-1835. He drew up the "Anti-Slavery Ordinance of 1787." Benton quotes from a speech by Daniel Webster: "At the foundation of the consitution of these new northwestern States, we are accustomed, sir, to praise the lawgivers of antiquity . . . but I doubt whether one single law of any lawgiver, ancient or modern, has produced effects of more distinct, marked, and lasting character, than the ordinance of '87. That instrument, was drawn by Nathan Dane. . . . It fixed, for ever, the character of the population in the vast regions northwest of the Ohio, by excluding them from involuntary servitude. . . . Now, sir, this great measure again was carried by the north, and by the north alone" [*TYV*, I, 134-135].

113. salt tax: This tax, imposed during a time of war, stayed on the books until President Jackson got rid of it. It wasn't easy. Benton has a chapter entitled "Repeal of the Salt Tax" [*TYV*, I, 143-148].

114. A. J.'s first message: "It has been already shown that General Jackson in his first annual message to Congress, called in question both the constitutionality and expediency of the national bank" [*TYV*, I, 158].

115. Maysville Road: [cf. 88 above].

116. To pull down . . . : Benton, writing on "Non-Renewal of Charter" of the Bank of the United States, said that it has "too much power" and should not "be allowed to exist in our country. But I knew it was not sufficient to pull down: We must build up also" [*TYV* I, 187].

117. hard money: The error made by those who refused to recharter the bank in 1811 was in not providing a substitute. Benton would avoid that error by proposing a gold coinage [ibid.].

118. France . . . : [cf. 89 above].

119. Parnells . . . : In the chapter on nonrenewal, Benton wrote: "In the speech which I delivered, I quoted copiously from British speakers—not the brilliant rhetoricians, but the practical, sensible, upright business men, to whom countries are usually indebted for all beneficial legislation: the Sir Henry Parnells, the Mr. Joseph Humes, the Mr. Edward Ellices, the Sir William Pulteneys [*sic*]" [*TYV*, I, 187-188].

120. laid on Table: Referring to the fate of an earlier resolution he had brought against the bank, Benton said, "This report came . . . just fourteen days before" the end of a six months' session. "It had no chance at all of getting the Senate's attention. The report was, therefore, laid upon the table unanswered, but was printed by order of the Senate . . ." [*TYV*, I, 188].

121. pawn-broker: The charter of the Bank of England was to expire about the same time as that of the Bank of the United States—1833. Nine years before that, debate about its renewal took place. Benton summarizes some points made in that debate: "Mr. Hume said . . . Let the country gentlemen recollect that the bank was now acting as pawn-broker on a large scale, and lending money on estates, a system entirely contrary to the original intention of that institution" [*TYV*, I, 189].

122. Ellice: Mr. Edward Ellice said: "It (the Bank of England) is a great monopolizing body, enjoying privileges which belonged to no other corporation [Pound's "contraption" may be intentional], and no other class of his majesty's subjects" [ibid.].

123. stock-holders: Defenders of the bank said the debate was unfair as it would diminish the value of their property. Benton said that was absurd, that American stockholders knew the charter had to come up for renewal [*TYV*, I, 190].

124. real estate: Said Benton of the stockholders: "They have been dividing seven per cent. per annum . . . and have laid up a real estate of three millions of dollars for future division" [ibid.].

125. at 46: Benton produced a case involving the bank which was decided by the Supreme Court. He read part of the case "showing that it was a case of usury at the rate of forty-six per cent" [ibid.].

126. SCIRE FACIAS: L, "Make cause to know." In law, "a judicial unit founded upon some matter of record and requiring the party proceeded against to show cause why the record should not be enforced, annulled, or vacated" [*Webster's*]; or "why letters patent, such as a charter, should not be revoked" [*Oxford Universal Dictionary*, 3d ed.]. Continuing from 125 above: "so that the bank, being convicted of taking usury, in violation of its charter, was liable to be deprived of its charter, at any time that a *scire facias* should issue against it" [ibid.].

127. institution: Said Benton: "Mr. President, I object to the renewal of the Charter of the Bank of the United States, because I look upon the bank as an institution too great and too powerful to be tolerated in a government of free and equal laws" [*TYV*, I, 191].

128. Vice President: The vice-president objected that Benton's statements were out of order under the motion he had made. Benton insisted he was in order as he had asked leave to bring in a joint resolution: "The Vice President then directed Mr. Benton to proceed" [ibid.].

129. Direct power: Benton proceeded: "The direct power of the bank is now prodigious, . . . and . . . must speedily become boundless and uncontrollable." Then listing its present power to issue notes up to "ninety million" with "an opening for an unlimited increase" with possible widening of powers, he said, "This opens the door to boundless emissions" [ibid.].

130. To whom . . . : Benton asks and answers these questions in his speech, showing that such power must make the bank "the absolute monopolist of American money" [ibid.].

131. Gt Britain: Benton illustrates: "I speak of what happened in Great Britian, in the year 1795, when the Bank of England, by a brief and unceremonious letter to Mr. Pitt . . . gave the proof of what a great moneyed power could do . . . to promote its own interest, in a crisis of national alarm and difficulty. I will read the letter." The short letter says: "It is the wish of the Court of Directors that the Chancellor of the Exchequer would settle his arrangements of finances for the present year, in such manner as not to depend upon any further assistance from them, beyond what is already agreed for" [*TYV*, I, 192].

132. Political . . . DEBT: Benton asks, "What are the tendencies of a great moneyed power, connected with the government, and controlling its fiscal operations? Are they not dangerous to every interest, public and private—political as well as pecuniary?" He answers: "Such a bank tends to subjugate the government. . . . It tends to collusion between the government and the bank in the terms of the loans . . . and insults upon the understanding, called three per cent loans, in which the government, for about £50 borrowed, became liable to pay £100. . . . It tends to create public debt, by facilitating public loans, and substituting unlimited supplies of paper, for limited supplies of coin" [*TYV*, I, 192-193].

133. 1694: Benton goes on: "The British debt is born of the Bank of England. That bank was chartered in 1694, and was nothing more nor less in the beginning, than an act of Parliament for the incorporation of a company of subscribers to a government loan. The loan was £1,200,000; the interest £80,000; and the expenses of management £4,000" [*TYV*, I, 193].

134. GERM: Benton: "And this is the birth and origin, the germ and nucleus of that debt, which is now £900,000,000" [ibid.].

135. It tends . . . : Benton: "It tends to beget and prolong unnecessary wars, by furnishing the means of carrying them on without recurrence to the people" [ibid.].

136. aggravate: Benton: "It tends to aggravate the inequality of fortunes; to make the rich richer, and the poor poorer. . . . It tends to make and to break fortunes, by the flux and reflux of paper" [ibid.].

137. "To carry . . . Monopoly: These 19 lines come from a 12-point summary of Benton's objections to renewal of the charter: "1. To carry on the trade of banking upon the revenue and credit, and in the name, of the United States of America. 2. To pay the revenues of the Union in their own promissory notes. 3. To hold the moneys of the United States in deposit, without making compensation for the undrawn balances. 4. To discredit and disparage the notes of other banks, by excluding them from the collection of the federal revenue. 5. To hold real estate, receive rents, and retain a body of tenantry. . . . 7. To establish branches in the States without their consent. 8. To be exempt from liability on the failure of the bank. 9. To have the United States for a partner. 10. To have foreigners for partners. 11. To be exempt from the regular administration of justice for the violations of their charter. 12. To have all these privileges secured to them as a monopoly, in a pledge of the public faith not to grant the like privileges to any other company" [*TYV*, I, 193-194].

138. Yeas: . . . Nays: The probank people expected to treat Benton's brilliant speech with contempt and silence and defeat his resolution with a show-of-hands vote. They were shocked to find they were defeated. Pound records the vote.

139. That it failed . . . (for the Bank): These 11 lines are based on Benton's summary of Jackson's remarks in his annual message of 1829 about the bank's practices. It "had failed in furnishing a uniform currency. . . . It had in fact issued an illegal and vicious kind of paper—authorized it to be issued at all the branches—in the shape of drafts or orders payable in Philadelphia, but voluntarily paid where issued, and at all the branches, and so made into a local currency, and constituting the mass of all its paper seen in circulation; and as the greatest quantity was usually issued at the most remote and inaccessible branches, the payment of the drafts were well protected by distance and difficulty; and being of small denominations, loitered and lingered in the hands of the laboring people until the 'wear and tear' became a large item of gain to the Bank, and the difficulty of presenting them at Philadelphia an effectual bar to their payment there" [*TYV*, I, 220].

140. It was invented: Benton continued: "The origin of this kind of currency was thus traced by me: It was invented by a Scotch banker of Aberdeen, who issued notes payable in London, always of small denominations, that nobody should take them up to London for redemption" [ibid.].

141. Mr Benton asked: "Mr. Benton rose to ask leave to bring in his promised resolution on the state of the currency. . . . He made his resolution joint in its character, that it might have the action of both Houses of Congress;" [*TYV*, I, 220-221].

142. "Are they signed . . . cost: These 10 lines are based on a summation Benton gave to show "the incompatibility between the characteristics of this currency, and the requisites of the charter" by asking and answering 14 rhetorical questions. Pound chooses 5 for emphasis. The "president" is the president of the bank [ibid.].

143. And as for the charter: The fight to prevent rechartering the bank went on with increased intensity, the proponents in both houses seeking to do it as quietly as possible. Benton wanted a public investigation into its activities to determine whether it had lived up to the terms of its charter. The proponents did not. Calls for investigations were treated to the parliamentary tricks of tabling or postponing. Finally, Benton wrote a list of "twenty-two heads of accusation" involving both violation of the charter and abuses of bank power. "Mr. Clayton, a new member from Georgia," read out to the House these accusations in defense of Mr. Polk's motion for an investigation. In reading, Clayton tried to conceal Benton's handwriting in the manner described [*TYV*, I, 235-238].

144. And/fifty/2: Pound saw the playing cards printed on the shirt of one of his visitors to St. Elizabeths. He interpreted it as an evil omen that the printer placed the Ace of Spades upside down" [EH, *Pai*, 2, 1, 143]. The lore of playing cards ramifies in all directions to many cultures, East and West. Here they echo the spring-autumn motif of "no righteous wars" [82/525; 78:139].

CANTO LXXXIX

Sources

Dante, *Par.* V, XXV, XX, XXIV; Thomas H. Benton, *Thirty Years' View* . . . , 2 vols., New York, Appleton, 1854 [*TYV*]; Martin Van Buren, *The Autobiography of Martin Van Buren*, ed. John C. Fitzpatrick, Washington, D.C., Government Printing Office, 1920 [MVB, *Auto*]; Allan Nevins, ed., *The Diary of John Quincy Adams, 1794-1845: American Political, Social and Intellectual Life from Washington to Polk*, New York, London, Toronto, 1928; Andrew Lipscomb and Albert Bergh, eds., *The Writings of Thomas Jefferson*, Vol. X, Washington, D.C., 1905; C. H. Douglas, *Economic Democracy*, New York, Harcourt, Brace and Howe, 1920; Alexander Del Mar, *History of Monetary Systems*, Chicago, Charles H. Kerr & Co., 1896 [*HMS*]; Alexander Del Mar, *Ancient Britain* . . . , New York, Cambridge Encyclopedia Co., 1900; Alexander Del Mar, *The Middle Ages Revisited* . . . , New York, Cambridge Encyclopedia Co., 1900; James Legge, *The Four Books,* Shanghai, 1923 [Legge], Elizabeth Benton Frémont *Recollections of Elizabeth Benton Frémont*, New York, Frederick H. Hitchcock, 1912 [Frémont, *Recollections*]; John Charles Frémont, *Memoirs of My Life*, Chicago, 1887 [*Memoirs*]; Sophocles, *Ajax*, 1105-1106; Homer, *Od.* I; Alexander Del Mar, *Money and Civilization* . . . , London, G. Bell & Sons, 1886; Jessie Frémont, *Souvenirs of My Time*, Boston, 1887 [Jessie Frémont, *Souvenirs*]; EP, *CON*, 59-60; James Parton, *Life of Andrew Jackson*, 3 vols., Houghton, Mifflin and Co., 1859-60.

Background

EP, *GK*, 274, 345, 254, 30, 31, 264, 47, 40-41; *SP*, 457-459, 327, 312, 344, 159, 307, 355; *SR*, 111; *IMP*, xiv; Emanuel Swedenborg, *Heaven and Its Wonders and Hell*, 1758: D. G. Bridson, "An Interview with Ezra Pound, "*New Directions* 17; M de R, *Discretions* 166, 190-192; Raphael Pumpelly, *My Reminiscences*, New York, 1918; Robert McNair Wilson, *The Mind of Napoleon: A Study of Napoleon, Mr. Roosevelt, and the Money Power*, G. Routledge & Sons, London, 1934 [Wilson, *Napoleon*]; William Cabell Bruce, *John Randolph of Roanoke*, 1773-1833, 2 vols., New York, G. P. Putnam's 1922 [Bruce, *Randolph*]; William M. Meigs, *The Life of Thomas Hart Benton*, Philadelphia, Lippincott, 1924 [Meigs, *Life of THB*]; JW, *Medieval Song: An Anthology of Hymns and Lyrics*, E. P. Dutton and Allen & Unwin; Christopher B. Coleman, *Treatise of Lorenzo Valla on the Donation of Constantine*, Yale Univ. Press, 1922 [*Donation*]; J. F. C. Fuller, *The Generalship of Alexander the Great*, London, 1958; Claude Bowers, *The Party Battles of the Jackson Period*, Houghton, Mifflin, 1922 [Bowers, *Party Battles*]; Marquis James, *The Life of Andrew Jackson*, Bobbs-Merrill, 1938 [James, *Jackson*].

Exegeses

CFT, Pai, 6-2, 227-229; Bosha, *Pai*, 4-1, 99-100; Grieve, *Pai*, 4-2 & 3, 471, 492; Korg, *Pai*, 4-2 & 3, 301-313; Michael Reck, *Ezra Pound: A Close-up*, New York, McGraw-Hill, 1967, 174-175.

Glossary

1. **Ideogram**: Shu [M5857] ; Ideogram: ching [M1123]. The odes collected by Confucius known as *The Book of History* or *The History Classic*; or variously (in French, 19th-century, Mathews, or other transcriptions) as *Chou King, Shoo King, Shu King,* or *Shu Ching*. Confucius believed that if one knew the histories one would know good from evil. Hao [M2062] means "good." Thus, Ching Hao says, the *Shu Ching* is good. Omar Pound tells me the sentiment rhymes with the Shakespear family motto "Fide sed cui vide" (L, "have faith but see in whom"). His source is marginalia made by DP in her copy of *The Cantos*.

2. **Chi crescerà**: I, "Who will increase." From "*Ecco chi crescerà li nostri amori*" ("Behold the man who will increase our loves") [*Par.* V, 105].

3. **Swedenborg**: [77:126]. In describing the division and arrangement of angels in heaven, Swedenborg wrote: "The angels of each heaven are not together in one place but are divided into larger and smaller societies. . . . Moreover, every society of heaven increases in number daily, and as it increases it becomes more perfect. Thus not only the society becomes more perfect, but also heaven in general, because it is made up of societies" [*Heaven and Its Wonder and Hell*, 23, 36].

4. **Mr. Jefferson** . . . : In a chapter entitled "Visit of Lafayette to the United States," Benton tells about a conversation he had with Jefferson in which TJ said Lafayette predicted the transition to a constitutional monarchy. That happened when Louis Philippe became the "citizen king" in 1830 [*TYV*, I, 31].

5. **M. de Tocqueville**: [88:84].

6. **Privilege**: Benton wrote of his early years in the Senate: "I felt it to be a privilege to serve in the Senate with three such senators as Mr. King, Mr. Macon, and John Taylor of Carolina, and was anxious to improve such an opportunity" [*TYV*, I, 57].

7. **King**: Rufus K. [62:134], U.S. Senator 1813-1825.

8. **Macon**: [88:15].

9. **John Taylor**: [67:112]. He was from Caroline County, Va.

10. **Entangling** . . . : A return to the conflict over the proposed Panama mission [88:5], in which those against the mission said the U.S. should avoid entangling alliances.

11. **would be** . . . : A repetition of Benton's theme that the state would derive more revenue from the donation of the wildlands to settlers than from their sale to the highest bidder [88:82, 96].

12. **Freedom** . . . : Benton: "Tenantry is unfavorable to freedom. . . . The farming tenant has, in fact, no country" [*TYV*, I, 103-104].

13. **Abbas Mirza**: [88:96].

14. **Indian treaty**: After the Cherokee Indians had been removed to the territory of Arkansas, a treaty to cede some territory to them was presented to Congress. Benton was against the treaty and raised several questions, such as "whether a law of Congress could be abolished by an Indian treaty?" [*TYV*, I, 107].

15. **"enlightened classes"**: Replying to Tocqueville's charges against Jackson [88:84] that the enlightened classes were opposed to him, Benton said: "but the mass

of the intelligence of the country was with him! and sustained him in retrieving the country from the deplorable condition in which the 'enlightened classes' had sunk it!" [*TYV*, I, 113].

16. grave yards: Benton eulogizes Macon [88:15, 101] for wanting his grave put where it would not waste good land [ibid., 114]. Pound found this to be a good Confucian attitude: "Nothing cd. be more false than the idea that Kung was preoccupied with the dead. He was concerned with the living. Cemeteries shd. be on high ground, hills least use for cultivation" [*GK*, 274].

17. Mr Webster: On a question of the availability of fertile lands to settlers, Mr. Benton supposes Webster was against a bill to give land to settlers and says, "The bare reading of these passages . . . shows how erroneous Mr. Webster was" [*TYV*, I, 134]. Since Webster was in favor of the bill, Benton is wrong.

18. Obit Picabia: Francis Picabia, the wealthy, French-born Cuban painter died Dec. 2, 1953, as reported in *Time* magazine as well as in other media. Pound thought highly of Picabia [cf. 87:31; *SP*, 457-459].

19. And paper . . . metals: A return to Benton's first speech against rechartering the bank [88:89].

20. Public debt increased: A return to the theme of government dependence on the bank [88:131] and the Bank of England's notice to the British government not to depend upon it for "further assistance" [*TYV*, I, 192].

21. Profuse issues . . . : Benton described the extraordinary effect a great moneyed power run by a few men in a private corporation could have on the nation. Profuse issues of paper money, followed by limitation of credit, could be dangerous.

22. power of "construction": Concerning the government's deposits in the bank and the bank's misuse of the funds, Benton said the bank had construed the intent of a previous bill into its opposite effect: "I wished to repeal this section, which had thus been construed into the reverse of its intention" [*TYV*, I, 195].

23. Branch forced on Alabama: From a Benton speech against the bank's practice of forcing branches on states that didn't want them [*TYV*, I, 199].

24. Hence WAR: Pound's opinion that the financiers of the North were a major cause of the War Between the States [88:28].

25. Prototype . . . : Said Benton: "Let no one say that the Bank of the United States is too great to fail. One greater than it, and its prototype, has failed, and that in our own day, and for twenty years at a time: the Bank of England failed in 1797, and the Bank of the United States was on the point of failing in 1819. The same cause, namely, stock jobbing and overtrading, carried both to the brink" [*TYV*, I, 200].

26. Our OWN money: About the way the U.S. Government acted as a partner with the bank, Benton said: "I pass over other instances of the damage suffered by the United States on account of this partnership; the immense standing deposits for which we receive no compensation; the loan of five millions of our own money, for which we have paid a million and a half in interest" [ibid.].

27. the POlitical: Benton said further that, from a money angle, troubles enough could accrue to the U.S. when borrower and lender got together. But there was a greater danger: "suppose they agree to drop rivalry, and unite their resources. Suppose they combine, and make a push for political power: how great is the mischief which they may not accomplish!" [ibid.].

28. hug . . . blow: Sir William Pulteney [88:119] had warned England against possible collusion between the bank and the government. Benton named Pulteney's object and said: "And this is my object also. I wish to secure the Union from all chance of harm from this bank. I wish to provide against its friendship, as well as its enmity–

against all danger from its hug, as well as from its blow" [*TYV*, I, 201].

29. Name . . . king: Benton: "I wish to provide against all risk, and every hazard; for, if this risk and hazard were too great to be encountered by King, Lords, and Commons . . . they must certainly be too great to be encountered by the people of the United States, who are but commons alone" [ibid.]. The line seems to be an echo of the "chêng ming" or "right name" concept, according to which a king should do things appropriate to a king. Benton, after quoting Pulteney, said: "The downright and upright people of that unsophisticated region [the West] believe that words mean what they signify, and that 'the Bank of the United States' is the Bank of the United States. How great then must be their astonishment to learn . . . that this bank . . . is just as much the bank of foreigners as it is of the federal government" [ibid.].

30. Ideogram: Wang [M7037], "a prince or king."

31. Foreigners . . . : Benton goes on: "the report of the Committee of Ways and Means . . . admits that foreigners own seven millions of the stock of this bank; and every body knows that the federal government owns seven millions also" [ibid.].

32. usury at 46: [88:125]. "It is a case of usury at the rate of forty-six per cent., in violation of the charter" [ibid., 202].

33. if beneficial . . . : In talking about the twelfth exclusive privilege held by the bank, Benton says: "To have all these unjust privileges secured to the corporators as a monopoly, by a pledge of the public faith to charter no other bank.—This is the most hideous feature in the whole mass of deformity. If these banks are beneficial institutions, why not several?" [ibid.].

34. Adams match . . . : In answering the charges of Tocqueville [88:84] that the House of Representatives was made up of incompetents whereas the Senate (then elected by state legislatures) had good men, Benton cites the case of JQA: "The late Mr. John Quincy Adams . . . after having been minister to half the great courts of Europe, a senator . . . Secretary of State, and President of the United States . . . was refused an election by the Massachusetts legislature to the United States Senate . . . he was taken up by the people, sent to the House of Representatives, and served there to octogenarian age—attentive, vigilant and capable—an example to all, and a match for half the House to the last" [*TYV*, 207; 34:71].

35. Randolph: "The brilliant, incorruptible, sagacious Randolph . . . scourge and foe to all corruption . . . had merely the same fate" [ibid.]. Benton fails to mention his own case. After 30 years in the Senate, he was refused re-election by the legislature but ran for the House and was elected by a big popular majority.

36. An advantage: In the political struggles between President Jackson and Vice-President Calhoun, Van Buren, the secretary of state, became a pawn. After Van Buren led the resignation of the cabinet [37:1], Jackson nominated him to be ambassador to Great Britain. He took up his post before confirmation by the Senate. Vice-President Calhoun engineered the vote of confirmation to be a tie so that he could cast the deciding ballot against him and cause the most embarrassment. Benton says: "[When] all the London newspapers heralded the rejection of the American minister, there was a great party at Prince Talleyrand's . . . Mr. Van Buren . . . was there, as if nothing had happened; and received distinguished attentions, and complimentary allusions. Lord Aukland . . . said to him, It is an advantage to a public man to be the subject of an outrage" [*TYV*, I, 218-219; see Van Buren, *Auto*, 457-458 for his version].

37. 2 buffer states . . . : [86:10].

38. Ca'our, tessitore: I, "Cavour, weaver." Since Cavour [cf. 39 below], was not literally a weaver, the epithet probably has a metaphorical intent to suggest Cavour's political adroitness in working his way through tangled webs spun to snare him. In "A Visiting Card" Pound wrote: "The Rothschilds financed the armies against the Roman Republic. Naturally. They tried to buy over Cavour. Naturally. Cavour accomplished the first stage towards Italian unity, allowing himself to be exploited according to the custom of his times, but he refused to be dominated by the exploiters" [*SP*, 327].

39. **Cavour**: Count Camillo Benso di Cavour, 1810-1861, Italian statesman who became premier (1852-1859). Just as Jackson had to accept Van Buren's resignation as secretary of state, King Victor Emmanuel II was forced to accept a similar resignation by Cavour [61:19]. Pound called himself a Cavourian [*SP*, 312].

40. **Auctor**: L, "author."

41. **Borah**: [84:6].

42. **"Borrowing . . .** : Recurrent theme in Pound. Benton said: "it is incontestable, that the United States have been borrowing these undrawn balances [the government's own money on deposit] from the bank, and paying an interest upon their own money" [*TYV*, I, 194].

43. **Randolph**: [87:10].

44. **Tariff . . .** : [88:93, 95]. Benton saw the idea of protective tariff as the source of the doctrine of nullification, "from which a serious division . . . between the North and the South" dated. He said: "The question of a protective tariff had now not only become political, but sectional" [*TYV*, I, 97].

45. **Excessive issues**: [88:18, 78].

46. **Treasury wd/pay . . .** : Part of the bank's ploy to retire stock of a revolutionary war debt at 100% on the dollar when it had obtained it for less: "it was clear that the treasury would pay one hundred cents on the dollar on what could be then purchased for sixty-odd, losing in the mean time the interest on the money with which it could be paid" [*TYV*, I, 242].

47. **As Indian silver . . .** : In "Gold and Work," Pound, in discussing how "Usurocracy makes wars" one after the other [88:28], wrote: "At one period, in fact, silver fell to 23 cents per ounce, and was later bought by certain American idiots at 75 cents per ounce, in order to please their masters and to '*save India*'" [*SP*, 344].

48. **Catron**: John C., ca. 1786-1865, American jurist who went from chief justice of Tennessee to an appointment by Jackson as associate justice of the U.S. Supreme Court. He was an early supporter of Jackson in the bank controversy. Says Marquis James: "Catron suggested a democratic substitute for Mr. Biddle's monopoly: all directors to be appointed by the President and Congress; branches to be set up only on petition of state legislatures . . ." [*Jackson*, 558].

49. **Ideogram**: Pi [M5109], "certainly, must."

50. **Andy Jackson**: Upon vetoing the recharter bill, Jackson listed a number of objections to the practices of the bank as well as to the idea of the U.S. government creating exclusive monopolies: "If our government must sell monopolies, it would seem to be its duty to take nothing less than their full value; and if gratuities must be made once in fifteen or twenty years, let them not be bestowed on the subjects of a foreign government, nor upon a designated or favored class of men in our own country" [*TYV*, I, 251].

51. **70 million**: Probank senators predicted that if the veto were sustained it would cause financial ruin on a national scale. Benton tried to show that the bank had engineered the conditions for panic in the West by increasing its debts most in the West, from $40,216,000 in Dec. of 1829 to $70,428,000 in 1832, showing "an increase of thirty millions in the short space of two years and four months" [ibid., 258].

52. **mehercule ventum!**: F, "by Hercules' wind." A Poundian oath [80:295].

53. **with bowie knives**: A reference to a barroom quarrel in 1813 between General

Jackson and Benton's brother Jesse, while the Bentons were living in Tennessee [cf. 266 below]. Although relations had been cool between the Jacksons and the Bentons for a while, their beliefs and philosophy of government and democracy eventually made them strong mutual supporters. Nonetheless, Clay brought up the old quarrel by innuendo twenty years later in his answer to Benton's defense of Jackson's veto of the bank recharter bill. Said Clay: "I never had any personal rencontre with the President of the United States . . . I never published any bulletins respecting his private brawls . . . I never complained, that while a brother of mine was down on the ground, senseless or dead, he received another blow . . . I never declared my apprehension and belief, that if he [Jackson] were elected, we should be obliged to legislate with pistols and dirks by our side." Benton declared that the allegation going the rounds in the press that he said such things was "an atrocious calumny" [*TYV*, I, 263-264].

54. pre- not ex-officio: In contrast to the Clay-Randolph duel [88:1-30], Pound notices that the Clay-Benton brawl took place before either were in office, not while in office.

55. Do our cottons: In arguing for tariff protection for cottons, Clay and his followers said that many U.S. products, "especially the cotton, were going abroad . . . ; and sustaining themselves . . . against all competition." Benton argued that if that were the case they didn't need any protection: "Surely, sir, our tariff laws . . . are not in force in Bengal and China . . . if our cottons can go to these countries, and be sold at a profit without any protection at all, they can stay at home, and be sold to our citizens, without loss" [*TYV*, I 372].

56. Aurelian: Benton cites Emperor Aurelian's order, "never to levy a contribution of salt upon a Roman citizen!" The wealth of the West went down the river past New Orleans, but the money for those goods went to the Northeast. According to a Benton note, a military station called "Aurelian" was later corrupted into "Orleans" [ibid., 273].

57. Mr. Taney: Roger Brooke T., 1777-1864, was first attorney general in Jackson's cabinet and then (1833-1834) secretary of the treasury. A former secretary refused to carry out Jackson's order to deposit U.S. money not in the Bank of the United States—which would not have its charter renewed—but in selected state banks. Taney carried out the orders and stood firmly with Van Buren and Jackson against the financial interests [37:76].

58. Burr . . . late: Aaron B., 1756-1836 [32:11]. Line is prob. a Pound opinion that if Burr had killed Hamilton in a duel in 1784 instead of 1804, he wouldn't have been able to get the first U.S. Bank, modeled on the Bank of England, started.

59. Monsieur Vebbstair . . . : F, "Mr. Webster liked to lounge." The line is prob. based on Van Buren's opinion that Webster, who may have worked hard when young, had reached the state that a lot of "weather beaten politicians" reach: "the enjoyment of public stations exempted . . . from the cares and sacrifices often inseparable from a punctilious discharge of the duties attached to them" [MVB, *Auto*, 706].

60. Ut moveat . . . dilectet: L, "To move, to instruct, to delight [delectet]." Pound attributes the phrase, in a different order, to Rodolfo Agricola [*ABCR*, 66].

61. J.Q.A.: During his final years as a member of the House of Representatives, Adams fought steadily and at an increasing tempo against slavery [*Pai*, 6-2, 227-229], as opposed to "Vebbstair," who liked to rest. Said JQA: "and what can I, upon the verge of my seventy-fourth birthday, with a shaking hand, a darkening eye, a drowsy brain . . . what can I do for the cause of God and man . . . for the supression of the African slave-trade?" [Nevins, *Diary of JQA*, 519].

62. Roman law: Pound interpolation concerning the two-third's majority required to stop debate which "hogswoggled" (prob. "tied up" or "prevented action by") the House. JQA labored to get the "gag-rule" repealed in the House and succeeded on Dec. 3, 1845. His diary account for that day ends: "The question was then put on the resolution to rescind the gag rule; and it was carried–108 to 80. Blessed, forever blessed, be the name of God!" [ibid., 573].

63. **Old John**: John Adams, JQA's father. On funding, he wrote: "Funds and banks I never approved, or was satisfied without fundings systems . . . it was contrived to enrich particular individuals at the public expense" [71:35]. John Adams was against paper currency because it depreciated. He wrote to his wife, Abigail, Feb. 8, 1794: "Borrowing of banks for trading capital is very unmercantile" [62:126]. "Vide infra": L, "see below."

64. **Mr Jefferson**: TJ wrote to William Crawford on June 20, 1816, the year before Crawford became Monroe's treasury secretary, a letter that contains statements Pound thinks are essential to any understanding of U.S. monetary history. TJ writes of three measures needed to insure lasting prosperity. The third measure "should insure resources of money by the suppression of all paper circulation during peace, and licensing that of the nation alone during war . . . and if the national bills issued, be bottomed . . . on pledges of specific taxes for their redemption . . . no interest on them would be necessary" [*GK*, 345; *SP*, 159].

65. **our own mines**: Benton believed that the mines of the United States could provide enough money in specie so that no paper need be circulated by private banks: "In the year 1824 the product was $5,000; in the last year [1833] the product, in coined gold was $868,000; in uncoined, as much more; and the product of the present year [1834] computed at two millions; with every prospect of continued and permanent increase . . . But the great source of supply, both for gold and silver, . . . was in our foreign commerce" [*TYV*, I, 439].

66. **Napoleon** . . . : When Napoleon was only a consul, he ordered specie payments to begin on a certain day, and they did. Benton said: "and a hard money currency has been the sole currency of France from that day to this" [ibid., 440].

67. **Mr. Hamilton** . . . : In 1792 AH fixed the gold-silver ratio at 15 to 1, while Europe and South American held to a 16-to-1 ratio. The result was to drain gold from the U.S. Complete extinction was delayed for a time: "The trade to the lower Mississippi continued to bring up from Natchez and New Orleans . . . a large supply of doubloons" [ibid., 442]. But the end was inevitable: "Gold goes where it finds its value . . . In Mexico and South America the value of gold is 16 to 1 over silver . . . It is not to be supposed . . . that our own gold will remain with us, when an exporter can gain a dollar upon every fifteen that he carries out" [ibid., 443].

68. **6 suspensions**: Benton showed Hamilton's plan was the eventual elimination of foreign coins, which would be replaced by an American currency. Since that didn't happen, and the law to exclude foreign coins didn't work, Congress suspended it for three years. Six further 3-year suspensions became necessary and they didn't end until 1819 [88:75].

69. **OU TIS**: H, "No one" [74:17]. Used here as an intensive.

70. **Nothing . . . West**: The prohibition of foreign coins had a devastating effect upon the West: "for the coinage of trade and exchanges, to carry money from the Atlantic States to the West" [*TYV*, I, 446].

71. **Brooks**: B. Adams, 1848-1927, son the Charles Francis A. and brother of Henry Adams, 1838-1918. Both were American historians. Pound said of B. Adams: "His cyclic version of the West shows us a consecutive struggle against four great rackets, namely the exploitation of the fear of the unknown (black magic, etc.), the exploitation of violence, the exploitation or the monopolisa-

tion of cultivable land, and the exploitation of money" [*SP*, 307].

72. **grandfather**: John Quincy Adams [34:passim].

73. **old John**: President John Adams [31:15]. Said Pound, "The tragedy of the U.S.A. over 160 years is the decline of Adamses. More and more we cd., if we examined events, see that John Adams had the corrective for Jefferson" [*GK*, 254].

74. **Under . . . four**: The effect of the law excluding foreign coinage even resulted in the export of U.S.-minted coins, which made the law "the curse and the nuisance of the country. . . . The custom-house returns showed the large exportation of domestic coins. . . . In the year 1832, it amounted to $2,058,474" [*TYV*, I, 447].

75. . . . **the highest**: Benton said that regulating the currency "was one of the highest and most delicate acts of sovereign power" [ibid., 449].

76. **tho charter**: The bank helped create the coinage vacuum so it could float its own paper money: "Although forbid by her charter to deal in coin, she has employed her branches to gather $40,040,000 of coin from the states; a large part of which she admits that she has sold and transported to Europe" [ibid., 448].

77. **POWER . . .** : The power to coin and regulate the currency is a constitutional question: "this power is vested in the federal government not in one department of it, but in the joint action of the three departments" [ibid., 449].

78. **Every city . . .** : "Every commercial city . . . should have an independent moneyed system—should be free from the control and regulation of a distant, possibly a rival city, in the means of carrying on its own trade" [ibid., 450]. This statement and its context is of special interest as it contains the germs of one of the major theses of Social Credit [Douglas, *Economic Democracy*, 112 ff.].

79. **Gold . . . issue**: In Del Mar's *History of Monetary Systems*, we read, "The right to coin money has always been and still remains the surest mark and announcement of sovereignty" [*HMS*, 66]. Del Mar [96:119] earlier said: "No language is more positive than that of Mommsen . . . in laying down the following institute: that Rome never permitted her vassals to strike gold." He develops in this chapter the use of other metals [ibid., 34-35]. In the Bridson interviews Pound reiterated one of his long-held theses: "Gold was under the Pontifex or the Empire; silver was a wangle farmed out to senators . . . and the bronze, the small coinage, was under certain privileged municipalities. That is to say, enough local control to prevent the local economic order being ruined from the center [Bridson, "An Interview," 179].

80. **Benton's . . .** : These lines refer to the power to issue. The answer to the question "when?" was, according to Benton, when the national government used its sovereignty and when there was national, regulated metal currency in circulation. "Why?" Because if the national government issued its own money it would not have to pay interest, as it did on the bank's paper money, and no public debt would build up and be owed to the bank [88:137, 139; and 26 above].

81. **Voltaire**: [65:108]. He said: "I have a friend . . . who is a director in the Bank of France, who writes to me when they are going to make money plenty, and make stocks rise, and then I give orders to my broker to sell; and he writes to me when they are going to make money scarce . . . and then I write to my broker to buy; and thus . . . without moving from my chair, I make money" [*TYV*, 450].

82. **Drove out . . .** : Del Mar believed Rome became subject to barbarian invasion because (among other things) it gave up its eclectic, polytheistic religion, began making emperors gods, and increased the burden of taxation to build temples [Del Mar, *Ancient Britain*, 55, 77-78, and passim].

83. Del Mar: Alexander D. M. [96:119].

84. "ratios . . . Orient.": After Julius Caesar conquered Egypt (48 B.C.), he found that the difference in the gold-silver ratio between Rome and the Orient made it possible for Roman money men to work the system by demanding silver in payment from foreign countries. Said Del Mar, "one reason was that the Roman government knew where to sell this silver at a usurer's profit" [*HMS*, 86-87].

85. Government wanted: To the chorus of complaints that the secretary of the treasury acted illegally when he deposited federal funds in state banks rather than branches of the U.S. Bank, Benton said that the U.S. Bank was using the deposits to create its own currency, whereas, "The government wanted banks of deposit, not of circulation; and . . . the State banks [under the charter] are made just as much banks of deposit for the United States as the Bank of the United States is" [*TYV*, I, 457].

86. Ideogram: I⁴ [M3002], "right conduct" or "righteousness."

87. black-out: A restatement of Pound's belief that munitions makers, usurers, and all their kind fostered war because it kept business and profits increasing, and that they could not get away with it if they did not keep their operations in the dark [*GK*, 30, 31, 264].

88. Taney: Roger Brooke T. [cf. 57 above] from a Maryland slaveholding family, which eventually led to a stormy career as a Supreme Court Justice. He was appointed to the court by Andrew Jackson as a reward for service in his cabinet in a number of posts, first as attorney general and then, at a critical moment in the struggle against the bank, as secretary of the treasury. Taney wrote most of Jackson's veto message on the rechartering bill.

89. showed an increase: The U.S. Bank created the panic of 1833-34 by curtailing all capital loans across the country. The Senate called upon Secretary Taney to report on the government's finances, expecting the country was close to ruin. But the reverse was true. "Far from showing the financial decline . . . it showed an increase in every branch of the revenue!" [*TYV*, I, 462].

90. Benton: [88:80]. In defending Taney's report to the Senate, he reviewed details of the history of the "war with the bank" and listed such propaganda as contained in these lines.

91. "Hid the books . . . ": The U.S. Bank created panic in the West by deliberately removing money from its branches, where it was needed by merchants to pay farmers, to Philadelphia, where it was not needed. They thus created a depression in the Midwest, which was done deliberately to obtain an outcry for renewal of the charter: "This fact, said Mr. B., would have been proved from the books of the banks, if they had been inspected. Failing in that, the proof was intelligibly found in the weekly returns" [ibid., 466].

92. "In specie . . . ": "If the gold bill passed, and raised gold sixteen to one, there would be more than that amount of gold in circulation in three months. The foreign coin bill, and the gold bill, would give the country many dollars in specie, without interest, for each paper dollar which the bank issues. . . . The Bank is now a nuisance" [ibid., 468].

93. 16 to 1 . . . dominions: This fact has relevance because it led finally to a bill to make the U.S. ratio 16 to 1: "And, eventually the bill was passed by a large majority" [ibid., 469].

94. Biddle: [88:92]. After the bank was not rechartered, it eventually was dissolved in 1841 as a result of wrongdoing. In the process, the bank itself sued Nicholas Biddle for "$1,018,000 paid out during his administration, for which no vouchers can be found" [ibid., 472].

95. Levari facias: L, "Give relief." *The Dictionary of English Law* defines the phrase thus: "A writ of execution which commanded the sheriff to levy a judgement debt on the lands and goods of the debtor by seizing and selling the goods, and seizing the rents and profits of the lands until the debt was satisfied." Such a writ was issued against the estate of Biddle [ibid., 472].

96. **Louis . . . language**: Since 1815 France had owed the U.S. money for its depredations against American ships from 1806-1812. France had not denied the debt but never came up with the money. Because the Bank of the United States had bought the debt and sold it to its English agents, who were now demanding payment for the French default from the U.S. treasury, the Jackson administration was embarrassed. But King Louis Philippe wanted it paid and suggested the only way the House of Deputies would appropriate the money would be by President Jackson being very firm. Jackson thus recommended that unless the next session of the House of Deputies appropriated the money, Congress should pass a law "authorizing reprisals upon French property." The French were offended and demanded apologies. The king was amused. The president wouldn't apologize. The situation worsened. The French press denounced Jackson as a tyrant. Ambassadors were recalled. Diplomatic relations were broken off. "The people of both countries were in the temper that precedes and provokes hostilities." Congress wouldn't vote money for Atlantic coast defence, "in spite of Jackson's warning that a French armed convoy was at that moment sailing toward the American continent, its intentions unknown." The British offered to mediate. Both parties agreed. Mediation began in February 1836 and was concluded May 10, when Jackson announced that "the four installments under our treaty with France have been paid to the agent of the United States" [*TYV*, I, 472, 477-479, 554-556, 569-572, 588-602; Parton, *Life of Jackson*, I.I, 563-579].

97. **Public debt**: The result of not renewing the bank's charter resulted quickly in the liquidation of the federal debt. Jackson announced the fact at the opening of the 1834 session of Congress [*TYV*, I, 479]. Pound sees a rhyme between the act of *levari facias* against Biddle and Jackson's firm stand against France.

98. **ho^2 . . . li^4**: Ho^2 [M2109], "Why?"; pi$^{4-5}$ [M5109], "must"; yüeh$^{4-5}$ [M7694], "to say"; li^4 [M3867], "profits." "Why must [the king] use the word profit?" [87:117]. The opening lines of *The Works of Mencius* concern a visit of Mencius to King Hwuy. The king said: "Venerable sir, since you have not counted it far to come . . . a thousand li, may I presume you are likewise provided with counsels to profit my kingdom?" Said Mencius, "Why must Your Majesty use the word 'profit'? What I am 'likewise' provided with, are *counsels* to benevolence and righteousness" [Legge, 430].

99. **Webster**: Daniel W. [34:72; cf. 59 above]. Unlike Mencius, Webster's vigorous support of Biddle and his bank shows that he had an enthusiastic attitude toward profit.

100. **Clay opposed . . .** : Benton has a chapter entitled "Branch mints at New Orleans, and in the Gold Regions of Georgia and North Carolina." A bill to establish such mints was hotly debated. Benton was for the bill, but it "was earnestly and perserveringly opposed by Mr. Clay" [*TYV*, I, 550].

101. **The Civil War . . .** : Pound's view, supported by many, was that it was not slavery but economic repression of the South by northern bankers which was the major cause of the Civil War. Benton probes these conditions in a chapter entitled ". . . Southern Discontent: Its True Cause" [*TYV*, II, 180-183].

102. **Philadelphia . . .** : Clay argued that the mint at Philadelphia was enough for the nation. Benton's forces argued that the Philadelphia coinage did not reach all sections of the country in an equitable fashion [*TYV*, I, 551].

103. **France . . .** : "Money was attracted to Philadelphia from the South and West, but not returned back again to those regions. Local mints alone could supply them.

France had ten branch mints; Mexico had eight; the United States not one" [ibid., 551].

104. Every citizen . . . : "Now the whole land is infested with a vile currency of small paper: and every citizen was more or less cheated" [ibid., 552].

105. . . . counterfeit: Because they were backed by nothing [ibid.].

106. French currency . . . : "Mr. B. held the French currency to be the best in the world . . . there was a gold and silver circulation of upwards of five hundred millions of dollars; a currency which had lately stood two revolutions and one conquest, without the least fluctuation in its quantity or value" [ibid., 552-553].

107. 20 millions . . . : The source shows it was the United States and not France that the "20 millions entered." That happened because "of the revival of the gold currency": "Near twenty millions of dollars had entered the country . . . for which, different from a bank paper currency, no interest was paid for its use, and no danger incurred of its becoming useless" [ibid., 573-574].

108. Land not safe . . . : A recurrent theme: The excessive "issue" by banks of paper not founded on anything made all business ventures unsafe [*TYV*, I, 550].

109. Sovreignty . . . : Rhyme with gold is of the Pontifex [cf. 79 above].

110. "All it . . . nothing": [88:78].

111. 600 banks . . . sorrow: Benton, in denouncing a Senate resolution censuring Jackson for his order to remove public deposits from the bank, said: "It was a plot against the government, and against the property of the country. The government was to be upset, and property revolutionized. Six hundred banks were to be broken—the general currency ruined—myriads bankrupted—all business stopped—all property sunk in value—all confidence destroyed! . . . These crimes . . . were to be accomplished by . . . a whole system of . . . subsidiary crime! . . . and the Senate chamber converted into a theatre for . . . woe" [ibid., 646].

112. "My fellow slave-holder": "[Randolph] was one of the large slaveholders of Virginia, but disliked the institution . . . . In the House, when the term 'slaveholder' would be reproachfully used, he would assume it, and refer to a member, not in the parliamentary phrase of colleague, but in the complimentary title of 'my fellow-slaveholder.'" He said to consignees of his tobacco who urged him to free his slaves: "Yes; you buy and set free to the amount of the money you have received from my father and his estate for these slaves, and I will set free an equal number" [ibid., 474-475].

113. (masnatosque liberavit): ML, "and he freed [his] household slaves" [6:35; 90:19].

114. Mr Bishop: Prob. either a Pisan prisoner or a fellow inmate at St. Elizabeths.

115. co-detenuto: I, "prisoner."

116. POPULUM . . . : L, "He edified the people" [8:43].

117. Sigismundo: [8:5]. Just as Sigismundo was villified and condemned by powerful interests (popes and rivals), so AJ was condemned by powerful bankers and politicians. Said Benton in a speech: "President Jackson has done more for the human race than the whole tribe of politicians put together; and shall he remain stigmatized and condemned?" [ibid., 646-648].

118. Commander Rogers: The commodore of the frigate *President*, who in the War of 1812 cruised against the British merchant fleet. In giving chase to a British frigate, Rogers knew he was on the right trail of a "fleet . . . of eighty-five sail. . . . Passing Newfoundland and finding the sea well sprinkled with the signs of West India fruit—orange peels, cocoanut shells . . . the Commodore knew" [*TYV*, II, 146].

119. Giles . . . read: William B. G., 1762-1830, American statesman from V. who opposed the bank. Benton writes of him after his death as "the most accomplished debater which his country had ever seen." He compares him to Charles Fox of Britain, also a great debater in the House of Commons, but they worked differently: "Mr. Fox, a ripe scholar, addicted to literature, and imbued with all the learning of all the classics in all time; Mr. Giles neither read nor studied, but talked incessantly with able men" [ibid., I, 682-683].

120. Young Jessie . . . : Benton's daughter, who married John C. Frémont, a young officer in the U.S. Army Topographical Corps [cf. 191 below]. His expedition to the West was ordered stopped because of arms his party carried. "[Jessie] read the countermanding orders, and detained them! and Frémont knew nothing of their existence until after he had returned from one of the most marvellous . . . expeditions of modern times—one to which the United States are indebted . . . for the present ownership of California" [*TYV*, II, 579].

121. The Collingwood . . . : In a long sequence of events involving the struggle by Indians, Mexico, and the British to control California, Frémont, not even knowing the Mexican War had broken out, acted on his own and raised the American flag over the key port at Monterey. On July 16, 1846 the British admiral who was under orders to take California arrived: "his flagship the Collingwood, of 80 guns, and his squadron the largest British fleet ever seen in the Pacific. To his astonishment he beheld the American flag flying over Monterey, the American squadron in its harbor, and Frémont's mounted riflemen encamped over the town. His mission was at an end. The prize had escaped him. He attempted nothing further, and Frémont and Stockton rapidly pressed the conquest of California to its conclusion" [ibid., 692].

122. "Madame Bileau . . . : Elizabeth Benton Frémont (young Jessie) had an aunt named Susie who spent much time in Paris. She eventually married a Frenchman named Boileau. Says Elizabeth in her *Recollections*: "My Aunt Susie later in life was Madame Boileau, and when she lived in Paris, often played at Rossini's musical Sundays—the musical event of the week. I have heard her say that when she was ready to play, Rossini would send his wife among the guests with the message: 'Madame Boileau is going to play; those who want to talk may now leave!' " [pp. 61-62].

123. "Trade . . . Lanier: Sidney Lanier's "The Symphony" has these lines: "O Trade! O Trade! would thou wert dead! / The Time needs heart—'tis tired of head: / We're all for love the violins said" [77:119].

124. Van Buren . . . : [95:13].

125. the elderly Aida: Prob. Ida or Adah Lee Mapel [91:80].

126. Sagetrieb: [85:194].

127. Ubaldo: [77:99]. M de R suggests that the remark reflects the admiral's conviction that "Mussolini did not have enough good men about him" [*Discretions*, 166].

128. Pumpelly: Raphael P., 1827-1923, American Geologist who, for the Carnegie Institute and others, made two expeditions into Turkestan. His digs there were to test the theory of Aryan migration. The excavations at Anau showed several levels of civilization. Identification was done partly by the bones of domesticated animals. The lower levels had only bones of wild animals. In his *Reminiscences* he gives a fascinating account of his work and discoveries. He says: "At the end of Anau I . . . there appeared a short-horned breed [of ox] which . . . may have been brought in by the newcomers of Anau II, along with the goat, dog, and camel" But below that level they found no dogs, goats, or other domesticated animals [II, 804-812].

129. Said Bonaparte: When young, Napoleon read some Rousseau and disagreed with it. He set forth his own ideas about how primitive man formed community: "Exchange had to be made. Wealth and taste followed. Imagination then emerged from the cave in which it had been a prisoner" [Wilson, *Napoleon*, 24-27].

130. 220 riflemen . . . : Frémont wrote to his father-in-law (T. H. Benton) on July 25, 1846 about his success in freeing Californian territory from "all Mexican authority." He describes the forces he had under him to march upon and take Monterey: "The registered force, actually in arms, under my orders, numbered two hundred and twenty riflement, with one piece of artillery, and ten men, in addition to the artillery of the garrison" [*Memoirs*, 525].

131. Mr Dix: John Adams D., 1798-1879, American statesman who served in the Senate (1845-1849). In a speech to the Senate he showed that if it had not been for Frémont the British would have had the U.S. surrounded by British colonies in Central America, Canada, and all the Pacific coast: "There is no doubt that his [Frémont's] rapid and decisive movements kept California out of the hands . . . of the British government . . . . We could not have failed to regard them [Britain's movements], considered in connection with her proceedings in Oregon, and more recently in Central America, as part of a deliberate design to environ us with her colonies, and especially to shut us out from the Pacific and its extending commerce" [*Memoirs*, 547-548].

132. "The irish are . . . : Father MacNamara, an apostolic missionary, had a "far-reaching plan to colonize California with emigrants from Ireland." In his application to the president he said: "The Irish people are devout Catholics, moral, industrious, sober, and brave" [ibid., 550-554]. To include "sober" is to suggest the good father had in mind a very special group of Irishmen not to be found in other places.

133. Kit Carson: This famous mountain man acted as a scout for Frémont in his military effort to locate and oust the Mexicans in lower California. But he and some of his men did better on land than on sea. Says Frémont: "By the time we had been a few hours at sea we were all very low in our minds. . . . Carson was among those who were badly worsted by this evening of landsmen, and many were the vows made to the winds that never again would they put trust in the fairweather promises of the ocean" [*Memoirs*, 563].

134. 3 days . . . : Frémont left a party of 10 men, all 20 years of age or so, to guard Santa Barbara, which soon came under attack by a party of 150. They refused to surrender. The ladies of Santa Barbara offered to hide them, but they took to the mountains, where in time, "They suffered greatly for want of food." The enemy tried to burn them out by setting fires on the mountain around them: "It took them three days to cross the first ridge of the mountains, during which time they had nothing but rosebuds to eat" [ibid., 596-597].

135. Che tolgo lo stato: I, "that I remove the condition." A half-line variant of a line in a canzone, "Song of Fortune," attributed (wrongly?) to Cavalcanti, in which Fortuna says, "Sono colei, che tolgo / e / dò stato" ("I am the one who gives and takes away") [*SR*, 111].

136. Don Jesus . . . : In the continual insurrections of Mexican forces, many were captured and some were paroled, including a leader, Don Jesus Pico: "Don Jesus had broken his parole, and was put before a court-martial and sentenced to be shot." But at the hour of execution when he was about to be led before the firing squad, his wife and several children burst in upon Frémont and begged for mercy. She said, "he did not know that he was committing such a crime. He went . . . because he was ashamed to stay behind." Frémont pardoned him. Don Jesus said Frémont had given him a new life and that he would dedicate it to him: "And he did it faithfully" [*Memoirs*, 598-599].

137. Guadalupe: The Treaty of Guadalupe Hidalgo of 1848 ended the war between the United States and Mexico.

138. von Humboldt: [97:130, 131].

139. Agassiz: [93:51].

140. Del Mar: [96:119]. Writing of Del Mar, Pound said: "Along with Louis Agassiz and Leo Frobenius, he builds upon Alexander von Humboldt's 'art of collecting and arranging a mass of isolated facts, and rising thence by a process of induction to general ideas.' " From a bulletin announcing the Square Dollar Series [NS, 556; CB-R, *ZBC*, 112]. The concept is basic to Pound's idea of a "sufficient phalanx of particulars [74/441].

141. Frobenius: [38:45].

142. Benton: [88:80]. Benton tells a sad story. After Frémont's successes, he returned to Washington to be court-martialed for exceeding his orders. He was found guilty and sentenced to loss of rank and dismissal from military service. President Polk pardoned him of some charges and restored him to the rank of Lt. Colonel, but Frémont said he wasn't guilty of any of them and resigned his commission in protest. Soon he was back on the trail west on a 4th expedition. As he was trying to cross the southern Rockies, however, a guide misled his party, which was caught in a blizzard high up. The 120 pack mules froze to death. They were ten days from any supplies and without food. Frémont sent the guide with a party of 2 to get food. After they had been gone 16 days, Frémont with 2 others went looking for them. The guide had died; his comrades had eaten part of him and were wandering around wild. He took them in tow and finally reached an Indian he knew, who gave them horses. He got supplies, went back for the survivors, and got there in time to save two-thirds of them: "finding the other third dead along the road, scattered at intervals as each had sunk exhausted and frozen." Benton says, "Frémont found himself in a situation which tries the soul—which makes the issue between despair and heroism—and leaves no alternative but to sink under fate or to rise above it" [*TYV*, II, 721]. This passage may be the one Pound thinks is in Benton.

143. Randolph . . . : [87:10]. JR applauded Jackson's veto of the bank bill, but he violently opposed the Nullification Ordinances of 1832. Although he was weak, he would not see the Constitution so mistreated: "he attended large meetings at the Charlotte Court House and again at Buckingham, fifty miles from his home, in so weak a condition that he could not stand to speak but was obliged to address them from his chair" [MVB, *Auto*, 424].

144. Henry's passion . . . : Thomas Jefferson, when asked about the mind and manners of Patrick Henry in 1759-60, wrote of him: "His manners had something of the coarseness of the society he had frequented; his passion was fiddling, dancing, and pleasantry" [ibid., 441]. Charlotte Courthouse was the scene of Patrick Henry's last speech, which engaged the beardless young John Randolph in his first attempt at public speaking [ibid., 436].

145. "We ought not . . . : The "old crump" is James Kent of New York who met Van Buren after he was no longer president and asked pardon for being against him and helping put a "wholly unfit" man in his place: "You made a very good President . . . you did nothing of which either of us has reason to be ashamed; and we ought not to have turned you out, without placing a more competent man in your place" [ibid., 63].

146. "Great blackguard . . . : AJ went to Richmond to be present at the Burr treason trial in 1807, which was presided over by John Marshall. AJ's boisterous conduct remained in the memory of one present: "As I was crossing the Court House Green, I heard a great noise at some distance off. Inquiring what it was, I was told it was a great blackguard from Tennessee, one Andrew Jackson, making a speech for Burr and damning Jefferson as a prosecutor" [Bruce, *Randolph*, 305-306].

147. "No auction . . . : Randolph would not enter the debate about the relation of the slave to his owner, but he vehemently protested a slave market in the heart of Washington, the nation's capital. So he called upon the House to put a stop to "a practice which . . . was not surpassed for abomination in any part of the earth; for in no part of it . . . was there so great and infamous a slave market as in this metropolis; in the very seat of government of this nation which prided itself on freedom" [ibid., 438-439].

148. Τὴν τῶν ὅλων ἀρχήν: H, "The beginning of all things" [Sophocles, *Ajax*, 1105-1106].

149. Slave labour . . . : Randolph, in a slave vs. antislave states debate, said in 1803: "[It is] the opinion of your committee, that the labor of slaves is not necessary to promote the growth and settlement of colonies in that region. That this labor, demonstrably the dearest of any, can only be employed to advantage in the cultivation of products more valuable than any known to that quarter of the United States" [*TYV*, II, 759-560].

150. But for Price: Exgovernor Rodman Price of New Jersey told the story of the raising of the flag at Monterey after Frémont had taken it. In those days Price was an officer serving under Commodore Sloat. Sloat had given him orders to go ashore but not to take part in any aid to Frémont whatsoever. He didn't know the people seemed to prefer the British to the Americans as rulers. When ashore, Price found the truth. Frémont was ready to raise the flag at San Francisco. In a nip-and-tuck situation, Price returned to the flagship, roused the commodore in the middle of the night, and in an impassioned plea asked him to ignore "the treaty obligations with Mexico" and raise the flag. Sloat was convinced. Price raised the flag at Monterey (July 7, 1848) and Frémont raised it at San Francisco: "The English admiral arrived a few days afterwards, and the first thing he said on receiving the Commodore was, 'Sloat, if your flag was not flying on shore I should have hoisted mine there' " [Frémont, *Memoirs*, 538-542].

151. Quam . . . regitur: L, "such small wisdom is hidebound." Randolph, in a speech ca. 1827 supporting Jackson against JQA, is prompted to recall other great statesmen: "Cardinal Richelieu was what? A priest. Yes, but what a priest! Oxenstierna was a chancellor. He it was who sent his son abroad to see—*Quam parva sapientia regitur mundus*—with how little wisdom this world is governed. This administration [JQA's] seemed to have thought that even less than little would do for us" [Bruce, *Randolph*, 547].

152. Ideogram: I[4] [M2952], "treat lightly."

153. Macauley . . . : Said Van Buren, speaking of Robert Peel as a great orator: "Lord Macauley, a competent judge, altho' certainly sometimes extravagant if not careless in his conclusions, ranks him [Peel] among the successors of Pitt" [MVB, *Auto*, 464].

154. Palmerston: Van Buren had much contact with Palmerston as secretary of state, as president, and as minister to Great Britain. Protesting anti-Palmerston sentiments in the U.S., he said: "In the course of the exciting and truly important discussions in which we have been involved I never had occasion to suspect him of professing opinions he did not sincerely believe. . . . During my recent visit to England, twenty-five years later than the period of which I am writing, I saw much of him and was pleased to find him at the head of government" [MVB, *Auto*, 465-466; 42:1].

155. Jury from . . . : MVB speaks of the ways of liberty which the U.S. and Britain have in common: "liberty of speech and of the press . . . liberty of conscience in matters of religious faith—securities and safeguards for the enjoyment of personal liberty, such as the Writ of Habeas Corpus, trial by a jury of the vicinage etc" [ibid., 480-481].

156. Disraeli sold: [48:19]. At a critical moment when Parliament was not in session, D (then prime minister) was dining at the Rothschild mansion when news came that shares controlling the Suez were available at Paris. D made a deal with the Rothschilds to transfer £4 million to the Egyptian Khedive's account. Other details of cost, etc, are hidden [86:61].

157. Tory not a Liberal: On the right to search suspicious vessels at sea, which the British under the liberals asserted in provocative tones of voice. With Robert Peel as prime minister, says MVB, "a great change had occurred in the tone of the English Ministry" [ibid., 528-529].

158. Galileo: [85:7].

159. 孟 : Meng[4] [M4428], "great, eminent"; 子 : tzu[3] [M6939], "a son, a philosopher." "Meng-tzu," Mencius ["Mang Tsze," *SP*, 81-97].

160. caliginem vespertinum: L, "evening fog" or "darkness."

161. *πύρωσιν* . . . *Θαλάττης*: H, "and he set fire to the sea."

162. Caleb . . . christening": Meigs says of THB: "Benton was . . . often outrageously personal in his criticisms." During the slave vs. free-state debates of 1849: "Claiborne Jackson and two other leading enemies attended one of his meetings and took front seats with a view to interrupting him with questions; but the interruption did not occur, after Benton early in his speech said, 'And here are Claib Jackson [and the others, naming them] . . . as demure as three prostitutes at a christening' " [Meigs, *Life of THB*, 456]. Pound's "Johnson" is an error.

163. Calhoun called . . . : Henry Clay in open Senate debate said Calhoun used this epithet for MVB. MVB drew up a bill proposing a national treasury system and Calhoun endorsed it: "What the drawer thinks of the indorser, his cautious reserve and stiffled enmity prevent us from knowing. But the frankness of the indorser has not left us in the same ignorance with respect to his opinion of the drawer. He has often expressed it upon the floor of the Senate. On one occasion . . . denying him any of the royal beast of the forest, he attributed to him those which belong to the most crafty, most skulking, and the meanest of the quadruped tribe" [*TYV*, II, 101].

164. Firm taste . . . : Clay's own opinion of MVB is different: "I do not . . . share with [Calhoun] . . . in this opinion of the President of the United States [MVB]. I have always found him . . . civil, courteous and gentlemanly; and he dispenses . . . a generous and liberal hospitality" [*TYV*, II, 101]. Frémont said of THB: "Mr. Benton always relaxed to the enjoyment of the interesting and cheerful dinner-table" [*Memoirs*, 414-415].

165. Domvile: [102:29].

166. Uberti: [77:99; cf. 127 above].

167. "His agreeable niece . . . : MVB as minister to Britain speaks of Prince Talleyrand: "I visited his house as often as the habits of society in relation to persons in his position would justify, and was always received with cordiality by himself and his agreeable niece the Duchesse de Dino" [MVB, *Auto*, 458].

168. Mihailovitch: Prob. Draza Mihajlovic, a Yugoslav adversary of Tito who believed Communism was a greater threat than Fascism. He was tried for treason in 1946 and executed [104:2].

169. Henriot: Prob. Philippe H., minister in Petain's Vichy government. Three weeks and a day after the Normandy invasion (June 28, 1944), he was shot to death by members of the French Resistance [Bosha, *Pai*, 4-1, 99-100; 84-39].

170. Gentile: Prob. Giovanni G., 1875-1944, who taught philosophy at several Italian universities. An early supporter of Mussolini, he was called "the philospher of Fascism."

171. "China . . . treaty: A would-be con man by the name of Caleb Cushing sought notoriety and fame by promoting a trade treaty between the U.S. and China. A bill sponsored in Congress for money to promote this unwise project was opposed by Benton and many others. The idea came because China had signed a peace treaty with Great Britain; but that treaty was in settlement of a conflict. Both China and wise men in this country said that trade between the two countries had increased amid fine relationships and no such formality or costly administrative arrangement was needed. In spite of this, President Tyler was charmed by

Cushing and his idea, so money was appropriated. Cushing was launched on his mission with three battleships "carrying altogether near two hundred guns; a formidable accompaniment for a peace mission seeking a commercial treaty" [*TYV*, II,515]. Fortunately, fire and disaster disabled some of the ships or Cushing might have caused a war. When he got to China, he demanded to see the emperor. "The Emperor's governor-general, Ching, replied that the Emperor would not give audience to a trade mission, and that it was the custom and law for foreign trade missions to conduct business outside the heavenly empire, at Canton" [Watts, unpub. 206]. Cushing persisted and threatened to sail up the river and hunt down the emperor, who was "insulting the dignity of the United States." Benton concludes that only the delay of the warships may have prevented Cushing blundering the U.S. into war–a result that seems to have been narrowly avoided. The lines focus on several arguments. Our trade with China had gone on with little bureaucratic interference or control. Benton outlines Ching's response: "With respect to the treaty of friendship and commerce, the governor declares there is no necessity for it–that China and America have traded together two hundred years in peace and friendship without a treaty–that all nations now had the benefit of the treaty with Great Britain, which treaty was necessary to establish relations after a war; and that the United States, having had no war with China, had no need for a treaty" [*TYV*, II, 516].

172. Cambreling: [Cambreleng]. Jackson appointed Samuel Swartwout, an old political ally, to be the customs collector of New York Harbor over the protests of his secretary of state, Van Buren, who considered resigning because he thought the appointment so unwise. His own choice was Churchill C. Cambreleng [37:58]. MVB decided, finally, to stay on but with the proviso that he be allowed to state his objections to his friends in New York. In response to his letters, Cambreleng ended a long reply: "and now mark me–if our Collector is not a defaulter in four years, I'll swallow the Treasury if it was all coined in coppers . . . C. C. Cambreleng" [MVB, *Auto*, 268]. It was discovered in 1838 that Swartwout had embezzled $1,250,000.

173. Tazewill . . . St James: Jackson wanted to appoint Randolph's friend Littleton W. Tazewell (senator from Virginia) as minister to England. MVB thought he was too old and unsuited to the pomp of English court life: "I am sure he derived more social enjoyment from his games at quoits with Chief Justice Marshall . . . and others . . . than he could promise himself abroad" [ibid., 259]. Tazewell declined the appointment.

174. "Of great . . . resolved on: Although Jackson had turned over office to MVB with the nation not only free of debts but with a surplus in the treasury, the politicians in consort with the bankers put up a big and destructive fight in the next round of bank battles. One thousand banks in all the states were empowered to issue paper money without specified specie reserves. Some went so far as to issue 20 times as much paper as they had specie to redeem it. Financial ruin loomed. Daniel Webster (a henchman of Biddle) and the bank were conniving to force the bank's rechartering. At a critical moment Webster made a famous speech to a large crowd in New York blaming Jackson and MVB for all the monetary troubles. Benton writes of the Webster performance and explains what he was up to: "It was the first formal public step which was to inaugurate the new distress, and organize the proceedings for shutting up the banks, and with them, the federal treasury, with a view to coerce the government into submission to the Bank of the United States and its confederate politicians. Mr. Van Buren was a man of great suavity and gentleness of deportment, and, to those who associated the idea of violence with firmness, might be supposed deficient in that quality. An experiment upon his nerves was resolved on–a pressure of public opinion, in the language of Mr. Webster, under which his gentle temperament was expected to yield" [*TYV*, II,

15-16]. MVB did not yield. He even managed to restore the situation and get federal notes issued backed by specie and taxes to resolve the crisis without rechartering the bank. But his acts were "political suicide." In 1840 the bankers and their cohorts mounted "the most scurrilous and fradulent campaign against a Presidential incumbent in American history." MVB was defeated by the innocuous Harrison, who would, they believed, restore the bank to power.

175. Had Crab . . . day: Pound's translation of Dante's "Sì che, se il Cancro avesse un tal cristallo, / L'inverno avrebbe un mese d'un sol dì" [*Par.* XXV, 101-102]. Guided by Beatrice, Dante comes to the Heaven of the fixed stars where he is questioned about his hopes. After his response, a splendid vision takes place in which the soul of St. John flashes across the heavens: "then one light among them shone out so bright that if the Crab had one such crystal, winter would have a month of one unbroken day" [Singleton].

176. mariners . . . : THB accounted the economic distress of the South vs. the North as partly due to the North's money, shipping, international trade, etc.: "continued unequal legislation in Congress; and increasing expenditures of the government, chiefly disbursed in the North, and defect of seamen in the South (for mariners cannot be made of slaves), all combined to retain the foreign trade" [*TYV*, II, 133].

177. Guinicelli: Guido G. [51:1], a Ghibelline poet from Bologna who was one of the most important influences on Cavalcanti and Dante. His most famous canzone ("Al Cor gentil ripara sempre Amore") has lines that Wilhelm translates: "Sun beats against the mud the livelong day; / Mud it remains; Sun does not lose its ray;" [JW, *Medieval Song*, 232; 51:2].

178. Mr Tyler: [37:39; 87:13].

179. Ideogram: [M3016]: "one"; [M3097]: "man." A rhyme with, "It may depend on one man" [86/563]. In the *Shoo King* we read: "The prosperity and unsettledness of a State may arise from one man. The glory and tranquillity of a State also may perhaps arise from the excellence of one man" [Grieve, *Pai*, 4-2 & 3, 471, 492].

180. "even if . . . : Source unknown, but the idea applies in all the significant political struggles of Cantos 87-89.

181. M. Hottinguer . . . : [Hottenguer]. A month after the bank was declared insolvent, Biddle and others were indicted as criminals for lending $30 million in unrecoverable loans to their friends, supporters, and others, in contravention of the bank's charter. In trying to cover their tracks, they had sought to raise money abroad, especially with their agents in Paris and London. But the "state of the accounts of the bank with its agents abroad did not warrant any large drafts upon them, expecially that of the Messrs. Hottinguer in Paris" [*TYV*, II, 370-372; 101-32].

182. Vicountess . . . transportation: Although the indictment against Biddle and his cohorts led to their arrest, they procured writs of habeas corpus and were "discharged in vacation by judges before whom they were brought." Benton compares this action with the action involving much smaller bank crimes in London in 1855: "three of the greatest bankers in London are receiving sentence of transportation for fourteen years for offences, neither in money nor morals, the hundredth part of the ruin and crime perpetrated by our American bank—bearing the name of the United States." Benton said, "The case presents too strong a contrast . . . to be omitted" So he doesn't: "one of them, Sir John Paul, was a baronet by descent, and allied to some of the highest nobility of England. He was first cousin to . . . Vicountess Barrington, Lady Bloomfield; and, above all, the honorable Mrs. Villiers. . . . These connections . . . did not save them from a criminal trial and utter disgrace. . . . The defendants appeared in court, attended by Sir Frederick Thesiger . . . and other almost equally eminent counsel. . . ." Benton thinks of the $30 million misappropriations as well as the multitude of other crimes the American bankers were guilty of, and almost sighs at the comparison: "For misappropriating sixty thousand dollars of one of their customers—using it [not to steal but] without his consent—these three great London bankers were sentenced to fourteen years' transportation: for misappropriating thirty-five millions, and sinking twenty-one millions more in other institutions, the wrong-doers go free in the United States" [ibid.].

183. The sub-treasury: In place of renewing the bank charters, MVB had proposed a sub-treasury system that would perform the same services. To accomplish this, the Independent Treasurer Act was passed in 1840, MVB's last year in office. The first thing the Whig-dominated Congress of 1841 did was repeal the act in a special session. But the regular session of that year revived it. Said Benton: "The measures passed, had no duration . . . were repealed by the same congress that passed them. . . . The sub-treasury system, believed to have been put to death, came to life again" [*TYV*, II, 372-373].

184. Louis Philippe: Tyler, in his second annual message, proposed another scheme for a quasi-public agency to issue paper currency. Benton opposed it and in doing so remarked on the soundness of French currency: "And here let me do justice to the wisdom and firmness of the present king of the French. The Bank of France lately resolved to reduce the minimum size of its notes to two hundred francs (say forty dollars). The king gave them notice that if they did it, the government would consider it an injury to the currency, and would take steps to correct the movement. The Bank rescinded its resolution; and Louis Philippe . . . showed himself to be a patriot king" [ibid., 391].

185. From '34 . . . : In praising the success of the hard-money policy adopted, Benton said: "The long . . . struggle between paper money and gold was now [1842] verging to a crisis. The gold bill, rectifying the erroneous valuation of that metal, had passed in 1834: an influx of gold coin followed. In seven years the specie currency had gone up from twenty millions to one hundred. . . . There was as much as the current business of the country and of the federal government could use: for these 100 million . . . in every ten hands that they passed through, would do the business of one thousand millions" [ibid., 406].

186. "ad valorem": L, "in proportion to the value." Tariffs were a longtime source of conflict between the North and the South. The North wanted them in order to protect their manufacturing interests. The South didn't because it decreased their markets. One plan was to go "to a uniform *ad valorem* duty of twenty per centum on all dutied articles." Those who knew could see this ploy would end in an increase in the tariff. Benton says: "The introduction of the universal *ad valorem* the exception." The trouble would be in hundred of customs officers trying to determine value, which would lead to legal actions: "So that this *ad valorem* system, besides its great expense, its chance for diversity of opinions among the appraisers, and its openness to corruption, also gave rise to differences among the highest administrative and law officers of the government, with resorts to courts of law, in nearly all of which the United States was the loser" [ibid., 189-190].

187. Wright: Silas W., 1795-1847, U.S. senator (1833-1844) and governor of New York (1844-1846). Benton made a eulogy to the Senate in memory of Wright in which he said: "His mind was clear and strong. . . . He spoke to the head, not to the passions: . . . In 1844 he left the Senate, to stand for the governorship of New York; and never did his self-sacrificing temper undergo a stronger trial. . . . He liked the Senate: he disliked the governorship. . . . But it was said to him . . . that the State would be lost to Mr. Polk, unless Mr. Wright was associated with him in the canvass: and to this argument he yielded. He stood the canvass for the governorship—carried it—and Mr. Polk with him; and saved the presidential election of that year" [ibid., 701].

188. Quiditas . . . : I, "essence." Dante used the word "quiditate" twice in the *Commedia* [*Par.* XX, 92; *Par.* XXIV, 66]. Translators variously render it as "essence" or "quiddity."

189. Under head of "medicine" . . . : Benton wrote about the navy's misappropriation of funds, saying that "the disorderly conduct of the Navy was notorious" and that its expenses in peace time (1843) were greater than they were during the war with England. Furthermore: "The honorable member [Meriwether of Georgia] showed . . . that under the head of medicine there had been purchased out of the same funds, whiskey, coal, clothing, spirits, harness, stationery, hay, corn, oats, stoves, beef, mutton, fish, bread, charcoal . . . and purchases of all articles were . . . made from particular persons, and double prices paid" [*TYV*, II, 484-485].

190. *δ . . . ἴδεν*: H, "of men he saw" [*Od.* I, 3]. The whole line translates: "and he saw the cities of many men, and knew their minds" [12:7].

191. Frémont . . . : John Charles F., 1813-1890, born in Savannah, Ga., the son of a French refugee. Attended Charleston College, taught math to naval cadets, and in 1838 was introduced to the West as a member of a surveying team. He eloped with Jessie Benton, daughter of THB, who became reconciled to him later and helped secure him command of several expeditions–Des Moines River, Rocky Mts., Oregon, and California. In 1845 when the Mexican War was brewing, he raised the revolt against the Mexican authorities in California and was court-martialed and found guilty of disobeying orders. President Polk pardoned him and in 1848 he was back on the exploration trail. He served briefly (1850-1851) as U.S. Senator from California and was even chosen by the Republicans as their presidential candidate in 1856. He lost, though he was considered a national hero. From that moment his fortune declined; he even became beggared in 1870 by an effort to build a railroad. But his wife gave him constant support. Although he was a controversial figure, he became a sort of folk hero by the end of his life and was known as "the Pathfinder." He finally received a government pension just before his death. The canto line here refers to the attempt to stop Frémont's expedition because, as he said, "in addition to ordinary arms, I had taken a howitzer with me." The plot was foiled when his wife didn't forward the dispatch [cf. 120 above].

192. So that . . . Geld: After Sept. 1943 Pound left Rome and traveled north to Gais to see his daughter, Mary, who was being brought up by Mr. and Mrs. Marcher. The villagers were suspicious of an American from Italy saying he was Mary's father so they formed a committee that came to the Marcher home to ask questions. The Marchers were frightened of men entering with rifles [M de R., *Discretions*, 190-192].

193. der Schwiegersohn: G, "the son-in-law." After the investigation was over they started to discuss politics. It was the brother-in-law who came in on the conversation.

194. "Was sagt er?": G, "What does he say?"

195. Der Jud will Geld: G, "The Jew wants money."

196. "Neither . . . fraud: One of Pound's "gists" under the heading "LAW" says: "The right aim of law is to prevent coercion either by force or fraud" [*SP*, 355].

197. Ἀθήνη . . . **jury**: H, "Athena" [87:40].

198. Ideogram: Tuan [M6541], "principles; doctrines." The four basic cornerstones of Confucianism: "love, duty, propriety, wisdom" [85:33].

199. Ideogram: Chen [M346], "upright."

200. ataraxia: L, "undisturbed in mind or by passion."

201. From Charlemagne's . . . : Said Pound:

"Charlemagne fights the Monopolists; he decrees a commodity denar, or a grain denar, and the significance escapes six hundred and more economists in a sequence of centuries" [*GK*, 47].

202. Venice . . . : Del Mar said: "The history of Venice commences with the reopening of the Suez route to India" After that its commerce developed because of well-founded specie [*Money and Civilization*, 23].

203. Hansa: Del Mar: "far more important . . . was the Hansa established at a very early epoch by the pagan Goths. . . . The Christian Hansa was the earliest trade corporation" [Del Mar, *HMS*, 264-265]. The point common to all three names is that the power to issue legal tender or specie should belong to the state: "Gold was under the Pontifex" [cf. 79 above and 231 below].

204. forged Donation . . . : The *Donation of Constantine* is one of the most famous forgeries employed in the struggles for power between the Eastern and Western empires. Written around the mid 8th century, it became incorporated as a part of the Pseudo-Isidorian Decretals and thence, in part, got into most medieval collections of canon law. The *Donation* purports that "Constantine the Great, reciting his baptism and the cure of his leprosy at the hands of Sylvester, Bishop of Rome 314-336, confirmed the privilege of that pontiff as head of all the clergy and supreme over the other four patriarchates . . . it tells how he, Constantine, recognized the superior dignity of the Pope by holding the bridle of his horse. . . . This remarkable document was almost universally accepted as genuine from the ninth to the fifteenth century" [Coleman, *Donation*, 1-2]. Del Mar believes the forgery was the Latin bishop's attempt to wrest authority from both Charlemagne and the basileus in the East: the documents "purported to be a donation from Constantine I, to the Bishop of Rome, of both the spiritual and temporal dominion of the western world" [*Middle Ages Revisited*, 200-201].

205. "Perchè . . . idee): I, "Why in order [do you wish to put your ideas]?" [87:4].

206. Thalers . . . Belgium: [86:79]. Morris says: "The coin which was known as the Maria Theresia [*sic*] thaler . . . was extensively used in trading outside Austria. . . . Besides furthering trade relations, the advantages of the coin itself were very helpful for its distribution. . . . The picture of the Empress . . . was artistically valuable. . . . Until recently, Austria provided parts of Africa with newly minted Maria Theresia thalers, and only last year [1935] . . . they were in circulation in Abyssinia" [*Maria Theresia*, 347-348; cf. 226 below].

207. The Emperor's furrow: [53:122; 86:78].

208. Antoninus: [46:42; 78:56; *GK*, 40-41].

209. Rock Drill: Pound took the name from a review by Wyndham Lewis entitled "The Rock-Drill," which Lewis quite likely derived from an Epstein sculpture [Korg, *Pai*, 4-2 & 3, 301-313].

210. Wd / have packed Hamburg . . . : [86:8].

211. young Windsor: [86:47].

212. Image (Selwyn): A well-known literary figure in Pound's early years in London who talked to him about Paris, "Old Verlaine," stained glass, and presumably Ruskin. In a letter home, 21 Feb. 1909, he said, "I think the Shakespears and Selwyn Image are about the most worth while out of the lot I have come across" [NS, *Life*, 94].

213. Ruskin: John R., 1819-1900, whose writings, such as *The Political Economy of Art* (1857), would be certain to interest Pound [see Robert Faulkner Casillo, "The Parallel Design in John Ruskin and Ezra Pound," Ph.D. dissertation, Johns Hopkins, 1978, University Microfilms International 78-6240].

214. Tasso: Torquato T., 1544-1595, Italian poet, author of *Jerusalem Delivered* (1575).

A blow on the head inflicted by an angry courtier rendered him recurrently insane and he was hospitalized for the rest of his life.

215. **Kidd**: Prob. Thomas Kyd, 1558-1594, English dramatist. For alleged unorthodox religious views, he was arrested and tortured.

216. **Raleigh**: Sir Walter R., 1552?-1618, English soldier, explorer, courtier, and man of letters. In and out of favor with Queen Elizabeth, he was imprisoned in the Tower in 1592. With the accession of James I, he was persona non grata for years. Convicted of treason and sentenced to death, he was reprieved to spend over 10 years in the Tower. He was released in 1616 to make another voyage to the Oronoco in search of gold with specific instructions not to aid the cause of Savoy against Spain. But he captured a Spanish town, and on his return was executed at the demand of the Spanish ambassador who had great influence because the question of marriage between the Infanta of Spain and James's son Charles was being explored.

217. **My father . . . window**: Elizabeth Benton Frémont wrote: "From the balcony of our Paris house we witnessed the triumphant entry of . . . Napoleon III, as the Emperor of the French" Napoleon III had ordered that no guard should surround him on his entry, saying "If I die at the hands of an assassin, I die alone!" The problem for the police was a difficult one, but they obtained the names of all people expected to be on the route. General Frémont gave his list of names, but was surprised when uninvited guests showed up. He gave those names to the police at the last minute: "detectives were sent to guard the unbidden guests . . . and thus a delicate situation was safely mastered." Said the General: "If there is to be any shooting it must not be done from my home" [Frémont, *Recollections* 54-56].

218. **My grandfather . . .** : Elizabeth B. Frémont (Benton's granddaughter) makes no mention of Morse or his telegraph, but Benton says: "Dr. Franklin first broached the idea of using electricity for communicating intelligence: Professor Morse gave practical application to his idea." And Jessie Frémont, Benton's daughter, wrote: "living close by were the Ellsworths, who were 'friends indeed' to Mr. Morse in the hard days when he could not get his idea of the electric telegraph launched. He was laughed at in Congress; his money gave out; his health was going, he was so worn out that his dead-white face and brilliant hollow eyes startled one . . . these ladies went among their friends whose husbands were in Congress and *made* them understand . . . and now it girdles the earth" [Jessie Frémont, *Souvenirs*, 61; 34:88].

219. **"Pige-moi . . . carthaginois**: F, "Just look at the character, said old Gustav, who will paint you a Carthaginian easy chair." "Old Gustav" is Flaubert, author of *Salammbô, a roman de Carthage*.

220. **Henry J. had Coburn**: Said Coburn: "it was my unique privilege in 1906-1907 to provide the frontispieces for each of the twenty-four volumes of the collected edition of Henry James' works" [*Alvin Langdon Coburn: Photographer*, 52].

221. **I need add nothing . . .** : Said MVB: "I entered the Senate . . . at the commencement of Mr. Monroe's second Presidential Term [1821]. John Gaillard, of South Carolina, was then, as he had been for many years, President *pro tem* of that body. I need add nothing to the eloquent description given of his character by Col. Benton . . . except the expression of my full concurrence in what has been so well said" [MVB, *Auto*, 115].

222. **"Good-bye Tazewell . . .** : [cf. 173 above]. A very complicated senatorial struggle between Randolph and both his friends and opponents developed because of the increasing vituperation in his speeches. This lack of temper would eventually lead to the Clay duel. Randolph himself expected not to be re-elected to the Senate. While the Senate was preparing to pass rules to curb him, he was preparing to go to England to get away from it all. At one moment of great drama,

Senator Lloyd of Mass. stood ready to duel to the death. Said MVB, "The Senate at this moment presented a striking *tableau* . . . every Senator present inclining . . . to take sides in the fray—when . . . Randolph moved deliberately from his place . . . and passed in front of the Chair to the door, exclaiming as he walked along, 'I will have no more of this! I am off for England! Good bye, Tazewell! Good bye Van Buren! They are all against me! . . . in Virginia too!'—and still uttering these words the doors of the Senate closed behind him" [MVB, *Auto*, 206-210].

223. **"on borrowed capital . . .**: [cf. 63 above].

224. **Judge Marshall**: [37:67].

225. **Agamemnon**: By killing a stag sacred to Diana and allowing the sacrifice of his daughter Iphigenia so that the Greeks, windbound at Aulis, might be freed to sail to Troy, Agamemnon himself became a "father of war."

226. **"Leave the Duke**: [50:28].

227. **quest'oggi**: I, "this very day" [cf. 205 above]. M de R. cites these several lines about forging the thalers and says that while the village committee was questioning Pound on his return to Gais [cf. 192-194 above], the "single dangling Thaler on the watch-chain [of the brother-in-law] shifted interest from paper money and stamp-scrip to the Thalers from Maria Theresa" [*Discretions*, 192].

228. **"Benton . . . (Randolph)**: After the duel [88/577], R wrote to a friend: "I cannot write. I tried yesterday to answer your letter, but I could not do it. My pen *choked*. . . . I am all but friendless. . . . Benton begins to understand and to love me. Nothing has stood in his way" [Bruce, *Randolph*, 524-525].

229. **In Venice . . . Danzig**: [cf. 203 above]. The stability of these two corporate states, Venice and the Hanseatic League, depended on their power to issue and control the money supply. With the rise of banks, that control was lost. Said Del Mar: "In 1268, owing to the severity of the taxes . . . particularly the corn duties, a bread riot occurred in Venice, and though the republic was in great financial distress, the obnoxious imposts were repealed" [*Money and Civilization*, 66].

230. **Alex said . . . paid**: Says Fuller: "Alexander also undertook to pay all debts incurred by his soldiers, and to find out how many debtors there were, he invited all who were in debt to enter their names and the amounts they owed in a register." The soldiers were afraid and most didn't, so Alexander changed the order. "He cancelled registration and ordered that all debts . . . were to be paid without . . . their names in writing" [*Generalship*, 136-137].

231. **Gold . . . Pontifex**: Says Del Mar: "The jealous monopoly of gold coinage by the sovereign-pontiff ascends to the Achimenides of Persia, that is to say, to Cyrus and Darius; in fact, it ascends to the Bramins of India. The Greek and Roman Republics broke it down; Caesar set it up again" [*HMS*, 70; cf. 79 above].

232. **Bezants . . .**: Bezants were Byzantine coins issued by the Basileus of the Eastern Empire: gold was then under the pontifex.

233. **Dandolo**: Enrico D., ca. 1108-1205, became doge of Venice in 1192. In the 4th crusade he diverted the attacking forces to Zara and then, in 1203, to Constantinople ("Stamboul"). Though old and blind, he commanded the victorious fleet. Thereafter, the coinage, which had been stable, passed into the hands of banks and merchants.

234. **arab uneasiness**: Between the basileus and the rulers of the Arab states bordering the Eastern Empire open conflict sometimes broke out over the coinage [97:6].

235. **The forgery**: [cf. 204 above].

236. **Valla**: Lorenzo V., ca. 1407-1457, Italian humanist and Greek scholar. His claim to fame rests on three things: (1) the exposure of the forgery; (2) the allegation that he was tortured by the Inquisition for the exposure,

which is untrue—he wasn't even imprisoned; and (3) his treatise *De Voluptate*—proving that he was given to paganism—which attacked chastity as an ideal [Coleman, *Donation*, passim].

237. **12 to one, Roma**: Says Del Mar: "From the accession of Julius to the fall of Constantinople, the ratio of value between gold and silver within the Roman empire, whether pagan or Christian, was always 1 to 12; whereas, during the same interval, it was 6 1/2 in India, as well as in the Arabian empires" [*HMS*, 79].

238. **And the Portagoose**: Said Pound: "Portagoose as SOON as got into Goa/ started uprooting spice trees/400 year ramp [age]" [letter to Denis Goacher, 10 Aug. 1954; unpublished letter to Simon Fraser University Special Collections, cat. no. 552/ 84; Watts, 256]. Afonso de Albuquerque and his Portuguese adventurers seized Goa and other territories on the west coast of India in 1510. Del Mar describes him debasing the coinage of Goa to obtain gold. "His professed object was to relieve a local dearth of coins . . . his real one to buy the gold which he might fail to plunder, and sell it (in Portugal) at cent per cent profit" [*HMS*, 388; 104:84].

239. **Orage**: [46:17; 80:322]. "The *New Age* traced the recession of power, away from the people into inner rooms inhabited by inner cliques" [*IMP*, xiv].

240. **Uncle George . . . Senate**: [74/433; 78/481; 80/509].

241. **"offensive, defensive"**: Said MVB: "With Nations who consider that their respective positions make it for their interest to bind themselves to mutual support . . . a treaty of alliance, offensive and defensive, is the usual mode by which that object is accomplished. But experience has greatly weakened the confident reliance of mankind on such safeguards. When the crisis arrrives it has been found that Nations are disposed to be governed by their apparent interests at the moment" [MVB, *Auto*, 485].

242. **"50 mocking birds . . .** : It was Dr. James Alexander of "Randolph's District" who wrote after Randolph's death: "The spring no longer coquets but embraces with Oriental voluptuousness. . . . Before breakfast, I counted fourteen species of birds known to me, and two unknown. There are about 50 mocking birds in and about this lawn, and 40 robins were counted on the grass at once" [Bruce, *Randolph*, II, 110-111].

243. **and "construe . . .** : John Marshall, chief justice of the Supreme Court, had to be operated on by a surgeon, who saved his life. Randolph in a speech afterwards said how glad he was that the surgeon "has restored the Chief Justice to his health, to his friends, to his country and to his seat on the bench of the supreme court where God knows he ought never have been put. He is a great man and a good man . . . and yet, if he should be Chief Justice thirty years longer, he will construe our liberties away from us" [Bruce, *Randolph*, II, 194-195].

244. **Mazzini**: Giuseppe M., 1805-1872, Italian nationalist and revolutionary. Said Pound: "As a Cavourian I long neglected the writings of Mazzini." He then quotes approvingly from Mazzini's *Duties of Man* and finds there constructive ideas consistent with the basic concepts of Social Credit: "The distribution of the *credit* . . . should not be undertaken by the Government, nor by a National Central Bank; but, with a vigilant eye on the National Power, *by local Banks administered by elective Local Councils*" [Pound's italics; *SP*, 312].

245. **Doveri**: I, "duties." Part of title of Mazzini's book.

246. Κατὰ σφαγάς": H, "against slaughter." Mazzini did not agree with Cavour's plan to get foreign power, France in particular, involved in fighting for Italian unification. He believed in the revolution, but his program was political, deeply social, religious, and moral. He was against needless slaughter.

247. **N'Yoleanz . . . 16**: Source unknown,

but the lines seem to pose a moral question relating to the political struggles over the tariff: one of the issues was that the concentration of sugar in the syrup of New Orleans was only half that in the syrup from the West Indies.

248. Catron . . . : [cf. 48 above].

249. "Shd / have shot Clay: Years after his retirement from politics, Jackson talked about his life to some of his friends, who later reported the conversation to one of the president's biographers: "Jackson talked, and the other listened. He told them of his two principal regrets—that he had never had an opportunity to shoot Clay or to hang Calhoun" [Bowers, *Party Battles*, 480].

250. Antoninus: [78:56].

251. semina motuum: [90:24]. L, "seeds of movement."

252. Ideogram: Chi [M411], "changes, motions; the origin of, the moving power of—as of the universe" This character occurs in a passage from the *Ta Hsio* which Pound translated thus: "one humane family can humanize a whole state; one courteous family can lift a whole state into courtesy; one grasping and perverse man can drive a nation to chaos. Such are the seeds of movement [*semina motuum*, the inner impulses of the tree]. That is what we mean by: one word will ruin the business, one man can bring the state to an orderly course" [80/500; *CON*, 59-60].

253. the old hawk: A friend of Jackson wrote to MVB in 1859 telling him about a siege Nicholas Biddle organized against Jackson during the war of the bank in the mid-1830s: "I spent the month of August . . . with the President at the Rip Raps. . . . Biddle had planned a most insidious mode of reaching him in this isolated spot. . . . He had organized a sort of siege . . . in the shape of letters entreating a surrender of the design of removing the Deposits [37:76]. In a word no man was ever so overwhelmed with such a deluge" [MVB, *Auto*, 607].

254. Mr Biddle . . . baby: Of the bank's insolvency of 1841, THB says: "The losses to the stockholders were deplorable, and in many instances attended with circumstances which aggravated the loss. Many were widows and children, their all invested where it was believed to be safe" [*TYV*, II, 369].

255. mr cummings: e. e. C., 1849-1962, American poet whose work Pound admired.

256. "Yes, Mr Van Buren . . . : MVB tells of visiting Jackson after his (MVB's) return from England and finding him "stretched on a sick-bed . . . but as always a hero in spirit." Then he says: "Holding my hand in one of his own and passing the other thro' his long white locks he said . . . 'the bank, Mr. Van Buren, is trying to kill me, but I will kill it!' " [MVB, *Auto*, 625].

257. Mr Taney's statement: [37:76]. Mr. Taney said in effect that the bank and its directors were able to use the money of depositors and the money of the government and public for their private purposes without public accountability of any kind. Said MVB: "Mr. Taney's statement was never refuted either by the bank or by its supporters in Congress, but, on the contrary, not only was a challenge . . . to go into the investigation of its truth declined but the investigation itself was . . . refused thro' the action of the friends of the bank" [ibid., 644]. MVB goes on to show how the bank used public funds to publish the bank's praises "avowedly for electioneering purposes." The government proposed an accounting should be made: "This proposition . . . was promptly voted down. . . . This took place in August 1833" [ibid., 648-649].

258. And as to expunging? . . . : The Senate passed a resolution of censure against Jackson, implying ciminality. Jackson responded by a letter of protest to be read before the Senate, which the Senate refused to hear. Great excitement ensued, which resulted in a motion to receive the protest. Having had about enough, THB moved that "The Expunging Resolution," ordering the original censure resolution be "expunged from the journals of the Senate" be adopted. The original resolution was adopted March 28, 1834. Benton offered his motion at each session of the Senate until, on January 14, 1837, it was finally passed at night in an atmosphere of great drama: "As the darkness of approaching night came on, and the great chandelier was lit up, splendidly illuminating the chamber, then crowded with the members of the House, and the lobbies and galleries filled to their utmost capacity by visitors and spectators, the scene became grand and impressive." Clay, Calhoun, and Webster indulged in the oratorical fireworks few but they could muster, but to no avail: "Midnight was now approaching . . . Mr. Webster concluded. No one rose. There was a pause, a dead silence, and an intense feeling." The question was called and passed. One part of the gallery was filled with henchmen of the bank, "sullen and menacing in their looks." Drama became danger, and firearms were brought in. "The presiding officer . . . gave the order to clear the gallery." Benton opposed the order, saying, "I hope the galleries will not be cleared, as many innocent persons will be excluded. . . . Let the ruffians who have made the disturbance alone be punished . . . seize the bank ruffians." Benton's demand was acted upon: "The ringleader was seized, and brought to the bar. This sudden example intimidated the rest; and the expunging process was performed in quiet." And so ended one chapter in the wars of the bank [*TYV*, I, 528-550, 717-731].

259. Securing . . . in 'elect: Daniel Webster in 1833, looking forward to becoming president in the next election, decided that forming an alliance with Jackson would be his best ploy. He thought they'd make a good team. Webster seemed to think he was "admirably qualified for a great adviser." Jackson's "heart to execute" would be abetted by "the majesty of his [Webster's] intellect" [MVB, *Auto*, 687-690]. Since there is no mention of Dante in the sources, nor evidence that either Webster or Jackson had read him, and since part of Webster's ploy was to assist Jackson in the next election, "Dante" is prob. a typo for "Dan'el."

260. "No . . . Knittl: Prob. John Knittel, 1891-1970, a prolific writer who lived in England 1910-1912. The quote about Russia is attributed in *Orientamenti* to a conversation with "the novelist Knitl." Pound wrote in *Meridiano di Roma* [7 June 1942]: "certainly the great civilizations are monuments and splendid and leave monuments because they have marble" [BK]. By this measurement, Russia, with "no stone," has no chance [97:259].

261. (Hrooshia): Russia [103:82].

262. Make distress . . . : In 1841, THB spoke against the repeal of the Independent Treasury Act, which would put the monetary power back in the hands of the banks: "the architects of the mischief–the political, gambling, and rotten part of the banks, headed by the Bank of the United States, and aided by a political party–set to work to make panic and distress, to make suspensions and revulsions, to destroy trade and business, to degrade and poison the currency; to harass the country until it would give them another national bank: and to charge all the mischief they created upon the democratic administration" [*TYV*, II, 228].

263. "The angrier . . . : Meigs writes: "All agree that he [Benton] was a terrible man in anger, but while some say that on such occasions he grew almost beside himself and became the helpless victim of his fury, both Wentworth and Dyer think that the higher his anger the cooler he was and he never lost his self-possession" [Meigs, *Life of THB*, 487].

264. one "assumption": [69:67, 76, 82,83]: "About one half of the States had contracted debts abroad which they were unable to pay when due, and in many instances were unable to pay the current annual interest. These debts at this time [1839] amounted to one hundred and seventy millions of dollars, and were chiefly due in Great Britain." Benton was against a proposal for the federal government to assume the debt: "We have had one assumption in our country . . . [and that] was attended by such evils as should deter posterity from imitating the example" [*TYV*, II, 171-175]. Benton opposed the "Assumption of the State Debts" and the measure did not pass.

265. English debt . . . posterity: In a speech against assumption, Benton said: "What is more unwise and more unjust than to contract debts on long time . . . thereby invading the rights and mortgaging the resources of posterity, and loading unborn generations with debts not their own? . . . The British national debt owes its existence entirely to this policy. It was but a trifle in the beginning of the last century, and might have been easily paid during the reigns of the first and second George; but the policy was . . . to pay the interest annually, and send down the principal to posterity" [ibid., 175].

266. "EXPUNGED": Over 20 years earlier, Jesse Benton, brother of Thomas Hart Benton, with the encouragement of gossip provoked Jackson into threatening to horsewhip him. On Sept 4, 1813, they met in a barroom in Nashville. Jackson went for him, "brandishing his whip," saying, "Now, defend yourself you damned rascal!" THB, then a colonel, came from the corridor and saw "Jackson's gun at his [brother's] breast." He whipped out his own gun and fired: "Jackson pitched forward, firing. . . . Thomas Benton fired twice at the falling form of Jackson and Jesse lunged forward to shoot again . . . . Jackson's wounds soaked two mattresses with blood. . . . He was nearly dead—his left shoulder shattered by a slug, and a ball embedded against the upper bone of the arm" [James, *Jackson*, 153]. Later on, when Benton was battling for Jackson as President, another "expunging" took place: "the President had to submit to a surgical operation for the extraction of the bullet which he had carried in his left arm ever since the time of the Benton affray, in Nashville, twenty years before. . . . The doctor made a bold incision into the flesh, gave the arm a squeeze, and out jumped the ball upon the floor." Parton says, "My informant does not state whether the General restored the ball to its rightful owner [Jesse Benton] or his representative [THB]" [Parton, *Life of Andrew Jackson*, III, 415-416].

267. I want Frémont . . .: Says THB: "[In August, 1842] attended by four of his men, he [Frémont] climbed the loftiest peak of the Rocky Mountains" [*TYV*, II, 478-479].

268. Reck: Michael R., who visited Pound often during the St. Elizabeths years, wrote: "In June 1954, I visited Fenollosa's grave at the Miidera, a temple overlooking Lake Biwa near Kyoto. . . . Fenollosa lies in a clearing among the trees, Biwa gracefully beneath: a stone urn resting on a concrete base. . . . I described my visit in a letter to Pound, and he recorded it in the last line of his Canto 89" [Reck, *Close-up*, 174-175].

CANTO XC

Sources

J. P. Migne, *Patrologiae Latina*, Tomus 196: *Opera Omnia Richardi A Sancto Victore; De praeparatione animi ad contemplationem (Benjamin Minor); De gratia contemplationis (Benjamin Major)* [Migne, column no.]; Luke 7.47; Dante, *Par.* I, 75; EP, *CON*, 179-181; Thaddeus Zielinski, "The Sibyl," *Edge*, no. 2, 1956; Juan Ramon Jimenez, *Animal de Fondo*, Buenos Aires, Editorial Pleamar, 1949; Ovid, *Meta.* V, 600 ff.

Background

EP, *SP*, 71-72; EM, *Difficult*, 306, ff.; CE *Ideas*, 109-113; Dekker, *The Cantos of Ezra Pound*, 74-86 [*Cantos*]; DD, *Sculptor*, 208-213; EH, *Approaches*, 25-27, 164-165, passim; CB-R, *ZBC*, 132, 203-204; Juan Ramon Jimenez, *Libros de Poesia*, Aguilar, 1959 [*Libros*].

Exegeses

D. J. Neault, *Pai*, 3-2, 219-227; WB, *Approaches*, 311; NS, *Exile*, 23-26; HK, *Gnomon: Essays on Contemporary Literature*, New York, 1958, 280-297; JW, *Pai*, 2-2, 178; DG, *Pai*, 3-2, 239-244; HK, *Era*, 368; MB, *Trace*, 259-277.

Glossary

1. **Animus . . . procedit**: L, "The human soul is not love, but love flows from it, and it delights not in the idea of itself but in the love which flows from it" [Richard of St. Victor, *Quomodo Spiritus sanctus est amor Patris et Filii* (Migne, 1012B); cf. DJN, *Pai*, 3-2, 222].

2. **"From the colour . . .** : Reference to the doctrine of signatures of John Heydon [87:82]. Just as the color, shape, and size of item and leaf are aspects of the "signature" of a particular plant, so "love" or the "ability to love," is the signature of the "soul" or the mark of the divine in man [WB, *Approaches*, 311].

3. **Ygdrasail**: [Yggdrasil]: The great ash tree in Eddic mythology [85:6]. Its roots reached to the center of the earth, and its branches supported the Heavens. It contained and expressed the universe.

4. **Baucis**: From a myth of gods disguised to test the charity of people by seeking food and drink. They were refused by all except Baucis and her husband Philemon, who gave them what they had. The gods flooded other houses away but transformed their cottage into a temple and granted Baucis and Philemon their wish to serve as keepers. Years later they were metamorphosed into two trees that grew twined together. A rhyme with the pines at Takasago and Ise [4:22, 23].

5. **Castalia**: A fountain dedicated to Apollo on Mr. Parnassus at Delphi. Pilgrims to the oracle purified themselves there. The various temples and shrines were built in niches cut

into the side of the mountain. Over all a great cliff beetles above a deep recess that seems like a fold in the mountain, whence the waters of Castalia flow. Known as the fount of poetic inspiration.

6. **Templum aedificans**: L, "Building the temple."

7. **"Amphion!"**: Son of Zeus. Hermes taught him to play the lyre so well that when he became king of Thebes he fortified the city with a wall magically conjured up by his music: at the sound of his lyre the stones moved into place by themselves.

8. **Ideogram**: San [M5415], "three"; Ideogram: ku [M3470], "alone." The San Ku was an inner council in ancient China. Pound associated it with the Eleusinian tradition that culminated in the Order of the Templars. It was a sort of Masonic council with an initiation rite called the Widow's Son, "which is also to be found in some of the Romance literature of the Middle Ages and in the modern Masonic ritual" [NS, *Exile*, 23-26]. [87:75].

9. **Poitiers**: Town in W central France. The reference is to a particular room in the town's Hotel de Ville ("once part of the home of Duke William IX of Aquitaine," [JW]), so constructed that one does not cast a shadow when standing in it [6:1, 2; 76:77].

10. **Sagetrieb**: "Passing on the tradition" from father to son, or transmitting civilization from one generation to the next [85:194]. In this context, the passing on by priests of the secrets of the Eleusinian mysteries.

11. **Jacques de Molay**: [87:77]. Last grand master of the Order of Templars, who was burnt at the stake for heresy. The Templars were associated with the Masons. The Golden Section of Pythagoras informs the concept of proportions [DD, *Pai*, 1-1, 58].

12. **Erigena**: Scotus E. [36:9; 74:90; 85:53]. The line suggests, "Was not Erigena also a member of the brotherhood of Eleusis?"

13. **Kuthera**: L, Aphrodite. She was called Kuthera because the island of Cythera (now Kythera) was sacred to her.

14. **δεινά**: H, "terrifying" or "fear-inspiring."

15. **sempiterna**: L, "everlasting."

16. **Ubi . . . oculus**: L, "Where love is, there is the eye" [Richard of St. Victor, *Benjamin Minor*, 13; DG, *Pai*, 2-3, 500; DJN, *Pai*, 2-3, 501; cf. 1 above].

17. **Vae qui cogitatis inutile**: L, "Woe to you who think without purpose." Pound correlates the three states, Hell, Purgatory, and Paradise, with Richard's three levels of intellectual activity. *Cogitatio*, in which "the mind flits aimlessly about the object" [*GK*, 77], is "a haphazard improvident looking about" [*Pai*, 2-3, 500-501]. "Woe" suggests the Hell-direction of those who do purposeless thinking. *Meditatio* correlates with Purgatory and *comtemplatio* with mystic and visionary aspirations for Paradise.

18. **quam in nobis . . . imago**: L, part of a sentence that correctly reads: "Bona voluntatis per quam in nobis divinae similitudinis imago reperietur," Pound translated it as: "The good things of will, through which an image of the divine likeness will be found in us" [*SP*, 71].

19. **Randolph**: John R. of Roanoke, Va., who "loved much," as the Greek in the next line reads [87:10]. His love of mankind led him to free his slaves by wills and several codicils between 1819 and 1831: "I give my slaves their freedom to which my conscience tells me they are justly entitled" [Bruce, *Randolph*, Vol. II, 49].

20. **ἠγάπησεν πολύ**: H, "she loved much." From the New Testament story of Jesus being tested by Simon the Pharisee [Luke 7.47]. While Jesus "sat at meat" at Simon's house, a woman who was a sinner "brought an alabaster box of ointment" and "began to wash his feet with tears, and did wipe them with the hairs of her head . . . and annointed them with the ointment." Simon thought

that if Jesus were really a prophet he would have known what the woman was and would not have allowed her to come near him. Knowing what was in Simon's heart, Jesus told the story of the creditor who had two debtors, one who owed much and one who owed little. The creditor, finding neither had money to pay, forgave them both. Jesus asked, "Tell me therefore, which of them will love him most?" Simon gave the right answer and Jesus then compared his actions with those of the sinner and concluded, "wherefore I say unto thee, her sins, which are many, are forgiven; for she loved much; but to whom little is forgiven, the same loveth little." The Greek phrase is thematic to this central Paradiso canto, the first half of which concerns the various ways divinity manifests itself through love: the woman's love is "a good thing of will" flowing from the soul, as was the love of Randolph in his act of manumission.

21. **liberavit masnatos**: L, "he freed his slaves." An act of humanitarian compassion which rhymes with that of Cunizza da Romano, who freed her slaves. The Latin phrase is also applied to her [6:34; 29:14].

22. **Castalia**: [cf. 5 above].

23. **Evita**: Prob. Eva Perón, wife of Juan P. then dictator of Argentina; but poss. Eva Braun, the mistress, consort, or companion of Hitler. While Pound was writing parts of this canto, *Life* magazine carried a picture of a breadline in Washington just at the time the Marshall Plan, with billions of dollars for Europe, was being announced. Eva Perón's response was to organize "a drive in Argentina for the poor *gringos* of the North" [EM, *Difficult*, 306]. The story, promoted by Lampman [97:60], caused Pound great amusement.

24. **semina motuum**: L, "seeds of motion." This Latin tag is used as a musical figure to express one of the most important religious concepts of *The Cantos*,–and one of the dimensions in which the mysterium is perceived similarly in both the East and the West. The good things of will (*directio voluntatis*) [77:57] flow from the soul as perceived by Richard of St. Victor, a Christian mystic, but Pound found a similar idea expressed by Confucius in the *Analects*. A few fragments of Tsze Tze's Third Thesis climax: "He who possesses this sincerity does not lull himself to somnolence. . . . Fulfilling himself he attains full manhood. . . . The inborn nature begets this activity naturally, this looking straight into oneself and thence acting. These two activities constitute the process which unites outer and inner . . . and thence constitutes a harmony with the seasons of earth and heaven. . . . Hence the highest grade of this clarifying activity has no limit, it neither stops nor stays. Not coming to a stop, it endures; continuing durable, it arrives at the minima [the seeds whence movement springs]. From these hidden seeds it moves forth slowly but goes far and with slow but continuing motion it penetrates the solid, penetrating the solid it comes to shine forth on high" [EP, *CON*, 179-181; see also *CON*, 59 and 89:252].

25. **Sibylla**: The all-seeing priestess of the oracle at Delphi. For a number of years Pound tried to get "The Sibyl" by Thaddeus Zielinski translated into English. It was finally finished and published in 1956 as the 2d number of *Edge*. The sibyl is mainly a prophetess but seems also to function as an intercessor [97:160]. Sheri Martinelli is understood to be the real-life sibyl at St. Elizabeths.

26. **m'elevasti**: I, "you lifted me up" [adapted from *Par*. I, 75], praise which Dante lovingly attributes to Beatrice.

27. **Erebus**: The dark place through which souls must pass on the way to Hades.

28. **Isis**: In Egyptian mythology, Isis, the earth goddess, was the wife of Osiris, god of the sun and the Nile–in which form he visited her as flooding water. Isis correlates with Ishtar, Demeter, and Ceres as the goddess of grain, renewal, and compassion. In the myth, she gathered up the limbs of Osiris and restored the god of light under Ra to his power. Early in his career Pound wrote a

series of articles that together are called, "I gather the Limbs of Osiris." They appeared in *New Age*, Dec. 7, 1911-Feb. 15, 1912 [*SP*, 21-43]. Here, at a particularly dramatic moment in *The Cantos*, Pound brings a key element in Western myth together in one image with the compassionate bodhisattva of the East, Kuanon.

29. **Kuanon**: [74:81].

30. **the blue serpent**: The uraeus, or blue cobra: the emblem of the sacred serpent in the headdress of Egyptian divinities. At this time Pound's interest in Egyptian analogues for his canto themes led Sheri Martinelli (the most immediate motivation for Canto 90) to do a painting entitled "Isis of the Two Kingdoms" [*Pai*, 3-2, 240]. About this painting David Gordon wrote: "Here is the faintly blue serpentine cobra just below the sun-disc of this composite Egyptian and Chinese goddess of compassion: 'the natural object is always the adequate symbol.' And it is she herself who is lifting the protagonist from the dust" [DG, *Pai*, 3-2, 241]—and from the dust to one of the most dramatic paradisal visions of the poem. Here the musical leitmotif "aram vult nemus" ("the grove needs its altar"), sounded several times earlier, [74:441; 78:91; 79:126] receives visionary fulfillment. Beginning with the viper and the blue serpent, all nature answers the call and comes from the depths of the ocean and out of the earth to the grove, where smoke and bright flame rise from the altar. Just as Dionysus at the moment of declaring his godhead evoked a furry assemblage out of the air [2/7-9]—lynx, leopard, and panther—so in the following lines the hieratic animals answer the call.

31. **lamps float**: Ceremony celebrating the death of Adonis. Every July at Rapallo, "votive lights [were] set adrift in the Golfo di Tigullio for the festival of Montallegre Madonna." EP associated it with primitive rites to Tammuz-Adonis [HK, *Era*, 368; 47:7].

32. **"De fondo"**: S, "of the depths."

33. **Juan Ramon**: J. R. Jimenez, 1881-1958, Spanish poet from Andalusia who received the Nobel Prize for Literature in 1956 while in Puerto Rico. The death of his father (which be observed in 1900) was a great trauma from which he never freed himself. During the remainder of his life, he traveled a lot and lived in the U.S., Puerto Rico, and Cuba. He lectured in Argentina in 1948. Returning to the U.S. by ship, he had the intense mystical experience that he tried to evoke in *Animal de Fondo* (1949). In this book, his obsession with nothingness and the fear of death, symbolized in earlier books by various sea and ocean metaphors, is resolved. *Animal de Fondo* is filled with joy, mystical aspirations, and the union of the "inner" and "outer" selves, realized by a perception of spirit as beauty, ecstasy, and light. Poem 29 in this volume ("Soy animal de fondo") is the immediate source of Pound's imagery [Jimenez, *Libros*, p. 1339].

34. **Castalia**: [Cf. 5 above]. Castalia was a water nymph who, pursued by Apollo, leaped into the spring at Delphi which bears her name. A rhyme with the myth of Arethusa.

35. **Arethusa**: A water nymph in the service of Diana [Ovid, *Meta*. V, 600 ff.]. As with Daphne [2:26] Pound changes some details in the myth. Arethusa, bathing naked in a still stream, inspired lust in a water-god, who pursued her. She fled far, but finally, feeling his heavy panting on her hair, she called for help to Diana, who spirited her into the earth so she could escape and brought her to light again as a fountain in Sicily. The poplars and willows of the source are changed to the elms of the lawn of St. Elizabeths, and Arethusa is seen as a lone nymph.

36. **Wei and Han**: Two Chinese rivers which join. This rhymes with the Arethusa myth: as a fountain Arethusa flowed together with the water-god Alpheus.

37. **Richardus**: Among the "gists" from Richard of St. Victor [85:52] Pound gives one that translates, "watch birds to understand how spiritual things move, animals to understand physical motion" [*SP*, 71]. The

free-flowing waters suggest the way thought ought to flow in the unburdened mind [DJN, *Pai*, 3-2, 225].

38. Gaio! . . . : I, "merry, merry."

39. rilievi: I, "reliefs." In sculpture.

40. Faunus: L, "woodland sprite." The Italian Pan.

41. sirenes: L, "sirens." Female sea-nymphs.

42. stone taking form: a rhyme with Dionysus's creation of the sacred cats "out of nothing" with "void air taking pelt" [2/8]. Here we have the vision of Zeus creating the stone altar of the grove out of the air in sculptured relief, as Amphion [cf. 7 above] called the stone walls into being with his lyre.

43. ac ferae: L, "and wild beasts."

44. cervi: L, "deer."

45. Pardus: L, "panther."

46. leopardi: I, "leopards" or "jaguars."

47. Bagheera: The name of the black panther in Kipling's *Jungle Book*; he educates Mowgli, the boy brought up by a wolf (*bagh* means "tiger" in Urdu).

48. *ἐπὶ χθονί*: H, "around [or "on"] the earth."

49. *οἱ χθόνιοι*: H, "spirits of the underworld." The spirit nature of the voices is indicated by the various butterfly wings [48:42, 50, 53; 113/788]

50. Palatine: One of the great hills of Rome.

51. pineta: I, "pinewood."

52. *χελιδών*: H, "swallow." An echo of l. 429 of *The Waste Land* and the Philomela of *Pervigilium Veneris*.

53. Corpus: L, "Body." Evokes rhyme with the church festival and procession on Corpus Christi day, the first Thursday after Trinity Sunday.

54. Erebus: Dark place in the netherworld. After the incantation, we have a vision of souls being delivered out of Hades and rising up out of the earth.

55. Tyro: Daughter of Salmoneus who became enamored with the divine river [2:12].

56. Alcmene: [Alcmena]: Wife of Jupiter and mother of Hercules.

57. e i cavalieri: I, "and the chevaliers, or cavalry."

58. *Ἠλέκτρα*: H, "Electra." Daughter of Agamemnon and Clytemnestra. Clytemnestra became the paramour of Aegisthus while Agamemnon was away at the Trojan War. After Clytemnestra murdered her husband, Electra joined with her brother Orestes to murder her mother.

59. Trees die & the dream remains: According to Sheri Martinelli, this line was evoked by a thought of Juan Ramon Jimenez [cf. 33 above]. Pound was struck by a line something like, "Love dies but the trees remain." Going a step beyond his own "What thou lovest well remains, the rest is dross" [81/521], it prompted him to "make it new" and evoke the dream, which for him is the vision still of *paradiso terrestre*.

60. ex animo: L, "from the soul."

61. UBI AMOR . . . : [Cf. 16 above].

CANTO XCI

Sources

Jean Beck, *Die Melodien der Troubadours und Trouvers*; Philostratus, *Life of Apollonius of Tyana*, trans. F. C. Conybeare (Loeb Classical library) [Apollonius]; L. A. Waddell, *Egyptian Civilization, Its Sumerian Origin*, London, 1930; Boris de Rachewiltz, *Papiro Magico Vaticano*, Rome, 1954, and *Massime degli antichi Egiziani*, Milan, 1954; John Heydon, *The Holy Guide*, 1662; Homer, *Odyssey* [*Od.*]; Dante, *Paradiso* [*Par.*]; José-Maria de Heredia, "Antoine et Cleopatre"; Horace, *Carmina* [*Carm.*]; Layamon, *Brut*, ed. Sir Frederick Madden, 3 vols., London, 1847; Julien Benda, *La trahison des clercs*, Paris, B. Grasset, 1927; Richard of St. Victor, *Tractatus de Gradibus Charitatis*; G. Cavalcanti, "Sonnet XVII"; Juan Ramon Jimenez, *Animal de Fondo*, Buenos Aires, 1949.

Background

EP, "Psychology and Troubadours," *SR*, 87-100; "Neo-Platonicks etc.," *GK*, 222-226; "Kulchur: Part One," *GK*, 127-132; *LE*, 150-155; *NPL*, 157; *SP*, 45, 53; *Instigations*, 62; NS, *Ezra Pound's Pennsylvania*, Toledo, Ohio, 1976; Gianfranco Ivancich, *Ezra Pound in Italy*, New York, Rizzoli, 1978; G.R.S. Mead, *The Doctrine of the Subtle Body*, London, 1919 [*Doctrine*]; John Read, *Through Alchemy to Chemistry*, London, 1957 [*Alchemy*]; Timothy Materer, *Vortex, Pound, Eliot, and Lewis*, Ithaca, N.Y. 1979, 184-197; E. A. Wallis Budge, *The Book of the Dead*, New York, Bell, 1960.

Exegeses

EH, *Pai*, 1-2, 272; HK, *Pai*, 2-2, 332-334; Peck, *Pai*, 1-1, 14, 21, 36; Surette, *Pai*, 2-3, 419-421; DD, *Sculptor*, 217-232; CFT, *Pai*, 2-3, 449-471; J. D. Neault, "Apollonius of Tyana," *Pai*, 4-1, 3-54; WB, "Secretary of Nature, J. Heydon," in EH, *Approaches*, 303-318; CB-R, "Lay Me by Aurelie," in EH, *Approaches*, 253-271, and *ZBC*, 185-203; JW, *Pai*, 2-2, 175-191, and *Later*, 83-101; MB, *Trace*, 278-302.

Glossary

1. **ab lo . . . vai**: P, "with the sweetness that comes to my heart." Conflation of several troubadour lines into one. Pound changed both the words and the music of his sources, so that we read "my heart" instead of "his heart" [HK, *Pai*, 2-2, 333-335]. Note the articulation with several important vortex-image metaphors: (1) the music of Janequin's birds [75/450]; (2) the numerous notations of birds on wires in different config-

urations throughout the *Pisan Cantos*; and (3) the new emphasis given to birds as metaphors for the spirit, drawn from Richard of St. Victor [90:37].

2. **the body of light**: The "tensile light" descending. The primal Neoplatonic light—the divine principle, or "the total light process—which manifests as intelligence in man [74:100]. With the word "body," Pound brings into *The Cantos* more specific allusions to the mystical symbolism of the alchemists as set forth in the summary work of G. R. S. Mead, *The Doctrine of the Subtle Body* [*Doctrine*]. Mead's work in the mystery religions covered a lifetime and was set forth in many volumes, such as *Simon Magus*, 1892,; *Thrice-greatest Hermes*, 3 vols., 1906; *Mysteries of Mithra*, 1907; and *Chaldaean Oracles*, 2 vols., 1908. *The Doctrine of the Subtle Body* is a brief work (109 pp.) which concentrates his theories in chapters entitled "The Spirit Body," "The Radiant-Body," and "The Resurrection-Body." Neoplatonists who occur often in the Pound canon are the subjects of detailed study by Mead: Orpheus, Porphyry, Psellos, Iamblicus, Hermes Trismegistus, John Heydon [*GK*, 225]. In "Psychology and Troubadours" (first published in Mead's journal *Quest*, then in *The Spirit of Romance*), Pound wrote [*SR*, 91n.]: "Let me admit at once that a recent lecture by Mr. Mead on Simon Magus has opened my mind to a number of new possibilities [cf. 10 below]. Later Pound came to speak of Mead as "Old Krore" [*GK*, 225] and certainly didn't accept any of his ideas about "resurrection body" after death, but Mead provided rhymes with the image Pound used from light-philosophers in the Neoplatonic tradition, which presumes a body of divine fire to be the procreative source of all life in both the macrocosm and the microcosm. Mead, using the ancient myth of a tree as an image of the total universe [cf. rhyme with Yggdrasil, 90:3], says: "Hidden in the seed of the tree is the principle (*ratio*, *logos*) of the tree. This is the formative power (*virtus, dynamis*) in the seed, the spermatic principle, which is called symbolically in Greek spintherismos . . . [which] means, literally, 'emission of sparks,' 'sparking,' 'Light-spark,' or light-emanation,' . . . [this spermatic principle] is used by a number of Gnostic schools as a symbolic expression for the 'germ' of the spritual man" [*Doctrine*, 84-85]. Quoting from the Stoics, Pound wrote: "From god the creative fire, went forth spermatic logoi" [*GK*, 128]. About a Hellenistic work admired by both Porphyry and Proclus, Mead says: "this famous poem sets forth a highly mystical doctrine concerning the nature of the subtle body . . . and purports to reveal the mystery of the divine paternal fire and the secret of the life of the great mother . . . a doctrine of the living fire and all its works" [*Doctrine*, 22-23]. Speaking of the chief document of the "Simonian [Simon the Magus] school" called *Great Announcement*, Mead says it "presents us with a highly developed doctrine of the divine fire and of the tree of life . . . entirely in keeping with the subtle body theory of psychical alchemy" [*Doctrine*, 24].

3. **the body of fire**: Helios, Apollo, the source of divinity or the operating intelligence in the created universe—in man and nature [5:10]. Speaking of how the essence of spirit and the divinity that were manifest in the works of early painters became lost in the carnality of Renaissance painting, Pound said: "The people are corpus, corpuscular, but not in the strict sense 'animate,' it is no longer the body of air clothed in the body of fire; it no longer radiates, light no longer moves from the eye" [*LE*, 153].

4. **your eyes . . . sunken**: A metaphor of eyes as the window of the "radiant divinity" buried deep within the human "persona" ("soul" and "body" cannot be used lest an endless number of sectarian or dogmatic associations, not intended, be evoked) [81:54]. Said Pound: "We have about us the universe of fluid force, and below us the germinal universe of wood alive, of stone alive. Man is . . . a mechanism rather like an electric appliance" [*SR*, 92]. Tracing parallels between electric phenomena and the contact of one human psyche and another,

in which "a spark will leap," he goes on to pose "a possibly subtler form of energy," which leads to ideas about "chivalric love" and sex, which in turn returns us to the divine fire and the body of light. "Sex is . . . of a double function . . . or, as we see in the realm of fluid force, one sort of vibration produces at different intensities, heat and light" [*SR*, 94]. The water images here and through the rest of this canto have rhymes in alchemical mysticism, in which the moon and water express the female principle, whereas the sun and fire express the male; but often in a wider sense the sphere of water connotes the ambience of the spirit. Mead says of the myth of souls imprisoned in the flesh: "they lose the direct vision they previously enjoyed . . . their bodies are now 'watery sphere,' and their organs of vision 'windows not eyes' [*Doctrine*, 40]. Says Pound: "Let us say quite simply that light is a projection from the luminous fluid, from the energy that is in the brain, down along the nerve cords which receive certain vibrations in the eye. Let us suppose man capable of exteriorizing a new organ, horn, halo, Eye of Horus" [*NPL*, 154]. Says Read: "Hermes Trismegistus, the patron of alchemy and alleged father of the Hermetic Art, was the Greek equivalent of the Egyptian god, Thoth, the personification of wisdom. The Egyptian triad, Osiris, Isis, and Horus, were all endowed with alchemical attributes. Osiris, the Sun-god, was a symbol of the active, masculine principle and vivifying force; Isis, the Mood-goddess [90:28], passive and fertile, bore an earthly significance; Horus, their annual offspring, was an image of the infant year and the process of growth and multiplication" [*Alchemy*, 62]. But "earthly" included the four elements, earth, water, air, and fire. Of these, fire and water had to combine with earth and air to give the combinations hot-dry, hot-moist, cold-dry, cold-moist, which were the qualities in various degrees of all creation. "The deep" in these lines leads in many directions: to the deepest reaches of the self, as well as to the waters of primal chaos. It metamorphoses into other forms in this canto: crystal and flowing crystal as well as the medium by which the golden sun-boat traverses the underworld to be reborn and made new [cf. 28 below].

5. Reina: Prob. the goddess Aphrodite, whom Pound wanted restored to her pedestal at Terracina (near Circeo), as well as a generalized epithet for "Isis-Persephone-Demeter-Kuanon." It links also with a poem by Bernart de Ventadorn composed for Eleanor of Aquitaine ("can vei la lauzeter mover," "When I see the lark on the wing"), in which the poet speaks of "the eyes of Eleanor as the mirrors in which the poet drowns, like Narcissus drowning in the pool that reflects his image" [EH, *Pai*, 1-2, 272].

6. qui laborat, orat: L, "he who works, prays." Variant of Latin tag *Orare est laborare*: "To work is to pray."

7. Undine: [Ondine]: Mythical sea-creature with sirenlike magical attraction for men, but "symbolically the inverse of sirens: in the latter, the fishy part of their body . . . [relates them to] the water (and the moon) and woman; with undines, it is the feminine—or perilous—nature of the waters which is symbolized" [Cirlot, 337]. When they are in the water, they may represent dangerous currents and torrents; when they are on a rock, the waters are placid.

8. Circeo: Town on the Ligurian coast of Italy near Terracina [74:208]. If the goddess were restored to her pedestal here (as Pound said he would do if he had the material means [*SP*, 53]), her stone eyes would again be looking seaward, and that would be "worth more than any metaphysical argument" [*SP*, 45].

9. Apollonius: A. of Tyana. A first-century mystic, man of wisdom, miracle-worker, and seer. A Pythagorean and a sun-worshipper [cf. 94 below; 94:42]. At the end of his trial [cf. 91-94 below], he metamorphosed into thin air, an act that rhymes with the transformation of Helen of Tyre by powers derived from Pythagoras. Said A. to the emperor, "Nay, you cannot even take my body." The source continues: "And with these words he vanished from the court" [*Apollonius*, Bk. VIII, chap. 5]. Thus, Apollonius.

10. Helen of Tyre: Pound wrote, "there would seem to be in the legend of Simon Magus and Helen of Tyre a clearer prototype of 'chivalric love' than in anything hereinafter discussed" [*SR*, 91]. Mead in his study entitled *Simon Magus*: *An Essay* [cf. 2 above] said of Helen of Troy that after the Trojan War she was changed by the angels into another form and "lived in a brothel in Tyre," where Simon Magus found her "and purchased her freedom" [Surette, *Pai*, 2-3, 419-421]. Pound lists her [*NPL*, 157] with "priestesses in the temple of Venus" and other female religious celebrants to support his thesis that sexuality and love are manifestations of the divine power in all nature including man, and that sexual congress, if so considered by the devotee, is a religious act. Such a belief contributed to the "mediterranean sanity" which he found in Provence: "I believe that a light from Eleusis persisted throughout the middle ages and set beauty in the song of Provence and Italy" [*SP*, 53]. Sex acts in the Eleusinian rites of initiation and celebration were conceived as acts of worship. Thus Pound says of "chivalric love" (which was by no means ascetic or platonic) that it "was, as I understand it, an art, that is to say, a religion" [*SR*, 87]. So Helen of Tyre takes her place among the servants of Aphrodite as a celebrant of the sanctity of love, a far better thing than the condition wrought by the usurers, who "brought whores for Eleusis" [45/230].

11. Pithagoras: [Pythagoras]: Greek philosopher of the 6th century B.C. His doctrines figure large in Neoplatonism. Pound values his ideas of order and usually lists him as one of the pre-Socratics in the tradition of Neoplatonism and the medieval philosophers of light and finds in their ideas rhymes with similar ones in Confucius [*GK*, 24, 25, 28, 121, 255, 333]. He used the "holy tetractys" of P. as an ordering or structural *forma* for the *Leopoldine*, *Chinese*, and *Adams* cantos. Mead said: "what we may call revived or Pythagorean Orphism spells already . . . a decided 'Oriental,' influence" [*Doctrine*, 40]. The final source of both Middle Eastern and Far Eastern esoteric doctrine was Indian.

12. Ocellus: O. Lucanus, Pythagorean philosopher of the 6th century to whom Pound attributes the phrase, "To build light" [87:43].

13. et libidinis expers: L, "and having no part in lust." Refers to the ascetic life of Helen of Tyre and the Pythagoreans. The phrase is in Lacharme's Latin description of the Confucian odes [59:6].

14. Justinian, Theodora: Justinian I, 483-565, Byzantine emperor, and his wife the Empress Theodora. Famous for codifying the laws and building the Hagia Sophia [65:126, 77:44, 94:45].

15. GREAT CRYSTAL: The great "acorn of light": Neoplatonic metaphor from Grosseteste's *de Luce*. The source of the primal creative force [74:249; 116/795]. It mirrors the pine as a reflection in water and thus doubles it. Pound found such ideas as paradigms of reality in Plato and the Platonists after him, who "have caused man after man to be suddenly conscious of the reality of the *nous*, of mind, apart from any man's individual mind, of the sea crystalline and enduring, of the bright as it were molten glass that envelops us, full of light" [*GK*, 44].

16. pensar . . . ripaus: P, "to think of her is my rest." From Arnaut's, "En breu brisral temps braus," which Pound translates: "Briefly bursteth season brisk" [*LE*, 135]. Connected with the "If I see her not" refrain [JW].

17. Miss Tudor: Elizabeth I, a historical figure who made a difference, as did Sigismundo, Justinian, and Theodora. It was the divine *nous* reflected in the depth of her eyes, the window of divinity flowing on in process, that animated Drake—referred to in "he saw it" [cf. 21 below].

18. compenetrans: L, "intensely penetrating."

19. Princess Ra-Set: Conflation of "two ancient Egyptian male divinities, Ra and Set . . . into a single female entity" [B de R, *Approaches*, 181], thus representing the full solar and lunar cycles. Ra, the sun-god, as good and Set, the moon-god, as evil. In the Osiris myth, Set, bound in chains by Horus, is liberated by Isis. Ra-Set thus connects with Isis-Kuanon [90:28]. The "cloud" in this passage has esoteric significance both sensual and spiritual. Says Mead: "Porphyry tells us that . . . souls who love the body attract a moist spirit to them, and condense it like a cloud (for the moist being condensed in air constitutes a cloud)" [*Doctrine*, 48].

20. convien . . . amando: I, "It is right that the mind should move by loving" [Par. XXVI, 34-35].

21. Drake: Sir Francis Drake, 1540-1596. The first Englishman to circumnavigate the globe. In the power struggle between Spain and England, Drake played a critical role. In 1587, he entered the port of Cadiz and destroyed the Spanish fleet there; in 1588, he was vice-admiral in the fleet that defeated the Armada. In him, the spirit of the Elizabethan age reached its height. A "luminous" persona who altered history.

22. ichor: H, "the fluid that flows in the veins of gods." An ethereal blood.

23. amor: L, "love." With "ichor" we have a metaphor: Love is not the soul but the divine fluid that flows from the soul [cf. 90:1]. Mead says, "Homer knew that blood was the food and aliment of spirit," and, "Diogenes Laërtius . . . attributes to Pythagoras the opinion 'that the *soul* is nourished by blood' " [*Doctrine*, 38n.].

24. J. Heydon: [90:2]

25. Apollonius: [Cf. 94 below].

26. Ocellus: [Cf. 12 above].

27. "to this khan": Source of quote unknown. A *khan* is an Oriental inn surrounding a courtyard, as well as the title of a ruler in Central Asia.

28. The golden sun boat: The vehicle by which the Egyptian sun-god Ra traversed the underworld during the night to reappear in the east at dawn, as set forth in the *Book of the Dead*. The journey is a rhyme with that of Helios [23:12-18].

29. Love moving . . . : Paraphrase of the last line of *The Divine Comedy*: "the Love which moves the sun and the other stars" [*Par*. XXXIII, 145].

30. *παρὰ βώμιον*: H, "beside the altar."

31. Tamuz!: The Babylonian name for the Dionysus-Bacchus-Zagreus-Adonis figure [74:12-15].

32. set lights now in the sea: Reference to the July celebration of the death of the vegetation god [90:31].

33. hide cocoons: Primitive vegetation rite, still practiced as part of Christian celebrations among old women on the Ligurian Coast.

34. hsien: [M2692]. "The tensile light" that flows from the divine [74:88]. A transliteration of the character beside it. The dualism of fire and light is repeated with fire connoting sensual experience and light, intelligence [cf. 2,3 above].

35. **Ἐλέναυς**: H, "Helen." Epithet for a number of great queens. Here, Elizabeth I.

36. Ra-Set: [Cf. 19 above]. Says Mead: "We find Porphyry elsewhere explaining the Egyptian symbolism of the boats or barques of the 'daimones' as being intended to represent not solid bodies, but the vehicles in which they 'sail on the moist' " [*Doctrine*, 47].

37. Queen's eye: In José-Maria de Heredia's *Antoine et Cléopatre*, Antony looked into Cleopatra's eyes and saw "Toute une mer immense où fuyient des galeres" ("A whole immense sea where galleons were fleeing); [Dekker, *Cantos*, 105].

38. ne quaesaris: L, "he asked not." EP's standard rendering of Horace's "ne quaesieris" [*Carm*. I, 11, 1], which he takes to mean unhesitating commitment [*SR*, 96].

39. He . . . hunting rite: The "he" is prob. the Trojan Brut of Layamon's *Brut*, who founded Albion after invoking the protection of Diana. Albion was the new Troy, a city of love associated with Montsegur. In Ur-Canto 3, Pound placed Layamon with Heydon.

40. sanctus: L, "holy" or "divine."

41. Leafdi . . . londe: OE, part of song sung to Diana by Brutus in Layamon's *Brut*: "Lady Diana, dear Diana / High Diana, help me in my need / Teach me through skill / where I might go / to a winsome land" [CB-R, *ZBC*, 190]. Brutus, great grandson of Aeneas, came to an island empty except for wild deer, where his men found a marble temple sacred to Diana. Unlike his men, Brutus was unafraid. He "entered the temple alone, with a vessel of red gold, full of milk from a white hind he had shot, and wine separately" [ibid.]. After an elaborate ritual, he uttered the prayer from which these lines are taken.

42. Rome th'ilke tyme was noght: OE, "Rome at this time was not [inhabited]." From Robert of Brunne [ibid.].

43. Lear: King Leir in Layamon.

44. Janus: Underworld god who rules the double gates of birth and death [47:10]. In Layamon, King Lear dies and is buried "inne Janies temple" (unlike his fate in Shakespeare).

45. Ideogram: Chên[4] [M315], "terrify, shake, or excite." Pound translates as, "timing the thunder."

46. Constance: Constantin the Fair, a monk of post-Roman Briton, brother of Aldroein of Britanny, who sends him to . . . the Britons who have asked for help. He is persuaded to "shed his hood" and become their king. Unable to govern, he is the victim of a plot and is beheaded. Vortiger, the crafty earl behind all these doings, becomes king. But he has trouble and loses his throne; he then asks for help from the Angles and Saxons, who thus come into the land.

47. Merlin's fader: Vortiger once fled to Wales, where he built a castle that kept falling down. A wise man told him that the clay needed "the blood of a man born of no father." He heard that the boy Merlin was "being taunted for having no father and a whore for a mother." Merlin's mother, who had become a nun, was sent for.

48. Lord, thaet scop the dayes lihte: OE, "Lord, who created the daylight." Slight modernization of a line from Aurelie's prayer before battle. Aurelie, the son of Constantin, was chosen by the people to be king after his father died [CB-R, *ZBC*, 190-194].

49. a spirit bright: Merlin's mother explained that she was the daughter of a king and that one night a fair figure "all clothed in gold" glided into her bedchamber and embraced her and afterwards she found she was with child [DG, *Pai*, 3-2, 242].

50. "By the white dragon . . . ": Merlin is sent for and explains that the castle keeps falling down because two dragons, red and white, fight at midnight under a stone beneath the castle. Merlin foretells that Aurelie will become king but will be poisoned.

51. Aurelie: Just before he dies from the poison, he makes a request. As translated by CB-R: "And lay me at the east end, in Stonehenge, where lie much of my kin." His brother, Uther, becomes king, and when he dies says (according to Pound), "Lay me by Aurelie." Uther is buried there.

52. And yilden . . . : OE, "And he began to rear gilds." An act attributed in Layamon to King Athelstan (924-940), who had peace guilds with judicial functions set up by the bishops and reeves of London. Not to be confused with later craft or trade guilds.

53. light . . . Ra-Set . . . crystal: [Cf. 36 above].

54. Sibile a boken isette: OE, "Sibyl set in a book." From the story of one Cadwalader, who had a vision. After his death, his wise men checked out his prophecy to see if it accorded with that of Merlin and Sibyl. They reported it did, saying, "Merlin said it in words, and Sibyl the wise set it in a book" [97:160].

55. ***kikery***: An opprobrious epithet Pound applies to usurers and financiers—who foster wars and depressions to make money—as well as to intellectuals in universities and the publishing world who appear to support them. Once, when asked how he could say he was not anti-Semitic when he used words such as "kike" and "kikery," he replied with some feeling: "There are Jew kikes and non-Jew kikes." Pound marked the passage in italics to be set in a somewhat smaller type: "carattere un poco piu piccolo" [MB, *Trace*, 296]. The passage is intended to rhyme with the 5 lines in *The Divine Comedy* where, at the summit of Paradise, St. Peter castigates "him who usurps my seat of earth" and says, "he has made of my burial place a cloaca of blood and filth" [*Par.* XXVII, 22-26]. Because there was no clear thought about the way divinity manifested in the world, such people as those listed allowed the inciting causes of WWI to operate in 1913. Marx and Freud need no glosses, but lest the reader jump to the wrong conclusion, see the index to *SP*, where Marx is listed 18 times and Freud 4. If one reads all Pound has said about Freud over the years, one concludes he has less quarrel with Freud than he does with Freudians, a rhyme with Christ and Christians or the Buddha and Buddhists [99:25]. Pound said: "People treated by Freudians, etc. get steadily more and more interested in their own footling interiors, and . . . less interesting to anyone else. . . . They are at the nadir from Spinoza's sane and hearty: the more perfect a thing is the more it acts and the less it suffers" [*NEW* May 2, 1935]. N.B.: The functional words in the 8 lines are, "no clear thought about holiness." A parallel to the unhappy custom of using racial epithets is found in Joyce's Leopold Bloom who, enraged by a money-lender named Dodd, said: "Now he's what you call a dirty jew." Dodd in fact wasn't a Jew and Bloom was [HK].

56. Maritain: Jacques M., 1882-1973, French philosopher who started out to be a scientist but changed to philosophy and wrote extensively on Thomism.

57. Hutchins: Robert Maynard H., 1899- , American educator famous for establishing novel degree requirements while chancellor of the University of Chicago. He championed intellectual attainment but is no hero to Pound.

58. Benda: Julien B., 1867-1956. French critic, novelist, and intellectual whose work Pound admired (fortunately Benda was a Jew). His *La trahison des clercs* [The treason of the intellectuals] (1927) contends that it is moral treason to deny intellectual freedom to political candidates. A rhyme with Mussolini's asserted credo: "freedom is not only a right, it is a duty."

59. "ecco il te": I, "here is the tea [74:488].

60. en calcaire . . . : F, "in limestone, forty-four steps." Reference to steps at the arena in Verona [4:48].

61. "Dodici Apostoli": I, "The Twelve Apostles." The name of one of the best restaurants in Verona.

62. (trattoria): "I, "restaurant."

63. putana: I, "prostitute." The affable "putana" at Verona wanted to change the spellings in Pound's edition of Cavalcanti's poems from the "Capitolare" ms.

64. Come . . . piccolo: I, "'How he resembles the martyr!' said the little boy." Prob. young Veronese boy thought Pound or someone resembled the martyr John the Baptist.

65. Battista martire: I, "Baptist, the martyr," applied to Battisti in 72 below.

66. Ortolo: I, "garden" [4:45].

67. San Zeno: I, "St. Zeno." The patron saint of Verona, he is buried at the finest

Romanesque church of northern Italy, San Pietro.

68. San Pietro: I, "St. Peter." The castle and church of St. Peter offer a magnificent panoramic view of Verona.

69. "quel naszhong": I, "what a nation." Remark in accent by French child upon seeing doors of San Zeno.

70. Ed: Edgar Williams, brother of the poet William Carlos Williams. In 1911 he was in Italy on an architectual scholarship and helped Pound find a column inscribed by the sculptor, "Adaminus." E. W. asked "how the hell *we* could have any architecture when we ordered our columns by the gross" [HK, *Era*, 323].

71. Nanni: A lawyer and journalist at Forli and one of the few socialists with whom Mussolini had maintained friendly relations since his youth. Torquato N. wrote the first full biographical sketch of Mussolini in 1924. But in 1934 Mussolini let his old friend be sent to prison for not bending to Fascist orthodoxy. Later he was restored to favor and became a member of Mussolini's in-group during the Salò Republic; he was among those who were captured and shot with him and his mistress, Clara Petacci, at Como in 1945.

72. Battista: Cesare Battisti. He ran a Socialist paper at Trent before WWI. When Mussolini was in Trent in 1909, he occasionally collaborated with Battisti by writing for the paper. Battisti was destined to die on the Austrian gallows for collaborating with the Italians in WWI. His fate influenced Mussolini to leave *Avanti!*, the official Socialist paper, and establish (Nov. 15, 1914) an "Intervention" paper: *Il Popolo d'Italia*: The Interventionists were a pro-Allied group in WWI.

73. Salò: The Salò Republic in Northern Italy, which Mussloini took over in 1943 as a subservient of Hitler after the fall of the Fascist government at Rome and his dismissal by King Emanuele III.

74. (Arpinati): Leandro A. One of the group captured with Mussolini during the attempted flight from Salò. Pound presumes he died in the manner described, but the historical data are ambiguous.

75. Farinata: F. degli Uberti [78:79]. "Pudg'd" prob. describes a statue.

76. Can Grande's grin: Can Grande della Scala, the great friend and patron of Dante. A statue of Can Grande in the square at Verona shows him with a very toothful smile. A photograph can be found in Ivancich, *Ezra Pound in Italy*.

77. Tommy Cochran: A boyhood friend who lived next door to Pound in Jenkintown. A photograph of the two sitting together can be seen in Stock's *Ezra Pound's Pennsylvania* [p. 24]. Can Grande's "grin" must have evoked a memory of a similar grin sported by Tommy Cochran when they were young. The same line appears in the *Pisan Cantos*, also associated with Farinata [78:79].

78. Plenod' alegreca: S, "full of mirth." the spelling may indicate a connotation of "in the Greek style."

79. Rapunzel: OG, "lamb's lettuce." The name of various plants used as salad greens. Also, the comic name of a Grimm's fairy tale. In "A Study in French Poets" [*Instigations*, 62], Pound described a Poem by Moréas: "Moréas was born in 1856, the year after Verhaeren, but his Madeline-aux-serpents might be William Morris on Rapunzel."

80. Adah Lee, Ida: In 1906 Pound met Miss Adah Lee and Miss Ida Lee Mapel, ladies from Virginia, with whom he maintained a friendship for over 40 years. In 1919 he and Dorothy stayed at Ida Lee's Paris flat. During the St. Elizabeths years, the Mapel ladies both lived in Washington and visited Pound regularly. Dorothy later described them to Stock as "two old ladies not used to having friends in gaol." She said that "they were invaluable" [NS, *Life*, 540].

81. Merlin's moder: [Cf. 49 above].

82. **quidity**: The essential nature or "whatness" of a thing which flows in "the process" from its *virtu*. Dante wrote: "Faith is the substance of things hoped for, / and the proof of things not apparent, / and this I take to be its quiddity" [*Par*. XXIV, 64-65; JW translation: *Pai*, 2-2, 190]. Pound adapted the Italian *quiditate* [93/631; 103:7].

83. **fire . . . crystal . . . light**: [Cf. 2, 3, 15 above].

4 **Rhea**: The female Titan, wife of Saturn (Cronos) and mother of the chief gods, including Ceres (Demeter). Her Latin name was Cybele. In works of art she is often depicted seated on a throne with lions at her side or sometimes riding in a chariot drawn by lions.

85. **Musonius**: A philosopher colleague of Apollonius of Tyana [94:42] who was forced by Nero to dig the Corinth Canal as a slave laborer—but he did it in defiance of tyranny. Hence, the "tough guy" epithet and the "honor" by Pound [94:114].

86. **Ideogram**: Tan [M6037], "dawn."

87. **The arcanum**: The mysterium, or final secrets, unrevealed in the rites of Eleusis except symbolically. Also, the final or secret aspirations of esoteric alchemy. Pound wrote: "The mysteries are *not* revealed, and no guide book to them has been or will be written" [*L*, 327].

88. **Κάδμου θυγάτηρ**: H, "Daughter of Cadmus."

89. **parapernalia**: Paraphernalia. Leucothea, daughter of Cadmus, in the form of a seabird flew over the foundering raft of Odysseus and told him to get rid of the clothes Calypso had given him [*Od*. V, 331-357; 95:32]

90. **Tlemousune**: H, "Misery to be suffered with patience."

91. **Domitian**: Titus Flavius D., 51-96, Roman emperor. D. was a strict moralist (for others, but a man of unrestrained sensuality himself) who executed many people for little reason and many for plotting against his tyranny. His wife finally joined others in a plot that resulted in his murder. At least twice he banished all philosophers from Rome, once while Apollonius, the traveling man of wisdom, was there. Apollonius, refusing to leave, was arrested and taken to court [*Apollonius*, Bk. VIII, chap. 3; Neault, *Pai*, 4-1, 4].

92. **"Is this a bath-house?"**: As Apollonius waited before court, a clerk said to him, "Man of Tyana, you must enter the court with nothing on you," meaning he should have no papers or books. A.'s response, taking the remark to mean "no clothes," resulted in a witty reply which Pound gives as, "Is this a bathouse . . . or a Court House?" [ibid.].

93. ἄλλοτε . . . διώκειν: H, "Has the east wind abandoned him for the west wind to play with?" [*Od*. V, 332]. Concerns the havoc the winds of Poseidon played with Odysseus's raft. Apollonius traveled much in the eastern countries and was always welcomed by kings and wise men and treated with great honor and respect. But in the west (Rome) his life was in danger.

94. **Apollonius**: Like many wise men of old, A. was supposedly able to converse with animals. In Egypt a "whining and fawning" lion approached him as he was sitting in the temple. He explained to bystanders: "This lion is begging me to make you understand that a human soul is within him" [*Pai*, 4-1, 27; 94:42].

95. **charitas insuperabilis**: L, "love invincible." From Richard of St. Victor's *Tractatus de Gradibus Charitatis* [Treatise on the steps of love].

96. **Heydon**: [87:82]. John Heydon, secretary of nature, author of *The Holy Guide*, where in Bk. I, Ch. II, we read: " . . . but if God would give you leave and power to ascend to those high places I meane to these heavenly thoughts and studies . . . " [p. 26]. And later: "for God, when he cast his mind upon the building of the world, he went to make a beautiful and goodly work, meet for the Power, Wisdome and Pleasure of such a Builder, and therefore a *stirring and change-*

able work, because there might be no cunning shown, no delight taken in one ever like or still thing; but *light fighting for speed*, is ever best in such a ground: let us away, and follow" [p. 28]. Heydon recommends that on should rule the desire for "honour and pleasure" and seek rather "Wisdome and Vertue" [pp. 31-32] and adds: "let us know first, that the minde of man being come from that high City of Heaven, desireth of her self to live still that heavenly life" [pp. 33-34]. A few pages later Heydon writes: "the whole Creation is concerned in this Number four" [p. 39]. In Bk. III Heydon writes: "And to say there is no such things as *Pulchritude*, and some say, there is no *way to felicity*" [p. 87]. Speaking of the vision of Euterpe, Heydon writes [Bk. VI]: "her hour to Translation was come, and taking as I thought our last leave, she *past before my eyes into the Aether of Nature*" [WB in EH, *Approaches*, 313-316].

97. Pythagoras: [Cf. 11 above]. Apollonius claimed himself to be a spiritual descendant of Pythagoras. Heydon claimed that both Pythagoras and Apollonius were able to be in two different places at the same time: hence, Apollonius "who was with Pythagoras at Taormina" while being elsewhere with others [Neault, *Pai*, 4-1, 17].

98. Taormina: A town that flourished as a Greek colony. In E Sicily at the foot of Mt. Etna above the Ionian Sea. Apollonius taught philosophy there.

99. Porphyrius: Prophyry, A.D. 232/3-305, a scholar-philosopher who studied under Longinus at Athens and became a devoted personal disciple of Plotinus at Rome. He edited the *Enneads* after 300. A prolific writer who adopted many Neoplatonic concepts.

100. Νυχτὸς . . . ἡμέρα: H, "But of the Night both day and skie were born" [Hesiod, *Theogony* II, 13 (Loeb)]. EP quotes the line from Heydon [Bk. II, Chapt. III, p. 13], who attributes it to Plato.

101. Ζηνὸς πυρὸς: H, "Wheat of Zeus." Pound added these words to Hesiod to get a third element "born of night" [Neault, *Pai*, 4-1, 15].

102. "my bikini . . . ": Pound paraphrases the words of Leucothea [*Od.* V, 339-350] when she told Odysseus to get rid of his water-logged clothes and raft and rely on her magic cloth: "kredemnon" [96:1].

103. celandine: Heydon believed that some beasts "have knowledge in the Virtue of Plants," so they will go to the right place for medicinal help [92:3].

104. before my eyes: [Cf. 96 above].

105. The water-bug's . . . : Pound sent the fragment that appears in *The Cantos* [p. 800] in a letter to Katue Kitasono. It ends with a variant of these lines. The letter contains a note about the "mittens": "If I were 30 years younger I would call 'em his boxing gloves. I wonder if it is clear that I mean the shadow of the 'mittens'? and can you ideograph it; very like petals of blossoms" [*L*, 348].

106. natrix: L, "water snake" [90:30].

107. NUTT: Nut, the Egyptian goddess Night, from which Day is born, is sometimes imaged as a cow arching over the earth. Budge renders a key inscription in this way: "[Hail] Osiris . . . living for ever, born of heaven, conceived of Nut. . . . Spreadeth herself thy mother Nut over thee in her name of 'Mystery of heaven', she granteth that thou mayest exist as a god to thy foes" [Budge, *Book of the Dead*, 16]. Note the mystery-arcanum motif.

108. "mand'io a la Pinella": I, "I send to Pinella."

109. Guido: G. Cavalcanti. Pound translated a line of his Sonnet XVII: "I send Pinella a river in full flood" [*T*, 58]. Pinella was a lady to whom Bernado da Bologna wrote a sonnet. Cavalcanti wrote a sonnet to Bernado in reply "and explains why they have sweet waters in Galicia" [ibid.]. Writing about Cavalcanti, Pound asks, "What is the magic river 'filled full of lamias' that Guido sends to Pinella in return for her caravan . . . ? [*LE*, 180].

110. "Ghosts . . . adorned": The source of the quote is unknown, but the intent seems clear: visions of other ladies adorn the memory when the divine spirit animates the mind and heart.

111. "Et Jehanne": L, "And Joan." Joan of Arc came from Lorraine. Can we call her visionary experience lost to the world? Pound's answer is, "Scarcely," if we allow the power of love to prevail.

112. O Queen Cytherea: Aphrodite, goddess of love.

113. che 'l terzo ciel movete: I, "which moves the third heaven" [*Par.* VIII, 37]. The whole line says "O you who knowing" does the moving. Pound makes the lines refer back to the goddess of love [JW, *Pai*, 2-2, 188].

CANTO XCII

Sources

Dante, *Pur.* I, XXVIII, *Inf.* X, *Par.* IX; Shakespeare, *The Tempest* I, ii; Cavalcanti, Ballata VII [*T*, 111]; Isaiah 1.11; Joshua 2.1-24; Sordello, *Le Poesie*, ed. Marco Bono, Bologna, 1954.

Background

EP, *NPL*, 152; *SR*, 92; *CON*, 188; *SP*, 265; *GK* 229; John Read, *The Alchemist in Life, Literature and Art*, Thomas Nelson and Sons, 1947; Desmond Fitzgerald, *Memoirs*, ed. Fergus Fitzgerald, London, 1968; Francesco Guicciardini, *Storia d'Italia*, ed. Rosini, 10 vols., Pisa, 1819; Roberto Ridolfi, *The Life of Francesco Guicciardini*, trans. Cecil Grayson, Knopf, 1968.

Exegeses

FR, *Pai*, 7-2 & 3, 41; Akiko Miyake, *Pai*, 7-2 & 3, 110; JW, *Pai*, 2-2, 176-181; J. Neault, *Pai*, 4-1, 35; EH, *Pai*, 2-3, 498-499; W. B. Michaels, *Pai*, 1-1, 51; CE, *Ideas*, 110-111; DD, *Sculptor*, 180-181; HK, *Era*, 51-53, 113, 412; MB, *Trace*, 303-310.

Glossary

1. Mount: The mount of Purgatory, at whose summit is a dense forest high up in the air, with plants of such potency that if struck they scatter their virtue and their seed abroad. The lady tells Dante that because of this, "the holy plain, where you are, is full of every seed" [*Pur.* XXVIII, 91-120]. Pound spoke of ideas as seeds: "the thought once born . . . does lead an independent life . . . blowing seeds, ideas from the paradisal garden at the summit of Dante's Mount Purgatory, capable of lodging and sprouting where they fall" [*NPL*, 152].

2. **plant . . . seed**: Pound wrote of certain men, "their consciousness is 'germinal.' Their thoughts are in them as the thought of the tree is in the seed, or in the grass, or the grain, or the blossom" [*SR*, 92].

3. **weasel . . . celandine**: Heydon [90:2] wrote: "Beasts have knowledge in the vertue of Plants. . . . The Weasel, when she is to encounter the Serpent, arms her self with eating of Rue. . . . The Swallows make use of Celandine" [WB, in EH, *Approaches*, 312]. Divine intelligence works in all living things, according to "the plan that is in nature / rooted." Pound said that beneath our kinship with animals "is our kinship to the vital universe, to the tree, and the living rock" [*SR*, 92].

4. **engraven . . . silver**: In the numerical system of the Pythagorean alchemist, metals had their numbers engraved on them [MB, *Trace*, 304].

5. **unity . . . frankincense**: Evokes the ambience of the alchemist's laboratory and provides a link with the opening of *Thrones* [96:3].

6. **a sea-change**: A metamorphosis as in Shakespeare's "suffer a sea-change / Into something rich and strange" [*Tempest*, I, ii]. Here, not base metal into gold but the material into the spiritual is queried.

7. **Fitzgerald**: Desmond F., 1888-1947, Irish nationalist who fought in the Easter rising in Dublin in 1916. In the later years of the revolution and after Ireland's independence was established, a test of whether a person was really a founder of the Irish Free State was whether he was present in the post office, the headquarters of the insurgents, during the rising. In the 20s and 30s a number of Irish patriots claimed they were there when they were not. Fitzgerald's "I was" is supported by fact. Three days after the post office was burned, he was arrested, but he was later released. After the new state was consolidated, he became the minister for external affairs and, later, minister for defence, but he lost office when Valera came to power in 1932. As a young man he was a member of the imagist group in London. According to Fitzgerald's son Fergus, it was his father and Florence Farr who introduced Pound to the imagist group [Fitzgerald, *Memoirs*].

8. **freed a man**: Grattan Freyer writes: "Fitzgerald was a fearless fighter, as well as poet and philosopher." When the post office was under fire he prob. did not take cover and was later accused of foolhardiness. In later years when people who falsely claimed to have been at the post office were exposed, D. F. "did his utmost to discourage recrimination against those who had played less heroic or divisive roles" [letter to editor].

9. **Signori . . . sentinella**: I, "Sirs, did I cover the sentinel? Or did I not cover the sentinel?"

10. **"Gran dispitto"**: I, "Great contempt" [*Inf.* X, 36]. Said by Farinata degli Uberti [91:75]. Here indicating the tone of voice of the questions in Italian.

11. **"A chi stima . . . l'onore assai"**: I, "to him who esteem . . . honor enough." From postscript by Guicciardini to Pound's *Confucius*: "Nothing is impossible to him who holds honor in sufficient esteem" [*CON*, 188].

12. **Guicciardini**: Francesco G., 1483-1540, the scion of one of the greatest Florentine families. Although trained in the law, he started his lifelong work as a writer with *The History of Florence* and *The History of Italy*. But he was a man of action too: he was ambassador to Spain, governor of Modena and Reggio, president of Romagna, lieutenant general of the papal forces in the League of Cognac, and governor of Bologna. A contemporary of Machiavelli, he was a supporter of the Medici power in Florence and instrumental in selecting Cosino de' Medici to succeed Alessandro after his assassination [5:33, 43, 45].

13. Ra-Set: [91:19].

14. e piove d'amor / in nui: I, "love is raining / within us." Phrases from Cavalcanti's Ballata VII [*T*, 111].

15. ghosts dipping . . . : [91:110].

16. Pinella: [91:109].

17. Hewlett: [80:417]. Besides novels, he wrote travel accounts of Italy (such as *The Road in Tuscany*), retold Icelandic sagas, and wrote a lot of narrative poetry. The quote is prob. a memory of the closing lines of "Leto's Child," by Hewlett, where from prison he sees his love "Snow-white on some peak blue and cold, / Moon-toucht, and see thy rapt soul hold / Communion; see thee, from my bars, / Drink, motionless, the eternal stars" [JE].

18. rain . . . silver: Replay of golden rain motif [4:33] with Diana, and echo of "love is raining within us" [cf. 14 above].

19. La Luna Regina: I, "The Moon Queen": Diana.

20. Ecbatan: [4:32]. City of "Dioce whose terraces are the color of stars" [74:8]. It was built on a hill and surrounded by 7 walls, each one higher than the other; the 6th wall was silver and the 7th, which contained the palace of the king, was gold.

21. Anubis: The Egyptian jackal god—his home was the cosmic mountain—who guarded the "tent of the ritual resurrection known as Osirification" [B de R, *Approaches*, 178]. Pound evoked Anubis in an early poem, "Before Sleep" [*P*, 147]. The "cellula" corresponds to the *sanctum sanctorum* of temples [Miyake, *Pai*, 7-1 & 2, 110].

22. Mont Ségur: P, "Secure Mountain" [23:25; 80:316].

23. Sanctus: L, "Consecrated."

24. no blood: "To what purpose is the multitude of your sacrifices unto me? saith the Lord. . . . I delight not in the blood of bullocks [Isaiah 1.11].

25. ex aquis nata: L, "born out of water." Ref. to Aphrodite.

26. *τά . . . γενόμενα*: H, "the birth out of the waters."

27. "in . . . appresso": I, "in this light nearby" [*Par.* IX, 112-113]. Taken from lines that read, "you would like to know who is *in this light* that *nearby* me here sparkles like the sun's ray in clear water." The speaker is Rehab [Joshua 2.1-24], the redeemed prostitute who was the Israelite spy [JW].

28. Folquet: Folco of Marseille, 1150-1232, a writer of troubadour love songs who later became bishop of Toulouse. He was reviled in the *Chanson de la croisade* for persecuting heretics. Dante placed him in his third heaven [*Par.* IX, 80-142] because he was a poet and a lover [DG].

29. nel terzo cielo: I, "in the third heaven."

30. "And if . . . thought": Repeat of Ventadorn lines [20:3].

31. Coeli Regina: I, "Queen of Heaven." The name of several churches and numerous paintings dedicated to the Virgin.

32. four altars: Perhaps the Santa Maria in Aracoeli in Rome is that place, but a number of places might qualify.

33. farfalla in tempesta: I, "butterfly in storm." Recall of lines [*Pur.* X, 125] where the soul on the way to the beatific vision is likened in difficulty to a worm seeking the form of an "angelic butterfly" [74:68; 90:49; Frags. 38, 39].

34. Nymphalidae: A family of handsome butterflies.

35. basilarch . . . erynnis: Each of the names is a genus of the family of Nymphalidae. Since the natural object is the adequate symbol, Pound wants to convey the qualities of different souls aspiring to reach paradise.

36. il tremolar . . . : I, "the trembling of the sea" [*Pur.* I, 116-117]. The end of a line that starts: "from afar [*di lontans*] I heard." From the dawn scene marking the first sight of light after the pilgrim's ascent from Hell [JW].

37. **chh . . . ch'u**: Onomatopoetic sounds of the sea.

38. **"fui . . . refulgo"**: I, "I was called and here I glow" [*Par.* IX, 32]. Cunizza da Romano [29:14; 76:16] is speaking in the third heaven of Venus.

39. **Le Paradis . . .** : F, "Paradise is not fictitious," meaning that it is real and around us always [Neault, *Pai*, 4-1, 35].

40. **Hilary**: Hilary of Poitiers [95:72]. Pound lists "The church of St. Hilaire in Poitiers" first in a list of art works that manifest degrees of light in "black festering darkness" [*SP*, 265].

41. ***improvisatore:*** I, "improviser."

42. **Omniformis**: L, "every shape" [23:1].

43. **Pontifex**: Pontifex Maximus, the high priest of the Pontifical College in ancient Rome [89:79].

44. **Margarethe**: Queen Margherita of Savoy [86:5].

45. **Uncle Carlo**: Carlo Delcroix [cf. 49 below].

46. **Rimini bas-reliefs**: [8:43; HK, *Era*, 253]. Sigismundo's "clean-up" of the prevailing art modes by his work at the Tempio seems implied.

47. **Semele**: Mother of Bacchus (Dionysus) by Jupiter. By the trickery of Juno, she was led to exact a promise from Jupiter that he would come to her in all his splendor. Since he swore by the river Styx, he had to so appear. The immortal radiance reduced her to ashes.

48. **"Io porto . . . la cecita**: I, "I carry the blindness."

49. **Delcroix**: Carlo D. [88:46]. He was blinded in the Fascist struggle. His work for war veterans was made difficult by the "Two evils": usury and theft. His will to act is indicated by his willingness to struggle with the bureaucracy [*GK*, 229, 249].

50. **un ministro**: I, "a minister."

51. **les soc / anonymes**: F, "anonymous societies": massive impersonal corporations.

52. **Bottai**: Guiseppi B., secretary of the ministry of corporations, 1927-1932. He helped draft the *Carta del Lavoro* that defined working norms for the state. From 1936 to the collapse of the government, he was minister of education. He is cited here for his quick phone call to Turin to help Pound get the Vivaldi manuscripts [JW].

53. **instanter**: L, "sudden."

54. **Torino**: Count di T.

55. **Vivaldi**: Antonio V., ca. 1675-1743. Pound and Olga Rudge helped to popularize his concerti and, even more, assisted in retrieving drafts of his compositions from Dresden before their destruction by WWII bombs.

56. **ministri**: I, "ministers."

57. **Marinetti**: Filippo Tommaso M., 1876-1944. He fought in Russia during WWI and was a political activist as well as a primary figure in the futurist movement. Pound mentioned him among the avant-garde in art during the 30s [*SP*, 396, 456, 459].

58. **Hans Sachs**: German meistersinger (1494-1576) and leading poet of the Nuremberg school. Although a shoemaker by trade, he educated himself, became master of his guild, and wrote 6000 songs, fables, and tales as well as 208 plays.

59. **Schnitz Brandt**: Hermann Carl George B., a professor at Hamilton nicknamed "Schnitz" ("Slice") by students.

60. **"war ein . . . dazu"**: G, "was a shoemaker and a poet as well." Pound liked poets who were good and careful craftsmen.

61. **the armada**: Return to Drake and sea battles [91:21].

62. **300 years**: Reina [91:4, 5].

63. **Nein! . . . Wolken**: G, "No! but in clouds."

64. **Yang tse**: The Yellow River, which used to flood seasonally [53:116].

65. **25 hundred**: Figure seems to derive from Antef's time [93:4]. And the "2 thousand years" from the time of Christ.

66. **Apollonius**: [91:9; 94:42].

67. **Erigena**: One of the most important light-philosophers [74:90], as are the others listed here.

68. **Avicenna**: [93:48].

69. **Richardus**: [85:52].

70. **Hilary**: [Cf. 40 above].

71. **brown . . . sweat**: Reference to post-Raphaelite painting, with its blurred lines and shadows.

72. **cannon . . . opium**: The British purportedly trained the Chinese to use opium and developed a lucrative trade in it during their 19th-century occupation of China.

73. **Portagoose**: Portuguese [89:238].

74. **Ari**: Aristotle [87:26]. The "common custom" is the formation of monopolies.

CANTO XCIII

Sources

Boris de Rachewiltz [B de R], *Massime degli antichi Egiziani*, Milan, 1954, and *Il Libro Egizio degli Inferi*, Rome, 1959; Bernart de Ventadorn, "Tant ai mo cor ple de joya," no. 44, Appel, 1915, 260-263: Dante, *Inf.* XX, XXVII, *Par.* III, V, *Pur.* XXVII, *Convivio* [*Conv.*]; EP, *Lustra*, 196.

Background

EP, *SP*, 452-457, 28, 25, 47-52; *SR*, 80. Boris de Rachewiltz [B de R], "Pagan and Magic Elements," in EH, *Approaches*, 174-197; E. A. Wallis Budge, *A History of Egypt*, Vol. III, Netherlands, 1968; Eustace Mullins, *This Difficult Individual, Ezra Pound* [EM, *Difficult*]; M de R. *Discretions*, 151; Allan Wade, ed., *The Letters of W. B. Yeats*, New York, 1955.

Exegeses

JW, *Pai*, 2-2, 183-187; J. Neault, *Pai*, 4-1, 7, 28; M de R, *Discretions*, 113-114; NS, *Reading*, 96-102; HK, *Era*, 364; BK, *Pai*, 5-1, 214; EH, *Pai*, 2-1, 143; CE, *Ideas* 157-158; CB-R, *ZBC*, 32, 140-143; HK, *Era*, 338-339, 530-531; MB, *Trace*, 310-324; Timothy Materer, "Ez to WynDAMN," in *Helix*, 13/14 (this double issue is devoted to Ezra Pound).

Glossary

1. **"A man's . . . "**: Trans. of the Egyptian hieroglyphics provided to Pound by his son-in-law, Boris de Rachewiltz. Pound was much elated to discover such secular wisdom recorded so early in history [B de R, in EH, *Approaches*, 178].

2. **Kati**: King Khati, an Egyptian ruler Pound encountered in a book by his son-in-law [ibid.].

3. **"panis angelicus"**: L, "angel-bread." From Dante's *Convivio* 1.1, 50-102 [cf. 60 below], where the writer promises to distribute the never-diminishing bread of angels among his readers, in keeping with the Neoplatonic tenet that the good always increases [JW]. Also, common phrase for the communion wafer.

4. **Antcf**: A minister "in the reign of Sesostris I (12th dynasty, ca. 1970-1936 B.C.)," who purportedly said, "Give bread to the hungry, beer to the thirsty" [cf. RO, *Pai*, 6-2, 181].

5. **two 1/2s of a seal**: [77:56]. The first half is the "panis angelicus" and the second is Antef's compassion for the destitute.

6. **his own mind**: A musical figure evoking Tiresias [80:30] and Odysseus, whose mind was such that the gods said "he must be one of us" [*L*, 270].

7. **Κάδμου . . .** : H, "daughter of Cadmus" [91:88].

8. **Apollonius**: [94:42].

9. **arcivescovo**: I, "archbishop." Archbishop Pisani [97:200]. Pound and his daughter Mary visited him at Rome before WWII. The next several lines concern his kind act of giving the child a roll of chocolates [M de R, *Discretions*, 113-114].

10. **"La Tour"**: F, "The Tower." A picture of a painting by Georges de la Tour on a box of Gianduja chocolates the archbishop gave to Mary. The box and the painting together suggest a cornucopia.

11. **Augustine**: St. Augustine [16:6]. It seems that the two lines are a detail from a story the archbishop told as the three walked from St. Peter's toward their carrozza.

12. **The Pope**: Augustine's conversion took place in 387. In 391 he moved to Hippo and in 395 became auxiliary bishop there. Since his most significant works, *The Confessions* (ca. 400) and *The City of God* (later than 412), were done after 395, the pope with whom he had such a dialog would most likely be St. Siricius (384-399), Anastasius (399-401), or Innocent I (401-417).

13. **St Peter's**: M de R wrote: "The first visit was to St. Peter's."

14. **carrozza**: I, "carraige." Wrote Mary: "It was a short walk to the *carrozza*." Afterwards, she received the gift.

15. **internal horrors**: Prob. referring to churches with interior design and art of the ersatz variety.

16. **Santa Sabina**: I, "Saint Sabine," a church in Rome: one of the best examples of good architecture.

17. **San Domenico**: I, "Saint Dominic" [44:9]. A church Pound was fond of at Siena. Wrote M de R: "His favorite walk was to Fontebranda and then up to San Domenico" [ibid., 133].

18. **Hyksos**: Asiatic invaders of Egypt around 2100 B.C. The Egyptologist Budge wrote: "The Hyksos destroyed much, but what they left undestroyed the native Egyptians neglected; through these causes the condition of the country was lamentable" [*Egypt*, III, 190; Neault, *Pai*, 4-1, 28]. A later ruler, Amasis I, started to restore the temples of the gods and to this end "had the quarries of Tura reopened, in order that 'good stone' might be hewed therein for the buildings" [ibid.].

19. **butchers . . .** : [87/573].

20. Classe: I, from the name of an Italian church, "Saint Appollinaire in Classe" ("St. Apollinaire by the fleet" or "at the harbor"), located just outside Ravenna. It is a marvel of Romanesque beauty [9:28]. Its incredible wall-long-length mosaics were prob. source of Yeats's "O sages, standing in God's holy fire / As in the gold mosaic of a wall."

21. Ondine: [91:7].

22. "The waves . . . there!": Pound's rendition of a Japanese haiku which he used in 1937 to illustrate the third element that is always suggested by two present. The haiku concerned a war hero. Here the waves and moonlight evoke a "you" that refers to the "Ondine" [*SP*, 453].

23. Old Grinell: Prob. a Pound acquaintance of his London years, when he was first interested in Japanese verse forms.

24. Olibanum: [2:20]. Frankincense, sacred to Dionysus [cf. 35 below].

25. "non fosse cive": I, "were not a citizen" [*Par.* VIII, 116]. In this scene Charles Martel asks Dante: "But tell me—would it be worse for man on earth, if he wasn't a citizen?" Dante, with civility, must say that it would [JW].

26. Avon: A river in England. People from its banks would not agree on matters of civility.

27. "dragons' spleens": Chatillon reports to King Philip concerning Englishmen on the warpath: "Rash, inconsiderate, fiery voluntaries, / With ladies' faces and fierce dragons' spleens, / Have sold their fortunes at their native homes, / . . . To make a hazard of new fotunes here" [*King John*, II, 1, 71-75].

28. "a pelting farm": John of Gaunt says: "This land of such dear souls, this dear dear land / —Is now leas'd out—I die pronouncing it— / Like to a tenement or a pelting farm" [*Richard II*, II, 1, 58-60].

29. alum: A double sulfate of aluminum and potassium widely used in medicine and in alchemical and chemical processes, as well as in the arts. A source of alum and related clays and bauxite meant wealth: here the solvency of the papacy seems to be indicated.

30. Tolfa: Prob. Le Tolfe, a hilly district north of Siena.

31. Medici: [8:38; 21:35].

32. "Te voilá . . . ": F, "There you are, my Bourienne."

33. Bourienne: [18:11]. Louis Bourrienne, private secretary to Napoleon the Great.

34. corrent' attrattiva: I, "attractive current." The magnetic attraction in alchemy and in sexuality are implied.

35. ureus . . . gold: [90:28]. Related to the Isis-Kuanon and the natrix [90:30]. Pound wrote to his son-in-law about the sacred snakes: "The turquoise, that is to say white belly turquoise shading, long diamond pattern, and sapphire back is a natrix, not a rock viper. . . . Some brute had needlessly slaughtered the one in memory, somewhere cross country from Caserta, or thereabout and left it on a loose stone division wall, by foot path or mulatiera. . . . Certainly servant of Iside. I suppose olibanum standard for usage, plus what else as salutation" [MB, *Trace*, 313].

36. Peitz . . . bionda: P, "I suffer worse the pain of love / Than did the lover Tristan / Who suffered many a grief / Because of Isolde, the blonde" [lines 45-48 of Bernart de Ventadorn's "Tant ai mo cor ple de joya" ("I have a heart so full of joy"), No. 44, Appel's 1915 edition, pp. 260-263]. Pound edited the poem himself, since his reading of *peitz* for *plus* and his Italian spelling of *bionda* for *blonda* can be found in no other edition [JW].

37. Castalia: [90:5].

38. c'est autre chose: F, "that's something else."

39. San Cristoforo: I, "St. Christopher."

Third-century Christian martyr, the patron of travelers.

40. little Christo: In legend, the saint carried a child (Christ) across a river and staggered because he also bore the weight of the world in his hands. In paintings he is pictured as a giant with the little Christ holding onto his neck or hair.

41. Gardesee: [76:91]. the German name of Lake Garda.

42. dove siede Peschiera: I, "where Peschiera sits" [*Inf.* XX, 70]. The passage concerns Virgil's account of the founding of his native city, Mantua. He says it was not because of the false prophetess Manto but because the River Adige provided an appropriate bank–thus underlining Pound's conviction that mythology, topography, and economics mesh.

43. Sorrento: A romantic city situated high on the hills overlooking the Bay of Naples.

44. Cortesia . . . : I, "Courtesy, honesty" [*Conv.* II, 10.8]. Dante is equating civilized behavior with these qualities.

45. Ureus: Uraeus. Emblem of the sacred serpent (*haje*) in the headdress of gods and kings in Egypt, symbolizing such things as wisdom, power, and compassion [cf. 35 above].

46. Nine knowledges: The 9 heavens of Dante's Paradise and their allegorical significance. The first 7 included the traditional trivium and quadrivium.

47. Ideogram: Chih^3 [M939], "stop," or "cease," or "to rest in." The 9 heavens turn around a center that is at rest–the still point of the turning world or the center of the multifoliate rose [85:9].

48. Avicenna: Ibn-Sina. Arabic philosopher, 980-1037, noted for his work in medicine (*The Canon*), theology, and alchemy (about which he wrote at least one book, and several others were falsely attributed to him). It was through his numerous works and the works of other Islamic scholars that the intellectual tradition of the classical world was preserved for the renaissance in the West. Dante cites him with Algazel and Plato [*Conv.* II, 14.5], linking the soul to Heaven and defining the 8th sphere (concerned with natural science) and the 9th (concerned with moral science), which Pound calls "agenda."

49. Algazel: Arabic philosopher, 1058-1111, who lived most of his life in Baghdad. A confirmed mystic and ascetic, he was fiercely critical of the rationalizing Aristotelian movement in Arabic thought: quite the opposite of the fun-loving life of enthusiastic debauchery often lived by Avicenna.

50. agenda: L, "things to be done."

51. Agassiz: Alexander Emanuel A., 1835-1910, American scientist born in Switzerland. He received a Harvard degree in 1855 and went on to study engineering, chemistry, and marine ichthyology. His interests spread to mining engineering, in which he made such a fortune that he endowed the Harvard Museum of Comparative Zoology. In 1875 he surveyed Lake Titicaca, looked at the copper mines of Peru and Chile, and collected Peruvian antiquities for the museum. Through all this, as well as dredging expeditions for the U.S. Coast Survey, he was a prolific writer. He is a Pound hero because of his close observation and accurate reporting. Writing about the curse of writers of abstract statement, Pound said: "They had no ideogrammic method or hadn't erected it into a system and hadn't heard about Professor Agassiz's fish [*ABCR*, 17-18], but to confuse a tendency to abstract statement with *tout bonnement* 'intelligence' is to sin against all those most admirable canons of nomenclature" [*LE*, 68]. Agassiz's place is in the 8th sphere of Paradise.

52. Kung: Confucius [13:1]. As he was concerned with moral science, Kung belongs to the highest realm of the empyrean, which is crystalline. [*Conv.* II, 13, 8].

53. Nephertari: The queen of Ramses II. A tomb fresco showed her being led by the goddess Isis [B de R, *Approaches*, 34]. The ancient Egyptians used incense as a medium to transform the material into the spiritual [NS, *Reading*, 96].

54. Isis: [90:28]. Pound is creating rhymes to show how the qualities of wisdom, reason, compassionate social action, moral aspiration, and love were common driving forces in all great cultures of the past and that they are essential to at least the mystery part of all great religions. These qualities will be developed in greater detail in *Thrones*.

55. "quest' . . . ama": I, "And this union [is what we call love, whereby we can know] what is inside the mind by seeing outside the thing it loves" [*Conv*. III, 2.9]. The words in brackets Pound leaves out [cf. 90:1].

56. Risplende . . . : I, "Shines" [Cavalcanti's *Donna Mi Prega*, 1.26; *T*, 132; cf. *LE*, 164].

57. degli occhi: I, [de li occhi]: "of the eyes" [*Conv*. III, 8.10]. The whole sentence reads: "Wherefore, since there are six emotions proper to the human soul . . . to wit grace, jealousy, pity, envy, love and shame, by none of these may the soul be impassioned without the semblance thereof appearing at the window of the eyes" [91:4].

58. Numa Pompilius: Second legendary king of Rome, 715-672 B.C. A Sabine from Cures, his wife was the nymph Egeria whom he used to meet by night in her sacred grove. The early religious instructions of Rome were almost all attributed to him: "He set up the worship of Terminus (the god of landmarks), appointed the festival of Fides (Faith), built the temple of Janus, reorganized the calendar and fixed days of business and holiday. He instituted the flamens (sacred priests) of Jupiter, Mars and Quirinus; the virgins of Vesta, to keep the sacred fire burning on the hearth of the city; the Salii, to guard the shield that fell from heaven; the pontifices and augurs, to arrange the rites and interpret the will of the gods; he also divided the handicraftsmen into nine gilds" [EB]. It seems that the wisdom, reason, civil compassion, and religious motivation of Pompilius rhyme with that of other early statesmen: the nine heavens of Dante also rhyme with the nine gilds. But historians assert that the accomplishments of Pompilius, essentially Italian in nature, should be attributed to some of his followers as well as to him [JW, *Pai*, 2-2, 186].

59. the Pitagora si chiamò: I, "who called himself Pythagoras" [*Conv*. III, 91.3]. The whole sentence reads: "Almost at the time of Numa Pompilius, second King of the Romans, there lived a very noble philospher, who called himself Pythagoras."

60. "non sempre": I, "not always" [*Conv*. III, 13.3]. The whole sentence reads: "I say therefore that people who are in love here, that is: in this life, feel it (intelligence) in their thought, not always, but when Love makes his peace felt." The "jagged" duality of Paradise may be blamed on the absence of love [JW].

61. Convivio: I, "*The Banquet*." In some ways a continuation of *Vita Nuova* [New life], *The Banquet* was written between 1304 and 1307. It consists of four treatises and a series of odes which deal with various subjects: theology, epistemology, allegory, symbolism, ethics, and literary criticism, to list only the most important. The treatises are divided into chapters with lines numbered according to the standard edition of G. Busnelli and G. Vandelli, Florence, 1934. Documentation herein gives treatise, chapter, and line.

62. l'amor . . . bella: I, "the love that makes you beautiful [*Conv*. III, 13.9].

63. "ut facias" . . . "pulchram": L, "[You love] so that you may become beautiful." The first line of a Latin sequence by Gottschalk contained in *Le Latin Mystique* by Remy de Gourmont [*SP*, 422].

64. Goddeschalk: Gottschalk [Godescalus, Gottescale], ca. 808-867?. A German theologian dedicated by his parents from infancy to the monastic life, from which he withdrew in 829 at the synod of Mainz. Because of his enthusiastic promotion of the idea of double predestination (including election to damnation), he was convicted of heresy several times and became the center of violent religious controversy until his death. Some of his writings were preserved by Erigena, including his *Sequaire*, containing the line cited.

65. **è forma . . .** : I, "is the form of philosophy" [DG, *Pai*, 5-2, 276; Singh, *Pai*, 3-2, 163-165; JW, *Pai*, 2-2, 183].

66. **Dant's**: Dante's.

67. **beltà . . .** : I, "beauty, that is, morality" [*Conv*. II, 3.63]; "piove fiammelle di foco" ("rains flakes of fire") continues the line. The beauty of philosophy defined by Dante as morality rhymes with "the golden rain of the sun in Neoplatonism and the lyrics of Arnaut Daniel" [JW].

68. **Jacopo Sellaio**: [20/90; 80/511]. Florentine painter, 1422-1493, who included knowledge as a necessary ingredient of technique [*P*, 73; HK, *Era*, 364].

69. **"e solo . . . diletta"**: I, "and in showing loyalty alone it [the soul] delights" [*Conv*. III, 4.131], when young [ages 20-40].

70. **e "d'udir . . . prode"**: I, "and to hear . . . the good" [ibid., 135]. Tractate 4 of the 3d canzone concerns what the soul delights in at various ages. In the third phrase of life [40-60], the soul is wedded to goodness, and is "prudent, just, and generous, delighting in itself and in hearing and speaking good of others."

71. **Beaumarchais**: Pierre de B., 1732-1799 [31:29].

72. **KATI**: [Cf. 2 above].

73. **"compagnevole . . . "**: I, "social animal" [*Conv*. IV, 4]. Speaking of Aristotle's *Nichomachean Ethics*, Dante says: "Thus the Philosopher says that man is naturally a social [or friendly] animal." The phrase comments on the hieroglyph, which in an idiogrammic way seems to place birds, animals, and man in a single continuum of nature [JW, *Pai*, 2-2, 185].

74. **Hieroglyph**: King Khaty. Pound associates him with the compassion toward others expressed in the *Convivio*.

75. **"Perché . . . ordine?"**: I, "Why do you wish to put your ideas in order?" [87:4].

76. **Boss**: Mussolini.

77. **"Pel mio poema"**: I, "For my poem." Pound's response to the question of Mussolini [*GK*, 105].

78. **bellezza**: I, "beauty," or "loveliness."

79. **Perugia**: Italian city, capital of the province of Umbria. Pound recalls the beautiful girl "on an ass-cart" outside this city [29/145].

80. **pargoletta**: I, "little girl."

81. **"onestade . . .,"**: I, "honor shines" [cf. 44 and 56 above].

82. **Dio . . . bontade**: I, "God, the first goodness" [*Conv*. III, 7, 2; JW, *Pai*, 2-2, 184; BK, *Pai*, 5-1, 214].

83. **Ideogram**: I4 [M3002], "right conduct." Other definitions include concepts such as morality, loyalty, patriotism, and concern with the public good. They rhyme with the nonmetaphysical circles of Dante's 9 spheres.

84. **Augustine**: [Cf. 11 above].

85. **Alessandro**: Alexander the Great [85:230].

86. **Saladin**: [6:15].

87. **Galasso di Montefeltro**: A famous Italian lord, related to the notorious Guido of Montefeltro [*Inf.* XXVII]. Dante mentions the three men in this line as examples of public generosity and liberality [*Conv*. IV, II, 14]. Other historians have not concurred.

88. **distributive justice**: This phrase is the heart of the matter. A central concern of the good state and the good, humane man and

ruler is to provide a just way to distribute food and other things to meet the needs of the people. The just price is one means to this good end [85:95]. The motif anticipates *Thrones*.

89. "cui . . . bontade": I, "which this goodness adorns" [*Conv.* III, 121]. This canzone states that the human soul wedded to goodness shows this adornment in all of its actions.

90. Know agenda: [Cf. 48, 50 above].

91. virtu: [74:87]. Pound wrote: "The soul of each man is compounded of all the elements of the cosmos of souls, but in each soul there is some one element which predominates, which is in some peculiar and intense way the quality or *virtu* of the individual; in no two souls is this the same. It is by reason of this *virtu* that a given work of art persists" [*SP*, 28].

92. und kein: G, "and not a." In the military a weekend pass was usually devoted to fun and / or entertainment.

93. Mr Hoepli: A publisher in Milan, the great-uncle of Vanni Scheiwiller who published Pound's wartime economic pamphlets. Tradition has it that Hoepli sent a copy of one such pamphlet to a banker friend in Switzerland, who wrote back saying it should be destroyed [EH, *Pai*, 2-1, 143].

94. "urgente": I, "urgent."

95. "e farlo sparire": I, "and make it vanish."

96. Shivers: A nickname for either Eisenhower (R) or Adlai Stevenson (D), who ran for president against each other in the elections of 1952 and 1956. They were both renominated in the conventions of 1955, and Stevenson was twice defeated. Prob. Eisenhower is meant. At his first nomination, Pound remarked, "Well, if this doesn't finish off the Republican Party, nothing else will" [EM, *Difficult*, 321].

97. "Alfalfa": The nickname of Alfred Landon, Republican nominee for president during the campaign of 1935. His overwhelming defeat assigned him to historical oblivion.

98. Grenfell: [87:21]. Both David Gordon and his wife Ellen remember quite vividly Pound's conviction that Grenfell had been murdered. One of the "some others" was James Forrestal (1892-1949), first secretary of defense, who committed suicide while under care at Bethesda Naval Hospital. The press reported that while the corpsman who was supposed to be guarding him was out of the room for a minute, Forrestal jumped out of a window. Pound suspected that he, too, was murdered. Grenfell's *Unconditional Hatred* was written by a man who approached complex international problems not with partisan passion but with good nature and civility.

99. The Bard . . . : [Cf. 27 and 28 above].

100. Dante: [Cf. 25 above].

101. abuleia: I, "paralysis of the will" [5:44; 54:192].

102. KATI: [Cf. 2 above].

103. Taffy: An engineer [18:25].

104. Zaharoff: Sir Basil Z., European munitions maker and predatory capitalist [38:2].

105. Aquarone: Duke Pietro Aquarone. Minister of the Italian royal household, who on July 26, 1943 with Marshall Pietro Badoglio ousted Mussolini by order of King Vittorio Emmanuele III.

106. Ub: Ubaldo degli Uberti [77:99; *Pai*, 6-2, 244]. A longtime friend of the poet [R. Uberti, *Italian Quarterly*, 95-107].

107. agitante calescemus: [calescimus]: L, "When he [the god in us] stirs we are set on fire" [Ovid, *Fasti* I, 5]. The phrase is preceded by "est deus in nobis" ("a god is in us"), which Pound associates with Richard of St. Victor's "Ignus quidquid in nobis est," which he himself translated, "There is a certain fire within us" [EH, *Pai*, 3-1, 136; *Pai*, 4-1, 30; *SP*, 72]. It is followed by a line containing the word *semina* which echoes the leitmotif *semina motuum* [90:24] : "impetus hic sacrae semina mentis habet" ("This impulse produces the sacred seeds of the intellect").

108. The autumn . . . autumn: The two lines framing the god stirring within give a Japanese tone to the awakening fire. The source could be any number of haiku with the traditional autumn tag.

109. Lux: L, "Light" [83:6].

110. in diafana: I, "in a transparency" [36:4]. The word has other associations in Pound usage. Talking about "the decline of the West . . . between the *Nicomachean Ethics* and the *Magna* (or fat) *Moralia*," and the need for Confucius, he wrote in a letter: "I am trying to get my American publisher to reprint the 'Mencius.' But don't think it contains much more on the present point (or diafana)" [*L*, 333].

111. Creatrix: L, "Mother."

112. oro: L, "I pray."

113. Ursula benedetta: I, "Blessed Ursula." Saint Ursula was a mythical late entry into the company of saints. Many legends flourished around her, most having to do with her martyrdom as a virgin along with numerous other virgins, numbered from a few up to thousands. Their slaughter presumably took place near Cologne, which resulted in the basilica of the sacred virgin there [*EB*].

114. per dilettevole ore: I, "through beloved hours."

115. Ysolt: Isolde, who languished in the absence of Tristan.

116. Ydone: "Ydoine," from the medieval romance *Amadis and Ydoine* which Pound cites in discussing love "lais" [*SR*, 80].

117. Picarda: Piccarda Donati [*Par.* III, 49], a beautiful lady whom Dante placed in the heaven of the moon because she had broken her vows.

118. Isis-Luna: Conflation of Isis [90:28] and Diana/Artemis, the moon goddess.

119. black panther: One of the hieratic cats, used to evoke a quality of paradisal yearning. In "Heather," an early poem, we read: "The black panther treads at my side, / And above my fingers / There float the petal-like flames. / The milk-white girls / Unbend from the holly-trees, / And their snow-white leopard / Watches to follow our traces" [EP, *Lustra*, 196].

120. J'ai . . . assez!: F, "I have had compassion for others. Not enough! Not enough!"

121. the child . . . : His daughter, Mary, whom he remembers most vividly during her years at Gais [77:102] and at moments in Rapallo during WWII. She wrote a poem then in Italian which contained the sentiment "For me nothing, stillness—stillness outlasting all wars" [M de R, *Discretions*, 151].

122. The light there . . . : Divinity manifested in natural intelligence . . . flowing.

123. Ideogram: Li^4 [M3920], "power" or "energy."

124. Ideogram: Hsing^2 [M2754], "to walk" or "act."

125. Ideogram: Chin^4 [M1061], "near to."

126. Ideogram: Hu^1 [M2154], "to" or "at."

127. Ideogram: Jen^2 [M3099], "benevolence." The five characters are from *The Unwobbling Pivot* [XX, 10]. Pound translates: "energy is near to benevolence" [*CON*, 155].

128. au bois dormant: F, "to the sleeping woods."

129. "Krr! Krr!": Onomatopoetic rendition of the bird's song.

130. "mai . . . ignoto": I, "never late . . . by the unknown." From "non e mai tardi per tentar l'ignoto" ("It is never too late to try the unknown"), a line from the third episode of *La Nave*, a political play by D'Annunzio which opened January 11, 1908 to an enthusiastic audience that included the king and queen. *La Nave* contained the usual horror scenes favored by D'Annunzio (Faledro and his four sons have their eyes and tongues torn out on stage), but it projected Italy's restoration as a great sea power with control of the Dalmatian coast. Pound approved of the daring and lyrical mysticism of the line early on, as he quoted it in "I Gather the Limbs of Osiris" in 1911 [*SP*, 25].

131. Ocellus: [87:43] Pound attributes to this Pythagorean philosopher the phrase "to build light," which he associates with T'ang's idea "to make it new" [cf. 91/610, 611; 94/642; 98/684; 107/762].

132. T'ang tub . . . : [53/265; 53:40, 43; *GK*, 278].

133. 見: Chien^{4} [M860], "to see." Pound sees in the character the eye mounted on running legs [*CON*, 23].

134. D'Annunzio: Gabriele d'A., 1863-1938, a popular Italian author who wrote poetry, plays, novels, and short stories. He was born and reared in primitive districts of the Abruzzi, which informed the dramatic physicality of his perception. His flamboyant personal life and addiction to splendor awed his public, many of whom tried to imitate him. His experiments with Greek and Latin verse forms and rhythms created a poetry alien to the normal Italian practice. He is noted for sharp, dramatic images and unusual musicality. His clamorous love affair with Eleanora Duse led him to become a playwright, especially when she decided to limit her repertoire to his works. Pound refers to his play *La Figlia di Jorio* [The daughter of Jorio] of 1904.

135. Brescia: City of N Italy noted for its lion sculptures [110/780].

136. Amphion!: [90:7].

137. Venus: for Aphrodite, goddess of love.

138. Roma: L, "Rome."

139. Rapicavoli: The name of a prominent Italian family [M de R], but which member is meant here is not known. Perhaps the horse jump took place in Libya.

140. Quarta Sponda: I, "Fourth Side." The Fascist name for Libya.

141. Carthage: The possibilities of what "waste" could refer to are numerous enough to discourage speculation.

142. Flora: L, goddess of flowers, whose festival was celebrated on April 28. "In the spring buds grow: only in autumn do petals of the flowers flow in the air."

143. Castalia: [90:5].

144. "pone metum, Cerinthe: L, "lay aside fear, Cerinthus" [25:35, 36].

145. Nec deus laedit: L, "God does not harm [lovers]" [25:38].

146. Lorraine girl: Joan of Arc.

147. volucres . . . auditum: L, "and flying dolphins to the hearing."

148. Ideogram: Hsien^{3} [M2692], "to manifest" [85:143].

149. nuova vita: I, "new life." Dante's *La Vita Nuova* concerned how his childhood encounters with Beatrice changed him finally from a lovesick troubadour to a man of great spiritual depth.

150. e ti fiammeggio: I, "and for you I burn" [*Par.* V, 1]. The words of Beatrice as she illuminates the mind of Dante and lightens his eyes. The flame here is the light of love.

151. e . . . Ciprigna: I, "and the beautiful Cyprian." Venus (Aphrodite) is associated with the sea caves [91:4, 5]. The copper recalls "orichalchi" [1:29].

152. alcun vestigio: I, "some trace."

153. (Kati): [Cf. 2 and 102 above].

154. quidity: [91:82].

155. "Oh you . . . ": Pound's translation of Dante line [Par. II, 1; 7:38].

156. incognita: L, "unknown things."

157. un . . . spiriti: I, "a light filled with spirits." From the opening to Cavalcanti's Ballata V [*T*, 106].

158. Persephone's . . . : The underworld–that Virgil led Dante through.

159. E "chi crescerà": I, "And 'who will increase'" [89:2].

160. Swedenborg: [89:3; 94:81].

161. "Blind eyes . . .": From an early Pound poem, "Ballatetta": "The light became her grace and dwelt among / Blind eyes and shadows that are formed as men; / Lo, how the light doth melt us into song" [*P*, 38].

162. to enter . . . velocities: Pound said in a letter [3 Feb. 1957] to Wyndham Lewis: "F. Masai on Plethon notes that gods are gods cause they got more hilaritas than the *animal electoral*, and also that they COMMUNICATE more rapidly with each other" [Materer, "Ez to WynDAMN," 156]. This vortex (a complex of images in a cone-whirling action) is a vitally important fugal leitmotif, which as it connects with other moments in the poem, expresses some of the Arabic-Moslem, Christian–Dante metaphors for the way to paradise, and climaxes with the "bridge over worlds" on the last page of the poem. The "gate" to the "way" is seen as the lost lane into heaven. One must find the narrow gate that opens onto a path leading up from the labyrinth to a corridor (1/2 inch wide? [105:14]) and thence to the narrowest of bridges. As Asin [*Islam and the Divine Comedy*] puts it: "Over a turbid river, in the Pauline vision, stretches a bridge *as fine as a hair* [italics Asin's], connecting this world with paradise; this bridge the righteous souls cross with ease, but the wicked fall into the river" [p. 183]. The gates at Canto 47/236-237 anticipate this passage, which anticipates others: the line at 94/634, "And that all gates are holy," as well as "bab,gate" [100:63], and TSO, the rope bridge between heaven and earth used by the Na-khi gods [101:51]. [For an analytical study see Colin McDowell, "Bridge Over Worlds," *Pai*, 13-1].

163. Ian Hamilton: General I. H., 1853-1947, an Irish officer who served in the English army. Yeats's opinion changed. In a letter to his father [Nov. 29, 1909] he said the general was "a man of the really finest culture, as fine as that of anybody I've ever met" [Wade, *Letters of Yeats*, 541]. But in a later letter to his father [Sept. 12, 1914], he wrote: "I hear that Ian Hamilton has written home that his men are heroic but can achieve nothing because all the officers are incompetent" [ibid., 588].

164. antennae: The sensitivity to the surrounding world: the body is in the soul, not the soul [only] in the body [98:20].

165. malevolence: As a real force, it is continuously operating, not as an external personification but as a tendency to the dilution of positive human emotions such as love and compassion. Said Pound: "The Lord of terrible aspect is real and no mere personification; there are some who either cannot or will not understand this."

166. Six ways . . . : Whereas some sectarian religions presume a transcedent personfied deity invoked only at specific times, Pound's religion assumes that divinity, which he calls "intimate essence" [*SP*, 49], operates through the persona continuously as a state of mind: "A god is an eternal state of mind . . . a god [is] manifest. . . . When the states of mind take form" [*SP*, 47].

167. Without guides: "Concerning the intimate essence of the universe we are utterly ignorant" [*SP*, 49].

168. Flora Castalia: [90:5]. The earlier reference implied spring. With the petals drifting in the air, the canto has come to autumn.

169. diafana: I, a "transcendent screen through which light can come, but through which one cannot see behind to the source of the light" [cf. 110 above].

170. e Monna Vanna: I, "and Madonna Giovanna," an endearing diminutive for Guido Cavalcanti's lady love.
171. tu mi fai rimembrar: I, "you call to mind." From Dante's picture of the Earthly Paradise, in the conversation (across a stream) with the nymph Matilda, to whom he says: "You call to mind where and what Proserpine was when her mother lost her and she the spring" [*Pur.* XXVII, 49-51].

CANTO XCIV

Sources

John Adams, *Old Family Letters*, compiled by Alexander Biddle, Philadelphia, 1892 [*Biddle*]; Charles Rollin, *The Ancient History of the Egyptians, Carthaginians, Assyrians, Babylonians, Medes and Persians, Grecians, and Macedonians*, 8 vols., Philadelphia, 1829; Raymond De Roover, *The Medici Bank*, New York University Press, 1948 [Roover, *Medici*]; S. P. Scott, trans., *Corpus Juris Civilis*. . . , vols. 2, 11, 12, 13, 16, 17, rpt. New York, AMS Press, 1973 [Scott]; *Corpo Del Diritto*, corredato delle note di Dionisio Gotofredo, e di C. E. Freiesleben, altrimenti Ferromontano. Per cura del consigliere Giovanni Vignali, Napoli: presso Vincenzo Pezzuti, editore, vols. 1, 2, 7, 8, 10, 1856 [*Vignali*]; Philostratus, *The Life of Apollonius of Tyana*, trans. F. C. Conybeare, 2 vols., Harvard University Press (Loeb 16) [P, *Life*]; L. A. Waddell, *Egyptian Civilization: Its Sumerian Origin*, London, 1930; G. R. S. Mead, *Apollonius of Tyana, The Philosopher–Reformer of the First Century A.D.*, London, 1901 [Mead, *A of T*]; Agnes Strickland, *Lives of the Queens of England*, London, 1864 [*Queens*].

Background

EP, *LE*, 160; *SP*, 333; *The Spur of Fame, Dialogues of John Adams and Benjamin Rush, 1805-1813*, ed. John A. Schutz and Douglass Adair, Huntington Library, 1966; Yogi Ramacharaka, *Hatha Yoga*, L. N. Fowler, London (continuous undated reprints); Eike Haberland, ed., *Leo Frobenius 1873-1983: An Anthology*, trans. Patricia Crampton, Franz Steiner, 1973.

Exegeses

DG, *Pai*, 11-1, 99-101; *Pai*, 3-2, 164; *Pai*, 4-2 & 3, 554; MSB, *Pai*, 3-3, 334; WF, *Pai*, 11-1, 39-49; J. Neault, *Pai*, 4-1, 3-36; JW, *Later*, 8-101; P. Surette, *Pai*, 2-2, 337-338; HK, "Under the

Larches of Paradise," in *Gnomon*: *Essays on Contemporary Literature*, New York, 1958; W. McNaughton, *Pai*, 3-3, 320; J. Neault, *Pai*, 3-2, 226; DD, *Pai*, 6-1, 101-107; A. Miyake, *Pai*, 7-1 & 2, 98-99; CE, *Ideas*, 158-159; MB *Trace*, 324-326.

Glossary

1. **Brederode**: Hendrik, Count of B., 1531-1568, Dutch nobleman who became a leader in the revolt of the Netherlands from Spain. In 1564 he joined other great nobles who began making demands upon Philip II of Spain. Most of the nobility, including Catholics, were appalled at the severity of the Inquisition against the Protestants. But many of the great nobles, including for a few years William, Prince of Orange, would do little more than appeal to Philip for compassion and leniency, which would mean a relaxation of edicts–something Philip would by no means sanction. When the greater nobles became divided, Brederode became an activist leader of the lesser nobles. A Calvinist attack on Catholic churches in 1566 led to military repression and a demand for an oath of allegiance from the nobility. Brederode refused the oath and began recruiting troops. "He became the chief military leader of the rebels when William, Prince of Orange (later William I, the Silent), wavered" [*EB* (Micropaedia), 1978].

2. **Rush**: Benjamin R. [65:56; 70:50], American physician and political figure, with whom John Adams had a lifelong correspondence. In a letter dated April 4, 1790, JA speculates on the way fame is given by history and asserts that "The History of our Revolution will be one continued Lye from one end to the other. The essence of the whole will be *that Dr. Franklin's electrical Rod, smote the Earth and out sprung General Washington. That Franklin electrified him with his rod–and thence forward these two conducted all the Policy, Negotiations, legislatures and War* [JA's italics]. These underscored Lines contain the whole Fable Plot and Catastrophy" [*Biddle*, 55]. To illustrate historical injustice, JA says: "But this my Friend . . . is the Fate of all ages and Nations; and there is no resource in human nature for a Cure. Brederode did more in the Dutch Revolution than William 1st Prince of Orange. Yet Brederode is forgotten and William [is called] the Savior, Deliverer and Founder" [ibid., 56].

3. **Blue Jay**: Prob. Sheri Martinelli, who during her visits to St. Elizabeths lived in nearby Alexandria, Va., which suggested the city of Alexandria in Egypt, which in turn may have suggested the following characters to describe the son of Philip of Macedon and then Rollin's historical works [cf. 7 below].

4. **T'ai:** [M6020], archaic Chinese King.

5. **Wu**: [M7195], "military" or "violent."

6. **Tzu**: [M6939], "son." The characters in this sequence do not occur elsewhere either in the works of Pound or in any of his known sources. Prob. Pound invented the phrase with two intents: (1) to suggest Alexander the Great, who Rollin says, "was of a violent, fiery temper" [*Ancient History*, Bk. XV, vol. 5, p. 16]; and (2) to suggest by sound the city of Dioce [74:8]. *T*, as in *tao*, has the sound of *d*; Pound may not have recalled that *t'* does not. A JA letter to Rush [Sept. 1807] evokes the notion and ties several references on this canto page together. JA, thinking by pen that Washington didn't have much education, wonders where he got what he had and comes up with a theory: "I will tell you what I conjecture. Rollins ancient History you know is very generally diffused through this Country, because it has been and is in England. The Reading of most of our Men of Letters extends little further than this Work. . . . From Rollin I suspect Washington drew his Wisdom . . . in the History of the Kingdom of the Medes, there are in the Character of

Dejoces, several strokes, which are very curious, as they resemble the Politicks of so many of our Countrymen, though the whole Character taken together is far inferiour in Purity and Magnanimity to that of Washington" [*Biddle*, 164-165]. In two pages of description JA traces the actions of Dioce until he is finally prevailed upon by the people to be their king. He consents to this only if they will build a capital city in a certain way: "'Within the last and smallest enclosure stood the Kings Palace. In the next were several appartments for lodging the officers. The Name of the City was Ecbatana'" [ibid., 166]. JA draws parallels between the building of Ecbatan [4:32] and the building of the city of Washington, which he (JA) had been dead set against. He closes his letter: "Read the Chapter in Rollin. Washington was more sincere than Dejoces; but I am persuaded he had read this description of him" [ibid., 167]. The association of the characters with Dioces was made by Pound to Sheri Martinelli [DG, *Pai*, 11-1, 99-101].

7. **Rollin**: Charles Rollin, 1661-1741, French educator who was rector of the University of Paris (1694-1695) and coadjutor of the Collège de Beauvais (1699-1711). He was removed from this position because of his sympathies with the Jansenists and was in later years restored, removed, and restored again. He is known to scholars for his *Traite des Études* (1726-1731), a book about the duties of a college rector. But he became famous through his popular works on ancient history [cf. sources above].

8. **re / Lincoln**: Benjamin L., 1733-1810, American general from Hingham, Mass., who was active in the provisional congresses and many battles of the revolutionary war. Washington appointed him to receive the sword of Cornwallis. Later he was a member of the commission that in 1789 formed a treaty with the Creek Indians. In his final years he took a great interest in science and wrote papers that received marked attention. He was an unselfish, dedicated public man. John Adams attended his funeral (he died May 9, 1810), and in a letter to Rush dated 14 May, bewailed the fact that the official obsequies had not been further enlarged: "The day before yesterday I went to Hingham to convoy to the tomb my . . . Friend Lincoln. . . . A cold unanimated and ignorant sketch of his life and Character was pronounced by his own Parson. . . . A long Train . . . of Relations and Neighbors walked in Procession. No Arms; No Militia, no Regulars! . . . Lincoln's Education, his Reading his general Knowledge, his Talent at Composition was superiour to Washingtons" [*Biddle*, 256].

9. **depreciations . . . people"**: In a letter to Rush dated June 21, 1811, JA says about banks and usurers and the arts they use in cheating the people: "But all these Arts are not equal to that of making immense fortunes . . . by a financiering operation, which substitutes a Paper Money, whose immense depreciations go into the Pocketts of a few individuals in Lieu of a Paper Money whose depreciations are in favour of the whole People" [*Biddle*, 288].

10. **Mr Adams**: The longer JA watched the iniquity of bankers the more outraged he became [71:101]. In many letters to Rush he indulged that outrage and castigated banks for using their power to defeat honest men at the polls [*Biddle*, 272, 276-277] and even to gull people into helping the bank to cheat them: "The Rage for Banks is a Fever a Mania. . . . Every Bank in America is an enourmous Tax upon the People for the Profit of Individuals. . . . Our Banks are the madness of the Many for the Profit of a Few. . . . Our Banks are all founded upon a fundamental Principle of Iniquity" [ibid., 281]. Thus he saw through their "hoax" to their responsibility for "the corruption of history," referred to at the top of the next canto page.

11. **Suvitch**: Fulvio Suvich (b. 1887), Italian statesman who helped negotiate the Franco-Italian Rome Agreement of 1935, which permitted M to go ahead in Ethiopia. He was well connected in Geneva and was led to believe that Britain would make no serious protest about extending Italian Somaliland

because of the primitive and brutalized state of the Ethiopian peasants [104:24]. But he so firmly opposed the rapprochement of Italy and Germany that he was sent as ambassador to Washington to get him out of the way. Pound himself was uncertain of the name. In a letter to Olivia Agresti [9 Aug. 1953] he said: "NO use creating such a panic and dither as THOUGHT did at that time in little Suvitch (if that was his name)." The occasion for Suvich's shattering response, said Pound, was "when I spoke of finance" [Folder 77, Beinecke; BK]. The implication is that if people really knew what banks were up to, it would create an explosion.

12. **dinamite**: I, "dynamite."

13. **the Medici . . .** : [45/230]. In *The Medici Bank* [Roover, *Medici*], Pound read: "As deposits poured in, it became increasingly difficult to find suitable investments. . . . Rather than refuse deposits, the Medici . . . [sought] an outlet for surplus cash in making dangerous loans to princes. This policy proved to be their undoing" [BK and TCDE, *Pai*, 11-2, 282]. But the problem was not that simple: "The Medici lost in more than one way: First because gold prices of commodities fell steadily, and secondly because much business was done with countries . . . whose silver currency was depreciating in terms of gold. . . . While assets thus tended to shrink in value, liabilities remained the same because the Medici owed gold . . . to depositors. As the purchasing power of gold increased, interest charges payable in gold became more and more burdensome. . . . The assets, as they declined in value, reduced the owner's equity, until there was nothing left" [Roover, *Medici*, 60].

14. **Alex . . . Biddle**: Alexander Williams B., 1856-1916, the son of Alexander Biddle and Julia Rush. Alex Biddle (not to be confused with Nicholas Biddle of the bank wars [34:70; 88:92]) was a medical doctor who practiced in Pennsylvania. His wife, a descendent of Benjamin Rush, engaged his interest in the JA-Rush correspondence, from which he made selections for publication.

15. **l'AMOR**: I, "Love." The "civic order" makes the lines into a Confucian concept [DG, *Pai*, 3-2, 164].

16. **Frate Egidio**: I, "Brother Egidio." Prob. the author of a treatise on *Donna mi Prega* consulted by Pound, who wrote: "Frate Egidio (Colonna, Romano, il beato, degli Agostiniani) goes round it [that is, a problem in the ms. of the *Donna*]. . . . He begins his commentary with a graceful description of a notable lady" [*LE*, 160].

17. **per la mente**: I, "through the mind." Source of the line "who shd / mistake . . . " is unkown, but the intent is a rhyme with the lack of precision in language as in "drive screws with a hammer" [104/741], as developed in "Axiomata" [*SP*, 49-52] and in the discrimination concerning *prana* in the next gloss.

18. **prana**: [pranja]: Skt, "absolute energy." A major concept of Hindu occultism: "We may consider it as the active principle—Vital Force, if you please. It is found in all forms of life, from the amoeba to man—from the most elementary form of plant life to the highest form of animal life. Prana is all pervading. . . . Prana must not be counfounded with the ego—that bit of Divine Spirit in every soul, around which clusters matter and energy. Prana is merely a form of energy used by the Ego in its material manifestation. When the Ego leaves the body, the prana, being no longer under its control, responds only to the orders of the individual atoms, or groups of atoms, forming the body, and as the body disintegrates and is resolved to its original elements, each atom takes with it sufficient prana . . . to form new combinations. . . . With the Ego in control, cohesion exists and the atoms are held together by the will of the Ego" [Ramacharaka, *Hatha Yoga*, 157-158]. The concept is seminal in Pound's thinking. It overlaps and reinforces other seminal concepts such as *virtu* and *directio voluntatis*. *Hatha Yoga* devotes two chapters to the subject, taken up in more detail in other books by Yogi Ramacharaka. The foregoing quote is from a chapter entitled "Pranic Energy." Another

chapter is called "Pranic Exercises" [ibid., 166-175]. Pound didn't talk much about yoga at St. Elizabeths, but he routinely did some of the rhythmic breathing exercises. He also assumed his version of the lotus position and did some of the mental rituals that correlate with Richard of St. Victor's final stage in *cogitatio, meditatio*, and *contemplatio* [*SP*, 333; 85:52]. To flow with the forces of divinity unfolding is to participate in the process [Booth, *Pai,* 3-3, 334; WF, *Pai*, 11-1, 39-49]. The process flows through the many stages described in the metaphors of light, crystal, and finally, jade.

19. **clover . . . time**: Restatement of recurrent theme: the green world alive outlasts any structure of the earth or creation of man—basalt: (1) a dense, dark volcanic rock; (2) a black, unglazed pottery. "Learn of the green world what can be thy place" [81/521] [DG, *Pai*, 4-2 & 3, 554].

20. **gates . . . holy**: Gates into life and out of life: deaths and entrances [47:10]. In *Pandects*, Bk. I, Title 8, we read that some things come under human law and others under divine law: "Sacred things are for example, walls and gates, which, to a certain extent, are under divine law" [for the Latin and commentary see DG, *Pai*, 11-2, 313-324].

21. **Pandects**: The *Pandecta* (or *Digests*) of Roman law produced by direction of Justinian I [cf. 45 below].

22. **Gaius**: A Roman jurist of the 2d century who did an early codification of the law. His *Institutes* formed the structural design of the *Digests*, which were organized into fifty books each with a differing number of subsections.

23. **divini . . .** : L, "communicating of human and divine law." A phrase from Bk. I, Title 8.

24. **Ius Italicum**: L, "Italian Law."

25. **Digest**: Bk. L, Title 15 concerns tax laws: "8 Paulus, On Taxation, Book II" contains this sentence: "The same privileges were conferred by the Divine Severus and Antoninus upon the city of Tyre" [Scott, vol. 2, 259].

26. **Antoninus**: [78:56]. Roman emperor, 137-166, who started the tradition of looking at law and money wisely.

27. **Tyre**: The "this" refers to the "Italian Law" of the time, which Paulus, the great jurist, gave to the city of Tyre.

28. **Paulus**: Julius P., 2d century A.D., a legal adviser of Septimius Severus and industrious author of some 300 books on the law of his time. The *Digests* of Justinian are almost one-sixth of his work.

29. **Consul**: One of the two chief magistrates ruling conjointly in the Roman republic. A prefect in ancient Rome acted as a magistrate, governor, or commander. Sources refer to Paulus as a prefect but not a consul. The "7th of December" is not in the sources.

30. **the "Code"**: It concerned bishops, other clergy, and superintendents of orphanages, hospitals, and charitable foundations for the aid and protection of old men, strangers, captives, and the sick. Grants of money were to be made: "For this, indeed, seems to be necessary, as the support and education of boys and poor persons depend upon these grants." These activities go beyond the call of "civic order" and indicate the compassion and wisdom of feeding the people, one of Pound's tests of a good ruler, as with the Egyptian Antef [93:4].

31. **The Bulgar**: The king or ruler of the Bulgars, one of the groups Justinian could not subdue by war, whose differences with the emperor concerned not only taxation but also Justinian's vigorous support of church dogma. The Bulgars dissension went back to the time of Constantine the Great and the founding of the Eastern Empire.

32. **Constantine**: C. the Great, 288?-337, who in the process of winning the throne of the empire saw a "flaming cross" in the sky, the sign by which he would win. He won handsomely. Thereafter, he set forth the Edict of Toleration of Christianity. Christi-

anity was not made a state religion and Constantine himself was not baptized until he was dying. But he convened the Council of Nicea, moved the capital to Byzantium, rebuilt the city as Constantinople, and by his very success displeased the Slavs and Bulgars to the north, who tried to discredit him. The Council of Nicea, after much argument and dissension, adopted the dogma of the Trinity. In the end all the bishops present (estimates vary from 225 to over 300) voted for it except two, who were banished along with Arius (the father of Arianism). Thereafter, those who objected to the idea of the Son being coequal with the Father said that many bishops voted under threats and pressures. The phrase "horse sense" may refer to the anti-Trinity feeling of the Bulgars and Slavs, whose territories were hotbeds of Arianism. In fact, Constantine convened the Council of Nicea in 325 in order to settle the question because the struggles between the Arians and their opponents were tearing the church apart and making it difficult to govern. But the council settled nothing: the struggles, sometimes violent, went on for centuries and contributed to the final split between the Eastern and Western churches. Pound calls Constantine a louse because of inhuman laws he made against the offspring of female slaves or prostitutes, dispossessing them of property and torturing them. The new law of Justinian (whose empress, Theodora, had been an actress and had given birth to an illegitimate child before he married her) changed all that. *Novel* (an amendment to Justinian's code) 127, Chap. IV says that "such women can contract marriage with men of every description . . . provided that dotal instruments are executed. . . . All others . . . can contract marriage through affection alone, provided the women with whom it is lawful for them to contract marriage are free" [DG, *Pai*, 11-2, 313-324].

33. **CODE V. 27**: The source of the data in the preceding gloss [Scott, vol. 13, 214].

34. **Code V. iv . . .**: Subsection 23,5 contains much detail about "daughters of women of this kind" directing how they can avoid previous harsh legal sanctions, so that, in the sense of "persistent" or "painstaking," "fuss-cat" is appropriate [DG, ibid.].

35. **Kung**: Confucius [13:1; 53:78].

36. **the Odes**: The Confucian odes.

37. **Mencius**: [54:66; 78:139]. Following the precepts of Kung, he practiced *chêng ming* and called things by their right name.

38. **Dante**: He used the language of the people and wrote *De Vulgari Eloquentia*, which showed the value of avoiding "abstract yatter."

39. **Agassiz**: [93:51]. He taught his students to look directly at a thing until they could finally see it [*ABCR*, 17], allowing the light to pour.

40. **Gestalt**: G, "form." The word is related to the idea of formative power, or the kind of intelligence that directs the cherry to become a cherry tree [113:43]. Also, to the *forma* or *concetta*, the divine force (the light pouring) in the universe [75:8].

41. **let the light**: [74/429]. Let the divine force of intelligence flow. Infections grow in the moist dark.

42. **Apollonius**: A. of Tyana, 4 B.C.-A.D.96?, was born in the Cappadocia of Greek Asia Minor and trained in philosophy. He traveled as a mendicant sage to most of the courts of the Mediterranean world, as far as India to the east and Spain to the west. He was a student of the lore of both Asclepius and the neo-Pythagorean school, to which he added a knowledge of oriental mysticism. The story of his life, by Philostratus, is so replete with miracles, some have regarded him as an imaginary character. "On his return to Europe [from the East] he was received with reverence as a magician. He himself claimed only the power of foreseeing the future. . . . It was said that he was accused of treason both by Nero and Domitian, but escaped by miraculous means. Finally, he set up a school at Ephesus, where he died, apparently aged 100. The work of

Philostratus is generally regarded as a religious work of fiction" [EB] [cf. 78 below].

43. made peace . . . : [91:9, 94; 93/623]. A natural affinity is supposed to have existed between animals and most holy men of the East both before and after the time of Christ. Of Apollonius, Conybeare wrote: "he professed to know all languages without ever having learned them . . . to understand the language of birds and animals . . . [and] shared the Pythagorean belief of the migrations of human souls from body to body, both of animals and of human beings" [P, *Life*, xii].

44. the Cyprian: Aphrodite. The altars sacred to her on the island of Cyprus were often stained by blood sacrifice. Apollonius, at age 16 began to follow a rigid ascetic rule. He renounced wine, refused to marry, would not eat flesh of any kind, and in particular "condemned the sacrifice of animals to the gods. . . . In antiquity hardly any meat was eaten which had not previously been consecrated by sacrifice to a god, . . . consequently the priest was the butcher of a village and the butcher the priest" [P, *Life*, ix]. The obverse of the Hyksos motif [93:18].

45. Justinian: Flavius Anicius Justinianus, 483-565, called "the Great," is the most famous emperor of the Eastern Roman Empire. He is famous for his new modes of administration, an advanced ecclesiastical policy, and his wisdom in war and foreign policy, but most of all for his extensive legal reforms. Before his reign the vast body of contradictory legal documents, including the *Perpetual Edict,* resulted in conflict and confusion in the courts. When he became emperor (528), he appointed 10 commissioners to study and edit all existing constitutions, retain what was practical, and get rid of what was wasteful. In 14 months they produced the *Codex constitutionum*, which was promulgated in 529, all imperial edicts not included becoming instantly repealed. This work was so successful that another commission of 16 was appointed in 530 to deal with the whole history of jurisprudence and the law, and to produce extracts from the best in order to make a practical, workable document. They were to discard as much as possible and retain nothing at variance with the new *Codex*. Their work in both Greek and Latin editions was to be contained in fifty books, each book to be divided into subtitles, the general order being that of the old *Perpetual Edict*. Justinian promulgated the fifty-book work December 16, 533. According to authorities this work is not only "the most precious monument of the legal genius of the Romans," but by the "influence it has exerted and still exerts the most remarkable law book the world has ever seen" [EB]. The Greek volume was called *Pandects* (*Πάνδεκτα*), the Latin the *Digests* (*Digesta*). While the *Code* (*Codex*) and the *Digests* were in process, Justinian conceived that a third book was needed: an easy, basic manual for beginners which would give an outline of the law in clear and simple words. This work, based on the previous outlines of Gaius, was published as the *Institutes of Justinian*. The emperor did not stop here: commissions were kept busy revising the work already done, such as the *Codex*. It is the first revision of the *Codex* (534) which has come down to us. Pound often lists Justinian as one of the great minds of the Western world who added to the "building up of social and economic criteria" [*SP*, 150, 156; *GK*, 40, 109, 275, 342].

46. the novel, 127: A *novel* was a new addition, an amendment to the *Codex*. Pound prob. meant 117 and not 127 because the phrase "from affection" occurs in 117 [DG, *Pai*, 11-2, 322n.].

47. Goth . . . Queen Ash: Pound's source for these four names is Waddell's *Egyptian Civilization*, which is historically inaccurate [B de R, in EH, *Approaches*, 188]. Goth, "the hawk-king," is supposed to be in the early dynastic line of Sargon the Great, whom Waddell believed was the father of Menes, the founder of the Egyptian dynasties.

48. Agdu: Says B de R: "Agadu or Agade is supposed to be shown by the Indian seals to be the capital city of Sargon and Menes(!)" [ibid.].

49. Prabbu of Kopt: Says B de R: " 'Prabhu' (Pound's Prabbu is a typographical error) was, according to Waddell, a form of the Sumerian title 'Par,' corresponding to 'Pharaoh': 'the form Prabhu adopted by the Indian scribes was presumably to make this "Pharaoh" title intelligent to Indian readers' " [ibid.].

50. Queen Ash: Supposedly, "the wife of Sargon, whose name, again according to Waddell, is found on the Abydos vases" [ibid.]. Says DG: "Regardless of L. A. Waddell's errors in Egyptology and the names of 'Prabbu of Kopt, Queen Ash,' their significance is perfectly clear: The Egyptian Pharaoh and his wife, as well as Eleanor of Castile and Edward I [cf. 146 below] are subject rhymes of Justinian and Theodora. And this theme continues from the 'gt / healing' with 'Justinian, Theodora' " [91:14].

51. Isis: [90:28].

52. Manis . . . silver: Waddell, the source of Menes' purchase of land, also defined the relative value: "One *bur* of land" [was] reckoned as worth sixty *gur* measures of grain, and one *mana* of silver [B de R, in EH, *Approaches*, 188].

53. black obelisk: "The famous black obelisk [the Tablet of Abydos] discovered by de Morgan at Susa in 1897 is likewise arbitrarily attributed to 'Menes.' " [ibid.]. It is a block of stone with inscriptions including the dates of 65 Egyptian rulers covering some 2200 years.

54. Abydos: Town in upper Egypt on the west bank of the Nile, the site of a temple of Osiris built by Seti I, which houses in numerous chambers and corridors most of the reliefs, including the Tablet of Abydos.

55. Hieroglyph: Sargon the Great. But Pound follows the errors of Waddell here and later. Waddell took the lower part of the seal to be a cartouche and the top part to be a falcon. Pound took the top figure *in* the cartouche to be the image of a temple, which becomes important in later cantos when there is the recurrent theme "the temple is not for sale" [97/676, 678, 679].

56. caligine: I, "darkness."

57. 1/2 year . . . tin: Source unknown, but the two "1/2" lines appear to articulate with the "Agada, Gana" line, which they bracket.

58. Agada, Gana: [cf. 48 above]. Pound may be rhyming the religious spirit that formed the city of Agdu, sacred to Osiris, with a similar spirit that formed the city sacred to Wagadu in "Gassire's Lute" [74:134], as found in Frobenius. Or he may be suggesting that Agdu, the city of Sargon, was actually the second Wagadu from that "Tale of the Sudan." The tale says: "Four times Wagadu was built and stood there in spendour. Four times it was destroyed so that there was no trace of it to be seen. Once it was lost through vanity, once through faith being broken, once through greed, and once through strife. Four times Wagadu changed its name. First it was Dierra, then Agada, then Ganna and finally Silla" [Haberland, *Frobenius*, 146]. As a metaphor, the tale articulates with *The Cantos*. Having destroyed Agada by broken faith, we may be at the Ganna stage, where greed is the destroyer: "Hoggers of harvest are the curse of the people" is a recurrent theme of the later cantos [88:44].

59. Swans . . . : As with other holy men, the birth of Apollonius was accompanied by marvels. His mother was told in a dream to go to a meadow and pick flowers. She did this and then fell asleep: "Thereupon the swans who fed in the meadow set up a dance around her as she slept, and lifting their wings . . . cried out aloud. . . . She then leaped up at the sound of their song and bore her child . . . just at the moment of the birth, a thunderbolt seemed about to fall to earth and then rose up into the air and disappeared" [P, *Life*, I, 14-15].

60. *πολλοὺς τιμῶν . . . ὀλιγόις*: H, "to respect many, and confide in few." [Conybeare's translation, P, *Life*, I, 109. The accents are incorrect in the canto text.]. This was A.'s answer to King Vardanes of Babylon, who asked him what was "the most stable and secure way of governing."

61. styrax . . . leopards: After leaving Babylon, A. and his friend Damis came to Pamphylia, a land fragrant with the odors that attracted leopards: "For these animals delight in fragrant odours . . . and traverse the mountains in search of the tear of gum of the *Styrax*" [P, *Life*, I, 121].

62. King Huey: King Hui of Liang. Since A. could speak all languages, he could have spoken in Chinese to King Hui if he had met him, but he hadn't. The advice Mencius gave to that king rhymes with the advice A. gave to King Vardanes about how he should use his money. Said A., "By spending it, for you are a king." Both sages were against hoarding. The Chinese characters say, "Hui of Liang, by wealth put to use not by wealth hoarded," but they occur in this sequence in none of Pound's known Chinese sources. Part of the statement occurs in the *Ta Hsio* (*The Great Digest*): "The Ch'u state does not go in for collecting wealth but counts fair-dealing its treasure" [*CON*, 75].

63. Ideogram: Leang [M3951], "Liang dynasty."

64. Ideogram: Hui [M2339], "kind, gracious," King Hui.

65. Ideogram: I [M2932], "by."

66. Ideogram: Ts'ai^2 [M6662], "wealth."

67. Ideogram: Fa [M1768], "issue stores."

68. Ideogram: Wu^2 [M7180], "without, none."

69. Ideogram: I [M2932], "by."

70. Ideogram: Pao^3 [M4956], "treasure."

71. Taxila: Country in India ruled by King Phraotes. The maxim in the characters is rhymed there, because this king spent his treasure for the good of the people and lived in a simple style much approved by A. who said to him: "I am delighted, O king, to find you living like a philosopher" [P, *Life*, I, 183].

72. Phraotes' . . . sun: It is said of a cub of the tigers of Taxila: "as soon as it is born, it lifts up its front paws to the rising sun" [P, *Life*, I, 189]. The gesture was taken as an act of worship.

73. *νυμφόληπτοι . . . νήφειν*: H, "rapt by the nymphs . . . bacchantic revellers in sobriety" [ibid., 217]. Part of A.'s way of telling the king about religious ecstasy brought about by drinking only water.

74. *ὕμνον ἡμέραν*: H, "daily hymn." From a description of some of the Brahman's religious rites. A. was amazed to discover statues of the Greek gods which the Indians had set up with their own and worshipped with their own: "and to the Sun they sing a hymn every day at midday" [ibid., 257].

75. *ξῶον . . . πάντα*: H, "a living creature . . . the universe . . . for it engenders all." After Phraotes, A. visited the chief Brahman of India, named Iarchas, who told him that the universe possessed a soul. Said A., "Am I to regard the universe as a living creature?" Said Iarchas, "Yes . . . for it engenders all living things" [ibid., 309].

76. III 34: Bk. III, chap. 34 of *The Life of Apollonius* [P, *Life*].

77. *ἐρωτά . . .*: H, "Love it has . . . and knits together." A. asked if the universe were then male or female. Iarchas said it was both: "for by commerce with itself it fulfills the role both of mother and father . . . ; and it is possessed by a love for itself more intense than any separate being has for its fellows, a passion which knits it together into harmony" [ibid.].

78. F. C. Conybeare: The prelector of Oxford who translated *The Life of Apollonius of Tyana* by Philostratus, which had "only been once translated in its entirety into English, as long ago as the year 1811." Said

Conybeare: "there is in it much that is very good reading and it is lightly written" [ibid., v].

79. **Richardus**: R. of St. Victor [85:52]. Many of Richard's ideas rhyme well with those of Iarchas [*SP*, 71].

80. Ἰάρχας: Iarchas, the Indian Brahman.

81. **Swedenborg**: Emanuel S. [89:3], who also believed that universal or divine love was the binding force of societies.

82. **griffins** . . . : "As to the gold which the griffins dig up, there are rocks which are spotted with drops of gold as with sparks, which this creature can quarry" [P, *Life*, I, 333].

83. **phoenix**: Iarchas said: "And the phoenix . . . is unique in that it gives out rays of sunlight and shines with gold." The Indians say that "the phoenix which is being consumed in its nest sings funeral strains for itself. And this is also done by the swans according to the account of those who have the wit to hear them" [ibid., 333-335].

84. προπεμπτηρίους . . . : H, "sings funeral strains for itself."

85. **universe is alive**: [75:8]. The music of the spheres, or, the harmony flowing in the cosmos, is part of the *forma* or the *concetta*. The song of the nymphs in ecstasy fulfills true harmony. Said Pound: "beneath this [the flesh] is our kinship to the vital universe, to the tree and the living rock. . . . We have about us the universe of fluid force, and below us the germinal universe of wood alive, of stone alive" [*SR*, 92].

86. ἐρωτά . . . : [Cf. 77 above].

87. **the Ganges** . . . : After 4 months with Iarchas, A. "was minded to go. . . . And . . . keeping the Ganges on his right hand . . . went down towards the sea a journey of ten days from the sacred ridge." On the way they saw many animals. "And in the usual discussion of what they saw they reached the sea. . . . And they say that the sea called Erythra 'or red' is of deep blue colour, but that it was so named from a king Erythras" [P, *Life*, I, 337].

88. ὑμᾶς . . . ἐρρωσθε: H, "you presented me with the sea farewell" [ibid.]. Iarchas had given A. camels to travel with. When A. reached Erythra, he sent the camels back to Iarchas with greetings, thanks, and a message that said: "I came to you on foot, and yet you presented me with the sea; but by sharing with me the wisdom which is yours, you have made it mine even to travel through the heavens" [ibid.].

89. **Balàra**: "They also touched at Balara, which is an emporium full of myrtles and date palms; and there they also saw laurels, and the place was well watered by springs" [ibid., 341].

90. παρὰ . . . τιμῶσιν: H, "among all lovers of wisdom." After travel to many other places, including Babylon, again, Nineveh, Seleucia, Cyprus, and Paphos, A. "then sailed to Ionia, where he excited much admiration and no little esteem among all lovers of wisdom" [ibid., 345].

91. **bell the boat**: A story of pearl fishing at Balàra ends thus: "they found the entire sea full of wild animals and it was crowded with seals; and the ships . . . carry bells . . . the sound of which frightens away these creatures" [ibid., 343].

92. **Grant, O Muses**: The people of Symrna sent a deputation to A. asking that he visit them. When A. asked why they wanted him, the legate said "to see him and be seen." A. said: "I will come, but O ye Muses, grant that we may also like one another" [ibid., 349-351].

93. καὶ . . . ἀλλήλων: H, "we may also like one another."

94. **Ephesus** . . . : A. went to Ephesus and urged the people there to devote themselves to study: "for they were devoted to dancers and taken up with pantomimes, and the whole city was full of pipers, and full of effeminate rascals, and full of noise" [ibid., 351].

95. Hugo Rennert: [20:9]. This favorite professor of Pound at the University of Pennsylvania once reacted to the administration's ballyhoo that "the plant" should not lie idle by saying: "But damn it *we* are the plant" [EP, *Impact* 239]. This sentiment rhymes with A's idea that a city is the people in it rather than a place. So he urged the people of Smyrna "to take pride in themselves rather than in the beauty of their city" [ibid., 357].

96. Homer: [1:23].

97. πολλαῖς . . . : H, "many shapes." Said A.: "Men who visit all regions of the earth may be well compared with the Homeric Zeus, who is represented by Homer under many shapes." A. Believes this is better than the "statue of Zeus wrought . . . by Pheidias," which is merely frozen in stone [ibid., 359]. A rhyme with "Otis, Soncino" [82:17, 18].

98. πράττειν . . . οἵ τι δύναται: H, "do best what he knows" [the source has the singular ὅ rather than the plural nominative οἵ]. A.'s argument about keeping the peace included a tolerance for differences of opinion and the idea that each man should be urged to employ his best talent: "To me it seems best that each man should do what he understands best and what he best can do" [ibid., 361].

99. ἐπι . . . ᾗδη: H, "on board the ship [for it was] already evening." [The source has ἤδη, an adverb of time meaning "now" or "already." With the subscript on the first *eta*, the word becomes a form of εἴδω, but since with the rough breathing it means nothing, we must assume an error of transcription.] At Ilium, A. said he "must spend a night on the mound of Achilles." So "he went up alone to the barrow; but they went on board ship, for it was already evening" [ibid., 369].

100. "master . . . fire": A. had gathered in his travels a large group of followers. As autumn drew on and bad weather could be expected at sea, they wanted to be on his boat: "They all then regarded Apollonius as one who was master of the tempest and of fire" [ibid., 371].

101. Palamedes: P. was the messenger sent to call Odysseus to the war against Troy. Thus his shrine was of concern to Achilles. A. commandeered a large boat to carry many of his followers and set out for Methymna: "For there it was, he said, that Achilles declared Palamedes lay." A. found the buried statue and "set it up again in its place, as I myself saw; and he raised a shrine around it . . . large enough for ten persons at once to sit and drink and keep good cheer in" [ibid., 373].

102. "It was not . . . ": As A's followers kept pestering him to tell about his talk with Achilles, he finally agreed and said: "Well, it was not by digging a ditch like Odysseus, nor by tempting souls with the blood of sheep, that I obtained a conversation with Achilles" [ibid., 377] [cf. 1/3-4].

103. Aeolis . . . : A. offered an Indian prayer to get Achilles to appear. When he did appear he granted A. the boon of answering 5 questions about the Trojan War. A.'s fifth question concerned Homer's reason for not mentioning Palamedes. Achilles said that Odysseus, to his shame, caused Palamedes' death and Homer didn't want to record that shame. Achilles said: "But you, O Apollonius, . . . must care for his tomb and restore the image of Palamedes . . . and it lies in Aeolis close to Methymna in Lesbos." Then A. said to his companions: "With these words . . . Achilles vanished with a flash of summer lightning, for indeed the cocks were already beginning their chant" [ibid., 383-385].

104. So that . . . margin: The source of these three lines is not known. They are not in Apollonius [cf. HK, "Under the Larches of Paradise," *Gnomon*].

105. a touchstone: As A. approached Rome, he was warned to keep away because Nero would doubtless have him imprisoned or put to death, as he did with other philosophers, so that young men were left without a teacher. A. said: "Well, of all the blessings which have been vouchsafed me by the gods . . . this present one . . . is the greatest . . .: for chance has thrown in my way a touchstone to test these young men . . . to prove . . . which of them are philosophers" [ibid., 335].

106. *γὰρ βάσανος*: H, "for a touchstone" [ibid., 434]. the remainder of the Greek line, if it occurs anywhere, must be part of a sentence that contains a transitive verb. *καθαρὸν* is an adjective in the objective case. It means, "pure, bright, clear." The other words may mean, "and far from anything mortal."

107. "Hic sunt leones": L, "here are lions." After Rome, A. traveled toward Gibraltar: "the extremity of Libya . . . furnishes a haunt to lions" [ibid., 467].

108. Calpis . . . : "But the promontory of Europe, known as Calpis, stretches along the inlet of the ocean on the right hand side" [ibid.]. And going west, right would be north.

109. Heliad's poplar: "At Gadeira," A. and Damis visited a shrine shaded by two trees: "they were a cross between the pitch tree and the pine, and formed a third species; and blood dripped from their bark, just as gold does from the Heliad poplar" [ibid. 473].

110. their pillars: They came then to a temple to Hercules: "the pillars in the temple were made of gold and silver smelted together . . . and their capitals were inscribed with letters which were neither Egyptian nor Indian" [ibid.]. Pound identifies the letters as Sumerian.

111. *δὲ . . . πράττουσι*: H, "for the doers of holiness" [ibid., 503].

112. *γῆν . . . ἀσφαλῆ*: H, "and the sea is all safe." A. said: "let us not forget that the whole earth affords secure ground for the doers of holiness, and that the sea is safely traversed not only by people in ships but even by people attempting to swin" [ibid.].

113. v. 17: Bk. V, chap. 17 of *The Life of Apollonius* [ibid., 501].

114. Musonius: A philosopher of Babylon whom Nero threw into prison "for the crime of being a sage." A. was told his story as a warning to himself as he approached Rome [ibid., 431]. Some years later at Athens, A. "met Demetrius the philosopher for after the episode of Nero's bath and of his speech about it [91:92], Demetrius continued to live at Athens." Demetrius told of how he, trying to console Musonius "took his spade and stoutly dug it into the earth." The phrase "raised our stele," not in the source, is a metaphor for "done honor to" [ibid., 505].

115. Five, twenty two: This chapter of *The Life of Apollonius* tells the story of a young man who spent his fortune on building a huge house with gardens and colonades but spent nothing on education. A. asked him whether men should be valued for themselves or for their wealth. Said the young man, "their wealth, for wealth has the most influence." A. finally says: "My good boy, it seems to me that it is not you that own the house, but the house that owns you." A.'s sentiment rhymes exactly with the preachments of Kung and Mencius. The first two characters are the core of the Kung adage, "Humane men use wealth to develop themselves; inhumane men use themselves to develop wealth" [55:9]. *Fa* [1-5] ("use") and *ts'ai*[2] ("wealth") are the core of the message to "King Huey" [Cf. 62 above].

116. 29-: At Alexandria A. had conversations with Vespasian, whose idea about wealth was the opposite of the young man of chapter twenty-two. V. used wealth to develop himself and others. In chap. 29, V. says to A.: "For I was never the slave of wealth that I know of even in my youth" [ibid., 529].

117. Chung: [M1504], "the mean" or "balance." Pound translated the Chinese classic *Chung Yung* [The doctrine of the mean] as *The Unwobbling Pivot* [*CON*, 95-188]. In discussing the duties of an emperor, A. told

Vespasian that Nero "disgraced the empire by letting the strings go too slack and drawing them too tight." V. thought this over and asked: "Then you would like a ruler to observe the mean?" A.'s answer was emphatic: "Not I but God himself, who has defined equity as consisting in the mean" [ibid., 527].

118. VESPASIAN: [78:55]. Titus Flavius Vespasianus, A.D. 9-79, Roman emperor (69-79). He made his way in the world by sheer work and talent. After the murder of Nero in 68, Galba succeeded and ruled a few months until he was killed and Otho succeeded. Meanwhile, Vitellius was proclaimed emperor by the armies in the north. He ruled until Otho was routed, but support for him melted away when Vespasian's troops from the east arrived. Vespasian asked A. whether he should be emperor and A. said he should. He seized Egypt, received help from his friends in Italy, and arrived in Rome in A.D. 69. His troops located Vitellius in hiding and killed him [ibid., 537-553].

119. formó . . . : S, "I made new records." Source unknown. The phrases summarize the reign of Vespasian, who set about restoring the state and its finances and gave an example of frugal living which contrasted greatly with the life of Nero.

120. BUT . . . Greece: Later on V. wrote A. many letters inviting him to attend his court at Rome. But A. refused because V. had taken away the freedom of the Greeks because of their "factitiousness." Thus, A. wrote to Vespasian: "You have taken such a dislike to the Hellenes, that you have enslaved them. . . . What then do you want with my company? Farewell" [ibid., 567].

121. ANTONINUS: A. Pius [78:56].

122. lex Rhodi: L, "law of Rhodes."

123. Daughter . . . TYana: Julia Domna, wife of Emperor Septimius Severus, was one of the most remarkable women of the classical world: "She possessed, even in an advanced age, the attractions of beauty . . . and strength of judgment, seldom bestowed on her sex" [Mead, *A of T*, 54]. She prob. exercised some restraint upon "the dark and jealous temper of her husband, but in her son's (Caracalla's) reign, she administered the principal affairs of the Empire. . . . She was the patroness of every art, and the friend of every man of genius." She had both the background and the reasons: "for the beautiful daughter of Bassianus, priest of the sun at Emesa, was an ardent collector of books from every part of the world. . . . It was at her request that Philostratus wrote the Life of Apollonius" [ibid. 55]. N.B.: Tyana is pronounced with the accent on the first syllable [Surette, *Pai*, 2-2, 337-338].

124. *τῶν . . . παίδων*: H, "of his own children." In convincing V. he should be emperor, A. said: "If however he accepts the throne, he will have the devoted service of his own children" [P, *Life*, 549].

125. *ὑπὸ τοῖς θεοῖς*: H, "by the gods." This phrase occurs a few lines after the first one, when A. says: "For myself I care little about constitutions, seeing that my life is governed by the gods" [ibid.]. The sense of A.'s page-long speech adds up to a lack of interest in abstract theory.

126. Ideograms: I 1-5 jen[2] [M3016 and M3097], "one man." A. said to V.: "For just as a single man pre-eminent in virtue transforms a democracy into the guise of a government of a single man who is the best; so the government of one man, if it provides all round for the welfare of the community, is popular government" [ibid.]. The immediate reason for the phrase came from a visit to St. Elizabeths of a Confucian scholar, Carson Chang. Pound said to him that 4 Confucians working together could save China. Chang replied, "Four? *One* is enough" [*Pai*, 3-3, 326].

127. V. 35: Bk V., chap. 35 contains the materials of the 3 foregoing glosses.

128. *ἐπὶ . . . εἰρήσεται*: H, "that he should say what he really thinks. A.'s idea of "a man of philosophic habit" [P, *Life*, I, 553].

129. *εἰ . . . ᾤκεις*: H, "if you were the tenant of my breast." V. "listened gladly" to all A. had to say and then said: "if you were the tenant of my breast, you could not more accurately report my inmost thoughts" [ibid.].

130. & do not mow: A.'s final advice to V. was: "mow not down the loftier stalks which overtop the rest for this maxim of Aristotle's is unjust; but try rather to pluck disaffection out of men's hearts" [ibid., 553-555].

131. Ideogram: Wang² [M7037], "king."

132. *ἑλληνίζοντας* . . . : H, "over Greeks those who can speak Greek." A.'s advice to V. included the idea that a ruler sent to rule a province should speak the language of that province: "I mean, that over Hellenes should be set men who can speak Greek, and Romans . . . " [ibid., 557].

133. Euphrates . . . : Said A. to V.: "O king, Euphrates and Dion . . . are at your door . . . call them in . . . for they are both of them wise men" [ibid., 535]. The king did, but A. was being devious for he wanted the king to see what bad advisers they had been: "You, my sovereign, have learned from these your good-for-nothing predecessors how not to rule" [ibid., 537]. But later, with the emperor not present, Euphrates attacked A., "in his anger resorting to coarse insults" [ibid., 565], thus proving himself a "schnorrer."

134. Dion . . . music: A. thought Dion was "too rhetorical and overmuch adapted to please and flatter," so A. said to Dion: "You should use a pipe and a lyre, if you want to tickle men's senses, and not speech" [ibid.].

135. sent the lion: In Egypt A. saw a man leading a tamed lion on a string. One day, the lion came earnestly fawning to A. so that bystanders thought it wanted food. But A. said: "This lion is begging me to make you understand that a human soul is within him, the soul namely of Amasis, the king of Egypt." Hearing this, the lion "gave a piteous and plaintive roar" and crouched down weeping. A. said he thought the lion should be cared for in a temple. So "the priests met and offered sacrifice to Amasis . . . and conveyed him up country into Egypt with pipings, hymns and songs composed in his honor" [ibid., 569-571].

136. *ἐπ' αὐτῷ ἄδοντες*: H, "in his honor."

137. Amasis: "Historically, Amasis I, Egyptian pharoah and founder of the XVIIIth Dynasty (c. 1700 B.C.), is famous as the king who finally delivered Egypt from the Hyksos [cf. 44 above] . . . who overran Egypt somtime around 2100 B.C." [Neault, *Pai*, 4-1, 27-28]. In *A History of Egypt*, Budge records the destruction caused by the Hyksos and the great good done by Amasis. Says Neault: "like Apollonius, Amasis becomes an embodiment of the moral precept, reaffirmed in Apollonius's identification of the lion, that was characteristic of an era of immanent gods when men lived in harmony with nature" [ibid.].

138. keeping the Nile . . . : Then A. set out for Ethiopia "to visit the naked sages." Through parable A. warned his many followers so that many remained behind: "but the rest, ten in number, I believe, offered prayer to the gods . . . departed straight for the pyramids, mounted on camels and keeping the Nile on their right hand" [P, *Life*, I, 573].

139. *μὴ . . . τέκῃ*: H, "one penny begets another penny."

140. book Six, chap. 2: In this chapter, A. praises the wisdom of the Egyptians and Ethiopians in their trading practices: "contrast our Helenes: they pretend they cannot live unless one penny begets another, and unless they can force up the price of their goods by chaffering or holding them back" [P, *Life*, II, 7].

141. Ἠῴῳ Μέμνονι: H, "Memnon of the Dawn." The statue was famous, "for when the sun's rays fell upon the statue, and this happened exactly at dawn . . . the lips spoke immediately the sun's rays touched them. . . . They . . . offered a sacrifice to . . . Memnon of the Dawn, for this the priests recommended them to do, explaining that the one name was derived from the words signifying 'to bùrn and be warm' and the other from his mother" [ibid., 15-17].

142. *ψυχὴ . . . τιμητέον*: This sentence does not appear in the source nor in any other of Pound's known sources. As written, it neither construes nor scans. The first two words in reverse order–*ἀθάνατος ψυχὴ*, "immortal soul"–do appear in the *Life* [p. 404]. If we read *ζωοῖσιν* for *ξωοῖσιν*, we could read "living things" or "the living." Perhaps "the immortal soul which must be honored among the living" is as close as one can come. The *τι*, although strangely placed, could function as an interrogative even though neuter.

143. Ideogram: Pen[3] [M5025], "root-origin-source."

144. thrones . . . Justice: A note foreshadowing *Thrones de Los Cantares*, a section thematically based on Dante's *Paradiso* [96:headnote]. The divine spirit that comes from the divine fire is the root and source and origin of justice.

145. Acre, again: City where the crusaders headquartered at times [6:10]. The first Acre Pound associates with Eleanor of Aquitaine [7:1] who landed there ca. 1150.

146. Eleanor: Eleanor of Castile (the great-great-granddaughter of Eleanor of Aquitaine), wife of Edward I of England, who landed at Acre in 1270 on the 7th crusade [DD, *Pai*, 6-1, 102]. While resting over winter at Cyprus, Edward was attacked and wounded by a hired assassin. The wound in his arm blackened so that he had to have painful surgery. "Eleanor was by his bedside at this dreadful crisis . . . and bewailed, with a passion of tears, the anguish about to be inflicted on her husband." He said that it was better for her to "scream and cry than all England mourn and lament." The operation was successful and Edward "always attributed his final recovery to the tender care of Eleanor; but if there had been any truth in the story of her sucking the poison from his wound, the narrators of the scene . . . would not have forgotten" [Strickland, *Queens*, 103]. Strickland's note says that the story got into the record by a man who lived 150 years after the siege of Acre.

147. via Padua: From Cyprus, Edward returned to England through Italy. At Padua he was honored by being made a member of the legal faculty of the university [T. F. Tout, *Edward the Exile*, London, 1903, 86] [BK].

148. thunderbolt: "At this juncture the life of Edward was preserved in a manner that he considered most miraculous. As he was sitting with his queen on a couch, in their palace at Bourdeaux, a flash of lightning killed two lords who were standing directly behind them, without injuring the royal pair" [*Queens*, 105]. The date was 1273, however.

149. Federico Secondo: Frederick the Second, I, 1272-1337, known as F. of Aragon [25:14], was king of Sicily 1296-1337. Although he was second, he called himself "the Third" because he was the third son of King Peter. His rule was tumultuous, as Sicily was subjected to the power plays of popes as well as the kings of France and Spain. But Frederick, a wise ruler, was devoted to justice and beloved of his people. In *The Cantos* he should not be confused with Frederick, king of Sicily (1198-1212), celebrated by Pound as author of *The Book of the Falcon* [97:272]; or Frederick II of Prussia [32:38; 62:117]; or Frederick II, holy Roman emperor, 1215-1250.

150. Alfonso: A. X, 1221-1284, king of Castile (1252-1284) and brother of Eleanora [cf. 145 above]. Although his reign was plagued by political and military turmoil, he is known for his advancement of culture, and for being the Justinian of Spain because he was largely responsible for *Las Siete Partidas*, a compilation of the legal knowldege of his time. A collection of poems for music is also attributed to him.

151. St Louis: Louis IX, 1214-1270, king of France (1226-1270), was the son of Blanche of Castile and thus the brother of Eleanora and Alfonso. He was a monarch dedicated to justice who sought to introduce uniform Roman law into France. He also abolished the judicial duel and extended the appellate jurisdiction of the crown to all cases.

152. **Magnus**: M. VI, 1238-1280, called "Magnus the Law Mender." As king of Norway (1263-1280), he made peace with Scotland by ceding islands to them. After that, he immediately undertook a general revision of the laws. His code introduced the concept that crime is an offense against the state. His acts in the name of justice greatly increased the power of the king by making the throne the source of justice.

153. **two years later . . .** : Eleanora died suddenly and unexpectedly on Nov. 29, 1290, while Edward was on his way to Scotland. He rushed back to her sickbed but arrived too late. "In the deepest grief, he followed her corpse in person, during thirteen days . . . to Westminster. . . . The king endowed the abbey . . . with many rich gifts. . . . Wax-lights perpetually burnt around her tomb, till the reformation extinguished them three hundred years afterwards" [*Queens*, 120-121]. Strickland says much about the continued sadness of her husband but nothing about his luck. The phrase is a musical figure used elsewhere [2/9; 11/51].

154. **Edwardus**: Edward I, 1239-1307, the king of England (1272-1307) who extended the power of the throne to include, for the first time, Wales and Scotland. His accomplishments in advancing learning, manners, architecture, education, and civilization were enormous, a program in which he was aided by the example of his queen, Eleanor of Castile, who introduced tapestry for the cold stone walls and forks to eat with. In *The Cantos*, Edward's name rhymes primarily with "thrones and justice." The consensus says: "more important, however, are those developments during his reign in law and constitution that have caused him to be praised as the English Justinian" [CE].

155. **Baliol . . . Bruce**: After the death of Alexander III, king of Scotland, such confusion reigned among the Scottish lords that they called upon Edward to arbitrate among the claimants to the throne. He agreed, if they would recognize him as their overlord. Both the claimants and the lords agreed. Thus, in 1292, Edward declared John Baliol as king of Scotland over Robert Bruce. Baliol did homage to Edward as agreed, but the rest of the Scots along with Bruce came to resent the arrangement, until finally John himself was left with little power and the Scots made an alliance with the French, who were also causing Edward trouble over Gascony. For some years Edward was at war with both France and Scotland. He conquered Scotland in 1296; but in 1297 the country arose in revolt under William Wallace and Edward had to reconquer it in 1298. He died attempting a 3d reconquest in 1307, this time facing another Robert Bruce, the grandson of the Bruce he rejected in 1292.

156. **stone**: The stone of Scone, or the coronation stone, was kept at the royal residence of Scottish kings from the time of the semi-legendary King Kenneth I. Tradition had it that no coronation could be valid without the stone. Thus, when Edward removed it to London, he thought he assured his overlordship. It didn't work. Scottish coronations took place at Scone without it. The Stone may now be seen at Westminster Abbey.

157. **PACTUM SERVA**: L, "slave agreement."

158. **Traist**: Ob., "safe" or "secure."

159. **As . . . corner**: We return to Apollonius, where Nilus, the youngest of the Naked Sages, a culture on the Nile, gives a long argument to A. defending his idea that he should leave his people and go over to A. He ends one speech on the idea that age "must not reject the claim that youth makes" by saying: "And anyone who takes the blessings bestowed upon him by fortune into a corner and there enjoys them by himself, violates their character as blessings, for he prevents

their sweetness from being enjoyed by as many as possible" [P, *Life*, II, 73].

160. the Cataracts: A. finally agrees that Nilus should join him. Then Nilus asks A. how long he plans to stay among the Naked Sages. A. says: "So long as the quality of their wisdom justifies . . . ; after that I shall take my way to the cataracts in order to see the springs of the Nile . . . [and] to listen to the roar of its waterfalls" [ibid., 75].

161. *καὶ . . . ἀκοῦσαι*: H, "but to listen to the roar [of its] waterfalls."

162. *φαντασία . . .* : H, "imagination wiser than imitation." Before leaving, A. has a long discussion with the chief of the Naked Sages about the images of their gods. A. objects to them being pictured as "grotesque" and "ignoble" animals. The elder sage says of the Greek artists such as Phidias, "they went up, I suppose, to heaven and took a copy of the forms of the gods." This irony does not impress A., who says there is a greater wisdom than such imitation: "Imagination wrought these works, a wiser and subtler artist by far than imitation" [ibid., 77-79].

163. baffled by terror: The elder questioned A. about the customs of Sparta under the law of Lycurgus, by which nobles and slaves were publicly beaten with whips until they were bloody. A. said the custom had a religious sanction and it was an improvement upon the old custom of human sacrifice: "It is not the scourging, but the sprinkling of the altar with human blood that is important." He said the Spartans were not terrified by the custom [ibid., 83].

164. Sparta: When the elder wanted to know why strangers were not allowed to settle in Sparta, A. said that Lycurgus, who made the law, "was not inspired . . . by mere boorish exclusiveness, but by a desire to keep the institutions of Sparta in their original purity by preventing outsiders from mingling in her life" [ibid., 85].

165. king . . . king: In a long discussion about the nature of justice and how it is obtained, A. shows that one necessary ingredient is for the king to guarantee it by being a just king [ibid., 89-99].

166. *μὴ ἐνομι λούντων*: H, "not mingling" and thus "not a melting pot."

167. Athens . . . Aristides: In his response, the elder sage uses the example of Aristides "to show the difference between one who is not unjust and one who is really just." When Aristides went to the islands he fixed their tribute according to their ability to pay, returning no richer than he was before he went. Afterwards the Athenians increased the tribute with dire results: "For when the Athenians exceeded his valuations and imposed heavier tributes upon the islands, their naval supremacy at once went to pieces" [ibid., 97].

168. Coke . . . : Sir Edward Coke [107:3], English jurist who fought for justice against James I and Charles I, even to imprisonment in the Tower. His work in defense of the *Magna Charta* is the anti-king gravamen of Cantos 107-109.

169. Ra-Set: [91:19].

170. To build light: The light descending that leads to the *paradiso terrestre* will be the result of justice for all put into practice, which will require new ways of doing things.

171. Ideogram: [53:42, 43]. Final words of legend on T'ang's bathtub, "Every day make it new."

172. Ocellus: [87:43]. Often in Pound's list of light-philosophers [Miyake, *Pai*, 7-1 & 2, 97-100].

CANTO XCV

Sources

J. P. Migne, *Patrologiae Latina*, vol. 90 [Migne, 90, column no.]; John Adams, *Old Family Letters*, compiled by Alexander Biddle, Philadelphia, 1892; Dante, *Conv*. IV, iv; Homer, *Od*. V, 325-376.

Background

EP, *SR*, 90; *SP*, 49-52, 71, 189, 378-383, 414, 434-435; *LE*, 150-154.

Exegeses

JE, *Pai*, 4-1, 181-182; JW, *Pai*, 2-2, 183; Morse, *Pai*, 10-3, 595-596; RO, *Pai*, 11-2, 283; WB, in EH, *Approaches*, 303-318; HK, *Era*, 327; CB-R, *ZBC*, 40, 141-145; George Kearns, *Guide to Ezra Pound's* Selected Cantos, Rutgers University Press, 1980; MB, *Trace*, 327-329.

Glossary

1. **LOVE . . . place**: The divine spirit flowing in the world [90:1]. Perhaps the "5000 years" goes back to Antef [93:4]. Pound's conviction that the best document about the Creation is the microcosm and the macrocosm, and that science is the best instrument to give us knowledge about the intelligence of divinity at work, is echoed here. The importance of the macrocosm in this spectrum is indicated by the comets and great stars, a rhyme with later references to the constellation Berenice [97:170; 102:42] and with many earlier references to the sun and stars [5:5; 37:72; 37/237; 74/425, etc.; *ABCR*, 17-27; "Hudson: Poet Strayed into Science," *SP*, 429-432].

2. **"Consonantium demonstratrix"**: L, "demonstration of harmonies." Miscopied from *Musica Theorica*, a section of the *Patrologiae Latina* [Migne, 90, 911C].

3. ἔφατ': H, "said."

4. **Beda**: L, "Bede." The Venerable Bede.

5. **Deus . . . mundi**: L, "God is the spirit of the world" [ibid., 987C].

6. **animal . . . sempiternum**: L, "[God is] best and everlasting being" [ibid., 987D].

7. **Tempus est ubique**: L, "time is everywhere" [ibid., 1050C].

8. **non motus**: L, "[time is] not motion" [ibid., 1050B].

9. **in vesperibus orbis**: L, for *in vepribus orbis*, "sphere among thornbushes" [ibid., 1186B]. Pound prob. thought his note concerned Hesperus, Vesper, or Venus as the evening star, which would climax the passage by a return to the opening theme of love [JE, *Pai*, 4-1, 182].

10. **Expergesci thalmis**: L, "to be awakened in the marriage bed" [ibid., 1190c].

11. **gravat serpella nimbus**: L, "mist weighs down the wild thyme" [ibid., 1192A].

12. **Delcroix**: [88:46]. Because Carlo D. was a lyric poet and wrote a peceptive study of Mussolini entitled *A Man and the People* (1924), Pound thought he had a perception

of Mussolini as a leader working "in favour of the whole people."

13. Van Buren . . . Talleyrand: In the 20s and 30s Pound had a dim view of Talleyrand [62:151] and his treatment of the U.S. ambassadors to France as well as his demand for bribes, but later he began to respect his intelligence as well as the difficulties he had with Napoleon. Then he noticed that his hero Van Buren expressed an attitude different from the one John Adams had during the time of the XYZ affair [70:16].

14. Adams to Rush: [94:9, 10; *Pai,* 9-3, 429].

15. guilds in Byzantium: A note foreshadowing *The Eparch's Book* [96:271].

16. "compagnevole animale": I, "friendly animal." Dante derived the phrase from Aristotle: "Thus, the philosopher says that man is a friendly animal" [*Conv.* IV. iv; cf. JW, *Pai*, 2-2, 183].

17. *πόλις πολιτική*: H, "city, community." Pound does not want these key words of Aristotle made into the idea of politics in the modern sense of trading in smoke-filled rooms [JW, *Pai*, 2-2, 184].

18. reproducteur: F, "stud animal." Taken from Remy de Gourmont's classification of the bourgeoisie into reproducing, taxpaying, and voting animals.

19. Paradis peint: F, "painted paradise."

20. *πολεύω*: H, "to plough."

21. *πολύγλωσσος*: H, "many-tongued, harmonious." The social-animal temper of pastoral politics may be suggested.

22. Benton: Thomas Hart B. [88:80]. Metal to coin money.

23. Van Buren: [Cf. 13 above].

24. J. A.: A recurrent theme of both John Adams and Pound is that devaluation of the currency hurts all the people [94:9, 10].

25. Alexander: A much-repeated motif [85:88; 85/549; 86/564].

26. Vicenza: I, the home town of Admiral Ubaldo degli Uberti [77:99].

27. stemma: I, "coat of arms."

28. "lapo . . . ": On returning to his home after the Mussolini government fell, Admiral Uberti wrote a letter to his son Riccardo, who said: "[I] received a letter from my father telling me that, arriving in Vincenza, he had seen . . . an arch with the old crest of the Uberti . . . [and] learned that it was the tomb of Lapo degli Uberti, who had died a Ghibelline exile in Vincenza six hundred years before. My father added in his letter, 'who knows if I too will not die a Ghibelline exile in Vencenza' for some *vento di siepe*! The latter is an Italian idiom, literally 'wind coming from the hedge,' which means, of course, a shot from an ambush. I wrote to Pound about it after the war, when he was writing *Section: Rock-Drill*" [*Italian Quarterly*, Spring 1973, 104].

29. Κάδμου *θυγάτηρ*: H, "Daughter of Cadmus" [91:88].

30. per diafana: I, "through diaphanousness" [36:4].

31. *λευκὸς*: H, "white."

32. *Λευκόθοε*: H, Pound's transcription of *Leucothea*, the white goddess Ino, daughter of Cadmus, who was metamorphosed into a sea-bird [91:89].

33. Nicoletti: Giachino N., the prefect at Gardone [74:52].

34. Ramperti: Marco R., an Italian journalist.

35. Desmond Fitzgerald: [92:7].

36. the crystal wave . . . solid: A recurrent paradisal motif [25/119; 40/201; 76/457; 76/459; 94:18].

37. Ideograms: [93:125-127].

38. YAO's worry: [53:14]. Legend says that he passed over his own son and named Shun as his successor, knowing that to carry on the middle kingdom would need the one man. Ideograms: "One man" [94:126].

39. Windsor: King Edward VIII. According to one account, he was instrumental in keeping WWII from starting [86:47; 89/601; 109:40; HK, *Pai*, 2-1, 41]. An example of what one man can do at a critical moment.

40. Saint Bertrand: [48:45]. A village that evokes for Pound the destruction of the light of Provence during the Albigensian Crusade [*SR*, 90].

41. Montrejeáu: Town in S France, in the department of Haute-Garonne, on the Garonne River some 27 miles SE of Tarbes. It marked the northern boundary of the Albigensian slaughter.

42. Elder Lightfoot: An elderly black gentleman at St. Elizabeths Pound was fond of. He entertained all with his cogent wit and pithy remarks, some of which concerned Darwin's ideas of natural selection. Lightfoot's observation was that evolution appeared to be going backwards [DG].

43. design: Intelligent design apparent in the universe is one of the central components in Pound's convictions that "the gods exist" [*SP*, 49-52]. Here used ironically about Elder's perceptions.

44. Miss Ida: Ida Mapel and her sister Adah, whom Pound met first in Spain in 1906; in 1919 he and Dorothy stayed at their Paris apartments. The two sisters visited him in jail in 1946 and at St. Elizabeths quite often [91:80].

45. "de Nantes . . . prisonnier": F, "There is a prisoner from Nantes." Line from a 17th-century song Pound found in a collection made by Yvette Guilbert and translated in 1912 [Kearns, *Guide*, 219].

46. periplum: L [59:10].

47. Madrid . . . 40 years: In 1906, when he first met the Mapel sisters.

48. Carrière show: [80:241]. Prob. a reference to a retrospective show of his works held either at the time of his death in 1906 or in 1946, 40 years later.

49. "Bret": Prob. the Hemingway "lost generation" heroine of *The Sun Also Rises.*

50. the jap girl: Prob. someone Pound heard going ecstatic over Rembrandt.

51. the russe: F, "in the Russian manner"; used here to describe a particular person, possibly the wife of Colonel Goleyevsky [74:172], who might have talked enthusiastically about Turgenev's novel *Smoke*, a favorite with the French and with Pound: "Turgenev in 'Fumée' and in the 'Nichee de Gentilshommes' digging out the stupidity of the Russian" [*SP*, 189].

52. Turgenev: [80:29]. Ivan T., 1818-1883, a Russian novelist who was one of the most famous and effective of "the Westernizers," as opposed to "the Slavophiles." In his mature years, he spent over half of his time in western Europe, most of it in Paris where he was a close friend of Flaubert. In his early London years Pound thought highly of him: "Galdos, Flaubert, Turgenev, see them all in a death struggle with provincial stupidity" [*L*, 25; cf. also *SP*, 414]. The Slavophiles would represent provincial stupidity.

53. Uncle William . . . Memory": W. B. Yeats [41:37; 77:163]. The ladies Pound recalls here from those pre-WWI years were doubtless so-called by Yeats (perhaps during his visits to Rapallo in the late 20s), who quoted a line from Blake: "The Muses are daughters of Memory" [74:439].

54. Pirandello: Luigi P., 1867-1936, one of the greatest of all Italian dramatists and novelists. One of his main literary concerns was the nature of reality and the impossiblity of catching it or fixing it. It must remain in memory, as in *Six Characters in Search of an Author* (1921) [*SP*, 434-435].

55. Pulitzer: Pound's outrage grew more intense because literary prizes such as the Pulitzer went to hacks and seldom to the real creative people who were "making it new."

56. historic blackout: A cue to Pound's increasing paranoia: he came to believe that, as in the past [cf. 74 below], a group of international conspirators were deliberately keeping the right information from the people and part of their object now was to destroy the Constitution as conceived by Adams and

Jefferson. Pound wrote, thinking of Upward [74:275] and Bunting [74:153], "All the resisters blacked out" [Knox, *Pai*, 3-1, 82].

57. Leucothae: [Cf. 32 above].

58. "My bikini . . .": [91:102].

59. And if I see . . . thought: [92:30].

60. Elsa Kassandra: Elsa von Freytag-Loringhoven, a post-WWI wild woman, who wrote for the *Little Review*. Dedicated to free love and free everything else, she once shocked W. C. Williams by telling him that what he ought to do to become great "was to contract syphilis from her and so free . . . [his] mind for serious art." Pound was sympathetic to her because she preached cosmopolitanism and antiprovincialism [Morse, *Pai*, 10-3, 595-596].

61. Dinklage: An author Pound remembered because of his dedication to the truth. In a letter to Reno Odlin about journalistic "lies in 1914 war," he says: "Von Dinklage demurred at A.B.C. for first grade frog kids" [RO, *Pai*, 11-2, 283].

62. what's his name: Prob. Robert Cowart, a young sailor who got caught in the ropes of the U.S. Navy dirigible *Akron* and was swept into the air. Two others who were also caught fell to their deaths, but "Cowart wrapped himself securely in the mooring line and held on" [Morse, *Pai*, 10-3, 597].

63. Hindoos . . . vacuity: Pound's not very sympathetic idea of the Hindu concept of nirvana; it's not the thing itself so much as its consequences Pound objects to. His associations inform the rest of this canto. The famous "We appear to have lost the radiant world" passage in "Cavalcanti" is followed by a description of two kinds of "the Hindoo disease, fanaticisms and excess that produce Savonarola, . . . [and] asceticisms that produce fakirs. . . . Between those diseases, existed the Mediterranean sanity . . . that gave the churches like St Hilaire . . . the clear lines and proportions" [*LE*, 154]. And again: "Against these European Hindoos we find the 'medieval clean line' " [*LE*, 150].

64. Gardasee: With the beautiful blues of Lago di Garda [76:91], who would want vacuity?

65. Mr Beddoes: Thomas Lovell B., 1803-1849, English poet often praised by Pound [see "Beddoes and Chronology," *SP*, 378-383], esp. for his "Death's Jest Book, or the Fool's Tragedy" (1825), where we read: "O world, world! the gods and fairies left thee, for thou were too wise, and now, thou Socratic star, thy demon, the Great Pan, Folly, is parting from thee" [ibid., 381].

66. Santayana: George S. [80:49]. To Pound's idea of intelligence in the cherry stone which made it able to create the cherry tree [113:43], he replied, in effect, that Pound had something there—but it would be intelligence of "an unconscious sort" [NS, *Life*, 429].

67. Responsus: L, "answer." The "something *there*" would not be a dead halt of the process as in stasis.

68. a hand . . . : The secret organized moneymen [cf. 55 above] hold all the face cards: they make the organized cowards.

69. something decent: The divine spirit or the "intimate essence" is that unnamable something [94:142], as reflected in Richard of St. Victor [*SP*, 71].

70. dicto millesimo: L, "at said date or time."

71. St Hilary: Prob. St. H. of Poitiers (8 saints named Hilary are listed in the *Dict. of Catholic Biography*), ca. 315-ca. 367, bishop and church father who became the major voice in the 4th century against Arianism [96:28], the most persistent heresy the church had to deal with for hundreds of years. His writings in defense of the dogma of the Trinity were informed, impassioned, and lyrical. Because of his beliefs he was exiled in 353 to Phrygia by Emperor Constantius II (who supported the Arians), not to be released until 361. His enemies called him "the sower of discord and the troublemaker of the Orient" [*New Catholic Encyclopedia*]. The Church of St. Hilaire at Poitiers [45:16], built in his honor, has the clean lines and the economy of form [HK, *Era*, 327] of the oak leaf of John Heydon, "secretary of nature" [87:82]. Pound would applaud one of his central teachings: "the existence of God can be known by reason, but his nature is incomprehensible" [ibid]. One can deduce from this premise that the human race is safer if it celebrates *mystery* as *mystery*, the *arcanum* as *arcanum*, than if it deduces, argumentatively, a lot of abstract dogma and starts burning and killing people in the name of such dogma. One of the reasons Pound praises the mysteries of Eleusis is that they maintained this distinction.

72. **an oak-leaf**: John Heydon said Hilary [92:40] looked at an oak leaf. A rhyme with "learn of the green world" and "the green casque has outdone your elegance" [81/521]: a central tenet of Pound's religion. One must marvel at both the elegance and the absolute economy of forms created in nature. Any plant distributes its branches and spreads its leaves in a mathematically precise way to obtain the optimum amount of sunlight. Since so precise a design implies a designer, Pound concurs with St. Hilary: "the *existence* of God can be known by reason" [109:49]. The point bears repeating as it is central to *The Cantos*. The "vine-leaf" evokes the god Dionysus, to discriminate him from the martyr Dionisis (hence the repetition of the line), but also because he was central to the Eleusinian mysteries.

73. **St Denys**: The Church of St. Denis, built in the 12th century on the spot in Montmartre where two missionaries, Dionisis and Eleutherio, were martyred by beheading in 273 [*Historia Francorum*, I, 31; CB-R, *ZBC*, 40].

74. **Calvin**: [14:16; 62:15]. His "logically developed" and fundamentalist belief that the Bible is the *sole* source of divine wisdom led to the burning of heretics, such as Michael Servetus in 1533. The point seems to be that Calvin did not succeed in destroying the names of the earlier martyrs by a blackout [89:87; cf. 56 above], because the flight of the Huguenots at the battle of St. Denis on Nov. 16, 1567 memorialized them [CB-R, ibid].

75. **the wave . . . sea-god**: The 10-line passage invokes again the Homeric scene where the raft of Odysseus is destroyed by the storm created by Poseidon and he is saved by Ino, daughter of Cadmus, who had been turned into Leucothea. She took pity on him with her kredemmon [*Od.* V, 325-376], which Pound called a "bikini" [cf. 91:102].

76. *νόστου . . . Φαιήκων*: H, "to reach the land of the Phaeacians" [ibid., 344-345].

CANTO XCVI

Sources

J. P. Migne, *Patrologiae Cursus Completus*, vol. 95, 1851: this volume contains *The Complete Works* of the Venerable Bede, and Paul the Deacon's *History of the Langobards* [Migne, column no.]; Alexander Del Mar, *History of Monetary Systems*, Chicago, 1896 [*HMS*]; *The Book of the Eparch of Leo The Wise*, trans. into modern Greek and Latin with a French translation by Professor Jules Nicole and published as *Le Livre du Prefet*, Geneva, 1893 [*EP. B*]; Cicero, *De Officiis*, 2; Catullus, *Carmen*, 93; Dante, *Pur.* I; Homer, *Od.* V, XIII.

Background

Max Gallo, *Mussolini's Italy*, trans. Charles Markmann, Macmillan, 1973; J. B. Bury, *History of the Later Roman Empire*, II, London, 1923 [*Later R.E.*]; *History of the Langobards* by Paul the Deacon, trans. William Dudley Foulke, Longmans, Green & Co., New York, 1906 [Foulke, *History*]; Constance Head, *Justinian II of Byzantium*, Univ. of Wisconsin Press, 1972 [Head, *J.II*]; John W. Barker, *Justinian and The Later Roman Empire*, Univ. of Wisconsin Press, 1966; Anthony Birley, *Septimius Severus*, Doubleday, 1972; Luigi Villari, *The Liberation of Italy*, C. C. Nelson, Wisconsin, 1959.

Exegeses

EP, *SP*, 231, 450; *GK*, 209; *LE*, 250; WB, in EH, *Approaches*, 312; Akiko Miyake, *Pai*, 7-1 & 2, 110; JW, *Pai*, 2-2, 176; *EH*, *Pai*, 2-3, 498; JW, *Later*, 102-132; Pearlman, *Pai*, 1-2, 163; Flory, *Pai*, 4-2 & 3, 325; CFT, *Pai*, 2-2, 223-242; Leo the Wise, *Pai*, 2-2, 245-311; MB, *Trace*, 304; DD, *Sculptor*, 239-240; CB-R, *ZBC*, 136, 146, 151, 258.

[As Cunizza says (*Par*. IX, 61-62): "Above are mirrors–you call them Thrones–by which the light of God as judge is reflected upon us." The source of divine wisdom is given as "pen yeh" at 94/640, followed by the comment, "That is of thrones, and above them: Justice." Said Pound: "*Thrones* concerns the states of mind of people responsible for something more than their personal conduct" (Don Hall, *Paris Review*, no. 28, 1962, p. 49)].

Glossary

1. **Κρήδεμνον**: H, "veil, scarf." What Leucothea [95:32, 75] threw to the drowning Odysseus to save him [*Od*. V, 351]: "So saying the goddess gave him the veil, and herself plunged again into the surging deep, like a sea-mew; and the dark wave hid her."

2. **Aestheticisme** . . . : F, "Aestheticism as church politics."

3. **hearth** . . . **diafana**: *Thrones* opens with a religious rite that is more than aesthetic. As indicated below, the name Tuscany (I, *Toscana*) derives from the Latin *thus, thuris* ("frankincense," "olibanum") and links the opening to the rhymes with Dionysus [2:20] at the end of Canto 95. The aromatic gum frankincense (pure incense) seems to derive from a variety of African cedar or juniper. The rite may be conceived as one of purification and linked forward to the Na-Khi [110:21; Eisenhauer, *Pai*, 9-2, 251].

4. **Aether** . . .**thure**: L, "The air rains down coins / the earth throws up corpses, / Tuscany which from incense" [Migne, 474, 492]. "Thusca" is a miscopying of Thuscia.

5. **ROMA** . . . : L, "Rome, which formerly. . . ."

6. **Sabines**: An ancient people living NE of Rome who were the source of many legends, including one about the rape of their women to supply wives for the followers of Romulus. For centuries they fought the Romans but

eventually became full Roman citizens. Their ensign had a picus (a woodpecker, rather than a crow). In time the Sabines spread north and east.

7. **Brennus**: A tribal chieftain from Gaul. Paul the Deacon [cf. 10 below] said [Migne, 495-496]: "And the reason why the Gauls came to Italy is represented to have been this: When they tasted the wine brought from that country, they were enticed by greed for this wine and passed over into Italy" [Foulke, *History*, 78].

8. **Bergamo . . . Ticino**: Cities eventually founded by other Celts. Ticino should be Pavia (from Latin *Ticinum*), the later Lombard capital, but perhaps the reference is to the Swiss canton of Ticino which is near Brescia, an Italian city near Lake Garda.

9. **Cunimundus**: King of the Gepidae, who "broke his treaty with the Langobards and chose war rather than peace." Alboin, king of the Langobards [cf. 17 below] entered into a treaty with the Avars, first called the Huns, and defeated them in two wars [Paul says one]: "In this battle Alboin killed Cunimund, and made out of his head, which he carried off, a drinking goblet. . . . And he led away as captive, Cunimund's daughter, Rosemund by name" [Migne, 476], whom he married by force. Rosemund murdered King Alboin after she learned the horror he did to her: "While he sat in merriment . . . with the cup which he made of the head of his father-in-law, King Cunimund, he ordered it to be given to the queen to drink wine, and he invited her to drink merrily with her father. Lest this should seem impossible to any one, I speak the truth in Christ. I saw King Ratchis holding this cup in his hand on a certain festal day to show it to his guest" [Migne, 498].

10. **Paulus**: Paul the Deacon, ca. 725-800, a Lombard historian, author of *Historia Miscella* [Mixed history] and *Historia Langobardorum* [History of the Langobards]. Both are sources of the opening of this canto.

11. **Tiberius Constantine**: A Byzantine emperor, 571-577. Directed by the divine, he discovered a great treasure of gold buried under slabs of the palace: "and the gold was carried away and distributed among the poor" [Migne, 509-511; cf. 106 below].

12. **Justinian**: A minor general whom the Empress Sophia Augusta tried to install as chief ruler after her husband, Justin II, died. It was during his rule (565-578) that the Lombards under Alboin invaded Italy. Not to be confused with the earlier Justinian I, called "the Great."

13. **Chosroes**: Or Khosru I, king of Persia (531-579). During the time of Justinian I and Justin II, he took part of Armenia and Caucasia from the Byzantine Empire. Thus Byzantium was threatened by powers from both north and south.

14. **Augustae Sophiae**: Empress, wife of Justin II.

15. **lumina mundi**: L, "lights of the world." From a note in Migne [517] quoting some verse in which Justinian and Sophia are called "pares duo lumina mundi" ("two equal lights of the world").

16. **ἐπικόμβια . . .** : H, "handouts . . . to the people." The emperor Mauricius [cf. 114 below] made a distribution of food when he took command in 577 [Migne, 517n.].

17. **Authar**: Authari, Lombard king (584-590) who, after the murder of Alboin, was elected by the Lombard dukes to end the anarchy that set in. By 586, "more or less," he had put the state in order, repelled several Frankish invasions, and instituted peace. Paul the Deacon wrote: "Mirabile in regno . . . nulla erat violentia" [Migne, 517], which in the canto becomes "marvelous reign, no violence."

18. **Vitalis beati**: L, "Vitale blessed." From a passage in Migne [520] describing the death and burial of Doctrulft, who was entombed "ante limina beati Vitalis martyris tribuentes" ("before the threshold assigned to the blessed martyrs in San Vitale").

19. **San Zeno**: Paul records that the church

in San Zeno had floodwaters up to its windows [Migne, 525].

20. Childibert: C. the Second, 570-596, son of Sigebert I and Brunhilda, king of Austrasia and Burgundy (575-596). But Paul reports it was Rome that had snakes in its granaries, and floods [Migne, 525].

21. Theodolinda: Empress of Bavaria. Her marriage to King Authar contributed to the power and stability of the Lombard throne. The translator says in a note: "An interesting question arises whether there is any connection between the characters and scenes in this Frankish drama of intrigue and revenge, and the legend of the Siegfried. . . . The resemblance of some of the names of the heroes is very striking; that of Sigispert . . . to Siegfried . . . Brunihilde to Brunhild. . . . It is well known that certain historical characters were actually introduced into legend: Etzel . . . was Attila the Hun, and Dietrich of Berne . . . was Theodoric the Great."

22. Theodoric: Called Theuderic by Paul. Grandson of Brunhilda and Sigebert I. Not to be confused with the earlier Theodoric the Great, 454-526.

23. Brunhilda: She ruled as regent for her young grandson Theodoric.

24. Roma caput Ecclesiae: L, "Rome the head of the Church." A declaration of Pope Boniface III made while (or, perhaps, because) the Persians were overrunning Jerusalem [Migne, 570].

25. my grand-dad . . . hungry: Paul the Deacon gives some of his own family history. He says the Huns forced his great-great-grandfather Lupicis to flee Pannonia (now, Yugoslavia) "using a wolf as guide" [Migne, 574]. JW sees a pun in the spelling of Jugoslavia, "because Paulus says his forebear was trying to escape the 'yoke (*jugum*) of captivity.' But when Lupicis (his own name resembles *lupus*, wolf) got too hungry, the animal became suspicious and fled" [JW, *Later*, 106].

26. comes itineris: L, "companion of the route," which is what Paulus calls the wolf [Migne, 574].

27. Rothar: Rothari (?-652), king of the Lombards, 636-652. "And he was brave and strong," said Paul, "and followed the path of justice; he did not, however, hold the right line of Christian belief, but was stained by the infidelity of the Arian heresy [103: 105]." Said Paul, "This king Rothari collected . . . the laws of the Langobards which they were keeping in memory only, and he directed this code to be called the Edict" [Migne, 581].

28. Arian heresy: A theological concept involving the nature of the Son in relation to the Father which as a major source of dissension, tore the early church apart for hundreds of years. Said Paul: "The Arians, indeed, say to their own ruin that the Son is less than the Father, and the Holy Spirit also is less than the Father and the Son. But we Catholics confess that the Father and Son and Holy Spirit are one and the true God in three persons, equal in power and the same in glory" [Migne, 582].

29. Ticino: Early name of Pavia, the seat of the one Arian bishop, "Anastasius by name," who finally became converted. Said Paul, "It was now indeed the seventy-seventh year from the time when the Langobards had come into Italy, as that king bore witness in a prologue to his Edict" [Migne, 582].

30. dope . . . murder: JW summarizes neatly: "no sooner does Rothar establish the law than Lombard society begins to show signs of decadence; dope is used (*talis potio*, 582); a snake cult is employed (585, note); and Chrothar debauches (*bacchatur*) with concubines (586). Things reach a nadir when an aristocrat is cut down brutally in the basilica of San Giovanni in Pavia (592)" [JW, *Later*, 107, nos. in parens refer to Migne].

31. Constans Augustus: Constantine IV, 631-685, became emperor at the age of 11 (642). His reign was fraught with violence and controversy. At one time, he captured many of the cities of the Langobards but, failing finally, "directed all the threats of his cruelty against his own followers, that is the Romans" [Migne, 602].

32. **Pantheon**: Constans was the first emperor to visit Rome for nearly two centuries–Pope Vitalian came out 6 miles to meet him. But Constans "pulled down everything that in ancient times had been made of metal for the ornament of the city, to such an extent that he even stripped off the roof of the church of the Blessed Mary which at one time was called the Pantheon . . . and he took away from there the bronze tiles and sent them with all the other ornaments to Constantinople" [Migne, 602].

33. **Constantinople**: Formerly Byzantium, headquarters of the emperor since the time of Constantine the Great.

34. **Siracusa**: Said Paul: "He [Constans] dwelt in Syracuse and put such afflictions upon the people . . . as were never heard of before . . . but at last he suffered the punishment of such great iniquities and while he was in the bath he was put to death by his own servants" [Migne, 603].

35. **Reyna**: Hieronymus Antonius R., a friend of Fridericus Lindenbrogius, who is the editor of the work. In a note [Migne, 620] the editor says his friend Reyna told him "that the Lombards of this period cast statues of their heroes in the name and cult of St. Michael" [JW, *Later*, 107].

36. **Migne**: Jacques Paul M., 1800-1875, a Roman Catholic priest who established a press in Paris and printed religious works. His principal work, in 3 series, was *Patrologiae*, a collection of the writings of all the Christian writers from the beginning to the 15th century. He did the Latin fathers in 221 vols., including indexes; the Greek fathers in Latin in 81 vols.; and the Greek fathers in both Greek and Latin in 166 vols. Vol. 95 contains the *Historia Langobardorum*.

37. **Cedwald**: Cedoaldus, an Anglo-Saxon who says Paul visited Rome for absolution and died there [Migne, 632].

38. **Architriclin**: L, "majordomo." A sort of "mayor of the palace" to whom the Merovingian kings yielded their power. As a result, the French rule passed into the hands of the Carolingians [Migne, 634]. Rhymes with the advice of Apollonius about what happens when the king will not be king [94:166].

39. **From the golden . . .** : Pound's translation of "Aureo ex fonte quiescunt in ordine regis," the epitaph on the sepulcher of King Cunibert, next to the basilica in Pavia.

40. **Cuningpert**: Cunibert. Paul calls him [Migne, 636] "*elegans*" ("elegant") and "audaxque bellator" ("a bold warrior").

41. **de partibus Liguriae**: L, "from the regions of the Ligurians."

42. **lubricus**: L, "slippery" or "deceitful." The epithet Paul applies to a duke from Liguia named Ferdulfus [Migne, 639].

43. **Aripert . . . gold**: The fate of King A. was to drown in the Ticino River while he was trying to escape to France. He might have gotten away if he hadn't loaded himself down with gold.

44. **auro gravatus**: L, "weighted down with gold." The irony prompts Pound's next two lines. Migne has "gravatus auro" [646].

45. **Via Lata**: L, "Broad Street."

46. **Ponte Milvio**: L, "Milvain Bridge." After listing minor mishaps, Paul recorded a real disaster in which most of Rome was flooded [Migne, 648].

47. **et quia Karolus**: L, "and whom Charles." From a chapter heading in Migne [648]: "De gente Anglorum, et rege Francorum Pippino, et bellis ejus, et quia ei Karolus suus filius successit" ("concerning the English people, and Pippin, king of the Franks, and his wars, and whom his son Charles [Charlemagne] followed").

48. **Pippin**: Pepin of Heristal (died ca. 714),

the father of Charles Martel and his wife Alpaide.

49. **Plectrude's**: A first wife of Pepin of Heristal whose sons were named Drogo and Grimvald.

50. **Martel**: Charles M., 688-741, ruler of the Franks, the natural son of Pepin of Heristal and grandfather of Charlemagne. He started to gain power as "mayor of the palace" [cf. 38 above], crushed all opposition, and extended his rule from Austrasia to Burgundy, Aquitaine, and Provence. He also subjugated a number of German tribes, encouraged the missionary work of St. Boniface, and consolidated enough power to halt the Moslem invasion of Europe at the battle of Tours in 732. Known as "Charles the Hammer," he never used the title *king*, but at his death he divided his lands between his sons Pepin the Short and Carolman.

51. **Pippin**: Pepin the Short. Paul's notes as well as his text is confusing, as the words "wait, wait" indicate. This Pepin was the father of Charlemagne.

52. **Charlemagne**: Charles the Great, 742-814, who became the greatest of the Carolingian kings.

53. **empty grave . . . San Zeno**: The reference is not in the source. DG's notes say it is a rhyme with "Y Yin sent the young king into seclusion" [85/546].

54. **another bloke in Milano**: Not in the source. Quite likely a reference to the funeral of Mussolini, which took place Aug. 31, 1957. The N.Y. *Times* for that date [pp. 1, 3] says that M's body had been hidden for 11 years in a box in a Capuchin monastary 15 miles NW of Milan. It was taken on this day to be buried in the family vault at the cemetery of San Casciano, at Predappio, M's home town. About 20 people were present with the widow: "members of her own and Mussolini's families." No mention is made of cardinals in this special report (sent by Arnold Cortesi) or in reports carried by the wire services.

55. **apud . . . Proenca**: Paul mentions [Migne, 659-660] two battles Charles Martel fought against the Saracens occupying Gaul: "uno in Aquitania apud Pictavium altero juxta Narbonam . . . postrerum in Provincia" ("one in Aquitania near Poitiers, the other next to Narbonne . . . later in Provence").

56. **Lombards pro Carolus**: L, "the Lombards [were] for Charles [Martel]."

57. **ACTUM . . . PALATIO**: L, "Decree in the palace of Ticinum." The heading of a document Paul quotes by which King Luitprand in his old age made his loyal assistant Hildebrand a coruler.

58. **et Arimniun**: L, "and Rimini." The phrase comes from a eulogy for Luitprand celebrating his victories (he also conquered Rimini).

59. **a stone in Modena**: The story that a sacred spear was given to the Lombard kings in their coronation rites is mentioned by Paul's editor, who says he saw this story engraved on "a stone on the back part [*ambon*] of the altarpiece in the basilica at Monza." Pound misreads *Monza* as *Modena* [Migne, 667].

60. **Luitprand**: King of Lombardy, died 744. He was the Charlemagne of Italy who succeeded in bringing all of the northern part of the country under a firm rule based on justice. He also expanded Lombardy's relations with surrounding kings and courts. Charles Martel thought highly enough of him to send his son to the Lombard court for a tonsorial rite [Migne, 659]: "and the king, cutting his hair, became a father to him and sent him back to his father enriched with many royal gifts" [Migne, 672].

61. **avars**: The Avars were a barbaric nomadic people who, driven from central Asia, laid siege to Constantinople in 626. They failed in that attempt but dominated the Hungarian plain until they were defeated by Charlemagne.

62. **verbo . . . corruscans**: L, "splendid in word and deed."

63. **Ideogram**: Hsin [in *K'ang Hsi Dictio-*

nary]. It is not in Mathews. The lower component is the word for *wood* and the upper components are flames: all denoting intense heat and light and connoting "passion and illumination" [Witemeyer, *Pai*, 4-243, 355]. For a king, perhaps "splendid" will do.

64. Wang: Chinese word for king, which Pound applies here to David Hsin-fu Wand because this Chinese poet was born into the distinguished Wang family. David Wand came to the U.S. in 1949 and corresponded with Pound first in 1955 [ibid., 333-335].

65. Eirene: The Byzantine empress Irene, 752-803. When her husband died (780), she became regent for her son, Constantine VI. She neglected the wars on all fronts and devoted much energy to religious problems. A military revolt forced her to retire from the regency in 790, but she was recalled by Constantine in 792 and made joint ruler. She encouraged his misconduct and cruelty, ordered him to be blinded, and got him deposed in 797. She was, in turn, deposed in 802 and died in exile.

66. Constans: An ambassador sent by Irene to propose a marriage between her son and the daughter of Carolus.

67. Carolus Magnus: Charlemagne. No marriage took place and thus the idea of uniting the Frankish Kingdom and the Byzantine Empire did not take place.

68. sardonix . . . rosis: L, "Parian sardonyx, lilies mixed with roses." From a verse epitaph for Queen Hildegard (d. 783), wife of Charlemagne. Sardonyx, a layered pink and white marble, is a metaphor for the queen's beauty. Paros, one of the Cyclades, was famous for its marble [Migne, 1602; with this line Pound leaves the *History of the Lombards* and goes to another book partly written by Paul, *Historia Miscella*].

69. Tyana: Birthplace of Apollonius [94:42]. The line may tie in with "Severus's wife" and Philostratus, mentioned below.

70. Diocletian: Caius Aurelius Valerius D., 245-313, Roman emperor (284-305). He came to power from a high military command. He consolidated the empire, restored Britain to it, and defeated the Persians. The later part of his reign was distinguished by persecution of the Christians, an advanced system of administration, and many wise economic measures. He believed it was better to tax conquered peoples than destroy them. In 301 he uttered *The Edict of Diocletian*, an economic measure meant to check speculation in commodity prices. In 305 he retired to live in a castle in Salona [Migne, 900-904].

71. Haud . . . Salonis: L, "Not far from Salo" [Migne, 903]. Salona is in Yugoslavia and should not be confused with the Salò Republic.

72. otio . . . senuit: L, "quietly aging" [Migne, 904].

73. Saturn . . . : The line is not in Migne. JW reports that "Diocletian and other emperors gave this tax-free money to the cities to circulate." If the gold and silver of the Pontifex [89:79] were taxed, this might have a beneficent economic effect [JW, *Later*, 112].

74. "changing . . . ": Not in Migne. Since one form of travertine is onyx marble, the line may mean changing from cottages to halls of marble, an idea that could apply to Diocletian or Vespasian: both came from poor families.

75. Vespasiano . . . : L, "under Vespasian [Migne, 871] ... cities rebuilt" [Migne, 874]. Roman emperor advised by Apollonius of Tyana [94:118]

76. Antoninus: A. Pius [78:56]

77. apud Eboricum: L, "near York." From "Ibique apud Eboracum [sic] oppidum" ("And there near the town of York"). Septimius Severus renewed the war in Britain and died there [Migne, 891].

78. Severus' wife: [94:123]. Julia Domna.

79. Philostratus: [94:123].

80. Galla Placidia: [110:46]. The beautiful woman who died 1165 years after the founding of the city of Rome, according to the old Roman calendar system, and was buried in one of the most beautiful tombs ever created [76:86]. The daughter of Theodosia, she became empress of the West at a time when there were disturbances throughout the empire.

81. Pictorum: L, "of the Picts." They created uprisings in Britain [Migne, 954].

82. Vandali: L, "the vandals." They created troubles in Spain [Migne, 955].

83. Bosphorus: Byzantium. Called *Bos* ("ox")-*phorus* ("ford") because of the tax exacted from all who passed through it.

84. treaty . . . Justinian: [94:45]. [Migne, 988].

85. Verona et Bruxia: L, "Verona and Bricia." Cities of Italy from which the Goths were finally expelled [Migne, 989].

86. all italian "reip.": From sentence in Migne [989] about Justinian: "universanque Italiam ad reip. jura reduxit" ("and he brought all Italy back to the laws of the republic").

87. Bernicoli: Unidentified, not in source. Prob. a memory of someone Pound saw in Ravenna.

88. that stuffed shirt: Prob. a contemporary reference.

89. embargo: Justinian [94:45] established embargoes to protect local business [Migne, 990].

90. Theodora: Wife of Justinian, who made her joint empress when he came to the throne in 527. She died in 548 in the 21st year of his reign.

91. Ablavius and Marcellus: Migne [992-994] calls these two conspirators "pecuniarum venditores" ("sellers of money"). They were apprehended before they succeeded. Says Bury (whose account is more complete than Migne's): "The conspirators were: Ablavius, son of Miltiades; Marcellus, Vitus, and Eusebius, bankers; . . . Marcellus, who was arrested as he entered the palace with a dagger . . . killed himself on the spot" [Bury, *Later R.E.*, 67-69]. Pound believes the plot was formed because of Justinian's tradition of tight control of money [Migne, 994].

92. two Abduls: Abdu-l-Malik, 646-705, the fith Omayyad caliph [685-705]: "At his accession Islam was torn by dissension and hard pressed by the Byzantine Empire." But he overthrew his rivals and united Islam. An able adminstrator, he introduced Arabic coins, improved postal facilities, made Arabic the official language, and reorganized the government [cf. 161 below]. The idea of "two" may be that one could do worse than have two such able rulers, even Orientals [cf. 93 below].

93. the third bahai: The first, Baha Ullah, 1817-1892, founder of Bahaism, said many remarkable things, as did his son, Sir Abdul Baha Bahai, 1844-1921, the second Bahai [46:22]. The third is not mentioned in encyclopedias. A rhyme with the several other occult religions Pound was interested in [94:18].

94. Edgar Wallace: Popular English novelist, 1875-1932, who wrote over 150 detective thrillers, as well as plays. Pound quotes him as saying, "Very few people are respected by anyone" [*SP*, 450]. Pound also said: "Mass culture insists on the fundamental virtues which are common to Edgar Wallace and to Homer. It insists on the part of technique which is germane to both these authors" [*SP*, 231]. And, "There is no faking in the arts. No artist can present what he hasn't got. Edgar Wallace triumphed by modesty" [*GK*, 209].

95. Caedual: Pound says "Cedwald" earlier [cf. 37 above]. His baptism and absolution took place at about the same time, on his visit to Rome. [Vol. 95 of Migne opens with Bede's *Ecclesiastical History*. At this point and for most of the next 15 lines, Pound leaves Paul the Deacon's account and turns to contemporaneous events in 7th century Britain.]

96. ΕΠΑΡΧΙΚΟΝ . . . : *The Eparch's Book.* Source of most of the last half of Canto 96 [cf. 271 below].

97. that sea gull: Ino of the bikini [cf. 1 above].

98. *θίνα θαλάσσης*: H, "beach of the sea." One of Pound's favorite Homeric phrases. At the moment Odysseus awakes on Ithaca, where the Phaeacians have beached him, he believes himself lost again and, moaning, walks *παρὰ θῖνα πολυφλοίσβοιο θαλάσσης* [*Od.* XIII, 220]. Pound translates, "the turn of the wave and the scutter of receding pebbles" [*L*, 274], leaving the literal sense to get the onomatopoetic effects he thought Homer had. Parts of the phrase occur often in both the prose and the poetry [98:17; *P*, 181; *LE*, 250].

99. ALDFRID: Alfred, king of Northumbria (d. 705) [Migne, 258]. Not to be confused with Alfred the Great, ca. 849-899, king of Wessex and areas of England.

100. Aldhelm: St. A., 640?-709, abbot of Malmesbury and author of a number of works in prose and verse, such as "De virginitate . . . versibus hexametris" ("concerning virginity . . . in hexameter verses"); *De Metaplasmo* [On the remolding]; and *De Sinalimpha* [On unclear waters]. Such works indicate that civilization was spreading to the outlands of the empire [Migne, 260, 261]. But most of Bede's commentary concerns such things as ecclesiastical tonsure rites—"fuss about hair-cuts"—[285, 288], comets facing north [282] and mere fads [JW, *Later*, 114]. After this entry, Pound returns to the *History of the Lombards* as continued after Paul the Deacon by Landulphus Sagax (Landulph).

101. Justin: Justin II, nephew and successor to Justinian I, and emperor (565-578). Early in his reign he and his wife carried on the policies of Justinian in the control of money and regulation of trade.

102. Sophia Augusta: Wife of Justin II.

103. pecuniarium . . . : L [pecuniarum], "money lenders." Sophia Augusta summoned the usurious money-lenders before her and ordered them to treat their debtors better. She restored mortgaged homes to their rightful owners and received great praise from the populace [Migne, 994].

104. the synagog: In the early years of his reign Justin maintained religious peace among all the warring factions, mostly Christian; but by 572, the 12th year of his reign, he began a severe persecution of the Monophysites and converted a synagogue into a church. Two years later he lost his mind completely and the rule passed to Tiberius [Migne, 996].

105. fads on Eleusis: Any doctrinal decoration of Christian belief or ceremony would appear to Pound a worsening of the simplicity of the rites of Eleusis.

106. TIBERIUS: Constantine II, emperor 571-577, squandered the money of the empire. He used himself to spend wealth rather than using wealth to develop himself, as the ideogram suggests [55:9].

107. Ideogram: Fa [M1768], "issue, spend."

108. Thrax: L, "Thrace." Mauricius overcame the Slavs there.

109. Cappadox: L, "Cappadocia," an ancient region in Asia Minor, the birthplace of Mauricius.

110. Lombards: [Cf. 59-60 above]. Overcome by Mauricius [Migne, 1000].

111. Avars: [cf. 61 above]. Overcome by Mauricius [Migne, 1001].

112. Theophanem sequitur: L, "follow Theophanes." A note in Migne [997, 998] tells the reader that the author is following the author of *Annals of the Greeks* in these details.

113. Lombards in Exarchate: Mauricius was a brilliant general who defeated the enemies of the Byzantine Empire in Persia, to the north and to the south; but he could not prevent the Lombards from entering the *exarchate* (adminstrative unit of the capital).

114. MAURICIUS . . . : L, "Emperor Maurice" (reigned 577-595). Tiberius II on his deathbed gave him his daughter in marriage and proclaimed him emperor. As he had been a successful general, he carried on as an excellent defender of the empire. But he "was killed, together with his sons . . . by Focas [Phocas] . . . . The Huns, too, who are also called Avars, were subjugated by his prowess" [Foulke, *History*, 168].

115. calamitatibus delectabantur: L, "delighted in calamities." Said of the Persians, "barbarians," whom Mauricius defeated. They delighted in anything bad that happened to Rome [Migne, 1004].

116. equestribus . . . : L, "speculating in horses" or "horse trading," a commercial venture developed to a fine art which Mauricius enjoyed. It was an activity of great importance in a city where the center of culture was the Hippodrome.

117. urbem splendidam reddidit: L, "he restored the shining city." Mauricius did this, says Migne, by dealings with the nobility [1005]. He also controlled the money and, according to Pound, provided "local freedom." The phrase must be understood not as freedom of the people in a democratic sense, but freedom from outside control.

118. local freedom . . . power: Since Mauricius carried on the kind of monetary controls established by his predecessors back to Justinian, which climaxed later in *The Eparch's Book* [cf. 271 below], Pound calls it "local control of local purchasing power," a primary tenet of Social Credit. The context is different, but enough alike to suggest Del Mar.

119. Del Mar: Alexander D. M., 1836-1926, a civil and mining engineer who spent a lifetime studying precious metals and monetary systems. His works include *A History of Money in Ancient States* (1881), *Money and Civilization* (1885), *The Science of Money* (1895), and many more. In a book entitled *Ancient Britain*, he developed an idea that occurs in several of his writings: "The sovereign pontiff monopolized the coinage of gold and fixed the weight-ratio of value between gold and silver at 1 to 12; a ratio remained unaltered for over 1200 years. He shared the coinage of silver with his subject kingdoms and left the coinage of bronze to the Senate and municipalities" [123; Pearlman, *Pai*, 1-2, 163; Flory, *Pai*, 4, 2-3, 325-326].

120. sanguinibus . . . : L, "the praise of bloodshed, love of murders, faithlessness, boasting and violence (of Hormisdas)" [Migne, 1006].

121. Hormisdae: Hormisdas IV (reigned 579-590), son of Chosroes. He continued the war with the Romans but was defeated first by Mauricius and then by Heraclius. He was blinded and later killed by the Persian aristocracy. He was the Asiatic king who ruled with "pleasure in blood, love of homicide, infidelity, vainglory and violence" [Migne, 1005].

122. Priscus: The *praetor* (city magistrate of ancient Rome who adminstered justice) of Mauricius. He caught the barbarian Musacius totally drunk at the funeral of his brother [Migne, 1011]. Phocus, or Focas [cf. 141 below], was his master of horse.

123. Musacius: King Musacius. Source: "Musacium barbarorum regem ebrietate corruptum: funebrem quippe proprii fratris celebrabat festivitatem" ("Musacius king of the barbarians as expected was totally drunk at the funeral festivities celebrated for his own brother") [Migne, 1010-1011].

124. aerumnae: L, "woes." From phrase that reads, "non defuerunt imperio variae, ac ingentes aerumnae" ("no absence of various great woes") [Migne, 1019]. The phrase is used to describe the result of Mauricius's dictatorial rule which led to his being deposed.

125. **Fortuna**: [86:93; for "pervanche" cf. 97:188].

126. **CHEN[4]**: [M315], "to tremble."

127. **e che permutasse**: I, "and who has changed entirely" [*Inf.* VII, 79]. Part of the answer to a question: "Master . . . this fortune which you touch on here, what is it, that has the goods of the world so in its clutches?" Virgil's answer is about the change of the good things of the world, under Fortune, from one person to another.

128. **Dei Matris**: L, "of the Mother of God."

129. **HERACLIUS**: H. I, ca. 575-641, Byzantine emperor (610-641), the son of an African governor. H. succeeded the tyrant Phocas after he deposed and executed him. He was threatened on all sides by Avars and Bulgars. He lost Syria, Palestine, and Egypt to the Persians in his early years but conquered them back in costly wars (622-628)–then lost them to the Moslem Arabs (629-641). Pound's date (602) comes from the "Mixed History," which is wrong. H. assumed power by coming to the city on castellated ships (*navibus castellatis*) that bore images of the Mother of God [Migne, 1023].

130. **imperator . . . sponsus**: L, "both commander and bridegroom."

131. **reip's business . . .** : Pound's rendition of "invenit dissoluta reip negotia" ("found the republic's business gone to pieces").

132. **Avars . . . desert**: [Cf. 61 above]. Trans. of "Europam Avares reddidere desertam" [Migne, 1024].

133. **Persians . . . Asia**: Trans. of "Asiam vero totam Persae exterminaverunt" [ibid.].

134. **Chosroes**: King Chosdroes II. This Persian king answered a message from Emperor Heraclius with these words: "I won't spare you until you deny the crucified one, whom you profess to be God, and adore the Sun" [Migne, 1025]. Heraclius could not stand this, so in order to defeat King Chosdroes he melted down candles and sacred vessels to get gold and silver coins. In a footnote the coins are called by their Greek names [Migne, 1026], given in the next line of the text.

135. *νομίσματα κὰι μιλιαρίσια*: H, "current coins and silver coins." The last word is not in Liddell-Scott. The closest form is *μιλιάριον*, which means a copper vessel to boil water in.

136. **nummos . . .** : L, "gold and silver coins" [Migne, 1026].

137. *εἰκόνος*: H, "sacred image." Heraclius swears on an icon shaped like "the virile figure of God" that he will fight Chosdroes to the death [Migne, 1026].

138. **Justinian**: [Cf. 12 above].

139. **Tiberius**: [Cf. 106 above].

140. **Mauricius**: [Cf. 114 above].

141. **Phocae**: Emperor of Byzantium, 595-610. His tyrannical regime led to his overthrow and execution.

142. **Heraclius**: So ends this historical review and summary. H. is a transitional figure.

143. **Deutschland unter**: G, "Germany under." The phrase takes off from "Deutschland über alles."

144. **Dulles**: John Foster D., 1888-1959, U.S. secretary of state, 1953-1959. While this canto was being written, he was much in the news with foreign policy formulations called "brinkmanship" and with the doctrine of "massive retaliation." In that post-WWII decade Dulles could almost dictate the foreign policy of the European nations that confronted the communist nations behind the iron curtain. Germany was a key to that policy, and a center of effort, after the construction of the Berlin Wall. On Jan. 22,

1954 Dulles arrived at the Berlin Conference with hopes of advancing the cause of the reunification of Germany. Over the years he promoted the "Baghdad Pact," a mutual defense alliance formed in 1955 between Turkey, Pakistan, and Iraq as a part of the bipartisan policy of communist containment.

145. over Euphrates: After the enemy burned a hemp bridge over the Euphrates River, Heraclius created a bridge by lashing a number of boats together [Migne, 1032].

146. Sebastia: An ancient name of Sivas, a city in central Turkey. While Heraclius passed the winter there, Chosdroes ruthlessly ransacked churches and robbed private citizens to build an elite army called the Golden Spears [JW, *Later*, 116]. He also tried to enlist the aid of a number of other enemies of the empire in the north, the Bulgars, Gespids, and "Hunnos," as well as the Turks, to move against the city called "Fu Lin" [Migne, 1033].

147. Χρυσολόχας: H, "Golden Spears."

148. quatenus Hunnos: L, "as far as the Hunnos."

149. Fu Lin: Chinese phrase for prefect's city: Constantinople.

150. Turcos . . . vocant: L, "Turks who are called Cazars."

151. superlaudabilis: L, with the "ultra praiseworthy" help of "God's Mother," a great hailstorm fell upon Chosdroes's army killing many of them, so that Heraclius's army won [Migne, 1036].

152. populus . . . glorificantes: L, "the people feasted sumptuously, glorifying God" [ibid.].

153. zinziber: L, "ginger."

154. tigrides . . . : L, "tigers of amazing hugeness." After their victory the Byzantines pushed on to Damastager and found Chosdroes's great palace there deserted. They found spices such as those mentioned and saw huge tigers, antelopes, and other beasts [Migne, 1037].

155. in sky . . . power: At the moment of final victory a warning came: a giant sword-like image, stretched in the sky from Mesembra to the star of Arcturus, predicted the Arabs were in the ascendant and would soon occupy all the Middle East [Migne, 1045].

156. Constans: Emperor, 642-668, the son and successor of Constantine III and grandson of Heraclius. Early in his reign the Moslems invaded Armenia and Asia Minor, took Cyprus, and threatened Constantinople and Sicily. The Latin source, "cinis e coelo descendit," "ashes descended from heaven," is a portent of other disasters to come [Migne, 1049].

157. Muhavis: A Moslem general who destroyed the famous Colossus of Rhodes, one of the seven wonders of the world, and sold 900 camel loads of its materials to a dealer named Emesenus [Migne, 1049].

158. mille . . . sexaginta: L, "one thousand, three hundred and sixty years" the Colossus had stood.

159. aere oneravit: L, "bronze-loaded."

160. seven years less: Pound follows the dating in the various books of Migne.

161. Habdimelich: Abd-l-Malik, 646-705, fifth Omayyad caliph (685-705), the son of Marwan [cf. 165 below]. When he became caliph, Islam was torn by internal troubles and hard pressed by the Byzantine Empire. His troubles could have been multiplied when Justinian II became emperor, so he made peace.

162. 2nd Justinian: Justinian II, 669-711, Byzantine emperor (685-711), the son and successor of Constantine IV. He fought against the Persians without success while his extravagance and the extortions of his ministers caused a revolution. J. II's nose was cut off (hence his name "Rhinotmetus"), and he was exiled to the Crimea. In 705 he was restored to the throne with the help of the

Bulgars, but he was finally deposed in 711. His enemies prevented a second return by cutting off his head.

163. contra Zubir: L, "against Zubir." Abd-l-Malik, by consolidating his own power, finally won against his chief rival, Zubir, and burned him alive along with his house and his idols [Migne, 1059].

164. sed susciperent: L, "but they should accept." That is, the emperor should accept coins paid in tribute to Rome with Abd-l-Malik's image on them.

165. Anno . . . Columnas: L. The passages in brackets restore the material in the source left out of the canto text, as indicated by ellipses. "In the sixth year of his rule Justinian foolishly broke the peace that he had made with Abd-l-Malik, and decided out of all reason to move both the whole island of Cyprus and its people, and refused to accept the formula sent to him from Abd-l-Malik since it was seen for the first time and had never before been used. [A great number of Cypriots while they were trying to get across were plunged into the water and perished from weakness. The survivors were in fact sent back to Cyprus.] And hearing all this, Abd-l-Malik, urged on by the devil, asked that the peace not be broken but that they (the Arabs) should issue their own currency since the Arabs would not use the mark of the Romans in their coinage. Because the weight of the gold was the same he said: the Romans would suffer no loss from the fact that the Arabs struck new coins. [But he (Justinian) thinking that the request had been made out of fear, did not consider it seriously, because it was their own wish, or that they were the leaders in suppressing the incursion of the Mardi, and in this way he dissolved the peace under the cover of a suppositious reason.] And so it was done, and Abd-l-Malik both sent Muchan to build a temple and determined to carry off the columns of St. Gethseman" [Migne, 1059, 1060]. (In line 5 of the quotation, Pound has *eum* for *cum*, and in lines 10-11, he has dropped the *e* out of *efficietur*.) This passage is critical as it concerns the early stage of the dissolution of the Eastern Empire. For Pound, the separate coinage is crucial. Justinian had refused the tribute because the form of address included an acknowledgement of the supremacy of Allah. [John Espey provided this translation and the substance of these notes.]

166. this item . . . : This item does locate what Pound called, before the long quote, "the crux of the matter"—a matter developed at length at the beginning of Canto 97. It concerns the sacred or "sacerdotal" nature of coinage. Prob. Pound first found the idea in *History of Monetary Systems* by Del Mar [cf. 119 above], who said that Gibbon in his 17th chapter "declares that by law the imperial taxes during the dark ages were payable in gold coins alone. . . . The custom of the period was that when gold coins were not paid, silver coins were accepted instead at the sacred weight ration of 12." Caesar had set that ratio centuries earlier, "and this alteration he sanctified and rendered permanent by stamping upon the coins the most sacred devices and solemn legends." Again, "It is not to be wondered that Justinian I rebuked Theodore the Frank for striking heretical gold coins, nor that Justinian II proclaimed war against Abd-l-Malik for presuming to pay his tribute in other heretical gold." The myth is important because it shows: "The sovereign-pontiff alone enjoyed the prerogative of coining gold throughout the Empire, and that the princes of the Empire respected this prerogative" [*HMS*, 91-93]. The idea that "gold was under the Pontifex" [89/602] is a recurrent motif [89/594; 92/620; 104/744]. It rhymes with all of Pound's monetary theories, including the theory that governmental units only should issue credit or money and should provide legal controls to prevent the people from exploitation, a subject central to the quotes from *The Eparch's Book* in the remainder of the canto.

167. Kemal: Mustafa K., 1880-1938, known as Ataturk, the founder of modern Turkey.

168. PANTA'REI: L, "Everything flows." A Latin transcription of a phrase from Heraclitus. The phrase is transitional between the first part of Canto 96 and the next part: the interchange of ideas about law and justice flows from one group of emperors and kings to the next. All things change with the divine fire, and even Byzantium rises and falls.

169. Du Bellay: Joachim Du B., 1522-1560, French poet of the *Pléiade* and friend of Ronsard. He dedicated himself to reforming French poetry, wrote Latin poems, and became a student and translator of the classics.

170. base . . . slide: Losing the imperial right to coinage was the base of Byzantium's loss of power over Asia Minor and eventually everywhere.

171. twenty thousand sclavons: To help him in his return to power Justinian II [cf. 162 above] persuaded a leader of the Slavs to support him with "viginti millibus Sclavorum" ("20,000 Slav troops"). J.II was overthrown by Leontius, who lasted as emperor only 3 years (695-698). He was overthrown by the navy, who put forward a naval officer named Aspimar, who as emperor called himself Tiberius, that being more Roman. J.II in time gathered enough support amongst the enemies of the empire to try a return to power. This he finally managed with the help of the Bulgars.

172. 7th Absimarus: Or Tiberius Aspimar, so-called because historians can't agree on whether he should be T.II or T.III (the question is whether the T. of Christ's time should be counted.) It was in the 7th year of his reign that J.II appeared with a large army outside the walls of Constantinople. Says Constance Head: "Then after the third night after their arrival, someone uncovered a secret passage under the city's walls. . . . The passageway was an old aqueduct or tunnel, and through this dark, underground channel, Justinian led a few of his trusted comrades." [Head, *J.II*, 111]. Or as Migne has it: "per aquaeductum ingressus" ("entering through the aqueduct"), an event that took place in 705, the year Abd-l-Malik died [1065].

173. Franks out of Thrace: Having recovered his throne with the help of the various tribes to the north, one of J.II's problems afterwards was to relieve the pressure of the Franks, who were challenging the territory of all southern Europe.

174. Watling Street: Ancient Roman military highway that reached from the English coast of Kent in SE England, through London, to Chester in the NW.

175. Hyacinthinis: L, "Vermilion" or "Crimson." Pound's source has now become *The Eparch's Book of Leo the Wise* [cf. 271 below].

176. μεγαλοζήλων: H, "of great majestic models." The fake purple is Pound's translation of the Latin in the line above. The idea is a comparison with royal purple because in the early years of cloth-dying only kings could afford it. In the *Analects* [B. XVII, chap. 18] Kung said: "I hate the way purple spoils Vermilion, I hate the way Chang sonority confuses the music of the Elegantiae, I hate sharp mouths (the clever yawp, mouths set on profits) that overturn states and families" [*CON*, 277].

177. Dr. Liddell's: Of the Liddell and Scott Greek dictionary.

178. chastised: Chap. 4 of *The Eparch's Book* [*Ep.B*], entitled "Merchants of Silk Stuffs," forbids them to sell to strangers silks colored with dyes reserved for royalty. If they did they should be chastised [CFT, *Pai*, 2-2, 228-242].

179. coom ben: Slang for L, *cum benis*, "caught with the goods."

180. verberator et bonis . . . : L, "flogged and liable to confiscation."

181. παιδευέσθω . . . : H, "flogged and liable to confiscation."

182. aurei: Roman coin.

183. δέκα νομισμάτων: H, "ten aurei."

184. purpureas vestes: L, "silk merchants." Professor Nicole's translation into Latin.

185. *τὰ βλαττία*: H, "silk merchants."

186. *ἀναιδῶς*: H, "shameless."

187. Dr. Nicole: Professor at the University of Geneva who discovered the manuscript of the book. In 1891 he translated it into both modern Greek and Latin in parallel columns.

188. *μὴ . . . τιμὴν*: H, "not to raise or lower the price."

189. *ἀλογίστους*: H, "thoughtless."

190. *καπηλεύων*: H, "retail dealers."

191. *στομύλος*: H, "hucksters"; *ἀγοραῖος*: H, "forensic."

192. λάλος: H, "babbler."

193. Ideograms: From the top, they are [M6954], "purple"; [M935], "to go to"; [M6433], "surpass"; and [M1346], "vermilion." Freely rendered they mean, "Purple goes far in surpassing red" [cf. 175, 176 above].

194. *ταραχώδης*: H, "quarrelsome."

195. Beaucaire: A town on the west bank of the Rhône roughly at the center of a triangle formed by Nîmes, Avignon, and Arles. On the east bank is a Tarascon, a small commercial town prob. filled with hucksters and quarrelsome babblers. Pound mentioned the town in a *Lustra* poem, "The Gypsy" [*P*, 119].

196. *μὴ . . . ἐσφραγισμένον*: H, "not stamped with the prefect's seal."

197. *βούλλη*: H, "seal."

198. *καμπανὸν . . .* : H, "steelyard . . .": from a chapter concerning rules for grocers who sell any article measured by steelyards rather than scales.

199. Ducange: Charles du Fresne Du Cange, 1610-1688, scholar and lexicographer who did basic glossaries of both medieval Greek and Latin.

200. *στατήρ*: H, "stater." The name of a coin.

201. *ἢ . . . ξέει*: H, "who files the coinage." *The Eparch's Book* lists a number of rules governing crimes in the marketplace, followed by the punishment, which is often a phrase such as "shall be flogged or shaved."

202. vel pactum . . . : L, "or raised the agreed price."

203. *καιρὸν . . .* : H, "hoard in a season of scarcity."

204. *ἐνοίκιον*: H, "house rent." In the next line, "house rent of others." The source reads: "Any grocer who . . . tries to raise the rent of another grocer shall be liable."

205. leather . . . : The source reads: "and will prepare hides for shoe leather and not for carriage equipment."

206. Xoirempers: H, "Pork Butchers." The source says: "[Sheep] butchers are forbidden to buy swine or store pork." And, "Any pork butcher introducing his animals into the house of an archon to sell them secretly shall be liable" [*Ep.B*, 16-4].

207. *οἶκον . . .* : H, "house of an archon."

208. ad pretium empti: L, "price to the buyer."

209. *κάτα τὴν . . . ἑνὸς*: H, "but for one *nomisma*." The source is concerned with bakers and bread sellers: "Bakers shall sell bread by weight fixed according to the price of corn. . . . They are to buy corn . . . by quantities . . . upon which the tax of one gold *nomisma* is payable . . . they shall calculate their remuneration at the rate of one *keration* plus two *miliaresia* per gold *nomisma*." "Bankers" is a misprint for *bakers* [*Ep.B* 18-1].

210. *μηδεμιᾷ . . .* : H, "but not for public service." Pound translates the word as "liturgy."

211. *οἰκονομία . . .* : H, "management . . . in a certain manner . . . to sell." The source for several lines reads: "When wine arrives in the city let the master . . . of the guild of innholders . . . warn the eparch so that he may fix the sale price. . . . The *sumponos* [deputy?] shall receive an order to compel innholders to settle their measures and vessels. . . . The measure shall contain 30 litres and what is called the *mina*, 3 litres" [*Ep.B*, 19-1].

212. *δευτέρας ὥρας*: H, "two hours."

213. *ἀσφαλίζειν*: H, "to lock up."

214. *σβεννύειν* . . . : H, "to quench the kettles"; *λέβης*: H, "kettle" or "cauldron."

215. *τοῦ οἴνου* . . . : H, "to take one's fill of wine" or "to get drunk."

216. **emphorio** . . . **vigors**: Pound transliterates certain Greek words and gives his translation.

217. **sunthema**: H, "guild."

218. *ἐκδιωκέσθωσαν*: H, "banished."

219. **ΠΕΡΙ** . . . : H, "Concerning the Deputy." The title of chap. 20 of *The Eparch's Book*, which Pound takes to be about foreign importers.

220. **ΒΟΘΡΩΝ**: H, "agents."

221. *διασημαίνεται*: H, "make known clearly."

222. *βοτόν, βοτήρ*: H, "beast, herdsman."

223. **Foro Amastriani**: L, "Forum." The name of the forum.

224. *τῶν ζώων τὰ αἰτίας*: H, "the vendors of the animals." The source adds: "Vendors are to declare the patent or latent vices of their animals" [*Ep.B*, 21-5].

225. **askothurarion**: H, prob. "of wineskins to carry outside."

226. ΛΕΠΤΟΥΡΓΩΝ: Title of chap 22: "Fine Workers." Freshfield gives, "Contractors."

227. *ἄυξει* . . . *λόγων*: H, "increase his wages by vain words in argument" [*Ep.B*, 22-3].

228. *στομυλία*: H, "muzzled."

229. **that louse G.**: Perhaps one of the henchmen of Nero Claudius Caesar, who as a captain of the Praetorian Guard under Tigullius (?) burned Rome in A.D. 64. Or it may be a reference to WWII, in which much was destroyed by bombing.

230. **Palatine**: One of the 7 hills of Rome rebuilt in magnificent fashion after the fire.

231. *ἀπληστία*: H, "insatiate desire."

232. *κακουργία*: H, "wickedness."

233. *θόλος*: H, "dome."

234. *καμάρα*: H, "anything with an arched covering."

235. *ἀσφάλειαν*: H, "stability."

236. *ἐμπειριάν*: H, "experienced."

237. *θεμέλιος*: H, "foundation."

238. *σαθρός*: H, "cracked."

239. **Justinian's boy**: In 532-537, Justinian I, the son of Justin I, built the Santa Sophia after two previous structures had been destroyed by fire because they were structurally weak. The present one was a fireproof structure, strong in foundation, domes, arches and everything else.

240. **Pearson**: Norman Holmes P., English professor at Yale, visited Pound at St. Elizabeths while he was working on *Thrones.*

241. *μὴ τὸ κτιζόμενον λοξὸν*: H, "not built on a slant."

242. **Morrison**: Robert M., 1782-1834, author of *Chinese Grammar* (1814) and *Chinese Dictionary* (6 vols., 1821).

243. **de Saumase**: F, "Claude de Saumaise," the French name of Salmasius [87:24]. In a note appended to Nicole's *Livre du Préfet* Pound read: "Ces leçons meilleures du Genevensis confirment certaines corrections des critiques modernes, de Saumaise et de Reitz." A rhyme with the names of several other people in *The Cantos* who, in justice, should be remembered for their contributions [MB, *Trace*, 364-365].

244. de Reitz: [Cf. 243 above]. The two names appeared in the essay of Julien d'Askalon [cf. 246 below].

245. *πυρὸς . . . γῆς*: H, "fire, air, water, and earth." For "hodatas" read *hydatos.*

246. Julien d'Askalon: J. d'Askalon, author of the *Collection of Extracts* appended to the Geneva ms Nicole edited. His comments were arranged under four headings: (1)precautions against fire; (2)airing of solid items to be sold; (3)the uses of water; and (4)the laws of land ownership.

247. *τραπέζιον*: H, "at the table." Because bankers leaned on the tables at which they changed money, the phrase became associated with the process: hence, the modern Greek word for banker is *trapezites*, or "exchange table keeper."

248. *βυρσοδέψαι*: H, "tanners."

249. *μαλακατάριοι*: H, "softeners."

250. *βυρσοποιοί*: H, not in Liddell and Scott; but *βυρσο* is "leather" and *ποιόι* is the plural of *ποιός* "of a certain kind."

251. *μάγκιπες*: H, not in Liddell and Scott, but related forms indicate, "a place run for cookery." The "four" is F for "oven."

252. No yugo-slav . . . : Not in *The Eparch's Book* but prob. a contemporary example of rules made to prevent foreigners from becoming citizens and competing in trade, which the work deals with in detail, especially in chap. 2, "Dealers in Bullion and Money-lenders" and Chap. 20, "Deputy of the Eparch," whose business it was to keep track of "any persons arriving in Constantinople." Any traders who stayed beyond their permitted time were punished: "they shall be flogged, shaved, their goods shall be confiscated and they shall be expelled from the city" [*Ep.B*, 20-2].

253. Ronnie: Prob. Ronald Duncan, a major poet in the Pound Tradition and a life-long farmer in North Devon, who had a lengthy correspondence with Pound during the St. Elizabeths years [OP].

254. *ἐγκύκλιος* . . . : H, "circular education."

255. Necephoras: Emperor N. Phocas, 963-969, who debased the coinage [cf. 114 above]. Pound says he "kolobozed" it.

256. episkeptiks . . . bánauson: The controllers of the currency fought against usorious bankers in an effort to keep interest rates under 12% [*Ep.B*, 2-notes]. The rates changed over time and according to the use of the money: "Basil I forbade interest to be asked or taken . . . Leo III . . . made the max official rate 4 per cent p.a. . . . maritime loan . . . 12%," etc.

257. *κατὰ . . . ζώων*): H, "for the quality of animals." Refers to a chapter concerned with butchers [*Ep.B*, 15-2].

258. *Χαῖρε* . . . : H, "Goodbye to the sun."

259. Clarore: L, "brightness." The system of defending the public by laws to maintain "the just price" and the integrity of the coinage was beginning to disintegrate.

260. And in the sixth . . . : Pound's rendition of part of the long quote from the *Patrologiae Latina* [cf. 165 above].

261. iustitiae . . . : L, "Justice . . . nothing more ancient." Part of quote from Cicero's *De Officiis* [86/565].

262. "Honest feathers": Dante [*Pur.* I, 42] describes Cato asking a question while "movendo quelle oneste piume" ("moving those dignified plumes"). Pound gives the last two words thus.

263. "Quid occidere?": L, "What about murder?" Cato asked this [86:77].

264. Pascere satis: L, "Raise [cattle] well." In Cicero's *De Officiis* Cato the elder answered the first question about how to run an estate profitably by these words.

265. humiles . . . improbi: L, "All humble people are not dishonest" [Cicero, *De Officiis*, 2.71].

266. An ater, an albus: L, "Or black, or white." Catullus said to Julius Caesar: "Do I care whether you're white or black?" [Catullus, *Carmen*, 93 has the words reversed]. The 3 men in these several lines all stood for justice against the injustice of the state.

267. **Tully**: Cicero.

268. **no such blue**: Lake Garda's blue water. The villa to which Catullus was banished was at Sirmio on this lake.

269. **Ocelle Veronensis**: L, "the eye of Verona." Description of the blue of the water.

270. **Leo**: L. the Sixth, known as "the Wise," Byzantine emperor (866-912). He modernized the works on the law done under Justinian I.

271. **ΕΠΑΡΧΙΚΟΝ** . . . : H, *The Eparch's Book*: The great legal document uttered by Leo the Wise, 866-912, to provide some measure of justice in the marketplace. The Byzantine-Greek version was discovered in 1891 by Professor Jules Nicole [cf. 187 above], who transcribed it into modern Greek and made both Latin and French translations, published in 1893 as *Le Livre du Préfet*. [The original ms and the Greek and Latin versions are reproduced in *Pai*, 2-2, 245-311.] The book has 22 short chapters each devoted to one part of the marketplace, including money, banking, food, clothing, and construction. The rules were designed to prevent one part of the public from victimizing another. This is the earliest known document to deal with such matters in specific detail. The *eparchy* was an administrative district reaching 100 miles in all directions from Constantinople. The book opens with a formulary preamble saying the work was done by direction of "the Serene Emepror following the examples of God for the good of all subjects, the tranquillity of the state."

272. *γαληνότης*: H, "tranquil." The formula includes "to stop one man from treading on another."

273. *πολιτικῶν σωματείων*: H, "Political Bodies." Part of the title of the Greek ms.

274. **"les arrhes du marché"**: F, "earnest-money for trade," or "option money." Nicole's annoyance seems to have been caused by the difficulty of finding words for Greek goods and processes no longer in existence.

275. *βασιλεῦσι Λέων*: H, "King Leo."

276. **notary**: Chap. one concerns the qualifications needed for and the duties of "tabularies," whose functions were similar to those of notaries.

277. **ni cuivre . . . lin**: L, "neither copper nor linen textiles." From chap. 2, "Bullion and Moneylenders." They are required by the notary to deal in silver and to keep out of other businessmen's business. The source reads: "It is forbidden to hoard these commodities so as to sell them at a period of dearth, or to exact an undue profit above what is fair when they are scarce."

278. *κατὰ δόλον* . . . : H, "cheat through increasing."

279. **"romaine"**: Prob. the name of a Roman scale.

280. **ergastorios**: H, "premises."

281. **Manuale**: *Manualis Legis*, L, "Book of Law."

282. **Basiliks**: A modernization of the Code of Justinian done by Leo the Wise.

283. **Handschrift**: G, "handwriting."

284. *θυμίαμα* . . . : H, "incense in the presence of the Lord."

285. *ου μὴν χαλκὸν*: H, "and not copper."

286. *ἐί τις*: H, "anyone."

287. *χειροκοπείσθω*: H, "let a hand be cut off."

288. **῾Ο** *δόλον* . . . : [change] the nature [of gold] by cunning adulterate.

289. *ἐν* . . . *τῆς* Μέσης: H, "on the main [business] street." A particular circular thoroughfare which functioned as the agora or marketplace.

290. *εἰδήσεως* . . . : H, "the knowing assent of the Eparch." The source has these words

preceded by "$\alpha\nu\epsilon\upsilon$," "without." Nicole's eyesight seems to have been better than Pound's here. *Aveu*: F, "consent, avowal." The Greek ν is similar to the Roman v, and the source of this pun.

291. Palace . . . castello: From Nicole's note describing the area of the agora.

292. δοῦλον: H, "slave."

293. Καταλλάκτης . . . : H, "The coinmeasurer [must guard against] counterfeit[s].

294. Habdimelich: [cf. 161 above]. The affair concerned the coinage. The Islamic ruler wanted to settle debts with his own coinage. But the ruler of the Byzantine Empire could not accept it for two reasons: (1) only the emperor had the authority to issue money; and (2) acceptance of the coins implied assent that Allah was the one God. All tradition demanded that "Gold was of the Pontifex" [89:79; cf. 166 above]. The point is basic to Pound's economics: the state not only *can* but *should* issue money. More than that, no other agency should be allowed to do it.

295. Anno . . . : L, "Year six of the rule."

296. "pacem": L, "peace."

CANTO XCVII

Sources

Alexander Del Mar, *History of Monetary Systems*, Chicago, 1896 [*HMS*]; John Hamill, *The Strange Case of Mr. Hoover Under Two Flags*, New York, 1931; Dante, *Par.* XIX, *Pur.* XXXIII, XXVI, *Inf.* VII; Homer, *Od.* X; William Carlos Williams, *Paterson* (author's note); *Lucilius and Laws of XII Tables*, in *Remains of Old Latin*, ed. and trans. E. H. Warmington (Loeb) [*Lucilius*]; J. P. Migne, *Patrologia Latina*, vol. 95 [Migne, col. no.]; Philostratus, *The Life of Apollonius of Tyana*, trans. F. C. Conybeare, 2 vols., Harvard University Press [P, *Life*].

Background

EP, *SR*, 176; *SP*, 179, 184, 307-309, 311, 319, 325, 339-341, 429-432, 448; *PD*, 6; *Imp*, 39; *J/M*, 113; *CON*, 27, 75, 248; Constance Head, *Justinian II of Byzantium*, Univ. of Wisconsin Press, 1972; Theodor Mommsen, *History of Rome*, New York, Scribner, 1895; Herbert Finer, *Dulles over Suez*, Chicago, 1964; John Robinson Beal, *John Foster Dulles*, Harper Bros., New York, 1957; Alexander Del Mar, *The Science of Money*, 1885, rpt. 1967 [*Science*]; Wyndham Lewis, ed., *Blast* I, 1914 (rpt. 1981); James A. Barnes, *John G. Carlisle, Financial Statesman*, Peter Smith, 1967 [*Carlisle*]; James G. Frazer, *The Golden Bough*, ed. Gaster, Criterion, 1959; H. J. Rose, trans., *The Roman Questions of Plutarch*, Oxford, 1924 [*Roman Questions*].

Exegeses

Eastman, *Ezra Pound's Cantos: The Story of the Text*, Orono, Me., 1979; DD, *Sculptor*, 239-240; BK and TCDE, *Pai*, 9-3, 505-507; EH, *Pai*, 4-1, 182-185; Peck, *Pai*, 1-1, 27-28; CB-R, *ZBC*, 198; FR, *P/J*, 273; MB, *Trace*, 365; B de R, in EH, *Approaches*, 187-188; HK, *Pai*, 2-3, 488; Peck, *Pai*, 2-2, 212; EH, *Pai*, 8-1, 53-54.

Glossary

1. **Melik**: Abd-el-Melik [96:92].

2. **Edward**: Edward III, king of England, 1327-1377. The source says that in A.D. 692 Abd-el-Melik, "determined to assert his independence from Rome . . . struck gold coins with his own effigy, holding a drawn sword, as afterwards did Edward III when he renounced the same dread authority. Abd-el-Melik's dinars [ancient Moslem gold coin] bore this challenging legend: 'The Servant of God, Abd-el-Melik, Emir-el-Moumenim' " [*HMS*, 134].

3. **six and . . . people**: The ratio of silver to gold used by Moslems, because after their conquests they owned most of the silver mines and planned [*HMS*, 134-140] to spread their empire to India, where the ratio had for centuries been 6 or 7 to 1. The Romans had fixed the ratio at 12 to 1 because it could then get "twice as much gold for silver in India as it paid for it in Europe" [*HMS*, 136]. The source says that the Moslem ratio "may have been due to the fact that in all the western countries conquered by the Moslem, silver was chiefly in the hands of the people, whilst gold was in those of their rulers; and the great alteration which was made in their relative value was a covert bribe to gain the suffrages of the former and reconcile them to Moslem government and religion" [*HMS*, 135].

4. **(Princess A.)**: "Princess Alice" is a marginal note in DP's annotated copy of *The Cantos* [OP]. Poss. the 3d child and 2d daughter of Queen Victoria, Alice Maud Mary (1843-1878), who later became the grand-duchesse of Hesse-Darmstadt, except that her exemplary life of public service would not suggest a concern for money. The source of the quotation is unknown.

5. **Spew Deal**: The "New Deal" of Franklin D. Roosevelt.

6. **one billion . . .** : Del Mar speculated on why abd-el-Melik went to 61/2 and finds it was to make money. He concludes the supposed train of thought thus: "Judging from the proportions of the metallic spoil thus far captured, we shall secure about twenty times as much (in weight of) silver as gold, and assuming that we eventually secure 100,000,000 marks of silver, and coin it at the Indian ration, our fund will amount to 1,120,000,000 dinars" [*HMS*, 137].

7. **Gothic 8**: "The ratio of 8 to 1 is Gothic" [*HMS*, 137].

8. **barleycorn . . . mithcal**: The source has: "In the earliest Moslem system (period of Mahomet) the mithcal [or dinar] was divided into 96 parts . . . : 96 barleycorns = 48 habbeh = 24 tussuj = 6 danik = 1 mithcal" [*HMS*, 141].

9. **Shafy and Hanbal**: A footnote [ibid.] reads: "Esh Shafy and Ibn Hanbal both affirm that the ratio was 12 in the time of the Prophet." This was the ratio adapted from the practice of the Romans.

10. **Roman Christers**: The Roman emperors and/or people after the conversion to Christianity.

11. **devlish ingenuity**: Prob. the long, ingenious argument Del Mar assigned to Abd-el-Melik which led him to the 61/2-12 ratio

[*HMS*, 137-138]. He concludes in part: "As we have driven the Romans from the Mediterranean, and will soon control the commerce of Maritime Europe, whither could our gold dinars go outside of the influence of our own trade? Answer–Nowhere" [*HMS*, 138].

12. **ut supra**: L, "as [mentioned] above."

13. **Paulus**: [96:10].

14. **Theophanus**: Theophanes the Confessor, ca. 758-818, a monk and scholar of the Eastern church. He is the source of the story that Justinian was highly offended that Abd-el-Melik wanted to pay his tribute in Arab coins, thus leading to the war [96:165]. Recent scholars believe the story is legendary [Head, *Justinian II*, 47-50].

15. **& went decimal**: Abd-el-Melik created a new system: "the mithcal was divided into 100 parts.... Both the Roman binary weights and the Roman ratio of silver to gold were now dropped. the weights became decimal" [*HMS*, 141-142].

16. **the Prophet . . .**: The source says: "The dinar was valued at 10 dirhems–a valuation derived from the ordinances of the Prophet, and one which it would have been sacrelegious to alter. The law of the Prophet levies a title on all possessions of the precious metals" [*HMS*, 142].

17. **"NOUCH KHOR" . . .**: A, "Feast in health!" The source quotes the Koran: "There are some who if you entrust them with a talent (quintar) give it back to you; and some if you entrust them with a dinar will not return it" [BK, *Pai*, 5-2, 349]. But Del Mar misunderstood the Koran passage. An Islamic authority says the verse [Imram's Family, iii, Medina, v. 60] is not about borrowing or lending money. It's about non-Moslems, some of whom are said to be trustworthy and some not [Mohammed Shaheen, *Pai*, 11-3, 420-428].

18. **a king's head . . . benevolence**: Stating that the prototype of the dinar was the Roman solidus, the source goes on: "The dirhem [ten to a dinar] . . . was based upon an average of the three sorts of silver coins then circulating in the Persian dominions. Those with the effigy of the king and legend NOUCH KHOR, or 'Feast in Health' weighed one mithcal" [*HMS*, 145].

19. **1859 . . . Bassora**: "In A.H. 1276 (A.D. 1859) a Persian, named Djevad, paid into the post office at Constantinople a dirhem struck at Bassora in A.H. 40. . . . Its weight is 36.13 English grains" [ibid.].

20. **A.H.**: L, "anno Hegirae" (from Arabic *hijrah*), meaning "in the year of the Hegira," the migration of Mohammed from Mecca to Medina in 622.

21. **Irak . . .**: Mohammed (or someone else of importance) boasted: "I have left to Irak its dinar, to Syria its dirhem" [*HMS*, 146].

22. **Percussum . . .**: L, "Struck leather, a specie of the republic." "The leather notes of archaic Rome are mentioned by Seneca: 'Corium forma publica percussum.' . . . some authors trace the Ies [*as* or *ace*, the earliest money of Rome] to Janus, whose face was stamped on the coins" [*HMS*, 18n].

23. **Said Lear**: King Lear, entering "fantastically dressed with flowers," says: "No, they cannot touch me for coining; I am the king himself" [*King Lear*, IV, vi, 84-85].

24. **(Seneca)**: [Cf. 22 above]. Lucius Annaeus S., ca. 4 B.C.-A.D. 41, who wrote, besides tragedies, satires, epigrams, and analyses of moral questions.

25. **Charisius . . .**: Flavius Sosipater C. (late 4th century A.D.). African grammarian. His work is valuable because of sections copied from others, such as Ennius, Lucilius, and Cato, which are not found elsewhere.

26. **Scaliger**: Joseph Justus S., 1540-1609, French classical scholar who wrote (among many other things) 3 Latin tracts, cited by Del Mar, on numismatics [*HMS*, 15].

27. **Andoleon**: Writing about early Roman silver coins, Del Mar says: "The type of some of the Capuan coins . . . is apparently

copied from the coins of Andoleon, king of Paeonia (in Macedon), about A.U. [for A.U.C. (*ab urbe condita*), which dates the founding of Rome ca. 753 B.C.] 470" [*HMS*, 27].

28. Gold scrupulum: "In A.U. 437 a notable addition was made to the monetary system of Rome by the issuance of a 'Roma' gold coin, called the 'scrupulum' which was valued at twenty aces." The word *scrupulum* was used early to mean the 9th, then 10th, then 12th part of anything: "At a still later date the game of draughts was played . . . with twelve men. . . . Hence in Rome during the fifth century of the city a scrupulum meant, not a weight, but the ninth of anything; and in the case of money it meant the ninth of the gold aureus" [*HMS*, 27-28].

29. B.C. 316: Del Mar gives a table of coins and their values, with a heading that says: "Roman coinage system about A.U. 437 or B.C. 316. Ratio of silver to gold 9 for 1" [ibid., 28].

30. "Outre . . . ": F, "Besides the book of weights." "With regard to the 'libra' of account, Gibbon says that, besides the libra weight, the Romans used a libra of account, which they called pondo" [ibid., 29].

31. 2000 aces . . . : Del Mar gives several tables of various dates which start by defining the *ace* in relation to other coins and end with the phrase: "Hence 2000 aces = 1 libra" [*HMS*, 31-34].

32. Gibbon . . . : Edward Gibbon, 1737-1794. Del Mar cites *The Decline and Fall of the Roman Empire* and *Miscellaneous Works* in his bibliography [ibid., 13].

33. Mommsen: Theodor M., 1817-1903, German historian whose *History of Rome* has been long available in English. He wrote authoritatively on Roman law and economics and received the Nobel Prize for literature in 1902.

34. Lenormant: Del Mar cites two of his works: *Monnaies et Medailles*, 1879, and *La Monnaie dans l'Antiquite* [*HMS*, 14]. Del Mar finds two grievous errors made by Mommsen and carried on by Lenormant: "The first one is that of mistaking the 'libra' of money . . . for a pound weight of silver metal; the second one is that of calculating the ratio from anachronical coins" [*HMS*, 38-39]. After dealing with the errors, Del Mar cites Gibbon, whose judgment he finds to be better than that of these later authorities.

35. "Qu'on décrie": F, "that they return." From a ballad in Villon's *Testament* about old, worn-out prostitutes: "Car vieilles n'ont ne cours ne estre / Ne que monnoye qu'on descrie." Pound translates: "For old they have not course nor status / More than hath money that's turned in" [*SR*, 176].

36. Caligula: Roman emperor, A.D. 37-41. "Upon the death of Caligula an attempt was made to reestablish the Republic" [*HMS*, 40-41].

37. Nero: Roman emperor, A.D. 54-68. "Upon the news of Nero's death many people . . . ran wildly through the streets . . . fomenting an excitement that ended by involving the Senate in their design, and the issuance of an Act proclaiming a Republican government. Among the first measures of the short-lived administration was the coinage of money, designed to announce the restoration" [*HMS*, 42-43].

38. June 9th, 68: "Besides the gold coins, there were struck silver and bronze ones. . . . All these must have been struck between June 9, A.D. 68, the date of Nero's death, and July 18, A.D. 69" [ibid., 43].

39. LIBERTATI: L, "For liberty." "A common type of these coins was a citizen clad in a toga, with a cap of Liberty on his head and a wreath of laurel in his right hand, and the legend LIBERTATI" [ibid.].

40. LIBERTAS RESTITUTA: L, "Liberty restored." One of 12 Latin phrases found on the reverse sides of various coins [ibid.].

41. Caracalla: Marcus Aurelius Antoninus, 188-217, the son of Septimius Severus, called

"Caracalla" because he wore a Gallic tunic. While Roman emperor (211-217) he raised taxes and used the money to bribe the army and people. "This system of Caracalla contains all the elements of the decimo-doudecimal or s.d. system" [*HMS*, 49].

42. Venice . . . silver: "Even after the Empire fell and the Western States, as Venice, Florence, Amalfi, Aragon, etc., began to coin gold, they maintained the same ratio of 12 to 1 in their coinages" [*HMS*, 59].

43. leather . . . (Aug.): In a table "of the earliest gold coinages of Christian Europe," one item reads: "1241. FAENZE, Sieze of.–Leather notes issued by Frederick, payable in gold augustals" [*HMS*, 76]. Another entry reads: "1250. FRANCE.–Gold agnels, or dinars, struck for Louis IX. by Blanche, his mother." A footnote to this entry contains the phrase: "(M. Paris, sub anno 1250, vol. II., pp. 342, 278, 280)" [ibid., 77]. "Aug." is an abbreviation of "augustals."

44. Avignon . . . : In the same table, another item reads: "1316. AVIGNON.–Sequino of Pope John XXII." A footnote to this item reads: "This pope is responsible for a treatise on the transmutation of metals, the prolific exemplar of many similar works" [ibid.].

45. Darius, and Targitaus: "For example, Targitaus, the first king of Scythia, a thousand years before Darius, the sacred king of Persia (this would make it about B.C. 1500), was the divine son of Jupiter. . . . In the kingdom of Targitaus gold was found in abundance, but being deemed sacred, it was reserved for the use of the sacred king" [*HMS*, 81].

46. Cicero . . . : "In B.C. 59, Cicero said: 'The Senate, on several different occasions, but more strictly during my consulship, prohibited the exportation of gold' " [ibid., 85].

47. "gravissime . . . : L, "more strictly during my consulship." The Latin for a part of the quote given in 46 above.

48. Theodosian Code: "The libra of money (not the whole triad of £ s.d.) is at least five hundred and may be fifteen hundred years older than Charlemagne, being clearly defined in the Theodosian Code (lib. xiii., tit. ii., II)" [*HMS*, 96]. Del Mar uses these facts in an argument to show that other writers are in error to suppose the English pound came from a pound of silver or of anything else.

49. Caracalla: Del Mar repeats the contribution of this emperor [cf. 41 above] to reinforce his argument that the pound originated in ratios of value rather than weight: "In the reign of Caracalla 24 denarii went to the aureus, the ratio of value between the metals remaining unchanged. Such is briefly the genesis of £ s.d." [*HMS*, 97].

50. first fish . . . maravedis: "The evolution of Norse monetary systems . . . usually proceeded in the following manner:–First, fish and vadmal (cloth) money; second, baug, or ring-money; third, imitations of pagan Roman coined money; fourth, Norse pagan coinage system (partly dervied from the Roman system) of stycas, scats, and oras; fifth, intrusion of the Moslem coinage system of dinars, maravedis and dirhems, sixth, replacement of the last by Christian Roman coinage system of £ s.d."

51. kelt coin . . . scat: "[Among Norsemen] Sild, hring, or herring, is still used to mean money, and the scad or scat (corrupted to scot), a fish of the same genus, has the same meaning in North Britain" [ibid., 115-116]. "Eight stycas went to the scat, and eight scats to the ora" [*HMS*, 121].

52. Del Mar: "Money is perhaps the mightiest engine to which man can lend intelligent guidance" [*HMS*, 5].

53. King Offa . . . : "Offa, king of Mercia, and perhaps other early English princes [put the ratio] at 61/2 silver for 1 gold" [*HMS*, 157].

54. Alfred . . . : A table shows the valuations of Alfred starting at 71/2 in 874, and going to 10 c. 878, finally to 12 in 901. The 12-1 ration given in the table is the "valuations of Athelstan, son of Edward, elder" [*HMS*, 158].

55. Canute: "Canute, the Christian but anti-papal king of Denmark and England, has left us a greater variety of coin-types than any other English prince before the Plantagenet dynasty" [*HMS*, 183-184].

56. 20 scads . . . accountancy: A table gives these values: "1 mancus, or dinar [=] 20 scats; 1 mark of account [=] 100 scats" [*HMS*, 162].

57. Edgar's leather . . . : "The reign of Edgar, king of Wessex, is marked by the issuance of leather moneys" [*HMS*, 181]. Del Mar gives Edgar's dates as 959-975 [p. 182] and Athelstan's as 925-941 [p. 158].

58. "thon yilden . . . ": "then he set up gilds" [91:52]. The reference is to "peace-gilds set up by the bishops and reeves of London for mutual protection against cattle-thieves (*Laws*, VI Athelstan), echoing Pound's idea of good government" [CB-R, *ZBC*, 198n.].

59. the president: F.D.R.

60. old Lampman: Rex Herbert L., a Washington newspaperman who had a nervous breakdown because of the confusion of Cissie Patterson's will, in which she bequeathed the Washington *Times Herald* to 7 of her employees. He was confined in a violent unit at St. Elizabeths at first but later could visit Pound during his time on the grounds and told him inside stories about Washington between the wars [EM, *Difficult*, 303-306].

61. Mencken: [81:31; 87:112].

62. the London judge: In a letter of Sept. 3, 1954, Pound wrote: "Yes, the high point in American dignity was when Hoover voted in W. 8 election AND simultaneously the British judge said: Mr. Hoover I am sorry that this has been brought as a civil, not a criminal action." Herbert Hoover was employed as a mining engineer by the defendants (a firm named Bewick, Moreing and Co.) in a suit "brought to trial before Justice Joyce in the Chancery Division of the High Court in London." The plaintiffs were a Chinese company who sued "because the value of their shares [in Bewick, Moreing] had been reduced by the issue of shares to the promoters of the company and their friends." Justice Joyce said: "I cannot set the matter right in this action, which was not framed and is not properly constituted for the purpose." Pound's source appears to be John Hamill's *The Strange Case of Mr. Hoover Under Two Flags* (New York, 1931). Hamill wrote: "The Judge was shocked. But his was not a Criminal Court but a Court of Equity and all he had to pass on was the claim before him" [p. 190]. Hoover was also associated with the "Youanme" mine in China [79:76]. Say Kimpel and Eaves, who located these facts and others at Beinecke (including an unpublished poem, "O, o, O the Yewenmee / Is a vurry fine gole mine companee"): "The point of the poem is that the only limit to the number of shares the company sells is the time it takes to print more" [BK and TCDE, *Pai*, 9-3, 505-507].

63. Missenden, Dunmore . . . : Source: "In 1362 the abbot of Missenden was convicted of coining and clipping groats and sterlings; in 1369 the canon of Dunmore was accused of counterfeiting gold and silver coins; and in 1371 the canon of St. Gilbert of Sempingham was charged with secretly conveying coins abroad contrary to law" [*HMS*, 192-193n.]. The canon's name appears to have been Lear.

64. Offa's gold . . . the Third: "The coinage of gold ceased when Christianity was introduced, and the last gold coins known to have been struck in England previous to the reign of Henry III, were the dinars of Offa" [*HMS*, 190]. Del Mar devotes a couple of pages to an outline of the continuous debasement of the coinage, including counterfeiting, until "a re-coinage was ordered in 1108, and the severest sentences were threatened to false coiners. In 1123, to lend effect to these threats, the power of Rome was invoked in aid of the crown, and the penalties of the Canon law were added to t[illegible]e of the civil . . . much of the base coining was done by a class of people who knew too much about the *crimen majestatis* to stand in fear of impeachment" [*HMS*, 192; the quote in 63 above is a footnote to this quote].

65. Crimen majestatis: L, "crime against sovereignty."

66. the plebs . . . : "Plebians." "It should not be forgotten that there were but four classes of people who had anything to do with public affairs—the imperial authorities, the royal authorities, the nobles, and the ecclesiastics. The adulteration of money was committed chiefly by the two last-named classes" [*HMS*, 194].

67. in 1914: Prob. a ploy on the part of the British banks at the outbreak of WWI. Scarcity at home could only force the government to meet the banks' demands in costs of credit.

68. Coins . . . Poitou: "In 1189, upon his accession to the throne, Richard [Coeur de Lion] weighed out more than 10,000 marks from his father's treasure . . . in 1190, . . . he found it necessary to command and exhort his followers to accept his money—a tolerably sure indication of coinage. . . . Coins which were struck in Poitou under his authority are still extant" [*HMS*, 203-204].

69. Caxton: "In 1192 Richard was taken prisoner. . . . In 1194 he was ransomed. . . . This ransom was collected in England and from the possessions of the English crown in France. . . . Caxton says that plate 'was molten and made into money' " [*HMS*, 204].

70. Polydore: "The old coin and bullion was prob. melted down [to pay the ransom] . . . and delivered to the German Emperor's legate—a supposition that precisely agrees with Polydore Vergil's account of the affair" [ibid., 204-205].

71. Villon: Not mentioned in the source [cf. 35 above].

72. "blanc": "During the Norman era farms were let . . . upon a money rent (*numero*) or bullion rent (*blanc*) . . . which Madox would lead us to infer were always made in silver" [*HMS*, 196]. "In explaining the use of the term 'blanc,' Madox confuses *blanc* silver and *blanc* money. The former was silver bullion, the latter a white money, sometimes called album [white] made wholly or for the most part of tin" [p. 206].

73. Bacchus . . . massacre: "Corrupt coins made their appearance in all directions. . . . In that age the solution of all monetary problems was found in torturing the Jews. Henry [III] had resorted to this measure [once] before the decision of the General Council [to lower the standard of royal silver coins in 1247]. He now resorted to it again [the 2d massacre of the Jews was in 1264] . . . but it did not work. With the second persecution of the Jews, the besants [coins worth 4s, and the most important in trade] became still scarcer. . . . One of the last in . . . besants . . . is a Hebrew bond and mortgage executed during the reign of Henry III. . . . The besants are therein called Iaku of gold . . . Iaku being the Hebrew form of the Greek Iacchus and Roman Bacchus" [*HMS*, 212-213].

74. wheat . . . perch: "The division of the pound of account into twenty parts, and each of these into twelve, was in this reign extended to the pound weight, used for the assize of bread. Still more strangely it was imitated in the subdivisions of the agrarian acre. By the Act 51 Henry III. (1266) it was provided . . . that 'when a quarter of wheat is 12d. per quarter, then wastel bread of a farthing shall weight £ 6 16s.'; by which we suppose was meant 64/5 pounds weight. A similar enactment was made as to acres. The acre was divided into 160 pence. . . . Thus . . . (a penny of land) meant a rod or perch" [*HMS*, 213].

75. grammar . . . prosody: "If the kings of England previous to Edward III were not vassals [of the emperor], why have we none of their ordinances? . . . It is not alone upon literary evidence that the argument relies; it stands also upon the far more certain evidence of coins and nummulary grammar" [*HMS*, 224-225].

76. *πρόσοδος* **. . .** : H, "the regular income of taxes."

77. *μεταθεμένων*: H, "changing" [cf. 74:343].

78. **Dandolo**: Henry C., "the aged and pious doge" of Venice [89:233]. The passage concerns the deterioration of the ratio and the standards of coinage. Dandolo worked with Innocent III to destroy and despoil Constantinople in 1204.

79. **the Third Edward**: The source continues from the quote in 75 above: "Many of these evidences have been already adduced. Those which will now be furnished relate chiefly to the sudden and frequent alterations of money which began after the fall of Constantinople, and culminated in the reign of Edward III."

80. **the VIIth**: Edward 1841-1910, king of England (1901-1910).

81. **Thus Dante**: Lines Pound oftens cites [*Par.* XIX, 118-119]: "il duol che sopra Senna / induce, falseggiando la moneta" ("the woe brought upon the Seine / by falsifying the coinage"). Dante's outcry against Philip the Fair's debasement of the coinage to finance his Flemish campaign in 1302 [38:1], part of the general debasement Pound is concerned with here [*SP*, 311].

82. **Villon**: [cf. 35 above].

83. **& in 1311** . . . : "In 1311 the Lords Ordainers enacted that no changes should be made in the value of the coins without the consent of the barons in paliament assembled" [*HMS*, 230].

84. **"coignagio stagminis"**: L, "tin coinage." "Edward II . . . commanded Richard Hywysh . . . to pay on his account . . . out of the profits of the tin coinage (*coignagis stagminis*)" [ibid.].

85. **religious men** . . . : "Among the earliest statutes of the new reign [of Edward III] were those of 1327, against the importing of light and counterfeit coins and of 1331, against the exportation of either coins or bullion. The penalty for the latter was first made death . . . and in 1335 the Act [with penalty lessened] was extended to 'religious men' as well as others" [*HMS*, 233].

86. **Almoravedis' . . . 9, 7, 9?**: "The maravedi [a Moorish gold coin] of that period [1150-1250] contained 40 to 43 grains of fine gold" [*HMS*, 236]. "The maravedi was first coined in Spain, during the dynasty of the Almoravedis, hence its name" [*HMS*, 237]. "The king's council advised the king . . . to issue a convention gold coin. . . . This advice was carried into effect in 1344 by the coinage of a gold double-florin, weighing 50 to the pound tower and 231/2 carats 0.979 1/6 fine, the old 'standard' for gold." A footnote says: "the expression 'old standard'. . . could only refer to the Byzantine or the Arabian standard for gold" [*HMS*, 240]. The question mark is prob. a printer's error for 1/6.

87. **Scanda . . . Laconics**: "Scanda was the name of a Getic city in Colchis and Scandea that of a Getic seaport at the extremity of Cythera, a large island off the southern coast of Greece. Pausanias in 'Laconics' " . . . [*HMS*, 254n.].

88. **2 doits . . . doits**: "The term merk [market] is still used by the Scots. In their ancient scale of moneys there were 2 doits (fingers) to a boodle, 2 boodles to a plack, 3 placks to a bawbee, and 131/3 bawbes, or 160 doits, to a merk" [*HMS*, 258n.]. The Pound text has a misprint [cf. Eastman, *Story*, 118-119].

89. **Capn. Wadsworth**: Joseph W., an ancestor of Pound's who in 1687 stole the Connecticut State Charter and hid it in an oak tree to protect it, "to the embarrassment of legitimist tyranny" [*PD*, 6].

90. **ED. Three** . . . : The gold double-florins [cf. 86 above] of 1344, "were the first English coins of any kind upon which were stamped the words 'Dei gratia.' Down to that time the kings of England coined by the grace of Caesar, or, as in John's case, the pope, his successor. Edward III. first coined by the grace of God" [*HMS*, 241].

91. **sand-paper ordered** . . . : Sandpaper was

used instead of clipping to remove small quantities of gold or silver from coins.

92. **Mons of Jute . . . record**: King Christian of Denmark, "a tyrant as well as a Zealot," and his minister, "who was little better than a wild beast," by "the grossest indignities . . . had fired the Gothic blood." The Pope's legate "by the sale of indulgences and other artifices . . . [had] managed to squeeze out of the poorest country in Europe nearly 'two millions of florins'. . . ." At this point, "It was not merely Norway and Sweden that rose up to throw off the shackles of Rome, it was all Scandinavia. . . . Jutland . . . transmitted to the tyrant of Denmark a demand of deposition which was read to him by a single unarmed man . . . whose act should never be permitted to fall into oblivion. This hero's name was Mons, and it deserves to be written over the gateway of every oppressor" [*HMS*, 278-279]. Justice, as in Dante's "Thrones," demands that he not be forgotten.

93. **Vasa klipped . . .** : "The unlooked-for result of Mons' brave act was the abdication and flight of the cowardly Christian. His uncle Frederick was chosen in his place but the real sovereign was Gustavus Vasa. . . . [King] Christian . . . had introduced the klippings for the sake of personal profit; Gustavus issued them for the benefit of his country" [*HMS*, 279].

94. **Lycurgus, nomisma**: "All the great enfranchisements of society have been accomplished with the aid of fiduciary money. The Spartans won their liberties with the iron discs of Lycurgus; the Athenians . . . rehabilitated the republic with 'nomisma,' a highly overvalued copper issue" [*HMS*, 279].

95. **"limitation . . . "**: "When the people take the government of a country into their own hands wealth naturally hides itself, and the first form of wealth to disappear is the precious metals. The moment a revolution or a civil war is declared gold and silver disappear [cf. 67 above]. Thereupon the emission of fiduciary money by the State becomes imperative" [*HMS*, 280]. A central thesis of Social Credit, Douglas, and *The Cantos*. But the key to preventing inflation is the proper relation of "fiduciary money" to tax policy and the production of goods and services, or "limitation": "These [are the] principles of money—namely, that Money is a Measure, . . . that the Unit of money is All Money within a given legal jurisdiction, [and] that the practical Essence of money is Limitation" [*HMS*, preface, 8; *Science*, 25-55].

96. **Goertz von Schlitz**: George Heinrich de Goertz, Baron von Schlitz, financial adviser to Charles XII of Sweden. "After the defeat of Charles XII. at Pultowa and his return from captivity money was scarce. . . ." Goertz had what seemed a good idea: issue copper dollars with the king's stamp as legal tender. The idea might have worked except for two factors: "First, government was too prostrate and weak to sustain a fiduciary money. Second, Goertz did not place any limitations upon the coinage. This (limitation) is the main principle and essence of money" [*HMS*, 295-296].

97. **executed**: After the death of King Charles in 1718, Goertz was charged with a dozen monetary crimes, including peculation and ruining the public credit. Del Mar quotes from another source: " 'the case went on without regard to formality or perhaps to equity. The court and the citizens seemed equally determined to hound him to death. . . . He was condemned to lose his head, and at a place appointed for the execution of felons' " [*Modern Univers. Hist.*, XXX, 288]. Del Mar concludes: "This cruel sentence was enforced March 3, 1719" [*HMS*, 297-298].

98. **Copjenhaven . . .** : "In 1745 it [the Bank of Copenhagen, founded in 1736] was released from the obligation of discharging its notes in coin. . . . This bank had issued paper to the amount of eleven millions of riksdalers, when the king returned their deposits to the shareholders and became himself the sole proprietor" [*HMS*, 303]. Then, "all further emission of notes was forbidden, and a progressive liquidation of the paper

was ordered." After that the king quit, and "a new bank was created which was . . . independent of the government." Then the bankers began their crooked deals over again [*HMS*, 303-304].

99. 15.08 . . . 1873: "The Scandinavian States practically demonetized silver. . . . 'The basis of conversion adopted was the proportion of silver to gold of 15.08 for 1'. . . . These provisions were adopted in the Danish, Swedish, and Norwegian laws of May 23, 1873" [*HMS*, 306].

100. Mr Benton: [88:80, 95:22].

101. Friesland . . . : In a chapter on the Netherlands, Del Mar traces the coinage of early centuries and relates it to the coinage of other states at the time. "I regard the silver pieces of Friesland . . . as typically quarter-dirhems . . . or half-deniers. It is of no practical consequence [which] . . . if as half-deniers, they should bear a ratio of 12 to the gold shilling of the empire, which they do not; whereas, if as quarter-dirhems, they should bear a ratio of 61/2 to the quarter-dinars of Saracenic Spain, which they do" [*HMS*, 312].

102. "The olde double-ducat: "During the Burgundian period, some of the Dutch ducats now called double ducats . . . were 23 carats 31/2 grains fine (Budelins, p. 249, 'Old Double Ducat')" [*HMS*, 315].

103. The olde turkish grouch": "There was also a silver dollar . . . the prototype of the existing German thaler, the old Turkish grouch, and many other coins" [ibid.].

104. Amsterdam . . . : "The 'Confederation of Bergers' was formed in 1566; the revolution was proclaimed in 1572; paper money was issued in 1574; the Jews of Amsterdam organized a sort of Wissel bank in 1607; and the bank of Amsterdam, which, under the authority of the city, imitated and then destroyed the Wissel bank and forbade the Jews from dealing in exchange, was established in 1609" [*HMS*, 321-322].

105. Del Mar . . . buyables: These four lines, not in the source, are Pound's summary of a central Social Credit thesis.

106. Ike, '55: Dwight D. Eisenhower, 1890-1969, president of the U.S., 1953-1961.

107. Baffico . . . papers: In "Economic Nature of the United States," Pound wrote: "A perfect example of instinctive monetary good sense is met today in this small town. The newsvendor, Mr. Baffico . . . because he lacked the necessary small change . . . has had some little tags printed which he now gives to his patrons" [*IMP*, 39; *SP*, 184].

108. giornali: I, "newspapers."

109. legat de Leicestre: L, "envoy from Leicester."

110. Thomas . . . Realm: In 1526 Henry VIII issued an ordinance to "Thomas, Cardinal of York, . . . legat de Leicestre of the See Apostolic. . . ." Since gold and silver coins, "in the realm of France, as also in the emperor's Low Countries," were bringing higher prices than they were in England, "the money of our realm is daily . . . conveyed out of this realm into parts beyonds the seas." Something had to be done to stop the flow. The king "determined that our coins . . . shall be . . . from henceforth made of such fineness . . . as may be equivalent . . . in outward parts" [*HMS*, 323].

111. "Ad perpetuam . . . memoriam": L, "In perpetual memory of their divine liberation from tyranny" [*HMS*, 327].

112. "Rien de ce monde": F, "nothing in this world."

113. "Godt behoede": D, "God protect."

114. Pugno pro patria: L, "Fight for [your] country." "The revolutionary moneys of Leyden were of white pasteboard, round, about 1 1/2 inches in diameter and stamped or embossed to resemble a coin. . . . Their deonominations were 24 and 40 stivers. The former bore on one side . . . 'Godt behoede Leyden,' or God protect Leyden. The latter had the city arms on one side, and 'Pugno propatria' " [*HMS*, 327n.].

115. degradations . . . resemblance: "Is it yet clearly understood that whatever degradation of money was committed by the emperors, whatever debasement was afterwards committed by the kings, these have since been vastly exceeded by the dishonest use made of 'individual' coinage and the control of bank issues? Not at all. The Emperors of Rome controlled emissions . . . for thirteen centuries, and the kings and dukes for nearly four centuries afterwards; whilst the usurers have held it to the present time, for about two centuries. . . . During these two centuries . . . more losses have been occasioned to the industrial classes . . . than were made by all the degradations and debasements of the Imperial and regal periods put together. . . . 'The control of money' says an eloquent writer on the subject, 'is the ground upon which an international or cosmopolitan combination "finances" the world and "farms" humanity.' " [*HMS*, 330-331].

116. Kitson, Fenton . . . : Del Mar has a footnote identifying the eloquent writer: "Reginald Fenton, Esq. formerly of Kimberly, South Africa, now of San Diego, California. 'The distribution of wealth and the exploitation of some men by others are dependent upon money.' Count Leo Tolstoi in his Essay on Money in Kitson's 'Scientific Solution of the Money Question' " [*HMS*, 331n.; EH, *Pai*, 4-1, 182-185].

117. Brooks Adams: American historian, 1848-1927, whose works, especially *The Law of Civilization and Decay*, were admired by Pound [*SP*, 307-309].

118. "Salzburg: Saltzburg. "In 1763 an imperial decree . . . established a convention coinage rate [for North German States] : . . . 360.8 grains fine silver to the riks thaler effectives . . . the Austrian 'effectives' struck under this convention actually contained but 353.7 grains . . . Saltzburg alone struck them of full weight" [*HMS*, 352].

119. The 1806 . . . years: "The paper notes of Prussia were nationalized in 1806 and are in circulation today" [*HMS*, 353].

120. Octonary sun-worshiping: Del Mar discusses two systems of weights for coinage in the 16th century and concludes: "To the experienced metrologist it is evident that both of these are hybrid systems, originating remotely in the octonary numbers and relations of the sun-worship practiced in the countries of the Baltic" [*HMS*, 356]. Pound uses it as a musical figure recalling the sunrites of Sargon the Great [94:55; cf. 240 below], already dealt with, and rites to come in later cantos [Peck, *Pai*, 1-1, 27-28].

121. 371 1/4 grains: "In Spain and America during the eighteenth century it [the thaler] never fell below 3711/4 grains fine, and there it stands today in the coinage of the United States" [*HMS*, 359].

122. as I have seen them: Pound's memory of watching men shoveling coins in a Philadelphia mint that he visited with his father at the age of 8. He wrote Sir Montagu Webb, a British businessman: "Silver I saw, as no Aladdin, for when Cleveland was elected there was the recount of four million in the Mint vaults, the bags had rotted, and the men half-naked with open gas flares, shovelled it into the counting-machines, with a gleam on tarnished discs" [NS, *Life*, 7].

123. Theresa's 390- . . . Salzburg: [Cf. 118 above]. Other data from the tables: "Austria, before 1753–390; . . . Saltzburg–3581/5; . . . Austria 1753 (nominally 361 gr) actually–3533/4" [*HMS*, 358].

124. Bryan: William Jennings B., 1850-1925. During Bryan's campaign for president in 1896, Arthur Kitson jumped on his free-silver bandwagon. Since Kitson was for demonetizing silver, that seemed strange. After Bryan's death, Kitson said Bryan understood "that the real issue was to gain presidential control of the national credit" [EH, *Pai*, 4-1, 183]. Pound wrote to Stock years later: "William J. Bryan admitted to Arthur Kitson many years ago that the 'Free Silver' campaign was window dressing" [ibid.].

125. Kitson: Arthur K., 1860-1937, one of Pound's favorite writers about monetary policy [*SP*, 179, 339, 341, 448]. Kitson wrote *A Scientific Solution of the Money Question*, Boston, 1894; *A Fraudulent Standard*, 1917, rpt. Omni Publications, 1972.

126. Legal . . . Zollverein: "From 1st January, 1841, the thaler . . . was to be the sole full legal-tender money of the Prussian States. . . . Besides this, a new coin . . . was to be struck, 7 to the mark fine, which should be legal in all the States of the Zollverein" [*HMS*, 359-360].

127. crisis: "In 1873 there was a crisis,[8]" note 8 says: "Paper money 106 millions more than previous year" [*HMS*, 363].

128. in vain did Hume: A great fear grew in the commercial world: so much gold would be mixed and become money that disastrous inflation, "that is disastrous to millionaires," would result. "In vain had Hume . . . shown that rises of prices occasioned by an increase of metallic money had benefited not only the poor, but the rich as well" [*HMS*, 370].

129. Hume: Joseph H., 1777-1855, a member of the House of Commons who made a number of speeches over the years on monetary questions, many of which were published, such as: "On the Banks of England; and the State of the Currency" (1839) and "Economy and Retrenchment" (1822).

130. in vain Von Humboldt: In vain had Von Humboldt, whose familiarity with history . . . and with mining should have entitled him to speak with some authority . . . assured the world that the vast disparity between the world's stock of coins of the precious metals, compared with any additions that might be made to it, rendered the latter a very trifling factor in the account . . . the money-lenders and usurers . . . knew better" [*HMS*, 370].

131. Von Humboldt: Alexander Freiherr von H., 1769-1859, German scientist, explorer, and natural philosopher, who served in the Prussian department of mines and afterwards made worldwide explorations. His 5-vol. *Cosmos* proved him one of the great minds of the 19th century. Del Mar calls him "this most illustrious of Germans and of savants" but says, "Von Humboldt's book, 'The Fluctuations of Gold,' was consigned to oblivion, and the essays of the Metallic School were hailed with applause, translated into all languages, and published in every country of Europe and America" [ibid.].

132. Such suckers . . . Liverpool: The "Metallic School" taught that "the unit of money is both the whole volume of money and each indivisible fraction of it; money is metal, and metal is money; finally, the national honor is subject to the comparative output of the gold and silver mines! All these and many other sophistries will be found in the essays of Harris, Chevalier and Lord Liverpool" [*HMS*, 371]. This issue involves a central doctrine of Social Credit, now several hundred years old. One must understand why Hume, Von Humboldt, Douglas, Kitson, Orage, Pound, and dozens of others found these arguments "sophistries" to understand the central thesis of Social Credit. To agree with the "Metallic School" is to agree that money is just a form of barter and not a legal instrument [Del Mar, *Science*, 25-56].

133. Cobden: "[These sophistries] led . . . Mr. Cobden to recommend corn rents and payments in kind." A footnote says: "Chevalier's essays were published . . . shortly after the opening of California. Most of the sophistries [are] . . . in the first chapter of his subsequent work 'The Fall in the Value of Gold,' translated by Cobden" [*HMS*, 371].

134. Von Schultz: Arguments to extend more power to banks to issue money, "in the interest of international circulation," were opposed by some: "the declaration of Von Schultz, that to sign away the independence of the State in reference to money would constitute an act of treason." A footnote to this statement says: "Sir Wm. Harcourt said he was 'not willing to place the currency of England at the mercy of foreign States' " [*HMS*, 378].

135. Frank Harris: 1854-1931, a famous editor, critic, novelist, playwright and autobiographer. In *Blast*, Pound includes him on the list of those to be blessed. Where or when he said this is not yet known. But the context suggests the banking industry's ability to create money based on ambiguous backing.

136. Albuquerque . . .Goa: "Albuquerque . . . raised the flag of Portugal upon the battlements of Goa." Right away he issued "an unauthorized and debased coinage of gold, silver and copper . . . to relieve [so he said] a local dearth of coins . . . [but in fact] to buy the gold . . . and sell it . . . at cent per cent profit" [*HMS*, 387-388].

137. 18, CHARLES . . . 5: An act of Charles II which to Pound was the climax of a long process that finally put the right of coinage into the hands of banks. "The British East India Company . . . struck idolatrous coins, under native permission, in 1620; and, with the door thus ajar to private coinage, it was easily pushed wide open. An intrigue with this object was introduced . . . during the reign of Charles I, which blossomed during that of his son, in the Act 18 Charles II., c. 5, an Act that bargained away the Measure of Value" [*HMS*, 388].

138. 1816: "In 1816 the Crown was persuaded to suspend the exercise of its power over the ratio. In this manner was silver demonetized. By the . . . Mint Act of 1870 [of Queen Victoria] . . . the last remnant of a prerogative whose exercise is essential to the autonomy of the State was innocently surrendered to private hands" [*HMS*, 389].

139. "Victoria . . . ": [35:48]. The caption under a Max Beerbohm cartoon.

140. Ideogram: I [M3002], "right conduct" or "public spirit."

141. Goldsmiths: Concerning the power of goldsmiths Del Mar says: "These tremendous powers have been wielded . . . in so narrow and selfish a spirit, that its arbiters have repeatedly plunged the commercial world into bankruptcy and confiscated . . . its accumulated earnings, either for their own benefit or else to save themselves from the effects of their own blundering" [*HMS*, 390].

142. *σοφία*: H, "wisdom"

143. *πίστις*: H, "trust [in others]." G. R. S Mead edited a Gnostic miscellany entitled *Pistis Sophia* [Peck, *Pai*, 1-1, 28].

144. Gansl . . . death: "Consult the writer's [Del Mar's] examination of Mr Albert Gansl, banker and agent of the Rothschilds before the U.S. Monetary Commission, printed . . . at Washington, 1876" [*HMS*, 391n.].

145. "Duped . . . ": "The States which in 1873 were duped into doubling their indebtedness [have dispensed] . . . with that mischief of Private Coinage. . . . Most of them now exercise . . . a more or less complete control over their own monetary systems" [*HMS*, 392].

146. "Portcullis . . . devices": In a table entitled *"Ratio of Silver to Gold in India,"* we read: "1677–East India Company authorized by the British Crown [then Charles II] to coin gold, silver, copper, or lead, with its own devices" [*HMS*, 396].

147. Assyria . . . somewhere: "Down to the epoch of Mahomet . . . every state in the West . . . [seemed] to value its gold coins at twice the quantity of silver for which they exchanged in the Orient. Such was the case with Assyria, Babylonia, Persia, Macedon . . . and Imperial Rome" [*HMS*, 393].

148. (abbreviare): L, I, "to abridge, shorten." Various tables in the source show that over the years [1650 B.C. to A.D. 1893] the differences between the Orient-to-West ratios became smaller [*HMS*, 394-400].

149. Steed: Henry Wickham S. (1871-1956), foreign ed. of the London *Times*, author of numerous books, lecturer on Central European history at King's College. Also owner and ed. of the *Review of Reviews*, founded by W. T. Stead in 1890 [100:107].

150. 1858 . . . : A table [cf. 146 above] has this entry: "1858–15.0–The British Crown resumes its prerogative of the government of India. End of the East India Company" [*HMS*, 397].

151. Sylla . . . Byzantium: A table entitled "The Roman Ratio" has these entries: "78 B.C.–9–Sylla. Social Wars." And, "A.D. 1204–Alexis IV, sovereign-pontiff. Fall of the [Byzantine] Empire" [ibid.].

152. "The signal . . . Marble": "In 1868, one of the two great national parties . . . [in favor of retaining] the greenback . . . was suddenly deserted by its leaders on the eve of the Presidential election and . . . defeated at the polls. . . . The signal of desertion, known as 'The Betrayal,' was given by Manton Marble, editor of *The New York World*, the trusted organ of the party" [*HMS*, 420].

153. Mr Carlyle: John Griffin Carlisle, 1835-1910, longtime congressman from Kentucky in both the House and the Senate. He was speaker of the House for 6 years and served in the Senate until Feb. 4, 1893, when he resigned to become secretary of the treasury during Grover Cleveland's second term. He is one of the unsung heroes in the long fight against the money barons. As early as 1878 he said: "The struggle now going on cannot cease, and ought not to cease, until all the industrial interests of the country are fully and finally emancipated from the heartless domination of the syndicates, stock exchanges, and other great combinations of money-grabbers in this country and in Europe" [Barnes, *Carlisle*, 36]. [As I write this, Dec. 23, 1982, a tragic irony is clear: the entire industrial world and the developing countries upon which we depend for materials and markets have been brought to the brink of monetary and fiscal disaster, not because the people cannot produce and distribute goods and services, but because of the operations of bankers and the vested interests that support them. Worst of all, no voice such as Carlisle's is heard in the media. The public debates concern "apples and oranges," while the solution to the problem is "preventive medicine"].

154. Geryon: [51:16].

155. novelle piante: I, "new plants" [*Pur.* XXXIII, 143-144]. The passage reads: "I turned myself remade like new plants with new leaves [*novella fronda*]". Dante, atop Mount Purgatory, faces a new life by cutting away the old [JW].

156. Ideogram: Hsin [M2737]. Part of "Make new, day by day make new" on T'ang's washbasin [53:40-43]. Pound said of this ideogram: "[It] shows the fascist ax for the clearing away of rubbish . . . the tree, organic vegetable renewal" [*J/M*, 113].

157. Ideogram: Ch'in[1] [M1107], "relatives" or "people." Pound translates the character, "the way people grow," in the *Ta Hio* [*CON*, 27].

158. Ideogram: Tan[4] [M6037], "dawn."

159. *οἶνος αἰθίοψ*: H, "wine-dark." Homeric epithet. "Gloss" is the reflected shining [Peck, *Pai*, 1-1, 21-23].

160. Sibilla . . . : OE, "Sibyl put it in a book" [91:54; CB-R, *ZBC*, 198].

161. ἁλιπόρφυρος: H, "of sea purple."

162. orixalxo: Form of orichalchi, "of copper" [1:29].

163. xaladines: The last line of the Merrill sonnet quoted earlier, "En casque de cristal rose les baladines" [80:205], ends with this rhyme [78:72]. Merrill and Pound use the word to suggest a certain rare color in the eyes of the goddess. [MB, *Trace*, 355-356, has good discussion.]

164. nature the sign: [90:2].

165. San Marco: Cathedral in St. Mark's Square with emblematic lions set on pillars at the front. In Canto 102, the "small lions are there in benevolence" [102/730].

166. Ideogram: Ling [M4071], "sensiblity" [85:1].

167. Kuanon: [90/606]. The compassionate bodhisattva, who has her own salvation boat. Here she replaces Ra-Set [91:19, 36].

168. διϊπετέος: H, "flowering from heaven," or the "celestial" Nile.

169. ἀίσσουσιν: H, "flitting about" [*Od.* X, 495, 102:41].

170. Bernice: Berenice, the wife of Ptolemy III, placed a lock of her hair in the shrine of her mother-in-law, Arsinoe, at Zephyrium as an earnest of her husband's return from war in Syria. The lock disappeared, but the court astronomer found it as a new constellation and called it Coma ["hair"] Berenices [106:57].

171. folc-loristica: I, "folkloristic."

172. reserpine: A tranquilizing drug once prepared from rauwolfia alkaloids.

173. Uncle William: W. B. Yeats. See such poems as "Dialogue of Self and Soul," and "Ego Dominus Tuus."

174. per esempio: I, "for example."

175. δολιχηρέτμοισι: H, "long-oared." Homeric epithet [*Od.*, passim].

176. Ideogram: Jen [M3099], "perfect virtue" or "unselfishness." Read left to right.

177. Ideogram: Wei [M7059], "to do or cause."

178. Ideogram: Ch'in [M1107]: "people" or "relatives."

179. Ideogram: Pao [M4956], "precious [stones]."

180. Ideogram: I [M2932], "by means of." Adapted from the *Ta Hio*, the six characters translate: "does not go in for wealth [treasuring porcelain, jewels, and money] but counts his humanity and love of people the true treasure" [*CON*, 75].

181. degli Uberti: Italian admiral [77:99]. Poss. the high admiral who built something at Zephyrium [106:54].

182. Fortuna: [86:93; 96:125].

183. splendor' mondan': I, "earthly splendors" [*Inf.* VII, 77]. Virgil says that God ordained a general minister and guide to preside over all earthly splendors, and she is Fortuna.

184. beata gode: I, "blessed, she enjoys" [*Inf.* VII, 96]. Virgil says of Fortuna that, though cursed by mankind, she "turns her sphere and enjoys her bliss [*beata si gode*]."

185. eel in sedge: Dante [*Inf.* VII, 84] describes the secret decisions of Fortuna as inscrutable to men: "hidden like a snake in the grass [*occulto come in erba l'angue*]."

186. hoc signo: L, "this sign."

187. Ideogram: Chen[1] [M346] (tone 1, not 4), "fortune" or "luck" [85:120].

188. pervanche: pervenche, I, F, "periwinkle"; a small marine snail whose shell has a distinctive violet-blue coloration; also myrtle, a flower of the dogbane family, which has a similar iris-purple blue. Since Pound is meticulous in distinguishing particular shades of blue, perhaps he changed the vowel to create a word for this color: blues have symbolic and religious significance [4:8]. Or perhaps it's a misspelling [96/656].

189. San Vio: Church in the field of San Vio in Venice [83:62]. The eyes of Old Ziovan's family stayed the same Adriatic color for three generations: violet or deep sea-green [83:60].

190. Pale sea-green . . . eyes: [91:4].

191. Raleigh remarked . . . : Sir Walter R. Says Eva Hesse: "In his works Raleigh refers to the defeat of Genoa at the hands of the Venetians but makes no comment on Genoa's loans or about the Genoese having 'had only their usury left' " [EH, *Pai*, 4-1, 182].

192. Führer of Macedon: Alexander the Great [85:88, 95:25]. He died at age ("aetat") 33, not 38.

193. ⊥⊥⊥: [94:110]. Three-columned facade of a temple.

194. George: George Tinkham [74:180], member of Congress, 1915-1943. Pound said: "Just as the Republican Party wd / be a happier institution if they had had the sense to nominate Uncle Geo. TINKHAM instead of the tin horn double twister Rip van Wilkie. Rip van winkle wobble the Wendle" [FR, *P/J*, 273]. The Line seems to give an ironic twist to a conversation reported or overheard.

195. lo jorn: P, "the day."

196. Der Tag: G, "the day."

197. Ideogram: "Dawn" [cf. 158 above].

198. Arnaut: Arnaut Daniel [20:12]. Dante allowed him to speak his native Provençal [*Pur.* XXVI, 140-147].

199. forsitan: L, "perhaps." Etymologically related to *fortuna* as to do with chance, luck, or the wheel of fortune.

200. Pisani: Archbishop of Rome [93:9].

201. abbreviare: L, I, "to shorten" [cf. 148 above]; here to shorten the time and increase the velocity of money.

202. faster . . . : A major premise of Social Credit. The present money and banking system produces goods and services faster than it distributes the money to buy them [38:49, 50].

203. Benton: [88:80].

204. 12 to 6 and one half: [Cf. 101 above].

205. T.C.P.: Thaddeus Coleman Pound, Pound's grandfather, once lt. gov. of Wisconsin, and three times elected to Congress. Pound wrote: "T.C.P. had already in 1878 been writing about . . . the same essentials of monetary and statal economics that I am writing about today" [*SP*, 325].

206. Adams to Rush: [94:10].

207. Vasa: [Cf. 93 above].

208. Pieire Cardinal: P. C. [or Cardenal], 1185-1275, a major poet during the waning period of troubadour verse, the time of the Albigensian Crusade [23:28]. His predominant subjects were war, usury, and corruption.

209. sempre biasmata: I, "always blamed." Third line of Cavalcanti's canzone to Fortuna, in which he says that this goddess of earthly mutability is "always blamed" for her turnings [JW].

210. gode: [Cf. 184 above].

211. Brancusi: [85:215].

212. "mais . . . faire": F, "But *we*, to get ourselves into the state of mind to do them." In the context of, "Works of art are not difficult to make."

213. "je peux . . . fi– – –nir!": F, "I can start something every day, but finish!" [86:13].

214. Griffith: [19:10].

215. Del Croix: [88:46].

216. Picabia: [87:31].

217. Art is local: W. C. Williams quotes John Dewey in the "Author's Note" to *Paterson*: "The local is the only universal, upon that all art builds."

218. Ike . . . : [cf. 106 above].

219. Started . . . suffrage: Primary tenet of Fascist ideology.

220. πανουργία: H, "villany."

221. Essad . . . gate-post: Pasha E., 1863-1920, Albanian military and political hero. During WWI, with the support of Italy, he created a dictatorship and maintained it until Albania was invaded by Austria. After WWI he was proclaimed King of Albania by a so-called national assembly, but he was assassinated at Paris in 1920.

222. houris: In Moslem belief, beautiful virgins allotted to the faithful who attain Paradise.

223. Aquinas . . . : [36:11]. He said: "Nothing hinders certain things from happening by fortune or by chance . . . but not if compared with Divine Providence" [*Summa*, P. 1, question 116, art. 1; JW].

224. beat' . . . : [Cf. 184 above].

225. **plenilune**: From I, *plenilunis*, "full moon." A description of Fortuna, whose rhythm of giving luck or taking it away appears to wax and wane.

226. **Dante . . . Canzone**: Cavalcanti's canzone "Fortuna."

227. **Hudson**: William Henry Hudson, 1841-1922, English naturalist and author of such books as *Green Mansions* and *A Naturalist in La Plata* [reviewed by EP, *SP* 429-432].

228. **Jonathan Edwards**: American Calvinist, 1703-1758, who preached damnation with burning passion in such sermons as "Sinners in the Hands of an Angry God."

229. **Twelve Tables**: *Lucilius and Laws of XII Tables* (Loeb, vol. III) [*Lucilius*].

230. **Lucilius**: Gaius L., ?-ca. 102 B.C., Latin satirist who "invented a new literary genre. . . . All that he says is colored by his personality. . . ." He wrote much, but about it "little can be said since the fragments are so meagre." [*OCD*, 622].

231. **Antoninus**: [78:56].

232. **Luigi**: The hunchbacked (*gobbo*) peddler Pound knew at Rapallo [104/741]. Pound saw him doing the mystery rite [106/753]. He was "somewhat crippled" but "not a hunchback." MB was told Luigi would come to Pound's house in San Ambrogio and "call after 'the poet' from a distance–then tell him of such wonders as the one recorded here" [MB, *Trace*, 365].

233. **ONE, ten, eleven**: Prob. a structural and vorticist cue, an arcane hint about the hub-turning world: 11011. Pound wrote a note for *The Unwobbling Pivot* which gives the immediate source of the numbers: "The ideogram *tan* . . . is found in the eleventh Ode of T'ang (Shih Ching, 1, 10, 11, 3)" [ibid]. The line is a central cue to the wheels-within-wheels and overlapping wheels of the basic structural units of 11 in *The Cantos*. The *0* is the still point around which the five cantos on either side turn.

234. **chi con me**: I, "who [goes] with me." Pound also made his dawn communion.

235. **Ideogram**: [Cf. 158 above]. "Dawn."

236. **chun tze**: Chun tze [M1715-19], "a man of complete virtue" who is "the beau-ideal of Confucianism." To Pound a much superior ethical system than is the Fall of Man premise of Christian dogma, which he thinks of as physically, mentally, and spiritually repressive.

237. **Aswins**: Asvins. In Hinduism the twin deities of light who were included among the nature gods of the *Veda*.

238. **Fou-Hi**: [53:3].

239. **keg of money**: Prob. an assertion of T. C. P. [cf. 205 above].

240. **Sargon . . .** : [94:55]. The other figures are not identifiable as hieroglyphs but bear some resemblance to early Chinese bone inscriptions and may suggest fields and plants.

241. **T'ang**: [53:40].

242. **Multan**: [or "Mooltan"]: An ancient city of the Near East. capital of the district of Multan, Punjab, Pakistan, near the Chenab River about 100 miles NE of its junction with the Indus River.

243. **li**: C, Na-khi [M3862]. One *li* is a bit less than one-third of a mile.

244. **Napat**: Napata. An ancient city of Ethiopia built on a hill overlooking the Nile. A temple of Amenhotep III is there.

245. **Panch**: Panchala. Name of a country and people of ancient India (the *Mahabharata* places it in the lower Doab), visited by Apollonius of Tyana, who called it "Patala" [P, *Life* I, 339].

246. **Tyanu**: "of Tyana" [94:123].

247. **lion head**: This hieroglyph (as do the others in the canto) comes from Waddell's errors of interpretation [B de R, *Approaches*, 187-188].

248. **Knoch Many**: "the hill of Many." The

supposed burial place near Clogher, Ireland, of King Menes: "Waddell . . . identifies Menes with Min or Minor of Crete and interprets the text on the ivory tablets found in Abydos to say that King Menes died in Ireland of a wasp's sting" [ibid., 188n.].

249. no blood: No blood sacrifices. A sign of an advanced civilization. Pound probes into the history of all religions, looking for their progress away from barbaric acts (such as human sacrifice [88:62-63]) to the rejoicing and celebration of the mysterium he believes to be a measure of civilization.

250. Ungaro: Filippo U., Italian journalist connected with *Il Secolo* [The age]. He was a member of the parliament during the Fascist era. Pound used the gesture, later, to describe the difference between Chinese and Japanese cultures [HK, *Pai*, 2-3, 488].

251. Ville d'Avray: A suburb of Paris, 7 miles from Notre Dame Cathedral, W of Sèvres. Ref. may be to a painting by Corot, *The Street of the Station*, at Ville d'Avray [National Gallery, Washington].

252. Pré Catalan: [76:44].

253. *μετά* . . . : H, "after the physics." Source of the word *metaphysical.*

254. Adams: John A. [71:28, 64].

255. artigianato: I, "artisan."

256. "Buckie": R. Buckminster Fuller, architect and poet who invented the geodesic dome.

257. "Luce . . . vuoi": I, "Kindly light, in your eyes, / What I want, do you want too? / You want it?" Prob. phrases from a popular song, or the rhythm of such a song as imitated in the next 5 lines, which render the rhythm of "Mid pleasures and palaces / Tho we may roam / Be it ever so humble, / There's no place like home." Prob. evoked by radio or TV at St. Elizabeths.

258. wode: OE/ME, "madly." Adverbial form of *wod.*

259. Knittl: [89:260].

260. TEMENOS: H, "a piece of land sacred to a god; the precincts of a temple."

261. PAUL: [96:10].

262. Upsala: [L, *Ubsola*]. According to Migne [col. 447], the northern limits of the territory from which the Lombards came. Now, Uppsala, city of eastern Sweden.

263. fane: Archaic: "sanctuary; temple." Migne has: "In hoc templo (Ubsola patrio sermone vocato) . . ." ["In this temple (called Upsala in native talk) . . ."].

264. ministrat virtutem . . . : Migne adds that in the temple the statues of three gods were venerated by the people. The first was Thor, the second Wodan: "Wodan . . . ministrat virtutem contra inimicos" ("did gallant deed against the enemy") [Migne, 448].

265. Fricco: L, "Tertius est Fricco pacem" ("The third is Fricco [devoted to] peace") [ibid.].

266. Priapo: "Voluptatemque . . . igenti Priapo" ("and Priapus creates desire") [ibid.].

267. Dea libertatis: L, "goddess of liberty" [ibid.].

268. Agelmund: Migne tells the story of how the Langobards were led from Scandinavia by their leaders Ibor and Aio, and being "unwilling to remain longer under mere chiefs (dukes), ordained a king for themselves like other nations. Therefore Agelmund, the son of Aio, first reigned over them . . . [and] held the sovereignty . . . for thirty years" [452-452].

269. PUER APULIUS: L, "Apulian boy." Frederick II of Sicily [cf. 272 below], who became king at the age of 4 and assumed the throne at 18 [DD, *Pai*, 6-1, 103].

270. "Fresca rosa": I, "fresh rose." The "Song of the Rose" was sung at Frederick II's court by Cielo d'Alcamo [107:1], "one of the first to write an Italianate Sicilian" [MB, *Trace*, 368]. "Cielo" is an Italinate spelling of "Ciullo."

271. Antoninus: [78:56].

272. **book of the Falcon**: "De Arte venandi cum avibus," known as "The Book of the Falcon." Written by the extraordinarily versatile Frederick II, emperor of Sicily, 1194-1250.

273. **Mirabile . . .** : L, "With marvelous brevity, he straightened out" [Migne, 1144]. Source has "mirabili." Said by Laudulphus Sagax, editor of the *Historia Miscella*, added to Migne, Vol. 95.

274. **Justinian**: [65:126; 94:45].

275. **Sta Sophia**: The church built by Justinian [96:239].

276. **Sapientiae Dei**: L, "wisdom of God."

277. **Ideograms**: Chêng ming [66:68], "right name." Justinian practiced this Confucian principle in his new legal codes.

278. **Verrius Flaccus**: Roman freedman and scholar who taught the grandsons of Emperor Augustus. His best known work is *Libri de Significatu Verborum*, in which several books are devoted to each letter of the alphabet.

279. **Festus**: Sextus Pompéius F., late 2d century A.D. The epitomizer of the *Libri . . . Verborum* of Flaccus, which he called *De Significatione Verborum . . .*, Festus was in turn epitomized by Paulus Diaconus, and Migne added Paul's work to vol. 95 of the *Patrologiae Latina* [1626-?].

280. ἀρσενικὰ: H, "masculine." (The feminine or neuter ending for the masculine ἀρσενικὸς is used by Leto.)

281. ἀνδρικὰ: H, "manly." Leto changed this Greek word used by Festus to the other, saying it was preferable [Peck, *Pai*, 1-1, 30] because more precise. Leto was thus practicing "chêng ming."

282. **Leto (Pomponio)**: A medieval lexicographer who worked with the texts of Flaccus and Festus.

283. θηλυκά: H, "feminine." Leto said ἀρσενικὰ, "masculine," was more elegant because it paired with this word.

284. **Deorum Manium**: L, "of gods of the souls of the dead." This phrase, as well as the others in the next 6 lines come from Migne [1611-1612].

285. **Flamen Dialis & Pomona**: L, "High priest of Jupiter and Pomona."

286. **aethera terrenaeque**: L, "earthly and heavenly things."

287. **Manes Di**: L, "spirits of the gods."

288. **manare credantur**: L, "are believed to remain."

289. ἐν . . . δαίμων: H, "in shady groves. But now some power brings down a ravenous lion" [*Il* XI, 479-480; trans. R. Fitzgerald]. Pound uses the ἔμβαλε of Leto rather than Homer's ἤγαγε, a 2d a. of ἄγω meaning "leads in" [Peck, *Pai*, 1-1, 30].

290. **Mount Taygeto**: The mountain in Lacedaemonia. In October, after a chariot race the "off horse of the winning team is sacrificed to Mars" [Rose, *Roman Questions*, 161].

291. **Campo Martio**: L, "field of Mars." A field near the Tiber used for sports, elections, military exercises, public sacrifices, etc. The Greeks variously sacrificed chariots and horses to Helios each year. The Rhodians flung them into the sea for the gods to use. "The Spartans performed the sacrifice on the top of Mount Taygetus, the beautiful range behind which they say the great luminary set every night" [Frazer, *Golden Bough*, 49].

292. **rubbing . . . parsley**: A custom at Quirinus [113:32] which Festus records [1125]. The question of *parsley* for Latin *persillum* or *persilium* is controversial [Peck, *Pai*, 2-2, 212].

293. **Flamen Portualis**: "Priest of Portunus," the god of harbors. Source has "Portunalis."

294. **"inter . . . sepulta"**: L, "words are now dead and buried." [JE: "Festus is referring to his researches and the number of words in

books that have fallen out of use (1626). *Intermortua* is a single word."]

295. **Ideogram**: Po [M4977], "old."

296. **Ideogram**: Ma [M4310], "horse."

297. **Ideogram**: Tsu [M6815], "god." The three characters signify Helios. In ancient China the Ma-tsu presided over sacrifices to protect or benefit the emperor's horses. With the two characters at the end of the canto, we read: "Old horse god doesn't lie down" [*Analects* XIII, ii].

298. **Athelstan**: [91:52].

299. **kadzu**: Transliteration from the Japanese for "ground ivy" [EH, *Pai* 8-1, 53-54].

300. **arachidi**: I, "peanuts." In a note dated 15 Sept. 1942 Pound wrote: "Peanuts could bring self-sufficiency in food to Italy or, rather to the empire, for these 'monkey nuts' would grow better in Cyrenaica" [*SP*, 319].

301. **acero**: I, "maple tree." During WWII Pound wanted the government to cultivate peanuts (for oil) and maple trees (for sugar) to relieve food shortages [ibid]. They didn't, but he did not "lie down" on the job: he imported maple trees himself.

302. **Ideogram**: Wu [M7180], "not."

303. **Ideogram**: Chuan [M1641], "fatigue." Pound translates these last two characters in the *Analects* as: "not lie down" [*CON*, 248].

CANTO XCVIII

Sources

Homer, *Od.* X, III; F. W. Baller, trans., *The Sacred Edict*, Shanghai, 1924, rpt. NPF, Orono, Me., 1979 [*Edict*]; Plotinus, *The Enneads*, trans. Stephen Mackenna, London, 1926 [*Enneads*]; Ovid, *Meta.* IV; Cavalcanti, *Donna mi prega*; Ciullo d' Alcamo, "Rosa fresca aulentissima," *SR*, 101; Frederick II, *The Book of the Falcon*, trans. C. A. Wood and F. Marjorie Fyfe, Stanford, 1943; P. Lacharme, *Confucii Chi-King*, Stuttgartiae et Tubingae, 1830 [Lacharme]; Dante, *Par.* XIII; Pliny, *History* XXXV, 36, 85-86 (Loeb IX, 323-325); Herman Diels, *Die fragmente der Vorsokratiker*; a companion to Diels trans. by Kathleen Freeman, Oxford, B. Blackwell, 1946 [Diels, frag no.].

Background

EP, *GK*, 260; *SP*, 73-97; JN, *Blossoms From the East*, Orono, Me., 1983.

Exegeses

CFT, *Pai*, 2-1, 79; CFT, *Pai*, 2-3, 451-453; Michaels, *Pai*, 1-1, 50; MB, *Trace*, 379; DG, *Pai*, 4-1, 121-168; DG, *Pai*, 3-2, 169-190; JW, *Later*, 133-147.

Glossary

1. **Ra-Set**: [91:19].

2. **Ocellus**: [94:172].

3. **Agada . . . Faasa**: [77:24].

4. **Ideogram**: Hsin[1] [97:156].

5. **Τὰ . . . φάρμακα**: H, "drugs from Egypt" [39:7]. Circe gave the men of Odysseus "evil drugs from Egypt" [*Od* X, 213].

6. **Leucothea . . .** : [95:32].

7. **Χρόνος**: H, "Time."

8. *πνεῦμα θεῶν*: H, "spirit of the gods."

9. *καὶ ἔρως σοφίας*: H, "and wisdom of love."

10. **(hieron)**: [97/678-681]. H, "temple."

11. **ne quaesaris**: L, "he asked not" [91:38] [see 100:81 for "sell a slave"].

12. **ius Italicum**: L, "Italian law."

13. **more Sabello**: L, "according to Sabellian custom." The Sabelli were a primitive tribe of Italy.

14. **Piazza**: I, "Square." The central public place of a town. Pound saw the custom of women parading their grief in black shawls around the square (an atavistic remnant from ancient vegetation rites) being destroyed by new Italian law under fascism.

15. **Demeter**: The Greek goddess, mother of Persephone, from whose black gown the mourning shawls were supposedly cut, in the most ancient belief [JW].

16. **"Ut . . . pulchram"**: L, "So that you make beauty."

17. *θῖνα θαλάσσης*: H, "by the sands of the sea" [96:98].

18. **Byzantium 12%**: Pound believed one of the reasons the Byzantine Empire lasted for a thousand years, whereas the Manchu dynasty in China did not, was the interest rate [CFT, *Pai*, 2-1, 79; cf. 160 below].

19. **Anselm**: [105:16]. Anselm's idea of the Trinity has two persons flowing from the nonphysical Father as Knower, but the third, awareness of the Knower, exists within the human body as well as without. The concept may be difficult to equate with that of Plotinus below. The metaphor of sunlight shining through a prism might help: in its flow, it is both outside and inside the prism.

20. **Plotinus**: [15:11]. In the "Preller-Ritter Extracts" appended to the *Enneads*, we read: "Plotinus does not allow that the authentic, the separable soul, is in the body: the body is in the soul" [CFT, *Pai*, 2-3, 451-553].

21. **Gemisto**: Georgias G., a Byzantine Neoplatonist sometimes called Plethon [8:31].

22. **hilaritas**: L, H, ἱλαρότης. A neologism Pound created to stand for one of the primary ways divinity manifests in the world. Combine gaiety, mirth, rejoicing, gladness, laughter, and other such words and collectively they yield the basic religious concept *hilaritas* [Michaels, *Pai*, 1-1, 50; 83:9].

23. **et . . . simiglianza**: I + L. Prob. intended to mean "and half-gliding [cadenza like] in misty clouds," or "their likeness in clouds."

24. *καθ ὁμοίωσιν*: H, "down in the manner." *Deorum*: L, "of the Gods."

25. **Herakleitos**: Fl. in Ephesus (500 B.C.) in the time of Confucius. H. equated the Logos with elemental fire and said the universe was a tension of opposites vibrating as the lyre under the bow. Said H.: "God is day-night, winter-summer, war-peace, satiety-famine" [Diels, frag. 67]. Hence in politics "the people must fight for the law as for a wall" [frag. 44].

26. **Leucothoe**: Daughter of Orchamus of Babylon, who buried her alive because of her love for Apollo. Her divine lover changed her into an incense bush [Ovid, *Meta*. IV, 238-297]. Not to be confused with Leucothea [cf. 6 above].

27. **Commissioner**: [cf. 49 below].

28. Est deus in nobis: L, "And god [is] in us."

29. that sea-gull: Leucothea.

30. Χρήδεμνον: H, "veil" or "scarf." Pound's "bikini" [95:75].

31. She . . . line: Leucothea, the daughter of Cadmus [4:4], was turned into a sea-bird [Ovid, *Meta.* IV, 670 ff].

32. lot of'em . . . : W. B. Yeats, Eliot, and W. Lewis had no firm ground in understanding money, economics, or political ideology, as Pound remembered the 20s and 30s.

33. Ideogram: Pu [M5379], "none." Picture of a bird in flight [85:179].

34. Orage: Alfred Richard O., 1873-1934, as editor of the *New Age* a promoter of Social Credit ideas [80:322].

35. Per ragione vale: I, "valid or worthy through reason." From Cavalcanti's *Donna mi prega*. Pound renders as, "deeming intention to be reason's peer and mate" [36/178].

36. Senator Cutting: Bronson C., 1888-1935, senator from New Mexico. In a letter Pound asked him, "How many literate senators are there?" Cutting "sent nine names, ending 'and I suppose Dwight L, Morrow' " [*GK*, 260]. Add Morrow and Cutting himself and you get "eleven."

37. μάω: H, a root that combines with other words to add the idea of "longing" or "desire."

38. Mohammed . . . : The Koran recognizes "desire" as a part of religion.

39. Sister . . . : Circe [1:1] was the sister of Aeetes and the daughter of Apollo.

40. "noi . . . borghesi: I, "we other middle-class citizens [bourgeois]."

41. Consigliere: I, "councillor."

42. in piazza": I, "in the square." In contrast with Mussolini, whose public speaking overwhelmed the masses.

43. Uncle William: W. B. Yeats: "When you are old and gray and full of sleep" is from Ronsard [MB, *Trace*, 379].

44. Ronsard: Pierre de R., 1525-1585, leading poet of the French Pléiade.

45. Ψεῦδος . . . πεπνύμενος: H, "he will not tell a lie for [he is], wise indeed" [*Od.* III, 20]. Athene is talking to Telemachus about old Nestor.

46. ich bin am Zuge: G, "I am on the march" or "I'll get there," meaning get to the *Sheng U* or *The Sacred Edict*, which is the source of most of the rest of this canto and of Canto 99 [cf. 60 below].

47. ἀρχή: H, "in the beginning."

48. Shensi: A province of old China.

49. Ouang: For "Wang," 王, the first character of the salt commissioner's name; the two following characters "Iu" and "p'uh," the rest of his name, are given in the text.

50. volgar' eloquio: I, "popular speech," an Italian rendering of Dante's Latin title *De Vulgari Eloquentia.*

51. The King: A pun on *wang*, which is the word for "king." Wang's job was to bring the wisdom of *The Sacred Edict* to the common man.

52. Sagetrieb: [85:194].

53. Hsuan: 暄 [M2870], "warmth."

54. Ideogram: Shih [M5788], "to manifest" or "to proclaim."

55. Ideogram: Pen [M5025], "root" or "source."

56. Ideogram: Yeh [M7321], "teachings" or "instruction." The heart of Neoconfucianism is the ethics of human relations in the family, in civil life, and in military life. From sunrise to sunset, the warmth of human relations should be the guide for all behavior. This central message of *The Sacred Edict* must be made manifest to the world. Combined with the art and skill to create things, it is the root and source of all good teaching [*Edict*, passim]. In order that the message be proclaimed continuously, the emperor required that the people of every town be called together once a month to hear it read. For over a century this was presumably done. [From here on, citations to the source will be given by chapter number of the *Edict* followed by the page number in the Baller edition. Cf. 124 below.]

57. *τέχνη*: H, "art" or "skill."

58. Ari: Aristotle said that philosophy was the business of old men who could base their conclusions on a sufficient phalanx of particulars.

59. *καθόλου*: H, "generally" or "on the whole."

60. Yong Tching: Yung Chêng [60:73]. Son of K'ang Hsi [59:21] and emperor of China, 1723-1735. There were 3 versions of the *Edict*: (1) The original document, made up of 16 7-character platitudes, which was set forth by Emperor K'ang Hsi; (2) the *Wen-li*, or literary text, done by Yung Chêng, which was a lengthy commentary explaining with examples the intentions of the original edict; and (3) a still later and more elaborate commentary done in the language of the people by Wang Iu-p'uh. The *Wen-li* asks a question of all Buddhists of Yung Chêng's time who were out begging money and gifts to build palaces for the Buddha to live in: Since Buddha himself (Gautama Siddhartha) abandoned the splendid palace of his father, the king, "and hid himself in the heights of a snowy mountain to practice asceticism," would he be likely to "prize the religious houses and monasteries you build?" [VII, 79].

61. Taoist priests . . . : The Neoconfucians were against the Buddhist priests because they seemed to encourage idleness and collected money by sending their followers out with begging bowls. But that was not an idea of Buddha himself. The main idea of Buddha was different: "What is Buddha? Buddha is the heart. . . . if your heart is good this *is* Buddha" [VII 74]. *The Sacred Edict* distinguishes the original ideas of founders from the practices of later followers. So with Taoism, which also preached asceticism in the beginning. Later, Taoist priests pretended to do miracles and to be able to produce "the Elixir of Gold, a mystical compound by means of which the Taoist alchemists professed themselves able to produce gold, and confer the gift of immortality" [VII, 75]. In a section called "Taoist Delusions," we read a list of such miracles, which, the *Edict* says, "is a pack of lies." People ought to show more sense because no one ever sees them do the things they promise, or if they do, "it is all a parcel of magic, a device for hoodwinking you" [VII, 84]. *The Sacred Edict* appeals to reason: "Who has seen them go to the Western Paradise? or fly up in broad daylight? manifestly it is all humbug!" [VII, 76].

62. 5 human relations: "From time immemorial to the present what has been orthodox? Nothing more than (the observance of) these Five Relationships—emperor and minister, father and son, husband and wife, elder and younger brother, friend and companion" [VII, 72].

63. mules . . . farmsteads: A long passage in the source concerns grandfathers who toiled, hoarded, and saved a fortune only to have children and grandchildren who, "having no sense, squander it at pleasure" and in keeping up appearances. "If they see this one wears silk, they must wear satin; if that one rides horseback, they must ride in a chair." After they squander the money, what then? "The next thing is to sell off the farmsteads" [V, 56-67]. How does this happen? In Chap. VI, entitled "The Value of Education," we have the answer: "If people are uneducated, though they dress well and live well, their minds are stupid and sordid; like mules or horses: (it is) all in vain they are saddled with good saddles, and trappings, they are still animals" [VI, 62-63].

64. Ideogram: Fu [M1982], "living priests" or "Bhud-foes" [DG, *Pai*, 3-2, 185].

65. Bhud-foés: Chap. VII, entitled "Orthodoxy," has a number of subsections with such titles as, "Evils of Promiscuous Meetings," "Follies of Idolatrous Ritual," "Buddhist Incantations," "Taoist Delusions," etc., all concluding that these heretical sects do not help with the emperor's work.

66. **external . . . gold pill**: "As to Taoism it speaks of plans for asceticism (such as) grasping mercury in lead; the dragon moaning; the tiger screaming; the internal and the external pill" [VII, 75].

67. **Is the Bhud likely . . . nunneries**: The emperor is at much pain to explain that the evil tactics and promises of the priests were not an idea of Buddha himself: "You ignoramuses are all ignorant that their Buddhist books say that Buddha was the Heir Apparent of the King of Fan. Grown weary of the cares of the world, he hid himself in the heights of a snowy mountain to practice asceticism. Parents, children, and wife he alike neglected: is it likely he will concern himself about all you people and expound his tenets to you? Besides, he gave up his Harem, the Dragon Chamber, and the Phoenix Hall; will he on the other hand prize the religious houses and monasteries you build?" A footnote explains that a "feng koh" is an abode of royalty [VII, 78-79].

68. **ch'i'd . . . 'em**: A play on the sound of the 2 characters following.

69. 棄 : Ch'i [M550], "abandon."

70. 捨 : She [M5700], "reject."

71. 嗎 : Ma [M4311], used as question mark. The left component is the character for "mouth," the right for "horse."

72. *φύσιν τοῦ θεοῦ*: H, "the nature [physics] of the god."

73. **Procopius**: D.ca. A.D. 562? Byzantine historian who is alleged to have written the scurrilous *Secret History* unmasking the evil life of Empress Theodora [96:90].

74. **old Peabody**: [101/724; 101:18].

75. **Antoninus**: [78:56].

76. **Leo**: [96:270].

77. **Stock**: Noel S., Australian poet and critic who, as a young man, wrote Pound at St. Elizabeths and for a time championed his ideas and causes and visited him in Italy after Pound's return there. Author of numerous articles about Pound, as well as *The Life of Ezra Pound, Reading The Cantos*, etc.

78. **god . . . gilded?**: "As to His Celestial Excellency [the Buddha] . . . he is taking it easy in paradise; do you suppose he needs you to model him a gilded image, and build him a house to live in?" [VII, 79].

79. **hua⁴ . . .** : Hua⁴ [M2215], "words"; t'ou² [M6489], "head"; [M2215-15]: "something to talk about."

80. **whiteness of bones**: The bones of those "Bhud-foes" or other devotees who have thrown themselves off a precipice [DG, *Pai*, 4-1, 135]. "Again, there is a set of extremely foolish people. It may be on account of their parents' illness they vow to devote their body. As soon as the parents are well, they go up to the mountain to publicly burn incense . . . On arriving at the summit, they throw themselves down the precipice, and are either killed, or maimed" [VII, 80].

81. **celestial . . . not get it**: "If he [the Buddha] is divine will he long to have your silver and . . . protect you in consequence? And if you fail to offer money . . . he will be angry. . . ? then he is a despicable fellow [a *hsiao jen*]" [VII, 81].

82. **Gemisto**: [23:3; 83:3].

83. **Ideogram**: Hsiao [M2605], "little."

84. **Ideogram**: Jen [M3097], "man."

85. **And the language . . .** : "But all the incantations of the Buddhist books are in the barbarous lingo of Buddha's country" [VII, 83].

86. **fan¹**: [M1790], "foreign."

87. **hua⁴**: [M2215], "talk."

88. **If you don't . . . out**: "If none of you people believe these heretical sects, they will

not wait to be driven out, they will become extinct naturally" [VII, 87].

89. Ideogram: Wang-iu [cf. 49 above], the salt commissioner. Wang-iu-p'uh . . . feeling that the style was still too abstruse . . . rendered this exposition [the *Wen-li*, cf. 128 below] into colloquial" [Baller, *Edict*, foreword, iii].

90. K'ang-hsi: [Cf. 60 above].

91. grits in the mortar: The *Wen-li* was done by a literary man whose language, making no connection with the real life of the people, contained impediments to understanding, so Wang Iu-p'uh, after this unintentionally ineffective effort, started over again [DG, *Pai*, 4-1, 137-139].

92. Ideograms: I^4 [M3002], "righteousness"; $shen^1$ [M5719], "profound."

93. Ideogram: Li^{3-4} [M3865], "inside."

94. Ideogram: $Yüan^2$ [M7725], "source." The characters are from the *Edict*: "The law contains a profound meaning and was primarily drawn up in accordance with . . . human nature" [VIII, 92]. The characters for "small . . . white . . . under cover" are components of *yüan*^{2}, all helping to express the idea that "justice issues from human nature" [DG, *Pai*, 4-1, 139].

95. Ideogram: $T'ai^4$ [M6020], "great."

96. Ideogram: $P'ing^2$ [M5303], "peace." "The peace of the Empire depends entirely upon the existence of good manners and customs" [IX, 99].

97. Earth and water . . . : Pound's visual reaction to some of the characters in the source: "All this is the result of climatic influences [Lit., imbued with the wind breath of the water and soil] hence it is spoken of as 'feng' [or breath of nature]" [IX, 99].

98. tso: [M6776], "is."

99. feng: 風 [M1890], "wind."

100. suh: [M5497], "customs." A footnote reads: "The Chinese attach great importance to the influence of climate and locality on character: suh, is composed of 'man' and 'a valley' " [ibid.].

101. feelings . . . nature: "Observe the well-bred man; he conforms to custom with both grace and sincerity; this is the real thing in courteousness" [IX, 102]. Again Pound relies on ideas elicited by some of the characters, as in the next line.

102. en^1: [M1743], "grace."

103. ch'ing^2: [M1170], "feelings."

104. Ford: Ford Madox F. [74:165].

105. "De tribus": L, "concerning tribe." Originally, "three." Refers to *De tribus impostoribus* [On the three imposters], attributed (prob. falsely) to Frederic II [97:272]. The great deceivers in the treatise are Moses, Christ, and Mohammed [JW].

106. "Aulentissima": [79:44].

107. "ver l'estate": The last half of the opening line of Alcamo's poem [97:270] is, "ch'apari inver' la state" ("which appears toward the summer"). Pound may have used "ver" rather than "inverno" because the word means "spring" in Latin [JW].

108. more solid . . . cassia: The continuous tradition that "a man's paradise is his own good nature," from Kati [93:2] to K'ang Hsi, is "more solid. . . ."

109. i^4: [M3002], "morality."

110. ch'i^4: [M554], "breath."

111. Kang: [M3278], "peace."

112. Hi: Hsi: [M2451], "bright." The name of the Manchu emperor. The characters together mean "the King of Peace."

113. two 1/2s . . . : As with the tally-sticks [77:56].

114. "De libro Chi-king": L, the Latin edition of the *Shih Ching* [59:2, 6] done by Lacharme [59:Sources].

115. his father: Shun Chih, the father of K'ang Hsi [59:20].

116. "Ostendit, incitaque: L, "show and incite." The odes do so "ad lumen rationis" ("by the light of reason") so that we may reach enlightenment, or "reap in the sunlight" [Lacharme, preface, xi].

117. Plotinus: [cf. 20 above].

118. Gemisto: [cf. 21 above]. Gemisto defined divinity as hilarity and speed in communication [DG, *Pai*, 3-2, 178; cf. 22 above].

119. Anselm: [105:16]. Anselm said that by mind, *mens ipsa sola*, one can understand the nature of divinity, "and that the presence of memory, intelligence and love in man is a mirror-image, *speculum*, of the Divine Trinity"[ibid.].

120. john barleycorn: An epithet for a farmer in England. Vegetation / mystery rites connections are implied [Moody, *Pai*, 4-1, 56-65; 88:62].

121. Je tzu: Je [M3094], "incite." Tzu [M6939], "son." A pun on the name Jesus.

122. Byzance: [Cf. 18 above].

123. Sagetrieb: [Cf. 52 above and inside front cover of the journal *Sagetrieb*].

124. Baller: Frederick William B., 1853-1922, member of the China Inland Mission, author of Chinese word lists, translator of *The Sacred Edict*.

125. volgar'eloquio: [Cf. 50 above].

126. Mathews: R. H. M., author of the *Chinese English Dictionary*, whose renderings of the characters struck Pound as lacking "verve" or "style."

127. Wang: The salt commissioner [cf. 49 above].

128. Uen-li: *Wen-li*. The literary rendition of *The Sacred Edict*.

129. Iong-ching: Yung Chêng. He wrote the *Wen-li*.

130. Baller's view: "The Chinese think in quotations; and he who can quote their ready-made expressions will add a vivacity to his style" [*Edict*, foreword, iv].

131. "Don't send . . . ": A Chinese proverb often quoted. "By all means go and pay your taxes yourself; don't commission somebody else to take them" [XIV, 151].

132. Delcroix: Carlo D. [88:46; 92:49].

133. Baller thought . . . : "Nothing but Divine motive power can raise fallen humanity" [*Edict*, foreword, iv].

134. ²muan ¹bpo: [112:6]. A Na-khi ceremony to be developed at length in Cantos 110-113.

135. meaning . . . Emperor: Each chapter of *The Sacred Edict* opens with this formula: "The meaning of the Emperor: (he) says." The first chapter goes on: "–Our Imperial Ancestor, the Benevolent Emperor ruled the empire for sixty-one years." A note to the word "Emperor" says: "Lit. Lord of 10,000 years" [I, 1].

136. heart's . . . say: Pound's literal rendering of several characters in the opening of *The Sacred Edict*: i^4 [M2960], "idea"; $hsin^1$ [M2735], "heart"; yin^1 [M7418], "tone"; szu^1 [M5580], "think"; $shuo^{1-5}$ [M5939], "say" [ibid.].

137. Ideogram: Ching: [M1138], "reverence"; *Ideogram:* hsiao [M2601], "filial piety." From which comes order in the state. The latter character is used with *Sagetrieb* [cf. 123 above] to mean passing on the tradition from father to son or from one generation to the next.

138. *τὸ καλόν*: H, "beauty."

139. "Parents . . . ": An exact quote from the *Edict* [I, 5].

140. cheng: [M351], "upright"; *king:* ching [M1123], "constant" or "classics."

141. The text . . . : Authorities differ about the meaning of these two characters in the Chinese classics. Some say they are the opposite of the characters used for "strange doctrines" or "flimsy foundations." Pound invites the reader to consider the terms from Kung's point of view.

142. men[3]: [M4418], "door" or "school." "Years ago the philosopher Tseng of the Confucian school said. . . ." A footnote says, "Lit., door; hence the entrance into a sect itself: cf. 'disciples of the Porch' " [I, 5].

143. and not cheat . . . : "If they act falsely and fraudulently in serving the Government, it is the same as defrauding their parents, and is undutiful" [I, 6].

144. Filial . . . : "It is evident from this passage . . . that the principle of filial piety is very inclusive" [ibid.].

145. Family . . . : "All the squabbles that arise among brethren . . . are on account of property. Some squabble about money, some about land, some about houses, some about food: all sorts of things" [I, 11].

146. II. Ten thousand . . . : A formulaic phrase meaning a very long time. An expression of good will is quite often, "May you live ten thousand years" [cf. 135 above]. The Roman numerals here and in the following indicate the chapter of the *Edict*.

147. have clans . . . : "All mankind have ancestors. Those who descend from them (like) the branching of a tree, are spoken of as the 'Nine clan relatives' " [II, 19].

148. There are districts: "From time immemorial there have been district communities" [III, 29].

149. Avoid litigation: The 7-character sentence of K'ang Hsi's original *Edict* precedes each of the 16 chapters. The slogan for Chap. III reads: "Pacify the Local Communities in order to put an end to Litigation" [ibid.]. The title of section 3 is "How to avoid Strife" [III, 3].

150. Without . . . : "But for sowing, whence would there be food to eat? but for silkworm culture whence should we have clothes to wear?" [IV, 42].

151. Imperial paradigm: "Observe that the Emperors of old all regarded farming . . . as a matter of the utmost importance. In spring time the Emperor went ploughing in person." A footnote reads: "Lit., in the interests of the Empire to set a good example" [IV, 43]. This notion was taken up in 17th-century Germany and France [86:78].

152. and then waste not: "The main thing is to recognize the difficulty of (obtaining) money, and not to waste and squander it" [V, 59].

153. Nor scrape iron . . . : The 6 characters involved mean literally: "needle–pointed–top–scrape–iron–[and a nonsyllabic]." Baller gives: "hoarding in a regular skin-flint fashion [V, 56; DG, *Pai*, 4-1, 154].

154. habits of scholars: "Attach Importance to Academies, in order to improve the Habits of Scholars" [VI, 62]. A rendition of the character slogan at the head of the chapter.

155. ox . . . mule . . . : [Cf. 63 above].

156. books you read . . . : "Study some classical works; cultivate intercourse with a few respectable companions" [VI, 65].

157. cheng king: [Cf. 140 above].

158. ut supra: L, "as above."

159. Sixteen bitched: The 16 chapters of *The Sacred Edict*, containing wisdom that should have made for a stable society, were, in Pound's opinion, destroyed by a usurious interest rate. "(Take for instance) the case of a poor villager. I ought to assist him, and if I give him a loan, must not take more than 36 percent interest" [III, 32].

160. Byzantium: [Cf. 18 above]. The Byzantine Romans lasted 1200 years, but the Manchus lasted only 300.

161. "from rib to cheek . . . ": Dante: "Then the light within which the wondrous life . . . had been narrated to me broke the silence . . . You believe that into the breast from which the rib was drawn to form her beautiful cheek whose palate costs so dear to all the world" [*Par.* XIII, 31-39; trans. Singleton].

162. Miss Mitford . . . : Prob. Mary Russell Mitford, 1789-1855, a popular writer of sketches, tales, poetry, and plays, who became quite a public figure after her dramas were performed by some of the great tragic actors of her time, including William Macready. Her plays included *Foscari, Julian, Rienzi,* and *Charles I*, as well as one of definite interest to Pound: *Inez de Castro* [3:23]. The source of the quote is unknown, but Miss Mitford would go far to avoid the taint of "gothic" in her work, which was based solidly on village and country life and historical fact. She was universally referred to as "Miss Mitford," in criticism of her work as well as in books about her. Other candidates could be the 20th-century Mitfords Nancy, Jessica, or Unity.

163. XIV: this light: Dante's "viva luce . . . che non si disuna" [*Par.* XIII, 55-56] : "vivid light . . . that is not disunited [from its Lucent Source] ." Correlates with Pound's light symbolism and the "total light process," functioning throughout the poem.

164. No . . . contraptions: "Extirpate Heresy and so exact Orthodoxy," K'ang's saying for Chap. VII. Again Pound uses his own reaction to the characters and gives an even more colloquial rendering than does the salt commissioner [VII, 72].

165. State the laws . . . : K'ang's statement heading Chap. VIII: "Explain the Law, to Warn the Foolish and Wayward" [VIII, 88].

166. Iu-an . . . fed it: An illustration of good manners and customs tells of a better way then stealing someone's cow: "There was a (man named) Kuan Iu-an; he also was most willing to give way to others. Somebody else's cow ate grain in his field. He was not in the least vexed; on the contrary he tied the cow up to a tree and brought it grass to eat" [IX, 108].

167. The Xth clause: "Let the People attend to their Proper Callings, that they may have Settled Determination" [X, 110]. Pound calls the K'ang 7-character slogan a clause.

168. pen yeh: [Cf. 55, 56 above].

169. ne ultra crepidam: Variation on a story told by Pliny about a shoemaker who criticized an artist's work because he had painted one too few loops in a sandal. The artist corrected it, which so encouraged the shoemaker that he then criticized the painting of the leg, whereupon the artist said, "a shoemaker in his criticism must not go beyond the sandal—a remark that has also passed into proverb." A footnote says: "Ne sutor ultra crepidam. 'Let the shoemaker stick to his last' " [Pliny, *History*, XXXV, 36, 85-86 (Loeb IX, 323-325)].

170. children . . . evil: "Consider—what do children know about good and evil? They are wholly dependent upon their elders to excite in them good affections" [XI, 121].

171. Not a fixed charge: The *Edict* has a long passage on the "Tithing System," which requires different payments (not a fixed charge) based on ability to pay [XV, 156-157].

172. Mang Tzu: Mencius. Pound wrote: "Mencius distinguishes a tax from a share, he is for an economy of abundance" ["Mang Tsze," *SP*, 86].

173. Ideogram: Meng [M4428], "Mencius."

174. Yield not . . . : The *Edict* has a subheading that reads, "Evils of Yielding to Anger." It is followed by many examples [XIV, 170 ff.].

175. those who lie . . . : K'ang's saying at the head of Chap. XII is, "Prevent False Accusations, and so shield the Law-abiding." But Chap. XII of the *Wen-li* of Yung Chêng [cf. 128 above] asked the people to listen and hear clearly: "You soldiers and civilians, give this (material) your most careful hearing and don't disregard it" [*Wen-li* XII, 203]. The characters can be seen in the upper right hand corner of p. 203 of the facsimile edition of Baller.

176. Ideogram: Wu [M7193], "don't."

177. Ideogram: Hu [M2194], "disregard."

178. colour of Nature: [90:2].

179. hsien: [M2692], "manifest" [85:143]. The character occurs often in the "light descending" passages.

180. ming: [M4534]. What Pound calls "the total light process . . . hence the intelligence" [*CON*, 20].

181. (Pitagora): Pythagoras [91:11].

182. non si disuna: [Cf. 163 above].

183. Splendor: [109:17]. Pound is prob. deliberately bringing together elements of Greek wisdom, in the tables of opposites of Pythagoras and the "coherence" of splendor in the *Women of Trachis*, with the Chinese yin-yang and other Confucian doctrines in the *Edict*, which in turn had later expression in Dante: "That which cannot die and that which can die is only the splendor of that Idea which in His love our Sire begets; for that living light which so streams from its Lucent Source that It is not disunited from It nor from the Love" [*Par*. XIII, 52-57].

184. 2nd year . . . : The 9 characters at the beginning of the *Wen-li*, on the upper left of p. 183 in the facsimile edition, read: "Yung Cheng, the 2nd year, the 2nd month, beginning the 2nd day."

185. Sheng: [M5753], "sacred"; yu [M7641], "edict."

186. "Each year . . . : The source is the *Wen-li*: "Each year in the first month of spring" [p. 182; DG, *Pai*, 4-1, 162-163].

187. The herald: "The herald with wooden-tongued bell goes all along the roads" [ibid.].

188. six rites: "The minister of education uses the six rites to form the character of the people" [ibid.].

189. not to lose life: "Suddenly in a fit of anger they quarrel with others, and either kill them, or are killed by them, and forfeit their lives in consequence" [XVI, 170].

CANTO XCIX

Sources

F. W. Baller, trans., *The Sacred Edict*, Shanghai, 1924, rpt. Orono, Me., 1979 pp. 182-211 [*Edict*]; Dante, *Par*. XIII, VIII; Homer, *Od*. XI, III; Pliny, *History* XXXV (Loeb IX); Diogenes Laertius, *Philosophers* VII (Loeb) [Diogenes]; Plotinus, *The Enneads*, trans. A. H. Armstrong, II, III (Loeb) [*Enneads*]; Dante, *Convivio* II [*Conv*.].

Background

EP, *LE*, 41-47, 178, 437-440; *SP*, 64-98; Frobenius, *Leo Frobenius 1873-1973: An Anthology*, ed. Eike Haberland, Wiesbaden, F. Steiner, 1973 [*Anthology*]; Charles Singleton, trans. *The Divine Comedy*, 6 vols., Bollingen Series LXXX, Princeton University Press, 1970; 3 vols. text and 3 vols. commentary [*Commentary*]; J. P. Migne, *Patrologiae Latina*, vol. 14 [Migne, column no.].

Exegeses

EP, *GK*, 290; CFT, *Pai*, 2-1, 69-112; DG, *Pai*, 3-2, 169-190; DG, *Pai*, 4-1, 121-168; DG, *Ezra Pounds's Use of the Sacred Edict*, in process [*EP: Edict*] ; JW, *Later*, 133-147.

[For most of Canto 98, Pound used the language of the salt commissioner. For most of Canto 99, he goes to the Wen-li (Literary Text) of Yung Chêng, analyzes all the components of the characters, and gives the results in his own idiomatic or colloquial English. His method will be illustrated in the first page or so; after that the lines will not be glossed unless the meaning in context is unclear. Translations from the *Wen-li* cited in the glosses are based on the work of David Gordon, which will appear in a book presently being edited.]

Glossary

1. **Till . . . air**: The *Wen-li* really says, "The Sacred Edict with Expanded Meanings . . . there is no better than this." A component of the character for "expanded" is the character for "yellow," and a component of "there is not" means "grass." From a line that reads, "The Edict dealt with . . . mulberry culture," the character for "mulberry tree" has components that look like leaves (叒) in a tree (木): 桑, sang [M5424]. [DG, *EP: Edict*].

2. **Iong Cheng**: [98:60].

3. **Kang Hi**: [98:111, 112].

4. **silk cords . . .** : In the character *hsien* [98:179], Pound sees silk threads, which he often relates to "light descending" or "intelligence." At the end of "The Unwobbling Pivot," we read, "As silky light, King Wen's virtue / Coming down with the sunlight, / what purity! . . . This unmixed is the tensile light, the Immaculata. There is no end to its action" [*CON*, 187].

5. **Non disunia**: [98:163].

6. **2nd year . . .** : [98:184]. Pound's cue to what he is translating or reacting to.

7. **SHENG U**: [98:185].

8. **Each year . . . converge**: [98:186-188].

9. **7 instructions**: *Wen-li*: "And the rites say: 'The Minister of Education attends to the six kinds of ceremonies in order to temper the character of the people, and he illuminates the seven teachings in order to uplift the peoples moral aim' " [*Edict*, 182]. The 7 instructions follow in the canto.

10. **tun^{1}**: [M6572], "to urge; cement friendly relations; to consolidate." Thus, Pound's "converge."

11. **pen^{3}**: [M5025], "root."

12. **shih$^{2-5}$**: [M5821], "solid." *Wen-li* has in this context *ch'ung*^{2} [M1526], for which Mathews gives several meanings: "to venerate; discriminate."

13. **Mohamed no popery**: The idea of venerating solid evidence or objective reality, or discriminating the realm of faith and reason, came into scholastic or medieval thought via Averroes [*LE*, 183-186] and was advanced by Siger de Brabant in the 13th century. The papal position and that of the Dominicans was championed by Aquinas; but the early Christian thinkers Pound celebrates are closer to the Mohammedan tradition as expressed by Averroes and Avicenna. Dante places Siger along with Bede and Richard of St. Victor as an eternal light in Paradise [*Par.* X, 136]. Singleton says of Siger: "He was no doubt one of those at whom in 1270, a general condemnation of Averroism was

aimed" [*Commentary*, 192]. The issue is by no means a minor one in Pound's religion. Faith based on the necessity of a continuous denial of reason and of solid objective evidence is destructive both to the religious sect that requires it and to the adherents of such a sect: such rhetorical dogma is "popery." [*LE*, 41-47].

14. **mu²**: [M4588], "to follow a pattern."

15. **fa¹ . . . szu¹**: Pound gives the meanings.

16. **Odysseus' old ma**: Anticlea [1:15] said: "Nay, it was longing for thee, and for thy counsels, glorious Odysseus . . . that robbed me of honey-sweet life" [*Od.* XI, 202-203].

17. **sinceritas**: L, "sincerity" [74:45].

18. **KOINE ENNOIA**: H, "Thoughts of the common people [public]."

19. **Chou**: [53:77]. Founder of 3d Dynasty.

20. **cognome . . .** : I, "name [and] address."

21. **Chên**: [M 316], "We, I. The emperor. Once a general pronoun, it was later appropriated to imperial use only.

22. **Yo el rey**: S, "I the king."

23. **Rats' . . . business**: *Wen-li*: "Therefore, when over a basket of food or bean soup the reason for strife doesn't arise, then the back-biting scandal-mongers have no cause to go to law. And then how can one contract hatreds, ruin property, waste time, and fail in business?" The components in the sequence of characters give Pound the names of animals and birds. Pound used to call the squirrels at St. Elizabeths "oak cats" [87:104].

24. **Nor scrape iron . . .** : [98:153].

25. **Bhud rot**: This phrase does *not* say "all Buddhists are rotten." If one respects the precise meaning of the words—according to the dictionary—it is clear that "to rot" means to disintegrate from a former pristine state. This is a judgment Pound makes against all the great organized religions: later practitioners reduce the vision of the founder into a tissue of absurd practices and superstitions.

26. **floaters**: Those sitting by the road with begging bowls instead of working on the land: a theme first sounded in Canto 13 [13:17].

27. **Redson**: Name contrived from two characters: *chu* [M1346], meaning "red," and *tzu* [M6939], meaning "son." Indicating the great Neoconfucian Chu Hsi [80:345].

28. **papists . . . calendar**: [60:1, 5, 15].

29. **Odysseus' . . .** : [Cf. 16 above].

30. **Nestor . . .** : Athene said to Telemachus: "But come now, go straightway . . . , let us learn what counsel he keepeth. . . . A lie he will not utter for he is wise indeed" [*Od.* III, 18-20].

31. **pen yeh**: [98:55, 56]. A recurrent leitmotif.

32. **Wang . . . incense**: *Wen-li*: "The mind of man, as given by heaven, was, in the first instance upright and free from depravity; but from no other reason than cupidity it has deviated into depraved courses. . . . If you fulfill your duty to your parents at home, what need is there to go to a distance to burn incense."

33. **INTENZIONE**: I, "Intention." Pound translates the word in *Donna mi prega* [36/178]: "Deeming intention to be reason's peer and mate." But he says there is "a mare's nest" in the word and allies it with a number of scholars in the Aristotelian tradition, including the Arabs Alfarabi and Averroes, and Albertus Magnus and Scotus Erigena in the European tradition [*LE*, 178]. The "mare's nest" includes such canto themes as *directio voluntatis* and reason as "the light descending."

34. **Han**: *Wen-li*: The Han scholars had a saying: "The nature of all people contains the five basic principles. But temperamentally some are energetic, some gentle, some

leisurely, some fast, just as pronunciations are not all alike. These things are influenced by water and earth."

35. **ne ultra . . . "**: [98:169].

36. **Mang Tzu**: Mencius.

37. **Crysippus**: An early minor philosopher who said: "Vices are forms of ignorance of those things where of the corresponding virtues are the knowledge" [Diogenes, 93].

38. **Simbabwe**: Frobenius wrote of the great Temple in Simbabwe–where human sacrifice was practiced, which seemed to be connected with social disintegration–symbolized by increasing droughts [*Anthology*, 204-210].

39. **se non fosse cive**: I, "if he were not a citizen" [*Par.* VIII, 116]. The end of a question that began, "Now tell me would it be worse for man or earth. . . ."

40. **Heaven . . . biceps**: *Wen-li*: "Now in the laws and statutes there are a thousand sections . . . and none go beyond the measure of affection and the calculation of reason."

41. **fa$^{3-5}$**: [M1762], 法, "law." This character has three components: 氵 = "water"; 土 = "earth"; and 厶 = "biceps."

42. **Crusaders' . . .** : Whatever good intent the crusaders may have had was undone by those who lusted for money.

43. **Normandy pawned . . .** : By kings, to go on the Crusades [6+7:passim].

44. **T. C. P '78**: Thaddeus Coleman Pound [97:205]. His credit memos in effect created "non-interest-bearing money" or, as Social Creditors would put it, "debt-free money."

45. **Khati**: [93:2].

46. **kuang**: [M3583], "light." Ming [M4534], "intelligence."

47. **Synesius**: S. of Cyrene, A.D. 370-413, Christian Neoplatonist who bewailed in letters and rhetorical discourses the decline of humane culture.

48. **Al Kindi**: Abu Yusuf Ya'qub ibn Ishaq . . . al-Kindi (L, Alkindus), ca.810-ca.873, born in Bazra, fl. in Baghdad. He became known as the philosopher of the Arabs because he was the first and only Arab philosopher. As an encyclopedic scientist, he transmitted Aristotle through the Neoplatonic traditions and became an influence on Avicenna and Averroes as well as Roger Bacon et al.

49. **Mencken**: [81:31].

50. **fromm**: G, "innocent" or "harmless."

51. **Han(IX, i.e. nine)**: *Wen-li*: "The scholars of the Han Dynasty have said, 'The principles of benevolence, right, propriety, knowledge and sincerity, are in the hearts of all the people. But of people born in different places. . . . All this is the result of climatic influences [Literally, imbued with the wind breath of the water soil]; hence it is spoke of as "Feng" (or Breath of Nature).' "

52. **Uen Ogn**: *Wen-li*: "In the Han Dynasty there was a certain Wen-ong, a Prefect in the province of Si-ch'uan. Perceiving that the place was boorish and untaught, he built colleges. . . . Whenever he went on circuit . . . he selected those who were competent . . . to accompany him. . . . The result was that the people became aware of the excellencies of study. . . . Now only Provincial Graduates . . . are employed to fill the post of Officer of Instructions who have . . . a literary degree. . . . Scholars on their part must . . . establish a character. First let the character be upright and then produce essays which are not mere paper talk."

53. **can't . . .** : Before this, candidates for office bought them.

54. **tuan^{1}**: [M6541], "upright"; cheng^{4} [M351], "upright."

55. **Four tuan**: [85:33].

56. **t'ung tree**: *Wen-li*: "The Phoenix rests

on the wu-T'ung tree, a favorable omen." A rhyme with an earlier statement about the Buddha: "Besides, he gave up his Harem, the Dragon Chamber, and the Phoenix Hall" [98:67].

57. **a mirrour . . .** : *Wen-li*: "If we can eschew all covetousness, anger, and foolish thoughts, all points will be as (clear as) flowers in a looking glass, as the moon in water—all suspense and fear will be no more: then will the heart be perfect."

58. **Chu Wan Kung**: *Wen-li*: "Hence Chu the Accomplished, of the Sung Dynasty, said, 'Buddhism does not concern itself with anything in the four corners of the universe, but simply with the heart.' "

59. **Bother . . . neither . . .** : Pound's great-uncle Albert used to say this to show his contempt for the Church of England because it did not concern itself with either politics or religion. Pound said that serious Victorians, from Hardy to Swinburne, thought likewise [*GK*, 290]. Such a dim sense of morality on the part of a state religion would be enough to give one a pain in various parts of one's anatomy.

60. **Plotinus . . .** : In Porphyry's brief life of P. at the opening of *The Enneads*, we read: "Plotinus was often distressed by an intestinal complaint, but declined clysters, pronouncing the use of such remedies unbecoming in an elderly man" [*Enneads* I, 1; *Pai* 2-3, 45]. At St. Elizabeths Pound used the French version of Emile Brehier (Paris, 1954) [DG].

61. **Body inside**: [98:20].

62. **Sd/Chu**: The late Taoist theories of an elixir of gold which would purify the soul leads to the rejoinder, "clean out the body"; then the soul would take care of itself.

63. **Tao talk**: On the Taoist promise of immortality [98:61], the *Wen-li* says: "It is simply to nourish well the animal spirits, and to prolong life a few years—that is all! Chu the Accomplished said, 'Taoism does but conserve a little vitality.' "

64. **"e basta"**: I, "and enough."

65. **ut supra**: L, "as above." *Wen-li*: "Again there is a class of people whose grandfather had to toil and labour . . . hoarding, in a regular skin-flint fashion, before thay made a fortune." The characters for hoarding are "scraping-the-iron-off-the-end-of-a-needle-fashion saving" [98:153].

66. **tuan^1 cheng^4**: [Cf. 54 above].

67. **amicitia**: [Amicizia] : I, "friendship."

68. **Four books**: *Great Learning, Analects, Doctrine of the Mean, Mencius.*

69. **5 relations**: [98:62].

70. **Mr. Baller**: [98:124].

71. **Canto whatever**: [28/136].

72. **The Papist . . .** : *Wen-li*: "Neither are the Papists orthodox, who speak of heaven and earth and the Invisible. It was simply because they understood astronomy, and were able to calculate the rules for astronomical tables, that the government made use of them to compile the Calendar. This is by no means to say their sect is good: you must on no account believe them."

73. **pu k'o hsin**: [M5379], "not"; [M3381], "can"; [M2748], "believe."

74. **hsin^1 shu$^{4-5}$ hai^4**: [M2735], "mind"; [M5889], "device"; [M2015], "injure": "mind's principles damaged."

75. **cheng^4**: [Cf. 66 above].

76. **huo$^{4-5}$ fu$^{2-5}$**: Huo$^{2-5}$ [not huo$^{4-5}$] [M2401], "2 incarnations of Buddha"; [M1982], 'Buddha." *Wen-li*: "If men were aware that at the present time there are two Living Buddhas [their parents] placed in their own homes, why need they go elsewhere to worship on the mountains and to seek happiness from idols?"

77. **Kuang Ming**: [Cf. 46 above].

78. **Khaty**: [Cf. 45 above].

79. **tien t'ang^2 hsin^1 li$^{3-5}$**: T'ien [M6361], "heaven"; [M6107], "temple"; [M2735];

"heart"; li$^{3-4}$ [not li$^{3-5}$] [M3865]; "in": "Heaven's temple is in the heart."

80. The phallos . . . : At least the Buddhists didn't create a whole spectrum of "sins of the flesh" as did the various Christian sects after Augustine and again after the 12th century.

81. chih^3: Chi'ih [M1037], "upper incisors"; [M1037-25], "gnash the teeth."

82. wo$^{4-5}$: [M7163], "paltry."

83. ch'o$^{4-5}$: [M1287], "grate the teeth."

84. kuan^3: [M3557], "control."

85. chao^4: [M238], "care for."

86. che yang ti jen: Che^4 [M265, "in this way"; yang^4 [M7256], "kind"; ti$^{4-5}$ [M6213], a particle; jen^2 [M3097], "man."

87. liu^2: [M4080], "flow."

88. pai lui: Pai^4 [M4866], "ruin"; lui^4 [M4244], "bad class." The components of lui^4 are 米, "rice"; 犬, "dog"; and 頁, "head."

89. An Ting: *Wen-li*: "In the Sung Dynasty there was one Hu-u'en called An-ting, a district officer of Instruction. . . ."

90. Wen^2 Weng^1: *Wen-li*: "In the Han Dynasty there was a certain Wen-ong, A Prefect in the Province of Se-ch'uan" [cf. 52 above].

91. pen yeh: [98:168]. *Yeh*$^{4-5}$ is also a musical instrument, which recalls Dolmetsch.

92. Ne ultra . . . : [98:169].

93. Dolmetsch: [81:48]. He carried on his family tradition of making great musical instruments, as the circus performers of the "Big Top" carried on their tradition.

94. hsiu^4 ts'an^2: [M2803], "cultivated talents"; ts'ai^2 [not ts'an^2] [M6660], "ability."

95. kuan^1 ch'ang^2: [M3552], "mandarin"; [M213], "excelling."

96. grain . . . : Hsiu^4 also means "grain in the ear."

97. Kiang Sheng: Meaning the *Sheng U* or *Sacred Edict*. The emperor required that it be read to all the people once a month.

98. Generation . . . : *Wen-li*: "The why and wherefore of these regulations no doubt is that mankind rely entirely upon their children to perpetuate their posterity."

99. hao hsin^2: Hao^3 hsin^1 [M2062], "good heartedness"; [M2735], "affections."

100. O$^{4-5}$: [M4809], "evil, foul." A rhyme with "There is no darkness but ignorance" [80:141]. Education is the cure for that.

101. huai: Huai^4 [M2232], "ruin" [cf. 88 above].

102. kids . . . homestead: [*Pai*, 2-1, 79; 7-1 & 2, 319].

103. Born . . . gong: The words come from components of the characters.

104. Yao: [53:14]. The "lovelies" are his two daughters.

105. Hsiang i . . . : Hsiang^3 [M2564], "think it over"; [M3016], "one."

106. hsiao^4: Hsiao^1 [not hsiao^4] [M2611], "put into circulation."

107. tsou: Tsou^4 [M6808], "memorialize the emperor."

108. k'ao ch'eng: [M3299-16], "settlement between a superior and a subordinate." The share of the harvest to be tithed, agreed upon through an argument between a landowner and a tenant.

109. Thiers: [100:115]. Pound felt Thiers offered valid criticism of the income tax which was an advance on the earlier ideas of Talleyrand.

110. Talleyrand: [101:22].

111. PANURGIA: H, "knavery."

112. SOPHIA: H, "wisdom." Pound discusses *sophia* and its relation to knowledge and will as conceived by Aristotle and finds that Aristotle's ideas will not do [*GK*, 326-328].

113. **scienza**: I, "science."

114. **XIV**: Chap. 14 of the *Edict* concerns an enlightened tax system: "The ten voices . . ." is a way of saying "from time immemorial" or "according to ancient customs."

115. **t'ien² ti⁴**: [M6362], "land"; [M6198], "soil."

116. **(liang²)**: [M3944], "taxes in kind."

117. **Yong (2.2.3)**: Yung Chêng. The numbers refer to the Wang text, Baller's translation, and the notes on the *Wen-li* text.

118. **Elkin Mathews**: [82:6]. As editor, he defined the requirements and length of W. L. Courtney's work [see 119 below]. Perhaps a statement of the value of literary criticism in England at the time. DG remembers Pound saying the phrase often at St. Elizabeths. HK thinks that was good pay for the time.

119. **Courtney's**: W. L. Courtney, editor of the *Fortnightly Review* during Pound's early years in London.

120. **Chou rite . . .** : *The Sacred Edict* was a last great expression of Neoconfucianism, which according to Kung himself, derived from the Chou dynasty [53:77-78].

121. **manesco**: I, "rough, brutal."

122. **the 9 arts**: Pound prob. meant "6 arts," as there is no such phrase as "9 arts" in China. But *lu*⁴·⁵ [M4189], "6 arts," is fundamental to Confucianism.

123. **chao¹**: [M236-6], "clear."

124. **CHÊN**: Chen⁴ [M316], "I."

125. **Yo el rey**: S, "I the king." Since some of the Jesuit missionaries to China were from Spain, perhaps K'ang Hsi or his son learned enough Spanish to say some things to them in their tongue.

126. **(logistica)**: I, "logistics." But Pound prob. wants to suggest "roots." *Wen-li*: "We have heard that nourishing the people is the basic root, consisting in clothing and food: farming and mulberry culture are the source for clothing and food."

127. **nung**: Nung² [M4768], "to farm."

128. **sang**: Sang¹ [M5424], "the mulberry tree."

129. **Empress**: *Wen-li*: "Anciently the emperor went in person to plough and the empress in person attended the mulberry trees. They personally enjoyed the highest prestige, and their not shirking from the heat of toil set the empire an example."

130. **Ideogram**: Ch'ao⁴ [M247], "an omen."

131. **ch'ang²**: [M213], "to show respect."

132. **chu**: Chu⁴ [M1581], "to assemble or meet together."

133. **wu² . . . li⁴**: [M7208], "do not"; [M4587-10], "love ardently"; [M514], "wonderful"; [M7483], "profit"; [M5000], "double profit"; [M3867], "interest on money."

134. **(Byzance . . .** : [98:18].

135. **Michelet**: Jules M., 1798-1874, French historian extraordinaire who did much to resurrect the past and explain it to his contemporaries.

136. **Ambrose**: St. Ambrose [88:45]. This bishop of Milan is a favorite of Pound's because of his attitude toward moneymakers: "hoggers of harvest are the curse of the people."

137. **"De Tobia"**: St. Ambrose wrote this commentary on the *Book of Tobias* which is a telling indictment of usury [Migne, 793-832].

138. **(que ça doure)**: F, the end of an idiomatic phrase, *pourvou que ça doure*: "while it lasts." Supposedly a habitual aside uttered by Donna Letizia, Napoleon's mother [RO].

139. **literate Confucians**: *Wen-li*: "Those

who were to become leaders in the land were especially attended to by appointed professors and scholars."

140. graceful bigots . . . phalloi: Perhaps a reference to Pound himself. David Gordon believes it is. He thinks Pound's anti-Semitism of the early 1950s gave way little by little until by the time of *Thrones* he could begin to see it objectively; especially since a number of people, including Gordon and John Espey, accused him over and over again of being a bigot. The "thundering phalloi" may refer to his continuous efforts to show that man's sexuality is divinely created and natural and has nothing to do with sin, as Gourmont showed in *The Natural Philosophy of Love* years earlier. Ethical questions involve treatment of others; sin comes from mistreatment of others, not from phallic expression in itself. Trying to get such an idea across to someone brainwashed for a lifetime by puritanism may require a kind of thundering repetition. One of the characters involved is *no*⁴, 懦 [M4750]: it has the component 忄, "heart," which Pound considered a drawing of the phallus, and right-hand components which are similar to 雷, "thunder." No⁴ means "weak." The lower part of the right component is not really "thunder"; hence, "mistranslation."

141. SAGE . . . : *Wen-li*: "Our meritorious ancestor even in old age was still stimulating others to goodness, and especially exalted schools and scholarship. In all things, therefore, that would feed the spirit of scholars and conduce to their educative disciplines he was circumspectly prepared."

142. anagogico: I, "anagogic." The highest of the four allegorical levels of meaning as described by Dante [*Conv*., 2.1.6], where it is called the "super-sense" and is related to a spiritual interpretation of the Bible. In Dante the anagogic relates the soul of the present to the heaven of the future. In Pound it means the wisdom of the ancestors for those of the present and the wisdom of the sages of the present for posterity.

143. en¹: [M1743-3], "bound by mutual ties, on the one side grace, and on the other loyalty." Pound used this character as the title-page seal in *Thrones*.

144. village usage: *Wen-li*: "Now because the scholar is considered as the first of the four classes of people, one expects quite a bit from him, and therefore the scholar's expectations of and demands on himself cannot be easy going. A scholar constantly practices the fundamentals and afterward the large and small villages regard him as a reliable mold of behavior."

145. chiao¹: [M702], "to communicate," "friendship." *Wen-li*: "And in regard to your studies, let them all be the classical books; in regard to friends, choose reliable officers."

146. raise ruin: *Wen-li*: "Be alert to preserve the honorable lest in establishing yourself you come to ruin and flaw your school's name." The components of one character mean "bird" and "mouth," which means "chirrp."

147. jen, i, li, chih: Jen² [M3099], "humanity"; i⁴ [M3002], "equity"; li³ [M3886], "propriety"; chih⁴ [M933], "wisdom." The four *tuan* [85:33].

148. worship . . . day!: *Wen-li*: "Then even ignorant people can apply the values of courtesy and justice to their plowing and weeding. And the decisive soldier can apply the values of the Shih Odes and the Shu History to his shield and helmet. A unifying principle of manners brought to Zenith. May we again see it in our day."

149. All . . . grows: *Wen-li*: "Only wanting to solidify the customs of the people, we first set out to rectify men's hearts; wanting to rectify men's hearts, we instituted a program of studies . . . now man receives the central principles of Heaven and Earth at his birth." The final lines of the canto are a comment on this key passage which is central to the Confucianism of both Mencius and Pound [*Pai*, inside front cover].

CANTO C

Sources

St. Ambrose, *De Moribus Brachmanorum,* in Migne XVII, 1176-1179; Brooks Adams, *The Theory of Social Revolutions,* N.Y., 1913 [BA, *Theory*] ; Brooks Adams, *The Law of Civilization and Decay,* N.Y., 1895 [BA, *Civilization*] ; Dante, *Par.* XVIII, IX, XIX, XX; Homer, *Od*, V; Paul de Rémusat, *Thiers*, trans. M. B. Anderson, Chicago, 1889 [*Thiers*] ; F. W. Baller, trans., *The Sacred Edict,* Shanghai, 1924, rpt. NPF, Orono, Me., 1979 [*Edict*] ; Charles de Rémusat, *Saint Anselme de Cantorbéry.* Paris, Didier, 1853; Alexander Del Mar, *History of Monetary Systems*, Chicago, 1896 [HMS] .

Background

W. B. Fowler, *British American Relations, 1917-1918; The Role of Sir William Wiseman,* Princeton, 1969 [Fowler, *Wiseman*] ; Lord Beaverbrook, *Men and Power, 1917-1918,* Duell, Sloan and Pearce, New York, 1956; Jesse D. Clarkson, *A History of Russia*, Random House, 1961 [*Russia*] ; Andrzef Walicki, *The Slavophile Controversy*, Oxford, 1975; James Cleugh, *The Medici; A Tale of Fifteen Generations*, Doubleday, 1975 [*Medici*] .

Exegeses

EP, *GK*, 227; *N. D. 17*, 174-175; R. Sieburth, *Pai*, 6-3, 386; NS, *Reading*, 110; DD, *Sculptor,* 239-241; EH, *Approaches*, 26-27, 31-32, 188-189; CB-R, *ZBC*, 153-154, 262-263; EH, *Pai,* 1-2, 273; CFT, *Pai*, 2-3, 451-452; MB, *Trace*, 338-340; William Cookson, *A Guide to the Cantos*, inedit [WC, *Guide*] .

Glossary

1. **Supreme Court**: Because the high court was systematically declaring the legislation of the New Deal unconstitutional, President Roosevelt proposed the court be increased from nine judges to twelve. His political enemies orchestrated a chorus of protest so that the proposal failed to carry.

2. **Senator Wheeler**: Burton Kendall W., 1882-1975, a Democrat from Montana elected to the U. S. Senate in 1922. After a brief flirtation with the Progressive party of Robert La Follette, he returned to the Democratic party and backed much of the New Deal legislation. But as war loomed in Europe, he became a leading exponent of isolationism and by 1940 had broken with Roosevelt because of his pro-Allied posture, his attempt to "pack the Supreme Court," and other matters.

3. **some Habsburg . . .** : [86:78] .

4. **Eu ZoOn**: H, "living well." The capitol *O* indicates the word has two syllables.

5. **Not . . . liberties**: Arguments about not tampering with the Supreme Court: the issue was not that the court should never in prin-

ciple be larger, but that at that historic juncture, such action could lead to infringement of liberties.

6. **Joffre** . . . : Joseph J. Cesaire J., 1852-1931, marshal of France and eventually chairman of the Allied War Council for WWI. After his setback at the battle of Verdun, he was promoted because of outmoded tactics. Prob. at Verdun he made the remark about Napoleon.

7. **Lenin**: Vladimir Ilyich L. [V. I. Ulyanov], 1870-1924, inciter and leader of the Bolshevik overthrow of the Mensheviks (minority party who engineered the October Revolution) in November 1917. Lenin's exposure of monopoly capitalism's technique of fostering the appreciation followed by the depreciation of money, finally led to the creation of the FDIC (Federal Deposit Insurance Corporation), which insures small bank accounts.

8. **increase of debt** . . . : The temporary expedient of the New Deal was the creation of money by debt, which is anathema to Social Creditors because the same effect could be managed without going into debt.

9. **Moslem**: Source unknown.

10. **Danton**: John Jacques D., 1759-1794, a leading statesman in the French Revolution. Said Brooks Adams: "Topino-Lebrun, the artist . . . sat on the jury which tried Danton, and observed that the heart of his colleague seemed failing him. Topino took the waverer aside, and said: "This is not a trial, it is a measure . . . " [BA, *Theory,* 223].

11. **Jo Skelton**: John S., ca. 1460-1529, the creator of Skeltonic verse, pilloried Cardinal Wolsey with unrestrained enthusiasm during the reign of Henry VIII but he was never "committed."

12. **Wiseman**: Sir William George Eden W. (b. 1885), served in WWI and was gassed at Ypres. In 1917, as chief of British Intelligence in the U. S., he so impressed Colonel House (Wilson's inside man) that he called him "one of the most efficient men of his age I ever met." During the complicated problems that evolved after the war was over, he acted as a behind-the-scenes adviser to all the most important people in both the British and American governments. Wilson much preferred to talk to him privately than to the official ambassador. Wiseman came to believe that it would be easier for England and the U. S. to coordinate actions leading to Versailles if Congress gave Wilson the power to act. During 1917 and 1918 he sent hundreds of cables to those who could influence events, such as Lord Reading, the British ambassador.

13. **Isaacs**: Rufus Daniel I., 1st earl Reading, 1860-1935, lord chief justice of England since 1913, he was appointed president of the Anglo-French Loan Mission to the U. S. in 1917 and ambassador to the U. S. in Jan. 1918. In a Cablegram [CXP 701, 16 August 1918] from Wiseman to Lord Reading, labeled "Personal & Very Secret," we read of a conversation between Wiseman and President Wilson with Colonel House present. The cable concerns ways of getting a powerful League of Nations and the necessity to avoid publicity before agreements were reached [Fowler, *Wiseman,* 278]. No such cable for Aug. 18 has yet been found.

14. **Francis**: F. the 1st, 1494-1547, king of France (1515-1547).

15. **S . . . W . . .** : Identified in Beinecke drafts as sumner Welles, 1892-1961, American diplomat and expert in Latin-American affairs, who under FDR became assistant and then undersecretary of state. After his retirement, he was found unconscious and half-frozen on his estate, where he had apparently fallen into a stream [BK: NY *Times,* 27 Dec. 1948]. Pound thought highly of Welles and thought if people had listened to him WWII might have been avoided [EP, *Speaking,* 306-308].

16. **Mazarin**: Jules M., 1602-1661, French statesman and cardinal who succeeded Richelieu in 1642. An effective negotiator who won concessions at the Peace of West-

phalia (1648), but his financial abuses led to trouble with the Fronde. He won but put the state into great debt.

17. **PERENNE BELLUM**: L, "Everlasting War."

18. **Code out of . . .** : The Napoleonic Code. N's contribution to civilization should be looked for not in his everlasting wars (he must always be going somewhere [34/165]) but in his codification of the laws.

19. **Peloponesus**: The western Greek peninsula dominated by Sparta, whence came the legal code of Lycurgus.

20. **Maison Quarree**: [Carree]: An ancient (ca. 2d cent.) building at Nimes, France, called by many the most perfect Roman temple to survive. It inspired President Jefferson in the design of Monticello [31:22].

21. **Gave . . . trade**: The Treaty of Utrecht in 1713 passed from France to England the monopoly (for 30 years) of supplying Negro slaves to the Spanish colonies. The contracts were earlier passed from the Dutch to the French. No special change is recorded for 1708.

22. **Gibraltar**: Controlled by the Turks, then by the Spanish, then by the Moors, and after 1462 by the Spanish again, it passed into the control of the English in 1704, which in effect gave them control over at least part of the slave trade.

23. **Medicis**: Marie de M., 1573-1642, queen of France, second wife of Henry IV. After he was assassinated (1610), she became regent for her son Louis XIII. She engaged in power struggles for over 30 years and was sometimes exiled, sometimes restored. Richelieu helped force her final exile in 1630, when she fled first to the Netherlands and then to England. Finally rejected by her son-in-law, King Charles of England, and by Philip IV of Spain, who would not allow her back into the Netherlands, she was accepted into the city of Cologne by a prince-archbishop who felt Christian sympathy for her misery [Cleugh, *Medici,* 314-330]. Her anti-Hapsburg posture during the Thirty Years' War (1618-1648) and her personal intriguing behind the scenes from Gibraltar to Compeigne, may have put her on the wrong side in Pound's mind.

24. **John Law**: 1671-1729, Scottish banker and financier who went to France, which chartered his Banque Generale in 1716 and allowed the bank to issue paper currency. After 1719 the bank's paper became guaranteed by the state, and the stock issued by it soared to ridiculous prices as the bank became involved in colonial speculation such as the Mississippi scheme. Before the bubble burst, insiders cleaned up by selling their stock. When it did burst, thousands of investors were left destitute, the government was weakened, and Law left in disgrace. He became a gambler in Venice and in 1729 died and was interred there in the churchyard of St. Moisé west of St. Mark's Square. It wasn't the idea of the state bank issuing currency that was bad, however—that worked beautifully and, for a brief time, created great prosperity. It was the unrestrained speculation of big money men—who misused both the bank and the state—that was disastrous. For Pound, Law demonstrated that the state could extend credit and create prosperity: thus, he should not lie in a grave unhonored.

25. **SUMBAINAI**: H, "coheres" [*WT*, 50: "What / SPLENDOUR / IT ALL COHERES"; 109:17; 116:20].

26. **Grevitch**: Inmate at St. Elizabeths [MSB, *Pai*, 3-3, 332].

27. **Young Labarre**: For a few schoolboy pranks involving "the desecration of crucifixes," this chevalier was sentenced to be tortured, mutilated, beheaded, and burned. Some of Voltaire's works were found in his possession, including the *Dictionnaire philosophique*, which "was burned with [Labarre's] corpse" [Sieburth, *Pai,* 6-3, 386].

28. **Cavour**: [61:19].

29. **Hohenlohe**: Chlodwig Karl Viktor, Fürst zu H., 1819-1901. As a premier of

Bavaria, he supported German unification and the program of Bismarck. He was ambassador to Paris after the War of 1870, and, later, governor of Alsace-Lorraine (1885-1894). Pound sees the settlement of that war as a wise one that maintained the peace in Europe until the usurers created WWI.

30. **Chez . . . civilizée**: F, "In our country the press is still very little civilized."

31. **Napoleon Third**: 1808-1873, president of the Second Republic, 1848-1852, emperor of the French, 1852-1870.

32. **'69: southern Slavs . . .** : By the terms of the Treaty of Paris (1856), Russia agreed to a neutralization of the Black Sea and to cease efforts to dominate the Slavic populations of the old Ottoman Empire. But by the late 60s, Russia was making serious efforts to control these areas and gain access to the southern seas. These efforts were rebuffed by a pan-Slavic movement, including a secret society formed in 1869. Led first by Bakunin as a revolutionary movement against the Tzar, it was used by the southern Slavs as a means of keeping out of the Russian empire. The movement caused only a reaction: the Black Sea clauses were repudiated by Russia in 1870 [Clarkson, *Russia,* 284-308].

33. **Zollverein**: G, "customs union:" The political unification of Germany was much assisted by the preceding economic unification called the Zollverein, in which, over a period of 30 years, the small German states dropped tariffs amongst themselves and erected a common tariff barrier against outside states. The success of this venture became one of the models for the post-WWII European Common Market.

34. **Ionides**: Luke I, [40:26]. A Greek Pound knew during his early London years [*GK*, 227].

35. **Count Usedom**: Ironic epithet created for Bismarck.

36. **Bismarck**: [86:3].

37. **(. . . no more wars . . .)**: To Bismarck, the Franco-Prussian War was to be the war to end all wars.

38. **Clodovic**: [Cf. 29 above].

39. **Ultramontaines**: L, "Beyond the mountains." Name given to Catholics whose first allegiance was to the pope, on the other side of the Alps, rather than to the king of France itself. They were opposed to the Gallicans, who said France first and pope after. The term was revived in 19th-century Germany and Austria and applied to the Old Catholics.

40. **aristos . . . ploots**: The Ultramontaines were generally aristocrats. Hence, their ignorance (of the way the usurocrats worked), combined with the similar illiteracy of the plutocrats, allowed France to be "bitched."

41. **"JESUS . . . for ."**: The reaction of Queen Elizabeth. The source is Brooks Adams [RO, *Pai*, 6-2, 181]; but her concern in Adams is with the number of clergy, not with money: "Jesus (quoth the queen) 13,000 it is not to be looked for, I thinke the time hath been, there hath not been 4. preachers in a diocesse, my meaning is not you should make choice of learned ministers only for they are not to be found, but of honest, sober, and wise men, and such as can read the scriptures and homilies well unto the people" [BA, *Civilization,* 225].

42. **ploughing . . . solid**: A central theme of the poem: Justice comes from the growing of food to feed the people and in using words precisely—in law, the press, the schoolroom, economics, and politics.

43. **Von Moltke**: Helmuth Karl Bernhard, Graf von M., 1800-1891, a great Prussian field marshal, who trained his armies so well he won the Danish War (1864), the Austro-Prussian War (1866), and the Franco-Prussian War (1870). He could also be charming at the court of Napoleon III at Fontainebleau.

44. **"In locis . . . viventia"**: "In desert places / we rejoice in the middle of the woods. / are sheared, you kill, they are milked / by which you till the land. / You

shed their blood / their flesh fills you inside / you thus become a living sepulchre of dead bodies." From a Latin translation of a Greek account of Alexander the Great's conversation with Indian Brahmins, done (prob.) by St. Ambrose, entitled *De Moribus Brachmanorum.*

45. **"That Virginia . . . with . . . "**: John Randolph [87:10] got some resolutions adopted at Charlotte Courthouse in 1833 which contained these phrases: "That *Virginia* 'is, and of right, ought to be, a free, sovereign and independent state.' . . . when . . . *Virginia* [joined] . . . the other twelve colonies . . . , she parted with *no portion* of her *sovereignity*" [BK, *Pai* 9-3, 425].

46. **Oh GAWD!!! . . .** : Supposedly, Pound's reaction upon discovering that Section X of the Constitution could be used as a barrier to some monetary reforms he thought essential, such as the Douglas concept of "local control of local purchasing power" [96:118; NS, *Reading,* 110].

47. **George Second encouraged . . .** : During his reign, the production of indigo in the U. S. was encouraged, but . . . [88:93].

48. **Barley . . . tax-free**: [88:96].

49. **hilaritas**: [83:9].

50. **Letizia**: I, "gladness" [*Par.* XVIII, 42].

51. **Virtù**: I, "spiritual power to love." Dante feels this power increasing after his delight, in the preceding line, of seeing Beatrice and doing well [*Par.* XVIII, 60].

52. **Buona . . . volontà**: I, "Will good in itself" [*Par.* XIX, 86-87]. "The primal will is good in itself, / and from itself, which is the highest good, it is never moved" [JW]. A rhyme with *directio voluntatis* [77:57].

53. **Lume non e . . .** : I, "There is no light, if not from the serene [nature of God]" [*Par.* XIX, 64].

54. **stone . . . descending**: From "I seem to hear the murmur of a river / that descends clearly from stone to stone" [*Par.* XX, 19-20].

55. **the sound . . . light**: From, "Where I saw begemmed the sixth light" [*Par.* XX, 17].

56. **lute[s neck**: From, "And as sound at the neck of lute / takes its form" [*Par.* XX, 22-23].

57. **Jackson . . . Adams**: [88:97].

58. **Tocqueville**: [88:84].

59. **Taney**: [37:58; 89:57]. President Jackson appointed him to replace Duane as secretary of the treasury in April 1834. But the Senate refused to confirm.

60. **Duane**: [34:43]. During the political conflicts over renewing the charter of the Bank of the U. S., Jackson appointed Duane as secretary of the treasury to replace Louis McLane, who had refused to remove government deposits to the state banks. Duane also refused to carry out the transfer and was replaced by Taney.

61. **Erebus**: [1:8; 90:27]. Just as Dante does, Pound places men groveling for money here [14:3, 4].

62. **all gates**: [47:10; 94:20].

63. **bab**: [bāb] A and Per, "gate". In mystical writings it means "the way" and is used to refer to Abdul Baha [96:93], the founder of the Bahai movement [93:162].

64. **Pandects . . . Gaius**: [94:21].

65. **Consul for . . .** : [94:29].

66. **Windsor**: Edward VIII [95:39].

67. **Agassiz, Kung**: [93:51, 52].

68. **maison close**: F, "closed [sealed or encircled] house."

69. **Lightfoot**: [95:42].

70. **Le Portel**: [80:422].

71. **KREDEMNON**: [96:1].

72. **DEXATO XERSI**: H, "received it in [her] hand" [*Od.* V, 462].

73. **AGERTHE**: H, "returned again." While dozens of other events are taking place in the poem, we recall that in Canto I Odysseus started his "Nostos" (journey home). At the end of *Rock-Drill,* Ino (Leucothea) saved him with her magic veil and protected him on his swim to Phaeacia. Here we note his arrival at the shores where Ino retrieves her magic veil and the hero goes ashore.

74. **two lies**: The red-herring technique Pound often deplored and from which he has suffered much. He said to Bridson: "Confusion is caused by package-words. You call a man a Manichaean or a Bolshevik, or something or other, and never find out what he is driving at. The technique of infamy is to start two lies at once and get people arguing which is the truth" [*N.D. 17,* 174-175].

75. **CODE**: [65:126; 94:45]. Justinian's Code.

76. **Gesetzbuch**: G, "law-book; code."

77. **Justin's village**: Prob. Justinian the Great [94:45; cf. 84 below].

78. **"Non della" (Verona)**: [78:18, 19].

79. **J. Austin**: John A., 1790-1859, English jurist and professor at the University of London and author of *Province of Jurisprudence Determined* (1832), in which he analyzed the principles on which all legal systems were based. He argued that the law expressed the will of the sovereign and should not be confused with the dictates of ethics or of religions.

80. **Frank Harris**: [97:135].

81. **No greek** . . . : Since other Mediterranean ethnic groups did sell their own people into slavery, perhaps this indicates for Pound an advanced civilization before Christ.

82. **Silk news** . . . : Sericulture passed from China to India before 1000 B.C. and, after that, slowly to Persia and the Middle East. Aristotle [*Hist. Anim.* V, 19(17), 11(6)] mentions the silkworm. Justinian conducted the silk trade as a state monopoly: "[He tried] to divert the trade from the Persian route . . . into the East of Europe. In this he failed, but two Persian monks . . . arrived at Constantinople and imparted their knowledge to the emperor" [*EB*, Vol. XXV, 11th ed., 97].

83. **monetary (218 A.D.)**: No data can be found for this date, but since Landulph's chronology is 7 years less than the accepted [JW, *Later*, 113], the reference may be to Caracalla's [97:41] new coinage system of A.D. 211 which established the silver-gold ratio at 12 for 1 [*HMS*, 49].

84. **Belisarius**: Ca. 505-565, Byzantine general under Justinian I. He suppressed the *Nika* sedition (532), defeated the Vandals of Africa (533-534), recovered Italy from the Ostragoths, took Naples and Rome (536), and so on. Since he was handicapped by Justinian's distrust and jealousy, he could only keep the enemy in check and so retired. But he returned to drive the Bulgars from Constantinople (559).

85. **NO . . . shares**: The anecdote concerns an Allied submarine which the Italian navy might have sunk but didn't because it was insured by the Trieste branch of Lloyd's, an international marine insurance underwriter made up of about 300 different syndicates. A rhyme with similar international munitions makers' acts of WWI [18:13].

86. **De Stael**: Anne Louise Germaine Necker, wife of Jacques Necker [68:96], baronne de Stael-Holstein, 1766-1817, whose defense of German culture and romanticism outraged Napoleon. His police caused her flight and exile to Russia and England, but she returned in 1815 to become a great influence on European thought and literature.

87. **Santayana**: [81:38; 95:66].

88. **Nel mezzo**: I, "in the middle." Translation of character [M 1504], "chung."

89. **Ideogram**: Fu$^{2-5}$ [M1982], "Buddha" or "the Buddhists" [98:64].

90. taozers: Followers of the Tao [98:61].

91. Ideogram: Pai jih [M3124-125], "day-light" [DG, *Pai*, 5-3, 398].

92. Alighieri . . . : The brilliant light of paradise was so blinding that Dante had to shade his eyes [JW, *Pai*, 2-2, 176].

93. Tyler . . . Van Buren: Prob. Noel Stock, in a letter written ca. 1957 from Australia [*Pai*, 9-3, 419].

94. "With the horned moon . . . your valley": These 16 lines are Pound's rendition of parts of Chap. VII ("Orthodoxy") of *The Sacred Edict* [98:67, 78, 81]. The chapter concludes: "If you recognize that reason is true, and know that the mind enlightened is heaven, the mind in darkness is hell—you will then as a matter of course have a ruling principle, and it will be impossible for you to be beguiled away by heretical sects. If your character is upright . . . the Empire will be at peace, and the people cheerful as a matter of course. If none of you people believe these heretical sects, they will not wait to be driven out, they will become extinct naturally" [*Edict*, 87]. "Wang" is the salt commissioner [98:49], "Sheng U," *The Sacred Edict*.

95. De Tribus . . . ver l'estate: [98:105, 107].

96. Fordie: [98:104].

97. Kuan Ming: Kuang Ming [M3583; M4534], "bright light." Rhyme with Dante's paradisal light [cf. 55 above].

98. Durch . . . kompromittiert: G, "Because of the Bankhouse, Pacelli compromised."

99. Pacelli: Eugenio P., 1876-1968, Pope Pius XII, 1939-1958.

100. B. Swan: Pound referred to B. Swan on a postcard to Ingrid Davies [25 March 1955] as "my murderer friend" who was on an oil boat [MS, Humanities Research Center, University of Texas, Austin]. Says BK: "That's all we know." The NY *Times* Index yields the name Benjamin Swan as an officer in a Swan-Finch Oil Co.; but no further data can be found. Or perhaps Byron L. Swan, 1892-1950, whose obit. [Sept. 28, 1950, NY *Times*] identifies him as "an investment manager for Wall Street concerns."

101. OLYMPIAD/236: The Olympic games, held every 4th year, were founded in 776 B.C. According to a list of winners drawn up by Julius Africanus and preserved by Eusebius, the 236th Olympiad was held in A.D. 165.

102. Peregrinus: Cynic philosopher, A.D. ca. 100-165, of Parium in Mysia. Because he was suspected of murdering his father, he fled to Palestine, where he became a Christian. For this act he was imprisoned. When he got out he became a restless wandering scholar (hence, *peregrinate*). In 165 he committed suicide by throwing himself onto the flames at the Olympic games.

103. Plarr: [16:18; 74:168].

104. Parion: For Parium, birthplace of Peregrinus (nicknamed Proteus).

105. Colelum . . . largitur: L, "The sky my roof, God does not sell; / the earth [is my] couch but He endows [me with wisdom]." Supposedly said to Alexander the Great by the Brachmani (Phaeacians) [Migne, XVII, 1176-79; MB, *Trace*, 389].

106. Caritas: L, "love; charity."

107. Stead: William Thomas S., 1849-1912, who pioneered modern journalistic methods in England and the U.S. He edited the *Pall Mall Gazette* and founded the *Review of Reviews* in 1890. An advocate of Naval reform, child welfare, and social legislation, he went to prison in 1885 for his attacks on government policy toward white slavery. In later years he became involved in psychical research; he died on the Titanic.

108. Douglas: [38:49].

109. "Mortal . . . ears": Says Dante of mortals who "wrongfully blame" Fortune, "she is blest and does not hear it" [*Inf.* VII, 93-94].

110. Rémusat: Charles François Marie R., 1797-1875, the son of Auguste Laurent, Comte de R., and Clare Elizabeth R. (referred to in *The Cantos* as Mme. de R.). All three of these people, as well as Paul de Rémusat, the grandson of Clare and the son of Charles, appear in the poem and can easily be confused. Charles is indicated here because as a writer of philosophical history he made studies of several people mentioned in the surrounding lines, such as Anselm [105:16] and Lord Herbert de Cherbury below.

111. "bien . . . à priori": F, "well accounted for knowledge [in a theological context] à priori." Rémusat wrote in a footnote in Chap. V of *Saint Anselme de Cantorbéry:* "Saint Thomas ne s'est jamais bien rendu compte des connaissances *à priori*" [p. 527].

112. Cocteau: [76:49].

113. Erigina: [74:90].

114. Cherbury: [Cf. 133 below].

115. Thiers: [101:11]. During the time of perils and "the conspiracies of Prince Louis Bonaparte in 1851, Thiers remained the most impassioned of Conservatives" [*Thiers,* 108]. In a book of 1848 (*Defence of Property*), he set forth his ideas of taxation, and in later speeches "he refuted Socialistic theories by the report of a committee appointed to examine . . . taxation, public credit, mortgage loans, paper money, and right to labor" [p. 109]. Throughout, his attitude was against taxation of income or wealth.

116. Psellos: [23:2].

117. Degas: [74:226].

118. Old what's-her-name: According to Michael Tsellos (called Psellos above), the Byzantine empress Zoe, whose one concern in her old age was to develop a new perfume. The braziers in her room in the summer made it unbearable for the servants, but the heat didn't bother her [*The Chronographia,* trans. E. R. A. Seurter, Yale, 1953, 137-138, Bk. IV, 64] [BK].

119. servitu: I, "servants."

120. Agra: One of the United Provinces of India.

121. Neque . . . diligunt: L, "Nor did any choose gold."

122. Gardner . . . specific: Gardner wrote in the *London Daily News* of Aug. 1, 1914: "If we crush Germany and make Russia dictator of Europe and Asia it will be the greatest disaster that has ever befallen Western Europe" [WC, *Guide*].

123. Beauclerc: Title given to Henry I of England in recognition of his scholarly interests.

124. Julian: [102:53].

125. 2 million . . . : The centuries-long struggle between the popes and the kings of Europe and England, over which should have the final power of investing both church and temporal authority, led to battles and wars in which millions died.

126. Autun: A town in E central France. Founded by Augustus, it became an early episcopal seat and a center of learning. It is famous for its Roman ruins and 12th-century cathedral.

127. Poictiers: [90:9].

128. Benevento: Small city in S Italy which under the Romans became an important commercial center on the Appian Way. From the 11th century until 1860, it was under the rule of the papacy most of the time.

129. et l'anneau: F, "ring," as the Pope's signet-ring.

130. 1075 . . . '87: Key dates in the struggle between church and state over "investiture." Gregory VII made the issue paramount during his papacy (1073-1085). The most famous dramatic moment was the submission of the young King Henry IV in 1077: he walked barefoot in the snow before the pope in order to receive forgiveness [see W. F. Barry, *The Papal Monarchy*; or any biography of Hildebrande (Gregory VII)].

131. et le prépuce: F, "and the foreskin."

132. **Puy en Vellay**: Le Puy (F, "conical hill") is a capital in Velay of S central France. It is famous for a bare rock 500 feet high topped by a 50-foot bronze statue of the Virgin, erected in 1860. It has a 12th-century cathedral of daring construction. After the 6th century, Le Puy began to grow because it was made an episcopal see. Among the relics at one time was the "prépuce de Christ."

133. **Herbert**: Lord H. of Cherbury, 1583-1648, the English philosopher and elder brother of metaphysical poet George H. He was ambassador to France (1619-1624) and was made Lord H. of Cherbury in 1629. He set forth his principles of natural religion in *De Veritate* (1624), *De religione laici* (1645), and *De religione gentilium* (1663). He laid the foundations for deism, which he also set forth in his own metaphysical poetry.

134. **(De Veritate)**: The full title of this work translates: *On Truth as distinguished from Revelation, from Probability, from Possibility, and from Falsehood*. Pound's sentence comes from a preface, "To the Candid Reader." The sentence translates: "The primary consideration of such men is to remain true to the role they have adopted, and to avoid expressing any other views" [Meyrich H. Carré edition, Bristol, 1937].

135. **come in subjecto**: I, "as in a subject ready." Pound's translation of a part of line 23 of Cavalcanti's *Donna mi prega* [*LE*, 156, 184-185n.]. The idea is that a comprehended seen form remains as a subject or ideal against which other visual images may be judged [JW].

136. **lisses . . . a tenir**: F, "smooth, lovingly tender, to cherish." From Villon's "Heaulmiere." The line concerns the hips of this once beautiful woman as she grieves the time of her youth," as V. did his own [*SR*, 175].

137. **EX . . . HYPOSTASIN**: H, "out of essence . . . hypostasis" [81:55]. From Plotinus.

138. **PERI EROTAS**: H, "Concerning Love." Title of a section of *The Enneads* [Loeb 442, p. 166].

139. **hieron**: H, "temple" [97/678-681].

140. **Nous . . . auton**: H, "the mind in itself most sacred." *Aristos* could be translated "noblest" or even "best," but since Pound's continuous theme states that the intelligence of man is the most exalted expression of divinity at work in the universe, "sacred" comes closest to his meaning.

141. **compenetrans**: I, "penetrating everywhere."

142. **pathema . . . aphistatai**: H, "affection . . . not separate [from mind]" [EH, *Pai*, 1-2, 273; CFT, *Pai*, 2-3, 451-452].

143. **Plotinus**: [98:20].

144. **per . . . diafana**: L, "through more diaphanes [layers of translucency]" [36:4].

CANTO CI

Sources

The Memoirs of Mme de Rémusat, trans. Mrs. Cashel Hoey and John Lillie, 2 vols., London, 1880 [*Memoirs*]; Joseph F. Rock, *The Ancient Na-khi Kingdom of Southwest China*, 2 vols., Harvard Univ. Press, 1947 [*Na-khi*, vol., p.]; Joseph F. Rock, "The ^{2}Muan ^{1}Bpo Ceremony or the Sacrifice to Heaven as Practiced by the ^{1}Na-^{2}khi," Vol. VIII, *Monumenta Serica*, Peiping, 1948, 1-160 [*Muan Bpo*, p.]; Joseph F. Rock, *The ²Zhi ³Ma Funeral Ceremony of the Na-khi of Southwest China*, vol. 9, Studia Instituti Anthropos, Viennae-Mödling, Austria, 1955; Joseph F. Rock, "The ¹D'a ³Nv Funeral Ceremony," *Anthropos*, L (1955): Paul de Rémusat, *Thiers*, trans. Melville B. Anderson, Chicago, A. C. McClung, 1889; Tacitus, *The Annals*, Bk. XIII, trans. John Jackson (Loeb 322).

Background

George K. Kennan, *Siberia and The Exile System*, 1891; Laurence Binyon, *The Flight of The Dragon*, London, 1911; R. Wilson McNair, *Promise to Pay*, London 1934; Plotinus, *The Enneads*, ed. Porphyry, trans. A. H. Armstrong, I, II, (Loeb, 440-441) [*Enneads*]; Peter Goulart, *Forgotten Kingdom*, London 1955; Paul H. Emden, *Money Powers of Europe in the Nineteenth and Twentieth Centuries*, New York, 1938 [Emden, *Powers*]; Osvald Sirén, *Chinese Painting*, New York, Ronald Press, 1956-1958; John Read, *Through Alchemy to Chemistry*, London, 1957 [Alchemy].

Exegeses

EP, *GK*, 274; DD, *Pai*, 1-1, 61; CFT, *Pai*, 3-1, 90-122; NS, *Reading*, 111; John Peck, *Agenda*, vol. 9, 2-3, 1971, pp. 26-69 [Peck, *Agenda*]; Jamila Ismail, ibid., pp. 70-87; Bridson Interview, *ND* 17, p. 175, 176.

Glossary

1. **Monsieur de Rémusat**: [100:110]. "M. de Talleyrand, finding scarcely any one but M. de Rémusat who could understand him, disclosed to him the political views with which the victories of our armies inspired him" [*Memoirs*, 301].

2. **junipers, . . .** : "Junipers love southern, dry exposure where the snow melts quickly, while northern exposures are always occupied by spruces, firs and hemlocks" [*Na-khi*, I, 270].

3. **Talleyrand**: [70:15, 20; 86:10; 95:13]. The change in Pound's attitude toward both Napoleon and his minister in the later cantos has been called by several scholars their rehabilitation.

4. **Chalais, Aubeterre**: These towns "Near Perigord" were part of the stronghold of the Talleyrand family since the early Middle Ages [DD, *Pai*, 1-1, 61].

5. **snow-flakes . . . rain**: "The wind was biting, and during the three months of autumn the mists and the rains obscured the view. Snowflakes were as large as the palm of the hand. It rained from morning to night" [*Na-khi*, II, 281].

6. **Trees . . . willows**: "The trees along the bank are mostly willows, while several species of oaks grow on the lower half of the mountain slopes" [*Na-khi*, II 298-299].

7. **Kublai . . . hither**: These lines concern a pagoda believed to have been built by Kublai Khan, on which an inscription written in Tibetan says, "Erected in the fire-female-sheep year, in the beginning of the year, in the third moon, on the 14th day, on a full

moon, on a Thursday." About this date, Rock [110:54] says: "the date given . . . can only be April 26, 1307, or the eleventh year of the period of Ta-te . . . of the Mongol Emperor Ch'eng Tsung . . . (Timur or Olcheitu). It could not have been the year 1247" [*Na-khi*, II, 298n.]. Pound prefers the earlier date.

8. **Forest . . . dawn . . .** : Perhaps Kublai's men coming from the forest, through mountain ice, back down to the emerald grass at dawn [CFT, *Pai*, 3-1 107].

9. **Ideogram**: [M6037], "dawn."

10. **larix . . . armandi**: Of a place called A-tun-tzu, Rock says: "The vegetation here is composed mostly of junipers, Larix, *Caragana jubata* . . . and Berberis. . . . A few li beyond we reach the hamlet of I-chia-p'o . . . two stages from A-tun-tzu, a distance of about 105 li [1 li - a bit less than 1/3 mile] . . . . Here the oak forest gives way to pines, *Pinus yunnanensis* and *Pinus Armandi*" [*Na-khi*, II, 344-345].

11. **Thiers**: Adolphe T., 1797-1877, French statesman, journalist, legal adviser, and historian. He was a moderate liberal whose work in the journal *National* helped bring about the July Revolution of 1830 [104: passim]. During a long life, he seems to have been involved in all the major events of the century, in a way that led once to his arrest and exile. If Napoleon III had listened to him, history would have been different, as in the Franco-Prussian War of 1870, which he strongly opposed.

12. **Simon**: Jules S., 1814-1896, French statesman and philosopher and author of *Le Gouvernement de M. Thiers* (2 vols.), Paris, 1878. He taught at the Sorbonne (1839-1852) but lost that job because he refused to swear allegiance to Louis Napoleon. From 1863 to 1875 he served as deputy and then was made a senator for life. A much more liberal man than Thiers, his admission of something proposed by Thiers, for example in monetary reform of taxation, would be an endorsement of its good sense.

13. **4 letters . . . horses**: The Mongol and Ming emperors, throughout "Eight Generations of Na-khi Chiefs," held ceremonies investing the chiefs with imperial power to govern. Documents and gifts, such as letters and seals, gold belts, and horses, were exchanged. [CFT, *Pai*, 3-1, 103].

14. **Mr. Kennan**: George K., 1845-1924, American authority on Siberia, who from 1864 on was the romantic image of an explorer and—through such books as *Tent Life in Siberia* (1870) and *Siberia and the Exile System* (1891)—an inspiration to the young.

15. **40 years . . .** : Prob. reference to Kennan's life of travel.

16. **(Del Pelo Pardi**: Guilio Del Pelo Pardi, Italian anthropologist and agricultural engineer; author of *Agricoltura e civilta* [Agriculture and civilization], 1923, and *Per la pace del mondo* [On the peace of the world], 1924. Pardi, who worked with Pound's son-in-law, Boris de Rachewiltz, discovered some ancient canals near Rome which he called "a perfectly engineered irrigation system" and said they "were far too old by many thousands of years to fit in with established chronology" [NS, *Reading*, III].

17. **cunicoli**: I, "subterranean passages."

18. **Peabody**: Prob. a patient at St. Elizabeths who was fond of saying, "to unscrew the inscrutable." The Peabody Coke and Coal Co. is now called the Peabody Holding Co., Inc. (301 N. Memorial Dr., St. Louis M. 63102]. The president of the company writes that a search has not revealed anybody in the records by the name of Warren G.

19. **"infini" . . . humaine"**: F, "endless . . . [is] human stupidity."

20. **Renan**: Ernest R., 1823-92, French historian and critic. Author of the 8-vol. *Histoire des origines christianisme*, of which the shocking *Vie de Jesus* was the first volume.

21. **one dollar's worth . . .** : The sentence starts with Peabody and ends with this illustration of inscrutable stupidity [98/688].

22. Talleyrand . . . : According to Mme. Rémusat, Talleyrand spent some hours reworking the hastily penned details Napoleon had written regarding the peace he had agreed to with the emperors Alexander (Russia) and Francis (Austria) after the battle of Austerlitz in 1805 [*Memoirs*, 304-305].

23. "90 francs . . . note": "Money had become still more scarce; in fact, it attained such a price that . . . I had to pay ninety francs merely for obtaining gold for a thousand-franc bank-note" [*Memoirs*, 321].

24. Cambacérès: Jean Jacques Regis de C., 1753-1824, French revolutionary who rose to be archchancellor of the empire. He helped formulate the Napoleonic Code and the constitutional relationship of Italy to the empire. He was made duke of Parma in 1808. Mme. de Rémusat mentions him several times as a vain and pompous man who returned flattery with favors [*Memoirs*, 321-322].

25. A constitution: "That portion of Italy [area of Genoa] was at once divided into new departments, and shortly afterwards [June 4, 1805] the new constitution was sent to the Italian Legislature and Prince Eugene was made Viceroy of the kingdom" (*Memoirs*, 264].

26. Xmas . . . maximum: The peace treaty after Austerlitz seems to Pound the height of N's power: "M. de Talleyrand returned to the Court after signing the treaty, and once more peace seemed restored to Europe—at any rate, for a time. Peace was signed on Christmas Day, 1805" [*Memoirs*, 320].

27. Marbois . . . Gaudin: "As soon as it became possible for him [Napoleon] to divert his attention . . . from foreign affairs, he devoted it to . . . finances. . . . M. Barbe-Marbois, Minister of the Treasury, having incurred his displeasure, was replaced by M. Mollien, who was a skillful financier. The Emperor was ably seconded by his Minister of Finance, Gaudin, whose perfect integrity and sound knowledge sustained credit and improved the system of taxation" [*Memoirs*, 345].

28. Mt Cenis, Simplon: "Roads over Mont Cenis and the Simplon were actively pushed on; bridges were built, roadways repaired" [ibid.].

29. Mme. Rémusat: "Madame de Rémusat writes on the 12th of December, 1806: 'We ought to be very cautious in our correspondence. . . . Peace! People scarce hope for it here. Depression and discontent prevail. . . . This feeling is, no doubt, unjust; for, after all, there are cases in which even men of the strongest mind are carried along by circumstances farther than they wish, and I can not believe that a great mind will seek for glory in war' " [*Memoirs*, 455n.].

30. Jena: "In the name of the Emperor. The University of Jena, its professors . . . its possessions . . . are placed under the special protection of the commanders of the French and allied troops. The course of study will be continued" [*Memoirs*, 481].

31. "Liberty . . . : Mme. R. says Napoleon used to say: "Liberty is needed by a small and privileged class, who are gifted by nature with abilities greater than those of the bulk of mankind. It can therefore be restricted with impunity" [*Memoirs*, 506].

32. Hottenguer: [89:181].

33. Neuflize: The Haute Banque Parisienne was a group of private banks which had connections with the Rothschild brothers. Among these groups were Mallet Frères and Henrotte & Muller, all with powerful resources. A subgroup called the Haute Banque Protestante was formed after 1800. This group included "*Hottinguer & Cie* . . . together with *de Neuflize & Cie*" [Emden, *Powers*, 394-395]. This group of private bankers undid the work of such people as Marbois and Mollien [cf. 27 above] and became their Nessus.

34. Nessus: [87:58]. The shirt-of-fire caused by the blood of Nessus became so painful to Hercules that he caused his mortal body to be consumed by the flames of a funeral pyre.

35. **Rémusat**: Source of remark unknown.

36. **Gaudin**: "Indirect taxes were ventured on to a greater extent than before; luxury, which would render these taxes more productive, was encouraged; and the heavy contributions which the Emperor had everywhere levied upon his conquered enemies afforded him the means, without burdening his people, of keeping up the strength of his army" [*Memoirs*, 345]. "M. Gaudin, the wise Minister of Finance, observed an order and regularity in the management of taxes and receipts which rendered him valuable to the Emperor" [ibid., 520].

37. **Kang Hi**: [98:111, 112].

38. **Mme d'Houdetot**: No one could possess more—I will not say goodness, but more kindness than Mme. d'Houdetot. Goodness implies the choice of good as against evil; it perceives the evil and forgives it. Mme. d'Houdetot never perceived evil in any one" [*Memoirs*, 681-682].

39. **Yeats**: Musical figure on a scene mentioned earlier and later [113/789; *Pai*, 1-1, 53].

40. **Tsung-Kuan . . .** : A native chief whom Rock [110:54] knew personally and remembered fondly. "The hospitality of Yung-ning chiefs, especially of the late Tsung-kuan . . . was unsurpassed. . . . It was a great loss . . . to all the poor and troubled chiefs, his neighbors . . . when he passed away . . . July 20th, 1933" [*Pai*, 3-1, 107-108; *Na-khi*, II, 418].

41. **Bears . . . fields**: "No hunting is permitted, and here roam many bears who live on the oaks, and often come to the fields of the villages and eat their broad beans and peas" [*Na-khi*, II, 418].

42. **Elzéard Bouffier**: A French farmer who during three years planted 100,000 trees in a wilderness, thereby creating a forest. Having lost his only son and his wife, he withdrew to a place he thought was dying for want of trees. So, "having no pressing business of his own, he . . . resolved to remedy this state of affairs" [Jean Giono, *Vogue*, 15 March, 1954, p. 157; MB, *Trace*, 401].

43. **Vergons**: A small Alpine village between Castellane and Annot on the Iscle River. The mountain-gorge atmosphere is a rhyme with Lion Mountain of the Na-khi [cf. 45 below].

44. **Kuanon's eye**: [90/606]. "On the top of this hill is a temple with a huge figure of Chenrezig with the thousand arms and eyes (Kuan-yin . . . of the Chinese). . . . The trail leads along . . . the edge of the larger basin up the pine and oak covered spur" [*Na-khi*, II, 412].

45. **Sengper ga-mu**: "One of the most conspicuous landmarks which confront the lake on the north, is the southern face of Shih-tzu Shan (Lion Mountain; Seng-ge ga-mu). . . . This mountain is mirrored in the lake, its broad face representing the lion's head . . . while its body extends to the north" [*Na-khi*, II, 418; several key plates from Rock are reproduced in *Pai*, 3-1, 110-116].

46. **To him we burn . . .** : "Immediately back of the main building is a shrine dedicated to the mountain goddess Seng-ge ga-mu . . . an incense burner in front of the shrine belches forth white smoke in the morning and evening, when pine branches are burnt as offering to the mountain goddess" [*Na-khi*, II, 426].

47. **The hills . . .** : "Junipers grow on all the lofty peaks of the district of Yen-yuan, giving the latter a blue-green tint. The dragon-like rivers flow zigzag over its land" [*Na-khi*, II, 444].

48. **Achilöos**: The longest Greek river, which flows through a similar mountainous landscape. In Pound's translation of *Trachiniae* (1954), Deianeira speaks of the wooer Akheloos as the river, rather than the river-god, which winds in serpentine fashion [Peck, *Agenda*, 49].

49. **one man . . .** : "It [a mountain trail] passes over the lofty peaks, covered with

fragrant junipers, can safely be guarded by one man" [*Na-khi*, II, 444].

50. Mt. Ségur: [87:101]. The stronghold of the Albigensians [23:28] had a similar narrow pass which they held against Simon de Montfort [23:26] in his crusade against them.

51. TSO: [M6784], "rope made from bamboo-splints." "The reason why so many places were called Tso (Bamboo rope) was because the aborigines used rope bridges to cross the large rivers" [*Na-khi*, II, 446].

52. land tax: "The territory pays an annual land-tax of 70 *Shih* . . . of buckwheat" [*Na-khi*, II, 454].

53. Tolosa: [80:186]. Rhyme with unadulterated food theme [45:5; 74/428; 80/493].

54. Gubbio: A town in Umbria, central Italy.

55. L'il Josephine: Prob. a local radio personality.

56. Wilson (McN.): R. McNair W., one of Pound's favorite writers on money and banking; author of *Promise To Pay: An Inquiry into the Principles and Practice of the Latter-Day Magic Called Sometime High Finance*, London, 1934.

57. KALON KAGATHON: H, "Noble and brave." Homeric epithet.

58. Marengo: A village in NW Italy which was the scene of a famous battle between Napoleon and the Austrians. Mme. R. says: "He [Napoleon] held a grand review on the battlefield of Marengo, and distributed crosses on that occasion." [*Memoirs*, 260]. They were prob. given to "noble and brave" soldiers.

59. This aura . . . crimson: Formulaic lines from alchemy found in many places: "Fire is the soul of the Great All. . . . Light-gold . . . fire in its concrete state . . . *Flamma!* Yes, fire that is all. The diamond exists already in the charcoal, gold in fire" [Read, *Alchemy* p. 90].

60. Apollonius: [94:42].

61. Porphery: A.D. 232/3-ca.305. Scholar and philosopher who eventually became a devoted follower of Plotinus. He wrote a life of Plotinus and edited his *Enneads*.

62. Anselm: [105:16].

63. Plotinus: [98/685, 690; 99/700].

64. EN . . . EXEI: H. By transliterating the 'ON into the genitive plural we have: "In the contemplation of which things the mind is engaged." In *The Enneads* II, 3, "On whether the stars are causes," Plotinus took a singleminded view of the function of the stars. His theory differed from the theories of astrologists of his time, which he considered well-meaning but a tangle of "basic absurdities": hence, the "unicorns" and "antelopes" [*Enneads* II (Loeb 441), 57-101].

65. HS'UAN TSUNG: Hsuan-tsung, 1398-1435, emperor (1425-1435) during the early years of the Ming dynasty, noted as a humanitarian as well as a promoter of the arts. "His own paintings represent . . . mostly domestic animals such as cats and dogs, but also goats and monkeys. The models are very closely observed and sometimes characterized with a touch of humour" [Sirén, 113].

66. natus: L, "born." The canto date is an error.

67. Joey: The young brother of Sheri Martinelli [90:25]. Said Pound: "Joey is La Martinelli's kid brother who was taken down to look at the paintings in the Mellon Gallery and asked, 'Are they for real?' and she couldn't make out what he was driving at' [Bridson Interview, *N.D.* 17, 176].

68. H.J.: Henry James.

69. With the sun . . . coat: Joseph Rock has a picture of Na-khi women in ceremonial costumes with images of the sun, moon, and stars sewn on the back [*Pai*, 3-1, 114].

70. Li Chiang . . . : A city enclosed on 3 sides by the Yangtze River loop. Plate 77 in Rock has a commentary which says in part, "View across the upper end of the Li Chiang plains." The snow range stands out starkly in the distance, as does the meadow in the foreground [ibid., 115].

71. **^{2}dto - ^{1}mba's face . . .** : A Na-khi priest pictured in one of the plates.

72. **muy simpático**: S, "very sympathetic."

73. **Stone Drum . . .** : The town of Shih-ku ("Stone Drum"), named "from a large stone drum on the slopes to the north" [*Na-khi*, II, 279]. The waters refer to the Yangtze, which flows by it.

74. **the two aces**: The leaders of two tribes who fought for the area: the leader of the T'u-fan, who was defeated, and the leader of the Na-khi [Peck, *Agenda*, 73].

75. **Mint . . . bracken**: The third inscription on the Stone Drum says in part: "The chiefs leading a million brave soldiers, their majestic air like that of a tiger and of a plumed bird bent on exterminating, they struck and roared like thunder" [*Pai*, 3-1, 118].

76. **Rossoni**: Edmondo R. (b.1884), minister of agriculture and forests in Mussolini government; editor of *La Stirpe* [The race] and author of such books as *The Political and Moral Aspects of New Corporate Economy in Italy*. Said Pound: "Of living men, Edmondo Rossoni, with his agricultural experts and his care for crops, is nearest the Confucian model" [*GK*, 274].

77. **"così lo stato . . . "**: I, "thus the state. . . ." Pound gives the intent of Rossoni's whole statement as, "that's where the state gets its cut." When he first heard about Gesell's stamp script, this was R.'s response [Bridson Interview, *N.D.* 17, 175].

78. **Delcroix**: [88:46].

79. **"che magnifica!"**: I, "how magificent!" Said Pound: "And another thing . . . I mean Delcroix, who was the head of the Italian Veterans . . . he beat his head with his little wooden artificial arms and said *'che magnifica idea'*—What a magnificent idea" [ibid., 176].

80. **(prescrittibile)**: I, "prescriptible." Used with *moneta* it means "stamp script" of the Gesell variety.

81. **"May their pond be full**: "We perform ch'er k'o [a medicinal rite] on the family; may heaven give it many sons and daughters, may their pond be full and may they only hear good tidings" [Rock, "D'a ^{3}Nv," 21].

82. **The son . . . hearing**: "[The ms has phrases] expressing the hope that there may be among descendants such ^{1}D'a (=courageous) sons: [the ceremony] is performed on his good hearing, keen sight, on his right arm, on his left arm . . ." [ibid.].

83. **noun graph . . . peace."**: A "very rare ms. entitled . . . The funeral of a rich warrior" has 3 Na-khi pictographs in a rectangular frame, which translate "rich-warrior funeral." The center one is an image of a man standing. The first one, meaning "rich," suggests two rows of teeth in a square mouth and appears to be sideways. The third looks like the mane of a horse as if seen from above [ibid.].

84. **"His horses . . . peace."**: In another Rock work entitled *The ^{2}Zhi ^{3}mä Funeral Ceremony*, we read: "You are on the way to the realm of the gods, your body and soul are at peace and the mane of your horse is beautiful" [p. 197].

CANTO CII

Sources

Homer, *Od.* I, II, III, IV, V, X; Ovid, *Meta.* IV; EP, *CON*; Sir Barry Domvile, *From Admiral to Cabin Boy*, London, 1947; Apollodorus, *The Library*, III (Loeb); Ammianus Marcellinus, *History*, II [*Mar.*].

Exegeses

EP, *ABCR*, 187; *SP*, 328; Peck, *Pai*, 1-1; MB, *Trace*, 408; NS, *Reading*, 111; JW, *Pai*, 3-2, 289; Peck, *Agenda*, vol. 9, 2-3, 1971.

Glossary

1. **Kalupso**: Calypso [20:67]. Hermes told her that Zeus said she should let Odysseus go [*Od.* V, 97 ff.].

2. **Hermes**: [12:8]. Here the messenger of Zeus.

3. **Dwight L. Morrow**: [86:105].

4. **the body elected . . .** : Unlike members of the English Parliament, U.S. senators must have a legal residence in the state they run in.

5. **Pallas**: P. Athena, disguised as the old woman Mentes, lied to Telemachus, saying that she had a ship whose cargo was iron [*Od.* I, 184].

6. **Penelope**: Around 1950 Pound wanted friends not to send clichéd Christmas cards but a question that would send people back to the classics, such as, "Why did Penelope wait for the return of Odysseus?" The answer is in *Od.* IV, 693 (not 639): *κεῖνος . . . ἐώργει*, which should tranliterate to, "keinos . . . eorgei." The whole line means, "Never at any time did that man do anyone harm" [HK, *Pai*, 4-1, 187].

7. **Leucothoe**: The daughter of King Orchamus of Babylon. She resisted the passion of Apollo, who turned her into "a sweet delightful tree of frankincense" [*Meta.* IV, 203-310]. Not to be confused with Leucothea [cf. 8 below].

8. **sea-gull**: Pound's name for the bird which Ino, the daughter of Cadmus, was changed into; she was thence called Leucothea. With the help of the veil ("bikini") she gave Odysseus, he reached the shores of the Phaeacians.

9. **Ideogram**: Pu [M5379], "not; a negative." Because his old artist friends did not see that ignorance of money and how it should be issued prevented the creation of a society in which the arts could flourish, they "had no ground to stand on" [98:33].

10. **Black shawls . . .** : [98:14, 15].

11. **OIOS . . . TE**: H, "so as to finish the job . . . and love." The original line [*Od.* II, 272] has *ἔπος*, "word," rather than EROS, "love." Thus Loeb has: "such a man was he to fulfill both deed and word."

12. *μάω*: A Greek root used here only for sound [98:37].

13. **Barley . . .** : Athena tells Telemachus to "make ready stores, and bestow all in vessels—wine in jars, and barley meal, the marrow of men, in stout skins" [*Od.* II, 289-291]. Also a rhyme with the Eleusinian grain-rites, and perhaps with Pound's early visits to Venice when gondolas "cost too much" and "he had to live upon barley soup" [MB, *Trace*, 408]. The strength-of-men-is-in-grain motif [106:4].

14. orzo: I, "barley." An *orzo* is an order of barley soup, which costs "40 centess'," or 40 centesimi, or 40% of one lira.

15. Procope: Restaurant at 13 rue de l'Ancienne Comédie on the Left Bank in Paris. It was founded in the 17th century by an Italian and patronized by writers, from Voltaire to Pound, because it served excellent food cheaply [JW].

16. Noi . . . borghesi: I, "we other common people."

17. We thought . . . : [98/686] : ". . . control Mussolini."

18. ye sail over . . . : The lines evoke the words of Tiresias and "the dark eyelids" of Aphrodite in Canto I.

19. Winkelmann: The French edition, *Histoire de l'art chez les anciens* (Paris, 1802), of the classic work by Johann Joachim Winckelmann: *Geschichte der Kunst des Altertums,* 1764. He said that the shape, heaviness, and arch of the eyelid in Venus are crucial to her beauty [Peck, *Pai*, 1-1, 26].

20. Ronsard: [80/505].

21. "jacques Père": Pun on Shakespeare. The Belgians would pronounce the *J* soft, as an *I* [*ABCR*, 187].

22. Le Portel: The Swinburne connection [82/523].

23. Freiheit: G, "Freedom." Eva Hesse: longtime friend and correspondent of Pound and official translator of *The Cantos* and other Pound works into German. His line [74/426], "that free speech without free radio speech is as zero," she translated: "dass Redefreiheit ohne Radiofreiheit gleich null ist."

24. The Changes: The *I Ching*. Confucius said: "If many years were added to me, I would give fifty to the study of The Book of Changes, and might therefore manage to avoid great mistakes" [*CON*, p. 221].

25. Swan: Unidentified, but clearly a man who showed heroism and unperturbability under pressure in the manner of Bud Cowart below.

26. another chap . . . : [95:62]. Bud Cowart, who got caught in the *Akron's* mooring ropes but held on while seeing two others fall to their deaths.

27. KatZe: G, "cat." Pound said of Frobenius, "He saw nothing ridiculous in a child's wanting to know if the last letter of the word *Katz* stood for the cat's tail, and the first one for its head. But to the school teacher . . . the child just seemed stupid" [*SP*, 328].

28. Dummheit: G, "stupidity."

29. (Ingrid): A London woman Pound corresponded with who said "she could not find anything by Sir Barry Domvile in local libraries" [NS, *Reading*, 111]. Pound believed this was deliberate suppression. According to Stock, "Pound was thinking specifically of Domvile's autobiography, *From Admiral to Cabin Boy*, a comparatively mild piece of anti-semitism published in 1947." It is the suppression of anti-Semitic data which Stock thinks explains "as was natural" [a poem by Domvile is in *PD*, 236-237].

30. "pseudos . . . pepneumenos": H, [98:45], "he won't lie . . . is much too clever" [*Od.* III, 20]. The intimation is that Domvile has been silenced because he was, like Nestor, "too intelligent to prevaricate" [99/697].

31. seed . . . (Lacedaemon): The Spartans (of Lacedaemonia) sacrificed a horse to Apollo on Mt. Taygetus [97:290]. Eurycleia, the nurse, lulled Penelope to sleep: "She then . . . went up to her upper chamber with her handmaids, and placing barley grains in a basket prayed to Athene" [*Od.* IV, 758-761].

32. Leucothoe: [Cf. 7, 8 above]. The divine intelligence that makes the cherrystone into a cherrytree is what makes the metamorphosed girl rise "as an incense bush."

33. "for my bitch eyes": Helen of Troy said to Menelaus, "when for the sake of shameless me ye Achaeans came . . ." [*Od.* IV, 144-145]. κυνώπης literally means "dog-eyed"–says Lidell-Scott, "i.e. shameless one." Lidell-Scott gives for the feminine, "the shameless woman," but adds: "also fierce-eyed, terrible." Pound prefers the latter and works the half-goddess into the fearful-eyes theme started with Aphrodite in Canto 1 and recurring in *Rock-Drill* and *Thrones* [81:54; 91:4].

34. **Atalant**: Says Apollodorus: "This Atalanta was exposed by her father, because he desired male children; and a she-bear came often and gave her suck. . . ." Thereafter, she "kept herself a virgin and became protected by Diana" [*The Library*, III, 9.2; Loeb, I, 399].

35. **aithiops . . . oinops**: H, "wine . . . dark-bright" [97:159]; Homeric variant of "wine-dark sea" [*Il.* I, 462; Peck, *Pai*, 1-1, 24; MB, *Trace*, 412].

36. **haliporphuros**: H, "sea purple." But Pound prefers the colors he lists.

37. **oriXalko**: H, "watery-copper."

38. **le xaladines**: [97:163]. The sound suggests the Greek καλι ("beautiful") and/or the sound of *copper* (above), in addition to Shakespeare's "multitudinous seas incarnadine" [*Macbeth*, II, 1].

39. **the nature, the sign**: [90:2].

40. **Small lions**: Animal statues atop tall columns of St. Mark's Cathedral in Venice [97:165].

41. **AISSOUSIN**: H, "flitting about" [97:169]. Odysseus tells of his visit to Tiresias and says: "To him even in death Persephone has granted reason, that he alone should have understanding; but the others flit about as shadows" [*Od.* X, 494-495].

42. **Berenice**: [97:170].

43. **"Same books" . . . brotherlike**: [88:67].

44. **south slope . . .** : [101:2; 110:20].

45. **Wild goose . . . coral**: Details of Na-khi landscape [Peck, *Agenda*, 9, p. 51].

46. **dead words . . .** : Applies to all the Na-khi religious ceremonies, and by extension, to many others.

47. **KAI ALOGA**: H, "and unspoken."

48. **APHANASTON**: H, "secret, inscrutable, or unknown" [cf. DG, *Pai*, 3-3, 420-421].

49. **the pine needles . . .** : A recurrent leitmotif in the Na-khi materials. Rock [110:54] mentions pine needles and cones burned in religious ceremonies a number of times. Both the red glow and the billowing smoke have significance. Pound believes such ceremonies performed by the Na-khi derive from the same spiritual essence as do similar ceremonies performed by various occult and alchemical sects in the West [91:2-5]. Both groups aspire to burst out of the universe. Recall the third subject-response of *The Cantos*, which Pound explained to his father: "The 'magic moment' or moment of metamorphosis, bust through from quotidien into 'divine or permanent world.' Gods, etc." [*L*, 210]. Note, too, the way images used early in the poem are repeated as we near the end: "There is a wine-red glow in the shallows" [2/7].

50. **OU THELEI . . . KOSMOU**: H. Pound's translation in the next line: "they want. . . ." But Pound neglects the negative, "OU." Peter Lori gives: "does not want to come into the world" [*Pai*, 3-2, 289]. For the phrase in Greek except for EAEAN, see 105/750.

51. **amnis . . . ripas**: L, "river-grass-banks" [JW, *Pai*, 3-2, 289].

52. **Antoninus**: [42:4; 78:56].

53. **Julian**: J. the Apostate, 331?-363, Roman emperor (361-363). He succeeded Constantius III, who had made him caesar with command of the Western Empire. But his success in Gaul as an idol of his troops and his reforms of the fiscal system in Rome, which allowed him to reduce the tax from

25 to 7 *solidi* per *caput*, made Constantius fearful of him as a rival. Constantius ordered him to bring his army east. Julian tried, but his troops refused and named him augustus. Then he marched east, but before the confrontation Constantius died of a fever [cf. 57 below].

54. **Marcellinus**: Ammianus M., ca. 300-ca. 400, Latin historian who was a great admirer of Julian. His 31-book history of Rome, in the manner of Tacitus, covered A.D. 96 to 378, but only books XIV-XXXI survive. Bk. XXIII, chap. 6, has this heading: "A description of the eighteen greater provinces of the Persian kingdom, with the cities of each and the customs of their inhabitants" [*Mar.*, II, 349]. This chapter does not contain the quotations about the many dead, but similar lines are found throughout the 3 vols. in the many battle scenes.

55. **Assyrios . . .** : L, "he passed the frontiers of Assyria" [*Mar.* XXIV, 1, Vol. II, p. 399]. Julian had sent a reserve army into Assyria, but on the way there himself in 363 was attacked by Persians and mortally wounded.

56. **sueta annona**: L, "usual high price."

57. **Quem . . . eripuit**: L, "whom a slight fever took from me." Refers to the death of Constantius.

58. **Domitian**: [91:91]. The increased intensity of his reign of terror resulted in his assassination.

59. **infaustus**: L, "unfortunate."

CANTO CIII

Sources

William Elliot Griffis, *Millard Fillmore*, Andrus and Church, Ithaca, N.Y., 1915 [*Fillmore*]; Roy Franklin Nichols, *Franklin Pierce*, Univ. of Penn., Philadelphia, 1931, rpt. 1958 [*Pierce*]; *Memoirs of the Prince de Talleyrand*, ed. duc de Broglie, trans. Raphael de Beaufort, 5 vols., G. P. Putnam, N.Y., 1891 [*Memoirs*, vol., p.]. Dante, *Inf.* XXV, *Pur.* V; Seraphin Couvreur, *Les Annales de la Chine*, Cathasia, Paris; George Ticknor Curtis, *Life of James Buchanan*, 2 vols., N.Y., 1883 [*Buchanan*, vol., p.]; Alexander Del Mar, *History of Monetary Systems*, Chicago, 1896 [*HMS*]; J. P. Migne, *Patrologiae Latina*, vol. 95 [Migne].

Background

David Donald, *Charles Sumner and the Coming of the Civil War*, Knopf, 1960, [*Sumner*]; David Donald, *Charles Sumner and the Rights of Man*, Knopf, 1970; B. L. Reid, *The Man from New York: John Quinn and His Friends*, Oxford Univ. Press, N.Y., 1968; EP, *SP*, 180; CON, 210; MB, *Trace*; Robert J. Rayback, *Millard Fillmore*, Buffalo Hist. Soc., N.Y., 1959 [Rayback, *Fillmore*];

Exegeses

EP, *Pai*, 3-3, 393; *New Directions 17*, 1961 [*ND* 17]; Eustace Mullins, *This Difficult Individual, Ezra Pound*, Fleet Pub. Corp., N.Y., 1961 [*Difficult*]; M de R, *Discretions*; BK & TC Duncan Eaves, *Pai*, 9-3, 428-439.

Glossary

1. **1850**: Upon the death of Zachary Taylor in 1850, Millard Fillmore became president. Because he broke with the branch of his party led by Weed and Seward and associated himself with the prosouthern Whigs, he was not nominated in 1852. The conflict paralyzed the government during his two years in office.

2. **'56, an M. C. . . .** : At a critical moment just before the nominating convention of 1856, Franklin Pierce, who had been a compromise candidate in 1852 because he was more acceptable to the South than any of the strong candidates (Marcy, Douglass, or Buchanan), faced great difficulty in being renominated by the Jacksonian Democrats. Stresses over sectionalism, slavery, and Central America made it nip-and-tuck. Pound's source [*Pierce*, 464] gives a 300-page background to the important moment and then shows, in a chapter entitled "The Calamities of a Month," how scandalous events ruined whatever chances Pierce may have had: "Few months have been more murderous, in peace times, than May 1856. Just as the cycle began [formation of forces for reelection], news came that some Kansans of Lawrence had shot Sheriff Jones, perhaps fatally. On May 8, Herbert, member of Congress from California, killed one of the waiters at the Willard [Headquarters of Pierce's party]. That same day, John P. Heiss, recently back from Nicaragua, assailed Wallach, the editor of the *Star*, for an article on Nicaragua. On the 15th there was a murder at the Navy Yard." As if all this weren't enough, then came Brooks. So did scandal alter the course of the nation.

3. **Brooks . . . others"**: On May 22, 1856, the nephew of Senator Butler, Preston S. Brooks, a congressman from South Carolina, entered the Senate chamber after it had adjourned and attacked Sumner with a cane and injured him severely. Brooks was tried for the offence in the House, but the two-thirds majority needed could not be mustered to oust him. On July 14 he made a speech in the House, during which he said he acted in defense of the rights of the South and of others and resigned. But he was overwhelmingly reelected and became a great hero in the slave states [Donald, *Sumner*, 294 ff.].

4. **"respectful . . . others"**: After the inauguration of Lincoln, Pierce continued to preach conciliation and the avoidance of war. Says Nichols: "On June 1 at an anniversary banquet given in Faneuil Hall . . . he was among the speakers and he lost no time in preaching to New England. We must learn to respect our own rights and the equally sacred rights of others" [*Pierce*, 508]. For expressing such views, he was not reelected.

5. **Homestead**: The Homestead Act, 1862, authorized the government to sell land to settlers in the West for revenue. Pound would approve of the government receiving money this way to be used for public services. Pound wrote to Mullins in 1950: "Del Mar's vast and exact erudition enabled him to correct Mommsen on various points. Mommsen's great merit as a teacher resided in his demonstration that the stability of the Roman Empire, in contrast to the various Mesopotamian despotisms, lay in Rome's planting its veterans in homesteads, as distinct from mere raids of pillage" [EM, *Difficult*, 311]. Land policy of this kind became central to Pound's criticism of Stalinism. In a note to *Strike* [Oct. 1955] he quoted

Mencius to show the Confucian idea of a reasonable balance between public and private lands and ownership: "A square li covers 9 squares of land, which 9 squares contain 900 mau. The central square is the public field, and 8 families, each having its private 100 mau, cultivate in common the public field. And not until the public work is finished, may they presume to attend to their private affairs" [*Pai*, 3-3, 393].

6. **kolschoz**: R, "collective farm" [104:113]. In the same issue of *Strike* [cf. 5 above], Pound went on: "We ask the 'Voice of America' if they are making full use of this idea in the fight against Communism in China. Bolshevism started off as an attack against loan-capital and quickly shifted into an attack against the homestead" [ibid.]. The idea stuck with Pound. In the Bridson interview, July 9, 1959, he said: "Lack of local government is an effect, not a cause. The contest is between the homestead and the *kolchos*. Mommsen noted that the Roman Empire endured longer than Oriental tyrannies because they settled veterans on the land. Civilization is from the homestead. The Russian Revolution was a fake: it pretended to attack capital–the general understanding being that that was loan capital–and it merely attacked landed property down to the peasant's cow" [*ND* 17, p. 179].

7. **Rome . . . Babylon**: In Rome "gold was under the Pontifex" [92:43]. In Babylon, the rulers did not perceive the "power inherent" [quiddity; 91:82] of gold to the state [cf. 5 above].

8. **The slaves . . . issuers**: Pound believed the American Civil War was fought not to free the slaves but to protect New York bankers, who had many great plantations under mortgage [*SP*, 180].

9. **Emerson . . . funeral**: Says Nichols: "On December 2, 1863, Mrs. Pierce died. Hawthorne came to him immediately and together they looked at the shrunken figure in the coffin, which strangely affected the author. . . . In the spring of 1864, death came again; this time to . . . Hawthorne. . . . The funeral was imposing because of those who attended: Emerson, Whittier, Lowell, Longfellow, Agassiz, and Alcott. . . . Pierce was there too" [*Pierce*, 524-525].

10. **Agassiz**: [93:51].

11. **Alcot**: Amos Bronson Alcott, 1799-1888, one of the New England Transcendentalists and once a nonresident member of Brook Farm.

12. **principal bond-holders**: The Spanish royal house was greatly in debt to most of the big banking houses of Europe, all of which had branches in the U.S. The problem of Cuba was one of the most difficult and treacherous of Pierce's administration. The South demanded that Cuba be "freed" from Spain. What really frightened them were rumors that Cuba was on the point of freeing its slaves, an idea which was anathema to all slave-state politicians in the U.S. Propositions to either conquer the island or buy it were in the works for years. The Gadsden Purchase had just passed by a narrow margin. In May 1854 a secret agent returned from Cuba and reported it was all true. Spain was getting ready to free Cuban slaves. An uproar ensued in the Senate. The situation was more complicated because of a movement in Spain itself to overthrow the government. This revolution in the making was being financed by Great Britain. Pierce was prepared to buy the island, but Congress would not pass the funds. Abolitionists in the North would by no means have Cuba entered into the Union as another slave state. At this point came the plan to borrow the purchase price [*Pierce*, 266-267, 329-330, passim].

13. **Belmont**: [40:18]. Says Nichols: "August Belmont had once suggested to Buchanan [now Minister to Great Britain] that the way to acquire Cuba was to use backstairs influence on the Spanish royal family and to call in the aid of the great European banking houses . . . the Barings, the Rothschilds, and other large holders of Spanish bonds who would be interested in having Spain sell

Cuba, because the large sum . . . would insure the payment of the debt." Belmont was appointed to a diplomatic post at The Hague. The negotiations were delicate and secrecy was essential. The abolitionists would consider the whole thing the underhanded deal it was. But Pierce was under the threat of powerful southerners that they'd take the island by force if need be. Says Nichols: "Into the midst of the puzzle came Mr. Sickles" [*Pierce*, 357-358].

14. Sickles: Daniel Edgar S., 1819-1914, early became a lawyer and a democratic politician and, by age 35, an ebullient charmer. At this moment he was the secretary of Buchanan's legation in London and arrived in New York with dispatches for Pierce. Says Nichols: "Pierce and Sickles were kindred spirits. Sickles talked too much in his usual vein. He had a great deal to say about the revolution in Spain" [*Pierce*, 358]. Pierce got him to return to Europe and explore other ways to obtain Cuba. He did, and bounced around Europe, and just before the fall elections of 1854 he talked freely to a group of Congressmen and others in Paris about his plans. The uproar that broke in the press thereafter guaranteed the party's defeat in the elections and the end of any plans to annex Cuba. Says Nichols: "Pierce's last Cuban card was thrown away by his agents" [366].

15. land . . . veterans: Toward the end of a chapter entitled "Salvaging the Program," Nichols lists a number of bills that failed, a few which the 33rd Congress passed: "It had voted 160 acres of land to all veterans, their widows or minors, a blanket grant which Pierce signed in spite of its size; he had a tender spot for old soldiers" [*Pierce*, 379]. The Mommsen reference [97:33] relates the act to the homestead acts [cf. 5, 6 above].

16. Hui: Tze-Kung was asked [*Anal.* Five, VIII]: "Who comprehends most, you or Hui?" He answered: "No comparison, Hui hears one point and relates it to ten . . . ; I hear one point and can only get to the next" [*CON*, 210]. Pound is asking the reader to act like Hui and see how many random things relate in a dramatic way; how states and governments rise and fall, not by the well-considered merits of their causes, but by what ought to be minor matters. It is a central theme of this and many other cantos.

17. cunicoli: [101:16].

18. canalesque: [canalisque]: L, "and conduits."

19. (min): C [M4508], "the people; mankind."

20. caelum renovabat: L, "he restored heaven."

21. manes: [60:43].

22. Protocol . . . : In the duc de Broglie's *Memoirs* there are a number of chapters concerned with efforts to restore the balance of power to Europe after the revolution of 1830. Much of the problem developed around the possibility of obtaining the neutrality of Belgium as a buffer state between France, to the south, and the powerful Netherlands, to the north. In a letter proposing neutrality, he has an introductory sentence: "In sending the protocol of this sitting to Paris on January 29th, I wrote as follows:" What follows is an outline of the problem and the proposal of the neutrality solution [*Memoirs*, IV, 26]. It should be noted that the problem was not solved quickly, nor in perpetuity.

23. (T. C. P.): Thaddeus Coleman Pound [97:205].

24. France . . . Europe: For some time Pound preferred the idea that, after Tallyrand, France started no war in Europe. When the facts dictated otherwise he blanked these two lines, but they were restored in the New Directions edition [MB, *Trace*, 417]. "No" was replaced by "one."

25. Bismarck: [86:3]. B's EMS Dispatch presumably insulted France into starting the Franco-Prussian War in 1870. B believed that was to be the "war to end all wars."

26. Casimir: C. Pierre Périer, 1777-1832,

French statesman from a wealthy family of bankers and financiers who became head of the ministry of Louis Philippe (1831). He opposed the *ancien régime* and supported the constitutional monarchy.

In Broglie we read: "Mr. Périer has just made an incalculable mistake, by the decree which replaces the statue of Buonaparte on the column in the Place Vendôme. The Buonapartist party, led by the Republicans and Monarchists, will gain fresh strength." A footnote reads: "See Casimer Périer's announcement which preceded the king's proclamation, ordering the statue of Napoleon to be replaced (*Journal des Débats*, April 12)." The document is headlined: "Paris, April 12th, 1831" [*Memoirs*, IV, 95].

27. **Mme de Lieven**: Dorothy de Benkendorf, 1784-1857, married the Prince de Lieven (1800) and was appointed lady-in-waiting to the empress of Russia (1828); she developed strong relationships with many powerful men. "Canning, and later on Lord Grey were the most constant attendants of her *salon*" [*Memoirs*, III, 279]. She was thus in a position to side with the Englishmen who were messing up Talleyrand's efforts to convince England to help him create a long-lasting balance of power in Europe. Broglie does not use a phrase such as "that bitch." But he does indicate the situation: "Lord Grey, influenced by Madame de Lieven, sought for pretexts to avoid all intervention of the part of England in a cause that was looked upon as lost" [*Memoirs*, IV, 164].

28. **Mme de Staël**: [100/717]. A similar situation applied.

29. **Bolivar**: Simón Bolívar, 1783-1830, South American revolutionist who was called "the Liberator." As president of Greater Columbia, he organized the government of Peru and created the state named after him, Bolivia. His death just at the wrong moment tended to destabilize South America and European interests there.

30. **Tolosa**: [101:53]. Town in the Basque provinces of N Spain.

31. **Gubbio**: [101:54].

32. **on pouvait manger**: F, "they can eat." Pound believed that the economic actions of Mussolini, following the dictate of all wise rulers to "Feed the people" [101/695], led to this result.

33. **Picabia**: [87:31, 32].

34. **T. to Broglie**: Achille C. L. Victor, duc de Broglie, 1785-1870, premier of France (1835-1836). Talleyrand wrote him a letter dated 9 April 1833 in which he said: "I am a little surprised to hear the public opinion of Vienna; my recollections and my actual knowledge of that place, led me to believe that there was no such thing as public opinion in Vienna; society there has an opinion, but society is one; it is not divided and M. de Metternich is its leading spirit" [*Memoirs*, V, 9].

35. **Metternich**: [50:13, 27]. Clemens Wenzel N. Lothar, Fürst von M., 1773-1859, Austrian statesman and the most compelling force at the Congress of Vienna. As a voice of conservatism he was anathema to liberals for over a hundred years, especially because of his endorsement and promotion of the Holy Alliance proposed by Alexander I of Russia.

36. **Maria Theresa**: 1717-1780, empress consort of Francis I of Bohemia and dowager empress on the accession of her son Joseph II in 1765, after which she carried out a series of agrarian reforms. During her time Vienna became a center of the arts and music. The only application possible is that Metternich, at the Congress of Vienna 35 years after her death, helped destroy her aspirations and the work she had done. She is not mentioned in Broglie.

37. **Maremma**: Italian coastal section of Tuscany famous for swamps, snakes, and malaria [*Inf.* XXV, 19-20]. T. S. Eliot made the place famous with his note to line 293 of *The Waste Land*, which cites "Siena mi fe', disfecemi Maremma" ("Siena made me, the Maremma undid me"), said by La Pia [*Pur.* V, 133].

38. **Hroosia**: Russia. If the phrases are put

into the mouth of Vienna personified, we would have the sequence "Maria made me, Metternich [with the contrivance of Alexander I of Russia] undid me."

39. **"tranne . . . re"**: I, "except in the house of the king."

40. **B. Mussolini**: A trap for M had been laid, which he expected. Says M de R: "Mussolini was prepared for treachery, but not on the King's doorstep" [*Discretions*, 184].

41. **Predappio**: Village of Romany, south of Forli; hometown of Mussolini, who made the remark above to a man from there.

42. **Knole**: Perhaps the family seat in *Knole and the Sackvilles*, by V. Sackville-West. The chronicle, beginning in Elizabethan times, is sad enough.

43. **Warsaw**: In a letter to Talleyrand (Dec. 12, 1830), Madame Adelaide expresses sadness about the situation brought about at the Congress of Vienna which eventually led to another partition of Poland: "how startling is the news of the Revolution at Warsaw. . . . Ah! if Prussia and Austria would only understand their own interests, how splendid it would be for England and ourselves, if we could obtain a fairer and more tolerable state of things for poor unhappy Poland! . . . The Powers are now reaping what the Holy Alliance sowed" [*Memoirs*, III, 321].

44. **de Vaux**: Louis de V., 1766-1841, who founded the *Journal des Debats*, which at first was interested in arts and literature. He lost this journal but edited others and seemed to conform to the tastes of the time. In 1830, however, he vigorously supported the monarchical party [*Memoirs*, IV, 51 ff.].

45. **(the Archbishop)**: This representative of the church is an ironic picture of an authority whose grasp of events in indicated by his belief that such things as sacred relics are significant [cf. 47 below].

46. **St Leu . . . Talleyrand**: These lines involve a detail that, ironically, complicated and delayed the resolution of the balance of power in Europe after the revolution of 1830. Napoleon I had made members of his family kings in various places. His eldest son, Charles, was known as the king of Rome (1811-1814); Napoleon I abdicated in 1814 in favor of Charles, who technically became Napoleon II. He became a sad creature known in literature as "L'Aiglet," and although he never ruled, he and his family had a strong political following all over Europe known as the Bonapartists. But others, including Broglie and T., were now supporting the Monarchist party, which meant maintaining in power the restored Bourbon, Louis XVIII. While king of Rome Napoleon II-to-be married Hortense de Beauharnais. When the family fell she lived as an exile in Switzerland, with her son, Louis Napoleon Bonaparte (1808-1873), who would eventually become Emperor Napoleon III (1852-1870). At a most inopportune moment, Charles, the presumptive heir, was killed fighting the war in the Papal States. That made the second son the heir; and he turned out to be in the last place he should be during delicate negotiations: Paris. In earlier years, when T. had served Napoleon I in a number of official capacities, he had done much for Hortense. During her exile she had taken the title of duchesse de Saint-Leu, a fiefdom that in better times T. had helped attain for her. She called upon him now for help in getting passports for herself and her entourage; but her son, Louis, was ill at an embarrassing moment. T. allowed her to stay in Paris, hoping to be unnoticed, until the health of the young prince improved enough to allow them to travel to London. But they were discovered, and the press had a field day. Broglie says of this contretemps: "Before continuing my dispatches, I must mention a matter of no great importance in itself, but which gave rise to the most absurd comments in certain newspapers" [*Memoirs*, IV, 120]. It seemed as if the public outcry might blow to bits all efforts to reach a resolution to the problem of a balance of power in Europe, and undo T.'s years of work. It didn't. The final irony, however, may be that the young prince's health im-

proved and he lived to undo T.'s work in 1870. (N.B.: Citizen Talleyrand of the 1st Republic, while serving Napoleon I, had helped confer upon Hortense the titles in the lines.)

47. **"a sapphire . . . skeleton**: Charlemagne [89:201], during the centuries after his death, grew into a mythic figure of enormous proportions. His accomplishments both real and imagined were behind the formation of the Holy Roman Empire. He was canonized in 1165 by the Antipope Paschal III. In 1215 his tomb was opened and his remains, including all the sacred relics, were transferred to a splendid shrine, where they were exhibited once every 6 years. His image and accomplishments were in Napoleon I's mind when he made himself emperor in 1804.

48. **Mme de Genlis**: [111:6]. Felicite Ducrest de Saint-Augin, marquise de Sillery, comtesse de Genlis, 1746-1830, married Charles Brulart, a captain in the navy, who was guillotined with the Girondists in 1793. The comtesse became an emigré in 1792 but returned in 1800 to be well received by the consular court. She became famous as the author of a number of novels and books on education. "under the Empire, she wrote every other week in different periodicals, at the request of Napoleon himself" [*Memoirs*, I, 123]. Broglie says much about the comtesse but mentions no paintings. He does say: "M. de Celles had married the daughter of General Vallence, who had married a daughter of Mdme. de Genlis. Mdme de Celles' sister was married to Marshal Gerard, who had been made War Minister after the revolution of July. Mdme. de Genlis' other daughter, the Marquise de Laevestine, married to a Belgian, had left a son, who had distinguished himself as one of the leaders of the Buonapartist party in France. It will be seen what great influence this relationship gave M. de Celles, through Mdme. de Genlis, with the Palais Royale, and through Marshal Gerard with the government. It was by these means that he intrigued and plotted, to secure the re-union of Belgium with France. . . . I have, perhaps, dwelt too long on this very uninteresting person, but this digression was necessary in order to expose the hot-bed of intrigue which impeded the progress of our affairs in England" [*Memoirs*, III, 309]. Pound would not call it a digression. He would call such things luminous details at the heart of the matter. During the decade in which these cantos were written, the same nations of Europe were struggling for position and power, as they always had been, only now the tentacles of intrigue reached into every corner of the world; and the U.S. was in the grip of such public panics as the McCarthy scandals, the Alger Hiss trials, and other cold-war battles. These considerations gave way at times to such things as the vicuna coat seen as a bribe to Eisenhower's chief of staff, Sherman Adams.

49. **Bismarck** . . . : [cf. 25 above]. He is credited with the unification of Germany, an accomplishment that made him believe he could defeat France. He was right at least in the Franco-Prussian War.

50. **Ivar Kreuger**: 1880-1932, a Swedish engineer and financial tycoon who came to the United States and set up construction companies and the firm of Kreuger and Toll. In 1913 he formed a match trust that expanded from steel into forests and mines. After WWI his empire became international and specialized in fraud, which made him a giant of usurocrats. He was discovered and committed suicide. The investigation showed he had bilked his investors of more than $1/2 billion.

51. **Lorrimer's paper**: George Horace Lorimer, 1867-1937, editor of the *Saturday Evening Post*, president of Curtis Publishing Co., and a neighbor of the Pounds at Wyncote. He lived 2 doors away and used to take a shortcut through their backyard. Lorimer would certainly think a crook like Kreuger a titan. Pound said: "Lorimer honestly didn't know that there ever had been a civilization" [*GK*, 89].

52. **Edishu** . . . : Pseudonym based on "Ed-

shu the Troublemaker" in Frobenius. Prob. Joachim von Ribbentrop or the journalist Alfred-Ingemar Berndt, who added a zero to the reported casualties of 5000 to get 50,000 [EH, *Pai*, 1-1, 86-88].

53. **1831** . . . : Says Griffis: "Two great measures, the abolition of imprisonment for debt and that of religious tests for witnesses in the Empire State, are to be credited to Millard Fillmore. The first [was] passed by the assembly, April 2nd, 1831" [*Fillmore*, 5].

54. **John Quinn**: [12:18]. A lawyer of Irish background, 1870-1924, who became a major supporter of artists in the 20th-century revolutions. His first law partner, Bainbridge Colby, was appointed by Wilson to be his new secretary of state in Feb. 1920. The furor in the press prompted Quinn (who hated Wilson and all he stood for) to volunteer his services to represent Colby before the Senate Foreign Relations Committee: "He worked hard for six consecutive days on the matter and apparently turned it into another oneman show, and a successful one. . . . Colby was painlessly instated on March 27" [Reid, *The Man from New York*, 460-461].

55. **Lansing's** . . . : Robert L., 1864-1928, secretary of state, 1915-1920, lost Wilson's favor by calling several meetings of the cabinet during Wilson's illness. Wilson asked for and got his resignation in early Feb. 1920 [ibid.].

56. **1841 Fillimore**: Millard Fillmore, 1800-1874, 13th president of the U.S. (1850-1853). In his struggle for primacy among New York Whigs in the 1830s, he lost the speakership of the House to Henry Clay; but as runner-up, he became chairman of the powerful Ways and Means Committee and thus, in 1841, was able to direct the finances of the nation. In addition to over a decade of squabbles about renewing the charter of the Bank of the United States, new conflicts arose over the use of the millions of dollars of income received from the sale of federal lands. A thirty-year struggle between "Free Soilers" and those who wanted to buy land cheap for speculation, as well as fights over tariffs, reached many climaxes: "In 1841 the industrial forces had reassembled their strength in the Whig party. . . . To lead them into battle . . . they had chosen . . . Millard Fillmore" [Rayback, *Fillmore*, 126].

57. **Wolverine** . . . : Also in 1841, MF took a statesmanlike stand on the "Caroline" affair: "During the Patriot War in Canada . . . a virtual invasion of the soil of the United States took place." On Dec 29, 1837, armed Canadians boarded the American steamer *Caroline*, set it afire, and headed it blazing for Niagara Falls. The British government took responsibility and knighted the instigator. Congress took to incendiary oratory. War seemed to loom. Knowing we had no naval forces on the Great Lakes, Fillmore pleaded for good sense saying, "The best way to avoid a war with Great Britain is to show that we are prepared to meet her." And while other Congressmen "vapored and threatened," he said: "Reasonable preparations for defense are better than gasconading" [*Fillmore*, 17]. "Not content with words, Mr. Fillmore on Feb. 25th, 1841, sought . . . to provide for American duplication of British Naval armaments on the lakes" [ibid., 18]. Eventually the first iron man-of-war, was built, which people expected to see sink at its launching. Named the *Wolverine*, it set forth to engage the British; but the British, daunted by such a unsinkable monster, decided peace would be a better option. Says Griffis: "The issue of the Caroline affair [guided by MF] was creditable to both nations. The treaty . . . created a precedent for the future, when war will be deemed barbarism. It dismantled every fort and dismounted every gun, American and British, along a frontier of three thousand miles" [ibid.].

58. **Telegraph bill**: In the years of struggle to get his invention patented in England and France, Morse came to Congress in 1842 for an appropriation of $30,000 to test his discovery on a forty-mile line between Washington and Baltimore. Sneers and ridicule pre-

vailed in the Congress. Said MF later: "I, however, advocated the bill, and though I could not say that the telegraph would do all its inventor had predicted . . . I thought it was possible, and even probable that it might . . . and $30,000 was not much for the nation to pay on a contingency of this kind, and the bill was passed and became law on the 3rd of March, 1843" [Griffis, *Fillmore*, 26].

59. Griffith: [78/481].

60. ut delectet: [delectat]: L, "for amusement."

61. Mat Quay: Matthew Stanley Q., 1833-1904, lawyer, Civil War veteran, Pa. politician; he became chairman of the Republican National Committee in 1888. As U.S. senator, 1887-1899, he faced serious charges of financial and political corruption, none of which seemed to go so far as the secret reading of Greek.

62. Mr. Beecher . . . Boston: [40:17]. Behind these lines lies the bizarre incident upon which the U.S. approached a state of war with Austria in 1849. Austrian refugees, led by one Louis Kossuth, fled to Turkey because of intolerable oppression. Kossuth mastered English and sent an address to the American people, which created "instant and sympathetic excitement because of its hope for liberty and justice." In 1849 President Taylor sent an envoy "to Austria and Hungary to get the real facts in the case." An Austrian envoy didn't arrive until after Taylor's death, but as soon as Fillmore was inaugurated, the envoy sent an official protest that accused the U.S. of sending a spy to Austria and, among other things, threatened war. Fillmore's answer was, "the Government of the United States is willing to take its chances and abide its destiny." He also said that, if the president's agent of inquiry were treated as a spy, "instant reprisal" would result, "to be waged to the utmost exertion of the Republic military and naval." Fillmore sent a ship to Turkey to rescue the fugitives; but when Kossuth got to the U.S. he turned out to be a flamboyant con man, rather than one "to touch the mind and heart of the thinking man . . . [or] to move the men worth moving." That did not include Henry Ward Beecher, for whom rabble-rousing was a favorite sport. He joined in the movement called "Kossuthism," which some aspirants to fame and power saw as a way to become the next president. Says Griffis: "When he lectured in Plymouth Church in Brooklyn, Mr. Beecher carried some rusty canon balls, alleged to be from Bunker Hill, into the pulpit. Other ministers went wild" [*Fillmore*, 77-84].

63. Nara . . . : First permanant capital of Japan (710-784), Nara is an ancient cultural and religious center with Buddhist temples and Shinto shrines. Says Griffis: "In 1854, the Japanese saw the first formal display of modern industries and inventions, by the seashore of a region which, in Nara days, was in their uncivilized 'far East.' " And, "This was a thousand years after that first exhibition in Japan of Greek, Persian, Hindoo, Korean and Chinese arts at Nara—and in a building erected A.D. 784 and still standing, the oldest wooden edifice in the world—which placed their island country at the head of all schools of art in Asia" [*Fillmore*, 85].

64. Perry: [88:74]. On July 14, 1853 he presented his papers, including a letter from President Millard Fillmore, to the emperor. On March 31, 1854 a treaty was concluded between Japan and the United States.

65. Sow-face: In 1944 (90 years after Perry's treaty) FDR was finishing his war against Japan: he is prob. intended by this epithet.

66. "the colossal . . . : Says Griffis: "Millard Fillmore, the real and executive author of the Japan Expedition of 1852, liberated a great stored-up force in Asia, for the good of the world. He helped to bring before the American people a social and racial problem, that is destined to shake the world. The 'white man' must now descend from his self-exalted throne to consider the claims of the intellectual equality of Asian men of color. . . . It is a common superstition, growing out of the colossal conceit of the average American, that Commodore Perry virtually created the New Japan. The scholar knows that the naval officer simply . . . set the interior machinery going" [ibid., 95].

67. Mr. Griffis: William Elliot Griffis, D.D., L.H.D., a pioneer educator in Japan (1870-1874) and the author of such books as *The Mikado's Empire, Brave Little Holland, China's Story*, etc. He dated the preface to *Millard Fillmore* January 1, 1915.

68. Heaven made . . . rule: Couvreur gives the Latin of the *Chou King*, Pt. III, Chap. II, sec. 2 [*Les Annales de la Chine*, 104], thus: "At coelum procreat acuto auditu acutoque visu (viros) qui regnant." Couvreur's French is: "Aussi le ciel fait naitre des hommes d'une intelligence supérieure et les charge de diriger les autres." In English we have, "Heaven caused men of superior intelligence to be born and charged them with the leadership of others." Pound's sense is the line in the text.

69. cheu i: C, "intelligent men." Couvreur's French transliteration of the Chinese characters for this sentence goes: "Wei t'ien cheng ts'oung ming cheu i." Pound changed the Latin verbal *regnant* to the French noun *regent*, "ruler."

70. Hia caeca . . . agebat: L, "Hia [53:44] acted in a manner blind to reason" (This sentence follows the one given from Couvreur in 68 above.) The cluster says, in effect: Because of Hsia's blindness to reason, Heaven, which wanted hearing and seeing men to rule, caused that dynasty to fall.

71. Chase: Salmon P. C., 1808-1873, longtime seeker of nomination for president. In 1861 he became Lincoln's secretary of the treasury, against the concerted resistance of southern politicians, who saw him, accurately, as an extreme abolitionist.

72. Stanton: Edward M. S., 1814-1869, secretary of war under Lincoln and Johnson (1862-1868). Concerning the losses during the attack on Fort Monroe, he wrote [June 12, 1861]: "the brother of General Butler has arrived . . . and reports the whole loss of our troops at fourteen killed and forty-four wounded. This is so greatly below the former reports, which set down our loss at over one thousand, that it affords great relief" [*Buchanan*, II, 554].

73. Buchanan: [34:84]. Three months earlier Buchanan had turned over the presidency to Lincoln.

74. Miss Lane: Harriet Lane was Buchanan's niece. He eventually made her an ornament of his household and of Washington society. Says Curtis: "To direct the education of this young girl, to form her religious and moral principles, to guard her against the temptations that beset an impulsive temperament, and to develop her into the character of a true woman, became one of the chief objects of Mr. Buchanan's busy life" [*Buchanan*, I, 532]. Many letters ended as does the letter of Stanton: "I beg you to present my compliments to Miss Lane"; another formula to end letters was "I hope Miss Lane is well," and sometimes Buchanan would end his letters thus: "P.S. Miss Lane desires to be kindly remembered" [ibid., 557].

75. Biddle for conscription: Nicholas B. [34:70; 37:43-54]. Buchanan described his own entrance into public life in 1814 as a member of the House of Representatives in the state legislature of Pennsylvania. Then he had to face the fight over a conscription bill because an attack upon Philadelphia seemed likely. One plan, "reported in the [State] Senate by Mr. Nicholas Biddle," proposed a sort of lottery system. Because, as he said, "this law is calculated to be very unjust and very unequal in its effects," Buchanan was against it [*Buchanan*, I, 8-9].

76. A.J. to Buchanan: In 1824 B. was a member of the House of Representatives when the Adams-Jackson election was thrown to it and Adams won [88:91-92]. But the election was followed by charges of deals and corruption on all sides. Afterwards, a friendly correspondence took place between B. and the general. One letter, dated the "Hermitage, April 8, 1826," says, concerning the complicated problem of the U.S. becoming involved in any Panama Treaty: "Let the primary interests of Europe be what they may, or let our situation vary as far as you please from that which we occupied when the immortal Washington retired from the councils of his country, I cannot see, for my part, how it follows that the primary interests of the United States will be safer in the hands of others than her own; or, in other words, that it can ever become necessary to form treaties, alliances, or any connections with the governments of South America, which may infringe upon the principles of equality among nations which is the basis of their independence, as well as all their international rights" [*Buchanan*, I, 47]. A vital principle that guided Jackson while he was president.

77. **Foreign . . . '32**: While minister to Russia, B. wrote: "I have not yet learned to submit patiently to the drudgery of etiquette. It is the most formal court in Europe and one must conform to its rules. Foreign ministers must drive a carriage and four with a postilion, and have a servant behind decked out in a more queer dress than our militia generals. This servant is called a 'chasseur' and has in his chapeau a plume of feathers. To this plume, as it passes, the detachment of soldiers present arms, and individual soldiers take off their hats. How absurd all this appears to a republican!" [*Buchanan*, I, 147].

78. **"I cannot** . . . : In a letter from St. Petersburg dated October 31, 1832, B. wrote: "I fear I cannot with truth defend the chastity of the Empress Catherine [the Great]. She was a disciple of the school of the French philosophers, and was therefore wholly destitute of religion—the surest safeguard of female virtue" [*Buchanan*, I, 154].

79. **Emperor** . . . : To the secretary of state, B. wrote, August 7, 1833: "On Monday last . . . I had my audience of leave of the emperor [Nicholas I]. . . . The conduct and conversation of his majesty throughout the interview were highly gratifying to myself." There follows a long account of what was said, in the middle of which we read: "The emperor afterwards observed that the English nation had, in his opinion, been acting very unwisely. They had got tired of a constitution under which they had risen to a high degree of greatness, and which had secured them many blessings, and he feared they were now about to prostrate their most valuable institutions" [*Buchanan*, I, 214]. The talk was about the Reform Bill of 1832.

80. **The French** . . . : In the same letter, B. said he would return to the U.S. via Paris: "I said I had no particular desire to visit Paris . . . but it would be considered strange for an American to return from Europe without. . . . He said I was quite right in my intention to visit Paris. The French were a singular people. They were so fickle in their character, and had such a restless desire to disturb the peace of the world that they were always dangerous" [ibid.].

81. **Napoleon's taxes** . . . : On his way home B. stopped at various places in Prussia where the people yearned for the good old days of Napoleon: "The old maitre d' hotel at Bergheim, who has kept a public house for years . . . told me that the taxes were not half so heavy under Napoleon as they were at present" [ibid., 219].

82. **Buchanan . . . hRooshuns**: B. undertook a series of frustrating negotiations, with ups and downs, to conclude a commercial treaty. On June 22, 1832 he wrote: "I am not without hope of succeeding in the negotiation" [ibid., 164]. On Dec. 20, 1832 he wrote: "I have now the pleasure of transmitting to you a treaty of commerce and navigation, which was signed on Tuedsay last . . . between the United States and Russia" [ibid., 171].

83. **bank system**: In 1838, now a U.S. senator, B. made a lengthy speech on the bank system, in which he referred to an earlier speech he had made: "It is true that at the special session I did endeavor to prove that the present banking system, under its existing regulations, was one of the very worst which the art of man could devise" [ibid.,

438]. B. was speaking in favor of a bill that would prevent the new Bank of the U.S. in Pa. from circulating notes of the old Bank of the United States, which no longer existed.

84. English income tax: In 1844 B. wrote about a proposed new income tax: "The income tax of England has never been resorted to except in cases of extreme necessity. That tax at present . . . imposes seven pence per pound upon the annual rent of land and houses, upon the income from titles." There follows a detailed list. Then: "The income tax has always been odious in England; and it will prove to be so, if carried to anything like the same extent in this country" [ibid., 527].

85. Vic's character: In 1853 (not 1852), as minister for Pierce to Great Britain, B. wrote a letter to his niece, Miss Lane, in which he described his presentation to the queen: "She has not many personal charms, but is gracious and dignified in her manners, and her character is without blemish" [*Buchanan*, II, 100].

86. Daily Telegraph: Problems about Central America, including Panama and the islands of the Caribbean, continued to raise hostile reactions in the British press. In 1856 B. wrote: "The *Times* is a mighty power in the state; and I have adopted means, through the agency of a friend, to prevent that journal from committing itself. . . . The tone of the other journals has not been satisfactory; and the *Daily Telegraph* has been evidently bought over, and become hostile to the United States" [*Buchanan*, II, 119].

87. (his "Inaugural"): In his inaugural address in March 1857, B. devoted much of his text to hopes that the slavery question for new territories seeking to become states had finally been resolved and that, on the question, the passions of the nation could be quieted. The recently adopted Kansas-Nebraska Act provided that the question would be decided by the people of a state itself. B. appealed to all to let the issue be: "Let every Union-loving man, therefore, exert his best influence to suppress this agitation, which since the recent legislation of Congress, is without any legitimate object. It is the evil omen of the times that men have undertaken to calculate the mere material value of the Union" [*Buchanan*, II, 190].

88. A grant from States: Later in his address, B. took a firm stand on another question of great controversy: "The Federal Constitution is a grant from the States to Congress of certain specific powers; and the question whether this grant should be liberally or strictly construed, has, more or less, divided political parties from the beginning. Without entering into the argument, I desire to state, at the commencement of my administration, that long experience and observation have convinced me that a strict construction of the powers of the Government is the only true, as well as the only safe, theory of the Constitution" [*Buchanan*, II, 192]. Ironically, the emphasis of states rights became one of the specific causes of the Civil War, which loomed darkly ahead.

89. nec Templum . . . rem: L, "he neither built the temple nor restored anything." Prob. a reference to Buchanan, a dedicated man filled with good intentions whose work came to naught.

90. Winter in Pontus: A place at the eastern edge of the Roman Empire, subject to military raids, to which Ovid was banished by Augustus, perhaps with the thought that he would not survive. His "Letters from Pontus" are filled with accounts of the dangers of the place and the miseries of the climate.

91. Sulmona: Town in central Italy, NE of Rome, the birthplace of Ovid. Pound makes several references to the lion sculptures there [105:8].

92. Federico . . . Falcon: [25:14].

93. Orsi: (I, "I am also an old Syracusan.") Paolo O., 1859-1935, Italian archaeologist out of Austria who pioneered in excavating and researching sites in Sicily and Italy. As director of the museum at Syracuse from 1888, he devoted himself to discovering and exploring dozens of new sites and established the four-period chronology of the area's early inhabitants from the prehistoric to the Byzantine. He published 300 titles and edited the *Bullettino di paleontologia italiana* and the *Archivia storico della Calabria e Lucania.*

94. **Arab . . . Sweden**: Said Del Mar: "A barbaric imitation of Byzantine coin of the fifth century was found in Mallgard, Gotland" [*HMS*, 119]. Gotland is an island of SE Sweden in the Baltic Sea.

95. **Fortuna**: [96/656].

96. **Raleigh . . . usury**: [97:191].

97. **Wodan . . .** : L, "Wodan has charge of power" [Migne, 95, 447-448].

98. **Frico**: [Fricco]: A major Lombardic god who presided over peace and sexual pleasures [ibid.].

99. **voluptatem**: L, "pleasure" [ibid.].

100. **Agelmund**: [97:268].

101. **quae . . . sacrificiis**: L, "which from frankincense they were accustomed in their sacrifices" [96:3].

102. **Roma**: [96:5].

103. **Brennus**: [96:7].

104. **Lupus . . .** : L, "a wolf companion of the journey" [96:25].

105. **Rothar . . .** : L, "Rothar of the Arian heresy" [96:27, 28].

106. **edicti prologo**: L, "with a prologue to the edict" [96:271]. The edict of Leo the Wise.

107. **dope . . . use**: Not in the source in this apparent sense. But Paul the Deacon mentions a drink that drove the king out of his mind [Migne, 582] [BK].

108. **Puteum . . .** : L, " 'I shall fill a well with the testicles of clerics,' said Alchis."

109. **Alchis**: The Brescian duke Alachis (or Alahis) tried to take power from King Cuningpert of Lombardy [96:40]. He uttered the line after he had killed an Arian-heretical prelate who he thought was the king [Migne, 620].

110. **Das Leihkapital**: G, "the loan-capital."

111. **Mensdorf letter**: A letter written by Count Albert Mensdorf [19:22] to Nicholas Murray Butler, 28 June, 1928, who was then Chairman of the Executive Committee of the Carnegie Endowment for Peace. Mensdorf recommended a study of the causes of wars and included a list as a starter [EH, *Pai*, 1-2, 273-275; *IMP*, 281-283]. A note in *Impact* says that Pound helped draft the letter.

CANTO CIV

Sources

Joseph Rock, *The Ancient Na-Khi Kingdom of Southwest China*, 2 vols., Harvard University Press, 1947 [Rock, vol., p.]; Séraphin Couvreur, *Chou King*, Cathasia, 1950; Ovid, *Fasti*, Vol. I, V; Allen Upward, *The Divine Mystery*, London, New York, 1910 [Upward, *Mystery*]; L. A. Waddell, *Indo-Summerian Seals Deciphered*, London, 1925 [*Seals*]; Dante, *Par.* XV, 70-87.

Background

EP, *Speaking*, 400; George H. Dunne, S.J., *Generation of Giants*, University of Notre Dame, 1962 [Dunne, *Giants*]; Julian Amery, *Approach March, A Venture in Autobiography*, Hutchinson, London, 1973; Viscount Templewood, *Nine Troubled Years*, Collins, London, 1954; Igantius Balla, *The Romance of the Rothschilds*, Eveleigh Nash, London, 1913; Virginia Cowles, *The Rothschilds, A Family of Fortune*, Knopf, New York, 1973; J. A. Symonds, *Renaissance in Italy*, London, 1897-99; M. von Wolff, *Lorenzo Valla*, Leipzig, 1893 [Wolff, *Valla*]; Bernard J. Poli, *Ford Madox Ford and the Transatlantic Review*, Syracuse, 1967.

Exegeses

John Peck, *Agenda*, vol. 9, nos. 2-3, 1971, 26-29; Jamila Ismail, *Agenda*, vol. 9, nos. 2-3, 1971, 70-87; CFT, *Pai*, 3-1, 90-122; NS, *Reading*, 111; MSB, *Pai*, 3-3, 332; John Peck, *Pai*, 2-1, 144; FR, P/J, 216-221; MB, *Trace*, 418-423; William Cookson, *A Guide to The Cantos*, inedit [WC, *Guide*].

Glossary

1. **Na Khi . . . game**: Source in Rock [110:54]: "The region here is wild, and not a breath of air is stirring in the forest . . . Not a human soul dwells here" [Rock, II, 235-6n.; *Pai*, 3-1, 105].

2. **Mihailovitch**: Draja Mikhailovitch, 1893?-1946, Serbian revolutionary who fought on the monarchist side against the axis, as did Croatian underground leader Marshall Josef Tito, who sided with the Communists. But M.'s guerilla group, the Chetniks, was in every way antithetical to Tito's Partisans. The ideological cross-purposes and confusions of all WWII alliances were played out in microcosm by the struggles of these two. Although M.'s force did not want to fight for any totalitarian power, it did sign up with the Communists to fight the Nazis. The situation behind the canto lines is complicated. In 1941 some people in the British Foreign Office ("F.O.") wanted to support M. rather than Tito because he had been pro-British in the Balkan Wars and in WWI and would be more reliable to deal with after the war than Tito would be. But the pro-Communist forces in the government won out and support went to Tito rather than M. M. was by all his acts an Allied hero, but after the war he was tried by Tito in a glare of publicity. In spite of worldwide protest, he was found guilty and executed. The world concluded that internal political considerations dictated the sentence rather than his guilt. Julian Amery in his autobiography, *Approach March*, has a polite but detailed statement of the affair [see "Mihailovitch, General Draja" in the index]. The "young lout" could be any member of the Communist party then high up in the British government (Burgess and Blunt come to mind); the "old lout" is prob. someone close to the foreign secretary or even to Churchill himself.

3. **young S.**: Unidentified, but poss. young Jan Smuts who is mentioned by Amery as pro-Mihailovitch. The connection between the "Na-Khi" lines and the "F.O." lines is one of time and theme: Dr. Rock in 1941 is exploring the paradisal scene of peace in the Mekong mountains; meanwhile, back in Europe, etc.

4. Lepanto: The naval battle in 1571 at which the Christian powers defeated the Turkish fleet and prevented the Ottoman Empire from controlling the Mediterranean and the Balkans. Pound's contention is that the banks in power (after the battle) controlled the outlets of money and depreciated the value of the printed currency. The connection between Lepanto and the WWII Balkans is "the same old story."

5. Ling: [85:1]. C, "sensibility." If the ethics of the West were grounded in *ling*, we would not have the conditions suggested by the preceding glosses.

6. semina: L, "seeds." A part of the musical figure *semina motuum* [90:24]: "seeds in motion." Paraphrase: Only by a great human sensibility will the seeds that might blossom into a paradisio terrestre be put into motion.

7. Ideogram: Wu [M7164], "ritual," the bottom component of *ling*.

8. And a $ . . . : The results of a managed and calculated depreciation of the currency.

9. Procope: [102:15].

10. Dondo: Mathurin Marius D., 1884-?, French playwright and poet who made adaptations of medieval pieces. Pound wrote in a letter to WCW, Dec. 1913: "Dondo has turned up again after years of exile. He is in Paris, has met De Gourmont. We printed a page of his stuff, verse, in *The N.F.* last week. I think he will do something" [*L*, 28].

11. Tabarin: [80:26]. French restaurant and nightclub.

12. Moulin Rouge: A nightclub favored by a number of the modernist painters as well as the *beau monde.*

13. Degas: H. G. Edgar D., 1834-1917, one of the most important of the impressionist painters.

14. La Concorde: The Degas painting *Place de la Concorde* (Paris, c. 1875) has a perspective from the center of the square to the Chamber of Deputies in the distance. A family group is in the right foreground. The painting shows only what the eye catches at a glimpse.

15. Seurat's": George S., 1859-1891, French post-impressionist painter whose pointillism (tiny dots of pure color) suggest "splintered light."

16. Pitagora: Pythagoras, the well-spring of Neoplatonic light-philosophy.

17. Disraeli . . . Parliament: [48:19; 89:156]. In one of his broadcasts Pound said: "Subversion was not invented in the days of Disraeli" [*Speaking*, 400]. But Pound believes that under his leadership and with his example it was brought to a point of perfection. The "bitching England"concerns D's deals with the house of Rothschild to buy the controlling interest of the Suez Canal [86:61].

18. Wolff: Henry Wolff (b. 1931), poet, writer, and perennial student (in 1982 at UC Berkeley). Sometime during the mid-fifties H. W. allowed John Kaspar, a close friend, to use his apartment in N.Y. Since Pound was writing to Kaspar often and addressing his letters c/o Henry Wolff, the name became familiar to him. Prob. the "double ff" indicated Jewish descent to Pound, even though the spelling does not indicate anything for certain. The association is prob. because of Pound's idea of Disraeli as a Jewish "Wolfman."

19. de l'audace: F, "the audacity of it!"

20. PANURGIA: H, "villany." The brutal drug-smuggling and slave-trading [cf. 24 below].

21. Xreia: H, "need."

22. Schmidt: [86/566]. Formerly recalled as Schwartz.

23. Rocke: An English colonel, "active on behalf of Italy during the Abyssinian war, who disseminated information that was being refused circulation in Britain and elsewhere" [NS, *Reading*, 111]. The other Rock is a botanist [110:54].

24. Sammy's nevvy . . . : Ted Press (the nephew of Sir Samuel Hoare), an employee of the Bank of Egypt who got from Addis Ababa all the gold Haile Selassie had hidden under his bed [80:307]. The Bank of Egypt was in effect a branch of the Bank of England, whose interest in the Lion of Judah diminished after they had the gold [BK, *Pai*, 12-2 &3]. Sir Samuel Hoare, British foreign secretary 1835-1836, was given the job of forestalling the Italian occupation of Ethiopa. Hoare said of Haile Selassie's rule: "The Amharic Government of Addis Ababa had little authority over the tribes and races of the south and west, Gallas, Somalis, Leiba and Shifta wandering gangs, disloyal Rases, anti-Christian Moslems, Arab slave traders and intriguing adventurers, who one and all did much as they liked in this remnant of Medieval Africa. However good the intentions of the Emperor, his writ scarcely ran beyond the limits of his palace" [Templewood, *Nine Troubled Years*, 150].

25. Londres' books . . . : Albert L. during the 20s and 30s published a series of well-written exposés of oppression and corruption, dealing with: black oppression (*Terre d'Ebène*, 1929); prison conditions (*Au Bague*, 1932); white slavery (*Le Chemin de Buenos Aires*, 1927); mental institutions (*Chez les fous*, 1925); drug traffic in China (*La Chine enfolie*, 1925). "His *Le juif errant est arrivé* (1930) is a sympathetic treatment of the Zionist cause which denounces the persecution of Jews in Central Europe" [Sieburth, *Pai*, 5-2, 293].

26. pine-needles: [101:46].

27. ^{2}muan ^{1}bpo: C, "sacrifice to heaven."

28. agitante . . . calescimus: L, "stirs us we are warmed" [93:107].

29. nos otros: S, "we others."

30. Murare, tradurre: I, "to build, to translate."

31. Pope Nicolo: Nicolò V, 1397-1455, who as pope (1447-1455) was a founder of the Vatican Library and a great patron of the humanities.

32. (Valla): Lorenzo V., c. 1407-1457, an Italian humanist who knew Greek well. Pope Nicholaș V chose him to translate Herodotus and Thucydides into Latin. He exposed the Donation of Constantine as a forgery [89:236] and was subject to suspicion because of his treatise *De Voluptate*, which attacked chastity as an ideal [89:204].

33. latinitas: L, "pure Latin" or "the spirit of latinity"; from Valla's *De Elegantiis Latinae Linguae* [Wolff, *Valla*; the "ff" spelling of Wolff's name (cf. 18 above) may have reminded Pound of this book].

34. Bassinio: Basinio da Parma, 1424-1457, an Italian scholar who died in Rimini and is buried in a sarcophagus next to Sigismundo Malatesta [9:7].

35. Uncle Carlo: [92:49].

36. (Wieland): Prob. Christoph Martin Wieland, 1733-1813, the great German poet, novelist, and critic, who after living long in Switzerland, was converted from pietism to a light-hearted romantic attitude of the scenic kind. Prob. a memory of a WWI scene of getting a torpedo boat overland suggested something in W.'s work.

37. The Pollok . . . sea": Sir Ian Hamilton [93:163], 1853-1947, who commanded the British Mediterranean Expeditionary Force in WWI and after became an adviser on Near Eastern affairs, told the Poles that if Germany invaded Poland they could expect help via the Black Sea. But the Soviet-Nazi pact intervened, which made it impossible to get to Poland via the Black Sea [WC, *Guide*].

38. Pitonessa: I, "Pythoness." Name of a woman seer, such as at the Oracle of Delphi, who became inspired by breathing intoxicating fumes: "[She] took her stand on a three-legged stool, or tripod, placed over a crack in the floor of a cave, and became literally inspired by the fumes that issued from the earth" [Upward, *Mystery*, 15].

39. Ideogram: Ling^{2} [85:1]. The top component stands for clouds. The repeated central component [M3434], "mouth," gives "the three voices," over the bottom component, which stands for a wizard or seer, such as the Pythoness.

40. And stopped . . . metals: Prob. the religious ecstasy that led some to dedicate themselves to values other than gold and silver.

41. Once gold . . . burrows: Waddell says: "The gold-digging 'ants' are described by Strabo as having 'skins as large as leopards.' They were evidently the large Tibetan rabbit-like Marmots, which burrowed in the auriferous sand and brought gold to the surface" [*Seals*, 13].

42. pao^{three}: [M4956], "treasure." Character as given.

43. pao^{three}: [M4953], "a bird said to be like the wild goose." Character not given.

44. pao^{four}: [M4954], "a leopard; a panther; a kind of wildcat." Character as given.

45. da radice torbida: I, "of turbid root."

46. maalesh: A colloquial Arabic expression that means "never mind," "don't worry about it," "take things as they come," "que sera sera," or all these things.

47. Adolf: A. Hitler. Pound seems to have believed that Hitler got onto the bankers and usurocrats; his perception of their international plot is what made him furious [Pound, *Speaking*, 49, 79, 433, passim]. But Pound also wrote, in a piece entitled "From Italy" [*NEW*, May 24, 1934]: "Adolphe is, an, almost, pathetic hysteric; . . . he is, so far as I can make out, a tool of *almost* the worst Huns."

48. they . . . : FDR, Churchill, and all those who were blind to what WWII was really all about.

49. "Beg the . . . him": The source of the remark is unknown, but clearly the speaker is a wonderful lady of the old school, who knows it is immoral to embarrass *anyone.*

50. And the cap . . . nuance: The lines are an enigma. This gloss number and space are reserved for the time when someone will have a reasonable clue.

51. 1910: Pears': Although China had claimed suzerainty over Tibet since 1720, the British began challenging that control in the 20th century. In 1904 they sent to Lhasa Sir Frances Younghusband, who by 1910 had managed to get a number of valuable trading rights. In those years Pears' soap was supposedly a measure of the civilization Britain was bringing to the "unwashed" world: it functioned as a symbol with ironic overtones, somewhat as Coca-Cola does today.

52. Les Douze: Prob. a Parisian literary group of the old school who met occasionally at a restaurant but were quite oblivious to the important things going on, such as Ford's new *Transatlantic Review.*

53. Fordie: Ford Madox F. [74:165]. In the early twenties, when he was editing the *Transatlantic Review* in Paris.

54. Ambro[i]se Paré: French army surgeon, ca. 1510-1590, famous for introducing humane methods into medicine. He did away with "the boiling oil treatment of wounds" (which sometimes caused death by shock), promoted the use of artificial limbs, and saved many lives by introducing the tourniquet.

55. before Zeus . . . bluejays: "The bluebird is regarded . . . as the outcome of aerial motion; that is, as a pure association of ideas" [*Cirlot*, 26]. In Hellenic folklore birds in general indicate the spiritual nature of man.

56. THEMIS: Greek goddess of justice.

57. Yo-Yo: A friendly inmate at St. Elizabeths whom Pound was fond of [MSB, *Pai*, 3-3, 332].

58. raise up guilds: [91:52]. Religious, not craft, orders.

59. the moon kings: Perhaps the early kings

of England, such as Athelstan or Lear, whose prayers were often to Diana [91/612-613].

60. "Wash . . . lan'.": Prob. remark of Elder Lightfoot [95:42].

61. Luigi . . . communion: [97:232]. Said Pound: "The religious man communes every time his teeth sink into a bread crust" [*SP*, 70].

62. lasso: [105:63].

63. Yseult . . . : Iseult Gonne MacBride, the daughter of Maud Gonne, to whom Yeats proposed in 1917 after Maud had turned him down finally [Schmitz, *Pai*, 3-2, 286; EH, *Pai*, 3-3, 416].

64. Walter: W. Morse Rummel [80:5] died in 1953 [ibid.].

65. Fordie: He died in 1939.

66. familiares: I, "intimate friends."

67. HOWells: William Dean H., 1837-1920, longtime dean of American letters. Pound is recalling a scene in which Henry James is reacting to a request to send some congratulations to be read at a dinner in honor of Howells. He did, but the American Academy suppressed them. Pound first wrote of it in a 1924 article on the Nobel Prize, in which he said (of James): "One can still hear the slow suave voice: 'Eh, I, eh, belong to a body, eh, doubtless you also belong to it . . . and there is another inner and more secret body . . .' etc. ending magnificently: 'and how my dear old friend . . . eh . . . Howells . . . !" [Peck, *Pai*, 2-1, 144; FR, *P/J*, 216-221].

68. Remy's: R. de Gourmont [87:88].

69. "milésiennes": F, "Milesian women." In citing lines from Gourmont's *Les Litanies de la Rose* to show his sense of "tonal variations," Pound gives one in particular: "Femmes, conservatrices des traditions milesiennes" [*LE*, 345]. Pound liked the word so much he wrote it in a letter to John Quinn to describe Maude Gonne [*L*, 140].

70. William's: W.B. Yeats.

71. monoceros: H, "unicorn." Yeats wrote of "Magical Unicorns" and "cloud-pale unicorns" in the last stanza of *The Tower*. His bookplate shows a rampant unicorn in heraldic style.

72. Gladstone: William Ewart G., 1809-1898, dominant personality of the British Liberal party and erstwhile prime minister toward end of the century. Earlier, as a young man, he served in the cabinet of Palmerston and may have tried to cultivate one of his important lady supporters, which may have been bad but was not as bad as Disraeli's act of selling the country.

73. Palmerston: [89:154].

74. Hollis: Author of *The Two Nations, A Financial Study of English History*, a book that exposed the "Whiggery" of the professorships as well as the diliberate and knowing creation of a nation of poverty in order to maintain a nation of wealth.

75. Regius: [46:29].

76. Coke: [107:3].

77. Von Bülow: Freidrich W., Freiherr von B., 1755-1816, the Prussian general who assisted in the defeat of Napoleon at Gross Beeren and at Waterloo (not to be confused with Bernhard von B. at 86:9 and 89/601).

78. (Wells): [42:2; 46/232].

79. Orage: [80:322; 89:239].

80. Nicht Bosheit . . . DUMMheit: G, "not cowardice . . . stupidity" [86:4].

81. Margherita Regina: [86:5].

82. Mirabeau: Honore G. Riquetti, Comte de M., 1749-1791, because of a wild and dissolute youth was repeatedly jailed. In 1785 he was in exile in England, and in 1786 he was sent on a secret mission to Prussia which failed. He published an account of the affair which some believed to be treasonous. After the revolution he acted as a moderate behind the scenes and collaborated to establish a constitutional monarchy. He predicted that, should the monarchy not be preserved, a violent course of revolution would materialize. It did, in all its horror, after his death at age 42.

83. **Ovid . . . Pontus**: [76/462]. Ovid was exiled, for reasons kept secret, to the far borders of the empire at Tomi on the Black Sea, where he suffered greatly. His *Epistulae ex Ponto* delineate his misery and plea for him to be allowed to return to Rome. But neither Augustus nor Tiberius would hear of it. He died at Pontus in A.D. 17.

84. **Goa**: Portuguese colony on the west coast of India founded by Afonso de Albuquerque in 1510, where St. Francis Xavier spent 10 years doing successful missionary work. Xavier's tomb is there. At first Goa was a center of trade for spices, but that trade declined in the 17th and 18th centuries [89:238]. The immediate effect of the arrival of Christian missionaries in this tropical paradise was a chain of destruction. Why? Money! [97/674].

85. **Intorcetta**: Prospero I., Jesuit missionary to China during the late Ming and early Manchu dynasties. He is still remembered in his native Sicily, to which he returned with artifacts in 1671 [Dunne, *Giants*, 174-175, 292].

86. **Webster, Voltaire and Leibnitz**: Grouped here as lexicographers and refiners of language. Voltaire: *Dictionnaire philosophique*. Leibnitz: *Monadology* (1714) and *Principles of Nature and Grace* (1714). Said Pound: "Leibniz was the last philosopher who 'got hold of something'... Up till Leibniz you can find men who really struggle with thought. After Leibniz the precedent kind of thought ceased to lead men" [*GK*, 74].

87. **phyllotaxis**: The biological laws that dictate the arrangement of leaves on a stem. The force that makes the cherry stone become a cherry tree, which to Pound is one of the ways divine intelligence works in the world. Its highest expression is through the mind of great thinkers such as those above [cf. Sieburth, *Pai*, 6-3, 383-384; 109:49].

88. **Selvo**: Domenigo Selvo [26:25, 26] doge of Venice (1071-1081); he put the first mosaics into the Cathedral of San Marco.

89. **Franchetti**: Luigi F., a Venetian friend of Pound's during the 1930s. In the context of a discussion of words and meaning ("Mankind's fog... comes from NOT defining one's terms. First the clear definition, then the clear articulation"), Pound draws parallels with musical composition and playing, and cites a comment of Franchetti to illustrate [*GK*, 248].

90. **"Very cleverly drained"**: Source unknown. Perhaps there is a connection with the discoveries of Del Pelo Pardi and his underground canals [101:16, 17]. Or Larranaga [cf. 106 below].

91. **Chauncey Alcot**: C. Olcott, 1860-1932, Irish actor and tenor who wrote "My Wild Irish Rose." He was so popular in the 1890s that the songwriting team of William Jerome and Jean Schwartz immortalized him in the chorus of a 1903 song of their own named "Bedelia," which starts: "Bedelia, I want to steal ya, / Bedelia, I love you so. / I'll be your Chauncey Olcott / If you'll be my Molly, O!" Pound prob. heard it at St. Elizabeths, either sung by another patient or in the media [M. Fournier, *Pai*, 12-2 & 3].

92. **Ionides**: [40:26]

93. **Pulchra documenta**: L, "beautiful examples."

94. **Bulow**: [cf. 77 above].

95. **Gold... 1204**: [89:79].

96. **El Melek**: [97:1-15].

97. **kalos kagathos**: H, "beautiful and well born" [33:11].

98. **Del Mar cites . . . :** [96:119]. Pound uses "ticket" to mean any piece of paper or chit or legal tender which people will accept in exchange: "money is a general sort of ticket, which is its only difference from a railway or theatre ticket" [*SP*, 290].

99. **Cythera PAGGKALA**: H, "All-beautiful

Cytherian": Aphrodite. The Greek *n* in *pan* ("all") becomes *g* before kappa, gamma, or chi.

100. Mond: Alfred Moritz M., 1868-1930, of a family famous for chemical research and manufacturing. In 1910 he bought the *English Review* (then being edited by F. M. Ford) for political purposes, and Ford was soon out of it. Said Pound: "no greater condemnation of the utter filth of the whole social system of the time can be dug up than the fact of that review's passing out of his hands" [HK, *Poetry*, 308]. It was Mond's brother who said, "it will not take 20 years to crwuth Mussolini" [*SP*, 313; 78:10]. The "interval" refers to the dozen years before Ford went to Paris to edit the *Transatlantic Review* [cf. 53 above].

101. . . . Quatorze: F, "fourteenth." The celebration of Bastille Day, July 14th, the national holiday of republican France.

102. Brits paid . . . : The first issue of the *Transatlantic Review* may be referred to. But "installment" may suggest some kind of war reparations.

103. Alex . . . : [89:230].

104. the king lost . . . : When coinage–once the right of the sovereign alone–was lost, such monetary chaos took place that even Del Mar is amazed. See his chapter entitled "Private Coinage," "Bank Suspensions under Coinage," and the analysis that starts: "From the day when the royal voluptuary resigned a prerogative . . ." [*HMS*, 389].

105. McNair Wilson: Robert M. W., author of dozens of books on dozens of subjects, including history, medicine, and money. Said Pound: "There is a body of sane writing in our time and/or a body of writing by enlightened men . . Larranaga, McNair Wilson, Christopher Hollis . . . Economic light in our time has not come from the HIRED . . . It has come from free men . . . Larranaga a builder of roads . . . Rossoni, Por, McN. Wilson–NONE of them in harness" [*GK*, 245-246]. "In harness" means "men hired by usurocrats to lie for pay."

106. Larranaga: Pedro Juan Manuel L., 1893-?, civil engineer and road builder. Author of *Gold, Glut, and Government: A New Economic Dawn*, G. Allen and Unwin, 1932, and *Successful Asphalt Paving*, London, 1926.

107. Tremaine: Poss. Herbert Tremaine, poet (*The Wide Garden and Other Poems*, London, 1917) and author of novels such as *The Tribal God* (London, 1921) and *The Feet of the Young Men*, a domestic war novel (London, 1917).

108. prescrittibile: I, "stamp script," as money [101:80; *SP*, 315].

109. False Middles: When the second or middle premise of a syllogism is false, the conclusion is false. A major premise of Pound's ideas about economists is that they base their reasoning on this kind of illogic. Thus, the acts of the state in taxing are ridiculous: "As ridiculous as . . . for someone who possessed a tin mine to go about collecting old tin cans" [*SP*, 315]. When one has understood completely the truth of this sentence, he will be on the way to knowing how needless, destructive, and cruel the international banking and monetary mess is. [Currently, Feb. 1982, the international bankers and oil men are "full of alarm" at the prospect of *declining* oil prices.]

110. NOOS: H, nous, "mind" [40/201]: "the ineffable crystal."

111. Stink Saunders': [87:123].

112. pen yeh: [98:55, 56].

113. Homestead . . . kolschoz: [103:5, 6].

114. tessera: I, "ticket" [cf. 98 above; *SP*, 310-311].

115. Monreale: Sicilian town near Palermo, site of famous cathedral in Norman-Sicilian style, which contains Byzantine mosaics.

116. Topaz: [88/581]. This jewel is the climax in a musical crescendo starting as early as the top of the previous page with, "Gold was in control of the Pontifex." In Dante's "Thrones," concerned with justice, he speaks to Cacciaguida overwhelmed by the jeweled light that flows from Beatrice: "I turned to Beatrice, and she heard before I spoke, and smiled to me a sign that made the wings of my desire increase. And I began . . . But I beseech you, living Topaz who are a gem in this precious jewel, that you satisfy me with your name" [*Par.* XV, 70-87]. It is appropriate that this note be struck as we approach the climax of the *Thrones* section of the poem, the special added section, 107-109, on the Magna Carta.

117. **Fetzen Papier**: G, "scrap paper."

118. **Where deer's feet . . . edge**: The last six lines of the canto return to ceremonial and paradisal themes like those found at the close of earlier paradisal cantos (e.g., 17, 47, 49, 90, 91). The lines here are based on evocative scenes in Couvreur, who says that at a certain moment when musicians are playing a musical background, "Ils s'arretent au signal donné par le tigre couché" [Couvreur, p. 58] Notes on this passage include a drawing of a tiger lying down. A moment later we read, "Les oiseaux et les quadrupèdes tressailent de joie" ("The birds and the beasts dance with joy"). Pound adds the specific detail of "deer" and conveys the ideal of dancing by "make dust." This scene rhymes with Pound's recurrent idea of appropriate religious celebration: "Religion? With no dancing girls at the altar?" [87/575]; or, "Come let us make joyful noise unto the lord"; or, "Be glad and rejoice for the lord is with you."

119. **curet . . . perennia**: L, "he cares about permanent things." Beware of "false middles": the process may be total flux, but a shape in the wave may be eternal.

120. **foung . . . i**: These four Chinese words in Couvreur are the last phrase of a sentence which follows the sentence given in gloss 118 above. In French, the whole sentence is, "Quand on exécute les neuf chants appelee *Siao chao*, les deux phénix viennent et s'agitent avec élégance." The 4 characters mean "come and dance with elegance." To accent the religious note, Pound has altered Couvreur's "lai i" to "li i," so the characters read, "with ceremony" [ibid.].

121. **Varnish . . . tribute**: The final 2 lines refer to another part of Couvreur concerned with the Hia dynasty, the first chapter of which is entitled "Tribut de IU." In sec. 5 we read: "Les habitants offrent en tribut a l'empereur du vernis et de la soie" ("The citizens offer as tribute to the emperor varnish and silk"). Note: This is a tribute in kind, not an indiscrimnate tax [ibid., 66].

122. **Iu's Weights . . .** : The lines in the source concern Iu's efforts to regulate weights and measures so that the people would not be cheated [ibid.].

CANTO CV

Sources

J. P. Migne, *Patrologiae Latina*: vol. 158, containing St. Anselm's *Monologium* and *Proslogion; Chronicon Centulense* vol. 174; William of Malmesbury's *The Deeds of the English Kings*, vol. 179.

Background

JW, *Seven Troubadours*, Pa. State Univ., 1970; A. Carlini, ed., *Compendio di storia della filosofia*, Villacchi, Florence, 1921-24; EP, *J/M*, 30-31; EP, *SR*, 166-178.

Exegeses

EP, *ND* 17, 173; JW, *Later*, 156-166; JW, *Pai*, 2-3, 399-407; HM, *Caged*, 69; Zapatka, *Pai*, 2-3, 423; EM, *Difficult*, 355.

Glossary

1. **Feb. 1956**: Date canto was started.

2. **Talleyrand**: [62:151; 95:13]. He tried to create a peace that would prevent further wars.

3. **Bismarck**: [86:3]. He believed the Franco-Prussian War was a war to end wars in Europe.

4. **rem salvavit**: I, "saved the thing." Phrase applied to Sigismundo [9:22], who was said to have saved the Florentine state.

5. **il salvabile**: I, "the savable." Reference to M's sending troops to assist Franco in 1936. Each of these three was betrayed by those he tried to help.

6. **Ideogram**: Chi [M411], "motions and origins: moving power of—as the universe."

7. **semina motuum**: L, "seeds of motion" [90:24; 89:252].

8. **Sulmona**: Birthplace of Ovid [103:91].

9. **Federico . . . hawk**: [97:272; 98:105].

10. **Il Marescalco**: *Libro di Marescalco* [or Mascalcia] : I, *Book of the Marshall.* A book of veterinary medicine written by Giordano Ruffo di Calabria, imperial marshall of the Holy Roman Empire, 1250-1260, and friend, earlier, of Frederico II [JW].

11. **Cesena . . . colonne**: I, "Cesena, Cesena of the beautiful columns." Romagnole dialect. [11:20].

12. **obit aetat [e]**: L, "died at the age of."

13. **Christian's . . .** : Pseudonym of Herbiet [80:319].

14. **the corridor 1/2 . . .** : Pound must have had a vital memory of Herbiet's portrait of a lady (?) with hat and gloves. He asked at 80/510, "What the deuce has . . . [he] done with . . . [it]?" and says here, "[it] must be somewhere." If one could find it, quite likely it would have in the background a narrow corridor with a window looking out onto a bridge in the far distance [93:162], which suggested to Pound "a bridge over worlds" [Frags./802].

15. **"moyens . . . inconnus"**: F, "means of existence unknown."

16. **Anselm**: St. A., c.1034-1109, archbishop of Canterbury (1093-1109), an Italian scholar who became a monk in France, where he was befriended by Lanfranc and followed him as prior at Bec in 1062; he later followed him to Canterbury in England. He was made archbishop against his will and became involved in the terrible problems of investiture but held out strongly against Henry I, who finally yielded. In his most notable work, *Monologium* (1063), he is one of the first theologians to argue the compatibility of faith and reason. Pound found him important, not only because of his rationality in discussing the Mysterium but also because he was a significant figure in the development of democratic freedoms. In the Bridson interview he said: "You can be damn well thankful to St. Anselm, because all your liberties back before 'Maggie Carter' as they used to call her in the law schools in America—I mean the fight between him and William Rufus, the dirty bandit—all your liberties come out of that" [*ND* 17, 173]. The connection Pound makes between Anselm and the Magna Carta is a comment on the structure of *The Cantos.* Canto 104 prepares the way for the great climax of the Magna Carta cantos, 107-109.

17. **scripsit**: L, "wrote."

18. **"non . . . sapientia"**: L, "not in space, but in knowing." A part of Anselm's ontolo-

gical argument: "our ability to conceive of an Infinite Being necessarily entails the existence of that being." Pound mentions this not because of some minor historical interest but because it is a vital part of his own religion, as is the idea of the compatibility of faith and reason. By the end of the 19th century, many had concluded it was "either/or": faith or reason. This conclusion is a false dichotomy. No "false middles," please! [104:109]. [Migne, vol. 158, chap. 2, col. 146-147; JW, *Pai*, 2-3, 400].

19. **non pares**: L, "not equal." From a statement in the *Monologium* which says that members of the Trinity are not equal in worth [ibid.].

20. **rerum naturas**: L, "nature of things." Taken from a passage in the *Monologium* which translates: "every created nature takes its place in a higher grade of the worth of essence, the more it seems to approach there" [ibid.]. That is, all things are not, as they are in pantheism, equally beautiful, valuable, or good: differences exist.

21. **Lanfranci** . . . : L, "They feared the wisdom of Lanfranci" [cf. 16 above].

22. **old Gallagher**: [87:134].

23. **Sodom . . . Napoleon**: Ref. to the trick the Rothschilds pulled on Napoleon to get gold to Arthur Wellesley during the penninsula campaign [86:56].

24. **Ideograms**: "Hou Chi," name of the minister of agriculture under Shun, later worshipped as the god of agriculture.

25. **stando . . . Terrestre**: I, "standing in the Earthly Paradise." In Dante's cosmography, on top of Mt. Purgatory.

26. **sheep on Rham** . . . : Some dialects are very difficult because the word for a "white dog" may have no etymologic connection at all with the word for "black dog," etc.

27. **"Meas nugas"**: L, "my trifles." Taken from Catullus's dedicatory poem 1.4. St. Anselm quotes the phrase to describe his own more frivolous writings: prob. his own poems [Migne, Vol. 158, chap. 2, col. 687 ff.].

28. **"L'adoravano . . . Lucia"**: I, "They adore it . . . like St. Lucy" (a town in SE Italy). The anecdote concerns a stone statue of the pagan god Cupid. Because the people adored it, the church official had to put it out of sight. Pound tells elsewhere the same story as taking place at Terracina [*J/M*, 30-31].

29. **Barocco, anima**: I, "baroque, soul."

30. **anima . . . vagula, tenula**: L, "soul . . . wandering, tenuous." Line from Hadrian's poem to his soul which Pound played with in one of his own early poems [*P*, 39].

31. **"non genitus" Caput 57, "discendendo"**: L, " 'not born' Chapter 57, 'descending.' " In chapters 56 and 57 of the *Monologium*, the point is made that the Father and Son, the Highest Nature, do not give birth to the Spirit of Love (Third Person of the Trinity): that spirit is inborn, a mysterious breathing-forth from the Highest Nature. Pound has changed the Latin *discedendo* ("removing") to a hybrid Latin-Italian word to suggest "descending" [JW, ibid.].

32. **Guido C.**: G. Cavalcanti [4:46].

33. **vera imago**: L, "true image." Anselm said that "the mind itself is a mirror [of Highest Nature] and its image." The word "true" is added later. The idea is implicit in Cavalcanti's *Donna Mi Prega* [36/177].

34. **via mind** . . . : A key statement in Pound's light-divinity imagery.

35. **"rationalem"**: L, "reason."

36. **"intenzione"**: I, "intended design."

37. **Ratio . . . imago**: L, "Reason, moon mirror is not the image." Anselm stresses the importance of reason but also its limitations, which cannot lead directly to total Memory, the Father. The words "mirrour, not image" may seem not to be from Anselm, who distinctly says that the mind is an image of what it sees; but Pound prob. intends: "the

mind mirrors the image but in itself is not the image." This construction aligns Anselm with antecedent Neoplatonic light-philosophers.

38. Sapor . . . pulchritudo: L, "flavor . . . beauty." Anselm's *Proslogion* [chaps. 17 and 18] says that a nonknower "looks around him and doesn't see beauty" and "tastes, yet doesn't know savour [saporem]" [Migne, vol. 158, cols. 236-237; JW, *Pai*, 2-3, 402].

39. ne . . . intellectu: L, "that it not be divisible in the intellect." An amalgam of phrases from several places in Anselm, who makes the point that wisdom is whole and entire in itself and cannot be reached by logic alone [JW, *Pai*, 2-3, 402].

40. (insulis fortunatis): L, "to the blessed isles."

41. fertur . . . amictus: L, "carried like bees . . . beehives of the sky-temple (Urania) with light as cloak." A pastiche of phrases enacting the flight of the mind to the Highest Nature, which Anselm compared to the flight of bees. A rhyme with the soul as sparks rising [5:6].

42. Puteus Cantauriensis: L, "Canterbury Well." Legend says that when, as archbishop of Canterbury, Anselm visited Liberi, 9 mi. E of Capua, to write *Cur Deus Homo* (*Why Did God Live*), there was a drought. The monks dug a well where Anselm told them to and it produced water with healing properties. Thereafter, the well was named after him [Migne, vol. 158, cols. 100-101].

43. a partridge: Anselm fell ill and wouldn't eat. The monks protested that he must until he finally said he might eat a partridge. The monks couldn't find one, but a stable boy found a *martyram* [marten: a kind of weasel ("martin" is a misprint)] with a partridge in its mouth. Anselm ate it and was cured [ibid., 112-113].

44. Ideograms: Kuei [M3634], "spirits"; chao [M239], "to appeal to."

45. et sake . . . woden: [OE/NF]. Proximate source, *Charter Hen. II* in *Anglia* VII. 220: "Saca & Socne, on strande & on Streame, on wudan & on feldan . . ." [JE]. But "Sake et soke appears to be a formulaic phrase denoting certain manorial privileges, derived from *Domesday Bk* [I. 225 b/2]: "Gitda tenuit cum saca & soca."; e.g., Stow says, "I . . . will and command, that they shall inioy the same well and quietly and honourably with sake and soke" [*Surv.* 36]. The words came to mean a district within a shire that could comprise a number of towns: "Coningsburg in Yorkshire . . . had twenty eight Towns and hamlets within its soke" [Blount, *Anc. Tenures* 9]. But the words came to have other meanings: "You send a sack of corn to the soakmill, and you get back half a sack of flour" [OED]. Says Donald Davie: "Soke persists in placenames; e.g. . . . Thorpe-le-Soken, and Kirby-le-Soken, both villages in Essex near where I lived between 1964 and 1968, which figure in the *Essex Poems* I wrote during those years". "Stronde" is a variant of "strande": "beach" or "broad traffic way." The last two words are translated in the next line.

46. liberates: L, "liberties."

47. consuetudines: L, "habitual rights." Such rights ultimately determined legal rights in English law [Migne, vol. 159, cols. 336, 337, 352, 375, 383].

48. Rochester: City in Kent, SE England, site of 12th-century cathedral built at place where St. Augustine founded a mission in 604.

49. Rufus: William II, "the Red," king of England (1087-1100). Opposed Anselm's stand on investiture on the grounds of state rights. He raised rents 8 times their original value (5 to 40) for use of the land ("*usu terrae*"). *Usu* suggests usury [JW, *Pai*, 2-3, 402].

50. Unitas Charitatis: L, "Unity of Charity."

51. consuetudo diversa: L, "diverse in customs." Anselm argued that people might be united as one in Christ under God and king, but they were diverse in their operations or customs; since they were so created they should have the liberties to be so.

52. **Khati**: [93:2].

53. **"ordine"**: I, "order"; L, "by order."

54. **Boamund**: Bohemond I, c. 1056-1111, prince of Antioch after its capture from the infidels in 1098 during the first crusade. A violent exponent of brute force, he double-crossed the Byzantine emperor Alexius I, who defeated and humiliated him in 1108.

55. **Alexis**: Alexius Comnenus, 1048-118, Byzantine emperor (1081-1118). He repelled the first crusade invaders, Robert Guiscard and Bohemond.

56. **Boniface**: Prob. Pope B. VIII, Dante's great enemy.

57. **Clermont**: The capital of the Puy-de-Dome [100:132] Dept. in SE France and long the center of religious activity [cf. 63 below]. It was also the center of the struggles between Boniface VIII and Philip IV of France. In these struggles the public did get excited at times. Once, when an emissary of Philip with an army behind him actually struck the pope, the outraged public literally drove the army away and rescued him.

58. **George Fifth**: 1865-1936, king of England (1910-1936). He was against England's becoming involved in WWI but loyally supported the government. Pound wrote about seeing him on Armistice Day, Nov. 11, 1918, with "the crowds cheering" and "the general enthusiasm for George on his drive through the drizzle in an open carriage, with no escort save a couple of cops. Poor devil was looking happy, I should think, for the first time in his life. I happened to be in Piccadilly about two feet from the carriage" [*L*, 141].

59. **the Bard's death**: Charles I was executed in 1649, 33 years after the death of Shakespeare: a king who also "willed no wrong."

60. **"Dalleyrand"**: Talleyrand, whose family came from Perigord near Hautefort (Altafort), the four-towered castle of Betrans de Born [cf. "Sestina: Altaforte" and "Near Perigord," *P*, 28, & 151-157]. The heavy dialect gives "Dalleyrand of Berigord," with the *D* and *B* initial sounds. *D* and *B* are also the initials of David Blumenthal, who bought the castle and lived there. Pound used to tell a story about Blumenthal's quick wit: "One evening at dinner a guest asked what the initials D.B. on the cutlery stood for. Blumenthal replied: "Dalleyrand Berigorrr' " [NS, *Reading*, 112].

61. **"en gatje"**: [85:87]: "en gatge": P, mortgage (the castle).

62. **Urban**: Pope Urban II (1088-1099). He preached the call for the first crusade at Clermont in 1095, which is seen by Pound to be a needless instigation of destructive wars against the infidels. He is also culpable for not taking a strong enough stand against ruthless rulers like William Rufus to prevent them from raising the rents [cf. 49 above].

63. **Charles of the Suevi**: L, "of the Swabians," called Charles the Fat, who became king of Spain in 876 and Frankish emperor (881-887). He witnessed a miraculous vision that caused him to abdicate the throne. The event is related in Migne in a chap. entitled "Visio Caroli" ("Vision of Charles"). He said he was led by a ball of light ("lucifluum glomus") looped over his shoulder ("jactavit super scapulas meas filum glomeris") to survey souls (especially those of priests) cast into dark perdition, his father in purgatorial pain, and his predecessors, Lothair I and his son Louis II, ensconced in paradisal joy, with Lothair on a rock of Topaz [104:116]. Said Charles: "suddenly I was seized by my spirit . . . and he held in his hand a solid ball emitting the brightest ray of light . . . and he began to unwind it and said to me: 'Take a thread of this brilliant light, and tie and knot it firmly around the thumb of your right hand, because you will be led by this through the labyrinthine punishments of Hell' " [JW, *Later*, 165].

64. **Antoninus**: [78:56].

65. **Athelstan**: Ruled 924-940. His distribu-

tions are recorded in William of Malmesbury's *Deeds of English Kings.*

66. **Ethelbald**: King E., 716-757. He ruled "ut omnia monasteria . . . a publicis vectigalibus . . . absolvantur" ("that all monasteries be absolved from public taxes").

67. **Egbert**: King of Wessex (802-839). Sometimes referred to as the first king of England, he really had control of only small areas of the island.

68. **consuetudiness**: [cf. 47 above].

69. **Paschal**: From letter 85, in which Pope Paschal II (1099-1118) wrote to Anselm telling him to withstand the efforts of English kings to control investiture of bishops [Migne, vol. 163, col. 106: "Unde Jesum . . ."].

70. **Guillaume**: William IX, 1071-1127 [6:2].

71. **Henry**: Henry I, 1068-1135, king of England (1100-1135), successor of William Rufus [cf. 49 above]. He continued the conflict between church and state. His economic program is recorded in William of Malmesbury's *New History*, where [1.14] we read: "fere ad centum millia libras; erant et vasa" ("almost 100,000 pounds; and there were vessels"). He left an important monetary record on the so-called Pipe Rolls.

72. **Maverick**: Lewis M., editor of *Kuan Tzu* [106:4].

73. **mosaic?**: Pound is suggesting that the ideogram he is putting together, a collection of "luminous details" about economic wisdom and repression, may well be called a mosaic.

74. *οὐ . . . κόσμον*: H, "You do not want to come into the world" [102:50].

75. **Charta Magna**: [107:passim].

76. **accensio**: L, "sparked, as in kindling, or to inflame"; but perhaps Pound meant *ascensio*, for "a lofty flight" [JW, *Later*, 163].

77. **Anselm . . . Rufus**: A question of the investiture of bishops as well as monetary matters.

78. **"Ugly? . . . whore!"**: adapted from one of Anselm's "nugas" called "Song on Contempt of the World." The lines translate: "If anyone has a base wife, he loathes and hates her; / If pretty, he anxiously fears adulterers" [*Migne*, vol 158, col. 697; JW, *Later*, 161].

79. **Anselm . . . weak**: Because of his exhausting struggles, A. had periods of depression, perhaps not helped by stomach trouble. A rhyme with Plotinus [99:60]?

80. **Trinity**: [cf. 31 above]. Pound despaired for years over the great destruction wreaked on some sects of the Christian church by other sects on just the one issue of what he called "the numbers game." One can refer to the three sides of a box and be clear only one box is at issue.

81. **Essentia . . .** : L, "Essence, feminine, immaculate, unstainable." Anselm sees the essence of all created things as part of the breath (*anima*) or loving spirit of the Father and Son and hence spotless and pure. The Latin words for "essence," and even "the Father," the highest nature (*summa natura*), all end in *-a* and are feminine. By grammar male and female become one.

82. **Ambrose**: St. A., 340?-397, bishop of Milan, father of the Church, and author of the apochryphal *De Tobia* [On Tobias] in which he attacked usury: the source of Pound's "Hoggers of harvest" [88:44] calling them "the curse of the people."

83. **Franks . . .** : William of Malmesbury, in *Deeds of the English Kings*, says of the Franks: "decenni vectigalium indulgentia" ("for ten years given tax indulgences"). They were called Franks because of their ferocity [1.68 ff].

84. **Valentinian**: V. III, 419-455, Roman emperor of the West (425-455), the son of Galla Placidia [96:80], who acted as regent. Her attempts to oust the Vandals and Alani

from France only led to their conquest of Africa in 429 [JW].

85. **Alani**: Nomadic peoples from the Caucasus who merged with the Vandals in France and Spain and eventually conquered North Africa.

86. **Omnia Gallia**: L, "All Gaul." Here refers to Faramond, the first king of the Franks in 425.

87. **Pepin** . . . : [96:51]. King of the Franks (751-768). He was crowned over an altar to Zagreus (Dionysus) at the Church of St. Denis in Paris [95:73]. He is thus linked with St. Dionysius [95:72].

88. **Ethelbald**: [Cf. 66 above].

89. **Charles**: Charlemagne, son of Pepin the Short.

90. **Offa**: King of Mercia (757-796). His laws became highly regarded and his coinage system was used for 500 years. Wm. of Malmesbury says Charlemagne gave him a "baltheum" ("belt") and a "gladium Huniscum" ("sword of the Huns") as part of the first recorded commercial treaty in English history [97:64].

91. **Quendrida . . . Kenelm**: In 821 the 7-year-old king of Mercia (later called St. Kenelm) was killed by his sister Quendrida [JW, *Later*, 163].

92. **Egbert**: [Cf. 67 above].

93. **looping the light** . . . : [Cf. 63 above].

94. **Hariulf's** . . . : Wm. of M. says he took the story of Charles of the Suevi's visions from H.'s *Chronicon Centulense* [Migne, vol. 174, col. 1211 ff].

95. **For a thousand . . . versa**: Pound's judgment of all the people and events he has been reading about and, in the canto, giving cues to.

96. **Alfred**: A. the Great (849-899?). He "instituted the tenth-parts called tithings" [JW, *Later*, 164].

97. **Erigena**: [36:9; 74:104]. Wm. of M. tells the story (much disputed) that he was murdered by his students, who stabbed him with pens while he was teaching.

98. **Athelstan** . . . : [91:52].

99. **Aunt Ethelfled**: Source says: "Took care of education by the great zeal of his aunt" [JW, *Later*, 164].

100. **Canute**: King of England (1017-1035). He is to be honored because he lightened the burden of both taxes and tolls.

101. **Gerbert**: A Frenchman who was installed as Pope Sylvester II (999-1003). He was educated in Spain in astronomy and mathematics, in the tradition of Averroes and Avicenna. Hence, the astrolabe, a new instrument that was an improvement over the tools of Ptolemy.

102. **A tenth tithe** . . . : A provision of Alfred to be honored because it was a share, not a blanket indiscriminate tax: a distinction related to Social Credit.

103. **Crommelyn . . .**: Admiral John Crommelin who got his ships out of Pearl Harbor before the Japanese attack. Also a staunch believer in the U.S. Constitution.

104. **del Valle**: Lt. Gen. Pedro A. del Valle, who commanded the U.S. Marines in the Battle of Okinawa, WWII. He became a staunch defender of Pound in the 1950s [EM, *Difficult*, 355]. David Horton, Rex Lampman, Harry Meacham, and others orchestrated a campaign of such heroes in their efforts to get Pound out of St. Elizabeths. They all saw him as a defender of the Constitution.

105. *πανουργία*: H, "knavery" [99/706].

106. **Guido**: G. Cavalcanti [4:46].

107. **Proslogion**: The major theological work of St. Anselm.

108. **Villon**: [97:35]. François V., 1431-1464?, one of Pound's favorite French poets [*SR*, 166-178].

CANTO CVI

Sources

Lewis Maverick, ed., *Economic Dialogues in Ancient China: Selections from the Kuan-tzu*, trans. T'an Po-fu and Wen Kung-wen, Carbondale, Ill., 1954 [*Kuan*]; *Analects* XIX, 18 [*CON*, 285]; Paul the Deacon, *History of the Langobards*, trans. William Dudley Foulke, N.Y. 1906 [Deacon, *Langobards*]; Ovid, *Meta*, VIII, 580-683; EP, *SR*, 34; *Hagoromo* [*CNTJ*, 103].

Background

EP, Bridson Interview, *ND 17*, 175; *SP*, 53.

Exegeses

EH, *Pai*, 10-3, 285-286; HK, *Era*, 107-108, 119, 185, 546; MB, *Trace*, 425-443; CFT, *Pai*, 2-3, 453-454.

Glossary

1. **her daughter**: Kore/Persephone. The opening pages of this canto are a sort of subject-response incantation between the Eleusinian mystery rites and the oriental wisdom that climaxed in Neoconfucianism, or "between Kung and Eleusis" [52:18].

2. **Demeter**: [98/684-685]. Mother of Persephone, who was abducted by Dis, the god of the underworld.

3. **Phlegethon**: [75:1].

4. **Ideograms**: Kuan[3] [M3557], "to govern"; tzu [M6939], "master"; together, the name of Kuan Chung, or Kuan I-Wu, prime minister of the state of Ch'i, 684-645 B.C. He was given the honorific title *tzu* ("master, teacher, philosopher") after his death. His extensive writings became known by his name. The book by Maverick [*Kuan*] has a selection of 32 essays, followed by a detailed commentary. All of the essays reflect the primacy of agriculture and appear to be a major source for Kung's thought 150 years later. Essay 1, titled "On Shepherding the People," starts: "Every ruler . . . should above all things adjust his administration to the four seasons. He should fill and watch over the granaries and public storehouses . . . When the granaries have been filled, then the people will obey the laws and the rules of courtesy" [*Kuan*, 31]. Later: "The ancient kings . . . enriched their subjects through the increased production of grain. The people cannot live without grain to eat" [*Kuan*, 70].

5. **NINE decrees** . . . : Essay 8, entitled "Basic Methods of Government," records decrees adopted by 9 assemblies. "At the first assembly, the following regulation was issued: 'Unless ordered by the God of the Sombre Heavens . . . none shall conduct a military campaign, even for only one day.' At the second assembly, this regulation: 'Take care of the aged who have lost their relatives; feed those who are permanently ill; give shelter to helpless persons' " [*Kuan*, 58]. The 9 together add up to a precis of the *Analects*.

6. **Venice shawls**: [98:14, 15].

7. **This Tzu** . . . : The guide in the final rites

of Eleusis, or a reference to Kuan Tzu above, or perhaps both.

8. **Kuan Chung**: [Cf. 4 above].

9. **Patera**: Patara. Legend has it that a cup of white gold preserved at the temple at Lyndos on the island of Rhodes was modelled on the breast of Helen. Pound first marvelled in print at the thought in 1917 [*PD*, 102]. Pound's spelling appears to come from Paul the Deacon [96:10], who said of the goblet Alboin made out of Cunimund's head: "This kind of goblet is called among them 'scala,' but in the Latin language 'patera'" [Deacon, *Langobards*, 51; EH, *Pai*, 10-3, 585-586].

10. ὁ θεός: H, "the god."

11. **Caledon**: Prob. a reference to the swift-footed Atalanta of Calydon, whose speed was like the wind but who was tricked by the golden apples to lose the race to Hippomenes; or perhaps the destruction of Calydon by fire after the death of Maleager at the hands of his mother / sister Althea [*Meta*. VIII, 580-683].

12. **Apeliota**: [74:304]. The East Wind.

13. **deep waters** . . . : [91:4]

14. **nueva lumbre**: P, "new reflections." From, "Y dar nueva lumbre las armes y hierros," in a canzon of Arnaut Daniel, which Pound translated: "And the arms irons give forth new (or strange) reflections" [*SR*, 34].

15. **the flame's barge**: [91:28].

16. **Amazon, Orinoco**: Great rivers in Brazil.

17. **Kuan Chung**: [Cf. 4 above]. Pound said: "Fuller [Buckminster] wrote me that he'd seen the *Kuan-tzu* three years ago and that it was the best book on economics he'd ever read . . . When Mencius and a few highbrows were objecting to Kuan Chung because he wasn't a saint, Confucius said, 'You cannot judge a man like that as you would any bum who could die in the gutter and nobody know it.' If it weren't for Kuan Chung, we'd still be dressing ourselves like barbarians" [Bridson, *ND* 17, 175].

18. **Antoninus** . . . : [78:56]. Paraphrase: If Antoninus got as far as Kuan Chung did in understanding economics, his knowledge has been hidden from us. Said Pound, "Now as I see it, billions of money are being spent to hide about seventeen historic facts" [ibid.; see contrary opinion in MB, *Trace*, 433].

19. **Ideogram**: Kuan¹ [M3571], "a frontier pass or gate . . . a customhouse; suburbs of a city." Not to be confused with *kuan³* [M3557] above: "to govern." Pound apparently confused the character for *gate* with that of *pi* [M5089]. It was an error he made earlier in translating the first line of Ode 1, "Hid! Hid!' the fish-hawk saith" [EP, *Confucian Odes*, 2; EH, *Letter to MB*, 9 Mar., 1977].

20. **Ad . . . donat**: L, "He gave the city to posterity." But the *-os* ending does not exist as an accusative or anything else. Perhaps by "posteros" Pound meant "gate."

21. **Artemis**: Prob. a coin uttered by Antoninus with the image of the goddess.

22. **400 . . . copper**: The *Kuan Tzu* says: "There are 467 mountains producing copper. . . . If there is cinnabar on the surface there will be copper and gold beneath" [*Kuan*, 145-146]. Cinnabar: the chief ore of mercury.

23. **Ko Lu**: "From the mountains in Ko Lu there came a flood, which washed down gold" [*Kuan*, 146].

24. **XREIA**: H, "gold." "So these minerals commanded high and stable prices. . . . 'When the demand for it becomes urgent, gold becomes heavy. . . .' The ancient kings estimated the degree of urgency, and issued decrees accordingly" [*Kuan*, 147].

25. **Yao . . . jade**: "The ancient kings . . . made use of their concentrated value. Pearls and jade were adopted as the superior money; gold the middle" [ibid.].

26. **the goddess . . . hypostasis**: These 20

lines are a reprise of the Eleusinian and grain-rite mysteries celebrated to evoke the earth's return to life in the spring.

27. **Luigi**: [97:232].

28. **Enna**: According to Ovid, the place where Persephone was abducted into the underworld [*Meta*. V, 485 ff.].

29. **Nyssa**: Where the abduction took place according the *Hymn to Demeter*.

30. **Circe**: [1:1]. Certain cantos in *Thrones* as well as *Drafts* contain an increasing number of thematic recapitulations reaching back to the beginning of the poem. Note the pines at Isé [4:23].

31. **Persephone**: [1:11, 3:8].

32. **juniper**: A holy bush of the Na-khi [101:2]. "In the centre / is / Juniper" [110/778].

33. **Athene Pronoia**: H, "Athena [who], knows the future."

34. **hypostasis**: [81:55].

35. **Helios, Perse**: Circe in her role of sexuality is seen as the daughter of the sun, and Perse[phone] is seen as earth-goddess.

36. **Zeus . . . Leto**: Zeus, in conjunction with Leto, sired both Helios (Apollo) and Artemis (Diana).

37. **Help me . . .** : [91:41]. "Help me in my need."

38. **Circeo . . . seaward**: The place near Terracina where Pound would have restored the goddess to her pedestal [*SP*, 53; 39:38].

39. **The temple . . . blossom**: These 12 lines are a visionary glimpse of paradise, with its strange, unearthly lights and colors and the hieratic animals [17/77].

40. **Carrara**: [74:80]. City in Tuscany noted for the purity of its white marble.

41. **Xoroi**: H, "dancers." "Religion? With no dancing girls at the altar?" [87/575].

42. **Sulmona**: [103/736; 105/746; for the lion and gold light, see 21:43].

43. **king-wings**: The "blue-grays" and the "king-wings" are butterflies [Frag/802]. The paradisal image of souls in flight, the final stage in the process from the earth: from egg to chrysalis to wings, as with the wasp [83/532-533].

44. **asphodel**: The flower of the Elysian Fields [*Aeneid* VI; 21:60; 78/482].

45. **broom-plant**: Prob. *Musa paradisiaca*, or plantain.

46. **Yao and Shun**: [Cf. 25 above].

47. **Whuder . . . lidhan**: ME, "Where I might go . . ." [91:41].

48. **acorn of light**: The primal unseen light from which all intelligence in the universe flows [CFT, *Pai*, 2-3, 453-454; 116/795].

49. **Aquileia**: A town in NE Italy, once a chief city of the Roman Empire.

50. **caffaris . . . cloud-wall**: Paradisal flora.

51. **three years peace . . . him**: [109:40]. Edward VIII, who according to Pound, delayed WWII for three years and was forced to abdicate for this, rather than for Wallis Simpson [86:47].

52. **violet . . . them**: The eyes motif [81:54; 83:61; 97:188-190].

53. **Buck stands . . .** : The ash, along with the oak, laurel, and cedar, is a sacred tree [*Cirlot*, 328]. To Pound, deer are hieratic animals, as in various paradiso passages [17/77; 104:118].

54. **Selena Arsinoe**: Queen Arsinoe II, of Egypt (316-270 B.C.), who married her brother Ptolemy II and became the mother-in-law of Berenice [97:170]. She died July 9 and was worshipped thereafter (as in life) as Arsinoe Aphrodite. She was also called Zephyritis after the temple Admiral Callicrates built in her honor at Zephyrium. An epigram of Posidippus may be Pound's source: "Propitiate . . . this temple of Cyprian Arsinoe

Philadelphus. . . . The admiral first placed there the goddess, lady of this beach of Zephyrium" [MB, *Trace*, 441]. The epithet "Selena" is a conflation with another young girl [cf. 60 below].

55. **Aedificavit**: L, "built."

56. **EUPLOIA**: H, "good voyage." The epigram continues: "She [Aphrodite] will grant a good voyage and in the midst of the storm becalm the sea in behalf of those who invoke her" [ibid.].

57. **an Aeolian**: Berenice. It was at this temple that B. offered a lock of her hair (as an earnest [*ex voto*]), which became the latest constellation [97:170; 102:42].

58. **Arsinoe Kupris**: H, "the Cyprian Arsinoe."

59. **Miwo**: The chorus in the *Hagaromo* says to Tennin (the aerial spirit): "O, you in the form of a maid, grant us the favour of your delaying. The pine-waste of Miwo puts on the color of spring" [*CNTJ*, 103]. Before this, the Tennin said: "The jeweled axe takes up the eternal renewing, the palace of the moon-god is being renewed with the jeweled axe" [ibid., 102].

60. **HREZEIN**: H, "knowing." From a phrase in Epigram 14 [cf. 54 above], *esthla hrezein* ("knowing virtue"), about Selenaia, a young girl born in Aeolian Smyrna who presented a nautilus to Arsinoe.

61. **Selena**: [Salenaia]: The "pearly nautilus," a spiral shell lined with mother of pearl, is a memora to the birth of Aphrodite out of the sea foam.

62. **Paros**: A Greek island of the central Cyclades.

63. **Xoroi**: [Cf. 41 above].

64. **Carrara's . . .** : Italian city famous for marble [74/428].

65. **God's eye . . . .** : [Cf. 113:43]. The divine essence operates as intelligence in man: it is through man's eyes that God sees.

66. **columns . . . boughs**: Items in a paradisal scene which Pound, as he nears the end of the poem, still sees as visionary [74:292].

CANTO CVII

Sources

Sir Edward Coke, *Second Institutes of the Laws of England*, 1797 [*Institutes*]; Catherine Drinker Bowen, *The Lion and the Throne*, Little, Brown, Boston 1956 [Bowen, *Lion*]; Dante, *Par.* X, 42, 136.

Background

EP, *SR*, 62, 101; EH *Approaches*, 173, 192; Bryce Lyon, *A Constitutional and Legal History of Medieval England*, Harpers, N.Y., 1960; William Stubbs, *The Constitutional History of England*, Vol. II, Oxford, 1887; William Sharp McKechnie, *Magna Carta*, rev., Burt Franklin, N.Y., 1958.

Exegeses

DD, *Sculptor*, 239-240; DG, *Pai*, 4-2 & 3, 223-299; DD, *Pai* 6-1, 101-107; HK, *Era*, 336; CFT, *Pai*, 5-1, 69-76; Materer, *Pai*, 4-2 & 3, 323; Moody, *Pai*, 4-1, 55-69; MB, *Trace*, 444-447; William Cookson, *A Guide to The Cantos*, inedit [WC, *Guide*].

[Documentation for the *Institutes* is difficult, as the numbering and subsectioning of the text is inconsistent. The chap. is given here, with section no. in parentheses if clear; if not, the p. no. of the 1797 edition is given.]

Glossary

1. **Selinunt**: Sicily. "The Sicilian rose of Ciulio D'Alcamo has grown into the English azalia" [DG, *Pai* 4-2 & 3, 249]. Frederick II, 1194-1250, king of Sicily, was a great legislator whose fame and work were known in the England of Henry III. Some of the precepts of the Magna Carta were maturing in Sicily under his direction [DD, *Pai*, 6-1, 104].

2. **Akragas**: Agrigento, capital of Agrigento Province, S Sicily. Founded in 580 B.C. as Acragas or Akragas by the Greek colonists of Gela, it became one of the most splendid cities of the Grecian world.

3. **Coke**: Sir Edward C., 1552-1634, one of the most famous of English jurists. He was member of Parliament, solicitor general, speaker of the House of Commons, and attorney-general under Elizabeth; under King James he was chief justice of common pleas and lord chief justice of England. In his long years of battle in defense of the rule of law and the primacy of Magna Carta against the prerogative of kings, he eventually spent much time imprisoned in the Tower during the last years of James and the first years of Charles I. His *Institutes of the Laws of England* became the backbone of English common law. Certain of his precepts, such as the primacy of Magna Carta and the tradition of common law, became vital to the American Revolution. Wrote Coke: "In many cases *the common law will control acts of Parliament* and sometimes adjudge them to be utterly void; for when an act of Parliament is against common right and reason, or repugnant, or impossible to be performed, the common law will control it and adjudge such acts to be void." This precept, issued in a trivial case, echoed down the centuries. Concerning the Stamp Act of 1765, passed by Parliament, James Otis shouted: "An act against natural equity is void." The Mass. Assembly declared the Stamp Act invalid, "against *Magna Carta* and the natural rights of Englishmen, and therefore, according to the Lord Coke, null and void" [Bowen, *Lion*, 315].

4. **Inst. 2**: *The Second Part of the Institutes of the Laws of England*, by Edward Coke. The "Proeme" says that, after King Edward I, Parliament ordained that the charters "should be sent under the great seale, as well to the justices of the forest, as to others, and to all sheriffes . . . and that the same charters should be sent to all the cathedrall churches, and that they should be read and published in every county four times in the yeare" [A6: p. 6 of the "Proeme"].

5. **20. H. 3**: The 20th year of the reign of Henry III. This was the year in which Henry removed "evil councill" and did "under his great seale confirme both *Magna Charta* and *Charta de Foresta*" [A9].

6. **mother . . . of repose**: Coke ends the "Proeme" to the *Institutes* by making a distinction between other glosses written by doctors and his expositions upon the Charter. Others contained private interpretations; but "our expositions or commentaries upon

Magna Charta . . . are the resolutions of judges in courts of justice in judiciall courses of proceeding . . . and shall (as we conceive) produce certainty, the mother and nurse of repose" [A13].

7. **scutage**: According to the *Institutes*: "Certain it is, that he that holdeth by castleguard shall pay no escuage, for escuage must be rated according to the quantity of the knights fees" [Chap II. pp. 9-10]. *Scutage* was a fee paid by a knight in lieu of military service.

8. **Milite**: L, "Soldier." Coke's name as author on the title page of the *Institutes* reads: "Authore EDWARDO COKE, Milite, J.C."

9. **Sigier**: Siger de Brabant, 13th-century French philosopher who was condemned in 1270 for Aristotelian teaching. His works reveal Averroes' concepts of Aristotle, as opposed to Thomas Aquinas's interpretations, which were accepted by the church. Siger held that men have but one intellectual spirit and that, although man is mortal, mankind is immortal. Undaunted by his condemnation, Dante Places Siger in Paradise among the orthodox thinkers in the "heaven of the sun" [*Par*. X, 136].

10. **Berengar**: Raymond Berenger, count of Provence, and father of Eleanor. The House of Berenger had extensive holdings in Provence and Toulouse and was linked through Eleanor of Aquitaine to the House of Plantagenet and England. After Eleanor of Provence married Henry III, she installed members of her family in high offices, thereby alienating the barons.

11. **Eleanor**: E. of Provence, d. 1291. Queen of Henry III. She had a benevolent effect upon the king and helped lead him from evil counselors to those who advised him to make confirmation of the charters.

12. **quod custod'** . . . : L, "such custody shall not be sold." This and the preceding line about "the land stored with ploughs" are taken from a section of the Magna Carta that concerns a "keeper" who is holding land in trust which is expected to return to rightful heirs. The sense of the passage is that the keeper, whether acting for the king or the church, must keep up the land and "the houses, parks, warrens, ponds, mills . . . and he shall deliver to the heir . . . all the land stored with ploughs, and all other things, at the least as he received it. The passage ends with the warning to the "Custodian" that "such custody shall not be sold" [Chap. V].

13. **Light, cubic**: Neoplatonic flow of light conceived by Pound as the "great acorn . . . bulging out" [106:48]. The "light descending" is intelligence, as in Kung.

14. **nel Sole**: I, "in the sun" [cf. 9 above].

15. **non . . . parvente**: I, "showing not by color but by light" [*Par*. X, 42]. The fourth heaven (of the sun) is inhabited by theologians, who are bathed in pure light.

16. **Custumier . . . de Normand**: Said Coke: "We have also . . . cited the Grand Custumier de Normandy . . . being a book compounded as well of the laws of England . . . which book was composed in the raign of King H.3." [A10-11].

17. **de la foresta**: F, "of the forest." Early English charters, such as the Coronation Charter of Henry I and "The Articles of the Barons" (signed by King John at Runnymede), which became known as "The Charter of Runnymede," included the *Charter de Foresta*, which in time, said Coke, was "called *Magna Charter de Foresta*" [A4]. This document collected all the laws concerned with the royal forests [CFT, *Pai*, 5-1, 70]. "14/H/3" indicates the 14th year in the reign of Henry III.

18. **yellow green**: May indicate permanence, as with "The Sacred Edict." The color rhymes with 99/694: "Till the blue grass turn yellow / and the yellow leaves float in air."

19. **king dies not**: Coke said: "These words being spoken in the politique capacity doe extend to the successors, for in judgement of law the king in his politique capacity dieth

not" [Chap. VIII, (1)]. The royal "we" encompasses the kings before us and the kings who will come after us, as implied in "The king is dead; long live the king."

20. **ancient eit franchies**: OF, "that it have its ancient liberties." From Coke's comment on this article, which reads: "The city of London shall have all the old liberties and customs, which it hath been used to have. Moreover we will and grant, that all other cities, boroughs, towns, and barons of the five ports, and all other ports, shall have all their liberties and free customs" [Chap. IX].

21. **ne injuste vexes**: OF, "not unjustly harass." Coke said: "No man shall be distrained to do more service for a knights fee, nor any freehold, than therefore is due." Coke says this concept was founded in ancient law, in "the form of the writ of *Ne injuste vexes*" [Chap. X].

22. **progressus ostendunt**: L, "progress [of things] reveals." From a note which says that, when a question cannot be settled by a justice or circuit, it can be taken to London. Coke cites an old Latin rule of law which translates: "But the progress of things reveals much that could not have been foreseen at the beginning" [Chap. XII, (4)b].

23. **periplum** . . . : English justices were required to go out throughout the kingdom to the local courts of assize to bring justice to the people. Here the concept is made to rhyme with the ideas of Kung (Confucius). Kung found the root in the process. Pound sees a similar root in Magna Carta. As in the Pisan Cantos, "periplum" simply indicates, in addition, moving from place to place [74/431, 443, 444].

24. **Ideogram**: Pen [M5025], "root, source, origin." Part of *pen yeh* [98:55, 56].

25. **Glanvil**: Ranulf de Glanvill[e], d. 1190. A chief justicier for Henry II of England. One of the great works of English law, *Tractatus de legibus et consuetudinibus regni Angliae* [Treatise on the laws and customs of the realm of England], has been ascribed to him. Coke said: "*It appeareth by Glanvile* that this act was made in affirmance of the common law" [Chap. XIV, (2)].

26. **saving his wainage**: One of Glanville's concepts, that no fine should be so severe that it would take away a man's means of making a living [DG, *Pai*, 4-2 & 3, 255].

27. **hominum . . . proborum**: L. An inversion of "Nisi per sacramentum proborum et legalium *hominum de vicineto*" ("But by the oath of honest and lawful men of the vicinage"). The article concerns fines or amerciaments and prescribes that "the punishment should fit the crime" and that no fine can be assessed except by the oath as indicated [Chap. XIV].

28. **laicum tenementum**: L, "lay-tenement." From a section which extends protection to church members: "No man of the church shall be amerced after the quantity of his spiritual benefice, but after his lay-tenament, and after the quantity of his offence" [Chap. XIV].

29. **de par le monde**: F, "somewhere."

30. **J'ai connu**: F, "I knew."

31. **books of a scholler**: Coke distinguishes the legal sense of the words "contenement" and "countenance" and ends: "countenance is used for contenement: the armor of a souldior is his countenance, the books of a scholler his countenance and the like" [Chap XIV, (2)].

32. **H. 2 E. 1**: Kings Henry II and Edward I, whom Coke praises for their dedication to justice.

33. **en temps** . . . : F, "in the time of King Henry Second."

34. **Jim First**: King James I. "When he drank, His thick tongue slobbered 'very uncomely, as if eating his drink, which came out into the cup on each side of his mouth . . .' " [Bowen, *Lion*, 228]. Because of his fondling of, and attachment to, a long series of handsome young men, James was known as a sodomist.

35. bitched our heritage: James I's long fight for the divine right of Kings and the royal prerogative as superior to the common law. Coke, who fought tirelessly against the concepts, ended up in the Tower. Thus the king is seen as one who undermined the legal heritage of the people.

36. Obit: L, "died."

37. Jacques Père: Shakespeare.

38. Noll: Nickname of Oliver Cromwell, who had King Charles I beheaded in 1649.

39. Puer Apulius: L, "the boy from Apulia," i.e., Frederick II. The words "Ver" and "L'estate" are from Ciullo d'Alcano's "Fresca rosa Aulentissima" [DD, *Pai*, 6-1, 101-107; *SR*, 62, 101].

40. Voltaire could not: Prob. "could not" conceive of a government that provided such protection to the people as Magna Carta provided.

41. Queen of Akragas: Prob. Athena, as goddess of wisdom and justice. Akragas [cf. 2 above] had a temple of Athena; even today a certain prominence is called "the Rock of Athena" [EB].

42. resistent: Prob. F, *resistant*, "strong."

43. templum aedificavit: L, "built a temple" [8:43]. Thus the lines construe: "built a temple to the strong goddess Athena."

44. Segesta: Ancient city of Sicily and bitter rival of Selinus [cf. 1 above]. Its ruins, with a temple to Artemis, are near modern Alcamo, and it is thus associated with the Sicilian poet Ciulio d'Alcamo, which Pound hopes will "evoke the enlightened legal Codes of Frederick II" of Sicily [DG, *Pai*, 4-2 & 3, 257].

45. II. Inst. XXI: This chapter of Magna Carta says: "No sheriff nor bailiff . . . shall take the horses or carts of any man to make carriage, except he pay the old price" In his commentary Coke says the statute applies to all nobility but "extendeth not to any person ecclisiasticall," and, "all this . . . was (. . . for the advancement and maintenance of that great peacemaker, and love-holder, hospitality) one of the auncient ornaments, and commendations of the kingdome of England" [Chap. XXI].

46. Nec alii boscum: L, "nor any other [take another man's] wood." Conflation of "nec nos, nec balivi nostri, nec alii, capiemus boscum alienum ad castra" ("not we, nor our bailiffs, nor any other, shall take any man's wood for our castles") [Chap. XXI].

47. high-wood is called saltus: In his commentary Coke writes: "High-wood is properly called *Saltus*" [ibid.].

48. Fleta: "It [boscum] is called in Fleta, *maeremium*" [ibid.]. The *Fleta* is a treatise on the English common law written by an unknown person in the 13th century. Tradition says it was written in the old Fleet Prison, hence the name "Fleta" or "Fleda."

49. qui utlagatus est: L, prob. *ut* + *legatus*, "who has a legal commission." The phrase occurs in a quote Coke makes from Glanville, as notes to an article in Magna Carta which reads: "We will not hold the lands of them that be convict of felony but one year and one day, and then those lands shall be delivered to the lords of the fee." At the end of his commentary Coke says: "hereby it also appeareth, how necessary the reading of auncient authors is for understanding of auncient statutes" [Chap. XXII].

50. kidells and skarkells: Names for "open weares [weirs] whereby fish are caught." Men were accustomed to spread weirs across rivers, which disrupted river traffic: "All wears from henceforth shall be utterly put down by Thames and Medway, and through all England, but only by the sea-coasts." Coke comments: "It was specially given in charge by the justices in eire, that all juries should enquire, *De hiis qui piscantur cum kidellis et skarkellis* [concerning those who were fishing with kidells and skarkells]" [Chap. XXIII].

51. sheepes back . . . : From a chapter on the uniform standards of weights and measures. Concerning "broade cloathes," Coke's note ends: "And this is the worthiest and richest commoditie of this kingdome, for divide our native commodities exported into tenne parts, and that which comes from the sheepes back, is nine parts in value of the tenne, and setteth great numbers of people on worke" [Chap. XXV].

52. **tonsured . . . untonsured**: These lines express the attitude of Coke during his struggles against the ecclesiastical courts, when they were taking jurisdiction in cases Coke believed should be tried under the common law. In King James's time both church people (tonsured) and nonchurch lawyers (untonsured) tried to play safe by pleasing the king, who promoted the ecclesiastical courts.

53. **vitex . . . market**: These 5 lines are a pastiche of memories cut into the canto. Pound translated the Chinese characters for a tree (*ch'ang-ts'o*) as "vitex negundo." DG associates this with Pound's earliest poem about turning into a tree and the process of metamorphosis. "Excideuil" returns us to his walking tour in Provence in the summer of 1919 [80:315; HK, *Era* 333-40]. At one point they were on a plateau so high, they were level with the tops of the poplar trees and the spire of a church. "From Val Cabrere, were two miles of roofs to San Bertrand" [48/243]. "Mme Pierre," prob. the old woman at Excideuil: "In the castle an old woman lived in a couple of rooms, and drew no water from the ill-kept well in the courtyard. Ezra bought a beam to lay across the well-curb (high on the castle bluff; level with the spire of St. Thomas)" [HK, *Era*, 336].

54. **Atque . . . belli**: L, "and for the public good, the laws of war are to be observed" [Chap. XXX, (1), 2].

55. **butlerage**: In ancient times import duties were paid to the king's butler—hence, *butlerage*.

56. **strangers**: Foreigners. From a regulation concerning the protection of foreign merchants, who "shall have their safe and sure conduct to depart out of England, to come into England, to tarry in and go through England, as well by land as by water . . . etc." [Chap. XXX].

57. **wooll woolfels & leather**: In this regulation—"And where some have supposed that there was a custom due to the king by the common law, as well of the stranger . . . viz for wools, wooll-fells, and leather . . ."—Coke shows that the custom was owing not to the common law but to a special act of a parliament of Edward III, granted for a limited time only [ibid.].

58. **hearth silver**: A tax Edward III imposed on the French after he took Aquitaine; it involved such an odious process of search, "an opening of kitchen doors to the king's officers," that it caused a revolt" [ibid.].

59. **naught new imposed . . .** : Concerns Coke's comment on the attempt of Queen Mary Tudor to impose an illegal duty on Malmsey wine: the duty was found to be illegal under the common law [ibid.].

60. **Scacarrio Rot. 319**: Queen Elizabeth set a custom in all the pope's dominions "upon every hundred weight of allome." The custom was challenged by some, but "judgement in the exchequer was given against them" [ibid.]. Custom: 3 shillings, 4 pence.

61. **on currants**: In the same chapter we read: "A judgement was given in the exchequer, for an imposition set upon currants, but the common opinion was, that that judgement was against law, and divers expresse acts of parliament. . . ." And: "To conclude this point, with two of the maximes of the common law. 1. Le common ley ad tielment admeasure les prerogatives le roy, que ilz ne tolleront, ne prejudiceront le inheritance dascun" ("The common law hath so admeasured the prerogatives of the king, that they should not take away, nor prejudice the inheritance of any") [Chap. XXX, (2), 3].

62. **ad mesure**: L, "measured out."

63. **Laws of Edgar**: Coke said: "And amongst the laws of King Edgar it is thus

concerning the sheriffes tourn provided." The "Sheriffs tourn" was the name of a circuit court [Chap. XXXV, (1)].

64. **ex omni satrapia**: L, "in all satrap-counties." The sense is, "all provinces which come under the jurisdiction of the courts." The judges traveled to all the counties to bring justice to the people.

65. **a circuit**: The law provided that "the bishop with the sheriffe did goe in circuit twice every yeare, by every hundred within the county . . . [such circuit] was called tour, or tourn, which signifieth a circuit or perambulation" [ibid.].

66. **sil ne fuit dizein**: OF, "if he were not of a group of ten." Coke citation from ancient law. The whole sentence in the source translates: "It was anciently ordered that no one could live in the realms if he did not pledge himself part of a group of ten" [ibid., (4)].

67. **quod trithinga teneatur integra**: L, "that the trithing be entirely kept." The trithing was a division between a shire and a hundred, and refers to the "group of ten" [ibid., (5)].

68. **decemvirale collegium**: L, "group of ten." The phrase was adapted from Roman law, in which it referred to the council of assistants to the praetor [ibid.].

69. **exceptis viris religiosis et . . .** : L, "except to religious institutions and." The source has "Judaeis" after "et," or "the Jews." Coke is citing Bracton, who said: "It is legal for a donor to make a gift of or sell land to anyone," except those named. DG believes Pound omitted the Jews because the point of the chapter is not aimed at any race but is "a definite separation of state affairs from all other institutions whatsoever" [Chap. XXXVI].

70. **vide Bracton**: L, "See B." Henry Bracton, d. 1268, was the author of *De Legibus et consuetudinibus Angliae* [On the laws and customs of England]. It was Coke's primary source of materials in his struggle against the king.

71. **sub colore donationis**: L, "under color of donation." A continuation of the gloss above which says the sale of land could not be made as if it were a gift [ibid.].

72. **his testibus**: The source reads: "hiis testibus": L, "these being witnesses." The last chapter of Magna Carta makes a general statement about the "customs and liberties" outlined and described earlier and concludes: "And we have granted into them [all subjects] . . . that neither we, nor our heirs, shall procure or do any thing whereby the liberties in this charter contained shall be infringed or broken; and if any thing be procured by any person contrary to the premisses, it shall be had of no force nor effect. These being witnesses; lord B. Archbishop of Canterbury, E. bishop of London, and others" [Chap. XXXVIII].

73. **chartae**: In his comment Coke said: "Those that had *hiis testibus*, were called *chartae*, as this charter is called *Magna Charta*, and so is *charta de foresta*, Etc. and those others." The others, from the time of Henry I in 1100, include the Coronation Charter, the Articles of the Barons, the Charter of Runnymede, the Charters of the Forest, etc. [CFT, *Pai*, 5-1, 69-76].

74. **PIVOT**: The center, base of process, unwobbling pivot, or "heart of the matter" from which our roots derive. The great English charters are our pivot.

75. **Statute de Merton . . .** : Coke's note to *Statutum de Merton, Editum anno 20 H. III*, so-called "because the Parliament was holden at the monastery of the canons regular of Merton, seven miles distant from the city of London" [DG, *Pai*, 4-2 & 3, 265].

76. **Bingham**: "And this is that monastery of Merton, the prior where of had a great case in law, which long depended between him and the Prior of Bingham" [ibid.].

77. **18 H. 3**: Eighteenth year of the reign of Henry III. Bracton misdates the feast of St. Vincent and the statute, which was actually in 1236 (not 1234). The statute concerned widows' dowers, wardships, enclosure of

commons, and usury, and is thus connected with the problem of Helianor.

78. **Helianor . . . Cantaur**: Eleanor of Provence, who married Henry III in 1236. A linkage with all the earlier Eleanors and Helen of Troy [2:7, 9; 7:1]. This Eleanor was the daughter of Raymond Beranger IV, count of Provence; her mother was the daughter of Thomas I, count of Savoy. She was thus the grand-daughter of the first troubadour, Duke William IX of Aquitaine [6:2]. Eleanor of Aquitaine's son, King John, is linked to the development of Magna Carta, and Henry III, under the influence of his wife, assisted in supporting it. Eleanor had no brothers; but her uncle, Boniface of Savoy (d. 1270), was elected archbishop of Canterbury (1241) through the influence of Henry III and Eleanor.

79. **Raymond Berengar**: The fourth of the counts of Provence. The House of Berenger were rulers in Barcelona and later had extensive holdings in Provence and Toulouse. The family was powerful enough to make marriages and concords or exercise influence over the royal houses of both France and England for over a century [cf. 10 above].

80. **de la plus beale**: OF, "of the fairest." Part of the name of a kind of dower: "fairest of the husband's tenements" [ibid.].

81. **the symbol**: Prob. the Christian cross.

82. **invasion of Bede's time**: The Venerable Bede, ?673-735; the invasions of the Norsemen in the 8th century.

83. **his version**: The King James Bible, 1611.

84. **lingua latina**: L, "Latin language." Pound uses 1850 to date the start of the process of ruining the schools.

85. **Alex**: Prob. Alexander the Great [89:230].

86. **Antoninus**: [78:56].

87. **Randolph**: [87:10].

88. **not to distreine**: The law says that the owner of the land in a widow's dower may get his due fo rent and services by taking "corn after it is reaped," but he "may not take the corn in sheaves" as a distraint for taxes [DG, *Pai*, 4-2 & 3, 266].

89. **Edward**: E. I, "Mirror of Princes," prohibited usury; but Coke notes in "Statute of Merton," Chap. V, that, nevertheless, England had great profit because of usury at a time when "the ounce of silver was five groats" [ibid.].

90. **forrein laws**: In a note on the legal problems of bastardy, Coke says that "forrein precedents are not to be objected against us because we are not subject to forrein laws" [ibid.].

91. **One thousand . . .** : In 1267, the 52d year of Henry III as king.

92. **Utas of St Martin**: The 8th day following the feast of St. Martin. On this day in 1267 was adopted the *Statutem de Marlebridge*, a general restatement of Magna Carta. After this, peace was once again restored to the people, "as well high as low" [ibid., 267].

93. **sapiens incipit a fine**: L, "A wise man begins at the end," or "anticipates the end." The Coke phrase seems to paraphrase the aphorism of Kung: "things have scopes and beginnings" [ibid.].

94. **Ideogram**: Chung [M1500], "the end."

95. **Ideogram**: Shih [M5772], "the beginning."

96. **Box hedge . . . basilicum**: Details of the house and gardens in Norwich where Coke went to Free Grammar School [Bowen, *Lion*, 48-54; DG, *Pai*, 4-2 & 3, 268].

97. **Allegre**: Rhyme with the lark song of Bernart de Ventadorn [117/802].

98. **1560**: One of the happiest acts of Elizabeth two years after she became queen was to call in all the debased coinage which was causing economic distress and issue a completely new and sound currency [DG, *Pai*, 4-2 & 3, 268].

99. '65, dutch weavers: As a boy of 13 years in Norwich, Coke saw the way the authorities dealt with a depression in the worsted industry. In 1565 they allowed weavers fleeing from religious persecution in Holland to settle in Norwich and produce fabrics, which allowed the "city to recapture its markets and regain its prestige" [ibid.].

100. at terms: The 4 terms of court each year related to 4 church festivals: Michaelmas from 9 Oct; Hilary from Jan 23; Trinity from May 22; and Easter. During terms the "women of uncertain profession" lingered around Westminster Hall," where their attendance was so regular that in those days they had the special name of 'termers.' " At Saint Paul's "every wench takes a pillar, as well as distinguished serjeant-at-law" [ibid., 269].

101. grain: After bad harvests, proclamations were issued to prohibit use of grain "for starching clothing or for any purpose except that of food" [Bowen, *Lion*, 319].

102. no more houses: The increasing crowding and growth of population led in both Elizabeth's and James's time to proclamations forbidding the construction of new buildings [ibid.].

103. de heretico comburendo: L, "of burning heretics." The name of a writ issued by a bishops court in 1612 sentencing Bartholomew Legate and Edward Wrightman to be burned as heretics. They were. Coke opposed the "monstrous writ," saying the bishops court did not have jurisdiction. Francis Bacon and others said conviction in bishops court would suffice [ibid., 296].

104. white sheet . . . sentence: In 1628 Coke's daughter, Frances, married to the brother of the powerful duke of Buckingham, was accused of adultery with Sir Robert Howard and tried before the Court of High Commission. The court judged her guilty, and Sir Henry Martin "fined her five hundred pounds and declared she must do public penance–walk barefoot, draped in a white sheet, from Paul's Cross to the Savoy and stand before the church for all to see" [Bowen, *Lion*, 531].

105. Invasion of rights: The duke of Buckingham, attempting to tax the people without sanction of Parliament, created a crisis in which Magna Carta was on the line. The king threatened to imprison anyone who did not pay the illegal tax. When Parliament met, March 17, 1628, Coke and his supporters went at once to the problem of the king's invasion of the rights of his subjects. Said Coke: "What doth this tend to but the utter subversion of the choice liberty and right belonging to every freeborn subject of this kingdom?" [Bowen, *Lion*, 485].

106. habeas: Parliament stood against the king for nearly 3 months, until Charles capitulated and granted habeas corpus against false imprisonment [ibid., 497-503].

107. B. 18: During WWII, the 18B regulations suspended habeas corpus to allow for the imprisonment of those who opposed the war [WC, *Guide*].

108. Chaise Dieu: F, "Throne of God" [23:24]. Mountains in the area had the shape of a throne. Pound may have been reminded of an earlier struggle of declared heretics against the absolute power of Innocent III in Charles I's repeated assertions of the divine right of Kings.

109. *μὴ ὄν*: H, "not being." Phrase of Aristotle used by Christopher Marlow's Faustus [I, V. 11]. Avon's man said, "To be or not to be."

110. Gaudier: Gaudier-Brzeska [16:26].

111. Nina: Nina Hamnett, an amateur painter who sat as GB's model for three different works [Materer, *Pai*, 4, 2 & 3, 323].

112. Diana: Artemis. Evidently Pound remembers a stone image of her in the Cathedral of Notre Dame des Champs which was crumbling with time. He supposes that a permanent bronze must exist somewhere.

113. Amphion: His music raised the walls of Troy [62:141; 90:7].

114. the great algae: May suggest that just as algae is the basic sustenance of life at the bottom of the great food chain, so the Great Charters and the Charters of Confirmation are the basic sustenance in the development of human rights and liberties.

115. color prediletto: colore prediletto: I, "favorite color."

116. *σῆραγξ*: H, "cave or rock hollowed out by the sea."

117. *Σειρήν*: H, "siren." One of those whose song lured sailors to their death.

118. hippocampi: hippocampe: F, "sea-horse."

119. *θελκτήριν*: H, "charm, spell, enchantment." As with the sirens.

120. god's antennae: Poss. poets, the "antennae of the race."

121. Norfolk tumbler: A gift Coke gave to his friend and supporter Robert Cecil as he was on his way to Bath to take the waters for his extreme ill-health. Because Cecil–a small hunchback but the son of Lord Burghley (the lord treasurer and the most powerful man in England)–used tricks to walk the thin line between king and Parliament, there may be a suggestion in Coke's giving this breed, which had "a trick of falling down to simulate injury while stalking game" [Bowen, *Lion*, 330].

122. Cecil: Robert C., 1563?-1612, earl of Salisbury. Trained by his father (the lifelong and most powerful adviser of Elizabeth) to statecraft, he came to power in 1596, first as secretary of state. He secretly prepared the way for James I to assume the throne. Known as the little pygmy, he maintained his position through ability and great financial skill.

123. Hatfield: Hatfield House, the name of the great Jacobean mansion Cecil built for himself. "The parks and gardens of Hatfield House were like a small friendly kingdom. Five hundred mulberry trees newly planted, thirty thousand grape vines sent from France" [ibid., 331].

124. enclosed: Cecil was a hero to most of the people, but he had at least one flaw: his "humbler neighbors did not love the place; enclosure of Hatfield wood had robbed their common pasture" [ibid., 332].

125. Gondemar: Count Gondemar, ambassador of Spain to the court of King James, whose charge was to cement a peace with England and arrange for the marriage of Prince Charles and the Infanta, which would advance the Catholic cause and–in Philip III's mind–eventually bring England back into the true church. On Oct 29, 1620 Sir Walter Raleigh was beheaded because of activities that harmed the cause of peace. Protestant England hated and feared all these procedings, and their wrath fell upon Gondemar. "On public holidays he did not dare venture into the streets. 'There goes the devil in a dungcart!' " an apprentice cried as he passed by. The youth and his friends were arrested and flogged through Fleet Street. James put out a proclamation: "No man by look or countenance to show irreverence to strangers, especially such as are ambassadors" [ibid., 417].

126. Flaccus' translator: The translations of Horace, Plutarch (on curiosity), and Boethius by Elizabeth I, mostly in her own hand and arranged in bundles dated 1593 and 1598, are to be found at the Public Record Office in London. The probable reason they were not included in any of the collections (Flügel, Pemberton, Bradner) is that they are written in paratactic prose and contain numerous errors of translation owing–as with Pound–to faulty eyesight or the use of inferior Renaissance editions of the classics. This was more or less common knowledge to students of Pound's generation, so he is not necessarily quoting from any particular source [EH][85:11].

127. The jew: Unidentified. Poss. Dr. Roderigo Lopez, Queen Elizabeth's physician, who was found guilty and executed for attempting to poison her. But Pound may have identified Gondomar as one of the Sephardim.

128. **The buggar**: Slang expression for sodomist. Refers either to James I or to the duke of Buckingham, who with the extraordinary power given to him by the king, undertook policies that, according to the party of Coke, tended to undermine the crown.

129. **Raleigh's head**: Sir Walter Raleigh was firmly opposed to the proposed marriage between Prince Charles and the Spanish Infanta. He had been condemned to the Tower in 1603 but was released in 1616 to sail to Guiana in search of gold. Raleigh gave his solemn promise that no Spaniard would be harmed; but he fought the battle of San Tomás, in which four Spaniards were killed, and returned with no gold. He was thus guilty of maliciously breaking the peace with Spain. The English public hated Gondomar because he actively sought the execution.

130. **That the dead**: In the continuing struggle of Parliament against the Spanish alliance, James I responded to a 2d petition of Commons "on the eleventh of December, 1621" but gave a response which in fact abrogated the privilege of free speech. In the ensuing parliamentary debate, there were those who would make fawning speeches designed to curry favor with the king. Coke was against further petitions but advised they go to Magna Carta and laws created by their ancestors and cite precedent and practice. "Best to ask counsel of the dead! For they will not flatter nor fawn to advance themselves, nor bribe nor dissemble" [Bowen, *Lion*, 451].

131. **Dante's view**: [Cf. 107/756].

132. **Kung**: [13:1; 52:18].

133. **Ocellus**: [87:43].

134. **Agassiz**: [93:51].

135. *ῥεῖ*: H, "flows." Part of PANTA 'REI [96:168].

136. **Three Ninas**: [Cf. 111 above].

137. **mania . . . veins**: Lusting after some distant mystic paradise, many cannot see clearly the details of the paradise around them.

138. **Wheat . . . days**: [45:5].

139. **(1.46 . . . midnight)**: Prob. Pound read this time as he was finishing the canto.

140. **Allen Upward**: [74:271]. Says David Moody: "Upward's place in this company is by virtue of more than his seal. . . . Sitalkas is the divinity in the wheat" [*Pai*, 4-1, 56]. Since Sitalkas is mentioned nowhere in Upward, Pound doubtless got the name from a poem by H.D. so titled. The importance of Upward and *The Divine Mystery* to Pound's sun-light-divinity-intelligence cannot be over emphasized. In reviewing the book [*New Freewoman*, 15 Nov. 1913], Pound wrote: "The first half of the book is planned . . . on the slow recognition of the sun . . . primitive man turns from his worship of the dead . . . to a worship of the life-giving Helios. The solar missionary says it is unnecessary to bury a man in the cornfield in order that crops shall rise by virtue of his spirit." This perception does away with the need of sacrificial victims and all practices against nature. The sun, not the buried slain, gives power to the seed and puts it in motion (*semina motuum*) and ends by "snatching the victim from the cross" [ibid., 58-59].

141. **Sitalkas**: [74:272]. Sitalkas was a warrior king of the tribe of the Odrysae inhabiting the Hebrus valley in southern Thrace. He reigned c. 431-424. Several Odrysian kings named Sitalkes seem to have derived from a Prince Sitalkes mentioned in Herodotus [IV, 80], Thucydides [I, 29], and Xenophon [*Anabasis* VI, I, 6]. The name may have derived from *σῖτο* and *αλ-αλκεῖν*, meaning "Protector of Grain" [EH].

142. **Coin . . . Ambracia**: Just as Sitalkas, the king of a tribe looked upon by the

Greeks as uncouth barbarians, was sophisticated enough to have his own seal, the tribal inhabitants of Ambracia were sophisticated enough to have a coinage of their own [EH].

143. Ambracia: City of ancient Greece, in Epirus on an inlet of the Ionian Sea. The modern Greek town or Arta.

144. Caelator: L, "carver."

145. Pythagora: Pythagorus: L, "Pythagoras" [91:97; 104:16].

CANTO CVIII

Sources

Sir Edward Coke, *Second Institutes of the Laws of England*, 1797 [*Institutes*]; Catherine Drinker Bowen, *The Lion and the Throne*, Little, Brown, Boston, 1956 [Bowen, *Lion*]; Dante, *Par.* X, 42, 136. Virgil, *Aeneid* I, 412; *Servii Commentarii*, Vol. I, Lipsiae, 1881.

Background

EP, *SR*, 62, 101; EH, *Approaches*, 173, 192; Bryce Lyon, *A Constitutional and Legal History of Medieval England*, Harpers, N.Y., 1960; William Stubbs, *The Constitutional History of England*, Vol. II, Oxford, 1887; William Sharp McKechnie, *Magna Carta*, rev., Burt Franklin, N.Y., 1958; J. M. Rigg, *Select Pleas, Starrs, and Other Records from the Rolls of the Exchequer of the Jews* London, B. Quaritch, 1902; M de R, *Discretions*, 58.

Exegeses

DD, *Sculptor*, 239-240; DG, *Pai*, 4-2 & 3, 223-299; DD, *Pai*, 6-1, 101-107; HK, *Era*, 336; CFT, *Pai*, 5-1, 69-76; Materer, *Pai*, 4, 2 & 3, 323; Moody, *Pai*, 4-1, 55-69; MB, *Trace*, 444-447; EH, *Pai*, 5-2, 354.

Glossary

1. COMMINUIT . . . BRUM: A phrase from Bk. I, 412, of *The Aeneid*, which is glossed [*Servii Commentarii*, 137] thus: "412. CIRCUM DEA FUDIT figura est tmesis, quae fit cum secto uno sermone aliquid interponimus, ut alibi *septem* subiecta *trioni*. sed hoc tolerabile est in sermone conposito, ceterum in simplici nimis est asperum; quod tamen faciebat antiquitas, ut saxo cere comminuit brum." ("CIRCUM DEA FUDIT [DEA CIRCUMFUDIT: "the goddess closely embraced"] is the figure tmesis, which is made when we interpose something in a split word, as elsewhere *septem* subiecta *trioni* [septemtrioni subiecta: "lying under the great bear"]. But this is permissible in a compound word, otherwise in a simple word it is too harsh: however, the ancients used to do this, such as SAXO CERE COMMINUIT BRUM [SAXO CEREBRUM COMMINUIT: "he split his head with a rock" /].") A gloss on SAXO in this passage in the *Servii* cites the *Annales* of Quintus Ennius [Enn. Ann. rel. 586 Vahl.]. To show that he was using the rhetorical figure tmesis Pound put the two Latin components into striking capitals and split them by an interpolation of two other striking figures. Pound told J. Laughlin that the cluster derived from Ennius, whom he admired as a precursor of e e cummings. HK [letter, 14 Oct. 1981] says of splitting the word: "EP likens this to the frost splitting the rock itself." Laughlin made use of the information in a poem he wrote in the 50s entitled "Saxo Cere," the first line of which is "Comminuit brum a rainy day" [*In Another Country, Poems 1935-1975*, selected by Robert Fitzgerald, City Lights, San Francisco, 1978]. This poem was noted as source by Eva Hesse [*Pai*, 5-2, 354].

2. 25 Edward III: This statute begins, "Loans against the will of the subjects are against reason and the franchises of the land." Coke quoted it in a House of Commons session during which Dudley Digges said: "meum and tuum . . . [is] the nurse of industry, the mother of courage; for if a man hath no property, he has no care to defend it" [DG, *Pai*, 4-2 & 3, 277].

3. "alla" at Verona: Part of "alla [I, "to thee"] non della" [I, "of thee"] in the *Programma di Verona* of Mussolini [86:63]: "e un diritto alla proprieta" (I, "it is a right to property"): a rhyme with statute 25 of Edward III.

4. pen yeh: [98:55, 56]: "source of knowledge."

5. Enrolled . . . her hands: Lyric evocation of pomona theme [79/490-492] and the fire of life in *semina motuum* [90:24].

6. Charter to . . . Petition: The instrument by which Coke finally won his battle against Buckingham (the man behind the scenes prompting Charles I) and achieved habeas corpus and other rights [107:105-107] was called "The Petition of Right." The king finally assented to it by the appropriate legal formula in June of 1628. The activities of Buckingham constituted a fundamental attack upon Magna Carta. The petition became a reaffirmation of all the charters. If the parliament had lost the battle for the petition, justice and freedom would have received a terrible setback.

7. DROIT FAIT: F. Key phrase in the formula by which the monarch had for centuries made acts of Parliament legal: "Soit droit fait comme il est desiré" ("Let right be done as it is desired"). Behind the phrase lies one of the most dramatic moments in the history of English and American law. For months Coke and the Commons had been petitioning the king to reaffirm the charter and stop his ministers, led by Buckingham, from taking peoples' property by forced loans, arresting them illegally, holding them in the tower without trial, and so on. The struggle between the Commons and the king was traditional and simple: he wanted taxes levied; the Commons refused until the Petition of Right was legally adopted. In May of 1628 the King began threatening to dissolve the Parliament if they did not get on with the royal business, saying always that the Commons need not worry because he had long since affirmed the charters and he existed to see justice done for all his people. Neither side gave in; but on June 2 great hope prevailed. The king came to Parliament and listened to the Petition of Right read in its entirety. After it was over, the day became known as "Black Thursday," because the lord keeper said, "The King Willeth that right be done according to the laws . . ." etc. Instantly, the Commons knew they had failed: the traditional *soit droit fait* was not spoken. After the king departed, the Commons continued to sit in uncertain sadness. On June 3d the king sent a message saying the session must end in a week. On June 4th the House continued to sit as if the message had not come. According to one member, there were "above a hundred weeping eyes" among strong men, some of whom had been tested by imprisonment. Then Coke had an idea. If the lords would join them, they could not lose. It had long been an axiom that no king could hold out against the Lords and Commons together. Since forced loans and false arrests had been made against the lords of the land, too, they did join. "After a brief conference with the Commons they dispatched a joint deputation to ask his Majesty for 'a clear and satisfactory answer', given in full Parliament [both houses] to their Petition of Right." The king assented. Somewhat after 4 o'clock on Saturday, June 6th, amid much pomp and circumstance, the king, lords, and Commons heard again the whole document: "their words as they had set them down, the confirmation of their ancient rights and liberties." When the clerk's voice ceased, the Commons broke into an applause, which was followed by an immediate hush as he stepped forward again to give the royal response. The clerk said: "*Soit droit fait comme il est desiré*." A great shout rang out which was repeated again and again. The news spread to the street, where it "broke out into ringing of bells." Says Bowen: "as the June dusk began to fall there were bonfires 'at every door . . .' " [*Lion*, 497-503].

8. **Statutum Tallagio**: A statute of 28 Edward I, *De tallagio non concedendo*, which states that no tax shall be levied except by the whole people through the elected members of Parliament. This statute was one of the basic sources of the Petition of Right [DG, *Pai*, 4-2 & 3, 278].

9. **Lambarde on Valla**: Coke sought to give precise definitions of key terms by resorting to etymology. At one point he tried to derive *parliament* from *parler le ment*, saying he got the idea "from the antiquarian Lambarde." But he thought better of it, saying: "But Laurence Valla misliketh that manner of Etymology, and therefore I will not stand upon it" [ibid.].

10. **"all monopolies"**: Says Coke: "Generally all monopolies are against the great Charter, because they are against the liberty and freedom of the subject and against the law of the land" [Chap. XXIX, (4)].

11. **"Nor against . . . Ireland**: Ireland is a personal matter here because when James I wanted Parliament to pass illegal taxes to fit out a fleet, he thought of sending Coke to Ireland to get him out of the way [Bowen, *Lion*, 460]. The *Institutes* says: "Therefore the king cannot send any subject of England against his will into Ireland to serve the king as his deputy there" [ibid., 461].

12. **autarchia**: H, [αὐτάρκεια]: "independence." Used by Coke in his concern for the independence of traders [Chap. XXX, 57-59].

13. **not cloth . . . Realm**: In the past, kings had imposed a custom on wool, to which Parliament had assented. The wool was converted into cloth and often exported. When attempts were made to extend this tariff to wool already made into cloth, they protested [Cap. XXX, 60-62].

14. **Owse . . . Tine**: Rivers of England which needed and received protection from the over-fishing of salmon: "Before the making of this act fishermen for a little lucre did very much harm, and destroyed the increase of salmons by fishing for them in unseasonable times" [DG, *Pai*, 4-2 & 3, 279].

15. **Post . . . disherisons**: L, "After the feast of St. Hilary many evils and disinheritings." An act passed in the year 1290 (the 18th year of the reign of Edward I) concerned property lost to legal heirs because of usury. It goes on to define limits to usury and leads to acts to protect Jews. King John had restricted Jews to any occupation except moneylending and then confiscated their property because they were guilty of usury. Edward I attempted to remedy such injustice [ibid., 280-282].

16. **ne curge . . . prochainement**: L, phrase from *que nul usury ne curge de S. Edward prochainement passe en avant*, "that no

usury will run from the feast of St. Edward next coming and afterwards" [ibid.].

17. **ne quis injuriam**: L, phrase from writ for the protection of Jews: *ne quis . . . injuriam, molestiam, damnum inferat, seu gravamen*, "no one will suffer injury, molestation, damage or trouble."

18. **salvum conductum**: L, "safe conduct." From a specific provision which guaranteed safe-conduct to Jews if they wanted to leave the country. DG summarizes passages from J. M. Rigg [*Select Pleas, Starrs, and Other Records from the Rolls of the Excheques of the Jews*] and others concerned with usury and the Jews in medieval England: "We shall see how much the English crown had been benefitting from the Jews. . . . This statute [Edward I] forbids usury but also forbids the persecution of the Jews. As Coke points out, many had decisively banished the Jews and discriminated against them racially but Edward I saw the injustice of this and merely made a law against usury." He also made a law assuring those Jews who wanted to leave England that "they might have the king's writ to the sherifes for their safe conduct" [ibid.].

19. **die decimoctave**: L, "18th day."

20. **was 15 000 three score**: The number of Jews who left the country under the anti-usury law.

21. **divers . . . exeuntibus**: In paraphrase, other kings had banished the Jews, but no king before Edward had forbidden usury itself. The three names are Coke's marginal citation of sources [ibid.].

22. **Uncle Carlo**: C. Delcroix [88:46].

23. **Margherita**: [86:5]. But possibly the person MB identifies thus: "Alias Val di Tures, in the environs of which P.'s daughter was raised" [*Trace*, 452].

24. **no officer . . .** : Opening of the statute *De tallagio* . . . [cf. 8 above].

25. **cujus bona**: For cui bono: I, early form for "for whose advantage?"

26. **Et Forestae . . . Edward**: NF, "[Concerning the liberties] and forests by the grace of God [Edward King] of England." A condensation of the first chapter of the Charter of Confirmation adopted in the 25th year of Edward I's reign. It says to the sheriffs that the charters have been confirmed in all points and they should be published throughout the realm.

27. **Devant . . . guier**: NF, "Before them in judgment . . . that is to know . . . amending our realm . . . have to guide." Key phrases in the chapter.

28. **nient tenus**: NF, "holden for nought." The context is, anything done contrary to the charter shall be undone and "holden for nought."

29. **per an, deux foits**: NF, "two times per year." A direction that the charters should be read before the people this many times.

30. **mises ne prises**: NF, "puts nor takes." A *mise* was a task or tallage a lord could "put" on his subject. A *prise* was something a king or lord could take from his tenant as a duty or a tax.

31. **precedent**: The charter said: "The king had obtained by free consent, and good will in parliament precedent aids, subsidies or tasks for the maintenance of his warres in forein parts, which howsoever they were graunted in full parliament . . ." [*Institutes*, 529; DG, *Pai*, 4-2 & 3, 284]. The point was that previous granting of aid should not be precedent, without consent of Parliament, for future grants.

32. **1272 . . . 1297**: Date of Edward's accession to the throne and the date of adoption of this Confimation Charter.

33. **Confirmationis . . .** : ML, "Confirmation of the Charter."

34. **Cap VI**: The chapter concerns no use of public funds without express consent of Parliament.

35. **Disraeli**: According to Pound, D's purchase of the Suez Canal was done behind the

back of Parliament [86:61]; but Parliament was not in session and the transaction had to be accomplished, if at all, with great speed and secrecy.

36. de la maletot . . . : NF, "of the sack of the laws 40 shillings." The source has "leynes": "wool."

37. nous lettres . . . 8 pence: NF, "In witness of which things we have caused these our letters to be made patents . . . [Witness Edward] our son at London the tenth day of October, the five and twentieth year of our reign" [*Institutes*, 530].

38. dimidium . . . pellibus: NF, "half a mark [about 6s. 8p.] for three hundred pelts." The amount of illegal tax Edward I assessed on the wool trade [*Institutes*, 530].

39. aliorum liberorum: NF, "of other free men." Part of "De Tallagio . . . " [cf. 8 above]. Tax could not be assessed on free men without consent "of other free men" [ibid., 532].

40. nullum tallagium: NF, "no tallage [customs charge]" [ibid., 534].

41. in pleno . . . : NF, part of, "this must be petitioned in a full parliament."

42. or to, or for . . . : Part of sentence about taxes which ends: "either to or for the king, or to or for any subject by the king's letters patents . . . is prohibited by the act" [ibid., 534].

43. et vacua nulla: NF, part of *vacua ut nulla sint*, "shall be void and frustrate for evermore" [ibid., 534].

44. nihil capiatur: NF, "nothing shall be taken" [ibid.,534].

45. Bohun: Humfrey le Bohun, earl of Hereford, was one of those who refused to pay the war tax of Edward I. He was, along with others, specifically pardoned by act of Parliament.

46. John de Ferraris: John Ferrers, also pardoned.

47. Felton: [Cf. 54 below]. His name is included among the others as one who risked and gave his life for a greater good.

48. Henry III . . . 1307: Sets forth the time and efforts in which the charters were perfected and approved, from the simple "Articles of the Barons" signed by King John at Runnymede, through the major additions demanded and approved by Parliament.

49. CESTASCAVOIR: NF, "that is to say." The opening of Chap. I of the Charter of Confirmation, which was "a son people," an inclusive phrase of the king and all his subjects.

50. 4 times a year: The number of times the document was required to be read.

51. Michael . . . John: The four church festivals during which it was to be read.

52. tried locally: The charter required each district to elect commissioners whose function it was to investigate any infringement of the charters. The sentences these courts could impose were limited to imprisonment, ransom, and amercement, "according to the trespass."

53. Charles . . . 41: Charles I kept Coke's work buried for 7 years. Then, on May 12, 1641, the Long Parliament ordered Coke's commentary upon *Magna Charta, The Second Institutes* be published [Bowen, *Lion*, 517, 551].

54. Felton: The source says: "On the twenty-third of August, a Saturday, the Duke was at Portsmouth, preparing to sail with the fleet. In a crowded hallway, a man—John Felton by name—walked up and stabbed Buckingham with a tenpenny knife. In fifteen minutes he was dead. . . . Everywhere the people showed their joy. Poems poured out upon the town . . . Felton's health was drunk. . . . Threatened by the Earl of Dorset with torture to make him disclose his accomplices, 'If I be put upon the rack,' said Felton, 'I will name you, my Lord of Dorset, and none but yourself.' Spared the rack, on November twenty-eighth

Felton was hanged at Tyburn" [Bowen, *Lion*, 522].

55. articuli . . . avisés: NF, "The articles of the Charter of 28th Edward will be administered [by the election of] three just men or other well-disposed-persons" [DG, *Pai*, 4-2 & 3, 288-289].

56. "Vierge": To stay within the "verge" was to stay within 6 miles of the person of the sovereign, either at court or traveling through the kingdom.

57. Fleta: One of Coke's oft-cited sources. The Fleta was a brief paraphrase of Bracton done around 1290.

58. Hastings . . . Sandwich: The original 5 ports of the "Cinque Ports," a group of maritime towns in Sussex and Kent.

59. Ideogram: Chi [M412], "royal domains." Rhyme with the king's house.

60. Ideogram: Pi [M5103], "silks." This ideogram "is used in the history to demonstrate the symbolic loyalty of the subjects to the king. . . . *Pi* later comes to stand for coin, 'the currency of the realm' " [ibid., 289].

61. sheriffs elective: Election of such a public office was a major step toward human freedom, "since in matters judicial, military and fiscal, the sheriff transacted all the business of the shire" [ibid., 290].

62. ou . . . de fee: NF, "where shrivality is not in fee [inherited]."

63. In those . . . sufficient": Source: "They shall put in those inquests and juries such as be next neighbours, most sufficient, and least suspicious" [*Institutes*, 561].

64. et malveyes procurers: NF, "and the packing of juries." [ibid., 562].

65. De lum . . . lauter: NF, "of the civil bench and criminal." Justices of both benches–Common Pleas and the King's Bench–are in this chapter directed to give justice quickly in any kind of conspiracy [DG *Pai*, 4-2 & 3, 290].

66. Elfynge . . . Com: Says DG: "Pound's marginalia is a tribute to H. Elfynge the clerk of the House of Commons who on a Wednesday inscribed that Coke's Commentaries on *Magna Charta* should be published in print" [ibid.].

67. William of Helmswell: The name of one who appeared to be involved in a conspiracy [cf. 65 above].

68. leopard's head: The monarch is responsible for the purity–legal fineness–of silver and gold. The sign of the leopard was the sign of the crown: "And that these standards be kept it is imperative that no sort of vessel of silver leaves a worker's hand unless it be marked with the leopard's head and that a goldsmith work no worse gold than that denoted by 'the touch of Paris' " [ibid., 291].

69. Articuli twenty: The "Cap xx" below. The article of the 28th year of Edward I concerned with standards of coinage.

70. Auxy . . . : NF, "Must be marked with the sign of the leopard."

71. King onely . . . : Coke said that it "pertains to the king onely to put a value on the coine," a rhyme with "Gold was under the Pontifex" [89:231].

72. 12 grains . . . : The English denar was defined as weighing the same as "twelve grains of wheat in mid spike" [ibid., 291].

73. frumento . . . : NF, Source has, "ponderabit 12 grano frumenti in medio spicae" ("will weigh 12 grains of wheat in mid spike") [ibid.].

74. Magnalia . . . : ML, Source has, "inter Magnalia et regalia coronae" ("among the important and regal rights of the king"). Concerns regulation of coinage [ibid.].

75. ELIZABETH: Queen E. the First. Although she did much to deserve the love of the English ("Angliae amor"), her greatest deed was to restore the coinage of the realm, which had been badly debased.

76. Ad valorem . . . : ML. Inscribed on E's tomb is the phrase *Moneta ad suum valorem reducta*, "she brought money back to its true value."

77. non . . . fundendam: ML. From Coke's phrases "a tempore quo non extat memoria" and "utilioribus boscis ad mireram regis ardendom & fundendam" ("from time out of memory" [for this long the king had]) ("had the use of wood for burning and melting regal metals / gold and silver") [ibid., 292].

78. souls . . . defrauded: Money left to the church to do things in the name of the departed was often sent to Rome.

79. that the seal . . . : The remedy noted was to take the seal from the prior and give it to 4 worthy men ("dignioribus") to administer.

80. Paragots: Coke notes that just one cardinal, Paragots, received more than 10,000 marks a year which in the end came from the "almes" of the people.

81. alienigenae . . . : ML, "alien superiors." Coke says that such aliens "had a third part of the possessions of the realm" [*Institutes*, 584].

82. brocars: ME, "brokers."

83. caitifes: NF, "wretches." Thus does education decay in the hands of the church.

84. Rot . . . 3: Coke's marginal note that tells when these bad customs were introduced in Rome.

85. grosbois . . . hornbeam: Coke's exposition upon tithes says that the timber trees listed here cannot be tithed because they take years to develop; but acorns can because they are renewable yearly. A rhyme with the grasslands of the Sienese bank, as well as a central thesis of Pound's economics: the acorns would be natural, legitimate interest, but to cut down the tree would be usury [*Institutes*, 639].

86. nel Tirolo: I, "in the Tyrol." One lira, a legitimate tithe, as a lamb is born every year [M de R, *Discretions*, 58].

87. dies solaris: L, "light of day." Coke is concerned with laws whereby the buyer can see the horse he is buying, so that the public can be protected from deception.

88. ut pena . . . perveniat: ML, "so that punishment of a few will serve as warning to the many."

89. 2 rights . . . : When 2 statutes conflicted Coke said the older should be preferred.

90. caveat emptor: L, "Let the buyer beware."

91. HORSFAIRE . . . no toll: A pastiche of details from a statute meant to help prevent fraud, especially in the sale of horses. The buyer should be allowed to ride the horse as at present a car-buyer is allowed to drive the car. "Phil" and "Mar" identify the statute: "2 & 3 Phil and Mac [sic] Cap 7." Fines are set as are other payments: "And for the bookkeeper only one penny, without toll, for every contract" [DG, *Pai*, 4-2 & 3, 294-295].

92. Iong Ching: Yung Chêng [60:73].

93. responsabili . . . ewe: NF, "responsibility for the increasing of the [water] flowing"

94. reparando: NF, "repairing."

95. Stat. . . . Eliz.: In an effort to prevent overcrowding and the growth of slums, this statute, entitled "Concerning Inmates," attempted to regulate open space around each dwelling [*Institutes*, 736].

96. Angliae amor: [Cf. 75 above].

CANTO CIX

Sources

Sir Edward Coke, *Second Institutes of the Laws of England*, 1797 [*Institutes*]; Catherine Drinker Bowen, *The Lion and the Throne*, Little, Brown, Boston, 1956 [Bowen, *Lion*]; Dante, *Par.* X, 42, 136; Virgil, *Aeneid* I, 412; *Servii Commentarii*, Vol. I, Lipsiae, 1881; Edward Coke, *The First Institute of the Laws of England*, London, 1897 [*First*]. Sophocles, *The Women of Trachis* [*WT*]; The Charter of Connecticut; Dante, *Par.* II, 1.

Background

EP, *SR*, 62, 101; EH, *Approaches*, 173, 192; Bryce Lyon, *A Constitutional and Legal History of Medieval England*, Harpers, N.Y., 1960; William Stubbs, *The Constitutional History of England*, Vol. II, Oxford, 1887; William Sharp McKechnie, *Magna Carta*, rev., Burt Franklin, N.Y., 1958; J. M. Rigg, Select *Pleas, Starrs, and Other Records from the Rolls of the Excheques of the Jews*; M de R, *Discretions*, 58; W. Keith Kavenagh, ed. *Foundations of Colonial America*, Chelsea House, N.Y., 1973 [WK, *Colonial*].

Exegeses

DD, *Sculptor*, 239-240; DG, *Pai*, 4-2 & 3, 223-299; DD, *Pai*, 6-1, 101-107; HK, *Era*, 336; CFT, *Pai*, 5-1, 69-76; Materer, *Pai*, 4, 2 & 3, 323; Moody, *Pai*, 4-1, 55-69; MB, *Trace*, 444-447; EH, *Pai*, 5-2, 354.

Glossary

1. **Pro Veritate**: L, "for truthfulness"

2. **curtilagia teneant**: ML, "[those] living in cottages." The statute prescribes the ideal and goes on to allow exceptions to some who cannot afford "4 acres" [108:95] or would otherwise be harmed.

3. **Idlenesse**: But the statute was against "unlawful houses," which Coke describes as "being nests to hatch idleness, the mother of pickings" [*Institutes*, 740].

4. **EPARXON**: Reference to *The Book of the Eparch* [96:271]

5. **Do sell . . . changed**: These 10 lines (with those before and after) indicate parallel concerns in ancient laws such as *The Eparch's Book* and a number of statutes throughout the legal history of England.

6. **Donaison, denizen**: NF, "Merchant strangers."

7. **(Littleton's)**: Coke's *First Institute* was in large part a commentary upon the legal work of Littleton.

8. **No wight . . .** : In his comment on Littleton, Coke quoted Chaucer's description of the "Sergeant of the Lawe": "Ther koude no wight pynche at his writyng."

9. vocabula artis: NF. "vocables of art." Coke said of "law French" that it "has grown to be vocables of art—vocabula artis, so apt and significant to express the sense of laws . . ." and "neither ought legal terms to be changed ["Proeme"].

10. Bracton: [107:70].

11. nemo omnia novit: L, "no one renews all." But prob. in NF, or what Coke called "law French," it means "without knowing all the details."

12. The Confessor's: Edward the Confessor, king 1042-1066. Coke's discovery of the phrase "excused jury service" implied that trial by jury must have existed before the Norman conquest.

13. Ambracia: City of ancient Greece on an inlet of the Ionian Sea, founded 7th century B.C.

14. veigne en Court: NF, "Vigne for short."

15. Sellaio: [20:17; 93:68], Florentine painter.

16. le Concord del fine: NF, "a fine which brings harmony because it [cannot omit] anything [*ascum chose*]."

17. *συμβαίναι*: [87:59]. Pound gives the whole phrase from *WT* as: "Splendour it all coheres!" [*WT*, 50].

18. solonques . . . dit): NF, "so long as the purpose holds, CHARTER said to be certain. / in which the earth lives / (the book says)." These phrases do not occur in Coke in any such form, but some parts occur in a variety of places.

19. "de ses vicines": NF [?], "of these neighborhoods [?]."

20. tempora non regum: ML, "times not of kings."

21. arundinetum: Source has this word followed by "where seeds grow" [Coke, *First*, 86a, 4b, 5b; DG, *Pai* 4-2 & 3, 296].

22. Si . . . nascitur: ML, "If the name of a thing is not known then knowledge of things perishes / No man is born an artist."

23. Ten families . . . : Early English community organization was arranged in units of ten under a leader who pledged allegiance to his leader: Modeled upon Roman precedents.

24. a city remaineth: Although Henry VIII expropriated the property of the church, London still went on.

25. Tuan: [85:33].

26. et consuetudo: L, "also custom."

27. Wadsworth: Joseph W., "who stole the Connecticut Charter and hid it in Charter Oak" [*PD*, 6]. He was publicly rewarded in 1715.

28. Charles . . . '62: From the preamble to the Charter of Connecticut, dated April 23, 1662: "Charles the Second, by the grace of God, King of England. . . ."

29. Brewen, Canfield: Among 19 persons listed in the Charter of Conn. to whose petition the king was responding in granting the charter: Henry Woolicott, John Talcott, Obedias Brewen, Mathew Camfeild, etc. The charter says: "Wee have thought fitt, and att the humble Petiçon of the Persons aforesaid, and are graciously pleased to create and make them a Body Pollitique . . ." [WK, *Colonial*, 111-112].

30. meere . . . : The charter says: "And accordingly Our Will and pleasure is, and of our especiall grace, certeine knowledge and meere moçon, wee have Ordeyned, Constituted and Declared, And by theis presents, for vs, our heires and Successors, Doe Ordeine, Constitute and Declare that they, the said. . . ." Here the 19 names are repeated and are followed by many phrases and conditions, including those in the canto lines, such as: "And further, that the said Governour and Company, and their Successors shall and may for ever hereafter have a Comon Seale. . . . there shall bee one Governour, one Deputy Governour and Twelve Assistants to bee . . . Elected. . . ." In the meantime, the king appointed such officers and said they were "to contynue in the said severall Offices respectively, untill the second Thursday which shall bee in the Moneth of October now next comeing" [ibid, 112-113].

31. **Oathes**: "All other Officers to be appointed . . . shall . . . take their severall and respective Corporall Oathes . . ." [ibid., 114]. The next two pages of text are devoted to the ritual of oaths.

32. **Ship** . . . : "And to every such Person . . . full power . . . to take, Ship, Transport and Carry away, for and towards the Plantaçon . . . such of our loveing subjects. . . ." etc. [ibid., 115].

33. **Under . . . seal**: "That all such Lawes . . . as shall bee soe made by the Governor . . . and Assistants . . . and published in writeing under their Comon Seale, shall carefully and duely bee observed . . ." [ibid., 116].

34. **hinder fishinge** . . . : "These presents shall not in any manner hinder any of our loveing Subjects whatsoever to use and exercise the Trade of Fishinge. . . . And to build . . . such . . . workehouses as shall bee necessary for the Salting, drying and keepeing of their Fish . . ." [ibid., 117].

35. **Narrowgancett** . . . : "And by theis presents . . . Doe give . . . unto the said Governor and Company . . . All that parte of our Dominions in Newe England . . . bounded on the East by Norrogancett . . . and on the South by the Sea . . ." [ibid.].

36. **Mynes . . . Silver**: "Together with all firme lands . . . Mynes, Mynerals, Precious Stones, Quarries, . . . To have and to hold . . . as of our Mannor of East Greenewich, in Free and Comon Soccage, and not in Capite . . . and Payinge therefore, to us, our heires and Successors, onely the Fifth parte of all the Oare of Gold and Silver . . . to bee to us . . . paid" [ibid., 117-118].

37. **23rd April**: [cf. 28 above].

38. **HOWARD**: The charter, ends: "In witnes whereof, wee have caused these our Letters to bee made Patent: Witnes our Selfe, att Westminster, the three and Twentieth day of Aprill . . . By Writt of Privy Seale. [Signed] Howard" [ibid., 118].

39. **Wing . . . Azaleas**: The 4 lines pick up the flora and fauna of the Na-khi, looking to the opening of Canto 110.

40. **Monro**: A foreign correspondent for Beaverbrook's *Evening Standard* stationed in Rome in the mid and late 30s. Pound appears to believe that Edward VIII, who acceded to the throne in 1936, was forced to abdicate by Baldwin not because of his marriage to Wallis Simpson but because he wouldn't have signed the papers of mobilization. Said Pound: "And that Eddie may have felt it was comin,' at any rate he hadn't the backbone to stick it [out]. And the traitors were afraid that he might balk at the last moment and refuse to sign on the dotted line, for mobilization" [EP, *Speaking*, 172-173]. Pound was still convinced at St. Elizabeths. Says *Mullins*: "There was one last-minute obstacle—'Eddie' refused to sign. . . . He had been through the veterans' hospitals just after the First World War, and . . . could not bring himself to send men into that kind of hell again" [EM, *Difficult*, 195].

41. **Jury trial**: [87:40].

42. **reparando**: [108:94].

43. **Stat de 31 Eliz**: [Cf. 2 above; 108:95].

44. **Angliae amor**: [108:75].

45. **false stone** . . . : [108/768].

46. **auxy sort** . . . : [108:68].

47. **Taormina**: [91:98].

48. **Selloi**: [87:83]. In the *Trachiniae* Heracles says: "The dead beast kills the living me / and that fits another odd forecast / breathed out at the Selloi's oak— / those fellows rough it . . ." [*WT*, 49]. Ten lines later we have the thematic declaration: "SPLENDOUR, IT ALL COHERES" [100/714].

49. **Phyllotaxis**: The arrangement of leaves around the stem of a plant or a tree is designed in such a way that the maximum amount of sunlight and energy is absorbed. To Pound this design is one more evidence of a divinity shaping all things in process. Also, the circular pattern of the stems around the main stem is one of the structural models for the poem [DG, *Pai*, 4-2 & 3, 299; 104:87].

50. **Ino . . . Kadmeia**: G, "Ino, daughter of Kadmus."

51. **Erigena**: [36:9; 74:90]

52. **Anselm**: [105:16].

53. **Herbert**: [100:133].

54. **Remusat**: [100:110].

55. Καλλιαστράγαλος: H, "beautiful ankles" [110/780].

56. **San Domenico, Santa Sabina**: [93:16, 17]. Ancient Roman churches about which Pound said earlier: "Where the spirit is clear in the stone," in contrast to the "internal horrors (mosaic)" of St. Peter's [93/623].

57. **Sta Maria**: Prob. the oldest church in Rome, supposedly consecrated in 222. A facade was added in the 12th century. The mosaics on the facade, dating from the 13th century, are only excelled by those within.

58. **Trastevere**: I, "Across the Tiber" [74:24]. The most colorful district of Rome, a sort of Soho or Left Bank scene.

59. **Cosmedin**: The name of a square in Constantinople. The church, Sta. Maria in Cosmedin, originally belonged to a Greek brotherhood which gave it this name.

60. **Le chapeau . . . St Pierre**: F, "The melon hat of St. Peter." Description of the dome of St. Peter's, which was built when the age of usury was far advanced and is thus not great architecture and design, as are the other churches built before usury had an effect.

61. **piccioletta**: I, "little boat" [*Par.* II, 1; 7:38; 93:155].

Drafts and Fragments

Sources

Ernest Fenollosa, *Epochs of Chinese and Japanese Art*, 2 vols., 1912; rpt. N.Y., 1963 [EF, *Epochs*]; Dante, *Inf.* V, 75; Joseph Rock, "The ²*Muan-¹bpö Ceremony, or the Sacrifice to Heaven as Practiced by the Na-khi*," *Monumenta Serica*, Vol. XIII, 1948 [Rock, "Ceremony"]; Joseph Rock, "The Romance of *K'a-²mä-¹gyu ²mi-gkyi*, A Na-khi Tribal Love Story," *Bulletin de l'Ecole Francaise d'Extreme-Orient*, XXXIX (1939), 1-152 [Rock, "Romance"]; Dante, *Inf.* XVII; Raphael Pumpelly, *Across America and Asia* (1869) and *My Reminiscences*, 2 vols., N.Y., 1918.

Background

EP, *SR*, 214-215; *CNTJ*, 131-121; *CON*, 232; M de R, *Discretions*, Little Brown, Boston, 1971; John Humphrey Noyes, II, *A*

History of American Socialism, Philadelphia, 1870 [Noyes, *Socialism*] ; W. Keith Kavenagh, *Foundations of Colonial America*, Chelsea House, N.Y., 1973 [WK, *Colonial*] .

Exegeses

Peck, *Agenda*, vol. 9, nos. 2-3, 26-69; Jamila Ismail, ibid., 70-87; CFT, *Pai*, 3-1, 91-123; EH, *Ezra Pound Letzte Texte*, Zurich, 1969 [EH, *Letzte*] ; Schmidt, *Pai*, 8-1, 55; JW, *Later*, 167-198; MB, *Trace*, 461-480.

CX

Glossary

1. **Thy quiet house**: The basilica of Torcello in the Venetian Lagoon, which has a mosaic Madonna "over the portal" [cf. 47 below; 116/795] .

2. **crozier's curve**: The crook in the staff carried before a Roman Catholic bishop.

3. **harl**: [herle] : ME, "fibers and filaments." Here prob. in a tuft, as in the crest of a bird [51/251] .

4. **Verkehr**: G, "commerce." An endorsement of what others have called "The free enterprise system."

5. **caracole**: In riding, a horseman's ceremonial half-turn to the left or right.

6. **panache**: F, "crest," or "plume of a helmet."

7. **Toba Sojo**: A Buddhist priest, 1052-1140, originally named Kakuyu. He became chief of the Enryaku-ji-temple of the Tendai sect and later returned to Toba, after which he got the name Toba Sojo. The pictures he painted were called, after him, Toba-e, and this designation later came to include the whole genre of caricature [EF, *Epochs*, 174-175] .

8. **che . . . vent'**: I, "who appear so on the wind." Adapted from Dante [*Inf.* V, 75] , where he speaks to the lovers Paolo and Francesca, "who seem so light on the wind." A lead-in to the Na-khi ceremony.

9. **^{2}Här-^{2}la-^{1}llü ^{3}k'ö**: The collective name for the 13 ceremonies performed by the Na-khi to expiate the spirits of suicides. When these ceremonies are not carried out, the spirits of suicides remain headless demons, or wind-demons, which draw hail and contagious diseases with them. When a person dies, it is of utmost importance that a relative see his last breath. Otherwise, a fowl must be strangled, whose last breath then stands for that of the suicide [Rock, "Ceremony," 1-156] .

10. **nine . . . seven**: "A man has nine fates, . . . a girl has seven." The lines and most of the Na-khi lines in this canto are based on the Romance of *^{2}K'a-^{2}mä-^{1}gyu-^{3}mi-^{2}gkyi*, which was used in the "Wind Sway" ceremonies [Rock, *Romance*, 20n.] .

11. **the black tree . . .** : As ^{2}K'a-^{2}ma (the young girl who is going to commit suicide with her lover rather than accept a forced marriage to someone else) approached her hanging tree, "the black crown of the tree waved, [her] heart was faint, the black tree was born dumb" [ibid., 42] .

12. **blue . . . turquoise**: Before coming to the tree, the young girl thought of throwing herself into the lake, which is "a deep blue"—like her eyes, except they are "turquoise" [ibid., 41] .

13. **the stag**: In the romance, a stag drinks

at a salt spring, but the taste or longing for the water stays with it; this leads the stag to commit *[1]yu-[2]vu* ("suicide"), as does the young girl [ibid., 47-48].

14. **gentian sprout**: The gentian is called the last bloom of summer and flowers when the shepherds are bringing their herds down from the high meadows [ibid., 50-51].

15. **coral . . . oak**: When K'a's lover sees her corpse, he says, among other things: "If I gave you turquoise and coral eyes, will you again be able to see? If I attach the roots of the pine and the oak, will you be able to walk" [ibid., 89].

16. **Yellow iris**: Peck says: "As Rock notes, the pictograph for "[2]k'a" . . . shows spring water flowing down a valley or gulch. Earlier in the text . . . the spring pictograph is a compound of 'water' and [1]ba or 'flower'—the picture of which resembles an iris" [Peck, *Agenda*, 56].

17. **Ideograms**: [M7696], "moon"; [M4534], "bright(ness)"; [M4557], "not"; [M2702], "former"; [M5054], "friend." Pound's grandson Walter glosses the passage thus: "The brightness of the moon . . . there are no former friends." MdeR says that "he must have asked his grandfather" [HK, *Pai*, 8-1, 51-52].

18. **Quercus**: "Oak" in Na-khi. The tree on which [2]K'a hangs herself.

19. **Mt Sumeru**: The holy mountain where the suicide of [2]K'a took place. Says Peck: "Mt. Sumeru rests at the earth's navel, and in Hindu cosmology is the heaven of Indra, terracing the cities of the gods up toward nothingness. . . . Its tree drips honey which, like Yggdrassil's, gives rise to a river" [Peck, *Agenda*, 55].

20. **juniper**: In the "Sacrifice to Heaven" rites, one prays first to Heaven, Earth, and the Juniper. Three small trees are erected on a platform where the sacrifice is made: "an oak, representing Heaven, a juniper, representing [1]K'aw, the emperor, and another oak . . . on the left, representing earth or [2]Ndaw" [Rock, "Ceremony," 13].

21. **The purifications . . .** : One of the "Sacrifices to Heaven" is called *[3]Ch'ou [3]Shu*, or "Impurities Smoke Out." By different acts, houses and the landscape are purified: "the former, a high mountain, was purified by the snow, the latter, a lower mountain, was purified by the rain" [Rock, "Ceremony," 23]. Different people went to do different ceremonial things: "the former went to a large Juniper, and the latter to a large oak and they purified themselves. . . . The former went into a ravine . . . the latter was purified by the dew" [ibid, 23-24]. Of another ceremony we read, "The three trees . . . are then placed in position on the altar . . . the tree of Heaven on the right, the Juniper in the center and the tree representing Earth on the left . . . underneath which . . . [2]bbue (*Artemisia*) twigs . . . had been laid [ibid., 30].

22. **Artemis**: Or Diana. Rhyme with Artemisia.

23. **Kuanon**: [74:81].

24. **Cozzaglio . . . (Gardesana)**: Italian engineers who built a road called the "Gardesana." Says EH: "The Occidental Gardesana, one of the most famous highways in Europe, begins in Riva along the western shore of Lake Garda. Its course for great stretches is blasted out of rocks, and more than 50 bridges lead over ravines, waterfalls and crevices. The Arc'd rock layers consist of 70 tunnels" [EH, *Letzte*, 88]. The waves of the lake may recall Canaletto's scenes of Venice.

25. **Savoia . . . that**: "that" refers to a cavalry attack the Italians made against the Russians [cf. 31 below].

26. **Un caso . . . memoria**: Pg, "A sad case and worthy of memory" [Camoëns, *Os Luisadas*, III, 118; *SR*, 214-215].

27. **Uncle G.**: George Holden Tinkham [74:180].

28. **Knox . . . Lodge**: [89/603].

29. Bettoni: Commander of the cavalry attack at Ibukerki.

30. Galliffet: [16:17].

31. (Ibukerki): "The steppes of Isbuschenskij in the Ukraine, where on August 24, 1942 the Savoia Cavalleria regiment attacked the Russians. The Italians had 32 dead (officially, 3), 52 wounded (officially, 5), and more than a hundred horses wounded or lost. The Russians–according to Italian figures–suffered 150 dead and 500 prisoners" [EH, *Letzte*, 90].

32. tracciolino: I, a Pound neologism deriving from *tracciare*, meaning something like "road-engineer."

33. Oleari: Italian theater of operations during WWI.

34. Divisione Sforzesca: I, "Special Force Division."

35. Felix nupsit: L, "a happy marriage." Allusion to the marriage of Pound's daughter [M de R, *Discretions*, 307].

36. Khaty: [93:2]. Boris de R., who married Mary, was an Egyptologist much taken with the pharaoh Akthoi (Khaty).

37. Euridices: The dead wife of Orpheus, the singer.

38. Laurel bark . . . : Reference to Dafne [2:26], who, fleeing from Apollo, was turned into a laurel tree.

39. Endymion: The lover of Artemis (Diana), the moon-goddess, for whom Artemisia [cf. 21 above] is named.

40. Kalliastragalos: [4:14; 109:55].

41. Ideogram: Hsin[1] [M2737], "make new" [53:42-43]. Used with "day by day" [cf. 53 below].

42. go forth by day: The Egyptian *Book of the Dead* was known as "The Sayings for Going Forth by Day" [Schmidt, *Pai*, 8-1, 55].

43. Awoi: Character in the Noh play *Awoi No Uye*. Her love, corrupted by jealousy, turns to hate [EP, *CNTJ*, 113-121; 77:21, 22].

44. La Tour . . . Voisin: Famous restaurants Pound remembers, 3 of which were in Paris and one (Dieudonné) in London [74/433; 76/453].

45. Byzance: Santa Fosca, a church of the 6th century with a Byzantine structure at Torcello [cf. 47 below]. Over its portal is the image of the Virgin Mary, to which Pound refers by the phrase "Thy quiet house."

46. Galla's Rest: The tomb of Galla Placidia [21:37; 76:86]. Said Pound: "Of religion it will be enough for me to say . . . 'every self-respecting Ravennese is procreated, or at least receives spirit or breath of life, in the Mausoleum of Galla Placidia' " [*SP*, 322].

47. Torcello: The sunken city (founded in 639) in the Venetian Lagoon, where two palaces and the cathedral Santa Maria Assunta (from the 7th century) are preserved. The cathedral has 12th- and 13th-century mosaics on its facade [EH, *Letzte*, 90].

48. Quos . . . : L, "which I Persephone." Based on Propertius VI, 26: "Three books will there be at my funeral, / Which I Persephone will bring, not a trifling gift."

49. Ideogram: Chih[3] [M939], "stop." A comment on *Analects* IX, 20: "Alas, I see him advance, I never see him stop (take a position)." Pound said: "There is no more important technical term in the Confucian philosophy than this Chih[3], the hitching post, position, place one is in, and works from" [*CON*, 232].

50. Bunting: [74:153].

51. Upward: [74:275].

52. fragments: [8:1].

53. Ideogram: Jih[4-5], "day" [53:42-43]. Used with "make new" [cf. 41 above].

54. Mr Rock: Dr. Joseph Rock, a research fellow of the Harvard Yenching Institute, who started work with the Na-khi in 1922 and returned there to make special studies for over 20 years. In the spring of 1943 he tried to ship over 700 manuscripts, all his 20 years' work ready for the printer, back to the States. The ship was torpedoed by a Japanese submarine and his work went with it to the bottom of the Arabian Sea. Said Rock with monumental restraint, "That I felt the loss keenly I need not waste time to tell" [Rock, "Ceremony," preface]. Dr. Rock returned after WWII to start the work over again (*Pai*, 3-1, 101].

55. **Mount Kinabalu**: Mountain in North Borneo, now called Sebah.

56. **Jesselton**: Formerly capital of North Borneo. After independence (1963), it was renamed Kota Kinabalu.

57. **Falling . . . tempest**: Perhaps a reference to the Dragon Boat Festival and the 5 poisons in Taoism: "spider, scorpion, lizard, snake and toad" [Ismail, *Agenda*, 75]. But perhaps a note of despair for one who set out to write a paradise and discovered all the evidence indicated he should be writing an apocolypse. Perhaps both.

58. **Lux enim**: L, "Light itself" [55:135; 83:6].

59. **The marble form . . .** : Evokes the "grove needs its altar" motif [90/607-609].

60. **Ideogram**: Ching[4] [M1138], "reverence." In a note to an Indian friend, Naresh Guha, Pound commented on this character, which names an essential quality of the fully humane Confucian man: "The grass, the sentence in root [艹] the beating on earth (with feet) (or drum) [攵] (to evoke) respect for the power . . ." [*Pai*, 3-1, 67-68]. The "beating on earth" implies ritual dance, as in certain Noh plays [88/581; 98/691] and other rituals [104:118]. Parallels exist in many primitive cultures [81:19].

61. **Awoi**: [Cf. 43 above].

62. **Komachi**: A character in the Noh play *Kayoi Kamachi*, which ends with a dance under the moon. Pound's final note to the play says: "The final dance means that the lovers are spirits fluttering in the grass" [*CNTJ*, 21].

Notes for CXI

Glossary

1. **Hui**: [103:16]

2. **Wadsworth**: Joseph W., a relative of Pound on his mother's side, who stole and preserved by hiding in an oak tree the Charter of Connecticut [109:27]. On May 15, 1715, at the Town House in Hartford, he was rewarded: "This assembly do, as token of their grateful resentment of such his faithful and good service, grant him out of the Colony treasury the sum of twenty shillings" [WK, *Colonial*, 42].

3. **au fond**: F, "in essence."

4. **Roche-Guyon**: Louis Alexandre duc de La R-G, 1743-1792. During the revolutionary events of June 20, 1792, he raised his voice in defense of the king and had to flee Paris. He was arrested in Forges and died Nov. 14, 1792, as a result of a stone thrown from the crowd as he was being transported through the town of Gisors.

5. **Austerlitz**: The battle Napoleon won against Alexander I of Russia and Franz II of Austria on Dec. 2, 1805. Pound called this point in N's career "Bonaparte's Maximum" [101:26], because at that time, he could have unified Italy.

6. **Mme de Genlis**: [103:48].

7. **Lannes**: Jean L., 1769-1809, marshal of France who fought under N in Egypt, Italy, and at Austerlitz.

8. **Talleyrand**: [95:13, 101:22].

9. **Wu . . . Szu**: C, "Have no twisty thoughts." The one sentence which Confucious said the anthology of 300 poems could be reduced to [*CON*, 197]. The "heart's field" should be next to "Wu."

10. **"in civilization"**: [97/680].

11. **Alexander**: Emperor of Russia (1801-1825), who was a significant voice at the Congress of Vienna ("Wien") in 1815.

12. **Quemoy**: An island off China occupied by Chiang K'ai-shek's troops which came under attack by the Chinese Communists. A sort of hit-and-run seige from the sea went on for months, which led to Dulles's threat of "massive retaliation" [96:144].

13. **Orage**: [80:322].

14. **compassione**: I, "pity."

15. **Amor**: L, "love."

16. **Geryon**: [15:4; 46:3, 5].

17. **Veritas**: L, "truth."

18. **come . . . riva**: I, "like a boat [or raft] at the shore." Variation on Dante's "Come tal volta stanno a riva i burchi" ("As boats sometimes lie at the shore") [*Inf.* XVII, 19].

19. **ex profundis**: L, "out of the deep."

20. **Anima into aura**: L, "soul into brightness." Alchemical term whose aim was to bring forth the *lumen natural* ("natural light") or the *quinta essentia* ("quintessence") in the shape of the philosopher's stone [76:217].

21. **Serenitas**: L, "brightness."

22. **Edictum prologo**: L, "Edict with prologue."

23. **Rothar**: [96:27]. This king of the Lombards compiled the civil rights of the Lombards into a code [cf. 22 above], fought against the Byzantines, and coined his own gold [JW, *Later*, 180].

From CXII

Glossary

1. **owl . . . fire-fox**: Among the birds and aminals which became purified in the Muan Bpö ceremonies [Rock, "Ceremony," 22 ff.].

2. **³huo -²hu**: NK, "A bay or sorrel horse" [ibid.].

3. **Amrta**: NK, "nectar of immortality." In Na-khi an elaborate ceremony to make it is prescribed. After 9 medicines are made over a period of time, with elaborate rituals (a rhyme with some formulas for making the philosopher's stone), they are put together and "there comes forth a pure, limpid one." This is Amrta: "some of the medicine (Amrta) reached Heaven, whereupon Heaven became blue; some of it reached the Earth, whereupon the Earth became yellow" [ibid., 38]. It is used throughout the ceremonies.

4. **³La ²mun ³mi**: NK, female figure involved in making Amrta. "From the head of the Celestial . . . ¹muan- ³mi . . . medicinal flowers sprouted, and from her eyes came forth liquid medicine. . . ." A footnote adds: "After three nights she caused a magic and from her breath there came forth 13 brilliant . . . Goddesses. ²La- ²mun is the Tibetan Lhamo, to which the Na-khi add the word ³mi = female" [ibid., 39].

5. **²Ndaw ¹bpo**: NK, "Sacrifice to Earth." "If we do not perform ²Ndaw ²bpö . . . all that we have accomplished will not be real" [ibid., 41].

6. **²Muan . . .** : NK. "If ²Muan ¹bpö is not performed, all that which we accomplished is not real" [ibid.]

7. **Agility** . . . : "The . . . family's livestock, grain . . . courage, agility, and long life are due to the Juniper" [ibid., 42].

8. **rice** . . . : "When rice is transplanted into the fields and it grows so that the ground is invisible, this is due to ¹O- ²mä-¹hä . . ." [ibid., 45].

9. **Li Chiang**: A ceremony called *³Gko ³ō*, or "Grain Throw Out," is held in many places, one of which is described thus: "This is a beautiful spot with many springs which issue from a gravelly flat . ,.; the springs themselves are called . . . pomegranate water, and are five li [1/3 mile] north of Li-chiang" [ibid, 65n.].

10. **Hsiang Shan**: "There are the many springs which issue at the foot of Hsiang Shan, or Elephant Mountain, immediately north of Li-Chiang" [ibid.].

11. **Lung Wang's**: "A Lung-wang Miao . . . or Dragon King Temple, has been built there with a large pond with sacred fish. The springs are called ²Ngu . . ., and their waters flow through the city of Li-chiang as the Yü ho . . . or Jade stream" [ibid.].

12. **Ideograms**: Yu⁴ [M7666], "jade"; ho² [M2111], "stream."

13. **Artemisia . . . Arundinaria**: The Na-khi *²Bbue* and *¹mun* are plants usedmuch in the purification ceremonies [ibid., 36]. They were conceived to have been born "before all other trees" [ibid., 144].

14. **Winnowed . . . tray**: The phrases and pictographs come from a ceremony called the "Pig Fate Offer." "The second is the picture of a large winnowing tray made of the small bamboo (*Arundianaria*) called ¹mun" [ibid., 67-68].

15. **neath luna**: Prob. a rhyming with moon ceremonies and Artemis themes in earlier cantos and at the end of Canto 110.

CXIII

Glossary

1. **12 Houses . . . sorry**: Signs of the Zodiac. The "seeing" and "tasting" lines are a statement of "the tale of the tribe" in brief: a reduction like Confucius's putting the 300 odes into "have no twisty thoughts" [111:9].

2. **Pater Helios**: And all transpires under the turning constellations and the sun.

3. **"Mortal . . . ears"**: Trans. of Dante [*Inf.* VII, 92].

4. **Θρῆνος**: H, "lament, esp. for the dead."

5. **Mozart**: [26:99].

6. **Agassiz**: [93:51].

7. **Linnaeus**: Karl von Linné, 1707-1778, Swedish botanist who founded the modern binomial method of designating plants and animals. Although he published over 180 books, his name is here because of the great reverence he showed toward all creation, as expressed in his *Philosophia Botanica* (1751).

8. **Marcella**: M. Spann, a constant visitor and friend during the late years at St. Elizabeths and one of the few people who returned with Pound to Italy in 1958. She edited, with Pound's encouragement and help, *Confucius to Cummings* (1964). The garden could be at Brunnenberg, on the lawn at St. Elizabeths, or both.

9. **Li Chiang**: [101:70].

10. **Rock's world**: [110:54].

11. **Paré** . . . : [104:54]. A French doctor famous for saying: "Je le pansay, Dieu le guarist" ("I dress it [the wound], God heals it") [EH, *Letzte*, 95].

12. Tweddel: Prob. Francis Tweddell, 1863-?, author of *How to Take Carre of the Baby; A Mother's Guide and a Manual for Nurses*, which went through a number of reprints from 1911 to 1915, as well as a book described in the National Union catalog as "Collected Papers on Tuberculosis."

13. Donnelly: Leo G. D., a medical friend of Pound's who in WWI served as an orthopedic surgeon in France. In 1935 he founded the Social Credit party in Detroit; in 1944 he was a presidential candidate for the Greenback party; in the 50s he allowed himself to be a candidate for the U.S. Congress. He died in 1958.

14. Pumpelly: [89:128]. In a book entitled *Across America and Asia*, he tells the stories of people he knew, such as a man named Parkyn: ' Parkyn knew what real adventure was . . . one of his stories recurs to me. Parkyn stayed one night at a wayside house in the 'bush.' He was eating when a man entered and handed the cook something wrapped in paper, telling him to cook it . . . When the man had emptied his dish, he leaned back and said: *'There! I told the damned---I'd eat his damned liver, and I've done it.'* " [Vol. I, 165].

15. Gobi: A 500,000 sq.-mi. desert in N China and Mongolia into which Pumpelly made explorations.

16. 17 Maggio: I, "17 May." This date, and the following "19th May '59," identify events in Pound's private life.

17. H.D.: Hilda Doolittle, 1886-1961, early love and lifelong friend of Pound's. She used the word "Serenitas" [111:20] about a translation from Sappho by her husband, Richard Aldington ("Atthis") [HK, *Era*, 57].

18. Dieudonne's: London restaurant [74:178].

19. long flank . . . : Reflections on the Sappho poem.

20. garofani: I, "carnations" or "clovetrees."

21. Portofino: Italian harbor town near Rapallo.

22. Hesperides: Daughters of Atlas and Hesperis who guarded the golden apples of a tree that the goddess Gea let sprout from her lap.

23. old countess: Perhaps the whoring countess of Vienna [35/173].

24. Stef: Stephanie Yankowska, a beautiful Polish girl Pound knew in Venice in 1908. When she read in the late 40s that a poet named Pound was locked up in St. Elizabeths, she wanted to know if it was the young man she had known. Finding it was, she began a long campaign to get him released and began a correspondence with EP which went on intensely during his St. Elizabeths years. As a wealthy Polish expatriate, she knew almost everyone in the diplomatic corps in the capitals of Western Europe. It was through her intercession with the sister of Dag Hammarskjöld that he cited lines from Pound in the General Assembly of the United Nations; and it was her intercession with Mrs. John Foster Dulles in 1957 that helped with the decision to release Pound in 1958 [data from Jerzy Niemojowski friend of the Yankowska family].

25. Sir Ian: Prob. General Ian Standish Monteith Hamilton [104:37], staff officer in the British Army. Pound repeated the story Stephanie told him of their escape during the Communist takeover of Poland.

26. Pétain: [79:18]. The lines refer to the Poles marching into the Ukraine in 1920. Pétain warned the Poles against this action as a dangerous challenge to the Soviet Union [EH, *Letzte*, 95].

27. Kalenda maja: "The feast of Venus Genetrix, which survives as Mayday [celebration]" [*SR*, 18]; also, "a famous Estampida of Raimbaut de Vacqueiras (1180-1207]: Kalenda maia / Ni flor de faira / Ni cant d'auzel'l" [EH, *Letzte*, 90]. Wilhelm calls the Raimbaut work "a rousing South French dance song (the music survives) . . .; it has much of the joy and verve that Pound associates with the pagan roots of Provençal song and the beautiful landscapes in Languedoc" (JW, *Later*, 188].

28. **Li Sao**: C, "Farewell to Sorrow," an elegy by the poet Ch'u Yuan (c.338-288 B.C.).

29. **intelligent . . .** : Since there is no word in any language to cover what Pound means, he resorts to this one. If he had lived to know of the extraordinary genetic coding of DNA, he would have been even more overwhelmed by the sense of design and the depth of the mystery of life in process.

30. **grass versus . . .** : A friend of mine, when asked what his brother was doing, said he was paving New Jersey. At the present rate, the entire nation may be paved more quickly than one might think.

31. **Schwundgeld**: G, technical term in Gesell's theory of money: "inflationary decrease in money value." Compared here with the Continental currency used to finance the American Revolution. As early as that, the currency devised proved that money could serve as both a *standard* and a *medium* of exchange. The desperate fact in Pound's mind was that neither economists nor politicians could learn this simple fact.

32. **Parsley . . .** : [97:292].

33. **body . . . soul**: [98:20].

34. **(Sac . . . guisto)**: Sac. L. P. Carioli wrote *Il Giusto Prezzo Medioevale: Studio Economica Politica* [The just price in the Middle Ages: Studies in political economy], pub. in 1913 [EH, *Letzte*, 83].

35. **Giustizia**: I, "justice."

36. **Mountain . . . seeping**: Return to Na-khi landscape [JP, *Agenda*, 9-2 & 3, 62].

37. **kind of ignorance" . . .** : [101/725].

38. **Article X**: Of the U.S. Constitution reads: "The powers not delegated to the United States by the Constitution, nor prohibited by it to the States, are reserved to the States respectively, or to the people." Pound conceived this article as justifying a major tenet of Social Credit: "local control of local purchasing power."

39. **As to sin . . .** : Pound believed that about the time of Pope Innocent III and therafter, the church, taking cues from Augustine and a few others, developed and accented the whole horror of sin, especially the so-called sins of the flesh, and the absurdity of hell-fire as a punishment, in order to dominate the minds of the people. Before that, in Provence and Italy, religious activity accented celebration and rejoicing, dancing and singing [114:28].

40. **malvagità**: I, "wickedness, nastiness."

41. **Limone**: Town on Lake Garda.

42. **(scala altrui)**: I, "the stairs of another." Cacciaguida says to Dante: "You will prove how salt is the taste of another's bread, how hard the way up and down the stairs of another man" [*Par*. XVII, 58-60].

43. **God's eye . . .** : A central thesis of the poem. Divinity, the light descending, works through the intelligence of man. God acting in the world is revealed at one pole by the intelligence in the cherry stone and, at the other pole, through the mind of man and man's perception of beauty (τὸ καλόν); his creative powers and his sense of humor (hilaritas); his powers of kindness, mercy, and justice; and his impulse to rejoice through dance and song.

44. **Daphne**: [2:26].

45. **Syrian onyx**: A vessel that contained embalming unguents. In *Homage to P.* Pound wrote: "Nor will you be weary of calling my name, nor too weary / To place the last kiss on my lips / When the Syrian onyx is broken" [*P*, 219].

46. **Ixion**: The overthrown sun-god who is bound to an eternally turning, fiery sun wheel in Tartarus [80:168].

CANTO CXIV

Glossary

1. **Pas . . . Fréron**: F, "Not even Freron, I hate no one, not even Freron."

2. **Fréron**: Eli F., 1718-1776, fought for throne and altar against the Philosophes and the Encyclopedists. His strongest attacks were aimed at Voltaire.

3. **Voltaire**: [65:108]. In *Le Pauvre Diable* [The poor devil] V. said: "The other day, at the bottom of a dale / A serpent bit Jean Fréron / What do you think happened? / It was the serpent who died" [EH, *Letzte*, 87].

4. **Mr. Law**: [100:24].

5. **Tom Pick**: Timothy Pickering [62:156; 63:7].

6. **respect a good book . . .** : Major tenet in Pound's ideas about literary criticism [*ABCR*, 28-35].

7. **O di . . . natura**: L, "O of the diversity of nature." From Dialog V, "Concerning Infinity," in *The Dialogs of Bruno* [Torino, 1932, p. 64]. The original has "e" ("and") instead of "o." The lines concern the multiplicity of heavenly bodies [JE, *Pai*, 3-3, 414-415].

8. **(Giordano Bruno)**: Italian philosopher, 1548-1600, who defied the religious thinking of his time and was arrested late in the Inquisition and burned at the stake by the Church of Rome. His central thesis, that deity is an infinite principle manifest in man and in all creation in a hierarchy of values, rhymes with Pound's own beliefs.

9. **belly-ache**: Bruno reasoned in a way different from Plotinus, who had stomach trouble [99/700].

10. **Ari**: Aristotle was employed by Philip of Macedon to educate his son, who was to become Alexander the Great. During those years and after, Aristotle became a marine biologist.

11. **bianco c(h)ade**: I, "white falls." From Cavalcanti's *Canzone d'amore* V, 8 [36:13; *MIN*, 394-395].

12. **Oneida**: Pound's Uncle Loomis, whom he associates on the one hand with the Oneida Colony (jealousy) and on the other with horse theft (property). The Oneida Colony (1847-1879) was founded by John Humphrey Noyes (1811-1886) on a collectivist basis. The commune practiced "complex marriage," a system in which all members were married to each other [Noyes, *Socialism*, passim; EH, *Pai*, 3-3, 413-414].

13. **Macleod**: Joseph Gordon M., Scottish poet who in 1936 called Pound's attention to the difference between property and possession [*L*, 279].

14. **(Sandro's, Firenze)**: "Botticelli's, Florence" [20:19].

15. **Mu$^{4.5}$**: [M4593] : "wood."

16. **Fu Hi**: Fu Hsi [53:3]. His emblem is the T-square. In the table of succession (or evolution), he belongs to the change cycle "wood," which corresponds to the "power of imagination and growth" [EH, *Letzte*, 88]. The "metal" in the table is associated with Shao-hao, Pound's "Chan" [53:35], hence the line [53/264] "Chan by metal."

17. **"Harve**: A relative of Pound's. Pound's grandmother (the Loomis side of Oneida County) provoked this memory: "I can remember no phrase of hers save that once in a discussion of conduct, she said 'Harve was *like* that.' The statement ended the matter" [*PD*, 11-12; 37].

18. **Sarah**: S. Angevine Loomis, Pound's grandmother: "the old cat-head."

19. **niente**: I, "nothing."

20. **tribù**: I, "stem (of a tree or family)."

21. **Armes et blasons!**: F, I, for "coat of arms" in heraldry.

22. **Al's**: Albert Pound, great-uncle of the poet called Amos in *Indiscretions* [*PD*, 33-34].

23. **Old Joel's**: Joel Pound, great-great-uncle of the poet: "Joel lived to ninety-six" [*PD*, 16] and "Joel also I approved" [*PD*, 44].

24. **"Locke"**: [50:9, 67:99].

25. **Del Mar**: [96:119].

26. **Tanagra Mia**: Town in Boeotia famous for female clay statues found there.

27. **Ambracia**: Town in ancient Epirus famous in the reign of Pyrrhus [107:143; 109:13].

28. **Fear . . .** : [113:39]. Pound's theory that demonology was part of a deliberate plot to "scare the hell out of" people, especially the young, in order to maintain control of the minds of men, even though such ethics are against all reason [*LE*, 42-43].

29. *τετραδάκτυλος*: H, "four-toed." July 14th is prob. a personal memory. Whoever made the remark about the lizard's feet perceived something that would strike Pound as memorable, a rhyme with the child who noticed the German word for cat looked like a cat's head and tail: "Katze" [102:27].

30. **Ubi amor . . .** : L, "where love is, there perception is" [90:16].

31. **hypostasis**: [81:55].

32. **Quelque toile . . .** : F, "on some painting, in the Louvre, on some painting."

33. **Boy in fruit shop . . .** : Memory of boy Pound saw in Italy.

34. **"bisogna . . . "**: I, "one must be inspired."

35. **William**: Yeats. Sligo was one of his favorite Irish scenes.

36. **Tigullio**: The gulf Rapallo overlooks.

FROM CXV

Glossary

1. **The scientists . . .** : Atomic weapons and the Russian "Sputnik" for a while had the whole human race terrified, or seemed to when these lines were written.

2. **Wyndham Lewis**: [16:30].

3. **garofani**: I, "carnations."

4. **Mozart, Linnaeus**: [113:5, 7].

5. **Sulmona**: [103/736; 105/746]. Birthplace of Ovid in province of Aquila.

6. **In meiner Heimat**: G, "In my homeland."

7. **living . . . cardboard**: Return to major theme of early cantos [7:32-37].

CANTO CXVI

Glossary

1. **Muss.**: Mussolini.

2. **Cuniculi**: I, "canals" or "underground passages" [101:16].

3. **An old "crank"**: Pound here is thinking of a dead "genius" in Virginia, from whom originates a theory about the origin of a giant footprint. This reminds him of Ode 245 in the *Shih-ching*, where an immaculate conception is mentioned: Chian Yüan, wife of the Emperor K'u, becomes pregnant when she steps in the big toe of a giant footprint. She bears a son, whom she exposes. The child is saved by a miracle and receives the name Hou Ch'i (*ch'i* means "someone exposed"). Ch'i, under the mythical original

ruler Yao, becomes leader of agriculture. At 98/690 he is mentioned as "john barleycorn Je Tzu" and at 105/747 as "Hou Je," with inadvertently exchanged Chinese characters [EH, *Letzte*, 85].

4. **The Madonna** . . . : [110:1, 45].

5. **(Mucchio di leggi)**: I, "a haystack of laws."

6. **Litterae** . . . : L, "literature which heals nothing" [33:25].

7. **Justinian's**: [94:45].

8. **Crystal . . . acorn of light**: Image from Neoplatonic light-philosophy seen through Grosseteste [*Pai*, 2-3, 454; 74:249].

9. **Twice beauty** . . . : Moments of great vision under the elms on the grounds of St. Elizabeths.

10. **"plus . . . chien"**: F, "the more I love dogs." Mme. Roland [*Letzte*, 97] had said this, prefaced by "the more I know men" [cf. *P*, 102].

11. **Ariadne**: The holy of holies at the center of the labyrinth.

12. **Disney**: Walt D., 1901-1966. Pound, a great movie fan, was fond of any Disney movie. In 1958 he saw the Disney film about a squirrel, *Perri* [Donald Hall, *Paris Review*, Summer-Fall 1962, 27].

13. **Laforgue**: Jules L., 1860-1887, French symbolist poet. He described the Berlin Aquarium as the symbol of Nirvana: "the mute depths, which only know eternity, for which spring, summer, fall, and winter don't exist" [*Moralité légendaire Salomé*, 1888].

14. **Spire**: Andre S. [77:134; 81:23].

15. **in proposito**: I, "for the intention."

16. **Linnaeus**: [113:7].

17. **chi crescera** . . . : [89:2].

18. **terzo**: I, "third."

19. **Venere**: I, "Venus."

20. **it coheres**: [*Pai*, 2-1, 35; 8-3, 567; 109:17].

21. **al poco . . . d'ombra**: I, "In the small hours with the darkness describing a huge circle" [5:53].

22. **(Torcello)**: [110/780].

23. **al . . . d'oro**: Street in Rapallo where at the intersection one can see a cross of blue sky.

24. **(Tigullio)**: [114:36].

Fragments of Cantos

Addendum for C

1. **neschek**: Heb, "usury" [JW, *Later*, 181-182].

2. **the serpent**: Geryon [14:3; 46:3; 51:13, 16].

3. **the defiler . . . race**: At the time this was written Pound was aware that he was being attacked for anti-Semitism, which he vigorously denied. Thus, he uses the Hebrew word to show that the Jews from the time of Moses had rules against usury. When writers in the *New English Weekly* and elsewhere in the 1930s were blaming the Jews for money problems in the Depression, Pound wrote: "Usurers have no race. How long the whole Jewish people is to be sacrificial goat for the usurer, I know not" [*SP*, 300]. But in the mid-years at St. Elizabeths the record shows clearly that he was anti-Semitic, at least emotionally and at times.

4. *τόκος*: H, "usury."

5. **hic . . . est**: L, "here is the center of evil."

6. **Fafnir**: [Fafner]. In Wagner's *Ring* the giant who turned into a dragon and became

a treasure stealer. In solar myth the darkness that steals the day.

7. **Hydra**: The nine-headed monster slain by Hercules.

8. **Paphos**: Daughter of Pygmalion and Galatea, whose union was blessed by Venus. The city and groves named Paphos are sacred to Venus. Thus a rhyme with usury defiling the bed of "the young bride and her bridegroom" [45/230].

9. Tὸ καλόν: H, "beauty."

10. **formosus . . . decens**: L, "is neither beautiful nor decent."

11. **eel-fisher's . . .** : [51:18]. Note that "Addendum for C" and Cantos 45 and 51 were all written about the same time.

12. Χαῖρη . . . : H, "Hail! O Dione, Hail." Dione was the mother of Venus.

13. **Light . . . clarity**: This impassioned prayer to the divine, is put in these terms so that it cannot be confused with what dogmatic and/or anthropomorphic religions intend when they say *God.*

14. **Sero**: L, "late." [25:40].

15. **Spain . . .** : The mercury idea is unclear.

16. **Finland . . .** : The nickel idea is unclear.

17. **S . . . R . . .** : Sassoon . . . Rothschild [RO].

18. **spilla**: I, "pin, brooch." Repeat from 20/93: "With the silver spilla, / the ball as of melted amber, coiled, caught up, and turned / Lotophagoi" [20:58, 59]. The opium smokers here are rhymed with the Odyssean lotus eaters.

19. **Jannequin**: [75:8].

20. **San Pantaleo**: A little church in Rapallo [M de R, *Discretions*, 117].

21. **"e mobile . . . un'e due . . . mobile"**: I, "[woman] is fickle . . . one and two . . . that the woman is fickle." From a song in the last act of Verdi's *Rigoletto.* Pound could hear the carillon song at his house at Sant 'Ambrogio in the hills above Rapallo.

22. **(videt et urbes)**: L, "and he sees cities."

23. **salita**: I, "hill path."

24. **water-bug's**: [91:105].

Notes for CXVII et seq.

25. **benedetta**: I, "blessed."

26. **Brancusi's bird**: A form in a tree on the lawn of St. Elizabeths reminded Pound of the famous statue.

27. **Rupe Tarpeia**: In ancient Rome, the Tarpeian Rock was the site on the Capitoline Hill from which criminals were thrown to their deaths [74/443].

28. **Zagreus**: [17:3; 77:195].

29. **Semele**: [92:47].

30. **M'amour . . .** : F, "My love, my love."

31. **The dreams clash . . .** : The last 3 sections of a book by Daniele Varè, erstwhile ambassador from Italy to the United States, are entitled "Harvesting of a Dream," "Shadows," and "The Dream Shattered." The book, *The Two Imposters*, records the personal memories of an Italian statesman whom Mussolini replaced with younger men. Its title comes from Kipling's "If" ("If you can meet with Triumph and Disaster / And treat those two imposters just the same") and explains Varè's intent: to show both the triumphs and disasters of Mussolini and his Fascism. Since Pound believed that Fascism promised to result in a corporate state with debt-free money which would result in the creation of a *paradiso terrestre*, it is appropriate that the shattered dream become part of the tragic ambience of the poem's close.

32. **La faillite**: F, "bankruptcy."

33. **Francois Bernouard**: A publisher and familiar literateur (friend of Remy de Gourmont, Fritz Vanderpyl, and Pound) in the Paris of the 20s. His firm became bankrupt in 1929 [Sieburth, *Pai*, 4-2, 3, 329-332].

34. Allegre: A town in S France associated with Bernart de Ventadorn.

35. "es laissa cader": P, [e.s laissa chazer]: "and let himself fall."

36. "de joi sas alas": P, "[I see the lark moving] his wings with joy." The quotes are from the first stanza of a Ventadorn song [*SR*, 41].

37. Two mice and a moth: Reaffirming the importance of Gourmont's *Physique de l'Amour* to Pound's vision.

38. farfalla: I, "butterfly." The soul-in-flight motif given throughout the poem in various winged insects from wasps to various other lapidoptera [48:50-53; 92:33-35].

39. The kings . . . : The Monarch butterfly; cf. "the king-wings in migration" [106/754]. This butterfly, which does live on poisonous milkweed, migrates in mid-September, "from artic Canada, along sky-ways that have been mapped" [DD, *Pai*, 11-3, 390].

40. arcanum: The final mystery in Pound's religious sense. A place or state about which nothing can be known or said: "the undiscovered country."

41. I have tried . . . : These lines were added to the poem in the 1975 edition to fill out the final design of 120 cantos. But in future editions they will be left out. Olga Rudge told J. Laughlin emphatically in 1981 that Pound wanted the poem to end in its unfinished form with the line: "To be men not destroyers."

Bibliography

Alexander, Michael. *The Poetic Achievement of Ezra Pound*. London, 1979.

Anderson, David. *Pound's Cavalcanti: An Edition of the Translations, Notes, and Essays*. Princeton, 1983.

Bacigalupo, Massimo. *The Forméd Trace: The Later Poetry of Ezra Pound*. New York, 1980.

Baumann, Walter. *The Rose in the Steel Dust: An Examination of the Cantos of Ezra Pound*. Bern, 1967; Coral Gables, 1970.

Bell, Ian F. A. *Critic as Scientist: The Modernist Poetics of Ezra Pound*. London and New York, 1981.

Bell, Ian F. A., ed. *Ezra Pound: Tactics for Reading*. London, 1982.

Benediktson, D. Thomas. *Propertius / Modernist Poet of Antiquity*. Carbondale, 1989.

Bernstein, Michael André. *The Tale of the Tribe: Ezra Pound and the Modern Verse Epic*. Princeton, 1980.

Berryman, Jo Brantley. *Circe's Craft: Ezra Pound's Hugh Selwyn Mauberley*. Ann Arbor, 1983.

Bischoff, Volker. *Ezra Pound Criticism 1905–1985 / A Chronological Listing of Publications in English*. Marburg, 1991.

Bornstein, George. *Ezra Pound Among the Poets*. Chicago, 1985.

———. *The Postromantic Consciousness of Ezra Pound*. Victoria, B.C., 1977.

Brooke-Rose, Christine. *A ZBC of Ezra Pound*. Berkeley, 1971; London, 1971.

Bush, Ronald. *The Genesis of Ezra Pound's Cantos*. Princeton, 1977.

Carpenter, Humphrey. *A Serious Character: The Life of Ezra Pound*. London, 1988.

Cookson, William. *A Guide to The Cantos of Ezra Pound*. Persea, 1985.

Cornell, Julien. *The Trial of Ezra Pound: A Documented Account of the Treason Case by the Defendant's Lawyer*. New York, 1966.

Craig, Cairns. *Yeats, Eliot and Pound and the Politics of Poetry*. London, 1982.

D'Epiro, Peter. *A Touch of Rhetoric: Ezra Pound's Malatesta Cantos*. Ann Arbor, 1983.

Dasenbrock, Reed Way. *The Literary Vorticism of Ezra Pound and Wyndham Lewis: Towards the Condition of Painting*. Baltimore, 1985.

Davenport, Guy. *Cities on Hills: A Study of I–XXX of Ezra Pound's Cantos*. Ann Arbor, 1983.

Davie, Donald. *Ezra Pound. New York, 1975*.

———. *Ezra Pound, Poet as Sculptor*. New York, 1964; London, 1965.

———. *Studies in Ezra Pound: Chronicle and Polemic*. Manchester, 1991.

Davis, Earle. *Vision Fugitive: Ezra Pound and Economics*. Lawrence, 1968.

Davis, Kay. *Fugue and Fresco: Structures in Pound's Cantos*. Orono, 1984.

de Nagy, N. Christoph. *Ezra Pound's Poetics and Literary Tradition: The Critical Decade*. Bern, 1966.

———. *The Poetry of Ezra Pound: The Pre-Imagist Stage*. Bern, 1960.

Dekker, George. *Sailing after Knowledge: The Cantos of Ezra Pound, a Critical Appraisal*. London and New York, 1963.

Dembo, Lawrence Sanford. *The Confucian Odes of Ezra Pound: A Critical Appraisal*. Berkeley and London, 1963.

Driscoll, John. *The China Cantos of Ezra Pound*. Stockholm, 1983.

Durant, Alan. *Ezra Pound: Identity in Crisis*. New York, 1981.

Eastham, Scott. *Paradise and Ezra Pound: The Poet as Shaman*. University Press of America, 1983.

Eastman, Barbara. *Ezra Pound's Cantos: The Story of the Text*. Orono, Maine, 1979.

Edwards, John Hamilton, and William V. Vasse. *Annotated Index to the Cantos of Ezra Pound: Cantos I-LXXXIV*. With the assistance of John J. Espey and Frederic Peachy. Berkeley, 1957; 2d ptg. (with additions and corrections), 1959.

Ellman, Maude. *The Poetics of Impersonality: T.S. Eliot and Ezra Pound*. Cambridge, 1987.

Emery, Clark. *Ideas into Action: A Study of Pound's Cantos*. Coral Gables, 1958.

Espey, John J. *Ezra Pound's Mauberley: A Study in Composition*. Berkeley and London, 1955.

Flory, Wendy Stallard. *The American Ezra Pound*. New Haven, 1989.

———. *Ezra Pound and The Cantos: A Record of Struggle*. New Haven, 1980.

Fogelman, Bruce. *Shapes of Power: The Development of Ezra Pound's Poetic Sequences*. Ann Arbor, 1988.

Fraser, G. S. *Ezra Pound*. Edinburgh and London, 1960; New York, 1961.

Froula, Christine. *A Guide to Ezra Pound's Selected Poems*. New York, 1983.

———. *To Write Paradise: Style and Error in Pound's Cantos*. New Haven, 1984.

Furia, Philip. *Pound's Cantos Declassified*. Philadelphia, 1984.

Gallup, Donald. *Ezra Pound: A Bibliography*. Charlottesville, 1983.

Géfin, Lazlo K. *Ideogram: History of a Poetic Method*. Austin, 1982.

Goodwin, K. L. *The Influence of Ezra Pound*. London, 1966.

Grover, Philip, ed. *Ezra Pound: The London Years, 1908–1920*. New York, 1978.

Harmon, William. *Time in Ezra Pound's Work*. Chapel Hill, 1977.

Hesse, Eva, ed. *New Approaches to Ezra Pound*. Berkeley and London, 1969.

Hoffman, Daniel, ed. *Ezra Pound and William Carlos Williams*. Philadelphia, 1983.

Hooley, Daniel M. *The Classics in Paraphrase: Ezra Pound and Modern Translators of Latin Poetry*. Selinsgrove, PA, 1988.

Hutchins, Patricia. *Ezra Pound's Kensington: An Exploration, 1885–1913*. London, 1965.

Ivancich, Gianfranco. *Ezra Pound in Italy*. New York, 1978.

Jackson, Thomas H. *The Early Poetry of Ezra Pound*. Cambridge, MA, 1969.

Kearns, George. *Guide to Ezra Pound's Selected Cantos*. New Brunswick, NJ, 1980.

Kenner, Hugh. *The Poetry of Ezra Pound*. New York and London, 1951.

———. *The Pound Era*. Berkeley and London, 1971.

Kodama, Sanehide. *American Poetry and Japanese Culture*. Seattle, 1984.

Laughlin, James. *The Master of Those Who Know*. San Francisco, 1986.
———. *Pound as Wuz*. St. Paul, MN, 1987.
Leary, Lewis, ed. *Motive and Method in the Cantos of Ezra Pound*. New York, 1954.
Lewis, Wyndham, ed. *Blast 1 & 2*. Santa Barbara, Rpt., 1981.
Lindberg, Kathryne V. *Reading Pound Reading: Modernism After Nietzsche*. New York, 1987.
Lindberg-Seyested, Brita, ed. *Pound / Ford: The Story of a Literary Friendship*. New York, 1982.
Longenbach, James. *Modern Poetics of History: Pound, Eliot, and the Sense of the Past*. Princeton, 1987.
———. *Stone Cottage: Pound, Yeats, and Modernism*. New York, 1988.
Makin, Peter. *Pound's Cantos*. London, 1985.
———. *Provence and Pound*. Berkeley, London, 1979.
Materer, Timothy, ed. *Pound / Lewis: The Letters of Ezra Pound and Wyndham Lewis*. New York, 1985.
Materer, Timothy. *Vortex: Pound, Eliot, and Lewis*. Ithaca, 1979.
Mayo, Robert. ed. *The Analyst*. A serial mimeographed newsletter containing source studies by different editors and writers. Evanston, 1953–1971.
Meacham, Harry. *The Caged Panther*. New York, 1967.
Miyake, Akiko. *Ezra Pound and the Mysteries of Love: A Plan for "The Cantos."* Durham, NC, 1991.
Mullins, Eustace Clarence. *This Difficult Individual, Ezra Pound*. New York, 1961.
Nolde, John. *Blossoms from the East: The China Cantos of Ezra Pound*. Orono, 1983.
Norman, Charles. *The Case of Ezra Pound*. New York, 1960.
———. *Ezra Pound: A Biography*. Rev. version of earlier ed. London, 1969.
O'Connor, William Van, and Edward Stone. *A Casebook on Ezra Pound*. New York, 1959.
Oderman, Kevin. *Ezra Pound and the Erotic Medium*. Durham, NC, 1986.
Pearce, Donald and Herbert Schneidau. *Ezra Pound / John Theobald: Letters*. Redding Ridge, CT, 1984.
Pearlman, Daniel S. *The Barb of Time*. New York and London, 1969.
Perloff, Marjorie. *The Dance of the Intellect: Studies in the Poetry of the Pound Tradition*. Cambridge, 1985.
Pound, Ezra and Rudd Fleming. *Elektra: A Play*. Princeton, 1989.
Pound, Ezra and Louis Zukofsky. *Pound / Zukofsky: Selected Letters of Ezra Pound and Louis Zukofsky*. Barry Ahearn, ed. New York, 1987.
Pound, Ezra. Mary DeRachewiltz, ed. & tr. *I Cantos*. Milano, 1985.
Pound, Omar and A. Walton Litz, eds. *Ezra Pound and Dorothy Shakespear: Their Letters 1909–1914*. New York, 1984.
Pound, Omar and Robert Spoo, eds. *Ezra Pound and Margaret Cravens: A Tragic Friendship, 1910–12*. Durham, NC, 1988.
Rabate, Jean Michel. *Language, Sexuality and Ideology in Ezra Pound's Cantos*. Albany, NY, 1986.
Rachewiltz, Mary de. *Discretions*. Boston and London, 1971.
———. *Ezra Pound: Father and Teacher* çPB of Discretions. New York, 1975.
Read, Forrest. *'76: One World and The Cantos of Ezra Pound*. Chapel Hill, 1980.
Redman, Tim. *Ezra Pound and Italian Fascism*. Cambridge, 1991.
Rosenthal, M. L. *A Primer of Ezra Pound*. New York, 1960.
Russell, Peter, ed. *Ezra Pound: A Collection of Essays to Be Presented to Ezra Pound on his 65th Birthday*. London, 1950; New York, 1950 (with title *An Examination of Ezra Pound: A Collection of Essays*).
Ruthven, K. K. *Ezra Pound as Literary Critic*. London and New York, 1990.
Ruthven, K. K. *A Guide to Ezra Pound's "Personae" (1926)*. Berkeley, 1969.
Schafer, R. Murray, ed. *Ezra Pound and Music: The Complete Criticism*. New York, 1978.
Schneidau, Herbert N. *Ezra Pound: The Image and the Real*. Baton Rouge, 1969.
Seelye, Catherine. *Charles Olson and Ezra Pound*. New York, 1975.
Sicari, Stephen. *Pound's Epic Ambition: Dante and the Modern World*. Albany, 1991.
Sieburth, Richard. *Instigations: Ezra Pound and Remy de Gourmont*. Cambridge, MA, 1978.
Stead, C. K. *Pound, Yeats, Eliot, and the Modernist Movement*. New Brunswick, NJ, 1986.
Stock, Noel. *The Life of Ezra Pound*. New York, 1970.
———. *Poet in Exile: Ezra Pound*. Manchester and New York, 1964.
———. *Reading the Cantos: A Study of Meaning in Ezra Pound*. New York, 1966.
Sullivan, J. P., ed. *Ezra Pound: A Critical Anthology*. Middlesex, England, 1970.
———. *Ezra Pound and Sextus Propertius: A Study in Creative Translation*. Austin, and London, 1964.
Surette, Leon. *A Light from Eleusis: A Study of Ezra Pound's Cantos*. Oxford, 1979.
Sutton, Walter, ed. *Ezra Pound: A Collection of Critical Essays*. Englewood Cliffs, NJ, 1963.
Terrell, Carroll F. *Ideas in Reaction: Byways to the Pound Arcana*. Orono, 1991.
Thomas, Ron. *The Latin Masks of Ezra Pound*. Ann Arbor, 1983.
Tryphonopoulos, Demetres P. *The Celestial Tradition: A Study of Ezra Pound's "The Cantos."* Waterloo, 1992.
Watts, Harold H. *Ezra Pound and the Cantos*. Chicago, 1952.
Wilhelm, J. J. *The American Roots of Ezra Pound*. New York, Inc., 1985.
———. *Dante and Pound: The Epic of Judgement*. Orono, 1975.
———. *Ezra Pound in London and Paris 1908–1925*. Philadelphia, 1990.
———. *The Later Cantos of Ezra Pound*. New York, 1977.
Woodward, Anthony. *Ezra Pound and the Pisan Cantos*. London, 1980.
Yeats, W. B. *A Packet for Ezra Pound*. Dublin, 1929.
Zinnes, Harriet, ed. *Ezra Pound and the Visual Arts*. New York, 1980.

Bibliography

Anderson, David. *Pound's Cavalcanti: An Edition of the Translations, Notes, and Essays.* Princeton: Princeton University Press, 1983.

Benediktson, D. Thomas. *Propertius / Modernist Poet of Antiquity.* Southern Illinois University Press, 1989.

Bischoff, Volker. *Ezra Pound Criticism 1905–1985 / A Chronological Listing of Publications in English.* Marburg: Universitätsbibliothek Marburg, 1991.

Bornstein, George. *Ezra Pound Among the Poets.* Chicago: University of Chicago Press, 1985.

Carpenter, Humphrey. *A Serious Character: The Life of Ezra Pound.* London: Faber and Faber, 1988.

Cookson, William. *A Guide to The Cantos of Ezra Pound.* Persea, 1985.

D'Epiro, Peter. *A Touch of Rhetoric: Ezra Pound's Malatesta Cantos.* UMI Research Press, 1983.

Dasenbrock, Reed Way. *The Literary Vorticism of Ezra Pound and Wyndham Lewis: Towards the Condition of Painting.* Baltimore: Johns Hopkins University Press, 1985.

Davenport, Guy. *Cities on Hills / A Study of I–XXX of Ezra Pound's Cantos.* UMI Research Press, 1983.

Davie, Donald. *Studies in Ezra Pound / Chronicles and Polemic.* Manchester, England: Carcanet, 1991.

Davis, Kay. *Fugue and Fresco: Structures in Pound's Cantos.* Orono: National Poetry Foundation, 1984.

Driscoll, John. *The China Cantos of Ezra Pound.* Stockholm: 1983.

Eastham, Scott. *Paradise and Ezra Pound / The Poet as Shaman.* University Press of America, 1983.

Ellman, Maude. *The Poetics of Impersonality / T.S. Eliot and Ezra Pound.* Cambridge: Harvard University Press, 1987.

Flory, Wendy Stallard. *The American Ezra Pound.* New Haven: Yale University Press, 1989.

Fogelman, Bruce. *Shapes of Power: The Development of Ezra Pound's Poetic Sequences.* UMI Research Press, 1988.

Froula, Christine. *To Write Paradise: Style and Error in Pound's Cantos.* New Haven: Yale University Press, 1984.

Furia, Philip. *Pound's Cantos Declassified.* Philadelphia: Pennsylvania State University Press, 1984.

Hoffman, Daniel [ed.]. *Ezra Pound and William Carlos Williams.* Philadelphia: University of Pennsylvania Press, 1983.

Hooley, Daniel M. *The Classics in Paraphrase: Ezra Pound and Modern Translators of Latin Poetry.* Susquehanna University Press and Associated University Presses, 1988.

Kodama, Sanehide. *American Poetry and Japanese Culture.* Archon, 1984.

Laughlin, James. *Pound as Wuz.* Graywolf, 1987.

Laughlin, James. *The Master of Those Who Know.* San Francisco: City Lights, 1986.

Lindberg, Kathryne V. *Reading Pound Reading: Modernism After Nietzsche.* New York: Oxford University Press, 1987.

Longenbach, James. *Modernist Poetics of History / Pound, Eliot, and the Sense of the Past*. Princeton: Princeton University Press, 1987.

Longenbach, James. *Stone Cottage: Pound, Yeats, and Modernism*. Oxford University Press, 1988.

Makin, Peter. *Pound's Cantos*. London: George Allen & Unwin, 1985.

Materer, Timothy, ed. *Pound / Lewis: The Letters of Ezra Pound and Wyndham Lewis*. New York: New Directions, 1985.

Miyake, Akiko. *Ezra Pound and the Mysteries of Love: A Plan for "The Cantos."* Duke University Press, 1991.

Nicholls, Peter. *Ezra Pound: Politics, Economics and Writing / A Study of "The Cantos."* Humanities Press, 1984.

Oderman, Kevin. *Ezra Pound and the Erotic Medium*. Duke University Press, 1986.

Pearce, Donald and Herbert Schneidau. *Ezra Pound / John Theobald: Letters*. Redding Ridge, CT: Black Swan Books Ltd., 1984.

Perloff, Marjorie. *The dance of the intellect / Studies in the poetry of the Pound tradition*. Cambridge University Press, 1985.

Pound, Ezra and Louis Zukofsky. *Pound / Zukofsky: Selected Letters of Ezra Pound and Louis Zukofsky*. Barry Ahearn, ed. New York: New Directions, 1987.

Pound, Ezra and Rudd Fleming. *Elektra: A Play*. Princeton University Press.

Pound, Ezra. *Je rassemble les membre d'Osiris*. Edited by Jean-Michel Rabate; translated by Jean-Paul Auxemery, Claude Miniere, Margaret Tunstill, Jean-Michel Rabate; commentary by Massimo Bacigalupo and Joel Peter Shapiro. Auch: Tristram, 1989.

Pound, Ezra. Mary DeRachewiltz, ed. & tr. *I Cantos*. Milano: Mondadori (I Meridiani), 1985.

Pound, Omar and A. Walton Litz (eds). *Ezra Pound and Dorothy Shakespear: Their Letters 1909–1914*. New York: New Directions, 1984.

Pound, Omar and Robert Spoo, eds. *Ezra Pound and Margaret Cravens: A Tragic Friendship, 1910–1912*. Duke University Press, 1988.

Rabate, Jean Michel. *Language, Sexuality and Ideology in Ezra Pound's Cantos*. State University of New York Press, 1986.

Redman, Tim. *Ezra Pound and Italian Fascism*. Cambridge: Cambridge University Press, 1991.

Ruthven, K.K. *Ezra Pound as Literary Critic*. London and New York: Routledge, 1990.

Sicari, Stephen. *Pound's Epic Ambition / Dante and the Modern World*. Albany: State University of New York, 19??.

Stead, C.K. *Pound, Yeats, Eliot, and the Modernist Movement*. Rutgers University Press, 1986.

Terrell, Carroll F. *Ideas in Reaction: Byways to the Pound Arcana*. Orono: Northern Lights, 1991.

Thomas, Ron. *The Latin Masks of Ezra Pound*. UMI Research Press, 1983.

Tryphonopoulos, Demetres P. *The Celestial Tradition / A Study of Ezra Pound's* The Cantos. Waterloo: Wilfrid Laurier University Press, 1992.

Wilhelm, J.J. *Ezra Pound in London and Paris 1908–1925*. Philadelphia: Pennsylvania State University Press, 1990.

Wilhelm, J.J. *The American Roots of Ezra Pound*. New York: Garland Publishing, Inc., 1985.

INDEX TO THE CANTOS

This index, designed to provide access to the *Companion* as well as to *The Cantos*, is divided into four parts. In the first part, all proper names or nouns in the poem are listed alphabetically. Variants in spelling are listed both correctly and by the variant; e.g., "Baastun" as Boston and "Ausstrians" as Austrians. Plurals are listed with the singular form if it occurs in the text. These exceptions are also listed: (1) words not capitalized but which in traditional practice should be, such as "Aethopians" at 40/199; (2) a slang expression involving nationality such as "frog-bassador" for French Ambassador at 78/444; and (3) certain words that Pound capitalizes for emphasis. In the second part all foreign words or phrases in the Roman alphabet are listed alphabetically, except for Chinese Romanization. In the third part, all Greek words are listed alphabetically. Finally, in the fourth part, the Chinese characters are indexed alphabetically by traditional Wade-Giles transliteration. This list has first the character, then the W-G translitera-tion, and finally Pound's variant usages. Each entry in all parts of the index is followed by page references to the common New Directions and Faber editions.

FOREIGN WORDS AND PHRASES IN ROMAN ALPHABET

WORDS AND PHRASES IN GREEK

CHINESE CHARACTERS

[Column I gives characters and Mathews numbers, in parenthesis if not found in text. Column II gives the standard Wade-Giles transliteration. Column III, Pound's transliteration in parenthesis. Column IV gives page numbers which are followed by an asterisk if not found in character form on that page.]

I	II	III	IV
(安 26)	An		704*
茶 101	Cha	(tcha)	341
諂 174	Ch'an		467, 476, 738
昌 206	Ch'ang		559
長 213	Ch'ang		532, 548, 704,* 709*
常 221	Ch'ang	(tch'âng)	562
(昭 236)	Chao		708*
(照 炤 238)	Chao		703
兆 247	Ch'ao		709
者 263	Che		290
(這 这 265)	Che		704*
震 315	Chen		566, 613, 656
(朕 316)	Chên		695,* 709*
忱 331	Ch'en		545
忱 331	Ch'en		545
陳 339	Ch'en		547
貞 346	Chen	(tchen)	547, 550, 562, 601, 676
正 351	Cheng	(tcheng; CH'ing; ching)	252, 333, 352, 382, 387, 400, 557, 682, 692,* 694,* 699,* 700,* 701,* 770*
(征 352)	Cheng		707*

CHINESE CHARACTERS – Continued

I	II	III	IV
成 379	Ch'eng	(tch'eng)	475, 476, 555, 568, 706*
誠 381	Ch'êng		454
機 411	Chi		603, 746
譏 412	Chi		767
既 453	Chi	(Kiue)	561
祭 465	Chi		467, 476
極 484	Chi		553
(積 500)	Chi	(tsi)	550*
稷 504	Chi		747
(奇 竒 514)	Ch'i		709*
其 525	Ch'i	(K'i)	467, 476, 554, 555*
棄 550	Ch'i		687
氣 554	Ch'i		690
齊 560	Ch'i	(t'si)	553
甲 610	Chia		544
戒 627	Chiai		547
(嬌 690)	Chiao		705*
(交 702)	Chiao		711*
教 719	Chiao	(Kiaó)	557, 559, 561
節 795	Chieh		468, 476
簡 837	Chien		561
監 839	Chien	(Kien)	554

CHINESE CHARACTERS – Continued

CHINESE CHARACTERS – Continued

I	II	III	IV
衷 1508	Chung		544
(種 1511)	Chung		696*
(崇 1528)	Ch'ung		697*
居 1535	Chü		548
(聚 1581)	Chü		709*
(曲 1623)	Ch'ü		702*
倦 1641	Chüan		683
犬 1650	Ch'üan		499
厥 1680	Chueh		544,* 548
俊 1727	Chun	(tsiun)	557
恩 1743	En		689, 710
貳 1752	Erh		556, 575*
而 1756	Erh		467, 476
法 1762	Fa		694,* 699
發 1768	Fa		290, 636, 639, 655
(番 1790)	Fan		688*
非 1819	Fei		467, 476, 566
(廢 1848)	Fei		696*
風 1890	Feng		689, 698*
(浮 1906)	Fou		699*
夫 1908	Fu		547, 712*
符 1922	Fu		468, 476
婦 1963	Fu		547
福 1978	Fu		338

CHINESE CHARACTERS – Continued

I	II	III	IV
佛 1982	Fu		687, 702, 718
(害 2015)	Hai		701*
漢 2039	Han		309, 704*
好 2062	Hao		544, 705*
何 2109	Ho		465, 476, 498, 595
河 2111	Ho		784
和 2115	Ho	(Houo)	567
後 2143	Hou		465, 476
后 2144	Hou	(heou)	544,* 552,* 747
厚 2147	Hou	(heóu)	558
乎 2154	Hu		629, 644
忽 2194	Hu		693
(般 2210)	Hu		695*
(話 / 譮 2215)	Hua		688*
(壞 2232)	Huai		705*
皇 2283	Huang	(houâng)	554
黃 2297	Huang		487
惠 2339	Hui		636
(鴻 2386(a))	Hung		695*
火 2395	Huo	(tcho)	555
(活 2401)	Huo		702*
獲 2412	Huo		547
熙 2451	Hsi	(Hi)	690, 694,* 725*

CHINESE CHARACTERS – Continued

I	II	III	IV
夏 2521	Hsia		265
(想 2564)	Hsiang		706*
(象 2568)	Hsiang		784*
詳 2579	Hsiang		560
(曉 2594)	Hsiao		695*
孝 2601	Hsiao		691
小 2605	Hsiao		688
(銷 2611)	Hsiao		706*
(邪 2625)	Hsieh		697*
賢 2671	Hsien		543
顯 2692	Hsien		429, 550, 552, 612, 630, 693
憲 2697	Hsien		562
先 2702	Hsien		465, 476, 778*
心 2735	Hsin		561, 573, 701,* 702,* 705*
新 2737	Hsin		265, 278, 571, 629, 642, 675, 684, 780
信 2748	Hsin		171, 564, 701*
行 2754	Hsing		629
(秀 2803)	Hsiu		704*
胥 2835	Hsü	(siu)	557
恤 2862	Hsü		560
(暄 2870)	Hsuan		686*
血 2901	Hsueh		553
以 2932	I		290, 544,* 547, 636, 676
(乂 2934)	I		735*

CHINESE CHARACTERS – Continued

CHINESE CHARACTERS – Continued

I	II	III	IV
孤 3470	Ku		572, 605
(官 3552)	Kuan		704*
管 3557	Kuan		703,* 752
瘝 3560	Kuan		553
關 3571	Kuan		753
光 3583	Kwang	(Kuan, Kuang)	698,* 699,* 702,* 719
鬼 3634	Kuei		467, 476, 748
(櫃 匱 鐀 3638)	Kuei		695*
(公 3701)	Kung		694,* 700*
供 3710	Kung		557
戾 3854	Li	("Min")	554
裏 3865	Li		689, 702*
利 3867	Li		575, 595, 709*
(禮 礼 3886)	Li		544,* 698,* 711*
力 3920	Li		628
(量 3943)	Liang		707*
梁 3951	Liang	(Leang)	636
林 4022	Lin		553
靈 4071	Ling		543, 551, 552, 555, 560, 675, 738, 740
(流 4080)	Liu		704*
(類 類 4244)	Lui		704*
呂 4280	Lu		562

CHINESE CHARACTERS – Continued

I	II	III	IV
慮 4292	Lü		549
(律 4297)	Lü		699*
(麻 4303)	Ma		696*
馬 4310	Ma		683
嗎 4311	Ma		688
貌 4368	Mao		563
冒 4373	Mao		559
門 4418	Men		691
(氓 甿 } 4424)	Mêng		695*
孟 4428	Meng		599, 692, 698*
(棉 4505)	Mien		696*
名 4524	Ming		252, 333, 382, 400, 682
明 4534	Ming		539, 552, 557, 558,* 693, 719, 697,* 699,* 702,* 778*
命 4537	Ming		558
莫 4557	Mo	(Moua)	430, 545,* 778*
([illegible] 4587)	Mu		709*
(模 4590)	Mu		694*
木 4593	Mu		792
穆 4601	Mu	(Mou)	562
乃 4612	Nai		553
尼 4654	Ni		272, 308
鳥 4688	Niao		487
(寧 寜 寍 } 4725)	Ning	(gning)	545*

CHINESE CHARACTERS – Continued

I	II	III	IV
辳 莀 4768	Nung		709*
我 4778	Ngo		557
惡 4809	O		705*
敗退 4866	Pai		704*
盤 4903	P'an		548
鴇 4953	Pao		740*
豹 4954	Pao		740
寶 4956	Pao		566, 636, 676, 740
白 4975	Pai		718
伯 4977	Pe		567, 683
備 4997	Pei		558
倍 5000	Pei		709*
配 5019	P'ei		554
本 5025	Pen		640, 686, 692, 694,* 697,* 698,* 704,* 744, 757, 764
朋 5054	P'eng		554, 778*
幣 5103	Pi		767
必 5109	Pi		592, 595
丕 5137	P'i		556
匹 5170	P'i		547
編 5231	Pien		695*
變 5245	Pien		313
偏 5246	P'ien		553

CHINESE CHARACTERS – Continued)

I	II	III	IV
秉 5291	Ping		559
平 5303	P'ing		689
(薄 5326)	Po		699*
樸 5354	P'o		686
不 5379	Pu	(Pou)	290, 545,* 556,* 575,* 685, 701,* 728
僕 5401	P'u		551
三 5415	San		572, 605
(桑 5424)	Sang		709*
(俗 5497)	Su		689,* 698*
(宋 5565)	Sung		700
(厶 5568)	Szu		694*
(私 5569)	Szu		694*
祀 5592	Szu	(séu)	546
(山 5630)	Shan		784*
上 5669	Shang		575
尚 5670	Shang		563
捨 5700	She		687
身 5718	Shen		290, 554
深 5719	Shen		689
生 5738	Sheng	(Chong)	558
聖 5753	Sheng		693, 694,* 704,* 719*
尸 5756	Shih		582
始 5772	Shih	(Chèu)	544,* 760
時 5780	Shih	(Cheu)	545, 550, 557

CHINESE CHARACTERS – Continued

I	II	III	IV
示 5788	Shih		686
(實 寔 5821)	Shih		694*
書 5857	Shu		590
(術 5889)	Shu		701*
舜 5936	Shun	(Chun)	263, 302, 309
達 5956	Ta		486
太 6020	T'ai		556, 633, 689
旦 6037	Tan		466, 476, 554, 615, 675, 677, 679, 723
亶 6048	Tan		552
湯 6101	T'ang		555
(堂 6107)	T'ang		702*
道 6136	Tao		482, 550, 700*
陶 6156	T'ao	(also Yao in ancient history)	264
德 6162	Te		546, 546,* 548, 574
(地 6198)	Ti		707*
(的 6213)	Ti	(te)	558,* 704*
體 6246	T'i		561
典 6347	Tien		560
甸 6350	Tien		555
(天 靝 6361)	T'ien		702*
田 6362	T'ien		691, 707*
丁 6381	Ting		556
(定 6393)	Ting		704*
奪 6433	To		659

CHINESE CHARACTERS – Continued

CHINESE CHARACTERS – Continued

I	II	III	IV
罔 7045	Wang		550,* 551
爲 7059	Wei		676
惟 7066	Wei		544,* 556
(文 7129)	Wen	(Wan)	700,* 704*
(翁 7146)	Weng		704*
(齷 7163)	Wo		702*
巫 7164	Wu		738
無 7180	Wu		636, 683
毋 7193	Wu		693
武 7195	Wu		552, 556, 633
戊 7197	Wu		556
勿 7208	Wu		532, 709*
(養 7254)	Yang		695*
(樣 7256)	Yang		704,* 707*
昜 7258	Yang		598
堯 7295	Yao		263, 302, 309, 695,* 706*
要 7300	Yao	(iao)	561
耀 7306	Yao		254
也 7312	Yeh		467, 476
業 7321	Yeh		687, 692, 697,* 698,* 704,* 744, 764
尹 7439	Yin		543
(嬴 7483)	Ying		709*
幽 7505	Yu	(Iou)	558,* 567
又 7539	Yu		686, 688

CHINESE CHARACTERS – Continued

I	II	III	IV
(雍 邕 7554)	Yung	(Iong)	694,* 707,* 770*
容 7560	Yung		558
(用 7567)	Yung	(jóung)	561*
于 7592	Yü		548
禹 7620	Yü		263, 302
諭 7641	Yü		693, 694
玉 7666	Yü		784
曰 7694	Yüeh	(iue)	550,* 554, 595
(月 7696)	Yueh		778*
(元 7707)	Yüan	(iuên)	547,* 552*
原 7725	Yuan		689
遠 7734	Yüan		465, 476, 498
允 7759	Yun	(iun)	546

Addendum†

I	II	III	IV
燊	Hsin		653: Made up of the radicals: 火 2395 X 3 = (火火火) = Huo: flame, and 木 4593 Mu(Muh): wood

†The only major Chinese dictionary that contains this character for Hsin is the K'ang Hsi Dictionary, the official dictionary of the Ch'ing (Manchu) Dynasty (1644-1911) [H. Witemeyer, *Pai*, 4-2+3, p. 333n].